POETRY EXPLICATION

A Checklist of Interpretation Since 1925
of British and American Poems
Past and Present

"POETRY EXPLICATION"

A Checklist of Interpretation Since 1925 of British and American Poems Past and Present

JOSEPH M. *Marshall* KUNTZ

NANCY C. MARTINEZ

G.K.HALL &CO.

70 LINCOLN STREET, BOSTON, MASS.

Library of Congress Cataloging in Publication Data

Kuntz, Joseph Marshall. 1911-
  Poetry explication.

  1. English poetry—Explication—Bibliography.
2. American poetry—Explication—Bibliography.
I. Martinez, Nancy Conrad, joint author.
II. Title.
Z2014.P7K8 1980 [PR502]   016.821'009
ISBN 0-8161-8313-9   80-10291

This publication is printed on permanent/durable acid-free paper
MANUFACTURED IN THE UNITED STATES OF AMERICA

Contents

Introduction

The third edition of <u>Poetry Explication: A Checklist</u> presents a comprehensive index of poetry explications printed during the period 1925-1977. It incorporates the checklists of 1950 and 1962 and, following the same aim, scope, and limitations established for the first editions, lists explications printed through 1977, with an occasional excursion into 1978.

An introduction in the first edition defines explication as "an examination of a work of literature for a knowledge of each part, for the relations of these parts to each other, and for their relations to the whole." In addition to the rather broad confines of this definition, we have observed the following limitations in compiling the <u>Checklist</u>: 1. We have limited ourselves for the most part to poems of not more than five hundred lines, although we have occasionally added a longer poem when the additional length is negligible or when the explications seem especially important or difficult to find in existing bibliographies. 2. We have omitted material devoted exclusively to sources and circumstances of composition, to literary parallels, or to a minor part of a poem. 3. We have generally omitted paraphrase and metrical analysis unless the authors relate their analyses to the total effect of the poem. 4. We have excluded explications from books devoted to single authors but have included reprints from those books that have appeared in collections or periodicals. For the most part we have included rather than excluded borderline explications.

Within these limitations we have listed explications from many different "schools" of criticism. The <u>Checklist</u> includes interpretations of poems by phenomenologists, new literary historians, Marxist or dialectical critics, psychological critics, linguists, stylistic experts, rhetoricians, and prosodists as well as by formalists and avowed "new critics." The large number of explications printed since 1960 (almost three times the number listed in the second edition) and the presence of explication in all kinds of critical writing attest to its continued importance in modern critical method.

Many studies of explication as an interpretative and as a critical tool continue to appear. Some recent discussions deserve special attention: Jonathan Culler, "Beyond Interpretation: The Prospects of Contemporary Criticism," <u>Comparative Literature</u>, 28 (Summer, 1976); Cleanth Brooks, "In Defence of 'Interpretation' and 'Literary History,'" <u>Mosaic</u>, 8 (Winter, 1975); Gemino H. Abad, <u>A Formal Approach to Lyric Poetry</u> (1978); Cleanth Brooks, <u>A Shaping Joy</u> (1971); David Clark, <u>Lyric Resonance</u> (1972); and Laurence Perrine, <u>The Art of Total Relevance</u> (1976).

We wish to acknowledge with thanks the assistance of several individuals. George Arms, who planned the original checklist and provided many of the entries for the first edition, has continued to advise us most generously. In addition, for help in compiling and preparing the final manuscript and for unfailing encouragement, we wish to thank Elizabeth Kuntz, Bonnie L. Conrad, and Joseph G. R. Martinez. The credit for much of the merit but none of the defects of the completed <u>Checklist</u> must go to them.

List of Abbreviations

ABR	American Benedictine Review
AI	American Imago
AL	American Literature
AN&Q	American Notes and Queries (New Haven, Conn.)
AQ	American Quarterly
AR	Antioch Review
ArielE	Ariel: A Review of International English Literature
ArQ	Arizona Quarterly
ASch	American Scholar
BlakeS	Blake Studies
BNYPL	Bulletin of the New York Public Library
BSUF	Ball State University Forum
BuR	Bucknell Review
CE	College English
CEA	CEA Critic
CEJ	California English Journal
CentR	The Centennial Review (Mich. State U.)
ChauR	The Chaucer Review (Penn. State U.)
ChiR	Chicago Review
CimR	Cimarron Review (Oklahoma State U.)
CL	Comparative Literature
CLAJ	College Language Association Journal (Morgan State Coll., Baltimore) - listed in holdings file as CLA Journal
CLQ	Colby Library Quarterly
CLS	Comparative Literature Studies (U. of Ill.)
CollL	College Literature
ColQ	Colorado Quarterly
ConL	Contemporary Literature (Supersedes WSCL)
ConnR	Connecticut Review
ContempR	Contemporary Review (London)
CP	Concerning Poetry (West. Wash. State Coll.) Not owned by msu
CQ	The Cambridge Quarterly
CritI	Critical Inquiry: A Voice for Reasoned Inquiry into Significant Creations of the Human Spirit
CritQ	Critical Quarterly
DHLR	The D. H. Lawrence Review (U. of Arkansas)
DR	Dalhousie Review
EA	Etudes Anglaises
EAL	Early American Literature
E&S	Essays and Studies by Members of the English Association annual - see title card catalog
ECS	Eighteenth-Century Studies (U. of Calif., Davis)
EIC	Essays in Criticism (Oxford)
EJ	English Journal
ELH	Journal of English Literary History listed as ELH

Abbreviations

ELN	English Language Notes (U. of Colo.)
ELR	English Literary Renaissance
ELT	English Literature in Transition (1880–1920)
ELWIU	Essays in Literature (Western Ill. Univ.)
EngR	English Record
ES	English Studies
ESQ	ESQ: Journal of the American Renaissance
Expl	Explicator
FMLS	Forum for Modern Language Studies (U. of St. Andrews, Scotland)
GaR	Georgia Review
HAB	The Humanities Association Review/La Revue de l'Association des Humanités (Formerly Humanities Association Bulletin)
HLQ	Huntington Library Quarterly
HudR	Hudson Review
IEY	Iowa English Bulletin: Yearbook
IowaR	Iowa Review
JAAC	Journal of Aesthetics and Art Criticism
JEGP	Journal of English and Germanic Philology
JHI	Journal of the History of Ideas
JJQ	James Joyce Quarterly (U. of Tulsa, Okla.)
JML	Journal of Modern Literature
JNT	Journal of Narrative Technique
KanQ	Kansas Quarterly (Formerly KM)
KSJ	Keats-Shelley Journal *annual - listed in title card catalog*
KSMB	Keats-Shelley Memorial Bulletin (Rome)
L&P	Literature and Psychology (Fairleigh Dickinson U.)
Lang&S	Language and Style
LitR	Literary Review (Fairleigh Dickinson U.)
McNR	McNeese Review (McNeese State Coll., La.)
MD	Modern Drama
MiltonQ	Milton Quarterly (Formerly MiltonN)
MinnR	Minnesota Review
MissQ	Mississippi Quarterly
MLN	Modern Language Notes
MLQ	Modern Language Quarterly
MLR	Modern Language Review
ModA	Modern Age (Chicago)
MP	Modern Philology
MPS	Modern Poetry Studies
MQ	Midwest Quarterly (Pittsburg, Kan.)
MQR	Michigan Quarterly Review
MR	Massachusetts Review (U. of Mass.)
MSE	Massachusetts Studies in English
N&Q	Notes and Queries
NConL	Notes on Contemporary Literature
NEQ	New England Quarterly
NLH	New Literary History (U. of Va.)
OhR	Ohio Review
PLL	Papers on Language and Literature
PMLA	Publications of the Modern Language Association of America *listed PMLA*
PQ	Philological Quarterly (Iowa City)
PR	Partisan Review
PrS	Prairie Schooner
QJS	Quarterly Journal of Speech
QQ	Queen's Quarterly
RenQ	Renaissance Quarterly

RES — Review of English Studies
RS — Research Studies (Wash. State U.)
SAQ — South Atlantic Quarterly
SatR — Saturday Review
SBHC — Studies in Browning and His Circle (Supersedes Browning Newsletter)
SBL — Studies in Black Literature
SCN — Seventeenth-Century News
SEL — Studies in English Literature, 1500-1900
ShakS — Shakespeare Studies (U. of Cincinnati) *annual - see title card catalog*
SHR — Southern Humanities Review
SIR — Studies in Romanticism (Boston U.)
SJS — San Jose Studies
SLitI — Studies in the Literary Imagination (Ga. State Coll.)
SoQ — The Southern Quarterly (U. of So. Miss.)
SoR — Southern Review (Louisiana State U.)
SP — Studies in Philology
SQ — Shakespeare Quarterly
SR — Sewanee Review
SSL — Studies in Scottish Literature (U. of So. Car.)
SWR — Southwest Review
TC — Twentieth Century
TCL — Twentieth Century Literature
TLS — (London) Times Literary Supplement
TQ — Texas Quarterly (U. of Texas)
TSE — Tulane Studies in English *annual - see card catalog - title*
TSL — Tennesse Studies in Literature *annual - see title card catalog*
TSLL — Texas Studies in Literature and Language
UCSLL — University of Colorado Studies in Language and Literature
UDQ — University of Denver Quarterly
UDR — University of Dayton Review
UMSE — University of Mississippi Studies in English
UTQ — University of Toronto Quarterly
UWR — University of Windsor Review (Windsor, Ontario)
VN — Victorian Newsletter
VP — Victorian Poetry (W. Va. U.)
VQR — Virginia Quarterly Review
VS — Victorian Studies (Ind. U.)
WC — Wordsworth Circle *v. 3-*
WHR — Western Humanties Review
WVUPP — West Virginia University Philological Papers *annual, see title card catalog*
WWR — Walt Whitman Review
YES — Yearbook of English Studies *annual - see title card catalog*
YR — Yale Review

Checklist of Interpretation

ADAMS, Robert Simson. "I Am No Prince of Darkness, Lord of Sorrow"
Adams, The Contexts of Poetry, pp. 8-12.

AGEE, James. "Sunday: Outskirts of Knoxville, Tenn."
Drew and Sweeney, Directions in Modern Poetry, pp. 243-247.

Drew, Poetry: A Modern Guide, pp. 211-214.

James A. Freeman, "Agee's 'Sunday' Meditation," CP, 3 (Fall, 1970), 37-39.

AIKEN. "The Crystal"
James Dickey, "A Gold-Mine of Consciousness," Poetry, 94 (April, 1959), 42-43.

_____. "Dead Leaf in May"
James Zigerell, Expl, 25 (Sept., 1966), 5.

_____. "Morning Song from 'Senlin'"
Perrine and Reid, 100 American Poems, pp. 143-144.

_____. "South End"
Perrine and Reid, 100 American Poems, p. 145.

_____. "Sursum Corda"
Donald A. Stauffer, "Genesis, or the Poet as Maker," Poets at Work, pp. 72-76.
    Rpt. Engle and Carrier, Reading Modern Poetry, pp. 240-241.

AKENSIDE. "Ode on the Winter Solstice"
William Frost, English Masterpieces, Vol. 6, Romantic and Victorian Poetry, pp. 3-4.

AMES, Richard. "The Folly of Love"
Felicity Nussbaum, "Juvenal, Swift, and The Folly of Love," ECS, 9 (Summer, 1976), 546-549.

AMMONS, A. R. "Corsons Inlet"
Guy Rotella, "Ghostlier Demarcations, Keener Sounds: A. R. Ammons' 'Corsons Inlet,'" CP, 10 (Fall, 1977), 25-33.

_____. "Hibernaculum"
Richard Pevear, "Poetry Chronicle," HudR, 26 (Spring, 1973), 217-218.

_____. "I Went to the Summit"
Bloom, A Map of Misreading, pp. 200-203.

_____. "Periphery"
Harold Bloom, "Dark and Radiant Peripheries: Mark Strand and A. R. Ammons," SoR, 8 n.s. (Winter, 1972), 145.

_____. "Play"
Lawrence Kramer, "The Wodwo Watches the Water Clock: Language in Post-modern British and American Poetry," ConL, 18 (Summer, 1977), 329-331.

ANDERSON, Patrick. "The Unfinished Hotel"
J. F. Nims, Poetry: A Critical Supplement, March, 1948, pp. 4-5.

ANDREWS, Bruce. "Bananas Are an Example"
Robert Pinsky, The Situation of Poetry: Contemporary Poetry and Its Traditions (Princeton, New Jersey: Princeton Univ. Press, 1976), pp. 87-89.

ANONYMOUS. "Adam Lay I-bowdyn"
Manning, Wisdom and Number, pp. 6-7.

Reiss, The Art of the Middle English Lyric, pp. 138-142.

Savage, The Personal Principle, pp. 48-49.

Sarah Stanbury Smith, "'Adam Lay I-Bowndyn' and the Vinculum Amoris," ELN, 15 (Dec., 1977), 98-101.

_____. "Advent"
Robert B. Burlin, The Old English "Advent": A Typological Commentary, New Haven: Yale Univ. Press, 1968.

_____. "A Gest' of Robyn Hode"
David Parker, "Popular Protest in 'A Gest of Robyn Hode,'" MLQ, 32 (March, 1971), 3-20.

_____. "Almsgiving"
Carl T. Berkhout, "Some Notes on the Old English 'Almsgiving,'" ELN, 10 (Dec., 1972), 81-85.

_____. "Als I Lay up-on a Nith"
Weber, Theology and Poetry in the Middle English Lyric, pp. 73-86.

_____. "Alysoun"
Moore, The Secular Lyric in Middle English, pp. 68-69.

_____. "A Prayer"
Barbara C. Raw, The Art and Background of Old English Poetry (London: Edward Arnold Ltd., 1978), pp. 123-126.

_____. "At a Sprynge-wel under a Thorn"
Douglas Gray, Themes and Images in the Medieval English Religious Lyric (London and Boston: Routledge & Kegan Paul, 1972), pp. 92-93.

_____. "The Bargain of Judas"
J. D. W. Crowther, "'The Bargain of Jauds,'" ELN, 13 (June, 1976), 245-249.

_____. "The Battle of Brunanburh"
W. F. Bolton, "'Variation' in The Battle of Brunanburh," RES, n.s. no. 76, 19 (Nov., 1968), 363-372.

Isaacs, Structural Principles in Old English Poetry, pp. 118-126.

Ann S. Johnson, "The Rhetoric of Brunanburh," PQ, 47 (Oct., 1968), 487-493.

Frances Randall Lipp, "Contrast and Point of View in The Battle of Brunanburh," PQ, 48 (April, 1969), 166-177.

_____. "The Battle of Maldon"
F. J. Battaglia, "Notes on "Maldon': Toward a Definitive Ofermod," ELN, 2 (June, 1965), 247-249.

N. F. Blake, "The Flyting in The Battle of Maldon," ELN, 13 (June, 1976), 242-45.

W. F. Bolton, "Byrhtnoth in the Wilderness," MLR 64 (July, 1969), 481-490.

George Clark, "The Battle of Maldon: A Heroic Poem," Speculum, 43 (Jan., 1968), 52-71.

J. E. Cross, "Mainly on Philogy and the Interpretative Criticism of Maldon," in Old English Studies in Honour of John C. Pope (Toronto and Buffalo: Univ. of Toronto Press, 1974), pp. 235-253.

David G. Hale, "Structure and Theme in The Battle of Maldon," N&Q, 15 (July, 1968), 242-243.

Isaacs, Structural Principles in Old English Poetry, pp. 159-166.

Louis G. Locke, Expl, 1 (Nov., 1942), 9.
    Rpt. The Explicator Cyclopedia, II, p. 1.

T. A. Shippey, Old English Verse (London: Hutchinson Univ. Library, 1972), pp. 107-110.

Michael J. Swanton, "The Battle of Maldon: A Literary Caveat," JEGP, 67 (July, 1968), 441-450.

_____. "Blodles and Bonles, Blod Has Nou Bon"
Manning, Wisdom and Number, p. 145.

_____. "Blow, Northerne Wynd"
Leo Spitzer, "Explication de Texte Applied to Three Great Middle English Poems," in Essays on English and American Literature by Leo Spitzer, pp. 195-216.

_____. "Bytuene Mersh and Aueril"
Reiss, The Art of the Middle English Lyric, pp. 58-65.

_____. "Christ I"
Earl R. Anderson, "Mary's Role as Eiron in Christ I," JEGP, 70 (April, 1971), 230-240.

Gardner, The Construction of Christian Poetry in Old English, pp. 107-110.

_____. "Christ I," Lyric 4
Earl R. Anderson, "Mary's Role as Eiron in Christ I," JEGP, 70 (April, 1971), 230-234.

_____. "Christ I," Lyric 7
Earl R. Anderson, "Mary's Role as Eiron in Christ I," JEGP, 70 (April, 1971), 234-239.

Isaacs, Structural Principles in Old English Poetry, pp. 93-99.

_____. "Christ I," Lyric 9
Earl R. Anderson, "Mary's Role as Eiron in Christ I," JEGP, 70 (April, 1971), 239-240.

_____. "Christ and Satan"
Spencer Cosmos, "Old English 'Limwaestin' ('Christ and Satan' 129)," N&Q, 22 (May, 1975), 196-198.

Robert Emmett Finnegan, Expl, 31 (Oct., 1972), 10.

Isaacs, Structural Principles in Old English Poetry, pp. 127-144.

_____. "Corpus Christi Carol"
Douglas Gray, Themes and Images in the Medieval English Religious Lyric (London and Boston: Routledge & Kegan Paul, 1972), pp. 164-167.

_____. "Crabbed Age and Youth"
Edward F. Nolan, Expl, 30 (May, 1972), 76.

_____. "Cristes Milde Moder, Seynte Marie" ("On God Ureisun of Ure Lefde")
Manning, Wisdom and Number, pp. 94-96.

_____. "Crist Makith to Man a Fair Present"
Manning, Wisdom and Number, pp. 27, 146-150.

_____. "Dame Sirith and the Weeping Bitch"
Nicolai Von Kreisler, "Satire in Dame Sirith and the Weeping Bitch," in Essays in Honor of Esmond Linworth Marilla, pp. 379-387.

_____. "Daniel"
Isaacs, Structural Principles in Old English Poetry, pp. 145-151.

_____. "The Death of Edgar"
Isaacs, Structural Principles in Old English Poetry, pp. 89-93.

_____. "De Clerico et Puella"
Patricia Abel, "The Cleric, the Kitchie Boy, and the Returned Sailor," PQ, 44 (Oct., 1965), 552-555.

Moore, The Secular Lyric in Middle English, pp. 70-72.

_____. "Deor"
James L. Boren, "The Design of the Old English Deor," in Anglo-Saxon Poetry, pp. 264-276.

Isaacs, Structural Principles in Old English Poetry, pp. 107-114.

K. S. Kiernan, "A Solution to the Maedhild-Geat Crux in Deor," ES, 56 (April, 1975), 97-99.

Alvin A. Lee, The Guest-Hall of Eden: Four Essays on the Design of Old English Poetry (New Haven and London: Yale Univ. Press, 1972), pp. 161-168.

Jerome Mandel, "Exemplum and Refrain: The Meaning of Deor," YES, 7 (1977), 1-9.

Murray F. Markland, "Deor:thaes Ofereode; thisses swa maeg," AN&Q, 11 (Nov., 1972), 35-36.

T. A. Shippey, Old English Verse (London: Hutchinson Univ. Library, 1972), pp. 75-78.

_____. "The Descent into Hell" ("Harrowing of Hell")
Thomas D. Hill, "Cosmic Stasis and the Birth of Christ: The Old English Descent into Hell, Lines 99-106," JEGP, 71 (July, 1972), 382-389.

_____. "The Dream of the Rood"
Robert B. Burlin, "The Ruthwell Cross, The Dream of the Rood and the Vita Contemplativa," SP, 65 (Jan., 1968), 23-43.

John Canuteson, "The Crucifixion and the Second Coming in The Dream of the Rood," MP, 66 (May, 1969), 293-297.

Robert R. Edwards, "Narrative Technique and Distance in The Dream of the Rood," PLL, 6 (Summer, 1970), 291-301.

Gardner, The Construction of Christian Poetry in Old English, pp. 98-105.

Willem Helder, "The Engel Dryhtnes in The Dream of the Rood," MP, 73 (Nov., 1975), 148-150.

Huppé, The Web of Words, pp. 75-112.

Isaacs, Structural Principles in Old English Poetry, pp. 3-18.

Alvin A. Lee, The Guest-Hall of Eden: Four Essays on the Design of Old English Poetry (New Haven and London: Yale Univ. Press, 1972), pp. 60-64.

Alvin A. Lee, "Toward a Critique of The Dream of the Rood," in Anglo-Saxon Poetry, pp. 163-191.

Faith H. Patten, "Structure and Meaning in The Dream of the Rood," ES, 49 (Oct., 1968), 385-401.

Richard C. Payne, "Convention and Originality in the Vision Framework of The Dream of the Rood," MP, 73 (May, 1976), 329-341.

Derek Pearsall, Old English and Middle English Poetry, The Routledge History of English Poetry, No. 1 (London: Routledge & Kegan Paul, 1977), pp. 46-48.

Barbara C. Raw, The Art and Background of Old English Poetry (London: Edward Arnold Ltd., 1978), pp. 127-132.

Raymond P. Tripp, Jr., "The Dream of the Rood: 9b and its Context," MP, 69 (Nov., 1971), 136-137.

F. H. Whitman, Expl, 33 (May, 1975), 70.

_____. "Edi Beo thu, Heuene Quene"
Manning, Wisdom and Number, pp. 97-100.

William Elford Rogers, Image and Abstraction: Six Middle English Religious Lyrics (Copenhagen: Rosenkilde and Bagger, 1972), pp. 41-51.

_____. "Edward"
Abad, A Formal Approach to Lyric Poetry, pp. 75-76; 77-78.

Beaty and Matchett, Poetry: From Statement to Meaning, pp. 145-149.

Brooks, Purser, and Warren, An Approach to Literature, pp. 435-437.
   Rpt. third edition, pp. 288-290.
   Rpt. fourth edition, pp. 290-292.

Daniels, The Art of Reading Poetry, pp. 151-154.

Arthur K. Moore, "The Literary Status of the English Popular Ballad," CL, 10 (Winter, 1958), 16.

_____. "Erthe toc of erthe"
Reiss, The Art of the Middle English Lyric, pp. 50-56.

_____. Exeter Riddle 1 "Storm" ("Hwylc is Haeleth a thaes Horsc")
Gardner, The Construction of Christian Poetry in Old English, pp. 42-44.

_____.   Exeter Riddle 2 "Storm" ("Hwilum Ic Gewite")
Gardner, The Construction of Christian Poetry in Old English, pp. 44-49.

_____.   Exeter Riddle 3 "Storm" ("Hwilum Mec Min Frea")
John F. Adams, "The Anglo-Saxon Riddle as Lyric Mode," Criticism, 7 (Fall, 1965), 345-347.

Gardner, The Construction of Christian Poetry in Old English, pp. 44-49.

Marie Nelson, "Time in the Exeter Book Riddles," PQ, 54 (Spring, 1975), 512-513.

_____.   Exeter Riddle 5 "Shield" ("Ic Eom Anhaga Iserne Wund")
Marie Nelson, "Time in the Exeter Book Riddles," PQ, 54 (Spring, 1975), 514-515.

_____.   Exeter Riddle 7 "The Swan" ("Hraegl Min Swigath")
John F. Adams, "The Anglo-Saxon Riddle as Lyric Mode," Criticism, 7 (Fall, 1965), 343-345.

_____.   Exeter Riddle 16 "The Anchor" ("Oft Ic Sceal With Waege Winnan")
John F. Adams, "The Anglo-Saxon Riddle as Lyric Mode," Criticism, 7 (Fall, 1965), 342-343.

_____.   Exeter Riddle 20 "Sword" ("Ic Eom Wunderlicu Wiht, on Gewin Scaepen")
Donald Kay, "Riddle 20: A Revaluation," TSL, 13 (1968), 133-138.

_____.   Exeter Riddle 25 "Onion" ("Ic Eom Wunderlicu Wiht, Wifum of Hyte")
Gardner, The Construction of Christian Poetry in Old English, pp. 41-42.

_____.   Exeter Riddle 39 ("Gewritu Secgath thaet Seo Wiht Sy")
Christopher B. Kennedy, "Old English Riddle No. 39," ELN, 13 (Dec., 1975), 81-85.

_____.   Exeter Riddle 45 "Dough" ("Ic on Wincle Gefraegn")
Edith Whitehurst Williams, "What's so New About the Sexual Revolution?" TQ, 18 (Summer, 1975), 49-50.

_____.   Exeter Riddle 47 "Book Moth" or "Bookworm" ("Mothe Word Fraet")
John F. Adams, "The Anglo-Saxon Riddle as Lyric Mode," Criticism, 7 (Fall, 1965), 337-340.

Fred C. Robinson, "Artful Ambiguities in the Old English 'Book-Moth' Riddle," in Anglo-Saxon Poetry, pp. 355-362.

Ann Harteman Stewart, "Old English Riddle 47 as Stylistic Parody," PLL, 11 (Summer, 1975), 227-241.

_____.   Exeter Riddle 60 ("Ic Waes Be Sonde")
Margaret E. Goldsmith, "The Enigma of The Husband's Message," in Anglo-Saxon Poetry, pp. 242-246.

F. H. Whitman, "Riddle 60 and Its Source," PQ, 40 (Jan., 1971), 108-115.

_____.   Exeter Riddle 61 ("Oft Mec Faeste Bileac")
Edith Whitehurst Williams, "What's so New About the Sexual Revolution?" TQ, 18 (Summer, 1975), 50-51.

_____.   Exeter Riddle 72 "Ox" ("Ic Waes Lytel")
Marie Nelson, "Time in the Exeter Book Riddles," PQ, 54 (Spring, 1975), 513-514.

_____. Exeter Riddle 74 ("Ic Waes Faemne Geong")
K. S. Kiernan, "The Mysteries of the Sea-eagle in Exeter Riddle 74," PQ, 54 (Spring, 1975), 518-522.

_____. Exeter Riddle 75 ("Ic Swiftne Geseah")
Thomas A. Reisner, Expl, 28 (May, 1970), 78.

_____. Exeter Riddle 85 "Fish and River" ("Nis Min Sele Swige")
John F. Adams, "The Anglo-Saxon Riddle as Lyric Mode," Criticism, 7 (Fall, 1965), 340-341.

_____. Exeter Riddle 91 ("Min Heafod Is...")
Edith Whitehurst Williams, "What's so New About the Sexual Revolution?" TQ, 18 (Summer, 1975), 51-54.

_____. Exeter Riddle 95 ("Ic Eom Indryhten")
K. S. Kiernan, "Cwene: The Old Profession of Exeter Riddle 95," MP, 72 (May, 1975), 384-389.

_____. "Exodus"
Isaacs, Structural Principles in Old English Poetry, pp. 151-159.

_____. "For Ou that Is So Feir ant Brist"
Manning, Wisdom and Number, pp. 126-132, 172.

_____. "The Fortunes of Men"
Barbara C. Raw, The Art and Background of Old English Poetry (London: Edward Arnold, 1978), pp. 73-74.

_____. "Fowles in the Frith"
Howell D. Chickering, Jr., "'Foweles in the frith': A Religious Art-Song," PQ, 50 (Jan., 1971), 115-120.

Daiches, A Study of Literature, pp. 151-152.

David Luisi, Expl, 25 (Feb., 1967), 47.

Edmund Reiss, "A Critical Approach to the Middle English Lyrics," CE, 27 (Feb., 1966), 376-377.

Reiss, The Art of the Middle English Lyric, pp. 18-22.

_____. "Frankie and Johnny"
Brooks, Purser, and Warren, An Approach to Literature, pp. 431-432.
    Rpt. third edition, pp. 285-286.
    Rpt. fourth edition, pp. 287-288.

_____. "Gabriel, Fram Evene-King"
Weber, Theology and Poetry in the Middle English Lyric, pp. 32-46.

_____. "Genesis B"
Michael D. Cherniss, Ingeld and Christ: Heroic Concepts and Values in Old English Christian Poetry (The Hague and Paris: Mouton, 1972), pp. 151-170.

Robert Emmett Finnegan, "Eve and 'Vincible Ignorance' in Genesis B," TSLL, 18 (Summer, 1976), 329-39.

Thomas D. Hill, "The Fall of Angels and Man in the Old English Genesis B," in Anglo-Saxon Poetry, pp. 279-290.

Eric Smith, Some Versions of the Fall: The Myth of the Fall of Man in English Literature (Pittsburgh, Pennsylvania: Univ. of Pittsburgh, 1973), pp. 69-91.

_____. "The Gifts of Men"
Barbara C. Raw, <u>The Art and Background of Old English Poetry</u> (London: Edward Arnold, Ltd., 1978), pp. 69-73.

Douglas D. Short, "The Old English 'Gifts of Men,' Line 13," <u>MP</u>, 71 (May, 1974), 388-89.

_____. "Glade Us Maiden, Moder Milde"
Weber, <u>Theology and Poetry in the Middle English Lyric</u>, pp. 156-164.

_____. "Gold and Al This Werdis Wyn"
Reiss, <u>The Art of the Middle English Lyric</u>, pp. 132-136.

_____. "Goosey-Goosey-Gander"
Robert Graves, "Mother Goose's Lost Goslings," <u>HudR</u>, 4 (Winter, 1951), 590-591.

_____. "The Grand Old Duke of York"
Robert Graves, "Mother Goose's Lost Goslings," <u>HudR</u>, 4 (Winter, 1951), 587.

_____. "The Grave"
Alvin A. Lee, <u>The Guest-Hall of Eden: Four Essays on the Design of Old English Poetry</u> (New Haven and London: Yale Univ. Press, 1972), pp. 153-155.

_____. "Haile Be Thu, Mari, Maiden Bright"
Manning, <u>Wisdom and Number</u>, pp. 75-77.

_____. "He Bare Him Vp, He Bare Hym Down"
Manning, <u>Wisdom and Number</u>, pp. 115-118.

_____. "Herodes, Thou Wikked Fo"
Manning, <u>Wisdom and Number</u>, pp. 118-120; 132.

_____. "He Yaf Himself as Good Felowe"
Manning, <u>Wisdom and Number</u>, pp. 121-122.

_____. "Heyl Be Thou, Marie, Milde Quene of Hevene"
Weber, <u>Theology and Poetry in the Middle English Lyric</u>, pp. 182-186.

_____. "He3e Louerd, Thou Here My Bone"
Manning, <u>Wisdom and Number</u>, pp. 51-55.

_____. "Homiletic Fragment I" (<u>Vercelli Book</u>)
Isaacs, <u>Structural Principles in Old English Poetry</u>, pp. 99-106.

_____. "The Hunting of the Cheviot"
Douglas Hamer, "Towards Restoring <u>The Hunting of the Cheviot</u>," <u>RES</u>, 20 (Feb., 1969), 1-21.

_____. "The Husband's Message"
Earl R. Anderson, "<u>The Husband's Message</u>: Persuasion and the Problem of <u>Genyre</u>," <u>ES</u>, 56 (Aug., 1975), 289-94.

Gardner, <u>The Construction of Christian Poetry in Old English</u>, p. 52.

Margaret E. Goldsmith, "The Enigma of <u>The Husband's Message</u>," in <u>Anglo-Saxon Poetry</u>, pp. 247-263.

Stanley B. Greenfield, <u>The Interpretation of Old English Poems</u> (London and Boston: Routledge & Kegan Paul, 1972), pp. 145-154.

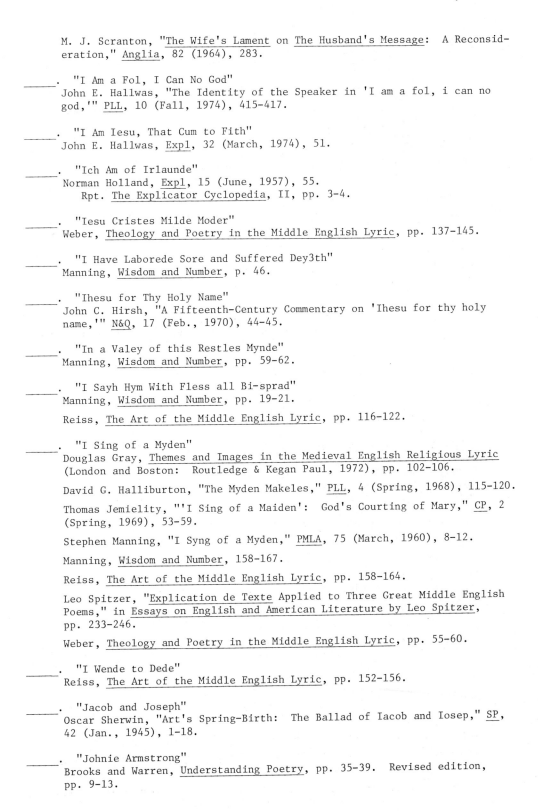

M. J. Scranton, "The Wife's Lament on The Husband's Message: A Reconsideration," Anglia, 82 (1964), 283.

_____. "I Am a Fol, I Can No God"
John E. Hallwas, "The Identity of the Speaker in 'I am a fol, i can no god,'" PLL, 10 (Fall, 1974), 415-417.

_____. "I Am Iesu, That Cum to Fith"
John E. Hallwas, Expl, 32 (March, 1974), 51.

_____. "Ich Am of Irlaunde"
Norman Holland, Expl, 15 (June, 1957), 55.
   Rpt. The Explicator Cyclopedia, II, pp. 3-4.

_____. "Iesu Cristes Milde Moder"
Weber, Theology and Poetry in the Middle English Lyric, pp. 137-145.

_____. "I Have Laborede Sore and Suffered Dey3th"
Manning, Wisdom and Number, p. 46.

_____. "Ihesu for Thy Holy Name"
John C. Hirsh, "A Fifteenth-Century Commentary on 'Ihesu for thy holy name,'" N&Q, 17 (Feb., 1970), 44-45.

_____. "In a Valey of this Restles Mynde"
Manning, Wisdom and Number, pp. 59-62.

_____. "I Sayh Hym With Fless all Bi-sprad"
Manning, Wisdom and Number, pp. 19-21.
Reiss, The Art of the Middle English Lyric, pp. 116-122.

_____. "I Sing of a Myden"
Douglas Gray, Themes and Images in the Medieval English Religious Lyric (London and Boston: Routledge & Kegan Paul, 1972), pp. 102-106.

David G. Halliburton, "The Myden Makeles," PLL, 4 (Spring, 1968), 115-120.

Thomas Jemielity, "'I Sing of a Maiden': God's Courting of Mary," CP, 2 (Spring, 1969), 53-59.

Stephen Manning, "I Syng of a Myden," PMLA, 75 (March, 1960), 8-12.

Manning, Wisdom and Number, 158-167.

Reiss, The Art of the Middle English Lyric, pp. 158-164.

Leo Spitzer, "Explication de Texte Applied to Three Great Middle English Poems," in Essays on English and American Literature by Leo Spitzer, pp. 233-246.
Weber, Theology and Poetry in the Middle English Lyric, pp. 55-60.

_____. "I Wende to Dede"
Reiss, The Art of the Middle English Lyric, pp. 152-156.

_____. "Jacob and Joseph"
Oscar Sherwin, "Art's Spring-Birth: The Ballad of Iacob and Iosep," SP, 42 (Jan., 1945), 1-18.

_____. "Johnie Armstrong"
Brooks and Warren, Understanding Poetry, pp. 35-39. Revised edition, pp. 9-13.

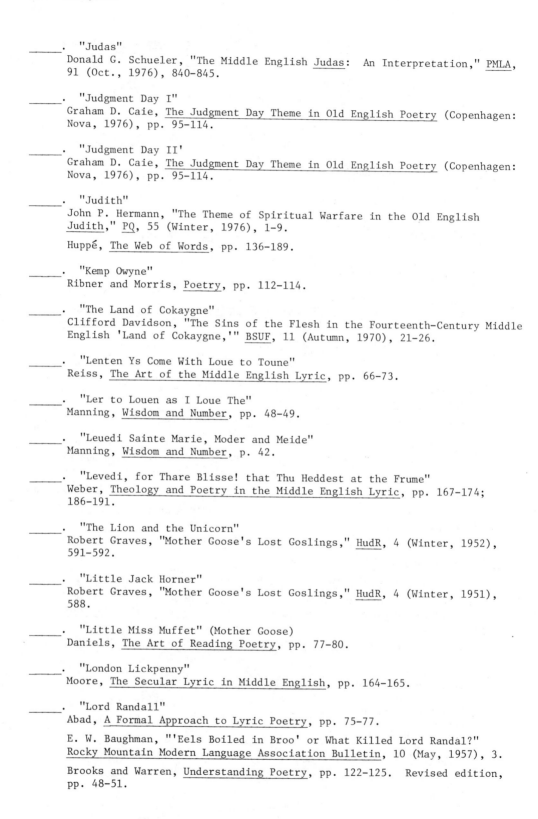

_____. "Judas"
Donald G. Schueler, "The Middle English Judas: An Interpretation," PMLA, 91 (Oct., 1976), 840-845.

_____. "Judgment Day I"
Graham D. Caie, The Judgment Day Theme in Old English Poetry (Copenhagen: Nova, 1976), pp. 95-114.

_____. "Judgment Day II'
Graham D. Caie, The Judgment Day Theme in Old English Poetry (Copenhagen: Nova, 1976), pp. 95-114.

_____. "Judith"
John P. Hermann, "The Theme of Spiritual Warfare in the Old English Judith," PQ, 55 (Winter, 1976), 1-9.

Huppé, The Web of Words, pp. 136-189.

_____. "Kemp Owyne"
Ribner and Morris, Poetry, pp. 112-114.

_____. "The Land of Cokaygne"
Clifford Davidson, "The Sins of the Flesh in the Fourteenth-Century Middle English 'Land of Cokaygne,'" BSUF, 11 (Autumn, 1970), 21-26.

_____. "Lenten Ys Come With Loue to Toune"
Reiss, The Art of the Middle English Lyric, pp. 66-73.

_____. "Ler to Louen as I Loue The"
Manning, Wisdom and Number, pp. 48-49.

_____. "Leuedi Sainte Marie, Moder and Meide"
Manning, Wisdom and Number, p. 42.

_____. "Levedi, for Thare Blisse! that Thu Heddest at the Frume"
Weber, Theology and Poetry in the Middle English Lyric, pp. 167-174; 186-191.

_____. "The Lion and the Unicorn"
Robert Graves, "Mother Goose's Lost Goslings," HudR, 4 (Winter, 1952), 591-592.

_____. "Little Jack Horner"
Robert Graves, "Mother Goose's Lost Goslings," HudR, 4 (Winter, 1951), 588.

_____. "Little Miss Muffet" (Mother Goose)
Daniels, The Art of Reading Poetry, pp. 77-80.

_____. "London Lickpenny"
Moore, The Secular Lyric in Middle English, pp. 164-165.

_____. "Lord Randall"
Abad, A Formal Approach to Lyric Poetry, pp. 75-77.

E. W. Baughman, "'Eels Boiled in Broo' or What Killed Lord Randal?" Rocky Mountain Modern Language Association Bulletin, 10 (May, 1957), 3.

Brooks and Warren, Understanding Poetry, pp. 122-125. Revised edition, pp. 48-51.

Arthur K. Moore, "The Literary Status of the English Popular Ballad," CL, 10 (Winter, 1958), 16.

_____. "Louerd Thu Clepedest Me"
Manning, Wisdom and Number, pp. 36-38.

_____. "Lovely Tear from Lovely Eye" (or "Thu Sikest Sore")
John E. Hallwas, "Thu Sikest Sore," Expl, 35 (Spring, 1977), 12-13.

_____. "Luf Es Lyf that Lastes Ay"
Manning, Wisdom and Number, pp. 58-59.

_____. "Maiden of the Moor"
Jane L. Curry, "Waking the Well," ELN, 2 (Sept., 1964), 1-4.
Richard Leighton Greene, "Troubling the Well-Waters," ELN, 4 (Sept., 1967), 4-6.

_____. "Maiden in the mor lay"
Reiss, The Art of the Middle English Lyric, pp. 98-106.

_____. "Man in the Moon"
Moore, The Secular Lyric in Middle English, pp. 95-97.

William Elford Rogers, Image and Abstraction: Six Middle English Religious Lyrics (Copenhagen: Rosenkilde and Bagger, 1972), pp. 52-68.

_____. "Maxims I"
Barbara C. Raw, The Art and Background of Old English Poetry (London: Edward Arnold Ltd., 1978), pp. 75-80.

_____. "Maxims II"
Stanley B. Greenfield and Richard Evert, "Maxims II: Gnome and Poem," in Anglo-Saxon Poetry, pp. 337-354.

_____. "Methingkit"
John C. Hirsh, Expl, 35 (Spring, 1977), 11.

_____. "Metrical Epilogue to the Pastoral Care"
Isaacs, Structural Principles in Old English Poetry, pp. 83-89.

_____. "Middelerd for Mon Wes Mad"
Ralph Hanna, "A Note on a Harley Lyric," ELN, 7 (June, 1970), 243-246.
Celia Townsend Wells, "Line 21 of 'Middelerd for Mon Wes Mad,'" ELN, 10 (March, 1973), 167-169.

_____. "The Milde Lomb Isprad o Rode"
Weber, Theology and Poetry in the Middle English Lyric, pp. 94-109.

_____. "Mirie It Is While Sumer Ilast"
David L. Jeffrey, The Early English Lyric & Franciscan Spirituality (Lincoln: Univ. of Nebraska Press, 1975), pp. 12-15.
Reiss, The Art of the Middle English Lyric, pp. 2-6.

_____. "Naueth My Saule Bute Fur and Ys"
Reiss, The Art of the Middle English Lyric, pp. 24-28.

_____. "Nou Goth Sonne Under Wod"
John L. Cutler, Expl, 4 (Oct., 1945), 7.
    Rpt. Readings for Liberal Education, II, 506-507.
    Rpt. The Explicator Cyclopedia, II, pp. 4-5.

Stephen Manning, "Nou Goth Sonne under Wod," MLN, 74 (Nov., 1959), 578-581.

Manning, Wisdom and Number, pp. 80-84.

Edmund Reiss, "A Critical Approach to the Middle English Lyrics," CE, 27
(Feb., 1966), 375-376.

Reiss, The Art of the Middle English Lyric, pp. 14-17.

C. G. Thayer, Expl, 11 (Feb., 1953), 25.
    Rpt. The Explicator Cyclopedia, II, pp. 5-6.

_____. "Nou Sprinketh Rose ant Lylie Flour"
Manning, Wisdom and Number, pp. 100-105.

_____. "Nou Sprinkes the Sprai"
Reiss, The Art of the Middle English Lyric, pp. 44-49.

_____. "Nutbrowne Mayde"
Moore, The Secular Lyric in Middle English, pp. 182-188.

_____. "Nu this Fules Singet Hand Maket Hure Blisse"
Weber, Theology and Poetry in the Middle English Lyric, pp. 48-55.

_____. "Ny Yh She Blostme Sprynge"
Manning, Wisdom and Number, pp. 22-23.

_____. "Of a Rose, A Lovely Rose"
Leo Spitzer, "Explication de Texte Applied to Three Great Middle English
Poems," in Essays on English and American Literature by Leo Spitzer,
pp. 216-233.

_____. "On the Author"
Leo Miller, Expl, 29 (Feb., 1971), 52.

_____. "The Order of the World"
Isaacs, Structural Principles in Old English Poetry, pp. 71-82.

_____. "O Western Wind"
Abad, A Formal Approach to Lyric Poetry, pp. 363-364.

_____. "The Parlement of the Three Ages"
John Speirs, "'Wynnere and Wastoure' and 'The Parlement of the Three
Ages,'" Scrutiny, 17 (Autumn, 1950), 221-252.

_____. "The Passionate Man's Pilgrimage"
Philip Edwards, "Who Wrote The Passionate Man's Pilgrimage?" ELR, 4
(Winter, 1974), 83-97.

_____. "Patience"
Malcolm Andrew, "Patience: The 'Munster Dor,'" ELN, 14 (March, 1977),
164-167.

F. N. M. Diekstra, "Jonah and Patience: The Psychology of a Prophet,"
ES, 55 (June, 1974), 205-217.

Charles Moorman, "The Role of the Narrator in 'Patience,'" MP, 61 (Nov.,
1963), 90-95.

Jay Schleusener, "History and Action in Patience," PMLA, 86 (Oct., 1971), 959-965.

David Williams, "The Point of Patience," MP, 68 (Nov., 1970), pp. 127-136.

_____. "Praise the Lord, Ye Heavens Adore Him"
Sr. M. Pauline Parker, "The Hymn as a Literary Form," ECS, 8 (Summer, 1975), 401-403; 407.

_____. "Quanne Hic Se on Rode"
Reiss, The Art of the Middle English Lyric, pp. 30-36.

_____. "Resignation"
Alvin A. Lee, The Guest-Hall of Eden: Four Essays on the Design of Old English Poetry (New Haven and London: Yale Univ. Press, 1972), pp. 147-149.

Barbara C. Raw, The Art and Background of Old English Poetry (London: Edward Arnold Ltd., 1978), pp. 126-127.

_____. "The Rhyming Poem"
Isaacs, Structural Principles in Old English Poetry, pp. 56-70.
John P. Hermann, Expl, 34 (Sept., 1975), 4.

Ruth P. M. Lehmann, "The Old English Riming Poem: Interpretation, Text, and Translation," JEGP, 69 (July, 1970), 437-449.

_____. "The Ruin"
James F. Doubleday, "The Ruin: Structure and Theme," JEGP, 71 (July, 1972), 369-381.

_____. "St. Erkenwald"
Vincent F. Petronella, "St. Erkenwald: Style as the Vehicle for Meaning," JEGP, 66 (Oct., 1967), 532-540.

_____. "Satire Against the Blacksmiths"
Moore, The Secular Lyric in Middle English, pp. 98-99.

_____. "The Seafarer"
Roberta Bux Bosse, "Aural Aesthetic and the Unity of The Seafarer," PLL, 9 (Winter, 1973), 3-14.

Michael D. Cherniss, Ingeld and Christ: Heroic Concepts and Values in Old English Christian Poetry (The Hague and Paris: Mouton, 1972), pp. 208-217.

W. A. Davenport, "The Modern Reader and the Old English Seafarer," PLL, 10 (Summer, 1974), 227-240.

I. L. Gordon, "Traditional Themes in The Wanderer and The Seafarer," RES, 5 n.s. (Jan., 1954), 1-13.

Martin Green, "Man, Time, and Apocalypse in The Wanderer, The Seafarer, and Beowulf," JEGP, 75 (Oct., 1975), 506-512.

Joyce M. Hill, "'This Deade Lif': A Note on The Seafarer, Lines 64-66," ELN, 15 (Dec., 1977), 95-97.

Isaacs, Structural Principles in Old English Poetry, pp. 19-34.

W. F. Klein, "Purpose and the 'Poetics' of The Wanderer and The Seafarer," in Anglo-Saxon Poetry, pp. 218-223.

Alvin A. Lee, The Guest-Hall of Eden: Four Essays on the Design of Old English Poetry (New Haven and London: Yale Univ. Press, 1972), pp. 143-146.

Bruce Moore, "Author Unknown: 'The Seafarer,' 11. 1-8a," Expl, 35 (Fall, 1976), 11-12.

T. A. Shippey, Old English Verse (London: Hutchinson Univ. Library, 1972), pp. 68-71.

Kenneth Sisam, "Seafarer, Lines 97-102," RES, 21 (Oct., 1945), 316-317.

Raymond P. Tripp, Jr., "The Narrator as Revenant: A Reconsideration of Three Old English Elegies," PLL, 8 (Fall, 1972), 352-356.

Phyllis Gage Whittier, "Spring in 'The Seafarer' 48-50," N&Q, 15 (Nov., 1968), 407-409.

Rosemary Woolf, "The Wanderer, The Seafarer and the Genre of Planctus," in Anglo-Saxon Poetry, pp. 202-206.

_____. "The Search for the Lost Husband"
Robert P. Fitgerald, "'The Wife's Lament' and 'The Search for the Lost Husband,'" JEGP, 62 (Oct., 1963), 769-777.

_____. "Shoot False Love I Care Not"
MacDonald Emslie, Expl, 13 (May, 1955), 44.
    Rpt. The Explicator Cyclopedia, II, pp. 7-8.

_____. "Sir Orfeo"
Francis P. Carpinelli, Expl, 19 (Nov., 1960), 13.
    Rpt. The Explicator Cyclopedia, II, pp. 9-10.

A. S. G. Edwards, Expl, 29 (Jan., 1971), 43.

_____. "Sir Patrick Spens"
Abad, A Formal Approach to Lyric Poetry, pp. 106-107.

Adams, The Contexts of Poetry, pp. 23-28.

Brooks, Purser, and Warren, An Approach to Literature, pp. 429-431.
    Rpt. third edition, pp. 283-284.
    Rpt. fourth edition, pp. 285-286.

Daniels, The Art of Reading Poetry, pp. 137-141.

Frankenberg, Invitation to Poetry, pp. 112-113.

Louis L. Martz, "The Teaching of Poetry," in Essays on the Teaching of English, pp. 254-255.

William H. Matchett, "The Integrity of 'Sir Patrick Spence,'" MP, 68 (Aug., 1970), 25-31.

Arthur K. Moore, "The Literary Status of the English Popular Ballad," CL, 10 (Winter, 1958), 11-13.

Van Doren, Introduction to Poetry, pp. 127-129.
    Rpt. Locke, Gibson, and Arms, Introduction to Literature, third edition, pp. 6-8.
    Rpt. fourth edition, pp. 8-10.
    Rpt. fifth edition, pp. 8-10.

Wheeler, The Design of Poetry, pp. 280-282; 283-287.

_____. "Sodenly Afraide/Half-waking, Half-slepyng"
Reiss, The Art of the Middle English Lyric, pp. 144-150.

_____. "Some is Commen Winter Gon"
Manning, Wisdom and Number, pp. 114-115.

_____. "Song of the Husbandman"
Moore, The Secular Lyric in Middle English, pp. 85-87.

_____. "Stod Ho There Neh"
Manning, Wisdom and Number, pp. 150-154.

_____. "Stond Wel, Moder, Vnder Rode"
Manning, Wisdom and Number, pp. 77-80.

Weber, Theology and Poetry in the Middle English Lyric, pp. 125-145.

_____. "Suete Sone, Reu on Me, & Brest Out of Thi Bondis"
Weber, Theology and Poetry in the Middle English Lyric, pp. 117-121.

_____. "Summer Is Icumen In"
Huntington Brown, Expl, 3 (Feb., 1945), 34.
        Rpt. The Explicator Cyclopedia, II, pp. 11-12.

Jeffrey A. Helterman, "The Antagonistic Voices of 'Sumer Is Icumen In,'"
TSL, 18 (1973), 13-17.

Theodore C. Hoepfner, Expl, 3 (Dec., 1944), 18, and 3 (June, 1945), 59.
        Rpt. The Explicator Cyclopedia, II, pp. 10-11.
        Rpt. The Explicator Cyclopedia, II, p. 12.

John S. Kenyon, Expl, 3 (March, 1945), 40.
        Rpt. The Explicator Cyclopedia, II, p. 12.

Stephen Manning, Expl, 18 (Oct., 1959), 2.
        Rpt. The Explicator Cyclopedia, II, pp. 12-13.

Moore, The Secular Lyric in Middle English, pp. 50-52.

Reiss, The Art of the Middle English Lyric, pp. 8-12.

Ribner and Morris, Poetry, pp. 35-36.

_____. "Swarte-Smekyd Smethes, Smateryd wyth Smoke"
Reiss, The Art of the Middle English Lyric, pp. 166-170.

_____. "Tam Lin"
John D. Niles, "Tam Lin: Form and Meaning in a Traditional Ballad," MLQ,
38 (Dec., 1977), 336-347.

_____. "That Lovely Lady Sat and Song"
Manning, Wisdom and Number, pp. 49-50.

_____. "Ther Is No Rose of Swych Vertu"
Douglas Gray, Themes and Images in the Medieval English Religious Lyric
(London and Boston: Routledge & Kegan Paul, 1972), pp. 88-89.

Manning, Wisdom and Number, pp. 155-158.

_____. "Thirty Days Hath September"
Theodore Spencer, "How to Criticize a Poem," The New Republic, 109 (Dec.
6, 1943), 816-817.
        Rpt. Readings for Liberal Education, II, 340-342.
        Rpt. Stallman and Watters, The Creative Reader, pp. 847-849.

_____. "Thomas Rymer"
Daniels, The Art of Reading Poetry, pp. 144–147.

_____. "The Three Ravens"
Brooks and Warren, Understanding Poetry, pp. 118–122. Revised edition, pp. 45–48.

Daniels, The Art of Reading Poetry, pp. 133–137.
   Rpt. Readings for Liberal Education, II, 363–366.

Tyrus Hillway, Expl, 5 (March, 1947), 36.
   Rpt. The Explicator Cyclopedia, II, p. 14.

Seymour Lainoff, Expl, 17 (May, 1959), 55.
   Rpt. The Explicator Cyclopedia, II, pp. 14–15.

Louis G. Locke, Expl, 4 (June, 1946), 54.
   Rpt. The Explicator Cyclopedia, II, pp. 13–14.

Rosenthal and Smith, Exploring Poetry, pp. 311–314.

_____. "The Twa Corbies"
Abad, A Formal Approach to Lyric Poetry, pp. 347–349.

Daniels, The Art of Reading Poetry, pp. 133–137.
   Rpt. Readings for Liberal Education, II, 363–366.

Bert Case Diltz, Sense or Nonsense: Contemporary Education at the Cross-roads (Toronto: McClelland and Stewart Ltd., 1972), pp. 63–69.

Drew, Poetry: A Modern Guide, pp. 93–94.

Arthur K. Moore, "The Literary Status of the English Popular Ballad," CL, 10 (Winter, 1958), 15–16.

_____. "Vndo Thi Dore, My Spuse Dere"
Manning, Wisdom and Number, pp. 125–126.

Reiss, The Art of the Middle English Lyric, pp. 124–130.

_____. "Vainglory"
Huppé, The Web of Words, pp. 8–26.

_____. "The Wanderer"
Robert O. Bowen, Expl, 13 (Feb., 1955), 26.
   Rpt. The Explicator Cyclopedia, II, pp. 15–16.

I. L. Gordon, "Traditional Themes in The Wanderer and The Seafarer," RES, 5 n.s. (Jan., 1954), 1–13.

Martin Green, "Man, Time, and Apocalypse in The Wanderer, The Seafarer, and Beowulf," JEGP, 74 (Oct., 1975), 506–512.

Stanley B. Greenfield, "The Wanderer: A Reconsideration of Theme and Structure," JEGP, 1 (Oct., 1951), 451–465.

B. F. Huppé, "The Wanderer: Theme and Structure," JEGP, 42 (Oct., 1943), 516–538.

Isaacs, Structural Principles in Old English Poetry, pp. 35–55.

W. F. Klein, "Purpose and the 'Poetics' of The Wanderer and The Seafarer," in Anglo-Saxon Poetry, pp. 212–218.

Alvin A. Lee, The Guest-Hall of Eden: Four Essays on the Design of Old English Poetry (New Haven and London: Yale Univ. Press, 1972), pp. 136–143.

Tony Millns, "The Wanderer 98: 'Weal Wundrum Heah Wyrmlicum fah,'" RES, 28 (Nov., 1977), 431-438.

Barbara C. Raw, The Art and Background of Old English Poetry (London: Edward Arnold Ltd., 1978), pp. 66-68.

D. W. Robertson, Jr., "Historical Criticism," English Institute Essays, 1950, pp. 18-22.

Mary Rohrberger, "A Psychoanalytical Reading of 'The Wanderer,'" CimR, 2 (Dec., 1967), 70-74.

James L. Rosier, "The Literal-Figurative Identity of the Wanderer," PMLA, 79 (Sept., 1964), 366-369.

Thomas C. Rumble, "From Eardstapa to Snotter On Mode: The Structural Principle of 'The Wanderer,'" MLQ, 19 (Sept., 1958), 225-230.

T. A. Shippey, Old English Verse (London: Hutchinson Univ. Library, 1972), pp. 56-60.

Raymond P. Tripp, Jr., "The Narrator as Revenant: A Reconsideration of Three Old English Elegies," PLL, 8 (Fall, 1972), 345-352.

Susie I. Tucker, "Return to The Wanderer," EIC, 8 (July, 1958), 229-237.

Rosemary Woolf, "The Wanderer, The Seafarer, and the Genre of Planctus," in Anglo-Saxon Poetry, pp. 196-202.

_____. "Wanne Mine Eyhnen Misten"
Manning, Wisdom and Number, pp. 15-17.

Reiss, The Art of the Middle English Lyric, pp. 88-92.

_____. "A Wayle Whyte ase Whalles Bon"
Moore, The Secular Lyric in Middle English, pp. 64-65.

_____. "Weep You No More, Sad Fountains"
Laurence Perrine, Expl, 34 (April, 1976), 61.

_____. "WEl, Qwa Sal Thir Hornes Blau"
Edmund Reiss, "A Critical Approach to the Middle English Lyrics," CE, 27 (Feb., 1966), 377-379.
Reiss, The Art of the Middle English Lyric, pp. 94-97.

_____. "Wen the Turuf Is Thi Tuur"
Reiss, The Art of the Middle English Lyric, pp. 83-87.

Ribner and Morris, Poetry, pp. 29-30.

_____. "Western Wind, When Wilt Thou Blow"
Bateson, English Poetry, p. 81.
    Abridged in The Case for Poetry, p. 13.

Brooks and Warren, Understanding Poetry, revised edition, pp. 177-178.

Ciardi, How Does a Poem Mean?, pp. 996-998.

Roberts W. French, "'Western Wind' and the Complexity of Poetry," EJ, 60 (Feb., 1971), 212-214.

Charles Frey, "Interpreting 'Western Wind,'" ELH, 43 (Fall, 1976), 259-78.

Walter Gierasch, Expl, 14 (April, 1956), 43.
    Rpt. The Explicator Cyclopedia, II, p. 6.

Greenfield and Weatherhead, eds., "Introductory Essay: The Experience of a Poem," in The Poem: An Anthology, pp. xxvii-xxxi.

Richard R. Griffith, Expl, 21 (May, 1963), 69.

Nat Henry, Expl, 16 (Oct., 1957), 5.
 Rpt. The Explicator Cyclopedia, II, p. 7.

Arthur O. Lewis, Jr., Expl, 15 (Feb., 1957), 28.
 Rpt. The Explicator Cyclopedia, II, pp. 6-7.

Moore, The Secular Lyric in Middle English, pp. 29-30.

Sanders, The Discovery of Poetry, pp. 163-164.

Douglas D. Short and Porter Williams, Jr., "'Westron Wynde': A Problem in Syntax and Interpretation," PLL, 13 (Spring, 1977), 187-192.

Stauffer, The Nature of Poetry, p. 63.
 Abridged in The Case for Poetry, p. 13.

Patric M. Sweeney, Expl, 14 (Oct., 1955), 6.
 Rpt. The Explicator Cyclopedia, II, p. 6.

Unger and O'Connor, Poems for Study, pp. 12-13.

Walsh, Doors into Poetry, pp. 4, 127.

R. P. Warren, "Pure and Impure Poetry," The Kenyon Review, 5 (Spring, 1943), 233-235.
 Rpt. Criticism, p. 369, and Critiques, pp. 89-90.
 Abridged in The Case for Poetry, p. 13.
 Rpt. West, Essays in Modern Literary Criticism, pp. 250-251.
 Rpt. The Kenyon Critics, pp. 22-24.

_____. "When Thi Hed Whaketh"
Manning, Wisdom and Number, pp. 17-19.

_____. "The Wife's Lament"
Rudolph C. Bambas, "Another View of the Old English Wife's Lament," JEGP, 62 (April, 1963), 303-309.

Thomas M. Davis, "Another View of 'The Wife's Lament,'" PLL, 1 (Fall, 1965), 291-304.

Gareth W. Dunleavy, "Possible Irish Analogues for 'The Wife's Lament,'" PQ, 35 (July, 1956), 211-213.

Robert P. Fitzgerald, "'The Wife's Lament' and 'The Search for the Lost Husband,'" JEGP, 62 (Oct., 1963), 769-777.

Joseph Harris, "A Note on eorthscr aef/eorthsele and Current Interpretations of The Wife's Lament," ES, 58 (June, 1977), 204-208.

P. L. Henry, "The Wife's Lament," in The Early English and Celtic Lyric (London: Unwin, 1967), p. 23.

Lee Ann Johnson, "The Narrative Structure of 'The Wife's Lament,'" ES, 52 (Dec., 1971), 497-501.

William Witherle Lawrence, "The Banished Wife's Lament," MP, 5 (Jan., 1908), 387-405.

Michael D. Patrick, Expl, 28 (Feb., 1970), 50.

Alain Renoir, "A Reading Context for The Wife's Lament," in Anglo-Saxon Poetry, pp. 224-241.

Alain Renoir, "A Reading of The Wife's Lament," ES, 58 (Feb., 1977), 4-19.

Thomas J. Rountree, Expl, 29 (Nov., 1970), 24.

M. J. Scranton, "The Wife's Lament on The Husband's Message: A Reconsideration," Anglia, 82 (1964), 283.

T. A. Shippey, Old English Verse (London: Hutchinson Univ. Library, 1972), pp. 73-75.

Robert D. Stevick, "Formal Aspects of 'The Wife's Lament,'" JEGP, 59 (Jan., 1960), 21-25.

Raymond P. Tripp, Jr., "The Narrator as Revenant: A Reconsideration of Three Old English Elegies," PLL, 8 (Fall, 1972), 356-360.

J. A. Ward, "'The Wife's Lament': An Interpretation," JEGP, 59 (Jan., 1960), 26-33.

_____. "The Wife of Usher's Well"
Abad, A Formal Approach to Lyric Poetry, pp. 108-109.

Brooks and Warren, Understanding Poetry, pp. 42-45. Revised edition, pp. 16-20.

Arthur K. Moore, "The Literary Status of the English Popular Ballad," CL, 10 (Winter, 1958), 13-14.

_____. "The Wind of the Moor"
D. W. Robertson, Jr., "Historical Criticism," English Institute Essays 1950, pp. 26-27.

_____. "With Faerstice"
Minna Doskow, "Poetic Structure and the Problem of the Smiths in 'With Faerstice,'" PLL, 12 (Summer, 1976), 321-326.

_____. "Wonder of Creation"
Huppé, The Web of Words, pp. 34-61.

_____. "Worldes Blisce, Haue God Day"
Reiss, The Art of the Middle English Lyric, pp. 38-42.

_____. "Wulf and Eadwacer"
Norman E. Eliason, "On Wulf and Eadwacer," in Old English Studies in Honour of John C. Pope, ed. Robert B. Burlin and Edward B. Irivng, Jr. (Toronto and Buffalo: Univ. of Toronto Press, 1974), pp. 225-234.

Isaacs, Structural Principles in Old English Poetry, pp. 114-117.

Harry E. Kauros, "A Note on 'Wulf and Eadwacer,'" ELN, 15 (Dec., 1977), 83-84.

Ruth P. M. Lehmann, "The Metrics and Structure of 'Wulf and Eadwacer,'" PQ, 48 (April, 1968), 151-165.

_____. "Wy Have Ye No Reuthe on My Child?"
Weber, Theology and Poetry in the Middle English Lyric, pp. 111-117.

_____. "Wynner and Wastoure"
Jerry D. James, "The Undercutting of Conventions in 'Wynnere and Wastoure,'" MLQ, 25 (Sept., 1964), 243-258.

John Speirs, "'Wynnere and Wastoure' and 'The Parlement of the Three Ages,'" Scrutiny, 17 (Autumn, 1950), 221-252.

_____. "Wynter Wakeneth al My Care"
David L. Jeffrey, The Early English Lyric & Franciscan Spirituality (Lincoln: Univ. of Nebraska Press, 1975), pp. 257-259.

Manning, Wisdom and Number, pp. 105-106; 133.

Lewis H. Miller, Jr., "Two Poems of Winter," CE, 28 (Jan., 1967), 316-317.

Reiss, The Art of the Middle English Lyric, pp. 74-81.

Ann Shannon, "The Meaning of grein in 'Winter wakeneth al my care,'" PQ, 53 (Summer, 1974), 425-427.

_____. "Young Waters"
Hardy, The Curious Frame, pp. 3-21.

ARNOLD. "The Buried Life"
Alice N. Stitelman, "Lyrical Process in Three Poems by Matthew Arnold," VP, 15 (Summer, 1977), 134-139.

David Trotter, "Hidden Ground Within: Matthew Arnold's Lyric and Elegiac Poetry," ELH, 44 (Fall, 1977), 549-552.

_____. "Cromwell"
John M. Wallace, "Landscape and 'The General Law': The Poetry of Matthew Arnold," Boston University Studies in English, 5 (Summer, 1961), 92-93.

_____. "Dover Beach"
Michael C. Andrews, "'Dover Beach': 'Bright Girdle' and 'Naked Shingles,'" CEA, 32 (March, 1970), 15.

Melvin W. Askew, "Form and Process in Lyric Poetry," SR, 62 (April-June, 1964), 293; 295-296.

Cleanth Brooks, "Irony and 'Ironic' Poetry," EJ, 37 (Feb., 1948), 59-60.

William Cadbury, "Coming to Terms with 'Dover Beach,'" Criticism, 8 (Spring, 1966), 126-138.

Chatman, An Introduction to the Language of Poetry, pp. 61-63.

Rodney Delasanta, Expl, 18 (Oct., 1959), 7.
    Rpt. The Explicator Cyclopedia, II, pp. 18-19.

Bert Case Diltz, Sense or Nonsense: Contemporary Education at the Cross-roads (Toronto: McClelland and Stewart Ltd., 1972); pp. 111-112.

Drew, Poetry: A Modern Guide, pp. 221-223.

Gerhard Friedrich, "A Teaching Approach to Poetry," EJ, 49 (Feb., 1960), 79-81.

Ellen S. Gahtan, "'Nor help for pain': Matthew Arnold and Sophocles' Philoctetes," VN, 48 (Fall, 1975), 22-26.

Richard M. Gollin, "'Dover Beach': The Background of Its Imagery," ES, 48 (Dec., 1967), 493-511.

Frederick L. Gwynn, Expl, 8 (April, 1950), 46.
    Rpt. The Explicator Cyclopedia, II, pp. 17-18.

Wendell V. Harris, "Freud, Form, and Fights by Night," VS, 10 (Sept., 1966), 70-76.

James L. Hill, "The Frame for the Mind: Landscape in 'Lines Composed a Few Miles Above Tintern Abbey,' 'Dover Beach,' and 'Sunday Morning,'" CentR, 18 (Winter, 1974), 39-43.

Norman H. Holland, "Freud and Form: Fact about Fiction," VS, 10 (Sept., 1966), 76-82.

Norman H. Holland, "Psychological Depths and 'Dover Beach,'" VS, 9, Supplement (Sept., 1965), 5-28.

Jerome, <u>Poetry: Premeditated Art</u>, pp. 147-153.

Wendell Stacy Johnson, "Matthew Arnold's Dialogue," <u>The University of Kansas City Review</u>, 27 (Winter, 1960), 112-113.

Wendell S. Johnson, "Some Functions of Poetic Form," <u>JAAC</u>, 13 (June, 1955), 501.

James M. Keech, "'Dover Beach' Again," <u>CEA</u>, 35 (Jan., 1973), 35-36.

J. P. Kirby, <u>Expl</u>, 1 (April, 1943), 42.
    Rpt. <u>Readings for Liberal Education</u>, II, 524-525.
    Rpt. <u>The Explicator Cyclopedia</u>, II, p. 16.

Murray Krieger, "'Dover Beach' and the Tragic Sense of Eternal Recurrence," <u>The University of Kansas City Review</u>, 23 (Autumn, 1956), 73-79.
    Rpt. <u>The Play and Place of Criticism</u>, pp. 69-77.

Lois T. Miller, "The Eternal Note of Sadness: An Analysis of Matthew Arnold's 'Dover Beach,'" <u>EJ</u>, 54 (May, 1965), 447-448.

Gene Montague, <u>Expl</u>, 18 (Nov., 1959), 15.
    Rpt. <u>The Explicator Cyclopedia</u>, II, pp. 19-20.

Theodore Morrison, "Dover Beach Revisited: A New Fable for Critics," <u>Harper's</u>, 180 (Feb., 1940), 235-244.
    Rpt. Stallman and Watters, <u>The Creative Reader</u>, pp. 863-873.

Laurence Perrine, "The Poet and the Pulpit," <u>SWR</u>, (Spring, 1974).
    Rpt. <u>The Art of Total Relevance</u>, pp. 141-143.

Ruth Pitman, "On Dover Beach," <u>EIC</u>, 23 (April, 1973), 109-136.

F. A. Pottle, <u>Expl</u>, 2 (April, 1944), 45.
    Rpt. <u>The Explicator Cyclopedia</u>, II, pp. 16-17.

John Racin, "'Dover Beach' and the Structure of Meditation," <u>VP</u>, 8 (Spring, 1970), 49-54.

Kristian Smidt, "The Beaches of Calais and Dover: Arnold's Counterstatement to Wordsworth's Confession of Faith," <u>VP</u>, 14 (Autumn, 1976), 256-257.

Stageberg and Anderson, <u>Poetry as Experience</u>, p. 492.

Norman C. Stageberg, <u>Expl</u>, 9 (March, 1951), 34.

Alice N. Stitelman, "Lyrical Process in Three Poems by Matthew Arnold," <u>VP</u>, 15 (Summer, 1977), 139-142.

William I. Thompson, "Collapsed Universe and Structured Poem: An Essay in Whiteheadian Criticism," <u>CE</u>, 28 (Oct., 1966), 34-35.

William B. Toole, III, "Arnold's 'Dover Beach,'" <u>CEA</u>, 30 (June, 1968), 8-9.

_____. "A Dream"
John M. Wallace, "Landscape and 'The General Law': The Poetry of Matthew Arnold," <u>Boston University Studies in English</u>, 5 (Summer, 1961), 104-105.

_____. "Empedocles on Etna"
Allan Brick, "Equilibrium in the Poetry of Matthew Arnold," <u>UTQ</u>, 30 (Oct., 1960), 53-55.

F. L. Burwich, "Hölderlin and Arnold: 'Empedocles on Etna,'" <u>CL</u>, 17 (Winter, 1965), 24-42.

Barbara T. Gates, "Arnold's <u>Empedocles</u> and the <u>Book of Common Prayer</u>," <u>Renascence</u>, 28 (Summer, 1976), 215-222.

Donald J. Gray, "Arthur, Roland, Empedocles, Sigurd, and the Despair of Heroes in Victorian Poetry," Boston University Studies in English, 5 (Spring, 1961), 10-13.

Kaplan, Miracles of Rare Device, pp. 124-142.

Kermode, Romantic Image, pp. 12-19.

Albert J. Lubell, "Matthew Arnold: Between Two Worlds," MLQ, 22 (Sept., 1961), 248-263.

Linda Lee Ray, "Callicles on Etna: The Other Mask," VP, 7 (Winter, 1969), 309-320.

Meredith B. Raymond, "Apollo and Arnold's 'Empedocles on Etna,'" A Review of English Literature, 8 (July, 1967), 22-32.

John M. Wallace, "Landscape and 'The General Law': The Poetry of Matthew Arnold," Boston University Studies in English, 5 (Summer, 1961), 98-99.

_____. "A Farewell"
Ball, The Heart's Events, pp. 42-44.

_____. "The Forsaken Merman"
Howard W. Fulweiler, "Matthew Arnold: The Metamorphosis of a Merman," VP, 1 (Autumn, 1963), 208-221.

Wendell Stacy Johnson, "Matthew Arnold's Dialogue," The University of Kansas City Review, 27 (Winter, 1960), 112.

_____. "Fragment of an 'Antigone'"
John M. Wallace, "Landscape and 'The General Law': The Poetry of Matthew Arnold," Boston University Studies in English, 5 (Summer, 1961), 95.

_____. "The Future"
John M. Wallace, "Landscape and 'The General Law': The Poetry of Matthew Arnold," Boston University Studies in English, 5 (Summer, 1961), 102-103.

_____. "Haworth Churchyard"
Marjorie Perloff, "Yeats and the Occasional Poem: 'Easter 1916,'" PLL, 4 (Summer, 1968), 314-320.

_____. "Human Life"
George Forbes, "Arnold's 'Oracles,'" EIC, 23 (Jan., 1973), 52-53.

_____. "In Harmony with Nature"
Albert Van Aver, "Disharmony in Arnold's 'In Harmony with Nature,'" The Personalist, 48 (Autumn, 1967), 573-578.

_____. "In Utrumque Paratus"
George Forbes, "Arnold's 'Oracles,'" EIC, 23 (Jan., 1973), 42-45.

Jan B. Gordon, "Disenchantment with Intimations: A Reading of Arnold's 'In Utrumque Paratus,'" VP, 3 (Summer, 1965), 192-196.

W. Stacy Johnson, Expl, 10 (May, 1952), 46.
    Rpt. The Explicator Cyclopedia, II, pp. 20-21.

_____. "Isolation: To Marguerite"
Drew, Poetry: A Modern Guide, pp. 145-147.

Stauffer, The Nature of Poetry, pp. 232-235.

Kathleen Tillotson, "'Yes: in the Sea of Life,'" RES, 3 n.s. (Oct., 1952), 346-364.

Wheeler, The Design of Poetry, pp. 124-126.

_____. "The Last Word"
Bloom, Philbrick, and Blistein, The Order of Poetry, pp. 83-84.

Daniels, The Art of Reading Poetry, p. 273.

_____. "Meeting"
Ball, The Heart's Events, pp. 36-37.

_____. "Memorial Verses"
Bateson, English Poetry and the English Language, pp. 106-108.

_____. "A Modern Sappho"
Allan Brick, "Equilibirum in the Poetry of Matthew Arnold," UTQ, 30 (Oct., 1960), 50-51.

_____. "Morality"
George Forbes, "Arnold's 'Oracles,'" EIC, 23 (Jan., 1973), 50-52.

_____. "Mycerinus"
Allan Brick, "Equilibrium in the Poetry of Matthew Arnold," UTQ, 30 (Oct., 1960), 49-50.

John M. Wallace, "Landscape and 'The General Law': The Poetry of Matthew Arnold," Boston University Studies in English, 5 (Summer, 1961), 94.

_____. "The Neckan"
Howard W. Fulwiler, "Matthew Arnold: The Metamorphosis of a Merman," VP, 1 (Autumn, 1963), 212-215.

_____. "Palladium"
Alice N. Stitelman, "Lyrical Process in Three Poems by Matthew Arnold," VP, 15 (Summer, 1977), 142-146.

_____. "Parting"
Ball, The Heart's Events, pp. 37-39.

_____. "Philomela"
Beaty and Matchett, Poetry: From Statement to Meaning, pp. 109-112.

_____. "Quiet Work"
George Forbes, "Arnold's 'Oracles,'" EIC, 23 (Jan., 1973), 48-49.

_____. "Religious Isolation"
George Forbes, "Arnold's 'Oracles,'" EIC, 23 (Jan., 1973), 47-48.

_____. "Requiescat"
Thomas and Brown, Reading Poetry, p. 639.

_____. "Resignation"
George Forbes, "The Reluctant Lover and the World: Structure and Meaning in Arnold's 'Resignation' and 'Stanzas in Memory of the Author of Obermann,'" SEL, 16 (Autumn, 1976), 662-670.

_____. "Rugby Chapel"
H. Kerpneck, "The Road to Rugby Chapel," UTQ, 34 (Jan., 1965), 178-196.

Jerrald Ranta, "The Metrics of 'Rugby Chapel,'" VP, 10 (Winter, 1972), 333-349.

John O. Waller, "Doctor Arnold's Sermons and Matthew Arnold's 'Rugby Chapel,'" SEL, 9 (Autumn, 1969), 633-646.

_____. "Scholar Gipsy"
Kenneth Allot, "Arnold's 'Tyrian Trader,'" TLS (Oct. 18, 1963), 827.

Brooks and Warren, Understanding Poetry, pp. 545-549. Revised edition, pp. 416-420.

David R. Carroll, "Arnold's Tyrian Trader and Grecian Coaster," MLR, 64 (Jan., 1969), 28-33.

Dennis Douglas, "Matthew Arnold's Historic Sense: The Conflict of Greek and Tyrian in 'The Scholar-Gipsy,'" RES, 25 (Nov., 1974), 422-36.

Douglas, Lamson, and Smith, The Critical Reader, pp. 46-49. Revised edition, pp. 658-661.

A. E. Dyson, Between Two Worlds: Aspects of Literary Form (London and Basingstoke: The Macmillan Press, 1972), pp. 41-52.

A. E. Dyson, "The Last Enchantments," RES, 8, n.s. (Aug., 1957), 257-265.

David L. Eggenschwiler, "Arnold's Passive Questers," VP, 5 (Spring, 1967), 5-9.

R. M. Gay, Expl, 2 (Feb., 1944), 28.
    Rpt. The Explicator Cyclopedia, II, pp. 22-23.

Clyde K. Hyder, Expl, 9 (Dec., 1950), 23.
    Rpt. The Explicator Cyclopedia, II, p. 22.

Johnson, The Alien Vision of Victorian Poetry, pp. 199-202.

William S. Knickerbocker, Expl, 8 (May, 1950), 51.
    Rpt. The Explicator Cyclopedia, II, pp. 21-22.

G. Wilson Knight, "'The Scholar Gypsy': An Interpretation," RES, 6, n.s. (Jan., 1955), 53-62.

Gene Montague, Expl, 18 (Nov., 1959), 15.
    Rpt. The Explicator Cyclopedia, II, pp. 19-20.

Laurence Perrine, Expl, 15 (Feb., 1957), 33.
    Rpt. The Explicator Cyclopedia, II, pp. 23-24.

Eric Smith, By Mourning Tongues: Studies in English Elegy (Ipswich and Totowa: The Boydell Press and Rowan and Littlefield, 1977), pp. 81-89.

Michael G. Sundell, "Life, Imagination and Art in Arnold's Oxford Elegies," Criticism, 15 (Fall, 1973), 310-316.

Roger B. Wilkenfeld, "The Argument of 'The Scholar Gipsy,'" VP, 7 (Summer, 1969), 117-128.

_____. "Self-Dependence"
George Forbes, "Arnold's 'Oracles,'" EIC, 23 (Jan., 1973), 49-50.

Frank Giordano, Jr., "Rhythm and Rhyme in 'Self-Dependence,'" ELN, 13 (Sept., 1975), 29-35.

_____. "Shakespeare"
F. A. Dudley, Expl, 4 (June, 1946), 57.
   Rpt. The Explicator Cyclopedia, II, pp. 24-25.

Frankenberg, Invitation to Poetry, pp. 93-94.

Robert A. Greenberg, "Patterns of Imagery: Arnold's 'Shakespeare,'" SEL, (Autumn, 1965), 723-733.

E. M. Halliday and Carlton F. Wells, Expl, 6 (Oct., 1947), 4.
   Rpt. The Explicator Cyclopedia, II, pp. 25-26.

Leavis, Education and the University, pp. 73-76.

F. A. Philbrick, Expl, 5 (Dec., 1946), 24.
   Rpt. The Explicator Cyclopedia, II, p. 25.

Tom J. Truss, Jr., Expl, 19 (May, 1961), 56.
   Rpt. The Explicator Cyclopedia, II, pp. 26-27.

_____. "The Sick King in Bokhara"
Allan Brick, "Equilibrium in the Poetry of Matthew Arnold," UTQ, 30 (Oct., 1960), 52.

John M. Wallace, "Landscape and 'The General Law': The Poetry of Matthew ARnold," Boston University Studies in English, 5 (Summer, 1961), 95.

_____. "Stanzas from the Grande Chartreuse"
Sr. Mary Richard Boo, Expl, 23 (May, 1965), 69.

David Trotter, "Hidden Ground Within: Matthew Arnold's Lyric and Elegiac Poetry," ELH, 44 (Fall, 1977), 542-545.

_____. "Stanzas in Memory of the Author of 'Obermann'"
George Forbes, "The Reluctant Lover and the World: Structure and Meaning in Arnold's 'Resignation' and 'Stanzas in Memory of the Author of Obermann.'" SEL, 16 (Autumn, 1976), 671-676.

_____. "The Strayed Reveller"
Kenneth Allott, "The 'Scythian' in 'The Strayed Reveller,'" VP, 11 (Summer, 1973), 163-166.

Leon A. Gottfried, "Matthew Arnold's 'The Strayed Reveller,'" RES, 11 (Nov., 1960), 403-409.

Dorothy M. Mermin, "The Two Worlds in Arnold's 'The Strayed Reveller,'" SEL, 12 (Autumn, 1972), 735-743.

M. G. Sundell, "Story and Context in 'The Strayed Reveller,'" VP, 3 (Summer, 1965), 161-170.

_____. "A Summer Night"
Ribner and Morris, Poetry, pp. 358-360.

David Trotter, "Hidden Ground Within: Matthew Arnold's Lyric and Elegiac Poetry," ELH, 44 (Fall, 1977), 537-539.

John M. Wallace, "Landscape and 'The General Law': The Poetry of Matthew Arnold," Boston University Studies in English, 5 (Summer, 1961), 101.

_____. "Switzerland"
Ronald E. Becht, "Matthew Arnold's 'Switzerland': The Drama of Choice," VP, 13 (Spring, 1975), 35-45.

_____. "Thyrsis"
David L. Eggenschwiler, "Arnold's Passive Questers," _VP_, 5 (Spring, 1967), 9-11.

Richard Giannone, "The Quest Motif in 'Thyrsis,'" _VP_, 3 (Spring, 1965), 71-80.

Johnson, _The Alien Vision of Victorian Poetry_, pp. 202-204.

Laurence Lerner, _The Uses of Nostalgia: Studies in Pastoral Poetry_ (New York: Schocken Books, 1972), 232-237.

Michael Macklem, "The Elegiac Theme in Housman," _QQ_, 59 (Spring, 1952), 48.

Eric Smith, _By Mourning Tongues: Studies in English Elegy_ (Ipswich and Totowa: The Boydell Press and Rowan and Littlefield, 1977), pp. 89-99.

Michael G. Sundell, "Life, Imagination, and Art in Arnold's Oxford Elegies," _Criticism_, 15 (Fall, 1973), 316-321.

_____. "To Marguerite-Continued"
Ball, _The Heart's Events_, pp. 39-42.

Peckham and Chatman, _Word, Meaning, Poem_, pp. 60-66.

_____. "The World and the Quietist"
George Forbes, "Arnold's 'The World and the Quietist' and the _Bhagavad Gita_," _CL_, 25 (Spring, 1973), 153-160.

Robert A. Greenberg, "Matthew Arnold's Mournful Rhyme: A Study of 'The World and the Quietist,'" _VP_, 1 (Winter, 1963), 284-290.

ASHBERY. "As You Came from the Holy Land"
Bloom, _A Map of Misreading_, pp. 204-206.

_____. "The Chateau Hardware"
Charles Molesworth, "'This Leaving-Out Business': The Poetry of John Ashbery," _Salmagundi_, 38-39, (Summer-Fall, 1977), 28-29.

_____. "Leaving the Atocha Station"
Carroll, _The Poem In Its Skin_, pp. 6-23.

Fred Moramarco, "John Ashbery and Frank O'Hara: The Painterly Poets," _JML_, 5 (Sept., 1976), 452-453.

_____. "The Painter"
Fred Moramarco, "John Ashbery and Frank O'Hara: The Painterly Poets," _JML_, 5 (Sept., 1976), 449-450.

_____. "The Skaters"
Fred Moramarco, "John Ashbery and Frank O'Hara: The Painterly Poets," _JML_, 5 (Sept., 1976), 453-455.

_____. "The Tennis Court Oath"
Fred Moramarco, "John Ashbery and Frank O'Hara: The Painterly Poets," _JML_, 5 (Sept., 1976), 451-452.

ASHLEY, Leonard R. N. "The Game"
Leonard R. N. Ashley, "The Rules of the Games," _CP_, 1 (Spring, 1968), 38-44.

AUDEN. "Address for a Prize-Day"
    Monroe K. Spears, "Late Auden: The Satirist as Lunatic Clergyman," SR,
    59 (Winter, 1951), 66.

_____. "The Alien"
    Evelyn A. Flory, "Auden and Eiseley: The Development of a Poem," CP, 8
    (Spring, 1975), 67-73.

_____. "And the Age Ended, and the Last Deliverer Died" from "In Time of War"
    Wheeler, The Design of Poetry, pp. 131-136.

_____. "Another Time"
    Joost Daalder, "W. H. Auden's 'Another Time,'"
    CP, 5 (Spring), 1972), 65-66.

_____. "As I Walked Out One Evening"
    Chatman, An Introduction to the Language of Poetry, pp. 76-78.

    Ellsworth Mason, Expl, 12 (May, 1954), 43.
      Rpt. The Explicator Cyclopedia, I, p. 2.

    Edward C. McAleer, "As Auden Walked Out," CE, 18 (Feb., 1957), 271-272.

_____. "Caliban to the Audience"
    Monroe K. Spears, "Late Auden: The Satirist as Lunatic Clergyman," SR,
    59 (Winter, 1951), 66-70.

_____. "Casino"
    Peckham and Chatman, Word, Meaning, Poem, pp. 286-295.

_____. "The Climbers"
    Maynard Mack, Leonard Dean, and William Frost, English Masterpieces,
    Vol. VII, Modern Poetry, pp. 21-22.

_____. "Crisis"
    Harold Morland, Expl, 5 (Nov., 1946), 17.
      Rpt. The Explicator Cyclopedia, I, p. 3.

    F. A. Philbrick, Expl, 5 (April, 1947), 45.
      Rpt. The Explicator Cyclopedia, I, pp. 3-4.

_____. "The Cultural Presupposition"
    Robert Bloom, "W. H. Auden's Bestiary of the Human," VQR, 42 (Spring,
    1966), 213-214.

_____. "Dame Kind"
    Robert Bloom, "W. H. Auden's Bestiary of the Human," VQR, 42 (Spring,
    1966), 228-231.

_____. "The Dance of Death"
    Brooks, Modern Poetry and the Tradition, pp. 133-135.

_____. "Dear, Though the Night Is Gone"
    Frankenberg, Invitation to Poetry, p. 172.

_____. "The Decoys" from The Orators
    Rosenthal, The Modern Poets, pp. 189-191.

_____. "The Diaspora"
    Robert E. Knoll, "The Style of Contemporary Poetry," PrS, 29 (Summer,
    1955), 122-124.

_____. "Doom Is Dark and Deeper than any Sea-Dingle"
Morton W. Bloomfield, "W. H. Auden and Sawles Warde," MLN, 63 (Dec.,
1948), 548-552.

_____. "The Fall of Rome"
W. P. Nicolet, Expl, 31 (Nov., 1972), 22.

_____. "Family Ghosts" ("The Strings' Excitement")
Sr. M. Cleophas, Expl, 7 (Oct., 1948), 1.
     Rpt. Engle and Carrier, Reading Modern Poetry, pp. 294-295.
     Rpt. The Explicator Cyclopedia, I, pp. 4-5.

_____. "Fish in the Unruffled Lakes"
Ruth H. Bauerle, Expl, 26 (March, 1968), 57.
Robert Bloom, "W. H. Auden's Bestiary of the Human," VQR, 42 (Spring,
1966), 214.

_____. "For the Time Being"
Maynard Mack, Leonard Dean, and William Frost, English Masterpieces,
Vol. VII, Modern Poetry, pp. 22-24.

Donald E. Morse, "'For the Time Being': Man's Response to the Incarnation," Renascence, 19 (Summer, 1967), 190-197.

Donald E. Morse, "The Nature of Man in Auden's 'For the Time Being,'"
Renascence, 19 (Winter, 1967), 93-100.

_____. "Foxtrot from a Play"
William Power, Expl, 16 (March, 1958), 32.
     Rpt. The Explicator Cyclopedia, I, pp. 5-6.

_____. "Fugal-Chorus"
William Frost, Expl, 11 (Dec., 1952), 21.
     Rpt. The Explicator Cyclopedia, I, pp. 6-7.

Frederick A. Pottle, Expl, 11 (April, 1953), 40.
     Rpt. The Explicator Cyclopedia, I, pp. 7-8.

_____. "Get There If You Can and See the Land You Once Were Proud to Own"
     (Poem 12 of Poems)
Savage, The Personal Principle, pp. 161-162.

_____. "Have a Good Time"
F. A. Philbrick, Expl, 4 (Dec., 1945), 21.
     Rpt. The Explicator Cyclopedia, I, pp. 8-9.

_____. "A Healthy Spot"
J. N. Satterwhite, Expl, 21 (March, 1963), 57.

_____. "Homage to Clio"
Robert Bloom, "W. H. Auden's Bestiary of the Human," VQR, 42 (Spring,
1966), 222-225.

_____. "Horae Canonicae"
Adams, Strains of Discord, pp. 125-127.

Monroe K. Spears, "Auden in the Fifties: Rites of Homage," SR, 69
(Summer, 1961), 385-388.

_____. "In Memory of W. B. Yeats (d. Jan., 1939)"
Abad, A Formal Approach to Lyric Poetry, pp. 59-64.

Dickinson, Suggestions for Teachers of "Introduction to Literature,"
fifth edition, ed. Locke, Gibson, and Arms, pp. 48-49. (Teacher's Manual)

Drew, Poetry: A Modern Guide, pp. 267-270.

Lucy S. McDiarmid, "Poetry's Landscape in Auden's Elegy for Yeats," MLQ,
38 (June, 1977), 167-177.

Edward W. Rosenheim, Jr., "The Elegiac Act: Auden's 'In Memory of W. B.
Yeats,'" CE, 27 (Feb., 1966), 422-425.

Robert Roth, "The Sophistication of W. H. Auden: A Sketch in Longinian
Method," MP, 48 (Feb., 1951), 198-202.

_____. "In Praise of Limestone"
Geoffrey Millard, "Auden's Common Prayer: In Praise of Limestone,"
English, 22 (Autumn, 1973), 105-109.

_____. "In Time of War," Sonnet 1
Robert Bloom, "W. H. Auden's Bestiary of the Human," VQR, 42 (Spring,
1966), 216-218.

_____. "It's No Use Raising a Shout"
George McFadden, Expl, 15 (Nov., 1956), 12.
    Rpt. The Explicator Cyclopedia, I, pp. 10-11.

J. H. Naterstad, "Auden's 'It's No Use Raising a Shout': A New Perspective," CP, 3 (Spring, 1970), 17-20.

Mark Rowan, Expl, 15 (Nov., 1956), 12.
    Rpt. The Explicator Cyclopedia, I, p. 9.

John H. Sutherland, Expl, 15 (Nov., 1956), 12.
    Rpt. The Explicator Cyclopedia, I, pp. 9-10.

_____. "It was Easter as I Walked in the Public Gardens"
Robert Bloom, "Auden's Essays at Man: Some Long Views in the Early
Poetry," Shenandoah, 18 (Winter, 1967), 28-30.

_____. "Kairos and Logos"
Beach, Obsessive Images, pp. 355-356.

_____. "Law Like Love"
Unger and O'Connor, Poems for Study, pp. 647-649.

_____. "Lay Your Sleeping Head, My Love"
Beaty and Matchett, Poetry: From Statement to Meaning, pp. 36-45.

Robert W. Caswell, Expl, 26 (Jan., 1968), 44.

Stephen Spender, "W. H. Auden and His Poetry," Atlantic Monthly, 192
(July, 1953), 79.

_____. "Letter to a Wound"
Monroe K. Spears, "Late Auden: The Satirist as Lunatic Clergyman,"
SR, 59 (Winter, 1951), 65-66.

_____. "Meiosis"
Gladys Garner Leithauser, "W. H. Auden's 'Meiosis,'" ELN, 8 (Dec., 1970),
120-126.

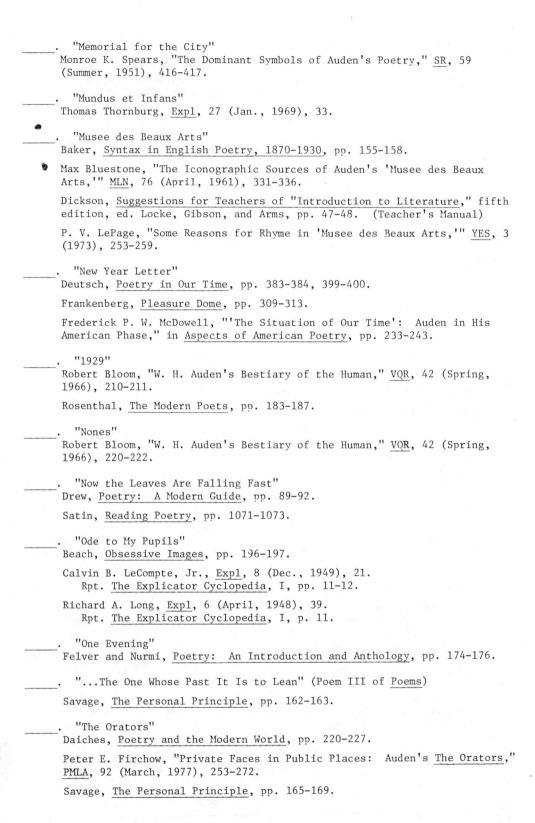

_____.   "Memorial for the City"
Monroe K. Spears, "The Dominant Symbols of Auden's Poetry," SR, 59 (Summer, 1951), 416-417.

_____.   "Mundus et Infans"
Thomas Thornburg, Expl, 27 (Jan., 1969), 33.

_____.   "Musee des Beaux Arts"
Baker, Syntax in English Poetry, 1870-1930, pp. 155-158.

Max Bluestone, "The Iconographic Sources of Auden's 'Musee des Beaux Arts,'" MLN, 76 (April, 1961), 331-336.

Dickson, Suggestions for Teachers of "Introduction to Literature," fifth edition, ed. Locke, Gibson, and Arms, pp. 47-48.   (Teacher's Manual)

P. V. LePage, "Some Reasons for Rhyme in 'Musee des Beaux Arts,'" YES, 3 (1973), 253-259.

_____.   "New Year Letter"
Deutsch, Poetry in Our Time, pp. 383-384, 399-400.

Frankenberg, Pleasure Dome, pp. 309-313.

Frederick P. W. McDowell, "'The Situation of Our Time': Auden in His American Phase," in Aspects of American Poetry, pp. 233-243.

_____.   "1929"
Robert Bloom, "W. H. Auden's Bestiary of the Human," VQR, 42 (Spring, 1966), 210-211.

Rosenthal, The Modern Poets, pp. 183-187.

_____.   "Nones"
Robert Bloom, "W. H. Auden's Bestiary of the Human," VQR, 42 (Spring, 1966), 220-222.

_____.   "Now the Leaves Are Falling Fast"
Drew, Poetry: A Modern Guide, pp. 89-92.

Satin, Reading Poetry, pp. 1071-1073.

_____.   "Ode to My Pupils"
Beach, Obsessive Images, pp. 196-197.

Calvin B. LeCompte, Jr., Expl, 8 (Dec., 1949), 21.
   Rpt. The Explicator Cyclopedia, I, pp. 11-12.

Richard A. Long, Expl, 6 (April, 1948), 39.
   Rpt. The Explicator Cyclopedia, I, p. 11.

_____.   "One Evening"
Felver and Nurmi, Poetry: An Introduction and Anthology, pp. 174-176.

_____.   "...The One Whose Past It Is to Lean" (Poem III of Poems)
Savage, The Personal Principle, pp. 162-163.

_____.   "The Orators"
Daiches, Poetry and the Modern World, pp. 220-227.

Peter E. Firchow, "Private Faces in Public Places: Auden's The Orators," PMLA, 92 (March, 1977), 253-272.

Savage, The Personal Principle, pp. 165-169.

W. H. Sellers, "New Light on Auden's The Orators," PMLA, 82 (Oct., 1967), 455-464.

_____. "Our Hunting Fathers Told the Story"
F. Cudworth Flint, Expl, 2 (Oct., 1943), 28.
    Rpt. The Explicator Cyclopedia, I, p. 15.

Tate, Reason in Madness, pp. 97-98.
    Rpt. On the Limits of Poetry, pp. 127-128.

_____. "O What Is That Sound"
Laurence Perrine and Jane Johnston, Expl, 30 (Jan., 1972), 41.

_____. "O Who Can Ever Gaze His Fill"
Robert Bloom, "Auden's Essays at Man: Some Long Views in the Early Poetry," Shenandoah, 23 (Winter, 1967), 41.

_____. "Oxford"
Bateson, English Poetry, pp. 240-245.

_____. "Paysage Moralisé"
Beach, Obsessive Images, pp. 104-114.
Virginia M. Hyde, "The Pastoral Formula of W. H. Auden and Piero di Cosimo," ConL, 14 (Summer, 1973), 339-342.

_____. "Petition"
Deutsch, Poetry in Our Time, pp. 381-382.

Dickinson, Suggestions for Teachers of "Introduction to Literature," fifth edition, ed. Locke, Gibson, and Arms, p. 48. (Teacher's Manual)

Melvin G. Williams, "Auden's 'Petition': A Synthesis of Criticism," The Personalist, 66 (Spring, 1965), 222-232.

_____. "Pleasure Island"
R. Mayhead, "The Latest Auden," Scrutiny, 18 (June, 1952), 316-318.

_____. "Poem XX"
Brooks, Modern Poetry and the Tradition, pp. 126-129.

_____. "Prime"
R. Mayhead, "The Latest Auden," Scrutiny, 18 (June, 1952), 315-316.

_____. "The Questioner Who Sits So Sly"
Seymour Chatman, Expl, 28 (Nov., 1969), 21.

Rosenthal, The Modern Poets, pp. 187-189.

_____. "Reflections in a Forest"
Robert Bloom, "W. H. Auden's Bestiary of the Human," VQR, 42 (Spring, 1966), 226-227.

_____. "The Sabbath"
Robert Bloom, "W. H. Auden's Bestiary of the Human," VQR, 42 (Spring, 1966), 227-228.

_____. "Schoolchildren"
Richard A. Long, Expl, 7 (Feb., 1949), 32.
    Rpt. The Explicator Cyclopedia, I, p. 12.

_____. "The Sea and the Mirror"
Frederick P. W. McDowell, "'The Situation of Our Time': Auden in His American Phase," in Aspects of American Poetry, pp. 243-253.

_____. "Secrets"
Robert Bloom, "W. H. Auden's Bestiary of the Human," VQR, 42 (Spring, 1966), 219-220.

_____. "September 1, 1939"
Phyllis Bartlett and John A. Pollard, Expl, 14 (Nov., 1955), 8.
    Rpt. The Explicator Cyclopedia, I, pp. 15-16.

Daphne N. Bennett, "Auden's 'September 1, 1939,'" QJS, 42 (Feb., 1956), 4-13.

Edwards, Imagination and Power, pp. 203-210.

Rosenthal, The Modern Poets, pp. 193-195.

_____. "The Shield of Achilles"
Feder, Ancient Myth in Modern Poetry, pp. 312-315.

_____. "Sir, No Man's Enemy, Forgiving All"
Brooks, Modern Poetry and the Tradition, pp. 1-2.

Wallace Cable Brown, Expl, 3 (March, 1945), 38.

D. A. Robertson, Jr., W. K. Wimsatt, Jr., and Hallet Smith, Expl, 3 (May, 1945), 51.
    Rpt. The Explicator Cyclopedia, I, pp. 13-14.

Charles Child Walcutt, The Explicator Cyclopedia, I, "Introduction," p. xiii.

_____. "Song for St. Cecilia's Day"
Deutsch, Poetry in Our Time, pp. 390-391.

Ingeborg Hough, Expl, 18 (March, 1960), 35.
    Rpt. The Explicator Cyclopedia, I, pp. 17-18.

_____. "Spain 1937"
Rosenthal, The Modern Poets, pp. 191-193.

Delmore Schwartz, "The Two Audens," The Kenyon Review, 1 (Winter, 1939), 43-44.

_____. "Their Lonely Betters"
Robert Bloom, "W. H. Auden's Bestiary of the Human," VQR, 42 (Spring, 1966), 218-219.

_____. "Tonight at Seven Thirty"
Edward Callan, "Auden's Goodly Heritage," Shenandoah, 17 (Winter, 1967), 65-67.

_____. "To T. S. Eliot On His Sixtieth Birthday"
Dennis A. Wentraug, Expl, 31 (May, 1973), 75.

_____. "Venus Will Now Say a Few Words"
Robert Bloom, "Auden's Essays at Man: Some Long Views in the Early Poetry," Shenandoah, 18 (Winter, 1967), 32-33.

Deutsch, Poetry in Our Time, pp. 380-381.

_____. "The Wanderer"
    Duncan Robertson, Expl, 28 (April, 1970), 70.

_____. "Which of You Waking Early and Watching Daybreak"
    Robert Bloom, "Auden's Essays at Man: Some Long Views in the Early
    Poetry, Shenandoah, 18 (Winter, 1967), 26-28.

_____. "Which Side Am I Supposed to Be On?" (or "Ode to My Pupils")
    C. B. LeCompte, Jr., Expl, 8 (Dec., 1949), 21.

    Richard A. Long, Expl, 6 (April, 1948), 39.

_____. "Woods"
    Virginia M. Hyde, "The Pastoral Formula of W. H. Auden and Piero de
    Cosimo," ConL, 14 (Summer, 1973), 333-7.

AVISON, Margaret. "Butterfly Bones; or Sonnet Against Sonnets"
    William H. New, "The Mind's Eyes (I's) (Ice): The Poetry of Margaret
    Avison," TCL, 16 (July, 1970), 191.

_____. "Natural/Unnatural"
    William H. New, "The Mind's Eyes (I's) (Ice): The Poetry of Margaret
    Avison," TCL, 16 (July, 1970), 199-200.

_____. "Prelude"
    William H. New, "The Mind's Eyes (I's) (Ice): The Poetry of Margaret
    Avison," TCL, 16 (July, 1970), 188-189.

BAKER, Karle W. "Courage"
    Sanders, The Discovery of Poetry, pp. 180-181.

BARAKA, Imamu A. (LeRoi Jones). "Black Art"
    Kathleen Gallagher, "The Art(s) of Poetry: Jones and MacLeish," MQ,
    12 (Summer, 1971), 383-392.

_____. "Black Dada Nihilismus"
    William C. Fischer, "The Pre-Revolutionary Writings of Imamu Amiri
    Baraka," MR, 14 (Spring, 1973), 290-292.

_____. "Hymn for Lanie Poo"
    William C. Fischer, "The Pre-Revolutionary Writings of Imamu Amiri
    Baraka," MR, 14 (Spring, 1973), 266-267.

_____. "In Memory of Radio"
    John Hakac, "Baraka's 'In Memory of Radio,'" CP, 10 (Spring, 1977), 85.

BAILEY. "Life's More Than Breath and the Quick Round of Blood" (from Festus)
    Richards, Practical Criticism, pp. 21-30.

BARCLAY. "The Towre of Vertue and Honoure," Eclogue IV
    R. J. Lyall, "Tradition and Innovation in Alexander Barclay's 'Towre
    of Vertue and Honoure,'" RES, 23 (Feb., 1972), 1-18.

BARKER, George. "The Amazons"
    David Daiches, "The Lyricism of George Barker," Poetry, 69 (March, 1947),
    337-339.

_____. "The Seagull, Spreadeagled, Splayed on the Wind"
Day Lewis, <u>The Poetic Image</u>, pp. 128-130.
Rpt. Engle and Carrier, <u>Reading Modern Poetry</u>, pp. 248-249.

_____. "Sonnet to My Mother"
Abad, <u>Formal Approach to Lyric Poetry</u>, pp. 349-356.

_____. "To Father Gerard Manley Hopkins, S.J."
Michael Routh, <u>Expl</u>, 33 (April, 1975), 65.

BARLOW. "Advice to a Raven in Russia"
Robert D. Arner, "Joel Barlow's Poetics: 'Advice to a Raven in Russia,'"
<u>ConnR</u>, 5 (April, 1972), 38-43.

James T. F. Tanner, "The 'Triple Ban' in Joel Barlow's 'Advice to a Raven
in Russia,'" <u>EAL</u>, 12 (Winter, 1977/1978), 294-295.

_____. "The Hasty Pudding"
Robert D. Arner, "The Smooth and Emblematic Song: Joel Barlow's <u>The Hasty
Pudding,</u>" <u>EAL</u>, 7 (Spring, 1972), 76-91.

BEATTIE. "The Hermit"
E. H. King, "James Beattie's <u>Retirement and The Hermit</u>, Two Early Romantic
Poems," <u>SAQ</u>, 72 (Autumn, 1973), 580-583.

_____. "Retirement"
E. H. King, "James Beattie's <u>Retirement and The Hermit</u>, Two Early Romantic
Poems," <u>SAQ</u>, 72 (Autumn, 1973), 576-580.

_____. "Verses Occasioned by the Death of the Revd Mr Charles Churchill"
E. H. King, "James Beattie's 'Verses Occasioned by the Death of the Revd
Mr Charles Churchill' (1765) and the Demise of Augustan Satire," <u>SSL</u>, 12
(April, 1975), 234-249.

BEAUMONT. "On the Tombs in Westminster Abbey"
John Robert Moore, <u>Expl</u>, 1 (Feb., 1943), 27.
Rpt. <u>The Explicator Cyclopedia</u>, II, p. 33.

BEDE. "Death-Song"
Howell D. Chickering Jr., " Some Contexts for Bede's <u>Death-Song</u>," <u>PMLA</u>,
91 (Jan., 1976), 91-100.

BELL. "Manicure"
Philip Hobsbaum, <u>Theory of Criticism</u> (Bloomington and London: Indiana
Univ. Press, 1970), pp. 172-176.

BELITT. "Double Poem"
Robert Weisberg, "Ben Belitt: Speaking Words Against the Word," <u>MPS</u>, 7
(Spring, 1976), 52-55.

_____. "Full Moon: The Gorge"
Robert Weisberg, "Ben Belitt: Speaking Words Against the Word," <u>MPS</u>, 7
(Spring, 1976), 57-59.

_____. "Xerox"
Robert Weisberg, "Ben Belitt: Speaking Words Against the Word," <u>MPS</u>, 7
(Spring, 1976), 48-49.

BENET, S. V. "Ode to Walt Whitman"
Morton D. Zabel, "The American Grain," Poetry, 48 (August, 1936), 279-281.

BERRY. "The Apple Tree"
John Ditsky, "Wendell Berry: Homage to the Apple Tree," MPS, 2 (Spring, 1971), 9.

_____. "The Return"
Robert Hass, "Wendell Berry: Finding the Land," MPS, 2 (Spring, 1971), 18-25.

_____. "The White and Waking of the House"
Robert Hass, "Wendell Berry: Finding the Land," MPS, 2 (Spring, 1971), 31-34.

BERRYMAN. "Desires of Men and Woman"
Richard Wilbur, "Poetry's Debt to Poetry," HudR, 26 (Summer, 1973), 290-293.

_____. "The Disciple"
Robert Fitzgerald, "Poetry and Perfection," SR, 56 (Autumn, 1948), 690-691.

_____. "The Dispossessed"
J. F. Nims, Poetry: A Critical Supplement, April, 1948, pp. 1-5.

_____. "Formal Elegy"
Ann Stanford, "The Elegy of Mourning in Modern American and English Poetry," SoR, 11 (April, 1975), 370-372.

_____. "A Strut for Roethke"
Jo Porterfield, Expl, 32 (Dec., 1973), 25.

_____. "Winter Landscape"
David M. Wyatt, "Completing the Picture: Williams, Berryman, and 'Spatial Form,'" CLQ, 13 (Dec., 1977), 257-261.

_____. "World's Fair"
Margaret M. McBride, Expl, 34 (Nov., 1975), 22.
J. F. Nims, Poetry: A Critical Supplement, April, 1948, p. 6.

BINYON. "The Supper"
James G. Southworth, "Laurence Binyon," SR, 43 (July-Sept., 1935), 343-346.

BISHOP, Elizabeth. "At the Fishhouses"
Sybil Estess, "'Shelters for What is Within': Meditation and Epiphany in the Poetry of Elizabeth Bishop," MPS, 8 (Spring, 1977), 53-59.

Crale D. Hopkins, "Inspiration as Theme: Art and Nature in the Poetry of Elizabeth Bishop," ArQ, 32 (Autumn, 1976), 204-205.

Nancy L. McNally, "Elizabeth Bishop: The Discipline of Description," TCL, 11 (Jan., 1966), 197-200.

Willard Spiegelman, "Landscape and Knowledge: The Poetry of Elizabeth Bishop," MPS, 6 (Winter, 1975), 204-208.

_____.   "The Bight"
Sybil P. Estess, "Elizabeth Bishop: The Delicate Art of Map Making,"
SoR, 13 (Oct., 1977), 717-718.

Willard Spiegelman, "Landscape and Knowledge: The Poetry of Elizabeth
Bishop," MPS, 6 (Winter, 1975), 209-211.

_____.   "Cape Breton"
Marjorie Perloff, "Elizabeth Bishop: The Course of a Particular," MPS, 8
(Winter, 1977), 188-190.

_____.   "The Colder the Air"
Karl F. Thompson, Expl, 12 (March, 1954), 33.
     Rpt. The Explicator Cyclopedia, I, p. 18.

_____.   "The Fish"
Sybil P. Estess, "Elizabeth Bishop: The Delicate Art of Map Making,"
SoR, 13 (Oct., 1977), 713-717.

Crale D. Hopkins,"Inspiration as Theme: Art and Nature in the Poetry of
Elizabeth Bishop," ArQ, 32 (Autumn, 1976), 200-202.

Nancy L. McNally, "Elizabeth Bishop: The Discipline of Description,"
TCL, 11 (Jan., 1966), 192-194.

Richard Moore, "Elizabeth Bishop: 'The Fish,'" Boston University Studies
in English, 2 (Winter, 1956-1957), 251-259.

Perrine and Reid, 100 American Poems, pp. 212-213.

_____.   "The Imaginary Iceberg"
Willard Spiegelman, "Landscape and Knowledge: The Poetry of Elizabeth
Bishop," MPS, 6 (Winter, 1975), 215-216.

_____.   "The Man-Moth"
Mills, Contemporary American Poetry, pp. 78-82.

_____.   "The Map"
Sybil P. Estess, "Elizabeth Bishop: The Delicate Art of Map Making,"
SoR, 13 (Oct., 1977), 708-713.

Frankenberg, Pleasure Dome, pp. 331-333.
     Rpt. Engle and Carrier, Reading Modern Poetry, pp. 228-229.

_____.   "Monument"
Nancy L. McNally, "Elizabeth Bishop: The Discipline of Description,"
TCL, 11 (Jan., 1966), 194-197.

Marjorie Perloff, "Elizabeth Bishop: The Course of a Particular," MPS, 8
(Winter, 1977), 185-187.

_____.   "Poem"
Sybil P. Estess, "Elizabeth Bishop: The Delicate Art of Map Making,"
SoR, 13 (Oct., 1977), 721-726.

_____.   "Quai d'Orleans"
Mills, Contemporary American Poetry, pp. 75-77.

_____.   "Questions of Travel"
Crale D. Hopkins, "Inspiration as Theme: Art and Nature in the Poetry of
Elizabeth Bishop," ArQ, 32 (Autumn, 1976), 208-212.

Willard Spiegelman, "Landscape and Knowledge: The Poetry of Elizabeth Bishop," _MPS_, 6 (Winter, 1975), 218-220.

_____. "The Sandpiper"
Sybil P. Estess, "Elizabeth Bishop: The Delicate Art of Map Making," _SoR_, 13 (Oct., 1977), 719-721.

BISHOP, John P. "Ballet"
    S. C. Moore, _Expl_, 23 (Oct., 1964), 12.

_____. "Behavior of the Sun"
    R. W. Stallman, _Expl_, 5 (Oct., 1946), 6.
        Rpt. _The Explicator Cyclopedia_, I, pp. 18-19.

    R. W. Stallman, "The Poetry of John Peale Bishop," _Western Review_, 11 (Autumn, 1946), 15-16.

_____. "Divine Nativity"
Joseph Frank, "Force and Form: A Study of John Peale Bishop," _SR_, 55 (Winter, 1947), 97-98.

_____. "O Let Not Virtue Seek"
Joseph Frank, "Force and Form: A Study of John Peale Bishop," _SR_, 55 (Winter, 1947), 91-93.

_____. "Perspectives are Precipices"
    R. W. Stallman, _Expl_, 5 (Nov., 1946), 8.
        Rpt. _The Explicator Cyclopedia_, I, pp. 19-20.

    R. W. Stallman, "The Poetry of John Peale Bishop," _Western Review_, 11 (Autumn, 1946), 17-19.

    Allen Tate, "A Note on Bishop's Poetry," _SoR_, 1 (Autumn, 1935), 362-363.

    Tate, _Reactionary Essays on Poetry and Ideas_, pp. 60-62.
        Rpt. _On the Limits of Poetry_, pp. 244-246.

_____. "A Recollection"
    R. W. Stallman, _Expl_, 19 (April, 1961), 43.
        Rpt. _The Explicator Cyclopedia_, I, pp. 20-21.

_____. "The Return"
    Allen Tate, "A Note on Bishop's Poetry," _SoR_, 1 (Autumn, 1935), 361-362.

    Tate, _Reactionary Essays on Poetry and Ideas_, pp. 58-60.
        Rpt. _On the Limits of Poetry_, pp. 243-244.

_____. "The Saints"
Joseph Frank, "Force and Form: A Study of John Peale Bishop," _SR_, 55 (Winter, 1947), 95-96.

_____. "Southern Pines"
    R. W. Stallman, _Expl_, 4 (April, 1946), 46.
        Rpt. _The Explicator Cyclopedia_, I, pp. 21-22.

    R. W. Stallman, "The Poetry of John Peale Bishop," _Western Review_, 11 (Autumn, 1946), 10-12.

_____. "Speaking of Poetry"
Deutsch, _Poetry in Our Time_, pp. 191-193.

Joseph Frank, "Force and Form: A Study of John Peale Bishop," _SR_, 55 (Winter, 1947), 83-86.

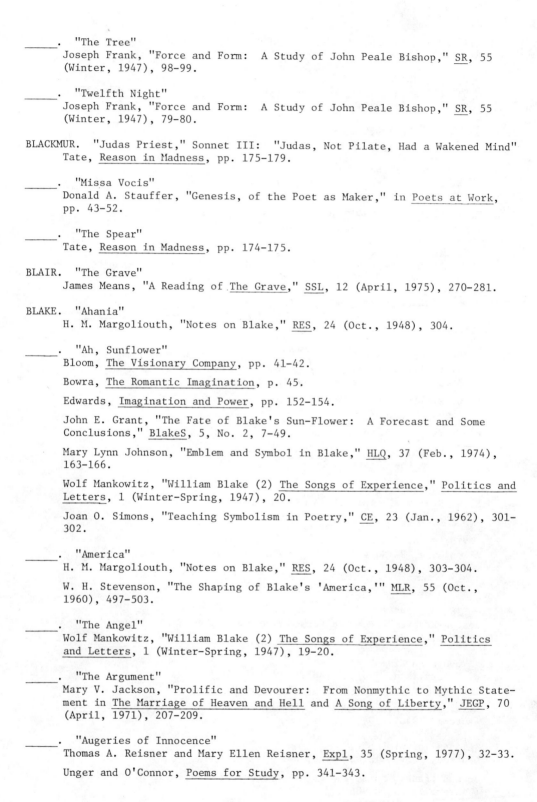

_____. "The Tree"
Joseph Frank, "Force and Form: A Study of John Peale Bishop," SR, 55 (Winter, 1947), 98-99.

_____. "Twelfth Night"
Joseph Frank, "Force and Form: A Study of John Peale Bishop," SR, 55 (Winter, 1947), 79-80.

BLACKMUR. "Judas Priest," Sonnet III: "Judas, Not Pilate, Had a Wakened Mind"
Tate, Reason in Madness, pp. 175-179.

_____. "Missa Vocis"
Donald A. Stauffer, "Genesis, of the Poet as Maker," in Poets at Work, pp. 43-52.

_____. "The Spear"
Tate, Reason in Madness, pp. 174-175.

BLAIR. "The Grave"
James Means, "A Reading of The Grave," SSL, 12 (April, 1975), 270-281.

BLAKE. "Ahania"
H. M. Margoliouth, "Notes on Blake," RES, 24 (Oct., 1948), 304.

_____. "Ah, Sunflower"
Bloom, The Visionary Company, pp. 41-42.

Bowra, The Romantic Imagination, p. 45.

Edwards, Imagination and Power, pp. 152-154.

John E. Grant, "The Fate of Blake's Sun-Flower: A Forecast and Some Conclusions," BlakeS, 5, No. 2, 7-49.

Mary Lynn Johnson, "Emblem and Symbol in Blake," HLQ, 37 (Feb., 1974), 163-166.

Wolf Mankowitz, "William Blake (2) The Songs of Experience," Politics and Letters, 1 (Winter-Spring, 1947), 20.

Joan O. Simons, "Teaching Symbolism in Poetry," CE, 23 (Jan., 1962), 301-302.

_____. "America"
H. M. Margoliouth, "Notes on Blake," RES, 24 (Oct., 1948), 303-304.

W. H. Stevenson, "The Shaping of Blake's 'America,'" MLR, 55 (Oct., 1960), 497-503.

_____. "The Angel"
Wolf Mankowitz, "William Blake (2) The Songs of Experience," Politics and Letters, 1 (Winter-Spring, 1947), 19-20.

_____. "The Argument"
Mary V. Jackson, "Prolific and Devourer: From Nonmythic to Mythic State-ment in The Marriage of Heaven and Hell and A Song of Liberty," JEGP, 70 (April, 1971), 207-209.

_____. "Augeries of Innocence"
Thomas A. Reisner and Mary Ellen Reisner, Expl, 35 (Spring, 1977), 32-33.

Unger and O'Connor, Poems for Study, pp. 341-343.

Janet Warner, "Blake's Auguries of Innocence," CLQ, 12 (Sept., 1976), 126-138.

_____. "The Bard's Song"
John H. Sutherland, "Blake's Milton: The Bard's Song," CLQ, 13 (June, 1977), 142-157.

Eve Teitelbaum, "Form as Meaning in Blake's Milton," BlakeS, 2, No. 1 (1970), 37-64.

Vogler, Preludes to Vision, pp. 43-47.

_____. "The Book of Thel"
Bloom, The Visionary Company, pp. 45-49.

Roland A. Duerksen, "The Life-in-Death Theme in The Book of Thel," BlakeS, 2 (Spring, 1970), 15-22.

Robert F. Gleckner, "Blake's 'Thel' and the Bible," BNYPL, 64 (Nov., 1960), 573-580.

Christopher Heppner, "'A Desire of Being': Identity and The Book of Thel," CLQ, 13 (June, 1977), 79-98.

Barbara F. Lefcowitz, "Blake and the Natural World," PMLA, 89 (Jan., 1974), 124.

Ann Kostelanetz Mellor, "Blake's Designs for The Book of Thel: An Affirmation of Innocence," PQ, 50 (April, 1971), 193-207.

Rodger L. Tarr, "'The Eagle' Versus 'The Mole': The Wisdom of Virginity in Comus and The Book of Thel," BlakeS, 3 (Spring, 1971), 187-194.

_____. "The Book of Urizen"
Bloom, The Visionary Company, pp. 66-75.

Marc Rosenberg, "Style and Meaning in The Book of Urizen," Style, 4 (Fall, 1970), 197-212.

_____. "The Chimney Sweeper" (Songs of Experience)
Abad, A Formal Approach to Lyric Poetry, pp. 223-225.

Brian Wilkie, "Blake's Innocence and Experience: An Approach," BlakeS, 6, No. 2, 123-125.

_____. "The Chimney Sweeper" (Songs of Innocence)
Paul D. McGlynn, Expl, 27 (Nov., 1968), 20.

Martin K. Nurmi, "Fact and Symbol in 'The Chimney Sweeper' of Blake's Songs of Innocence," BNYPL, 68 (1964), 249-255.

Brian Wilkie, "Blake's Innocence and Experience: An Approach," BlakeS, 6, No. 2, 123-125.

Porter Williams, Jr., "'Duty' in Blake's 'The Chimney Sweeper' of Songs of Innocence," ELN, 12 (Dec., 1974), 92-96.

_____. "The Clod and the Pebble"
Abad, A Formal Approach to Lyric Poetry, pp. 302-303.

Arthur Dickson, Expl, 2 (Nov., 1943), 12.
    Rpt. The Explicator Cyclopedia, II, p. 34.

Edwards, Imagination and Power, pp. 154-156.

Jean H. Hagstrum, "William Blake's 'The Clod and the Pebble,'" in Restoration and Eighteenth Century Literature: Essays in Honor of Alan Dugald McKillop, ed. Charles Camden (Chicago: Univ. of Chicago Press, 1963), pp. 381-388.

Wolf Mankowitz, "William Blake (2) The Songs of Experience," Politics and Letters, 1 (Winter-Spring, 1947), 18-19.

"Olybrius," Expl, 1 (Feb., 1943), 32.
    Rpt. The Explicator Cyclopedia, II, pp. 33-34.

Max F. Schulz, "Point of View in Blake's 'The Clod and the Pebble,'" PLL, 2 (Summer, 1966), 217-224.

Brian Wilkie, "Blake's Innocence and Experience: An Approach," BlakeS, 6, No. 2, 129-130.

_____. "A Cradle Song"
Sanders, The Discovery of Poetry, pp. 162-163.

_____. "The Crystal Cabinet"
Bloom, The Visionary Company, pp. 52-54.

John Sutherland, "Blake: A Crisis of Love and Jealousy," PMLA, 87 (May, 1972), 429-430.

_____. "The Divine Image"
Bloom, The Visionary Company, pp. 38-39.

David J. Smith, Expl, 25 (April, 1967), 69.

_____. "Earth's Answer"
Wolf Mankowitz, "William Blake (2) The Songs of Experience," Politics and Letters, 1 (Winter-Spring, 1947), 16-17.

_____. "The Echoing Green"
Tillyard, Poetry Direct and Oblique, pp. 9-12.
    Rpt. Criticism, pp. 286-288.

_____. "Europe"
D. Aers, "William Blake and the Dialectics of Sex," ELH, 44 (Fall, 1977), 507-508.

_____. "The Everlasting Gospel"
David V. Erdman, "'Terrible Blake in His Pride': An Essay on The Everlasting Gospel," in From Sensibility to Romanticism, pp. 331-352.

Michael Tolley, "Blake's 'Edens Flood' Again," N&Q, 15 (Jan., 1968), 11-19.

Michael Tolley, "William Blake's Use of the Bible in a Section of 'The Everlasting Gospel,'" N&Q, 9 (May, 1962), 171-176.

_____. "The Fly"
F. W. Bateson, "An Editorial Postscript," EIC, 11 (April, 1961), 162-163.

Robert F. Glecker, "Blake Gray, and the Illustrations," Criticism, 19 (Spring, 1977), 127-140.

John E. Grant, "Interpreting Blake's 'The Fly,'" BNYPL, 67 (Nov., 1963), 593-612.

John E. Grant, "Misreadings of 'The Fly,'" EIC, 11 (Oct., 1961), 481-487.

Leo Kerschbuam, Blake's 'The Fly,'" _EIC_, 11 (April, 1961), 154-162.

C. N. Manlove, "Engineered Innocence: Blake's 'The Little Black Boy' and 'The Fly,'" _EIC_, 27 (April, 1977), 117-119.

Robert Mikkelsen, "William Blake's Revisions of the Songs of Innocence and Of Experience," _CP_, 2 (Fall, 1969), 63-64.

Warren Stevenson, "Artful Irony in Blake's 'The Fly,'" _TSLL_, 10 (Spring, 1968), 77-82.

Michael J. Tolley, "Blake's Blind Man," _BlakeS_, 2, No. 1 (1970), 77-84, 86-88.

_____. "For the Sexes: The Gates of Paradise"
Gail Kmetz, "A Reading of Blake's The Gates of Paradise," _BlakeS_, 3 (Spring, 1971), 171-185.

_____. "The Ghost of Abel"
Leslie Tannenbaum, "Lord Byron in the Wilderness: Biblical Tradition in Byron's Cain and Blake's The Ghost of Abel," _MP_, 72 (May, 1975), 350-364.

_____. "Hear the Voice of the Bard"
Bateson, English Poetry, pp. 37-39.

Bodkin, Archetypal Patterns in Poetry, pp. 317-323.

_____. ⤶ "Holy Thursday" (Songs of Innocence)
Bloom, The Visionary Company, pp. 37-38.

Robert F. Gleckner, "Point of View and Context in Blake's Songs," _NYPLL_, 61 (Nov., 1957), 534-535.

Robert Mikkelsen, "William Blake's Revisions of the Songs of Innocence and Of Experience," _CP_, 2 (Fall, 1969), 61-62.

_____. "How Sweet I Roam'd"
W. B. Carnochan, Confinement and Flight: An Essay on English Literature of the Eighteenth Century (Berkeley: Univ. of Calif. Press, 1977), pp. 183-187.

Bert Case Diltz, Sense or Nonsense: Contemporary Education at the Cross-roads (Toronto: McClelland and Stewart Ltd., 1972), pp. 71-75.

_____. "The Human Abstract"
Bloom, The Visionary Company, p. 39.

Edwards, Imagination and Power, pp. 145-149.

_____. "I Asked a Thief"
Rosenthal and Smith, Exploring Poetry, pp. 455-458.

_____. "Imitation of Pope: A Compliment to the Ladies"
M. E. Bacon, _Expl_, 28 (May, 1970), 79.

_____. "In Englands Green & Pleasant Land"
Nancy M. Goslee, "'In Englands Green & Pleasant Land': The Building of Vision in Blake's Stanzas from Milton," _SIR_, 13 (Spring, 1974), 105-125.

_____. "Infant Sorrow"
Wolf Mankowitz, "William Blake (2) The Songs of Experience," _Politics and Letters_, 1 (Winter-Spring, 1947), 21-22.

_____. "Introduction" (Songs of Experience)
Bateson, English Poetry, pp. 37-39.

Bodkin, Archetypal Patterns in Poetry, pp. 317-323.

Northrop Frye, "Blake's Introduction to Experience," HLQ, 21 (Nov., 1957), 57-67.

Robert F. Gleckner, "Point of View and Context in Blake's Songs," BNPYL, 61 (Nov., 1957), 535-537.

Philip Hobsbaum, Theory of Criticism (Bloomington and London: Indiana Univ. Press, 1970), pp. 119-124.

Wolf Mankowitz, "William Blake (2) The Songs of Experience," Politics and Letters, 1 (Winter-Spring, 1947), 15.

Rene Wellek, "A Letter," The Importance of Scrutiny, pp. 24-25. First published in Scrutiny, 1937.

_____. "Introduction" (Songs of Innocence)
William R. Bowden, Expl, 11 (April, 1953), 41.
    Rpt. The Explicator Cyclopedia, II, pp. 36-37.

Frankenberg, Invitation to Poetry, pp. 64-65.

Margaret Giovannini, Expl, 8 (Oct., 1949), 5.
    Rpt. The Explicator Cyclopedia, II, pp. 34-35.

Howard Justin, Expl, 11 (Oct., 1952), 1.
    Rpt. The Explicator Cyclopedia, II, pp. 35-36.

Arthur Wormhoudt, Expl, 7 (May, 1949), 55.
    Rpt. The Explicator Cyclopedia, II, p. 34.

_____. "I Saw a Chapel All of Gold"
Abad, A Formal Approach to Lyric Poetry, pp. 306-307.

_____. "The Lamb"
Bloom, The Visionary Company, pp. 31, 34-35.

Jim S. Borck, "Blake's 'The Lamb': The Punctuation of Innocence," TSL, 19 (1974), 163-175.

_____. "The Lilly"
Mary Lynn Johnson, "Emblem and Symbol in Blake," HLQ, 37 (Feb., 1974), 166-169.

Wolf Mankowitz, "William Blake (2) The Songs of Experience," Politics and Letters, 1 (Winter-Spring, 1947), 20.

Brian Wilkie, "Blake's Innocence and Experience: An Approach," BlakeS, 6, No. 2, 122-123.

_____. "The Little Black Boy"
Jacob H. Adler, "Symbol and Meaning in 'The Little Black Boy," MLN, 72 (June, 1957), 412-415.

Bloom, The Visionary Company, pp. 35-37.

Ralph D. Eberly, Expl, 15 (April, 1957), 42.
    Rpt. The Explicator Cyclopedia, II, 38-39.

Howard H. Hinkel, "From Pivotal Idea to Poetic Ideal: Blake's Theory of Contraries and 'The Little Black Boy,'" PLL, 11 (Winter, 1975), 39-45.

Lloyd N. Jeffrey, Expl, 17 (Jan., 1959), 27.
    Rpt. The Explicator Cyclopedia, II, pp. 39-40.

Kremen, The Imagination of the Resurrection, pp. 142-143.

C. N. Manlove, "Engineered Innocence: Blake's 'The Little Black Boy' and 'The Fly,'" EIC, 27 (April, 1977), 112-117.

Van Doren, Introduction to Poetry, pp. 111-115.

J. E. Whitesell, Expl, 5 (April, 1947), 42.
    Rpt. The Explicator Cyclopedia, II, pp. 37-38.

_____. "The Little Boy Lost" and "The Little Boy Found"
Thomas E. Connolly and George R. Levine, "Pictorial and Poetic Design in Two Songs of Innocence," PMLA, 82 (May, 1967), 257-264.

J. G. Keogh, Thomas E. Connolly and George R. Levine, "Two Songs of Inno-cence," PMLA, 84 (Jan., 1968), 137-140.

_____. "The Little Girl Found"
Kremen, The Imagination of the Resurrection, pp. 147-148.

Barbara F. Lefcowitz, "Blake and the Natural World," PMLA, 89 (Jan., 1974), 128.

_____. "The Little Girl Lost"
Kremen, The Imagination of the Resurrection, pp. 147-148.

Barbara F. Lefcowitz, "Blake and the Natural World," PMLA, 89 (Jan., 1974), 127-128.

Stuart Peterfreund, "The Name of Blake's Lyca Re-Examined," AN&Q, 13 (May, 1975), 135-136.

Joseph Anthony Wittreich, Expl, 27 (April, 1969), 61.

_____. "The Little Girl Lost" and "The Little Girl Found"
Wolf Mankowitz, "William Blake (2) The Songs of Experience," Politics and Letters, 1 (Winter-Spring, 1947), 20.

_____. "The Little Vagabond"
Rodney M. Baine, Expl, 27 (Sept., 1968), 6.

Robert F. Gleckner, "Point of View and Context in Blake's Songs," BNYPL, 61 (Nov., 1957), 534.

_____. "London"
William Blissett, "Poetic Wave and Poetic Particle," UTQ, 24 (Oct., 1954), 5-6.

Bloom, Philbrick, and Blistein, The Order of Poetry, pp. 89-92.

Bloom, Poetry and Repression, pp. 34-44.

Bloom, The Visionary Company, pp. 42-43.

Bowra, The Romantic Imagination, pp. 42-43.

Brooks, Purser, and Warren, An Approach to Literature, pp. 496-498.
    Rpt. third edition, pp. 387-390.
    Rpt. fourth edition, pp. 383-385.

Edwards, Imagination and Power, pp. 141-144.

Donald Hall, The Pleasures of Poetry (New York: Harper & Row, 1971), 56-60.

Archibald Hill, Constituent and Pattern in Poetry (Austin: Univ. of Texas Press, 1976), 73-82.

Wolf Mankowitz, "William Blake (2) The Songs of Experience," Politics and Letters, 1 (Winter-Spring, 1947), 21.

John D. Rosenberg, "Varieties of Infernal Experience," HudR, 23 (Autumn, 1970), 458-459.

Rosenthal and Smith, Exploring Poetry, pp. 693-695.
   Rpt. Locke, Gibson, and Arms, Introduction to Literature, third
   edition, p. 77.
   Rpt. fourth edition, pp. 73-74.
   Rpt. fifth edition, pp. 71-72.

W. K. Wimsatt, "Genesis: A Fallacy Revisited," in The Disciplines of
Criticism: Essays in Literary Theory, Interpretation, and History, ed.
Peter Demetz, Thomas Greene, and Lowry Nelson, Jr. (New Haven and London:
Yale Univ. Press, 1968), pp. 216-220.

W. K. Wimsatt, Hateful Contraries: Studies in Literature and Criticism
(Lexington: Univ. of Kentucky Press, 1965), pp. 230-238.

_____. "Mad Song"
H. J. C. Grierson, "Blake and Macpherson," TLS, April 7, 1945, p. 163.

Geoffrey Keynes, "Blake's 'Poetical Sketches'--I," TLS, March 10, 1945,
p. 120.

Bloom, The Visionary Company, pp. 14-15.

_____. "Memory"
Vivante, English Poetry, p. 91.

_____. "The Mental Traveller"
Arthur Adamson, "Structure and Meaning in Blake's 'The Mental Traveller,'"
Mosaic, 7 (Summer, 1974), 41-58.

Bloom, The Visionary Company, pp. 54-60.

Gerald E. Enscoe, "The Content of Vision: Blake's 'Mental Traveller,'"
PLL, 4 (Fall, 1968), 400-413.

Martin K. Nurmi, "Joy, Love, and Innocence in Blake's 'The Mental Traveller,'" SIR, 3 (Winter, 1964), 109-117.

Morton D. Paley, "The Female Babe and 'The Mental Traveller,'" SIR, 1
(Winter, 1962), 97-104.

John H. Sutherland, "Blake's 'Mental Traveller,'" ELH, 22 (June, 1955),
136-147.

James B. Twitchell, "'The Mental Traveller,' Infinity and the 'Arlington
Court Picture,'" Criticism, 17 (Winter, 1975), 1-8.

_____. "My Pretty Rose Tree"
Robert F. Gleckner, Expl, 13 (May, 1955), 43.
   Rpt. The Explicator Cyclopedia, II, pp. 40-41.

Robert F. Gleckner, "Point of View and Context in Blake's Songs," BNYPL,
61 (Nov., 1957), 531-532.

Mary Lynn Johnson, "Emblem and Symbol in Blake," HLQ, 37 (Feb., 1974),
163.

_____. "My Spectre Around Me...Night & Day"
John Sutherland, "Blake: A Crisis of Love and Jealousy," PMLA, 87
(May, 1972), 427-429.

_____. "Never Pain to Tell Thy Love"
G. J. Finch, "'Never Pain to Tell Thy Love,' Blake's Problem Poem,"
BlakeS, 4 (Fall, 1971), 73-79.

_____. "Night the First"
Barbara F. Lefcowitz, "Blake and the Natural World," PMLA, 89 (Jan., 1974), 126.

_____. "Night the Eighth"
Barbara F. Lefcowitz, "Blake and the Natural World," PMLA, 89 (Jan., 1974), 127.

_____. "Night the Ninth"
Barbara F. Lefcowitz, "Blake and the Natural World," PMLA, 89 (Jan., 1974), 124.

_____. "Nurse's Song" (Songs of Innocence)
Robert Mikkelsen, "William Blake's Revisions of the Songs of Innocence and Of Experience," CP, 2 (Fall, 1969), 60-61.

_____. "O Earth, O Earth, Return"
Bowra, The Romantic Imagination, pp. 46-47.

_____. "A Poison Tree"
Phillip J. Gallagher, "The Word Made Flesh: Blake's 'A Poison Tree' and the Book of Genesis," SIR, 16 (Spring, 1977), 237-249.

Barbara F. Lefcowitz, "Blake and the Natural World," PMLA, 89 (Jan., 1974), 126-127.

T. O. Mabbott and Edward C. Sampson, Expl, 6 (Dec., 1947), 19.
    Rpt. The Explicator Cyclopedia, II, p. 41.

Robert Mikkelsen, "William Blake's Revisions of the Songs of Innocence and Of Experience," CP, 2 (Fall, 1969), 69-70.

_____. "A Pretty Epigram for the Entertainment of Those Who Have Paid Great Sums in the Venetian and Flemish Ooze"
M. E. Bacon, Expl, 28 (May, 1970), 79.

_____. "The Scoffers"
Brooks and Warren, Understanding Poetry, pp. 579-582.
    Revised edition, pp. 423-427.

_____. "The Shepherd"
Dyson and Lovelock, Masterful Images, pp. 131-133.

_____. "The Sick Rose"
Adams, The Contexts of Poetry, pp. 174-175.
H. L. Anshutz and D. W. Cummings, Expl, 29 (Dec., 1970), 32.

Bloom, The Visionary Company, pp. 40-41.

Bowra, The Romantic Imagination, p. 44.
    Abridged in The Case for Poetry, p. 25.

Brower, The Fields of Light, pp. 6-11.

Ralph G. Dillon, "Source for Blake's 'The Sick Rose,'" AN&Q, 12 (May/June, 1974), 157-158.

Drew, Discovering Poetry, pp. 63-64.

Dyson and Lovelock, Masterful Images, pp. 134-135.

Edwards, Imagination and Power, pp. 156-158.

Felver and Nurmi, Poetry: An Introduction and Anthology, pp. 73-76.

Jerome, Poetry: Premeditated Art, pp. 142-143.

F. R. Leavis, "'Thought' and Emotional Quality," Scrutiny, 13 (Spring, 1945), 69-70.

Wolf Mankowitz, "William Blake (2) The Songs of Experience," Politics and Letters 1 (Winter-Spring, 1947), 17-18.

E. H. W. Meyerstein, "'A True Maid' and 'The Sick Rose,'" TLS, June 22, 1946, p. 295.

Laurence Perrine, "The Nature of Proof in the Interpretation of Poetry," EJ, 51 (Sept., 1962), 398.
    Rpt. The Art of Total Relevance, pp. 17-19.

Rosenthal and Smith, Exploring Poetry, pp. 501-502.

Tillyard, Poetry Direct and Oblique, pp. 168-170.
    Abridged in The Case for Poetry, p. 25.

Brian Wilkie, "Blake's Innocence and Experience: An Approach," BlakeS, 6 No. 2, 130-134.

_____. "Song: How Sweet I Roam'd from Field to Field"
Bloom, The Visionary Company, pp. 13-14.

_____. "Song: My Silks and Fine Array"
Cleanth Brooks, "Current Critical Theory and the Period Course," CEA, 12 (Oct., 1950), 1, 5-6.

_____. "A Song of Liberty"
Mary V. Jackson, "Prolific and Devourer: From Nonmythic to Mythic State-ment in The Marriage of Heaven and Hell and A Song of Liberty," JEGP, 70 (April, 1971), 215-219.

Allan Kline, Expl, 15 (Oct., 1956), 4.
    Rpt. The Explicator Cyclopedia, II, pp. 41-42.

_____. "The Song of Los"
David V. Erdman, "The Symmetries of The Song of Los," SIR, 16 (Spring, 1977), 179-188.

_____. "Songs of Innocence"
Wallace Jackson, "William Blake in 1789: Unorganized Innocence," MLQ, 33 (Dec., 1972), 396-404.

_____. "Stanzas from Milton"
Nancy M. Goslee, "'In Englands Green & Pleasant Land': The Building of Vision in Blake's Stanzas from Milton," SIR, (Winter, 1974), 105-125.

L. G. Locke, Expl, 1 (March, 1943), 38.
    Rpt. The Explicator Cyclopedia, II, p. 42.

_____. "The Tyger"
M. E. Bacon, Expl, 26 (Dec., 1967), 35.

Mary B. and Rodney M. Baine, "Blake's Other Tigers, and 'The Tyger,'" SEL, 15 (Autumn, 1975), 563-578.

Rodney M. Baine, "Blake's 'The Tyger': The Nature of the Beast," PQ, 46 (Oct., 1967), 488-498.

Basler, Sex, Symbolism, and Psychology in Literature, pp. 19-24.

Beaty and Matchett, Poetry: From Statement to Meaning, pp. 242-244.

Bloom, Poetry and Repression, pp. 44-51.

Bloom, The Visionary Company, pp. 31-35.

Robert O. Bowen, Expl, 7 (June, 1949), 62.
   Rpt. The Explicator Cyclopedia, p. 44.

Bowra, The Romantic Imagination, pp. 47-49.

Joseph X. Brennan, "The Symbolic Framework of Blake's 'The Tyger,'" CE, (March, 1961), 406-407.

William S. Doxey, "William Blake and William Herschel: The Poet, The Astronomer, and 'The Tyger,'" BlakeS, 2 (Spring, 1970), 5-13.

Drew, Discovering Poetry, p. 160.

R. D. Eberly, Expl, 8 (Nov., 1949), 12.
   Rpt. The Explicator Cyclopedia, II, p. 44.

John E. Grant and Fred C. Robinson, "Tense and the Sense of Blake's 'The Tyger,'" PMLA, 81 (Dec., 1966), 596-603.

John E. Grant, "The Art and Argument of 'The Tiger,'" TSLL, 2 (Spring, 1960), 38-60.

James Hazen, "Blake's Tyger and Milton's Beasts," BlakeS, 3 (Spring, 1971), 163-170.

Philip Hobsbaum, Theory of Criticism (Bloomington and London: Indiana Univ. Press, 1970), pp. 67-71.

Fred Kaplan, "'The Tyger' and Its Maker: Blake's Vision of Art and the Artist," SEL, 7 (Autumn, 1967), 617-628.
   Rpt. Miracles of Rare Device, pp. 17-28.

Christopher Keane, "Blake and O'Neill: A Prophecy," BlakeS, 2 (Spring, 1970), 23-34.

T. O. Mabbott, N&Q, 188 (Nov., 1945), 211-212.

Wolf Mankowitz, "William Blake (2) The Songs of Experience," Politics and Letters, 1 (Winter-Spring, 1947), 22-23.

Robert Mikkelsen, "William Blake's Revisions of the Songs of Innocence and Of Experience," CP, 2 (Fall, 1969), 64-69.

Paul Miner, "'The Tyger': Genesis and Evolution in the Poetry of William Blake," Criticism, 4 (Winter, 1962), 59-73.

Elizabeth Nitchie, Expl, 1 (Feb., 1943), 34.
   Rpt. The Explicator Cyclopedia, II, pp. 43-44.

Martin K. Nurmi, "Blake's Revisions of The Tyger," PMLA, 71 (Sept., 1956), 669-683.

Morton D. Paley, "Tiger of Wrath," PMLA, 81 (Dec., 1966), 540-551.

Eli Pfefferkorn, "The Question of the Leviathan and the Tiger," BlakeS, 3, No. 1, 53-60.

Frederick A. Pottle, Expl, 8 (March, 1950), 39.
   Rpt. The Explicator Cyclopedia, II, p. 44.

Ribner and Morris, Poetry: A Critical and Historical Introduction, pp. 249-251.

Rosenthal and Smith, Exploring Poetry, pp. 185-187.
   Rpt. The Explicator Cyclopedia, II, p. 43.

Warren Stevenson, "'The Tyger' as Artefact," BlakeS, 2, No. 1 (1970), 5-19.

George Winchester Stone, Jr., Expl, 1 (Dec., 1942), 19.

L. J. Swingle, "Answers to Blake's 'Tyger': A Matter of Reason or of Choice?" <u>CP</u>, 2 (Spring, 1969), 61-70.

Wheeler, <u>The Design of Poetry</u>, pp. 72-75.

Winters, <u>Forms of Discovery</u>, pp. 161-162.

_____. "To Autumn"
Irene H. Chayes, "Blake and the Seasons of the Poet," <u>SIR</u>, 11 (Summer, 1972), 233-237.

Robert F. Gleckner, "Blake's Seasons," <u>SEL</u>, 5 (Summer, 1965), 544-546.

_____. "To Spring"
Irene H. Chayes, "Blake and the Seasons of the Poet," <u>SIR</u>, 11 (Summer, 1972), 228-229.

Robert F. Gleckner, "Blake's Seasons," <u>SEL</u>, 5 (Summer, 1965), 541-542.

Vivante, <u>English Poetry</u>, pp. 89-90.

W. K. Wimsatt, Jr., "The Structure of Romantic Nature Imagery," <u>The Age of Johnson</u> (New Haven: Yale University Press, 1949), pp. 300-301.
     Rpt. <u>The Verbal Icon</u>, pp. 112-113.

_____. "To Summer"
Irene H. Chayes, "Blake and the Seasons of the Poet," <u>SIR</u>, 11 (Summer, 1972), 229-233.

Robert F. Gleckner, "Blake's Seasons," <u>SEL</u>, 5 (Summer, 1965), 542-544.

_____. "To the Accuser Who Is the God of the World"
E. J. Rose, <u>Expl</u>, 22 (Jan., 1964), 37.

Stauffer, <u>The Nature of Poetry</u>, pp. 53-54.

_____. "To the Muses"
Vivante, <u>English Poetry</u>, p. 92.

_____. "To Tirzah"
Bloom, <u>The Visionary Company</u>, pp. 43-44.

Thomas A. Reisner, <u>Expl</u>, 33 (Sept., 1974), 3.

_____. "To Winter"
Irene H. Chayes, "Blake and the Seasons of the Poet," <u>SIR</u>, 11 (Summer, 1972), 237-240.

Robert F. Gleckner, "Blake's Seasons," <u>SEL</u>, 5 (Summer, 1965), 546-551.

_____. "Visions of the Daughters of Albion"
D. Aers, "William Blake and the Dialectics of Sex," <u>ELH</u>, 44 (Fall, 1977), 500-507.

Bloom, <u>The Visionary Company</u>, pp. 49-52.

Roland A. Duerksen, "The Life of Love: Blake's Oothoon," <u>CLQ</u>, 13 (Sept., 1977), 186-194.

Barbara F. Lefcowitz, "Blake and the Natural World," <u>PMLA</u>, 89 (Jan., 1974), 122.

Jane E. Peterson, "The <u>Visions of the Daughters of Albion</u>: A Problem in Perception," <u>PQ</u>, 52 (April, 1973), 252-264.

Henry H. Wasser, "Notes on the <u>Visions of the Daughters of Albion</u>," <u>MLQ</u>, 9 (Sept., 1948), 292-297.

_____. "William Bond"
John Sutherland, "Blake: A Crisis of Love and Jealousy," PMLA, 87 (May, 1972), 426-427.

BLUNDEN. "A Summer's Fancy"
Robert Penn Warren, Poetry, 48 (Feb., 1934), 287-288.

_____. "Thomasine"
Anonymous, "Menander's Mirror: Mr. Blunden's 'Thomasine,'" TLS, Jan. 20, 1945, p. 27.

BLY. "Driving Toward the La Qui Parle River"
Lacey, The Inner War, pp. 39-41.

_____. "Like the New Moon I Will Live My Life"
George S. Lensing and Ronald Moran, Four Poets and the Emotive Imagination: Robert Bly, James Wright, Louis Simpson, and William Stafford (Baton Rouge: Louisiana State Univ. Press, 1976), p. 81.

_____. "Meeting the Man Who Wants Me"
Michael Atkinson, "Robert Bly's Sleepers Joining Hands: Shadow and Self," IowaR, 7 (Fall, 1976), 142-145.

_____. "Night Journey in the Cooking Pot"
Michael Atkinson, "Robert Bly's Sleepers Joining Hands: Shadow and Self," IowaR, 7 (Fall, 1976), 145-148.

_____. "The Teeth Mother Naked at Last"
Michael Atkinson, "Robert Bly's Sleepers Joining Hands: Shadow and Self," IowaR, 7 (Fall, 1976), 138-141.

Lacey, The Inner War, pp. 51-55.

_____. "Watering the Horse"
Lacey, The Inner War, pp. 38-39.

BOGAN. "The Dream"
Perrine and Reid, 100 American Poems, pp. 146-147.

_____. "The Exhortation"
Winters, Forms of Discovery, pp. 279-281.

_____. "Simple Autumnal"
Winters, Forms of Discovery, pp. 278-279.

_____. "Solitary Observations..."
Daniels, The Art of Reading Poetry, pp. 199-200.

BOWERS. "Adam's Song to Heaven"
Helen P. Trimpi, "Contexts for 'Being,' 'Divinity,' and 'Self' in Valéry and Edgar Bowers," SoR, 13 n.s. (Winter, 1977), 65-66.

_____. "The Astronomers of Mont Blanc"
Winters, Forms of Discovery, pp. 284-286.

_____. "Autumn Shade"
Helen P. Trimpi, "Contexts for 'Being,' 'Divinity,' and 'Self' in Valéry and Edgar Bowers," SoR, 13 n.s. (Winter, 1977), 69-70, 72-80.

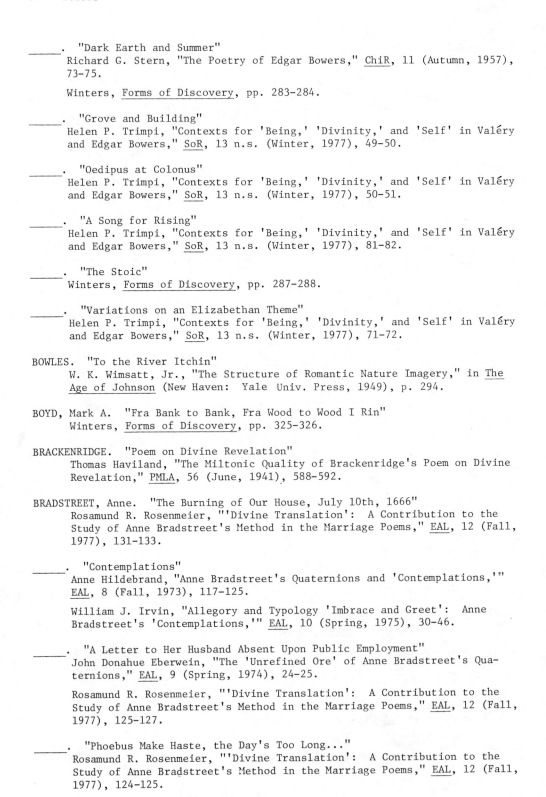

_____. "Dark Earth and Summer"
Richard G. Stern, "The Poetry of Edgar Bowers," ChiR, 11 (Autumn, 1957),
73-75.

Winters, Forms of Discovery, pp. 283-284.

_____. "Grove and Building"
Helen P. Trimpi, "Contexts for 'Being,' 'Divinity,' and 'Self' in Valéry
and Edgar Bowers," SoR, 13 n.s. (Winter, 1977), 49-50.

_____. "Oedipus at Colonus"
Helen P. Trimpi, "Contexts for 'Being,' 'Divinity,' and 'Self' in Valéry
and Edgar Bowers," SoR, 13 n.s. (Winter, 1977), 50-51.

_____. "A Song for Rising"
Helen P. Trimpi, "Contexts for 'Being,' 'Divinity,' and 'Self' in Valéry
and Edgar Bowers," SoR, 13 n.s. (Winter, 1977), 81-82.

_____. "The Stoic"
Winters, Forms of Discovery, pp. 287-288.

_____. "Variations on an Elizabethan Theme"
Helen P. Trimpi, "Contexts for 'Being,' 'Divinity,' and 'Self' in Valéry
and Edgar Bowers," SoR, 13 n.s. (Winter, 1977), 71-72.

BOWLES. "To the River Itchin"
W. K. Wimsatt, Jr., "The Structure of Romantic Nature Imagery," in The
Age of Johnson (New Haven: Yale Univ. Press, 1949), p. 294.

BOYD, Mark A. "Fra Bank to Bank, Fra Wood to Wood I Rin"
Winters, Forms of Discovery, pp. 325-326.

BRACKENRIDGE. "Poem on Divine Revelation"
Thomas Haviland, "The Miltonic Quality of Brackenridge's Poem on Divine
Revelation," PMLA, 56 (June, 1941), 588-592.

BRADSTREET, Anne. "The Burning of Our House, July 10th, 1666"
Rosamund R. Rosenmeier, "'Divine Translation': A Contribution to the
Study of Anne Bradstreet's Method in the Marriage Poems," EAL, 12 (Fall,
1977), 131-133.

_____. "Contemplations"
Anne Hildebrand, "Anne Bradstreet's Quaternions and 'Contemplations,'"
EAL, 8 (Fall, 1973), 117-125.

William J. Irvin, "Allegory and Typology 'Imbrace and Greet': Anne
Bradstreet's 'Contemplations,'" EAL, 10 (Spring, 1975), 30-46.

_____. "A Letter to Her Husband Absent Upon Public Employment"
John Donahue Eberwein, "The 'Unrefined Ore' of Anne Bradstreet's Quaternions," EAL, 9 (Spring, 1974), 24-25.

Rosamund R. Rosenmeier, "'Divine Translation': A Contribution to the
Study of Anne Bradstreet's Method in the Marriage Poems," EAL, 12 (Fall,
1977), 125-127.

_____. "Phoebus Make Haste, the Day's Too Long..."
Rosamund R. Rosenmeier, "'Divine Translation': A Contribution to the
Study of Anne Bradstreet's Method in the Marriage Poems," EAL, 12 (Fall,
1977), 124-125.

BRAUN, Richard E. "Against Nature"
  Jerome Mazzaro, "Putting It Together: The Poetry of Richard Emil Braun,"
  MPS, 5 (Winter, 1974), 256-258.

BRIDGES. "Eros"
  Rosenthal and Smith, Exploring Poetry, pp. 183-185.

  Winters, Primitivism and Decadence, pp. 66-71. Also in Defense of Reason,
  pp. 77-82, and in The Forms of Discovery, pp. 198-199.

_____. "In the Summer House on the Mound"
  Yvor Winters, "Traditional Mastery," Hound and Horn, 5 (Jan.-March, 1932),
  324-325.

_____. "London Snow"
  Lindon Stall, "Robert Bridges and the Laws of English Stressed Verse,"
  Agenda, 11 (Spring-Summer, 1973), 98-100.

_____. "Low Barometer"
  Yvor Winters, "The Poetry of Gerard Manley Hopkins (1)," HudR, 1 (Winter,
  1948), 458-460.
     Rpt. The Function of Criticism, pp. 105-107.
     Rpt. The Forms of Discovery, pp. 196-198.

_____. "Nightingales"
  Beaty and Matchett, Poetry: From Statement to Meaning, pp. 21-27.

  Brooks and Warren, Understanding Poetry, pp. 198-200.
     Revised edition, pp. 95-97.

  Daniels, The Art of Reading Poetry, p. 375.

  Bert Case Diltz, Sense or Nonsense: Contemporary Education at the Cross-
  roads (Toronto: McClelland and Stewart Ltd., 1972), pp. 101-103.

  Lindon Stall, "Robert Bridges and the Laws of English Stressed Verse,"
  Agenda, 11 (Spring-Summer, 1973), 105-106.

_____. "Ode to Music"
  Andrew J. Green, "Bridges' Odes for Music," SR, 49 (Jan.-March, 1941),
  30-38.

_____. "On a Dead Child"
  Lindon Stall, "Robert Bridges and the Laws of English Stressed Verse,"
  Agenda, 11 (Spring-Summer, 1973), 102-103.

BRINNIN. "The Alps"
  David Daiches, "Some Notes on Contemporary American Poetry," in Modern
  American Poetry, ed. B. Rajan, pp. 113-114.

_____. "The Fortunate Isles"
  Beach, Obsessive Images, pp. 136-137.

_____. "Goodnight, When the Door Swings"
  David Daiches, "Some Notes on Contemporary American Poetry," in Modern
  American Poetry, ed. B. Rajan, p. 114.

_____. "Islands: A Song"
  Beach, Obsessive Images, pp. 135-136.

_____. "A Sail"
Beach, Obsessive Images, pp. 166-168.

_____. "Second Sight"
Beach, Obsessive Images, pp. 168-169.

_____. "Skin Diving in the Virgins"
Perrine and Reid, 100 American Poems, p. 239.

_____. "Views of the Favorite Colleges"
Sr. Mary Humiliata, I.H.M., Expl, 14 (Jan., 1956), 20.
    Rpt. The Explicator Cyclopedia, I, pp. 22-23.

_____. "The Worm in the Whirling Cross"
J. F. Nims, Poetry: A Critical Supplement, Nov., 1947, pp. 1-15.
    Rpt. in part in Friar and Brinnin, Modern Poetry, pp. 447-449.

John Theobald, "The World in a Cross Word," Poetry, 71 (Nov., 1947), 82-90.

BRONTE, Emily. "Cold in the Earth"
F. R. Leavis, "Reality and Sincerity: Notes in the Analysis of Poetry,"
Scrutiny, 19 (Winter, 1952-3), 90-92, 93-94.

_____. "No Coward Soul is Mine"
Mark Roberts, The Tradition of Romantic Morality (London and Basingstoke:
Macmillan Press, 1973), 187-188.

Lawrence J. Starzyk, "The Faith of Emily Bronte's Immortality Creed,"
VP, 11 (Winter, 1973), 295-305.

BROOKE. "The Soldier"
Daniels, The Art of Reading Poetry, pp. 270-272.

BROOKS, Gwendolyn. "The Chicago Picasso"
William H. Hansell, "Aestheticism Versus Political Militancy in Gwendolyn
Brooks's 'The Chicago Picasso' and 'The Wall,'" CLA, 17 (Sept., 1973),
11-13.

_____. "The Children of the Poor"
Hayden Carruth, Poetry: A Critical Supplement, March, 1949, pp. 13-15.

_____. "A Light and Diplomatic Bird"
Hayden Carruth, Poetry: A Critical Supplement, March, 1949, pp. 16-18.

_____. "The Third Sermon on the Warpland"
William H. Hansell, "The Role of Violence in Recent Poems of Gwendolyn
Brooks," SBL, 5 (Summer, 1974), 22-25.

_____. "The Wall"
William H. Hansell, "Aestheticism Versus Political Militancy in Gwendolyn
Brooks's 'The Chicago Picasso' and 'The Wall,'" CLA, 17 (Sept., 1973),
13-15.

_____. "We Real Cool"
Barbara B. Sims, Expl, 34 (April, 1976), 58.

BROWN, Harry. "Fourth Elegy: The Poet Compared to an Unsuccessful General"
Hayden Carruth, "The Poet with Wounds," Poetry, 71 (Jan., 1948), 217-221.

J. F. Nims, Poetry: A Critical Supplement, Jan., 1948, pp. 2-12.

BROWN, Thomas E. "My Garden"
    Daniels, The Art of Reading Poetry, p. 261.

BROWNE. "Epitaph on the Countess Dowager of Pembroke"
    Abad, A Formal Approach to Lyric Poetry, pp. 42-43.

    Tate, Reason in Madness, pp. 95-96.
        Rpt. On the Limits of Poetry, p. 125.

    Allen Tate, "Understanding Modern Poetry," CE, 1 (April, 1940), 570.

BROWNING, E. B. "A Curse for a Nation"
    Leonid M. Arenshtein, "'A Curse for a Nation': A Controversial Episode
    in Elizabeth Barrett Browning's Political Poetry," RES, 20 (Feb., 1969),
    33-42.

_____. Sonnet 6 from Sonnets from the Portuguese
    Carol McGinnis Kay, "An Analysis of Sonnet 6 in Sonnets from the Portu-
    guese," CP, 4 (Spring, 1971), 17-21.

_____. Sonnet 22 from Sonnets from the Portuguese
    Robert M. Gay, Expl, 1 (Dec., 1942), 24.
        Rpt. The Explicator Cyclopedia, II, p. 379.

_____. Sonnet 43 from Sonnets from the Portuguese
    William T. Going, Expl, 11 (June, 1953), 58.
        Rpt. The Explicator Cyclopedia, II, pp. 45-46.

    Robert B. Heilman, Expl, 4 (Oct., 1945), 3.
        Rpt. Readings for Liberal Education, II, pp. 213-214.
        Rpt. Locke, Gibson, and Arms, Introduction to Literature, third edi-
    tion, pp. 116-117.
        Rpt. fourth edition, pp. 115-116.
        Rpt. The Explicator Cyclopedia, II, p. 45.

BROWNING, Robert. "Abt Vogler"
    Alan Bishop and John Ferns, "'Art in Obedience to Laws': Form and Meaning
    in Browning's 'Abt Vogler,'" VP, 12 (Spring, 1974), 25-32.

    Bloom, Poetry and Repression, pp. 186-191.

    Langbaum, The Poetry of Experience, pp. 140-143.

    Emerson R. Marks, Expl, 16 (Feb., 1958), 29.
        Rpt. The Explicator Cyclopedia, II, pp. 46-47.

    P. M. Plunkett, S.J., Expl, 25 (Oct., 1966), 14.

    George M. Ridenour, "Browning's Music Poems: Fancy and Fact," PMLA, 78
    (Sept., 1963), 374-375.

_____. "Andrea Del Sarto"
    Abad, A Formal Approach to Lyric Poetry, pp. 116-119.

    Elizabeth Bieman, "An Eros Manqué: Browning's 'Andrea del Sarto,'" SEL,
    10 (Autumn, 1970), 651-668.

    Bloom, Poetry and Repression, pp. 191-194.

    Paul A. Cundiff, "'Andrea del Sarto,'" TSL, 13 (1968), 27-38.

    Mario L. D'Avanzo, "King Francis, Lucrezia, and the Figurative Language
    of 'Andrea del Sarto,'" TSLL, 9 (Winter, 1968), 523-536.

    George V. Griffith, "'Andrea del Sarto' and the New Jerusalem," VP, 15
    (Winter, 1977), 371-372.

Langbaum, The Poetry of Experience, pp. 148-151, 152-155.

Sydney Mendel, Expl, 22 (May, 1964), 77.

Kaplan, Miracles of Rare Device, pp. 94-108.

Charles Child Walcutt, The Explicator Cyclopedia, I, "Introduction,"
p. xii.
_____. "Any Wife to Any Husband"
Richard Kelly, "The Dramatic Relationship Between 'By the Fire-side' and
'Any Wife to Any Husband,'" VN, 39 (Spring, 1971), 20-21.

_____. Balaustion's Adventure
Clyde de L. Ryals, "Balustion's Adventure: Browning's Greek Parable,"
PMLA, 88 (Oct., 1973), 1040-1048.

_____. "Bishop Blougram's Apology"
John Britton, S.J., Expl, 17 (April, 1959), 50.
    Rpt. The Explicator Cyclopedia, II, pp. 47-48.

William Irvine, "Four Monologues in Browning's Men and Women," VP, 2
(Autumn, 1964), 158-160.

Langbaum, The Poetry of Experience, pp. 100-102.

William O. Raymond, "Browning's Casuists," SP, 37 (Oct., 1940), 648-653.

C. E. Tanzy, VS, 1 (March, 1958), 255-266.

C. N. Wenger, "The Masquerade in Browning's Dramatic Monologues," CE, 3
(Dec., 1941), 228-229.

_____. "The Bishop Orders His Tomb at St. Praxed's Church"
Abad, A Formal Approach to Lyric Poetry, pp. 78-80.

Francis W. Bonner, Expl, 22 (March, 1964), 57.

Frank J. Chiarenza, Expl, 19 (Jan., 1961), 22.

Daniels, The Art of Reading Poetry, pp. 99-101.

Ernest L. Fontana, "Browning's St. Praxed's Bishop: A Naturalistic View,"
VP, 10 (Autumn, 1972), 278-282.

Robert A. Greenberg, "Ruskin, Pugin, and the Contemporary Context of 'The
Bishop Orders His Tomb,'" PMLA, 84 (Oct., 1969), 1588-1594.

Virgil F. Grillo, "Browning's Cuckold of St. Praxed's?" VP, 11 (Spring,
1973), 66-68.

Nathaniel I. Hart, Expl, 19 (Jan., 1971), 36.

Jerome, Poetry: Premeditated Art, pp. 236-242.

Vincent M. Milosevich, Expl, 27 (May, 1969), 67.

George Monteiro, "The Apostasy and Death of St. Praxed's Bishop," VP, 8
(Autumn, 1970), 209-218.

Laurence Perrine, "Family Relationships at Saint Praxed's," VP, 12
(Summer, 1974), 175-177.

Laurence Perrine, Expl, 24 (Oct., 1965), 12.

Charles T. Phipps, S.J., "The Bishop as Bishop: Clerical Motif and
Meaning in 'The Bishop Orders His Tomb at St. Praxed's Church,'" VP, 8
(Autumn, 1970), 199-208.

Heide Ziegler, Expl, 32 (Feb., 1974), 45.

_____. "Caliban Upon Setebos"
E. K. Brown, "The First Person in 'Caliban Upon Setebos,'" MLN, 66 (June, 1951), 392-395.

Christ, The Finer Optic, pp. 73-80.

John Howard, "Caliban's Mind," VP, 1 (Winter, 1963), 249-257.

Laurence Perrine, "Browning's 'Caliban Upon Setebos': A Reply," VP, 2 (Summer, 1964), 124-127.

Michael Rimko, "Browning Upon Butler; or, Natural Theology in the English Isle," Criticism, 7 (Spring, 1965), 141-150.

Arnold Shapiro, "Browning's Psalm of Hate: 'Caliban Upon Setebos,' Psalm 50, and The Tempest," PLL, 8 (Winter, 1972), 53-62.

_____. "Childe Roland to the Dark Tower Came"
George Arms, "'Childe Roland' and 'Sir Galahad,'" CE, 6 (Feb., 1945), 258-262.

Thomas J. Assad, "Browning's 'Childe Roland to the Dark Tower Came,'" TSE, 21 (1974), 67-76.

Bloom, A Map of Misreading, pp. 106-122.

Harold Bloom, "How to Read a Poem: Browning's Childe Roland," GaR, 28 (Fall, 1974), 404-418.

Bloom, Poetry and Repression, pp. 198-201.

Harold Bloom, The Ringers in the Tower: Studies in Romantic Tradition (Chicago and London: Univ. of Chicago Press, 1971), pp. 157-167.

William Cadbury, "Lyric and Anti-Lyric Forms: A Method for Judging Browning," UTQ, 34 (Oct., 1964), 55-58.

C. C. Clarke, "Humor and Wit in 'Childe Roland,'" MLQ, 23 (Dec., 1962), 323-336.

David V. Erdman, "Browning's Industrial Nightmare," PQ, 36 (Oct., 1957), 427-435.

Donald J. Gray, "Arthur, Roland, Empedocles, Sigurd, and the Despair of Heroes in Victorian Poetry," Bosotn University Studies in English, 5 (Spring, 1961), 8-9.

R. E. Hughes, "Browning's 'Childe Roland' and the Broken Taboo," L&P, 9 (Spring, 1959), 18-19.

Eugene R. Kintgen, "Childe Roland and the Perversity of the Mind," VP, 4 (Autumn, 1966), 253-258.

Langbaum, The Poetry of Experience, pp. 192-200.

John King McComb, "Beyond the Dark Tower: Childe Roland's Painful Memories," ELH, 42 (Fall, 1975), 460-470.

Joyce S. Meyers, "'Childe Roland to the Dark Tower Came': A Nightmare Confrontation With Death," VP, 8 (Winter, 1970), 335-339.

Philip Raisor, "The Failure of Browning's Childe Roland," TSL, 17 (1972), 99-110.

Arnold Shapiro, "'Childe Roland,' Lear and the Ability to See," PLL, (Winter, 1975), 88-94.

Clarice Short, "Childe Roland, Pedestrian," VP, 6 (Summer, 1968), 175-177.

Lionel Stevenson, "The Pertinacious Victorian Poets," UTQ, 21 (April, 1952), 239-240.

Leslie M. Thompson, "Biblical Influence in 'Childe Roland to the Dark Tower Came,'" PLL, 3 (Fall, 1967), 339-353.

Judith Weissman, "Browning's Politics of Hell: 'Childe Roland to the Dark Tower Came' and 'The Statue and the Bust,'" CP, 10 (Fall, 1977), 13-19.

John W. Willoughby, "Browning's 'Childe Roland to the Dark Tower Came,'" VP, 1 (Nov., 1963), 291-299.

_____. "Cleon"
William Irvine, "Four Monologues in Browning's Men and Women," VP, 2 (Autumn, 1964), 162-163.

Young F. Lee, "The Human Condition: Browning's 'Cleon,'" VP, 7 (Spring, 1969), 56-62.

Edward C. McAleer, "Browning's 'Cleon' and Auguste Comte," CL, 8 (Spring, 1956), 143-145.

_____. "Clive"
Mark Siegchrist, "Narrative Obtuseness in Browning's 'Clive,'" SBHC, 3 (Spring, 1975), 53-60.

_____. "Count Gismond"
Frank Allen, "Ariosto and Browning: A Reexamination of 'Count Gismond,'" VP, 11 (Spring, 1973), 15-25.

Christ, The Finer Optic, pp. 117-119.

John V. Hagopian, "The Mask of Countess Gismond," PQ, 40 (Jan., 1961), 153-156.

Sr. Marcella Holloway, "A Further Reading of 'Count Gismond.'" SP, 60 (April, 1963), 549-553.

Ina B. Sessions, "The Dramatic Monologue," PMLA, 62 (June, 1947), 510-511.

John W. Tilton and R. Dale Tuttle, "A New Reading of 'Count Gismond,'" SP, 59 (Jan., 1962), 83-95.

Michael Timko, "Ah, Did You Once See Browning Plain?" SEL, 6 (Autumn, 1966), 731-742.

_____. "Cristina"
Clyde S. Kilby, Expl, 2 (Nov., 1943), 16.
    Rpt. The Explicator Cyclopedia, II, pp. 48-49.

_____. "A Death in the Desert"
Elinor Shaffer, "Browning's St. John: The Casuistry of Higher Criticism," VS, 16 (Dec., 1972), 205-221.

_____. "A Dialogue Between Apollo and the Fates" Prologue, Parleyings
Mark Siegchrist, "Type Needs Antitype: The Structure of Browning's Parleyings," VN, 5 (Fall, 1976), 3-4.

_____. "Dis Aliter Visum; or Le Byron de Nos Jours"
Kaplan, Miracles of Rare Device, pp. 115-123.

_____. "The Englishman in Italy"
Christ, The Finer Optic, pp. 66-69, 72-73.

_____. "An Epistle Containing the Strange Medical Experience of Karshish, the
Arab Physician"
James R. Bennett, "Lazarus in Browning's 'Karshish,'" VP, 3 (Summer,
1965), 189-191.

Wilfred L. Guerin, "Irony and Tension in Browning's 'Karshish,'" VP, 1
(Summer, 1963), 132-139.

William Irvine, "Four Monologues in Browning's Men and Women," VP, 2
(Autumn, 1964), 160-162.

Roma A. King, Jr., "Karshish Encounters Himself: An Interpretation of
Browning's 'Epistle,'" CP, 1 (Spring, 1968), 23-33.

Mary K. Mishler, "God Versus God: The Tension in 'Karshish,'" ELN, 13
(Dec., 1975), 132-137.

Maureen Wright, "An Epistle Containing the Strange Medical Experience of
Karshish, the Arab Physician," TLS, May 1, 1953, p. 285.

_____. "Evelyn Hope"
George O. Marshall, Jr., "Evelyn Hope's Lover," VP, 4 (Winter, 1966),
32-34.

Susan Radnor, "Love and the Lover in Browning's 'Evelyn Hope,'" L&P, 16
(Spring, 1966), 115-116.

Ina B. Sessions, "The Dramatic Monologue," PMLA, 62 (June, 1947), 515.

C. E. Tanzy, "Madness and Hope in Browning's 'Evelyn Hope,'" L&P, 17,
Nos. 2 and 3 (1967), 155-158.

_____. "Flute Music: With an Accompaniment"
George M. Ridenour, "Browning's Music Poems: Fancy and Fact," PMLA, 78
(Sept., 1963), 272-273.

_____. "Fra Lippo Lippi"
Michael H. Bright, "John the Baptist in Browning's 'Fra Lippo Lippi,'"
VP, 15 (Spring, 1977), 75-77.

Edwin M. Everett, Expl, 16 (Dec., 1957), 18.
    Rpt. The Explicator Cyclopedia, II, p. 51.

C. M. Hudson, Jr., and Edward H. Weatherly, "The Survey Course at the
University of Missouri," CE, 8 (March, 1947), 323-327.

William Irvine, "Four Monologues in Browning's Men and Women," VP, 2
(Autumn, 1964), 156-158.

Boyd Litzinger, "Incident as Microcosm: The Prior's Niece in 'Fra Lippo
Lippi,'" CE, 22 (March, 1961), 409-410.

Boyd A. Litzinger, "The Prior's Niece in 'Fra Lippo Lippi,'" N&Q, 8
(Sept., 1961), 344-345.

R. G. Malbone, Expl, 25 (Nov., 1966), 20.

Glen Omans, "Browning's 'Fra Lippo Lippi,' A Transcedentalist Monk," VP,
7 (Summer, 1969), 129-145.

John Ower, "The Abuse of the Hand: A Thematic Motif in Browning's 'Fra
Lippo Lippi,'" VP, 14 (Summer, 1976), 135-141.

Margaret W. Pepperdene, Expl, 15 (Feb., 1957), 34.
   Rpt. The Explicator Cyclopedia, II, pp. 49-50.

Laurence Perrine, Expl, 16 (Dec., 1957), 18.
   Rpt. The Explicator Cyclopedia, II, pp. 50-51.

W. David Shaw, "Character and Philosophy in 'Fra Lippo Lippi,'" VP, 2 (Spring, 1964), 127-132.

David Sonstroem, "On Resisting Brother Lippo," TSLL, 15 (Winter, 1974), 721-734.

C. S. Vogel, "Browning's Salome: An Allusion in 'Fra Lippo Lippi,'" VP, 14 (Winter, 1976), 346-348.

_____. "The Glove"
Louise Schutz Boas, Expl, 2 (Nov., 1943), 13.
   Rpt. The Explicator Cyclopedia, II, p. 51.

Louis S. Friedland, Expl, 1 (May, 1943), 54.
   Rpt. The Explicator Cyclopedia, II, p. 51.

Louis S. Friedland, Expl, 2 (Feb., 1944), 30.
   Rpt. The Explicator Cyclopedia, II, p. 52.

Neil D. Isaacs and Richard M. Kelly, "Dramatic Tension and Irony in Browning's 'The Glove,'" VP, 8 (Summer, 1970), 157-159.

David Sonstroem, "'Fine Speeches like Gold' in Browning's 'The Glove,'" VP, 15 (Spring, 1977), 85-90.

Bennett Weaver, "Primer Study in Browning's Satire," CE, 16 (Nov, 1952), 80.

R. W. Whidden, Expl, 2 (Dec., 1943), 23.
   Rpt. The Explicator Cyclopedia, II, p. 52.

_____. "A Grammarian's Funeral"
Richard D. Altick, "'Grammarian's Funeral': Browning's Praise of Folly?" SEL, 3 (Autumn, 1963), 449-460.

William Cadbury, "Lyric and Anti-Lyric Forms: A Method for Judging Browning," UTQ, 34 (Oct., 1964), pp. 54-55.

Robert L. Kelly, "Dactyls and Curlews: Satire in 'A Grammarian's Funeral,'" VP, 5 (Summer, 1967), 105-112.

George Monteiro, "A Proposal for Settling the Grammarian's Estate," VP, 3 (Autumn, 1965), 266-270.

J. Mitchell Morse, "Browning's Grammarian, Warts and All," CEA, 20 (Jan., 1958), 1, 5.

Thomas Frederick Scheer, "Mythopoeia and the Renaissance Mind: A Reading of A Grammarian's Funeral," JNT, 4 (May, 1974), 119-128.

Robert C. Schweik, "The Structure of 'A Grammarian's Funeral,'" CE, 22 (March, 1961), 411-412.

Martin J. Svaglic, "Browning's Grammarian: Apparent Failure or Real?" VP, 5 (Summer, 1967), 93-103.

_____. "The Guardian Angel"
A. P. Antippas, "Browning's 'The Guardian Angel': A Possible Early Reference to Ruskin," VP, 11 (Winter, 1973), 342-344.

_____. "Holy-Cross Day"
Barbara Melchiori, "Browning and the Bible: An Examination of 'Holy
Cross Day,'" A Review of English Literature, 7 (April, 1966), 20-42.

Bennet Weaver, "Primer Study in Browning's Satire," CE, 16 (Nov., 1952),
79-80.

_____. "Home-Thoughts, from the Sea"
Frederick L. Gwynn, Expl, 12 (Nov., 1953), 12.
Rpt. Locke, Gibson, and Arms, Introduction to Literature, third edition,
pp. 131-132.
   Rpt. fourth edition, pp. 130-131.
   Rpt. The Explicator Cyclopedia, II, pp. 52-53.

_____. "How Its Strikes a Contemporary"
Susan Hardy Aiken, "On Clothes and Heroes: Carlyle and 'How It Strikes a
Contemporary,'" VP, 13 (Summer, 1975), 99-109.

Charline R. Kvapil, "'How It Strikes a Contemporary': A Dramatic Monologue," VP, 4 (Autumn, 1966), 279-283.

_____. "How They Brought the Good News from Ghent to Aix"
Francis V. Lloyd, Jr., Expl, 6 (March, 1948), 35.
   Rpt. The Explicator Cyclopedia, II, pp. 53-54.

Francis V. Lloyd, Jr., Expl, 12 (March, 1954), 31.
   Rpt. The Explicator Cyclopedia, II, p. 54.

Adrian Van Sinderen, Expl, 7 (Oct., 1948), 10.
   Rpt. The Explicator Cyclopedia, II, p. 54.

Charles D. Smith, Expl, 11 (April, 1953), 42.
   Rpt. The Explicator Cyclopedia, p. 54.

_____. "In a Balcony"
P. G. Mudford, "The Artistic Consistency of Browning's In a Balcony," VP,
7 (Spring, 1969), 31-40.

Elmer E. Stoll, "Browning's 'In a Balcony,'" MLQ, 3 (Sept., 1942), 407-
415.

_____. "In a Year"
Robert J. Cornet, "Irony Without Positive Norms: Robert Browning's 'In
a Year,'" in Aeolian Harps: Essays in Honor of Maurice Browning, ed.
Donna G. Fricke and Douglas C. Fricke (Bowling Green, Ohio: Bowling
Green Univ. Press, 1976), pp. 149-166.

_____. "The Inn Album"
J. T. Foster, Expl, 10 (Dec., 1951), 18.
   Rpt. The Explicator Cyclopedia, II, pp. 54-55.

_____. "The Italian in England"
Bernadine Brown, "Robert Browning's 'The Italian in England,'" VP, 6
(Summer, 1968), 179-183.

_____. "James Lee's Wife" 1 "Speaks at the Window"
Ball, The Heart's Events, pp. 147-149.

Francine Gomberg Russo, "Browning's 'James Lee's Wife': A Study in
Neurotic Love," VP, 12 (Autumn, 1974), 220-222.

_____. "James Lee's Wife" 2 "By the Fireside"
Ball, The Heart's Events, pp. 149-150.

Christ, The Finer Optic, pp. 119-124.

Richard Kelley, "The Dramatic Relationship Between 'By the Fire-side' and 'Any Wife to Any Husband,'" VN, 39 (Spring, 1970), 20.

Jean Stirling Lindsay, "The Central Episode of Browning's 'By the Fire-side,'" SP, 39 (July, 1942), 571-579.

Francine Gomberg Russo, "Browning's 'James Lee's Wife': A Study in Neurotic Love," VP, 12 (Autumn, 1974), 222-223.

V. S. Seturaman, "Browning's 'By the Fireside': 'The Path Gray Heads Abhor,'" N&Q, 9 (August, 1962), 297-298.

Geoffrey Tillotson, "A Word for Browning," SR, 72 (July-Sept., 1964), 394-397.

_____. "James Lee's Wife" 3 "In the Doorway"
Ball, The Heart's Events, pp. 150-152.

Francine Gomberg Russo, "Browning's 'James Lee's Wife': A Study in Neurotic Love," VP, 12 (Autumn, 1974), 223-224.

_____. "James Lee's Wife" 4 "Along the Beach"
Ball, The Heart's Events, pp. 152-155.

Francine Gomberg Russo, "Browning's 'James Lee's Wife': A Study in Neurotic Love," VP, 12 (Autumn, 1974), 225-226.

_____. "James Lee's Wife" 5 "On the Cliff"
Ball, The Heart's Events, pp. 155-156.

Francine Gomberg Russo, "Browning's 'James Lee's Wife': A Study in Neurotic Love," VP, 12 (Autumn, 1974), 226-228.

_____. "James Lee's Wife" 6 "Reading a Book Under the Cliff"
Ball, The Heart's Events, pp. 156-159.

Francine Gomberg Russo, "Browning's 'James Lee's Wife': A Study in Neurotic Love," VP, 12 (Autumn, 1974), 228-230.

_____. "James Lee's Wife" 7 "Among the Rocks"
Ball, The Heart's Events, pp. 159-160.

Francine Gomberg Russo, "Browning's 'James Lee's Wife': A Study in Neurotic Love," VP, 12 (Autumn, 1974), 230.

_____. "James Lee's Wife" 8 "Beside the Drawing Board"
Ball, The Heart's Events, pp. 160-162.

Francine Gomberg Russo, "Browning's 'James Lee's Wife': A Study in Neurotic Love," VP, 12 (Autumn, 1974), 230-232.

G. Robert Stange, Expl, 17 (Feb., 1959), 32.
    Rpt. The Explicator Cyclopedia, II, pp. 55-56.

_____. "James Lee's Wife" 9 "On Deck"
Ball, The Heart's Events, pp. 162-165.

Francine Gomberg Russo, "Browning's 'James Lee's Wife': A Study in Neurotic Love," VP, 12 (Autumn, 1974), 232-234.

_____. "Johannes Agricola in Meditation"
George Wasserman, Expl, 24 (March, 1966), 59.

John W. Willoughby, Expl, 21 (Sept., 1962), 5.

_____. "The King"
John Grube, "Browning's 'The King,'" UTQ, 37 (Oct., 1967), 69-74.

_____. "The Laboratory"
Daniels, The Art of Reading Poetry, pp. 92-95.

Neil D. Isaacs, "Browning's 'Laboratory,'" AN&Q, 7 (Oct., 1968), 21-23.

Lionel Stevenson, "The Pertinacious Victorian Poets," UTQ, 21 (April, 1952), 243-244.

_____. "La Saisiaz"
F. E. L. Priestley, "A Reading of 'La Saisiaz,'" UTQ, 25 (Oct., 1955), 47-59.

_____. "The Last Ride Together"
Richard D. Altick, "Memo to the Next Annotator of Browning," VP, 1 (Spring, 1963), 64.

Russell M. Goldfarb, "Sexual Meaning in 'The Last Ride Together,'" VP, 3 (Autumn, 1965), 255-261.

Russell M. Goldfarb, Sexual Repression and Victorian Literature (Lewisburg: Bucknell Univ. Press, 1970), pp. 68-81.

_____. "Love Among the Ruins"
William Cadbury, "Lyric and Anti-Lyric Forms: A Method for Judging Browning," UTQ, 34 (Oct., 1964), 58-66.

David V. Erdman, "Browning's Industrial Nightmare," PQ, 36 (Oct., 1957), 425-426.

Philip Raisor, "'Palmyra's Ruined Palaces!': The Influence of Shelley's Queen Mab in Browning's 'Love Among the Ruins,'" VP, 14 (Summer, 1976), 142-149.

_____. "Master Hugues of Saxe-Gotha"
Richard D. Altick, "The Symbolism of Browning's 'Master Hugues of Saxe-Gotha,'" VP, 3 (Winter, 1965), 1-7.

Bloom, Poetry and Repression, pp. 178-181.

Langbaum, The Poetry of Experience, pp. 144-146.

George M. Ridenour, "Browning's Music Poems: Fancy and Fact," PMLA, 78 (Sept., 1963), 375-376.

Bennett Weaver, "A Primer Study in Browning's Satire," CE, 16 (Nov., 1952), 78-79.

_____. "Meeting at Night"
Abad, A Formal Approach to Lyric Poetry, pp. 44-46.

Bloom, Philbrick, and Blistein, The Order of Poetry, pp. 80-82.

Ralph W. Condee, Expl, 12 (Feb., 1954), 23.
    Rpt. The Explicator Cyclopedia, II, p. 57.

Christ, The Finer Optic, pp. 113-114.

Frankenberg, Invitation to Poetry, p. 231.

Walter Gierasch, Expl, 1 (May, 1943), 55.
    Rpt. The Explicator Cyclopedia, II, pp. 56-57.

F. R. Leavis, "Imagery and Movement," Scrutiny, 13 (Sept., 1945), 130-131.

Perrine, Sound and Sense, pp. 41-42.
    Rpt. second edition, pp. 46-47.

_____. "Meeting at Night," "Parting at Morning"
Brown and Olmstead, Language and Literature, pp. 199-201.

James McNally, "Suiting Sight and Sound to Sense in 'Meeting at Night'
and 'Parting at Morning,'" VP, 5 (Autumn, 1967), 219-224.

_____. "My Last Duchess"
Abad, A Formal Approach to Lyric Poetry, pp. 341, 346-347.

Adams, The Contexts of Poetry, pp. 145-148.

Joshua Adler, "Structure and Meaning in Browning's 'My Last Duchess,'"
VP, 15 (Autumn, 1977), 219-227.

Beaty and Matchett, Poetry: From Statement to Meaning, pp. 85-90.

Brooks, Purser, and Warren, An Approach to Literature, pp. 437-439.
    Rpt. third edition, pp. 292-293.
    Rpt. fourth edition, pp. 295-296.

R. F. Fleissner, "Browning's Last Lost Duchess: A Purview," VP, 5
(Autumn, 1967), 217-219.

Louis S. Friedland, "Ferrara and 'My Last Duchess,'" SP, 33 (Oct., 1936),
656-684.

B. R. Jerman, "Browning's Witless Duke," PMLA, 72 (June, 1957), 488-493.

Patrick E. Kilburn, Expl, 19 (Feb., 1961), 31.
    Rpt. The Explicator Cyclopedia, II, pp. 57-58.

Kirk and McCutcheon, An Introduction to the Study of Poetry, pp. 17-24.

Langbaum, The Poetry of Experience, pp. 82-85.

George Monteiro, "Browning's 'My Last Duchess,'" VP, 1 (Autumn, 1963),
234-237.

Leonard Nathanson, Expl, 19 (June, 1961), 68.
    Rpt. The Explicator Cyclopedia, II, p. 58.

Laurence Perrine, "Browning's Shrewd Duke," PMLA, 74 (March, 1959), 157-
159.

Sanford Pinsker, "'As if she were alive': Rhetorical Anguish in 'My Last
Duchess,'" CP, 9 (Fall, 1976), 71-73.

John D. Rea, "My Last Duchess," SP, 29 (Jan., 1932), 120-122.

Ina B. Sessions, "The Dramatic Monologue," PMLA, 62 (June, 1947), 508-
510.

Joseph Solimine, Jr., Expl, 26 (Sept., 1967), 11.

Lionel Stevenson, "The Pertinacious Victorian Poets," UTQ, 21 (April,
1952), 240-242.

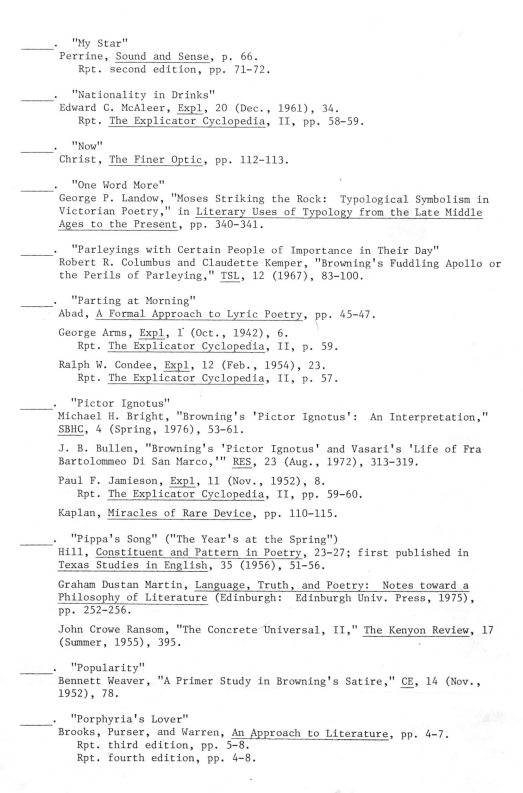

_____. "My Star"
Perrine, Sound and Sense, p. 66.
    Rpt. second edition, pp. 71-72.

_____. "Nationality in Drinks"
Edward C. McAleer, Expl, 20 (Dec., 1961), 34.
    Rpt. The Explicator Cyclopedia, II, pp. 58-59.

_____. "Now"
Christ, The Finer Optic, pp. 112-113.

_____. "One Word More"
George P. Landow, "Moses Striking the Rock: Typological Symbolism in
Victorian Poetry," in Literary Uses of Typology from the Late Middle
Ages to the Present, pp. 340-341.

_____. "Parleyings with Certain People of Importance in Their Day"
Robert R. Columbus and Claudette Kemper, "Browning's Fuddling Apollo or
the Perils of Parleying," TSL, 12 (1967), 83-100.

_____. "Parting at Morning"
Abad, A Formal Approach to Lyric Poetry, pp. 45-47.

George Arms, Expl, 1 (Oct., 1942), 6.
    Rpt. The Explicator Cyclopedia, II, p. 59.

Ralph W. Condee, Expl, 12 (Feb., 1954), 23.
    Rpt. The Explicator Cyclopedia, II, p. 57.

_____. "Pictor Ignotus"
Michael H. Bright, "Browning's 'Pictor Ignotus': An Interpretation,"
SBHC, 4 (Spring, 1976), 53-61.

J. B. Bullen, "Browning's 'Pictor Ignotus' and Vasari's 'Life of Fra
Bartolommeo Di San Marco,'" RES, 23 (Aug., 1972), 313-319.

Paul F. Jamieson, Expl, 11 (Nov., 1952), 8.
    Rpt. The Explicator Cyclopedia, II, pp. 59-60.

Kaplan, Miracles of Rare Device, pp. 110-115.

_____. "Pippa's Song" ("The Year's at the Spring")
Hill, Constituent and Pattern in Poetry, 23-27; first published in
Texas Studies in English, 35 (1956), 51-56.

Graham Dustan Martin, Language, Truth, and Poetry: Notes toward a
Philosophy of Literature (Edinburgh: Edinburgh Univ. Press, 1975),
pp. 252-256.

John Crowe Ransom, "The Concrete Universal, II," The Kenyon Review, 17
(Summer, 1955), 395.

_____. "Popularity"
Bennett Weaver, "A Primer Study in Browning's Satire," CE, 14 (Nov.,
1952), 78.

_____. "Porphyria's Lover"
Brooks, Purser, and Warren, An Approach to Literature, pp. 4-7.
    Rpt. third edition, pp. 5-8.
    Rpt. fourth edition, pp. 4-8.

David Eggenschwiler, "Psychological Complexity in 'Porphyria's Lover,'" VP, 8 (Spring, 1970), 39-48.

Willis D. Jacobs, "Browning's 'Porphyria's Lover,'" Rocky Mountain Modern Language Association Bulletin, 5 (May, 1952), 8.

Max Keith Sutton, "Language as Defense in 'Porphyria's Lover,'" CE, 31 (Dec., 1969), 280-289.

_____. "Prospice"
George Arms, Expl, 2 (May, 1944), 53.
    Rpt. The Explicator Cyclopedia, II, pp. 60-61.

Harry M. Campbell, Expl, 3 (Oct., 1944), 2.
    Rpt. The Explicator Cyclopedia, II, p. 61.

_____. "Rabbi Ben Ezra"
David Fleisher, "'Rabbi Ben Ezra,' 49-72: A New Key to an Old Crux," VP, 1 (Spring, 1963), 46-52.

Philip Darrough Ortega, "Robert Browning's 'Rabbi Ben Ezra,'" CEA, 30 (March, 1968), 6-7.

Roger L. Slakey, "A Note on Browning's 'Rabbi Ben Ezra,'" VP, 5 (Winter, 1967), 291-294.

_____. "Respectability"
Laurence Perrine, "Browning's 'Respectability,'" CE, 14 (March, 1953), 347-348.

Bennett Weaver, "A Primer Study in Browning's Satire," CE, 14 (Nov, 1952), 79.

_____. "St. Martin's Summer"
Kenneth Leslie Knickerbocker, "An Echo from Browning's Second Courtship," SP, 32 (Jan., 1935), 120-124.

_____. "Saul"
Joseph E. Baker, "Religious Implications in Browning's Poetry," PQ, 36 (Oct., 1957), 440.

Elizabeth Bieman, "The Ongoing Testament in Browning's 'Saul,'" UTQ, 43 (Winter, 1974), 151-168.

Kaplan, Miracles of Rare Device, pp. 145-155.

J. H. McClatchey, "Browning's 'Saul' as a Davidic Psalm of the Praise of God: The Poetics of Prophecy," SBHC, 4 (Spring, 1976), 62-83.

Victor A. Neufeldt, "Browning's 'Saul' in the Context of the Age," JEGP, 73 (Jan., 1974), 48-59.

W. David Shaw, "The Analogical Argument of Browning's 'Saul,'" VP, 2 (Winter, 1964), 277-282.

_____. "A Serenade at the Villa"
Arthur Dickson, Expl, 9 (June, 1951), 57.
    Rpt. The Explicator Cyclopedia, II, pp. 62-63.

Walter Gierasch, Expl, 8 (March, 1950), 37.
    Rpt. The Explicator Cyclopedia, II, pp. 61-62.

T. O. Mabbott, Expl, 8 (Dec., 1949), Q6.

_____. "Sibrandus Schafnaburgensis"
Christ, The Finer Optic, pp. 67-68.

Bennett Weaver, "A Primer Study in Browning's Satire," CE, 16 (Nov., 1952), 77-78.

_____. "Soliloquy of the Spanish Cloister"
Virginia H. Adair, Expl, 22 (Dec., 1963), 24.

Richard D. Altick, "Memo to the Next Annotator of Browning," VP, 1 (Spring, 1963), 62-63.

Wayne C. Booth, A Rhetoric of Irony (Chicago and London: Univ. of Chicago Press, 1974), pp. 142-150.

Robert A. Day, Expl, 24 (Dec., 1965), 33.

Fred A. Dudley, "'Hy, Zy, Hine,'" RS, 25 (March, 1957), 63-68.

Lucy Dickinson Fryxell, Expl, 22 (Dec., 1963), 24.

Patrick W. Gainer, "'Hy, Zy, Hine,'" VP, 1 (Summer, 1963), 158-160.

Thomas C. Kishler, "A Note on Browning's 'Soliloquy of the Spanish Cloister,'" VP, 1 (Spring, 1963), 70-71.

James F. Loucks, "'Hy, Zy, Hine,' and Peter of Abano," VP, 12 (Summer, 1974), 165-169.

Raymond Gates Malbone, "That Blasted Rose-Acacia: A Note on Browning's 'Soliloquy of the Spanish Cloister,'" VP, 4 (Summer, 1966), 218-221.

Charles T. Phipps, S.J., "Browning's 'Soliloquy of the Spanish Cloister': Lines 71-72," VP, 7 (Summer, 1969), 158-159.

Ina B. Sessions, "The Dramatic Monologue," PMLA, 62 (June, 1947), 512.

Roger L. Slakey, Expl, 21 (Jan., 1963), 42.

David Sonstroem, "Animal and Vegetable in the Spanish Cloister," VP, 6 (Spring, 1968), 70-73.

Miriam K. Starkman, "The Manichee in the Cloister," MLN, 75 (May, 1960), 399-405.

Charles Child Walcutt, "Introduction," in The Explicator Cyclopedia, I, p. xiii.

Richard Wear, "Further Thoughts on Browning's Spanish Cloister," VP, 12 (Spring, 1974), 67-70.

_____. "The Statue and the Bust"
R. P. Basler, Dudley Fitts, and DeLancey Ferguson, Expl, 3 (June, 1945) 62.
    Rpt. The Explicator Cyclopedia, II, p. 63.

Frances Bridges Carleton, The Dramatic Monologue: Vox Humana, Salzburg Studies in English Literature, No. 64 (Salzburg, Austria: Institut für Englische Sprache und Litteratur, 1977), pp. 180-184.

Wendell Stacy Johnson, Sex and Marriage in Victorian Poetry (Ithaca and London: Cornell Univ. Press, 1975), pp. 208-212.

W. O. Raymond, "Browning's 'The Statue and the Bust,'" UTQ, 28 (April, 1959), 233-249.

Judith Weissman, "Browning's Politics of Hell: 'Childe Roland to the Dark Tower Came' and 'The Statue and the Bust,'" CP, 10 (Fall, 1977), 11-13.

_____. "Thamuris Marching" (Aristophanes' Apology)
George M. Ridenour, "Browning's Music Poems: Fancy and Fact," PMLA, 78 (Sept., 1963), 371-372.

_____. "A Toccata of Galuppi's"
Roy P. Basler, Expl, 2 (June, 1944), 60.
    Rpt. The Explicator Cyclopedia, II, pp. 64-65.

Bloom, Poetry and Repression, pp. 181-186.

Arthur Dickson, Expl, 3 (Nov., 1944), 15.
    Rpt. The Explicator Cyclopedia, II, pp. 65-66.

Edgar H. Duncan, Expl, 5 (Oct., 1946), 5.
    Rpt. The Explicator Cyclopedia, II, p. 68.

William Frost, English Masterpieces, Vol. VI, Romantic and Victorian Poetry, pp. 13-14.

Edgar F. Harden, "A New Reading of Browning's 'A Toccata of Galuppi's,'" VP, 11 (Winter, 1973), 330-336.

Frederick A. Pottle, Expl, 2 (Feb., 1944), 25.
    Rpt. The Explicator Cyclopedia, II, p. 64.

George M. Ridenour, "Browning's Music Poems: Fancy and Fact," PMLA, 78 (Sept., 1963), 373-374.

Stauffer, The Nature of Poetry, p. 178.

William D. Templeman and Frederick A. Pottle, Expl, 2 (Feb., 1944), 25.
    Rpt. The Explicator Cyclopedia, II, pp. 63-64.

Bennett Weaver, "A Primer Study in Browning's Satire," CE, 16 (Nov., 1952), 80-81.

_____. "Too Late"
Laurence Perrine, "Browning's 'Too Late': A Re-Interpretation," VP, 7 (Winter, 1969), 339-345.

_____. "Transcendentalism"
Richard D. Altick, "Browning's 'Transcendentalism,'" JEGP, 58 (Jan., 1959), 24-28.

_____. "Two in the Compagna"
Richard D. Altick, "Lovers' Finiteness: Browning's 'Two in the Compagna,'" PLL, 3 (Winter, 1967), 75-80.

Christ, The Finer Optic, pp. 114-117.

Day Lewis, The Poetic Image, pp. 78-80.

Peckham and Chatman, Word, Meaning, Poem, pp. 190-207.

_____. "Up at a Villa-Down in the City"
Richard Fleck, "Browning's 'Up at a Villa-Down in the City' as Satire," VP, 7 (Winter, 1969), 345-349.

_____. "With Charles Avison" (Parleyings With Certain People of Importance in Their Day)
George M. Ridenour, "Browning's Music Poems: Fancy and Fact," PMLA, 78 (Sept., 1963), 369-370.

Mark Siegchrist, "Type Needs Antitype: The Structure of Browning's Parleyings," VN, 5 (Fall, 1976), 8.

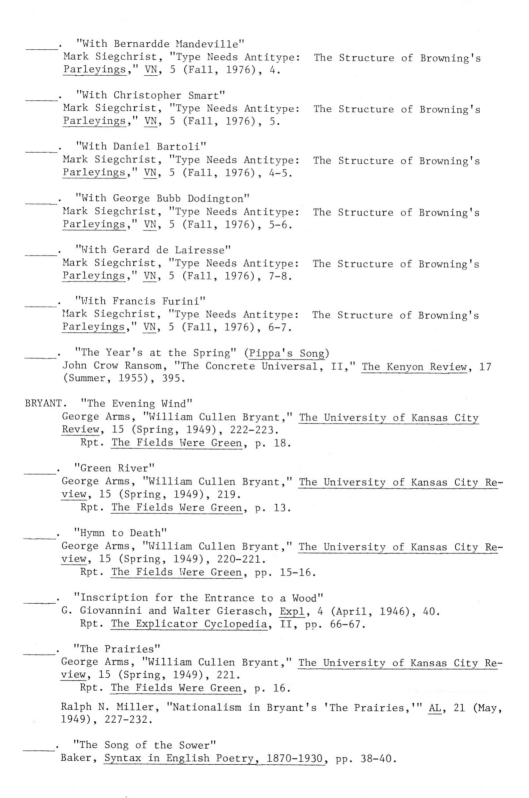

_____. "With Bernardde Mandeville"
Mark Siegchrist, "Type Needs Antitype: The Structure of Browning's
Parleyings," VN, 5 (Fall, 1976), 4.

_____. "With Christopher Smart"
Mark Siegchrist, "Type Needs Antitype: The Structure of Browning's
Parleyings," VN, 5 (Fall, 1976), 5.

_____. "With Daniel Bartoli"
Mark Siegchrist, "Type Needs Antitype: The Structure of Browning's
Parleyings," VN, 5 (Fall, 1976), 4-5.

_____. "With George Bubb Dodington"
Mark Siegchrist, "Type Needs Antitype: The Structure of Browning's
Parleyings," VN, 5 (Fall, 1976), 5-6.

_____. "With Gerard de Lairesse"
Mark Siegchrist, "Type Needs Antitype: The Structure of Browning's
Parleyings," VN, 5 (Fall, 1976), 7-8.

_____. "With Francis Furini"
Mark Siegchrist, "Type Needs Antitype: The Structure of Browning's
Parleyings," VN, 5 (Fall, 1976), 6-7.

_____. "The Year's at the Spring" (Pippa's Song)
John Crow Ransom, "The Concrete Universal, II," The Kenyon Review, 17
(Summer, 1955), 395.

BRYANT. "The Evening Wind"
George Arms, "William Cullen Bryant," The University of Kansas City
Review, 15 (Spring, 1949), 222-223.
    Rpt. The Fields Were Green, p. 18.

_____. "Green River"
George Arms, "William Cullen Bryant," The University of Kansas City Review, 15 (Spring, 1949), 219.
    Rpt. The Fields Were Green, p. 13.

_____. "Hymn to Death"
George Arms, "William Cullen Bryant," The University of Kansas City Review, 15 (Spring, 1949), 220-221.
    Rpt. The Fields Were Green, pp. 15-16.

_____. "Inscription for the Entrance to a Wood"
G. Giovannini and Walter Gierasch, Expl, 4 (April, 1946), 40.
    Rpt. The Explicator Cyclopedia, II, pp. 66-67.

_____. "The Prairies"
George Arms, "William Cullen Bryant," The University of Kansas City Review, 15 (Spring, 1949), 221.
    Rpt. The Fields Were Green, p. 16.

Ralph N. Miller, "Nationalism in Bryant's 'The Prairies,'" AL, 21 (May,
1949), 227-232.

_____. "The Song of the Sower"
Baker, Syntax in English Poetry, 1870-1930, pp. 38-40.

_____. "Thanatopsis"
George Arms, "William Cullen Bryant," The University of Kansas City Review, 15 (Spring, 1949), 220.
    Rpt. The Fields Were Green, pp. 14-15.

E. Miller Budick, "'Visible' Images and the 'Still Voice': Transcendental
Vision in Bryant's 'Thanatopsis,'" ESQ, 22 (Second Quarter, 1976), 71-77.

Thomas O. Mabbott, Expl, 11 (Dec., 1952), 15.
    Rpt. The Explicator Cyclopedia, II, pp. 67-68.

Albert F. McLean, Jr., "Bryant's 'Thanatopsis': A Sermon in Stone," AL,
31 (Jan., 1960), 474-479.

_____. "To a Waterfowl"
George Arms, "William Cullen Bryant," The University of Kansas City Review, 15 (Spring, 1949), 221-222.
    Rpt. The Fields Were Green, pp. 17-18.

Donald Davie, Interpretations, ed. John Wain, pp. 130-137.

BUCHANAN, Robert. "The Ballad of Judas Iscariot"
    C. C. Cunningham, Literature as a Fine Art: Analysis and Interpretation,
    pp. 98-99.

BURKE, Kenneth. "Three Seasons of Love"
    John Ciardi, "The Critic of Love," Nation, 181 (Oct. 8, 1955), 307.

BURNS. "Address to the Deil"
    Daiches and Charvat, Poems in English, pp. 688-689.

_____. "Death and Dr. Hornbook"
William Frost, English Masterpieces, Vol. VI, Romantic and Victorian
Poetry, pp. 13-14.

_____. "Epistle to John Lapraik"
Raymond Bentman, "Robert Burns's Use of Scottish Diction," in From Sensibility to Romanticism, pp. 246-248.

_____. "Holy Willie's Prayer"
Daiches and Charvat, Poems in English, pp. 687-688.

_____. "John Anderson My Jo, John"
Kilby, Poetry and Life, pp. 19-25.

_____. "The Jolly Beggars"
Allan H. MacLaine, "Burns' 'Jolly Beggars'--A Mistaken Interpretation,"
N&Q, 198 (Nov., 1953), 486-487.

Allan H. MacLaine, "Radicalism and Conservatism in Burns's The Jolly
Beggars," SSL, 13 (Columbia, S.C.: Univ. of South Carolina Press, 1978),
125-143.

_____. "The Lea-Rig"
Raymond Bentman, "Robert Burns's Use of Scottish Diction," in From Sensibility to Romanticism, pp. 254-255.

_____. "Mary Morison"
Van Doren, Introduction to Poetry, pp. 9-12.

_____. "Tam O'Shanter"
James Kinsley, "A Note on Tam O'Shanter," English, 16 (Autumn, 1967), 213-217.

Allan H. MacLaine, "Burns's Use of Parody in 'Tam O' Shanter,'" Criticism, 1 (Fall, 1959), 308-316.

Richard Morton, "Narrative Irony in Robert Burns's 'Tam O'Shanter,'" MLQ, 22 (March, 1961), 12-20.

W. K. Thomas, Expl, 28 (Dec., 1969), 33.

_____. "To a Mouse"
Raymond Bentman, "Robert Burns's Use of Scottish Diction," in From Sensibility to Romanticism, pp. 248-250.

Cleanth Brooks and Robert P. Heilman, Understanding Drama (New York: Henry Holt and Company, 1945), pp. 19-22.

_____. "Ye Flowery Banks o'Bonie Doon"
Stauffer, The Nature of Poetry, pp. 164-166.
    Rpt. Locke, Gibson, and Arms, Introduction to Literature, third edition, pp. 79-80.

BUTLER. "The Ladies Answer"
Miner, The Restoration Mode from Milton to Dryden, pp. 190-194.

BYNNER. "Eden Tree"
R. P. Blackmur, "Versions of Solitude," Poetry, 39 (Jan., 1932), 217-221.

BYRON. "By the Rivers of Babylon"
Thomas L. Ashton, "Byronic Lyrics for David's Harp: The Hebrew Melodies," SEL, 12 (Autumn, 1972), 673.

_____. "Darkness"
George M. Ridenour, "Byron in 1816: Four Poems from Diodati," in From Sensibility to Romanticism, pp. 458-459.

_____. "The Destruction of Sennacherib"
Ogden Nash, "Very Like a Whale," The Face is Familiar (Garden City, 1941), pp. 104-105.

_____. "The Dream"
George M. Ridenour, "Byron, in 1816: Four Poems from Diodati," in From Sensibility to Romanticism, pp. 459-461.

_____. "Epistle to Augustus"
George M. Ridenour, "Byron in 1816: Four Poems from Diodati," in From Sensibility to Romanticism, pp. 455-458.

_____. "A Fragment" ("Could I Remount the River of My Years")
George M. Ridenour, "Byron in 1816: Four Poems from Diodata," in From Sensibility to Romanticism, pp. 462-463.

_____. "The Harp the Monarch Minstrel Swept"
Thomas L. Ashton, "Bryonic Lyrics for David's Harp: The Hebrew Melodies," SEL, 12 (Autumn, 1972), 673-675.

_____. "If that High World"
Thomas L. Ashton, "Byronic Lyrics for David's Harp: The Hebrew Melodies,"
SEL, 12 (Autumn, 1972), 676-677.

_____. "My Soul is Dark"
Thomas L. Ashton, "Byronic Lyrics for David's Harp: The Hebrew Melodies,"
SEL, 12 (Autumn, 1972), 672-673.

_____. "On This Day I Complete My Thirty-Sixth Year"
Arthur Dickson, Expl, 5 (Nov., 1946), 15.
    Rpt. The Explicator Cyclopedia, II, p. 70.

Frederick L. Jones, "Byron's Last Poem," SP, 31 (July, 1934), 487-489.

T. O. Mabbott, Expl, 4 (March, 1946), 36.
    Rpt. The Explicator Cyclopedia, II, p. 69.

_____. "The Prisoner of Chillon"
Gordon E. Slethaug, "Patterns of Imagery in 'The Prisoner of Chillon,'"
QQ, 78 (Autumn, 1971), 449-455.

Gerald C. Wood, "Nature and Narrative in Byron's 'The Prisoner of Chillon,'" KSJ, 24 (1975), 108-117.

_____. "Prometheus"
Bloom, The Visionary Company, pp. 239-242.

Michael G. Cooke, The Romantic Will (New Haven and London: Yale Univ.
Press, 1976), pp. 39-41.

_____. "Soul"
Thomas L. Ashton, "Byronic Lyrics for David's Harp: The Hebrew Melodies,"
SEL, 12 (Autumn, 1972), 670-671.

_____. "Song of Saul Before His Last Battle"
Thomas L. Ashton, "Byronic Lyrics for David's Harp: The Hebrew Melodies,"
SEL, 12 (Autumn, 1972), 675.

_____. "Stanzas to the Po"
Bloom, The Visionary Company, pp. 269-271.

_____. "The Vision of Judgment"
Bloom, The Visionary Company, pp. 265-269.

Leavis, Revaluation, pp. 148-153.

Edmund Miller, Expl, 33 (Sept., 1974), 4.

_____. "Waltz: An Apostrophic Hymn"
William Childers, "Byron's Waltz: The Germans and Their Georges," KSJ,
18 (1969), 85-95.

CALLANAN, Jeremiah J. "The Outlaw of Loch Lene"
    B. S. Lee, "Callanan's 'The Outlaw of Loch Lene,'" ArielE, 1 (July,
    1970), 89-100.

CAMPBELL, Joseph. "The Dancer"
    Clark, Lyric Resonance, pp. 85-90.

CAMPION. "My Sweetest Lesbia"
    Walter R. Davis, "Melodic and Poetic Structure: The Examples of Campion
    and Dowland," Criticism, 4 (Spring, 1962), 91-93.

_____. "Now Winter Nights Enlarge"
    John T. Irwin, "Thomas Campion and the Musical Emblem," SEL, 10 (Winter,
    1970), 121-141.

    Yvor Winters, "The Sixteenth Century Lyric in England," Poetry, 54 (April,
    1939), 37.
        Rpt. Forms of Discovery, pp. 37-39.

_____. "There Is a Garden in Her Face"
    Beaty and Matchett, Poetry: From Statement to Meaning, pp. 200-201.

    Laurence Perrine, "Four Forms of Metaphor," CE, 33 (Nov., 1971), 133-134.
        Rpt. The Art of Total Relevance, pp. 58-59.

_____. "Tune Thy Musicke to Thy Hart" (The First Book of Ayres, viii)
    Walter R. Davis, "Melodic and Poetic Structure: The Examples of Campion
    and Dowland," Criticism, 4 (Spring, 1962), 96-97.

_____. "When Thou Must Home to Shades of Under Ground"
    Tuve, Elizabethan and Metaphysical Imagery, p. 16.

_____. "When to Her Lute Corinna Sings"
    Walter R. Davis, "Melodic and Poetic Structure: The Examples of Campion
    and Dowland," Criticism, 4 (Spring, 1962), 97-98.

    Tuve, Elizabethan and Metaphysical Imagery, pp. 15-16.

CANE. "April Flurry"
    Melville Cane, "Snow: Theme with Variations," ASch, 20 (Winter, 1952-53),
    101-102.

_____. "Deep in Wagon-Ruts"
    Melville Cane, "Snow: Theme with Variations," ASch, 22 (Winter, 1952-53),
    97.

_____. "Hither and Thither"
    Melville Cane, "Snow: Theme with Variations," ASch, 22 (Winter, 1952-53),
    99-101.

_____. "Hopkinson"
    Melville Cane, "Concerning 'Hopkinson,'" The University of Kansas City
    Review, 17 (Summer, 1951), 288-293.

_____. "January Garden"
    Melville Cane, "Snow: Theme with Variations," ASch, 22 (Winter, 1952-53),
    97-98.

_____. "Last Night It Snowed"
    Melville Cane, "Snow: Theme with Variations," ASch, 22 (Winter, 1952-53),
    98-99.

_____. "Presence of Snow"
    Melville Cane, "Snow: Theme with Variations," ASch, 22 (Winter, 1952-53),
    104-105.

_____. "Snow in April"
Melville Cane, "Snow: Theme with Variations," ASch, 22 (Winter, 1953-53),
102-104.

_____. "White Fog"
Melville Cane, "Snow: Theme with Variations," ASch, 22 (Winter, 1952-53),
96-97.

CAREW. "Ask Me No More Where Jove Bestows"
Brooks, Modern Poetry and the Tradition, pp. 21-22.
   Rpt. fourth edition, pp. 354-356.

Brooks, Purser, and Warren, An Approach to Literature, pp. 486-488.
   Rpt. third edition, pp. 362-363.

Daniels, The Art of Reading Poetry, pp. 364-366.

Miner, The Cavalier Mode from Jonson to Cotton, pp. 135-137.

Ribner and Morris, Poetry: A Critical and Historical Introduction,
pp. 145-148.

Van Doren, Introduction to Poetry, pp. 3-8.
   Rpt. Stallman and Watters, The Creative Reader, pp. 854-856.

_____. "Celia Singing"
D. F. Rauber, "Carew Redivivus," TSLL, 13 (Spring, 1971), 26-28.

_____. "The Complement"
Sloan, The Rhetoric of Renaissance Poetry, pp. 22-23.

_____. "Disdain Returned"
Donald C. Baker, Expl, 11 (June, 1953), 54.
   Rpt. The Explicator Cyclopedia, II, p. 70.

MacDonald Emslie, Expl, 12 (Oct., 1953), 4.
   Rpt. The Explicator Cyclopedia, II, pp. 70-72.

_____. "A Divine Mistress"
Miles, The Primary Language of Poetry in the 1640's, pp. 5-6.

_____. "Mediocritie in Love Rejected"
D. F. Rauber, "Carew Redivivus," TSLL, 13 (Spring, 1971), 25-26.

_____. "Perswasions to Enjoy"
D. F. Rauber, "Carew Redivivus," TSLL, 13 (Spring, 1971), 23-25.

_____. "The Spring"
Robert E. Jungman, "The Ending of Thomas Carew's 'The Spring,'" CP, 8
(Fall, 1975), 49-50.

_____. "A Rapture"
Paula Johnson, "Carew's 'A Rapture': The Dynamics of Fantasy," SEL, 16
(Winter, 1976), 145-155.

_____. "To A. L.: Persuasions to Love"
D. F. Rauber, "Carew Redivivus," TSLL, 13 (Spring, 1971), 20-23.

Tuve, Elizabethan and Metaphysical Imagery, p. 260.

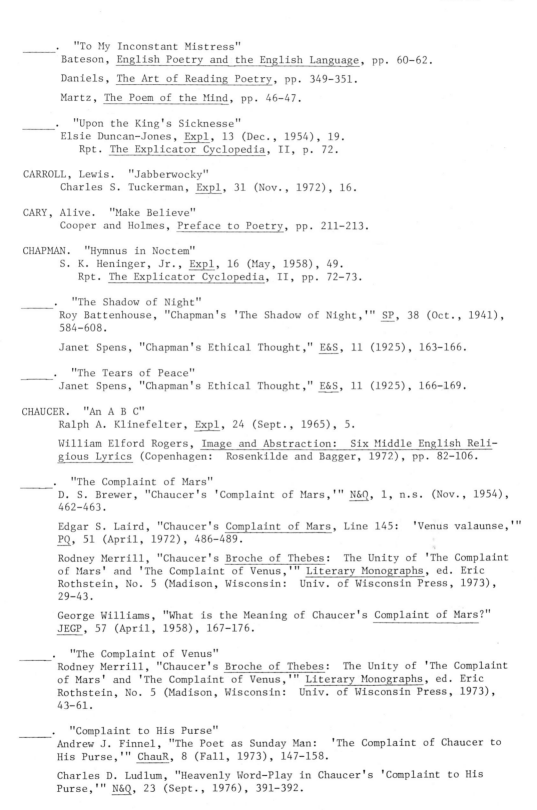

_____. "To My Inconstant Mistress"
Bateson, <u>English Poetry and the English Language</u>, pp. 60-62.

Daniels, <u>The Art of Reading Poetry</u>, pp. 349-351.

Martz, <u>The Poem of the Mind</u>, pp. 46-47.

_____. "Upon the King's Sicknesse"
Elsie Duncan-Jones, <u>Expl</u>, 13 (Dec., 1954), 19.
    Rpt. <u>The Explicator Cyclopedia</u>, II, p. 72.

CARROLL, Lewis. "Jabberwocky"
Charles S. Tuckerman, <u>Expl</u>, 31 (Nov., 1972), 16.

CARY, Alive. "Make Believe"
Cooper and Holmes, <u>Preface to Poetry</u>, pp. 211-213.

CHAPMAN. "Hymnus in Noctem"
S. K. Heninger, Jr., <u>Expl</u>, 16 (May, 1958), 49.
    Rpt. <u>The Explicator Cyclopedia</u>, II, pp. 72-73.

_____. "The Shadow of Night"
Roy Battenhouse, "Chapman's 'The Shadow of Night,'" <u>SP</u>, 38 (Oct., 1941),
584-608.

Janet Spens, "Chapman's Ethical Thought," <u>E&S</u>, 11 (1925), 163-166.

_____. "The Tears of Peace"
Janet Spens, "Chapman's Ethical Thought," <u>E&S</u>, 11 (1925), 166-169.

CHAUCER. "An A B C"
Ralph A. Klinefelter, <u>Expl</u>, 24 (Sept., 1965), 5.

William Elford Rogers, <u>Image and Abstraction: Six Middle English Reli-</u>
<u>gious Lyrics</u> (Copenhagen: Rosenkilde and Bagger, 1972), pp. 82-106.

_____. "The Complaint of Mars"
D. S. Brewer, "Chaucer's 'Complaint of Mars,'" <u>N&Q</u>, 1, n.s. (Nov., 1954),
462-463.

Edgar S. Laird, "Chaucer's <u>Complaint of Mars</u>, Line 145: 'Venus valaunse,'"
<u>PQ</u>, 51 (April, 1972), 486-489.

Rodney Merrill, "Chaucer's <u>Broche of Thebes</u>: The Unity of 'The Complaint
of Mars' and 'The Complaint of Venus,'" <u>Literary Monographs</u>, ed. Eric
Rothstein, No. 5 (Madison, Wisconsin: Univ. of Wisconsin Press, 1973),
29-43.

George Williams, "What is the Meaning of Chaucer's <u>Complaint of Mars?</u>"
<u>JEGP</u>, 57 (April, 1958), 167-176.

_____. "The Complaint of Venus"
Rodney Merrill, "Chaucer's <u>Broche of Thebes</u>: The Unity of 'The Complaint
of Mars' and 'The Complaint of Venus,'" <u>Literary Monographs</u>, ed. Eric
Rothstein, No. 5 (Madison, Wisconsin: Univ. of Wisconsin Press, 1973),
43-61.

_____. "Complaint to His Purse"
Andrew J. Finnel, "The Poet as Sunday Man: 'The Complaint of Chaucer to
His Purse,'" <u>ChauR</u>, 8 (Fall, 1973), 147-158.

Charles D. Ludlum, "Heavenly Word-Play in Chaucer's 'Complaint to His
Purse,'" <u>N&Q</u>, 23 (Sept., 1976), 391-392.

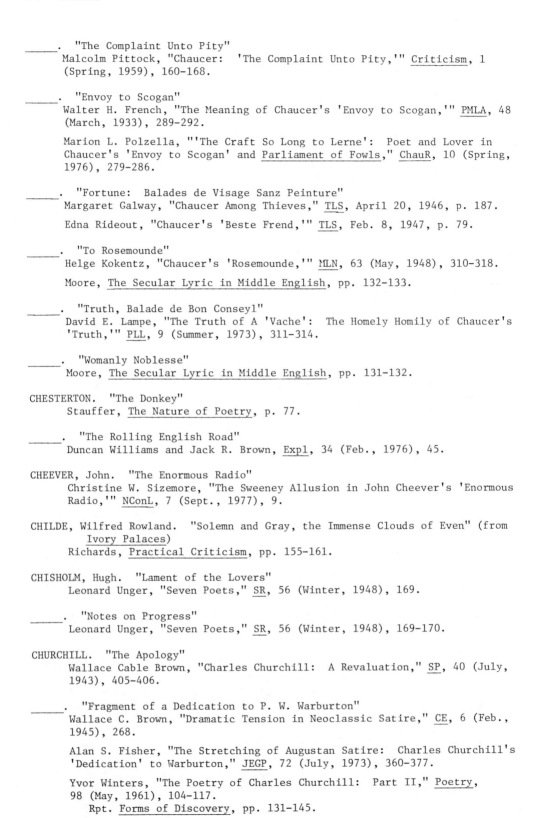

_____. "The Complaint Unto Pity"
Malcolm Pittock, "Chaucer: 'The Complaint Unto Pity,'" Criticism, 1
(Spring, 1959), 160-168.

_____. "Envoy to Scogan"
Walter H. French, "The Meaning of Chaucer's 'Envoy to Scogan,'" PMLA, 48
(March, 1933), 289-292.

Marion L. Polzella, "'The Craft So Long to Lerne': Poet and Lover in
Chaucer's 'Envoy to Scogan' and Parliament of Fowls," ChauR, 10 (Spring,
1976), 279-286.

_____. "Fortune: Balades de Visage Sanz Peinture"
Margaret Galway, "Chaucer Among Thieves," TLS, April 20, 1946, p. 187.

Edna Rideout, "Chaucer's 'Beste Frend,'" TLS, Feb. 8, 1947, p. 79.

_____. "To Rosemounde"
Helge Kokentz, "Chaucer's 'Rosemounde,'" MLN, 63 (May, 1948), 310-318.

Moore, The Secular Lyric in Middle English, pp. 132-133.

_____. "Truth, Balade de Bon Conseyl"
David E. Lampe, "The Truth of A 'Vache': The Homely Homily of Chaucer's
'Truth,'" PLL, 9 (Summer, 1973), 311-314.

_____. "Womanly Noblesse"
Moore, The Secular Lyric in Middle English, pp. 131-132.

CHESTERTON. "The Donkey"
Stauffer, The Nature of Poetry, p. 77.

_____. "The Rolling English Road"
Duncan Williams and Jack R. Brown, Expl, 34 (Feb., 1976), 45.

CHEEVER, John. "The Enormous Radio"
Christine W. Sizemore, "The Sweeney Allusion in John Cheever's 'Enormous
Radio,'" NConL, 7 (Sept., 1977), 9.

CHILDE, Wilfred Rowland. "Solemn and Gray, the Immense Clouds of Even" (from
Ivory Palaces)
Richards, Practical Criticism, pp. 155-161.

CHISHOLM, Hugh. "Lament of the Lovers"
Leonard Unger, "Seven Poets," SR, 56 (Winter, 1948), 169.

_____. "Notes on Progress"
Leonard Unger, "Seven Poets," SR, 56 (Winter, 1948), 169-170.

CHURCHILL. "The Apology"
Wallace Cable Brown, "Charles Churchill: A Revaluation," SP, 40 (July,
1943), 405-406.

_____. "Fragment of a Dedication to P. W. Warburton"
Wallace C. Brown, "Dramatic Tension in Neoclassic Satire," CE, 6 (Feb.,
1945), 268.

Alan S. Fisher, "The Stretching of Augustan Satire: Charles Churchill's
'Dedication' to Warburton," JEGP, 72 (July, 1973), 360-377.

Yvor Winters, "The Poetry of Charles Churchill: Part II," Poetry,
98 (May, 1961), 104-117.
Rpt. Forms of Discovery, pp. 131-145.

_____. "Night"
Wallace Cable Brown, "Charles Churchill: A Revaluation," SP, 40 (July, 1943), 421-423.

CIARDI. "Letter to Virginia Johnson"
Harvey Curtis Webster, "Humanism as the Father Face," Poetry, 70 (June, 1947), 146-150.

_____. "Metropolitan Ice Co."
Hayden Carruth and John Ciardi, Poetry: A Critical Supplement, April, 1949, pp. 15-18.

_____. "The Size of Song"
Edward Cifelli, "The Size of John Ciardi's Song," CEA, 36 (Nov., 1973), 22-27.

_____. "Tenzone"
Edward J. Gallagher, Expl, 27 (Dec., 1968), 28.

Laurence Perrine, Expl, 28 (May, 1970), 82.

_____. "To Judith"
J. F. Nims, Poetry: A Critical Supplement, Feb., 1948, pp. 10-16.

_____. "To Judith Asleep"
Hayden Corruth, Poetry: A Critical Supplement, April, 1949, pp. 18-19.

CLANVOWE, Sir John. "The Cuckoo and the Nightingale"
David E. Lampe, "Tradition and Meaning in The Cuckoo and the Nightingale," PLL, 3 (Supplement) (Summer, 1967), 49-62.

A. C. Spearing, Medieval Dream-Poetry (London: Cambridge Univ. Press, 1976), pp. 176-181.

CLARE, John. "Badger"
Abad, A Formal Approach to Lyric Poetry, pp. 263-265.

Rosenthal and Smith, Exploring Poetry, pp. 284-285.

Janet M. Todd, "'Very Copys of Nature': John Clare's Descriptive Poetry," PQ, 53 (Jan., 1974), 96.

_____. "Birds' Nests"
Thomas R. Frosch, "The Descriptive Style of John Clare," SIR, 10 (Spring, 1971), 138-139.

_____. "The Hedgehog"
Janet M. Todd, "'Very Copys of Nature': John Clare's Descriptive Poetry," PQ, 53 (Jan., 1974), 97-98.

_____. "I Am"
Bloom, The Visionary Company, pp. 443-444.

_____. "I Hid My Love"
Bloom, The Visionary Company, pp. 435-436.

_____. "An Invite to Eternity"
Bloom, The Visionary Company, pp. 441-443.

_____. "The Lark's Nest"
Thomas R. Frosch, "The Descriptive Style of John Clare" <u>SIR</u>, 10 (Spring, 1971), 138-139.

_____. "Love and Beauty"
Mark Storey, <u>Expl</u>, 28 (March, 1970), 60.

_____. "Mouse's Nest"
Janet M. Todd, "'Very Copys of Nature': John Clare's Descriptive Poetry,"
<u>PQ</u>, 53 (Jan., 1974), 97.

_____. "The Nightingale's Nest"
Janet M. Todd, "'Very Copys of Nature': John Clare's Descriptive Poetry,"
<u>PQ</u>, 53 (Jan., 1974), 88-90.

_____. "Sand Martin"
Janet M. Todd, "'Very Copys of Nature': John Clare's Descriptive Poetry,"
<u>PQ</u>, 53 (Jan., 1974), 91-92.

_____. "Schoolboys in Winter"
Frankenberg, <u>Invitation to Poetry</u>, p. 235.

_____. "The Skylark"
L. J. Swingle, "Stalking the Essential John Clare: Clare in Relation to His Romantic Contemporaries," <u>SIR</u>, 14 (Summer, 1975), 277-278.

Janet M. Todd, "'Very Copys of Nature': John Clare's Descriptive Poetry,"
<u>PQ</u>, 53 (Jan., 1974), 92-94.

_____. "The Sorrows of Love"
Ian Gregor, "The Last Augustan," <u>The Dublin Review</u>, 229 (First Quarter, 1955), 46-48.

_____. "A Vision"
Bloom, <u>The Visionary Company</u>, pp. 444-445.

_____. "The Woodman"
L. J. Swingle, "Stalking the Essential John Clare: Clare in Relation to His Romantic Contemporaries," <u>SIR</u>, 14 (Summer, 1975), 282-283.

CLARK, David R.   "The Bee Space"
Clark, <u>Lyric Resonance</u>, pp. 210-211.

_____. "Mountain Ash"
Clark, <u>Lyric Resonance</u>, pp. 211-215.

_____. "Robin"
Clark, <u>Lyric Resonance</u>, pp. 204-206.

_____. "Tree"
Clark, <u>Lyric Resonance</u>, pp. 207-210.

CLEVELAND.   "The Hecatomb to His Mistress"
H. M. Richmond, "The Intangible Mistress," <u>MP</u>, 56 (May, 1959), 221.

Williamson, <u>The Proper Wit of Poetry</u>, pp. 73-75.

_____. "The Senses Festival"
Williamson, <u>The Proper Wit of Poetry</u>, pp. 75-76.

CLOUGH. "Blank Misgivings of a Creature Moving about in Worlds not Realized"
Richard D. McGhee, "'Blank Misgivings': Arthur Hugh Clough's Search for
Poetic Form," _VP_, 7 (Summer, 1969), 110-115.

_____. "Blessed Are Those Who Have Not Seen"
Bruce Berlind, "A Curious Accomplishment," _Poetry_, 82 (April, 1953), 28-
30.

_____. "Epi-Strauss-Ium"
R. A. Forsyth, "Herbert, Clough, and Their Church-Windows," _VP_, 7 (Spring,
1969), 17-30.

_____. "Is It True, Ye Gods, Who Treat Us"
Michael Timko, "The Satiric Poetry of Arthur Clough," _VP_, 1 (Summer,
1963), 107-108.

_____. "Love and Reason"
Frederick Mulhauser, Jr., "Clough's 'Love and Reason,'" _MP_, 42 (Feb.,
1945), 174-186.

_____. "Say Not the Struggle Naught Availeth"
Burke, _Language as Symbolic Action_, pp. 445-447.

Cooper and Holmes, _Preface to Poetry_, pp. 177-181.

William Howard, _Expl_, 15 (March, 1957), 39.
Rpt. _The Explicator Cyclopedia_, II, pp. 81-82.

Millett, _Reading Poetry_, pp. 17-18.

COFFIN, Robert. "Love, the Leaves Are Falling Round Thee"
Adams, _The Contexts of Poetry_, pp. 15-18.

COHEN, Leonard. "Go By Brooks, Love"
Don Gutteridge, "The Affective Fallacy and the Student's Response to
Poetry," _EJ_, 61 (Feb., 1972), 217-221.

COLERIDGE. "The Ballad of the Dark Ladié"
Heather Dubrow Ousby, "Coleridge's 'The Ballad of the Dark Ladié,'"
Expl, 35 (Fall, 1976), 21-22.

_____. "Christabel"
John Adlard, "The Quantock _Christabel_," _PQ_, 50 (April, 1971), 230-238.

Douglas Angus, "The Theme of Love and Guilt in Coleridge's Three Major
Poems," _JEGP_, 59 (Oct., 1960), 661-663.

Roy P. Basler, "Christabel," _SR_, 51 (Winter, 1943), 73-95.

Basler, _Sex, Symbolism, and Psychology in Literature_, pp. 25-51.

L. D. Berkoben, "'Christabel': A Variety of Evil Experience," _MLQ_, 25
(Dec., 1964), 400-411.

Bloom, _The Visionary Company_, pp. 206-211.

Bostetter, _The Romantic Ventriloquist_, pp. 118-132.

Paul Edwards and MacDonald Emslie, "Thoughts So All Unlike Each Other:
The Paradoxical in _Christabel_," _ES_, 52 (June, 1971), 236-246.

MacDonald Emslie and Paul Edwards, "The Limitations of Langdale: A
Reading of _Christabel_," _EIC_, 20 (Jan., 1970), 57-70.

Warren G. French, Expl, 13 (June, 1955), 48.
    Rpt. The Explicator Cyclopedia, II, pp. 82-83.

Constance Hunting, "Another Look at 'The Conclusion to Part II' of
Christabel," ELN, 12 (March, 1975), 171-176.

Annabel Wetzel Kitzhaber, "David Hartley in Christabel," RS, 9 (Sept.,
1941), 213-222.

Knight, The Starlit Dome, pp. 83-84 et passim.

A. H. Nethercot, "Coleridge's 'Christabel' and LeFanu's 'Carmilla,'"
MP, 47 (Aug., 1949), 32-39.

Terry Otten, "Christabel, Beatrice, and the Encounter with Evil," BuR,
17 (May, 1969), 20-24; 29-30.

Raymond Smith, "Christabel and Geraldine: The Marriage of Life and
Death," BuR, 13 (March, 1965), 63-71.

Jonas Spatz, "The Mystery of Eros: Sexual Initiation in Coleridge's
'Christabel,'" PMLA, 90 (Jan., 1975), 107-116.

Tomlinson, Interpretations, ed. John Wain, pp. 103-112 .

James Twitchell, Expl, 35 (Winter, 1976), 28-29.

Carl Woodring, "Christabel of Cumberland," A Review of English Literature, 7 (Jan., 1966),.43-52.

Wormhoudt, The Demon Lover, pp. 17-29; 42-47.

_____. "Dejection: An Ode"
Bloom, The Visionary Company, pp. 216-223.

Bostetter, The Romantic Ventriloquist, pp. 132-133.

Charles S. Bouslog; "Structure and Theme in Coleridge's 'Dejection: An
Ode,'" MLQ, 24 (March, 1963), 42-52.

Bowra, The Romantic Imagination, pp. 85-92 passim.

Panthea Reid Broughton, "The Modifying Metaphor in 'Dejection: An Ode,'"
WC, 4 (Autumn, 1973), 241-249.

Irene H. Chayes, "Rhetoric as Drama: An Approach to the Romantic Ode,"
PMLA, 79 (March, 1964), 69-71.

Michael G. Cooke, The Romantic Will (New Haven and London: Yale Univ.
Press, 1976), pp. 13-16.

Ethel F. Cornwell, The "Still Point," pp. 81-86.

W. Paul Elledge, "Fountains Within: Motivation in Coleridge's 'Dejection:
An Ode,'" PLL, 7 (Summer, 1971), 304-308.

A. Harris Fairbanks, "The Form of Coleridge's Dejection Ode," PMLA, 90
(Oct., 1975), 874-884.

Richard H. Fogle, "The Dejection of Coleridge's Ode," ELH, 17 (March,
1950), 71-77.
    Rpt. The Permanent Pleasure, pp. 53-59.

R. M. Gay, Expl, 2 (Nov., 1943), 14.
    Rpt. The Explicator Cyclopedia, II, p. 83.

John O. Hayden, "Coleridge's 'Dejection: An Ode,'" ES, 52 (April, 1971),
132-136.

Knight, The Starlit Dome, pp. 105-107 et passim.

M. J. Lupton, "The Dark Dream of 'Dejection,'" L&P, 18, No. 1 (1968),
39-47.

M. J. Lupton, "The Dark Dream of 'Dejection,'" L&P, 18, No. 1 (1968), 39-47.

Morley J. Mays, Expl, 2 (Feb., 1944), 27.
    Rpt. The Explicator Cyclopedia, II, pp. 83-84.

James Smith, "The Poetry of Coleridge," Scrutiny, 8 (March, 1940), 416-420.

J. L. Simmons, "Coleridge's 'Dejection: An Ode': A Poet's Regeneration," The University of Kansas City Review, 23 (March, 1967), 212-218.

Newton Phelps Stallknecht, "The Doctrine of Coleridge's Dejection and Its Relation to Wordsworth's Philosophy," PMLA, 49 (March, 1934), 196-207.

William I. Thompson, "Collapsed Universe and Structured Poem: An Essay in Whiteheadian Criticism," CE, 28 (Oct., 1966), 26-29.

Ronald C. Wendling, "Dramatic Reconciliation in Coleridge's Conversation Poems," PLL, 9 (Spring, 1973), 150-152; 157-159.

_____. "The Destiny of Nations"
Knight, The Starlit Dome, pp. 136-142.

_____. "The Eolian Harp"
James D. Boulger, "Imagination and Speculation in Coleridge's Conversation Poems," JEGP, 64 (Oct., 1965), 693-699.

Bloom, The Visionary Company, pp. 194-196.

Burke, The Philosophy of Literary Form, pp. 93-98.

Richard H. Fogle, "Coleridge's Conversation Poems," TSE, 5 (1955), 108-109.
    Rpt. The Permanent Pleasure, pp. 23-25.

Albert Gerard, "Counterfeiting Infinity: The Eolian Harp and the Growth of Coleridge's Mind," JEGP, 60 (July, 1961), 411-419.

Albert Gerard, "The Systolic Rhythm: The Structure of Coleridge's Conversation Poems," EIC, 10 (July, 1960), 310-319.

William H. Marshall, "The Structure of Coleridge's 'The Eolian Harp,'" MLN, 76 (March, 1961), 229-232.

Jill Rubenstein, "Sound and Silence in Coleridge's Conversation Poems," English, 21 (Summer, 1972), 55-56.

E. San Juan, Jr., "Coleridge's 'The Eolian Harp' as Lyric Paradigm," The Personalist, 48 (Winter, 1967), 79-88.

William H. Scheuerle, "A Reexamination of Coleridge's 'The Eolian Harp,'" SEL, 15 (Autumn, 1975), 591-599.

Ronald C. Wendling, "Coleridge and the Consistency of 'The Eolian Harp,'" SIR, 8 (Autumn, 1968), 26-42.

_____. "Fears in Solitude"
Knight, The Starlit Dome, pp. 130-131 et passim.

_____. "France: An Ode"
Bloom, The Visonary Company, pp. 215-216.

_____. "Frost at Midnight"
Ronald A. Audet, "'Frost at Midnight': The Other Coleridge," EJ, 59 (Nov., 1970), 1080-1085.

Bloom, Philbrick, and Blistein, The Order of Poetry, pp. 39-41.

Bloom, The Visionary Company, pp. 196-199.

James D. Boulger, "Imagination and Speculation in Coleridge's Conversation Poems," JEGP, 64 (Oct., 1965), 705-711.

Morris Dickstein, "Coleridge, Wordsworth, and the 'Conversation Poems,'" CentR, 16 (Fall, 1972), 372-373.

Richard H. Fogle, "Coleridge's Conversation Poems," TSE, 5 (1955), 110. Rpt. The Permanent Pleasure, pp. 25-26.

Langbaum, The Poetry of Experience, pp. 45-46.

Kaplan, Miracles of Rare Device, pp. 44-61.

Jill Rubenstein, "Sound and Silence in Coleridge's Conversation Poems," English, 21 (Summer, 1972), 58-59.

Michael J. Sundell, "The Theme of Self-Realization in 'Frost at Midnight,'" SIR, 7 (Autumn, 1967), 34-39.

Ronald C. Wendling, "Dramatic Reconciliation in Coleridge's Conversation Poems," PLL, 9 (Spring, 1973), 156-157.

_____. "The Garden of Boccaccio"
Knight, The Starlit Dome, pp. 117-119.

_____. "The Hymn Before Sunrise, in the Vale of Chamouni"
Knight, The Starlit Dome, pp. 107-109.

A. P. Rossiter, "Coleridge's 'Hymn Before Sunrise,'" TLS, Sept. 28, 1951, p. 613.

A. P. Rossiter, "Coleridge's 'Hymn Before Sunrise,'" TLS, Oct. 26, 1951, p. 677.

_____. "Kubla Khan"
N. B. Allen, "A Note on Coleridge's 'Kubla Khan,'" MLN, 57 (Feb., 1942), 108-113.

Douglas Angus, "The Theme of Love and Guilt in Coleridge's Three Major Poems," JEGP, 59 (Oct., 1960), 663-668.

Bloom, The Visionary Company, pp. 212-215.

Bodkin, Archetypal Patterns in Poetry, pp. 90-116.

Bostetter, The Romantic Ventriloquist, pp. 84-91.

Bernard R. Breyer, "Towards an Interpretation of 'Kubla Khan,'" in English Studies in Honor of James Southall Wilson, pp. 227-290.

Brooke, Purser, and Warren, An Approach to Literature, third edition, pp. 376-378.
    Rpt. fourth edition, pp. 370-372.

Burke, Language as Symbolic Action, pp. 201-222.

Irene H. Chayes, "'Kubla Khan' and the Creative Process,' SIR, 6 (Autumn, 1966), 1-21.

A. B. England, "'Kubla Khan' Again: The Ocean, the Caverns, and the Ancestral Voices," ArielE, 4 (Oct., 1973), 63-72.

Felver and Nurmi, Poetry: An Introduction and Anthology, pp. 19-24.

Richard H. Fogle, "The Romantic Unity of 'Kubla Khan,'" CE, 18 (Oct., 1951), 13-18.
    Rpt. The Permanent Pleasure, pp. 43-52.

Frankenberg, Invitation to Poetry, pp. 45-48.

Richard Gerber, "Keys to 'Kubla Khan,'" ES, 44 (Oct., 1963), 321-341.

S. K. Heninger, Jr., "A Jungian Reading of 'Kubla Khan,'" JAAC, 18 (March, 1960), 358-367.

Knight, The Starlit Dome, pp. 90-97 et passim.

Alicia Martinez, "Coleridge, 'Kubla Khan,' and the Contingent," CP, 10 (Spring, 1977), 59-61.

Hans Heinrich Meier, "Xanaduvian Residues," ES, 48 (April, 1967), 145-155.

Dorothy F. Mercer, "The Symbolism of 'Kubla Khan,'" JAAC, 12 (Sept., 1953), 44-65.

R. H. Milner, "Coleridge's 'Sacred River,'" TLS, May 18, 1951, p. 309.

Charles I, Patterson, Jr., "The Daemonic in Kubla Khan: Toward Interpretation," PMLA, 89 (Oct., 1974), 1033-42.

H. W. Piper, "The Two Paradises in Kubla Khan," RES, 27 (May, 1976), 148-158.

Alan C. Purves, "Formal Structure in 'Kubla Khan,'" SIR, 1 (Spring, 1962), 187-191.

Kathleen Raine, "Traditional Symbolism in 'Kubla Khan,'" SR, 72 (Autumn, 1964), 626-642.

Ribner and Morris, Poetry: A Critical and Historical Introduction, pp. 304-307.

Duane B. Schneider, "The Structure of Kubla Khan," AN&Q, 1 (Jan., 1963), 68-70.

Elisabeth Schneider, "The 'Dream' of Kubla Khan," PMLA, 60 (Sept., 1945), 784-801.

John Shelton, "The Autograph Manuscript of 'Kubla Khan' and an Interpretation," A Review of English Literature, 7 (Jan., 1966), 32-42.

Eugene H. Sloane, "Coleridge's Kubla Khan: The Living Catacombs of the Mind," AI, 29 (Summer, 1972), 97-122.

James Smith, "The Poetry of Coleridge," Scrutiny, 8 (March, 1940), 411-414.

Nathan Comfort Starr, "Coleridge's Sacred River," PLL, 2 (Spring, 1966), 117-125.

Warren Stevenson, "'Kubla Khan' as Symbol," TSLL, 14 (Winter, 1973), 605-630.

Marshall Suther, "On the Interpretation of 'Kubla Khan,'" BuR, 7 (May, 1957), 1-19.

George Watson, "The Meaning of 'Kubla Khan,'" A Review of English Literature, 2 (Jan., 1961), 21-29.

M. A. Taylor, "'Kubla Khan': The Well-Ordered Fragment," CEA, 37 (March, 1975), 8-9.

Carl R. Woodring, "Coleridge and the Khan," EIC, 9 (Oct., 1959), 361-368.

_____. "Lewti"
C. L. Joughlin, "Coleridge's Lewti: The Biography of a Poem," Texas
Studies in English, 1943 (Austin: Univ. of Texas Press, 1943), pp. 66-93.

_____. "Limbo"
Bloom, The Visionary Company, pp. 227-230.

_____. "Lines Written at Shurton Bars"
Geoffrey Little, "'Lines Written at Shurton Bars...': Coleridge's First
Conversation Poem?" SoR, 2, No. 2 (1966), 137-147.

_____. "Monody on the Death of Chatterton"
I. A. Gordon, "The Cast History of Coleridge's Monody on the Death of
Chatterton," RES, 18 (Jan., 1942), 49-71.

_____. "The Nightingale"
Bloom, The Visionary Company, pp. 199-201.

Morris Dickstein, "Coleridge, Wordsworth, and the 'Conversation Poems,'"
CentR, 16 (Fall, 1972), 380-382.

R. H. Hopkins, "Coleridge's Parody of Melancholy Poetry, in 'The Nightingale': A Conversation Poem," ES, 49 (Oct., 1968), 436-441.

Jill Rubenstein, "Sound and Silence in Coleridge's Conversation Poems,"
English, 21 (Summer, 1972), 59-60.

_____. "No Plus Ultra"
Bloom, The Visionary Company, pp. 230-231.

_____. "Ode on the Departing Year"
Louise Schutz Boas, Expl, 9 (Nov., 1950), 15.
    Rpt. The Explicator Cyclopedia, II, p. 85.

Arthur Dickson, Expl, 9 (Nov., 1950), 15.
    Rpt. The Explicator Cyclopedia, II, pp. 85-86.

Walter Gierasch, Expl, 8 (March, 1950), 34.
    Rpt. The Explicator Cyclopedia, II, pp. 84-85.

F. H. Heidbrink, Expl, 2 (Dec., 1943), 21.
    Rpt. The Explicator Cyclopedia, II, p. 84.

Knight, The Starlit Dome, pp. 129-130.

Arthur H. Nethercot, Expl, 1 (June, 1943), 64.
    Rpt. The Explicator Cyclopedia, II, p. 84.

Max F. Schulz, "Coleridge's 'Ode on the Departing Year' and the Sacred
Theory of Earth: A Case for Analogical Criticism," CP, 1 (Spring, 1968),
45-53.

_____. "On Donne's Poetry"
Frankenberg, Invitation to Poetry, pp. 87-88.

_____. "The Pang More Sharp than All"
Knight, The Starlit Dome, pp. 120-121.

_____. "The Picture"
Knight, The Starlit Dome, pp. 116-117 et passim.

_____. "Reflections on Having Left a Place of Retirement"
Jill Rubenstein, "Sound and Silence in Coleridge's Conversation Poems,"
English, 21 (Summer, 1972), 56-57.

_____. "Religious Musings"
Bostetter, The Romantic Ventriloquist, pp. 94-96.

Knight, The Starlit Dome, pp. 131-132.

_____. "The Rime of the Ancient Mariner"
Douglas Angus, "The Theme of Love and Guilt in Coleridge's Three Major
Poems," JEGP, 59 (Oct., 1960), 660-661; 665-666.

Beach, A Romantic View of Poetry, pp. 8-22.

Marius Bewley, "The Poetry of Coleridge," The Importance of Scrutiny,
pp. 169-174. Published in Scrutiny, 1940.

Bloom, The Visionary Company, pp. 201-206.

Louise Schutz Boas, Expl, 2 (May, 1944), 52.
     Rpt. The Explicator Cyclopedia, II, pp. 86-87.

Bodkin, Archetypal Patterns in Poetry, pp. 26-89.

Edward E. Bostetter, "The Nightmare World of The Ancient Mariner," SIR,
1 (Summer, 1962), 241-254.

Bostetter, The Romantic Ventriloquist, pp. 108-118; 123.

James D. Boulger, "Christian Skepticism in The Rime of the Ancient
Mariner," in From Sensibility to Romanticism, pp. 439-451.

Hoyt E. Bowen, Expl, 15 (Nov., 1956), 9.
     Rpt. The Explicator Cyclopedia, II, p. 90.

Bowra, The Romantic Imagination, pp. 52-75.
     Abridged in The Case for Poetry, pp. 63, 65.

Burke, The Philosophy of Literary Form, pp. 22-25 et passim.

Kenneth Burke, "Towards Objective Criticism," Poetry, 70 (April, 1947),
42-47.

Brett, Reason and Imagination, pp. 78-107.

A. M. Buchan, "The Sad Wisdom of the Mariner," SP, 61 (Oct., 1964),
669-688.

Alice Chandler, "Structure and Symbol in 'The Rime of the Ancient Mariner,'" MLQ, 26 (Sept., 1965), 401-413.

Irene H. Chayes, "A Coleridgean Reading of 'The Ancient Mariner,'" SIR,
4 (Winter, 1965), 81-103.

Ciardi, How Does a Poem Mean? pp. 721-722.

Michael G. Cooke, The Romantic Will (New Haven and London: Yale Univ.
Press, 1976), pp. 30-39.

Howard Creed, "'The Rime of the Ancient Mariner': A Re-reading," EJ,
49 (April, 1960), 215-222; 228.

Abe Delson, "The Symbolism of the Sun and Moon in The Rime of the Ancient
Mariner," 15 (Winter, 1974), 709-720.

Arthur Dickson, Expl, 6 (June, 1948), 52.
     Rpt. The Explicator Cyclopedia, II, pp. 87-88.

Sarah Dyck, "Perspective in 'The Rime of the Ancient Mariner,'" SEL, 13
(Autumn, 1973), 591-604.

Dyson and Lovelock, Masterful Images, pp. 175-192.

Frances Ferguson, "Coleridge and the Deluded Reader: 'The Rime of the Ancient Mariner,'" GaR, 31 (Fall, 1977), 617-635.

Richard Harter Fogle, "The Genre of The Ancient Mariner," TSE, 7 (1957), 111-124.
     Rpt. in The Permanent Pleasure, pp. 27-42.

Newell F. Ford, "Kenneth Burke and Robert Penn Warren: Criticism by Obsessive Metaphor," JEGP, 53 (April, 1954), 172-177.

Lorne J. Forstner, "Coleridge's 'The Ancient Mariner' and the Case for Justifiable 'Mythocide': An Argument on Psychological, Epistemological, and Formal Grounds," Criticism, 18 (Summer, 1976), 211-229.

O. Bryan Fulmer, "The Ancient Mariner and the Wandering Jew," SP, 66 (Oct., 1969), 797-815.

Edward E. Gibbons, "Point of View and Moral in 'The Rime of the Ancient Mariner,'" The University of Kansas City Review, 35 (Summer, 1969), 257-261.

Elliott B. Gose, Jr., "Coleridge and the Luminous Gloom: An Analysis of the 'Symbolical Language' in 'The Rime of the Ancient Mariner,'" PMLA, 75 (June, 1960), 238-244.

D. W. Harding, "The Rime of the Ancient Mariner," The Importance of Scrutiny, pp. 174-181. Published in Scrutiny, 1941.

Lynn H. Harris, Expl, 6 (March, 1948), 32.
     Rpt. The Explicator Cyclopedia, II, p. 87.

Lloyd N. Jeffrey, "'Human Interest and a Semblance of Truth' in the Slaying of Coleridge's Albatross," CEA, 30 (Feb., 1968), 3-5.

Leo Kirschbaum, Expl, 7 (Oct., 1948), 5.
     Rpt. The Explicator Cyclopedia, II, pp. 88-89.

Knight, The Starlit Dome, pp. 84-90 et passim.

Kreuzer, Elements of Poetry, pp. 18-21.

Murray Krieger, "Ekphrasis and the Still Movement of Poetry: or, Laokoön Revisited," in The Poet as Critic, pp. 20-22.

Raphael Levy, Expl, 22 (May, 1964), 74.

Mark Littmann, "The Ancient Mariner and Initiation Rites," PLL, 4 (Fall, 1968), 370-389.

Florence Marsh, "The Ocean-Desert: 'The Ancient Mariner' and 'The Waste Land,'" EIC, 9 (April, 1959), 126-133.

William H. Marshall, "Coleridge, The Mariner, and Dramatic Irony," The Personalist, 42 (Oct., 1961), 524-532.

Daniel McDonald, "Too Much Reality: A Discussion of 'The Rime of the Ancient Mariner,'" SEL, 4 (Autumn, 1964), 543-554.

B. R. McElderry, Jr., "Coleridge's Revision of 'The Ancient Mariner,'" SP, 29 (Jan., 1932), 68-94.

Raimonda Modiano, "Words and 'Languageless' Meanings: Limits of Expression in The Rime of the Ancient Mariner," MLQ, 38 (March, 1977), 40-61.

Elizabeth Nitchie, "The Moral of the Ancient Mariner Reconsidered," PMLA, 48 (Sept., 1933), 867-876.

Olson, Critics and Criticism, Crane, ed., pp. 138-144.
    Abridged in The Case for Poetry, p. 67.

Charles A. Owen, "Structure in 'The Ancient Mariner,'" CE, 23 (Jan., 1962), 261-267.

Ward Pafford, "Coleridge's Wedding-Guest," SP, 60 (Oct., 1963), 618-629.

Frederick A. Pottle, "Modern Criticism of The Ancient Mariner," in Essays on the Teaching of Literature, pp. 261-269.

J. W. R. Purser, "Interpretation of the Ancient Mariner," RES, 8, n.s. (Aug., 1957), 249-256.

Maren-Sofie Rostvig, "'The Rime of the Ancient Mariner' and the Cosmic System of Robert Fludd," TSL, 12 (1967), 69-81.

Sewell, The Structure of Poetry, pp. 178-182.

Gayle S. Smith, "A Reappraisal of the Moral Stanzas in The Rime of the Ancient Mariner," SIR, 3 (Autumn, 1963), 42-52.

James Smith, "The Poetry of Coleridge," Scrutiny, 8 (March, 1940), 406-411.

Lionel Stevenson, "The Ancient Mariner as a Dramatic Monologue," The Personalist, 30 (Jan., 1949), 34-44.
    Abridged in The Case for Poetry, pp. 67, 69.

E. E. Stoll, "Symbolism in Coleridge," PMLA, 63 (March, 1948), 214-229.

Milton Teichman, "The Marriage Metaphor in The Rime of the Ancient Mariner," BNYPL, 73 (Jan., 1969), 40-48.

Tillyard, Five Poems, 1470-1870, pp. 66-86.

James Twitchell, "The World Above the Ancient Mariner," TSLL, 17 (Spring, 1975), 103-117.

Robert Penn Warren, "A Poem of Pure Imagination (Reconsiderations VI)," The Kenyon Review, 8 (Summer, 1946), 391-427.
    Abridged in The Case for Poetry, pp. 65, 67.

Wells, The Ballad Tree, pp. 313-314.

George Whalley, "The Mariner and the Albatross," UTQ, 16 (July, 1947), 381-398.

Alison White, Expl, 13 (Nov., 1954), 11.
    Rpt. The Explicator Cyclopedia, II, pp. 89-90.

J. Edwin Whitesell, "'The Rime of the Ancient Mariner,' Line 142," N&Q, 3, n.s. (Jan., 1956), 34-35.

Stewart C. Wilcox, "The Arguments and Motto of 'The Ancient Mariner,'" MLQ, 22 (Sept., 1961), 264-268.

Stewart C. Wilcox, Expl, 7 (Feb., 1949), 28.
    Rpt. The Explicator Cyclopedia, II, p. 89.

Stewart C. Wilcox, "The Water Imagery of The Ancient Mariner," The Personalist, 35 (Summer, 1954), 285-292.

Kenneth Wolman, "The Ancient Mariner's Unethical World," EngR, 23 (Spring, 1973), 34-39.

Carl Woodring, "The Mariner's Return," SIR, 11 (Fall, 1972), 375-380.

Wormhoudt, The Demon Lover, pp. 29-42.

_____. "This Lime-Tree Bower My Prison"
James D. Boulger, "Imagination and Speculation in Coleridge's Conversation Poems,'" JEGP, 64 (Oct., 1965), 699-705.

Morris Dickstein, "Coleridge, Wordsworth, and the 'Conversation Poems,'" CentR, 16 (Fall, 1972), 371-372.

R. A. Durr, "'This Lime-Tree Bower My Prison': and a Recurrent Action in Coleridge," ELH, 26 (Dec., 1959), 515-530.

Jill Rubenstein, "Sound and Silence in Coleridge's Conversation Poems," English, 21 (Summer, 1972), 57-58.

A. W. Rudrum, "Coleridge's 'This Lime-Tree Bower My Prison,'" Southern Review (Australia), 1, No. 2 (1964), 30-42.

Ronald C. Wendling, "Dramatic Reconciliation in Coleridge's Conversation Poems," PLL, 9 (Spring, 1973), 153-156.

_____. "The Three Graves"
Bostetter, The Romantic Ventriloquist, pp. 104-108.

_____. "Time, Real and Imaginary"
John R. Byers, Jr., Expl, 19 (April, 1961), 46.
    Rpt. The Explicator Cyclopedia, II, pp. 91-92.

F. H. Heidbrink, Expl, 3 (Oct., 1944), 4.
    Rpt. The Explicator Cyclopedia, II, pp. 90-91.

A. A. Raven, Expl, 3 (Feb., 1945), 33.
    Rpt. The Explicator Cyclopedia, II, p. 91.

_____. "To the River Otter"
W. K. Wimsatt, Jr., "The Structure of Romantic Nature Imagery," in The Age of Johnson (New Haven: Yale Univ. Press, 1949), pp. 296-298.
    Rpt. The Verbal Icon, pp. 108-110.

_____. "To William Wordsworth"
Bloom, The Visionary Company, pp. 223-227.

A. Reeve Parker, "Wordsworth's Whelming Tide: Coleridge and the Art of Analogy," in Forms of Lyric: Selected Papers from the English Institute (New York: Columbia Univ. Press, 1970), 75-102.

COLLINS. "Ode on the Poetical Character"
Bloom, The Visionary Company, pp. 3-10.

E. L. Brooks, "William Collins's 'Ode on the Poetical Character,'" CE, 17 (April, 1956), 403-404.

Winifred Lynskey, Expl, 19 (Feb., 1961), 33.
    Rpt. The Explicator Cyclopedia, II, p. 92.

Patricia Meyer Spacks, "Collins' Imagery," SP, 62 (Oct., 1965), 722-728.

Spacks, The Poetry of Vision, pp. 66-74.

Unger and O'Connor, Poems for Study, pp. 325-329.

Steve J. Van Der Weele, "Proverbs 8 and William Collins's 'Ode on the Poetical Character,'" PLL, 12 (Spring, 1976), 197-200.

Earl R. Wasserman, "Collins' 'Ode on the Poetical Character,'" ELH, 39 (March, 1967), 92-115.

A. S. P. Woodhouse, "The Poetry of Collins Reconsidered," in From Sensibility to Romanticism, pp. 100-108.

_____. "Ode on the Popular Superstitions of the Highlands of Scotland Consid-
ered as the Subject for Poetry,"
Patricia Meyer Spacks, "Collins' Imagery," SP, 62 (Oct., 1965), 731-736.

Spacks, The Poetry of Vision, pp. 78-82, 211-212.

_____. "Ode to Evening"
Abad, A Formal Approach to Lyric Poetry, p. 254.

Melvin W. Askew, "Form and Process in Lyric Poetry," SR, 72 (Spring,
1964), 281-299.

Merle E. Brown, "On William Collins' 'Ode to Evening,'" EIC, 11 (April,
1961), 136-153.

Daniels, The Art of Reading Poetry, pp. 360-364.

William Frost, English Masterpieces, Vol. VI, Romantic and Victorian
Poetry, p. 4.

Geoffrey H. Hartman, "Romantic Poetry and the Genius Loci," in The Disciplines of Criticism: Essays in Literary Theory, Interpretation, and
History, ed. Peter Demetz, Thomas Greene, and Lowry Nelson, Jr. (New Haven
and London: Yale Univ. Press, 1968), 299-303.

Peckham and Chatman, Word, Meaning, Poem, pp. 240-252.

Peter A. Stitt, "William Collins' 'Ode to Evening,'" CP, 5 (Spring, 1972),
27-33.

Winters, Forms of Discovery, pp. 152-155.

_____. "Ode to Fear"
John R. Crider, "Structure and Effect in Collins' Progress Poems," SP, 60
(Jan., 1963), 61-63.

Patricia Meyer Spacks, "Collins' Imagery," SP, 62 (Oct., 1965), 729-731.

Spacks, The Poetry of Vision, pp. 75-78, 209-210.

_____. "Ode to Liberty"
John R. Crider, "Structure and Effect in Collins' Progress Poems," SP, 60
(Jan., 1963), 69-72.

_____. "Ode to Pity"
Benjamin Boyce, "Sounding Shells and Little Prattlers in the Mid-
Eighteenth-Century English Ode," ECS, 8 (Spring, 1975), 246-249, 260-263.

John R. Crider, "Structure and Effect in Collins' Progress Poems," SP,
60 (Jan., 1963), 58-63.

Spacks, The Poetry of Vision, pp. 74-75, 208.

_____. "Ode to Simplicity"
John R. Crider, "Structure and Effect in Collins' Progress Poems," SP,
60 (Jan., 1963), 62-69.

_____. "Sonnet" ("When Phoebe Form'd a Wanton Smile")
Spacks, The Poetry of Vision, pp. 83-84.

CONGREVE. "Song: False Though She Be to Me and Love"
Bateson, English Poetry and the English Language, pp. 62-63.

CORBET, Richard. "The Fairies' Farewell"
    Cleanth Brooks, "The New Criticism and Scholarship," in Twentieth Century
    English, ed. William S. Knickerbocker (New York: The Philosophical
    Library, 1946), pp. 371-383.

COTTON. "Bacon's Epitaph, Made by His Man"
    Roy P. Basler, Expl, 2 (Dec., 1943), 20.
        Rpt. The Explicator Cyclopedia, II, pp. 92-93.

_____. "To Chloris. Stanzes Irreguliers"
    Miner, The Cavalier Mode from Jonson to Cotton, pp. 7-10.

COWLEY, Abraham. "Destinie"
    William D. McGaw, "The Civil War in Cowley's Destinie," ELN, 14 (June,
    1977), 268-270.

_____. "Hymn: to Light:
    Allen Tate, "Tension in Poetry," SoR, 4 (Summer, 1938), 105-108.
        Rpt. Tate, Reason in Madness, pp. 67-69; On the Limits of Poetry,
        pp. 78-81; Critiques, pp. 57-60.
        Rpt. West, Essays in Modern Literary Criticism, pp. 270-272.

_____. "The Muse"
    Harvey D. Goldstein, "Discordia Concors, Decorum, and Cowley," ES, 49
    (Dec., 1968), 486-487.

_____. "Of Wit"
    Harvey D. Goldstein, "Discordia Concors, Decorum, and Cowley," ES, 49
    (Dec., 1968), 481-486.

_____. "On the Queen's Reparing Somerset House"
    Charles Larson, "The Somerset House Poems of Cowley and Waller," PLL,
    10 (Spring, 1974), 127-131.

_____. "The Request"
    Miles, The Primary Language of Poetry in the 1640's, pp. 46-48.

_____. "The Resurrection"
    Harvey D. Goldstein, "Discordia Concors, Decorum, and Cowley," ES, 49
    (Dec., 1968), 488-489.

COWLEY, Malcolm. "The Long Voyage"
    Perrine and Reid, 100 American Poems, p. 172.

    Perrine, The Art of Total Relevance, pp. 122-124.

_____. "The Source"
    J. F. Nims, Poetry: A Critical Supplement, April, 1948, pp. 12-13.

COWPER. "The Castaway"
    Lodwick Hartley, Expl, 5 (Dec., 1946), 21.
        Rpt. The Explicator Cyclopedia, II, p. 93.

_____. "The Flatting Mill"
    Thomas A. Reisner, Expl, 32 (Nov., 1973), 22.

_____. "Hark My Soul It Is the Lord"
    Sr. Pauline Parker, "The Hymn as a Literary Form," ECS, 8 (Summer, 1975),
    414-415.

_____. Olney Hymns IX, "The Contrite Heart"
Spacks, The Poetry of Vision, pp. 166-167.

_____. Olney Hymns XI, "Jehovah Our Righteousness"
Spacks, The Poetry of Vision, pp. 167-169.

_____. "To Mary Unwin"
Kilby, Poetry and Life, pp. 19-25.

COXE, Louis O. "Gunner's Mate"
Leonard Unger, "Seven Poets," SR, 56 (Winter, 1948), 160-161.

CRABBE. "Abel Keene"
Ian Gregor, "The Last Augustan," The Dublin Review, 229 (First Quarter, 1955), 43-46.

_____. "Peter Grimes"
Gavin Edwards, "The Grimeses," EIC, 27 (April, 1977), 122-140.

_____. "Procrastination"
Ian Gregor, "The Last Augustan," The Dublin Review, 229 (First Quarter, 1955), 49-50.

_____. "The Village"
Ian Gregor, "The Last Augustan," The Dublin Review, 229 (First Quarter, 1955), 38-42.

Ronald B. Hatch, "George Crabbe and the Tenth Muse," ECS, 7 (Spring, 1974), 277-294.

CRANE, Hart. "The Air Plant"
O'Connor, Sense and Sensibility in Modern Poetry, p. 148.

Eric J. Sundquist, "Bringing Home the Word: Magic, Lies, and Silence in Hart Crane," ELH, 44 (Summer, 1977), 394-395.

_____. "And Yet This Great Wink of Eternity"
Drew, Directions in Modern Poetry, pp. 212-217.

_____. "Atlantis"
Clark, Lyric Resonance, pp. 141-145.

Friar and Brinnin, Modern Poetry, pp. 453-455.

Eric J. Sundquist, "Bringing Home the Word: Magic, Lies, and Silence in Hart Crane," ELH, 44 (Summer, 1977), 392-393.

Vogler, Preludes to Vision, pp. 191-194.

_____. "At Melville's Tomb"
Brooks and Warren, Understanding Poetry, pp. 477-482. Revised edition, pp. 333-336.

Clark, Lyric Resonance, pp. 152-158.

Hart Crane, quoted in Hart Crane by Brom Weber.
   Rpt. The Critic's Notebook, pp. 242-247.

Eastman, The Literary Mind, pp. 94-97.

Philip Furia, Expl, 33 (May, 1975), 73.

R. W. B. Lewis, "Crane's Visionary Lyric: The Way to The Bridge," MR, 7 (Spring, 1966), 242-248.

Harriet Monroe and Hart Crane, "A Discussion with Hart Crane," Poetry, 29 (Oct., 1926), 34-41.
   Rpt. Locke, Gibson, and Arms, Introduction to Literature, third edition, pp. 229-234.
   Rpt. fourth edition, pp. 231-236.
   Rpt. fifth edition, pp. 214-219.

Peter J. Sheehan, "Hart Crane and the Contemporary Search," EJ, 60 (Dec., 1971), 1212-1213.

Richard Strier, "The Poetics of Surrender: An Exposition and Critique of New Critical Poetics," CritI, 2 (Autumn, 1975), 182-186.

_____. "Ave Maria"
Friar and Brinnin, Modern Poetry, pp. 451-452.

Vogler, Preludes to Vision, pp. 149-153.

_____. "Belle Isle"
Evelyn J. Hinz, "Hart Crane's 'Voyages' Reconsidered," ConL, 13 (Summer, 1972), 325-333.

_____. "Black Tambourine"
Gray, American Poetry, pp. 219-220.

Milne Holton, "'A Boudelairesque Thing': The Direction of Hart Crane's 'Black Tambourine,'" Criticism, 9 (Summer, 1967), 215-228.

Edward Kessler, Expl, 29 (Sept., 1970), 4.

Peter J. Sheehan, "Hart Crane and the Contemporary Search," EJ, 60 (Dec., 1971), 1210-1211.

_____. "The Bridge"
Joseph J. Arpad, "Hart Crane's Platonic Myth: The Brooklyn Bridge," AL, 39 (March, 1967), 75-86.

Joseph Warren Beach, "The Cancelling Out--A Note on Recent Poetry," Accent, 7 (Summer, 1947), 245-246.

Stanley K. Coffman, "Symbolism in The Bridge," PMLA, 66 (March, 1951), 65-77.

Lawrence Dembo, "The Unfractioned Idiom of Hart Crane's Bridge," AL, 27 (May, 1955), 203-224.

Deutsch, Poetry in Our Time, pp. 322-328.

Deutsch, This Modern Poetry, pp. 141-148.

Joseph Frank, "Hart Crane: American Poet," SR, 62 (Winter, 1949), 157-158.

Brewster Ghiselin, "Bridge into the Sea," PR, 16 (July, 1949), 679-686.

Gordon K. Grigsby, "Hart Crane's Doubtful Vision," CE, 24 (April, 1963), 518-523.

Hoffman, The Twenties, pp. 229-239.

Hilton Landry, "Of Prayer and Praise: The Poetry of Hart Crane," in The Twenties, pp. 20-24.

James McMichael, "Hart Crane," SoR, 8 (April, 1972), 290-309.

Howard Moss, "Disorder as Myth: Hart Crane's The Bridge," Poetry, 62 (April, 1943), 32-45.

O'Connor, Sense and Sensibility in Modern Poetry, pp. 19-25.

Pearce, The Continuity of American Poetry, pp. 102-111.

Quinn, The Metamorphic Tradition, pp. 147-165.

Rosenthal, The Modern Poets, pp. 169-176.

Richard H. Rupp, "Hart Crane: Vitality as Credo in 'Atlantis,'" MQ, 3 (April, 1962), 265-275.

Bernice Slote, "Structure of Hart Crane's The Bridge," The University of Kansas City Review, 24 (Spring, 1958), 225-238.
    Rpt. Miller, Shapiro, and Slote, Start With the Sun, pp. 137-155.

Bernice Slote, "Transmutation in Crane's Imagery in The Bridge," MLN, 73 (Jan., 1958), 15-23.
    Rpt. Miller, Shapiro, and Slote, Start With the Sun, pp. 155-165.

Alan Swallow, "Hart Crane," The University of Kansas City Review, 16 (Winter, 1949), 114, 116-118.
    Rpt. Swallow, An Editor's Essays of Two Decades, pp. 183-184, 189-192.
    Rpt. UDQ, 1 (Spring, 1967), 115-117.

Tate, On The Limits of Poetry, pp. 228-237. First published in Hound and Horn and Poetry.

Tate, Reactionary Essays on Poetry and Ideas, pp. 30-42.
    Rpt. Zabel, Literary Opinion in America, revised edition, pp. 230-236.

John Unterecker, "The Architecture of The Bridge," Wisconsin Studies in Contemporary Literature, 3 (Spring-Summer, 1962), 5-20.

Albert Van Nostrand, "'The Bridge' And Hart Crane's 'Span of Consciousness,'" in Aspects of American Poetry, pp. 173-202.

Thomas A. Vogler, "A New View of Hart Crane's Bridge," SR, 73 (Summer, 1965), 381-408.

Waggoner, The Heel of Elohim, pp. 157-158, 171-190.

Wells, New Poets from Old, pp. 116-128.

Yvor Winters, "The Progress of Hart Crane," Poetry, 36 (June, 1930), 153-165.

Yvor Winters, "The Significance of The Bridge, by Hart Crane," in In Defense of Reason, pp. 577-603.

_____. "The Bridge of Estador"
Maurice Kramer, "Hart Crane's 'Reflexes,'" TCL, 13 (Oct., 1967), 134.

_____. "The Broken Tower"
Marius Bewley, "Hart Crane's Last Poem," Accent, 19 (Spring, 1959), 75-85.

Henry Braun, "Hart Crane's 'The Broken Tower,'" Boston University Studies in English, 5 (Autumn, 1961), 167-177.

Friar and Brinnin, Modern Poetry, p. 449.

Muriel Rukeyser, The Life of Poetry (New York: A. A. Wyn, 1949), pp. 32-33.

Eric J. Sundquist, "Bringing Home the Word: Magic, Lies, and Silence in Hart Crane," _ELH_, 44 (Summer, 1977), 395-396.

M. D. Uroff, "The Imagery of Violence in Hart Crane's Poetry," _AL_, 43 (May, 1971), 211-213.

_____. "C 33"
Maurice Kramer, "Hart Crane's 'Reflexes,'" _TCL_, 13 (Oct., 1967), 134.

_____. "Cape Hatteras"
Brooks, Lewis, and Warren, _American Literature_, pp. 2216-2217.

Karl Shapiro, "The Meaning of the Discarded Poem," in _Poets at Work_, pp. 111-118.

Eric J. Sundquist, "Bringing Home the Word: Magic, Lies, and Silence in Hart Crane," _ELH_, 44 (Summer, 1977), 389-390.

Vogler, _Preludes to Vision_, pp. 170-176.

_____. "Chaplinesque"
Deutsch, _Poetry in Our Time_, pp. 317-318.

Gray, _American Poetry_, pp. 220-221.

Robert L. Perry, "Critical Problems in Hart Crane's 'Chaplinesque,'" _CP_, 8 (Fall, 1975), 23-27.

Frank Porter, "'Chaplinesque' An Explication," _EJ_, 57 (Feb., 1968), 191-192, 195.

Peter J. Sheehan, "Hart Crane and the Contemporary Search," _EJ_, 60 (Dec., 1971), 1211-1212.

_____. "Cutty Sark"
Eric J. Sundquist, "Bringing Home the Word: Magic, Lies, and Silence in Hart Crane," _ELH_, 44 (Summer, 1977), 387-388.

Vogler, _Preludes to Vision_, pp. 166-170.

_____. "The Dance"
Clark, _Lyric Resonance_, pp. 176-184.

James McMichael, "Hart Crane," _SoR_, 8 (April, 1972), 300-309.

Eric J. Sundquist, "Bringing Home the Word: Magic, Lies, and Silence in Hart Crane, _ELH_, 44 (Summer, 1977), 383-386.

Vogler, _Preludes to Vision_, pp. 162-165.

Winters, _Primitivism and Decadence_, pp. 30-32.
   Rpt. _In Defense of Reason_, pp. 44-45, 52, and _Criticism_, pp. 295-298.

_____. "Eternity"
M. D. Uroff, "The Imagery of Violence in Hart Crane's Poetry," _AL_, 43 (May, 1971), 209-210.

_____. "The Fernery"
Robert L. Perry, "Critical Problems in Hart Crane's 'The Fernery,'" _Expl_, 35 (Fall, 1976), 3-5.

_____. "For the Marriage of Faustus and Helen"
Bruce Bassoff, "Rhetorical Pressures in 'For the Marriage of Faustus and Helen,'" _CP_, 5 (Fall, 1972), 40-48.

Bruce Bassoff, Expl, 31 (March, 1973), 53.

Clark, Lyric Resonance, pp. 159-173.

Roger Dickinson-Brown, Expl, 31 (April, 1973), 66.

Joseph Frank, "Hart Crane: American Poet," SR, 57 (Winter, 1949), 155-156.

Gray, American Poetry, pp. 221-224.

Will C. Jumper, Expl, 17 (Oct., 1958), 8.
   Rpt. The Explicator Cyclopedia, I, pp. 23-24.

Maurice Kramer, "Hart Crane's 'Reflexes,'" TCL, 13 (Oct., 1967), 134-135.

Robert K. Martin, "Hart Crane's 'For the Marriage of Faustus and Helen':
Myth and Alchemy," CP, 9 (Spring, 1976), 59-62.

Patricia McClintock, "A Reading of Hart Crane's 'For the Marriage of
Faustus and Helen,'" MSE, 1 (Fall, 1967), 39-43.

Savage, The Personal Principle, pp. 115-118.

Philip R. Yannella, "'Inventive Dust': The Metamorphoses of 'For the
Marriage of Faustus and Helen,'" ConL, 15 (Winter, 1974), 102-122.

_____. "The Harbor Dawn"
Edward Brunner, "'Your Hands Within My Hands are Deeds': Poems of Love
in The Bridge," IowaR, 4 (Winter, 1973), 112-118.

Friar and Brinnin, Modern Poetry, pp. 452-453.

Perrine and Reid, 100 American Poems, pp. 179-180.

Eric J. Sundquist, "Bringing Home the Word: Magic, Lies, and Silence in
Hart Crane," ELH, 44 (Summer, 1977), 382-383.

Vogler, Preludes to Vision, pp. 153-156.

_____. "The Hurricane"
M. D. Uroff, "The Imagery of Violence in Hart Crane's Poetry," AL, 43
(May, 1971), 210-211.

_____. "Indiana"
Vogler, Preludes to Vision, pp. 165-166.

_____. "Key West"
Kingsley Widmer, Expl, 18 (Dec., 1959), 17.
   Rpt. The Explicator Cyclopedia, I, pp. 24-25.

_____. "Lachrymae Christi"
Blackmur, The Double Agent, pp. 135-137.
   Rpt. Language as Gesture, pp. 312-314.

Barbara Herman, "The Language of Hart Crane," SR, 58 (Winter, 1950),
62-65.

Martin Staples Shockley, "Hart Crane's 'Lachrymae Christi,'" The University of Kansas City Review, 16 (Autumn, 1949), 31-36.
   Rpt. Engle and Carrier, Reading Modern Poetry, pp. 321-328.

M. D. Uroff, "The Imagery of Violence in Hart Crane's Poetry," AL, 43
(May, 1971), 206-207.

Philip R. Yannella, "Toward Apotheosis: Hart Crane's Visionary Lyrics,"
Criticism, 10 (Fall, 1968), 317-320.

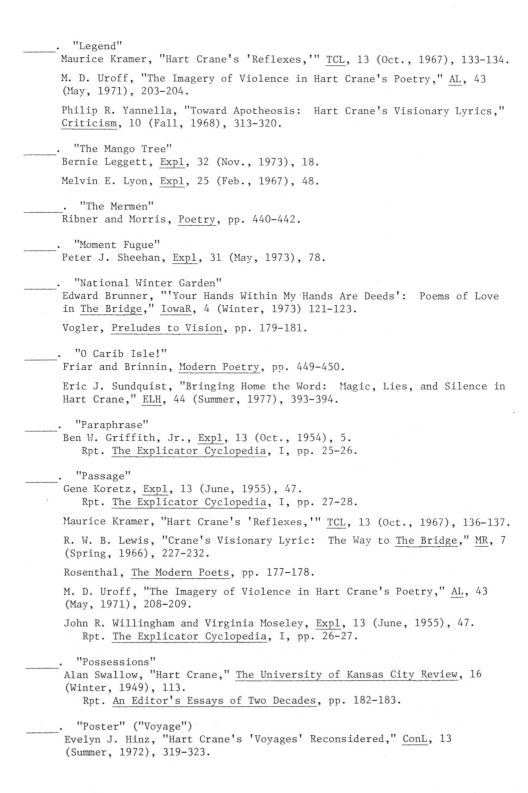

_____. "Legend"
Maurice Kramer, "Hart Crane's 'Reflexes,'" TCL, 13 (Oct., 1967), 133-134.

M. D. Uroff, "The Imagery of Violence in Hart Crane's Poetry," AL, 43 (May, 1971), 203-204.

Philip R. Yannella, "Toward Apotheosis: Hart Crane's Visionary Lyrics," Criticism, 10 (Fall, 1968), 313-320.

_____. "The Mango Tree"
Bernie Leggett, Expl, 32 (Nov., 1973), 18.

Melvin E. Lyon, Expl, 25 (Feb., 1967), 48.

_____. "The Mermen"
Ribner and Morris, Poetry, pp. 440-442.

_____. "Moment Fugue"
Peter J. Sheehan, Expl, 31 (May, 1973), 78.

_____. "National Winter Garden"
Edward Brunner, "'Your Hands Within My Hands Are Deeds': Poems of Love in The Bridge," IowaR, 4 (Winter, 1973) 121-123.

Vogler, Preludes to Vision, pp. 179-181.

_____. "O Carib Isle!"
Friar and Brinnin, Modern Poetry, pp. 449-450.

Eric J. Sundquist, "Bringing Home the Word: Magic, Lies, and Silence in Hart Crane," ELH, 44 (Summer, 1977), 393-394.

_____. "Paraphrase"
Ben W. Griffith, Jr., Expl, 13 (Oct., 1954), 5.
    Rpt. The Explicator Cyclopedia, I, pp. 25-26.

_____. "Passage"
Gene Koretz, Expl, 13 (June, 1955), 47.
    Rpt. The Explicator Cyclopedia, I, pp. 27-28.

Maurice Kramer, "Hart Crane's 'Reflexes,'" TCL, 13 (Oct., 1967), 136-137.

R. W. B. Lewis, "Crane's Visionary Lyric: The Way to The Bridge," MR, 7 (Spring, 1966), 227-232.

Rosenthal, The Modern Poets, pp. 177-178.

M. D. Uroff, "The Imagery of Violence in Hart Crane's Poetry," AL, 43 (May, 1971), 208-209.

John R. Willingham and Virginia Moseley, Expl, 13 (June, 1955), 47.
    Rpt. The Explicator Cyclopedia, I, pp. 26-27.

_____. "Possessions"
Alan Swallow, "Hart Crane," The University of Kansas City Review, 16 (Winter, 1949), 113.
    Rpt. An Editor's Essays of Two Decades, pp. 182-183.

_____. "Poster" ("Voyage")
Evelyn J. Hinz, "Hart Crane's 'Voyages' Reconsidered," ConL, 13 (Summer, 1972), 319-323.

_____. "Praise for an Urn"
Alan Swallow, "Hart Crane," The University of Kansas City Review, 16 (Winter, 1949), 115.
    Rpt. An Editor's Essays of Two Decades, pp. 185-186.

Van Doren, Introduction to Poetry, pp. 103-107.

_____. "Proem: To Brooklyn Bridge"
Edward Brunner, "'Your Hands Within My Hands Are Deeds': Poems of Love in The Bridge," IowaR, 4 (Winter, 1973), 108-111.

Friar and Brinnin, Modern Poetry, pp. 427-428, 450-451.

Eric J. Sundquist, "Bringing Home the Word: Magic, Lies, and Silence in Hart Crane," ELH, 44 (Summer, 1977), 379-381.

_____. "Quaker Hill"
Eric J. Sundquist, "Bringing Home the Word: Magic, Lies, and Silence in Hart Crane," ELH, 44 (Summer, 1977), 376.

Vogler, Preludes to Vision, pp. 182-185.

_____. "Recitative"
Maurice Kramer, "Hart Crane's 'Reflexes,'" TCL, 13 (Oct., 1967), 134-135.

M. D. Uroff, "Hart Crane's 'Recitative,'" CP, 3 (Spring, 1970), 22-27.

M. D. Uroff, "The Imagery of Violence in Hart Crane's Poetry," AL, 43 (May, 1971), 205.

Philip R. Yannella, "Toward Apotheosis: Hart Crane's Visionary Lyrics," Criticism, 10 (Fall, 1968), 322-323.

_____. "Repose of Rivers"
Clark, Lyric Resonance, pp. 148-151.

R. W. B. Lewis, "Crane's Visionary Lyric: The Way to The Bridge," MR, (Spring, 1966), 249-253.

Rosenheim, What Happens in Literature, pp. 140-160.

Sanders, The Discovery of Poetry, pp. 11-12.

_____. "The Return"
Thomas E. Sanders, Expl, 10 (Dec., 1951), 20.
    Rpt. The Explicator Cyclopedia, I, pp. 28-29.

M. D. Uroff, "The Imagery of Violence in Hart Crane's Poetry," AL, 43 (May, 1971), 211.

_____. "The River"
Perrine and Reid, 100 American Poems, pp. 177-178.

Vogler, Preludes to Vision, pp. 160-162.

_____. "The Sad Indian"
John R. Scarlett, Expl, 29 (April, 1971), 69.

_____. "Southern Cross"
Edward Brunner, "'Your Hands Within My Hands Are Deeds': Poems of Love in The Bridge," IowaR, 4 (Winter, 1973), 123-125.

Vogler, Preludes to Vision, pp. 177-179.

_____. "Three Songs"
Eric J. Sundquist, "Bringing Home the Word: Magic, Lies, and Silence in Hart Crane," ELH, 44 (Summer, 1977), 390-391.

J. R. Willingham, "'Three Songs' of Hart Crane's The Bridge: A Reconsideration," AL, 27 (March, 1955), 64-68.

_____. "The Tunnel"
Robert K. Martin, Expl, 34 (Oct., 1975), 16.

Vogler, Preludes to Vision, pp. 185-191.

_____. "Van Winkle"
Eric J. Sundquist, "Bringing Home the Word: Magic, Lies, and Silence in Hart Crane," ELH, 44 (Summer, 1977), 382-383.

Vogler, Preludes to Vision, pp. 156-160.

_____. "Virginia"
Edward Brunner, "'Your Hands Within My Hands Are Deeds': Poems of Love in The Bridge," IowaR, 4 (Winter, 1973), 118-121.

Vogler, Preludes to Vision, pp. 181-182.

_____. "Voyages"
Friar and Brinnin, Modern Poetry, pp. 455-456.

Maurice Kramer, "Six Voyages of a Derelict Seer," SR, 73 (Summer, 1965), 410-423.

H. C. MOrris, "Crane's 'Voyages' as a Single Poem," Accent, 14 (Autumn, 1954), 291-299.

Rosenthal, The Modern Poets, pp. 179-182.

Philip R. Yannella, "Toward Apotheosis: Hart Crane's Visionary Lyrics," Criticism, 10 (Fall, 1968), 324-333.

_____. "Voyages," I
Evelyn J. Hinz, "Hart Crane's 'Voyages' Reconsidered," ConL, 13 (Summer, 1972), 323-325, 327-329.

_____. "Voyages," II
Brooks, Lewis, and Warren, American Literature, p. 2211.

Robert A. Day, "Image and Idea in 'Voyages II,'" Criticism, 7 (Summer, 1965), 224-234.

Clark, Lyric Resonance, pp. 138-140.

Deutsch, Poetry in Our Time, pp. 319-321.

Judith S. Friedman and Ruth Perlmutter, Expl, 19 (Oct., 1960), 4.
    Rpt. The Explicator Cyclopedia, I, pp. 31-32.

John T. Irwin, "Naming Names: Hart Crane's 'Logic of Metaphor,'" SoR, 11 (April, 1975), 286-289.

O'Connor, Sense and Sensibility in Modern Poetry, pp. 73-75.

A. Poulin, Jr., Expl, 28 (Oct., 1969), 15.

Sidney Richman, "Hart Crane's 'Voyages II': An Experiment in Redemption," Wisconsin Studies in Contemporary Literature, 3 (Spring-Summer, 1962), 65-78.

Max F. Schulz, Expl, 14 (April, 1956), 46.
    Rpt. The Explicator Cyclopedia, I, pp. 32-33.

Richard Strier, "The Poetics of Surrender: An Exposition and Critique of New Critical Poetics," CritI, 2 (Autumn, 1975), 187-188.

Unger and O'Connor, Poems for Study, pp. 637-641.

_____. "Voyages," V
Evelyn J. Hinz, "Hart Crane's 'Voyages' Reconsidered," ConL, 13 (Summer, 1972), 328.

_____. "Voyages," VI
Brooks, Lewis, and Warren, American Literature, p. 2212.

Evelyn J. Hinz, "Hart Crane's 'Voyages' Reconsidered," ConL, 13 (Summer, 1972), 329-333.

M. D. Uroff, "Hart Crane's 'Voyages VI,' Stanza 6," ELN, 8 (Sept., 1970), 46-48.

Charles C. Walcutt, Expl, 4 (May, 1946), 53.
    Rpt. The Explicator Cyclopedia, I, pp. 33-34.

James Zigerell, Expl, 13 (Nov., 1954), 7.
    Rpt. The Explicator Cyclopedia, pp. 29-30.

_____. "The Wine Menagerie"
Blackmur, The Double Agent, pp. 130-134.
    Rpt. Language as Gesture, pp. 309-312.
    Rpt. The Critic's Notebook, pp. 106-110.

Maurice Kramer, "Hart Crane's 'Reflexes,'" TCL, 13 (Oct., 1967), 136.

R. W. B. Lewis, "Crane's Visionary Lyric: The Way to The Bridge," MR, 7 (Spring, 1966), 233-239.

Philip R. Yanella, "Toward Apotheosis: Hart Crane's Visionary Lyrics," Criticism, 10 (Fall, 1968), 320-322.

CRANE, Stephen. "Charity, Thou Art a Lie"
George Monteiro, "Stephen Crane and the Antinomies of Christian Charity," CentR, 16 (Winter, 1972), 95-97.

_____. "I Was in the Darkness"
Clarence O. Johnson, Expl, 34 (Sept., 1975), 6.

_____. "A Man Adrift on a Slim Spar"
George Monteiro, Expl, 32 (Oct., 1973), 14.

_____. "A Man Said to the Universe"
Charles Wegelin, Expl, 20 (Sept., 1961), 9.
    Rpt. The Explicator Cyclopedia, I, pp. 34-35.

_____. "War Is Kind"
Evelyn E. Miller, "A Trilogy of Irony," EJ, 59 (Jan., 1970), 60-61.

CRAPSEY. "Niagara"
Sanders, The Discovery of Poetry, pp. 75-76.

_____. "November Night"
Sanders, The Discovery of Poetry, pp. 79-80.

_____. "Song: I Make My Shroud, but No One Knows--"
Sanders, <u>The Discovery of Poetry</u>, pp. 328-333.

_____. "Suzanna and the Elders"
Sanders, <u>The Discovery of Poetry</u>, pp. 76-77.

_____. "Triad"
Daniels, <u>The Art of Reading Poetry</u>, p. 53.

Sanders, <u>The Discovery of Poetry</u>, p. 79.

CRASHAW. "An Apology for the Precedent Hymn"
A. F. Allison, "Crashaw and St. Francis de Sales," <u>RES</u>, 24 (Oct., 1948),
296-300.

_____. "Epiphany Hymn"
A. R. Cirillo, "Crashaw's 'Epiphany Hymn': The Dawn of Christian Time,"
<u>SP</u>, 67 (Jan., 1970), 67-88.

_____. "Epithalamium"
R. V. LeClercq, "Crashaw's <u>Epithalamium</u>: Pattern and Vision," <u>Literary</u>
<u>Monographs</u>, ed. Eric Rothstein and Joseph Anthony Wittreich, Jr., No. 6
(Madison, Wisconsin: Univ. of Wisconsin Press, 1975), 73-108.

_____. "The Flaming Heart"
A. F. Allison, "Crashaw and St. Francis de Sales," <u>RES</u>, 24 (Oct., 1948),
300-301.

_____. "The Glorious Epiphanie of Our Lord God"
Michael McCanles, "The Rhetoric of the Sublime in Crashaw's Poetry," in
<u>The Rhetoric of Renaissance Poetry</u>, pp. 198-202.

_____. "The Holy Nativity"
Michael McCanles, "The Rhetoric of the Sublime in Crashaw's Poetry," in
<u>The Rhetoric of Renaissance Poetry</u>, pp. 195-196.

_____. "Hymn in the Nativity"
Kerby Neill, "Structure and Symbol in Crashaw's <u>Hymn in the Nativity</u>,"
<u>PMLA</u>, 63 (March, 1948), 101-113.

_____. "A Hymn to the Name and Honor of the Admirable Saint Teresa"
Anthony E. Farnham, "Saint Teresa and the Coy Mistress," <u>Boston Univer-</u>
<u>sity Studies in English</u>, 2 (Winter, 1956-1957), 231-239.

Unger and O'Connor, <u>Poems for Study</u>, pp. 171-175.

_____. "In Memory of the Vertuous and Learned Lady Madre de Teresa..."
Robert G. Collmer, "Crashaw's 'Death More Misticall and High,'" <u>JEGP</u>,
55 (July, 1956), 373-380.

_____. "In the Glorious Epiphany of Our Lord God"
Martin Turnell, "Richard Crashaw After Three Hundred Years," <u>Nineteenth</u>
<u>Century and After</u>, 146 (Aug., 1949), 110-113.

_____. "The Mother of Sorrows"
A. F. Allison, "Crashaw and St. Francis de Sales," <u>RES</u>, 24 (Oct., 1948),
301-302.

_____. "Music's Duel"
William G. Madsen, "A Reading of 'Musicks Duell,'" in Studies in Honor of
John Wilcox, pp. 39-50.

_____. "On Our Crucified Lord, Naked and Bloody"
Adams, Strains of Discord, pp. 133-134.

Robert M. Adams, "Taste and Bad Taste in Metaphysical Poetry: Richard
Crashaw and Dylan Thomas," HudR, 8 (Spring, 1955), 67.

_____. "On the Wounds of Our Crucified Lord"
Adams, Strains of Discord, pp. 134-135.

Frank J. Fabry, "Crashaw's 'On the Wounds of Our Crucified Lord,'" CP, 10
(Spring, 1977), 51-58.

_____. "Prayer"
Martin Turnell, "Richard Crashaw After Three Hundred Years," Nineteenth
Century and After, 146 (Aug., 1949), 104-106.

_____. "Suppose He Had Been Tabled at Thy Teates"
Adams, Strains of Discord, p. 136.

Robert M. Adams, "Taste and Bad Taste in Metaphysical Poetry: Richard
Crashaw and Dylan Thomas," HudR, 8 (Spring, 1955), 68-69.

Russell M. Goldfarb, Expl, 19 (March, 1961), 35.
   Rpt. The Explicator Cyclopedia, II, 95.

_____. "The Tear"
Martin Turnell, "Richard Crashaw After Three Hundred Years," Nineteenth
Century and After, 146 (Aug., 1949), 106-107.

_____. "To the Name Above Every Name, the Name of Jesus"
Martz, The Poetry of Meditation, pp. 62-64, 338-352.

_____. "To the Noblest and Best of Ladies, the Countess of Denbigh" (1652
   and 1653 versions)
Richard Strier, "Crashaw's Other Voice," SEL, 9 (Winter, 1969), 135-151.

George W. Williams, Expl, 6 (May, 1948), 48.
   Rpt. The Explicator Cyclopedia, II, pp. 94-95.

_____. "Upon the Bleeding Crucifix"
George W. Williams, "Textual Revision in Crashaw's 'Upon the Bleeding
Crucifix,'" PBSA (Univ. of Virginia), 1 (1948-1949), 191-193.

_____. "The Weeper"
Adams, Strains of Discord, pp. 131-133, 136-137.

Robert M. Adams, "Taste and Bad Taste in Metaphysical Poetry: Richard
Crashaw and Dylan Thomas," HudR, 8 (Spring, 1955), 66-67, 69-71.

Leland Chambers, "In Defense of 'The Weeper,'" PLL, (Spring, 1967),
111-121.

Paul M. Levitt, Expl, 32 (March, 1974), 56.

Stephen Manning, "The Meaning of 'The Weeper,'" ELH, 22 (March, 1955),
34-47.

Paul A. Parrish, "Crashaw's Two Weepers," CP, 10 (Fall, 1977), 47-59.

John Peter, "Crashaw and 'The Weeper,'" <u>Scrutiny</u>, 19 (Oct., 1953), 259-273.

Peter Schwenger, "Crashaw's Perspectivist Metaphor," <u>CL</u>, 28 (Winter, 1976), 65-74.

Winters, <u>The Anatomy of Nonsense</u>, pp. 209-210.
    Also <u>In Defense of Reason</u>, pp. 538-540.

CRAWFORD. "The Canoe"
    Frank Bessai, "The Ambivalence of Love in the Poetry of Isabella Valancy Crawford," <u>QQ</u>, 77 (Autumn, 1970), 411-412.

_____. "The Dark Stag"
    Frank Bessai, "The Ambivalence of Love in the Poetry of Isabella Valancy Crawford," <u>QQ</u>, 77 (Autumn, 1970), 408-409.

_____. "The Lily Bed"
    Frank Bessai, "The Ambivalence of Love in the Poetry of Isabella Valancy Crawford," <u>QQ</u>, 77 (Autumn, 1970), 409-410.

CREELEY, Robert. "The Dishonest Mailmen"
    Charles Altieri, "The Unsure Egoist: Robert Creeley and the Theme of Nothingness," <u>ConL</u>, 13 (Spring, 1972), 169-170.

_____. "The Flower"
    Charles Altieri, "The Unsure Egoist: Robert Creeley and the Theme of Nothingness," <u>ConL</u>, 13 (Spring, 1972), 167-168.

Jerry R. Bacon, "Closure in Robert Creeley's Poetry," <u>MPS</u>, 8 (Winter, 1977), 234-235.

_____. "For W. C. W."
    Charles Altieri, "The Unsure Egoist: Robert Creeley and the Theme of Nothingness," <u>ConL</u>, 13 (Spring, 1972), 174-175.

_____. "I Know a Man"
    Charles Altieri, "The Unsure Egoist: Robert Creeley and the Theme of Nothingness," <u>ConL</u>, 13 (Spring, 1972), 163-164.

_____. "The Innocence"
    Allen Barry Cameron, "'Love Comes Quietly': The Poetry of Robert Creeley," <u>ChiR</u>, 19, No. 2 (1967), 24.

_____. "The Kind of Act Of"
    Cid Corman, "A Requisite Commitment," <u>Poetry</u>, 83 (March, 1954), 340-342.

_____. "The Language"
    Charles Altieri, "The Unsure Egoist: Robert Creeley and the Theme of Nothingness," <u>ConL</u>, 13 (Spring, 1972), 176-177.

_____. "La Noche"
    Allen Barry Cameron, "'Love Comes Quietly': The Poetry of Robert Creeley," <u>ChiR</u>, 19, No. 2 (1967), 100.

_____. "Le Fou"
    Jerry R. Bacon, "Closure in Robert Creeley's Poetry," <u>MPS</u>, 8 (Winter, 1977), 232-233.

_____. "Love Comes Quietly"
Allen Barry Cameron, "'Love Comes Quietly': The Poetry of Robert Creeley," ChiR, 19, No. 2 (1967), 98-99.

_____. "The Rhyme"
Charles Altieri, "The Unsure Egoist: Robert Creeley and the Theme of Nothingness," ConL, 13 (Spring, 1972), 164-165.

_____. "They"
Charles Altieri, "The Unsure Egoist: Robert Creeley and the Theme of Nothingness," ConL, 13 (Spring, 1972), 184-185.

_____. "A Wicker Basket"
Carroll, The Poem In Its Skin, pp. 31-38.

_____. "Zero"
Charles Altieri, "The Unsure Egoist: Robert Creeley and the Theme of Nothingness," ConL, 13 (Spring, 1972), 182-183.

CULLEN, Countee. "Incident"
Perrine and Reid, 100 American Poems, p. 191.

_____. "The Shroud of Color"
Ronald Primeau, "Countee Cullen and Keats's 'Vale of Soul-Making,'" PLL, 12 (Winter, 1976), 78-80.

CUMMINGS. "262"
Nat Henry, Expl, 21 (May, 1963), 72.

_____. "275"
Nat Henry, Expl, 20 (April, 1962), 63.
    Rpt. The Explicator Cyclopedia, I, p. 48.

_____. "303 (nor woman)"
Nat Henry, Expl, 22 (Sept., 1963), 2.

_____. "305"
Nat Henry, Expl, 20 (Feb., 1962), 49.
    Rpt. The Explicator Cyclopedia, I, p. 49.

W. Yeaton Wagener, Expl, 21 (Oct., 1962), 18.

_____. "All in Green Went My Love Riding"
William V. Davis, "Cummings' 'All in Green Went My Love Riding,'" CP, 3 (Fall, 1970), 65-67.

Will C. Jumper, Expl, 26 (Sept., 1967), 6.

Cora Robey, Expl, 27 (Sept., 1968), 2.

Barry Sanders, Expl, 25 (Nov., 1966), 23.

_____. "among these red pieces of"
John Arthos, "The Poetry of E. E. Cummings," AL, 14 (Jan., 1943), 386-387.
John Peale Bishop, "The Poems and Prose of E. E. Cummings," SoR, 4 (Summer, 1938), 176-177.

Eastman, The Literary Mind, pp. 59-62.

Riding and Graves, A Survey of Modernist Poetry, pp. 84-89.

_____. "anyone and noone"
Clark, Lyric Resonance, pp. 187-194.

_____. "anyone lived in a pretty how town"
Herbert C. Barrows, Jr., and William R. Steinhoff, Expl, 9 (Oct., 1950),
1. Abridged in The Case for Poetry, p. 95.
    Rpt. The Explicator Cyclopedia, I, pp. 35-36.

Arthur Carr, Expl, 11 (Nov., 1952), 6. Abridged in The Case for Poetry,
pp. 95-96.
    Rpt. The Explicator Cyclopedia, I, pp. 36-37.

James P. Dougherty, "Language as a Reality in E. E. Cummings," BuR, 16
(May, 1968), 119-122.

George Haines, IV, " : : 2 : 1--The World and E. E. Cummings," SR,
59 (Spring, 1951), 216-217.

Perrine and Reid, 100 American Poems, pp. 153-155.

Charles L. Squier, Expl, 25 (Dec., 1966), 37.

Walsh, Doors into Poetry, pp. 132-133.

Robert C. Walsh, Expl, 22 (May, 1964), 72.

Stallman and Watters, The Creative Reader, pp. 886-887.

_____. ("applaws)"
Joseph Axelrod, "Cummings and Phonetics," Poetry, 65 (Nov., 1944), 88-94.

Karl Shapiro, "Prosody as the Meaning," Poetry, 73 (March, 1949), 338-
340 et passim.

_____. "because you go away i give roses"
Riding and Graves, A Survey of Modernist Poetry, pp. 60-64.

_____. "Bells"
John W. Crowley, "Visual-aural Poetry: The Typography of E. E. Cummings,"
CP, 5 (Fall, 1972), 51-54.

_____. "! blac"
S. V. Baum, "E. E. Cummings: The Technique of Immediacy," SAQ, 53 (Jan.,
1954), 87-88.

_____. "brIght"
Robert M. McIlvaine, Expl, 30 (Sept., 1971), 6.

_____. "Buffalo Bill's/Defunct"
Adam Berkley, "Buffalo Bill's Defunct," CEA, 29 (March, 1967), 13-14.

Louis J. Budd, Expl, 11 (June, 1953), 55.
    Rpt. The Explicator Cyclopedia, I, pp. 37-38.

Earl J. Diaz, "Buffalo Bill's Defunct," CEA, 24 (March, 1967), 14.

Earl J. Dias, "e. e. cummings and Buffalo Bill," CEA, 29 (Dec., 1966),
6-7.

Norman Friedman and David Ray, "Pan and Buffalo Bill," CE, 23 (May, 1962),
672.

David Ray, "The Irony of E. E. Cummings," CE, 23 (Jan., 1962), 282, 287-
290.

Rosenthal, The Modern Poets, pp. 148-149.

John E. Unterecker, "Buffalo Bill Revisited," 29 (April, 1967), 1.

_____. "Chansons Innocentes I: in just-spring"
Brooks, A Shaping Joy, pp. 93-94.

Marvin Felheim, Expl, 14 (Nov., 1955), 11.
    Rpt. The Explicator Cyclopedia, I, pp. 38-39.

R. D. Mayo, English "A" Analyst, No. 2, pp. 1-4.
    Rpt. Engle and Carrier, Reading Modern Poetry, pp. 133-136.

Sanders, The Discovery of Poetry, pp. 243-246.

C. Steven Turner, Expl, 24 (Oct., 1965), 18.

_____. "darling! because my blood can sing"
Frankenberg, Invitation to Poetry, pp. 281-282.

_____. "death is more than certain"
Norman Friedman, "Diction, Voice, and Tone: The Poetic Language of E. E.
Cummings," PMLA, 62 (Dec., 1957), 1057-1058.

Riding and Graves, A Survey of Modernist Poetry, pp. 244-247.

_____. "floatfloafloflf"
Richard Crowder, Expl, 16 (April, 1958), 41.
    Rpt. The Explicator Cyclopedia, I, pp. 47-48.

_____. "goodbye Betty, don't remember me"
Rosenthal, The Modern Poets, pp. 150-151.

_____. "the greedy, the people"
Perrine and Reid, 100 American Poems, pp. 156-157.

_____. "I"
James E. White, Expl, 21 (Sept., 1962), 4.

_____. "if everything happens that can't be done"
Norman Friedman, "Diction, Voice, and Tone: The Poetic Language of
E. E. Cummings," PMLA, 62 (Dec., 1957), 1050-1051.

James M. Reid, John Ciardi, and Laurence Perrine, Poetry: A Closer Look
(New York: Harcourt, Brace & World, 1963), 45-49.
    Rpt. The Art of Total Relevance, pp. 70-73.

_____. "if up's the word; and a world grows greener'
Perrine and Reid, 100 American Poems, pp. 151-152.

_____. "(IM)C-A-T(MO)"
Vincent L. Heinrichs, Expl, 27 (April, 1969), 59.

_____. "Impression"
Adams, The Contexts of Poetry, pp. 4-8.

_____. "in heavenly realms of hellas"
Laurence Perrine, "Cumming's 'in heavenly realms of hellas,'" NConL, 1
(Jan., 1971), 9.

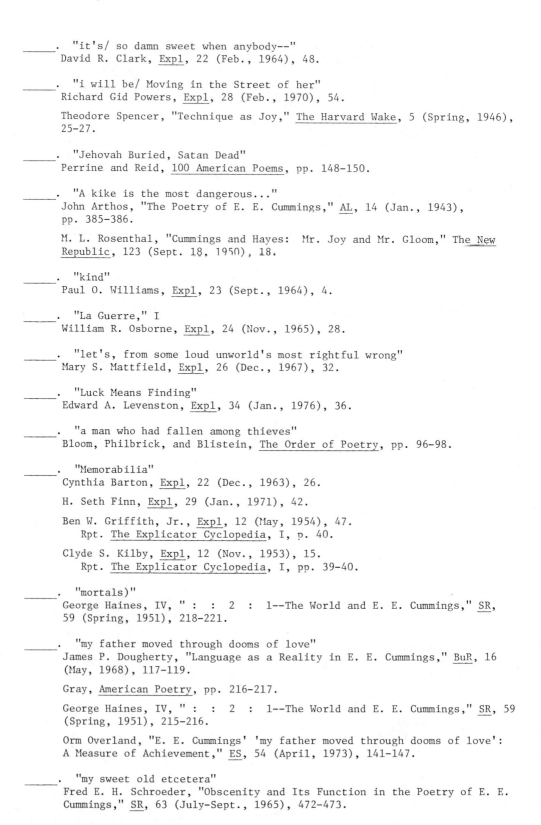

_____. "it's/ so damn sweet when anybody--"
David R. Clark, Expl, 22 (Feb., 1964), 48.

_____. "i will be/ Moving in the Street of her"
Richard Gid Powers, Expl, 28 (Feb., 1970), 54.

Theodore Spencer, "Technique as Joy," The Harvard Wake, 5 (Spring, 1946), 25-27.

_____. "Jehovah Buried, Satan Dead"
Perrine and Reid, 100 American Poems, pp. 148-150.

_____. "A kike is the most dangerous..."
John Arthos, "The Poetry of E. E. Cummings," AL, 14 (Jan., 1943), pp. 385-386.

M. L. Rosenthal, "Cummings and Hayes: Mr. Joy and Mr. Gloom," The New Republic, 123 (Sept. 18, 1950), 18.

_____. "kind"
Paul O. Williams, Expl, 23 (Sept., 1964), 4.

_____. "La Guerre," I
William R. Osborne, Expl, 24 (Nov., 1965), 28.

_____. "let's, from some loud unworld's most rightful wrong"
Mary S. Mattfield, Expl, 26 (Dec., 1967), 32.

_____. "Luck Means Finding"
Edward A. Levenston, Expl, 34 (Jan., 1976), 36.

_____. "a man who had fallen among thieves"
Bloom, Philbrick, and Blistein, The Order of Poetry, pp. 96-98.

_____. "Memorabilia"
Cynthia Barton, Expl, 22 (Dec., 1963), 26.

H. Seth Finn, Expl, 29 (Jan., 1971), 42.

Ben W. Griffith, Jr., Expl, 12 (May, 1954), 47.
    Rpt. The Explicator Cyclopedia, I, p. 40.

Clyde S. Kilby, Expl, 12 (Nov., 1953), 15.
    Rpt. The Explicator Cyclopedia, I, pp. 39-40.

_____. "mortals)"
George Haines, IV, " :   :   2   :   1--The World and E. E. Cummings," SR, 59 (Spring, 1951), 218-221.

_____. "my father moved through dooms of love"
James P. Dougherty, "Language as a Reality in E. E. Cummings," BuR, 16 (May, 1968), 117-119.

Gray, American Poetry, pp. 216-217.

George Haines, IV, " :   :   2   :   1--The World and E. E. Cummings," SR, 59 (Spring, 1951), 215-216.

Orm Overland, "E. E. Cummings' 'my father moved through dooms of love': A Measure of Achievement," ES, 54 (April, 1973), 141-147.

_____. "my sweet old etcetera"
Fred E. H. Schroeder, "Obscenity and Its Function in the Poetry of E. E. Cummings," SR, 63 (July-Sept., 1965), 472-473.

_____. "next to of course god america i"
William V. Davis, "Cummings' 'next to of course god america i,'" CP, 3
(Spring, 1970), 14-15.

Friedman and McLaughlin, Poetry: An Introduction to Its Form and Art,
pp. 96-97.

_____. "Nobody Loses All the Time"
William V. Davis, "Cummings' 'Nobody Loses All the Time,'" AN&Q, 9
(April, 1971), 119-120.

_____. "no man, if men are gods"
Frankenberg, Invitation to Poetry, p. 74.

_____. "nonsun blob a"
Richard Gunter, "Sentence and Poem," Style, 5 (Winter, 1971), 26-36.

_____. "The Noster Was a Ship of Swank"
Luther S. Luedtke, Expl, 26 (March, 1968), 59.

_____. "no time ago"
William V. Davis, "Cummings' 'no time ago,'" RS, 41 (Sept., 1973),
205-207.

Norman Friedman, "Diction, Voice and Tone: The Poetic Language of E. E.
Cummings," PMLA, 62 (Dec., 1957), 1058.

_____. "(one!)"
George C. Brauer, Jr., Expl, 16 (Dec., 1957), 14.
    Rpt. The Explicator Cyclopedia, I, p. 4.

Louis C. Rus, Expl, 15 (March, 1957), 40.
    Rpt. The Explicator Cyclopedia, I, pp. 40-41.

_____. "1x1"
Jack Steinberg, Expl, 8 (Dec., 1949), 17.
    Rpt. The Explicator Cyclopedia, I, p. 46-47.

_____. "one's not half two"
Norman Friedman, "Diction, Voice, and Tone: The Poetic Language of E. E.
Cummings," PMLA, 62 (Dec., 1957), 1041.

_____. "o pr"
Sheridan Baker, "Cummings and Catullus," MLN, 74 (March, 1959), 231-234.

_____. "the people who"
G. J. Weinberger, "E. E. Cummings' 'the people who,'" RS, 39 (Dec., 1971),
313-315.

_____. "pity this busy monster, manunkind"
John Britton, Expl, 18 (Oct., 1959), 5.
    Rpt. The Explicator Cyclopedia, I, pp. 41-42.

James W. Gargano, Expl, 20 (Nov., 1961), 21.
    Rpt. The Explicator Cyclopedia, I, p. 42.

Nat Henry, Expl, 27 (May, 1969), 68.

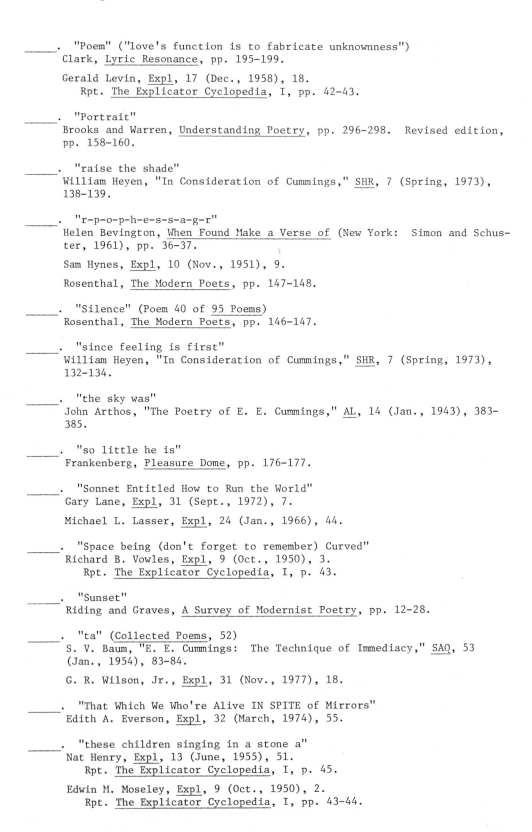

_____. "Poem" ("love's function is to fabricate unknownness")
Clark, Lyric Resonance, pp. 195-199.

Gerald Levin, Expl, 17 (Dec., 1958), 18.
    Rpt. The Explicator Cyclopedia, I, pp. 42-43.

_____. "Portrait"
Brooks and Warren, Understanding Poetry, pp. 296-298. Revised edition,
pp. 158-160.

_____. "raise the shade"
William Heyen, "In Consideration of Cummings," SHR, 7 (Spring, 1973),
138-139.

_____. "r-p-o-p-h-e-s-s-a-g-r"
Helen Bevington, When Found Make a Verse of (New York: Simon and Schuster, 1961), pp. 36-37.

Sam Hynes, Expl, 10 (Nov., 1951), 9.

Rosenthal, The Modern Poets, pp. 147-148.

_____. "Silence" (Poem 40 of 95 Poems)
Rosenthal, The Modern Poets, pp. 146-147.

_____. "since feeling is first"
William Heyen, "In Consideration of Cummings," SHR, 7 (Spring, 1973),
132-134.

_____. "the sky was"
John Arthos, "The Poetry of E. E. Cummings," AL, 14 (Jan., 1943), 383-
385.

_____. "so little he is"
Frankenberg, Pleasure Dome, pp. 176-177.

_____. "Sonnet Entitled How to Run the World"
Gary Lane, Expl, 31 (Sept., 1972), 7.

Michael L. Lasser, Expl, 24 (Jan., 1966), 44.

_____. "Space being (don't forget to remember) Curved"
Richard B. Vowles, Expl, 9 (Oct., 1950), 3.
    Rpt. The Explicator Cyclopedia, I, p. 43.

_____. "Sunset"
Riding and Graves, A Survey of Modernist Poetry, pp. 12-28.

_____. "ta" (Collected Poems, 52)
S. V. Baum, "E. E. Cummings: The Technique of Immediacy," SAQ, 53
(Jan., 1954), 83-84.

G. R. Wilson, Jr., Expl, 31 (Nov., 1977), 18.

_____. "That Which We Who're Alive IN SPITE of Mirrors"
Edith A. Everson, Expl, 32 (March, 1974), 55.

_____. "these children singing in a stone a"
Nat Henry, Expl, 13 (June, 1955), 51.
    Rpt. The Explicator Cyclopedia, I, p. 45.

Edwin M. Moseley, Expl, 9 (Oct., 1950), 2.
    Rpt. The Explicator Cyclopedia, I, pp. 43-44.

_____ . "a thrown a"
S. V. Baum, "E. E. Cummings: The Technique of Immediacy," SAQ, 53 (Jan., 1954), 85-86.

_____ . "up into the silence of the green"
John Arthos, "The Poetry of E. E. Cummings," AL, 14 (Jan., 1943), 385-386.

_____ . "the way to hump a cow is not"
Fred E. H. Schroeder, "Obscenity and Its Function in the Poetry of E. E. Cummings," SR, 63 (July-Sept., 1965), 473.

_____ . "what a proud dreamhorse pulling (smooth-loomingly) through"
Frankenberg, Invitation to Poetry, pp. 257-260.

_____ . "what if a much of a which of a wind"
Laurel Maureen O'Neal, Expl, 32 (Sept., 1973), 6.

Stephen E. Whicher, Expl, 12 (Nov., 1953), 14.
    Rpt. The Explicator Cyclopedia, I, pp. 45-46.

_____ . "When Faces Called Flowers Float Out of the Ground"
Alan M. Nadel, Expl, 32 (Feb., 1974), 47.

_____ . "When God Lets My Body Be"
Doris Dundas, Expl, 29 (May, 1971), 79.

_____ . "when you are silent, shining host by guest"
G. J. Weinberger, "E. E. Cummings's Benevolent God: A Reading of 'when you are silent, shining host by guest,'" PLL, 16 (Winter, 1974), 70-75.

_____ . ")when what hugs stopping earth than silent is"
G. J. Weinberger, "Cummings' ')when what hugs stopping earth than silent is,'" RS, 41 (June, 1973), 136-139.

_____ . "who are these (wraith a clinging with a wraith)"
Norman Friedman, "Diction, Voice, and Tone: The Poetic Language of E. E. Cummings," PMLA, 62 (Dec., 1957), 1047.

_____ . "Yes Is a Pleasant Country"
Gary Lane, Expl, 31 (Oct., 1972), 11.

CUNNINGHAM. "The Chase"
John Williams, "J. V. Cunningham: The Major and the Minor," ArQ, 6 (Summer, 1950), 140-141.

_____ . "Doctor Drink Epigram #1"
Robert Pinsky, The Situation of Poetry: Contemporary Poetry and Its Traditions (Princeton, New Jersey: Princeton Univ. Press, 1976), pp. 136-139.

_____ . "Meditation on Statistical Method"
Yvor Winters, "The Poetry of J. V. Cunningham," TCL, 6 (Jan., 1961), 163-164.

_____ . "Passion"
John Williams, "J. V. Cunningham: The Major and the Minor," ArQ, 6 (Summer, 1950), 142-144.

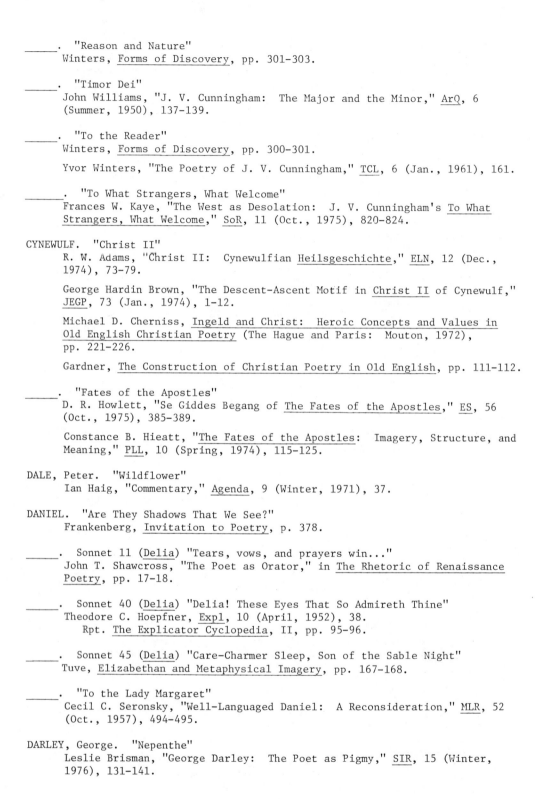

_____. "Reason and Nature"
Winters, <u>Forms of Discovery</u>, pp. 301-303.

_____. "Timor Dei"
John Williams, "J. V. Cunningham: The Major and the Minor," <u>ArQ</u>, 6 (Summer, 1950), 137-139.

_____. "To the Reader"
Winters, <u>Forms of Discovery</u>, pp. 300-301.

Yvor Winters, "The Poetry of J. V. Cunningham," <u>TCL</u>, 6 (Jan., 1961), 161.

_____. "To What Strangers, What Welcome"
Frances W. Kaye, "The West as Desolation: J. V. Cunningham's <u>To What Strangers, What Welcome</u>," <u>SoR</u>, 11 (Oct., 1975), 820-824.

CYNEWULF. "Christ II"
R. W. Adams, "Christ II: Cynewulfian <u>Heilsgeschichte</u>," <u>ELN</u>, 12 (Dec., 1974), 73-79.

George Hardin Brown, "The Descent-Ascent Motif in <u>Christ II</u> of Cynewulf," <u>JEGP</u>, 73 (Jan., 1974), 1-12.

Michael D. Cherniss, <u>Ingeld and Christ: Heroic Concepts and Values in Old English Christian Poetry</u> (The Hague and Paris: Mouton, 1972), pp. 221-226.

Gardner, <u>The Construction of Christian Poetry in Old English</u>, pp. 111-112.

_____. "Fates of the Apostles"
D. R. Howlett, "Se Giddes Begang of <u>The Fates of the Apostles</u>," <u>ES</u>, 56 (Oct., 1975), 385-389.

Constance B. Hieatt, "<u>The Fates of the Apostles</u>: Imagery, Structure, and Meaning," <u>PLL</u>, 10 (Spring, 1974), 115-125.

DALE, Peter. "Wildflower"
Ian Haig, "Commentary," <u>Agenda</u>, 9 (Winter, 1971), 37.

DANIEL. "Are They Shadows That We See?"
Frankenberg, <u>Invitation to Poetry</u>, p. 378.

_____. Sonnet 11 (<u>Delia</u>) "Tears, vows, and prayers win..."
John T. Shawcross, "The Poet as Orator," in <u>The Rhetoric of Renaissance Poetry</u>, pp. 17-18.

_____. Sonnet 40 (<u>Delia</u>) "Delia! These Eyes That So Admireth Thine"
Theodore C. Hoepfner, <u>Expl</u>, 10 (April, 1952), 38.
    Rpt. <u>The Explicator Cyclopedia</u>, II, pp. 95-96.

_____. Sonnet 45 (<u>Delia</u>) "Care-Charmer Sleep, Son of the Sable Night"
Tuve, <u>Elizabethan and Metaphysical Imagery</u>, pp. 167-168.

_____. "To the Lady Margaret"
Cecil C. Seronsky, "Well-Languaged Daniel: A Reconsideration," <u>MLR</u>, 52 (Oct., 1957), 494-495.

DARLEY, George. "Nepenthe"
Leslie Brisman, "George Darley: The Poet as Pigmy," <u>SIR</u>, 15 (Winter, 1976), 131-141.

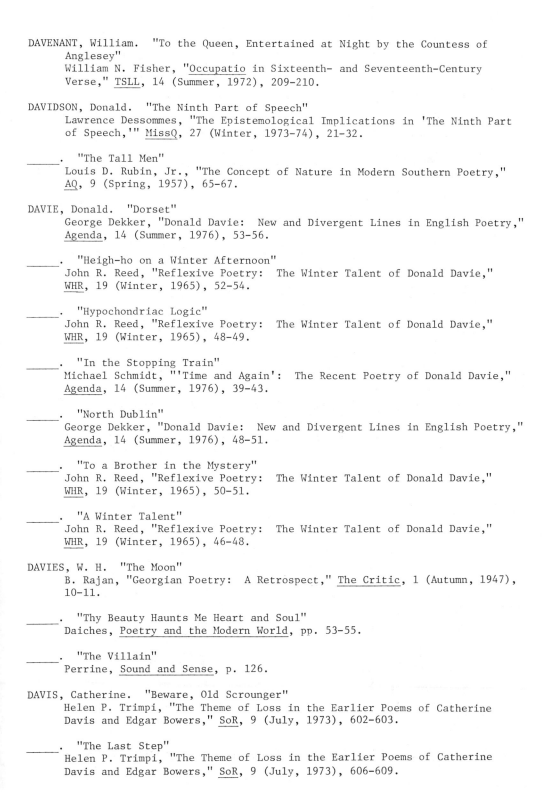

DAVENANT, William. "To the Queen, Entertained at Night by the Countess of
     Anglesey"
     William N. Fisher, "Occupatio in Sixteenth- and Seventeenth-Century
     Verse," TSLL, 14 (Summer, 1972), 209-210.

DAVIDSON, Donald. "The Ninth Part of Speech"
     Lawrence Dessommes, "The Epistemological Implications in 'The Ninth Part
     of Speech,'" MissQ, 27 (Winter, 1973-74), 21-32.

_____. "The Tall Men"
     Louis D. Rubin, Jr., "The Concept of Nature in Modern Southern Poetry,"
     AQ, 9 (Spring, 1957), 65-67.

DAVIE, Donald. "Dorset"
     George Dekker, "Donald Davie: New and Divergent Lines in English Poetry,"
     Agenda, 14 (Summer, 1976), 53-56.

_____. "Heigh-ho on a Winter Afternoon"
     John R. Reed, "Reflexive Poetry: The Winter Talent of Donald Davie,"
     WHR, 19 (Winter, 1965), 52-54.

_____. "Hypochondriac Logic"
     John R. Reed, "Reflexive Poetry: The Winter Talent of Donald Davie,"
     WHR, 19 (Winter, 1965), 48-49.

_____. "In the Stopping Train"
     Michael Schmidt, "'Time and Again': The Recent Poetry of Donald Davie,"
     Agenda, 14 (Summer, 1976), 39-43.

_____. "North Dublin"
     George Dekker, "Donald Davie: New and Divergent Lines in English Poetry,"
     Agenda, 14 (Summer, 1976), 48-51.

_____. "To a Brother in the Mystery"
     John R. Reed, "Reflexive Poetry: The Winter Talent of Donald Davie,"
     WHR, 19 (Winter, 1965), 50-51.

_____. "A Winter Talent"
     John R. Reed, "Reflexive Poetry: The Winter Talent of Donald Davie,"
     WHR, 19 (Winter, 1965), 46-48.

DAVIES, W. H. "The Moon"
     B. Rajan, "Georgian Poetry: A Retrospect," The Critic, 1 (Autumn, 1947),
     10-11.

_____. "Thy Beauty Haunts Me Heart and Soul"
     Daiches, Poetry and the Modern World, pp. 53-55.

_____. "The Villain"
     Perrine, Sound and Sense, p. 126.

DAVIS, Catherine. "Beware, Old Scrounger"
     Helen P. Trimpi, "The Theme of Loss in the Earlier Poems of Catherine
     Davis and Edgar Bowers," SoR, 9 (July, 1973), 602-603.

_____. "The Last Step"
     Helen P. Trimpi, "The Theme of Loss in the Earlier Poems of Catherine
     Davis and Edgar Bowers," SoR, 9 (July, 1973), 606-609.

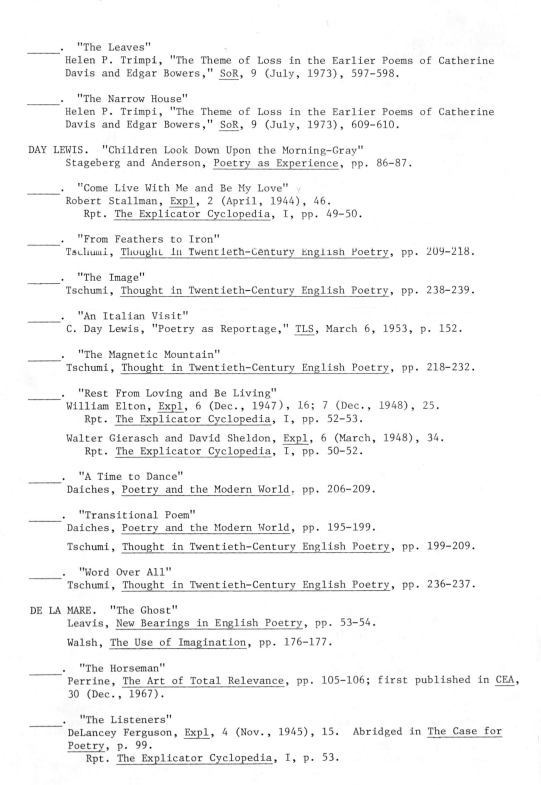

_____. "The Leaves"
Helen P. Trimpi, "The Theme of Loss in the Earlier Poems of Catherine
Davis and Edgar Bowers," SoR, 9 (July, 1973), 597-598.

_____. "The Narrow House"
Helen P. Trimpi, "The Theme of Loss in the Earlier Poems of Catherine
Davis and Edgar Bowers," SoR, 9 (July, 1973), 609-610.

DAY LEWIS. "Children Look Down Upon the Morning-Gray"
Stageberg and Anderson, Poetry as Experience, pp. 86-87.

_____. "Come Live With Me and Be My Love"
Robert Stallman, Expl, 2 (April, 1944), 46.
    Rpt. The Explicator Cyclopedia, I, pp. 49-50.

_____. "From Feathers to Iron"
Tschumi, Thought in Twentieth-Century English Poetry, pp. 209-218.

_____. "The Image"
Tschumi, Thought in Twentieth-Century English Poetry, pp. 238-239.

_____. "An Italian Visit"
C. Day Lewis, "Poetry as Reportage," TLS, March 6, 1953, p. 152.

_____. "The Magnetic Mountain"
Tschumi, Thought in Twentieth-Century English Poetry, pp. 218-232.

_____. "Rest From Loving and Be Living"
William Elton, Expl, 6 (Dec., 1947), 16; 7 (Dec., 1948), 25.
    Rpt. The Explicator Cyclopedia, I, pp. 52-53.

Walter Gierasch and David Sheldon, Expl, 6 (March, 1948), 34.
    Rpt. The Explicator Cyclopedia, I, pp. 50-52.

_____. "A Time to Dance"
Daiches, Poetry and the Modern World. pp. 206-209.

_____. "Transitional Poem"
Daiches, Poetry and the Modern World, pp. 195-199.

Tschumi, Thought in Twentieth-Century English Poetry, pp. 199-209.

_____. "Word Over All"
Tschumi, Thought in Twentieth-Century English Poetry, pp. 236-237.

DE LA MARE. "The Ghost"
Leavis, New Bearings in English Poetry, pp. 53-54.

Walsh, The Use of Imagination, pp. 176-177.

_____. "The Horseman"
Perrine, The Art of Total Relevance, pp. 105-106; first published in CEA,
30 (Dec., 1967).

_____. "The Listeners"
DeLancey Ferguson, Expl, 4 (Nov., 1945), 15. Abridged in The Case for
Poetry, p. 99.
    Rpt. The Explicator Cyclopedia, I, p. 53.

Frankenberg, <u>Invitation to Poetry</u>, p. 139.

Frederick Gwynn and Ralph W. Condee, <u>Expl</u>, 12 (Feb., 1954), 26.
Abridged in <u>The Case for Poetry</u>, pp. 99-100.
 Rpt. <u>The Explicator Cyclopedia</u>, I, pp. 53-54.

Robert M. Pierson, "The Meter of 'The Listeners,'" <u>ES</u>, 45 (Oct., 1964),
373-381.

J. M. Purcell, <u>Expl</u>, 3 (March, 1945), 42; 4 (Feb., 1946), 31. Abridged
in <u>The Case for Poetry</u>, p. 99.
 Rpt. <u>The Explicator Cyclopedia</u>, I, p. 53.

_____. "Maerchen"
Elisabeth Schneider, <u>Expl</u>, 4 (Feb., 1946), 29.
 Rpt. <u>Readings for Liberal Education</u>, II, 526.
 Rpt. Locke, Gibson, and Arms, <u>Introduction to Literature</u>, third
 edition, p. 178.
 Rpt. <u>The Explicator Cyclopedia</u>, I, pp. 54-55.

_____. "The Mocking Fairy"
Daniels, <u>The Art of Reading Poetry</u>, pp. 57-59.

_____. "Nostalgia"
E. K. Brown, "The Epilogue to Mr. de la Mare's Poetry," <u>Poetry</u>, 68
(May, 1946), 90-92.

DENHAM. "Cooper's Hill"
John Wilson Foster, "The Measure of Paradise: Topography in Eighteenth-
Century Poetry," <u>ECS</u>, 9 (Winter, 1975-76), 235-244.

Brendan O. Hehir, "Vergil's First 'Georgic' and Denham's 'Cooper's Hill,'"
<u>PQ</u>, 42 (Oct., 1963), 542-547.

Wasserman, <u>The Subtler Language</u>, pp. 45-88.

DENNEY, Reuel. "The Rememberer"
Hayden Carruth, <u>Poetry: A Critical Supplement</u>, April, 1949, pp. 11-14.

DENT, Peter. "Movement (For F. C.)"
Eileen Labrom, "Commentary," <u>Agenda</u>, 9 (Winter, 1971), 33.

DEUTSCH, Babette. "Visit to the Zoo"
Frank Jones, <u>Poetry: A Critical Supplement</u>, Nov., 1949, pp. 11-14.

DICKEY, James. "Adultery"
Constance Pierce, "Dickey's 'Adultery': A Ritual of Renewal," <u>CP</u>, 9
(Fall, 1976), 67-69.

_____. "Approaching Prayer"
H. L. Weatherby, "The Way of Exchange in James Dickey's Poetry," <u>SR</u>, 74
(July-Sept., 1966), 672-673.

_____. "A Dog Sleeping on My Feet"
H. L. Weatherby, "The Way of Exchange in James Dickey's Poetry," <u>SR</u>, 74
(July-Sept., 1966), 669-672.

_____. "The Driver"
Charles C. Tucker, "Knowledge Up, Down, and Beyond: Dickey's 'The
Driver' and 'Falling,'" <u>CEA</u>, 38 (May, 1976), 5-7.

H. L. Weatherby, "The Way of Exchange in James Dickey's Poetry," SR, 74 (July-Sept., 1966), 675.

_____. "The Eye-Beaters"
Joyce Carol Oates, "Out of Stone into Flesh: The Imagination of James Dickey," MPS, 5 (Autumn, 1974), 136-137.

_____. "Falling"
Charles C. Tucker, "Knowledge Up, Down, and Beyond: Dickey's 'The Driver' and 'Falling,'" CEA, 38 (May, 1976), 7-10.

John Vernon, The Garden and the Map: Schizophrenia in Twentieth-Century Literature and Culture (Urbana: Univ. of Illinois Press, 1973), pp. 134-142.

_____. "The Firebombing"
Joyce Carol Oates, "Out of Stone into Flesh: The Imagination of James Dickey," MPS, 5 (Autumn, 1974), 113-118.

_____. "The Heaven of Animals"
Carroll, The Poem In Its Skin, pp. 43-49.

William Heyen, ed., "A Conversation with James Dickey," SoR, 9 (Winter, 1973), 142-145.

_____. "In Pursuit from Under"
Daniel L. Guillory, "Water Magic in the Poetry of James Dickey," ELN, 8 (Dec., 1970), 135.

_____. "Inside the River"
Daniel L. Guillory, "Water Magic in the Poetry of James Dickey," ELN, 8 (Dec., 1970), 136-137.

_____. "The Lifeguard"
Perrine and Reid, 100 American Poems, pp. 279-280.

_____. "Mary Sheffield"
Daniel L. Guillory, "Water Magic in the Poetry of James Dickey," ELN, 8 (Dec., 1970), 132.

_____. "Orpheus Before Hades"
David C. Berry, "Harmony With the Dead: James Dickey's Descent into the Underworld," SoQ, 12 (April, 1974), 234-235.

_____. "The Owl King"
Daniel L. Guillory, "Water Magic in the Poetry of James Dickey," ELN, 8 (Dec., 1970), 133-134.

_____. "The Performance"
William Heyen, ed., "A Conversation with James Dickey," SoR, 9 (Winter, 1973), 136-138.

_____. "Sled Burial, Dream Ceremony"
William Heyen, ed., "A Conversation with James Dickey," SoR, 9 (Winter, 1973), 149-150.

_____. "Turning Away"
Joyce Carol Oates, "Out of Stone into Flesh: The Imagination of James Dickey," MPS, 5 (Autumn, 1974), 139-142.

DICKINSON. "The Admirations--and--Contempts--of Time--"
Roland Hagenbuchle, "Precision and Indeterminacy in the Poetry of Emily Dickinson," ESQ, No. 20 (1st Quarter, 1974), 45.

_____. "After Great Pain a Formal Feeling Comes"
Beaty and Matchett, Poetry: From Statement to Meaning, pp. 28-34.

Brooks and Warren, Understanding Poetry, pp. 468-471. Revised edition, pp. 325-327.

Drew, Poetry: A Modern Guide, pp. 124-125.

William Bysshe Stein, "Emily Dickinson's Parodic Masks," The University of Kansas City Review, 36 (Autumn, 1969), 54-55.

_____. "Apparently With No Surprise"
Herbert R. Coursen, Jr., "Nature's Center," CE, 24 (March, 1963), 468-469.

Perrine, Sound and Sense, pp. 126-127.
   Rpt. second edition, pp. 138-139.

_____. "As By the Dead We Love to Sit"
Edgar F. Daniels, Expl, 35 (Winter, 1976), 10-11.

Nat Henry, Expl, 31 (Jan., 1973), 35.

Nat Henry, Expl, 35 (Winter, 1976), 26-27.

Robert L. Lair, Expl, 25 (March, 1967), 58.

Laurence Perrine, Expl, 33 (Feb., 1975), 49.

_____. "As Imperceptibly as Grief"
Blair, The Literature of the United States, II, p. 751.

_____. "At Half Past Three, a Single Bird"
Robert W. Russell, Expl, 16 (Oct., 1957), 3.
   Rpt. The Explicator Cyclopedia, I, pp. 55-56.

_____. "As Watchers Hang Upon the East"
Brenda Ann Catto, Expl, 33 (March, 1975), 55.

Laurence Perrine, Expl, 35 (Winter, 1976), 4-5.

_____. "Aurora Is the Effort"
Kenneth B. Newell, Expl, 20 (Sept., 1961), 5.
   Rpt. The Explicator Cyclopedia, I, pp. 56-57.

_____. "Because I Could Not Stop for Death"
Abad, A Formal Approach to Lyric Poetry, pp. 141-143.

Blair, The Literature of the United States, II, p. 750.

Bloom, A Map of Misreading, pp. 184-186.

H. A. Bouraoui, "'Leaning Against the Sun': Emily Dickinson, the Poet as Seer," RS, 37 (Sept., 1969), 208-217.

Richard Chase, abridged in The Case for Poetry, pp. 105-106 from Emily Dickinson (New York: William Sloane Associates, 1951), pp. 249-251.

Daiches and Charvat, Poems in English, p. 727.

Bert Case Diltz, <u>Sense or Nonsense: Contemporary Education at the Cross-roads</u> (Toronto: McClelland and Stewart Ltd., 1972), pp. 83-89.

Eunice Glenn, "Emily Dickinson's Poetry: A Revaluation," <u>SR</u>, 51 (Autumn, 1943), 585-588.

Theodore Hoepfner, "'Because I Could Not Stop for Death,'" <u>AL</u>, 29 (March, 1957), 96.

John F. Lynen, "Three Uses of the Present: The Historian's, the Critic's, and Emily Dickinson's," <u>CE</u>, 28 (Nov., 1966), 134-135.

Martz, <u>The Poem of the Mind</u>, pp. 94-95.

Sanders, <u>The Discovery of Poetry</u>, pp. 344-346.

Tate, <u>Reactionary Essays on Poetry and Ideas</u>, pp. 13-16.
    Rpt. <u>On the Limits of Poetry</u>, pp. 205-208.
    Rpt. <u>Readings for Liberal Education</u>, II, 173-174.
    Abridged in <u>The Case for Poetry</u>, p. 105.
    Rpt. Feidelson and Brodtkorb, <u>Interpretations of American Literature</u>, pp. 204-205.
    Rpt. Locke, Gibson, and Arms, <u>Introduction to Literature</u>, third edition, pp. 158-159.

Tate, Reason in Madness, pp. 14-15.

Unger and O'Connor, <u>Poems for Study</u>, pp. 547-548.

J. S. Wheatcroft, "Emily Dickinson's White Robes," <u>Criticism</u>, 5 (Spring, 1963), 144-145.

Wheeler, <u>The Design of Poetry</u>, pp. 172-175.

Winters, <u>Maule's Curse</u>, pp. 154-156. Also <u>In Defense of Reason</u>, pp. 288-290. Abridged in <u>The Case for Poetry</u>, p. 105.

_____. "Before I Got My Eye Put Out"
B. J. Rogers, "The Truth Told Slant: Emily Dickinson's Poetic Mode," <u>TSLL</u>, 14 (Summer, 1972), 333.

_____. "Before the Ice Is in the Pools"
J. S. Wheatcroft, "Emily Dickinson's White Robes," <u>Criticism</u>, 5 (Spring, 1963), 136.

_____. "A Bird Came Down the Walk"
Frederic I. Carpenter, "Emily Dickinson and the Rhymes of Dream," <u>The University of Kansas City Review</u>, 20 (Winter, 1953), 119-120.

J. P. Kirby, <u>Expl</u>, 2 (June, 1944), 61.
    Rpt. <u>The Explicator Cyclopedia</u>, I, p. 57.

Eleanor Wilner, "The Poetics of Emily Dickinson," <u>ELH</u>, 38 (March, 1971), 147-154.

_____. "Blazing in Gold"
Lois A. Cuddy, "The Influence of Latin Poetics on Emily Dickinson's Style," <u>CLS</u>, 13 (Sept. 1976), 221-224.

_____. "The Bustle in a House"
Raymond J. Jordan, <u>Expl</u>, 21 (Feb., 1963), 49.

_____. "The Butterfly Obtains"
Donald E. Houghton, <u>Expl</u>, 27 (Sept., 1968), 5.

_____. "Came a Wind Like a Bugle"
Mario L. D'Avanzo, "'Came a Wind Like a Bugle': Dickinson's Poetic
Apocalypse," Renascence, 17 (Fall, 1964), 29-31.

_____. "A Clock Stopped--Not the Mantel's"
Donald W. Bolin, Expl, 22 (Dec., 1963), 27.

Earl Roy Miner, Expl, 13 (Dec., 1954), 18.
    Rpt. The Explicator Cyclopedia, I, pp. 57-58.

Laurence Perrine, Expl, 14 (Oct., 1955), 4.
    Rpt. The Explicator Cyclopedia, I, p. 59.

William Rossky, Expl, 22 (Sept., 1963), 3.

B. A. Sheffler, "Emily Dickinson's 'A Clock Stopped,'" MSE, 1 (Fall,
1967), 52-54.
_____. "The Crickets Sang"
Simon Tugwell, Expl, 23 (Feb., 1965), 46.

_____. "Crumbling Is Not an Instant's Act"
Charles R. Anderson, "The Conscious Self in Emily Dickinson's Poetry,"
AL, 31 (Nov., 1959), 297-298.

_____. "Dear Sue, Your--Riches--Taught Me--Poverty!"
Rebecca Patterson, "Emily Dickinson's Jewel Imagery," AL, 42 (Jan., 1974),
516-519.

_____. "Death Is a Dialogue Between"
Virginia H. Adair, Expl, 27 (March, 1969), 52.

Perrine, The Art of Total Relevance, pp. 120-121.

_____. "Elysium Is As Far As To"
Roland Hagenbüchle, "Precision and Indeterminacy in the Poetry of Emily
Dickinson," ESQ, No. 20 (1st Quarter, 1974), 48-49.

John F. Lynen, "Three Uses of the Present: The Historican's, the
Critic's, and Emily Dickinson's," CE, 28 (Nov., 1966), 135.

Stephen Whicher, Expl, 19 (April, 1961), 45.
    Rpt. The Explicator Cyclopedia, I, p. 59.

_____. "Except the Smaller Size"
Charles R. Anderson, "The Conscious Self in Emily Dickinson's Poetry,"
AL, 31 (Nov., 1959), 295-296.

_____. "'Faith' Is a Fine Invention"
Paul Witherington, Expl, 26 (April, 1968), 62.

_____. "Farther in Summer Than the Birds"
Frederic I, Carpenter, "Emily Dickinson and the Rhymes of Dream," The
University of Kansas City Review, 20 (Winter, 1953), 118.

Frederick I. Carpenter, Expl, 8 (March, 1950), 33.
    Rpt. The Explicator Cyclopedia, I, pp. 59-60.

Robert H. Elias and Helen L. Elias, Expl, 11 (Oct., 1952), 5.

Rene Rapin, Expl, 12 (Feb., 1954), 24.
    Rpt. The Explicator Cyclopedia, I, pp. 60-61.

Sidney E. Lind, "Emily Dickinson's 'Farther in Summer than the Birds' and Nathaniel Hawthorn's 'The Old Manse,'" AL, 39 (May, 1967), 163-169.

Marshall Van Deusen, Expl, 13 (March, 1955), 33.
    Rpt. The Explicator Cyclopedia, I, pp. 61-64.

Charles Child Walcutt, The Explicator Cyclopedia, I, "Introduction," pp. xvii-xviii.

Winters, Maule's Curse, pp. 158-159. Also In Defense of Reason, pp. 292-293.
    Rpt. The Literature of the United States, II, p. 752.

_____. "The Feet of People Walking Home"
Ted-Larry Pebworth and Jay Jay Claude Summers, Expl, 27 (May, 1969), 76,

_____. "For Every Bird A Nest"
Barton Levi St. Armand, "Dickinson's 'For Every Bird a Nest,'" Expl, 35 (Spring, 1977), 34-35.

_____. "Go Not Too Near a House of Rose"
Warren Beck, "Poetry's Chronic Disease," EJ, 33 (Sept., 1944), 362-363.

Macklin Thomas, "Analysis of the Experience in Lyric Poetry," CE, 9 (March, 1948), 320-321.

David W. Thompson, "Interpretative Reading as Symbolic Action," QJS, 42 (Dec., 1956), 395.

_____. "The Harm of Years Is on Him"
Charles R. Anderson, "The Conscious Self in Emily Dickinson's Poetry," AL, 31 (Nov., 1959), 296-297.

_____. "The Heart Asks Pleasure First"
Frederic I. Carpenter, "Emily Dickinson and the Rhymes of Dream" The University of Kansas City Review, 20 (Winter, 1953), 115.

_____. "He Put the Belt Around My Life"
Eunice Glenn, "Emily Dickinson's Poetry: A Revaluation," SR, 51 (Autumn, 1943), 580-582.

_____. "Hope Is a Strange Invention"
Charles R. Anderson, "The Conscious Self in Emily Dickinson's Poetry," AL, 31 (Nov., 1959), 301-302.

_____. "A House upon the Height"
Eleanor Wilner, "The Poetics of Emily Dickinson," ELH, 38 (March, 1971), 140-141.

_____. "I Asked No Other Thing"
Vivian R. Pollack, "'That Fine Prosperity': Economic Metaphors in Emily Dickinson's Poetry," MLQ, 34 (June, 1973), 169-170.

_____. "I Cannot Dance upon My Toes"
Norman Talbot, "The Child, the Actress, and Miss Emily Dickinson," The Southern Review, (Australia), 5 (June, 1972), 108.

_____. "I Cannot Live With You"
Eunice Glenn, "Emily Dickinson's Poetry: A Revaluation," SR, 51 (Autumn, 1943), 582-585.

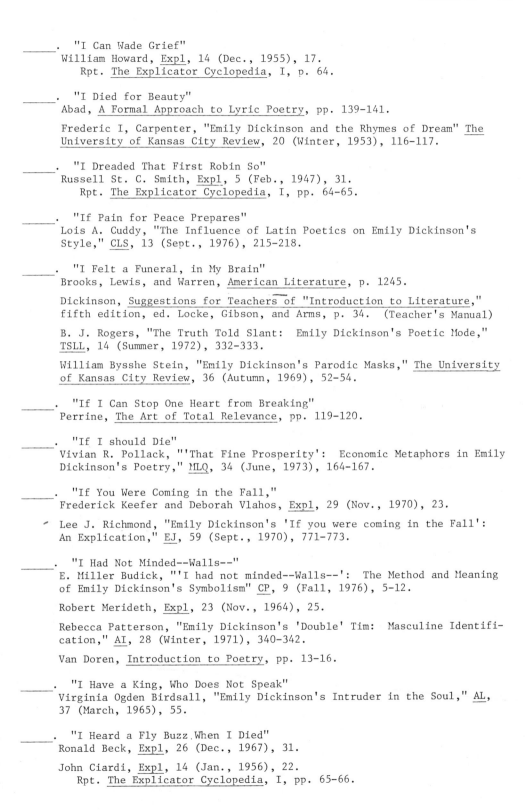

_____. "I Can Wade Grief"
William Howard, Expl, 14 (Dec., 1955), 17.
    Rpt. The Explicator Cyclopedia, I, p. 64.

_____. "I Died for Beauty"
Abad, A Formal Approach to Lyric Poetry, pp. 139-141.

Frederic I, Carpenter, "Emily Dickinson and the Rhymes of Dream" The
University of Kansas City Review, 20 (Winter, 1953), 116-117.

_____. "I Dreaded That First Robin So"
Russell St. C. Smith, Expl, 5 (Feb., 1947), 31.
    Rpt. The Explicator Cyclopedia, I, pp. 64-65.

_____. "If Pain for Peace Prepares"
Lois A. Cuddy, "The Influence of Latin Poetics on Emily Dickinson's
Style," CLS, 13 (Sept., 1976), 215-218.

_____. "I Felt a Funeral, in My Brain"
Brooks, Lewis, and Warren, American Literature, p. 1245.

Dickinson, Suggestions for Teachers of "Introduction to Literature,"
fifth edition, ed. Locke, Gibson, and Arms, p. 34. (Teacher's Manual)

B. J. Rogers, "The Truth Told Slant: Emily Dickinson's Poetic Mode,"
TSLL, 14 (Summer, 1972), 332-333.

William Bysshe Stein, "Emily Dickinson's Parodic Masks," The University
of Kansas City Review, 36 (Autumn, 1969), 52-54.

_____. "If I Can Stop One Heart from Breaking"
Perrine, The Art of Total Relevance, pp. 119-120.

_____. "If I should Die"
Vivian R. Pollack, "'That Fine Prosperity': Economic Metaphors in Emily
Dickinson's Poetry," MLQ, 34 (June, 1973), 164-167.

_____. "If You Were Coming in the Fall,"
Frederick Keefer and Deborah Vlahos, Expl, 29 (Nov., 1970), 23.

Lee J. Richmond, "Emily Dickinson's 'If you were coming in the Fall':
An Explication," EJ, 59 (Sept., 1970), 771-773.

_____. "I Had Not Minded--Walls--"
E. Miller Budick, "'I had not minded--Walls--': The Method and Meaning
of Emily Dickinson's Symbolism" CP, 9 (Fall, 1976), 5-12.

Robert Merideth, Expl, 23 (Nov., 1964), 25.

Rebecca Patterson, "Emily Dickinson's 'Double' Tim: Masculine Identification," AI, 28 (Winter, 1971), 340-342.

Van Doren, Introduction to Poetry, pp. 13-16.

_____. "I Have a King, Who Does Not Speak"
Virginia Ogden Birdsall, "Emily Dickinson's Intruder in the Soul," AL,
37 (March, 1965), 55.

_____. "I Heard a Fly Buzz.When I Died"
Ronald Beck, Expl, 26 (Dec., 1967), 31.

John Ciardi, Expl, 14 (Jan., 1956), 22.
    Rpt. The Explicator Cyclopedia, I, pp. 65-66.

James T. Connelly, Expl, 25 (Dec., 1966), 34.

Thomas W. Ford, "Thoreau's Cosmic Mosquito and Dickinson's Terrestrial Fly," NEQ, 48 (Dec., 1975), 487-504.

Gerhard Friedrich, Expl, 13 (April, 1955), 35.
    Rpt. The Explicator Cyclopedia, I, p. 65.

Eugene Hollahan, Expl, 25 (Sept., 1966), 6.

Caroline Hogue, Expl, 20 (Nov., 1961), 26.
    Rpt. The Explicator Cyclopedia, I, p. 66.

B. J. Rogers, "The Truth Told Slant: Emily Dickinson's Poetic Mode," TSLL, 14 (Summer, 1972), 333-334.

Benjamin T. Spencer, "Criticism: Centrifugal and Centrepetal," Criticism, 8 (Spring, 1966), 141-143.

Wheeler, The Design of Poetry, pp. 189-192.

_____. "I Know Some Lonely Houses Off the Road"
Virginia Ogden Birdsall, "Emily Dickinson's Intruder in the Soul," AL, 37 (March, 1965), 56-59.

Myron Ochshorn, Expl, 11 (Nov., 1952), 12.
    Rpt. The Explicator Cyclopedia, I, pp. 66-67.

_____. "I Like to See It Lap the Miles"
Abad, A Formal Approach to Lyric Poetry, pp. 342-344.

George Arms, Expl, 2 (May, 1944), Q31.

F. J. Hoffman, "The Technological Fallacy in Contemporary Poetry," AL, 21 (March, 1949), 97.
    Rpt. Stageberg and Anderson, Poetry as Experience, p. 460.

Robert E. Lowrey, "'Boanerges': An Encomium for Edward Dickinson," ArQ, 26 (Spring, 1970), 54-58.

Walsh, Doors into Poetry, pp. 15-18.

_____. "I'll Tell You How the Sun Rose"
Jerome, Poetry: Premeditated Art, p. 144.

Wilbur Scott, Expl, 7 (Nov., 1948), 14.
    Rpt. The Explicator Cyclopedia, I, pp. 67-68.

Suzanne M. Wilson, "Structural Patterns in the Poetry of Emily Dickinson," AL, 35 (March, 1963), 56-57.

_____. "I Meant to Have but Modest Needs"
Vivian R. Pollack, "'That Fine Prosperity': Economic Metaphors in Emily Dickinson's Poetry," MLQ, 34 (June, 1973), 170-171.

_____. "Immured in Heaven!"
Thomas H. Johnson, Expl, 11 (March, 1953), 36.

_____. "I Never Hear the One is Dead"
Myron Ochshorn, "In Search of Emily Dickinson," New Mexico Quarterly Review, 23 (Spring, 1953), 101-102, 104.

_____. "I Never Lost As Much But Twice"
Allen D. Lackey, Expl, 34 (Nov., 1975), 18.

George Monteiro, Expl, 30 (Sept., 1971), 7.

Vivian R. Pollack, "'That Fine Prosperity': Economic Metaphors in Emily Dickinson's Poetry," MLQ, 34 (June, 1973), 168-169.

René Rapin, Expl, 31 (March, 1973), 52.

_____. "I Never Saw a Moor"
W. Herget, Expl, 30 (March, 1972), 55.

William Howard, Expl, 21 (Oct., 1962), 13.

Robert Meredith, "Emily Dickinson and the Acquisitive Society," NEQ, 37 (Dec., 1964), 448-451.

Thomas Werge, "'Checks' in 'I Never Saw a Moor,'" AN&Q, 12 (March, 1974), 101-102.

_____. "I Should Have Been Too Glad, I See"
Myron Ochshorn, "In Search of Emily Dickinson," New Mexico Quarterly Review, 23 (Spring, 1953), 103-106.

_____. "I Started Early--Took My Dog"
Virginia Ogden Birdsall, "Emily Dickinson's Intruder in the Soul," AL, 37 (March, 1965), 61-64.

Eric W. Carlson, Expl, 20 (May, 1962), 72.
    Rpt. The Explicator Cyclopedia, I, pp. 69-70.

Kate Flores, Expl, 9 (May, 1951), 47.
    Rpt. The Explicator Cyclopedia, pp. 68-69.

George S. Lensing, Expl, 31 (Dec., 1972), 30.

Laurence Perrine, Expl, 10 (Feb., 1952), 28.
    Rpt. The Explicator Cyclopedia, I, p. 69.

Winters, Forms of Discovery, pp. 267-268.

_____. "I Taste a Liquor Never Brewed"
Hennig Cohen, Expl, 33 (Jan., 1975), 41.

Lloyd M. Davis, Expl, 23 (March, 1965), 53.

Wallace W. Douglas, English "A" Analyst, No. 4, pp. 1-3.

Cecil D. Eby, "'I Taste a Liquor Never Brewed': A Variant Reading," AL, 36 (Jan., 1965), 516-518.

A. Scott Garrow, "A Note on Manzanilla," AL, 35 (Nov., 1963), 366.

Charles J. Hauser, Expl, 31 (Sept., 1972), 2.

Raymond G. Malbone, Expl, 26 (Oct., 1967), 14.

William Bysshe Stein, "Emily Dickinson's Parodic Masks," The University of Kansas City Review, 36 (Autumn, 1969), 49-52.

_____. "It Dropped So Low--In My Regard"
Archibald A. Hill, "Figurative Structure and Meaning: Two Poems by Emily Dickinson," TSLL, 16 (Spring, 1974), 206-208.
    Rpt. Constituent and Pattern in Poetry (Austin: Univ. of Texas Press, 1976), pp. 133-135.

Ted-Larry Pebsorth, "The Lusterward of Dickinson's Silver Shelf," AN&Q, 12 (Oct., 1973), 18.

_____. "It's Easy to Invent a Life"
Vivian R. Pollack, "'That Fine Prosperity': Economic Metaphors in Emily
Dickinson's Poetry," MLQ, 34 (June, 1973), 167-168.

_____. "It Was Not Death, for I Stood Up"
B. J. Rogers, "The Truth Told Slant: Emily Dickinson's Poetic Mode,"
TSLL, 14 (Summer, 1972), 334-335.

_____. "I've Dropped My Brain--My Soul Is Numb"
Charles R. Anderson, "The Conscious Self in Emily Dickinson's Poetry,"
AL, 31 (Nov., 1959), 299-301.

_____. "I Years Had Been from Home"
Steven Axelrod, "Terror in the Everyday: Emily Dickinson's 'I Years had
been from Home,'" CP, 6 (Spring, 1973), 53-56.

James E. Miller, Jr,, "Emily Dickinson: The Thunder's Tongue," MinnR, 2
(Spring, 1962), 299-303.

_____. "The Lamp Burns Sure Within"
Stuart Lewis, Expl, 28 (Sept., 1969), 4.

_____. "The Last Night that She Lived"
Abad, A Formal Approach to Lyric Poetry, pp. 160-164.

Harry Modean Campbell, Expl, 8 (May, 1950), 54.
    Rpt. The Explicator Cyclopedia, I, pp. 70-71.

_____. "The Malay--Took the Pearl--"
Eleanor Wilner, "The Poetics of Emily Dickinson," ELH, 38 (March, 1971),
143-144.

_____. "A Mien to Move a Queen"
F. DeWolfe Miller, "Emily Dickinson: Self-Portrait in the Third Person,"
NEQ, 46 (March, 1973), 119-124.

_____. "A Mine There Is No Man Would Own"
Vivian R. Pollack, "'That Fine Prosperity': Economic Metaphors in Emily
Dickinson's Poetry," MLQ, 34 (June, 1973), 177-178.

_____. "The Moon Upon Her Fluent Route"
Winters, Forms of Discovery, pp. 270-271.

_____. "More Life Went Out, When He Went"
R. P. Blackmur, "Emily Dickinson: Notes on Prejudice and Fact," SoR, 3
(Autumn, 1937), 337-341.

Blackmur, Expense of Greatness, pp. 126-130.
    Rpt. Language as Gesture, pp. 40-43.

_____. "Much Madness Is Divinest Sense"
Abad, A Formal Approach to Lyric Poetry, pp. 133-134.

_____. "My Life Had Stood--a Loaded Gun--"
    Albert Gelpi, "Emily Dickinson and the Deerslayer: The Dilemma of the
Woman Poet in America," SJS, 2 (May, 1977), 81-90.

Laurence Perrine, Expl, 21 (Nov., 1962), 21.

The Poetry Workshop, Columbus, Georgia, Expl, 15 (May, 1957), 51.
    Rpt. The Explicator Cyclopedia, I, pp. 71-72.

_____. "My Wheel Is in the Dark!"
Mabel Howard, William Howard, and Emily Harvey, Expl, 17 (Nov., 1958), 12.
    Rpt. The Explicator Cyclopedia, I, pp. 72-73.

_____. "The Nearest Dream Recedes--Unrealized--"
Norman Talbot, "The Child, the Actress, and Miss Emily Dickinson," The
Southern Review (Australia), 5 (June, 1972), 107-108.

_____. "No Brigadier Throughout the Year"
Sr. Victoria Marie Forde, S.C., Expl, 27 (Feb., 1969), 41.

_____. "No Rack Can Torture Me"
Eunice Glenn, "Emily Dickinson's Poetry: A Revaluation," SR, 51 (Autumn,
1943), 577-578.

B. J. Rogers, "The Truth Told Slant: Emily Dickinson's Poetic Mode,"
TSLL, 14 (Summer, 1972), 332.

_____. "Not With a Club the Heart is Broken"
Mordecai Marcus, Expl, 20 (March, 1962), 54.
    Rpt. The Explicator Cyclopedia, I, pp. 73-74.

_____. "Of All the Souls that Stand Create"
Abad, A Formal Approach to Lyric Poetry, pp. 137-139.

_____. "Of Bronze--and Blaze--"
Robert Gillespie, "A Circumference of Emily Dickinson," NEQ, 46 (June,
1973), 258-260.

David Hiatt, Expl, 21 (Sept., 1962), 6.

Jo C. Searles, "The Art of Dickinson's 'Household Thought,'" CP, 6
(Spring, 1973), 46-51.

_____. "Of Death I Try to Think Like This"
Nancy McClaran, Expl, 35 (Winter, 1976), 18-19.

_____. "One Blessing Had I Than the Rest"
Vivian R. Pollack, "'That fine Prosperity': Economic Metaphors in Emily
Dickinson's Poetry," MLQ, 34 (June, 1973), 178-179.

_____. "One Day Is There of the Series"
Paul O. Williams, Expl, 23 (Dec., 1964), 28.

_____. "One Dignity Delays for All--"
Erhardt H. Essig, Expl, 23 (Oct., 1964), 16.

Pierre Michel, "The Last Stanza of Emily Dickinson's 'One Dignity Delays
for All--,'" ES, 50 (Feb., 1969), 98-100.

_____. "One Life of So Much Consequence"
Rebecca Patterson, "Emily Dickinson's Jewel Imagery," AL, 42 (Jan.,
1971), 514-515.

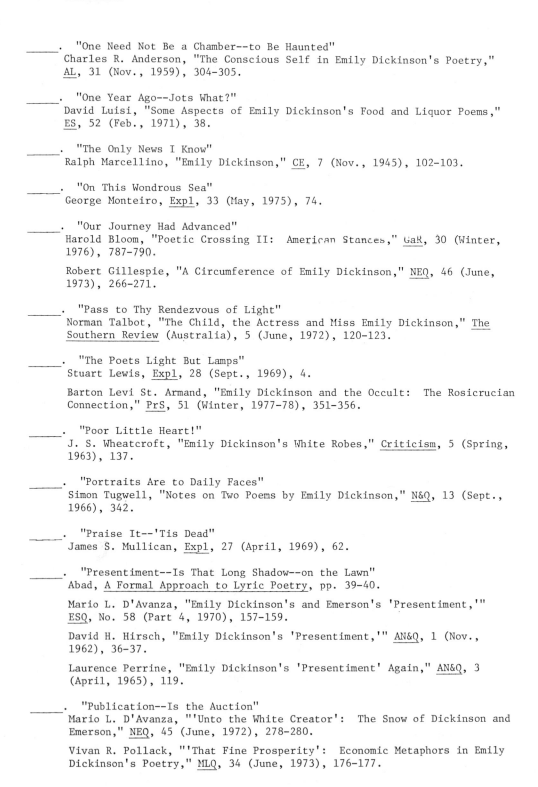

_____. "One Need Not Be a Chamber--to Be Haunted"
Charles R. Anderson, "The Conscious Self in Emily Dickinson's Poetry,"
AL, 31 (Nov., 1959), 304-305.

_____. "One Year Ago--Jots What?"
David Luisi, "Some Aspects of Emily Dickinson's Food and Liquor Poems,"
ES, 52 (Feb., 1971), 38.

_____. "The Only News I Know"
Ralph Marcellino, "Emily Dickinson," CE, 7 (Nov., 1945), 102-103.

_____. "On This Wondrous Sea"
George Monteiro, Expl, 33 (May, 1975), 74.

_____. "Our Journey Had Advanced"
Harold Bloom, "Poetic Crossing II: American Stances," GaR, 30 (Winter,
1976), 787-790.

Robert Gillespie, "A Circumference of Emily Dickinson," NEQ, 46 (June,
1973), 266-271.

_____. "Pass to Thy Rendezvous of Light"
Norman Talbot, "The Child, the Actress and Miss Emily Dickinson," The
Southern Review (Australia), 5 (June, 1972), 120-123.

_____. "The Poets Light But Lamps"
Stuart Lewis, Expl, 28 (Sept., 1969), 4.

Barton Levi St. Armand, "Emily Dickinson and the Occult: The Rosicrucian
Connection," PrS, 51 (Winter, 1977-78), 351-356.

_____. "Poor Little Heart!"
J. S. Wheatcroft, "Emily Dickinson's White Robes," Criticism, 5 (Spring,
1963), 137.

_____. "Portraits Are to Daily Faces"
Simon Tugwell, "Notes on Two Poems by Emily Dickinson," N&Q, 13 (Sept.,
1966), 342.

_____. "Praise It--'Tis Dead"
James S. Mullican, Expl, 27 (April, 1969), 62.

_____. "Presentiment--Is That Long Shadow--on the Lawn"
Abad, A Formal Approach to Lyric Poetry, pp. 39-40.

Mario L. D'Avanza, "Emily Dickinson's and Emerson's 'Presentiment,'"
ESQ, No. 58 (Part 4, 1970), 157-159.

David H. Hirsch, "Emily Dickinson's 'Presentiment,'" AN&Q, 1 (Nov.,
1962), 36-37.

Laurence Perrine, "Emily Dickinson's 'Presentiment' Again," AN&Q, 3
(April, 1965), 119.

_____. "Publication--Is the Auction"
Mario L. D'Avanza, "'Unto the White Creator': The Snow of Dickinson and
Emerson," NEQ, 45 (June, 1972), 278-280.

Vivan R. Pollack, "'That Fine Prosperity': Economic Metaphors in Emily
Dickinson's Poetry," MLQ, 34 (June, 1973), 176-177.

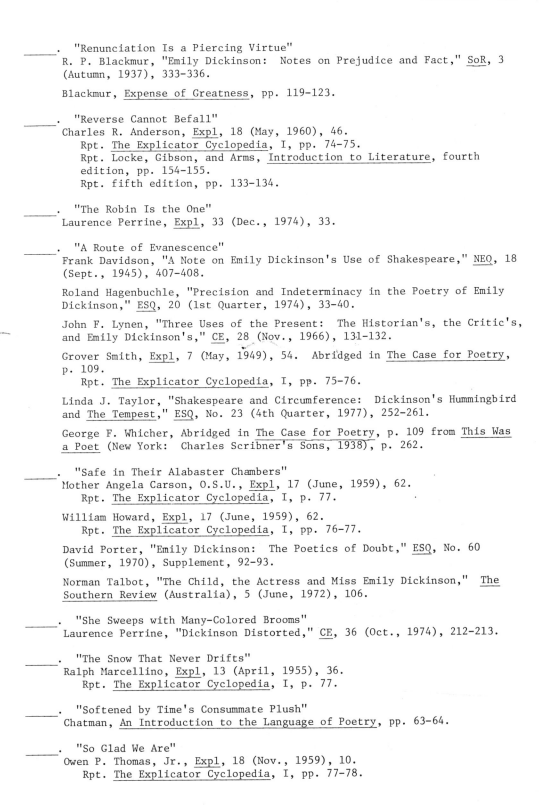

_____. "Renunciation Is a Piercing Virtue"
R. P. Blackmur, "Emily Dickinson: Notes on Prejudice and Fact," SoR, 3 (Autumn, 1937), 333-336.

Blackmur, Expense of Greatness, pp. 119-123.

_____. "Reverse Cannot Befall"
Charles R. Anderson, Expl, 18 (May, 1960), 46.
    Rpt. The Explicator Cyclopedia, I, pp. 74-75.
    Rpt. Locke, Gibson, and Arms, Introduction to Literature, fourth edition, pp. 154-155.
    Rpt. fifth edition, pp. 133-134.

_____. "The Robin Is the One"
Laurence Perrine, Expl, 33 (Dec., 1974), 33.

_____. "A Route of Evanescence"
Frank Davidson, "A Note on Emily Dickinson's Use of Shakespeare," NEQ, 18 (Sept., 1945), 407-408.

Roland Hagenbuchle, "Precision and Indeterminacy in the Poetry of Emily Dickinson," ESQ, 20 (1st Quarter, 1974), 33-40.

John F. Lynen, "Three Uses of the Present: The Historian's, the Critic's, and Emily Dickinson's," CE, 28 (Nov., 1966), 131-132.

Grover Smith, Expl, 7 (May, 1949), 54. Abridged in The Case for Poetry, p. 109.
    Rpt. The Explicator Cyclopedia, I, pp. 75-76.

Linda J. Taylor, "Shakespeare and Circumference: Dickinson's Hummingbird and The Tempest," ESQ, No. 23 (4th Quarter, 1977), 252-261.

George F. Whicher, Abridged in The Case for Poetry, p. 109 from This Was a Poet (New York: Charles Scribner's Sons, 1938), p. 262.

_____. "Safe in Their Alabaster Chambers"
Mother Angela Carson, O.S.U., Expl, 17 (June, 1959), 62.
    Rpt. The Explicator Cyclopedia, I, p. 77.

William Howard, Expl, 17 (June, 1959), 62.
    Rpt. The Explicator Cyclopedia, I, pp. 76-77.

David Porter, "Emily Dickinson: The Poetics of Doubt," ESQ, No. 60 (Summer, 1970), Supplement, 92-93.

Norman Talbot, "The Child, the Actress and Miss Emily Dickinson," The Southern Review (Australia), 5 (June, 1972), 106.

_____. "She Sweeps with Many-Colored Brooms"
Laurence Perrine, "Dickinson Distorted," CE, 36 (Oct., 1974), 212-213.

_____. "The Snow That Never Drifts"
Ralph Marcellino, Expl, 13 (April, 1955), 36.
    Rpt. The Explicator Cyclopedia, I, p. 77.

_____. "Softened by Time's Consummate Plush"
Chatman, An Introduction to the Language of Poetry, pp. 63-64.

_____. "So Glad We Are"
Owen P. Thomas, Jr., Expl, 18 (Nov., 1959), 10.
    Rpt. The Explicator Cyclopedia, I, pp. 77-78.

_____. "A Solemn Thing Within the Soul"
David Luisi, "Some Aspects of Emily Dickinson's Food and Liquor Poems,"
ES, 52 (Feb., 1971), 38-39.

_____. "Some Arrows Slay but Whom They Strike"
J. S. Wheatcroft, "Emily Dickinson's White Robes," Criticism, 5 (Spring,
1963), 139-140.

_____. "The Soul Has Bandaged Moments--"
Peckham and Chatman, Word, Meaning, Poem, pp. 303-311.

_____. "The Soul Selects Her Own Society"
Abad, A Formal Approach to Lyric Poetry, pp. 135-138.

Elizabeth Bowman, Expl, 29 (Oct., 1970), 13.

Paul Faris, Expl, 25 (April, 1967), 65.

Archibald A. Hill, "Figurative Structure and Meaning: Two Poems by
Emily Dickinson," TSLL, 16 (Spring, 1974), 196-206.
   Rpt. Constituent and Pattern in Poetry (Austin: Univ. of Texas Press,
   1976), pp. 123-133.

Will C. Jumper, Expl, 29 (Sept., 1970), 5.

Henry F. Pommer, Expl, 3 (Feb., 1945), 32.
   Rpt. The Explicator Cyclopedia, I, p. 78.

Larry Rubin, Expl, 30 (April, 1972), 67.

Simon Tugwell, Expl, 27 (Jan., 1969), 37.

Van Doren, Introduction to Poetry, pp. 39-42.

Paul Witherington, "The Neighborhood Humor of Dickinson's 'The Soul
Selects Her Own Society,'" CP, 2 (Fall, 1969), 5-8.

_____. "The Soul Should Always Stand Ajar"
Virginia Ogden Birdsall, "Emily Dickinson's Intruder in the Soul," AL, 37
(March, 1965), 59-60.

_____. "The Soul's Superior Instants"
Suzanne M. Wilson, "Emily Dickinson and the Twentieth-Century Poetry of
Sensibility," AL, 36 (Nov., 1964), 351-352.

_____. "Success Is Counted Sweetest"
Abad, A Formal Approach to Lyric Poetry, pp. 134-135.

_____. "Summer Has Two Beginnings"
Lawrence A. Walz, Expl, 33 (Oct., 1974), 16.

_____. "Superflous Were the Sun"
Brita Lindberg, "Further Notes on a Poem by Emily Dickinson," N&Q, 15
(May, 1968), 179-180.

_____. "There Are Two Ripenings"
Laurence Perrine, Expl, 31 (April, 1973), 65.

_____. "There Came a Day at Summer's Full"
Mother Mary Anthony, "Emily Dickinson's Scriptural Echoes," MR, 2
(Spring, 1961), 557-561.

Caroline Hogue, <u>Expl</u>, 11 (Dec., 1952), 17.
   Rpt. <u>The Explicator Cyclopedia</u>, I, pp. 78-79.

William Howard, <u>Expl</u>, 12 (April, 1954), 41.
   Rpt. <u>The Explicator Cyclopedia</u>, I, pp. 80-81.

_____. "There Is No Frigate Like a Book"
Perrine, <u>Sound and Sense</u>, p. 32.
   Rpt. second edition, p. 38.

_____. "There's A Certain Slant of Light"
George Monteiro, <u>Expl</u>, 31 (Oct., 1972), 13.

Elizabeth F. Perlmutter, "Hide and Seek: Emily Dickinson's Use of the
Existential Sentence," <u>Lang&S</u>, 10 (Spring, 1977), 110-114.

Laurence Perrine, <u>Expl</u>, 11 (May, 1953), 50.
   Rpt. <u>The Explicator Cyclopedia</u>, I, p. 80.

_____. "These Are the Days When Birds Come Back"
George Arms, <u>Expl</u>, 2 (Feb., 1944), 29.
   Rpt. <u>The Explicator Cyclopedia</u>, I, pp. 80-81.

Robert L. Berner, <u>Expl</u>, 30 (May, 1972), 78.

Marshall Van Deusen, <u>Expl</u>, 12 (April, 1954), 40.
   Rpt. <u>The Explicator Cyclopedia</u>, I, pp. 81-82.

_____. "This Consciousness That Is Aware"
Charles R. Anderson, "The Conscious Self in Emily Dickinson's Poetry,"
<u>AL</u>, 31 (Nov., 1959), 304-305.

_____. "This Was a Poet"
George E. Fortenberry, <u>Expl</u>, 35 (Spring, 1977), 26-27.

_____. "Those Not Live Yet"
Dorothy Waugh, <u>Expl</u>, 15 (Jan., 1957), 22.
   Rpt. <u>The Explicator Cyclopedia</u>, I, pp. 82-83.

_____. "The Thought Beneath So Slight a Film"
James E. White, "Emily Dickinson: Metaphysician and Miniaturist," <u>CEA</u>,
29 (March, 1967), 17-18

_____. "The Tint I Cannot Take Is Best"
Sr. Ellen Fitzgerald, <u>Expl</u>, 28 (Nov, 1969), 29.

_____. "Title Divine Is Mine"
Eunice Glenn, "Emily Dickinson's Poetry: A Revaluation," <u>SR</u>, 51 (Autumn,
1943), 578-580.

Laurence Perrine, "Dickinson Distorted," <u>CE</u>, 36 (Oct., 1974), 213.

_____. "To Hear an Oriole Sing"
B. J. Rogers, "The Truth Told Slant: Emily Dickinson's Poetic Mode,"
<u>TSLL</u>, 14 (Summer, 1972), 331-332.

_____. "To Lose One's Faith"
Friedman and McLaughlin, <u>Poetry: An Introduction to Its Form and Art</u>,
pp. 47-48, 75-76, 120-121.

_____. "To Undertake Is to Achieve"
Richard B. Sewall, Expl, 6 (June, 1948), 51.
    Rpt. The Explicator Cyclopedia, I, pp. 83-84.

_____. "'Twas Like a Maelstrom, with a Notch"
Dickinson, Suggestions for Teachers of "Introduction to Literature,"
fifth edition, ed. Locke, Gibson, and Arms, 34.   (Teacher's Manual)

Martha Fodaski, Expl, 19 (Jan., 1961), 24.
    Rpt. The Explicator Cyclopedia, I, pp. 84-86.

Myron Ochshorn, "In Search of Emily Dickinson," New Mexico Quarterly
Review, 23 (Spring, 1953), 103-106.

_____. "'Twas Warm at First Like Us"
Winters, Forms of Discovery, pp. 268-269.

_____. "Two Butterflies Went Out at Noon"
Frederick Asals, "Dickinson's 'Two Butterflies Went Out at Noon," ESQ,
No. 63 (Spring, 1971), 29-31.

Laurence Perrine, "The Importance of Tone in the Interpretation of Literature," CE, 24 (Feb., 1963), 390.
    Rpt. The Art of Total Relevance, pp. 20-21.

_____. "Water Makes Many Beds"
James S. Mullican, Expl, 27 (Nov., 1968), 23.

_____. "We play at Paste--"
Norman Talbot, "The Child, the Actress, and Miss Emily Dickinson," The
Southern Review (Australia), 5 (June, 1972), 107.

_____. "We Should Not Mind So Small a Flower"
Kenneth B. Newell, Expl, 19 (June, 1961), 65.

_____. "What Care the Dead, for Chanticleer"
Rebecca Patterson, "The Cardinal Points of Symbolism of Emily Dickinson,"
MQ, 14 (Summer, 1973), 308.

_____. "What Soft Cherubic Creatures"
Brooks, Lewis, and Warren, American Literature, p. 1241.

Robert Franicevich, Expl, 35 (Fall, 1976), 5-6.

Nancy Lenz Harvey, Expl, 28 (Oct., 1969), 17.

Dwight H. Purdy, Expl, 33 (April, 1975), 67.

_____. "When I Hoped I Feared"
Wilson O. Clough, Expl, 10 (Nov., 1951), 10.
    Rpt. The Explicator Cyclopedia, I, pp. 86-87.

Caroline Hogue, Expl, 10 (May, 1952), 49.
    Rpt. The Explicator Cyclopedia, I, pp. 87-88.

_____. "Where Ships of Purple Gently Toss"
Laurence Perrine, "The Nature of Proof in the Interpretation of Poetry,"
EJ, 51 (Sept., 1962), 394-396.
    Rpt. The Art of Total Relevance, pp. 12-14, 18.

_____. "A Wife--at Daybreak I Shall Be"
Norman Talbot, "The Child, the Actress, and Miss Emily Dickinson," The
Southern Review (Australia), 5 (June, 1972), 111.

_____. "Wild Nights--Wild Nights"
James T. Connelly, Expl, 25 (Jan., 1967), 44.

Christ of Wegelin, Expl, 26 (Nov., 1967), 25.

Suzanne M. Wilson, "Emily Dickinson and the Twentieth-Century Poetry of
Sensibility," AL, 36 (Nov., 1964), 353-354.

_____. "The Wind Drew Off"
Connie M. Doyle, "Emily Dickinson's 'The Wind Drew Off,'" ELN, 12 (March,
1975), 182-184.

_____. "The Wind--Tapped Like a Tired Man"
Virginia Ogden Birdsall, "Emily Dickinson's Intruder in the Soul," AL, 37
(March, 1965), 60-61.

_____. "Wonder Is Not Precisely Knowing"
Friar and Brinnin, Modern Poetry, pp. 456-457.

_____. "You're Right--'The Way Is Narrow'"
Vivian R. Pollack, "'That Fine Prosperity': Economic Metaphors in Emily
Dickinson's Poetry," MLQ, 34 (June, 1973), 167.

_____. "Your Riches--Taught Me--Poverty"
Vivain R. Pollack, "'That Fine Prosperity': Economic Metaphors in Emily
Dickinson's Poetry," MLQ, 34 (June, 1973), 174-175.

DODGSON. "Jabberwocky"
Ciardi, How Does a Poem Mean? pp. 705-709.

Charles S. Tuckerman, Expl, 31 (Nov., 1972), 16.

DONNE. "Aire and Angels"
John M. Couper and William D. McGaw, "Aire and Angels," AN&Q, 15
(April, 1977), 104-106.

William Empson, "Donne the Space Man," The Kenyon Review, 19 (Summer,
1957), 381-389.

Gardner, The Business of Criticism, pp. 62-75.

Frank L. Huntley, Expl, 6 (June, 1948), 53.
   Rpt. The Explicator Cyclopedia, II, p. 97.

Katherine Mauch, "Angel Imagery and Neoplatonic Love in Donne's 'Air and
Angels,'" SCN, 35 (Winter, 1977), 106-111.

Kerby Neill, Expl, 6 (Nov., 1947), 8.
   Rpt. The Explicator Cyclopedia, II, pp. 96-97.

Murray Prosky, Expl, 27 (Dec., 1968), 27.

A. J. Smith, "New Bearings in Donne: 'Aire and Angels,'" English, 13
(Summer, 1960), 49-53.

Martin Turnell, "John Donne and the Quest for Unity," Nineteenth Century,
147 (April, 1950), 266-267.

Unger, The Man in the Name, pp. 64-67.
  Rpt. from Donne's Poetry and Modern Criticism (Chicago: Regnery, 1950), pp. 42-44.

Unger and O'Connor, Poems for Study, pp. 119-121.

Wanamaker, Discordia Concors, pp. 16-17.

George Williamson, "Textual Difficulties in the Interpretation of Donne's Poetry," MP, 38 (August, 1940), 42-45.

Williamson, The Proper Wit of Poetry, p. 34.

_____. "The Anniversarie" ("All Kings, and all their favorites")
Ferry, All in War with Time, pp. 101-106.

Dickinson, Suggestions for Teachers of "Introduction to Literature," fifth edition, ed. Locke, Gibson, and Arms, p. 6.   (Teacher's Manual)

Peterson, The English Lyric from Wyatt to Donne, pp. 329-330.

Frank J. Warnke, Expl, 16 (Nov., 1957), 12.
  Rpt. The Explicator Cyclopedia, II, pp. 97-98.

Williamson, The Proper Wit of Poetry, p. 36.

_____. "The Anniversaries"   see also "The First Anniversary" "The Second Anniversary"
Richard E. Hughes, "The Woman in Donne's Anniversaries," ELH, 34 (March, 1967), 307-326.

Patrick Mahony, "The Anniversaries: Donne's Rhetorical Approach to Evil," JEGP, 68 (July, 1969), 407-413.

Dennis Quinn, "Donne's Anniversaries as Celebration," SEL, 9 (Winter, 1969), 97-105.

George Williamson, "The Design of Donne's Anniversaries," MP, 60 (Feb., 1963), 188-191.

_____. "The Apparition"
Robert G. Collmer, "Another Look at 'The Apparition,'" CP, 7 (Fall, 1974), 34-40.

Empson, Seven Types of Ambiguity, pp. 184-186; (1947 ed.), 146-147.

William Everson, Expl, 4 (June, 1946), 56.
  Rpt. The Explicator Cyclopedia, II, p. 99.

Stanley Friedman, Expl, 30 (Oct., 1971), 15.

Allan H. Gilbert, Expl, 4 (June, 1946), 56.
  Rpt. The Explicator Cyclopedia, II, p. 99.

Donald L. Guss, "Donne's Petrarchism," JEGP, 64 (Jan., 1965), 17-28.

C. William Miller and Dan S. Norton, Expl, 4 (Feb., 1946), 24.
  Rpt. The Explicator Cyclopedia, II, pp. 98-99.

Laurence Perrine, "On Donne's 'The Apparition,'" CP, 9 (Sring, 1976), 21-24.

"At the Round Earth's Imagin'd Corners Blow" see "Holy Sonnet 1"
"The Autumnall" see "Elegy 9"
_____. "The Blossom"
Brooks and Warren, Understanding Poetry, revised edition, pp. 247-250.

Silvia Ruffo-Fiore, "The Unwanted Heart in Petrarch and Donne," CL, 24 (Fall, 1972), 321-324.

Tillyard, The Metaphysicals and Milton, pp. 14-20.

"Batter my heart, three person'd God" see "Holy Sonnet 14"

"The Bracelet" see "Elegy 11"

_____. "The Broken Heart"
Silvia Ruffo-Fiore, "The Unwanted Heart in Petrarch and Donne," CL, 24 (Fall, 1972), 324-327.

G. R. Wilson, Jr., "The Interplay of Perception and Reflection: Mirror Imagery in Donne's Poetry," SEL, 9 (Winter, 1969), 116-117.

_____. "The Calme"
Linda Mizejewski, "Darkness and Disproportion: A Study of Donne's 'Storme' and 'Calme,'" JEGP, 76 (April, 1977), 226-230.

B. F. Nellist, "Donne's 'Storm' and 'Calm' and the Description Tradition," MLR, 59 (Oct., 1964), 511-515.

Carolyn H. Reeves, Expl, 32 (Sept., 1973), 3.

Gary Storhoff, "Metaphors of Despair in Donne's 'The Storme' and 'The Calme,'" CP, 9 (Fall, 1976), 44-45.

_____. "The Canonization"
John Bernard, "Orthodoxia Epidemica: Donne's Poetics and 'A Valediction of My Name in the Window,'" SAQ, 71 (Summer, 1972), 382-383.

Frances Bridges Carleton, The Dramatic Monologue: Vox Humana, Salzburg Studies in English Literature, No. 64 (Salzburg, Austria: Institut für Englische Sprache und Litteratur, 1977), pp. 68-69.

Cleanth Brooks, "The Language of Paradox," in The Language of Poetry, ed. Allen Tate, pp. 46-61.
    Rpt. Criticism, pp. 361-365.

Brooks, The Well Wrought Urn, pp. 10-17.
    Rpt. Critiques, pp. 71-76. Abridged in The Case for Poetry, p. 113.
    Rpt. American Literary Criticism, pp. 523-538.

A. B. Chambers, "The Fly in Donne's 'Canonization,'" JEGP, 65 (April, 1966), 252-259.

A. R. Cirillo, "The Fair Hermaphrodite: Love Union in the Poetry of Donne and Spenser," SEL, 9 (Winter, 1969), 93-94.

John A. Clair, "Donne's 'The Canonization,'" PMLA, 80 (June, 1965), 300-302.

Carvel Collins, Expl, 12 (Oct., 1953), 3.
    Rpt. The Explicator Cyclopedia, II, pp. 99-100.

Fernand Corin, "A Note on Donne's 'Canonization,'" ES, 50 (Feb., 1969), 89-93.

Daiches and Charvat, Poems in English, pp. 657-658.

Ferry, All in War with Time, pp. 113-125.

Donald L. Guss, "Donne's Petrarchism," JEGP, 64 (Jan., 1965), 17-28.

Kremen, The Imagination of the Resurrection, pp. 105-107.

Krieger, The New Apologists for Poetry, pp. 13-18.

Albert C. Labriola, "Donne's 'The Canonization': Its Theological Context and Its Religious Imagery," HLQ, 36 (Aug., 1973), 327-339.

Pierre Legouis, abridged in The Case for Poetry, pp. 112-113 from Donne The Craftsman (Paris: Henry Didier, 1928), pp. 55-61.

William H. Matchett, "Donne's 'Peece of Chronicle,'" RES, 18 (Aug., 1967), 290-292.

McCanles, Dialectical Criticism, pp. 63-66.

Peckham and Chatman, Word, Meaning, Poem, pp. 126-139.

William J. Rooney, "'The Canonization'--the Language of Paradox Reconsidered," ELH, 23 (March, 1956), 36-47.

Lewis Sawin, Expl, 13 (March, 1955), 31.
    Rpt. The Explicator Cyclopedia, II, p. 100.

Unger, The Man in the Name, pp. 49-53.
    Rpt. from Donne's Poetry and Modern Criticism (Chicago: Regnery, 1950), pp. 26-30.

G. R. Wilson, Jr., "The Interplay of Perception and Reflection: Mirror Imagery in Donne's Poetry," SEL, 9 (Winter, 1969), 113-115.
    "Change." see "Elegy 3"
_____. "Communitie"
William Rockett, "Donne's Libertine Rhetoric," ES, 52 (Dec., 1971), 511.

Silvia Ruffo-Fiore, "Donne's 'Parody' of the Petrarchan Lady," CLS, 9 (Dec., 1972), 401-402.

Unger, The Man in the Name, pp. 63-64.
    Rpt. from Donne's Poetry and Modern Criticism (Chicago: Regnery, 1950), pp. 41-42.

Elizabeth L. Wiggins, "Logic in the Poetry of John Donne," SP, 42 (Jan., 1945), 54; 58.

_____. "The Computation"
Lee Ball, Jr., Expl, 8 (April, 1950), 44.
    Rpt. The Explicator Cyclopedia, II, pp. 100-101.

Floyd E. Eddleman, Expl, (April, 1972), 71.

_____. "Confined Love"
Carol Marks Sicherman, "The Mocking Voices of Donne and Marvell," BuR, 17 (May, 1969), 35-36.

_____. "The Cross"
William Empson, "Donne the Space Man," The Kenyon Review, 19 (Summer, 1957), 379-380.

George Williamson, "Textual Difficulties in the Interpretation of Donne's Poetry," MP, 38 (Aug., 1940), 64-66.

_____. "Crucyfying"
Edgar F. Daniels, Expl, 30 (Nov., 1971), 25.

_____. "The Curse"
Robert A. Bryan, "John Donne's Use of the Anathema," JEGP, 61 (April, 1962), 310.

_____. "The Dampe"
Gerald Gallant and A. L. Clements, "Harmonized Voices in Donne's 'Songs and Sonets': 'The Dampe,'" SEL, 15 (Winter, 1975), 71-82.
    "Death be not proud" see "Holy Sonnet 10"
_____. "The Dissolution"
Jay Arnold Levine, "'The Dissolution': Donne's Twofold Elegy," ELH, 28 (Dec., 1961), 301-315.

_____. "The Dreame" (From Songs and Sonnets)
Partridge, The Language of Renaissance Poetry, pp. 245-248.

"The Dreame" see "Elegy 10"

_____. "The Ecstasy"
Adams, Strains of Discord, pp. 108-109.

Adams, The Contexts of Poetry, pp. 79-80.

Robert J. Bauer, "The Great Prince in Donne's 'The Extasie,'" TSL, 14 (1969), 93-100.

Brower, The Fields of Light, pp. 79-83.

John Carey, "Notes on Two of Donne's Songs and Sonets," RES, 16 (Feb., 1965), 50-53.

Frances Bridges Carleton, The Dramatic Monologue: Vox Humana, Salzburg Studies in English Literature No. 64 (Salzburg, Austria: Institut für Englische Sprache und Litteratur, 1977), pp. 66-68.

A. R. Cirillo, "The Fair Hermaphrodite: Love Union in the Poetry of Donne and Spenser," SEL, 9 (Winter, 1969), 90-92.

Frank A. Doggett, "Donne's Platonism," SR, 42 (July-Sept., 1934), 284-290.

William Empson, "Donne the Space Man," The Kenyon Review, 19 (Summer, 1957), 368-369.

Empson, English Pastoral Poetry, pp. 132-136.

Rene Graziani, "John Donne's 'The Extasie' and Ecstasy," RES, 19 (May, 1968), 121-136.

Merrit Y. Hughes, "Some of Donne's 'Ecstasies,'" PMLA, 75 (Dec., 1960), 509-518.

Susan C. Kemper, Expl, 35 (Winter, 1976), 2-3.

Kremen, The Imagination of the Resurrection, pp. 99-103.

Barbara K. Lewalski, "A Donnean Perspective on 'The Exstasie,'" ELN, 10 (June, 1973), 258-262.

Arthur F. Marotti, "Donne and 'The Extasie,'" in The Rhetoric of Renaissance Poetry, pp. 140-173.

John Marshall, "The Extasie," Hound and Horn, 3 (Oct.-Dec., 1929), 121-124.

McCanles, Dialectical Criticism, pp. 67-69.

Michael McCanles, "Distinguish in Order to Unite: Donne's 'The Extasie,'" SEL, 6 (Winter, 1966), 59-75.

Elizabeth McLaughlin, "'The Extasie'--Deceptive or Authentic?" BuR, 18 (Winter, 1970), 55-78.

Miner, The Metaphysical Mode from Donne to Cowley, pp. 76-83, 171-172.

Charles Mitchell, "Donne's 'The Extasie': Love's Sublime Knot," SEL, 8 (Winter, 1968), 91-101.

Charlotte F. Otten, Expl, 32 (April, 1974), 58.

M. K. Paffard, Expl, 22 (Oct., 1963), 13.

G. R. Potter, "Donne's Extasie, Contra Legouis," PQ, 15 (July, 1936), 247-253.

C. Schaar, "'Balme' in Donne's 'Extasie,'" ES, 53 (June, 1972); 224-225.

Raman Selden, "John Donne's 'Incarnational Conviction,'" CritQ, 17 (Spring, 1975), 61-64.

Spitzer, A Method of Interpreting Literature, pp. 5-21.
    Rpt. Essays on English and American Poetry by Leo Spitzer, pp. 142-153.

Thomas R. Thornburg, "Donne's The Extasie: a Definition of Love," BSUF, 11 (Autumn, 1970), 66-69.

Tillyard, The Metaphysicals and Milton, pp. 79-84.

Martin Turnell, "John Donne and the Quest for Unity," Nineteenth Century, 147 (April, 1950), 267-268.

Wheelwright, The Burning Fountain, pp. 72-73.

George Williamson, "Textual Difficulties in the Interpretation of Donne's Poetry," MP, 38 (Aug., 1940), 55-58.

G. R. Wilson, Jr., "The Interplay of Perception and Reflection: Mirror Imagery in Donne's Poetry," SEL, 9 (Winter, 1969), 111-113.

_____. Elegy 1 "Jealosie"
Alan Armstrong, "The Apprenticeship of John Donne: Ovid and the 'Elegies,'" ELH, 44 (Fall, 1977), 426-427.

_____. Elegy 3 "Change"
William Rockett, "John Donne: The Ethical Argument of Elegy III," SEL, 15 (Winter, 1975), 57-69.

_____. Elegy 4 "The Perfume"
Miner, The Metaphysical Mode from Donne to Cowley, pp. 223-231.

Arthur Minton, Expl, 4 (May, 1946), 50.
    Rpt. The Explicator Cyclopedia, II, p. 116.

Henry Ten Enck Perry, Expl, 5 (Nov., 1956), 10.
    Rpt. The Explicator Cyclopedia, II, pp. 116-117.

Carol Marks Sicherman, "The Mocking Voices of Donne and Marvell," BuR, 17 (May, 1969), 37-38.

_____. Elegy 5 "His Picture"
Helen L. Gardner, "John Donne: A Note on Elegie V, 'His Picture,'" MLR, 39 (Oct., 1944), 333-337.

_____. Elegy 7 "Natures Lay Ideot, I Taught Thee to Love"
Edgar F. Daniels and Wanda J. Dean, Expl, 24 (Dec., 1965), 34.

_____. Elegy 9 "The Autumnall"
Alan Armstrong, "The Apprenticeship of John Donne: Ovid and the 'Elegies,'" ELH, 44 (Fall, 1977), 435-439.

Carol Marks Sicherman, "Dionne's Discoveries," SEL, 11 (Spring, 1971), 74-78.

_____. Elegy 10 "The Dream"
Fredson T. Bowers, "An Interpretation of Donne's Tenth Elegy," MLN, 54 (April, 1939), 280-282.

Seymour Chatman, "Mr. Stein on Donne," in Discussions of Poetry: Rhythm and Sound, ed. George Hemphill (Boston: D. C. Heath and Company, 1961), pp. 95-98.

Partridge, <u>The Language of Renaissance Poetry</u>, pp. 242-245.

Elias Schwartz, <u>Expl</u>, 19 (June, 1961), 67.
   Rpt. <u>The Explicator Cyclopedia</u>, II, pp. 101-102.

Arnold Stein, "Structures of Sound in Donne's Verse," <u>The Kenyon Review</u>, 13 (Spring, 1951), 261-264.
   Rpt. in part, "Donne's Prosody," in <u>Discussions of Poetry: Rhythm and Sound</u>, ed. George Hemphill (Boston: D. C. Heath and Company, 1961), pp. 92-94.

_____. Elegy 11 "The Bracelet"
Alan Armstrong, "The Apprenticeship of John Donne: Ovid and the 'Elegies,'" <u>ELH</u>, 44 (Fall, 1977), 427-430.

Robert A. Bryan, "John Donne's Use of the Anathema," <u>JEGP</u>, 61 (April, 1962), 310-311.

William Rockett, "Donne's Libertine Rhetoric," <u>ES</u>, 52 (Dec., 1971), 514-517.

Edwin Thumboo, <u>Expl</u>, 27 (Oct., 1968), 14.

Elegy 12   see HA's file

_____. Elegy 14 "A Tale of a Citizen and His Wife"
Robin Skelton, "The Poetry of John Donne," in <u>Elizabethan Poetry</u>, pp. 205-207.

_____. Elegy 15 "The Expostulation"
Robert A. Bryan, "John Donne's Use of the Anathema," <u>JEGP</u>, 61 (April, 1962), 311-312.

Arthur W. Pitts, Jr., "Proverbs as Testimony in Donne's Style," in <u>Essays in Honor of Esmond Linworth Marilla</u>, pp. 49-51.

_____. Elegy 17 "Variety"
Peterson, <u>The English Lyric from Wyatt to Donne</u>, pp. 307-321.

_____. Elegy 18 "Loves Progress"
Edgar F. Daniels, <u>Expl</u>, 35 (Summer, 1977), 2-3.

Roberts W. French, <u>Expl</u>, 34 (Sept., 1975), 5.

William Rockett, "Donne's Libertine Rhetoric," <u>ES</u>, 52 (Dec., 1971), 513.

Robin Skelton, "The Poetry of John Donne," in <u>Elizabethan Poetry</u>, pp. 207-209.

_____. Elegy 19 "To His Mistress Going to Bed"
Edgar F. Daniels, <u>Expl</u>, 33 (May, 1975), 71.

Jonathan E. Deitz, <u>Expl</u>, 32 (Jan., 1974), 36.

William Empson, "Donne the Space Man," <u>The Kenyon Review</u>, 19 (Summer, 1957), 362-367.

Richard F. Giles, <u>Expl</u>, 33 (May, 1975), 71.

E. R. Gregory, Jr., "The Balance of Parts: Imagistic Unity in Donne's 'Elegie XIX,'" <u>The University of Kansas City Review</u>, 35 (Autumn, 1968), 51-54.

Philip K. Jason, <u>Expl</u>, 34 (Oct., 1975), 14.

Harold Love, <u>Expl</u>, 26 (Dec., 1967), 33.

W. W. Main, Expl, 10 (Nov., 1951), 14.
    Rpt. The Explicator Cyclopedia, II, pp. 102-103.

Robin Skelton, "The Poetry of John Donne," in Elizabethan Poetry,
pp. 209-210.

_____. Elegy 20 "Loves Warre"
Alan Armstrong, "The Apprenticeship of John Donne: Ovid and the 'Elegies,'" ELH, 44 (Fall, 1977), 421-426.

_____. "Elegy on the Lady Marckham"
W. M. Lebans, "The Influence of the Classics in Donne's Epicedes and
Obsequies," RES, 23 (May, 1972), 128.

_____. "Elegy on the L. C."
Miles, The Primary Langauge of Poetry in the 1640's, pp. 90-92.

_____. "Elegy on Mistress Boulstred"
Tuve, Elizabethan and Metaphysical Imagery, pp. 201-202.

_____. "Elegie Upon the Untimely Death of the Incomparable Prince Henry"
Charlotte F. Otten, Expl, 33 (March, 1975), 59.

Leonard D. Tourney, "Convention and Wit in Donne's Elegie on Prince
Henry," SP, 71 (Oct., 1974), 473-483.

Ruth C. Wallerstein, "Rhetoric in the English Renaissance: Two Elegies,"
English Institute Essays, 1948, pp. 166-170.

_____. "Epithalamion Made at Lincolnes Inne"
Heather Dubrow Ousby, Expl, 32 (Feb., 1974), 49.

Virginia Tufte, The Poetry of Marriage: The Epithalamium in Europe and
Its Development in England (Los Angeles: Tinnon-Brown, 1970), 218-222.

_____. "Farewell to Love"
Katherine T. Emerson, "Two Problems in Donne's 'Farewell to Love,'" MLN,
72 (Feb., 1957), 93-95.

Helen Gardner, "A Crux in Donne," TLS, June 10, 1949, p. 381.

Leslie Hotson, "A Crux in Donne," TLS, April 16, 1949, p. 249.

J. C. Maxwell, "A Crux in Donne," TLS, May 6, 1949, p. 297.

Marvin Morillo, "Donne's 'Farewell to Love': The Force of Shutting Up,"
TSE, 13 (1963), 33-40.

D. F. Rauber, "Donne's 'Farewell to Love': a Crux Revisited," CP, 3
(Fall, 1970), 51-63.

George Williamson, "Donne's 'Farewell to Love,'" MP, 36 (Feb., 1939),
301-303.
    Cf. ibid, 38 (August, 1940), 39-41.

_____. "A Fever"
Unger, The Man in the Name, pp. 74-75.
    Rpt. from Donne's Poetry and Modern Criticism (Chicago: Regnery,
    1950), pp. 54-55.

_____. "The First Anniversary" ("An Anatomy of the World") see also "The Anniversar

Raymond A. Anselment, "'Ascensio Mendax, Descensio Crudelis': The Image of Babel in the Anniversaries," ELH, 38 (June, 1971), 192-198.

Antony F. Bellette, "Art and Imitation in Donne's Anniversaries," SEL, 15 (Winter, 1975), 86-88.

Marius Bewley, "Religious Cynicism in Donne's Poetry," The Kenyon Review, 14 (Autumn, 1952), 621-635.

Cruttwell, The Shakespearean Moment, pp. 73-94.

Leonard Dean, English Masterpieces, Vol, III, Renaissance Poetry, p. 13.

Ruth A. Fox, "Donne's 'Anniversaries' and the Art of Living," ELH, 38 (Dec., 1971), 532-538.

Ernest B. Gilman, The Curious Perspective: Literary and Pictorial Wit in the Seventeenth Century (New Haven and London: Yale Univ. Press, 1978), pp. 179-183.

Hardison, The Enduring Monument, pp. 170-179.

Harold Love, "The Argument of Donne's First Anniversary," MP, 64 (Nov., 1966), 121-131.

L. L. Martz, "John Donne in Meditation," ELH, 14 (Dec., 1947), 248-262.

Martz, The Poetry of Meditation, pp. 221-231.

Miner, The Metaphysical Mode from Donne to Cowley, pp. 63-69, 182-186.

Nicolson, The Breaking of the Circle, pp. 65-104.

Paul A. Parrish, Expl, 33 (April, 1975), 64.

I. A. Richards, "The Interaction of Words," in The Language of Poetry, ed. Allen Tate, pp. 75-87.
    Rpt. Modern Literary Criticism, pp. 85-93.

Carol M. Sicherman, "Donne's Timeless Anniversaries," UTQ, 39 (Jan., 1970), 129-133.

P. G. Stanwood, "'Essentiall Joye' in Donne's Anniversaries," TSLL, 13 (Summer, 1971), 227-238.

Wanamaker, Discordia Concors, pp. 26-28.

Elizabeth L. Wiggins, "Logic in the Poetry of John Donne," SP, 42 (Jan., 1945), 52-54 et passim.

Beaty and Matchett, Poetry: From Statement to Meaning, pp. 81-84.

_____. "The Flea"
H. David Brumble III, "John Donne's 'The Flea': Some Implications of the Enclyclopedic and Poetic Flea Traditions," CritQ, 15 (Summer, 1973), 147-154.

Toshihiko Kawasaki, "Donne's Microcosm," in Seventeenth-Century Imagery: Essays on Uses of Figurative Language from Donne to Farquhar, ed. Earl Miner (Berkeley: Univ. of California Press, 1971), pp. 33-34.

Patricia Meyer Spacks, "In Search of Sincerity," CE, 29 (May, 1968), 593-594.

Tuve, Elizabethan and Metaphysical Imagery, pp. 172-173.

Unger, The Man in the Name, pp. 79-80.
    Rpt. from Donne's Poetry and Modern Criticism (Chicago: Regnery, 1950).

_____. "The Funeral Elegie"
Adams, Strains of Discord, p. 109.

J. E. V. Crofts, "John Donne," Essays and Studies, 22 (1936), 141-142.

Kilby, Poetry and Life, p. 160.

Stauffer, The Nature of Poetry, pp. 86-87.

Allen Tate, "Poetry and the Absolute," SR, 35 (Jan., 1927), 41-48.

Ruth A. Fox, "Donne's 'Anniversaries' and the Art of Living," ELH, 38 (Dec., 1971), 530-532.

Paul A. Parrish, "Donne's 'A Funerall Elegie,'" PLL, 11 (Winter, 1975), 83-87. "Go and Catch a Falling Star" see "Song..."
"Going to Bed" See "Elegy 19"

_____. "Good Friday, 1613. Riding Westward"
Rosalie Beck, "A Precedent for Donne's Imagery in 'Good Friday, 1613, Riding Westward,'" RES, 19 (May, 1968), 166-169.

Anthony F. Bellette, "'Little Worlds Made Cunningly,': Significant Form in Donne's Holy Sonnets and 'Goodfriday, 1613,'" SP, 72 (July, 1975), 342-347.

W. Nelson Francis, Expl, 13 (Feb., 1955), 21.
    Rpt. The Explicator Cyclopedia, II, pp. 103-104.

Donald M. Friedman, "Memory and the Art of Salvation in Donne's Good Friday Poem," ELR, 3 (Autumn, 1973), 418-442.

Jonathan Goldberg, "Donne's Journey East: Aspects of a Seventeenth-Century Trope," SP, 68 (July, 1971), 470-483.

George Herman, Expl, 14 (June, 1956), 60.
    Rpt. The Explicator Cyclopedia, II, pp. 104-105.

Kremen, The Imagination of the Resurrection, pp. 114-115.

Martz, The Poetry of Meditation, pp. 54-56.

Rosenthal and Smith, Exploring Poetry, pp. 479-483.

Carol Marks Sicherman, "Donne's Discoveries," SEL, 11 (Spring, 1971), 69-74.

George Williamson, "Textual Difficulties in the Interpretation of Donne's Poetry," MP, 38 (August, 1940), 66-69.

_____. "The Good Morrow"
Brooks, Purser, and Warren, An Approach to Literature, third edition, pp. 374-376.
    Rpt. fourth edition, pp. 366-368.

Daiches and Charvat, Poems in English, pp. 656-657.

Dickinson, Suggestions for Teachers of "Introduction to Literature," fifth edition, ed. Locke, Gibson, and Arms, p. 5. (Teacher's Manual)

William Empson, "Donne the Space Man," The Kenyon Review, 19 (Summer, 1957), 358-362.

Ferry, All in War with Time, pp. 71-78.

Dennis Grunes, "John Donne's 'The Good-Morrow,'" AI, 33 (Fall, 1976), 261-265.

Myrl G. Jones, Expl, 33 (Jan., 1975), 37.

Toshihiko Kawasaki, "Donne's Microcosm," in Seventeenth-Century Imagery: Essays on Uses of Figurative Language from Donne to Farquhar, ed. Earl Miner (Berkeley: Univ. of California Press, 1971), p. 28.

William E. Morris, "Donne's Use of Enallage in 'The Good-Morrow,'" AN&Q, 11 (Oct., 1972), 19-20.

Alfred W. Satterthwaite, Expl, 34 (March, 1976), 50.

Robin Skelton, "The Poetry of John Donne," in Elizabethan Poetry, pp. 212-216.

James Smith, "On Metaphysical Poetry," Scrutiny, II (Dec., 1933), 229-230.

Unger, The Man in the Name, pp. 46-49.
    Rpt. from Donne's Poetry and Modern Criticism (Chicago: Regnery, 1950).

G. R. Wilson, Jr., "The Interplay of Perception and Reflection: Mirror Imagery in Donne's Poetry," SEL, 9 (Winter, 1969), 109-111.
"His Parting from Her" see HA's file "His Picture" see "Elegy 5"

_____. "Holy Sonnets"
Douglas L. Peterson, John Donne's Holy Sonnets and the Anglican Doctrine of Contrition," SP, 56 (July, 1959), 504-518.

_____. "Holy Sonnet" 1: "Thou Hast Made Me, and Shall Thy Work Decay?"
Antony F. Bellette, "'Little Worlds Made Cunningly': Significant Form in Donne's Holy Sonnets and 'Goodfriday, 1613,'" SP, 72 (July, 1975), 334-335, 337.

Philip C. McGuire, "Private Prayer and English Poetry in the Early Seventeenth Century," SEL, 14 (Winter, 1974), 67-68.

Elias Schwartz, "Mimesis and the Theory of Signs," CE, 29 (Feb., 1968), 351-352.

Yvor Winters, "The Poetry of Gerard Manley Hopkins (1)," HudR, 1 (Winter, 1948), 457-460.
    Rpt. The Function of Criticism, pp. 105-107.

_____. "Holy Sonnet" 2: "As Due By Many Titles I Resign"
Antony F. Bellette, "'Little Worlds Made Cunningly': Significant Form in Donne's Holy Sonnets and 'Goodfriday, 1613," SP, 72 (July, 1975), 328-330.

_____. "Holy Sonnet" 5: "I Am a Little World Made Cunningly"
Paul Delany, "Donne's Holy Sonnet V, Lines 13-14," AN&Q, 9 (Sept., 1970), 6-7.

William Empson, "Donne the Space Man," The Kenyon Review, 19 (Summer, 1957), 374-379.

Empson, English Pastoral Poetry, pp. 74-76.

_____. "Holy Sonnet" 6: "This Is My Play's Last Scene, Here Heavens Appoint"
Antony F. Bellette, "'Little Worlds Made Cunningly': Significant Form in Donne's Holy Sonnets and 'Goodfriday, 1613,'" SP, 72 (July, 1975), 335-337.

J. Max Patrick, Expl, 31 (Oct., 1972), 12.

Arthur W. Pitts, Jr., Expl, 29 (Jan., 1971), 39.

_____. "Holy Sonnet" 7: "At the Round Earth's Imagined Corners Blow"
Antony F. Bellette, "'Little Worlds Made Cunningly': Significant Form in Donne's Holy Sonnets and 'Goodfriday, 1613,'" SP, 72 (July, 1975), 336-337.

Brower, The Fields of Light, pp. 67-70.
    Rpt. Locke, Gibson, and Arms, Introduction to Literature, third edition, pp. 29-32.
    Rpt. fourth edition, pp. 27-30.
    Rpt. fifth edition, pp. 26-29.

Martz, The Poetry of Meditation, pp. 50-52.

David I. Masson, "Thematic Analysis of Sound in Poetry," in Essays on the Language of Literature, ed. Seymour Chatman and Samuel R. Levin (Boston: Houghton Mifflin Company, 1967), pp. 60-61.

Richards, Practical Criticism, pp. 42-51 et passim.

Stauffer, The Nature of Poetry, pp. 139-140.

_____. "Holy Sonnet" 8: "If Faithful Soules Be Alike Glorified"
M. E. Grenander, "Holy Sonnets VIII and XVII: John Donne," Boston University Studies in English, 4 (Summer, 1960), 96-100.

_____. "Holy Sonnet" 9: "If Poisonous Minerals, and If That Tree" *See also first line*
Stanley Archer, Expl, 30 (Sept., 1971), 4.

Martz, The Poetry of Meditation, p. 52.

_____. "Holy Sonnet" 10: "Death Be Not Proud, Though Some Have Called Thee"
Daniels, The Art of Reading Poetry, pp. 275-278.

Sanders, The Discovery of Poetry, pp. 352-354.

Elizabeth Ward, English "A" Analyst, No. 12, pp. 1-4.

_____. "Holy Sonnet" 11: "Spit in My Face Ye Jews, and Pierce My Side"
Antony F. Bellette, "'Little Worlds Made Cunningly,': Significant Form in Donne's Holy Sonnets and 'Goodfriday, 1613,'" SP, 72 (July, 1975), 340-341.

Martz, The Poetry of Meditation, pp. 49-50.

_____. "Holy Sonnet" 12: "Why Are We by All Creatures Waited On?"
M. E. Grenander, Expl, 13 (May, 1955), 42.
  Rpt. The Explicator Cyclopedia, II, pp. 105-106.

Martz, The Poetry of Meditation, pp. 53-54.

Arthur L. Simpson, Jr., Expl, 27 (May, 1969), 75.

_____. "Holy Sonnet" 13: "What If This Present Were the World's Last Night?"
Antony F. Bellette, "'Little Worlds Made Cunningly': Significant Form in Donne's Holy Sonnets and 'Goodfriday, 1613,'" SP, 72 (July, 1975), 339-340.

Empson, Seven Types of Ambiguity, pp. 183-184; (1947 ed.), pp. 145-146.

John E. Parish, Expl, 22 (Nov., 1963), 19.

_____. "Holy Sonnet" 14: "Batter My Heart, Three-Personed God; for, You"
Antony F. Bellette, "'Little Worlds Made Cunningly': Significant Form in Donne's Holy Sonnets and 'Goodfriday, 1613,'" SP, 72 (July, 1975), 330-331.

Arthur L. Clements, "Donne's Holy Sonnet XIV," MLN, 76 (June, 1961), 484-489.

David K. Cornelius, Expl, 24 (Nov., 1965), 25.

Drew, Poetry: A Modern Guide, pp. 58-60.

Michael Gregory, "A Theory of Stylistics--Exemplified: Donne's 'Holy Sonnet XIV,'" Lang&S, 7 (Spring, 1974), 108-118.

George Herman, Expl, 12 (Dec., 1953), 18.
  Rpt. The Explicator Cyclopedia, II, pp. 106-107.

Jerome, Poetry: Premeditated Art, pp. 301-302.

William Kerrigan, "The Fearful Accommodations of John Donne," ELR, 4 (Autumn, 1974), 351-356.

George Knox, Expl, 15 (Oct., 1956), 2.
    Rpt. The Explicator Cyclopedia, II, pp. 108-109.

Kremen, The Imagination of the Resurrection, pp. 108-110.

P. C. Levenson, Expl, 11 (March, 1953), 31.
    Rpt. The Explicator Cyclopedia, II, p. 106.

P. C. Levenson, Expl, 12 (April, 1954), 36.
    Rpt. The Explicator Cyclopedia, II, pp. 107-108.

William R. Mueller, "Donne's Adulterous Female Town," MLN, 76 (April, 1961), 312-314.

John E. Parish, "No. 14 of Donne's Holy Sonnets," CE, 24 (Jan, 1963), 299-302.

Lucio R. Ruotolo, "The Trinitarian Framework of Donne's Holy Sonnet XIV," JHI, 27 (July-Sept., 1966), 445-446.

Elias Schwartz, Expl, 26 (Nov., 1967), 27.

Stauffer, The Nature of Poetry, pp. 135-136.

Thomas J. Steele, Expl, 29 (May, 1971), 74.

Walsh, Doors into Poetry, pp. 59-60.

Mary Tenney Wanninger, Expl, 28 (Dec., 1969), 37.

_____. "Holy Sonnet" 16: "Father, Part of His Double Interest"
George Williamson, Textual Difficulties in the Interpretation of Donne's Poetry," MP, 38 (Aug., 1940), 62-64.

_____. "Holy Sonnet" 17: "Since She Whom I Loved Hath Paid Her Last Debt"
Eleanor Faulkner and Edgar F. Daniels, Expl, 34 (May, 1976), 68.

Helen Gardner, "Another Note on Donne: 'Since She Whom I Lov'd,'" MLR, 52 (Oct., 1957), 564-565.

M. E. Grenander, "Holy Sonnets VIII and XVII: John Donne," Boston University Studies in English, 4 (Summer, 1960), 100-105.

Harry Morris, "John Donne's Terrifying Pun," PLL, 9 (Spring, 1973), 133-135.

Tillyard, The Metaphysicals and Milton, pp. 4-7, 77-78.

_____. "Holy Sonnet" 18: "Show Me Dear Christ, Thy Spouse, So Bright and Clear"
Brower, The Fields of Light, pp. 24-25.

William Kerrigan, "The Fearful Accomodations of John Donne," ELR, 4 (Autumn, 1974), 356-360.

_____. "Holy Sonnet" 19: "Oh, to Vex Me, Contraries Meet in One:"
Antony F. Bellette, "'Little Worlds Made Cunningly': Significant Form in Donne's Holy Sonnets and 'Goodfriday, 1613,'" SP, 72 (July, 1975), 331-332.

Norman E. Carlson, Expl, 32 (Nov., 1973), 19.

McCanles, Dialectical Criticism, pp. 70-71.

_____. "A Hymn to Christ, at the Author's Last Going into Germany"
Harry Morris, "John Donne's Terrifying Pun," PLL, 9 (Spring, 1973), 135-136.

Philip C. McGuire, "Private Prayer and English Poetry in the Early Seventeenth Century," SEL, 14 (Winter, 1974), 71-72.

Partridge, The Language of Renaissance Poetry, pp. 255-258.

_____. "Hymn to God, My God, in My Sickness"
Don Cameron Allen, "John Donne's 'Paradise and Calvarie,'" MLN, 60 (June, 1945), 398-400.

Donald K. Anderson, Jr., "Donne's 'Hymne to God my God in my Sicknesse' and T-in-O Maps," SAQ, 71 (Autumn, 1972), 465-472.

Harry M. Campbell, "Donne's 'Hymn to God, My God, in My Sickness,'" CE, 5 (Jan., 1944), 192-196.
    Rpt. Readings for Liberal Education, II, 500-504.

Dickinson, Suggestions for Teachers of "Introduction to Literature," fifth edition, ed. Locke, Gibson, and Arms, p. 7. (Teacher's Manual)

Conrad Hilberry, "The First Stanza of Donne's 'Hymne to God My God, In My Sicknesse,'" N&Q, 4, n.s. (Aug., 1957), 336-337.

Kremen, The Imagination of the Resurrection, pp. 111-113.

Barbara K. Lewalski, "Typological Symbolism and the 'Progress of the Soul' in Seventeenth-Century Literature," in Literary Uses of Typology from the Late Middle Ages to the Present, pp. 86-87.

Terrence L. Lisbeth, Expl, 29 (April, 1971), 66.

Martz, The Poem of the Mind, pp. 40-43.

Wheeler, The Design of Poetry, pp. 192-195.

_____. "A Hymn to God the Father"
Philip C. McGuire," Private Prayer and English Poetry in the Early Seventeenth Century," SEL, 14 (Winter, 1974), 70-71.

Harry Morris, "John Donne's Terrifying Pun," PLL, 9 (Spring, 1973), 129-130, 136-137.

Kester Svendsen, Expl, II, (June, 1944), 62.
    Rpt. The Explicator Cyclopedia, II, pp. 109-110.

_____. "A Hymn to the Saints and to Marquis Hamilton"
Elizabeth L. Wiggins, "Logic in the Poetry of John Donne," SP, 42 (Jan., 1945), 44-45. "If Faithful Souls Be Alike Glorified" see "Holy Sonnet 8'

_____. "If Poisonous Minerals" See also "Holy Sonnet 9"
Brooks and Warren, Understanding Poetry, pp. 520-524. Revised edition, pp. 380-386.

_____. "The Indifferent"
Miner, The Metaphysical Mode from Donne to Cowley, pp. 15-18.

Silvia Ruffo-Fiore, "Donne's 'Parody' of the Petrarchan Lady," CLS, 9 (Dec., 1972), 402-405.

Williamson, The Proper Wit of Poetry, pp. 32-33.

_____. "A Jet Ring Sent"
Ray L. Armstrong, Expl, 30 (May, 1972), 77.

Edgar F. Daniels, Expl, 30 (May, 1972), 77.

Myrtle Pihlman Pope, Expl, 34 (Feb., 1976), 44.

Tuve, Elizabethan and Metaphysical Imagery, pp. 290-291.

Thomas J. Wertenbaker, Expl, 35 (Summer, 1977), 27-28.

_____. "La Corona"
A. B. Chambers, "The Meaning of the 'Temple' in Donne's La Corona,"
JEGP, 59 (April, 1960), 212-217.

_____. "Lecture upon the Shadow"
M. A. Goldberg, Expl, 14 (May, 1956), 50.
    Rpt. The Explicator Cyclopedia, II, p. 110.

Nat Henry, Expl, 20 (March, 1962), 60.
    Rpt. The Explicator Cyclopedia, II, pp. 111-112.

Frederick Kiley, "A Larger Reading of Donne's 'Lecture upon the Shadow,'"
CEA, 30 (April, 1968), 16-17.

McCanles, Dialectical Criticism, pp. 61-63.

Peter R. Moody, Expl, 20 (March, 1962), 60.
    Rpt. The Explicator Cyclopedia, II, pp. 112-113.

Olivia Murray Nichols, Expl, 32 (March, 1974), 52.

Laurence Perrine, Expl, 21 (Jan., 1963), 40.

John D. Russell, Expl, 27 (Nov., 1958), 9.
    Rpt. The Explicator Cyclopedia, II, pp. 110-111.

Unger, The Man in the Name, pp. 76-77.
    Rpt. from Donne's Poetry and Modern Criticism, (Chicago: Regnery,
    1950).

Van Doren, Introduction to Poetry, pp. 27-31.

_____. "The Legacie"
S. A. Cowan, Expl, 19 (May, 1961), 58.
    Rpt. The Explicator Cyclopedia, II, p. 113.

_____. "Letters to the Lady Carey and Mrs. Essex Riche, from Amyens"
Laurence Stapleton, "The Theme of Virtue in Donne's Verse Epistles," SP,
55 (April, 1958), 197-198.

_____. "The Litanie"
James E. Wellington, "The Litany in Cranmer and Donner," SP, 68 (April,
1971), 177-199.

_____. "Lovers Infinitenesse"
William Freedman, Expl, 31 (Sept., 1972), 6.

McCanles, Dialectical Criticism, pp. 59-61.

Dennis Quinn, "Donne and the Wane of Wonder," ELH, 36 (Dec., 1969), 634.

Stauffer, The Nature of Poetry, pp. 240-241.

Tillyard, The Metaphysicals and Milton, pp. 30-35.

Martin Turnell, "John Donne and the Quest for Unity," Nineteenth Century,
147 (April, 1950), 264.

_____. "Love's Alchemy"
Leslie A. Fiedler, "Archetype and Signature: A Study of the Relationship between Biography and Poetry," SR, 60 (Spring, 1952), 265-266.

W. A. Murray, "Donne and Paracelsus: An Essay in Interpretation," RES, 25 (April, 1949), 115–118.

Wanamaker, Discordia Concors, pp. 15–16.

_____. "Love's Deity"
John L. Sweeney, "Basic in Reading," The Kenyon Review, 5 (Winter, 1943), 55–59.

_____. "Love's Diet"
John V. Hagopian, Expl, 17 (Oct., 1958), 5.
    Rpt. The Explicator Cyclopedia, II, pp. 113–114.

Laurence Perrine, Expl, 35 (Spring, 1977), 20–21.

Unger, The Man in the Name, pp. 75–76.
    Rpt. from Donne's Poetry and Modern Criticism, (Chicago: Regnery, 1950), pp. 55-56.

_____. "Love's Growth"
Sr. Mary Alphones, O.P., Expl, 25 (Jan., 1967), 43.

John Bernard, "Orthodoxia Epidemica: Donne's Poetics and 'A Valediction of my Name in the Window,'" SAQ, 71 (Summer, 1972), pp. 380–381.

Alan Blankenship, Expl, 31 (May, 1973), 73.

Judy Z. Kronenfeld, "The Asymmetrical Arrangement of Donne's 'Love's Growth' as an Emblem of its Meaning," CP, 9 (Fall, 1976), 53–58.

Alan MacColl, "A Note on Donne's 'Loves Growth,'" ES, 56 (Aug., 1975), 314–315.

Peterson, The English Lyric from Wyatt to Donne, pp. 303–305.

Stephen D. Ring, Expl, 29 (March, 1971), 58.

Arnold Stein, "Structures of Sound in Donne's Verse," The Kenyon Review, 13 (Spring, 1951), 260–261.

Barbara Traister, Expl, 34 (April, 1976), 60.

Tuve, Elizabethan and Metaphysical Imagery, pp. 174–175.
    "Love's Infiniteness" See "Lovers Infiniteness"
_____. "Love's Usury"
Marius Bewley, "Religious Criticism in Donne's Poetry," The Kenyon Review, 14 (Autumn, 1952), 638–639.

Robert F. Gleckner and Gerald Smith, Expl, 8 (April, 1950), 43.
    Rpt. The Explicator Cyclopedia, II, pp. 114–115.

Larry D. Tjarks, "Donne's 'Loves Usury' and a Self-Deceived Persona," SoQ, 14 (April, 1976), 207–213.

Unger, The Man in the Name, p. 77.
    Rpt. from Donne's Poetry and Modern Criticism (Chicago: Regnery, 1950).
    "Loves War" See "Elegy 20"
_____. "The Message"
John T. Shawcross, "The Poet as Orator," in The Rhetoric of Renaissance Poetry, pp. 24–25.
    "Metempsychosis" See "Progress of the Soul"
_____. "Nativity" (La Coronoa 3)
A. B. Chambers, "Christmas: The Liturgy of the Church and English Verse of the Renaissance," Literary Monographs, ed. Eric Rothstein and Joseph Anthony Wittreich, Jr., Vol. 6 (Madison, Wisconsin: Univ. of Wisconsin Press, 1975), 118–120

_____. "Negative Love"
Walter Gierasch, Expl, 9 (Nov., 1950), 13.
     Rpt. The Explicator Cyclopedia, II, pp. 115-116.

H. M. Richmond, "The Intangible Mistress," MP, 56 (May, 1959), 219-220.

_____. "A Nocturnal upon St. Lucy's Day"
William Empson, "Donne the Space Man," The Kenyon Review, 19 (Summer,
1957), 390-391.

Frank Kermode, Shakespeare, Spenser, Donne: Renaissance Essays (New
York: The Viking Press, 1971), pp. 130-132.

Leishman, The Metaphysical Poets, pp. 56-58.

Carol Marks Sicherman, "Donne's Discoveries," SEL, 11 (Spring, 1971),
81-83.

Martz, The Poem of the Mind, pp. 17-20.

Miner, The Metaphysical Mode from Donne to Cowley, pp. 57-58.

W. A. Murray, "Donne and Paracelsus: An Essay in Interpretation," RES,
25 (April, 1949), 118-123.

Peterson, The English Lyric from Wyatt to Donne, pp. 326-329.

Troy Dale Reeves, Expl, 34 (Nov., 1975), 26.

John T. Shawcross, Expl, 23 (March, 1965), 56.

Richard Sleight, Interpretations, ed. John Wain, pp. 32-58.

James L. Spenko, "Circular Form in Two Donne Lyrics," ELN, 13 (Dec.,
1975), 106-107.

Tillyard, The Metaphysicals and Milton, pp. 20-22.

Martin Turnell, "John Donne and the Quest for Unity," Nineteenth Century,
147 (April, 1950), 265-266.

Unger, The Man in the Name, pp. 67-71.
     Rpt. from Donne's Poetry and Modern Criticism, (Chicago: Regnery,
     1950), pp. 46-50

Elizabeth L. Wiggins, "Logic in the Poetry of John Donne," SP, 42 (Jan.,
1945), 51-52.

Williamson, The Proper Wit of Poetry, pp. 36-37.

_____. "Obsequies to the Lord Harrington"
Philip C. Kolin, "Donne's 'Obsequies to the Lord Harrington,': Theme,
Structure, and Image," SoQ, 13 (Oct., 1974), 65-82.

W. M. Lebans, "The Influence of the Classics in Donne's Epicedes and
Obsequies," RES, 23 (May, 1972), 134-137.

"The Perfume"
_____. "The Primrose"
E. D. Cleveland, Expl, 8 (Oct., 1949), 4.
     Rpt. The Explicator Cyclopedia, II, pp. 117-118.

R. A. Durr, "Donne's 'The Primrose,'" JEGP, 59 (April, 1960), 218-222.

Charlotte F. Otten, "Donne's Manna in 'The Primrose,'" ELN, 13 (June,
1976), 260-262.

Raman Selden, "John Donne's 'Incarnational Conviction,'" CritQ, 17
(Spring, 1974), 68-70.

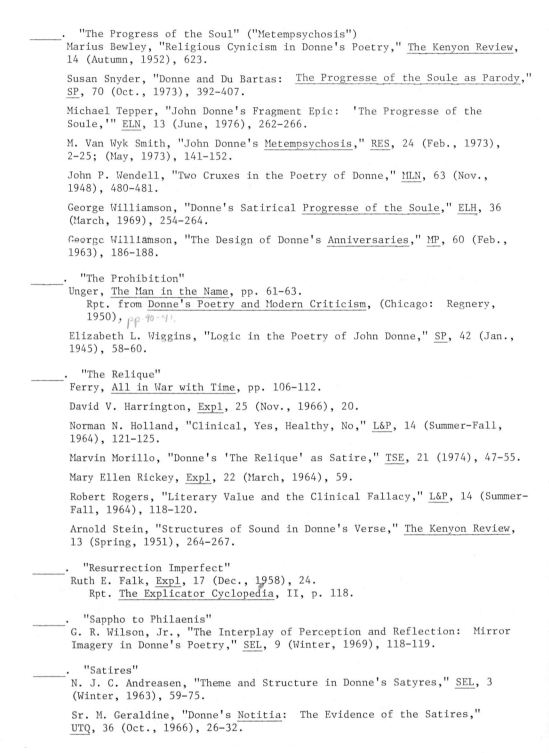

_____. "The Progress of the Soul" ("Metempsychosis")

Marius Bewley, "Religious Cynicism in Donne's Poetry," The Kenyon Review, 14 (Autumn, 1952), 623.

Susan Snyder, "Donne and Du Bartas: The Progresse of the Soule as Parody," SP, 70 (Oct., 1973), 392-407.

Michael Tepper, "John Donne's Fragment Epic: 'The Progresse of the Soule,'" ELN, 13 (June, 1976), 262-266.

M. Van Wyk Smith, "John Donne's Metempsychosis," RES, 24 (Feb., 1973), 2-25; (May, 1973), 141-152.

John P. Wendell, "Two Cruxes in the Poetry of Donne," MLN, 63 (Nov., 1948), 480-481.

George Williamson, "Donne's Satirical Progresse of the Soule," ELH, 36 (March, 1969), 254-264.

George Williamson, "The Design of Donne's Anniversaries," MP, 60 (Feb., 1963), 186-188.

_____. "The Prohibition"

Unger, The Man in the Name, pp. 61-63.
    Rpt. from Donne's Poetry and Modern Criticism, (Chicago: Regnery, 1950), pp. 40-41.

Elizabeth L. Wiggins, "Logic in the Poetry of John Donne," SP, 42 (Jan., 1945), 58-60.

_____. "The Relique"

Ferry, All in War with Time, pp. 106-112.

David V. Harrington, Expl, 25 (Nov., 1966), 20.

Norman N. Holland, "Clinical, Yes, Healthy, No," L&P, 14 (Summer-Fall, 1964), 121-125.

Marvin Morillo, "Donne's 'The Relique' as Satire," TSE, 21 (1974), 47-55.

Mary Ellen Rickey, Expl, 22 (March, 1964), 59.

Robert Rogers, "Literary Value and the Clinical Fallacy," L&P, 14 (Summer-Fall, 1964), 118-120.

Arnold Stein, "Structures of Sound in Donne's Verse," The Kenyon Review, 13 (Spring, 1951), 264-267.

_____. "Resurrection Imperfect"

Ruth E. Falk, Expl, 17 (Dec., 1958), 24.
    Rpt. The Explicator Cyclopedia, II, p. 118.

_____. "Sappho to Philaenis"

G. R. Wilson, Jr., "The Interplay of Perception and Reflection: Mirror Imagery in Donne's Poetry," SEL, 9 (Winter, 1969), 118-119.

_____. "Satires"

N. J. C. Andreasen, "Theme and Structure in Donne's Satyres," SEL, 3 (Winter, 1963), 59-75.

Sr. M. Geraldine, "Donne's Notitia: The Evidence of the Satires," UTQ, 36 (Oct., 1966), 26-32.

_____. "Satire" 1: "Away Thou Fondling Motley Humourist"
S. F. Johnson, Expl, 11 (June, 1953), 53.
    Rpt. The Explicator Cyclopedia, II, pp. 118-119.

John R. Lauritsen, "Donne's Satyres: The Drama of Self-Discovery," SEL,
16 (Winter, 1976), 120-123.

Barbara L. Parker and J. Max Patrick, "Two Hollow Men: The Pretentious
Wooer and the Wayward Bridegroom of Donne's 'Satyre I,'" SCN, 33 (Spring,
1975), 10-14.

Carol Marks Sicherman, "The Mocking Voices of Donne and Marvell," BuR,
17 (May, 1969), 38-40.

_____. "Satire" 2: "Sir; Though (I Thank God for It) I Do Hate"
Lucille S. Cobb, Expl, 14 (March, 1956), 40.
    Rpt. The Explicator Cyclopedia, II, pp. 120-121.

Lucille S. Cobb, Expl, 15 (Nov., 1956), 8.
    Rpt. The Explicator Cyclopedia, II, pp. 119-120.

Vernon Hall, Jr., Expl, 15 (Jan., 1957), 24.
    Rpt. The Explicator Cyclopedia, II, p. 121.

John R. Lauritsen, "Donne's Satyres: The Drama of Self-Discovery,"
SEL, 16 (Winter, 1976), 123-125.

T. O. Mabbott, Expl, 16 (Dec., 1957), 19.
    Rpt. The Explicator Cyclopedia, II, pp. 121-122.

_____. "Satire" 3: "Kind Pity Chokes My Spleen"
Adams, Strains of Discord, pp. 11-13.

Edgar F. Daniels, Expl, 28 (Feb., 1970), 52.

M. Thomas Hester, "John Donne's 'Hill of Truth,'" ELN, 14 (Dec., 1976),
100-105.

John R. Lauritsen, "Donne's Satyres: The Drama of Self-Discovery," SEL,
16 (Winter, 1976), 125-127.

Thomas V. Moore, "Donne's Use of Uncertainty as a Vital Force in Satyre
III," MP, 67 (Aug., 1969), 41-49.

Camille Slights, "'To Stand Inquiring Right': The Casuistry of Donne's
'Satyre III,'" SEL, 12 (Winter, 1972), 85-101.

Smith, Elizabethan Poetry, pp. 224-225.

_____. "Satire" 4: "Well; I May Now Receive, and Die"
John R. Lauritsen, "Donne's Satyres: The Drama of Self-Discovery," SEL,
16 (Winter, 1976), 127-129.

_____. "Satire" 5: "Thou Shalt Not Laugh in This Leaf, Muse"
John R. Lauritsen, "Donne's Satyres: The Drama of Self-Discovery," SEL,
16 (Winter, 1976), 129-130.

_____. "The Second Anniversary" ("Of the Progress of the Soul") see also "The Anniversarie
Raymond A. Anselment, "'Ascensio Mendax, Descensio Crudelis': The Image
of Babel in the Anniversaries," ELH, 38 (June, 1971), 198-205.

Antony F. Bellette, "Art and Imitation in Donne's Anniversaries," SEL,
15 (Winter, 1975), 89-96.

Marius Bewley, "Religious Cynicism in Donne's Poetry," The Kenyon Review, 14 (Autumn, 1952), 621-635.

Cruttwell, The Shakespearean Moment, pp. 73-94.

Ruth A. Fox, "Donne's 'Anniversaries' and the Art of Living," ELH, 38 (Dec., 1971), 538-541.

Ernest B. Gilman, The Curious Perspective: Literary and Pictorial Wit in the Seventeenth Century (New Haven and London: Yale Univ. Press, 1978), pp. 183-188.

Jonathan Goldberg, "Hesper-Vesper: Aspects of Venus in a Seventeenth-Century Trope," SEL, 15 (Winter, 1975), 51-55.

Hardison, The Enduring Monument, pp. 179-186.

Kremen, The Imagination of the Resurrection, pp. 118-121.

Barbara K. Lewalski, "Typological Symbolism and the 'Progress of the Soul' in Seventeenth-Century Literature," in Literary Uses of Typology from the Late Middle Ages to the Present, pp. 88-89.

L. L. Martz, "John Donne in Meditation," ELH, 14 (Dec., 1947), 262-273.

Martz, The Poetry of Meditation, pp. 236-248.

Miner, The Metaphysical Mode from Donne to Cowley, pp. 69-75, 182-186 et passim.

Nicolson, The Breaking of the Circle, pp. 65-104.

Carol M. Sicherman, "Donne's Timeless Anniversaries," UTQ, 39 (Jan., 1970), 133-141.

P. G. Stanwood, "'Essentiall Joye' in Donne's Anniversaries," TSLL, 13 (Summer, 1971), 227-238.

Wanamaker, Discordia Concors, pp. 28-36.

Elizabeth L. Wiggins, "Logic in the Poetry of John Donne," SP, 42 (Jan., 1945), 48-49 et passim.

"Show me dear Christ" See "Holy Sonnet 18"   "Since she whom I lov'd" s "Holy Sonnet 17"

_____. "Song. Go and Catch a Falling Star"
L. G. Locke, Expl, 1 (Feb., 1943), 29.
     Rpt. Stageberg and Anderson, Poetry as Experience, pp. 472-473.
     Rpt. The Explicator Cyclopedia, II, p. 122.

M. L. Rosenthal, W. C. Hummel, and V. E. Leighty, Effective Reading (Boston: Houghton Mifflin Company, 1944), pp. 406-413.

Silvia Ruffo-Fiore, "Donne's 'Parody' of the Petrarchan Lady," CLS, 9 (Dec., 1972), 397-399.

_____. "Sonnet. The Token"
Francis Manley, "Chaucer's Rosary and Donne's Bracelet: Ambiguous Coral," MLN, 74 (May, 1959), 385-389.

"Spit in my face, ye Jews ..." see "Holy Sonnet 11"

_____. "The Storme"
Clayton D. Lein, "Donne's 'The Storme': The Poem and the Tradition," ELR, 4 (Winter, 1974), 137-163.

Linda Mizejewski, "Darkness and Disproportion: A Study of Donne's 'Storme' and 'Calme,'" JEGP, 76 (April, 1977), 219-226.

B. F. Nellist, "Donne's 'Storm' and 'Calm' and the Descriptive Tradition,"
MLR, 59 (Oct., 1964), 511-515.

Gary Storhoff, "Metaphors of Despair in Donne's 'The Storme' and 'The
Calme,'" CP, 9 (Fall, 1976), 41-44.

Eaird W. Whitlock, "Donne's 'First Letter,'" TLS, Aug., 22, 1952, p. 556.

_____. "The Sun Rising"
Glen J. Christensen, Expl, 7 (Oct., 1948), 3.
   Rpt. The Explicator Cyclopedia, II, pp. 123-124.

Leonard Dean, English Masterpieces, Vol. III, Renaissance Poetry, p. 11.

Dickinson, Suggestions for Teachers of "Introduction to Literature,"
fifth edition, ed. Locke, Gibson, and Arms, pp. 5-6. (Teacher's Manual)

Drew, Poetry: A Modern Guide, pp. 199-200.

Dyson and Lovelock, Masterful Images, pp. 21-28.

Ferry, All in War with Time, pp. 78-84.

Frankenberg, Invitation to Poetry, p. 212.

Robert L. Gale, Expl, 15 (Dec., 1956), 14.
   Rpt. The Explicator Cyclopedia, II, p. 124.

Walter Gierasch, Expl, 6 (May, 1948), 47.
   Rpt. The Explicator Cyclopedia, II, pp. 122-123.

Kremen, The Imagination of the Resurrection, pp. 103-105.

William E. Morris, Expl, 23 (Feb., 1965), 45.

Elizabeth Pomeroy, Expl, 27 (Sept., 1968), 4.

Rosenthal and Smith, Exploring Poetry, pp. 477-479.

Martin Turnell, "John Donne and the Quest for Unity," Nineteenth Century,
147 (April, 1950), 263-264.

Unger, The Man in the Name, pp. 60-61.
   Rpt. from Donne's Poetry and Modern Criticism (Chicago: Regnery,
1950).

Wanamaker, Discordia Concors, p. 19.

_____. "To E. of D. with Six Holy Sonnets"
Thomas O. Sloan, "The Crossing of Rhetoric and Poetry in the English
Renaissance," in The Rhetoric of Renaissance Poetry, pp. 223-225.

_____. "To Mr. Roland Woodward"
Gary P. Storhoff, "Social Mode and Poetic Strategies: Donne's Verse
Letters to His Friends," ELWIU, 4 (Spring, 1977), 12.

_____. "To Sir Henry Goodyer"
Gary P. Storhoff, "Social Mode and Poetic Strategies: Donne's Verse
Letters to His Friends," ELWIU, 4 (Spring, 1977), 15-17.

_____. "To Sir Henry Wotton" ("Sir, More Than Kisses")
Gary P. Storhoff, "Social Mode and Poetic Strategies: Donne's Verse
Letters to His Friends," ELWIU, 4 (Spring, 1977), 14-15.

_____. "To Sir Henry Wotton, at His Going Ambassador to Venice"
Gary P. Storhoff, "Social Mode and Poetic Strategies: Donne's Verse
Letters to His Friends," ELWIU, 4 (Spring, 1977), 13-14.

_____. "To Sir Rowland Woodward"
Laurence Stapleton, "The Theme of Virtue in Donne's Verse Epistles," SP,
55 (April, 1958), 194-195.

_____. "To the Countess of Bedford" ("To Have Written Then")
Dan S. Collins, Expl, 31 (Nov., 1972), 19.

_____. "To the Countess of Huntingdon" ("Man to Gods Image...")
Robert Harrison, Expl, 25 (Dec., 1966), 33.

Elizabeth Lewis Wiggins, "Logic in the Poetry of John Donne," SP, 42
(Jan., 1945), 49-50.

_____. "Twicknam Garden"
Adams, The Contexts of Poetry, pp. 86-89.

John Boal Donds, "Donne's Technique of Dissonance," PMLA, 52 (Dec.,
1937), 1052-1054, 1056-1057.

Martz, The Poem of the Mind, pp. 16-17.

Unger, The Man in the Name, pp. 53-59.
   Rpt. from Donne's Poetry and Modern Criticism (Chicago: Regnery,
1950).

_____. "The Undertaking"
James L. Spenko, "Circular Form in Two Donne Lyrics," ELN, 13 (Dec.,
1975), 105-106.

Wanamaker, Discordia Concors, pp. 17-18.

_____. "Upon the Annunciation and Passion Falling upon One Day, 1608"
Hugh Kirkpatrick, Expl, 30 (Jan., 1972), 39.

_____. "A Vadediction: Forbidding Mourning"
Abad, A Formal Approach to Lyric Poetry, pp. 327-332.

Adams, Strains of Discord, pp. 109-111.

Adams, The Contexts of Poetry, pp. 80-82.

Brooks, The Well Wrought Urn, pp. 222-223.

Ciardi, How Does a Poem Mean? pp. 873-875.

Kitty Datta, "Love and Asceticism in Donne's Poetry: The Divine Analogy," CritQ, 19 (Summer, 1977), 20-21.

Daniels, The Art of Reading Poetry, pp. 213-216.

Jay Dean Divine, "Compass and Circle in Donne's 'A Valediction: Forbidding Mourning,'" PLL, 9 (Winter, 1973), 78-80.

Edgar H. Duncan, Expl, 1 (June, 1943), 63.
   Rpt. The Explicator Cyclopedia, II, p. 124.

William Empson, "Donne the Space Man," The Kenyon Review, 19 (Summer,
1957), 391-394.

Ferry, All in War with Time, pp. 90-101.

Fowler, Conceitful Thought, pp. 103-104.

John Freccero, "Donne's 'Valediction: Forbidding Mourning,'" ELH, 30 (Dec., 1963), 335-376.

David Goldknopf, "The Disintegration of Symbol in a Meditative Poet," CE, 30 (Oct., 1968), 50.

Jerome, Poetry: Premeditated Art, pp. 135-139.

Brother, Joseph, F.S.C., Expl, 16 (April, 1958), 43.
    Rpt. The Explicator Cyclopedia, II, p. 125.

Urmilla Khanna, "Donne's 'A Valediction: Forbidding Mourning--Some Possible Alchemical Allusions," N&Q, 17 (Feb., 1970), 404-405.

Kreuzer, Elements of Poetry, pp. 84-86.

Millett, Reading Poetry, pp. 62-63.

Raman Selden, "John Donne's 'Incarnational Conviction,'" CritQ, 17 (Spring, 1975), 66-67.

Carol Marks Sicherman, "Donne's Discoveries," SEL, 11 (Spring, 1971), 79-81.

James Smith, "On Metaphysical Poetry," in Determinations, pp. 28-29.

James Smith, "On Metaphysical Poetry," Scrutiny, II (Dec., 1933), 230-231.

Patricia Meyer Spacks, "In Search of Sincerity," CE, 29 (May, 1968), 594-595.

Arnold Stein, "Structures of Sound in Donne's Verse," The Kenyon Review, 12 (Spring, 1951), 267-268.

Allen Tate, "The Point of Dying: Donne's 'Virtuous Men,'" SR, 61 (Winter, 1953), 76-81.
    Rpt. West, Essays in Modern Literary Criticism, pp. 273-275.

Allen Tate, "Tension in Poetry," SoR, 4 (Summer, 1938), 109-111.
    Rpt. Reason in Madness, pp. 73-75, 90-91; On the Limits of Poetry,
    pp. 84-85; Critiques, pp. 61-62.

Unger, The Man in the Name, pp. 73-74.
    Rpt. from Donne's Poetry and Modern Criticism (Chicago: Regnery,
    1950).

Charles Child Walcutt, The Explicator Cyclopedia, I, "Introduction,"
p. xiv.

Walsh, Doors into Poetry, pp. 140-144.

Wheelwright, The Burning Fountain, pp. 103-104.

Anthony Whiting, Expl, 31 (March, 1973), 56.

Williamson, The Proper Wit of Poetry, pp. 34-35.

Yvor Winters, "Poetic Styles, Old and New," in Four Poets on Poetry,
pp. 45-47.
Rpt. Forms of Discovery, pp. 72-74.

_____. "A Valediction: Of My Name in the Window"
John Bernard, "Orthodoxia Epidemica: Donne's Poetics and 'A Valediction
of my Name in the Window,'" SAQ, 71 (Summer, 1972), 384-389.

Brooks, Modern Poetry and the Tradition, pp. 24-25.

Peterson, _The English Lyric from Wyatt to Donne_, pp. 321-326.

Unger, _The Man in the Name_, pp. 80-81.
    Rpt. from _Donne's Poetry and Modern Criticism_ (Chicago: Regnery, 1950).

G. R. Wilson, Jr., "The Interplay of Perception and Reflection: Mirror Imagery in Donne's Poetry," _SEL_, 9 (Winter, 1969), 117-118.

_____. "A Valediction: Of the Book"
Rhodes Dunlap, "Donne As Navigator," _TLS_, Dec. 28, 1946, p. 643.

Unger, _The Man in the Name_, pp. 77-78.
    Rpt. from _Donne's Poetry and Modern Criticism_ (Chicago: Regnery, 1950).

_____. "A Valediction: Of Weeping"
John Carey, "Notes on Two of Donne's Songs and Sonets," _RES_, 16 (Feb., 1965), 50-53.

J. E. V. Crofts, "John Donne," _Essays and Studies_, 22 (1936), 142-143.

Daniels, _The Art of Reading Poetry_, pp. 216-217.

Empson, _Seven Types of Ambiguity_, pp. 175-183; (1947 ed.), pp. 139-145.

Ferry, _All in War with Time_, pp. 86-90.

Toshihiko Kawasaki, "Donne's Microcosm," in _Seventeenth-Century Imagery: Essays on Uses of Figurative Language from Donne to Farquhar_, ed. Earl Miner (Berkeley: Univ. of California Press, 1971), pp. 29-31.

Frank M. Kerins, _Expl_, 32 (May, 1974), 71.

Ribner and Morris, _Poetry: A Critical and Historical Introduction_, pp. 161-164.

Arnold Stein, "Structures of Sound in Donne's Verse," _The Kenyon Review_, 13 (Spring, 1951), 264-265.

Martin Turnell, "John Donne and the Quest for Unity," _Nineteenth Century_, 147 (April, 1950), 266.

G. R. Wilson, Jr., "The Interplay of Perception and Reflection: Mirror Imagery in Donne's Poetry," _SEL_, 9 (Winter, 1969), 119-120.

_____. "The Will"
Hanford Henderson, _Expl_, 7 (June, 1949), 57.
    Rpt. _The Explicator Cyclopedia_, II, p. 125.

Don A. Keister, _Expl_, 8 (May, 1950), 55.
    Rpt. _The Explicator Cyclopedia_, II, p. 126.

T. O. Mabbott, _Expl_, 8 (Feb., 1950), 30.
    Rpt. _The Explicator Cyclopedia_, II, pp. 125-126.

Tuve, _Elizabethan and Metaphysical Imagery_, pp. 170-171.

Unger, _The Man in the Name_, pp. 78-79.
    Rpt. from _Donne's Poetry and Modern Criticism_ (Chicago: Regnery, 1950).

_____. "Witchcraft by a Picture"
G. R. Wilson, Jr., "The Interplay of Perception and Reflection: Mirror Imagery in Donne's Poetry," _SEL_, 9 (Winter, 1969), 115-116.

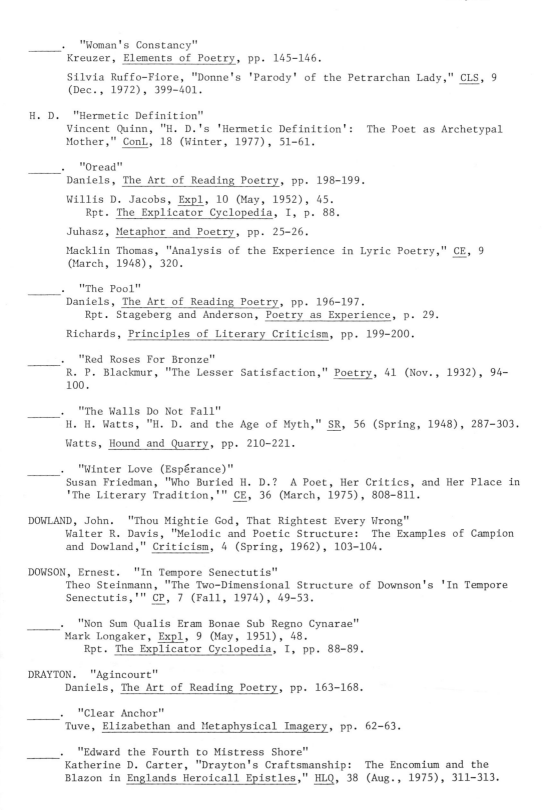

_____. "Woman's Constancy"
Kreuzer, Elements of Poetry, pp. 145-146.

Silvia Ruffo-Fiore, "Donne's 'Parody' of the Petrarchan Lady," CLS, 9 (Dec., 1972), 399-401.

H. D. "Hermetic Definition"
Vincent Quinn, "H. D.'s 'Hermetic Definition': The Poet as Archetypal Mother," ConL, 18 (Winter, 1977), 51-61.

_____. "Oread"
Daniels, The Art of Reading Poetry, pp. 198-199.

Willis D. Jacobs, Expl, 10 (May, 1952), 45.
   Rpt. The Explicator Cyclopedia, I, p. 88.

Juhasz, Metaphor and Poetry, pp. 25-26.

Macklin Thomas, "Analysis of the Experience in Lyric Poetry," CE, 9 (March, 1948), 320.

_____. "The Pool"
Daniels, The Art of Reading Poetry, pp. 196-197.
   Rpt. Stageberg and Anderson, Poetry as Experience, p. 29.

Richards, Principles of Literary Criticism, pp. 199-200.

_____. "Red Roses For Bronze"
R. P. Blackmur, "The Lesser Satisfaction," Poetry, 41 (Nov., 1932), 94-100.

_____. "The Walls Do Not Fall"
H. H. Watts, "H. D. and the Age of Myth," SR, 56 (Spring, 1948), 287-303.

Watts, Hound and Quarry, pp. 210-221.

_____. "Winter Love (Espérance)"
Susan Friedman, "Who Buried H. D.? A Poet, Her Critics, and Her Place in 'The Literary Tradition,'" CE, 36 (March, 1975), 808-811.

DOWLAND, John. "Thou Mightie God, That Rightest Every Wrong"
Walter R. Davis, "Melodic and Poetic Structure: The Examples of Campion and Dowland," Criticism, 4 (Spring, 1962), 103-104.

DOWSON, Ernest. "In Tempore Senectutis"
Theo Steinmann, "The Two-Dimensional Structure of Downson's 'In Tempore Senectutis,'" CP, 7 (Fall, 1974), 49-53.

_____. "Non Sum Qualis Eram Bonae Sub Regno Cynarae"
Mark Longaker, Expl, 9 (May, 1951), 48.
   Rpt. The Explicator Cyclopedia, I, pp. 88-89.

DRAYTON. "Agincourt"
Daniels, The Art of Reading Poetry, pp. 163-168.

_____. "Clear Anchor"
Tuve, Elizabethan and Metaphysical Imagery, pp. 62-63.

_____. "Edward the Fourth to Mistress Shore"
Katherine D. Carter, "Drayton's Craftsmanship: The Encomium and the Blazon in Englands Heroicall Epistles," HLQ, 38 (Aug., 1975), 311-313.

_____. "King John to Matilda"
Katherine D. Carter, "Drayton's Craftsmanship: The Encomium and the
Blazon in Englands Heroicall Epistles," HLQ, 38 (Aug., 1975), 107-311.

_____. "Like an Adventurous Sea-Farer Am I"
Tuve, Elizabethan and Metaphysical Imagery, pp. 61-62.

_____. "Love's Farewell" ("Since There's No Help")
Paul O. Clark, "Other Visits to Love's Deathbed," CEA, 37 (Nov., 1974),
30-31.

David Leon Higdon, "Love's Deathbed Revisited," CEA, 36 (Nov., 1973), 35.

Owen J. Reamer, "Come Back to Love's Deathbed," CEA, 37 (Nov., 1974),
28-29.

_____. "Mary, the French Queene, to Charles Brandon, Duke of Suffolke"
Katherine D. Carter, "Drayton's Craftsmanship: The Encomium and the
Blazon in Englands Heroicall Epistles," HLQ, 38 (Aug., 1975), 308-309.

_____. "Owen Tudor to Queene Katherine"
Katherine D. Carter, "Drayton's Craftsmanship: The Encomium and the
Blazon in Englands Heroicall Epistles," HLQ, 38 (Aug., 1975), 302-305.

_____. "Richard the Second to Queene Isabel"
Katherine D. Carter, "Drayton's Craftsmanship: The Encomium and the
Blazon in Englands Heroicall Epistles," HLQ, 38 (Aug., 1975), 297-299.

_____. "The Shepheards Garland"
Michael D. Bristol, "Structural Patterns in Two Elizabethan Pastorals,"
SEL, 10 (Winter, 1970), 43-48.

_____. "Since There's No Help, Come Let Us Kiss and Part"
Walter R. Davis, "'Fantastically I Sing': Drayton's Idea of 1619," SP,
66 (April, 1969), 214-215.

Leonard Dean, English Masterpieces, Vol, III, Renaissance Poetry, p. 4.

Laurence Perrine, "A Drayton Sonnet," CEA, 25 (June, 1963), 8.

John S. Phillipson, "A Drayton Sonnet," CEA, 25 (April, 1963), 3.

_____. "To the Virginian Voyage"
Michael D. West, "Drayton's 'To the Virginian Voyage': From Heroic
Pastoral to Mock-Heroic," RenQ, 24 (Winter, 1971), 501-506.

DRUMMOND, William. "Epilogue" to "For the King"
John T. Shawcross, "The Poet as Orator," in The Rhetoric of Renaissance
Poetry, pp. 18-19.

DRYDEN. "Alexander's Feast"
John Dawson Carl Buck, "The Ascetic's Banquet: The Morality of Alexander's Feast," TSLL, 17 (Fall, 1975), 573-590.

Thomas H. Fujimura, "The Personal Element in Dryden's Poetry," PMLA, 89
(Oct., 1974), 1019-1022.

Bessie Proffitt, "Political Satire in Dryden's 'Alexander's Feast,'"
TSLL, 11 (Winter, 1970), 1307-1316.

_____. "Astrea Redux"
Jacob Leed, "A Difficult Passage in 'Astraea Redux,'" ES, 47 (1966),
128-

Larry M. Maupin, Expl, 31 (April, 1973), 64.

Steven N. Zwicker, "The King and Christ: Figural Imagery in Dryden's
Restoration Panegyrics," PQ, 50 (Oct., 1971), 585-591.

_____. "Baucis and Philemon"
D. W. Hopkins, "Dryden's 'Baucis and Philemon,'" CL, 28 (Spring, 1976),
135-143.

_____. "Eleonora"
Donald R. Benson, "Platonism and Neoclassic Metaphor: Dryden's Eleonora
and Donne's Anniversaries," SP, 68 (July, 1971), 340-356.

Barbara K. Lewalski, Donne's Anniversaries and the Poetry of Praise: The
Creation of a Symbolic Mode (Princeton: Princeton Univ. Press, 1973),
pp. 348-354.

_____. "Epilogue Spoken to the King...at Oxford...1681"
Sanford Budick, Poetry of Civilization: Mythopoeic Displacement in the
Verse of Milton, Dryden, Pope and Johnson (New Haven and London: Yale
Univ. Press, 1974), pp. 83-86.

_____. "Epistle to Charleton"
Wasserman, The Subtler Language, pp. 15-33.

_____. "Heroique Stanzas...to...Oliver late Lord Protector of this Commonwealth
        (1659)
Michael West, "Shifting Concepts of Heroism in Dryden's Panegyrics," PLL,
10 (Fall, 1974), 379-382.

_____. "Mac Flecknoe"
Stanley Archer, Expl, 26 (Dec., 1967), 37.

John R. Clark, "Anticlimax in Satire," SCN, 33 (Spring-Summer, 1975),
24-26.

John R. Clark, Expl, 29 (March, 1971), 56.

Jerome Donnelly, "Movement and Meaning in Dryden's MacFlecknoe," TSLL,
12 (Winter, 1971), 569-582.

Mother Mary Eleanor, S.H.C.J., "'Anne Killigrew' and 'Mac Flecknoe,'" PQ,
43 (Jan., 1964), 47-54.

David Farley-Hills, The Benevolence of Laughter: Comic Poetry of the
Commonwealth and Restoration (London and Basingstoke: The Macmillan
Press, 1974), pp. 111-114.

David P. French, Expl, 21 (Jan., 1963), 39.

Giles Y. Gamble, Expl, 26 (Jan., 1968), 45.

Goodman, The Structure of Literature, pp. 117-126.

Tav Holmes, "Poppies in John Dryden's 'MacFlecknoe,'" N&Q, 24 (May-June,
1977), 219.

Maynard Mack, English Masterpieces, Vol. V, The Augustans, pp. 5-6.

Thomas E. Maresca, "Language and Body in Augustan Poetic," ELH, 37
(Sept., 1970), 374-378.

Nancy Conrad Martinez, "Little Epics: More Lively and Choleric," Diss. Univ of New Mexico, 1976, pp. 94-107.

George McFadden, "Elkanah Settle and the Genesis of 'MacFlecknoe,'" PQ, 43 (Jan., 1964), 55-72.

Miner, The Restoration Mode from Milton to Dryden, pp. 318-320.

Robert C. Olson, Expl, 35 (Fall, 1976), 14-16.

Christopher, R. Reaske, "A Shakespearean Backdrop for Dryden's Mac Flecknoe?" SQ, 25 (Summer, 1974), 358.

Michael Wilding, "Allusion and Innuendo in MacFlecknoe," EIC, 19 (Oct., 1969), 355-370.

Williamson, The Proper Wit of Poetry, pp. 131-133.

Robert F. Willson, Jr., "The Feral Vision in Mac Flecknoe," Satire News-letter, 8 (Fall, 1970), 1-4.

_____. "Ode: To the Pious Memory of Mrs. Anne Killigrew"
Robert Daly, "Dryden's Ode to Anne Killigrew and the Communal Work of Poets," TSLL, 18 (Summer, 1976), 184-197.

Mother Mary Eleanor, S.H.C.J., "'Anne Killigrew' and 'MacFlecknoe,'" PQ, 43 (Jan., 1964), 47-54.

Thomas H. Fujimura, "The Personal Element in Dryden's Poetry," PMLA, 89 (Oct., 1974), 1012-1015.

Barbara K. Lewalski, Donne's Anniversaries and the Poetry of Praise: The Creation of a Symbolic Mode (Princeton: Princeton Univ. Press, 1973), pp. 345-348.

I. A. Richards, "The Interaction of Words," in The Language of Poetry, pp. 75-87.
   Rpt. Modern Literary Criticism, pp. 85-93.

Tillyard, Five Poems, 1470-1870, pp. 49-65.
   Rpt. West, Essays in Modern Literary Criticism, pp. 353-465.

David M. Vieth, "Irony in Dryden's 'Ode to Anne Killigrew,'" SP, 62 (Jan., 1965), 91-100.

_____. "On the Marriage of...Mrs. Anastasia Stafford"
Miner, The Restoration Mode from Milton to Dryden, pp. 523-524.

_____. "Religio Laici"
William Empson, "Dryden's Apparent Scepticism," EIC, 20 (Oct., 1970), 172-181.

Phillip Harth, "Empson's Interpretation of Religio Laici," EIC, 20 (Oct., 1970), 446-450.

_____. "The Secular Masque"
Alan H. Roper, "Dryden's 'Secular Masque,'" MLQ, 23 (March, 1962), 29-40.

_____. "Song for St. Cecilia's Day, 1687"
H. James Jensen, "Comparing the Arts in the Age of Baroque," ECS, 6 (Spring, 1973), 341-347.

Jay Arnold Levine, "Dryden's 'Song for St. Cecilia's Day, 1687,'" PQ, 44 (Jan., 1965), 38-50.

Douglas Murray, "The Musical Structure of Dryden's 'Song for St. Cecilia's Day,'" ECS, 10 (Spring, 1977), 326-334.

Earl Wasserman, "Pope's 'Ode for Musick,'" ELH, 28 (June, 1961), 169-186.

_____. "To His Sacred Majesty"
Steven N. Zwicker, "The King and Christ: Figural Imagery in Dryden's Restoration Panegyrics," PQ, 50 (Oct., 1971), 591-598.

_____. "To Honor Dryden"
Terence Brown, "Dryden as Puritan Cavalier in his 'Letter to Honor Dryden,'" CP, 9 (Fall, 1976), 35-39.

_____. "To My Dear Friend Mr Congreve"
Thomas H. Fujimura, "The Personal Element in Dryden's Poetry," PMLA, 89 (Oct., 1974), 1015-1019.

_____. "To My Honored Friend, Dr. Charleton"
Samuel A. Golden, Expl, 24 (Feb., 1966), 53.

_____. "To My Honored Friend, Sir Robert Howard"
David M. Vieth, "Irony in Dryden's Verses to Sir Robert Howard," EIC, 22 (July, 1972), 239-243.

_____. "To My Honoured Kinsman, John Driden"
J. Douglas Canfield, "The Image of the Circle in Dryden's 'To My Honour'd Kinsman,'" PLL, 11 (Spring, 1975), 168-176.

_____. "To the Memory of Mr. Oldham"
Wallace Cable Brown, "The 'Heresy' of the Didactic," The University of Kansas City Review, 11 (Spring, 1945), 182-184.

John R. Clark, "'To the Memory of Mr. Oldham': Dryden's Disquieting Lines," CP, 3 (Spring, 1970), pp. 43-49.

Daniels, The Art of Reading Poetry, pp. 377-379.

Thomas H. Fujimura, "The Personal Element in Dryden's Poetry," PMLA, 89 (Oct., 1974), 1009-1012.

Dustin Griffin, "Dryden's 'Oldham' and the Perils of Writing," MLQ, 37 (June, 1976), 133-150.

Van Doren, Introduction to Poetry, pp. 93-98.

_____. "To Sir Godfrey Kneller"
Miner, The Restoration Mode from Milton to Dryden, pp. 438-439.

_____. "To William Congreve"
Miner, The Restoration Mode from Milton to Dryden, pp. 535-539.

_____. "Upon the Death of the Lord Hastings"
Barbara K. Lewalski, Donne's Anniversaries and the Poetry of Praise: The Creation of a Symbolic Mode (Princeton: Princeton Univ. Press, 1973), pp. 343-345.

Miles, The Primary Language of Poetry in the 1640's, pp. 92-94.

Tuve, Elizabethan and Metaphysical Imagery, pp. 318-319.

_____. "Zambra Dance" (The Conquest of Granada)
Betty Gay Coshow, Expl, 16 (Dec., 1957), 16.
    Rpt. The Explicator Cyclopedia, II, pp. 130-131.

Bruce King, Expl, 18 (Dec., 1959), 18.
    Rpt. The Explicator Cyclopedia, II, pp. 131-132.

DU BOIS, W. E. B. "Children of the Moon"
Wilson J. Moses, "The Poetics of Ethiopianism: W. E. B. Du Bois and
Literary Black Nationalism," AL, 47 (Nov., 1975), 418-420.

DUNBAR. "The Golden Targe"
Gerald B. Kinneavy, "Metaphors of the Poet and His Craft in William Dun-
bar," in Aeolian Harps: Essays in Honor of Maurice Browning Cramer, ed.
Donna G. Fricke and Douglas C. Fricke (Bowling Green, Ohio: Bowling
Green Univ. Press, 1976), pp. 61-63.

R. T. Lyall, "Moral Allegory in Dunbar's 'Golden Targe,'" SSL, 11 (July-
Oct., 1973), 47-65.

Walter Scheps, "'The Golden Targe': Dunbar's Comic 'Psychomachia,'"
PLL, 11 (Fall, 1975), 339-356.

E. Allen Tilley, "The Meaning of Dunbar's 'The Golden Targe,'" SSL, 10
(April, 1973), 220-231.

_____. "Hale, Sterne Superne! Hale, in Eterne"
Manning, Wisdom and Number, pp. 63-64.

_____. "Lament for the Makaris"
Cunningham, Tradition and Poetic Structure, pp. 50-53.

Gerald B. Kinneavy, "Metaphors of the Poet and His Craft in William
Dunbar," in Aeolian Harps: Essays in Honor of Maurice Browning Cramer,
ed. Donna G. Fricke and Douglas C. Fricke (Bowling Green, Ohio: Bowling
Green Univ. Press, 1976), pp. 58-60.

_____. "Meditation in Wintir"
Gerald B. Kinneavy, "Metaphors of the Poet and His Craft in William Dun-
bar," in Aeolian Harps: Essays in Honor of Maurice Browning Cramer, ed.
Donna G. Fricke and Douglas C. Fricke (Bowling Green, Ohio: Bowling
Green Univ. Press, 1976), p. 61.

Moore, The Secular Lyric in Middle English, pp. 207-209.

John Speirs, "William Dunbar," Scrutiny, 7 (June, 1938), 67-68.

_____. "My Heid Did Yak Yesternicht"
Moore, The Secular Lyric in Middle English, pp. 205-207.

_____. "Petition of the Gray Horse"
Moore, The Secular Lyric in Middle English, pp. 209-213.

_____. "The Thrissil and the Rois"
A. C. Spearing, Medieval Dream-Poetry (London: Cambridge Univ. Press,
1976), pp. 192-196.

_____. "To a Lady"
Walter Gierasch, Expl, 6 (Dec., 1947), 21.
    Rpt. The Explicator Cyclopedia, II, pp. 132-133.

Moore, The Secular Lyric in Middle English, pp. 201-203.

John Speirs, "William Dunbar," Scrutiny, 7 (June, 1938), 59.

_____. "The Twa Maritt Weman and the Wedo"
Allan Rodway, English Comedy: Its Role and Nature from Chaucer to the
Present Day (London: Chatto & Windus, 1975), pp. 76-79.

John Speirs, "William Dunbar," Scrutiny, 7 (June, 1938), 59-61.

_____. "Strains of Sight"
M. L. Rosenthal, "Dynamics of Form and Motive in Some Representative
Twentieth-Century Lyric Poems," ELH, 37 (March, 1970), 141-144.

DURRELL, Lawrence. "At Epidaurus"
Friar and Brinnin, Modern Poetry, pp. 457-458.

_____. "Song for Zarathustra"
Norman Silverstein and Arthur L. Lewis, Expl, 21 (Oct., 1962), 10.

_____. "To Argos"
Friar and Brinnin, Modern Poetry, pp. 457-458.

DYER. "A Modest Love"
Dorothy Petitt, "To Deepen Delight through Study," EJ, 53 (Jan., 1964),
57-58.

EBERHART. "Experience Evoked"
Seamus Cooney, Expl, 32 (Jan., 1974), 39.

Richard Eberhart, Expl, 32 (May, 1974), 76.

_____. "From Letter I"
J. F. Nims, Poetry: A Critical Supplement, April, 1948, p. 11.

_____. "The Fury of Aerial Bombardment"
Jo Allen Bradham, Expl, 22 (May, 1964), 71.

Ciardi, How Does a Poem Mean? pp. 999-1002.

_____. "Grave Piece"
Richard Eberhart, Expl, 6 (Feb., 1948), 23.
     Rpt. Engel and Carrier, Reading Modern Poetry, pp. 273-274.
     Rpt. The Explicator Cyclopedia, I, pp. 89-90.

_____. "The Groundhog"
Abad, A Formal Approach to Lyric Poetry, pp. 54-59.

Aerol Arnold, Expl, 15 (Oct., 1956), 3.
     Rpt. The Explicator Cyclopedia, I, pp. 90-91.

Harry J. Cargas, Daniel Berrigan and Contemporary Protest Poetry (New
Haven: College & Univ. Press, 1972), pp. 23-26.

Deutsch, Poetry in Our Time, pp. 216-217.

Sydney Mendel, Expl, 17 (June, 1959), 64.
     Rpt. The Explicator Cyclopedia, I, pp. 91-92.

Perrine and Reid, 100 American Poems, pp. 193-194.

Rosenthal, The Modern Poets, p. 247.

M. L. Rosenthal, "Three Poets in Focus," New Republic, 125 (Dec. 10,
1951), 27.

Wright, The Poet in the Poem, pp. 55-57.

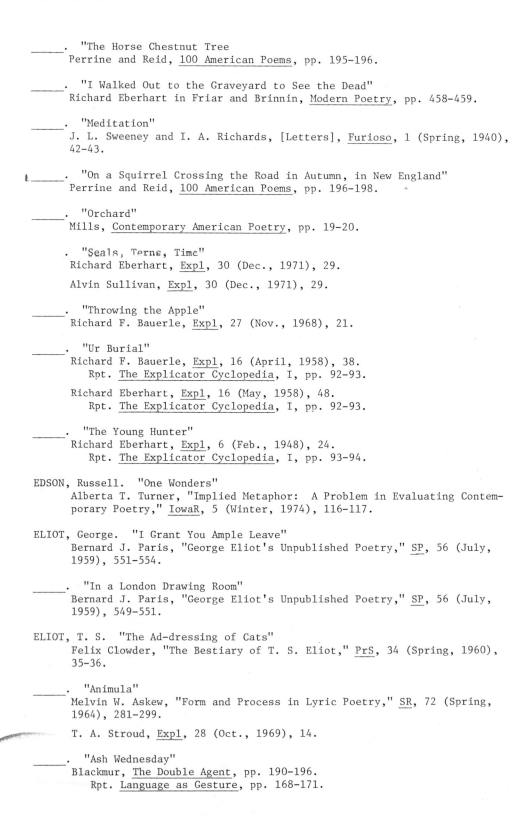

_____. "The Horse Chestnut Tree
        Perrine and Reid, 100 American Poems, pp. 195-196.

_____. "I Walked Out to the Graveyard to See the Dead"
        Richard Eberhart in Friar and Brinnin, Modern Poetry, pp. 458-459.

_____. "Meditation"
        J. L. Sweeney and I. A. Richards, [Letters], Furioso, 1 (Spring, 1940),
        42-43.

_____. "On a Squirrel Crossing the Road in Autumn, in New England"
        Perrine and Reid, 100 American Poems, pp. 196-198.

_____. "Orchard"
        Mills, Contemporary American Poetry, pp. 19-20.

       . "Seals, Terns, Time"
        Richard Eberhart, Expl, 30 (Dec., 1971), 29.

        Alvin Sullivan, Expl, 30 (Dec., 1971), 29.

_____. "Throwing the Apple"
        Richard F. Bauerle, Expl, 27 (Nov., 1968), 21.

_____. "Ur Burial"
        Richard F. Bauerle, Expl, 16 (April, 1958), 38.
            Rpt. The Explicator Cyclopedia, I, pp. 92-93.

        Richard Eberhart, Expl, 16 (May, 1958), 48.
            Rpt. The Explicator Cyclopedia, I, pp. 92-93.

_____. "The Young Hunter"
        Richard Eberhart, Expl, 6 (Feb., 1948), 24.
            Rpt. The Explicator Cyclopedia, I, pp. 93-94.

EDSON, Russell. "One Wonders"
        Alberta T. Turner, "Implied Metaphor: A Problem in Evaluating Contem-
        porary Poetry," IowaR, 5 (Winter, 1974), 116-117.

ELIOT, George. "I Grant You Ample Leave"
        Bernard J. Paris, "George Eliot's Unpublished Poetry," SP, 56 (July,
        1959), 551-554.

_____. "In a London Drawing Room"
        Bernard J. Paris, "George Eliot's Unpublished Poetry," SP, 56 (July,
        1959), 549-551.

ELIOT, T. S. "The Ad-dressing of Cats"
        Felix Clowder, "The Bestiary of T. S. Eliot," PrS, 34 (Spring, 1960),
        35-36.

_____. "Animula"
        Melvin W. Askew, "Form and Process in Lyric Poetry," SR, 72 (Spring,
        1964), 281-299.

        T. A. Stroud, Expl, 28 (Oct., 1969), 14.

_____. "Ash Wednesday"
        Blackmur, The Double Agent, pp. 190-196.
            Rpt. Language as Gesture, pp. 168-171.

Gwenn R. Boardman, "'Ash Wednesday': Eliot's Lenten Mass Sequence," Renascence, 15 (Autumn, 1962), 28-36.

Cleanth Brooks and Robert Penn Warren, "The Reading of Modern Poetry," The American Review, 7 (Feb., 1937), 445-446.

Sr. M. Cleophas, "Ash Wednesday: The Purgatorio in a Modern Mode," CL, 11 (Fall, 1959), 329-339.

Paul J. Dolan, "Ash Wednesday: A Catechumenical Poem," Renascence, 19 (Summer, 1967), 198-207.

Daniel N. Dwyer, S.J., Expl, 9 (Oct., 1950), 5.
    Rpt. The Explicator Cyclopedia, I, p. 95.

F. Peter Dzwonkoski, Jr., "'The Hollow Men' and Ash-Wednesday: Two Dark Night," ArQ, 30 (Spring, 1974), 23-42.

Genevieve W. Foster, "Archetypal Imagery of T. S. Eliot," PMLA, 60 (June, 1945), 580-582.

Vincent Freimarck, Expl, 9 (Oct., 1950), 6.
    Rpt. The Explicator Cyclopedia, I, pp. 94-95.

Friar and Brinnin, Modern Poetry, pp. 465-472.

Nancy D. Hargrove, "Landscape as Symbol in T. S. Eliot's Ash-Wednesday," ArQ, 30 (Spring, 1974), 53-62.

Hugh Kenner, "Eliot's Moral Dialectic," HudR, 2 (Autumn, 1949), 439-446.

Leavis, New Bearings in English Poetry, pp. 117-128.

Miller, Poets of Reality, pp. 182-184.

Theodore Morrison, "Ash Wednesday: A Religious History," NEQ, 11 (June, 1938), 266-286.

Pottle, The Idiom of Poetry, pp. 89-91; (1946 ed.), pp. 96-99.

B. Rajan, "The Overwhelming Question," SR, 74 (Jan.-March, 1966), 368-370.

Eleanor M. Sickels, Expl, 9 (Oct., 1950), 4.

Sr. Margaret Patrice Slattery, "Structural Unity in Eliot's 'Ash Wednesday,'" Renascence, 20 (Spring, 1968), 147-152.

Gordon Symes, "T. S. Eliot and Old Age," Fortnightly, 169 (March, 1951), 188-191.

Allen Tate, "Irony and Humility," Hound and Horn, 4 (Jan.-March, 1931), 290-297.

Tate, Reactionary Essays on Poetry and Ideas, pp. 210-220.
    Rpt. On the Limits of Poetry, pp. 344-349.

Tschumi, Thought in Twentieth-Century English Poetry, pp. 144-146.

Leonard Unger, "Notes on Ash Wednesday," SoR, 4 (Spring, 1939), 745-770.

Unger, The Man in the Name, pp. 141-166.

Leonard Unger, "T. S. Eliot's Images of Awareness," SR, 74 (Jan.-March, 1966), 207, 211-212.

Leonard Unger, "T. S. Eliot's Rose Garden: a Persistent Theme," SoR, 7 (Spring, 1942), 675-676.

Eugene Webb, The Dark Dove: The Sacred and Secular in Modern Literature (Seattle and London: Univ. of Washington Press, 1975), pp. 203-220.

William Carlos Williams, "The Fatal Blunder," Quarterly Review of Literature, 2, No. 2, 125-126.

Carl Wooton, "The Mass: 'Ash Wednesday's' Objective Correlative," ArQ, 17 (Spring, 1961), 31-42.

_____. "Aunt Helen"
Abad, A Formal Approach to Lyric Poetry, pp. 159-160, 164.

_____. "The Boston Evening Transcript"
W. C. Brown, "'A Poem Should Not Mean But Be,'" The University of Kansas City Review, 15 (Autumn, 1948), 61-62.

_____. "Burbank with a Baedeker: Bleistein With a Cigar"
Robert F. Coheen, "'Burbank with a Baedeker': The Third Stanza," SR, 61 (Winter, 1953), 109-119.

L. G. Locke, Expl, 3 (May, 1945), 53.
   Rpt. The Explicator Cyclopedia, pp. 95-96.

Riding and Graves, A Survey of Modernist Poetry, pp. 235-242.

Theodore Spencer, "The Poetry of T. S. Eliot," Atlantic Monthly, 151 (Jan., 1933), 61-62.

Richard C. Turner, "Burbank and Grub-Street: A Note on T. S. Eliot and Swift," ES, 52 (Aug., 1971), 347-348.

Jane Worthington, "The Epigraphs to the Poetry of T. S. Eliot," AL, 21 (March, 1949), 6-7.

_____. "Burnt Norton"
Mother Mary Anthony, "Verbal Pattern in 'Burnt Norton I,'" Criticism, 2 (Winter, 1960), 81-89.

C. A. Bodelsen, "Two 'Difficult' Poems by T. S. Eliot," ES, 34 (Feb., 1953), 17-21.

Daiches and Charvat, Poems in English, pp. 741-742.

Elizabeth Drew in Locke, Gibson, and Arms, Introduction to Literature, third edition, pp. 216-222.
   Rpt. from Drew, T. S. Eliot: The Design of His Poetry (New York: Charles Scribner's Sons, 1950), 151-162.
   Rpt. fourth edition, pp. 218-224.
   Rpt. fifth edition, pp. 200-207.

Drew and Sweeney, Directions in Modern Poetry, pp. 138-140.

Barbara Everett, "A Visit to Burnt Norton," CritQ, 16 (Autumn, 1974), 199-224.

Friar and Brinnin, Modern Poetry, pp. 461-465.

C. O. Gardner, "Some Reflections on the Opening of Burnt Norton," CritQ, 12 (Winter, 1970), 326-329.

Harvey Gross, "Music and the Analogue of Feeling: Notes on Eliot and Beethoven," CentR, 3 (Summer, 1959), 272-274.

Leavis, Education and the University, pp. 94-98.

F. R. Leavis, "Eliot's Later Poetry," Scrutiny, 11 (Summer, 1942), 65-67.

A. O. Lewis, Jr., Expl, 8 (Nov., 1949), 9.
   Rpt. The Explicator Cyclopedia, I, pp. 98-99.

Maynard Mack, Leonard Dean, and William Frost, English Masterpieces,
Vol. VII, Modern Poetry, pp. 15-16.

Walter J. Ong, "'Burnt Norton' in St. Louis," AL, 33 (Jan., 1962), 522-526.

Mark Reisenberg, "A Footnote to Four Quartets," AL, 21 (Nov, 1949), 342-344.

Linda Bradley Salamon, "The Orchestration of 'Burnt Norton II,'" UTQ, 45
(Fall, 1975), 51-66.

Schneider, Poems and Poetry, pp. 498-499.

Tschumi, Thought in Twentieth-Century English Poetry, pp. 149-154.

Unger, The Man in the Name, pp. 177-181.

Leonard Unger, "T. S. Eliot's Rose Garden: a Persistent Theme," SoR, 7
(Spring, 1942), 677-681.

Philip Wheelwright, "The Burnt Norton Trilogy," Chimera, 1 (1942), 7-18.

Jane Worthington, "The Epigraphs to the Poetry of T. S. Eliot," AL, 21
(March, 1949), 16-17.

_____. "Cape Ann"
Erik Arne Hansen, "T. S. Eliot's 'Landscapes,'" ES, 50 (Aug., 1969), 374-376.

_____. "A Cooking Egg"
Drew, Discovering Poetry, pp. 113-115.

Peckham and Chatman, Word, Meaning, Poem, pp. 320-322.

Richards, Principles of Literary Criticism, pp. 293-294.

Grover Smith, Jr., "Getting Used to T. S. Eliot," EJ, 49 (Jan., 1960),
8-9.

Sherna S. Vinograd, "The Accidental: A Cue to Structure in Eliot's
Poetry, " Accent, 9 (Summer, 1949), 231-232.

Jane Worthington, "The Epigraphs to the Poetry of T. S. Eliot," AL, 21
(March, 1949), 9-10.

_____. "Coriolan"
Edwards, Imagination and Power, pp. 197-203.

Feder, Ancient Myth in Modern Poetry, pp. 312-315.

Donald F. Theall, "Traditional Satire in Eliot's 'Coriolan,'" Accent, 11
(Autumn, 1951), 194-206.

_____. "The Cultivation of Christmas Trees"
Hugh Kenner, "A Plea for Metrics," Poetry, 86 (April, 1955), 42-45.

_____. "Dans le Restaurant"
William Arrowsmith, "Daedal Harmonies: A Dialogue on Eliot and the
Classics," SoR, 13, (Winter, 1977), 1-47.

Jeanne Flood, "T. S. Eliot's Dans Le Restaurant," AI, 33 (Summer, 1976),
155-173.

Frankenberg, Pleasure Dome, pp. 72-76.

Unger, The Man in the Name, pp. 169-171.

Leonard Unger, "T. S. Eliot's Rose Garden: a Persistent Theme," SoR, 7 (Spring, 1942), 669-671.

_____. "A Dedication to My Wife"
Leonard Unger, "T. S. Eliot's Images of Awareness," SR, 74 (Jan.-March, 1966), 222-224.

_____. "The Dry Salvages"
John D. Boyd, S.J., "The Dry Salvages: Topography as Symbol," Renascence, 20 (Spring, 1968), 119-132.

John Bugge, "Rhyme as Onomatopoeia in 'The Dry Salvages,'" PLL, 10 (Summer, 1974), 312-316.

Jack L. Davis, "Transcendental Vision in 'The Dry Salvages,'" ESQ, No. 62 (Winter, 1971), 38-44.

F. Peter Dzwonkoski, Jr., "Time and the River, Time and the Sea: A Study of T. S. Eliot's 'Dry Salvages,'" CimR, 30 (Jan., 1975), 48-57.

Harvey Gross, "Music and the Analogue of Feeling: Notes on Eliot and Beethoven," CentR, 3 (Summer, 1959), 277.

Leavis, Education and the University, pp. 99-103.

F. R. Leavis, "Eliot's Later Poetry," Scrutiny, 11 (Summer, 1942), 68-71.

Audrey T. Rodgers, "The Mythic Perspective of Eliot's 'The Dry Salvages,'" ArQ, 30 (Spring, 1974), 81-93.

Unger, The Man in the Name, pp. 186-188.

Leonard Unger, "T. S. Eliot's Rose Garden: a Persistent Theme," SoR, 7 (Spring, 1942), 687-689.

Waggoner, The Heel of Elohim, pp. 91-99.

Philip Wheelwright, "The Burnt Norton Trilogy," Chimera, 1 (1942), 7-18.

_____. "East Coker"
Beaty and Matchett, Poetry: From Statement to Meaning, pp. 235-236.

Curtis Bradford, "Footnotes to East Coker: A Reading," SR, 52 (Jan.-March, 1944), 169-175.

D. Bosley Brotman, "T. S. Eliot: The Music of Ideas," UTQ, 18 (Oct., 1948), 22-29.

Harvey Gross, "Music and the Analogue of Feeling: Notes on Eliot and Beethoven," CentR, 3 (Summer, 1959), 274-275.

H. W. Hausermann, "'East Coker' and The Family Reunion," Life and Letters, 8 (Oct., 1945), 32-38.

Jack Kligerman, "An Interpretation of T. S. Eliot's 'East Coker,'" ArQ, 18 (Summer, 1962), 101-112.

Scott, Rehearsals of Discomposure, pp. 237-243.

F. J. Smith, "A Reading of 'East Coker,'" Thought, 21 (June, 1946), 272-286.

James Johnson Sweeney, "East Coker: a Reading," SoR, 6 (Spring, 1941), 771-791.

Unger, The Man in the Name, pp. 185-186.

Leonard Unger, "T. S. Eliot's Rose Garden: a Persistent Theme," SoR, 7 (Spring, 1942), 686-687.

_____. "Four Quartets"
Joseph Beaver, Expl, 11 (March, 1953), 37.
   Rpt. The Explicator Cyclopedia, I, pp. 97-98.

William Bissett, "The Argument of T. S. Eliot's Four Quartets," UTQ, 15 (Jan., 1946), 115-126.

Blackmur, Language as Gesture, pp. 193-220.

R. P. Blackmur, "Unappeasable and Peregrine: Behavior and the 'Four Quartets,'" Thought, 26 (Spring, 1951), 50-76.

Bornstein, Transformations of Romanticism, pp. 154-160.

Bowra, The Creative Experiment, pp. 22-23.

John M. Bradbury, "Four Quartets: The Structural Symbolism," SR, 59 (Spring, 1951), 254-270.

Curtis B. Bradsford. "Journeys to Byzantium," VQR, 25 (Spring, 1949), 216-224.

R. L. Brett, "Mysticism and Incarnation in Four Quartets," English, 16 (Autumn, 1966), 94-99.

Brett, Reason and Imagination, pp. 119-135.

P. H. Butler, "Four Quartets: Some yes-buts to Dr. Leavis," CritQ, 18 (Spring, 1976), 31-40.

Merrel D. Clubb, Jr., "The Heraclitean Element in Eliot's Four Quartets," PQ, 40 (Jan., 1961), 19-33.

Ethel F. Cornwell, The "Still Point," pp. 17-61.

Elizabeth S. Dallas, "Canon Cancrizans and the 'Four Quartets,'" CL, 17 (Summer, 1965), 193-208.

Donald Davie, "T. S. Eliot: The End of an Era," TC, 159 (April, 1956), 350-362.

De Sola Pinto, Crisis in English Poetry, pp. 180-184.

Deutsch, Poetry in Our Time, pp. 164-167, 170-172, 177-180.

Arnold P. Drew, "Hints and Guesses in Four Quartets," The University of Kansas City Review, 20 (Spring, 1954), 171-175.

R. W. Flint, "The 'Four Quartets' Reconsidered," SR, 56 (Winter, 1948), 69-81.

Joseph Frank, "Force and Form: A Study of John Peale Bishop," SR, 55 (Winter, 1947), 102-103.

Frankenberg, Pleasure Dome, pp. 98-117.

Friar and Brinnin, Modern Poetry, pp. 426-427, 459-461.

B. H. Fussell, "Structural Methods in Four Quartets," ELH, 22 (Sept., 1955), 212-241.

Paul Fussell, Jr., "The Gestic Symbolism of T. S. Eliot," ELH, 22 (Sept., 1955), 201-208.

Helen L. Gardner, "'Four Quartets': A Commentary."
   Rpt. Critiques, pp. 181-197.

Sr. Mary Gerard, "Eliot of the Circle and John of Cross," Thought, 34 (Spring, 1959), 107-127.

Harvey Gross, "Music and the Analogue of Feeling: Notes on Eliot and Beethoven," CentR, 3 (Summer, 1959), 276-277, 282-288.

George A. Knox "Quest for the Word in Eliot's Four Quartets," ELH, 18 (Dec., 1951), 310-321.

James E. Miller, Jr., "Whitman and Eliot: The Poetry of Mysticism," SWR, 43 (Spring, 1958), 114-123.

Arthur Mizener, "To Meet Mr. Eliot," SR, 65 (Winter, 1957), 45-49.

William T. Moynihan, "Character and Action in 'The Four Quartets,'" Mosaic, 6 (Fall, 1972), 203-228.

George L. Musacchio, "A Note on the Fire-Rose Synthesis of T. S. Eliot's Four Quartets," ES, 45 (June, 1964), 238.

David Perkins, "Rose Garden to Midwinter Spring: Achieved Faith in the Four Quartets," MLQ, 23 (March, 1962), 41-45.

M. Gilbert Porter, "Narrative Stance in Four Quartets: Choreography and Commentary," The University of Kansas City Review, 26 (Autumn, 1969), 57-66.

Quinn, The Metamorphic Tradition, pp. 143-147.

B. Rajan, "The Overwhelming Question," SR, 74 (Jan.-March, 1966), 370-372.

Thomas R. Rees, "The Orchestration of Meaning in T. S. Eliot's Four Quartets," JAAC, 28 (Fall, 1969), 63-69.

Julia M. Reibetanz, "Traditional Meters in Four Quartets," ES, 56 (Oct., 1975), 409-420.

Rosenthal, The Modern Poets, pp. 88-89, 94-103.

James P. Sexton, "Four Quartets and the Christian Calendar," AL, 43 (May, 1971), 279-281.

T. B. Shepherd, "The Four Quartets Re-examined," The London Quarterly and Holborn Review, 175 (July, 1950), 228-239.

Gordon Symes, "T. S. Eliot and Old Age," Fortnightly, 169 (March, 1951), 192-193.

Leonard Unger, "T. S. Eliot's Image of Awareness," SR, (Special Issue), 74 (Jan.-March, 1966), 212-215.

Robert D. Wagner, "The Meaning of Eliot's Rose Garden," PMLA, 69 (March, 1954), 22-33.

Watts, Hound and Quarry, pp. 226-238.

A. Kingsley Weatherhead, "Four Quartets: Setting Love in Order," Wisconsin Studies in Contemporary Literature, 3 (Spring-Summer, 1962), 32-49.

Eugene Webb, The Dark Dove: The Sacred and Secular in Modern Literature (Seattle: Univ. of Washington Press, 1975) pp. 221-236.

Morris Weitz, "T. S. Eliot: Time as a Mode of Salvation, SR, 60 (Winter, 1952), 49-52, 55-64.

Wheelwright, The Burning Fountain, pp. 332-336, 350-364.

George T. Wright, "Eliot Written in a Country Churchyard: The Elegy and Four Quartets," ELH, 43 (Summer, 1976), 227-243.

_____. "Gerontion"
R. P. Blackmur, "T. S. Eliot," Hound and Horn, 1 (March, 1928), 201-203.

Brooks, Lewis, and Warren, American Literature, pp. 2107-2111.

Robert M. Brown and Joseph B. Yokelson, Expl, 15 (Feb., 1957), 31.
    Rpt. The Explicator Cyclopedia, I, pp. 103-104.

Alec Brown, "The Lyric Impulse in the Poetry of T. S. Eliot," Scrutinies,
II, pp. 7-12.

Taylor Culbert, Expl, 17 (Dec., 1958), 20.
    Rpt. The Explicator Cyclopedia, I, pp. 104-105.

Daiches and Charvat, Poems in English, pp. 738-740.

David Daiches, "Some Aspects of T. S. Eliot," CE, 9 (Dec., 1947), 117-120.

Edgar F. Daniels, Expl, 17 (May, 1959), 58.
    Rpt. The Explicator Cyclopedia, I, p. 106.

Douglas, Lamson, and Smith, The Critical Reader, pp. 125-130.

Drew and Sweeney, Directions in Modern Poetry, pp. 42-44.

F. Dye, Expl, 18 (April, 1960), 39.
    Rpt. The Explicator Cyclopedia, I, pp. 102-103.

William R. Eshelman, Expl, 4 (April, 1946), 44.
    Rpt. The Explicator Cyclopedia, I, pp. 99-101.

Feder, Ancient Myth in Modern Poetry, pp. 308-311.

Armin Paul Frank, Expl, 30 (March, 1972), 53.

Frankenberg, Pleasure Dome, pp. 51-56.

G. S. Fraser, TLS, June 11, 1970.

Friar and Brinnin, Modern Poetry, pp. 497-498.

Clark Griffith, Expl, 21 (Feb., 1963), 46.

Harvey Gross, "Gerontion and the Meaning of History," PMLA, 73 (June,
1958), 299-304.

Robert B. Kaplan and Richard J. Wall, Expl, 19 (March, 1961), 36.
    Rpt. The Explicator Cyclopedia, I, pp. 106-107.

Elsie Leach, "'Gerontion' and Marvell's 'The Garden,'" ELN, 13 (Sept.,
1975), 45-48.

Leavis, New Bearings on English Poetry, pp. 79-87.

Maynard Mack, Leonard Dean, and William Frost, English Masterpieces,
Vol. VII, Modern Poetry, p. 22.

John M. Major, "Eliot's 'Gerontion' and As You Like It," MLN, 74 (Jan.,
1959), 29-31.

Arthur Mizener, "To Meet Mr. Eliot," SR, (Winter, 1957), 42-44.

George Monteiro, Expl, 18 (Feb., 1960), 30.
    Rpt. The Explicator Cyclopedia, I, pp. 105-106.

Myrtle P. Pope, Expl, 6 (May, 1948), Q16.
    Rpt. The Explicator Cyclopedia, I, p. 101.

Frederick A. Pottle, Expl, 4 (June, 1946), 55.

B. Rajan, "The Overwhelming Question," SR, 74 (Jan.-March, 1966), 365-
367.

John Crowe Ransom, "Gerontion" SR, 74 (Spring, 1966) 389-414.

Rosenthal and Smith, Exploring Poetry, pp. 638-644.

Rosenthal, The Modern Poets, pp. 85-88.

E. San Juan, Jr., "Form and Meaning in 'Gerontion,'" Renascence, 22 (Spring, 1970), 115-126.

Daniel R. Schwarz, "The Unity of Eliot's 'Gerontion': The Failure of Meditation," BuR, 19 (Spring, 1971), 55-76.

Grover Smith, Expl, 7 (Feb., 1949), 26.
    Rpt. The Explicator Cyclopedia, I, pp. 101-102.

Gordon Symes, "T. S. Eliot and Old Age," Fortnightly, 169 (March, 1951), 189-190.

Allen Tate, "Poetry Modern and Unmodern: A Personal Recollection," HudR, 21 (Summer, 1968), 258-260.

Zohreh Tawakuli Sullivan, "Memory and Meditative Structure in T. S. Eliot's Early Poetry," Renascence, 29 (Winter, 1977), 102-105.

Leonard Unger, "T. S. Eliot's Rose Garden: a Persistent Theme," SoR, 7 (Spring, 1942), 672-673.

Unger, The Man in the Name, pp. 172-173.

Sherna S. Vinograd, "The Accidental: A Clue to Structure in Eliot's Poetry," Accent, 9 (Summer, 1949), 233-235.

Wheelwright, The Burning Fountain, pp. 336-338.

Mervyn W. Williamson, "T. S. Eliot's 'Gerontion,'" University of Texas Studies in English, 36 (1957), 111-126.

Jane Worthington, "The Epigraphs to the Poetry of T. S. Eliot," AL, 21 (March, 1949), 5-6.

_____. "Gus: The Theatre Cat"
Priscilla Preston, "A Note on T. S. Eliot and Sherlock Holmes," MLR, 54 (Oct., 1959), 399.

_____. "The Hippopotamus"
Abad, A Formal Approach to Lyric Poetry, pp. 306-307.

Herbert Marshall McLuhan, Expl, 2 (May, 1944), 50.
    Rpt. The Explicator Cyclopedia, I, p. 107.

Christine Meyer, Expl, 8 (Oct., 1949), 6.
    Rpt. The Explicator Cyclopedia, I, p. 108.

Robert Sprich, "Theme and Structure in Eliot's 'The Hippopotamus,'" CEA, 31 (April, 1969), 8.

Francis Lee Utley, Expl, 3 (Nov., 1944), 10.
    Rpt. The Explicator Cyclopedia, I, pp. 107-108.

Jane Worthington, "The Epigraphs to the Poetry of T. S. Eliot," AL, 21 (March, 1949), 10-11.

_____. "The Hollow Men"
Donald R. Benson, "Eliot's and Conrad's Hollow Men," CEA, 29 (Jan., 1967), 10.

R. P. Blackmur, "T. S. Eliot," Hound and Horn, 1 (March, 1928), 203-205.

Harold F. Brooks, "Between The Waste Land and the First Ariel Poems: 'The Hollow Men,'" English, 16 (Autumn, 1966), 89-93.

Drew and Sweeney, Directions in Modern Poetry, pp. 134-136.

F. Peter Dzwonkoski, Jr., "'The Hollow Men' and <u>Ash Wednesday</u>:   Two Dark Nights," <u>ArQ</u>, 30 (Spring, 1974), 16-23.

Feder, <u>Ancient Myth in Modern Poetry</u>, pp. 232-236.

Genevieve W. Foster, "Archetypal Imagery of T. S. Eliot," <u>PMLA</u>, 60 (June, 1945), 576-578.

Paul Fussell, Jr., "The Gestic Symbolism of T. S. Eliot," <u>ELH</u>, 22 (Sept., 1955), 198-203.

Everett A. Gillis, Lawrence V. Ryan, Friederich W. Strothman, "Hope for Eliot's Hollow Men?" <u>PMLA</u>, 75 (Dec., 1960), 635-638.

Everett A. Gillis, "The Spiritual Status of T. S. Eliot's Hollow Men," <u>TSLL</u>, 2 (Winter, 1961), 464-475.

J. G. Keogh, "Eliot's <u>Holow Men</u> as Graveyard Poetry," <u>Renascence</u>, 21 (Spring, 1969), 115-118.

Robert S. Kinsman, <u>Expl</u>, 8 (April, 1950), 48.
   Rpt. <u>The Explicator Cyclopedia</u>, I, pp. 108-109.

Sydney J. Krauss, "Hollow Men and False Horses," <u>TSLL</u>, 2 (Winter, 1961), 368-377.

Miller, <u>Poets of Reality</u>, pp. 180-182.

Lawrence V. Ryan and Friedrich W. Strothman, "Hope for T. S. Eliot's 'Empty Men,'" <u>PMLA</u>, 32 (Sept., 1968), 426-432.

Grover Smith, Jr., "Getting Used to T. S. Eliot," <u>EJ</u>, 49 (Jan., 1960), 9.

Gordon Symes, "T. S. Eliot and Old Age," <u>Fortnightly</u>, 159 (March, 1951), 191-192.

John B. Vickery, "Eliot's Poetry: The Quest and the Way," (Part I), <u>Renascence</u>, 10 (Autumn, 1957), 8-9.

Jane Worthington, "The Epigraphs to the Poetry of T. S. Eliot," <u>AL</u>, 21 (March, 1949), 14-15.

. "Hysteria"
Henry Christian, "Thematic Development in T. S. Eliot's 'Hysteria,'" <u>TCL</u>, 7 (July, 1960), 76-80.

. "Jellicle Cats"
Felix Clowder, "The Bestiary of T. S. Eliot," <u>PrS</u>, 34 (Spring, 1960), 31-33.

. "Journey of the Magi"
R. D. Brown, "Revelation in T. S. Eliot's 'Journey of the Magi,'" <u>Renascence</u>, 24 (Spring, 1972), 136-140.

Margaret Church, <u>Expl</u>, 18 (June, 1960), 55.
   Rpt. <u>The Explicator Cyclopedia</u>, I, pp. 110-111.

Drew, <u>Poetry: A Modern Guide</u>, pp. 237-240.

Genevieve W. Foster, "Archetypal Imagery of T. S. Eliot," <u>PMLA</u>, 60 (June, 1945), 578-580.

Rosemary Franklin, "The Satisfactory Journey of Eliot's Magus," <u>ES</u>, 49 (Dec., 1968), 559-561.

Perrine and Reid, <u>100 American Poems</u>, pp. 133-134.

T. A. Smailes, <u>Expl</u>, 29 (Nov., 1970), 18.

John Howard Wills, Expl, 12 (March, 1954), 32.
    Rpt. The Explicator Cyclopedia, I, pp. 109-110.

_____. "La Figlia Che Piange"
J. H. Hagstrum, English "A" Analyst, No. 3, pp. 1-7.

Vernon Hall, Jr., Expl, 5 (Nov., 1946), 16.
    Rpt. The Explicator Cyclopedia, I, p. 111.

Martin Scofield, "'A gesture and a pose': T. S. Eliot's Images of Love," CritQ, 18 (Autumn, 1976), 11-14.

Jane Worthington, "The Epigraphs to the Poetry of T. S. Eliot," AL, 21 (March, 1949), 4-5.

_____. "Lines to Ralph Hodgson Esgre"
Robert H. Sykes, Expl, 30 (May, 1972), 79.

_____. "Little Gidding"
Brooks, Lewis, and Warren, American Literature, pp. 2130-2137.

F. O. Matthiessen, "Eliot's Quartets," The Kenyon Review, 5 (Spring, 1943), 173-175.

Rosenthal and Smith, Exploring Poetry, pp. 696-704.

John Shand, "Around 'Little Gidding,'" The Nineteenth Century and After, 136 (Sept., 1944), 120-132.

James Johnson Sweeney, "Little Gidding: Introductory to a Reading," Poetry, 62 (July, 1943), 216-223.

_____. "The Love Song of J. Alfred Prufrock"
Adams, Strains of Discord, pp. 112-113.

Charles Altieri, "Objective Image and Act of Mind in Modern Poetry," PMLA, 91 (Jan., 1976), 106-107.

Russell Ames, "Decadence in the Art of T. S. Eliot," Science and Society, 16 (Summer, 1952), 198-221.

Roy P. Basler, "Psychological Pattern in 'The Love Song of J. Alfred Prufrock,'" in Twentieth Century English, ed. William S. Knickerbocker (The Philosophical Library, 1946), pp. 384-400.
    Rpt. Basler, Sex, Symbolism, and Psychology in Literature, pp. 203-221.

Vereen M. Bell, "A Reading of 'Prufrock,'" ES, 50 (Supplement, 1969), lxviii-lxxiv.

R. P. Blackmur, "T. S. Eliot," Hound and Horn, 1 (March, 1928), 209-212.

Margaret Morton Blum, "The Fool in 'The Love Song of J. Alfred Prufrock,'" MLN, 72 (June, 1957), 424-426.

Bornstein, Transformation of Romanticism, pp. 130-134.

Jon Bracker, Expl, 25 (Nov., 1966), 21.

Brooks, Lewis, and Warren, American Literature, pp. 2099-2102.

Brooks and Warren, Understanding Poetry, pp. 589-596. Revised edition, pp. 433-444.
    Rpt. Stallman and Walters, The Creative Reader, pp. 881-885.

Gordon Browning, Expl, 31 (Feb., 1973), 49.

Chatman, An Introduction to the Language of Poetry, pp. 32-33.

R. G. Collingwood, The Principles of Art (Oxford: Oxford University Press, 1938), pp. 310-311.

Robert G. Cook, "Emerson's 'Self-Reliance,' Sweeney and Prufrock," AL, 42 (May, 1970), 223-226.

Ian S. Dunn, Expl, 22 (Sept., 1963), 1.

Daniel N. Dwyer, S.J., Expl, 9 (March, 1951), 38.

Paul Engle, Engle and Carrier, Reading Modern Poetry, pp. 167-174.

Paul Engle, "Why Modern Poetry," CE, 15 (Oct., 1953), 8.

Barbara Everett, "In Search of Prufrock," CritQ, 16 (Summer, 1974), 101-121.

Feder, Ancient Myth in Modern Poetry, pp. 219-222.

Clifford J. Fish, Expl, 8 (June, 1950), 62.
    Rpt. The Explicator Cyclopedia, I, pp. 111-112.

Robert F. Fleissner, "Prufrock's Peach," RS, 44 (June, 1976), 121-125.

Robert F. Fleissner, "Prufrock's 'Ragged Claws,'" ES, 53 (June, 1972), 247-248.

Frankenberg, Pleasure Dome, pp. 40-42, 45-49.

John Halverson, "Prufrock, Freud, and Others," SR, 76 (Autumn, 1968), 571-588.

Versa R. Harvey, "T. S. Eliot's 'The Love Song of J. Alfred Prufrock,'" IEY, No. 6 (Fall, 1961), 29-31.

Eugene Hollahan, "A Structural Dantean Parallel in Eliot's 'The Love Song of J. Alfred Prufrock,'" AL, 42 (March, 1970), 91-93.

James L. Jackson, Expl, 18 (May, 1960), 48.
    Rpt. The Explicator Cyclopedia, I, pp. 113-114.

Willis D. Jacobs, "T. S. Eliot's 'The Love Song of J. Alfred Prufrock,'" Rocky Mountain Modern Language Association Bulletin, 8 (Oct., 1954), 5-6.

Jerome, Poetry: Premeditated Art, pp. 164-168.

Hugh Kenner, "Prufrock of St. Louis," PrS, 31 (Spring, 1957), 24-30.

James F. Knapp, "Eliot's 'Prufrock' and the Form of Modern Poetry," ArQ, 30 (Spring, 1974), 5-14.

Langbaum, The Poetry of Experience, pp. 189-192, 197, 200-202.

Frederick W. Locke, "Dante and T. S. Eliot's 'Prufrock,'" MLN, 78 (Jan., 1963), 51-59.

Minor Wallace Major, "A St. Louisan's View of Prufrock," CEA, 23 (March, 1961), 5.

Joseph Margolis, Interpretations, ed. John Wain, pp. 183-193.

Miller, Poets of Reality, pp. 138-141.

Conny Nelson, "T. S. Eliot, Michelangelo, and John Webster," RS, 38 (Dec., 1970), 304-306.

Perrine and Reid, 100 American Poems, pp. 110-112.

John C. Pope, "Prufrock and Raskolnikov," AL, 17 (Nov., 1945), 213-230; 18 (Jan., 1947), 319-321.

Lyall H. Powers, Expl, 14 (March, 1956), 39.
   Rpt. The Explicator Cyclopedia, I, p. 113.

Edward Proffitt, "Bald Narcissus: The Drowning of J. Alfred Prufrock," NConL, 8 (Nov., 1978), 3-4.

B. Rajan, "The Overwhelming Question," SR, 74 (Jan.-March, 1966), 362-364.

John Crowe Ransom, "Gerontion," SR, 74 (April-June, 1966), 391-394.

Rosenthal and Smith, Exploring Poetry, pp. 376-377.

Thomas C. Rumble, "Some Grail Motifs in Eliot's 'Prufrock,'" in Studies in American Literature, ed. Waldo McNeir and Leo B. Levy (Baton Rouge: Louisiana State University Press, 1960), pp. 95-103.

Schneider, Poems and Poetry, pp. 491-495.

Martin Scofield, "'A gesture and a pose': T. S. Eliot's Images of Love," CritQ, 18 (Autumn, 1976), 9-11.

C. M. Shanahan, "Irony in LaForgue, Corbiére, and Eliot," MP, 53 (Nov., 1955), 119.

Robert C. Slack, "Victorian Literature as It Appears to Contemporary Students," CE, 22 (Feb., 1961), 345-347.

Gerald Smith, Expl, 21 (Oct., 1962), 17.

Grover Smith, Jr., "Getting Used to T. S. Eliot," EJ, 49 (Jan., 1960), 6-7.

William J. Stuckey, Expl, 20 (Sept., 1961), 10.

Gordon Symes, "T. S. Eliot and Old Age," Fortnightly, 169 (March, 1951), 188-189.

Zohreh Tawakuli Sullivan, "Memory and Meditative Structure in T. S. Eliot's Early Poetry," Renascence, 29 (Winter, 1977), 94-100.

Thomas and Brown, Reading Poems: An Introduction to Critical Study, pp. 698-700.

Tschumi, Thought in Twentieth-Century English Poetry, pp. 127-132.

W. A. Turner, "The Not So Coy Mistress of J. Alfred Prufrock," SAQ, 54 (Oct., 1955), 516-522.

John Virtue, Expl, 13 (Nov., 1954), 10.
   Rpt. The Explicator Cyclopedia, I, pp. 112-113.

Charles C. Walcutt, "Eliot's 'The Love Song of J. Alfred Prufrock,'" CE, 19 (Nov., 1957), 71-72.

Leon Waldoff, "Prufrock's Defenses and Our Responses," AI, 26 (Summer, 1969), 182-193.

Walsh, Doors into Poetry, pp. 118-126, 130.

Arthur E. Waterman, Expl, 17 (June, 1959), 67.
   Rpt. The Explicator Cyclopedia, I, p. 114.

Weitz, Philosophy of the Arts, pp. 94-107, 145.

Morris Weitz, "T. S. Eliot: Time as a Mode of Salvation," SR, 60 (Winter, 1952), 53-54.

Wheeler, The Design of Poetry, pp. 17-40, 168-171, 274.

Robert White, Expl, 20 (Nov., 1961), 19.

Arthur Wormhoudt, "A Psychoanalytic Interpretation of 'The Love Song of J. Alfred Prufrock,'" Perspective, 2 (Winter, 1949), 109-117.

Jane Worthington, "The Epigraphs to the Poetry of T. S. Eliot," AL, 21 (March, 1949), 1-2.

_____. "Macavity: The Mystery Cat"
Priscilla Preston, "A Note on T. S. Eliot and Sherlock Holmes," MLR, 54 (Oct., 1959), 398-399.

_____. "Marina"
Richard Abel, "The Influence of St. John Perse on T. S. Eliot," ConL, 14 (Spring, 1973), 235-237.

W. J. Barnes, "T. S. Eliot's 'Marina,'" The University of Kansas City Review, 29 (Summer, 1963), 297-305.

Michael Black, "The Musical Analogy," English, 25 (Summer, 1976), 125-132.

Elspeth Cameron, "T. S. Eliot's 'Marina': An Exploration," QQ, 77 (Summer, 1970), 180-189.

Daiches and Charvat, Poems in English, p. 741.

Deutsch, Poetry in Our Time, p. 175.

Paul J. Dolan, "Eliot's Marina: A Reading," Renascence, 21 (Summer, 1969), 203-206, 222.

Genevieve W. Foster, "Archetypal Imagery of T. S. Eliot," PMLA, 60 (June, 1945), 582-583.

Leavis, Education and the University, pp. 90-92.

F. R. Leavis, "Eliot's Later Poetry," Scrutiny, 11 (Summer, 1942), 61-63.

Leavis, New Bearings on English Poetry, pp. 129-131.

Martin Scofield, "'A gesture and a pose': T. S. Eliot's Images of Love," CritQ, 18 (Autumn, 1976), 22-25.

Jane Worthington, "The Epigraphs to the Poetry of T. S. Eliot," AL, 21 (March, 1949), 15-16.

_____. "Mr. Apollinax"
Alec Brown, "The Lyric Impulse in the Poetry of T. S. Eliot," Scrutinies, II, pp. 29-31.

Grover Smith, Jr., "Getting Used to T. S. Eliot," EJ, 49 (Jan., 1960), 8.

Floyd C. Watkins, "T. S. Eliot's Mysterious 'Mr. Apollinax,'" RS, 38 (Sept., 1970), 193-200.

Jane Worthington, "The Epigraphs to the Poetry of T. S. Eliot," AL, 21 (March, 1949), 3-4.

_____. "Mr. Eliot's Sunday Morning Service"
Abad, A Formal Approach to Lyric Poetry, pp. 332-336.

Anselm Atkins, "Mr. Eliot's Sunday Morning Parody," Renascence, 21 (Autumn, 1968), 41-43, 54.

Orvid Shulenberger, Expl, 10 (Feb., 1952), 29.
    Rpt. The Explicator Cyclopedia, I, pp. 114-115.

Floyd C. Watkins, "T. S. Eliot's Painter of the Umbrian School," AL, 36 (March, 1964), 72-75.

Jane Worthington, "The Epigraphs to the Poetry of T. S. Eliot," AL, 21 (March, 1949), 11-12.

_____. "The Naming of Cats"
Felix Clowder, "The Bestiary of T. S. Eliot," PrS, 34 (Spring, 1960), 34-35.

_____. "New Hampshire"
Brendon Galvin, "A Note on T. S. Eliot's 'New Hampshire' As a Lyric Poem," MSE, 1 (Fall, 1967), 44-45.

Eric Arne Hansen, "T. S. Eliot's 'Landscapes,'" ES, 50 (Aug., 1969), 365-367.

_____. "Ode of Dejection"
E. P. Bollier, "T. S. Eliot's 'Lost' Ode of Dejection," BuR, 16 (March, 1968), 1-17.

_____. "Old Deuteronomy"
Felix Clowder, "The Bestiary of T. S. Eliot," PrS, 34 (Spring, 1960), 33-34.

_____. "Old Possum's Book of Practical Cats"
Felix Clowder, "The Bestiary of T. S. Eliot," PrS, 34 (Spring, 1960), 36-37.

_____. "Portrait of a Lady"
Sar de Saussure Davis, "Two Portraits of a Lady: Henry James and T. S. Eliot," ArQ, 32 (Autumn, 1976), 367-380.

Richard J. Giannone, "Eliot's 'Portrait of a Lady' and Pound's 'Portrait d'une Femme,'" TCL, 5 (Oct., 1959), 131-134.

C. M. Shanahan, "Irony in LaForgue, Corbiére, and Eliot," MP, 53 (Nov., 1955), 123-124.

Patricia Meyer Spacks, "In Search of Sincerity," CE, 29 (May, 1968), 599-601.

W. A. Turner, "The Not So Coy Mistress of J. Alfred Prufrock," SAQ, 54 (Oct., 1955), 517-518.

Leonard Unger, "T. S. Eliot's Images of Awareness," SR, 74 (Jan.-March, 1966), 209-211, 217-218.

Philip Waldron, "T. S. Eliot, Mr. Whiteside, and 'The Psychobiographical Approach,'" The Southern Review (Australia), 6 (June, 1973), 138-141.

Jane Worthington, "The Epigraphs to the Poetry of T. S. Eliot," AL, 21 (March, 1949), 2-3.

_____. "Preludes"
Miller, Poets of Reality, pp. 144-145, 172-173.

Perrine and Reid, 100 American Poems, p. 105.

Grover Smith, Jr., "Getting Used to T. S. Eliot," EJ, 49 (Jan., 1960), 6.

Walsh, Doors into Poetry, pp. 27-30.

_____. "Rannoch, by Glencoe"
Erik Arne Hansen, "T. S. Eliot's 'Landscapes,'" ES, 50 (Aug., 1969), 373-374.

_____. "Rhapsody on a Windy Night"
Cleanth Brooks and Robert Penn Warren, "The Reading of Modern Poetry,"
The American Review, 7 (Feb., 1937), 442-445.

William Harmon, "T. S. Eliot's Raids on the Inarticulate," PMLA, 91 (May,
1976), 452-453.

Miller, Poets of Reality, p. 146.

Rosenthal, The Modern Poets, pp. 6-7.

Zohreh Tawakuli Sullivan, "Memory and Meditative Structure in T. S.
Eliot's Early Poetry," Renascence, 29 (Winter, 1977), 101-102.

_____. "A Song for Simeon"
Malcolm S. Glass, "T. S. Eliot: Christian Poetry Through Liturgical
Allusion," in The Twenties, pp. 42-45.

Hugh Kenner, "Eliot's Moral Dialectic," HudR, 2 (Autumn, 1949), 424-428.

_____. "Sweeney Agonistes"
Morris Freedman, "Jazz Rhythms and T. S. Eliot," SAQ, 51 (July, 1952),
420-423, 428-432.

Morris Freedman, "The Meaning of T. S. Eliot's Jew," SAQ, 55 (April,
1956), 200-201.

Charles L. Holt, "On Structure and Sweeney Agonistes," MD, 10 (May, 1967),
43-47.

Sears Jayne. "Mr. Eliot's Agon," PQ, 34 (Oct., 1955), 395-414.

William V. Spanos, "'Wanna Go Home, Baby?': Sweeney Agonistes as Drama
of the Absurd," PMLA, 85 (Jan., 1970), 8-20.

_____. "Sweeney Among the Nightingales"
Brooks, Lewis, and Warren, American Literature, pp. 2104-2105.

Cleanth Brooks, "T. S. Eliot as a 'Modernist' Poet," in Literary Theory
and Structure: Essays in Honor of William K. Wimsatt, ed. Frank Body,
John Palmer, and Martin Price (New Haven: Yale Univ. Press, 1973),
pp. 366-369.

James Davidson, "The End of Sweeney," CE, 27 (Feb., 1966), 400-403.

Deutsch, Poetry in Our Time, pp. 168-170.

Elizabeth Drew, abridged in The Case for Poetry, pp. 133-135 from T. S.
Eliot: The Design of His Poetry (New York: Charles Scribner's Sons,
1949), pp. 44-46.

Elizabeth Rudisill Homann, Expl, 17 (Feb., 1959), 34.
   Rpt. The Explicator Cyclopedia, I, pp. 117-118.

Stanley E. Hyman, "Poetry and Criticism: T. S. Eliot," ASch, 30 (Winter,
1961), 43-55.

Charles Kaplan, "Eliot Among the Nightingales: Fair and Foul," New
Mexico Quarterly Review, 24 (Summer, 1954), 228.

Leo Kerschbaum and Roy P. Basler, Expl, 2 (Dec., 1943), 18.
   Rpt. The Explicator Cyclopedia, I, pp. 115-116.

P. G. Mudford, "Sweeney Among the Nightingales," EIC, 19 (July, 1969),
285-290.

J. Ower, "Pattern and Value in 'Sweeney Among the Nightingales,'" Renascence, 23 (Spring, 1971), 151-158.

Stauffer, The Nature of Poetry, pp. 78-80. Abridged in The Case for Poetry, p. 135.

Charles C. Walcutt, Expl, 2 (April, 1944), 48.
     Rpt. The Explicator Cyclopedia, I, pp. 116-117.

George Williamson, abridged in The Case for Poetry, p. 133 from A Reader's Guide to T. S. Eliot (New York: The Noonday Press, 1953), pp. 97-98.

Jane Worthington, "The Epigraphs to the Poetry of T. S. Eliot," AL, 21 (March, 1949), 13.

_____. "Sweeney Erect"
Chatman, An Introduction to the Language of Poetry, pp 67-73.

Robert G. Cook, "Emerson's 'Self-Reliance,' Sweeney and Prufrock," AL, 42 (May, 1970), 222-223.

Arthur Mizener, "To Meet Mr. Eliot," SR, 65 (Winter, 1957), 41-42.

Glen W. Singer, Expl, 34 (Sept., 1975), 7.

Charles Child Walcutt, Expl, 35 (Winter, 1976), 31-32.

Jane Worthington, "The Epigraphs to the Poetry of T. S. Eliot," AL, 21 (March, 1949), 7-9.

_____. "Triumphal March" (from the unfinished Coriolan)
Daniels, The Art of Reading Poetry, pp. 406-409.

Leavis, Education and the University, pp. 92-93.

F. R. Leavis, "Eliot's Later Poetry," Scrutiny, 11 (Summer, 1942), 63-64.

_____. "Usk"
Erik Arne Hansen, "T. S. Eliot's 'Landscapes,'" ES, 50 (Aug., 1969), 370-373.

_____. "Virginia"
Erik Arne Hansen, "T. S. Eliot's 'Landscapes,'" ES, 50 (Aug., 1969), 367-370.

_____. "The Waste Land"
Conrad Aiken, "An Anatomy of Melancholy," SR (Special Issue), 74 (Jan.-March, 1966), 188-196.

Robert J. Andreach, "Paradise Lost and the Christian Configuration of The Waste Land," PLL, 5 (Summer, 1969), 296-309.

John Ross Baker, Expl, 14 (Jan., 1956), 27.
     Rpt. The Explicator Cyclopedia, I, p. 124.

Belgion, Reading for Profit, pp. 258-286, passim.

A. F. Beringause, "Journey through The Waste Land," SAQ, 56 (Jan., 1957), 79-90.

R. P. Blackmur, "T. S. Eliot," Hound and Horn, 1 (March, 1928), 190-196.

William Blissett, "Wagner in The Waste Land," in The Practical Vision: Essays in English Literature in Honour of Flora Roy, ed. Jane Campbell and James Doyle (Waterloo, Ontario: Wilfrid Laurier Univ. Press, 1978), 1-85.

Bodkin, Archetypal Patterns in Poetry, pp. 310-315.

Bowra, The Creative Experiment, pp. 159-188.

Brooks, Lewis, and Warren, American Literature, pp. 2118-2127.

Cleanth Brooks, Jr., "'The Waste Land': An Analysis," SoR, 3 (Summer, 1937), 106-136.
  Rpt. Brooks and Warren, Understanding Poetry, revised edition, pp. 645-667.

Alec Brown, "The Lyric Impulse in the Poetry of T. S. Eliot," Scrutinies, II, pp. 34-48.

Oscar Cargill, "Death in a Handful of Dust," Criticism, 11 (Summer, 1969), 275-296.

Richard Chase, "The Sense of the Present," The Kenyon Review, 7 (Spring, 1945), 225-231.

Albert Cook, Expl, 6 (oct., 1947), 7.
  Rpt. The Explicator Cyclopedia, I, p. 125.

C. B. Cox, "T. S. Eliot at the Cross-Roads," CritQ, 12 (Winter, 1970), 307-310, 316-319.

David Craig, The Real Foundations: Literature and Social Change (London: Chatto & Windus, 1973), 195-212.

Daiches, The Place of Meaning in Poetry, pp. 49-55.

Robert Gorham Davis, et al., "The New Criticism," ASch, 20 (Spring, 1951), 225-226.

Robert A. Day, "The 'City Man' in The Waste Land: The Geography of Reminiscence," PMLA, 80 (June, 1965), 285-291.

De Sola Pinto, Crisis in English Poetry, pp. 170-174.

Deutsch, Poetry in Our Time, pp. 160-164.

Deutsch, This Modern Poetry, pp. 118-127.

Marjorie Donker, "The Waste Land and the Aeneid," PMLA, 89 (Jan., 1974), 164-173.

Drew and Sweeney, Directions in Modern Poetry, pp. 40-44 et passim.

Barbara Everett, "Eliot In and Out of The Waste Land," CritQ, 17 (Spring, 1975), 7-30.

William J. Farrell, "The Waste Land as Rhetoric," Renascence, 22 (Spring, 1970), 127-140.

Feder, Ancient Myth in Modern Poetry, pp. 128-135, 222-231.

Rene E. Fortin, Expl, 21 (Dec., 1962), 32.

Genevieve W. Foster, "Archetypal Imagery of T. S. Eliot," PMLA, 60 (June, 1945), 571-576.

D. C. Fowler, "The Wasteland: Mr. Eliot's 'Fragments,'" CE, 14 (Jan., 1953), 234-235.

Frankenberg, Pleasure Dome, pp. 64-77.

Friar and Brinnin, Modern Poetry, pp. 425-426, 472-497.

A. L. French, "Criticism and The Waste Land," The Southern Review (Australia), 1, No. 2, (1964), 69-81.

Paul Fussell, Jr., "The Gestic Symbolism of T. S. Eliot," ELH, 22 (Sept., 1955), 194-211, et passim.

A. M. Gibbs, "Mr. French's Mr. Eliot," The Southern Review (Australia), 1, No. 2, (1964), 82-85.

William M. Gibson, "Sonnets in T. S. Eliot's 'The Waste Land,'" AL, 32 (Jan., 1961), 465-466.

William Harmon, "T. S. Eliot's Raids on the Inarticulate," PMLA, 91 (May, 1976), 453-454.

Hoffman, The Twenties, pp. 291-303.

Florence Jones, "T. S. Eliot Among the Prophets," AL, 38 (Nov., 1966), 285-302.

G. W. Knight, "Thoughts on 'The Waste Land,'" UDQ, 7 (Summer, 1972), 1-13.

Herbert Knust, "What's the Matter with One-Eyed Riley?" CL, 17 (Fall, 1975), 289-298.

Herbert Knust, Expl, 23 (May, 1965), 74.

Jacob Korg, "Modern Art Techniques in The Waste Land," JAAC, 18 (June, 1966), 456-463.

Dale Kramer, Expl, 24 (April, 1966), 74.

Robert Langbaum, The Mysteries of Identity: A Theme in Modern Literature (New York: Oxford Univ. Press, 1977), pp. 88-105.

Nancy K. Lawlor, "Eliot's Use of Rhyming Quatrains in The Waste Land," Poet and Critic, 4 (Fall, 1967), 29-37.

Leavis, New Bearings in English Poetry, pp. 90-114.

John Lucas and William Myers, "II, The Waste-Land Today," EIC, 19 (April, 1969), 193-209.

Maynard Mack, Leonard Dean, and William Frost, English Masterpieces, Vol. VII, Modern Poetry, p. 21.

Florence Marsh, "The Desert-Ocean: 'The Ancient Mariner' and 'The Waste Land,'" EIC, 9 (April, 1959), 126-133.

William H. Marshall, Expl, 17 (March, 1959), 42.
    Rpt. The Explicator Cyclopedia, I, pp. 124-125.

Peter A. Martin, "'Son of Man' in the Book of Ezekiel and T. S. Eliot's The Wasteland," ArQ, 33 (Autumn, 1977), 197-215.

Timothy Materer, "Chantecler in 'The Waste Land,'" N&Q, 24 (Oct., 1977), 451.

Juliet McLauchlan, "Allusion in The Waste Land," EIC, 19 (Oct., 1969), 454-460.

Giorgio Melchiori, "Echoes in The Waste Land," ES, 32 (Feb., 1951), 1-11.

James D. Merritt, Expl, 23 (Dec., 1964), 31.

Milton Miller, "What The Thunder Meant," ELH, 36 (June, 1969), 440-454.

Marion Montgomery, "The Awful Daring: The Self Surrendered in The Waste Land," ArQ, 30 (Spring, 1974), 43-52.

Charles Moorman, "Myth and Organic Unity in The Waste Land," SAQ, 57 (Spring, 1958), 194-203.

L. K. Morris, "Marie, Marie, Hold on Tight," PR, 21 (March-April, 1954), 231-233.

George W. Nitchie, "Eliot's Borrowing: A Note," MR, 6 (Winter-Spring, 1965), 403-406.

Gabriel Notola, "'The Waste Land': Symbolism and Structure," L&P, 18, No. 4 (1968), 205-212.

Palmer, Post-Victorian Poetry, pp. 312-322.

Pearce, The Continuity of American Poetry, pp. 306-312.

Marion Perret, "Eliot, the Naked Lady, and the Missing Link," AL, 46 (Nov., 1974), 289-303.

Perrine and Reid, 100 American Poems, pp. 130-132.

John Peter, "A New Interpretation of The Waste Land (1952) with Post-script (1969)," EIC, 19 (April, 1969), 140-175.

Sanford Pinsker, "Eliot's 'Falling Towers' and the Death of Language: A Note on The Waste Land," CP, 10 (Fall, 1977), 75.

Linda Ray Pratt, "The Holy Grail: Subversion and Revival of Tradition in Tennyson and T. S. Eliot," VP, 11 (Winter, 1973), 307-321.

William H. Pritchard, "I. Reading The Waste Land Today," EIC, 19 (April, 1969), 176-192.

Quinn, The Metamorphic Tradition, pp. 130-142.

B. Rajan, "The Overwhelming Question," SR, 74 (Jan.-March, 1966), 367-368.

John Crowe Ransom, "The Inorganic Muses," The Kenyon Review, 5 (Spring, 1943), 298-300.

D. F. Rauber, "The Notes on The Waste Land," ELN, 7 (June, 1970), 287-294.

Lee J. Richmond, Expl, 30 (Nov., 1971), 23.

Riding and Graves, A Survey of Modernist Poetry, pp. 50-58 et passim.

Audrey T. Rodgers, "'He Do the Police In Different Voices': The Design of The Waste Land," CollL, 1 (Winter, 1974), 48-63.

William N. Rogers II, "'Laquearia' in The Waste Land," AN&Q, 13 (March, 1975), 105-106.

Rosenthal, The Modern Poets, pp. 88-94.

Harry M. Schwalb, Expl, 11 (April, 1953), 46.

Delmore Schwartz, "T. S. Eliot as the International Hero," PR, 12 (Spring, 1945), 200-206.

Scott, Rehearsals of Discomposure, pp. 203-225.

C. M. Shanahan, "Irony in LaForgue, Corbiére, and Eliot," MP, 53 (Nov., 1955), 125-127.

Irene Simon, "Echoes in 'The Waste Land,'" ES, 34 (April, 1953), 64-72.

Theodore Spencer, "The Poetry of T. S. Eliot," Atlantic Monthly, 151 (Jan., 1933), 64-65.

Ronald Tamplin, "The Tempest and The Waste Land," AL, 39 (Nov., 1967), 352-372.

Tate, On the Limits of Poetry, pp. 299-302, 344-345. First published in Hound and Horn and The American Review.

Thomas and Brown, Reading Poems: An Introduction to Critical Study, pp. 716-731, 749-751.

Tschumi, Thought in Twentieth-Century English Poetry, pp. 132-144.

Leonard Unger, "T. S. Eliot's Images of Awareness," SR, 74 (Jan.-March, 1966), 202-203.

John B. Vickery, "Eliot's Poetry: The Quest and the Way," (Part I), Renascence, 10 (Autumn, 1957), 5-8.

Charles Child Walcutt, The Explicator Cyclopedia, I, "Introduction," p. xv.

Helen Watson-Williams, "The Blackened Wall: Notes on Blake's 'London' and Eliot's 'The Waste Land,'" English, 10 (Summer), 181-184.

Margaret C. Weirick, "Myth and Water Symbolism in T. S. Eliot's 'The Waste Land,'" TQ, 10 (Spring, 1967), 97-104.

Wheelwright, The Burning Fountain, pp. 338-351.

George Williamson, "The Structure of The Waste Land," MP, 47 (Feb., 1950), 191-206.

Edmund Wilson, Axel's Castle, pp. 104-111.
    Rpt. Literary Opinion in America, pp. 186-193. Revised edition, pp. 213-218.

Winters, The Anatomy of Nonsense, pp. 162-167. Also In Defense of Reason, pp. 497-501.

Jane Worthington, "The Epigraphs to the Poetry of T. S. Eliot," AL, 21 (March, 1949), 13-14.

_____. "The Waste Land I, The Burial of the Dead"
Beaty and Matchett, Poetry: From Statement to Meaning, pp. 71-77.

Lyman A. Cotten, Expl, 9 (Oct., 1950), 7.
    Rpt. The Explicator Cyclopedia, I, p. 121.

Lyle Glazier, Expl, 8 (Feb., 1950), 26.
    Rpt. The Explicator Cyclopedia, I, pp. 118-119.

Lysander Kemp, Expl, 7 (June, 1949), 60.
    Rpt. The Explicator Cyclopedia, I, p. 121.

Lysander Kemp, Expl, 8 (Feb., 1950), 27.
    Rpt. The Explicator Cyclopedia, I, p. 122.

Anthony Low, "The Friendly Dog: Eliot and Hardy," AN&Q, 12 (March, 1974), 106-108.

Eleanor M. Sickels, Expl, 9 (Oct., 1950), 4.
    Rpt. The Explicator Cyclopedia, I, p. 119.

Ray Smith, Expl, 9 (Oct., 1950), 8.
    Rpt. The Explicator Cyclopedia, I, pp. 121-122.

Willie T. Weathers, Expl, 9 (Feb., 1951), 31.
    Rpt. The Explicator Cyclopedia, I, pp. 119-120.

_____. "The Waste Land II, A Game of Chess"
Drew, Discovering Poetry, pp. 119-120.

Empson, Seven Types of Ambiguity (1947 ed.) pp. 77-78.

Harry M. Schwalb, Expl, 11 (April, 1953), 46.
    Rpt. The Explicator Cyclopedia, I, pp. 123-124.

Eleanor M. Sickels, Expl, 7 (Dec., 1948), 20.
  Rpt. The Explicator Cyclopedia, I, p. 123.

_____. "The Waste Land IV, Death by Water"
Grover Smith, "Observations, on Eliot's 'Death by Water,'" Accent, 6
(Summer, 1946), 257-263.

_____. "The Waste Land V, What the Thunder Said"
R. P. Blackmur, "T. S. Eliot," Hound and Horn, 1 (March, 1928), 197-201.

M. E. Gerander and K. S. Narayana Rao, "The Waste Land and the Upanishads:
What Does the Thunder Say?" Indian Literature (Calcutta), 14 (March,
1971), 85-98.

_____. "Whispers of Immortality"
R. P. Blackmur, "T. S. Eliot," Hound and Horn, 1 (March, 1928), 207-208.

Brooks, Lewis, and Warren, American Literature, pp. 2105-2106.

Cleanth Brooks, "T. S. Eliot as a 'Modernist' Poet," in Literary Theory
and Structure: Studies in Honor of William K. Wimsatt, ed. Frank Brady,
John Palmer, and Martin Price (New Haven: Yale Univ. Press, 1973),
pp. 365-366.

Sr. M. Cleophas, R.S.M., Expl, 8 (Dec., 1949), 22.
  Rpt. The Explicator Cyclopedia, I, pp. 126-127.

Empson, Seven Types of Ambiguity, (1947) ed., pp. 78-79.

Victor Strandberg, Expl, 17 (May, 1959), 53.
  Rpt. The Explicator Cyclopedia, I, pp. 127-128.

Charles C. Walcutt, Expl, 7 (Nov., 1948), 11.
  Rpt. The Explicator Cyclopedia, I, pp. 125-126.

EMERSON. "The Adirondacs"
Carl F. Strauch, "The Mind's Voice: Emerson's Poetic Styles," ESQ, No.
60 (Summer, 1970), Supplement, 55-57.

_____. "Bacchus"
Bernard Paris, "Emerson's 'Bacchus,'" MLQ, 23 (June, 1962), 150-159.

_____. "The Bohemian Hymn"
Richard E. Amacher, Expl, 5 (June, 1947), 55.
  Rpt. The Explicator Cyclopedia, II, pp. 133-134.

Eric W. Carlson, "Emerson's 'The Bohemian Hymn,'" ESQ, 6 (First Quarter,
1957), pp. 6-7.

_____. "Brahma"
Abad, A Formal Approach to Lyric Poetry, p. 131.

Marilyn Baldwin, Expl, 20 (Dec., 1961), 29.
  Rpt. The Explicator Cyclopedia, II, p. 135.

Dickinson, Suggestions for Teachers of "Introduction to Literature,"
fifth edition, ed. Locke, Gibson, and Arms, pp. 26-27. (Teacher's
Manual)

Robert Frost, "A Poet, Too, Must Learn the Magic Way of Poetry," N.Y.
Times, March 21, 1954, p. 1.

Richard Greenleaf, "Emerson and Wordsworth," Science and Society, 22 (Summer, 1958), 229.

Gaylord C. LeRoy, Expl, 20 (Dec., 1961), 29.
　　Rpt. The Explicator Cyclopedia, II, pp. 135-136.

Andrew M. McLean, "Emerson's Brahma as an Expression of Brahman," NEQ, 42 (March, 1969), 115-122.

John Russell, Expl, 20 (Dec., 1961), 29.
　　Rpt. The Explicator Cyclopedia, II, p. 134.

William Bysshe Stein, Expl, 20 (Dec., 1961), 29.
　　Rpt. The Explicator Cyclopedia, II, p. 134.

Van Doren, Introduction to Poetry, pp. 90-93.

Robert L. White, Expl, 21 (April, 1963), 63.

_____. "Compensation"
Richard VanDerBeets, "Compensatory Imagery in Emerson's Poem 'Compensation,'" ESQ, No. 63 (Spring, 1971), 12-13.

_____. "Concord Hymn"
George Arms, Expl, 1 (Dec., 1942), 23.
　　Rpt. The Explicator Cyclopedia, II, p. 136.

_____. "Days"
George Arms, Expl, 4 (Nov., 1945), 8. Abridged in The Case for Poetry, p. 140.
　　Rpt. The Explicator Cyclopedia, II, pp. 136-137.

Dickinson, Suggestions for Teachers of "Introduction to Literature," fifth edition, ed. Locke, Gibson, and Arms, pp. 25-26. (Teacher's Manual)

Edward G. Fletcher, Expl, 5 (April, 1947), 41.
　　Rpt. The Explicator Cyclopedia, II, p. 138.

Seymour L. Gross, "Emerson and Poetry," SAQ, 54 (Jan., 1955), 93-94.

Frances Hernández, Expl, 33 (Feb., 1975), 44.

Tyrus Hillway, Expl, 34 (May, 1976), 69.

Joseph Jones, Expl, 4 (April, 1946), 47. Abridged in The Case for Poetry, p. 140.
　　Rpt. The Explicator Cyclopedia, II, pp. 138-139.

Kirk and McCutcheon, An Introduction to the Study of Poetry, pp. 35-36. Abridged in The Case for Poetry, p. 139.

Matthiessen, American Renaissance, pp. 59-60.

_____. "Each and All"
George Arms, "The Dramatic Movement in Emerson's 'Each and All,'" ELN, 1 (March, 1964), 207-211.

Walter Blair and Clarence Faust, "Emerson's Literary Method," MP, 42 (Nov., 1944), 89-91.

Mario L. D'Avanzo, "Seeing and Hearing in 'Each and All,'" ESQ, No. 19 (Fourth Quarter, 1973), 231-235.

S. L. Gross, "Emerson and Poetry, SAQ, 54 (Jan., 1955), 89-91.

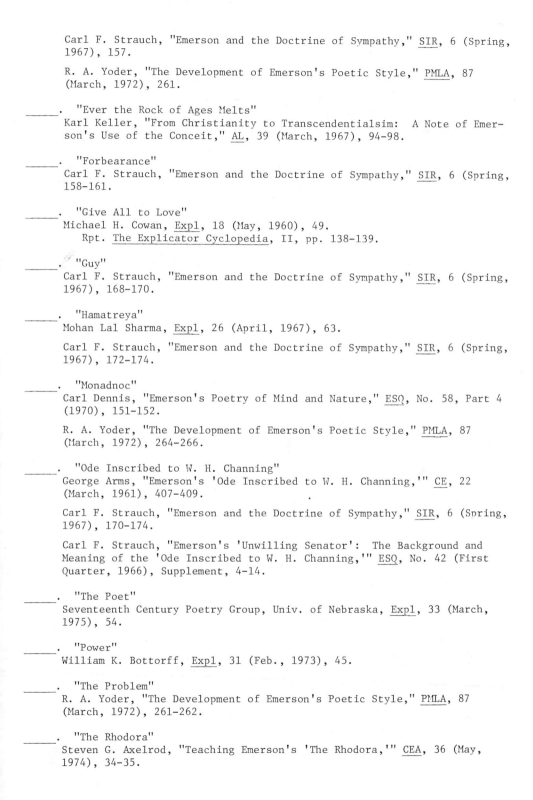

Carl F. Strauch, "Emerson and the Doctrine of Sympathy," SIR, 6 (Spring, 1967), 157.

R. A. Yoder, "The Development of Emerson's Poetic Style," PMLA, 87 (March, 1972), 261.

_____. "Ever the Rock of Ages Melts"
Karl Keller, "From Christianity to Transcendentialsim: A Note of Emerson's Use of the Conceit," AL, 39 (March, 1967), 94-98.

_____. "Forbearance"
Carl F. Strauch, "Emerson and the Doctrine of Sympathy," SIR, 6 (Spring, 158-161.

_____. "Give All to Love"
Michael H. Cowan, Expl, 18 (May, 1960), 49.
    Rpt. The Explicator Cyclopedia, II, pp. 138-139.

_____. "Guy"
Carl F. Strauch, "Emerson and the Doctrine of Sympathy," SIR, 6 (Spring, 1967), 168-170.

_____. "Hamatreya"
Mohan Lal Sharma, Expl, 26 (April, 1967), 63.

Carl F. Strauch, "Emerson and the Doctrine of Sympathy," SIR, 6 (Spring, 1967), 172-174.

_____. "Monadnoc"
Carl Dennis, "Emerson's Poetry of Mind and Nature," ESQ, No. 58, Part 4 (1970), 151-152.

R. A. Yoder, "The Development of Emerson's Poetic Style," PMLA, 87 (March, 1972), 264-266.

_____. "Ode Inscribed to W. H. Channing"
George Arms, "Emerson's 'Ode Inscribed to W. H. Channing,'" CE, 22 (March, 1961), 407-409.

Carl F. Strauch, "Emerson and the Doctrine of Sympathy," SIR, 6 (Spring, 1967), 170-174.

Carl F. Strauch, "Emerson's 'Unwilling Senator': The Background and Meaning of the 'Ode Inscribed to W. H. Channing,'" ESQ, No. 42 (First Quarter, 1966), Supplement, 4-14.

_____. "The Poet"
Seventeenth Century Poetry Group, Univ. of Nebraska, Expl, 33 (March, 1975), 54.

_____. "Power"
William K. Bottorff, Expl, 31 (Feb., 1973), 45.

_____. "The Problem"
R. A. Yoder, "The Development of Emerson's Poetic Style," PMLA, 87 (March, 1972), 261-262.

_____. "The Rhodora"
Steven G. Axelrod, "Teaching Emerson's 'The Rhodora,'" CEA, 36 (May, 1974), 34-35.

S. L. Gross, "Emerson and Poetry, SAQ, 54 (Jan., 1955), 91-93.

Matthiessen, American Renaissance, pp. 49-50.

R. A. Yoder, "The Development of Emerson's Poetic Style," PMLA, 87 (March, 1972), 257.

_____. "The Snow-Storm"
Matthiessen, American Renaissance, pp. 138-139.
    Rpt. Stageberg and Anderson, Poetry as Experience, pp. 485-486.

Sr. Paula Reiten, O.S.B., Expl, 22 (Jan., 1964), 39.

_____. "The Sphinx"
Carl Dennis, "Emerson's Poetry of Mind and Nature," ESQ, No. 58, Part 4 (1970), 150-151.

E. J. Rose, "Melville, Emerson, and the Sphinx," NEQ, 36 (June, 1963), 249-258.

Melvin G. Storm, Jr., "The Riddle of 'The Sphinx': Another Approach," ESQ, No. 62, (Winter, 1971), 44-48.

Carl F. Strauch, "Emerson and the Doctrine of Sympathy," SIR, 6 (Spring, 1967), 154-156.

Charles Child Walcutt, Expl, 31 (Nov., 1972), 20.

Thomas R. Whitaker, "The Riddle of Emerson's 'Sphinx,'" AL, 27 (May, 1955), 179-195.

R. A. Yoder, "The Development of Emerson's Poetic Style," PMLA, 87 (March, 1972), 264.

_____. "Terminus"
August H. Mason, Expl, 4 (March, 1946), 37.
    Rpt. The Explicator Cyclopedia, II, p. 139.

_____. "Threnody"
Walter Blair and Clarence Faust, "Emerson's Literary Method," MP, 42 (Nov., 1944), 91-95.

N. A. Brittin, "Emerson and the Metaphysical Poets," AL, 8 (March, 1936), 15.

David Porter, "'Threnody' and Emerson's Poetics of Failure," ESQ, No. 22 (First Quarter, 1976), 1-13.

_____. "The Titmouse"
Carl Dennis, "Emerson's Poetry of Mind and Nature," ESQ, No. 58, Part 4 (1970), 148-149.

John K. McKee, "The Identity of Emerson's 'Titmouse,'" AN&Q, 13 (June, 1975), 151-152.

Carl F. Strauch, "The Mind's Voice: Emerson's Poetic Styles," ESQ, No. 60 (Summer, 1970), Supplement, 53-55.

_____. "Woodnotes"
Carl Dennis, "Emerson's Poetry of Mind and Nature," ESQ, No. 58, Part 4 (1970), 147-148.

Carl F. Strauch, "Emerson and the Doctrine of Sympathy," SIR, 6 (Spring, 1967), 161-167.

EMPSON. "The Ants"
 John Wain, Professing Poetry (London: MacMillan London Limited, 1977),
 pp. 284-290.

_____. "Arachne"
 John Wain, Professing Poetry (London: MacMillan London Limited, 1977),
 pp. 296-298.

_____. "The Beautiful Train"
 Hartmut Breitkreuz, Expl, 31 (Oct., 1972), 9.

_____. "Flighting for Duck"
 William Empson in Friar and Brinnin, Modern Poetry, p. 499.

_____. "Four Legs, Two Legs, Three Legs"
 William Empson in Friar and Brinnin, Modern Poetry, p. 499.
   Rpt. from The Gathering Storm (London: Faber and Faber, 1940),
   pp. 63-64.

 William L. Hedges, "The Empson Treatment," Accent, 17 (Autumn, 1957),
 231-241.

_____. "High Dive"
 Veronica Forrest-Thompson, "Rational Artifice: Some Remarks on the
 Poetry of William Empson," YES, 4 (1974), 232-234.

_____. "Ignorance of Death"
 Jerome, Poetry: Premeditated Art, pp. 52-53.

_____. "Invitation to Juno"
 David Ormerod, Expl, 25 (Oct., 1966), 13.

_____. "Legal Fiction"
 Drew and Sweeney, Directions in Modern Poetry, pp. 204-207.

_____. "Let It Go"
 Anonymous, "Not Wrongly Moved...," TLS, Oct. 7, 1955, p. 588.

_____. "Missing Dates"
 Drew, Poetry: A Modern Guide, pp. 138-140.

 William Empson in Friar and Brinnin, Modern Poetry, pp. 498-499.

 Robert D. Spector, "Form and Content in Empson's 'Missing Dates,'" MLN,
 74 (April, 1959), 310-311.

_____. "Note on Local Flora"
 Drew and Sweeney, Directions in Modern Poetry, pp. 81-83 (quoting
 Empson's own explanation).

 Jeremy Hawthorn, Identity and Relationship: A Contribution to Marxist
 Theory of Literary Criticism (London: Lawrence & Wishart, 1973), pp. 87-
 90.

_____. "Success"
 John Wain, Professing Poetry (London: MacMillan London Limited, 1977),
 pp. 312-314.

_____. "The Teasers"
G. S. Fraser, Interpretations, ed. John Wain, pp. 225-234.

_____. "This Last Pain"
Richard Eberhart, "Empson's Poetry," Accent, 4 (Summer, 1944), 203-206.

_____. "Ufa Nightmare"
Richard Eberhart, "Empson's Poetry," Accent, 4 (Summer, 1944), 199-200.

_____. "Value Is in Activity"
John Wain, Professing Poetry (London: MacMillan London Limited, 1977),
pp. 294-296.

EVERSON, William (Brother Antinous). "Jacob and the Angel"
Lacey, The Inner War, pp. 99-101.

EWING. "American Miracle"
Irving N. Rothman, "Structure and Theme in Samuel Ewing's Satire, the
'American Miracle,'" AL, 40 (Nov., 1968), 294-308.

FEARING. "Ad"
Walsh, Doors into Poetry, pp. 56-57.

_____. "The Face in the Bar Room Mirror"
J. F. Nims, Poetry: A Critical Supplement, Oct., 1947, pp. 16-17.

_____. "Green Light"
Macha Rosenthal, "The Meaning of Kenneth Fearing's Poetry," Poetry, 64
(July, 1944), 211-212.

Rosentahl, The Modern Poets, pp. 237-238.

_____. "Obituary"
Macha Rosenthal, "The Meaning of Kenneth Fearing's Poetry," Poetry, 64
(July, 1944), 214.

_____. "Portrait"
Perrine and Reid, 100 American Poems, pp. 185-186.

_____. "Radio Blues"
Macha Rosenthal, "The Meaning of Kenneth Fearing's Poetry," Poetry, 64
(July, 1944), 220.

_____. "What if Mr. Jesse James Should Someday Die?"
Macha Rosenthal, "The Meaning of Kenneth Fearing's Poetry," Poetry, 64
(July, 1944), 214-215.

_____. "Yes, the Serial Will Be Continued"
Walter Gierasch, "Reading Modern Poetry," CE, 2 (Oct., 1940), 34-35.

FERGUSSON. "Auld Reekie"
David Daiches, "Eighteenth-Century Vernacular Poetry," in Scottish
Poetry: A Critical Survey, pp. 183-184.

_____. "The Daft-Days"
David Daiches, "Eighteenth-Century Vernacular Poetry," in Scottish Poetry:
A Critical Survey, pp. 172-173.

_____. "The Farmer's Ingle"
David Daiches, "Eighteenth-Century Vernacular Poetry," in Scottish
Poetry: A Critical Survey, pp. 180-181.

_____. "The King's Birthday in Edinburgh"
David Daiches, "Eighteenth-Century Vernacular Poetry," in Scottish
Poetry: A Critical Survey, pp. 175-176.

FERLINGHETTI, Lawrence. "A Coney Island of the Mind"
Br. Edward Kent, O.S.F., "Daredevil Poetics: Ferlinghetti's Definition
of a Poet," EJ, 59 (Dec., 1970), 1243-1244, 1251.

FIELD, Eugene. "Little Boy Blue"
Laurence Perrine, "Are Tears Made of Sugar or Salt?" IEY, No. 8 (Fall,
1963), 19-21.

Laurence Perrine, The Art of Total Relevance, pp. 125-129.

FIELDS, James T. "The Captain's Daughter"
Daniels, The Art of Reading Poetry, pp. 85-88.

FINCH, Anne, Countess of Winchelsea. "An Affliction"
Reuben A. Brower, "Lady Winchelsea and the Poetic Tradition of the Seventeenth Century," SP, 42 (Jan., 1945), 65-66.

FISKE, John. "Upon the Much-To-Be Lamented Desease of the Reverend Mr. John
Cotton..."
Astrid Schmitt-v. Mühlenfels, "John Fiske's Funeral Elegy on John Cotton,"
EAL, 12 (Spring, 1977), 49-62.

FLETCHER, Giles. "Christ's Victory and Triumph"
Rosenthal and Smith, Exploring Poetry, pp. 507-509.

FLINT, F. S. "The Swan"
Suzanne Juhasz, Metaphor and the Poetry of Williams, Pound, and Stevens
(Lewisburg: Bucknell Univ. Press, 1974), pp. 24-25.

FRANCIS, Robert. "The Big Tent"
J. F. Nims, Poetry: A Critical Supplement, Nov., 1948, pp. 17-18.

FRANKENBERG. "I Lazarus"
Nelson Algren, "Lloyd Frankenberg's Poems," Poetry, 56 (April, 1940),
47-48.

FRENEAU. "The American Village"
William L. Andrews, "Goldsmith and Freneau in 'The American Village,'"
EAL, 5 (Fall, 1970), 14-23.

_____. "The Beauties of Santa Cruz"
Jane Donahue Eberwein, "Freneau's 'The Beauties of Santa Cruz,'" EAL, 12
(Winter, 1977/78), 271-276.

_____. "The Indian Burying Ground"
George Arms, Expl, 2 (May, 1944), 55.
    Rpt. The Explicator Cyclopedia, II, p. 144.

George R. Wasserman, Expl, 20 (Jan., 1962), 43.
    Rpt. The Explicator Cyclopedia, II, pp. 141-142.

_____. "The Wild Honey Suckle"
Robert D. Arner, "Neoclassicism and Romanticism: A Reading of Freneau's
'The Wild Honey Suckle,'" EAL, 9 (Spring, 1974), 53-61.

Brooks, Lewis, and Warren, American Literature, pp. 207-208.

FROST, Frances. "Cradle Song"
John Cardi, "Sensitivity Without Discipline," The Nation, 179 (Dec. 4,
1954), 490-492.

FROST, Robert. "Accidentally on Purpose"
Claude M. Simpson, "Robert Frost and Man's 'Royal Role,'" in Aspects of
American Poetry, pp. 135-136.

_____. "Acquainted with the Night"
Malcolm Brown, "The Sweet Crystalline Cry," Western Review, 16 (Summer,
1952), 266.

Joseph H. Friend, "Teaching the 'Grammar of Poetry,'" CE, 27 (Feb.,
1966), 363-365.

Nat Henry, Expl, 35 (Spring, 1977), 28-29.

Wallace Martin, Expl, 26 (April, 1968), 64.

Laurence Perrine, Expl, 25 (Feb., 1967), 50.

_____. "After Apple Picking"
Brooks, Modern Poetry and the Tradition, pp. 114-116.

Brooks and Warren, Understanding Poetry, revised edition, pp. 389-397.

Cardwell, Readings, from the Americas, pp. 776-777.

Reginald L. Cook, "Frost as a Parablist," Accent, 10 (Autumn, 1949), 36.

Peter W. Dowell, "Counter-Images and Their Function in the Poetry of
Robert Frost," TSL, 14 (1969), 18-20.

Joe M. Ferguson, Jr., Expl, 22 (March, 1964), 53.

George Monteiro, Expl, 30 (March, 1972), 62.

William B. Stein, "'After Apple-Picking': Echoic Parody," The University
of Kansas City Review, 35 (Summer, 1969), 301-305.

_____. "And All We Call American"
Claude M. Simpson, "Robert Frost and Man's 'Royal Role,'" in Aspects of
American Poetry, pp. 126-128.

_____. "Away!"
Richard Eberhart, "Robert Frost in the Clearing," SoR, 11 (Spring,
1975), 264-266.

_____. "The Axe-Helve"
James R. Vitelli, "Robert Frost: The Contrarieties of Talent and Tradition," NEQ, 47 (Sept., 1974), 363-364.

Floyd C. Watkins, "The Poetry of the Unsaid--Robert Frost's Narrative and
Dramatic Poems," TQ, 15 (Winter, 1972), 90-92.

_____. "The Bear"
H. H. Watts, "Robert Frost and the Interrupted Dialogue," AL, 27 (March,
1955), 76-77.

Winters, The Function of Criticism, pp. 166-167.

_____. "Beech"
Harold E. Toliver, Pastoral: Forms and Attitudes (Berkeley: Univ. of
Calif. Press, 1971), pp. 338-340.

_____. "Bereft"
Clark Griffith, "Frost and the American View of Nature," AQ, 20 (Spring,
1968), 32-34.

_____. "Birches"
Jeffrey Hart, "Frost and Eliot," SR, 84 (July-Sept., 1976), 435-437.

Lewis H. Miller, Jr., "The Poet as Swinger: Fact and Fancy in Robert
Frost," Criticism, 16 (Winter, 1947), 59-63.

Perrine and Reid, 100 American Poems, pp. 35-36.

_____. "The Birthplace"
Peter W. Dowell, "Counter-Images and Their Function in the Poetry of
Robert Frost," TSL, 14 (1969), 17-18.

_____. "The Black Cottage"
Peter W. Dowell, "Counter-Images and Their Function in the Poetry of
Robert Frost," TSL, 14 (1969), 27-28.

_____. "Bond and Free"
Mordecai Marcus, "Robert Frost's 'Bond and Free': Structure and Meaning,"
CP, 8 (Spring, 1975), 61-64.

_____. "A Boy's Will"
Donald T. Haynes, "The Narrative Unity of A Boy's Will," PMLA, 87 (May,
1972), 452-464.

_____. "Brown's Descent"
Walter Gierasch, Expl, 11 (June, 1953), 60.
    Rpt. The Explicator Cyclopedia, I, pp. 128-129.

_____. "The Cocoon"
Richard Poirier, "Soundings for Home: Frost's Poetry of Extravagance and
Return," GaR, 31 (Summer, 1977), 299-300.

_____. "Come In"
Brooks, Purser, and Warren, An Approach to Literature, fourth edition,
p. 426.

Deutsch, Poetry in Our Time, pp. 75-76.

Robert Kern, "Toward a New Nature Poetry," CentR, 19 (Summer, 1975), 208-
210.

Robert Ornstein, Expl, 15 (June, 1957), 61.
    Rpt. The Explicator Cyclopedia, I, p. 129.

_____. "A Concept Self-Conceived"
Joseph Kau, Expl, 35 (Spring, 1977), 19.

_____. "The Death of the Hired Man"
C. M. Bowra, "Reassessments I: Robert Frost, Adelphi, 27 (Nov., 1950),
46-64.

Robert P. Tristram Coffin, (Review), AL, 14 (Jan., 1943), 438-439.

C. C. Cunningham, Literature as a Fine Art: Analysis and Interpretation, pp. 106-110.

Bess C. Hopkins, "A Study of 'The Death of the Hired Man,'" EJ, 43 (April, 1954), 175-176.

Jerome, Poetry: Premeditated Art, pp. 196-207.

Perrine and Reid, 100 American Poems, pp. 31-33.

Charles C. Walcutt, Expl, 3 (Oct., 1944), 7.
    Rpt. The Explicator Cyclopedia, I, pp. 129-130.

_____. "The Demiurge's Laugh"
Walter Blair, The Literature of the United States, II, 933.

Robert F. Fleissner, "Frost's Response to Keats' Risibility," BSUF, 11 (Winter, 1970), 40-43.

_____. "Desert Places"
R. P. Blackmur, "The Instincts of a Bard," The Nation, 142 (June 24, 1936), 819.

Brooks and Warren, Understanding Poetry, pp. 193-194. Revised edition, pp. 87-88.

W. C. Brown, "'A Poem Should Not Mean But Be,'" The University of Kansas City Review, 15 (Autumn, 1948), 62-63.

Chatman, An Introduction to the Language of Poetry, pp. 11-13.

Friedman and McLaughlin, Poetry: An Introduction to Its Form and Art, pp. 29-32, 51-53, 70-74, 93-95, 118-120, 143-148, 162-164, 179-181.

Charles B. Hands, "The Hidden Terror of Robert Frost," EJ, 58 (Nov., 1969), 1166-1168.

Carol M. Lindner, "Robert Frost: Dark Romantic," ArQ, 29 (Autumn, 1973), 243-244.

Lewis H. Miller, Jr., "Two Poems of Winter," CE, 28 (Jan., 1967), 314-316.

_____. "Design"
Drew, Poetry: A Modern Guide, pp. 186-188.

Randall Jarrell, "To the Laodiceans," The Kenyon Review, 14 (Autumn, 1952), 543-545.

Jerome, Poetry: Premeditated Art, pp. 54-57.

Carl M. Lindner, "Robert Frost: Dark Romantic," ArQ, 29 (Autumn, 1973), 240-243.

Perrine and Reid, 100 American Poems, pp. 46-47.

_____. "Devotion"
Walter Gierasch, Expl, 10 (May, 1952), 50.
    Rpt. The Explicator Cyclopedia, I, p. 130.

_____. "Directive"
Marie Borroff, "Robert Frost's New Testament: Language and the Poem," MP, 69 (Aug., 1971), 50-53.

Margaret M. Blum, "Robert Frost's 'Directive': A Theological Reading," MLN, 76 (June, 1961), 524-525.

Pearlanna Briggs, Expl, 21 (May, 1963), 71.

Clark, Lyric Resonance, pp. 106-117.

James M. Cox, "Robert Frost and the Edge of the Clearing," VQR, 35 (Winter, 1959), 85-87.

Deutsch, Poetry in Our Time, p. 75.

Dickinson, Suggestions for Teachers of "Introduction to Literature," fifth edition, ed. Locke, Gibson, and Arms, p. 42.   (Teacher's Manual)

James P. Dougherty, "Robert Frost's 'Directive' to the Wilderness," AQ, 18 (Summer, 1966), 208-219.

Drew, Poetry: A Modern Guide, pp. 229-233.

Mildred E. Hartsock, Expl, 16 (April, 1958), 42.
   Rpt. The Explicator Cyclopedia, I, pp. 130-131.

Anna K. Juhnke, "Religion in Robert Frost's Poetry: The Play for Self-Possession," AL, 36 (May, 1964), 163-164.

V. Y. Kantak, "Poetic Ambiguity in Frost," WHR, 28 (Winter, 1974), 42-44.

George Knox, "A Backward Motion toward the Source," The Personalist, 47 (Summer, 1966), 365-381.

Robert Peters, "The Truth of Frost's 'Directive,'" MLN, 75 (Jan., 1960), 29-32.

Gregory Waters, "'Directive': Frost's Magical Mystery Tour," CP, 9 (Spring, 1976), 33-38.

_____. "The Discovery of the Madeiras"
Yvor Winters, "Robert Frost: Or, The Spiritual Drifter as Poet," SR, 56 (Autumn, 1948), 593-594.
   Rpt. The Function of Criticism, pp. 184-185.

_____. "Doom to Bloom"
Claude M. Simpson, "Robert Frost and Man's 'Royal Role,'" in Aspects of American Poetry, pp. 128-129.

_____. "The Draft Horse"
Eben Bass, "Frost's Poetry of Fear," AL, 43 (Jan., 1972), 613-615.

Margaret M. Blum, Expl, 24 (May, 1966), 79.

Paul Burrell, Expl, 25 (March, 1967), 60.

Frederick L. Gwynn, "Analysis and Synthesis of Frost's 'The Draft Horse,'" CE, 26 (Dec., 1964), 223-225.

Laurence Perrine, Expl, 24 (May, 1966), 79.

_____. "Dust of Snow"
Norbert Artzt, "The Poetry Lesson," CE, 32 (April, 1971), 740-742.

Edgar H. Knapp, Expl, 28 (Sept., 1969), 9.

Elizabeth Nitchie, "The Language of Men," CentR, 3 (Winter, 1959), 193-194.

Laurence Perrine, Expl, 29 (March, 1971), 61.

H. G. Widdowson, Stylistics and the Teaching of Literature (London: Longman Group Ltd., 1975), pp. 38-39, 104-107.

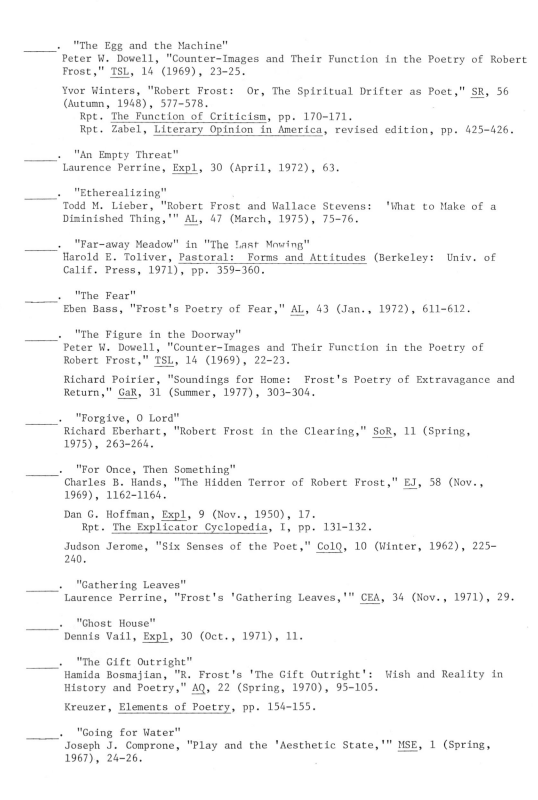

_____. "The Egg and the Machine"
Peter W. Dowell, "Counter-Images and Their Function in the Poetry of Robert Frost," TSL, 14 (1969), 23-25.

Yvor Winters, "Robert Frost: Or, The Spiritual Drifter as Poet," SR, 56 (Autumn, 1948), 577-578.
    Rpt. The Function of Criticism, pp. 170-171.
    Rpt. Zabel, Literary Opinion in America, revised edition, pp. 425-426.

_____. "An Empty Threat"
Laurence Perrine, Expl, 30 (April, 1972), 63.

_____. "Etherealizing"
Todd M. Lieber, "Robert Frost and Wallace Stevens: 'What to Make of a Diminished Thing,'" AL, 47 (March, 1975), 75-76.

_____. "Far-away Meadow" in "The Last Mowing"
Harold E. Toliver, Pastoral: Forms and Attitudes (Berkeley: Univ. of Calif. Press, 1971), pp. 359-360.

_____. "The Fear"
Eben Bass, "Frost's Poetry of Fear," AL, 43 (Jan., 1972), 611-612.

_____. "The Figure in the Doorway"
Peter W. Dowell, "Counter-Images and Their Function in the Poetry of Robert Frost," TSL, 14 (1969), 22-23.

Richard Poirier, "Soundings for Home: Frost's Poetry of Extravagance and Return," GaR, 31 (Summer, 1977), 303-304.

_____. "Forgive, O Lord"
Richard Eberhart, "Robert Frost in the Clearing," SoR, 11 (Spring, 1975), 263-264.

_____. "For Once, Then Something"
Charles B. Hands, "The Hidden Terror of Robert Frost," EJ, 58 (Nov., 1969), 1162-1164.

Dan G. Hoffman, Expl, 9 (Nov., 1950), 17.
    Rpt. The Explicator Cyclopedia, I, pp. 131-132.

Judson Jerome, "Six Senses of the Poet," ColQ, 10 (Winter, 1962), 225-240.

_____. "Gathering Leaves"
Laurence Perrine, "Frost's 'Gathering Leaves,'" CEA, 34 (Nov., 1971), 29.

_____. "Ghost House"
Dennis Vail, Expl, 30 (Oct., 1971), 11.

_____. "The Gift Outright"
Hamida Bosmajian, "R. Frost's 'The Gift Outright': Wish and Reality in History and Poetry," AQ, 22 (Spring, 1970), 95-105.

Kreuzer, Elements of Poetry, pp. 154-155.

_____. "Going for Water"
Joseph J. Comprone, "Play and the 'Aesthetic State,'" MSE, 1 (Spring, 1967), 24-26.

_____. "The Grindstone"
Reginald L. Cook, "Frost as Parablist," Accent, 10 (Autumn, 1949), 37-38.

_____. "Happiness Makes up in Height"
W. G. O'Donnell, "Robert Frost and New England: A Revaluation," YR, 37
(Summer, 1948), 698-712.

_____. "The Hill Wife"
Floyd C. Watkins, "The Poetry of the Unsaid--Robert Frost's Narrative and
Dramatic Poems," TQ, 15 (Winter, 1972), 92-94.

_____. "Home Burial"
Abad, A Formal Approach to Lyric Poetry, pp. 81-93.

Eben Bass, "Frost's Poetry of Fear," AL, 43 (Jan., 1972), 608-609.

Randall Jarrell, "Robert Frost's 'Home Burial,'" in The Moment of Poetry,
pp. 99-132.

Laurence J. Sasso, Jr., "Robert Frost: Love's Question," NEQ, 42 (March,
1969), 100-102.

Robert H. Swennes, "Man and Wife: The Dialogue of Contraries in Robert
Frost's Poetry," AL, 42 (Nov., 1970), 366-367.

Floyd C. Watkins, "The Poetry of the Unsaid--Robert Frost's Narrative and
Dramatic Poems," TQ, 15 (Winter, 1972), 86-87, 89-90.

_____. "In the Home Stretch"
Richard Foster, "Leaves Compared with Flowers: A Reading in Robert
Frost's Poems," NEQ, 46 (Sept., 1973), 411-412.

_____. "In Time of Cloudburst"
Peckham and Chatman, Word, Meaning, Poem, pp. 254-260.

_____. "In White and Design"
David Hiatt, Expl, 28 (Jan., 1970), 41.

_____. "I Will Sing You One-O"
Anna K. Juhnke, "Religion in Robert Frost's Poetry: The Play for Self-
Possession," AL, 36 (May, 1964), 154-155.

Laurence Perrine, Expl, 34 (Feb., 1976), 48.

_____. "Kitty Hawk"
Claude M. Simpson, "Robert Frost and Man's 'Royal Role,'" in Aspects of
American Poetry, pp. 136-147.

_____. "The Last Mowing"
Walter Gierasch, Expl, 10 (Feb., 1952), 25.
     Rpt. The Explicator Cyclopedia, I, pp. 132-133.

Yvor Winters, "Robert Frost: Or, The Spiritual Drifter as Poet," SR, 56
(Autumn, 1948), 589-590.
     Rpt. The Function of Criticism, pp. 181-182.
     Rpt. Zabel, Literary Opinion in America, revised edition, pp. 434-435.

_____. "A Leaf Treader"
Brooks, Purser, and Warren, An Approach to Literature, fourth edition.
pp. 423-424.

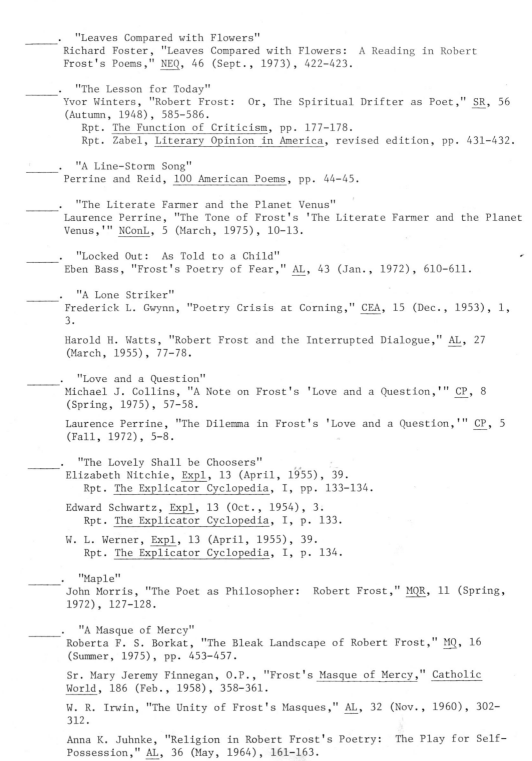

_____. "Leaves Compared with Flowers"
Richard Foster, "Leaves Compared with Flowers: A Reading in Robert
Frost's Poems," NEQ, 46 (Sept., 1973), 422-423.

_____. "The Lesson for Today"
Yvor Winters, "Robert Frost: Or, The Spiritual Drifter as Poet," SR, 56
(Autumn, 1948), 585-586.
    Rpt. The Function of Criticism, pp. 177-178.
    Rpt. Zabel, Literary Opinion in America, revised edition, pp. 431-432.

_____. "A Line-Storm Song"
Perrine and Reid, 100 American Poems, pp. 44-45.

_____. "The Literate Farmer and the Planet Venus"
Laurence Perrine, "The Tone of Frost's 'The Literate Farmer and the Planet
Venus,'" NConL, 5 (March, 1975), 10-13.

_____. "Locked Out: As Told to a Child"
Eben Bass, "Frost's Poetry of Fear," AL, 43 (Jan., 1972), 610-611.

_____. "A Lone Striker"
Frederick L. Gwynn, "Poetry Crisis at Corning," CEA, 15 (Dec., 1953), 1,
3.

Harold H. Watts, "Robert Frost and the Interrupted Dialogue," AL, 27
(March, 1955), 77-78.

_____. "Love and a Question"
Michael J. Collins, "A Note on Frost's 'Love and a Question,'" CP, 8
(Spring, 1975), 57-58.

Laurence Perrine, "The Dilemma in Frost's 'Love and a Question,'" CP, 5
(Fall, 1972), 5-8.

_____. "The Lovely Shall be Choosers"
Elizabeth Nitchie, Expl, 13 (April, 1955), 39.
    Rpt. The Explicator Cyclopedia, I, pp. 133-134.

Edward Schwartz, Expl, 13 (Oct., 1954), 3.
    Rpt. The Explicator Cyclopedia, I, p. 133.

W. L. Werner, Expl, 13 (April, 1955), 39.
    Rpt. The Explicator Cyclopedia, I, p. 134.

_____. "Maple"
John Morris, "The Poet as Philosopher: Robert Frost," MQR, 11 (Spring,
1972), 127-128.

_____. "A Masque of Mercy"
Roberta F. S. Borkat, "The Bleak Landscape of Robert Frost," MQ, 16
(Summer, 1975), pp. 453-457.

Sr. Mary Jeremy Finnegan, O.P., "Frost's Masque of Mercy," Catholic
World, 186 (Feb., 1958), 358-361.

W. R. Irwin, "The Unity of Frost's Masques," AL, 32 (Nov., 1960), 302-
312.

Anna K. Juhnke, "Religion in Robert Frost's Poetry: The Play for Self-
Possession," AL, 36 (May, 1964), 161-163.

_____. "A Masque of Reason"
Roberta F. S. Borkat, "The Bleak Landscape of Robert Frost," MQ, 16
(Summer, 1975), 453-467.

H. C. Hatfield, Expl, 4 (Nov., 1945), 9.
   Rpt. The Explicator Cyclopedia, I, pp. 134-135.

W. R. Irwin, "The Unity of Frost's Masques," AL, 32 (Nov., 1960), 302-
312.

Anna K. Juhnke, "Religion in Robert Frost's Poetry: The Play for Self-
Possession," AL, 36 (May, 1964), 160-161.

Ruth Todasco, "Dramatic Characterization in Frost: A Masque of Reason,"
The University of Kansas City Review, 29 (March, 1963), 227-230.

H. H. Waggoner, Expl, 4 (March, 1946), 32.
   Rpt. The Explicator Cyclopedia, I, p. 135.

_____. "Meeting and Passing"
Laurence J. Sasso, Jr., "Robert Frost: Love's Question," NEQ, 42 (March,
1969), 106-107.

Thomas Shalvey, S.J., "Valery and Frost: Two Views of Subjective Reality," Renascence, 11 (Summer, 1959), 188.

_____. "Mending Wall"
Joseph Warren Beach, "Robert Frost," YR, 43 (Winter, 1953), 210-211.

Marie Borroff, "Robert Frost's New Testament: Language and the Poem,"
MP, 69 (Aug., 1971), 37-44.

J. K. Bowen, "The Persona in Frost's 'Mending Wall': Mended or Amended,"
CEA, 31 (Nov., 1968), 14.

John C. Broderick, Expl, 14 (Jan., 1956), 24.
   Rpt. The Explicator Cyclopedia, I, pp. 135-136.

Joseph J. Comprone, "Play and the 'Aesthetic State,'" MSE, 1 (Spring,
1967), 26-28.

Deutsch, This Modern Poetry, pp. 42-44.

S. L. Dragland, Expl, 25 (Jan., 1967), 39.

Carson Gibb, Expl, 20 (Feb., 1962), 48.
   Rpt. The Explicator Cyclopedia, I, pp. 136-137.

Jeremy Hawthorn, Identity and Relationship: A Contribution to Marxist
Theory of Literary Criticism (London: Lawrence & Wishart, 1973),
pp. 78-82.

Edward Jayne, "Up Against the 'Mending Wall': The Psychoanalysis of a
Poem by Frost," CE, 34 (April, 1973), 934-951.

Frank Lentricchia, "Experience as Meaning: Robert Frost's 'Mending Wall,'"
CEA, 34 (May, 1972), 8-12.

George Monteiro, "Robert Frost's Linked Analogies," NEQ, 46 (Sept.,
1973), 466-468.

George Monteiro, "Unlinked Myth in Frost's 'Mending Wall,'" CP, 7 (Fall,
1974), 10-11.

Marion Montgomery, "Robert Frost and His Use of Barriers: Man vs. Nature
Toward God," SAQ, 57 (Summer, 1958), 349-350.

William H. Pritchard, "The Grip of Frost," HudR, 29 (Summer, 1976), 190-192.

Rosenthal and Smith, Exploring Poetry, pp. 5-6.

Thomas Shalvey, S.J., "Valery and Frost: Two Views of Subjective Reality," Renascence, 11 (Summer, 1959), 187.

William S. Ward, "Lifted Pot Lids and Unmended Walls," CE, 27 (Feb., 1966), 428-429.

Charles N. Watson, Jr., "Frost's Wall: The View from the Other Side," NEQ, 44 (Dec., 1971), 653-656.

Wheeler, The Design of Poetry, p. 53.

_____. "Moon Compasses"
Robert F. Fleissner, Expl, 32 (May, 1974), 66.

_____. "The Most of It"
Robert Pinsky, The Situation of Poetry: Contemporary Poetry and Its Traditions (Princeton, New Jersey: Princeton Univ. Press, 1976), pp. 65-68.

Richard Poirier, "Soundings for Home: Frost's Poetry of Extravagance and Return," GaR, 31 (Summer, 1977), 304-312.

William H. Pritchard, "The Grip of Frost," HudR, 29 (Summer, 1976), 200-203.

Thomas Shalvey, S.J., "Valery and Frost: Two Views of Subjective Reality," Renascence, 11 (Summer, 1959), 188.

Yvor Winters, "Robert Frost: Or, The Spiritual Drifter as Poet," SR, 56 (Autumn, 1948), 591-592.
    Rpt. The Function of Criticism, pp. 182-183.
    Rpt. Zabel, Literary Opinion in America, revised edition, pp. 435-436.

_____. "The Mountain"
Laurence Perrine, "Frost's 'The Mountain': Concerning Poetry," CP, 4 (Spring, 1971), 5-11.

_____. "Mowing"
Marie Borroff, "Robert Frost's New Testament: Language and the Poem," MP, 69 (Aug., 1971), 46-47.

Seymour Chatman, "Robert Frost's 'Mowing': An Inquiry into Prosodic Structure," in Discussions of Poetry: Rhythm and Sound, ed. George Hemphill (Boston: D. C. Heath and Comapny, 1961), pp. 85-92.

Lewis H. Miller, Jr., "The Poet as Swinger: Fact and Fancy in Robert Frost," Criticism, 16 (Winter, 1974), 64-67.

Harold E. Toliver, Pastoral: Forms and Attitudes (Berkeley: Univ. of Calif. Press, 1971), pp. 344-345.

_____. "Nature's First Green is Gold"
Southworth, Some Modern American Poets, pp. 84-85.

_____. "The Need of Being Versed in Country Things"
Brooks, Purser, and Warren, An Approach to Literature, third edition, pp. 346-347.
    Rpt. fourth edition, pp. 344-345.

_____. "Neither Out Far Nor in Deep"
Harold H. Corbin, Jr., and Cecilia Hennel Hendricks, Expl, 1 (May, 1943), 58.
    Rpt. The Explicator Cyclopedia, I, p. 137.

Clark Griffith, "Frost and the American View of Nature," AQ, 20 (Spring, 1968), 30-32.

Cecilia Hennel Hendricks, Expl, 1 (May, 1943), 58.
    Rpt. The Explicator Cyclopedia, I, pp. 137-138.

Randall Jarrell, "To the Laodiceans," The Kenyon Review, 14 (Autumn, 1952), 539-540.

D. J. Lepore, "Robert Frost--The Middle Ground: An Analysis of 'Neither Out Far Nor in Deep,'" EJ, 53 (March, 1964), 215-216.

Laurence Perrine, Expl, 7 (April, 1949), 46.
    Rpt. The Explicator Cyclopedia, I, p. 138.

R. W. Stallman, "The Position of Poetry Today," EJ, 46 (May, 1957), 247-248.

_____. "Never Again Would Birds' Song Be the Same"
Richard Poirier, "Soundings for Home: Frost's Poetry of Extravagance and Return," GaR, 31 (Summer, 1977), 313-314.

_____. "New Hampshire"
Jeffrey Hart, "Frost and Eliot," SR, 84 (July-Sept., 1976), 429-432.

James R. Vitelli, "Robert Frost: The Contrarieties of Talent and Tradition," NEQ, 47 (Sept., 1974), 361-362.

_____. "Not All There"
Morton W. Bloomfield, "The Two Cognitive Dimensions of the Humanities," Daedalus, 99 (Spring, 1970), 256-267.

Robert F. Fleissner, Expl, 31 (Jan., 1973), 33.

_____. "Nothing Gold Can Stay"
Charles R. Anderson, Expl, 22 (April, 1964), 63.

Warren Beck, "Poetry's Chronic Disease," EJ, 33 (Sept., 1944), 363.

Walter Sutton, "The Contextualist Dilemma--or Fallacy?" JAAC, 17 (Dec., 1958), 225-226.

_____. "October"
Southworth, Some Modern American Poets, pp. 69-71.

_____. "The Oft-Repeated Dream"
Felver and Nurmi, Poetry: An Introduction and Anthology, pp. 78-79.

_____. "An Old Man's Winter Night"
Charles G. Davis, Expl, 27 (Nov., 1968), 19.

_____. "On a Tree Fallen Across the Road"
Peter W. Dowell, "Counter-Images and Their Function in the Poetry of Robert Frost," TSL, 14 (1969), 25-27.

_____. "Once by the Pacific"
Clark Griffith, "Frost and the American View of Nature," AQ, 20 (Spring, 1968), 34-36.

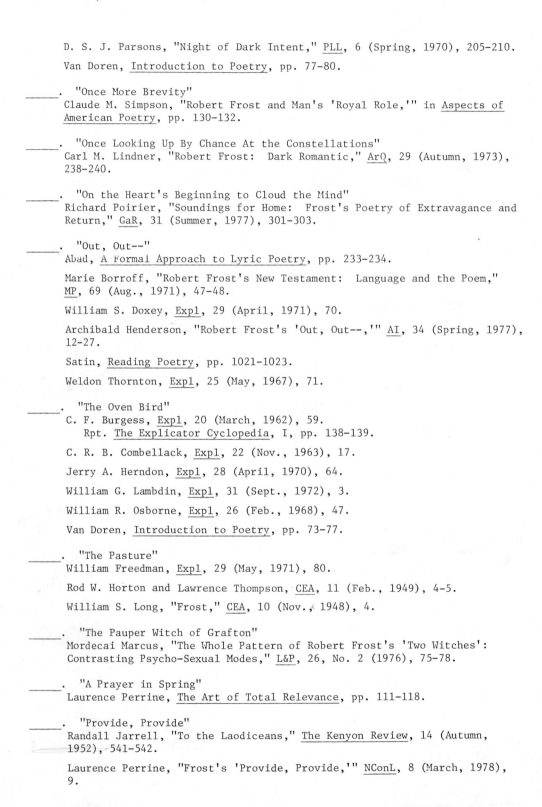

D. S. J. Parsons, "Night of Dark Intent," PLL, 6 (Spring, 1970), 205-210.

Van Doren, Introduction to Poetry, pp. 77-80.

_____. "Once More Brevity"
Claude M. Simpson, "Robert Frost and Man's 'Royal Role,'" in Aspects of American Poetry, pp. 130-132.

_____. "Once Looking Up By Chance At the Constellations"
Carl M. Lindner, "Robert Frost: Dark Romantic," ArQ, 29 (Autumn, 1973), 238-240.

_____. "On the Heart's Beginning to Cloud the Mind"
Richard Poirier, "Soundings for Home: Frost's Poetry of Extravagance and Return," GaR, 31 (Summer, 1977), 301-303.

_____. "Out, Out--"
Abad, A Formal Approach to Lyric Poetry, pp. 233-234.

Marie Borroff, "Robert Frost's New Testament: Language and the Poem," MP, 69 (Aug., 1971), 47-48.

William S. Doxey, Expl, 29 (April, 1971), 70.

Archibald Henderson, "Robert Frost's 'Out, Out--,'" AI, 34 (Spring, 1977), 12-27.

Satin, Reading Poetry, pp. 1021-1023.

Weldon Thornton, Expl, 25 (May, 1967), 71.

_____. "The Oven Bird"
C. F. Burgess, Expl, 20 (March, 1962), 59.
    Rpt. The Explicator Cyclopedia, I, pp. 138-139.

C. R. B. Combellack, Expl, 22 (Nov., 1963), 17.

Jerry A. Herndon, Expl, 28 (April, 1970), 64.

William G. Lambdin, Expl, 31 (Sept., 1972), 3.

William R. Osborne, Expl, 26 (Feb., 1968), 47.

Van Doren, Introduction to Poetry, pp. 73-77.

_____. "The Pasture"
William Freedman, Expl, 29 (May, 1971), 80.

Rod W. Horton and Lawrence Thompson, CEA, 11 (Feb., 1949), 4-5.

William S. Long, "Frost," CEA, 10 (Nov., 1948), 4.

_____. "The Pauper Witch of Grafton"
Mordecai Marcus, "The Whole Pattern of Robert Frost's 'Two Witches': Contrasting Psycho-Sexual Modes," L&P, 26, No. 2 (1976), 75-78.

_____. "A Prayer in Spring"
Laurence Perrine, The Art of Total Relevance, pp. 111-118.

_____. "Provide, Provide"
Randall Jarrell, "To the Laodiceans," The Kenyon Review, 14 (Autumn, 1952), 541-542.

Laurence Perrine, "Frost's 'Provide, Provide,'" NConL, 8 (March, 1978), 9.

_____. "Putting in the Seed"
Daniel R. Barnes, Expl, 31 (April, 1973), 59.

_____. "Quandary"
Thomas K. Hearn, Jr. "Making Sweetbreads Do: Robert Frost and Moral
Empiricism," NEQ, 49 (March, 1976), 73-75.

_____. "Range-Finding"
Peter W. Dowell, "Counter-Images and Their Function in the Poetry of
Robert Frost," TSL, 14 (1969), 20-22.

Darrel Mansell, Expl, 24 (March, 1966), 63.

_____. "Reluctance"
Dickinson, Suggestions for Teachers of "Introduction to Literature,"
fifth edition, ed. Locke, Gibson, and Arms, p. 40. (Teacher's Manual)

_____. "The Road Not Taken"
William B. Bache, "Rationalization in Two Frost Poems," BSUF, 11 (Winter,
1970), 33-34.

Daniels, The Art of Reading Poetry, pp. 347-349.

Robert W. French, "Reading Frost: 'The Road Not Taken,'" EngR, 26
(Spring, 1975), 91-93.

Ben W. Griffith, Jr., Expl, 12 (June, 1954), 55.
   Rpt. The Explicator Cyclopedia, I, pp. 139-140.

R. G. Malbone, Expl, 24 (Nov., 1965), 27.

Laurence Perrine, Expl, 19 (Feb., 1961), 28.
   Rpt. The Explicator Cyclopedia, I, p. 140.

Eleanor M. Sickels, Expl, 19 (Feb., 1961), 28.
   Rpt. The Explicator Cyclopedia, I, pp. 140-141.

Southworth, Some Modern American Poets, pp. 74-75.

Walsh, Doors into Poetry, pp. 52-53.

_____. "The Rose Family"
Laurence Perrine, Expl, 26 (Jan., 1968), 43.

_____. "The Runaway"
Charles B. Hands, "The Hidden Terror of Robert Frost," EJ, 58 (Nov.,
1969), 1165-1166.

Mark Van Doren, "The Permanence of Robert Frost," ASch, 5 (Spring,
1936), 190-198.

_____. "Sand Dunes"
Laurence Perrine, Expl, 14 (March, 1956), 38.
   Rpt. The Explicator Cyclopedia, I, p. 141.

R. W. Stallman, "The Position of Poetry Today," EJ, 46 (May, 1957),
246-247.

_____. "The Self-Seeker"
Laurence Perrine, "The Sense of Frost's 'The Self-Seeker,'" CP, 7 (Fall,
1974), 5-8.

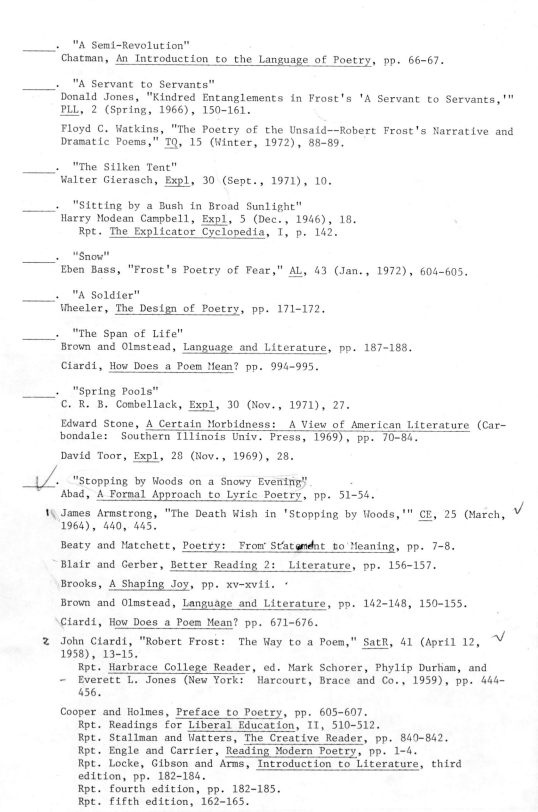

_____. "A Semi-Revolution"
Chatman, An Introduction to the Language of Poetry, pp. 66-67.

_____. "A Servant to Servants"
Donald Jones, "Kindred Entanglements in Frost's 'A Servant to Servants,'"
PLL, 2 (Spring, 1966), 150-161.

Floyd C. Watkins, "The Poetry of the Unsaid--Robert Frost's Narrative and
Dramatic Poems," TQ, 15 (Winter, 1972), 88-89.

_____. "The Silken Tent"
Walter Gierasch, Expl, 30 (Sept., 1971), 10.

_____. "Sitting by a Bush in Broad Sunlight"
Harry Modean Campbell, Expl, 5 (Dec., 1946), 18.
    Rpt. The Explicator Cyclopedia, I, p. 142.

_____. "Snow"
Eben Bass, "Frost's Poetry of Fear," AL, 43 (Jan., 1972), 604-605.

_____. "A Soldier"
Wheeler, The Design of Poetry, pp. 171-172.

_____. "The Span of Life"
Brown and Olmstead, Language and Literature, pp. 187-188.

Ciardi, How Does a Poem Mean? pp. 994-995.

_____. "Spring Pools"
C. R. B. Combellack, Expl, 30 (Nov., 1971), 27.

Edward Stone, A Certain Morbidness: A View of American Literature (Carbondale: Southern Illinois Univ. Press, 1969), pp. 70-84.

David Toor, Expl, 28 (Nov., 1969), 28.

_____. "Stopping by Woods on a Snowy Evening".
Abad, A Formal Approach to Lyric Poetry, pp. 51-54.

James Armstrong, "The Death Wish in 'Stopping by Woods,'" CE, 25 (March,
1964), 440, 445.

Beaty and Matchett, Poetry: From Statement to Meaning, pp. 7-8.

Blair and Gerber, Better Reading 2: Literature, pp. 156-157.

Brooks, A Shaping Joy, pp. xv-xvii.

Brown and Olmstead, Language and Literature, pp. 142-148, 150-155.

Ciardi, How Does a Poem Mean? pp. 671-676.

John Ciardi, "Robert Frost: The Way to a Poem," SatR, 41 (April 12,
1958), 13-15.
    Rpt. Harbrace College Reader, ed. Mark Schorer, Phylip Durham, and
    Everett L. Jones (New York: Harcourt, Brace and Co., 1959), pp. 444-
    456.

Cooper and Holmes, Preface to Poetry, pp. 605-607.
    Rpt. Readings for Liberal Education, II, 510-512.
    Rpt. Stallman and Watters, The Creative Reader, pp. 840-842.
    Rpt. Engle and Carrier, Reading Modern Poetry, pp. 1-4.
    Rpt. Locke, Gibson and Arms, Introduction to Literature, third
    edition, pp. 182-184.
    Rpt. fourth edition, pp. 182-185.
    Rpt. fifth edition, 162-165.

- 3 Herbert R. Coursen, Jr., "The Ghost of Christmas Past: 'Stopping by Woods on a Snowy Evening,'" CE, 24 (Dec., 1962), 236-238.

- 4 James M. Cox, "Robert Frost and the Edge of the Clearing," VQR, 35 (Winter, 1959), 82-84.

  Daniels, The Art of Reading Poetry, pp. 16-18.
      Rpt. Stallman and Watters, The Creative Reader, pp. 857-878.

5 Virginia Faulkner, "More Frosting on the Woods," CE, 24 (April, 1963), 560-561.

- 6 Robert F. Fleissner, "Stopping Yet Again by Frost's Woods," RS, 45 (March, 1977), 45-49.

- 7 Charles B. Hands, "The Hidden Terror of Robert Frost," EJ, 58 (Nov, 1969), 1164-1165.

  Nat Henry, Expl, 32 (Jan., 1974), 33.

8 Selwyn Kittredge, "'Stopping By Woods on a Snowy Evening'--Without Tugging at the Reins," EngR, 23 (Fall, 1972), 37-39.

  Charles A. McLaughlin, "Two Views of Poetic Unity," The University of Kansas City Review, 22 (Summer, 1956), 312-315.

  Perrine, Sound and Sense, pp. 117-118, 124-125.
      Rpt. second edition, pp. 126-127, 136-137.

  Perrine and Reid, 100 American Poems, pp. 24-26.

- 9 Stanley Poss, "Low Skies, Some Clearing, Local Frost," NEQ, 41 (Sept., 1968), 438-442.

10 E. H. Rosenberry, "Toward Notes for 'Stopping by Woods': Some Classical Analogs," CE, 24 (April, 1963), 526-528.

- 11 W. H. Shurr, "Once More to the 'Woods': A New Point of Entry into Frost's Most Famous Poem," NEQ, 47 (Dec., 1974), 584-594.

12 Elmer F. Suderman, "The Frozen Lake in Frost's 'Stopping by Woods on a Snowy Evening,'" BSUF, 11 (Winter, 1970), 22.

  Unger and O'Connor, Poems for Study, pp. 597-600.

- 13 Charles Child Walcutt, "Interpreting the Symbol," CE, 14 (May, 1953), 450.

14 Richard Wilbur, "Poetry's Debt to Poetry," HudR, 26 (Summer, 1973), 292-293.

  Earl Wilcox, Expl, 27 (Sept., 1968), 7.

_____. "Storm Fear"
  Carl M. Lindner, "Robert Frost: Dark Romantic," ArQ, 29 (Autumn, 1973), 236-238.

_____. "The Subverted Flower"
  Howard Munford, Expl, 17 (Jan., 1959), 31.
      Rpt. The Explicator Cyclopedia, I, pp. 144-145.

  Donald B. Stauffer, Expl, 15 (March, 1957), 38.
      Rpt. The Explicator Cyclopedia, I, pp. 142-144.

_____. "The Thatch"
  Clark, Lyric Resonance, pp. 117-133.

  Laurence J. Sasso, Jr., "Robert Frost: Love's Question," NEQ, 42 (March, 1969), 102-104.

_____. "To Earthward"
Brooks, Purser, and Warren, An Approach to Literature, fourth edition,
p. 425.

Wilbur S. Scott, Expl, 16 (Jan., 1958), 23.
    Rpt. The Explicator Cyclopedia, I, p. 145.

_____. "To the Thawing Wind"
Bruce Stillians, Expl, 31 (Dec., 1972), 31.

_____. "Tree at My Window"
R. W. Stallman, "The Position of Poetry Today," EJ, 46 (May, 1957), 248-
249.

_____. "Trespass"
Marjorie Cook, "The Complexity of Boundaries: 'Trespass' by Robert
Frost," NConL, 5 (Jan., 1975), 2-5.

_____. "The Tuft of Flowers"
George Monteiro, "Robert Frost's Linked Analogies," NEQ, 46 (Sept., 1973),
464-466.

Laurence Perrine, "Four Forms of Metaphor," CE, 33 (Nov., 1971), 131-132.
    Rpt. The Art of Total Relevance, pp. 55-56.

Thomas Shalvey, S.J., "Valery and Frost: Two Views of Subjective Reality," Renascence, 11 (Summer, 1959), 187-188.

Sr. Mary Anthony Weinig, "A Note on Robert Frost's 'Tuft of Flowers,'"
CP, 2 (Spring, 1969), 79.

_____. "Two Look at Two"
Laurence J. Sasso, Jr., "Robert Frost: Love's Question," NEQ, 42 (March,
1969), 105-106.

_____. "Two Tramps in Mud Time"
Abad, A Formal Approach to Lyric Poetry, pp. 185-186, 232-233.

William B. Bache, "Rationalization in Two Frost Poems," BSUF, 11 (Winter,
1970), 34-35.

Walter Blair, The Literature of the United States, II, 940.

Albert Braverman and Bernard Einbond, Expl, 29 (Nov., 1970), 25.

Brooks, Modern Poetry and the Tradition, pp. 112-113.

Joseph J. Comprone, "Play and the 'Aesthetic State,'" MSE, 1 (Spring,
1967), 28-29.

Richard Foster, "Leaves Compared with Flowers: A Reading in Robert
Frost's Poems," NEQ, 46 (Sept., 1973), 418-420.

Charles Kaplan, Expl, 12 (June, 1954), 51.
    Rpt. The Explicator Cyclopedia, I, pp. 145-146.

Laurence Perrine, "'Two Tramps in Mud Time' and The Critics," AL, 44
(Jan., 1973), 671-676.

Floyd C. Watkins, "The Poetry of the Unsaid--Robert Frost's Narrative and
Dramatic Poems," TQ, 15 (Winter, 1972), 96-97.

George F. Whicher, "Frost at Seventy," ASch, 14 (Autumn, 1945), 412-414.

_____. "Unharvested"
Harold E. Toliver, Pastoral: Forms and Attitudes (Berkeley: Univ. of
Calif. Press, 1971), pp. 346-348.

_____. "The Vanishing Red"
C. M. Bowra, "Reassessments I: Robert Frost," Adelphi, 27 (Nov., 1950), 46-64.

_____. "West-Running Brook"
Joseph Warren Beach, "Robert Frost," YR, 43 (Winter, 1953), 212.

Richard D. Lord, "Frost and Cyclicism," Renascence, 10 (Autumn, 1957), 20-25, 31.

Patrick Morrow, "The Greek Nexus in Robert Frost's 'West-Running Brook,'" The Personalist, 49 (Winter, 1968), 24-33.

Laurence Perrine, Expl, 35 (Summer, 1977), 26-27.

Laurence J. Sasso, Jr., "Robert Frost: Love's Question," NEQ, 42 (March, 1969), 98-100.

Robert H. Swennes, "Man and Wife: The Dialogue of Contraries in Robert Frost's Poetry," AL, 42 (Nov., 1970), 369-371.

H. H. Watts, "Robert Frost and the Interrupted Dialogue," AL, 27 (March, 1955), 70-74 et passim.

H. T. Webster, Expl, 8 (Feb., 1950), 32.
    Rpt. The Explicator Cyclopedia, I, pp. 146-148.

_____. "Wild Grapes"
Helen Bacon, "For Girls: From 'Birches' to 'Wild Grapes,'" YR, 67 (Oct., 1977), 13-29.

_____. "A Wishing Well"
A. R. Ferguson, "Frost, Sill, and 'A Wishing Well,'" AL, 33 (Nov., 1961), 370-373.

Claude M. Simpson, "Robert Frost and Man's 'Royal Role,'" in Aspects of American Poetry, pp. 133-135.

_____. "The Witch of Coös"
Eben Bass, "Frost's Poetry of Fear," AL, 43 (Jan., 1972), 612-613.

Mordecai Marcus, "The Whole Pattern of Robert Frost's 'Two Witches': Contrasting Psycho-Sexual Modes," L&P, 26, No. 2 (1976), 69-74.

Perrine and Reid, 100 American Poems, pp. 41-43.

Fred C. Schutz, Expl, 33 (Nov, 1974), 19.

Camille Slights and William Slights, Expl, 27 (Feb., 1969), 40.

Thomas R. Thornburg, "Mother's Private Ghost: A Note on Frost's 'The Witch of Coös,'" BSUF, 11 (Winter, 1970), 16-20.

Floyd C. Watkins, "The Poetry of the Unsaid--Robert Frost's Narrative and Dramatic Poems," TQ, 15 (Winter, 1972), 96.

_____. "A Witness Tree"
Alvin S. Ryan, Expl, 7 (March, 1949), 39.
    Rpt. The Explicator Cyclopedia, I, p. 148.

_____. "The Wood-Pile"
Ferman Bishop, Expl, 18 (June, 1960), 58.
    Rpt. The Explicator Cyclopedia, pp. 148-149.

Brooks, Modern Poetry and the Tradition, pp. 113-114.

Brooks, Purser, Warren, <u>An Approach to Literature</u>, pp. 453-454.
   Rpt. third edition, pp. 305-307.
   Rpt. fourth edition, pp. 421-423.

Alexander C. Kern, <u>Expl</u>, 28 (Feb., 1970), 49.

Laurence Lerner, "An Essay on Pastoral," <u>EIC</u>, 20 (July, 1970), 275-277.

Laurence Lerner, <u>The Uses of Nostalgia: Studies in Pastoral Poetry</u> (New York: Schocken Books, 1972), 11-13.

Lewis H. Miller, Jr., "The Poet as Swinger: Fact and Fancy in Robert Frost," <u>Criticism</u>, 16 (Winter, 1974), 67-72.

Robert D. Narveson, "On Frost's 'The Wood-Pile,'" <u>EJ</u>, 57 (Jan., 1968), 39-40.

Richard Poirier, "Soundings for Home: Frost's Poetry of Extravagance and Return," <u>GaR</u>, 31 (Summer, 1977), 288-292.

_____. "A Young Birch"
Mario L. D'Avanzo, "Frost's 'A Young Birch': A Thing of Beauty," <u>CP</u>, 3 (Fall, 1970), 69-70.

FRY, Christopher. "Venus Observed"
Robert C. Fox, <u>Expl</u>, 16 (May, 1958), 47.

GARDNER, Isabella. "Summer Remembered"
Perrine and Reid, <u>100 American Poems</u>, pp. 236-237.

_____. "The Widow's Yard"
Carroll, <u>The Poem in Its Skin</u>, pp. 51-62.

GARRIGUE. "Dialog for Belvedere"
Joseph Warren Beach, "The Cancelling Out--A Note on Recent Poetry," <u>Accent</u>, 7 (Summer, 1947), 246-248.

GARTH, Samuel. "The Dispensary"
Nancy Conrad Martinez, "Little Epics: More Lively and Choleric," Diss. University of New Mexico, 1976, pp. 107-121.

John F. Sena, "Samuel Garth's <u>The Dispensary</u>," <u>TSLL</u>, 15 (Winter, 1974), 639-648.

GASCOIGNE, George. "The Constancy of a Lover Hath Thus Sometimes Been Briefly Declared"
Sloan, <u>The Rhetoric of Renaissance Poetry</u>, pp. 13-14.

_____. "Gascoigne's Woodmanship"   _____.
Peterson, <u>The English Lyric from Wyatt to Donne</u>, pp. 154-159.

Yvor Winters, "The 16th Century Lyric in England: Part I," <u>Poetry</u>, 53 (Feb., 1939), 269-272.
   Rpt. <u>Forms of Discovery</u>, pp. 17-19.

_____. "Good Morrow"
Malcolm M. Ross, "History and Poetry: Decline of the Historical Concrete," <u>Thought</u>, 26 (Autumn, 1951), 437-438.

_____. "The Lullaby of a Lover"
Leonard Nathan, "Gascoigne's 'Lullaby' and Structures in the Tudor Lyric," in <u>The Rhetoric of Renaissance Poetry</u>, pp. 65-71.

Peterson, <u>The English Lyric from Wyatt to Donne</u>, pp. 160-162.

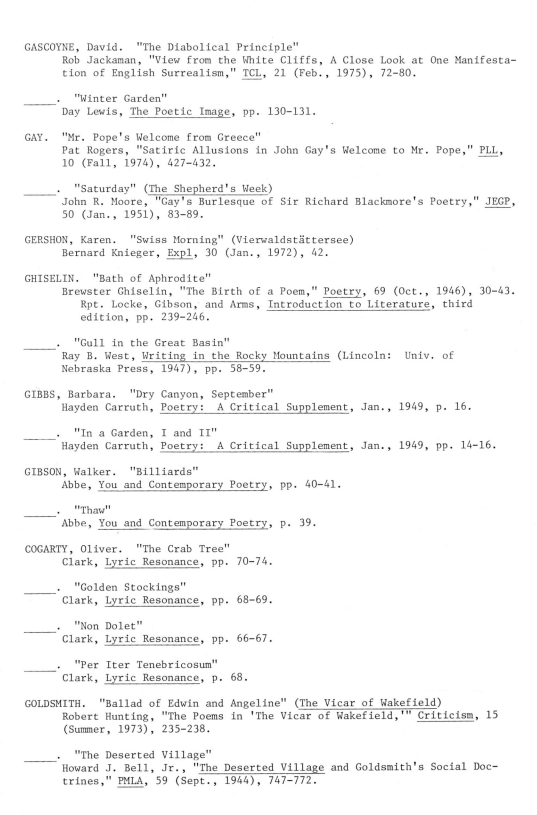

GASCOYNE, David. "The Diabolical Principle"
　　　Rob Jackaman, "View from the White Cliffs, A Close Look at One Manifesta-
　　　tion of English Surrealism," TCL, 21 (Feb., 1975), 72-80.

_____. "Winter Garden"
　　　Day Lewis, The Poetic Image, pp. 130-131.

GAY. "Mr. Pope's Welcome from Greece"
　　　Pat Rogers, "Satiric Allusions in John Gay's Welcome to Mr. Pope," PLL,
　　　10 (Fall, 1974), 427-432.

_____. "Saturday" (The Shepherd's Week)
　　　John R. Moore, "Gay's Burlesque of Sir Richard Blackmore's Poetry," JEGP,
　　　50 (Jan., 1951), 83-89.

GERSHON, Karen. "Swiss Morning" (Vierwaldstättersee)
　　　Bernard Knieger, Expl, 30 (Jan., 1972), 42.

GHISELIN. "Bath of Aphrodite"
　　　Brewster Ghiselin, "The Birth of a Poem," Poetry, 69 (Oct., 1946), 30-43.
　　　　　Rpt. Locke, Gibson, and Arms, Introduction to Literature, third
　　　　　edition, pp. 239-246.

_____. "Gull in the Great Basin"
　　　Ray B. West, Writing in the Rocky Mountains (Lincoln: Univ. of
　　　Nebraska Press, 1947), pp. 58-59.

GIBBS, Barbara. "Dry Canyon, September"
　　　Hayden Carruth, Poetry: A Critical Supplement, Jan., 1949, p. 16.

_____. "In a Garden, I and II"
　　　Hayden Carruth, Poetry: A Critical Supplement, Jan., 1949, pp. 14-16.

GIBSON, Walker. "Billiards"
　　　Abbe, You and Contemporary Poetry, pp. 40-41.

_____. "Thaw"
　　　Abbe, You and Contemporary Poetry, p. 39.

COGARTY, Oliver. "The Crab Tree"
　　　Clark, Lyric Resonance, pp. 70-74.

_____. "Golden Stockings"
　　　Clark, Lyric Resonance, pp. 68-69.

_____. "Non Dolet"
　　　Clark, Lyric Resonance, pp. 66-67.

_____. "Per Iter Tenebricosum"
　　　Clark, Lyric Resonance, p. 68.

GOLDSMITH. "Ballad of Edwin and Angeline" (The Vicar of Wakefield)
　　　Robert Hunting, "The Poems in 'The Vicar of Wakefield,'" Criticism, 15
　　　(Summer, 1973), 235-238.

_____. "The Deserted Village"
　　　Howard J. Bell, Jr., "The Deserted Village and Goldsmith's Social Doc-
　　　trines," PMLA, 59 (Sept., 1944), 747-772.

Donald Davie, "The Deserted Village: Poem as Virtual History," TC, 156 (Aug., 1954), 168-174.

Edwards, Imagination and Power, pp. 129-136.

Morris Golden, "The Broken Dream of The Deserted Village," L&P, 9 (Summer & Fall, 1959), 41-44.

Laurence Goldstein, "The Auburn Syndrome: Change and Loss in 'The De-serted Village' and Wordsworth's Grasemere," ELH, 40 (Fall, 1973), 354-359.

Richard J. Jaarsma, "Ethics in the Wasteland: Image and Structure in Goldsmith's The Deserted Village," TSLL, 13 (Fall, 1971), 447-459.

Robert Mahony, "Lyrical Antithesis: The Moral Style of The Deserted Village," ArielE, 8 (April, 1977), 33-47.

Desmond Pacey, "The Goldsmith's and their Villages," UTQ, 21 (Oct., 1951), 27-38.

Richard Quintana, "The Deserted Village: Its Logical and Rhetorical Elements," CE, 26 (Dec., 1964), 204-214.

_____. "An Elegy on the Death of a Mad Dog"
Robert Hunting, "The Poems in 'The Vicar of Wakefield,'" Criticism, 15 (Summer, 1973), 238-240.

_____. "Retaliation"
Charles Duffey, Expl, 7 (Oct., 1948), 6.
    Rpt. The Explicator Cyclopedia, II, p. 144.

_____. "The Traveller, or a Prospect of Society"
Richard J. Jaarsma, "Satire, Theme, and Structure in The Traveller," TSL, 16 (1971), 47-65.

GOODYERE, Sir Henry. "Elegie on the Untimely Death of the Incomparable Prince, Henry"
Barbara Kiefer Lewalski, Donne's Anniversaries and the Poetry of Praise: The Creation of a Symbolic Mode (Princeton: Princeton Univ. Press, 1973), 323-324.

GOOGE, Barnabe. "Cupido Conquered"
William E. Sheidley, "A Timely Anachronism: Tradition and Theme in Barnabe Googe's 'Cupido Conquered,'" SP, 69 (April, 1972), 150-166.

GRAHAM. "The White Threshold"
Leonie Adams, "First Poems of Celebration," Poetry, 82 (Aug., 1953), 275-276.

GRAVES. "Apple Island"
David Ormerod, Expl, 32 (March, 1974), 53.

_____. "The Bard"
Hoffman, Barbarous Knowledge, pp. 166-168.

_____. "The Castle"
Hoffman, Barbarous Knowledge, pp. 172-173.

_____. "The Cool Web"
Hoffman, Barbarous Knowledge, pp. 178-179.

_____. "Ecstasy of Chaos"
Patrick J. Callahan, "Toward Yet Unvisited Harbors," PrS, 44 (Spring, 1970), 176–177.

_____. "Pure Death"
Hoffman, Barbarous Knowledge, pp. 187–188.

_____. "The Return of the Goddess Artemis"
Robert Graves, Poetry: A Critical Supplement, April, 1948, pp. 18–21.

J. F. Nims, Poetry: A Critical Supplement, Oct., 1947, pp. 14–16.

_____. "Rocky Acres"
Hoffman, Barbarous Knowledge, pp. 164–165.

_____. "Saint"
Patricia Lacerva, Expl, 29 (Dec., 1970), 31.

_____. "The Second Fated"
Hoffman, Barbarous Knowledge, pp. 10–13.

_____. "Sick Love"
Hoffman, Barbarous Knowledge, pp. 188–189.

_____. "To Juan at the Winter Solstice"
Robert Graves in Friar and Brinnin, Modern Poetry, pp. 500–501.

Hoffman, Barbarous Knowledge, pp. 214–217.

Bruce A. Rosenberg, Expl, 21 (Sept., 1962), 3.

_____. "What Did You Say?"
Patrick J. Callahan, "Toward Yet Unvisited Harbors," PrS, 44 (Spring, 1970), 174–175.

_____. "The White Goddess"
Feder, Ancient Myth in Modern Poetry, pp. 366–367.

GRAY. "The Bard"
Patricia M. Spacks, "Artful Strife: Conflict in Gray's Poetry," PMLA, 81 (March, 1966), 66–67.

Spacks, The Poetry of Vision, pp. 110–112.

_____. "Elegy Written in a Country Churchyard"
Bateson, English Poetry, pp. 181–193.

Frank Brady, "Structure and Meaning in Gray's Elegy," in From Sensibility to Romanticism, pp. 177–187.

Brooks, The Well Wrought Urn, pp. 96–113. Abridged in The Case for Poetry, pp. 157–159.

Chatman, An Introduction to the Language of Poetry, pp. 5–7, 19–22.

Daiches and Charvat, Poems in English, p. 684.

A. E. Dyson, "The Ambivalence of Gray's 'Elegy,'" EIC, 7 (July, 1957), 257–261.

Edwards, Imagination and Power, pp. 120–129.

Frank H. Ellis, "Gray's Elegy: The Biographical Problem in Literary Criticism," PMLA, 66 (Dec., 1951), 984-1008. Abridged in The Case for Poetry, pp. 161-163.

Empson, English Pastoral Poetry, p. 4.
   Rpt. Brooks and Warren, Understanding Poetry, pp. 514-515.

William Empson, "Thy Darling in an Urn," SR, 55 (Oct.-Dec., 1957), 692. Abridged in The Case for Poetry, p. 159.

William Frost, English Masterpieces, Vol. VI, Romantic and Victorian Poetry, pp. 19-20.

Lyle Glazier, "Gray's Elegy: 'The Skull Beneath the Skin,'" The University of Kansas City Review, 19 (Spring, 1953), 174-180.

James M. Kuist, "The Conclusion of Gray's Elegy," SAQ, 70 (Spring, 1971), 203-214.

Richard Leighton Greene, Expl, 24 (Jan., 1966), 47.

Curt Hartog, "Psychic Resolution in Gray's Elegy," L&P, 25, No. 1 (1975), 5-16.

Theodore C. Hoepfner, Expl, 8 (March, 1950), 35.
   Rpt. The Explicator Cyclopedia, II, p. 145.

Ian Jack, "Gray's Elegy Reconsidered," in From Sensibility to Romanticism, pp. 155-167.

Bertrand H. Johnson, "On a Special Decorum in Gray's Elegy," in From Sensibility to Romanticism, pp. 171-176.

E. D. Mackerness, "Thomas Gray," ContempR, 174 (Sept., 1948), 168-169.

Rene Rapin, Expl, 9 (Nov., 1950), 14.
   Rpt. The Explicator Cyclopedia, II, p. 145.

Eric Smith, By Mourning Tongues: Studies in English Elegy (Ipswich and Totowa: The Boydell Press and Rowan and Littlefield, 1977), pp. 40-54.

Patricia M. Spacks, "Artful Strife: Conflict in Gray's Poetry," PMLA, 81 (March, 1966), 68-69.

Spacks, The Poetry of Vision, pp. 115-116.

Stageberg and Anderson, Poetry as Experience, pp. 195-197,

Herbert W. Starr, "'A Youth to Fortune and to Fame Unknown': A Re-Estimation," JEGP, 48 (Jan., 1949), 97-107.

Richard P. Sugg, "The Importance of Voice: Gray's Elegy," TSL, 19 (1974), 115-120.

P. E. Vernon, "The Structure of Gray's Early Poems," EIC, 15 (Oct., 1965), 390-393.

Vivante, English Poetry, pp. 80-82.

George Watson, "The Voice of Gray," CritQ, 19 (Winter, 1977), 51-57.

Winters, Forms of Discovery, pp. 155-157.

George T. Wright, "Stillness and the Argument of Gray's Elegy," MP, 74 (May, 1977), 381-389.

_____. "Ode on a Distant Prospect of Eton College"
Frank H. Ellis, "Gray's Eton College Ode: The Problem of Tone," PLL, 5 (Spring, 1969), 130-138.

Geoffrey H. Hartman, "Romantic Poetry and the Genius Loci," in The Disciplines of Criticism: Essays in Literary Theory, Interpretation, and History, eds. Peter Demetz, Thomas Greene, and Lowry Nelson, Jr. (New Haven and London: Yale Univ. Press, 1968), pp. 293-299.

Patrica M. Spacks, "Statement and Artifice in Thomas Gray," SEL, 5 (Summer, 1965), 527-532.

Spacks, The Poetry of Vision, pp. 98-103.

Karl F. Thompson, Expl, 9 (Feb., 1951), 28.
   Rpt. The Explicator Cyclopedia, II, pp. 145-146.

P. E. Vernon, "The Structure of Gray's Early Poems," EIC, 15 (Oct., 1965), 387-390.

Frederick C. Wilkins, Expl, 25 (April, 1967), 66.

_____. "Ode on the Death of a Favorite Cat Drowned in a Tub of Gold Fishes"
Empson, Seven Types of Ambiguity, pp. 97-99, 154-155; (1947 ed.), pp. 77, 121-123.

_____. "Ode I: On the Spring"
Robert F. Gleckner, "Blake, Gray, and the Illustrations," Criticism, 19 (Spring, 1977), 121-127.

Peckham and Chatman, Word, Meaning, Poem, pp. 224-238.

Patricia M. Spacks, "Statement and Artifice in Thomas Gray," SEL, 5 (Summer, 1965), 520-524.

Spacks, The Poetry of Vision, pp. 91-95.

P. E. Vernon, "The Structure of Gray's Early Poems," EIC, 15 (Oct., 1965), 382-387.

_____. "The Progress of Poesy"
Arthur Dickson, Expl, 9 (May, 1951), 49.
   Rpt. The Explicator Cyclopedia, II, p. 146.

John S. Phillipson, Expl, 29 (May, 1971), 78.

Patricia M. Spacks, "Artful Strife: Conflict in Gray's Poetry," PMLA, 81 (March, 1966), 63-66.

Spacks, The Poetry of Vision, pp. 103-110.

_____. "Sonnet On the Death of Richard West"
William B. Bache, "Gray's 'Sonnet: On the Death of Richard,'" CEA, 31 (Nov., 1968), 12.

Joseph Foladare, "Gray's 'Frail Memorial' to West," PMLA, 75 (March, 1960), 61-65.

Donald C. Mell, Jr., "Form as Meaning in Augustan Elegy: A Reading of Thomas Gray's 'Sonnet on the Death of Richard West,'" PLL, 4 (Spring, 1968), 131-143.

Patricia M. Spacks, "Statement and Artifice in Thomas Gray," SEL, 5 (Summer, 1965), 524-527.

Spacks, The Poetry of Vision, pp. 95-98.

GREENE. "The Shepherd Wife's Song"
   Ribner and Morris, Poetry, pp. 81-83.

_____. "Sweet Are the Thoughts"
George Arms and L. G. Locke, Expl, 3 (Feb., 1945), 27.
    Rpt. The Explicator Cyclopedia, II, p. 147.

GREGORY. "Bridgewater Jones: Impromptu in a Speakeasy"
    Robert K. Morris, "The Resurrected Vision: Horace Gregory's Thirties
    Poems," MPS, 4 (Spring, 1973), 82-83.

_____. "Chorus for Survival"
    Robert K. Morris, "The Resurrected Vision: Horace Gregory's Thirties
    Poems," MPS, 4 (Spring, 1973), 96-99.

_____. "O Metaphysical Head"
    Robert K. Morris, "The Resurrected Vision: Horace Gregory's Thirties
    Poems," MPS, 4 (Spring, 1973), 81-82.

_____. "O Mors Acterna"
    Robert K. Morris, "The Resurrected Vision: Horace Gregory's Thirties
    Poems," MPS, 4 (Spring, 1973), 84-85.

_____. "Under the Stone I Saw Them Flow" (from Chorus for Survival)
    Walter Gierasch, "Reading Modern Poetry," CE, 2 (Oct., 1940), 33-34.

    Walter Gierasch, Expl, 3 (June, 1945), 63.
        Rpt. The Explicator Cyclopedia, I, pp. 149-150.

GREVILLE, Fulke. "All My Senses, Like Beacons Flame"
    Winters, Forms of Discovery, pp. 46-48.

_____. "Caelica," Sonnet 2
Gary L. Litt, "'Images of Life': A Study of Narrative and Structure in
Fulke Greville's Caelica," SP, 69 (April, 1972), 223-224.

_____. "Caelica," Sonnet 7
Gary L. Litt, "'Images of Life': A Study of Narrative and Structure in
Fulke Greville's Caelica," SP, 69 (April, 1972), 218-219.

_____. "Caelica," Sonnet 16
Sloan, The Rhetoric of Renaissance Poetry, pp. 19-21.

_____. "Caelica," Sonnet 22
Williamson, The Proper Wit of Poetry, pp. 28-29.

_____. "Caelica," Sonnet 38
Peter Heidtmann, "The Lyrics of Fulke Greville," OhR, 10 (1968), 34-36.

_____. "Caelica," Sonnet 69
Williamson, The Proper Wit of Poetry, pp. 29-30.

_____. "Caelica," Sonnet 87
De Mourgues, Metaphysical Baroque & Precieux Poetry, pp. 24-25.

_____. "Caelica," Sonnet 99
Peter Heidtmann, "The Lyrics of Fulke Greville," OhR, 10 (1968), 38-40.

_____. "Caelica," Sonnet 100
Ernest B. Gilman, The Curious Perspective: Literary and Pictorial Wit in
the Seventeenth Century (New Haven and London: Yale Univ. Press, 1978),
pp. 198-201.

_____. "Down in the Depth of Mine Iniquity"
Winters, Forms of Discovery, pp. 49-51.

GUNN, Thom. "The Corridor"
Lawrence R. Ries, Wolf Masks: Violence in Contemporary Poetry (Port
Washington, N.Y.: Kennikat Press, 1977), pp. 79-80.

_____. "Elegy on the Dust"
Merle E. Brown, "A Critical Performance of Thom Gunn's 'Misanthropos,'"
IowaR, 4 (Winter, 1973), 81-83.

_____. "On the Move"
Lawrence R. Ries, Wolf Masks: Violence in Contemporary Poetry (Port
Washington, N.Y.: Kennikat Press, 1977), pp. 73-75.

_____. "The Wound"
John Miller, "The Stipulative Imagination of Thom Gunn," IowaR, 4 (Winter,
1973), 58.

HALL, Donald. "The Body of Politics"
Perrine and Reid, 100 American Poems, pp. 273-274.

_____. "Cold Water"
Ralph J. Mills, Jr., "Donald Hall's Poetry," IowaR, 2 (Winter, 1971),
108-111.

_____. "Exile"
Ralph J. Mills, Jr., "Donald Hall's Poetry," IowaR, 2 (Winter, 1971), 85-86.

_____. "The Grass"
Ralph J. Mills, Jr., "Donald Hall's Poetry," IowaR, 2 (Winter, 1971), 98-
99.

_____. "The Snow"
Ralph J. Mills, Jr., "Donald Hall's Poetry," IowaR, 2 (Winter, 1971), 96-
98.

_____. "The Stump"
Ralph J. Mills, Jr., "Donald Hall's Poetry," IowaR, 2 (Winter, 1971), 102-
104.

_____. "Swan"
Ralph J. Mills, Jr., "Donald Hall's Poetry," IowaR, 2 (Winter, 1971), 117-
120.

_____. "Wedding Party"
Ralph J. Mills, Jr., "Donald Hall's Poetry," IowaR, 2 (Winter, 1971), 86-
87.

_____. "Wells"
Ralph J. Mills, Jr., "Donald Hall's Poetry," IowaR, 2 (Winter, 1971), 105-
106.

HALLEY, Anne. "Dear God, the Day is Grey"
Perrine and Reid, 100 American Poems, pp. 288-289.

HARDY. "According to the Mighty Working"
John Crowe Ransom, "Honey and Gall," SoR, 6 (Summer, 1940), 10-11.

_____. "After a Journey"
David Holbrook, <u>Lost Bearings in English Poetry</u> (London: Vision Press, 1977), pp. 208-216.

F. R. Leavis, "Reality and Sincerity: Notes in the Analysis of Poetry," <u>Scrutiny</u>, 19 (Winter, 1953), 92-98.

Maire A. Quinn, "The Personal Past in the Poetry of Thomas Hardy and Edward Thomas," <u>CritQ</u>, 16 (Spring, 1974), 12-13.

_____. "After the Last Breath"
Ribner and Morris, <u>Poetry</u>, pp. 417-419.

_____. "Afterwards"
Charles Mitchell, "Hardy's 'Afterwards,'" <u>VP</u>, 1 (Spring, 1963), 68-70.

_____. "An Ancient to Ancients"
Deutsch, <u>Poetry in Our Time</u>, pp. 7-8.

_____. "At Castle Boterel"
Donald Davie, "Hardy's Virgilian Purples," <u>Agenda</u>, 10 (Spring-Summer, 1972), 154-155.

_____. "Beeny Cliff"
Donald Davie, "Hardy's Virgilian Purples," <u>Agenda</u>, 10 (Spring-Summer, 1972), 138-144.

_____. "Channel Firing"
Gerhard T. Alexis, <u>Expl</u>, 24 (March, 1966), 61.

Brooks and Warren, <u>Understanding Poetry</u>, pp. 309-311. Revised edition, pp. 164-166.

Deutsch, <u>Poetry in Our Time</u>, pp. 9-10.

Arthur W. Pitts, Jr., <u>Expl</u>, 26 (Nov., 1967), 24.

John Crowe Ransom, "Thomas Hardy's Poems and the Religious Difficulties of a Naturalist," <u>The Kenyon Review</u>, 22 (Spring, 1960), 170-173.

_____. "A Commonplace Day"
F. R. Leavis, "Hardy the Poet," <u>SoR</u>, 6 (Summer, 1940), 95-97.

_____. "The Contretemps"
Charles E. May, "Thomas Hardy and the Poetry of the Absurd," <u>TSLL</u>, 12 (Spring, 1970), 72.

_____. "The Convergence of the Twain"
Brooks, Purser, and Warren, <u>An Approach to Literature</u>, pp. 490-491.
   Rpt. third edition, pp. 380-382.
   Rpt. fourth edition, pp. 376-377.

John R. Combs, "Cleaving in Hardy's 'The Convergence of the Twain,'"<u>CEA</u>, 37 (Nov., 1974), 22-23.

Dickinson, <u>Suggestions for Teachers of "Introduction to Literature,"</u> fifth edition, ed. Locke, Gibson, and Arms, pp. 36-37. (Teacher's Manual)

Nat Henry, <u>Expl</u>, 31 (Sept., 1972), 4.

Wendell S. Johnson, "Some Functions of Poetic Form," <u>JAAC</u>, 13 (June, 1955), 503-504.

Donat O'Donnell, "Poetry, Inspiration, and Criticism," Spectator, 195 (July 8, 1955), 53.

Paul N. Siegel, Expl, 11 (Nov., 1952), 13.
   Rpt. The Explicator Cyclopedia, I, p. 150.

David S. Thatcher, Expl, 29 (Dec., 1970), 34.

_____. "The Darkling Thrush"
Beaty and Matchett, Poetry: From Statement to Meaning, pp. 94-98.

R. A. Burns, "Imagery in Hardy's 'The Darkling Thrush,'" CP, 10 (Spring, 1977), 87-89.

Charles E. May, "Hardy's 'Darkling Thrush': The 'Nightingale' Grown Old," VP, 11 (Spring, 1973), 62-65.

John Peck, "Hardy and the Figure in the Scene," Agenda, 10 (Spring-Summer, 1972), 121.

_____. "Doom and She"
Charles E. May, "Thomas Hardy and the Poetry of the Absurd," TSLL, 12 (Spring, 1970), 68-69.

_____. "A Dream or No"
Albert J. Guerard, "The Illusion of Simplicity: The Shorter Poems of Thomas Hardy," SR, 62 (July-Sept., 1964), 386-388.

_____. "A Drizzling Easter Morning"
Delmore Schwartz, "Poetry and Belief in Thomas Hardy," SoR, 6 (Summer, 1940), 73-74.
   Rpt. Critiques, p. 342.
   Rpt. in part The Critic's Notebook, pp. 201-203.
   Rpt. Modern Literary Criticism, pp. 347-348.

_____. "Drummer Hodge"
Dickinson, Suggestions for Teachers of "Introduction to Literature," fifth edition, ed. Locke, Gibson, and Arms, p. 36. (Teacher's Manual)

Van Doren, Introduction to Poetry, pp. 99-102.

_____. "During Wind and Rain"
Thom Gunn, "Hardy and the Ballads," Agenda, 10 (Spring-Summer, 1972), 28-32.

Donald Hall, The Pleasures of Poetry (New York: Harper & Row, 1971), 5-7.

Kreuzer, Elements of Poetry, pp. 162-164.

Mordecai and Erin Marcus, Expl, 19 (Dec., 1960), 14.
   Rpt. The Explicator Cyclopedia, I, pp. 150-151.

_____. "The Fallow Deer at the Lonely House"
Kilby, Poetry and Life, pp. 5-6.

_____. "Former Beauties"
Peter F. Neumeyer, "The Transfiguring Vision," VP, 3 (Autumn, 1965), 263-266.

_____. "Friends Beyond"
John Crowe Ransom, "Hardy--Old Poet," New Republic, 126 (May 12, 1952), 30-31.

_____. "The Garden Seat"
John Crowe Ransom, "Honey and Gall," SoR, 6 (Summer, 1940), 7-9.

_____. "George Meredith"
Richards, Practical Criticism, pp. 146-153 et passim.

_____. "God-Forgotten"
Laurence Perrine, "Thomas Hardy's 'God-Forgotten,'" VP, (Summer, 1968), 187-188.

_____. "The Going"
Dwayne Howell, "Dogma and Belief in the Poetry of Thomas Hardy," ELT, 19, No. 1 (1976), 10-11.

William W. Morgan, "Form, Tradition, and Consolation in Hardy's 'Poems of 1912-13,'" PMLA, 89 (May, 1974), 497-498.

_____. "He Abjures Love"
V. H. Collins, "The Love Poetry of Thomas Hardy," Essays and Studies, 28 (1942), 71-72.

Peckham and Chatman, Word, Meaning, Poem, pp. 80-88.

_____. "Her Father"
Lawrence Richard Holmes, Expl, 14 (May, 1956), 53.
    Rpt. The Explicator Cyclopedia, I, p. 152.

_____. "I Found Her Out There"
Albert J. Guerard, "The Illusion of Simplicity: The Shorter Poems of Thomas Hardy," SR, 62 (July-Sept., 1964), 383-386.

_____. "If You Had Known"
Albert J. Guerard, "The Illusion of Simplicity: The Shorter Poems of Thomas Hardy," SR, 62 (July-Sept., 1964), 369-372.

_____. "I Leant upon a Coppice Gate"
John Bayley, "Separation and Non-Communication as Features of Hardy's Poetry," Agenda, 14 (Autumn, 1976), 47-50.

_____. "The Impercipient at a Cathedral Service"
John E. Parish, "Thomas Hardy on the Evidence of Things Unseen," VP, 2 (Autumn, 1964), 203-205.

_____. "In Tenebris, I"
Walter Gierasch, Expl, 4 (April, 1946), 45.
    Rpt. The Explicator Cyclopedia, I, p. 152.

_____. "In the Days of Crinoline"
Blackmur, Expense of Greatness, pp. 62-64.
    Rpt. Language as Gesture, pp. 70-71.

_____. "In Time of 'The Breaking of Nations'"
DeLancey Ferguson, Expl, 4 (Feb., 1946), 25.

Thom Gunn, "Hardy and the Ballads," Agenda, 10 (Spring-Summer, 1972), 20-21.

_____. "The Lacking Sense"
Gilbert Neiman, "Was Hardy Anthropomorphic?" TCL, 2 (July, 1956), 86-91.

_____. "The Last Words to a Dumb Friend"
Blackmur, Expense of Greatness, pp. 68-72 et passim.
    Rpt. Language as Gesture, pp. 76-78.

_____. "The Man He Killed"
Perrine, Sound and Sense, pp. 21-22.
    Rpt. second edition, pp. 21-22.

_____. "The Masked Face"
Delmore Schwartz, "Poetry and Belief in Thomas Hardy," SoR, 6 (Summer,
1940), 72-72.
    Rpt. Critiques, pp. 340-341.
    Rpt. Modern Literary Criticism, pp. 345-346.
    Rpt. in part in The Critic's Notebook, pp. 202-203.

_____. "The Milkmaid"
Paul Zietlow, "Thomas Hardy and William Barnes: Two Dorset Poets," PMLA,
84 (March, 1969), 294-295.

_____. "The Missed Train"
Wheeler, The Design of Poetry, pp. 107-110, 279.

_____. "The Moth-Signal"
Blackmur, The Expense of Greatness, pp. 59-61.
    Rpt. Language as Gesture, pp. 68-69.

R. D. Blackmur, "The Shorter Poems of Thomas Hardy," SoR, 6 (Summer,
1940), 36-38.

_____. "Nature's Questioning"
J. O. Bailey, "Evolutionary Meliorism in the Poetry of Thomas Hardy,"
SP, 60 (April, 1963), 572-573.

H. M. Campbell, "Tate on Hardy: The Critic as Moralist," CEA, 29 (Nov.,
1966), 8-9.

Charles E. May, "Thomas Hardy and the Poetry of the Absurd," TSLL, 12
(Spring, 1970), 68.

Allen Tate, "Hardy's Philosophic Metaphors," SoR, 6 (Summer, 1940), 104-
107.

Tate, Reason in Madness, pp. 125-129.
    Rpt. On the Limits of Poetry, pp. 191-194.
    Rpt. Criticism, pp. 185-186.

_____. "Near Lanivet, 1872"
Thom Gunn, "Hardy and the Ballads," Agenda, 10 (Spring-Summer, 1972), 35-
37.

_____. "Neutral Tones"
Brooks, Purser, and Warren, An Approach to Literature, pp. 460-461.
    Rpt. third edition, pp. 329-331.
    Rpt. fourth edition, pp. 327-328.

Paul C. Doherty and E. Dennis Taylor, "Syntax in Hardy's 'Neutral Tones,'"
VP, 12 (Autumn, 1974), 285-290.

Albert J. Guerard, "The Illusion of Simplicity: The Shorter Poems of
Thomas Hardy," SR, 72 (Summer, 1964), 368-372.

James Hazen, "The God-Curst Sun: Love in 'Neutral Tones,'" VP, 9 (Autumn, 1971), 331-336.

William W. Morgan, "Syntax in Hardy's 'Neutral Tones,' Lines Seven and Eight," <u>VP</u>, 11 (Summer, 1973), 167-168.

John Crowe Ransom, "Hardy--Old Poet," <u>New Republic</u>, 126 (May 12, 1952), 16, 30.

_____. "A Night in November"
Maire A. Quinn, "The Personal Past in the Poetry of Thomas Hardy and Edward Thomas," <u>CritQ</u>, 16 (Spring, 1974), 10-11.

_____. "Nobody Comes"
Unger and O'Connor, <u>Poems for Study</u>, pp. 574-575.

_____. "On a Heath"
Walter F. Wright, "A Hardy Perennial," <u>PrS</u>, 48 (Fall, 1974), 255-257.

_____. "On an Invitation to the United States"
Brooks, Purser, and Warren, <u>An Approach to Literature</u>, pp. 464-467.
   Rpt. third edition, pp. 337-340.
   Rpt. fourth edition, pp. 334-338.

_____. "On the Departure Platform"
Walter Gierasch, <u>Expl</u>, 4 (Nov., 1945), 10.
   Rpt. <u>The Explicator Cyclopedia</u>, I, p. 153.

_____. "The Oxen"
Deutsch, <u>Poetry in Our Time</u>, p. 11.

Delmore Schwartz, "Poetry and Belief in Thomas Hardy," <u>SoR</u>, 4 (Summer, 1940), 70-71.
   Rpt. <u>Critiques</u>, pp. 339-340.
   Rpt. <u>Modern Literary Criticism</u>, pp. 344-345.

Paul Zietlow, "Thomas Hardy and William Barnes: Two Dorset Poets," <u>PMLA</u>, 84 (March, 1969), 300.

_____. "Postponement"
A. F. Cassis, "Self-Revelation in Hardy's Early Love Poems," <u>CLQ</u>, 9 (March, 1971), 263-264.

_____. "The Revisitation"
Paul Zietlow, "Thomas Hardy and William Barnes: Two Dorset Poets," <u>PMLA</u>, 84 (March, 1969), 301-302.

_____. "The Roman Road"
Van Doren, <u>Introduction to Poetry</u>, pp. 107-110.

_____. "The Sacrilege"
Richard L. Purdy, <u>Expl</u>, 3 (Feb., 1945), 28.
   Rpt. <u>The Explicator Cyclopedia</u>, I, p. 153.

_____. "Seen by the Waits"
Blackmur, <u>The Expense of Greatness</u>, pp. 61-62.
   Rpt. <u>Language as Gesture</u>, pp. 69-70.

_____. "The Shadow on the Stone"
Maire A. Quinn, "The Personal Past in the Poetry of Thomas Hardy and Edward Thomas," <u>CritQ</u>, 16 (Spring, 1974), 11.

_____. "She to Him"
R. P. Blackmur, "The Shorter Poems of Thomas Hardy," SoR, 6 (Summer, 1940), 25-27.

_____. "The Sign-Seeker"
Charles E. May, "Thomas Hardy and the Poetry of the Absurd," TSLL, 12 (Spring, 1970), 69.

_____. "The Subalterns"
John Crowe Ransom, "Thomas Hardy's Poems and the Religious Difficulties of a Naturalist," The Kenyon Review, 22 (Spring, 1960), 173-178.

_____. "The Telegram"
Blackmur, The Expense of Greatness, pp. 56-59.
    Rpt. Language as Gesture, pp. 66-67.

_____. "To a Motherless Child"
Paul Zietlow, "Thomas Hardy and William Barnes: Two Dorset Poets," PMLA, 84 (March, 1969), 292-293.

_____. "To an Unborn Pauper Child"
Day Lewis, The Poetic Image, pp. 150-153.
    Rpt. Engle and Carrier, Reading Modern Poetry, pp. 48-50.

_____. "To My Father's Violin"
Dwayne Howell, "Dogma and Belief in the Poetry of Thomas Hardy," ELT, 19, No. 1 (1976), 7-9.

_____. "Transformations"
Donald Hall, The Pleasures of Poetry (New York: Harper & Row, 1971), 68-74.

_____. "The Two Wives"
Charles E. May, "Thomas Hardy and the Poetry of the Absurd," TSLL, 12 (Spring, 1970), 72.

_____. "The Voice"
Leavis, New Bearings on English Poetry, pp. 59-60.

Maire A. Quinn, "The Personal Past in the Poetry of Thomas Hardy and Edward Thomas," CritQ, 16 (Spring, 1974), 11-12, 15-16.

_____. "Wessex Heights"
Charles E. May, "Thomas Hardy and the Poetry of the Absurd," TSLL, 12 (Spring, 1970), 70-71.

J. Hillis Miller, "'Wessex Heights': The Persistence of the Past in Hardy's Poetry," CritQ, 10 (Winter, 1968), 339-359.

_____. "Who's in the Next Room?"
Thom Gunn, "Hardy and the Ballads," Agenda, 10 (Spring-Summer, 1972), 22-24.

_____. "The Woman I Met"
Frank R. Giordano, Jr., "The Repentant Magdalen in Thomas Hardy's 'The Woman I Met,'" ELT, 15, No. 2 (1972), 136-143.

_____. "Your Last Drive"
Dwayne Howell, "Dogma and Belief in the Poetry of Thomas Hardy," ELT, 19, No. 1 (1976), 11-13.

HART, Richard. "Letter from Madrid"
    J. F. Nims, Poetry: A Critical Supplement, Jan., 1948, p. 13.

HARVEY. "Gloss"
    Hale Moore, "Gabriel Harvey's References to Marlowe," SP, 23 (July, 1926),
    343-357.

_____. "Sonnet: Gorgon, or the Wonderful Year"
    Hale Moore, "Gabriel Harvey's References to Marlowe," SP, 23 (July, 1926),
    343-357.

_____. "A Stanza Declarative: To the Lovers of Admirable Works"
    Hale Moore, "Gabriel Harvey's References to Marlowe," SP, 23 (July, 1926),
    343-357.

_____. "The Writer's Postscript: Or a Friendly Caveat to the Second Shakerley
        of Powles"
    Hale Moore, "Gabriel Harvey's References to Marlowe," SP, 23 (July, 1926),
    343-357.

HAY. "Jim Bludso"
    Daniels, The Art of Reading Poetry, pp. 88-92.

HAYDEN, Robert. "The Diver"
    Maurice J. O'Sullivan, Jr., "The Mask of Allusion in Robert Hayden's 'The
    Diver,'" CLAJ, 17 (Sept., 1973), 85-92.

    Wilburn Williams, Jr., "Covenant of Timelessness & Time: Symbolism &
    History in Robert Hayden's Angle of Ascent," MR, 18 (Winter, 1977), 732-
    733.

_____. "Frederick Douglass"
    Fred M. Fetrow, "Robert Hayden's 'Frederick Douglass': Form and Meaning
    in a Modern Sonnet," CLAJ, 17 (Sept., 1973), 79-84.

_____. "Full Moon"
    Wilburn Williams, Jr., "Covenant of Timelessness & Time: Symbolism &
    History in Robert Hayden's Angle of Ascent," MR, 18 (Winter, 1977), 743-
    745.

_____. "The Peacock Room"
    Wilburn Williams, Jr., "Covenant of Timelessness & Time: Symbolism &
    History in Robert Hayden's Angle of Ascent," MR, 18 (Winter, 1977), 746-
    747.

_____. "The Rabbi"
    Wilburn Williams, Jr., "Covenant of Timelessness & Time: Symbolism &
    History in Robert Hayden's Angle of Ascent," MR, 18 (Winter, 1977), 741-
    742.

HAYES, Alfred. "The Shrunken Head"
    J. F. Nims, Poetry: A Critical Supplement, Nov., 1948, pp. 7-8.

HECHT, Anthony. "Ostia Antica"
    Nicholas Joost, Expl, 20 (Oct., 1961), 13.
        Rpt. The Explicator Cyclopedia, I, p. 154.

HELWIG, David. "The Best Name of Silence"
  D. G. Jones, "David Helwig's New Timber: Notes on 'The Best Name of
  Silence,'" QQ, 81 (Summer, 1974), 202-214.

HENLEY. "Invictus"
  Herbert Marshall McLuhan, Expl, 3 (Dec., 1944), 22.
   Rpt. Stallman and Watters, The Creative Reader, pp. 874-875.
   Rpt. The Explicator Cyclopedia, I, p. 155.

  J. M. Purcell, Expl, 4 (Nov., 1945), 13.
   Rpt. The Explicator Cyclopedia, I, pp. 155-156.

  Sanders, The Discovery of Poetry, pp. 342-343.

_____. "Space and Dread and the Dark"
  George Herman, Expl, 22 (Oct., 1963), 14.

_____. "The Ways of Death"
  Ray L. Armstrong, Expl, 14 (Jan., 1956), 21.
   Rpt. The Explicator Cyclopedia, I, pp. 156-157.

  Daniels, The Art of Reading Poetry, pp. 268-269.

HENRYSON, Robert. "The Annunciation"
  Charles A. Hallett, "Theme and Structure in Henryson's 'The Annunciation,'"
  SSL, 10 (Jan., 1973), 165-174.

  John Stephens, "Devotion and Wit in Henryson's 'The Annunciation,'" ES, 51
  (Aug., 1970), 323-331.

_____. "The Preaching of the Swallow"
  J. A. Burrow, "Henryson: The Preaching of the Swallow," EIC, 25 (Jan.,
  1975), 25-37.

_____. "Robene and Makyne"
  Moore, The Secular Lyric in Middle English, pp. 188-194.

_____. "Sum Practysis of Medecyne"
  Denton Fox, "Henryson's 'Sum Practysis of Medecyne,'" SP, 69 (Oct., 1972),
  453-460.

_____. "Testament of Cresseid"
  Christopher Dean, Expl, 31 (Nov., 1972), 21.

HERBERT, George. "Aaron"
  H. Andrew Harnack, "George Herbert's 'Aaron': The Aesthetics of Shaped
  Typology," ELN, 14 (Sept., 1976), 25-32.

  William J. Scheick, "Typology and Allegory: A Comparative Study of George
  Herbert and Edward Taylor," ELWIU, 2 (Spring, 1975), 78-79.

_____. "Affliction, I"
  Empson, Seven Types of Ambiguity (1947 ed.), pp. 183-184.

  Barbara Leah Harman, "George Herbert's 'Affliction (I)': The Limits of
  Representation," ELH, 44 (Summer, 1977), 267-285.

  Knights, Explorations, pp. 141-144.

  L. C. Knights, "George Herbert (1)," Scrutiny, 12 (Spring, 1944), 180-183.

  Bill Smithson, "Herbert's 'Affliction' Poems," SEL, 15 (Winter, 1975),
  125-130.

Hermine J. Van Nuis, "Herbert's 'Affliction' Poems: A Pilgrim's Progress," <u>CP</u>, 8 (Fall, 1975), 8-11.

_____. "Affliction, II'
Bill Smithson, "Herbert's 'Affliction' Poems," <u>SEL</u>, 15 (Winter, 1975), 137-138.

Hermine J. Van Nuis, "Herbert's 'Affliction' Poems: A Pilgrim's Progress," <u>CP</u>, 8 (Fall, 1975), 11-12.

_____. "Affliction, III"
Thomas F. Merrill, <u>Christian Criticism: A Study of Literary God-Talk</u> (Amsterdam: Editions Rodopi N.V., 1976), pp. 60-62.

Bill Smithson, "Herbert's 'Affliction' Poems," <u>SEL</u>, 15 (Winter, 1975), 138-139.

Hermine J. Van Nuis, "Herbert's 'Affliction' Poems: A Pilgrim's Progress," <u>CP</u>, 8 (Fall, 1975), 12-13.

_____. "Affliction, IV"
Bill Smithson, "Herbert's 'Affliction' Poems," <u>SEL</u>, 15 (Winter, 1975), 134-137.

Hermine J. Van Nuis, "Herbert's 'Affliction' Poems: A Pilgrim's Progress," <u>CP</u>, 8 (Fall, 1975), 13-14.

_____. "Affliction, V"
Bill Smithson, "Herbert's 'Affliction' Poems," <u>SEL</u>, 15 (Winter, 1975), 131-134.

Hermine J. Van Nuis, "Herbert's 'Affliction' Poems: A Pilgrim's Progress," <u>CP</u>, 8 (Fall, 1975), 15-16.

_____. "The Agonie"
Edgar F. Daniels, <u>Expl</u>, 30 (Oct., 1971), 16.

B. P. Lamba and R. Jeet Lamba, <u>Expl</u>, 28 (Feb., 1970), 51.

Martz, <u>The Poetry of Meditation</u>, pp. 84-85.

Rene Rapin, <u>Expl</u>, 30 (Oct., 1971), 16.

_____. "The Altar"
Stanley E. Fish, "Letting Go: The Reader in Herbert's Poetry," <u>ELH</u>, 37 (Dec., 1970), 485-494.

Barbara K. Lewalski, "Typological Symbolism and the 'Progress of the Soul' in Seventeenth Century Literature," in <u>Literary Uses of Typology from the Late Middle Ages to the Present</u>, pp. 91-93.

Barbara K. Lewalski, "Typology and Poetry: A Consideration of Herbert, Vaughan, and Marvell," in <u>Illustrious Evidence: Approaches to English Literature of the Early Seventeenth Century</u>, ed. Earl Miner (Berkeley: Univ. of California Press, 1975), pp. 45-47, 48-49.

Philip C. McGuire, "Private Prayer and English Poetry in the Early Seventeenth Century," <u>SEL</u>, 14 (Winter, 1974), 75-76.

Florence Sandler, "Herbert's Use of the Images of the New Covenant," <u>PLL</u>, 8 (Spring, 1972), 154.

William J. Scheick, "Typology and Allegory: A Comparative Study of George Herbert and Edward Taylor," <u>ELWIU</u>, 2 (Spring, 1975), 83.

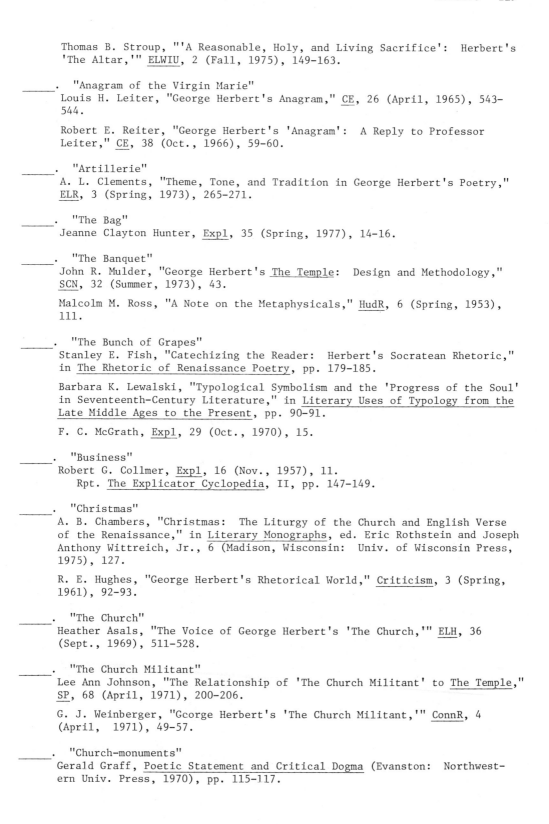

Thomas B. Stroup, "'A Reasonable, Holy, and Living Sacrifice': Herbert's 'The Altar,'" _ELWIU_, 2 (Fall, 1975), 149-163.

_____. "Anagram of the Virgin Marie"
Louis H. Leiter, "George Herbert's Anagram," _CE_, 26 (April, 1965), 543-544.

Robert E. Reiter, "George Herbert's 'Anagram': A Reply to Professor Leiter," _CE_, 38 (Oct., 1966), 59-60.

_____. "Artillerie"
A. L. Clements, "Theme, Tone, and Tradition in George Herbert's Poetry," _ELR_, 3 (Spring, 1973), 265-271.

_____. "The Bag"
Jeanne Clayton Hunter, _Expl_, 35 (Spring, 1977), 14-16.

_____. "The Banquet"
John R. Mulder, "George Herbert's _The Temple_: Design and Methodology," _SCN_, 32 (Summer, 1973), 43.

Malcolm M. Ross, "A Note on the Metaphysicals," _HudR_, 6 (Spring, 1953), 111.

_____. "The Bunch of Grapes"
Stanley E. Fish, "Catechizing the Reader: Herbert's Socratean Rhetoric," in _The Rhetoric of Renaissance Poetry_, pp. 179-185.

Barbara K. Lewalski, "Typological Symbolism and the 'Progress of the Soul' in Seventeenth-Century Literature," in _Literary Uses of Typology from the Late Middle Ages to the Present_, pp. 90-91.

F. C. McGrath, _Expl_, 29 (Oct., 1970), 15.

_____. "Business"
Robert G. Collmer, _Expl_, 16 (Nov., 1957), 11.
    Rpt. _The Explicator Cyclopedia_, II, pp. 147-149.

_____. "Christmas"
A. B. Chambers, "Christmas: The Liturgy of the Church and English Verse of the Renaissance," in _Literary Monographs_, ed. Eric Rothstein and Joseph Anthony Wittreich, Jr., 6 (Madison, Wisconsin: Univ. of Wisconsin Press, 1975), 127.

R. E. Hughes, "George Herbert's Rhetorical World," _Criticism_, 3 (Spring, 1961), 92-93.

_____. "The Church"
Heather Asals, "The Voice of George Herbert's 'The Church,'" _ELH_, 36 (Sept., 1969), 511-528.

_____. "The Church Militant"
Lee Ann Johnson, "The Relationship of 'The Church Militant' to _The Temple_," _SP_, 68 (April, 1971), 200-206.

G. J. Weinberger, "George Herbert's 'The Church Militant,'" _ConnR_, 4 (April, 1971), 49-57.

_____. "Church-monuments"
Gerald Graff, _Poetic Statement and Critical Dogma_ (Evanston: Northwestern Univ. Press, 1970), pp. 115-117.

Elissa S. Guralnick, Expl, 35 (Summer, 1977), 12-14.

Martz, The Poetry of Meditation, pp. 141-143.

Winters, Forms of Discovery, pp. 83-87.

_____. "The Church Porch"
Robert Higbie, "Images of Enclosure in George Herbert's The Temple," TSLL,
15 (Winter, 1974), 628-630.

Martz, The Poetry of Meditation, pp. 290-292.

McCanles, Dialectical Criticism, pp. 77-79

_____. "The Collar"
G. P. V. Akrigg, "George Herbert's 'Collar,'" N&Q, 1, n.s. (Jan., 1954),
17.

Jack M. Bickham, Expl, 10 (Dec., 1951), 17.
     Rpt. The Explicator Cyclopedia, II, p. 151.

Dickinson, Suggestions for Teachers of "Introduction to Literature,"
fifth edition, ed. Locke, Gibson, and Arms, p. 9.   (Teacher's Manual)

Jeffrey Hart, "Herbert's 'The Collar' Re-Read," Boston University Studies
in English, 5 (Summer, 1961), 65-73.

R. J. Handscombe, "George Herbert's 'The Collar': A Study in Frustration,"
Lang&S, 3 (Winter, 1970), 29-37.

Robert Higbie, "Images of Enclosure in George Herbert's The Temple," TSLL,
15 (Winter, 1974), 637.

Jerome, Poetry: Premeditated Art, pp. 294-300.

Paul M. Levitt and Kenneth G. Johnston, "Herbert's 'The Collar': A Nau-
tical Metaphor," SP, 66 (April, 1969), 217-224.

Day Lewis, The Poetic Image, pp. 80-81.

T. O. Mabbott, Expl, 3 (Nov., 1944), 12.
     Rpt. The Explicator Cyclopedia, II, p. 150.

Thomas F. Merrill, Christian Criticism: A Study of Literary God-Talk
(Amsterdam: Editions Rodopi N.N., 1976), pp. 63-68.

Dan S. Norton, Expl, 2 (April, 1944), 41.
     Rpt. The Explicator Cyclopedia, II, pp. 149-150.

Dan S. Norton, Expl, 3 (April, 1945), 46.
     Rpt. The Explicator Cyclopedia, II, pp. 150-151.

_____. "Confession"
Robert Higbie, "Images of Enclosure in George Herbert's The Temple," TSLL,
15 (Winter, 1974), 631-632.

_____. "The Cross"
Martz, The Poetry of Meditation, pp. 134-135.

_____. "Dialogue"
McCanles, Dialectical Criticism, pp. 83-86.

_____. "Discipline"
Jacob H. Adler, "Form and Meaning in Herbert's 'Discipline,'" N&Q, 5, n.s.
(June, 1958), 240-243.

_____. "Dooms Day"
Conrad Hilberry, Expl, 16 (Jan., 1958), 24.
     Rpt. The Explicator Cyclopedia, II, pp. 151-152.

_____. "Easter"
H. Neville David, "Sweet Music in Herbert's 'Easter,'" N&Q, 15 (March, 1968), 95-96.

R. E. Hughes, "George Herbert's Rhetorical World," Criticism, 3 (Spring, 1961), 93-94.

_____. "Easter-Wings"
C. C. Brown and W. P. Ingoldsby, "George Herbert's 'Easter-Wings,'" HLQ, 35 (Feb., 1972), 131-142.

_____. "The Flower"
Knights, Explorations, pp. 146-147.

L. C. Knights, "George Herbert (1)," Scrutiny, 12 (Spring, 1944), 185-186.

Thomas F. Merrill, Christian Criticism: A Study of Literary God-Talk (Amsterdam: Editions Rodopi N.V., 1976), pp. 27-39.

Miner, The Metaphysical Mode from Donne to Cowley, pp. 237-246.

Van Doren, Introduction to Poetry, pp. 70-73.

Helen Vendler, "The Re-invented Poem: George Herbert's Alternatives," in Forms of Lyric, pp. 35-42.

_____. "The Foil"
John R. Mulder, "George Herbert's The Temple: Design and Methodology," SCN, 32 (Summer, 1973), 42.

Philip J. Gallagher, "George Herbert's 'The Forerunners,'" ELN, 15 (Sept., 1977), 14-18.

Helen Vendler, "The Re-invented Poem: George Herbert's Alternatives," in Forms of Lyric, pp. 33-34.

_____. "Frailtie"
Sr. Sara William Hanley, C.S.J., Expl, 25 (Oct., 1966), 18.

_____. "The Glimpse"
Saad El-Gabalawy, "A Seventeenth-Century Reading of George Herbert," PLL, 7 (Spring, 1971), 166.

_____. "Grief"
Helen J. Schwartz, Expl, 31 (Feb., 1973), 43.

_____. "The Holdfast"
Stanley E. Fish, "Letting Go: The Reader in Herbert's Poetry," ELH, 37 (Dec., 1970), 480-482.

_____. "The Holy Communion"
Malcolm M. Ross, "A Note on the Metaphysicals," HudR, 6 (Spring, 1953), 110-111.

_____. "Home"
Robert Higbie, "Images of Enclosure in George Herbert's The Temple," TSLL, 15 (Winter, 1974), 637.

_____. "I Gave to Hope a Watch of Mine"
Empson, Seven Types of Ambiguity, pp. 150-153; (1947 ed.), pp. 118-120.

_____. "The Invitation"
Helen Vendler, "The Re-invented Poem: George Herbert's Alternatives," in
Forms of Lyric, pp. 25-27.

_____. "Jordan"
Frances Eldredge, Expl, 11 (Oct., 1952), 3.
    Rpt. The Explicator Cyclopedia, II, pp. 152-153.

Sheldon P. Zitner, Expl, 9 (Nov., 1950), 11.
    Rpt. The Explicator Cyclopedia, II, p. 152.

_____. "Jordan I"
MacDonald Emslie, Expl, 12 (April, 1954), 35,
    Rpt. The Explicator Cyclopedia, II, pp. 153-154.

Anthony Low, "Herbert's 'Jordan (I)' and the Court Masque," Criticism, 14
(Spring, 1972), 109-118.

Wanamaker, Discordia Concors, pp. 42-44.

_____, "Life"
Martz, The Poetry of Meditation, pp. 58-59.

_____. "Love"
Adams, Strains of Discord, pp. 123-124.

Brower, The Fields of Light, pp. 28-30.

Drew, Poetry: A Modern Guide, pp. 245-247.

Helen Vendler, "The Re-invented Poem: George Herbert's Alternatives," in
Forms of Lyric, pp. 43-44.

_____. "Love I"
Wanamaker, Discordia Concors, p. 41.

_____. "Love II"
Wanamaker, Discordia Concors, pp. 41-42.

_____. "Love III"
Robert Higbie, "Images of Enclosure in George Herbert's The Temple," TSLL,
15 (Winter, 1974), 635-636.

McCanles, Dialectical Criticism, pp. 75-76.

Nicholas Sharp, Expl, 33 (Nov., 1974), 26.

James Thorpe, Expl, 24 (Oct., 1965), 16.

Wanamaker, Discordia Concors, pp. 52-53.

_____. "Love-Joy"
Stanley E. Fish, "Catechizing the Reader: Herbert's Socratean Rhetoric,"
in The Rhetoric of Renaissance Poetry, pp. 177-178.

James J. Kirkwood, "Anneal'd as Baptism in Herbert's 'Love-Joy,'" AN&Q, 4
(Sept., 1965), 3-4.

_____. "Love Unknown"
Saad El-Gabalawy, "A Seventeenth-Century Reading of George Herbert," PLL,
7 (Spring, 1971), 165-166.

_____. "Man"
Lawrence J. Dessner, "A Reading of George Herbert's 'Man,'" CP, 5 (Spring, 1972), 61-63.

Martz, The Poetry of Meditation, pp. 59-61.

Peckham and Chatman, Word, Meaning, Poem, pp. 208-222.

_____. "The Odour"
Thomas F. Merrill, Christian Criticism: A Study of Literary God-Talk (Amsterdam: Editions Todopi N.V., 1976), pp. 68-72.

_____. "Paradise"
R. Darby Williams, "Two Baroque Game Poems on Grace: Herbert's 'Paradise' and Milton's 'On Time,'" Criticism, 12 (Summer, 1970), 181-186.

_____. "A Parodie"
Raymond J. Wilson, III, "George Herbert's 'A Parodie': Its Double Meanings," AI, 34 (Summer, 1977), 154-157.

_____. "Peace"
Michael West, "Ecclesiastical Controversy in George Herbert's 'Peace,'" RES, 22 (Nov., 1971), 445-451.

_____. "The Pearl"
Robert Higbie, "Images of Enclosure in George Herbert's The Temple," TSLL, 15 (Winter, 1974), 631.

Stephen Manning, Expl, 14 (Jan., 1956), 25.
    Rpt. The Explicator Cyclopedia, II, p. 154.

_____. "The Pilgrimage"
Saad El-Gabalawy, "The Pilgrimage: George Herbert's Favourite Allegorical Technique," CLAJ, 13 (June, 1970), 410-413.

Empson, Seven Types of Ambiguity, pp. 163-165; (1947 ed.), pp. 129-131.

Knights, Explorations, pp. 135-137.

Martz, The Poetry of Meditation, pp. 304-306.

_____. "Prayer"
Daniels, The Art of Reading Poetry, pp. 201-205.

E. B. Greenwood, "George Herbert's Sonnet 'Prayer': A Stylistic Study," EIC, 15 (Jan., 1965), 27-45.

Martz, The Poetry of Meditation, pp. 298-300.

Helen Vendler, "The Re-invented Poem: George Herbert's Alternatives," in Forms of Lyric, pp. 28-31.

_____. "Prayer II"
John Mulder, "George Herbert's The Temple: Design and Methodology," SCN, 32 (Summer, 1973), 39.

_____. "Providence"
Gideon Cohen, Expl, 35 (Winter, 1976), 2.

McCanles, Dialectical Criticism, pp. 89-93.

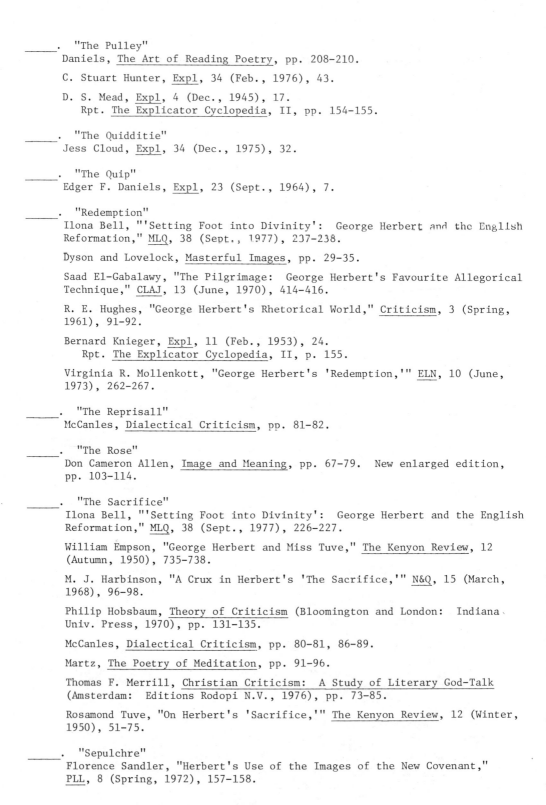

_____. "The Pulley"
Daniels, The Art of Reading Poetry, pp. 208-210.

C. Stuart Hunter, Expl, 34 (Feb., 1976), 43.

D. S. Mead, Expl, 4 (Dec., 1945), 17.
    Rpt. The Explicator Cyclopedia, II, pp. 154-155.

_____. "The Quidditie"
Jess Cloud, Expl, 34 (Dec., 1975), 32.

_____. "The Quip"
Edger F. Daniels, Expl, 23 (Sept., 1964), 7.

_____. "Redemption"
Ilona Bell, "'Setting Foot into Divinity': George Herbert and the English
Reformation," MLQ, 38 (Sept., 1977), 237-238.

Dyson and Lovelock, Masterful Images, pp. 29-35.

Saad El-Gabalawy, "The Pilgrimage: George Herbert's Favourite Allegorical
Technique," CLAJ, 13 (June, 1970), 414-416.

R. E. Hughes, "George Herbert's Rhetorical World," Criticism, 3 (Spring,
1961), 91-92.

Bernard Knieger, Expl, 11 (Feb., 1953), 24.
    Rpt. The Explicator Cyclopedia, II, p. 155.

Virginia R. Mollenkott, "George Herbert's 'Redemption,'" ELN, 10 (June,
1973), 262-267.

_____. "The Reprisall"
McCanles, Dialectical Criticism, pp. 81-82.

_____. "The Rose"
Don Cameron Allen, Image and Meaning, pp. 67-79. New enlarged edition,
pp. 103-114.

_____. "The Sacrifice"
Ilona Bell, "'Setting Foot into Divinity': George Herbert and the English
Reformation," MLQ, 38 (Sept., 1977), 226-227.

William Empson, "George Herbert and Miss Tuve," The Kenyon Review, 12
(Autumn, 1950), 735-738.

M. J. Harbinson, "A Crux in Herbert's 'The Sacrifice,'" N&Q, 15 (March,
1968), 96-98.

Philip Hobsbaum, Theory of Criticism (Bloomington and London: Indiana
Univ. Press, 1970), pp. 131-135.

McCanles, Dialectical Criticism, pp. 80-81, 86-89.

Martz, The Poetry of Meditation, pp. 91-96.

Thomas F. Merrill, Christian Criticism: A Study of Literary God-Talk
(Amsterdam: Editions Rodopi N.V., 1976), pp. 73-85.

Rosamond Tuve, "On Herbert's 'Sacrifice,'" The Kenyon Review, 12 (Winter,
1950), 51-75.

_____. "Sepulchre"
Florence Sandler, "Herbert's Use of the Images of the New Covenant,"
PLL, 8 (Spring, 1972), 157-158.

_____. "The Sinner"
Florence Sandler, "Herbert's Use of the Images of the New Covenant," PLL, 8 (Spring, 1972), 156-157.

Wanamaker, Discordia Concors, pp. 37-38.

_____. "Sinnes Round"
Jay Ruud, Expl, 34 (Jan., 1976), 35.

_____. "The Sonne"
Frederick von Ende, "George Herbert's 'The Sonne': In Defense of the English Language," SEL, 12 (Winter, 1972), 173-182.

_____. "The Temper"
Fredson Bowers, "Herbert's Sequential Imagery: 'The Temper,'" MP, 59 (Feb., 1962), 202-213.

_____. "The Temper I"
Helen Vendler, "The Re-invented Poem: George Herbert's Alternatives," in Forms of Lyric, pp. 31-33.

_____. "The Thanksgiving"
Ilona Bell, "'Setting Foot into Divinity': George Herbert and the English Reformation," MLQ, 38 (Sept., 1977), 228-236.

_____. "They Did Accuse Me of Great Villainy"
Empson, Seven Types of Ambiguity, pp. 286-295; (1947 ed), pp. 226-233.

_____. "To All Angels and Saints"
Martz, The Poetry of Meditation, pp. 97-98.

_____. "Trinity Sunday"
Joseph H. Summers, Expl, 10 (Feb., 1952), 23.
    Rpt. The Explicator Cyclopedia, II, pp. 155-156.

_____. "A True Hymne"
Stanley E. Fish, "Letting Go: The Reader in Herbert's Poetry, ELH, 37 (Dec., 1970), 482-485.

Frankenberg, Invitation to Poetry, p. 63.

_____. "Ungratefulnesse"
A. B. Chambers, "Christmas: The Liturgy of the Church and English Verse of the Renaissance," in Literary Monographs, ed. Eric Rothstein and Joseph Anthony Wittreich, Jr., 6 (Madison, Wisconsin: Univ. of Wisconsin Press, 1975), 128-130.

_____. "Vanitie"
Ronald Gaskell, "Herbert's 'Vanitie,'" CritQ, 3 (Winter, 1961), 313-315.

_____. "Virtue"
Edwin B. Benjamin, Expl, 9 (Nov., 1950), 12.
    Rpt. The Explicator Cyclopedia, II, p. 157.

Dan S. Collins, Expl, 27 (March, 1969), 50.

Roberts W. French, Expl, 26 (Sept., 1967), 4.

Herbert Marshall McLuhan, Expl, 2 (Oct., 1943), 1.
    Rpt. Readings for Liberal Education, II, pp. 534-535.
    Rpt. The Explicator Cyclopedia, II, pp. 156-157.

Rosenthal and Smith, _Exploring Poetry_, pp. 416-417.

Harold E. Toliver, _Pastoral: Forms and Attitudes_ (Berkeley: Univ. of California Press, 1971), pp. 126-128.

Helen Vendler, "George Herbert's 'Vertue,'" _ArielE_, 1 (April, 1970), 54-70.

_____. "The Windows"
Brower, _The Fields of Light_, pp. 45-47.

R. A. Forsyth, "Herbert, Clough, and Their Church-Windows," _VP_, 7 (Spring, 1969), 17-30 _et passim_.

Ronald G. Shafer, "Herbert's Poetic Adaptation of St. Paul's Image of the Glass," _SCN_, 35 (Spring-Summer, 1977), 10-11.

_____. "The World"
Edward C. Jacobs, "Herbert's 'The World': A Study of Grace," _CP_, 8 (Fall, 1975), 71-74.

_____. "A Wreathe"
William N. Fisher, "_Occupatio_ in Sixteenth- and Seventeenth-Century Verse," _TSLL_, 14 (Summer, 1972), 218-219.

HERBERT, Edward. "Tears, Flow No More"
John T. Cross, "The Poet as Orator," in _The Rhetoric of Renaissance Poetry_, pp. 26-27.

_____. "To Her Hair"
John T. Cross, "The Poet as Orator," in _The Rhetoric of Renaissance Poetry_, pp. 27-28.

HERBERT, William. "What Ys He, Thys Lordling, That Cometh Vrom the Vyth"
Reiss, _The Art of the Middle English Lyric_, pp. 108-114.

HERRICK. "All Things Decay and Die"
Judith K. Gardiner, _Expl_, 33 (May, 1975), 76.

_____. "Another Grace for a Child"
Anna Jean Mill, _Expl_, 3 (June, 1945), 61.
    Rpt. _The Explicator Cyclopedia_, II, p. 157.

_____. "The Apparition of His Mistress Calling Him to Elysium"
Rosenthal and Smith, _Exploring Poetry_, pp. 251-252.

_____. "The Argument of His Book"
A. B. Chambers, "Herrick and the Trans-shifting of Time," _SP_, 72 (Jan., 1975), 112-114.

Edward L. Hirsh, _Expl_, 2 (Nov., 1943), 11.
    Rpt. _The Explicator Cyclopedia_, II, p. 158.

John L. Kimmey, "Robert Herrick's Persona," _SP_, 67 (April, 1970), 222-223.

_____. "The Bracelet: To Julia"
Charles A. Huttar, _Expl_, 24 (Dec., 1965), 35.

Kilby, _Poetry and Life_, p. 15.

_____. "Care a Good Keeper"
Heather Asals, "King Solomon in the Land of the Hesperides," TSLL, 18
(Fall, 1976), 372.

_____. "The Carkanet"
Charles A. Huttar, Expl, 24 (Dec., 1965), 35.

Charles Sanders, Expl, 23 (Nov., 1964), 24.

_____. "Cherry-Ripe"
Daiches, A Study of Literature, pp. 148-150.

_____. "The Coming of Good Luck"
Bateson, English Poetry, pp. 82-83.

_____. "Corinna's Going A-Maying"
Brooks, The Well Wrought Urn, pp. 62-73.
    Rpt. West, Essays in Modern Literary Criticism, pp. 327-335.

Roy Harvey Pearce, "'Pure' Criticism and the History of Ideas," JAAC, 7
(Dec., 1948), 126-129.

J. Rea, "Persephone in 'Corinna's Going A-Maying,'" CE, 26 (April, 1965),
544-546.

Roger B. Rollin, "The Decorum of Criticism and Two Poems by Herrick,"
CEA, 31 (Jan., 1969), 4-7.

_____. "Counsell"
Heather Asals, "King Solomon in the Land of the Hesperides," TSLL, 18
(Fall, 1976), 370-371.

_____. "This Crosse-Tree Here"
John L. Kimmey, "Order and Form in Herrick's Hesperides," JEGP, 70
(April, 1971), 261-262.

_____. "Delight in Disorder"
F. W. Bateson, English Poetry and the English Language, pp. 42-43.
    Rpt. Brooks and Warren, Understanding Poetry, p. 328. 259
    Rpt. Unger and O'Connor, Poems for Study, p. 147.
    Rpt. Locke, Gibson, and Arms, Introduction to Literature, fourth
    edition, pp. 35-36. Rpt. fifth edition, pp. 34-35.

Drew, Poetry: A Modern Guide, pp. 78-79.

Friedman and McLaughlin, Poetry: An Introduction to Its Form and Art,
pp. 45-47, 121-122.

Kilby, Poetry and Life, pp. 14-15.

Rosenheim, What Happens in Literature, pp. 32-48.

Leo Spitzer, "Herrick's 'Delight in Disorder,'" MLN, 76 (March, 1961),
209-214.
    Rpt. Essays on English and American Literature by Leo Spitzer,
    pp. 132-138.

_____. "Divination by a Daffadill"
Ronald Berman, "Herrick's Secular Poetry," ES, 52 (Feb., 1971), 27.

_____. "Empires of Kings"
Heather Aslas, "King Solomon in the Land of the Hesperides," TSLL, 18
(Fall, 1976), 372.

_____. "The Fairie Temple: or, Oberons Chappell"
A. B. Chambers, "Herrick and the Trans-shifting of Time," SP, 72 (Jan., 1975), 91-94.

_____. "The Faerie Temple"
Daniel H. Woodward, "Herrick's Oberon Poems," JEGP, 64 (April, 1965), 276-279.

_____. "Farwell Frost, or Welcome the Spring"
Miner, The Cavalier Mode from Jonson to Cotton, pp. 177-179.

_____. "The Funeral Rites of the Rose"
Robert H. Deming, "Herrick's Funereal Poems," SEL, 9 (Winter, 1969), 153-158.

Empson, Seven Types of Ambiguity (1947 ed.), pp. 162-163.

T. R. Whitaker, "Herrick and the Fruits of the Garden," ELH, 22 (March, 1955), 16-23.

_____. "Good Friday: Rex Tragicus"
A. B. Chambers, "Herrick and the Trans-shifting of Time," SP, 72 (Jan., 1975), 87.

_____. "His Age, Dedicated to His Peculiar Friend, Master John Wickes, under the Name of Posthumus"
John L. Kimmey, "Robert Herrick's Persona," SP, 67 (April, 1970), 226-227.

_____. "His Farewell to Sack"
Peckham and Chatman, Word, Meaning, Poem, pp. 22-36.

_____. "His Grange, or Private Wealth"
John L. Kimmey, "Order and Form in Herrick's Hesperides," JEGP, 70 (April, 1971), 264-265.

_____. "His Poetrie His Pillar"
John L. Kimmey, "Order and Form in Herrick's Hesperides," JEGP, 70 (April, 1971), 262.

_____. "His Winding-Sheet"
T. R. Whitaker, "Herrick and the Fruits of the Garden," ELH, 22 (March, 1955), 26-29.

_____. "The Hock-Cart, or Harvest Home"
Paul O. Clark, Expl, 24 (April, 1966), 70.

Richard E. Hughes, "Herrick's 'Hock Cart': Companion Piece to 'Corinna's Gone a-Maying,'" CE, 27 (Feb., 1966), 420-422.

Robert Lougy, Expl, 23 (Oct., 1964), 13.

Roger B. Rollin, "The Decorum of Criticism and Two Poems by Herrick," CEA, 31 (Jan., 1969), 4-7.

_____. "How Roses Came Red"
Edgar Smith Rose, The Anatomy of Imagination," CE, 27 (Feb., 1966), 350.

_____. "Julia's Petticoat"
Anthony Low, "The Gold in 'Julia's Petticoat': Herrick and Donne," SCN, 34 (Winter, 1976), 88-89.

J. Max Patrick, "The Golden Leaves and Star in 'Julia's Petticoat,': A Reply to Anthony Low," SCN, 34 (Winter, 1976), 89-91.

Tuve, Elizabethan and Metaphysical Imagery, p. 93.

_____. "The Kisse. A Dialogue"
Heather Asals, "King Solomon in the Land of the Hesperides," TSLL, 18 (Fall, 1976), 368-369.

_____. "Love"
Heather Aslas, "King Solomon in the Land of the Hesperides," TSLL, 18 (Fall, 1976), 372.

_____. "The Mad Maid's Song"
Mario L. D'Avanzo, "Herrick's 'The Mad Maid's Song,'" AN&Q, 4 (Dec., 1965), 55.

William Van O'Connor, "Tension and Structure of Poetry," SR, 51 (Oct.-Dec., 1943), 557-558.

Unger and O'Connor, Poems for Study, p. 145.

_____. "A Meditation for His Mistresse"
Alison Heinemann, "Balme in Herrick's 'A Meditation for his Mistresse,'" ELN, 8 (March, 1971), 176-180.

_____. "The Night Piece, to Julia"
Douglas, Lamson, and Smith, The Critical Reader, pp. 83-86. Revised edition, pp. 699-701.

_____. "No Spouse but a Sister"
Heather Asals, "King Solomon in the Land of the Hesperides," TSLL, 18 (Fall, 1976), 367-368.

_____. "A Nuptiall Song"
Ronald Berman, "Herrick's Secular Poetry," ES, 52 (Feb., 1971), 20-25.

_____. "Oberon's Feast"
Daniel H. Woodward, "Herrick's Oberon Poems," JEGP, 64 (April, 1965), 279-280.

_____. "An Ode for Him" ("Ah Ben")
John L. Kimmey, "Order and Form in Herrick's Hesperides," JEGP, 70 (April, 1971), 262-263.

_____. "The Pillar of Fame"
John L. Kimmey, "Order and Form in Herrick's Hesperides," JEGP, 70 (April, 1971), 263-264.

_____. "The School or Perl of Putney...Mistresse Portman"
Heather Asals, "King Solomon in the Land of the Hesperides," TSLL, 18 (Fall, 1976), 373.

_____. "The Sick Rose"
Edgar Smith Rose, "The Anatomy of Imagination," CE, 27 (Feb., 1966), 350-352.

_____. "A Ternary of Littles Upon a Pipkin of Jelly Sent to a Lady"

Archibald Hill, <u>Constitutent and Pattern in Poetry</u> (Austin: Univ. of
Texas Press, 1976), 88–90.
    Rpt. from <u>English Studies Today</u>, third series (Edinburgh: Edinburgh
    Univ. Press, 1962), 41–50.

_____. "A Thanksgiving to God, for His House"
John L. Kimmey, "Order and Form in Herrick's <u>Hesperides</u>," <u>JEGP</u>, 70
(April, 1971), 265.

_____. "This Great Realme of Poetry"
Heather Aslas, "King Solomon in the Land of the <u>Hesperides</u>," <u>TSLL</u>, 18
(Fall, 1976), 371–372.

_____. "To Anthea Lying in Bed"
Tuve, <u>Elizabethan and Metaphysical Imagery</u>, pp. 11–12.

_____. "To Blossoms"
Ronald Berman, "Herrick's Secular Poetry," <u>ES</u>, 52 (Feb., 1971), 28–29.

Brooks and Warren, <u>Understanding Poetry</u>, pp. 368–370; 374. Revised
edition, pp. 246–247.

_____. "To Daffodils"
Beaty and Matchett, <u>Poetry: From Statement to Meaning</u>, pp. 223–224.

Sigurd Burckhardt and Roy Harvey Pearce, "Poetry, Language, and the Condition of Modern Man," <u>CentR</u>, 4 (Winter, 1960), 4–6.

A. B. Chambers, "Herrick and the Trans-shifting of Time," <u>SP</u>, 72 (Jan.,
1975), 101–105.

Thomas and Brown, <u>Reading Poems: An Introduction to Critical Study</u>,
pp. 650–651, 695–697.

_____. "To Electra"
Hennig Cohen, <u>Expl</u>, 17 (March, 1959), 44.
    Rpt. <u>The Explicator Cyclopedia</u>, II, p. 158.

_____. "To His Mistresse Objecting to Him Neither Toying nor Talking"
Heather Asals, "King Solomon in the Land of the <u>Hesperides</u>," <u>TSLL</u>, 18
(Fall, 1976), 369–370.

_____. "To Live Merrily and to Trust to Good Verses"
Frankenberg, <u>Invitation to Poetry</u>, pp. 49–50.

John L. Kimmey, "Robert Herrick's Persona," <u>SP</u>, 67 (April, 1970), 226.

_____. "To M. Denham, On His Prospective Poem"
R. E. Tyner, <u>Expl</u>, 23 (May, 1965), 72.

_____. "To Meadows"
Van Doren, <u>Introduction to Poetry</u>, pp. 66–69.

_____. "To Perilla"
Robert H. Deming, "Herrick's Funereal Poems," <u>SEL</u>, 9 (Winter, 1969),
158–160.

_____. "To Sylvia"
Heather Asals, "King Solomon in the Land of the <u>Hesperides</u>," <u>TSLL</u>, 18
(Fall, 1976), 372–373.

_____.   "To the Reverend Shade of His Religious Father"
Robert H. Deming, "Herrick's Funereal Poems," _SEL_, 9 (Winter, 1969), 160-162.

_____.   "To the Virgins to Make Much of Time"
George Arms, _Expl_, 1 (Oct., 1942), 2.
    Rpt. _The Explicator Cyclopedia_, II, pp. 158-159. *no*

William B. Bache, "Experiment With a Poem," _Col1L_, 1 (Winter, 1974), 64-66.
    College literature

Richard J. Ross, "Herrick's Julia in Silks," _EIC_, 15 (April, 1965), 177-179.   *EMW*   *Essays in Criticism*

Tillyard, _The Metaphysicals and Milton_, pp. 53-57.

_____.   "The Transfiguration"
A. B. Chambers, "Herrick and the Trans-shifting of Time," _SP_, 72 (Jan., 1975), 97-100.

_____.   "Upon Julia's Clothes"
Abad, _A Formal Approach to Lyric Poetry_, pp. 166-167, 174-175.

Bateson, _English Poetry_, p. 46.

Montgomery Belgion, "The Poetic Name," _SR_, 54 (Oct.-Dec., 1946), 643-644.

Lawrence Coffin, "'Liquefaction' in Herrick's 'Upon Julia's Clothes,'" _CP_, 6 (Spring, 1973), 56-59.

Earl Daniels, _Expl_, 1 (March, 1943), 35.
    Rpt. Stallman and Watters, _The Creative Reader_, pp. 852-853.   Abridged in _The Case for Poetry_, p. 175.
    Rpt. _The Explicator Cyclopedia_, II, p. 159.

Donald Hall, _The Pleasures of Poetry_ (New York: Harper & Row, 1971), 18-20.

William O. Harris, _Expl_, 21 (Dec., 1962), 29.

Nat Henry, _Expl_, 5 (April, 1947), 46.
    Rpt. _The Explicator Cyclopedia_, II, pp. 159-160.

Nat Henry, _Expl_, 14 (Dec., 1955), 15.
    Rpt. _The Explicator Cyclopedia_, II, p. 161.

Louis H. Leiter, _Expl_, 25 (Jan., 1967), 41.

C. S. Lewis, "An Open Letter to Dr. Tillyard," _Essays and Studies_, 22 (1936), 160-161.

C. S. Lewis, "The Personal Heresy in Criticism," _Essays and Studies_, 19 (1933), 9-11 _et passim_.

Michael J. Preston, _Expl_, 30 (May, 1972), 82.

Richard J. Ross, "Herrick's Julia in Silks," _EIC_, 15 (April, 1965), 171-176.

Elisabeth Schneider, _Expl_, 13 (March, 1955), 30.
    Rpt. _The Explicator Cyclopedia_, II, pp. 160-161.

J. D. Schuchter, _Expl_, 25 (Nov., 1966), 27.

Stauffer, _The Nature of Poetry_, pp. 162-163.

E. M. W. Tillyard, "The Personal Heresy in Criticism: A Rejoinder,"
Essays and Studies, 20 (1934), 17-20. Abridged in The Case for Poetry,
p. 175.

L. E. Weeks, "Julia Unveiled: A Note on Herrick's 'Upon Julia's Clothes,'"
CEA, 25 (June, 1963), 8.

Gail S. Weinberg, Expl, 27 (Oct., 1968), 12.

_____. "Upon Julia's Voice"
Perrine, Sound and Sense, p. 171.
    Rpt. second edition, pp. 183-184.

_____. "Upon Julia Weeping"
Wheeler, The Design of Poetry, pp. 49-51.

_____. "Upon Prig"
Robert W. Halli, Jr., Expl, 35 (Summer, 1977), 22.

_____. "Upon Sylvia"
Tuve, Elizabethan and Metaphysical Imagery, p. 129.

_____. "The Vine"
Heather Asals, "King Solomon in the Land of the Hesperides," TSLL, 18
(Fall, 1976), 376.

_____. "The Vision"
Tuve, Elizabethan and Metaphysical Imagery, pp. 87-88.

_____. "The Watch"
Felver and Nurmi, Poetry: An Introduction and Anthology, pp. 31-32.

HEYWARD, DuBose. "A Yoke of Steers"
Baker, Syntax in English Poetry, 1870-1930, pp. 147-150.

HILBERRY, Conrad. "Hamster Cage"
Margaret A. Larson, "Instructive Destructive," EJ, 61 (April, 1972),
508-509.

HILL, Geoffrey. "Funeral Music"
A. K. Weatherhead, "Geoffrey Hill," IowaR, 8 (Fall, 1977), 106-109.

_____. "Lachrimae Verae"
Jeffrey Wainwright, "Geoffrey Hill's 'Lachrimae,'" Agenda, 13 (Autumn,
1975), 33.

_____. "The Martyrdom of Saint Sebastian"
A. K. Weatherhead, "Geoffrey Hill," IowaR, 8 (Fall, 1977), 104-105.

_____. "Pavana Dolorosa" "Lachrimae Sonnet II"
Jeffrey Wainwright, "Geoffrey Hill's 'Lachrimae,'" Agenda, 13 (Autumn,
1975), 32-33.

_____. "Picture of a Nativity"
Lawrence Kramer, "The Wodwo Watched the Water Clock: Language in Post-
modern British and American Poetry," ConL, 18 (Summer, 1977), 323-325.

_____. "September Song"
Jeremy Hawthorn, Identity and Relationship: A Contribution to Marxist
Theory of Literary Criticism (London: Lawrence & Wishart, 1973), pp. 124-
127.

Jon Silkin, "The Poetry of Geoffrey Hill," IowaR, 3 (Summer, 1972), 110-
111.

HODGSON, Ralph. "February"
Darrell Abel, "How to Teach Students to Read a Poem," CE, 16 (Nov., 1955),
90-92.

_____. "The Muse and the Mastiff"
Anonymous, "Ralph Hodgson: A Poet's Journey in Time," TLS, Feb. 13,
1959, p. 78.

_____. "The Skylark"
Anonymous, "Ralph Hodgson: A Poet's Journey in Time," TLS, Feb. 13,
1959, p. 77.

_____. "Time"
Anonymous, "Ralph Hodgson: A Poet's Journey in Time," TLS, Feb. 13,
1959, p. 78.

_____. "To Deck a Woman"
Anonymous, "Ralph Hodgson: A Poet's Journey in Time," TLS, Feb., 13,
1959, pp. 77-78.

HODGSON, William Noel. "By All the Glories of the Day"
Palmer, Post-Victorian Poetry, pp. 229-231.

HOLMES, John. "Herself"
Doris Holmes, Expl, 28 (May, 1970), 77.

HOLMES, O. W. "The Chambered Nautilus"
George Arms, Expl, 4 (June, 1946), 51.
    Rpt. The Explicator Cyclopedia, II, pp. 161-162.

Arms, The Fields Were Green, pp. 108-110.

_____. "The Deacon's Masterpiece"
Arms, The Fields Were Green, pp. 112-113.

Howard Webb, Expl, 24 (Oct., 1965), 17.

_____. "The Living Temple"
George Arms, Expl, 2 (Nov., 1943), 15.
    Rpt. The Explicator Cyclopedia, II, pp. 162-163.

Arms, The Fields Were Green, pp. 104-105.

_____. "The Peau de Chagrin of State Street"
Arms, The Fields Were Green, p. 102.

_____. "Two Sonnets: Harvard"
Arms, The Fields Were Green, pp. 113-114.

_____. "The Two Streams"
Arms, The Fields Were Green, pp. 97-99.

George Arms, "'To Fix the Image All Unveiled and Warm,'" <u>NEQ</u>, 19 (Dec., 1946), 534-537.

HOOD. "Autumn"
Audrey Jennings, "Hood's 'Autumn,'" <u>TLS</u>, June 26, 1953, p. 413.

_____. "The Death Bed"
Beaty and Matchett, <u>Poetry: From Statement to Meaning</u>, pp. 139-140.

_____. "Ruth"
June Seligman, in Sanders, <u>The Discovery of Poetry</u>, p. 38.

HOPE, A. D. "Agony Column"
Laurence Perrine, "A. D. Hope's 'Agony Column,'" <u>NConL</u>, 2 (May, 1972), 2-3.

HOPKINS. "The Alchemist in the City"
James Leggio, "Hopkins and Alchemy," <u>Renascence</u>, 29 (Spring, 1977), 117-119.

_____. "As Kingfishers Catch Fire"
Kent Beyette, "Grace and Time in the Poetry of Hopkins," <u>TSLL</u>, 16 (Winter, 1975), 709-714.

Hartman, <u>The Unmediated Vision</u>, pp. 58-59.

Boyd Litzinger, "The Pattern of Ascent in Hopkins," <u>VP</u>, 2 (Spring, 1964), 45.

Walsh, <u>The Use of Imagination</u>, pp. 127-128.

_____. "Binsey Poplars Felled 1879"
Jerome D. Cartwright, <u>Expl</u>, 33 (May, 1975), 72.

_____. "The Blessed Virgin Compared to the Air We Breathe"
Tad W. Guzie, "Are Modern Poets Morbid?" <u>Catholic World</u>, 185 (April, 1957), 27-32.

_____. "The Caged Skylark"
Friar and Brinnin, <u>Modern Poetry</u>, pp. 503-504.

Margaret Giovannini, <u>Expl</u>, 14 (March, 1956), 35.
    Rpt. <u>The Explicator Cyclopedia</u>, I, pp. 157-158.

Sr. Mary John Bosco Houle, B.V.M., "Readings of Two Victorian Poems," <u>IEY</u>, No. 12 (Fall, 1965), 51-52.

Frank Jordan, Jr., <u>Expl</u>, 28 (May, 1970), 80.

Maynard Mack, Leonard Dean, and William Frost, <u>English Masterpieces</u>, Vol. VII, <u>Modern Poetry</u>, pp. 20-21.

_____. "The Candle Indoors"
Bell Gale Chevigny, "Instress and Devotion in Hopkins," <u>VS</u>, 9 (Dec., 1965), 149-150.

Denis Donoghue, "Technique in Hopkins," <u>Studies</u>, 44 (Winter, 1955), 452.

Sr. Rosemarie Julie Gavin, S.N.D. de N., <u>Expl</u>, 20 (Feb., 1962), 50.
    Rpt. <u>The Explicator Cyclopedia</u>, I, pp. 158-159.

_____. "Carrion Comfort"
Kent Beyette, "Grace and Time in the Poetry of Hopkins," TSLL, 16 (Winter, 1975), 715-716.

J. Angela Carson, "The Metaphor of Struggle in 'Carrion Comfort,'" PQ, 49 (Oct., 1970), 547-557.

Marie Cornelia, "Images and Allusion in Hopkins' 'Carrion Comfort,'" Renascence, 27 (Autumn, 1974), 51-55.

Friar and Brinnin, Modern Poetry, p. 502.

Ann Louise Hentz, "Language in Hopkins' 'Carrion Comfort,'" VP, 9 (Autumn, 1971), 343-347.

Jerome, Poetry: Premeditated Art, p. 51.

Leavis, New Bearings on English Poetry, pp. 190-191.

James Leggio, "Hopkins and Alchemy," Renascence, 29 (Spring, 1977), 125-126.

Christina J. Murphy, "Inverted Religious Imagery in Hopkins' 'Carrion Comfort,'" UMSE, 13 (1972), 1-5.

Philip Page, "Unity and Subordination in 'Carrion Comfort,'" VP, 14 (Spring, 1976), 25-32.

Betrand F. Richards, "Meaning in Hopkins' 'Carrion Comfort,'" Renascence, 27 (Autumn, 1974), 45-50.

Alan M. Rose, "Hopkins' 'Carrion Comfort': The Artful Disorder of Prayer," VP, 15 (Autumn, 1977), 207-217.

Malcolm H. Villarubia, S.J., "Two Wills Unwound in the 'Terrible' Sonnets," Renascence, 27 (Winter, 1975), 73-75.

Wells, New Poets from Old, pp. 153-154.

Patricia A. Wolfe, "The Paradox of Self: A Study of Hopkins' Spiritual Conflict in the 'Terrible' Sonnets," VP, 6 (Summer, 1968), 91-93.

_____. "Duns Scotus's Oxford,"
Yvor Winters, "The Poetry of Gerard Manley Hopkins (2)," HudR, 2 (Spring, 1949), 64.
    Rpt. The Function of Criticism, pp. 126-127.

_____. "The Escorial"
Donald Sutherland, "Hopkin's Again," PrS, 35 (Fall, 1961), 197-242.

_____. "Felix Randal"
Bell Gale Chevigny, "Instress and Devotion in Hopkins," VS, 9 (Dec., 1965), 149.

Joseph Eble, "Levels of Awareness: A Reading of Hopkins' 'Felix Randal,'" VP, 13 (Summer, 1975), 129-135.

Paul L. Mariani, "Hopkins' 'Felix Randal' as Sacramental Vision," Renascence, 19 (Summer, 1967), 217-220.

_____. "God's Grandeur"
Todd K. Bender, Expl, 21 (March, 1963), 55.

Bell Gale Chevigny, "Instress and Devotion in Hopkins," VS, 9 (Dec., 1965), 145-146.

John R. Combs, "The Trinity in Hopkins' 'God's Grandeur,'" CEA, 35 (May, 1973), 27.

Terry Eagleton, "Nature and the Fall in Hopkins: A Reading of 'God's Grandeur,'" EIC, 23 (Jan., 1973), 68-75.

Charlotte K. Gafford, Expl, 29 (Nov., 1970), 21.

Margaret Giovannini, Expl, 24 (Dec., 1965), 36.

Tad W. Guzie, "Are Modern Poets Morbid?" The Catholic World, 185 (April, 1957), 27-32.

Robert Irwin, Expl, 31 (Feb., 1973), 46.

George E. Montag, "Hopkins' 'God's Grandeur' and 'The Ooze of Oil' Crushed," VP, 1 (Winter, 1963), 302-303.

Sr. Mary Noel, S.C., "Gathering to a Greatness: A Study of 'God's Grandeur,'" EJ, 53 (April, 1964), 285-287.

Hugh Pendexter, III, Expl, 23 (Sept., 1964), 2.

Edward Prottitt, "Hopkins' 'Ooze of Oil/Crushed' Once More," CP, 10 (Fall, 1977), 61-64.

Donald H. Reiman, "Hopkins' 'Ooze of Oil' Rises Again," VP, 4 (Winter, 1966), 39-42.

Rosenthal and Smith, Exploring Poetry, pp. 94-97.

Roger L. Slakey, "The Grandeur in Hopkins' 'God's Grandeur,'" VP, 7 (Summer, 1969), 159-163.

Michael Taylor, Expl, 25 (April, 1967), 68.

Thomas L. Watson, Expl, 22 (Feb., 1964), 47.

Gertrude M. White, "Hopkins' 'God's Grandeur': A Poetic Statement of Christian Doctrine," VP, 4 (Autumn, 1966), 284-287.

Brooks Wright, Expl, 10 (Oct., 1951), 5.
    Rpt. The Explicator Cyclopedia, I, pp. 159-160.

_____. "The Habit of Perfection"
Francis J. Greiner, Expl, 21 (Nov., 1962), 19.

John Hardy, Expl, 30 (Dec., 1971), 32.

Boyd Litzinger, Expl, 16 (Oct., 1957), 1.
    Rpt. The Explicator Cyclopedia, I, pp. 160-161.

_____. "Harry Ploughman"
Day Lewis, The Poetic Image, pp. 125-128.

Stageberg and Anderson, Poetry as Experience, pp. 222-229.

_____. "Heaven-Haven"
Anonymous, "Poet and Priest," TLS, June 10, 1944, p. 282.

E. L. Epstein, "Hopkins's 'Heaven-Haven': A Linguistic-Critical Description," EIC, 23 (April, 1973), 137-145.

Allan Rodway, "Hopkins's 'Heaven-Haven,'" EIC, 23 (Oct., 1973), 430-434.

John Surple, F. Giles, and S. James, "Three Critics: One Poem," Agenda, 14 (Autumn, 1976), 93-95.

_____. "Henry Purcell"
Christ, The Finer Optic, pp. 93-98.

_____. "Hurrahing in Harvest"
Bloom, Philbrick, and Blistein, The Order of Poetry, pp. 130-134.

Bell Gale Chevingy, "Instress and Devotion in Hopkins," VS, 9 (Dec., 1965), 147-148.

Friar and Brinnin, Modern Poetry, p. 504.

Peckham and Chatman, Word, Meaning, Poem, pp. 334-342.

_____. "Inversnaid"
Humphrey Tonkin, "Hopkins' 'Inversnaid' and Its Stylistic Devices," Lang&S, 3 (Fall, 1970), 274-292.

_____. "I Wake and Feel the Fell of Dark, Not Day"
Alexander W. Allison, Expl, 17 (May, 1959), 54.
    Rpt. The Explicator Cyclopedia, I, pp. 161-162.

Friar and Brinnin, Modern Poetry, pp. 502-503.

S. C. Pepper, The Basis of Criticism in the Arts (Cambridge: Harvard Univ. Press, 1945), pp. 127-140.

Malcolm H. Villarubia, S.J., "Two Wills Unwound in the 'Terrible' Sonnets," Renascence, 27 (Winter, 1975), 75-76.

Walsh, The Use of Imagination, pp. 133-135.

Patricia A. Wolfe, "The Paradox of Self: A Study of Hopkins' Spiritual Conflict in the 'Terrible' Sonnets," VP, 6 (Summer, 1968), 98-100.

_____. "The Leaden Echo and the Golden Echo"
Leavis, New Bearings on English Poetry, pp. 172-175.

_____. "The Loss of Eurydice"
Richard J. O'Dea, "'The Loss of Eurydice': A Possible Key to the Reading of Hopkins," VP, 4 (Autumn, 1966), 291-293.

_____. "Margaret Clitheroe"
R. J. Schoeck, "Peine Forte et Dure and Hopkins' 'Margaret Clitheroe,'" MLN, 74 (March, 1959), 220-225.

_____. "The May Magnificat"
John D. Ratliff, Expl, 16 (Dec., 1957), 17.
    Rpt. The Explicator Cyclopedia, II, p. 162.

_____. "My Own Heart Let Me More Have Pity On"
Elisabeth Schneider, Expl, 5 (May, 1947), 51; and 7 (May, 1949), 49.
    Rpt. The Explicator Cyclopedia, I, 163-164.

Malcolm H. Villarubia, S.J., "Two Wills Unwound in the 'Terrible Sonnets," Renascence, 27 (Winter, 1975), 78-79.

Patricia A. Wolfe, "The Paradox of Self: A Study of Hopkins' Spiritual Conflict in the 'Terrible' Sonnets," VP, 6 (Summer, 1968), 101-103.

_____. "Nothing Is So Beautiful as Spring"
Susan A. Hallgarth, "A Study of Hopkins' Use of Nature," VP, 5 (Summer, 1967), 87.

_____. "No Worst, There Is None"
Kent Beyette, "Grace and Time in the Poetry of Hopkins," TSLL, 16 (Winter, 1975), 714-715.

Robert A. Durr, Expl, 11 (Nov., 1952), 11.
    Rpt. The Explicator Cyclopedia, I, p. 164.

Friar and Brinnin, Modern Poetry, p. 502.

Sr. Marcella M. Holloway, C.S.J., Expl, 14 (May, 1956), 51.
    Rpt. The Explicator Cyclopedia, I, pp. 165-166.

Sr. Mary Humiliata, "Hopkins and the Prometheus Myth," PMLA, 70 (March, 1955), 58-68.

Yvor Winters, "The Poetry of Gerard Manley Hopkins (1)," HudR, 1 (Winter, 1948), 460-466.
    Rpt. The Function of Criticism, pp. 107-113.

Patricia A. Wolfe, "The Paradox of Self: A Study of Hopkins' Spiritual Conflict in the 'Terrible' Sonnets," VP, 6 (Summer, 1968), 93-96.

_____. "On a Piece of Music"
Yvor Winters, "The Poetry of Gerard Manley Hopkins (2)," HudR, 2 (Spring, 1949), 87-88.
    Rpt. The Function of Criticism, pp. 137-138, 152-153.

_____. "Patience, Hard Thing"
Malcolm H. Villarubia, S.J., "Two Wills Unwound in the 'Terrible' Sonnets," Renascence, 27 (Winter, 1975), 77-78.

Patricia A. Wolfe, "The Paradox of Self: A Study of Hopkins' Spiritual Conflict in the 'Terrible' Sonnets," VP, 6 (Summer, 1968), 100-101.

_____. "Pied Beauty"
Miguel A. Bernard, S.J., "Hopkins' 'Pied Beauty': A Note on Its Ignatian Inspiration," EIC, 12 (April, 1962), 217-220.

John Britton, S.J., "'Pied Beauty' and the Glory of God," Renascence, 11 (Winter, 1959), 72-75.

Jerome Bump, "Hopkins, the Humanities, and the Environment," GaR, 28 (Summer, 1974), 230-232.

Christ, The Finer Optic, pp. 101-103.

Frankenberg, Invitation to Poetry, pp. 294-296.

Samuel Kliger, "God's 'Plenitude' in the Poetry of Gerard Manley Hopkins," MLN, 59 (June, 1944), 408-410.

Boyd A Litzinger, "Hopkins's 'Pied Beauty' Once More," Renascence, 13 (Spring, 1961), 136-138.

Boyd Litzinger, "The Pattern of Ascent in Hopkins," VP, 2 (Spring, 1964), 44-45.

Amy Lowenstein, "Seeing 'Pied Beauty': A Key to Theme and Structure," VP, 14 (Spring, 1976), 64-66.

Walsh, The Use of Imagination, pp. 121-123, 129.

_____. "The Shepherd's Brow"
Thomas K. Beyette, "Hopkins' Phenomenology of Art in 'The Shepherd's Brow,'" VP, 11 (Autumn, 1973), 207-213.

Sr. M. Mary Hugh Campbell, S.C.M.M., "The Silent Sonnet: Hopkins' 'Shepherd's Brow,'" Renascence, 15 (Spring, 1963), 133-142.

Robert Boykin Clark, S.J., "Hopkins's 'The Shepherd's Brow,'" VN, No. 28 (Fall, 1965), 16-18.

Paul L. Mariani, "The Artistic and Tonal Integrity of Hopkins' 'The Shepherd's Brow,'" VP, 6 (Spring, 1968), 63-68.

_____. "Soliloquy of One of the Spies Left in the Wilderness"
George P. Landow, "Moses Striking the Rock: Typological Symbolism in Victorian Poetry," in Literary Uses of Typology from the Late Middle Ages to the Present, pp. 328-330.

_____. "Sonnet to St. Alphonsus Rodriguez"
Herbert Marshall McLuhan, "The Analogical Mirrors," The Kenyon Review, 6 (Summer, 1944), 329-330.

_____. "Soul, Self; Come, Poor Jackself, I Do Advise"
Riding and Graves, A Survey of Modernist Poetry, pp. 90-94.

_____. "Spelt from Sibyl's Leaves"
Thomas J. Assad, "Hopkins' 'Spelt from Sibyl's Leaves," TSE, 22 (1977), 103-115.

Michael Black, "The Musical Analogy," English, 25 (Summer, 1976), 114-124.

Jerome Bump, "Hopkins, the Humanities, and the Environment," GaR, 28 (Summer, 1974), 241-242.

Francis Doherty, "A Note on 'Spelt from Sibyl's Leaves,'" EIC, 14 (Oct., 1964), 428-432.

Denis Donoghue, "Technique in Hopkins," Studies, 44 (Winter, 1955), 454.

Friar and Brinnin, Modern Poetry, p. 503.

Andor Gomme, "A Note on Two Hopkins' Sonnets," EIC, 14 (July, 1966), 327-333.

Leavis, New Bearings on English Poetry, pp. 182-186.

I. A. Richards, "Gerard Hopkins," The Dial, 81 (Sept., 1926), 199-201.

William J. Rooney, "'Spelt from Sibyl's Leaves'--a Study in Contrasting Methods of Evaluation," JAAC, 13 (June, 1955), 507-519.

Raymond V. Schoder, "Spelt from Sibyl's Leaves," Thought, 19 (Dec., 1944), 634-648.

H. C. Sherwood, Expl, 15 (Oct., 1956), 5.
   Rpt. The Explicator Cyclopedia, I, pp. 166-167.

Sr. Therese, S.N.D., Expl, 17 (April, 1959), 45.
   Rpt. The Explicator Cyclopedia, I, pp. 167-168.

Norman White, Expl, 30 (Nov., 1971), 24.

Norman White, "Hopkins' 'Spelt from Sibyl's Leaves,'" VN, No. 36 (Fall, 1969), 27-28.

Norman E. White, "'Hearse' in Hopkins' 'Spelt from Sibyl's Leaves,'" ES, 49 (Dec., 1968), 546-547.

_____. "Spring"
Bell Gale Chevigny, "Instress and Devotion in Hopkins," VS, 9 (Dec., 1965), 146.

Herbert F. Tucker, Jr., "Hopkins: Bloomfall and Inthought," PQ, 55 (Winter, 1976), 136-137.

Walsh, The Use of Imagination, p. 133.

_____. "Spring and Fall: To a Young Child"
Beaty and Matchett, Poetry: From Statement to Meaning, pp. 61-66.

Sigurd Burckhardt and Roy Harvey Pearce, "Poetry, Language and the Condition of Modern Man," CentR, 4 (Winter, 1960), 6-9.

Deutsch, Poetry in Our Time, p. 294.

Bert Case Diltz, Sense or Nonsense: Contemporary Education at the Crossroads (Toronto: McClelland and Stewart, 1972), pp. 76-82.

Paul C. Doherty, "Hopkins' 'Spring and Fall: To a Young Child,'" VP, 5 (Summer, 1967), 140-143.

Drew, Poetry. A Modern Guide, pp. 107-109.

John P. Driscoll, S.J., Expl, 24 (Nov., 1965), 26.

Empson, Seven Types of Ambiguity, pp. 187-188; (1947 ed.), pp. 148-149.

Sr. Robert Louise, O.P., Expl, 21 (April, 1963), 65.

John A. Myers, Jr., "Intimations of Mortality: An Analysis of Hopkins' 'Spring and Fall,'" EJ, 51 (Nov., 1962), 585-587.

John Nist, "Gerald Manley Hopkins and Textured Intensity: A Linguistic Analysis," CE, 22 (April, 1961), 497-500.

Julian Smith, Expl, 27 (Jan., 1969), 36.

Richards, Practical Criticism, pp. 80-91 et passim.

Herbert F. Tucker, Jr., "Hopkins: Bloomfall and Inthought," PQ, 55 (Winter, 1976), 137-138.

Charles Child Walcutt, The Explicator Cyclopedia, I, "Introduction," p. xiii.

_____. "The Starlight Night"
Yvor Winters, "The Poetry of Gerard Manley Hopkins (2)," HudR, 2 (Spring, 1949), 63.
    Rpt. The Function of Criticism, pp. 125-126.

_____. "That Nature Is a Heraclitean Fire"
Bell Gale Chevigny, "Instress and Devotion in Hopkins," VS, 9 (Dec., 1965), 152-153.

Winston Collins, "Tennyson and Hopkins," UTQ, 38 (Oct., 1968), 85-87.

Friar and Brinnin, Modern Poetry, pp. 501-502.

Susan A. Hallgarth, "A Study of Hopkins' Use of Nature," VP, 5 (Summer, 1967), 91-92.

Michael L. Johnson, "Hopkins, Heraclitus, Cosmic Instress and of the Comfort of the Resurrection," VP, 10 (Autumn, 1972), 235-242.

James Leggio, "Hopkins and Alchemy," Renascence, 29 (Spring, 1977), 126-129.

Boyd Litzinger, "The Pattern of Ascent in Hopkins," VP, 2 (Spring, 1964), 46-47.

Sr. Mary Doniic Stevens, O.P., Expl, 22 (Nov., 1963), 18.

_____. "Thee, God, I Come From, to Thee Go"
Denis Donoghue, "Technique in Hopkins," Studies, 44 (Winter, 1955), 451-453.

_____. "Thou Art Indeed Just, Lord, If I Contend"
Brower, The Fields of Light, pp. 26-27.

Drew, Discovering Poetry, pp. 140-141.

Andor Gomme, "A Note on Two Hopkin's Sonnets," EIC, 14 (July, 1964), 330-331.

_____. "Tom's Garland"
Deutsch, This Modern Poetry, pp. 178-180.

Henry Silverstein, "On 'Tom's Garland,'" Accent, 7 (Winter, 1947), 67-81.

_____. "To Oxford II"
Bernard Richards, Expl, 33 (Nov., 1974), 24.

_____. "To R. B."
Kent Beyette, "Grace and Time in the Poetry of Hopkins," TSLL, 16 (Winter, 1975), 716-717.

William M. Gibson, Expl, 6 (Nov., 1947), 12.
   Rpt. The Explicator Cyclopedia, I, pp. 168-169.

Stauffer, The Nature of Poetry, pp. 40-41.

_____. "To Seem the Stranger Lies My Lot, My Life"
Patricia A. Wolfe, "The Paradox of Self: A Study of Hopkins: Spiritual Conflict in the 'Terrible' Sonnets," VP, 6 (Summer, 1968), 96-98.

_____. "The Windhover, to Christ Our Lord"
Anonymous, "Difficult Poetry," TLS, June 24, 1955, p. 349.

Anonymous, "Hopkinsiana," TLS, Oct. 29, 1954, p. 689.

Anonymous, "Passionate Science," TLS, March 18, 1955, p. 165.

Anonymous, "'Pied Beauty' in Spanish," TLS, Aug. 13, 1954, p. 510.

Anonymous, "Poet and Priest," TLS, June 10, 1944, p. 282.

Thomas J. Assad, "Hopkins' 'The Windhover,'" TSE, 11 (1961), 87-95.

Eugene R. August, "Hopkins' Dangerous Fire," VP, 1 (Spring, 1963), 72-74.

Robert W. Ayers, "Hopkins' 'The Windhover': A Further Simplification," MLN, 71 (Dec., 1956), 577-584.

Ronald Bates, "Downdolphinry," UTQ, 36 (April, 1967), 229-236.

Ronald Bates, "'The Windhover,'" VP, 2 (Spring, 1964), 63-64.

Ralph C. Baxter, "Shakespeare's Dauphin and Hopkins' Windhover," VP, 7 (Spring, 1969), 71-75.

Robert Boyle, S.J., "Time and Grace in Hopkins' Imagination," Renascence, 29 (Autumn, 1976), 20-22.

Leslie F. Chard, II, "Once More Into The Windhover," ELN, 2 (June, 1965), 282-285.

Bell Gale Chevigny, "Instress and Devotion in Hopkins," VS, 9 (Dec., 1965), 146-147.

Deutsch, Poetry in Our Time, pp. 295-300.

Denis Donoghue, "The Bird as Symbol: Hopkins' Windhover," Studies, 44 (Autumn, 1955), 291-299.

Drew, Discovering Poetry, pp. 248-252.

Leon V. Driskell, "The Progressive Structure of 'The Windhover,'" Renascence, 19 (Fall, 1966), 30-36.

William Empson, "Hopkinsiana," TLS, Oct., 1, 1954, p. 625.

Empson, Seven Types of Ambiguity, pp. 284-286.

William Empson, "'The Windhover,'" TLS, May 20, 1955, p. 269.

Friar and Brinnin, Modern Poetry, p. 504.

W. H. Gardner, "The Religious Problem in G. M. Hopkins," Scrutiny, 6 (June, 1937), 35-38.
    Rpt. Critiques, pp. 349-353.
    Rpt. Engle and Carrier, Reading Modern Poetry, pp. 337-341.

W. H. Gardner, "'The Windhover,'" TLS, June 24, 1955, p. 349.

Frederick L. Gwynn, "Hopkins' 'The Windhover': A New Simplification," MLN, 66 (June, 1951), 366-370.

Susan A. Hallgarth, "A Study of Hopkins' Use of Nature," VP, 5 (Summer, 1967), 88.

Hartman, The Unmediated Vision, pp. 49-67, 162.

Ann S. Haskell, "An Image of 'The Windhover,'" VP, 6 (Spring, 1968), 75-77.

Archibald A. Hill, "An Analysis of 'The Windhover': An Experiment in Structural Method," PMLA, 70 (Dec., 1955), 968-978.
    Rpt. Constituent and Pattern in Poetry (Austin: Univ. of Texas Press, 1976), 28-38.

John D. Howard, "Letter to the Editor," CE, 19 (April, 1958), 312.

John F. Huntley, "Hopkins' 'The Windhover' as a Prayer of Request," Renascence, 16 (Spring, 1964), 154-162.

Kilby, Poetry and Life, pp. 208-209.

Edward A. Kopper, Expl, 22 (March, 1964), 54.

Langbaum, The Poetry of Experience, pp. 66-69.

F. N. Lees, "Hopkinsiana," TLS, Sept. 3, 1954, p. 557.

F. N. Lees, "Hopkinsiana," TLS, Oct., 22, 1954, p. 673.

F. N. Lees, "'The Windhover,'" Scrutiny, 17 (Spring, 1950), 32-38.

Peter Lisca, "The Return of 'The Windhover,'" CE, 19 (Dec., 1957), 124-126.

Boyd Litzinger, "Once More, 'The Windhover,'" VP, 5 (Autumn, 1967), 228-230.

Herbert Marshall McLuhan, "The Analogical Mirrors," The Kenyon Review, 6 (Summer, 1944), 326-329.

Bruce E. Miller, "On 'The Windhover,'" VP, 2 (Summer, 1964), 115-119.

Arthur Mizener, "Victorian Hopkins," The Kenyon Review, 6 (Autumn, 1944), 604.

George E. Montag, "'The Windhover,'" Crucifixion and Redemption," VP, 3 (Spring, 1965), 109-118.

Edwin Morgan, "A Hopkins Phrase," TLS, May 27, 1949, p. 347.

B. De Bear Nicol, "A Hopkins Phrase," TLS, May 13, 1949, p. 313.

Gerald L. Nolan, "'The Windhover,'" TLS, June 24, 1955, p. 349.

I. A. Richards, "Gerard Hopkins," The Dial, 81 (Sept., 1926), 197-199.

Jean Georges Ritz, "'The Windhover,'" TLS, May 6, 1955, p. 237.

Rosenthal, The Modern Poets, pp. 24-25.

Clive Sansom, "A Hopkins Phrase," TLS, May 20, 1949, p. 329.

Elisabeth Schneider, Expl, 18 (Jan., 1960), 22.
   Rpt. The Explicator Cyclopedia, I, pp. 169-171.
   Rpt. Locke, Gibson, and Arms, Introduction to Literature, fourth
   edition, pp. 162-164.
   Rpt. fifth edition, pp. 141-143.

Schneider, Poems and Poetry, pp. 470-471.

F. X. Shea, S.J., "Another Look at 'The Windhover,'" VP, 2 (Winter, 1964), 219-239.

Stageberg and Anderson, Poetry as Experience, pp. 493-496.

Stauffer, The Nature of Poetry, pp. 41-42 et passim.

Daniel Stempel, "A Reading of the Windhover," CE, 23 (Jan., 1962), 305-307.

Alfred Thomas, "G. M. Hopkins: 'The Windhover'; Sources, 'Underthought,' and Significance," MLR, 70 (July, 1975), 497-507.

Alfred Thomas, Expl, 33 (Dec., 1974), 31.

J. D. Thomas, Expl, 20 (Dec., 1961), 31.
   Rpt. The Explicator Cyclopedia, I, p. 171.

C. J. Tweedy, "A Note on Gerard Manley Hopkins: 'The Windhover,'" CritQ, 19 (Summer, 1977), 88-89.

Bruce Wallis, "Hopkins' 'Dapple-Dawn-Drawn' Charioteer," VN, 44 (Fall, 1973), 26-28.

Bruce Wallis, "'The Windhover' and the Patristic Exegetical Tradition," UTQ, 41 (Spring, 1972), 246-255.

Walsh, The Use of Imagination, pp. 135-136.

Dennis Ward, Interpretations, ed. John Wain, pp. 138-151.

J. L. Winter, "Notes on 'The Windhover,'" VP, 4 (Summer, 1966), 212-213.

Winters, The Function of Criticism, pp. 127-135.

Carl R. Woodring, "Once More 'The Windhover,'" The Western Review, 15 (Autumn, 1951), 61-64.

_____. "The Wreck of the Deutschland"
Robert Boyle, S.J., "Hopkins' Use of 'Fancy,'" VP, 10 (Spring, 1972), 17-27.

Robert Boyle, S.J., "Time and Grace in Hopkins' Imagination," Renascence, 29 (Autumn, 1976), 7-20.

M. H. Bright, "Homiletic Structure of The Wreck of the Deutschland," Renascence, 25 (Winter, 1973), 95-102.

Jerome Bump, "'The Wreck of the Deutschland' and the Dynamic Sublime," ELH, 41 (Spring, 1974), 106-129.

Winston Collins, "Tennyson and Hopkins," UTQ, 38 (Oct., 1968), 92-95.

James F. Cotter, "Inscaping: "The Wreck of the Deutschland," Renascence, 21 (Spring, 1969), 124-133, 166.

Deutsch, Poetry in Our Time, p. 290-292.

Denis Donoghue, "Techniques in Hopkins," Studies, 44 (Winter, 1955), 449.

John P. Driscoll, S.J., "'The Wreck of the Deutschland': Stanza 33," VP, (Summer, 1975), 137-142.

John Ferns, "'The Wreck of the Deutschland': Voice and Structure," VP, 9 (Winter, 1971), 383-393.

George F. Freije, "Grace in Hopkins's 'Deutschland,'" ELN, 13 (Sept., 1975), 37-38.

W. H. Gardner, "The Wreck of the Deutschland," Essays and Studies, 21 (1935), 124-152.

Susan A. Hallgarth, "A Study of Hopkins' Use of Nature," VP, 5 (Summer, 1967), 84-85.

Eileen Kennedy, "Lightning, Lashed Rod, and Dove in 'The Wreck of the Deutschland,'" VP, 11 (Autumn, 1973), 247-251.

Thomas Kretz, S.J., "Advents Three for Three: A Study of 'The Wreck of the Deutschland,'" VP, 11 (Autumn, 1973), 252-254.

F. R. Leavis, "Gerard Manley Hopkins," Scrutiny, 12 (Spring, 1944), 82-93.

Leavis, New Bearings on English Poetry, pp. 175-180.

Boyd Litzinger, Expl, 18 (Dec., 1959), 19.
    Rpt. The Explicator Cyclopedia, I, pp. 174.

Boyd Litzinger, Expl, 20 (Sept., 1961), 7.
    Rpt. The Explicator Cyclopedia, I, pp. 171-172.

M. B. McNamee, "Mastery and Mercy in 'The Wreck of the Deutschland,'" CE, 23 (Jan., 1962), 267-276.

J. Hillis Miller, "'Orion' in 'The Wreck of the Deutschland,'" MLN, 76 (June, 1961), 509-514.

Arthur Mizener, "Victorian Hopkins," The Kenyon Review, 6 (Autumn, 1944), 603-606.

Arthur W. Pitts, Expl, 24 (Sept., 1965), 7.

Edward Proffit, "'The Wreck of the Deutschland': Stanzas 25-28," ELN, 14 (March, 1977), 201-206.

Alvan S. Ryan, Expl, 34 (March, 1976), 53.

Elisabeth Schneider, Expl, 16 (May, 1958), 46.
    Rpt. The Explicator Cyclopedia, I, p. 172.

Elisabeth W. Schneider, "Sprung Rhythm: A Chapter in the Evolution of Nineteenth-Century Verse," PMLA, 80 (June, 1965), 237-253.

Elisabeth W. Schneider, "The Wreck of the Deutschland: A New Reading," PMLA, 81 (March, 1966), 110-122.

Brother Adelbert Scheve, F.S.C., Expl, 17 (June, 1959), 60.
Rpt. The Explicator Cyclopedia, I, pp. 172-173.

Francis B. Thornton, "Essays on 'The Wreck of the Deutschland,'" The Catholic World, 160 (Oct., 1944), 41-46.

HOSKINS, John. "Absence"
Cleanth Brooks, Jr., "Three Revolutions in Poetry," SoR, 1 (Autumn, 1935), 330.

Brooks, Modern Poetry and the Tradition, pp. 22-24.

Williamson, The Proper Wit of Poetry, pp. 16-18.

_____. "Of the Loss of Time"
Williamson, The Proper Wit of Poetry, pp. 14-15.

HOUSMAN. "Be Still, My Soul, Be Still" (Shropshire Lad, 48)
Gordon Pitts, "Housman's 'Be Still, My Soul,'" VP, 3 (Spring, 1965), 137-138.

_____. "Bredon Hill" (Shropshire Lad, 21)
Cleanth Brooks, "Alfred Edward Housman," Anniversary Lectures, 1959, pp. 46-48.

Brooks, A Shaping Joy, pp. 300-302.

_____. "The Carpenter's Son" (Shropshire Lad, 47)
S. G. Andrews, Expl, 19 (Oct., 1960), 3.
Rpt. The Explicator Cyclopedia, I, pp. 174-175.

_____. "The Chestnut Casts His Flambeaux" (Last Poems, 9)

F. A. Philbrick, Expl, 4 (Dec., 1945), 20.
Rpt. The Explicator Cyclopedia, I, p. 176.

Warren Taylor, Expl, 3 (June, 1945), 64.
Rpt. The Explicator Cyclopedia, I, pp. 175-176.

_____. "Crossing Alone the Nighted Ferry" (More Poems, 23)
Randall Jarrell, "Texts from Housman," The Kenyon Review, 1 (Summer, 1939), 261-266.

_____. "Eight O'Clock" (Last Poems, 15)
Cleanth Brooks, "Alfred Edward Housman," Anniversary Lectures, 1959, pp. 42-43.

Brooks, A Shaping Joy, pp. 296-297.

Richard H. Fogle, "Empathic Imagery in Keats and Shelley," PMLA, 61 (March, 1946), 169-170.

Rosenthal and Smith, Exploring Poetry, pp. 69-71.

HOUSMAN. "1887" (Shropshire Lad, 1)
Cleanth Brooks, "Alfred Edward Housman," Anniversary Lectures, 1959, pp. 48-51.

Brooks, A Shaping Joy, pp. 302-307.

T. S. K. Scott-Craig, Charles C. Walcutt and Cleanth Brooks, Jr., Expl, 2 (March, 1944), 34.
   Rpt. The Explicator Cyclopedia, I, pp. 191-193.

Charles Child Walcutt, "Housman and the Empire: An Analysis of '1887,'" CE, 5 (Feb., 1944), 255-258.
   Rpt. Readings for Liberal Education, II, 418-423.
   Rpt. Engle and Carrier, Reading Modern Poetry, pp. 20-26.

W. L. Werner, "Housman's '1887'--No Satire," CE, 6 (Dec., 1944), 165-166.

_____. "Epitaph on an Army of Mercenaries" (Last Poems, 37)

Cleanth Brooks, "Alfred Edward Housman," Anniversary Lectures, 1959, pp. 40-41.

Vincent Freimarck, "Further Notes on Housman's Use of the Bible," MLN, 67 (Dec., 1952), 549-550.

W. L. Werner, Expl, 2 (March, 1944), 38.
   Rpt. The Explicator Cyclopedia, I, pp. 176-177.

Richard Wilbur, "Round about a Poem of Housman's," in The Moment of Poetry, pp. 78-92.

_____. "Fancy's Knell" (Last Poems, 41)
Wheeler, The Design of Poetry, pp. 137-142, 223-225.

_____. "Farewell to Barn and Stack and Tree" (Shropshire Lad, 8)

George Arms, Expl, 1 (April, 1943), Q29.

Wilbur S. Scott, Expl, 5 (Nov., 1946), 11.
   Rpt. The Explicator Cyclopedia, I, pp. 177-178.

Frank Sullivan, Expl, 2 (March, 1944), 36.
   Rpt. The Explicator Cyclopedia, I, p. 177.

_____. "The Farms of Home Lie Lost in Even" (More Poems, 14)
Ellen Friedman, "The Divided Self in the Poems of A. E. Housman," ELT, 20, No. 1 (1977), 32-33.

_____. "Hell Gate" (Last Poems, 31)
John Hawley Roberts, Expl, 5 (April, 1947), 44.
   Rpt. The Explicator Cyclopedia, I, p. 178.

_____. "Here in the Beechen Forest"
Tom B. Haber, "A Poem of Beeches from the Notebooks of A. E. Housman," DR, 31 (Autumn, 1951), 196-197.

_____. "Her Strong Enchantments Failing" (Last Poems, 3)
Clyde K. Hyder, Expl, 4 (Nov., 1945), 11.
   Rpt. The Explicator Cyclopedia, I, pp. 178-179.

_____. "He Standing Hushed" (More Poems, 28)
Robert B. Pearsall, "Housman's 'He Standing Hushed,'" VP, 7 (Spring, 1969), 62-64.

_____. "If It Chance Your Eye Offend You" (Shropshire Lad, 45)
Robert I. Strozier, "A. E. Housman: Image, Illogic and Allusion," CLQ, 7 (June, 1966), 260.

_____. "I Hoed and Trenched and Weeded" (Shropshire Lad, 63)
Donald A. Stauffer, "Genesis, or the Poet as Maker," in Poets at Work, pp. 41-43.

_____. "The Immortal Part" (Shropshire Lad, 43)
Louise Schutz Boas, Expl, 2 (March, 1944), 37.
   Rpt. The Explicator Cyclopedia, I, p. 179.

Cleanth Brooks, "Alfred Edward Housman," Anniversary Lectures 1959, pp. 45-46.

Brooks, A Shaping Joy, pp. 299-300.

Brooks and Warren, Understanding Poetry, revised edition, pp. 617-622.

Harry M. Campbell, "Conflicting Metaphors: A Poem by A. E. Housman," CEA, 22 (Jan., 1960), 4.

_____. "Into My Heart an Air that Kills" (Shropshire Lad, 40)
Stauffer, The Nature of Poetry, pp. 22-24, 156-157, 158-159, et passim.

_____. "Is My Team Plowing?" (Shropshire Lad, 27)
Robert Brainard Pearsall, "Housman Versus Vaughan Williams: 'Is My Team Plowing?'" VP, 4 (Winter, 1966), 42-44.

_____. "It Nods and Curtseys and Recovers" (Shropshire Lad, 16)
Bateson, Essays in Critical Dissent, pp. 109-110.

Randall Jarrell, "Texts from Housman," The Kenyon Review, 1 (Summer, 1939), 266-270.

_____. "I To My Perils" (More Poems, 6)
Ellen Friedman, "The Divided Self in the Poems of A. E. Housman," ELT, 20, No. 1 (1977), 29-30.

_____. "The Lent Lily" (Shropshire Lad, 29)
Michael Macklem, "The Elgiac Theme in Housman," QQ, 59 (Spring, 1952), 50-51.

_____. "Loveliest of Trees" (Shropshire Lad, 2)
Abad, A Formal Approach to Lyric Poetry, pp. 47-48, 197.

George Arms, Expl, 1 (May, 1943), 57.

Beaty and Matchett, Poetry: From Statement to Meaning, pp. 220-222.

Dickinson, Suggestions for Teachers of "Introduction to Literature," fifth edition, ed. Locke, Gibson, and Arms, pp. 37-38. (Teacher's Manual)

B. J. Leggett, "The Poetry of Insight: Persona and Point of View in Housman," VP, 14 (Winter, 1976), 329-331.

Winifred Lynskey, Expl, 4 (June, 1946), 59.
   Rpt. The Explicator Cyclopedia, I, pp. 179-180.

Michael Macklem, "The Elegiac Theme in Housman," QQ, 59 (Spring, 1952), 41.

Laurence Perrine, "Housman's Snow: Literal or Metaphorical?" CEA, 35 (Nov., 1972), 26-27.

Patrick Story, "Housman's Cherry Trees: Toward the Practice of Marxist Explication," MinnR, 5 n.s. (Fall, 1975), 81-88.

William L. Werner, Expl, 1 (June, 1943), 69.
    Rpt. The Explicator Cyclopedia, I, p. 180.

William L. Werner, Expl, 5 (Oct., 1946), 4.

_____. "March" (Shropshire Lad, 10)
Robert I. Strozier, "A. E. Housman: Image, Illogic and Allusion," CLQ,
7 (June, 1966), 259.

_____. "The Merry Guide" (Shropshire Lad, 42)
Louise Schutz Boas, Expl, 3 (Oct., 1944), 6.
    Rpt. The Explicator Cyclopedia, I, p. 180.

_____. "The Night Is Freezing Fast" (Last Poems, 20)
Cleanth Brooks, "Alfred Edward Housman," Anniversary Lectures 1959,
pp. 44-45.

Brooks, A Shaping Joy, pp. 297-298.

Kreuzer, Elements of Poetry, pp. 220-221.

B. J. Leggett, "The Poetry of Insight: Persona and Point of View in
Housman," VP, 14 (Winter, 1976), 335-336.

_____. "Now Dreary Dawns the Eastern Light" (Last Poems, 28)
Ellen Friedman, "The Divided Self in the Poems of A. E. Housman," ELT,
20, No. 1 (1977), 31-32.

_____. "Now Hollow Fires Burn Out to Black" (Shropshire Lad, 60)
Tom Burns Haber, Expl, 11 (March, 1953), 35.
    Rpt. The Explicator Cyclopedia, I, p. 181.

_____. "The Olive"
Laurence Perrine, "Housman's 'The Olive,'" VP, 11 (Winter, 1973), 340-341.

_____. "On Moonlit Heath and Lonesome Bank" (Shropshire Lad, 9)
Perrine, The Art of Total Relevance, pp. 79-88.

_____. "On Wenlock Edge" (Shropshire Lad, 31)
Dickinson, Suggestions for Teachers of "Introduction to Literature," fifth
edition, ed. Locke, Gibson, and Arms, p. 38. (Teacher's Manual)

DeLancey Ferguson, Expl, 4 (Nov., 1945), 15.
    Rpt. The Explicator Cyclopedia, I, p. 182.

Spiro Peterson, Expl, 15 (April, 1957), 46.
    Rpt. The Explicator Cyclopedia, I, pp. 182-183.

Jack E. Reese, "Sound and Sense: The Teaching of Prosody," CE, 27 (Feb.,
1966), 371-372.

Robert Wooster Stallman, Expl, 3 (Feb., 1945), 26.
    Rpt. The Explicator Cyclopedia, I, pp. 181-182.

_____. "The Oracles" (Last Poems, 25)
Brewster Ghiselin, Expl, 4 (March, 1946), 33.
    Rpt. The Explicator Cyclopedia, I, p. 184.

Clyde K. Hyder, Expl, 4 (Oct., 1945), 5.
    Rpt. The Explicator Cyclopedia, I, pp. 183-184.

Edward Spiney, Expl, 21 (Jan., 1963), 44.

_____. "Others, I Am Not the First" (<u>Shropshire Lad</u>, 30)
B. J. Leggett, "The Poetry of Insight: Persona and Point of View in
Housman," <u>VP</u>, 14 (Winter, 1976), 332-333.

_____. "The Recruit" (<u>Shropshire Lad</u>, 3)
B. J. Leggett, <u>Expl</u>, 25 (Nov., 1966), 25.

_____. "Reveille" (<u>Shropshire Lad</u>, 8)
F. R. Leavis, "Imagery and Movement," <u>Scrutiny</u>, 13 (Sept., 1945), 132-134.

Stauffer, <u>The Nature of Poetry</u>, pp. 140-147.

_____. "Revolution" (<u>Last Poems</u>, 36)
F. A. Philbrick and Ralph P. Boas, <u>Expl</u>, 2 (March, 1944), 35 (cf. also
"Announcements," April, 1944).
    Rpt. <u>The Explicator Cyclopedia</u>, I, p. 184.

John W. Stevenson, "The Martyr as Innocent: Housman's Lonely Lad," <u>SAQ</u>,
57 (Winter, 1958), 78-79.

_____. "Tell Me Not Here; It Needs Not Saying" (<u>Last Poems</u>, 40)
Cleanth Brooks, "Alfred Edward Housman," <u>Anniversary Lectures 1959</u>,
pp. 53-56.

Brooks, <u>A Shaping Joy</u>, pp. 310-313.

_____. "Terence, This Is Stupid Stuff" (<u>Shropshire Lad</u>, 62)
Ronald E. McFarland, "The Tune the Old Cow Died of': An Allusion in
Housman," <u>VP</u>, 11 (Spring, 1973), 60-61.

Douglas John McReynolds, <u>Expl</u>, 31 (Jan., 1973), 39.

John W. Stevenson, "The Pastoral Setting in the Poetry of A. E. Housman,"
<u>SAQ</u>, 55 (Oct., 1956), 494-496.

W. J. Swanson, <u>Expl</u>, 29 (April, 1971), 67.

_____. "To an Athlete Dying Young" (<u>Shropshire Lad</u>, 19)
William Bache, <u>Expl</u>, 10 (Oct., 1951), 6.
    Rpt. <u>The Explicator Cyclopedia</u>, I, p. 185.

Beaty and Matchett, <u>Poetry: From Statement to Meaning</u>, pp. 173-174,
238-239.

Brooks and Warren, <u>Understanding Poetry</u>, pp. 385-387. Revised edition,
pp. 267-269.

C. R. B. Combellack, <u>Expl</u>, 10 (March, 1952), 31.
    Rpt. <u>The Explicator Cyclopedia</u>, I, pp. 185-187.

Nat Henry, <u>Expl</u>, 12 (May, 1954), 48.
    Rpt. <u>The Explicator Cyclopedia</u>, I, pp. 188-189.

B. J. Leggett, "The Poetry of Insight: Persona and Point of View in
Housman," <u>VP</u>, 14 (Winter, 1976), 336-337.

Walter L. Meyers, <u>Expl</u>, 11 (Feb., 1953), 23.
    Rpt. <u>The Explicator Cyclopedia</u>, I, pp. 182-188.

Elizabeth Nitchie, <u>Expl</u>, 10 (June, 1952), 57.
    Rpt. <u>The Explicator Cyclopedia</u>, I, p. 187.

Schneider, <u>Poems and Poetry</u>, pp. 24-25.

Charles Child Walcutt, "Interpreting the Symbol," <u>CE</u>, 14 (May, 1953),
449-451.

_____. "This Time of Year a Twelvemonth Past" (<u>Shropshire Lad</u>, 25)
Robert I. Strozier, "A. E. Housman: Image, Illogic and Allusion," <u>CLQ</u>,
7 (June, 1966), 261-262.

_____. "The True Lover" (<u>Shropshire Lad</u>, 53)
Darrel Abel, <u>Expl</u>, 8 (Dec., 1949), 23.
   Rpt. <u>The Explicator Cyclopedia</u>, I, p. 189.

Brooks, Purser, and Warren, <u>An Approach to Literature</u>, pp. 442-443.
   Rpt. third edition, pp. 296-297.
   Rpt. fourth edition, p. 298.

Maude M. Hawkins, <u>Expl</u>, 8 (June, 1950), 61.
   Rpt. <u>The Explicator Cyclopedia</u>, I, pp. 189-190.

_____. "We'll to the Woods No More" (<u>Last Poems</u>, Preface)
Elisabeth Schneider, <u>Aesthetic Motive</u>, pp. 97-103.
   Rpt in part <u>The Critic's Notebook</u>, p. 225.

_____. "When I Came Last to Ludlow" (<u>Shropshire Lad</u>, 58)
Ellen Friedman, "The Divided Self in the Poems of A. E. Housman," <u>ELT</u>,
20, No. 1 (1977), 27-29.

_____. "When Israel Out of Egypt Came" (<u>More Poems</u>, 2)
L. G. Locke, <u>Expl</u>, 2 (March, 1944), 39.
   Rpt. <u>The Explicator Cyclopedia</u>, I, pp. 190-191.

_____. "When Smoke Stood up from Ludlow" (<u>Shropshire Lad</u>, 7)
Stauffer, <u>The Nature of Poetry</u>, pp. 217-218.

Robert I. Strozier, "A. E. Housman: Image, Illogic and Allusion," <u>CLQ</u>,
7 (June, 1966), 258-259.

_____. "White in the Moon the Long Road Lies" (<u>Shropshire Lad</u>, 36)
Kreuzer, <u>Elements of Poetry</u>, pp. 132-134.

_____. "With Rue My Heart is Laden" (<u>Shropshire Lad</u>, 54)
Winifred Lynskey, "A Critic in Action: Mr. Ransom," <u>CE</u>, 5 (Feb., 1944),
239-242.

Tracey Peterson, "A. E. Housman's 'With Rue My Heart is Laden': A Sug-
gestion for Interpretation," <u>PLL</u>, 7 (Winter, 1971), 94-95.

John Crowe Ransom, "Honey and Gall," <u>SoR</u>, 6 (Summer, 1940), 7-8.

Thomas and Brown, <u>Reading Poems: An Introduction to Critical Study</u>,
pp. 754-756.

_____. "With Seed the Sowers Scatter" (<u>More Poems</u>, 32)
William Empson, "Emotions in Words Again," <u>The Kenyon Review</u>, 10 (Autumn,
1948), 587-589.
   Rpt. <u>The Kenyon Critics</u>, pp. 133-135.

HOWARD, Richard. "Waiting for Ada"
Thomas Woll, "Stasis Within Flux: Richard Howard's Findings," <u>MPS</u>, 4
(Winter, 1973), 263-264.

HOWES, Barbara. "The Heart of Europe"
Hayden Carruth, <u>Poetry: A Critical Supplement</u>, Feb., 1949, pp. 7-8.

_____. "In the Cold Country"
Hayden Carruth, <u>Poetry: A Critical Supplement</u>, Feb., 1949, pp. 3-7.

_____. "Portrait of an Artist"
Hayden Carruth, <u>Poetry: A Critical Supplement</u>, Feb., 1949, p. 9.

HUGHES, Langston. "Daybreak in Alabama"
    R. Baxter Miller, "'A Mere Poem': 'Daybreak in Alabama,' A Resolution
    to Langston Hughes's Theme of Music and Art," <u>Obsidian: Black Literature
    in Review</u>, 2 (Summer, 1976), 30-37.

_____. "Theme for English B"
Gary F. Scharnhorst, <u>Expl</u>, 32 (Dec., 1973), 27.

HUGHES, Ted. "A Childish Prank"
    Marjorie Perloff, "Poetry Chronicle: 1970-71," <u>ConL</u>, 14 (Winter, 1973), 121.

_____. "Full Moon and Little Frieda"
David Holbrook, <u>Lost Bearings in English Poetry</u> (London: Vision Press,
1977), pp. 127-128.

_____. "Gog"
David Holbrook, <u>Lost Bearings in English Poetry</u> (London: Vision Press,
1977), pp. 110-126.

_____. "The Hawk in the Rain"
Lawrence R. Ries, <u>Expl</u>, 33 (Dec., 1974), 34.

Lawrence R. Ries, <u>Wolf Masks: Violence in Contemporary Poetry</u> (Port
Washington, N.Y.: Kennikat Press, 1977), pp. 110-112.

_____. "Pike"
Dickinson, <u>Suggestions for Teachers of "Introduction to Literature</u>, fifth
edition, ed. Locke, Gibson, and Arms, pp. 53-54. (Teacher's Manual)

Stuart Hirschberg, "An Encounter with the Irrational in Ted Hughes's
'Pike,'" <u>CP</u>, 9 (Spring, 1976), 63-64.

_____. "Wodwo"
Lawrence R. Ries, <u>Wolf Masks: Violence in Contemporary Poetry</u> (Port
Washington, N.Y.: Kennikat Press, 1977), pp. 112-113.

HUMPHRIES. "Little Fugue"
    Harold E. Cook, <u>Expl</u>, 14 (Dec., 1955), 14.
        Rpt. <u>The Explicator Cyclopedia</u>, I, pp. 193-195.

_____. "Polo Grounds"
Perrine and Reid, <u>100 American Poems</u>, pp. 169-171.

HUNT. "Abou Ben Adhem"
    Ernest E. Leisy, <u>Expl</u>, 5 (Nov., 1946), 9.
        Rpt. <u>The Explicator Cyclopedia</u>, II, p. 163.

    T. O. Mabbott, <u>Expl</u>, 5 (March, 1947), 39.
        Rpt. <u>The Explicator Cyclopedia</u>, II, p. 163.

_____. "Jenny Kissed Me"
Abad, <u>A Formal Approach to Lyric Poetry</u>, pp. 325-326.

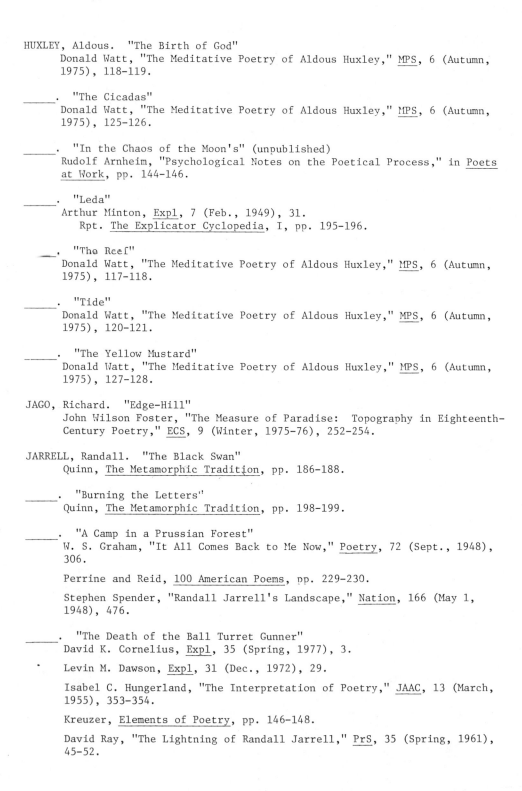

HUXLEY, Aldous. "The Birth of God"
Donald Watt, "The Meditative Poetry of Aldous Huxley," <u>MPS</u>, 6 (Autumn, 1975), 118-119.

_____. "The Cicadas"
Donald Watt, "The Meditative Poetry of Aldous Huxley," <u>MPS</u>, 6 (Autumn, 1975), 125-126.

_____. "In the Chaos of the Moon's" (unpublished)
Rudolf Arnheim, "Psychological Notes on the Poetical Process," in <u>Poets at Work</u>, pp. 144-146.

_____. "Leda"
Arthur Minton, <u>Expl</u>, 7 (Feb., 1949), 31.
    Rpt. <u>The Explicator Cyclopedia</u>, I, pp. 195-196.

_____. "The Reef"
Donald Watt, "The Meditative Poetry of Aldous Huxley," <u>MPS</u>, 6 (Autumn, 1975), 117-118.

_____. "Tide"
Donald Watt, "The Meditative Poetry of Aldous Huxley," <u>MPS</u>, 6 (Autumn, 1975), 120-121.

_____. "The Yellow Mustard"
Donald Watt, "The Meditative Poetry of Aldous Huxley," <u>MPS</u>, 6 (Autumn, 1975), 127-128.

JAGO, Richard. "Edge-Hill"
John Wilson Foster, "The Measure of Paradise: Topography in Eighteenth-Century Poetry," <u>ECS</u>, 9 (Winter, 1975-76), 252-254.

JARRELL, Randall. "The Black Swan"
Quinn, <u>The Metamorphic Tradition</u>, pp. 186-188.

_____. "Burning the Letters"
Quinn, <u>The Metamorphic Tradition</u>, pp. 198-199.

_____. "A Camp in a Prussian Forest"
W. S. Graham, "It All Comes Back to Me Now," <u>Poetry</u>, 72 (Sept., 1948), 306.

Perrine and Reid, <u>100 American Poems</u>, pp. 229-230.

Stephen Spender, "Randall Jarrell's Landscape," <u>Nation</u>, 166 (May 1, 1948), 476.

_____. "The Death of the Ball Turret Gunner"
David K. Cornelius, <u>Expl</u>, 35 (Spring, 1977), 3.

Levin M. Dawson, <u>Expl</u>, 31 (Dec., 1972), 29.

Isabel C. Hungerland, "The Interpretation of Poetry," <u>JAAC</u>, 13 (March, 1955), 353-354.

Kreuzer, <u>Elements of Poetry</u>, pp. 146-148.

David Ray, "The Lightning of Randall Jarrell," <u>PrS</u>, 35 (Spring, 1961), 45-52.

Rosenthal and Smith, Exploring Poetry, pp. 547-549.

Rosenthal, The Modern Poets, p. 245.

_____. "Eighth Air Force"
Cleanth Brooks, "Irony as a Principle of Structure," in Literary Opinion in America, ed. M. D. Zabel, revised edition, pp. 738-741.

Brooks, Purser, and Warren, An Approach to Literature, third edition, pp. 397-399.
    Rpt. fourth edition, pp. 396-398.

Frances C. Ferguson, "Randall Jarrell and the Flotations of Voice," GaR, 28 (Fall, 1974), 436-438.

_____. "The Emancipators"
Mordecai and Erin Marcus, Expl, 16 (Feb., 1958), 26.
    Rpt. The Explicator Cyclopedia, I, pp. 196-198.

_____. "The Girl Dreams That She Is Giselle"
Quinn, The Metamorphic Tradition, pp. 188-191.

_____. "Hohensalzburg"
Hayden Carruth, Poetry: A Critical Supplement, April, 1949, pp. 1-10.

Quinn, The Metamorphic Tradition, pp. 174-175, 178-181.

_____. "Hope"
Perrine and Reid, 100 American Poems, pp. 231-233.

_____. "The House in the Wood"
Robert Weisberg, "Randall Jarrell: The Integrity of His Poetry," CentR, 17 (Summer, 1973), 251-252.

_____. "A Hunt"
Robert Weisberg, "Randall Jarrell: The Integrity of His Poetry," CentR, 17 (Summer, 1973), 248-250.

_____. "Jerome"
Frances C. Ferguson, "Randall Jarrell and the Flotations of Voice," GaR, 28 (Fall, 1974), 431-435.

_____. "King's Hunt"
Quinn, The Metamorphic Tradition, pp. 192-193.

_____. "Losses"
James L. Jackson, Expl, 19 (April, 1961), 49.

_____. "The Lost World"
Robert Weisberg, "Randall Jarrell: The Integrity of His Poetry," CentR, 17 (Summer, 1973), 244-247.

_____. "Love in Its Separate Being"
Joseph Warren Beach, "The Cancelling Out--A Note on Recent Poetry," Accent, 7 (Summer, 1947), 248-249.

_____. "The Metamorphosis"
Quinn, The Metamorphic Tradition, pp. 200-201.

_____. "The Night Before the Night Before Christmas"
Quinn, The Metamorphic Tradition, pp. 182-185.

_____. "On the Railway Platform"
Beach, <u>Obsessive Images</u>, pp. 178-182.

_____. "A Quilt-Pattern"
Quinn, <u>The Metamorphic Tradition</u>, pp. 193-195.

_____. "A Rhapsody on Irish Themes"
Quinn, <u>The Metamorphic Tradition</u>, p. 191.

_____. "Seele im Raum"
Russell Fowler, "Randall Jarrell's 'Eland': A Key to Motive and Technique
in His Poetry," <u>IowaR</u>, 5 (Spring, 1974), 119-123.

Bertrand R. Richards, <u>Expl</u>, 33 (Nov., 1974), 22.

_____. "The Sleeping Beauty: Variation of the Prince"
Quinn, <u>The Metamorphic Tradition</u>, pp. 175-177.

_____. "Soul"
Quinn, <u>The Metamorphic Tradition</u>, pp. 172-173.

_____. "Thinking of the Lost World"
Robert Weisberg, "Randall Jarrell: The Integrity of His Poetry," <u>CentR</u>,
17 (Summer, 1973), 252-255.

_____. "The Venetian Blind"
Quinn, <u>The Metamorphic Tradition</u>, pp. 191-192.

_____. "A Well-to-do Invalid"
Robert Weisberg, "Randall Jarrell: The Integrity of His Poetry," <u>CentR</u>,
17 (Summer, 1973), 242-243.

JEFFERS. "Christmas Card"
Deutsch, <u>Poetry in Our Time</u>, pp. 21-22.

_____. "Fire on the Hills"
George Arms, <u>Expl</u>, 1 (May, 1943), 59.
    Rpt. <u>The Explicator Cyclopedia</u>, I, pp. 198-199.

_____. "Give Your Heart to the Hawks"
Frajam Taylor, "The Enigma of Robinson Jeffers: II, The Hawk and the
Stone," <u>Poetry</u>, 55 (Oct., 1939), 39-44.

_____. "Greater Grandeur"
J. F. Nims, <u>Poetry: A Critical Supplement</u>, Oct., 1947, pp. 5-6.

_____. "Hurt Hawks"
Gray, <u>American Poetry</u>, p. 205.

_____. "Margrave"
Waggoner, <u>The Heel of Elohim</u>, pp. 121-129.

_____. "Meditation on Saviours"
W. S. Johnson, "The 'Savior' in the Poetry of Robinson Jeffers," <u>AL</u>, 15
(May, 1943), 163-164.

_____. "Nova"
Perrine and Reid, <u>100 American Poems</u>, pp. 91-92.

_____. "Ocean"
Perrine and Reid, <u>100 American Poems</u>, pp. 89-90.

_____. "The Purse-Seine"
Perrine and Reid, 100 American Poems, pp. 93-94.

Rosenthal, The Modern Poets, pp. 157-158.

_____. "Roan Stallion"
Gray, American Poetry, pp. 201-205.

Karl Keller, "California, Yankees, and the Death of God: The Allegory
in Jeffers' Roan Stallion," TSLL, 12 (Spring, 1970), 111-120.

_____. "Science"
Delmore Schwartz, "The Enigma of Robinson Jeffers: I, Sources of Violence," Poetry, 55 (Oct., 1939), 34-38.

_____. "Shine, Perishing Republic"
Walsh, Doors into Poetry, pp. 30-31.

JEROME. "Aubade"
Judson Jerome, "Rivalry with Madmen," YR, 48 (March, 1959), 345-350.

_____. "From Beowulf to Thomas Hardy"
Judson Jerome, "Rivalry with Madmen," YR, 48 (March, 1959), 352-353.

JOHNSON, Lionel. "By the Statue of King Charles at Charing Cross"
F. R. Leavis, "'Thought' and Emotional Quality," Scrutiny, 13 (Spring,
1945), 62-66.

_____. "Comely and Calm He Rides"
H. P. Collins, "A Note on the Classical Principle in Poetry," The Criterion, 3 (April, 1925), 391-394.

_____. "The Dark Angel"
Iain Fletcher, Interpretations, ed. John Wain, pp. 155-178.

_____. "Oxford"
Bateson, English Poetry, pp. 235-239.

JOHNSON, Samuel. "London"
J. P. Hardy, Reinterpretations: Essays on Poems by Milton, Pope, and
Johnson (London: Routledge & Kegan Paul, 1971), pp. 103-123.

R. G. Peterson, "Samuel Johnson at War with the Classics," ECS, 9 (Fall,
1975), 81-83.

_____. "On the Death of Dr. Robert Levet"
Donald C. Mell, "Johnson's Moral Elegiacs: Theme and Structure in 'On
the Death of Robert Levet,'" Genre, 5 (Sept., 1972), 293-306.

Susie I. Tucker and Henry Gifford, Expl, 15 (April, 1957), 45.
   Rpt. The Explicator Cyclopedia, II, pp. 163-164.

_____. "The Vanity of Human Wishes"
J. M. Aden, "'Rasselas' and 'The Vanity of Human Wishes,'" Criticism, 3
(Fall, 1961), 295-303.

George T. Amis, "The Style of The Vanity of Human Wishes," MLQ, 35
(March, 1974), 16-29.

Anonymous, "Vanity of Human Wishes, Lines 15-20," N&Q, 4, n.s., (Aug.,
1957), 353-354.

Edward A. Bloom, "The Vanity of Human Wishes: Reason's Images," EIC, 15 (April, 1965), 181-192.

Wallace C. Brown, "Dramatic Tension in Neoclassic Satire," CE, 6 (Feb., 1945), 266-267.

Sanford Budick, Poetry of Civilization: Mythopoeic Displacement in the Verse of Milton, Dryden, Pope and Johnson (New Haven and London: Yale Univ. Press, 1974), pp. 156-172.

W. B. Carnochan, Confinement and Flight: An Essay on English Literature of the Eighteenth Century (Berkeley: Univ. of California Press, 1977), pp. 162-167.

MacDonald Emslie, Expl, 12 (Nov., 1953), 8.
    Rpt. The Explicator Cyclopedia, II, pp. 165-166.

Henry Gifford, "'The Vanity of Human Wishes,'" RES, 6 n.s. (April, 1955), 157-165.

Donald Greene, "On Misreading Eighteenth-Century Literature: A Rejoinder," ECS, 9 (Fall, 1975), 108-118.

Frederick W. Hilles, "Johnson's Poetic Fire," in From Sensibility to Romanticism, pp. 67-76.

Lawrence Lipking, "Learning to Read Johnson: The Vision of Theodore and The Vanity of Human Wishes," ELH, 43 (Winter, 1976), 527-535.

Paul D. McGlynn, "Rhetoric as Metaphor in The Vanity of Human Wishes," SEL, 15 (Summer, 1975), 473-482.

Edward P. Partridge, Expl, 6 (Feb., 1948), 28.
    Rpt. The Explicator Cyclopedia, II, pp. 164-165.

R. G. Peterson, "Samuel Johnson at War with the Classics," ECS, 9 (Fall, 1975), 83-85.

Mark Roberts, The Tradition of Romantic Morality (London and Basingstoke: Macmillan Press, 1973), 27-81.

Donald T. Siebert, Jr., Expl, 32 (April, 1974), 63.

Susie I. Tucker and Harry Gifford, "Johnson's Poetic Imagination," RES, 8, n.s. (Aug., 1957), 241-248.

Susie I. Tucker, "'The Steeps of Fate' Vanity of Human Wishes, I, 125," N&Q, 4, n.s. (Aug., 1957), 354.

Unger and O'Connor, Poems for Study, pp. 308-312.

Ian White, "The Vanity of Human Wishes," CQ, 6 No. 2 (1974), 115-125.

_____   "The Vision of Theodore"
Lawrence Lipking, "Learning to Read Johnson: The Vision of Theodore and The Vanity of Human Wishes," ELH, 43 (Winter, 1976), 517-527.

JONES, David. "Rite and Fore-Time"
    Thomas R. Dilworth, "David Jones's Use of a Geology Text for The Anathemata," ELN, 15 (Dec., 1977), 115-119.

_____.   "The Tribune's Visitation"
    John Heath-Stubbs, "New Writings," PoetryR, 61 (Summer, 1970), 168-170.

JONSON. "A Celebration of Charis"
    R. V. Leclercq, "The Reciprocal Harmony of Jonson's 'A Celebration of Charis,'" TSLL, 16 (Winter, 1975), 627-650.

Richard S. Peterson, "Virtue Reconciled to Pleasure: Jonson's 'A Celebration of Charis,'" SLitI, 6 (April, 1973), 219-268.

Sara Van Den Berg, "The Play of Wit and Love: Demetrius' On Style and
Jonson's 'A Celebration of Charis,'" ELH, 41 (Spring, 1974), 26-36.

G. J. Weinberger, "Jonson's Mock-Encomiastic 'Celebration of Charis,'"
Genre, 4 (Dec., 1971), 305-328.

_____. "A Celebration of Charis 1" "His Excuse for Loving"
Ferry, All in War with Time, pp. 157-161.

_____. "A Celebration of Charis 4" "Her Triumph"
Marie Borroff, "The Triump of Charis: Through Swards, not Swords," ELN,
8 (June, 1971), 257-259.

Ferry, All in War with Time, pp. 130-133.

William V. Spanos, "The Real Toad in the Jonsonian Garden: Resonance in
the Nondramatic Poetry," JEGP, 68 (Jan., 1969), 13-15.

_____. "Come, My Celia, Let Us Prove"
William Sylvester, Expl, 22 (Jan., 1964), 35.

_____. "Though Beautie be the Marke of Praise" "An Elegie"
Ferry, All in War with Time, pp. 168-172.

Judith K. Gardiner, "Syntax and the Platonic Ladder: Jonson's 'Though
Beautie be the Marke of Praise,'" CP, 8 (Spring, 1975), 35-40.

Miner, The Cavalier Mode from Jonson to Cotton, pp. 11-12.

Yvor Winters, "Poetic Styles, Old and New," in Four Poets on Poetry,
pp. 62-65.
    Rpt. Forms of Discovery, pp. 64-67.

_____. "Elegy on the Death of Lady Jane Pawlet"
Hardison, The Enduring Monument, pp. 142-145.

_____. "An Epistle Mendicant"
George B. Johnston, "'An Epistle Mendicant' by Ben Jonson," N&Q, 1,
n.s. (Nov., 1954), 471.

_____. "An Epistle to a Friend, To Perswade Him to the Warres"
Richard C. Newton, "'Goe, quit 'hem all': Ben Jonson and Formal Verse
Satire," SEL, 16 (Winter, 1976), 108-114.

_____. "Epistle to Elizabeth Countesse of Rutland"
James D. Garrison, "Time and Value in Jonson's 'Epistle to Elizabeth
Countesse of Rutland,'" CP, 8 (Fall, 1975), 53-58.

_____. "An Epistle to Katherine, Lady Aubigny"
Miner, The Cavalier Mode from Jonson to Cotton, pp. 170-171, 306-308.

_____. "Epistle to Mr. Arthur Squib"
Randolph L. Wadsworth, Jr., Expl, 33 (Jan., 1975), 42.

_____. "Epitaph on Elizabeth, L. H."
Howard S. Babb, "'The Epitaph on Elizabeth, L. H.' and Ben Jonson's
Style," JEGP, 62 (Oct., 1963), 738-744.

Hardison, The Enduring Monument, pp. 124-126.

J. M. Major, "A Reading of Jonson's 'Epitaph on Elizabeth, L. H.,'" SP, 73 (Jan., 1976), 62-86.

Stephen E. Tabachnick, Expl, 29 (May, 1971), 77.

_____. "Epitaph on Solomon Pavy"
Louis F. May, Expl, 20 (Oct., 1961), 16.
    Rpt. The Explicator Cyclopedia, II, p. 166.

_____. "Eupheme: Or, The Faire Fame Left to Posteritie of that Truly Noble Lady, the Lady Venetia Digby"

Barbara Kiefer Lewalski, Donne's Anniversaries and the Poetry of Praise: The Creation of a Symbolic Mode (Princeton: Princeton Univ. Press, 1973), pp. 339-342.

_____. "A Fit of Rime Against Rime"
George Hemphill, Expl, 12 (June, 1954), 50.
    Rpt. The Explicator Cyclopedia, II, pp. 166-167.

_____. "A Hymne on the Nativitie of My Saviour"
A. B. Chambers, "Christmas: The Liturgy of the Church and English Verse of the Renaissance," in Literary Monographs, ed. Eric Rothstein and Joseph Anthony Wittreich, Jr. No. 6 (Madison, Wisconsin: Univ. of Wisconsin Press, 1975), 140-141.

_____. "Hymn to Diana"
Winters, Forms of Discovery, pp. 114-115.

_____. "A Hymne to God the Father"
Philip C. McGuire, "Private Prayer and English Poetry in the Early Seventeenth Century," SEL, 14 (Winter, 1974), 68-70.

_____. "Inviting a Friend to Supper"
Leonard Dean, English Masterpieces, Vol. III, Renaissance Poetry, p. 14.

Jack Shadoian, "'Inviting a Friend to Supper': Aspects of Jonson's Craft and Personality," CP, 3 (Fall, 1970), 29-35.

_____. "It Was a Beauty That I Saw"
Daniels, The Art of Reading Poetry, pp. 200-201

_____. "My Answer. The Poet to the Painter"
Ferry, All in War with Time, pp. 149-151.

Mary L. Livingston, "Ben Jonson: The Poet to the Painter," TSLL, 18 Fall, 1976), 387-391.

_____. "My Picture Left in Scotland"
Ferry, All in War with Time, pp. 173-176.

Mary L. Livingston, "Ben Jonson: The Poet to the Painter," TSLL, 18 (Fall, 1976), 383.

_____. "An Ode: High Spirited Friend"
Sara Van Den Berg, Expl, 35 (Winter, 1976), 24-26.

Walter R. Davis, Expl, 32 (May, 1973), 70.

_____. "On a Lover's Dust Made Sand for an Hour Glass"
Miles. The Primary Language of Poetry in the 1640's, pp. 67-68.

_____. "On Lucy Countesse of Bedford"
Ferry, All in War with Time, pp. 143-149.

Harris Friedberg, "Ben Jonson's Poetry: Pastoral, Georgic, Epigram,"
ELR, 4 (Winter, 1974), 114-117.

_____. "On My First Daughter"
Roberts W. French, "Reading Jonson: Epigrammes 22 and 45," CP, 10
(Spring, 1977), 6-9.

_____. "On My First Son"
William B. Bache, "Verbal Complexity in 'On My First Son,'" CEA, 32
(Jan., 1970), 12.

L. A. Beaurline, "The Selective Principle in Jonson's Shorter Poems,"
Criticism, 8 (Winter, 1966), 65-70.

Ferry, All in War with Time, pp. 179-182.

Robert W. French, "Reading Jonson: Epigrammes 22 and 45," CP, 10
(Spring, 1977), 9-10.

W. David Kay, "The Christian Wisdom of Ben Jonson's 'On My First Sonne,'"
SEL, 11 (Winter, 1971), 125-136.

Leonard Nathan, "The Private 'I' in Contemporary Poetry," Shenandoah, 22
(Summer, 1971), 82-83.

Sharon Sanders Rando, "'On My First Sonne': The Aesthetic Radical of
Cavalier Poetry," CP, 9 (Spring, 1976), 27-30.

Kathryn Walls, "The 'Just Day' in Jonson's 'On My First Sonne,'" N&Q,
24 (March-April, 1977), 136.

_____. "On Something That Walkes Some-where"
Edgar F. Daniels, Expl, 33 (March, 1975), 58.

Ronald E. McFarland, Expl, 31 (Dec., 1972), 26.

Laurence Perrine, Expl, 32 (Dec., 1973), 30.

_____. "Pan's Anniversary"
Empson, Seven Types of Ambiguity, pp. 35-36; (1947 ed.), p. 27.

_____. "The Pattern of Piety"
Percy Simpson, "A Westminster Schoolboy and Ben Jonson," TLS, Nov. 27,
1953, p. 761.

_____. "The Picture of the Body"
Mary L. Livingston, "Ben Jonson: The Poet to the Painter," TSLL, 18
(Fall, 1976), 384-387.

_____. "Queene and Huntresse" ("Hymn," Cynthia's Revels)
Phyllis Rackin, "Poetry without Paradox" Jonson's 'Hymne' to Cynthia,"
Criticism, 4 (Summer, 1962), 186-196.

_____. "A Song"
Peter Steese, Expl, 21 (Dec., 1962), 31.

_____. "To Celia: Drink to Me Only With Thine Eyes"
L. A. Beaurline, "The Selective Principle in Jonson's Shorter Poems,"
Criticism, 8 (Winter, 1966), 72-73.

A. D. Fitton Brown, "Drink to Me, Celia," MLR, 54 (Oct., 1959), 554-557.

Gerald Bullett, "Drink to me only...," _TLS_, June 1, 1956, p. 329.

Empson, _Seven Types of Ambiguity_, pp. 306-307; (1947 ed.), pp. 242-243.

E. A. Horsman, "Drink to me only...," _TLS_, June 8, 1956, p. 345.

Gerald Sanders and Ralph P. Boas, _Expl_, 1 (Feb., 1943), 28.
      Rpt. _The Explicator Cyclopedia_, II, pp. 167-168.

Marshall Van Deusen, "Criticism and Ben Jonson's 'To Celia,'" _EIC_, 7 (Jan., 1957), 96-103.

_____. "To Heaven"
Judith K. Gardiner, "'To Heaven,'" _CP_, 6 (Fall, 1973), 26-36.

William Kerrigan, "Ben Jonson Full of Shame and Scorn," _SLitI_, 6 (April, 1973), 204-214.

Philip C. McGuire, "Private Prayer and English Poetry in the Early Seventeenth Century," _SEL_, 14 (Winter, 1974), 72-75.

Yvor Winters, "Poetic Styles, Old and New" in _Four Poets on Poetry_, pp. 65-69.
      Rpt. _Forms of Discovery_, pp. 67-70.

_____. "To His Lady, Then Mrs. Cary"
Ferry, _All in War with Time_, pp. 134-135, 137-138.

_____. "To John Donne"
Frederick M. Combellack, _Expl_, 17 (Oct., 1958), 6.
      Rpt. _The Explicator Cyclopedia_, II, p. 168.

Stanley M. Wiersma, _Expl_, 25 (Sept., 1966), 4.

_____. "To Mary Lady Wroth"
Peter Fellowes, _Expl_, 32 (Jan., 1973), 36.

Ferry, _All in War with Time_, pp. 139-142.

Harris Friedberg, "Ben Jonson's Poetry: Pastoral, Georgic, Epigram," _ELR_, 4 (Winter, 1974), 113, 125.

_____. "To Penshurst"
Paul M. Cubeta, "A Jonsonian Ideal: 'To Penshurst,'" _PQ_, 42 (Jan., 1963), 14-24.

Fowler, _Conceitful Thought_, pp. 114-134.

Harris Friedberg, "Ben Jonson's Poetry: Pastoral, Georgic, Epigram," _ELR_, 4 (Winter, 1974), 127-136.

Jeffrey Hart, "Ben Jonson's Good Society," _ModA_, 7 (Winter, 1962-1963), 62-68.

William A. McClung, Jr., _Expl_, 33 (May, 1975), 78.

Elizabeth McCutcheon, _Expl_, 25 (Feb., 1967), 52.

_____. "To Sir Lucklesse Woo-all"
Robert Early, "Sir Luckless Woo-all's 'Wast Wife' and the OED (Jonson's _Epigramme_ XLVI)," _ELN_, 12 (June, 1975), 265-268.

_____. "To the Immortall Memorie, and Friendship of that Noble Paire, Sir Lucius Cary, and Sir H. Morison"
Ian Donaldson, "Jonson's Ode to Sir Lucius Cary and Sir H. Morison," _SLitI_, 6 (April, 1973), 139-152.

Judith K. Gardiner, Expl, 33 (May, 1975), 76.

George Held, "Jonson's Pindaric on Friendship," CP, 3 (Spring, 1970), 29-41.

Miner, The Cavalier Mode from Jonson to Cotton, pp. 71-74.

Mary I. Oates, Expl, 33 (Sept., 1974), 6.

Mary I. Oates, "Jonson's 'Ode Pindarick' and the Doctrine of Imitation," PLL, 11 (Spring, 1975), 126-148.

Peckham and Chatman, Word, Meaning, Poem, pp. 90-125.

_____. "To the Memory of My Beloved, the AUTHOR Mr. William Shakespeare"
Fred M. Fetrow, "Disclaimers Reclaimed: A Consideration of Jonson's Praise of Shakespeare," ELWIU, 2 (Spring, 1975), 24-31.

Miner, The Cavalier Mode from Jonson to Cotton, pp. 137-140.

_____, "Why I Write Not of Love"
Ferry, All in War with Time, pp. 163-168.

JOYCE. "Alone"
Frankenberg, Invitation to Poetry, p. 171.

_____. Chamber Music 36"
Laurence Perrine, "Interpreting Poetry--Two Ways of Going Wrong," CEJ, 1 (Winter, 1965), 49-52.
    Rpt. The Art of Total Relevance, pp. 99-102.

_____. "Ecce Puer"
Marvin Fisher, "James Joyce's 'Ecce Puer,'" The University of Kansas City Review, 25 (Summer, 1959), 265-271.

Lawrence Richard Holmes, Expl, 13 (Nov., 1954), 12.
    Rpt. The Explicator Cyclopedia, I, pp. 200-201.

Richard M. Kain, Expl, 14 (Feb., 1956), 29.
    Rpt. The Explicator Cyclopedia, I, p. 201.

_____. "I Hear an Army"
Laurence Perrine, "Interpreting Poetry--Two Ways of Going Wrong," CEJ, 1 (Winter, 1965), 49-52.

JUHÁSZ, Ferenc. "The Boy Changed into a Stag"
Marjorie G. Perloff, "Poetry Chronicle: 1970-71," ConL, 14 (Winter, 1973), 119-121.

KAHN, Hannah. "Ride a Wild Horse"
Sanders, The Discovery of Poetry, pp. 165-167.

KAUFMAN, Wallace. "Smethport, Pennsylvania"
K. Crowhurst, "Comment," Agenda, 9 (Winter, 1971), 35.

KAVANAGH, Patrick. "Advent"
Daniel J. Casey, "Kavanagh's Calculations and Miscalculations," CLQ, 12 (June, 1976), 74-76.

_____. "Primrose"
Dudley Fitts, New York Times Book Review, Aug. 24, 1947, p. 10.

KEATS.   "La Belle Dame Sans Merci"
Abad, A Formal Approach to Lyric Poetry, pp. 109-115.

Bloom, The Visionary Company, pp. 375-378.

Bernard Breyer, Expl, 6 (Dec., 1947), 18.
Rpt. The Explicator Cyclopedia, II, pp. 176-177.

H. E. Briggs, "Keats, Robertson, and 'That Most Hateful Land,'" PMLA, 59 (March, 1944), 195-197.

Jane Rabb Cohen, "Keats's Humor in 'La Belle Dame Sans Merci,'" KSJ, 17 (1968), 10-13.

Cohen, Writing About Literature, pp. 16-19, 120.

Daniels, The Art of Reading Poetry, pp. 157-160.

Dickinson, Suggestions for Teachers of "Introduction to Literature," fifth edition, ed. Locke, Gibson, and Arms, p. 25.   (Teacher's Manual)

Don A. Keister, Expl, 5 (Feb., 1947), 29.
Rpt. The Explicator Cyclopedia, II, pp. 175-176.

L. G. Locke, Expl, 5 (Oct., 1946), 1.
Rpt. The Explicator Cyclopedia, II, pp. 174-175.

T. O. Mabbott, Expl, 5 (May, 1947), 50.
Rpt. The Explicator Cyclopedia, II, p. 176.

Millet, Reading Poetry, pp. 64-65.

Perkins, The Quest for Permanence, pp. 259-263.

David Simpson, "Keats's Lady, Metaphor, and the Rhetoric of Neurosis," SIR, 15 (Spring, 1976), 269-288.

J. M. Sinclair, "When Is a Poem like a Sunset?" A Review of English Literature, 6 (April, 1965), 76-91.

Bernice Slote, "La Belle Dame as Naiad," JEGP, 60 (Jan., 1961), 22-30.

James Twitchell, "La Belle Dame as Vampire," CEA, 37 (May, 1975), 31-33.

Francis L. Utley, "The Infernos of Lucretius and of Keats's 'La Belle Dame Sans Merci,'" ELH, 25 (June, 1958), 105-121.

Wormhoudt, The Demon Lover, pp. 75-76.

_____.   "Bright Star"
Bateson, English Poetry, pp. 10-11.

Bloom, The Visionary Company, pp. 425-427.

Brooks, Purser, and Warren, An Approach to Literature, pp. 481-482.
Rpt. third edition, pp. 358-359.

Jeremy Hawthorn, Identity and Relationship: A Contribution to Marxist Theory of Literary Criticism (London: Lawrence & Wishart, 1973), pp. 170-173.

Dell H. Hymes, "Phonological Aspects of Style: Some English Sonnets," in Essays on the Language of Literature, ed. Seymour Chatman and Samuel R. Levin (Boston: Houghton Mifflin Company, 1967), p. 47.

Knight, The Starlit Dome, pp. 304-305.

David Ormerod, "Nature's Eremite: Keats and the Liturgy of Passion," KSJ, 16 (Winter, 1967), 73-77.

Perkins, The Quest for Permanence, pp. 231-233.

_____. "Epistle to Charles Cowden Clarke"
Ciardi, How Does a Poem Mean? p. 783.

_____. "Epistle to John Hamilton Reynolds"
Bhabatosh Chatterjee, "The Enchanted Castle in Keats's' 'Epistle to Reynolds,'" N&Q, 15 (Sept., 1968), 334-335.

Louise Z. Smith, "The Material Sublime: Keats and Isabella," SIR, 13
(Fall, 1974), 301-304.

Stuart M. Sperry, "Keats's Epistle to John Hamilton Reynolds," ELH, 26
(Sept., 1969), 562-574.

_____. "The Eve of St. Agnes"
G. Douglas Atkins, "The Eve of St. Agnes Reconsidered," TSL, 18 (1973),
113-132.

Roy P. Basler, Expl, 3 (Oct., 1944), 1.
    Rpt. The Explicator Cyclopedia, II, pp. 172-173.

Arthur H. Bell, "'The Depth of Things': Keats and Human Space," KSJ, 23
(1974), 82-87.

Edward A. Bloom, Expl, 20 (Sept., 1961), 3.
    Rpt. The Explicator Cyclopedia, II, pp. 170-171.

Bloom, The Visionary Company, pp. 369-375.

James D. Boulger, "Keats' Symbolism," ELH, 28 (Sept., 1961), 254-259.

C. F. Burgess, "'The Eve of St. Agnes': One Way to the Poem," EJ, 54
(May, 1965), 389-394.

Arthur Carr, "John Keats' Other 'Urn,'" The University of Kansas City
Review, 20 (Summer, 1954), 237-242.

Ciardi, How Does a Poem Mean? pp. 772-774.

Marian H. Cusac, "Keats as Enchanter: An Organizing Principle of 'The
Eve of St. Agnes,'" KSJ, 17 (1968), 113-119.

R. H. Fogle, "A Reading of Keats's 'Eve of St. Agnes,'" CE, 6 (March,
1945), 325-328.

Katherine Garvin, "The Christianity of St. Agnes' Eve: Keats' Catholic
Inspiration," Dublin Review, 234 (Winter, 1960), 356-364.

William J. Grace, "Teaching Poetic Appreciation Through Quantitative
Analysis," CE, 1 (Dec., 1939), 222-226.

Barry Edward Gross, "The Eve of St. Agnes and Lamia: Paradise Won,
Paradise Lost," BuR, 13 (May, 1965), 47-57.

Peter Grudin, "Keats' 'The Eve of Saint Agnes,'" CEA, 37 (March, 1975),
10-11.

Elmo Howell, Expl, 14 (Feb., 1956), 28.
    Rpt. The Explicator Cyclopedia, II, pp. 171-172.

Knight, The Starlit Dome, pp. 279-280.

Kreuzer, Elements of Poetry, pp. 14-16, 125-132.

Terry Otten, "Porphyro's Feat in The Eve of St. Agnes," Serif, 5 (March,
1968), 22-24.

Michael Ragussis, The Subterfuge of Art: Language and the Romantic Tradition (Baltimore and London: The Johns Hopkins Univ. Press, 1978),
pp. 70-84.

Evelyn H. Scholl, Expl, 20 (Dec., 1961), 33.
    Rpt. The Explicator Cyclopedia, II, p. 172.

Stuart M. Sperry, Jr., "Romance as Wish-Fulfillment: Keats's The Eve of St. Agnes," SIR, 10 (Winter, 1971), 27-43.

Jack Stillinger, "The Hoodwinking of Madeline: Scepticism in 'The Eve of St. Agnes,'" SP, 58 (July, 1961), 533-555.

Leon Waldoff, "Porphyro's Imagination and Keats's Romanticism," JEGP, 76 (April, 1977), 177-194.

W. S. Ward, "A Device of Doors in The Eve of St. Agnes," MLN, 73 (Feb., 1958), 90-91.

Wheeler, The Design of Poetry, pp. 287-292.

Reginald R. Whidden, Expl, 1 (June, 1943), 66.
    Rpt. The Explicator Cyclopedia, II, p. 170.

J. E. Whitesell, Expl, 1 (Nov., 1942), 13.
    Rpt. The Explicator Cyclopedia, II, pp. 169-170.

Wormhoudt, The Demon Lover, pp. 71-77.

Herbert G. Wright, "Has Keats's 'Eve of St. Agnes' a Tragic Ending? MLR, 40 (April, 1945), 90-94.

_____. "The Eve of St. Mark"
Walter E. Houghton, "The Meaning of Keats' 'Eve of St. Mark,'" ELH, 13 (March, 1946), 64-78.

Jack Stillinger, "The Meaning of 'Poor Cheated Soul' in Keats's 'The Eve of Saint Mark,'" ELN, 5 (March, 1968), 193-196.

_____. "Fairy's Song"
J. Burke Severs, Expl, 14 (Oct., 1955), 3.
    Rpt. The Explicator Cyclopedia, II, pp. 173-174.

_____. "The Fall of Hyperion"
Arthur H. Bell, "'The Depth of Things': Keats and Human Space," KSJ, 23 (1974), 91-94.

Bloom, Poetry and Repression, pp. 113-142.

Bloom, The Visionary Company, pp. 411-421.

Bostetter, The Romantic Ventriloquist, pp. 136-140, 165-171.

Irene H. Chayes, "Dreamer, Poet, and Poem in The Fall of Hyperion," PQ, 46 (Oct., 1967), 499-515.

Anne K. Mellor, "Keats's Face of Moneta: Source and Meaning," KSJ, 25 (1976), 65-80.

Perkins, The Quest for Permanence, pp. 276-282.

Michael Ragussis, The Subterfuge of Art: Language and the Romantic Tradition (Baltimore and London: The Johns Hopkins Univ. Press, 1978), pp. 53-62.

Herbert Read, "The True Voice of John Keats," HudR, 6 (Spring, 1953), 98-104.

K. K. Ruthven, "Keats and Dea Moneta," SIR, 15 (Summer, 1976), 445-459.

Elizabeth Sewell, The Human Metaphor (Notre Dame, Indiana: Univ. of Notre Dame Press, 1964), pp. 127-136, 150.

Paul D. Sheats, "Stylistic Discipline in The Fall of Hyperion," KSJ, 17 (1968), 75-88.

Vogler, Preludes to Vision, pp. 122-141.

Walsh, The Use of Imagination, pp. 92-94.

Brian Wicker, "The Disputed Lines in The Fall of Hyperion," EIC, 7 (Jan., 1957), 28-41.

Wilkie, Romantic Poets and Epic Tradition, pp. 178-187.

_____. "Hyperion"
Bloom, The Visionary Company, pp. 381-389.

Bostetter, The Romantic Ventriloquist, pp. 136-137, 149, 154-155.

James Ralston Caldwell, "The Meaning of Hyperion," PMLA, 51 (Dec., 1936), 1080-1097.

Paul De Man, "Keats and Holderlin," CL, 8 (Winter, 1956), 37-45.

Helen E. Haworth, "The Titans, Apollo, and the Fortunate Fall in Keats's Poetry," SEL, 10 (Autumn, 1970), 637-649.

Hungerford, Shores of Darkness, pp. 137-162.

Michael Ragussis, The Subterfuge of Art: Language and the Romantic Tradition (Baltimore and London: The Johns Hopkins Univ. Press, 1978), pp. 41-53.

Herbert Read, "The True Voice of John Keats," HudR, 6 (Spring, 1953), 94-99.

John Hawley Roberts, "Poetry of Sensation or of Thought?" PMLA, 45 (Dec., 1930), 1134-1137.

Martha Hale Shackford, "Hyperion," SP, 22 (Jan., 1925), 48-60.

Pierre Vitoux, "Keats's Epic Design in Hyperion," SIR, 14 (Spring, 1975), 165-183.

Wilkie, Romantic Poets and Epic Tradition, pp. 145-178.

_____. "If by Dull Rhymes Our English Must Be Chained"
Mario L. D'Avenza, "Keats' 'If by Dull Rhymes,'" RS, 38 (March, 1970), 29-35.

_____. "Isabella; or the Pot of Basil"
Bradford A. Booth, Expl, 7 (May, 1949), 52.
   Rpt. The Explicator Cyclopedia, II, p. 174.

Knight, The Starlit Dome, pp. 280-282.

Louise Z. Smith, "The Material Sublime: Keats and Isabella," SIR, 13 (Fall, 1974), 304-311.

Jack Stillinger, "Keats and Romance," SEL, 8 (Autumn, 1968), 593-605.

_____. "I Stood Tip-toe"
Marjorie Norris, "Phenomenology and Process: Perception in Keats's 'I Stood Tip-toe,'" KSJ, 25 (1976), 43-54.

_____. "Lamia"
Adams, Strains of Discord, pp. 62-63.

Beach, A Romantic View of Poetry, pp. 123-131.

Arthur H. Bell, "'The Depth of Things': Keats and Human Space," KSJ, 23 (1974), 88-90.

Bloom, The Visionary Company, pp. 378-381.

Bostetter, The Romantic Ventriloquists, pp. 161-164.

James D. Boulger, "Keats' Symbolism," ELH, 28 (Sept., 1961), 248-254.

Barry Edward Gross, "The Eve of St. Agnes and Lamia: Paradise Won, Paradise Lost," BuR, 13 (May, 1965), 47-57.

D. B. Hardison, Jr., "The Decorum of Lamia," MLQ, 19 (March, 1958), 33-42.

Perkins, The Quest for Permanence, pp. 263-276.

Donald H. Reiman, "Keats and the Humanistic Paradox: Mythological History in Lamia," SEL, 11 (Autumn, 1971), 659-669.

Satyanarain Singh, Expl, 33 (April, 1975), 68.

William Curtis Stephenson, "The Fall from Innocence in Keats's 'Lamia,'" PLL, 10 (Winter, 1974), 35-50.

Warren Stevenson, "Lamia: A Stab at the Gordian Knot," SIR, 11 (Summer, 1972), 241-252.

Garrett Stewart, "Lamia and the Language of Metamorphosis," SIR, 15 (Winter, 1976), 3-41.

Wormhoudt, The Demon Lover, pp. 77-82.

_____. "Nebuchadnezzar's Dream"
Aileen Ward, "Keats's Sonnet, 'Nebuchadnezzar's Dream,'" PQ, 34 (April, 1955), 177-188.

_____. "Ode on a Grecian Urn"
M. H. Abrams, "Belief and Disbelief," UTQ, 27 (Jan., 1958), 124-127.

Adams, Strains of Discord, pp. 68-71.

Robert M. Adams, "Trompe-L'Oeil in Shakespeare and Keats," SR, 61 (Spring, 1953), 251-253.

Allen Austin, "Keats's Grecian Urn and the Truth of Eternity," CE, 25 (March, 1964), 434-436.

Roy P. Basler, Expl, 4 (Oct., 1945), 6.
    Rpt. The Explicator Cyclopedia, II, pp. 177-178.

Bateson, English Poetry, pp. 217-222.

Gillian Beer, "Aesthetic Debate in Keats's Odes," MLR, 64 (Oct., 1969), 747-748.

John Bellairs, Philip Waldron, and Manfred MacKenzie, "Variations on a Vase," The Southern Review (Australia), 1, No. 4 (1965), 58-73.

Robert Berkelman, "Keats and the Urn," SAQ, 57 (Summer, 1958), 354-358.
    Rpt. A Grammar of Motives, pp. 447-463.
    Rpt. West, Essays in Modern Literary Criticism, pp. 396-411.

Marius Bewley, "Kenneth Burke as a Literary Critic," Scrutiny, 15 (Dec., 1948), 270-273.

Pratap Biswas, "Keats' Cold Pastoral," UTQ, 47 (Winter, 1977-78), 95-111.

Bloom, The Visionary Company, pp. 406-410.

Bostetter, The Romantic Ventriloquist, pp. 156-158.

Bowra, The Romantic Imagination, pp. 126-148.

Cleanth Brooks, Jr., "History Without Footnotes: An Account of Keats' Urn," SR, 52 (Winter, 1944), 89-101.

Brooks, Purser, and Warren, An Approach to Literature, fourth edition, pp. 416-418.

Brooks, The Well Wrought Urn, pp. 139-152.

C. F. Burgess, Expl, 23 (Dec., 1964), 30.

Kenneth Burke, "Symbolic Action in a Poem by Keats," Accent, 4 (Autumn, 1943), 30-42.

Irene H. Chayes, "Rhetoric as Drama: An Approach to the Romantic Ode," PMLA, 79 (March, 1964), 78-79.

C. R. B. Combellack, "Keats's Grecian Urn as Unravished Bride," KSJ, 11 (Winter, 1962), 14-15.

David K. Cornelius, Expl, 20 (March, 1962), 57.
   Rpt. The Explicator Cyclopedia, II, pp. 183-184.

Dyson and Lovelock, Masterful Images, pp. 205-217.

William Empson, "Emotions in Words Again," The Kenyon Review, 10 (Autumn, 1948), 580-581.

Empson, The Structure of Complex Words, pp. 368-374.

William Empson, "Thy Darling in an Urn," SR, 55 (Oct.-Dec., 1947), 693-697.

Richard H. Fogle, "Empathic Imagery in Keats and Shelley," PMLA, 61 (March, 1946), 184-187.

Newell F. Ford, "Keats, Empathy, and the 'Poetical Character,'" SP, 45 (July, 1948), 488-489.

Robert C. Fox, Expl, 14 (June, 1956), 58.
   Rpt. The Explicator Cyclopedia, II, pp. 182-183.

Robert J. Fusco, "The Concrete Versus the Abstract in 'Ode on a Grecian Urn,'" MSE, 2 (Spring, 1969), 22-28.

R. M. Gay, Expl, 6 (April, 1948), 43.
   Rpt. The Explicator Cyclopedia, II, p. 178.

Albert Gerard, "Romance and Reality: Continuity and Growth in Keats's View of Art," KSJ, 11 (Winter, 1962), 23-29.

T. S. Gregory, "John Keats and Apocalypse," The Dublin Review, 225 (Third Quarter, 1951), 28-37.

Eugene Green and Rosemary M. Green, "Keats's Use of Names in Endymion and in the Odes," SIR, 16 (Winter, 1977), 31-32.

Martin Halpern, "Keats's Grecian Urn and the Singular 'Ye,'" CE, 24 (Jan., 1963), 284-288.

K. M. Hamilton, "Time and the Grecian Urn," DR, 34 (Autumn, 1954), 246-254.

Victor M. Hamm, Expl, 3 (May, 1945), 56.
    Rpt. The Explicator Cyclopedia, II, p. 177.

R. D. Havens, "Concerning the 'Ode on a Grecian Urn,'" MP, 24 (Nov.,
1926), 209-214.

Archibald A. Hill, "Some Points in the Analysis of Keats' Grecian Urn,"
in Studies in Language, Literature, and Culture of the Middle Ages and
Later, ed. E. Bagby Atwood and Archibald A. Hill (Austin: Univ. of
Texas, 1969), pp. 357-366.
    Rpt. Constituent and Pattern in Poetry (Austin: Univ. of Texas Press,
    1976), 104-114.

Virgil Hutton, Expl, 19 (March, 1961), 40.
    Rpt. The Explicator Cyclopedia, II, pp. 181-182.

Blair G. Kenney, Expl, 27 (May, 1969), 69.

Knight, The Starlit Dome, pp. 294-296.

Alice Fox Kornbluth, Expl, 16 (June, 1958), 56.
    Rpt. The Explicator Cyclopedia, II, pp. 179-181.

Murray Krieger, "Ekphrasis and the Still Movement of Poetry; or, Laokoön
Revisited," in The Poet as Critic, pp. 7-8, 15-17.

F. R. Leavis, "Keats (Revaluations IX)," Scrutiny, 4 (March, 1936), 384-
388.

Darrel Mansell, "Keats' Urn: 'On' and On," Lang&S, 7 (Fall, 1974), 235-
244.

Marco Mincoff, "Beauty is Truth--Once More," MLR, 65 (April, 1970), 267-
271.

Patrick Parrinder, Authors and Authority: A Study of English Literary
Criticism and Its Relation to Culture: 1750-1900 (London: Routledge &
Kegan Paul, 1977), pp. 95-97.

Charles I. Patterson, "Passion and Performance in Keats' 'Ode on a Grecian Urn,'" ELH, 21 (Sept., 1954), 208-220.

Perkins, The Quest for Permanence, pp. 233-242.

R. C. Pettigrew, Expl, 5 (Nov., 1946), 13.
    Rpt. The Explicator Cyclopedia, II, p. 178.

Krishna Rayan, "The Grecian Urn Re-read," Mosaic, 11 (Fall, 1977), 15-20.

John Reibetanz, "'The Whitsun Weddings': Larkin's Reinterpretation of
Time and Form in Keats," ConL, 17 (Autumn, 1976), 528-540.

Jean-Claude Salle, "The Pious Frauds of Art: A Reading of the 'Ode on a
Grecian Urn,'" SIR, 11 (Spring, 1972), 79-93.

James Shokoff, "Soul-Making in 'Ode on a Grecian Urn,'" KSJ, 24 (1975),
102-107.

David Simpson, "Keats's Lady, Metaphor, and the Rhetoric of Neurosis,"
SIR, 15 (Spring, 1976), 265-269.

Peter Skutcher, "Keats' Grecian Urn and Myth," IEY, No. 8 (Fall, 1963),
45-50.

Leo Spitzer, "The 'Ode on a Grecian Urn,' or Content Vs. Metagrammar,"
CL, 7 (Summer, 1955), 203-225.
    Rpt. Essays on English and American Literature by Leo Spitzer, pp. 67-
    97.

Royall Snow, "Heresy Concerning Keats," PMLA, 43 (Dec., 1928), 1142-1149.

R. W. Stallman, "Keats the Apollinian," UTQ, 16 (Jan., 1947), 155-156. Rpt. in part The Critic's Notebook, pp. 188-189.

Swallow, An Editor's Essays of Two Decades, pp. 71-73.

Ray Arthur Swanson, "Form and Content in Keats's 'Ode on a Grecian Urn,'" CE, 23 (Jan., 1962), 302-305.

Wylie Sypher, "Portrait of the Artist as John Keats," VQR, 25 (Summer, 1949), 422-423.

Allen Tate, "A Reading of Keats (II)," ASch, 15 (Spring, 1946), 194-197. Rpt. On the Limits of Poetry, pp. 177-180.

Nathaniel Teich, "Criticism and Keats's Grecian Urn," PQ, 44 (Oct., 1965), 496-502.

Thomas and Brown, Reading Poems: An Introduction to Critical Study, p. 660.

Harold E. Toliver, Pastoral: Forms and Attitudes (Berkeley: Univ. of California Press, 1971), pp. 267-270.

Unger and O'Connor, Poems for Study, pp. 457-459.

Helen Vendler, "The Experiential Beginnings of Keats's Odes," SIR, 12 (Summer, 1973), 598-602.

Vivante, English Poetry, pp. 196-203.

Charles Child Walcutt, The Explicator Cyclopedia, I, "Introduction," pp. xxiii-xiv.

Walsh, The Use of Imagination, pp. 113-119.

Wayne Warncke, Expl, 24 (Jan., 1966), 40.

Wheeler, The Design of Poetry, pp. 128-129.

Alvin Whitley, "The Message of the Grecian Urn," KSMB, Rome, 5 (1953), 1-3.

Jacob D. Wigod, "Keats's Ideal in the Ode on a Grecian Urn," PMLA, 62 (March, 1957), 113-121.

Stewart C. Wilcox, Expl, 6 (Oct., 1947), 2; and 7 (April, 1949), 47. Rpt. The Explicator Cyclopedia, II, pp. 178-179.

Stewart C. Wilcox, "The Unity of 'Ode on a Grecian Urn,'" Personalist, 31 (Spring, 1950), 149-156.

_____. "Ode on Indolence"

Bloom, The Visionary Company, pp. 410-411.

Bostetter, The Romantic Ventriloquist, pp. 155-156.

Irene H. Chayes, "Rhetoric as Drama: An Approach to the Romantic Ode," PMLA, 79 (March, 1964), 78.

Howard H. Hinkel, "Growth Without Toil: Generative Indolence in Keats," TSL, 20 (1975), 26-36.

Knight, The Starlit Dome, p. 296.

Margaret Yeates Robertson, "The Consistency of Keats's 'Ode on Indolence,'" Style, 4 (Spring, 1970), 133-143.

Monroe M. Stearns, _Expl_, 1 (May, 1943), 53.
    Rpt. _The Explicator Cyclopedia_, II, p. 184.

William F. Zak, "The Confirmation of Keat's Belief in Negative Capability: The 'Ode on Indolence,'" _KSJ_, 25 (1976), 55-64.

_____. "Ode on Melancholy"
M. Ray Adams, _Expl_, 14 (May, 1956), 49.
    Rpt. _The Explicator Cyclopedia_, II, pp. 185-186.

Beach, _A Romantic View of Poetry_, pp. 91-94.

Michael Black, "The Musical Analogy," _English_, 25 (Summer, 1976), 111-
134.

Bloom, _The Visionary Company_, pp. 403-406.

Brooks, Purser, and Warren, _An Approach to Literature_, pp. 479-481.
    Rpt. third edition, pp. 355-358.
    Rpt. fourth edition, pp. 349-352.

Irene H. Chayes, "Rhetoric as Drama: An Approach to the Romantic Ode,"
PMLA, 79 (March, 1964), 77-78.

Richard D. Eberly, _Expl_, 6 (April, 1948), 38.
    Rpt. Stallman and Watters, _The Creative Reader_, pp. 857-858.
    Rpt. _The Explicator Cyclopedia_, II, pp. 184-185.

Empson, _Seven Types of Ambiguity_, pp. 272-275; (1947 ed.), pp. 214-217.

Arthur Freeman, "Keats's 'Ode on Melancholy,' 24," _N&Q_, 9 (May, 1962),
184.

Eugene Green and Rosemary M. Green, "Keats's Use of Names in _Endymion_ and
in the Odes," _SIR_, 16 (Winter, 1977), 30.

Martin Halpern, "Keats and the 'Spirit that Laughest,'" _KSJ_, 15 (Winter,
1966), 75-78.

Knight, _The Starlit Dome_, pp. 296-298.

F. R. Leavis, "Keats (Revaluations IX)," _Scrutiny_, 4 (March, 1936), 390-
393.

Leavis, _Revaluation_, pp. 260-262.

G. L. Little, _Expl_, 25 (Feb., 1967), 46.

Perkins, _The Quest for Permanence_, pp. 283-290.

Horace G. Posey, Jr., "Keats's 'Ode on Melancholy': Analogue of the
Imagination," _CP_, 8 (Fall, 1975), 61-69.

Ribner and Morris, _Poetry_, pp. 295-297.

Robert Rogers, "Keats's Stenuous Tongue: A Study of 'Ode on Melancholy,'"
_L&P_, 17, No. 1 (1967), 2-12.

Barbara H. Smith, "'Sorrow's Mysteries': Keats's 'Ode on Melancholy,'"
SEL, 6 (Autumn, 1966), 679-691.

Helen Vendler, "The Experiential Beginnings of Keats's Odes," _SIR_, 12
(Summer, 1973), 595-598.

Aileen Ward, "The Psychoanalytic Theory of Poetic Form: A Comment," _L&P_,
17, No. 1 (1967), 33-35.

_____. "Ode to a Nightingale"

Adams, Strains of Discord, pp. 65-68.

Adams, The Contexts of Poetry, pp. 136-140.

Robert M. Adams, "Trompe-L'Oeil in Shakespeare and Keats," SR, 61 (Spring, 1953), 248-251.

E. H. Auden and N. H. Pearson, Poets of the English Language, IV (New York: The Viking Press, 1950), xix-xx.

Beaty and Matchett, Poetry: From Statement to Meaning, pp. 61, 90-94, 97-98.

Gillian Beer, "Aesthetic Debate in Keats's Odes," MLR, 64 (Oct., 1969), 744-747.

Arthur H. Bell, "'The Depth of Things': Keats and Human Space," KSJ, 23 (1974), 90-91.

Harry Belshaw, "Keats on the Mount of Transfiguration," The London Quarterly and Holborn Review, 175 (Oct., 1950), 320-324.

Blair and Chandler, Approaches to Poetry, pp. 552-556.

Bloom, The Visionary Company, pp. 397-403.

Bostetter, The Romantic Ventriloquist, pp. 158-159.

James D. Boulger, "Keats' Symbolism," ELH, 28 (Sept., 1961), 245-248.

Bowra, The Romantic Imagination, pp. 136-137.

Brooks, Modern Poetry and the Tradition, p. 31.

Brooks, Purser, and Warren, An Approach to Literature, fourth edition, pp. 412-415.

Brooks and Warren, Understanding Poetry, pp. 409-415. Revised edition, pp. 338-345.

Irene H. Chayes, "Rhetoric as Drama: An Approach to the Romantic Ode," PMLA, 79 (March, 1964), 74-77.

Michael G. Cooke, The Romantic Will (New Haven and London: Yale Univ. Press, 1976), pp. 166-170.

Daniels, The Art of Reading Poetry, pp. 366-372.

Drew, Poetry: A Modern Guide, pp. 178-179.

David Eggenschwiler, "Nightingales and Byzantine Birds, Something Less Than Kind," ELN, 8 (March, 1971), 186-191.

R. H. Fogle, "A Note on Keats's Ode to a Nightingale," MLQ, 8 (March, 1947), 81-84.

R. H. Fogle, "Keats's Ode to a Nightingale," PMLA, 68 (March, 1953), 211-222.
    Rpt. The Permanent Pleasure, pp. 100-115.

Newell F. Ford, "Keats, Empathy, and the 'Poetical Character,'" SP, 45 (July, 1948), 489-490.

Gerald Graff, Poetic Statement and Critical Dogma (Evanston: Northwestern Univ. Press, 1970), pp. 128-131.

Eamon Grennan, "Keats's Contemptus Mundi: A Shakespearian Influence on the 'Ode to a Nightingale,'" MLQ, 36 (Sept., 1975), 272-292.

Albert Guerard, Jr., "Prometheus and the Aeolian Lyre," YR, 33 (Spring, 1944), 495-496.

Eugene J. Harding, "A Possible Pun in Keats's 'Ode to a Nightingale,'" KSJ, 24 (1975), 15-17.

Thomas P. Harrison, "Keats and a Nightingale," ES, 41 (Dec., 1960), 353-359.

Anthony Hecht, "Shades of Keats and Marvell," HudR, 15 (Spring, 1962), 57-66.

Don A. Keister, Expl, 6 (March, 1948), 31.
    Rpt. The Explicator Cyclopedia, II, pp. 188-189.

Clyde S. Kilby, Expl, 5 (Feb., 1947), 27.
    Rpt. The Explicator Cyclopedia, II, pp. 186-187.

Knight, The Starlit Dome, pp. 298-300.

Murray Krieger, "Ekphrasis and the Still Movement of Poetry; or Laokoön Revisited," in The Poet as Critic, pp. 19-20.

Victor J. Lams, Jr., "Ruth, Milton, and Keats's 'Ode to a Nightingale,'" MLQ, 34 (Dec., 1973), 417-435.

Marghanita Laski, "The Language of the Nightingale Ode," Essays and Studies, 19 (1966), 60-73.

F. Matthey, "Interplay of Structure and Meaning in the Ode to a Nightingale," ES, 49 (Aug., 1968), 303-317.

F. R. Leavis, "Keats (Revaluations IX)," Scrutiny, 4 (March, 1936), 378-384.

Leavis, Revaluation, pp. 244-252.

Herbert Marshall McLuhan, "Aesthetic Pattern in Keats' Odes," UTQ, 12 (Jan., 1943), 167-179.

Caroline W. Mayerson, Expl, 25 (Nov., 1966), 29.

Lowry Nelson, Jr., "The Rhetoric of Ineffability: Toward a Definition of Mystical Poetry," CL, 8 (Fall, 1956), 332-335.

Peckham and Chatman, Word, Meaning, Poem, pp. 344-370.

Perkins, The Quest for Permanence, pp. 244-257.

Robert Pinsky, The Situation of Poetry: Contemporary Poetry and Its Traditions (Princeton, New Jersey: Princeton Univ. Press, 1976), 47-52.

S. M. Pitcher, Expl, 3 (March, 1945), 39.
    Rpt. The Explicator Cyclopedia, II, pp. 187-188.

W. O. Raymond, "'The Mind's Internal Heaven' in Poetry," UTQ, 20 (April, 1951), 229-230.

Rosenthal and Smith, Exploring Poetry, pp. 505-507.

Swallow, An Editor's Essays of Two Decades, pp. 73-75.

Wylie Sypher, "Portrait of the Artist as John Keats," VQR, 25 (Summer, 1949), 425.

Allen Tate, "A Reading of Keats (II)," ASch, 15 (Spring, 1946), 189-194.
    Rpt. On the Limits of Poetry, pp. 171-177 et passim.

Thomas and Brown, Reading Poems: An Introduction to Critical Study, pp. 658-660.

Dorothy Van Ghent, "The Passion of the Groves," SR, 52 (Spring, 1944), 226-246.

Helen Vendler, "The Experiential Beginnings of Keats's Odes," SIR, 12 (Summer, 1973), 592-595.

Vivante, English Poetry, pp. 193-195.

Donald Wesling, "The Dialectical Criticism of Poetry: An Instance from Keats," Mosaic, 5 (Winter, 1971-72), 81-96.

Wheeler, The Design of Poetry, pp. 129-130.

_____. "Ode to Psyche"
Adams, Strains of Discord, pp. 63-65.

Robert M. Adams, "Trompe-L'Oeil in Shakespeare and Keats," SR, 61 (Spring, 1953), 247-248.

Kenneth Allott, "Keats's 'Ode to Psyche,'" EIC, 6 (July, 1956), 278-301.

Gillian Beer, "Aesthetic Debate in Keats's Odes," MLR, 64 (Oct., 1969). 743-744.

Bloom, A Map of Misreading, pp. 152-156.

Bloom, The Visionary Company, pp. 389-397.

James H. Bunn, "Keats's Ode to Psyche and the Transformation of Mental Landscape," ELH, 37 (Dec., 1970), 581-594.

Irene H. Chayes, "Rhetoric as Drama: An Approach to the Romantic Ode," PMLA, 79 (March, 1964), 78-79.

Knight, The Starlit Dome, pp. 301-304.

Perkins, The Quest for Permanence, pp. 222-228.

Henry Pettit, "Scientific Correlatives of Keats' 'Ode to Psyche,'" SP, 40 (Oct., 1943), 560-566.

Max F. Schulz, "Keats's Timeless Order of Things: A Modern Reading of 'Ode to Psyche,'" Criticism, 2 (Winter, 1960), 55-65.

Wylie Sypher, "Portrait of the Artist as John Keats," VQR, 25 (Summer, 1949), 425-426.

Leon Waldoff, "The Theme of Mutability in the 'Ode to Psyche,'" PMLA, 92 (May, 1977), 410-419.

George Yost, Jr., "An Identification in Keats' 'Ode to Psyche,'" PQ, 26 (Oct., 1957), 496-499.

_____. "On First Looking into Chapman's Homer"
Joseph Warren Beach, "Keats's Realms of Gold," PMLA, 49 (March, 1934), 246-257.

H. E. Briggs, "Swift and Keats," PMLA, 41 (Dec., 1946), 1104-1105.

Cohen, Writing About Literature, pp. 55-58, 68-69, 81-82.

Thomas Cook, "Keats's Sonnet 'To Homer,'" KSJ, 11 (Winter, 1962), 8-12.

Daniels, The Art of Reading Poetry, pp. 210-212.

B. Ifor Evans, "Keats's Approach to the Chapman Sonnet," Essays and Studies, 16 (1930), 26-52.

G. Giovannini, "Keats' Elysium of Poets," MLN, 63 (Jan., 1948), 19-25.

Lynn H. Harris, Expl, 4 (March, 1946), 35.
    Rpt. The Explicator Cyclopedia, II, p. 189.

T. O. Mabbott, _Expl_, 5 (Dec., 1946), 22.
    Rpt. _The Explicator Cyclopedia_, II, pp. 189-190.

Douglad M. MacEachen, "Letter to the Editor," _CE_, 18 (Oct., 1956), 56.

Louis L. Martz, "The Teaching of Poetry," in _Essays on the Teaching of Literature_, pp. 252-263.

J. Middleton Murray, "When Keats Discovered Homer," _Hibbert Journal_, 27 (Oct., 1928), 93-110, and _Bookman_, 68 (Dec., 1928), 391-401.

R. W. Stallman, "Keats the Apollinian," _UTQ_, 16 (Jan., 1947), 153-154.

Bernice Slote, "Of Chapman's Homer and Other Books," _CE_, 23 (Jan., 1962), 256-260.

Stauffer, _The Nature of Poetry_, pp. 36-38.

Wylie Sypher, "Portrait of the Artist as John Keats," _VQR_, 25 (Summer, 1949), 423-424.

Charles C. Walcutt, _Expl_, 5 (June, 1947), 56.
    Rpt. _The Explicator Cyclopedia_, II, p. 190.

C. V. Wicker, "Cortez--Not Balboa," _CE_, 17 (April, 1956), 383-387.

Melvin G. Williams, "To Be or to Have Been: The Use of Verbs in Three Sonnets by John Keats," _CEA_, 32 (Dec., 1969), 12.

_____. "On Seeing the Elgin Marbles for the First Time"
Benjamin W. Griffith, _Expl_, 31 (May, 1973), 76.

Melvin G. Williams, "To Be or to Have Been: The Use of Verbs in Three Sonnets by John Keats," _CEA_, 32 (Dec., 1969), 12.

_____. "On Sitting Down to Read King Lear Once Again"
Jeremy Hawthorn, _Identity and Relationship: A Contribution to Marxist Theory of Literary Criticism_ (London: Lawrence & Wishart, 1973), pp. 108-109.

Porter William, Jr., _Expl_, 29 (Nov., 1970), 26.

_____. "On Visiting the Tomb of Burns"
George Yost, Jr., "A Source and Interpretation of Keats's Minos," _JEGP_, 57 (April, 1958), 220-229.

_____. "Sleep and Poetry"
Bloom, _The Visionary Company_, pp. 354-359.

Bostetter, _The Romantic Ventriloquist_, pp. 144-145.

Knight, _The Starlit Dome_, pp. 265-267 _et passim_.

Archibald Lampman, "The Character of the Poetry of Keats," _UTQ_, 15 (July, 1946), 351-363.

John Hawley Roberts, "Poetry of Sensation or of Thought?" _PMLA_, 45 (Dec., 1930), 1129-1130.

_____. "To Autumn"
Bloom, _The Visionary Company_, pp. 421-425.

Brooks, Purser, and Warren, _An Approach to Literature_, fourth edition, pp. 419-420.

Brower, The Fields of Light, pp. 39-41.

Irving H. Buchen, "Keats's 'To Autumn': The Season of Optimum Form," CEA, 31 (Nov., 1968), 11.

Michael G. Cooke, The Romantic Will (New Haven and London: Yale Univ. Press, 1976), pp. 170-174.

Robert Daniel and Monroe C. Beardsley, "Reading Takes a Whole Man," CE, 17 (Oct., 1955), 31-32.

Eugene Green and Rosemary M. Green, "Keats's Use of Names in Endymion and in the Odes," SIR, 16 (Winter, 1977), 32-34.

Norman Hampson, "Keats and Ourselves," TLS, Dec. 22, 1945, p. 607.

Geoffrey H. Hartman, "Poem and Ideology: A Study of Keats's 'To Autumn,'" in Literary Theory and Structure: Essays in Honor of William K. Wimsatt, ed. Frank Brady, John Palmer, and Martin Price (New Haven: Yale Univ. Press, 1973), pp. 305-330.

Knight, The Starlit Dome, pp. 300-301.

F. R. Leavis, "Keats (Revaluations IX)," Scrutiny, 4 (March, 1936), 392-393.

Leavis, Revaluation, pp. 262-264.

James Lott, "Keats's To Autumn: The Poetic Consciousness and the Awareness of Process," SIR, 9 (Winter, 1970), 71-81.

Anna Jean Mill, "Keats and Ourselves," TLS, Feb. 2, 1946, p. 55.

Donald Pearce, "Thoughts on the Autumn Ode of Keats," ArielE, 6 (July, 1975), 3-19.

Perkins, The Quest for Permanence, pp. 290-294.

Rosenheim, What Happens in Literature, pp. 42-59.

Satin, Reading Poetry, pp. 1102-1104.

B. C. Southam, "The Ode 'To Autumn,'" KSJ, 9, Part 2 (Autumn, 1960), 91-98.

Leonard Unger, "Keats and the Music of Autumn," Western Review, 14 (Summer, 1950), 275-284.
    Rpt. The Man in the Name, pp. 18-29.

Unger and O'Connor, Poems for Study, pp. 454-456.
    Rpt. Locke, Gibson, and Arms, Introduction to Literature, fourth edition, pp. 109-110.
    Rpt. fifth edition, pp. 102-103.

Walsh, The Use of Imagination, pp. 119-120.

_____. "To Sleep"
Dell H. Hymes, "Phonological Aspects of Style: Some English Sonnets," in Essays on the Language of Literature, ed. Seymour Chatman and Samuel R. Levin (Boston: Houghton Mifflin Company, 1967), pp. 47-48.

W. K. Thomas, Expl, 26 (March, 1968), 55.

_____. "To_____: What Can I Do to Drive Away Remembrance from My Eyes"
A. D. Atkinson, "Lines to Fanny," TLS, Nov. 25, 1949, p. 771.

Harold E. Briggs, "Keats, Robertson, and 'That Most Hateful Land,'" PMLA, 59 (March, 1944), 184-195.

John R. Moore, "Lines to Fanny," TLS, Dec. 23, 1949, p. 841.

J. Middleton Murry, "Lines to Fanny," TLS, Nov. 18, 1949, p. 751.

Ronald Primeau, "Chaucer's Troilus and Criseyde and the Rhythm of Experience in Keats's 'What can I do to drive away,'" KSJ, 23 (1974), 106-118.

_____. "What the Thrush Said"
Michael G. Cooke, The Romantic Will (New Haven and London: Yale Univ.
Press, 1976), pp. 158-161.

_____. "When I Have Fears That I May Cease to Be"
Thomas E. Connolly, Expl, 13 (Dec., 1954), 14.
    Rpt. The Explicator Cyclopedia, II, pp. 191-192.

Daniel Gibson and Morley J. Hays, Expl, 1 (April, 1943), 47.
    Rpt. The Explicator Cyclopedia, II, pp. 190-191.

M. A. Goldberg, "The 'Fears' of John Keats," MLQ, 18 (June, 1957), 125-
131.

Dell H. Hymes, "Phonological Aspects of Style: Some English Sonnets,"
Essays on the Language of Literature, ed. Seymour Chatman and Samuel R.
Levin, (Boston: Houghton Mifflin Company, 1967), pp. 46-47.

Melvin G. Williams, "To Be or to Have Been: The Use of Verbs in Three
Sonnets by John Keats," CEA, 32 (Dec., 1969), 12.

Zitner, Kissane, and Liberman, A Preface to Literary Analysis, pp. 93-100.

_____. "Why Did I Laugh Tonight? No Voice Will Tell"
Martin Halpern, "Keats and the 'Spirit that Laughest,'" KSJ, 15 (Winter,
1966), 78-80.

_____. "Written in the Cottage Where Burns Was Born"
Dell H. Hymes, "Phonological Aspects of Style: Some English Sonnets,"
in Essays on the Language of Literature, ed. Seymour Chatman and Samuel R.
Levin, (Boston: Houghton Mifflin Company, 1967), p. 47.

KEBLE, John. "Easter Eve"
George P. Landow, "Moses Striking the Rock: Typological Symbolism in
Victorian Poetry," in Literary Uses of Typology from the Late Middle Ages
to the Present, pp. 333-334.

KEES, Weldon. "The Locusts, the Plaza, the Room"
J. F. Nims, Poetry: A Critical Supplement, Oct., 1947, pp. 10-11.

KENNEDY, Rev. G. A. Studdert. "There Was Rapture of Spring in the Morning"
    ("Woodbine Willie") (More Rough Rhymes of a Padre)
Richards, Practical Criticism, pp. 53-61, 262-266.

KILMER. "Trees"
Brooks and Warren, Understanding Poetry, pp. 387-391. Revised edition,
pp. 274-278.

Jeffrey Fleece, "Further Notes on a 'Bad' Poem," CE, 12 (March, 1951),
314-320.

KING, Henry. "The Exequy"
Robert F. Gleckner, Expl, 12 (May, 1954), 46.
    Rpt. The Explicator Cyclopedia, II, pp. 192-194.

Williamson, The Proper Wit of Poetry, pp. 56-57.

Winters, Forms of Discovery, pp. 88-90.

_____. "The Labyrinth"
Tuve, Elizabethan and Metaphysical Imagery, p. 357.

KINNELL, Galway. "The Bear"
William V. Davis, "The Rank Flavor of Blood: Galway Kinnell's 'The Bear,'"
NConL, 7 (March, 1977), 4-6.

John Hobbs, "Galway Kinnell's 'The Bear': Dream and Technique," MPS, 5
(Winter, 1974), 237-250.

J. T. Ledbetter, Expl, 33 (April, 1975), 63.

_____. "The Descent"
Ralph J. Mills, Jr., "A Reading of Galway Kinnell," IowaR, 1 (Winter,
1970), 78-82.

_____. "Easter"
Ralph J. Mills, Jr., "A Reading of Galway Kinnell," IowaR, 1 (Winter,
1970), 72-73.

_____. "First Communion"
Ralph J. Mills, Jr., "A Reading of Galway Kinnell," IowaR, 1 (Winter,
1970), 68-69.

_____. "First Song"
James R. Hurt, Expl, 20 (Nov., 1961), 23.
    Rpt. The Explicator Cyclopedia, I, pp. 203-204.

Gene H. Koretz, Expl, 15 (April, 1957), 43.
    Rpt. The Explicator Cyclopedia, I, pp. 202-203.

Melvin Walker LaFollette, Expl, 14 (April, 1956), 48.
    Rpt. The Explicator Cyclopedia, I, pp. 201-202.

_____. "How Many Nights"
Philip L. Gerber and Robert J. Gemmett, ed., "Deeper Than Personality:
A Conversation With Galway Kinnell," IowaR, 1 (Spring, 1970), 125-126.

_____. "The Porcupine"
Ralph J. Mills, Jr., "A Reading of Galway Kinnell: Part 2," IowaR, 1
(Spring, 1970), 117-119.

_____. "Seven Streams of Nevis"
Ralph J. Mills, Jr., "A Reading of Galway Kinnell," IowaR, 1 (Winter,
1970), 73-76.

_____. "Spindrift"
Linda Wagner, "Spindrift: The World in a Seashell," CP, 8 (Spring,
1975), 5-9.

_____. "The Supper After the Last"
Ralph J. Mills, Jr., "A Reading of Galway Kinnell," IowaR, 1 (Winter,
1970), 82-86.

_____. "The Thief"
Ralph J. Mills, Jr., "A Reading of Galway Kinnell: Part 2," IowaR, 1
(Spring, 1970), 115-117.

_____. "To Christ Our Lord"
Ralph J. Mills, Jr., "A Reading of Galway Kinnell," IowaR, 1 (Winter, 1970), 70-71.

_____. "Vapor Trail Reflected in the Frog Pond"
Philip L. Gerber and Robert J. Gemmett, ed., "Deeper Than Personality: A Conversation with Galway Kinnell," IowaR, 1 (Spring, 1970), 129-131.

_____. "Where the Track Vanishes"
Ralph J. Mills, Jr., "A Reading of Galway Kinnell," IowaR, 1 (Winter, 1970), 76-78.

KINSELLA, Thomas. "Downstream"
Clark, Lyric Resonance, pp. 91-102.

_____. "First Light:
Bruce Kellner, "The Wormwood Poems of Thomas Kinsella," WHR, 26 (Summer, 1972), 225-227.

_____. "Navigators"
Dickinson, Suggestions for Teachers of "Introduction to Literature," fifth edition, ed. Locke, Gibson, and Arms, p. 53. (Teacher's Manual)

KIPLING, Rudyard. "Danny Deever"
Abad, A Formal Approach to Lyric Poetry, pp. 227-229.

Louis S. Friedland, Expl, 2 (Oct., 1943), 9.
   Rpt. The Explicator Cyclopedia, I, p. 204.

_____. "M'Andrew's Hymn"
Deutsch, Poetry in Our Time, p. 29.

KUNITZ, "Among the Gods"
George P. Elliott, "The Poetry of Stanley Kunitz," Accent, 18 (Autumn, 1958), 270.

_____. "Careless Love"
George P. Elliot, "The Poetry of Stanley Kunitz," Accent, 18 (Autumn, 1958), 268-269.

_____. "Geometry of Moods"
Mills, Contemporary American Poetry, pp. 37-39.

_____. "Hermetic Poem"
Mills, Contemporary American Poetry, pp. 39-40.

_____. "Journal for My Daughter"
Marjorie G. Perloff, "The Testing of Stanley Kunitz," IowaR, 3 (Winter, 1972), 94-99.

_____. "Night Letter"
Mills, Contemporary American Poetry, pp. 44-47.

_____. "Prophecy on Lethe"
Robert Weisberg, "Stanley Kunitz: The Stubborn Middle Way," MPS, 6 (Spring, 1975), 67-69.

_____. "The Science of the Night"
Mills, Contemporary American Poetry, pp. 33-35.

_____. "The Scourge"
Robert Weisberg, "Stanley Kunitz: The Stubborn Middle Way," MPS, 6
(Spring, 1975), 65-66.

_____. "The Surgeons"
Mills, Contemporary American Poetry, pp. 41-43.

_____. "The Testing-Tree"
Cynthia Davis, "Stanley Kunitz's 'The Testing-Tree,'" CP, 8 (Spring,
1975), 43-46.

LAMB. "The Old Familiar Faces"
Leo Spitzer, SoR, 6 (Winter, 1941), 586-588.

LANDOR. "Dirce"
Abad, A Formal Approach to Lyric Poetry, pp. 37-38.

_____. "Mild is the Parting Year and Sweet"
Mary Ellen Rickey, Expl, 13 (Oct., 1954), 2.
     Rpt. The Explicator Cyclopedia, II, pp. 194-195.

_____. "Mother I Cannot Mind My Wheel"
Abad, A Formal Approach to Lyric Poetry, pp. 43-44.

_____. "On Lucretia Borgia's Hair"
Abad, A Formal Approach to Lyric Poetry, p. 38.

_____. "Proud Word You Never Spoke"
Kirk and McCutcheon, An Introduction to the Study of Poetry, pp. 15-16.

_____. "Rose Aylmer"
Brooks and Warren, Understanding Poetry, pp. 270-273. Revised edition,
pp. 145-147.

R. H. Super, Expl, 3 (Feb., 1945), 31.
     Rpt. The Explicator Cyclopedia, II, p. 195.

Robert Penn Warren, "Pure and Impure Poetry," The Kenyon Review, 5
(Spring, 1943), 235-237.
     Rpt. Criticism, pp. 369-370.
     Rpt. Critiques, pp. 90-92.
     Rpt. The Kenyon Critics, pp. 24-26.
     Rpt. West, Essays in Modern Literary Criticism, pp. 251-253.

_____. "Yes; I Write Verses Now and Then"
Laurence Perrine, "The Importance of Tone in the Interpretation of Literature," CE, 24 (Feb., 1963), 393-395.

Satin, Reading Poetry, pp. 1076-1077.

LANIER. "Corn"
Edd Winfield Parks, "Lanier as Poet," in Essays on American Literature,
ed. Clarence Gohdes, pp. 189-190.

_____. "The Marshes of Glynn"
Philip Graham, "Sidney Lanier and the Pattern of Contrast," AQ, 11 (Winter, 1959), 506-507.

Edd Winfield Parks, "Lanier as Poet," in Essays on American Literature, ed. Clarence Gohdes, pp. 196-198.

Owen J. Reaner, "Lanier's 'The Marshes of Glynn' Revisited," MissQ, 23 (Winter, 1969-1970), 57-63.

Robert H. Ross, "'The Marshes of Glynn': A Study of Symbolic Obscurity," AL, 32 (Jan., 1961), 403-416.

Allen Tate, New Republic, 76 (August 30, 1933), 67-70.

R. P. Warren, "The Blind Poet: Sidney Lanier," The American Review, 2 (Nov., 1933), 42-45.

_____. "My Springs"
Brooks and Warren, Understanding Poetry, pp. 442-445. Revised edition, pp. 299-302.

_____. "Night and Day"
Edd W. Parks, "Lanier's 'Night and Day,'" AL, 30 (March, 1958), 117-118.

_____. "Sunrise"
Philip Graham, "Sidney Lanier and the Pattern of Contrast," AQ, 11 (Winter, 1959), 506.

Edd Winfield Parks, "Lanier as Poet," in Essays on American Literature, ed. Clarence Gohdes, pp. 199-200.

_____. "The Symphony"
C. H. Edwards, Jr., Expl, 31 (Dec., 1972), 27.

Elisabeth J. Hogenes, Expl, 16 (Oct., 1957), 4.
    Rpt. The Explicator Cyclopedia, II, pp. 195-196.

Edd Winfield Parks, "Lanier as Poet," in Essays on American Literature, ed. Clarence Gohdes, pp. 190-193.

LARKIN, Philip. "Absences"
Merle Brown, "Larkin and His Audience," IowaR, 8 (Fall, 1977), 117-119.

_____. "Arrival"
Roger Bowen, "Poet in Transition: Philip Larkin's XX Poems," IowaR, 8 (Winter, 1977), 93-94.

_____. "An Arundel Tomb"
Hermann Peschmann, "Philip Larkin: Laureate of the Common Man," English, 24 (Summer, 1975), 54-55.

_____. "At Grass"
Roger Bowen, "Poet in Transition: Philip Larkin's XX Poems," IowaR, 8 (Winter, 1977), 101.

Joan E. Hartman, "Teaching Poetry: An Exercise in Practical Criticism," CE, 35 (Oct., 1973), 17-30.

_____. "Deceptions"
Roger Bowen, "Poet in Transition: Philip Larkin's XX Poems," IowaR, 8 (Winter, 1977), 92-93.

_____. "The Dedicated"
Roger Bowen, "Poet in Transition: Philip Larkin's XX Poems," IowaR, 8 (Winter, 1977), 98-99.

_____. "Dry-Point"
Margaret Blum, Expl, 32 (Feb., 1974), 48.

Stuart Hirschberg, "Larkin's 'Dry-Point': Life Without Illusion," NConL, 8 (Jan., 1978), 5-6.

Rosenthal, The Modern Poets, p. 223.

_____. "Going"
Roger Bowen, "Poet in Transition: Philip Larkin's XX Poems," IowaR, 8 (Winter, 1977), 100.

_____. "Here"
Merle Brown, "Larkin and His Audience," IowaR, 8 (Fall, 1977), 127-130.

_____. "How Distant"
John Wain, Professing Poetry (London: MacMillan London Limited, 1977), pp. 160-162.

_____. "Modesties"
Roger Bowen, "Poet in Transition: Philip Larkin's XX Poems," IowaR, 8 (Winter, 1977), 90-91.

_____. "Next, Please"
Alun R. Jones, "The Poetry of Philip Larkin: A Note on Transatlantic Culture," WHR, 16 (Spring, 1962), 149.

_____. "Poem VII' (from XX Poems)
Roger Bowen, "Poet in Transition: Philip Larkin's XX Poems," IowaR, 8 (Winter, 1977), 94-95.

_____. "Reasons for Attendance"
Alun R. Jones, "The Poetry of Philip Larkin: A Note on Transatlantic Culture," WHR, 16 (Spring, 1962), 148-149.

_____. "Solar"
Merle Brown, "Larkin and His Audience," IowaR, 8 (Fall, 1977), 119-122.

_____. "Toads"
Alun R. Jones, "The Poetry of Philip Larkin: A Note on Transatlantic Culture," WHR, 16 (Spring, 1962), 147-148.

_____. "Coda" to The North Ship "Waiting for breakfast, while she brushed her hair"
James Naremore, "Philip Larkin's 'Lost World,'" ConL, 15 (Summer, 1974), 334-335.

_____. "Wants"
Merle Brown, "Larkin and His Audience," IowaR, 8 (Fall, 1977), 125-126.

_____. "The Witsun Weddings"
Merle Brown, "Larkin and His Audience," IowaR, 8 (Fall, 1977), 130-133.

James Naremore, "Philip Larkin's 'Lost World,'" ConL, 15 (Summer, 1974), 339-343.

John Reibetanz, "'The Whitsun Weddings': Larkin's Reinterpretation of Time and Form in Keats," ConL, 17 (Autumn, 1976), 528-540.

LATTIMORE. "Witness to Death"
     Ford T. Swetnam, Expl, 25 (March, 1967), 59.

LAUGHLIN, James. "Go West Young Man"
     Laurence Perrine, Expl, 28 (March, 1970), 61.

LAWRENCE, D. H. "Baby Tortoise"
     Harold Bloom, The Ringers in the Tower: Studies in Romantic Tradition
     (Chicago and London: Univ. of Chicago Press, 1971), pp. 200-201.

     Keith Sagar, "'Little Living Myths': A Note on Lawrence's Tortoises,"
     DHLR, 3 (Summer, 1970), 162-164.

_____. "Bavarian Gentians"
     David Cavitch, "Solipsism and Death in D. H. Lawrence's Late Works," MR,
     7 (Summer, 1966), 505-508.

_____. "Corot"
     Blackmur, The Double Agent, pp. 112-115.
        Rpt. Language as Gesture, pp. 294-295.

_____. "End of Another Home Holiday"
     Savage, The Personal Principle, pp. 135-136.

_____. "The Enkindled Spring"
     Skelton, The Poetic Pattern, pp. 104-105.

_____. "Fish"
     Del Ivan Janik, "Toward 'Thingness': Cézanne's Painting and Lawrence's
     Poetry," TCL, 19 (April, 1973), 124-127.

_____. "Gipsy"
     Blackmur, The Double Agent, pp. 108-109.
        Rpt. Language as Gesture, pp. 290-291.

_____. "Gloire de Dijon"
     Del Ivan Janik, "Toward 'Thingness': Cézanne's Painting and Lawrence's
     Poetry, TCL, 19 (April, 1973), 123.

_____. "The Hands of the Betrothed"
     Del Ivan Janik, "Toward 'Thingness': Cézanne's Painting and Lawrence's
     Poetry," TCL, 19 (April, 1973), 122-123.

_____. "Lotus and Frost"
     Skelton, The Poetic Pattern, pp. 103-104.

_____. "Love on the Farm"
     Abad, A Formal Approach to Lyric Poetry, pp. 233-240, 360-363.

_____. "Medlars and Sorb Apples"
     Harold Bloom, The Ringers in the Tower: Studies in Romantic Tradition
     (Chicago and London: Univ. of Chicago Press, 1971), pp. 199-200.

_____. "New Heaven and Earth"
     Rosenthal, The Modern Poets, pp. 165-167.

_____. "Piano"
F. R. Leavis, "'Thought' and Emotional Quality," Scrutiny, 13 (Spring, 1945), 55-58.

Richards, Practical Criticism, pp. 104-117.

Macklin Thomas, "Analysis of the Experience in Lyric Poetry," CE, 9 (March, 1948), 318-319.

_____. "Snake"
Deutsch, Poetry in Our Time, pp. 89-91.

L. B. Mittleman, "Lawrence's 'Snake' Not Sweet Georgia Brown," ELT, 9 No. 1 (1966), 45-46.

_____. "Song of a Man Who Has Come Through"
Donald Hall, The Pleasure of Poetry (New York: Harper & Row, 1971), 64-66.

Robert Hogan, Expl, 17 (April, 1959), 51.
   Rpt. The Explicator Cyclopedia, I, pp. 204-205.

Raphael Levy, Expl, 22 (Feb., 1964), 44.

Rosenthal, The Modern Poets, pp. 164-165.

_____. "Tortoise Shout"
Harold Bloom, The Ringers in the Tower: Studies in Romantic Tradition (Chicago and London: Univ. of Chicago Press, 1971), pp. 202-204.

Keith Sagar, "'Little Living Myths': A Note on Lawrence's Tortoises," DHLR, 3 (Summer, 1970), 165-166.

_____. "Whether or Not"
Deutsch, Poetry in Our Time, pp. 5-6.

_____. "The Wild Common"
Blackmur, The Double Agent, pp. 110-111.
   Rpt. Language as Gesture, pp. 291-292.

Del Ivan Janik, "Toward 'Thingness': Cézanne's Painting and Lawrence's Poetry," TCL, 19 (April, 1973), 121.

LEAR, Edward. "The Dong with a Luminous Nose"
Daiches, A Study of Literature, pp. 201-202.

A. E. Dyson, "Method in Madness: A Note on Edward Lear," English, 10 (Autumn, 1955), 221.

_____. "Jumblies"
A. E. Dyson, "Method in Madness: A Note on Edward Lear," English, 10 (Autumn, 1955), 222-223.

_____. "The Owl and the Pussycat"
Edmund Miller, "Two Approaches to Edward Lear's Nonsense Songs," VN, 44 (Fall, 1973), 5-6.

_____. "The Pobble Who Has No Toes"
Edmund Miller, "Two Approaches to Edward Lear's Nonsense Songs," VN, 44 (Fall, 1973), 6-7.

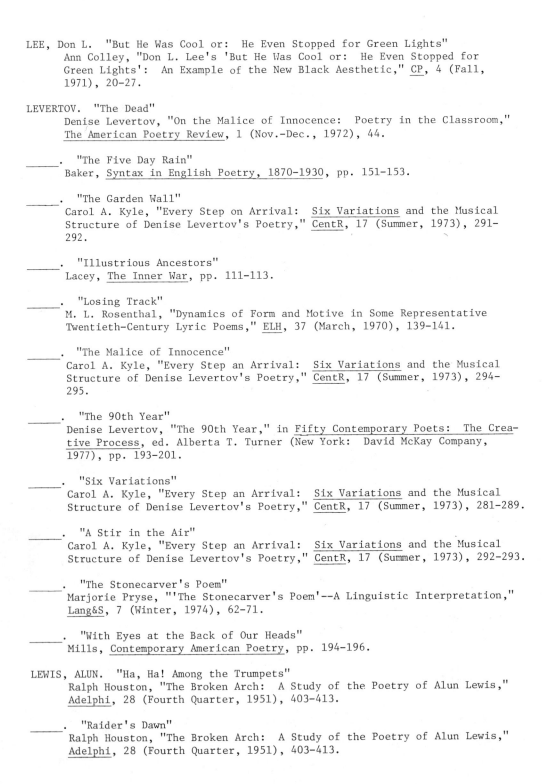

LEE, Don L. "But He Was Cool or: He Even Stopped for Green Lights"
     Ann Colley, "Don L. Lee's 'But He Was Cool or: He Even Stopped for
     Green Lights': An Example of the New Black Aesthetic," CP, 4 (Fall,
     1971), 20-27.

LEVERTOV. "The Dead"
     Denise Levertov, "On the Malice of Innocence: Poetry in the Classroom,"
     The American Poetry Review, 1 (Nov.-Dec., 1972), 44.

_____. "The Five Day Rain"
     Baker, Syntax in English Poetry, 1870-1930, pp. 151-153.

_____. "The Garden Wall"
     Carol A. Kyle, "Every Step on Arrival: Six Variations and the Musical
     Structure of Denise Levertov's Poetry," CentR, 17 (Summer, 1973), 291-
     292.

_____. "Illustrious Ancestors"
     Lacey, The Inner War, pp. 111-113.

_____. "Losing Track"
     M. L. Rosenthal, "Dynamics of Form and Motive in Some Representative
     Twentieth-Century Lyric Poems," ELH, 37 (March, 1970), 139-141.

_____. "The Malice of Innocence"
     Carol A. Kyle, "Every Step an Arrival: Six Variations and the Musical
     Structure of Denise Levertov's Poetry," CentR, 17 (Summer, 1973), 294-
     295.

_____. "The 90th Year"
     Denise Levertov, "The 90th Year," in Fifty Contemporary Poets: The Crea-
     tive Process, ed. Alberta T. Turner (New York: David McKay Company,
     1977), pp. 193-201.

_____. "Six Variations"
     Carol A. Kyle, "Every Step an Arrival: Six Variations and the Musical
     Structure of Denise Levertov's Poetry," CentR, 17 (Summer, 1973), 281-289.

_____. "A Stir in the Air"
     Carol A. Kyle, "Every Step an Arrival: Six Variations and the Musical
     Structure of Denise Levertov's Poetry," CentR, 17 (Summer, 1973), 292-293.

_____. "The Stonecarver's Poem"
     Marjorie Pryse, "'The Stonecarver's Poem'--A Linguistic Interpretation,"
     Lang&S, 7 (Winter, 1974), 62-71.

_____. "With Eyes at the Back of Our Heads"
     Mills, Contemporary American Poetry, pp. 194-196.

LEWIS, ALUN. "Ha, Ha! Among the Trumpets"
     Ralph Houston, "The Broken Arch: A Study of the Poetry of Alun Lewis,"
     Adelphi, 28 (Fourth Quarter, 1951), 403-413.

_____. "Raider's Dawn"
     Ralph Houston, "The Broken Arch: A Study of the Poetry of Alun Lewis,"
     Adelphi, 28 (Fourth Quarter, 1951), 403-413.

LEWIS, James F. "Dawn in the Study"
    Mary Graham Lund, Expl, 18 (Nov., 1959), 12.
       Rpt. The Explicator Cyclopedia, I, p. 205.

_____. "In Memoriam"
    Mary Graham Lund, Expl, 18 (Jan., 1960), 23.
       Rpt. The Explicator Cyclopedia, I, pp. 205-206.

LIMÓN, José. "Frost in the Rio Grande Valley"
    Albert D. Trevino, '"Frost in the Rio Grande Valley' by José Limón," EJ,
    66 (March, 1977), 69.

LINDSAY. "Abraham Lincoln Walks at Midnight"
    Perrine and Reid, 100 American Poems, p. 25.

_____. "The Congo"
    A. J. Bader, "Lindsay Explains 'The Congo,'" PQ, 27 (April, 1948), 190-
    192.

    William Blair, The Literature of the United States, II, 946.

    Perrine and Reid, 100 American Poems, pp. 61-64.

    Austin Warren, "The Case of Vachel Lindsay," Accent, 6 (Summer, 1946),
    237-239.

_____. "General William Booth Enters into Heaven"
    Walter Blair, The Literature of the United States, II, 944.

    Austin Warren, "The Case of Vachel Lindsay," Accent, 6 (Summer, 1946),
    237.

_____. "The Santa Fe Trail"
    Richard E. Amacher, Expl, 5 (March, 1947), 33.
       Rpt. The Explicator Cyclopedia, I, pp. 206-207.

    Richard E. Amacher, "Off 'The Santa Fe Trail,'" AL, 20 (Nov., 1948), 337.

    A. L. Bader, "Vachel Lindsay and 'The Santa Fe Trail,'" AL, 19 (Jan.,
    1948), 360-362.

LISTER, R. P. "Target"
    Laurence Perrine, "The Importance of Tone in the Interpretation of Liter-
    ature," CE, 24 (Feb., 1963), 391-392.

LODGE. "Satire 5" (from A Fig for Momus)
    Sidney H. Atkins, "Dyer at Woodstock," TLS, Feb. 3, 1945, p. 55.

LOGAN, John. "Big Sur: Partington"
    Charles Altieri, "Poetry as Resurrection: John Logan's Structures of
    Metaphysical Solace," MPS, 3 (1972), 211-213.

_____. "A Century Piece for Poor Heine"
    Carroll, The Poem in Its Skin, pp. 116-136.

_____. "Lines for Michael in the Picture"
    Charles Altieri, "Poetry as Resurrection: John Logan's Structures of
    Metaphysical Solace," MPS, 3 (1972), 219-220.

_____. "The Picnic"
    Charles Altieri, "Poetry as Resurrection: John Logan's Structures of
    Metaphysical Solace," MPS, 3 (1972), 205-207.

_____. "The Rescue"
Charles Altieri, "Poetry as Resurrection: John Logan's Structures of
Metaphysical Solace," MPS, 3 (1972), 195-198.

_____. "Shore Scene"
Charles Altieri, "Poetry as Resurrection: John Logan's Structures of
Metaphysical Solace," MPS, 3 (1972), 207-208.

_____. "A Trip to Four or Five Towns"
Charles Altieri, "Poetry as Resurrection: John Logan's Structures of
Metaphysical Solace," MPS, 3 (1972), 203-205.

LONGFELLOW. "Aftermath"
Arms, The Fields Were Green, pp. 213-214.

_____. "Chaucer"
Nancy L. Tenfelde, Expl, 22 (March, 1964), 55.

_____. "The Cross of Snow"
Robert A. Durr, Expl, 13 (March, 1955), 32.
    Rpt. The Explicator Cyclopedia, II, pp. 196-197.

_____. "Divina Commedia," Sonnet I
George Arms, Expl, 2 (Oct., 1943), 7.
    Rpt. The Explicator Cyclopedia, II, p. 197.

Arms, The Fields Were Green, p. 211.

_____. "The Falcon of Ser Federigo"
Arms, The Fields Were Green, pp. 218-219.

_____. "The Fire of Drift-Wood"
Arms, The Fields Were Green, p. 212.

_____. "Helen of Tyre"
Richard P. Benton, Expl, 16 (June, 1958), 54.
    Rpt. The Explicator Cyclopedia, II, pp. 197-198.

_____. "Hymn to the Night"
George Arms, Expl, 1 (Oct., 1942), 7.
    Rpt. The Explicator Cyclopedia, II, p. 198.

_____. "In the Churchyard at Cambridge"
Arms, The Fields Were Green, pp. 208-209.

Richard, Practical Criticism, pp. 162-178 et passim.

_____. "Jugurtha"
Richard E. Amacher, Expl, 6 (Feb., 1948), 29.
    Rpt. The Explicator Cyclopedia, II, pp. 198-199.

Arms, The Fields Were Green, p. 215.

_____. "Killed at the Ford"
Arms, The Fields Were Green, pp. 221-222.

_____. "My Lost Youth"
George Arms, "The Revision of 'My Lost Youth,'" MLN, 61 (June, 1946),
389-392.

_____. "The Occultation of Orion"
M. Zimmerman, "War and Peace: Longfellow's 'The Occultation of Orion,'"
AL, 38 (Jan., 1967), 540-546.

_____. "Paul Revere's Ride"
N. H. Pearson, "Both Longfellows," The University of Kansas City Review,
16 (Summer, 1950), 247.

_____. "Seaweed"
Arms, The Fields Were Green, pp. 209-211.

_____. "Serenade"
Arms, The Fields Were Green, pp. 220-221.

G. Thomas Tanselle, Expl, 23 (Feb., 1965), 48.

_____. "Snow-Flakes"
Arms, The Fields Were Green, pp. 207-208.

N. H. Pearson, "Both Longfellows," The University of Kansas City Review,
16 (Summer, 1950), 252-253.

_____. "The Tide Rises, The Tide Falls"
Dickinson, Suggestions for Teachers of "Introduction to Literature,"
ᵗfifth edition, ed. Locke, Gibson, and Arms, p. 28. (Teacher's Manual)

LOVELACE. "Advice to my best Brother. Coll: Francis Lovelace"
Miner, The Cavalier Mode from Jonson to Cotton, pp. 120-122.

Randolph L. Wadsworth, Jr., "Comment and Rebuttal," CE, 31 (March, 1970),
637-639.

_____. "Ant"
Miner, The Cavalier Mode from Jonson to Cotton, pp. 112-114.

_____. "A Black Patch on Lucasta's Face"
C. F. Williamson, "Two Notes on the Poems of Richard Lovelace," MLR, 52
(April, 1957), 229.

_____. "Cupid Far Gone"
Thomas Clayton, Expl, 33 (Dec., 1974), 32.

_____. "Elinda's Glove"
Paulina Palmer, "Lovelace's Treatment of Some Marinesque Motifs," CL, 29
(Fall, 1977), 302-306.

_____. "The Falcon"
Raymond A. Anselment, "'Griefe Triumphant' and 'Victorious Sorrow': A
Reading of Richard Lovelace's 'The Falcon,'" JEGP, 70 (July, 1971), 404-
417.

_____. "The Grasshopper"
Don Cameron Allen, "An Explication of Lovelace's 'The Grass-Hopper,'"
MLQ, 18 (March, 1957), 35-43.
    Rpt. Allen, Image and Meaning, p. 80-92. New enlarged edition.
    pp. 152-164.

Bruce King, "Green Ice and a Breast of Proof," CE, 26 (April, 1965),
511-515.

Bruce King, "The Grasshopper and Allegory," _ArielE_, 1 (April, 1970), 71-82.

Miner, _The Cavalier Mode from Jonson to Cotton_, pp. 64-65, 286-295.

_____. "Gratiana Dancing and Singing"
Paulina Palmer, "Lovelace's Treatment of Some Marinesque Motifs," _CL_, 29 (Fall, 1977), 309-312.

John T. Shawcross, "The Poet as Orator: One Phase of His Judicial Pose," in _The Rhetoric of Renaissance Poetry_, pp. 30-31.

_____. "La Bella Bona-Roba"
Marius Bewley, "The Colloquial Mode of Byron," _Scrutiny_, 16 (March, 1949), 12-14.

. "The Scrutinie"
Norman N. Holland, "Literary Value: A Psychoanalytic Approach," _L&P_, 14 (Spring, 1964), 44-50.

Robert Rogers, "Literary Value and the Clinical Fallacy," _L&P_, 14 (Summer-Fall, 1964), 117-118.

_____. "The Snayl"
Randolph L. Wadsworth, Jr., "On 'The Snayl' by Richard Lovelace," _MLR_, 65 (Oct., 1970), 750-760.

_____. "Song: No, No, Fair Heretic. It Needs Must Be"
Kreutzer, _Elements of Poetry_, p. 153.

_____. "Song: To Amarantha, that she would dishevell her haire"
Paulina Palmer, "Lovelace's Treatment of Some Marinesque Motifs," _CL_, 29 (Fall, 1977), 306-309.

_____. "To Althea, from Prison"
Empson, _Seven Types of Ambiguity_, pp. 266-267; (1947 ed.), pp. 209-211.

_____. "To Lucasta"
Norman N. Holland, "Literary Value: A Psychoanalytic Approach," _L&P_, 14 (Spring, 1964), 50-54.

Kirk and McCutcheon, _An Introduction to the Study of Poetry_, pp. 12-14.

Norman Holmes Pearson, _Expl_, 7 (June, 1949), 58.
    Rpt. Locke, Gibson, and Arms, _Introduction to Literature_, third edition, pp. 48-49.
    Rpt. _The Explicator Cyclopedia_, II, pp. 199-200.

Robert Rogers, "Literary Value and the Clinical Fallacy," _L&P_, 14 (Summer-Fall, 1964), 118.

John T. Shawcross, "The Poet as Orator: One Phase of His Judical Pose," in _The Rhetoric of Renaissance Poetry_, pp. 29-30.

Van Doren, _Introduction to Poetry_, pp. 22-26.

_____. "To My Dear Friend Mr. E. R."
C. F. Williamson, "Two Notes on the Poems of Richard Lovelace," _MLR_, 52 (April, 1957), 227-228.

LOWELL, Amy. "Meeting-House Hill"
Brooks, Lewis, and Warren, _American Literature_, pp. 2056-2057.

_____. "Night Clouds"
Cooper and Holmes, Preface to Poetry, pp. 141-142.

_____. "Patterns"
Brooks and Warren, Understanding Poetry, pp. 139-143. Revised edition,
pp. 58-61.

Perrine and Reid, 100 American Poems, pp. 51-52.

_____. "Sunshine"
Daniels, The Art of Reading Poetry, pp. 196-197.

LOWELL, James R. "Agassiz"
Arms, The Fields Were Green, pp. 124-126.

_____. "Auspex"
Richard E. Amacher, Expl, 9 (March, 1951), 37.
    Rpt. The Explicator Cyclopedia, II, p. 200.

Arms, The Fields Were Green, pp. 133-134.

_____. "The Cathedral"
Arms, The Fields Were Green, pp. 135-138.

_____. "The Courtin'"
Milledge B. Seigler, Expl, 8 (Nov., 1949), 14.
    Rpt. The Explicator Cyclopedia, II, pp. 200-201.

_____. "Fitz Adam's Story"
Arms, The Fields Were Green, pp. 130-132.

_____. "Ode Recited at the Harvard Commemoration"
Arms, The Fields Were Green, pp. 138-140.

_____. "To the Dandelion"
Arms, The Fields Were Green, pp. 132-133.

LOWELL, Robert. "Adam and Eve"
Mills, Contemporary American Poetry, pp. 144-146.

_____. "After Surprising Conversions"
John Akey, Expl, 9 (June, 1951), 53.
    Rpt. The Explicator Cyclopedia, I, p. 209.

G. Giovannini, Expl, 9 (June, 1951), 53.
    Rpt. The Explicator Cyclopedia, I, pp. 207-208.

John McCluhan, Expl, 9 (June, 1951) 53.
    Rpt. The Explicator Cyclopedia, I, p. 208.

Roy Harvey Pearce, Expl, 9 (June, 1951), 53.
    Rpt. The Explicator Cyclopedia, I, p. 209.

Dallas E. Wiebe, "Mr. Lowell and Mr. Edwards," Wisconsin Studies in Contemporary Literature, 3 (Spring-Summer, 1962), 26-29.

_____. "As a Plane Tree by the Water"
De Sales Standerwick, "Notes on Robert Lowell," Renascence, 8 (Winter,
1955), 80.

_____. "At the Indian Killer's Grave"
De Sales Standerwick, "Notes on Robert Lowell," Renascence, 8 (Winter, 1955), 78-79.

Austin Warren, "A Double Discipline," Poetry, 70 (Aug., 1947), 265.

_____. "Between the Porch and the Altar"
Marius Bewley, "Aspects of Modern American Poetry," Scrutiny, 17 (March, 1951), 345-347.

Rosenthal, The Modern Poets, pp. 228-229.

Thomas Vogler, "Robert Lowell: Payment Gat He Nane," IowaR, 2 (Summer, 1971), 78-82.

_____. "Beyond the Alps"
Clauco Cambon, "Dea Roma and Robert Lowell," Accent, 20 (Winter, 1960), 51-61.

Gray, American Poetry, pp. 243-245.

Mills, Contemporary American Poetry, pp. 149-151.

_____. "Caligula"
Joan Bobbitt, "Lowell and Plath: Objectivity and the Confessional Mode," ArQ, 33 (Autumn, 1977), 312-313.

_____. "Children of Light"
Rosenthal, The Modern Poets, pp. 227-228.

_____. "Colloquy in Black Rock"
Richard J. Fein, "Lord Weary's Castle Revisited," PMLA, 89 (Jan., 1974), 39.

Mills, Contemporary American Poetry, pp. 139-141.

_____. "Commander Lowell 1887-1950"
George McFadden, "'Life Studies'--Robert Lowell's Comic Breakthrough," PMLA, 90 (Jan., 1975), 100.

_____. "The Death of the Sheriff"
Thomas Vogler, "Robert Lowell: Payment Gat He Nane," IowaR, 2 (Summer, 1971), 84-90.

_____. "The Dolphin"
Steven Gould Axelrod, "Lowell's The Dolphin as a 'Book of Life,'" ConL, 18 (Autumn, 1977), 473-474.

_____. "The Drinker"
Marie Borroff, "Words, Language, and Form," in Literary Theory and Structure, ed. Frank Brady, John Palmer, and Martin Price (New Haven: Yale Univ. Press, 1973), pp. 71-73.

_____. "Dunbarton"
George McFadden, "'Life Studies'--Robert Lowell's Comic Breakthrough," PMLA, 90 (Jan., 1975), 100.

Phillips, The Confessional Poets, pp. 27-29.

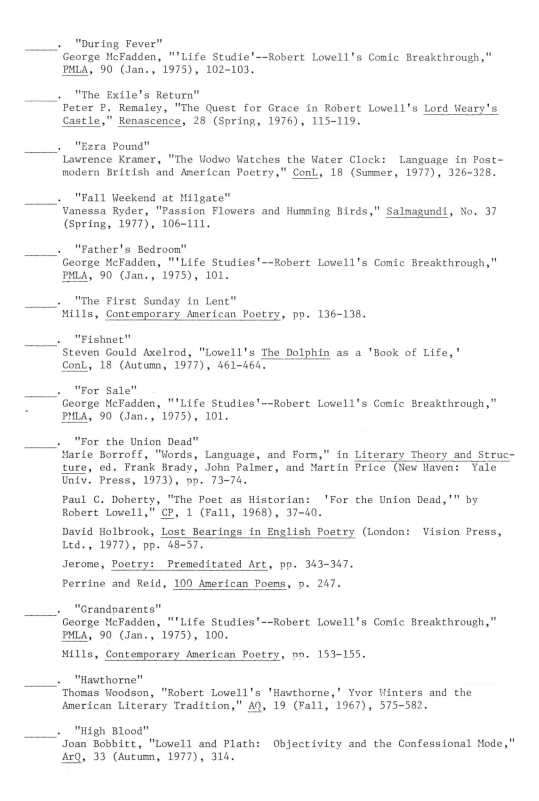

_____. "During Fever"
George McFadden, "'Life Studie'--Robert Lowell's Comic Breakthrough,"
PMLA, 90 (Jan., 1975), 102-103.

_____. "The Exile's Return"
Peter P. Remaley, "The Quest for Grace in Robert Lowell's Lord Weary's
Castle," Renascence, 28 (Spring, 1976), 115-119.

_____. "Ezra Pound"
Lawrence Kramer, "The Wodwo Watches the Water Clock: Language in Post-
modern British and American Poetry," ConL, 18 (Summer, 1977), 326-328.

_____. "Fall Weekend at Milgate"
Vanessa Ryder, "Passion Flowers and Humming Birds," Salmagundi, No. 37
(Spring, 1977), 106-111.

_____. "Father's Bedroom"
George McFadden, "'Life Studies'--Robert Lowell's Comic Breakthrough,"
PMLA, 90 (Jan., 1975), 101.

_____. "The First Sunday in Lent"
Mills, Contemporary American Poetry, pp. 136-138.

_____. "Fishnet"
Steven Gould Axelrod, "Lowell's The Dolphin as a 'Book of Life,'
ConL, 18 (Autumn, 1977), 461-464.

_____. "For Sale"
George McFadden, "'Life Studies'--Robert Lowell's Comic Breakthrough,"
PMLA, 90 (Jan., 1975), 101.

_____. "For the Union Dead"
Marie Borroff, "Words, Language, and Form," in Literary Theory and Struc-
ture, ed. Frank Brady, John Palmer, and Martin Price (New Haven: Yale
Univ. Press, 1973), pp. 73-74.

Paul C. Doherty, "The Poet as Historian: 'For the Union Dead,'" by
Robert Lowell," CP, 1 (Fall, 1968), 37-40.

David Holbrook, Lost Bearings in English Poetry (London: Vision Press,
Ltd., 1977), pp. 48-57.

Jerome, Poetry: Premeditated Art, pp. 343-347.

Perrine and Reid, 100 American Poems, p. 247.

_____. "Grandparents"
George McFadden, "'Life Studies'--Robert Lowell's Comic Breakthrough,"
PMLA, 90 (Jan., 1975), 100.

Mills, Contemporary American Poetry, pp. 153-155.

_____. "Hawthorne"
Thomas Woodson, "Robert Lowell's 'Hawthorne,' Yvor Winters and the
American Literary Tradition," AQ, 19 (Fall, 1967), 575-582.

_____. "High Blood"
Joan Bobbitt, "Lowell and Plath: Objectivity and the Confessional Mode,"
ArQ, 33 (Autumn, 1977), 314.

_____. "Home After Three Months Away"
Sr. Madeline DeFrees, "Pegasus and Six Blind Indians," EJ, 59 (Oct., 1970), 935-937.

George McFadden, "'Life Studies'--Robert Lowell's Comic Breakthrough," PMLA, 90 (Jan., 1975), 103-104.

Phillips, The Confessional Poets, pp. 35-37.

_____. "In Memory of Arthur Winslow"
Marjorie Perloff, "Death by Water: The Winslow Elegies of Robert Lowell," ELH, 34 (March, 1967), 117-124.

Stanley M. Wiersma, Expl, 30 (Oct., 1971), 12.

_____. "July in Washington"
Edwards, Imagination and Power, pp. 221-224.

_____. "Man and Wife"
Marjorie G. Perloff, "Realism and the Confessional Mode of Robert Powell," ConL, 11 (Autumn, 1970), 472-482.

Phillips, The Confessional Poets, pp. 38-39.

_____. "Mary Winslow"
John J. McAleer, Expl, 18 (Feb., 1960), 29.
     Rpt. The Explicator Cyclopedia, I, pp. 209-210.

_____. "Memories of West Street and Lepke"
George Lensing, "'Memories of West Street and Lepke': Robert Lowell's Associative Mirror," CP, 3 (Fall, 1970), 23-26.

George McFadden, "'Life Studies'--Robert Lowell's Comic Breakthrough," PMLA, 90 (Jan., 1975), 104.

_____. "Mother Marie Therese"
De Sales Standerwick, "Notes on Robert Lowell," Renascence, 8 (Winter, 1955), 81-82.

_____. "Mr. Edwards and the Spider"
Perrine and Reid, 100 American Poems, pp. 243-244.

Dallas E. Wiebe, "Mr. Lowell and Mr. Edwards," Wisconsin Studies in Contemporary Literature, 3 (Spring-Summer, 1962), 21-26.

_____. "My Last Afternoon with Uncle Devereux Winslow"
Richard James Calhoun, Expl, 23 (Jan., 1965), 38.

George McFadden, "'Life Studies'--Robert Lowell's Comic Breakthrough," PMLA, 90 (Jan., 1975), 98-100.

Marjorie Perloff, "Death by Water: The Winslow Elegies of Robert Lowell," ELH, 34 (March, 1967), 130-136.

Phillips, The Confessional Poets, pp. 24-26.

_____. "Napoleon Crosses the Berezina"
De Sales Standerwick, "Notes on Robert Lowell," Renascence, 8 (Winter, 1955), 79.

_____. "Near the Ocean"
G. S. Fraser, "'Near the Ocean,'" Salmagundi, No. 37 (Spring, 1977), 77-83.

_____. "The Neo-Classical Urn"
Joan Bobbitt, "Lowell and Plath: Objectivity and the Confessional Mode,"
ArQ, 33 (Autumn, 1977), 313.

_____. "Nostaligie de la Boue"
Paul Schwaber, "Robert Lowell in Mid-Career," WHR, 25 (Autumn, 1971),
348-350.

_____. "A Prayer for My Grandfather to Our Lady"
Marius Bewley, "Aspects of Modern American Poetry," Scrutiny, 17 (March,
1951), 344-345.

_____. "The Public Garden"
Rudolph L. Nelson, "A Note on the Evolution of Robert Lowell's 'The
Public Garden,'" AL, 41 (March, 1969), 108-110.

_____. "The Quaker Graveyard in Nantucket"
Paul J. Dolan, "Lowell's Quaker Graveyard: Poem and Tradition," Renascence, 21 (Summer, 1969), 171-180, 194.

Paul Engle, "Five Years of Pulitzer Poets," EJ, 38 (Feb., 1949), 64.

Friar and Brinnin, Modern Poetry, pp. 520-521.

Philip Furia, "'Is, the Whited Monster': Lowell's Quaker Graveyard Revisited," TSLL, 17 (Winter, 1976), 837-854.

Mills, Contemporary American Poetry, pp. 141-144.

Marjorie Perloff, "Death by Water: The Winslow Elegies of Robert Lowell,"
ELH, 34 (March, 1967), 124-130.

Sr. Mary Terese Rink, "The Sea in Lowell's 'Quaker Graveyard in Nantucket,'" Renascence, 20 (Autumn, 1967), 39-43.

Rosenthal, The Modern Poets, pp. 229-230.

De Sales Standerwick, "Notes on Robert Lowell," Renascence, 8 (Winter,
1955), 76-78.

_____. "Sailing Home from Rapallo"
George McFadden, "'Life Studies'--Robert Lowell's Comic Breakthrough,"
PMLA, 90 (Jan., 1975), 101-102.

_____. "Skunk Hour"
George McFadden, "'Life Studies'--Robert Lowell's Comic Breakthrough,"
PMLA, 90 (Jan., 1975), 105.

Phillips, The Confessional Poets, pp. 40-42.

_____. "The Slough of Despond"
Thomas Vogler, "Robert Lowell: Payment Gat He Nane," IowaR, 2 (Summer,
1971), 82-83.

_____. "Soft Wood"
Marjorie Perloff, "Death by Water: The Winslow Elegies of Robert Lowell,"
ELH, 34 (March, 1967), 136-140.

_____. "'Sunthin' in the Pastoral Line"
John C. Broderick, "Lowell's 'Sunthin' in the Pastoral Line,'" AL, 31
(May, 1959), 163-172.

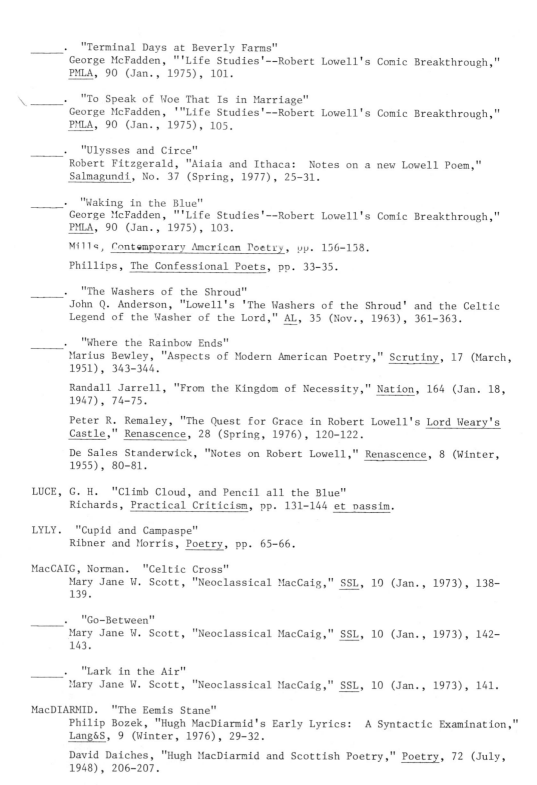

_____. "Terminal Days at Beverly Farms"
George McFadden, "'Life Studies'--Robert Lowell's Comic Breakthrough,"
PMLA, 90 (Jan., 1975), 101.

_____. "To Speak of Woe That Is in Marriage"
George McFadden, "'Life Studies'--Robert Lowell's Comic Breakthrough,"
PMLA, 90 (Jan., 1975), 105.

_____. "Ulysses and Circe"
Robert Fitzgerald, "Aiaia and Ithaca: Notes on a new Lowell Poem,"
Salmagundi, No. 37 (Spring, 1977), 25-31.

_____. "Waking in the Blue"
George McFadden, "'Life Studies'--Robert Lowell's Comic Breakthrough,"
PMLA, 90 (Jan., 1975), 103.

Mills, Contemporary American Poetry, pp. 156-158.

Phillips, The Confessional Poets, pp. 33-35.

_____. "The Washers of the Shroud"
John Q. Anderson, "Lowell's 'The Washers of the Shroud' and the Celtic
Legend of the Washer of the Lord," AL, 35 (Nov., 1963), 361-363.

_____. "Where the Rainbow Ends"
Marius Bewley, "Aspects of Modern American Poetry," Scrutiny, 17 (March,
1951), 343-344.

Randall Jarrell, "From the Kingdom of Necessity," Nation, 164 (Jan. 18,
1947), 74-75.

Peter R. Remaley, "The Quest for Grace in Robert Lowell's Lord Weary's
Castle," Renascence, 28 (Spring, 1976), 120-122.

De Sales Standerwick, "Notes on Robert Lowell," Renascence, 8 (Winter,
1955), 80-81.

LUCE, G. H. "Climb Cloud, and Pencil all the Blue"
Richards, Practical Criticism, pp. 131-144 et passim.

LYLY. "Cupid and Campaspe"
Ribner and Morris, Poetry, pp. 65-66.

MacCAIG, Norman. "Celtic Cross"
Mary Jane W. Scott, "Neoclassical MacCaig," SSL, 10 (Jan., 1973), 138-
139.

_____. "Go-Between"
Mary Jane W. Scott, "Neoclassical MacCaig," SSL, 10 (Jan., 1973), 142-
143.

_____. "Lark in the Air"
Mary Jane W. Scott, "Neoclassical MacCaig," SSL, 10 (Jan., 1973), 141.

MacDIARMID. "The Eemis Stane"
Philip Bozek, "Hugh MacDiarmid's Early Lyrics: A Syntactic Examination,"
Lang&S, 9 (Winter, 1976), 29-32.

David Daiches, "Hugh MacDiarmid and Scottish Poetry," Poetry, 72 (July,
1948), 206-207.

_____. "Ex Vermibus"
Ann E. Boutelle, "Language and Vision in the Early Poetry of Hugh MacDiarmid," ConL, 12 (Autumn, 1971), 504-506.

_____. "Farmer's Death"
Ann E. Boutelle, "Language and Vision in the Early Poetry of Hugh MacDiarmid," ConL, 12 (Autumn, 1971), 496-499.

_____. "Gairmscoile"
Ann E. Boutelle, "Language and Vision in the Early Poetry of Hugh MacDiarmid," ConL, 12 (Autumn, 1971), 499-501.

_____. "Lourd on My Hert as Winter Lies"
David Daiches, "Hugh MacDiarmid and Scottish Poetry," Poetry, 72 (July,
1948), 209-210.

_____. "The Man in the Moon"
Philip Bozek, "Hugh MacDiarmid's Early Lyrics: A Syntactic Examination,"
Lang&S, 9 (Winter, 1976), 32-34.

_____. "Moonstruck"
David Daiches, "Hugh MacDiarmid and Scottish Poetry," Poetry, 72 (July,
1948), 211.

_____. "O Wha's Been Here Afore Me, Lass"
Rosenthal, The Modern Poets, pp. 132-134.

_____. "The Skeleton of the Future"
Philip Bozek, "Hugh MacDiarmid's Early Lyrics: A Syntactic Examination,"
Lang&S, 9 (Winter, 1976), 39-41.

_____. "Somersault"
Philip Bozek, "Hugh MacDiarmid's Early Lyrics: A Syntactic Examination,"
Lang&S, 9 (Winter, 1976), 34-36.

_____. "The Spur of Love"
Ann E. Boutelle, "Language and Vision in the Early Poetry of Hugh MacDiarmid," ConL, 12 (Autumn, 1971), 501-504.

_____. "The Watergaw"
Philip Bozek, "Hugh MacDiarmid's Early Lyrics: A Syntactic Examination,"
Lang&S, 9 (Winter, 1976), 36-39.

_____. "Yet Ha'e I Silence Left, the Croon o' A'"
David Daiches, "Hugh MacDiarmid and Scottish Poetry," Poetry, 72 (July,
1948), 210.

MacDONALD, Cynthia. "Departure"
R. L. Widmann, "The Poetry of Cynthia MacDonald," CP, 7 (Spring, 1974),
24-26.

_____. "Inventory"
R. L. Widmann, "The Poetry of Cynthia MacDonald," CP, 7 (Spring, 1974),
21-24.

_____. "Objects d'Art"
R. L. Widmann, "The Poetry of Cynthia MacDonald," CP, 7 (Spring, 1974),
20-21.

McKAY, Claude.   "If We Must Die"
    Robert A. Lee, "On Claude McKay's 'If We Must Die,'" CLAJ, 18 (Dec.,
    1974), 216-221.

MacLEISH.   "...& Forty-Second Street"
    Ivar L. Myhr, Expl, 3 (April, 1945), 47.
        Rpt. The Explicator Cyclopedia, I, p. 211.

_____.   "Ars Poetica"
    David J. Kressler, "Resolution in 'Ars Poetica,'" CP, 10 (Spring, 1977),
    73.

    Sanders, The Discovery of Poetry, pp. 49-52.

    Victor P. Staudt, "'Ars Poetica' and the Teacher," CE, 19 (Oct., 1957),
    28-29.

    Stauffer, The Nature of Poetry, pp. 121-125.
        Rpt. Engle and Carrier, Reading Modern Poetry, pp. 99-101.

    Harry R. Sullivan, "MacLeish's 'Ars Poetica,'" EJ, 56 (Dec., 1967), 1280-
    1283.

_____.   "'Dover Beach'--A Note to That Poem"
    Kreuzer, Elements of Poetry, pp. 183-189, 191-192.

    James Zigerell, Expl, 17 (March, 1959), 38.
        Rpt. The Explicator Cyclopedia, I, pp. 210-211.

_____.   "Dr. Sigmund Freud Discovers the Sea Shell"
    Perrine and Reid, 100 American Poems, pp. 161-162.

_____.   "Einstein"
    Hoffman, The Twenties, pp. 287-288.

    Waggoner, The Heel of Elohim, pp. 143-146.

_____.   "Eleven"
    Deutsch, Poetry in Our Time, p. 147.

_____.   "The End of the World"
    Perrine and Reid, 100 American Poems, 163.

_____.   "Epistle to Be Left in the Earth"
    Waggoner, The Heel of Elohim, pp. 146-148.

_____.   "The Hamlet of A. MacLeish"
    Waggoner, The Heel of Elohim, pp. 141-143.

_____.   "Hypocrite Auteur"
    Nicholas Joost, Expl, 11 (May, 1953), 47.
        Rpt. The Explicator Cyclopedia, I, pp. 211-213.

_____.   "L'An Trentiesme de Mon Eage"
    Richard E. Amacher, Expl, 6 (April, 1948), 42.
        Rpt. The Explicator Cyclopedia, I, pp. 213-214.

_____.   "Lines for an Interment"
    Kreuzer, Elements of Poetry, pp. 141-143.

_____. "Memorial Rain"
Brooks, <u>Modern Poetry and the Tradition</u>, pp. 122-124.

_____. "Men"
Brooks, <u>Modern Poetry and the Tradition</u>, pp. 117-118.

_____. "'Not Marble nor the Gilded Monuments'"
Beaty and Matchett, <u>Poetry: From Statement to Meaning</u>, pp. 187-192.

_____. "Pony Rock"
Gerald Sanders, <u>Expl</u>, 2 (Oct., 1943), 8.
    Rpt. <u>The Explicator Cyclopedia</u>, I, p. 214.

_____. "You, Andrew Marvell"
Brooks, <u>Modern Poetry and the Tradition</u>, p. 122.

Brown and Olmstead, <u>Language and Literature</u>, pp. 194-197.

Guy A. Cardwell, <u>Readings from the Americas</u> (New York: Ronald Press Co.,
1947), pp. 790-791.

Drew, <u>Poetry: A Modern Guide</u>, pp. 104-105.

Louis L. Martz, "The Teachings of Poetry," <u>Essays on the Teaching of Lit-
erature</u>, pp. 249-252.

Perrine and Reid, <u>100 American Poems</u>, pp. 159-160.

Perrine, <u>Sound and Sense</u>, pp. 68-69.
    Rpt. second edition, pp. 74-75.

MacNEICE. "Autumn Journal"
S. G. Brown, "Some Poems of Louis MacNeice," <u>SR</u>, 51 (Winter, 1943), 68-72.

_____. "Eclogue from Iceland"
Beach, <u>Obsessive Images</u>, pp. 152-154.

_____. "Entirely"
Donald A. Stauffer, "Genesis, or the Poet as Maker," <u>Poets at Work</u>,
pp. 70-72.

_____. "Leaving Barra"
S. G. Brown, "Some Poems of Louis MacNeice," <u>SR</u>, 51 (Winter, 1943), 64-66.

_____. "Les Sylphides"
Drew and Sweeney, <u>Directions in Modern Poetry</u>, pp. 247-249.

_____. "Meeting Point"
A. J. Minnis, "Louis MacNeice: The Pattern and the Poem," <u>YES</u>, 5 (1975),
237.

_____. "The Pale Panther"
William T. McKinnon, "MacNeice's Pale Panther: An Exercise in Dream
Logic," <u>EIC</u>, 23 (Oct., 1973), 388-398.

_____. "Perseus"
John E. Cope, <u>Expl</u>, 26 (Feb., 1968), 48.

Drew and Sweeney, <u>Directions in Modern Poetry</u>, pp. 87-88 (quoting
MacNeice's explanation).

_____. "Prayer Before Birth"
Deutsch, <u>Poetry in Our Time</u>, pp. 365-366.

_____. "The Riddle"
James F. Dorrill, _Expl_, 29 (Sept., 1970), 7.

_____. "Snow"
Marie Barroff, "What a Poem Is: For Instance 'Snow,'" _EIC_, 8 (Oct., 1958), 393-404.

Sr. M. Martin Barry, O.P., _Expl_, 16 (Nov., 1957), 10.
     Rpt. _The Explicator Cyclopedia_, I, pp. 214-215.

Drew, _Poetry: A Modern Guide_, pp. 226-228.

A. J. Minnis, "Louis MacNeice: The Pattern and the Poem," _YES_, 5 (1975), 235-236.

_____. "The Streets of Laredo"
John T. Irwin, "MacNeice, Auden, and the Art Ballad," _ConL_, 11 (Winter, 1970), 58-74.

_____. "The Sunlight on the Garden"
Thomas and Brown, _Reading Poems: An Introduction to Critical Study_, pp. 686-697.

_____. "These Days Are Misty"
Stageberg and Anderson, _Poetry as Experience_, pp. 216-221.

_____. "Western Landscape"
A. J. Minnis, "Louis MacNeice: The Pattern and the Poem," _YES_, 5 (1975), 238-240.

_____. "You Who Will Soon be Unrecapturable"
S. G. Brown, "Some Poems of Louis MacNeice," _SR_, 51 (Winter, 1943), 66-67.

MAGEE, J. G. "High Flight"
Stageberg and Anderson, _Poetry as Experience_, p. 4.

MAHONY. "The Bells of Shandon"
Brooks and Warren, _Understanding Poetry_, pp. 222-224. Revised Edition, pp. 114-116.

MAIDSTONE, Richard. "The Fifty-First Psalm"
William Elford Rogers, _Image and Abstraction: Six Middle English Religious Lyrics_ (Copenhagen: Rosenkilde and Bagger, 1972), pp. 107-124.

MALLALIEU, H. B. "Lines from Europe"
J. F. Nims, _Poetry: A Critical Supplement_, April, 1947, pp. 14-16.

MANIFOLD, John. "Fife Tune"
Rosenthal and Smith, _Exploring Poetry_, pp. 549-550.

MARKHAM. "The Man With the Hoe"
Lynn H. Harris, _Expl_, 3 (March, 1945), 41.
     Rpt. _The Explicator Cyclopedia_, I, p. 215.

MARLOWE. "The Passionate Shepherd to His Love"
Boulton, _The Anatomy of Poetry_, pp. 160-163.

Louis H. Leiter, "Deification Through Love: Marlowe's 'The Passionate Shepherd to His Love,'" _CE_, 27 (March, 1966), 444-449.

MARSTON. "Cras" (Satire 4)
    D. C. Gunby, "Marston, Mecho, and Supererogation," ELN, 14 (Dec., 1976), 98–99.

    _____. "The Metamorphosis of Pygmalion's Image"
    John Scott Colley, "'Opinion' and the Reader in John Marston's The Meta-morphosis of Pigmalions Image," ELR, 3 (Spring, 1973), 221–231.

    Gustav Cross, "Marston's 'Pygmalion's Image': Mock-Epyllion," EA, 13 (July-Sept., 1960), 333–336.

    Philip J. Finkelpearl, "From Petrarch to Ovid: Metamorphoses in John Marston's 'Metamorphosis of Pygmalion's Image,'" ELH, 32 (Sept., 1965), 333–348.

MARVELL. "Bermudas"
    Edwin B. Benjamin, "'Bermudas,'" CEA, 30 (Oct., 1967), 10, 12.

    R. M. Cummings, "The Difficulty of Marvell's 'Bermudas,'" MP, 67 (Feb., 1970), 331–340.

    Tay Fizdale, "Irony in Marvell's 'Bermudas,'" ELH, 42 (Summer, 1975), 203–213.

    C. B. Hardman, "Marvell's Rowers," EIC, 27 (April, 1977), 93–99.

    John E. Parish, "Back to the 'Bermudas,'" CEA, 30 (Oct., 1967), 10, 12.

    Annabel Patterson, "'Bermudas' and 'The Coronet': Marvell's Protestant Poetics," ELH, 44 (Fall, 1977), 486–490.

    Michael Wilding, "Apples in Marvell's 'Bermudas,'" ELN, 6 (June, 1969), 254–257.

    Williamson, The Proper Wit of Poetry, pp. 98–99.

    J. B. Winterton, "Some Notes on Marvell's 'Bermudas,'" N&Q, 15 (March, 1968), 102.

    _____. "Clorinda and Damon"
    John D. Rosenberg, "Marvell and the Christian Idiom," Boston University Studies in English, 4 (Autumn, 1960), 153–158.

    _____. "Coronet"
    William N. Fisher, "Occupatio in Sixteenth- and Seventeenth- Century Verse," TSLL, 14 (Summer, 1972), 220–222.

    Hardy, The Curious Frame, pp. 46–60.

    Bruce King, "A Reading of Marvell's 'The Coronet,'" MLR, 68 (Oct., 1973), 741–749.

    Annabel Patterson, "'Bermudas' and 'The Coronet': Marvell's Protestant Poetics," ELH, 44 (Fall, 1977), 490–496.

    _____. "Damon the Mower"
    Elaine Hoffman Baruch, "Theme and Counterthemes in 'Damon the Mower,'" CL, 26 (Summer, 1974), 242–259.

    John Creaser, "Marvell's Effortless Superiority," EIC, 20 (Oct., 1970), 406–409.

    David Kalstone, "Marvell and the Fictions of Pastoral," ELR, 4 (Winter, 1974), 175–183.

    Ruth Nevo, "Marvell's 'Songs of Innocence and Experience,'" SEL, 5 (Winter, 1965), 18–20.

Don Perry Norford, "Marvell and the Arts of Contemplation and Action," ELH, 41 (Spring, 1974), 67-70.

Carol Marks Sicherman, "The Mocking Voices of Donne and Marvell," BuR, 17 (May, 1969), 43-45.

Jeffrey B. Spencer, Heroic Nature: Ideal Landscape in English Poetry from Marvell to Thomson (Evanston: Northwestern Univ. Press, 1973), pp. 86-89.

Joseph H. Summers, "Marvell's 'Nature,'" ELH, 20 (June, 1953), 128.

Wanamaker, Discordia Concors, pp. 77-78.

_____. "Daphnis and Chloe"
M. C. Bradbrook and M. G. Floyd Thomas, "Marvell and the Concept of Metamorphosis," The Criterion, 18 (Jan., 1939), 237-238.

Ruth Nevo, "Marvell's 'Songs of Innocence and Experience,'" SEL, 5 (Winter, 1965), 15-17.

_____. "The Definition of Love"
Ann Evam Berthoff, "The Allegorical Metaphor: Marvell's 'The Definition of Love,'" RES, 17 (Feb., 1966), 16-29.

F. W. Bradbrook, "The Poetry of Andrew Marvell," in From Donne to Marvell, ed. Boris Ford (Baltimore: Penguin Books, 1956), pp. 197-199.

Brooks and Warren, Understanding Poetry, pp. 437-440. Revised edition, pp. 294-297.

Nora C. Crook, Expl, 32 (May, 1974), 73.

Dennis Davison, "Marvell's 'The Definition of Love,'" RES, 6, n.s. (April, 1955), 141-146.

Dickinson, Suggestions for Teachers of "Introduction to Literature," fifth edition, Locke, Gibson, and Arms, pp. 12-13.   (Teacher's Manual)

Angela G. DorenKamp, "Marvell's Geometry of Love," ELN, 9 (Dec., 1971), 111-115.

Drew, Poetry: A Modern Guide, pp. 201-203.

Ferry, All in War with Time, pp. 239-249.

Katherine Hanley, C.S.J., "Andrew Marvell's 'The Definition of Love,'" CP, 2 (Fall, 1969), 73-74.

Miner, The Metaphysical Mode from Donne to Cowley, pp. 138-140.

Maren-Sofie Røstvig, "Images of Perfection," in Seventeenth-Century Imagery: Essays on Uses of Figurative Language from Donne to Farquhar, ed. Earl Miner (Berkeley: Univ. of Calif. Press, 1971), pp. 16-17.

Dean Morgan Schmitter and Pierre Legouis, "The Cartography of 'The Definition of Love,'" RES, 12 (Feb., 1961), 49-54.

Harold Earl Toliver, "Marvell's 'Definition of Love' and the Poetry of Self-Exploration," BuR, 10 (May, 1962), 263-274.

Geoffrey Walton, "The Poetry of Andrew Marvell: A Summing Up," Politics and Letters, 1 (Summer, 1948), 27-28.

Williamson, The Proper Wit of Poetry, pp. 101-102.

Lauri Zwicky, Expl, 22 (March, 1964), 52.

_____. "A Dialogue Between the Resolved Soul and the Created Pleasure"
F. W. Bradbrook, "The Poetry of Andrew Marvell," in From Donne to Marvell, ed. Boris Ford (Baltimore: Penguin Books, 1956), pp. 193-195.

Harold E. Toliver, "The Strategy of Marvell's Resolve Against Created Pleasure," SEL, 4 (Winter, 1964), 57-69.

_____. "A Dialogue Between the Soul and the Body"
Peter Berk, "The Voices of Marvell's Lyrics," MLQ, 32 (June, 1971), 144-147.

F. R. Leavis, "The Responsible Critic: Or the Function of Criticism at Any Time," Scrutiny, 19 (Spring, 1953), 163-170.

Laurence Lerner, The Uses of Nostalgia: Studies in Pastoral Poetry (New York: Schocken Books, 1972), 195-196.

Tuve, Elizabethan and Metaphysical Imagery, pp. 207-208 et passim.

_____. "An Epitaph Upon_____"
William N. Fisher, "Occupatio in Sixteenth- and Seventeenth-Century Verse," TSLL, 14 (Summer, 1972), 217-218.

_____. "Eyes and Tears"
Edgar F. Daniels, Expl, 35 (Spring, 1977), 8.

Empson, Seven Types of Ambiguity, pp. 217-220; (1947 ed.), pp. 171-173.

_____. "The First Anniversary"
Nicholas Guild, "Marvell's 'The First Anniversary of the Government Under O.C.,'" PLL, 11 (Summer, 1975), 242-253.

Annabel Patterson, "Against Polarization: Literature and Politics in Marvell's Cromwell Poems," ELR, 5 (Spring, 1975), 257-268.

Joseph H. Summers, The Heirs of Donne and Jonson (New York: Oxford Univ. Press, 1970), pp. 168-171.

John M. Wallace, "Andrew Marvell and Cromwell's Kingship: 'The First Anniversary,'" ELH, 30 (Sept., 1963), 209-235.

A. J. N. Wilson, "Andrew Marvell's 'The First Anniversary of the Government Under Oliver Cromwell': The Poem and Its Frame of Reference," MLR, 69 (April, 1974), 254-273.

James Winny, "A Marvell Foundation," TLS, Oct. 2, 1956, p. 626.

Steven N. Zwicker, "Models of Governance in Marvell's 'The First Anniversary,'" Criticism, 16 (Winter, 1974), 1-12.

Steven N. Zwicker, "Politics and Panegyric: The Figural Mode from Marvell to Pope," in Literary Uses of Typology from the Late Middle Ages to the Present, pp. 124-127.

_____. "Fleckno, an English Priest at Rome"
Miner, The Restoration Mode from Milton to Dryden, pp. 398-400.

_____. "The Gallery"
Charles H. Hinnant, "Marvell's Gallery of Art," RenQ, 24 (Spring, 1971), 26-37.

Edmund Miller, "Marvell's Pastoral Ideal in 'The Gallery,'" CP, 8 (Spring, 1975), 49-50.

Frank J. Warnke, "Play and Metamorphosis in Marvell's Poetry," SEL, 5 (Winter, 1965), 23-26.

_____.   "The Garden"

F. W. Bradbrook, "The Poetry of Andrew Marvell," in From Donne to Marvell, ed. Boris Ford (Baltimore: Penguin Books, 1956), pp. 199-201.

M. C. Bradbrook and M. G. Floyd Thomas, "Marvell and the Concept of Metamorphosis," The Criterion, 18 (Jan., 1939), 236-244.

Margaret Ann Carpenter, "Marvell's 'Garden,'" SEL, 10 (Winter, 1970), 155-169.

Daiches and Charvat, Poems in English, pp. 662-663.

Daniels, The Art of Reading Poetry, pp. 261-264.

Douglas, Lamson, and Smith, The Critical Reader, pp. 68-72. Revised edition, pp. 680-684.

Empson, English Pastoral Poetry, pp. 119-132.
    Rpt. Criticism, pp. 342-352.
    Rpt. West, Essays in Modern Literary Criticism, pp. 335-353.

William Empson, "Marvell's 'Garden,'" in Determinations, pp. 46-56.

William Empson, "Marvell's 'Garden,'" Scrutiny, (Dec., 1932), 236-240.

Ferry, All in War with Time, pp. 210-219.

William L. Godshalk, "Marvell's 'Garden' and the Theologians," SP, 66 (July, 1969), 639-653.

Geoffrey H. Hartman, "Marvell, St. Paul, and the Body of Hope," ELH, 31 (June, 1961), 175-188.

Anthony Hecht, "Shades of Keats and Marvell," HudR, 15 (Spring, 1962), 51-57.

Dale Herron, "Marvell's 'Garden' and the Landscape of Poetry," JEGP, 73 (July, 1974), 328-337.

Philip Hobsbaum, Theory of Criticism (Bloomington and London: Indiana Univ. Press, 1970), pp. 135-142.

Kenneth Holditch, Expl, 23 (Sept., 1964), 5.

Lawrence W. Hyman, "Marvell's 'Garden,'" ELH, 25 (March, 1958), 13-22.

David Kalstone, "Marvell and the Fictions of Pastoral," ELR, 4 (Winter, 1974), 184-187.

Don A. Keister, Expl, 10 (Feb., 1952), 24.
    Rpt. The Explicator Cyclopedia, II, p. 203.

Milton Klonsky, "A Guide Through the Garden," SR, 58 (Winter, 1950), 16-35.

McCanles, Dialectical Criticism, pp. 101-106.

John McChesney, Expl, 10 (Oct., 1951), 4.
    Rpt. The Explicator Cyclopedia, II, 202-203.

Miner, The Metaphysical Mode from Donne to Cowley, pp. 84-91.

Don Parry Norford, "Marvell and the Arts of Contemplation and Action," ELH, 41 (Spring, 1974), 53-56, 73.

John M. Potter, "Another Porker in the Garden of Epicurus: Marvell's 'Hortus' and 'The Garden,'" SEL, 11 (Winter, 1971), 137-151.

John Crowe Ransom, "Mr. Empson's Muddles," SoR, 4 (Autumn, 1938), 331-334.

Maren-Sofie Røstvig, "Andrew Marvell's 'The Garden': A Hermetic Poem," ES, 40 (April, 1959), 65-77.

John N. Serio, "Andrew Marvell's 'The Garden': An Anagogic Reading," OhR, 12, 1 (1970), 68-76.

John Edward Siemon, "Generic Limits in Marvell's 'Garden,'" PLL, 8 (Summer, 1972), 261-272.

Jeffrey B. Spencer, Heroic Nature: Ideal Landscape in English Poetry from Marvell to Thomson (Evanston: Northwestern Univ. Press, 1973), pp. 80-85.

Daniel Stempel, "'The Garden': Marvell's Cartesian Ecstasy," JHI, 28 (Jan.-March, 1967), 99-114.

Joseph H. Summers, "Marvell's 'Nature,'" ELH, 20 (June, 1953), 125.

Joseph H. Summers, "Reading Marvell's 'Garden,'" CentR, 13 (Winter, 1969), 18-37.
    Rpt. The Heirs of Donne and Jonson (New York: Oxford Univ. Press, 1970), pp. 130-155.

Jim Swan, "At Play in the Garden of Ambivalence: Andrew Marvell and the Green World," Criticism, 17 (Fall, 1975), 295-307.
    Rpt. The Practice of Psychoanalytic Criticism, ed. Leonard Tennenhouse (Detroit: Wayne State Univ. Press, 1975), pp. 189-201.

Unger, The Man in the Name, pp. 126-128.

Van Doren, Introduction to Poetry, pp. 61-65.

Charles C. Walcutt, Expl, 24 (Jan., 1966), 48.

Geoffrey Walton, "The Poetry of Andrew Marvell: A Summing Up," Politics and Letters, 1 (Summer, 1948), 30-31.

Wanamaker, Discordia Concors, pp. 79-86.

Williamson, The Proper Wit of Poetry, pp. 102-103.

_____. "An Horation Ode"
F. W. Bradbrook, "The Poetry of Andrew Marvell," in From Donne to Marvell, ed. Boris Ford (Baltimore: Penguin Books, 1956), pp. 201-203.

Cleanth Brooks, "A Note on the Limits of 'History' and the Limits of 'Criticism,'" SR, 61 (Winter, 1953), 129-133.

Cleanth Brooks, "Criticism and Literary History: Marvell's 'Horation Ode,'" SR, 55 (April-June, 1947), 199-222.

Cleanth Brooks, "Literary Criticism," English Institute Essays 1946, pp. 127-158.

Brooks and Warren, Understanding Poetry, revised edition, pp. 667-682.

John S. Coolidge, "Marvell and Horace," MP, 63 (Nov., 1965), 111-120.

Thomas N. Corns, Expl, 35 (Winter, 1976), 11-12.

David K. Cornelius, Expl, 35 (Spring, 1977), 18-19.

E. E. Duncan-Jones, "The Erect Sword in Marvell's Horation Ode," EA, 15 (April-June, 1962), 172-174.

Edwards, Imagination and Power, pp. 66-81.

Albert S. Gerard, _Expl_, 20 (Nov., 1961), 22.
  Rpt. _The Explicator Cyclopedia_, II, pp. 203-204.

L. D. Lerner, _Interpretations_, ed. John Wain, pp. 62-74.

Annabel Patterson, "Against Polarization: Literature and Politics in Marvell's Cromwell Poems," _ELR_, 5 (Spring, 1975), 254-256.

John M. Wallace, "Marvell's 'Horatian Ode,'" _PMLA_, 77 (March, 1962), 33-45.

Geoffrey Walton, "The Poetry of Andrew Marvell: A Summing Up," _Politics and Letters_, 1 (Summer, 1948), 32-33.

_____. "The Loyall Scott"
James Quivey, "Rhetoric and Frame: A Study of Method in Three Satires by Marvell," _TSL_, 18 (1973), 83-87.

____. "Mourning"
Paul Delany, "Marvell's 'Mourning,'" _MLQ_, 33 (March, 1972), 30-36.

_____. "The Mower Against Gardens"
Marcia E. Allentuck, "Marvell's 'Pool of Air,'" _MLN_, 74 (Nov., 1959), 587-589.

Dean R. Baldwin, _Expl_, 35 (Spring, 1977), 25-26.

Peter Berek, "The Voices of Marvell's Lyrics," _MLQ_, 32 (June, 1971), 147-151.

A. M. Cinquemani, _Expl_, 20 (May, 1962), 77.
  Rpt. _The Explicator Cyclopedia_, II, pp. 204-205.

Kitty Datta, "Marvell and Wotton: A Reconsideration," _RES_, 19 (Nov., 1968), 403-405.

Don Parry Norford, "Marvell and the Arts of Contemplation and Action," _ELH_, 41 (Spring, 1974), 61-62.

John D. Rosenberg, "Marvell and the Christian Idiom," _Boston University Studies in English_, 4 (Autumn, 1960), 158-161.

Nicholas A. Salerno, "Andrew Marvell and the Grafter's Art," _EA_, 21 (April-June, 1968), 125-132.

Carol Marks Sicherman, "The Mocking Voices of Donne and Marvell," _BuR_, 17 (May, 1969), 40-43.

Joseph H. Summers, "Marvell's 'Nature,'" _ELH_, 20 (June, 1953), 125-126.

Robert Wilcher, "Marvell's Cherry: A Reply to Mr. Salerno," _EA_, 23 (Oct.-Dec., 1970), 406-409.

_____. "Mower Poems"
Dean R. Baldwin, _Expl_, 35 (Spring, 1977), 25-26.

____. "The Mower's Song"
Barbara Everett, "Marvell's 'The Mower's Song,'" _CritQ_, 4 (Autumn, 1962), 219-224.

Geoffrey H. Hartman, "Marvell, St. Paul, and the Body of Hope," _ELH_, 31 (June, 1964), 189-192.

Ferry, _All in War with Time_, pp. 219-228.

Don Parry Norford, "Marvell and the Arts of Contemplation and Action," _ELH_, 41 (Spring, 1974), 66-67.

Joseph H. Summers, "Marvell's 'Nature,'" _ELH_, 20 (June, 1953), 127.

_____. "The Mower to the Glo-Worms"
John Creaser, "Marvell's Effortless Superiority," EIC, 20 (Oct., 1970), 409-412.

William Leigh Godshalk, Expl, 25 (Oct., 1966), 12.

Charles Mitchell, Expl, 18 (May, 1960), 50.
   Rpt. The Explicator Cyclopedia, II, p. 205.

Don Parry Norford, "Marvell and the Arts of Contemplation and Action," ELH, 41 (Spring, 1974), 63-65.

Jeffrey B. Spencer, Heroic Nature: Ideal Landscape in English Poetry from Marvell to Thomson (Evanston: Northwestern Univ. Press, 1973), pp. 89-93.

Tillyard, The Metaphysicals and Milton, pp. 32-35.

_____. "Musicks Empire"
Jonathan Goldberg, "The Typology of 'Musicks Empire,'" TSLL, 13 (Fall, 1971), 421-430.

_____. "The Nymph Complaining for the Death of Her Faun"
Allen, Image and Meaning, pp. 93-1194. New enlarged edition, pp. 165-186.

Don Cameron Allen, "Marvell's 'Nymph,'" ELH, 23 (June, 1956), 92-111.

Peter Berek, "The Voice of Marvell's Lyrics," MLQ, 32 (June, 1971), 151-153.

M. C. Bradbrook and M. G. Floyd Thomas, "Marvell and the Concept of Metamorphosis," The Criterion, 18 (Jan., 1939), 252-253.

Ruel E. Foster, "A Tonal Study: Marvell," The University of Kansas Review, 22 (Autumn, 1955), 73-78.

Nicholas Guild, "Marvell's 'The Nymph Complaining for the Death of Her Faun,'" MLQ, 29 (Dec., 1968), 385-394.

Geoffrey H. Hartman, "'The Nymph Complaining for the Death of Her Faun': A Brief Allegory," EIC, 18 (April, 1968), 131-135.

Evan Jones, Expl, 26 (May, 1968), 73.

Edward S. LeComte, "Marvell's 'The Nymph Complaining for the Death of Her Faun,'" MP, 50 (Nov., 1952), 97-101.

Pierre Legouis, "Marvell's 'Nymph Complaining for the Death of Her Faun': A Mise au Point," MLQ, 21 (March, 1960), 30-32.

Laurence Lerner, The Uses of Nostalgia: Studies in Pastoral Poetry (New York: Schocken Books, 1972), 192-195.

Earl Miner, "The Death of Innocence in Marvell's 'Nymph Complaining for the Death of Her Faun,'" MP, 65 (Aug., 1967), 9-16.

Miner, The Metaphysical Mode from Donne to Cowley, pp. 249-270.

Ruth Nevo, "Marvell's 'Songs of Innocence and Experience,'" SEL, 5 (Winter, 1965), 5-15.

Don Parry Norford, "Marvell and the Arts of Contemplation and Action," ELH, 41 (Spring, 1974), 56-60.

René Rapin, Expl, 28 (April, 1970), 71.

Jack E. Reese, "Marvell's 'Nymph' in a New Light," EA, 18 (Oct.-Dec., 1965), 398-401.

Leo Spitzer, "Marvell's 'Nymph Complaining for the Death of Her Faun': Sources Versus Meaning," MLQ, 19 (Sept., 1958), 231-243.
   Rpt. Essays on English and American Literature by Leo Spitzer, pp. 98-115.

Williamson, The Proper Wit of Poetry, pp. 100-101.

_____. "On a Drop of Dew"
Beaty and Matchett, Poetry: From Statement to Meaning, p. 56.

Empson, Seven Types of Ambiguity (1947 ed.), p. 80.

Ruth Nevo, "Marvell's 'Songs of Innocence and Experience,'" SEL, 5 (Winter, 1965), 1-3.

Wanamaker, Discordia Concors, pp. 88-97.

_____. "The Picture of Little T. C. in a Prospect of Flowers"
Peter Berek, "The Voices of Marvell's Lyrics," MLQ, 32 (June, 1971), 154-157.

Elsie Duncan-Jones, "T. C. of A Prospect of Flowers," TLS, Oct. 30, 1953, p. 693.

Dyson and Lovelock, Masterful Images, pp. 37-46.

Ferry, All in War with Time, pp. 200-210.

J. L. Simmons, Expl, 22 (April, 1964), 62.

Jeffrey B. Spencer, Heroic Nature: Ideal Landscape in English Poetry from Marvell to Thomson (Evanston: Northwestern Univ. Press, 1973), pp. 63-68.

Joseph H. Summer, "Marvell's 'Nature,'" ELH, 20 (June, 1953), 130-134.

Tillyard, Poetry Direct and Oblique, pp. 203-206.

Frank J. Warnke, "Play and Metamorphosis in Marvell's Poetry," SEL, 5 (Winter, 1965), 26-28.

Annabel Patterson, "Against Polarization: Literature and Politics in Marvell's Cromwell Poems," ELR, 5 (Spring, 1975), 268-272.

_____. "To His Coy Mistress"
B. O. Aboyade, Expl, 34 (May, 1976), 66.

Adams, The Contexts of Poetry, pp. 89-93.

Russell Ames, "Decadence in the Art of T. S. Eliot," Science and Society, 16 (Summer, 1952), 198-221.

Bateson, English Poetry, p. 9.

Michael Baumann, Expl, 31 (May, 1973), 72.

F. W. Bradbrook, "The Poetry of Andrew Marvell," in From Donne to Marvell, ed. Boris Ford (Baltimore: Penguin Books, 1956), pp. 196-197.

M. C. Bradbrook and M. G. Floyd Thomas, "Marvell and the Concept of Metamorphosis," The Criterion, 18 (Jan., 1939), 245-246.

Brooks, Purser, and Warren, An Approach to Literature, pp. 504-506.
   Rpt. third edition, pp. 393-395.
   Rpt. fourth edition, pp. 389-392.

Brown and Olmstead, Language and Literature, pp. 190-194.

John J. Carroll, "The Sun and the Lovers in 'To His Coy Mistress,'" MLN, 74 (Jan., 1959), 4-7.

Thomas Clayton, "'Morning Glew' and Other Sweat Leaves in the Folio Text of Andrew Marvell's Major Pre-Restoration Poems," ELR, 2 (Autumn, 1972), 365-375.

Cunningham, Tradition and Poetic Structure, pp. 41-48.

Robert Daniel, Expl, 1 (March, 1943), 37.
   Rpt. The Explicator Cyclopedia, II, p. 207.

Dickinson, Suggestions for Teachers of "Introduction to Literature," fifth edition, ed. Locke, Gibson, and Arms, pp. 11-12.   (Teacher's Manual)

Barbara DuBois, Expl, 34 (Jan., 1976), 39.

Anthony E. Farnham, "Saint Teresa and the Coy Mistress," Boston University Studies in English, 2 (Winter, 1956-1957), 226-231.

Ferry, All in War with Time, pp. 186-199.

Frederick L. Gwynn, Expl, 11 (May, 1953), 49.
   Rpt. The Explicator Cyclopedia, II, pp. 208-209.

Joan Hartwig, "The Principle of Measure in 'To His Coy Mistress,'" CE, 25 (May, 1964), 572-575.

Cherrill P. Heaton, Expl, 30 (Feb., 1972), 48.

Patrick G. Hogan, Jr., "Marvell's 'Vegetable Love,'" SP, 60 (Jan., 1963), 1-11.

Jerome, Poetry: Premeditated Art, pp. 110-113.

J. G. Keogh, Expl, 28 (Oct., 1969), 13.

Bruce King, "Irony in Marvell's 'To His Coy Mistress,'" SoR, 5 (Summer, 1969), 689-703.

Anthony Low and Paul J. Pival, "Rhetorical Pattern in Marvell's 'To His Coy Mistress,'" JEGP, 68 (July, 1969), 414-421.

Joseph J. Moldenhauer, "The Voices of Seduction in 'To His Coy Mistress': A Rhetorical Analysis," TSLL, 10 (Summer, 1968), 189-206.

Clarence H. Miller, "Sophistry and Truth in 'To His Coy Mistress,'" CollL, 2 (Spring, 1975), 97-104.

John Crowe Ransom, The New Criticism, pp. 311-313.

John Hawley Roberts, Expl, 1 (Dec., 1942), 17.
   Rpt. Readings for Liberal Education, II, 516-517.
   Rpt. The Explicator Cyclopedia, II, pp. 205-206.

Lawrence A. Sasek, Expl, 14 (April, 1956), 47.
   Rpt. The Explicator Cyclopedia, II, p. 208.

Roger Sharrock, "The Date of Marvell's 'To His Coy Mistress,'" TLS, Jan. 16, 1959, p. 33.

Stanley Stewart, "Marvell and the Ars Moriendi," in Seventeenth-Century Imagery: Essays on Uses of Figurative Language from Donne to Farquhar, ed. Earl Miner (Berkeley: Univ. of Calif. Press, 1971), pp. 133-150.

W. A. Turner, "The Not So Coy Mistress of J. Alfred Prufrock," SAQ, 54 (Oct., 1955), 520.

Geoffrey Walton, "The Poetry of Andrew Marvell: A Summing Up," Politics and Letters, 1 (Summer, 1948), 28-29.

Wanamaker, Discordia Concors, pp. 74-75.

Wheelwright, The Burning Fountain, pp. 112-113.

Williamson, The Proper Wit of Poetry, p. 101.

_____. "Tom May's Death"
Christine Rees, "'Tom May's Death' and Ben Jonson's Ghost: A Study of Marvell's Satiric Method," MLR, 71 (July, 1976), 481-488.

_____. "The Unfortunate Lover"
Ann Evans Berthoff, "The Voices of Allegory: Marvell's 'The Unfortunate Lover,'" MLQ, 27 (March, 1966), 41-50.

Ferry, All in War with Time, pp. 228-239.

J. Max Patrick, Expl, 20 (April, 1962), 65.
   Rpt. The Explicator Cyclopedia, II, pp. 208-209.

Nicholas A. Salerno, Expl, 18 (April, 1960), 42.

Peter T. Schwenger, "Marvell's 'Unfortunate Lover' as Device," MLQ, 35 (Dec., 1974), 364-375.

_____. "Upon the Death of the Lord Hastings"
Empson, Seven Types of Ambiguity, pp. 212-217; (1947 ed.), pp. 168-171.

_____. "Upon the Hill and Grove at Bill-borow"
Jeffrey B. Spencer, Heroic Nature: Ideal Landscape in English Poetry from Marvell to Thomson (Evanston: Northwestern Univ. Press, 1973), pp. 57-62.

MASEFIELD. "Cargoes"
   George Arms, Expl, 1 (Nov., 1942), 15.
      Rpt. The Explicator Cyclopedia, I, pp. 215-216.

   Blair and Gerber, Better Reading 2: Literature, pp. 176-177.

   Arthur Dickson, Expl, 2 (Nov., 1943), 12.
      Rpt. The Explicator Cyclopedia, I, p. 216.

   Roger P. McCutcheon, Expl, 2 (Feb., 1944), 31.
      Rpt. The Explicator Cyclopedia, I, p. 216.

   Clifford A. Nault, Jr., Expl, 16 (Feb., 1958), 31.
      Rpt. The Explicator Cyclopedia, I, pp. 216-217.

_____. "C. L. M."
   Walter Gierasch, Expl, 13 (Feb., 1955), 25.
      Rpt. The Explicator Cyclopedia, I, pp. 217-218.

_____. "The Racer"
   Cooper and Holmes, Preface to Poetry, pp. 170-173.

_____. "Sea Fever"
   Cunningham, Literature as a Fine Art: Analysis and Interpretation, pp. 160-164.

   Francis V. Lloyd, Jr., Expl, 3 (March, 1945), 36.
      Rpt. The Explicator Cyclopedia, I, p. 218.

_____. "Alfred Noir"
   Herb Russell, Expl, 31 (March, 1973), 54.

_____.   "The Lost Orchard"
    Richard E. Amacher, Expl, 7 (March, 1949), 38.
       Rpt. The Explicator Cyclopedia, I, pp. 218-219.

    Mary B. Deaton, Expl, 8 (Nov., 1949), 16.
       Rpt. The Explicator Cyclopedia, I, pp. 219-220.

MELVILLE.   "America, I"
    George Monteiro, Expl, 32 (May, 1974), 72.

_____.   "The Apparition: A Retrospect"
    Robert Penn Warren, "Melville the Poet," The Kenyon Review, 8 (Spring,
    1946), 216-218.

_____.   "Art"
    Leo Hamalian, Expl, 8 (March, 1950), 40.
       Rpt. The Explicator Cyclopedia, II, pp. 209-210.

_____.   "The Berg"
    Lawrence H. Martin, Jr., "Melville and Christianity: The Late Poems,"
    MSE, 2 (Spring, 1969), 14-15.

_____.   "Billy in the Darbies"
    Brooks, Lewis, and Warren, American Literature, pp. 929-930.

_____.   "Commemorative of a Naval Victory"
    Brooks, Purser, and Warren, An Approach to Literature, third edition,
    pp. 344-345.
       Rpt. fourth edition, pp. 342-343.

_____.   "The Conflict of Convictions"
    Robert Penn Warren, "Melville the Poet," The Kenyon Review, 8 (Spring,
    1946), 213-214 et passim.

_____.   "The Haglets"
    Richard Harter Fogle, "The Themes of Melville's Later Poetry," TSE, 11
    (1961), 72-73.

    Lawrence H. Martin, Jr., "Melville and Christianity: The Late Poems,"
    MSE, 2 (Spring, 1969), 13-14.

_____.   "In a Bye-Canal"
    Robert Penn Warren, "Melville the Poet," The Kenyon Review, 8 (Spring,
    1946), 209-211.

_____.   "The Little Good Fellows"
    William Bysshe Stein, "Melville's Poetry: Two Rising Notes," ESQ, No.
    27, (Second Quarter, 1962), 12-13.

_____.   "The Maldive Shark"
    Lawrence H. Martin, Jr., "Melville and Christianity: The Late Poems,"
    MSE, 2 (Spring, 1969), 14.

    Robert Penn Warren, "Melville the Poet," The Kenyon Review, 8 (Spring,
    1946), 218 et passim.

_____.   "Monody"
    Charles N. Watson, Jr., "The Estrangement of Hawthorne and Melville,"
    NEQ, 46 (Sept., 1973), 380-402.

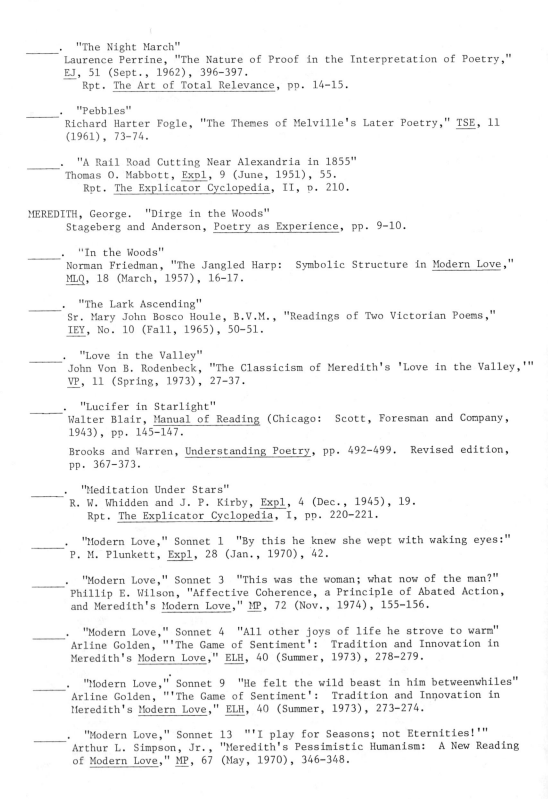

_____ . "The Night March"
Laurence Perrine, "The Nature of Proof in the Interpretation of Poetry,"
EJ, 51 (Sept., 1962), 396-397.
　　Rpt. The Art of Total Relevance, pp. 14-15.

_____ . "Pebbles"
Richard Harter Fogle, "The Themes of Melville's Later Poetry," TSE, 11
(1961), 73-74.

_____ . "A Rail Road Cutting Near Alexandria in 1855"
Thomas O. Mabbott, Expl, 9 (June, 1951), 55.
　　Rpt. The Explicator Cyclopedia, II, p. 210.

MEREDITH, George. "Dirge in the Woods"
Stageberg and Anderson, Poetry as Experience, pp. 9-10.

_____ . "In the Woods"
Norman Friedman, "The Jangled Harp: Symbolic Structure in Modern Love,"
MLQ, 18 (March, 1957), 16-17.

_____ . "The Lark Ascending"
Sr. Mary John Bosco Houle, B.V.M., "Readings of Two Victorian Poems,"
IEY, No. 10 (Fall, 1965), 50-51.

_____ . "Love in the Valley"
John Von B. Rodenbeck, "The Classicism of Meredith's 'Love in the Valley,'"
VP, 11 (Spring, 1973), 27-37.

_____ . "Lucifer in Starlight"
Walter Blair, Manual of Reading (Chicago: Scott, Foresman and Company,
1943), pp. 145-147.

Brooks and Warren, Understanding Poetry, pp. 492-499. Revised edition,
pp. 367-373.

_____ . "Meditation Under Stars"
R. W. Whidden and J. P. Kirby, Expl, 4 (Dec., 1945), 19.
　　Rpt. The Explicator Cyclopedia, I, pp. 220-221.

_____ . "Modern Love," Sonnet 1 "By this he knew she wept with waking eyes:"
P. M. Plunkett, Expl, 28 (Jan., 1970), 42.

_____ . "Modern Love," Sonnet 3 "This was the woman; what now of the man?"
Phillip E. Wilson, "Affective Coherence, a Principle of Abated Action,
and Meredith's Modern Love," MP, 72 (Nov., 1974), 155-156.

_____ . "Modern Love," Sonnet 4 "All other joys of life he strove to warm"
Arline Golden, "'The Game of Sentiment': Tradition and Innovation in
Meredith's Modern Love," ELH, 40 (Summer, 1973), 278-279.

_____ . "Modern Love," Sonnet 9 "He felt the wild beast in him betweenwhiles"
Arline Golden, "'The Game of Sentiment': Tradition and Innovation in
Meredith's Modern Love," ELH, 40 (Summer, 1973), 273-274.

_____ . "Modern Love," Sonnet 13 "'I play for Seasons; not Eternities!'"
Arthur L. Simpson, Jr., "Meredith's Pessimistic Humanism: A New Reading
of Modern Love," MP, 67 (May, 1970), 346-348.

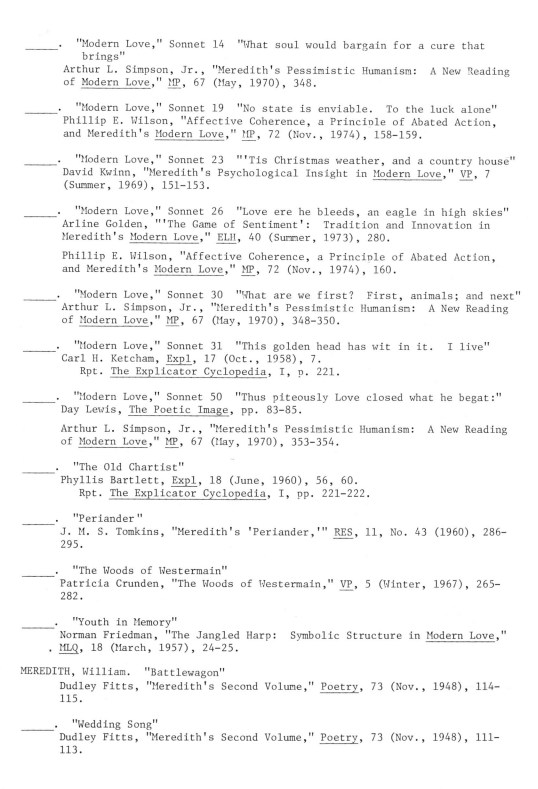

_____. "Modern Love," Sonnet 14   "What soul would bargain for a cure that brings"
Arthur L. Simpson, Jr., "Meredith's Pessimistic Humanism: A New Reading of Modern Love," MP, 67 (May, 1970), 348.

_____. "Modern Love," Sonnet 19   "No state is enviable. To the luck alone"
Phillip E. Wilson, "Affective Coherence, a Principle of Abated Action, and Meredith's Modern Love," MP, 72 (Nov., 1974), 158-159.

_____. "Modern Love," Sonnet 23   "'Tis Christmas weather, and a country house"
David Kwinn, "Meredith's Psychological Insight in Modern Love," VP, 7 (Summer, 1969), 151-153.

_____. "Modern Love," Sonnet 26   "Love ere he bleeds, an eagle in high skies"
Arline Golden, "'The Game of Sentiment': Tradition and Innovation in Meredith's Modern Love," ELH, 40 (Summer, 1973), 280.

Phillip E. Wilson, "Affective Coherence, a Principle of Abated Action, and Meredith's Modern Love," MP, 72 (Nov., 1974), 160.

_____. "Modern Love," Sonnet 30   "What are we first? First, animals; and next"
Arthur L. Simpson, Jr., "Meredith's Pessimistic Humanism: A New Reading of Modern Love," MP, 67 (May, 1970), 348-350.

_____. "Modern Love," Sonnet 31   "This golden head has wit in it. I live"
Carl H. Ketcham, Expl, 17 (Oct., 1958), 7.
   Rpt. The Explicator Cyclopedia, I, p. 221.

_____. "Modern Love," Sonnet 50   "Thus piteously Love closed what he begat:"
Day Lewis, The Poetic Image, pp. 83-85.

Arthur L. Simpson, Jr., "Meredith's Pessimistic Humanism: A New Reading of Modern Love," MP, 67 (May, 1970), 353-354.

_____. "The Old Chartist"
Phyllis Bartlett, Expl, 18 (June, 1960), 56, 60.
   Rpt. The Explicator Cyclopedia, I, pp. 221-222.

_____. "Periander"
J. M. S. Tomkins, "Meredith's 'Periander,'" RES, 11, No. 43 (1960), 286-295.

_____. "The Woods of Westermain"
Patricia Crunden, "The Woods of Westermain," VP, 5 (Winter, 1967), 265-282.

_____. "Youth in Memory"
Norman Friedman, "The Jangled Harp: Symbolic Structure in Modern Love," . MLQ, 18 (March, 1957), 24-25.

MEREDITH, William. "Battlewagon"
Dudley Fitts, "Meredith's Second Volume," Poetry, 73 (Nov., 1948), 114-115.

_____. "Wedding Song"
Dudley Fitts, "Meredith's Second Volume," Poetry, 73 (Nov., 1948), 111-113.

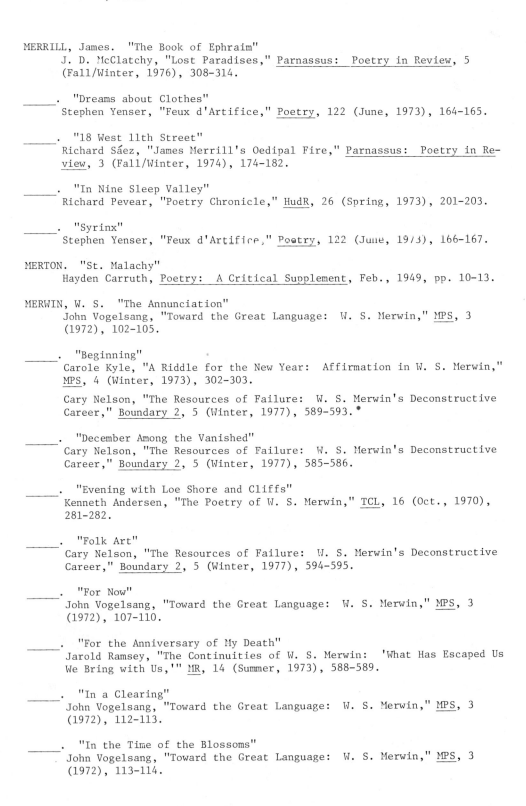

MERRILL, James. "The Book of Ephraim"
        J. D. McClatchy, "Lost Paradises," Parnassus: Poetry in Review, 5
        (Fall/Winter, 1976), 308-314.

_____. "Dreams about Clothes"
        Stephen Yenser, "Feux d'Artifice," Poetry, 122 (June, 1973), 164-165.

_____. "18 West 11th Street"
        Richard Sáez, "James Merrill's Oedipal Fire," Parnassus: Poetry in Re-
        view, 3 (Fall/Winter, 1974), 174-182.

_____. "In Nine Sleep Valley"
        Richard Pevear, "Poetry Chronicle," HudR, 26 (Spring, 1973), 201-203.

_____. "Syrinx"
        Stephen Yenser, "Feux d'Artifice," Poetry, 122 (June, 1973), 166-167.

MERTON. "St. Malachy"
        Hayden Carruth, Poetry: A Critical Supplement, Feb., 1949, pp. 10-13.

MERWIN, W. S. "The Annunciation"
        John Vogelsang, "Toward the Great Language: W. S. Merwin," MPS, 3
        (1972), 102-105.

_____. "Beginning"
        Carole Kyle, "A Riddle for the New Year: Affirmation in W. S. Merwin,"
        MPS, 4 (Winter, 1973), 302-303.

        Cary Nelson, "The Resources of Failure: W. S. Merwin's Deconstructive
        Career," Boundary 2, 5 (Winter, 1977), 589-593. *

_____. "December Among the Vanished"
        Cary Nelson, "The Resources of Failure: W. S. Merwin's Deconstructive
        Career," Boundary 2, 5 (Winter, 1977), 585-586.

_____. "Evening with Loe Shore and Cliffs"
        Kenneth Andersen, "The Poetry of W. S. Merwin," TCL, 16 (Oct., 1970),
        281-282.

_____. "Folk Art"
        Cary Nelson, "The Resources of Failure: W. S. Merwin's Deconstructive
        Career," Boundary 2, 5 (Winter, 1977), 594-595.

_____. "For Now"
        John Vogelsang, "Toward the Great Language: W. S. Merwin," MPS, 3
        (1972), 107-110.

_____. "For the Anniversary of My Death"
        Jarold Ramsey, "The Continuities of W. S. Merwin: 'What Has Escaped Us
        We Bring with Us,'" MR, 14 (Summer, 1973), 588-589.

_____. "In a Clearing"
        John Vogelsang, "Toward the Great Language: W. S. Merwin," MPS, 3
        (1972), 112-113.

_____. "In the Time of the Blossoms"
        John Vogelsang, "Toward the Great Language: W. S. Merwin," MPS, 3
        (1972), 113-114.

_____. "Learning a Dead Language"
John Vogelsang, "Toward the Great Language: W. S. Merwin," MPS, 3
(1972), 105-107.

_____. "Lemuel's Blessing"
Carroll, The Poem in Its Skin, pp. 142-152.

_____. "Memory of Spring"
John Vogelsang, "Toward the Great Language: W. S. Merwin," MPS, 3
(1972), 114.
Evan Watkins, The Critical Act: Criticism and Community (New Haven:
Yale Univ. Press, 1978), p. 224.

_____. "Odysseus"
Cheri Colby Davis, "Merwin's Odysseus," CP, 8 (Spring, 1975), 25-27.

_____. "The Port"
Cheri Colby Davis, "Time and Timelessness in the Poetry of W. S. Merwin,"
MPS, 6 (Winter, 1975), 229-231.

_____. "The Prodigal Son"
John Vogelsang, "Toward the Great Language: W. S. Merwin," MPS, 3
(1972), 99-105.

_____. "Psalm: Our Fathers"
John Vogelsang, "Toward the Great Language: W. S. Merwin," MPS, 3
(1972), 116-118.

_____. "Signs"
John Vogelsang, "Toward the Great Language: W. S. Merwin," MPS, 3
(1972), 115.

_____. "Under Black Leaves"
Cheri Colby Davis, "Time and Timelessness in the Poetry of W. S. Merwin,"
MPS, 6 (Winter, 1975), 232-235.

_____. "Whenever I Go There"
Robert Pinsky, The Situation of Poetry: Contemporary Poetry and Its
Traditions (Princeton, New Jersey: Princeton Univ. Press, 1976),
pp. 92-95.

_____. "When You Go Away"
Jan B. Gordon, "The Dwelling of Disappearance: W. S. Merwin's The Lice,"
MPS, 3 (1972), 129-130.

METCALFE, James. "Pray in May"
    Perrine, The Art of Total Relevance, pp. 111-118.

MIDDLETON, Christopher. "Male Torso"
    Wallace D. Martin, "Beyond Modernism: Christopher Middleton and Geoffrey
    Hill," ConL, 12 (Autumn, 1971), 422.

MILLAY. "Euclid Alone Has Looked on Beauty Bare"
    Bradford A. Booth, Expl, 6 (Oct., 1947), 5.
        Rpt. The Explicator Cyclopedia, I, p. 223.

    Cooper and Holmes, Preface to Poetry, pp. 46-53.

Arthur Dickson, Expl, 3 (Dec., 1944), 23.
  Rpt. The Explicator Cyclopedia, I, pp. 222-223.

Arthur Dickson, Expl, 6 (May, 1948), 49.
  Rpt. The Explicator Cyclopedia, I, pp. 223-224.

Drew and Sweeney, Directions in Modern Poetry, pp. 207-208.
  Rpt. Douglas, Lamson, Smith, The Critical Reader, pp. 110-111.

Carl A. Niemeyer and Robert M. Gay, Expl, 1 (Nov., 1942), 16.

_____. "God's World"
Sanders, The Discovery of Poetry, pp. 132-138.

_____. "Memorial to D. C.: Elegy"
Walter Gierasch, Expl, 2 (May, 1944), 23.
  Rpt. The Explicator Cyclopedia, I, p. 224.

_____. "Oh, Oh, You Will Be Sorry for that Word"
Perrine and Reid, 100 American Poems, pp. 165-166

_____. "Oh, Sleep Forever in the Latmian Cave"
John Crowe Ransom, "The Poet as Woman," SoR, 2 (Spring, 1937), 788-790.

Ransom, The World's Body, pp. 83-86.

_____. "On Hearing a Symphony of Beethoven"
Perrine and Reid, 100 American Poems, pp. 167-168.

_____. "The Return"
John Crowe Ransom, "The Poet as Woman," SoR, 2 (Spring, 1937), 804-806.

Ransom, The World's Body, pp. 107-110.

_____. "What's This of Death, from You Who Never Will Die?"
William Elton, Expl, 7 (March, 1949), 37.
  Rpt. The Explicator Cyclopedia, I, pp. 224-225.

Richards, Practical Criticism, pp. 62-79 et passim.

MILTON. "L'Allegro"
Victor Erlich, "Milton's Early Poetry: Its Christian Humanism," AI, 32 (Spring, 1975), 92-96.

H. Wendell Howard, Expl, 24 (Sept., 1965), 3.

C. Harold Hurley, "Comment and Controversy," ELN, 12 (March, 1975), 193-194.

C. Harold Hurley, "The Cheerful Man's Sorrow: A Key to the Meaning of 'L'Allegro,'" ELN, 11 (June, 1974), 275-278.

John M. Major, "Comment and Controversy," ELN, 12 (Dec., 1974), 124-125.

Edith Riggs, Expl, 23 (Feb., 1965), 44.

Mark L. Scher, "Milton's 'Fallows Gray': L'Allegro 71," ES, 52 (Dec., 1971), 518-520.

P. B. Tillyard, "What is a Beck?" TLS, July 25, 1952, p. 485.

George Walton Williams, Expl, 34 (Oct., 1975), 15.

_____. "L'Allegro" and "Il Penseroso"
Lawrence Babb, "The Background of 'Il Penseroso,'" SP, 37 (April, 1940), 257-273.

Leslie Brisman, "'All Before Them Where to Choose': 'L'Allegro and 'Il Penseroso,'" JEGP, 71 (April, 1972), 226-240.

Brooks, The Well Wrought Urn, pp. 47-61.

Nan Cooke Carpenter, "The Place of Music in L'Allegro and Il Penseroso," UTQ, 22 (July, 1953), 354-367.

T. S. Eliot, "A Note on the Verse of John Milton," Essays and Studies, 21 (1935), 34-35.

Michael Fixler, "The Orphic Technique of 'L'Allegro' and 'Il Penseroso,'" ELR, 1 (Spring, 1971), 165-177.

George L. Geckle, "Miltonic Idealism: L'Allegro and Il Penseroso," TSLL, 9 (Winter, 1968), 455-473.

J. P. Hardy, Reinterpretations: Essays on Poems by Milton, Pope, and Johnson (London: Routledge Kegan Paul, 1971), pp. 1-27.

John F. Huntley, "The Poet-Critic and His Poem-Culture in 'L'Allegro' and 'Il Penseroso,'" TSLL, 13 (Winter, 1972), 541-553.

Knight, The Burning Oracle, pp. 59-63.

Bridget Gellert Lyons, Voices of Melancholy: Studies in Literary Treatments of Melancholy in Renaissance England (New York: Barnes & Noble, 1971), pp. 151-161.

Phyllis MacKenzie, "Milton's Visual Imagination: An Answer to T. S. Eliot," UTQ, 15 (Oct., 1946), 18-20.

David M. Miller, "From Delusion to Illumination: A Larger Structure for L'Allegro-Il Penseroso," PMLA, 86 (Jan., 1971), 32-39.

Vincent F. Petronella, Expl, 28 (Jan., 1970), 40.

Gary Stringer, "The Unity of 'L'Allegro' and 'Il Penseroso,'" TSLL, 12 (Summer, 1970), 221-229.

Kathleen M. Swaim, "Time and Structure in L'Allegro and Il Penseroso," TSLL, 18 (Fall, 1976), 422-432.

Kester Svendsen, Expl, 8 (May, 1950), 49.
  Rpt. The Explicator Cyclopedia, II, pp. 212-214.

Marilyn L. Williamson, "The Myth of Orpheus in 'L'Allegro' and 'Il Penseroso,'" MLQ, 32 (Dec., 1971), 377-386.

_____. "At a Solemn Music"
Sharon Cumberland and Lynn Veach Sadler, "Phantasia: A Pattern in Milton's Early Poems," MiltonQ, 8 (May, 1974), 52.

Donald Friedman, "Harmony and the Poet's Voice in Some of Milton's Early Poems," MLQ, 30 (Dec., 1969), 533-534.

Arnold Stein, "A Note on Meter," in Discussions of Poetry: Rhythm and Sound, ed. George Hemphill (Boston: D. C. Heath and Company, 1961), pp. 100-106.

_____. "At a Vacation Exercise in the College"
Gordon Campbell, "The Satire on Aristotelian Logic in Milton's 'Vacation Exercise,'" ELN, 15 (Dec., 1977), 106-110.

Donald Friedman, "Harmony and the Poet's Voice in Some of Milton's Early Poems," MLQ, 30 (Dec., 1969), 527-528.

_____. "An Epitaph on the Marchioness of Winchester"
Donald Friedman, "Harmony and the Poet's Voice in Some of Milton's Early Poems," MLQ, 30 (Dec., 1969), 530-531.

Gayle Edward Wilson, "Decorum and Milton's 'An Epitaph on the Marchioness of Winchester,'" MiltonQ, 8 (March, 1974), 11-14.

_____. "Cyriack, this three years day these eys" (Sonnet 22)
William McCarthy, "The Continuity of Milton's Sonnets," PMLA, 92 (Jan., 1977), 104, 106.

_____. "How Soon Hath Time" (Sonnet 7)
"On His Having Arrived at the Age of Twenty-Three"

D. C. Dorian, Expl, 8 (Nov., 1949), 10.
     Rpt. The Explicator Cyclopedia, II, p. 218.

Roberts W. French, "Reading a Poem: Two Sonnets by Milton," CP, 2 (Fall, 1969), 11-16.

Donald Friedman, "Harmony and the Poet's Voice in Some of Milton's Early Poems," MLQ, 30 (Dec., 1969), 532-533.

William McCarthy, "The Continuity of Milton's Sonnets," PMLA, 92 (Jan., 1972), 100.

Partridge, The Language of Renaissance Poetry, pp. 268-270.

Kester Svendsen, Expl, 7 (May, 1949), 53.
     Rpt. The Explicator Cyclopedia, II, pp. 217-218.

_____. "I Did But Prompt the Age to Quit Their Clogs" (Sonnet 12)
W. R. Parker, Expl, 8 (Oct., 1949), 3.

D. F. Rauber, "Milton's Sonnet XII--'I Did But Prompt...,'" PQ, 49 (Oct., 1970), 561-564.

_____. "Lady that in the prime of earliest youth" (Sonnet 9)
William McCarthy, "The Continuity of Milton's Sonnets," PMLA, 92 (Jan., 1977), 101.

_____. "Lawrence of Virtuous Father Virtuous Son" (Sonnet 20)
Ralph W. Condee, "Milton's Gawdy-Day with Lawrence," in Directions in Literary Criticism: Contemporary Approaches to Literature, ed. Stanley Weintraub and Philip Young (Univ. Park and London: Penn. State Univ. Press, 1973), pp. 86-92.

William McCarthy, "The Continuity of Milton's Sonnets," PMLA, 92 (Jan., 1977), 103-104, 106.

Frank Nieman, "Milton's Sonnet XX," PMLA, 64 (June, 1949), 480-483.

_____. "Lycidas"
Richard P. Adams, "The Archetypal Pattern of Death and Rebirth in Milton's Lycidas," PMLA, 64 (March, 1949), 183-188.

Robert Martin Adams, "Bounding 'Lycidas,'" HudR, 23 (Summer, 1970), 293-304.

Barbara Currier Bell, "'Lycidas' and the Stages of Grief," L&P, 25, No. 4 (1975), 166-174.

Brett, Reason and Imagination, pp. 39-50.

J. B. Broadbent, "Milton's Rhetoric," MP, 56 (May, 1959), 224-242.

David K. Cornelius and Kathryn Thompson, Expl, 31 (Dec., 1972), 25.

Daiches, A Study of Literature, pp. 170-195.

Edgar F. Daniels, "Climactic Rhythms in 'Lycidas,'" AN&Q, 6 (March, 1968), 100-101.

Edgar F. Daniels, Expl, 21 (Jan., 1963), 43.

Victor Erlich, "Milton's Early Poetry: Its Christian Humanism," AI, 32 (Spring, 1975), 106-111.

David R. Fabian, "The 'Blind Mouths' Passage in Lycidas," AN&Q, 6 (May, 1968), 136-137.

James F. Forrest, "The Significance of Milton's 'Mantle Blue,'" MiltonQ, 8 (May, 1974), 41-48.

Robert C. Fox, Expl, 9 (June, 1951), 54.
    Rpt. The Explicator Cyclopedia, II, pp. 216-217.

J. Milton French, "The Digressions in Milton's 'Lycidas,'" SP, 50 (July, 1953), 485-490.

Roberts W. French, "Voice and Structure in Lycidas," TSLL, 12 (Spring, 1970), 15-25.

Christopher Grose, "Lucky Words: Process of Speech in Lycidas," JEGP, 70 (July, 1971), 383-403.

John Edward Hardy, "REconsideration I: Lycidas," The Kenyon Review, 7 (Winter, 1945), 99-113.

J. P. Hardy, Reinterpretations: Essays on Poems by Milton, Pope, and Johnson (London: Routledge & Kegan Paul, 1971), pp. 28-49.

Hardy, The Curious Frame, pp. 27-44.

Ralph E. Hone, "The Pilot of the Galilean Lake," SP, 56 (Jan., 1959), 55-62.

Leon Howard, "'That Two-Handed Engine' Once More," HLQ, 15 (Feb., 1952), 173-184.

R. E. Hughes, "'That Two-Handed Engine'--Again," N&Q, 2, n.s. (Feb., 1955), 58-59.

Ellen Zetzel Lambert, Placing Sorrow: A Study of the Pastoral Elegy Convention from Theocritus to Milton (Chapel Hill: Univ. of N.C. Press, 1976), pp. 154-186.

Marcia Landy, "Language and Mourning in 'Lycidas,'" AI, 30 (Fall, 1973), 294-312.

Steven J. Lautermilch, "'That Fatal and Perfidious Bark': A Key to the Double Design and Unity of Milton's Lycidas," RenQ, 30 (Summer, 1977), 201-216.

Jon S. Lawry, "'The Faithful Herdman's Art' in Lycidas," SEL, 13 (Winter, 1973), 111-125.

Michael Lloyd, "The Two Worlds of 'Lycidas,'" EIC, 11 (Oct., 1961), 390-402.

Winifred Lynskey, "A Critic in Action: Mr. Ransom," CE, 5 (Feb., 1944), 242-243.

Thomas O. Mabbott, Expl, 5 (Feb., 1947), 26.
    Rpt. The Explicator Cyclopedia, II, pp. 215-216.

Maynard Mack, English Masterpieces, Vol. IV, Milton, pp. 9-11.

Michael Macklem, "The Elegiac Theme in Housman," QQ, 59 (Spring, 1952), 46-47.

William G. Madsen, "The Voice of Michael in 'Lycidas,'" SEL, 3 (Winter, 1963), 1-7.

Emerson R. Marks, Expl, 9 (April, 1951), 44.
    Rpt. The Explicator Cyclopedia, II, pp. 214-215.

George O. Marshall, Jr., Expl, 17 (June, 1959), 66.
    Rpt. The Explicator Cyclopedia, II, p. 215.

Caroline W. Mayerson, "The Orpheus Image in Lycidas," PMLA, 64 (March, 1949), 189-207.

Miles, The Primary Language of Poetry in the 1640's, pp. 88-90.

Paul Elmer More, "How to Read 'Lycidas,'" The American Review, 8 (May, 1936), 140-158.
    Rpt. Criticism, pp. 539-545.
    Rpt. Zabel, Literary Opinion in America, revised edition, pp. 146-156.

Partridge, The Language of Renaissance Poetry, pp. 276-289.

Renato Poggioli, The Oaten Flute: Essays on Pastoral Poetry and the Pastoral Ideal (Cambridge, Mass.: Harvard Univ. Press, 1975), 83-104.

Balachandra Rajan, "Lycidas: The Shattering of the Leaves," SP, 64 (Jan., 1967), 51-64.

John H. Raleigh, "Lycidas: 'Yet Once More,'" PrS, 42 (Winter, 1969), 303-318.

John Crowe Ransom, "A Poem Nearly Anonymous," The American Review, 1 (May, Sept., 1933), 179-203, 444-467.
    Rpt. Criticism, pp. 333-342.

Ransom, The World's Body, pp. 1-54.

Joanne M. Riley, "Milton's 'Lycidas': New Light on the Title," N&Q, 24 (Dec., 1977), 545.

Harry F. Robins, "Milton's 'Two-Handed Engine at the Door' and St. Matthew's Gospel," RES, 6 (Jan., 1954), 25-36.

Malcolm M. Ross, "Milton and the Protestant Aesthetic: The Early Poems," UTQ, 17 (July, 1948), 358-360.

J. W. Saunders, "Milton, Diomede, and Amaryllis," ELH, 22 (Dec., 1955) 255-256, 260-261.

Edward C. Schweitzer, Expl, 28 (Oct., 1969), 18.

Wayne Shumaker, "Flowerets and Sounding Seas: A Study of the Affective Structure of Lycidas," PMLA, 66 (June, 1951), 485-494.

Eric Smith, By Mourning Tongues: Studies in English Elegy (Ipswich and Totowa: The Boydell Press and Rowan and Littlefield, 1977), pp. 22-39.

Edward E. Sullivan, Jr., "'Sweet Societies That Sing': The Voice of the Saints in Lycidas," ELWIU, 3 (Spring, 1976), 32-40.

Kathleen M. Swaim, "Lycidas and the Dolphins of Apollo," JEGP, 72 (July, 1973), 340-349.

Thomas and Brown, Reading Poems: An Introduction to Critical Study, pp. 692-694.

Claude Adelbert Thompson, "'That Two-Handed Engine' Will Smite: Time Will Have a Stop," SP, 59 (April, 1962), 184-200.

Tillyard, Poetry Direct and Oblique, pp. 208-213.

Harold E. Toliver, Pastoral: Forms and Attitudes (Berkeley: Univ. of Calif. Press, 1971), pp. 170-176.

Alberta Turner, "The Sound of Grief: A Reconsideration of the Nature and Function of the Unrhymed Lines in Lycidas," MiltonQ, 10 (Oct., 1976), 67-73.

W. Arthur Turner, "Milton's Two-Handed Engine," JEGP, 49 (Oct., 1950), 562-565.

Edward Wagenknecht, "Milton in 'Lycidas,'" CE, 7 (April, 1946), 393-397.

Ruth C. Wallerstein, "Rhetoric in the English Renaissance: Two Elegies," English Institute Essays 1948, pp. 170-178.

Joseph Anthony Wittreich, Jr., Expl, 26 (Oct., 1967), 17.

Joseph Anthony Wittreich, Jr., "Milton's 'Destined Urn': The Art of Lycidas," PMLA, 84 (Jan., 1969), 60-70.

_____. "Methought I Saw My Late Espoused Saint" (Sonnet 23)
John Huntley, "Milton's 23rd Sonnet," ELH, 34 (Dec., 1967), 468-481.

Edward S. Le Comte, "The Veiled Face of Milton's Wife," N&Q, 1, n.s. (June, 1954), 245-246.

William McCarthy, "The Continuity of Milton's Sonnets," PMLA, 92 (Jan., 1977), 106-107.

Ribner and Morris, Poetry: A Critical and Historical Introduction, pp. 176-178.

Leo Spitzer, "Understanding Milton," The Hopkins Review, 4 (Summer, 1951), 16-27.
   Rpt. Essays on English and American Literature by Leo Spitzer, pp. 116-131.

Tillyard, The Metaphysicals and Milton, pp. 7-11.

John C. Ulreich, "Typological Symbolism In Milton's Sonnet XXIII," MiltonQ, 8 (March, 1974), 7-10.

Vivante, English Poetry, pp. 73-74.

Thomas Wheeler, "Milton's Twenty-third Sonnet," SP, 58 (July, 1961), 510-515.

_____. "On His Blindness" (Sonnet 19) "When I consider how my light is spent"
Cooper and Holmes, Preface to Poetry, pp. 231-234.

Daniels, The Art of Reading Poetry, pp. 34-36. Abridged in The Case for Poetry, pp. 273-274.

Donald C. Dorian, Expl, 10 (Dec., 1951), 16. Abridged in The Case for Poetry, p. 274.
   Rpt. The Explicator Cyclopedia, II, p. 217.

Dixon Fiske, "Milton in the Middle of Life: Sonnet XIX," ELH, 41 (Spring, 1974), 37-49.

Roberts W. French, "Reading a Poem: Two Sonnets by Milton," CP, 2 (Fall, 1969), 11-16.

Goodman, The Structure of Literature, pp. 204-215.

Ann Gossman and George W. Whiting, "Milton's First Sonnet on His Blindness," RES, 12, 48 (1961), 364-372.

Evelyn J. Hinz, "New Light 'On His Blindness,'" MSE, 2 (Spring, 1969), 1-10.

John F. Huntley, "The Ecology and Anatomy of Criticism: Milton's Sonnet 19 and the Bee Simile in Paradise Lost, I, 768-778," JAAC, 24 (Spring, 1966), 386-388.

J. L. Jackson and W. E. Weese, "'...Who Only Stand and Wait': Milton's Sonnet 'On His Blindness,'" MLN, 72 (Feb., 1957), 91-93.

Jerome, Poetry: Premeditated Art, pp. 294-300.

Lysander Kemp, "On a Sonnet by Milton," The Hopkins Review, 6 (Fall, 1952), 80-83.
     Rpt. in The Case for Poetry, pp. 274-275.

William McCarthy, "The Continuity of Milton's Sonnets," PMLA, 92 (Jan., 1977), 103.

George Monteiro, Expl, 24 (April, 1966), 67.

William R. Parker, "The Dates of Milton's Sonnets on His Blindness," PMLA, 73 (June, 1958), 199-200.

Harry R. Robins, "Milton's First Sonnet on His Blindness," RES, 7, n.s. (Oct., 1956), 362-366.

Murray Roston, The Soul of Wit: A Study of John Donne (Oxford: Clarendon Press, 1974), pp. 61-62.

Roger L. Slakey, "Milton's Sonnet 'On His Blindness,'" ELH, 27 (June, 1960), 122-130.

Thomas B. Stroup, "'When I Consider': Milton's Sonnet XIX," SP, 69 (April, 1972), 242-258.

_____. "On Shakespeare 1630"
Partridge, The Language of Renaissance Poetry, pp. 266-268.

_____. "On the Death of a Fair Infant Dying of a Cough"
Jackson E. Cope, "Fortunate Falls as Form in Milton's 'Fair Infant,'" JEGP, 63 (Oct., 1964), 660-674.

Donald Friedman, "Harmony and the Poet's Voice in Some of Milton's Early Poems," MLQ, 30 (Dec., 1969), 526-527.

Victor Erlich, "Milton's Early Poetry: Its Christian Humanism," AI, 32 (Spring, 1975), 77-87.

Hugh N. MacLean, "Milton's 'Fair Infant,'" ELH, 24 (Dec., 1957), 296-305.

_____. "On the Late Massacre in Piedmont" (Sonnet 18)
David S. Berkeley, Expl, 15 (June, 1957), 58.

Sheila Blanchard, "Milton's Foothill: Pattern in the Piedmont Sonnet," Genre, 4 (March, 1971), 39-44.

Sanford Budick, <u>Poetry of Civilization: Mythopoeic Displacement in the</u>
<u>Verse of Milton, Dryden, Pope, and Johnson</u> (New Haven and London: Yale
Univ. Press, 1974), pp. 42-45.

Charles E. Goldstein, "The Hebrew Element in Milton's Sonnet XVIII,"
<u>MiltonQ</u>, 9 (Dec., 1975), 111-114.

William McCarthy, "The Continuity of Milton's Sonnets," <u>PMLA</u>, 92 (Jan.,
1977), 102-103.

Kester Svendson, "Milton's Sonnet on the Massacre in Piedmont," <u>The</u>
<u>Shakespeare Association Bulletin</u>, 20 (Oct., 1945), 147-155.

Van Doren, <u>Introduction to Poetry</u>, pp. 121-123.

_____. "On The Lord General Fairfax, at the Siege of Colchester" (Sonnet 15)
William McCarthy, "The Continuity of Milton's Sonnets," <u>PMLA</u>, 92 (Jan.,
1977), 101-102.

John T. Shawcross, "Milton's 'Fairfax' Sonnet," <u>N&Q</u>, 2, n.s. (May, 1955),
195-196.

_____. "Nativity Ode"
Stephen C. Behrendt, "Blake's Illustrations to Milton's <u>Nativity Ode</u>,"
<u>PQ</u>, 55 (Winter, 1976), 65-95.

_____. "On the Morning of Christ's Nativity Composed 1629"
A. B. Chambers, "Christmas: The Liturgy of the Church and English Verse
of the Renaissance," in <u>Literary Monographs</u>, ed. Eric Rothstein and Joseph
Anthony Wittreich, Jr., Vol. 6 (Madison, Wis.: Univ. of Wisconsin Press,
1975), 142-153.

Sharon Cumberland and Lynn Veach Sadler, "Phantasia: A Pattern in Milton's Early Poems," <u>MiltonQ</u>, 8 (May, 1974), 50-52.

Daiches and Charvat, <u>Poems in English</u>, pp. 665-667.

H. Neville Davies, "Laid Artfully Together: Stanzaic Design in Milton's
'On the Morning of Christ's Nativity,'" in <u>Fair Forms: Essays in English</u>
<u>Literature from Spenser to Jane Austen</u>, ed. Maren-Sofie Røstvig (Totowa,
New Jersey: Rowan and Littlefield, 1975), 85-117.

Victor Erlich, "Milton's Early Poetry: Its Christian Humanism," <u>AI</u>, 32
(Spring, 1975), 87-92.

Donald Friedman, "Harmony and the Poet's Voice in Some of Milton's Early
Poems," <u>MLQ</u>, 30 (Dec., 1969), 528-529.

Laurence H. Jacobs, "'Unexpressive Notes': The Decorum of Milton's Nativity Ode," <u>ELWIU</u>, 1 (Fall, 1974), 166-177.

Knight, <u>The Burning Oracle</u>, pp. 59, 61.

Maynard Mack, <u>English Masterpieces</u>, Vol. IV, <u>Milton</u>, pp. 5-7.

T. K. Meier, "Milton's 'Nativity Ode': Sectarian Discord," <u>MLR</u>, 65 (Jan.,
1970), 7-10.

David B. Morris, "Drama and Stasis in Milton's 'Ode on the Morning of
Christ's Nativity,'" <u>SP</u>, 68 (April, 1971), 207-222.

Ivar L. Myhr, <u>Expl</u>, 4 (Dec., 1945), 16.
   Rpt. <u>The Explicator Cyclopedia</u>, II, pp. 210-211.

Mother M. Christopher Pecheux, "The Image of the Sun in Milton's 'Nativity
Ode,'" <u>HLQ</u>, 38 (Aug., 1975), 315-333.

Renato Poggioli, The Oaten Flute: Essays on Pastoral Poetry and the Pastoral Ideal (Cambridge, Mass.: Harvard Univ. Press, 1975), 124-134.

Balanchandra Rajan, "In Order Serviceable," MLR, 63 (Jan., 1968), 13-22.

Malcolm M. Ross, "Milton and the Protestant Aesthetic: The Early Poems," UTQ, 17 (July, 1948), 349-352.

Maren-Sofie Røstvig, "Elaborate Song: Conceptual Structure in Milton's 'On the Morning of Christ's Nativity,'" in Fair Forms: Essays in English Literature from Spenser to Jane Austen, ed. Maren-Sofie Røstvig (Totowa, New Jersey: Rowan and Littlefield, 1975), pp. 54-84.

Lynn Veach Sadler, "Magic and the Temporal Scheme in 'On the Morning of Christ's Nativity,'" BSUF, 17 (Spring, 1976), 3-9.

Laurence Stapleton, "Milton and the New Music," UTQ, 23 (April, 1954), 217-236.

Kathleen M. Swaim, "'Mighty Pan': Tradition and an Image in Milton's Nativity Hymn," SP, 68 (Oct., 1971), 484-495.

Joan Webber, "The Son of God and Power of Life in Three Poems by Milton," ELH, 37 (June, 1970), 176-180.

_____. "On the University Carrier" and "Another on the Same"
Joan Ozark Holmer, "Milton's Hobson Poems: Rhetorical Manifestation of Wit," MiltonQ, 11 (March, 1977), 16-21.

_____. "On Time"
R. Darby Williams, "Two Baroque Game Poems on Grace: Herbert's 'Paradise' and Milton's 'On Time,'" Criticism, 12 (Summer, 1970), 186-192.

_____. "Paraphrase of Psalm 114"
Jack Goldman, "Milton's Intrusion of Abraham and Isaac upon Psalm 114," PQ, 55 (Winter, 1976), 117-126.

_____. "The Passion"
Sharon Cumberland and Lynn Veach Sadler, "Phantasia: A Pattern in Milton's Early Poems," MiltonQ, 8 (May, 1974), 52-53.

Philip J. Gallagher, "Milton's 'The Passion': Inspired Mediocrity," MiltonQ, 11 (May, 1977), 44-50.

_____. "Il Penseroso"
Victor Erlich, "Milton's Early Poetry: Its Christian Humanism," AI, 32 (Spring, 1975), 94-99.

_____. "To Mr. Lawrence"
Van Doren, Introduction to Poetry, pp. 123-125.

_____. "To Mr. H. Lawes, on his Aires" (Sonnet 13)
Nan Cooke Carpenter, "Milton and Music: Henry Lawes, Dante, and Casella," ELR, 2 (Spring, 1972), 237-242.

_____. "To the Lord General Cromwell" (Sonnet 16)
William McCarthy, "The Continuity of Milton's Sonnets," PMLA, 92 (Jan., 1977), 101-102.

_____. Upon the Circumcision"
A. B. Chambers, "Milton's 'Upon the Circumcision': Backgrounds and Meanings," TSLL, 17 (Fall, 1975), 687-697.

_____. "When the Assault Was Intended to the City" (Sonnet 8)
William McCarthy, "The Continuity of Milton's Sonnets," PMLA, 92 (Jan., 1977), 101.

MOMADAY, N. Scott. "Angle of Geese"
Kenneth Fields, "More Than Language Means," SoR, 6 (Jan., 1970), 197-200.

_____. "The Bear"
Winters, Forms of Discovery, pp. 289-290.

_____. "Before an Old Painting of the Crucifixion"
Winters, Forms of Discovery, pp. 291-294.

_____. "Buteo Regalis"
Winters, Forms of Discovery, pp. 290-291.

MONRO. "The Garden"
Stephen Spender, (Review), The Criterion, 12 (July, 1933), 681-682.

MONROE, Harold. "Trees"
Skelton, The Poetic Pattern, pp. 122-128.

MOODY. "Ode in Time of Hesitation"
R. P. Blackmur, "Moody in Retrospect," Poetry, 38 (Sept., 1931), 334-335.

MOORE, Marianne. "Apparition of Splendor"
Sr. Mary Cecilia, "The Poetry of Marianne Moore," Thought, 38 (Autumn, 1963), 367.

Rebecca Price Parkin, "Certain Difficulties in Reading Marianne Moore: Exemplified in Her 'Apparition of Splendor,'" PMLA, 81 (June, 1966), 167-172.

Rebecca Price Parkin, "Some Characteristics of Marianne Moore's Humor," CE, 27 (Feb., 1966), 406-407.

_____. "Bird-Witted"
Sr. Mary Cecilia, "The Poetry of Marianne Moore," Thought, 38 (Autumn, 1963), 367-369.

Frankenberg, Pleasure Dome, pp. 137-141.

Lloyd Frankenberg, "The Imaginary Garden," Quarterly Review of Literature, 4, No. 2, 210-212.

_____. "Black Earth"
Blackmur, The Double Agent, pp. 150-154.

Charles Tomlinson, "Abundance, Not Too Much: The Poetry of Marianne Moore," SR, 65 (Autumn, 1957), 677-682.

_____. "Camillia Sabina"
Rosenthal, The Modern Poets, pp. 141-142.

_____. "A Carriage from Sweden"
Perrine and Reid, 100 American Poems, pp. 97-98.

_____. "Critics and Connoisseurs"
Perrine and Reid, 100 American Poems, pp. 99-100.

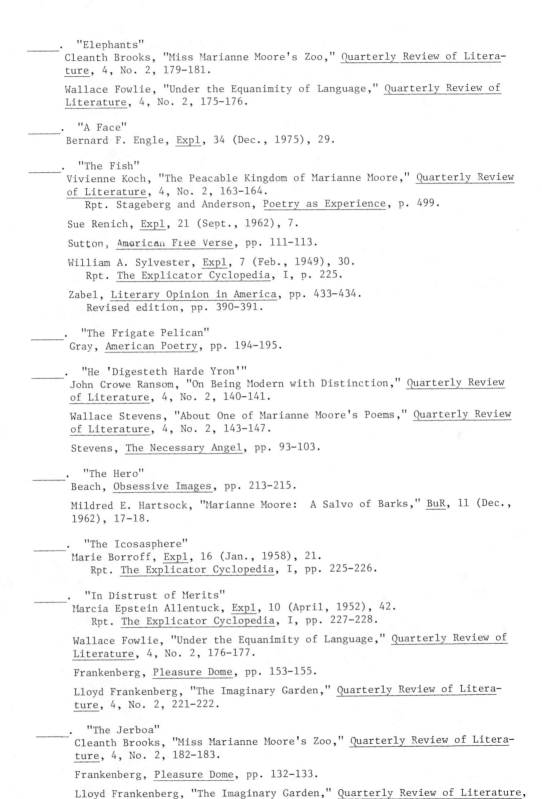

_____. "Elephants"
Cleanth Brooks, "Miss Marianne Moore's Zoo," Quarterly Review of Literature, 4, No. 2, 179-181.

Wallace Fowlie, "Under the Equanimity of Language," Quarterly Review of Literature, 4, No. 2, 175-176.

_____. "A Face"
Bernard F. Engle, Expl, 34 (Dec., 1975), 29.

_____. "The Fish"
Vivienne Koch, "The Peacable Kingdom of Marianne Moore," Quarterly Review of Literature, 4, No. 2, 163-164.
    Rpt. Stageberg and Anderson, Poetry as Experience, p. 499.

Sue Renich, Expl, 21 (Sept., 1962), 7.

Sutton, American Free Verse, pp. 111-113.

William A. Sylvester, Expl, 7 (Feb., 1949), 30.
    Rpt. The Explicator Cyclopedia, I, p. 225.

Zabel, Literary Opinion in America, pp. 433-434.
    Revised edition, pp. 390-391.

_____. "The Frigate Pelican"
Gray, American Poetry, pp. 194-195.

_____. "He 'Digesteth Harde Yron'"
John Crowe Ransom, "On Being Modern with Distinction," Quarterly Review of Literature, 4, No. 2, 140-141.

Wallace Stevens, "About One of Marianne Moore's Poems," Quarterly Review of Literature, 4, No. 2, 143-147.

Stevens, The Necessary Angel, pp. 93-103.

_____. "The Hero"
Beach, Obsessive Images, pp. 213-215.

Mildred E. Hartsock, "Marianne Moore: A Salvo of Barks," BuR, 11 (Dec., 1962), 17-18.

_____. "The Icosasphere"
Marie Borroff, Expl, 16 (Jan., 1958), 21.
    Rpt. The Explicator Cyclopedia, I, pp. 225-226.

_____. "In Distrust of Merits"
Marcia Epstein Allentuck, Expl, 10 (April, 1952), 42.
    Rpt. The Explicator Cyclopedia, I, pp. 227-228.

Wallace Fowlie, "Under the Equanimity of Language," Quarterly Review of Literature, 4, No. 2, 176-177.

Frankenberg, Pleasure Dome, pp. 153-155.

Lloyd Frankenberg, "The Imaginary Garden," Quarterly Review of Literature, 4, No. 2, 221-222.

_____. "The Jerboa"
Cleanth Brooks, "Miss Marianne Moore's Zoo," Quarterly Review of Literature, 4, No. 2, 182-183.

Frankenberg, Pleasure Dome, pp. 132-133.

Lloyd Frankenberg, "The Imaginary Garden," Quarterly Review of Literature, 4, No. 2, 202-203.

Nicholas Joost, "The Pertinence of the Notes to Marianne Moore's 'The Jerboa,'" Delta Epsilon Sigma Bulletin, 7 (May, 1962), 1-30.

Philip Legler, "Marianne Moore and the Idea of Freedom," Poetry, 83 (Dec., 1953), 158-167.

_____. "Marriage"
Mildred E. Hartsock, "Marianne Moore: A Salvo of Barks," BuR, 11 (Dec., 1962), 14-37.

Vivienne Koch, "The Peacable Kingdom of Marianne Moore," Quarterly Review of Literature, 4, No. 2, 167.

_____. "The Mind Is an Enchanting Thing"
Frankenberg, Invitation to Poetry, pp. 389-390.

_____. "The Monkeys"
Blackmur, The Double Agent, pp. 166-167.
   Rpt. Language as Gesture, p. 281.

_____. "Nevertheless"
Frankenberg, Pleasure Dome, p. 125.

Lloyd Frankenberg, "The Imaginary Garden," Quarterly Review of Literature, 4, No. 2, 195-196.

_____. "No Swan So Fine"
Brooks, Lewis, and Warren, American Literature, pp. 2177-2178.

Gray, American Poetry, pp. 193-194.

_____. "Novices"
Vivienne Koch, "The Peacable Kingdom of Marianne Moore," Quarterly Review of Literature, 4, No. 2, 157.

_____. "An Octopus"
Mildred E. Hartsock, "Marianne Moore: A Salvo of Barks," BuR, 11 (Dec., 1962), 31-32.

_____. "O To Be a Dragon"
Rebecca Price Parkin, "Some Characteristics of Marianne Moore's Humor," CE, 27 (Feb., 1966), 406.

_____. "The Pangolin"
Rebecca Price Parkin, "Some Characteristics of Marianne Moore's Humor," CE, 27 (Feb., 1966), 403-406.

Sutton, American Free Verse, pp. 106-107.

_____. "The Past Is the Present"
Blackmur, The Double Agent, pp. 142-149.

_____. "Poetry"
Frankenberg, Pleasure Dome, pp. 137-141.

Lloyd Frankenberg, "The Imaginary Garden," Quarterly Review of Literature, 4, No. 2, 207-209.

Gray, American Poetry, pp. 195-196.

_____. "Roses Only"
Brower, The Fields of Light, pp. 48-50.

_____. "See in the Midst of Fair Leaves"
Dan G. Hoffman, Expl, 10 (March, 1952), 34.
   Rpt. Locke, Gibson, and Arms, Introduction to Literature, third
   edition, pp. 203-204.
   Rpt. fourth edition, pp. 204-205.
   Rpt. fifth edition, pp. 187-188.
   Rpt. The Explicator Cyclopedia, I, pp. 228-229.

_____. "Tell Me, Tell Me"
Rebecca Price Parkin, "Some Characteristics of Marianne Moore's Humor,"
CE, 27 (Feb., 1966), 407.

_____. "Silence"
Blackmur, The Double Agent, 154-160.
   Rpt. Language as Gesture, pp. 271-276.

Barbara Charlesworth Gelpi, "From Colonial to Revolutionary: The Modern
American Woman Poet," SJS, 2 (Nov., 1976), 41-42.

_____. "Snakes, Mongooses, Snake-charmer and the Like"
Rosenthal and Smith, Exploring Poetry, pp. 250-251.

_____. "Spenser's Ireland"
Maurice J. O'Sullivan, Jr., "Native Genius for Disunion: Marianne Moore's
'Spenser's Ireland,'" CP, 7 (Fall, 1974), 42-47.

_____. "The Steeple-Jack"
Louise Bogan, "Reading Contemporary Poetry," CE, 14 (Feb., 1953), 257-260.

Denis Donoghue, "Technique in Hopkins," Studies, 44 (Winter, 1955), 452.

Gray, American Poetry, pp. 192-193.

Sutton, American Free Verse, pp. 110-111.

Charles Tomlinson, "Abundance, Not Too Much: The Poetry of Marianne
Moore," SR, 65 (Autumn, 1957), 677-682.

_____. "Then The Ermine"
Rebecca Price Parkin, "Some Characteristics of Marianne Moore's Humor,"
CE, 27 (Feb., 1966), 407.

_____. "To a Snail"
Francis W. Warlow, Expl, 26 (Feb., 1968), 51.

_____. "Tom Fool at Jamaica"
Marie Borroff, "'Tom Fool at Jamaica' by Marianne Moore: Meaning and
Structure," CE, 17 (May, 1956), 466-469.

Elder Olson, "The Poetry of Marianne Moore," ChiR, 11 (Spring, 1957),
103-104.

_____. "What Are Years"
Gray, American Poetry, pp. 198-199.

O'Connor, Sense and Sensibility in Modern Poetry, pp. 229-230 (quoting
Lloyd Frankenberg, The Saturday Review of Literature, 39 (March 23,
1946).

Perrine and Reid, 100 American Poems, pp. 101-102.

_____. "The Wood-Weasel"
Cleanth Brooks, "Miss Marianne Moore's Zoo," Quarterly Review of Literature, 4, No. 2, 182.

MOORE, Merrill. "Granny Weeks"
    Dudley Fitts, "The Sonnets of Merrill Moore," SR, 47 (April-June, 1939),
    278-279.

_____. "The Gun Barrel Looked at Him With Love in Its Single Eyehole"
    Dudley Fitts, "The Sonnets of Merrill Moore," SR, 47 (April-June, 1939),
    274-275.

_____. "The Sound of Time Hangs Heavy in My Ears"
    Dudley Fitts, "The Sonnets of Merrill Moore," SR, 47 (April-June, 1939),
    291-292.

MOORE, Nicholas. "Alteration"
    John Berryman, Poetry: A Critical Supplement, Dec., 1949, pp. 11-12.

_____. "Unity Quitbread at Eltham"
    John Berryman, Poetry: A Critical Supplement, Dec., 1949, pp. 10-11.

MOORE, Rosalie. "The Grasshopper Man"
    J. F. Nims and Rosalie Moore, Poetry: A Critical Supplement, May, 1949,
    pp. 1-11.

MOORE, T. Sturge. "Love's Faintness Accepted"
    Frederick L. Gwynn, Expl, 7 (April, 1949), 45.
        Rpt. The Explicator Cyclopedia, I, p. 229.

_____. "To Silence"
    Winters, Primitivism and Decadence, pp. 86-89. Also In Defense of Reason,
    pp. 96-99. Also in The Forms of Discovery, pp. 243-245.
        Rpt. West, Essays in Modern Literary Criticism, pp. 224-225.

MOORE, Thomas. "The Song of Fionnuala"
    Brendan P. O. Hehir, Expl, 15 (Jan., 1957), 23.
        Rpt. The Explicator Cyclopedia, II, pp. 230-231.

MORDAUNT. "Sound, Sound the Clarion"
    George Arms, Expl, 1 (Dec., 1942), 20.
        Rpt. The Explicator Cyclopedia, II, p. 231.

MORRIS, William. "The Chapel in Lyoness"
    Curtis Dahl, "Morris's 'The Chapel in Lyoness': An Interpretation," SP,
    51 (July, 1954), 482-491.

_____. "The Defence of Guenevere"
    Dennis R. Balch, "Guenevere's Fidelity to Arthur in 'The Defence of
    Guenevere' and 'King Arthur's Tomb,'" VP, 13 (Fall-Winter, 1975), 61-70.

    Mother Angela Carson, O.S.U., "Morris's Guenevere: A Further Note," PQ,
    42 (Jan., 1963), 131-134.

    John Hollow, "William Morris and the Judgment of God," PMLA, 86 (May,
    1971), 447-450.

    Laurence Perrine, "Morris's Guenevere: An Interpretation," PQ, 39 (April,
    1960), 234-241.

    C. G. Silver, "The Defense of Guenevere: A Further Interpretation," SEL,
    9 (Autumn, 1969), 695-702.

    Hartley S. Spatt, "William Morris and the Uses of the Past," VP, 13
    (Fall-Winter, 1975), 5-7.

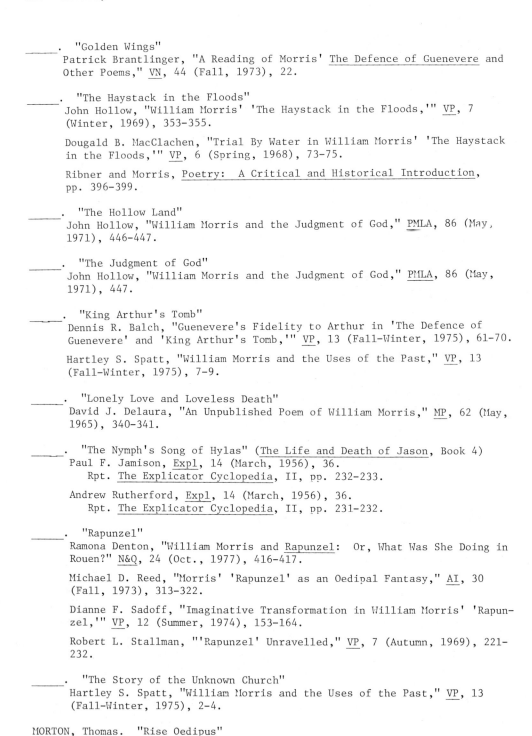

_____. "Golden Wings"
Patrick Brantlinger, "A Reading of Morris' The Defence of Guenevere and
Other Poems," VN, 44 (Fall, 1973), 22.

_____. "The Haystack in the Floods"
John Hollow, "William Morris' 'The Haystack in the Floods,'" VP, 7
(Winter, 1969), 353-355.

Dougald B. MacClachen, "Trial By Water in William Morris' 'The Haystack
in the Floods,'" VP, 6 (Spring, 1968), 73-75.

Ribner and Morris, Poetry: A Critical and Historical Introduction,
pp. 396-399.

_____. "The Hollow Land"
John Hollow, "William Morris and the Judgment of God," PMLA, 86 (May,
1971), 446-447.

_____. "The Judgment of God"
John Hollow, "William Morris and the Judgment of God," PMLA, 86 (May,
1971), 447.

_____. "King Arthur's Tomb"
Dennis R. Balch, "Guenevere's Fidelity to Arthur in 'The Defence of
Guenevere' and 'King Arthur's Tomb,'" VP, 13 (Fall-Winter, 1975), 61-70.

Hartley S. Spatt, "William Morris and the Uses of the Past," VP, 13
(Fall-Winter, 1975), 7-9.

_____. "Lonely Love and Loveless Death"
David J. Delaura, "An Unpublished Poem of William Morris," MP, 62 (May,
1965), 340-341.

_____. "The Nymph's Song of Hylas" (The Life and Death of Jason, Book 4)
Paul F. Jamison, Expl, 14 (March, 1956), 36.
     Rpt. The Explicator Cyclopedia, II, pp. 232-233.

Andrew Rutherford, Expl, 14 (March, 1956), 36.
     Rpt. The Explicator Cyclopedia, II, pp. 231-232.

_____. "Rapunzel"
Ramona Denton, "William Morris and Rapunzel: Or, What Was She Doing in
Rouen?" N&Q, 24 (Oct., 1977), 416-417.

Michael D. Reed, "Morris' 'Rapunzel' as an Oedipal Fantasy," AI, 30
(Fall, 1973), 313-322.

Dianne F. Sadoff, "Imaginative Transformation in William Morris' 'Rapunzel,'" VP, 12 (Summer, 1974), 153-164.

Robert L. Stallman, "'Rapunzel' Unravelled," VP, 7 (Autumn, 1969), 221-
232.

_____. "The Story of the Unknown Church"
Hartley S. Spatt, "William Morris and the Uses of the Past," VP, 13
(Fall-Winter, 1975), 2-4.

MORTON, Thomas. "Rise Oedipus"
     Robert D. Arner, "Mythology and the Maypole of Merrymount: Some Notes on
     Thomas Morton's 'Rise Oedipus,'" EAL, 6 (Fall, 1971), 156-164.

MOSS, Howard. "The City Lion"
     J. F. Nims, Poetry: A Critical Supplement, Nov., 1948, p. 9.

MUIR, Edwin. "The Animals"
Dickinson, Suggestions for Teachers of "Introduction to Literature,"
fifth edition, ed. Lock, Gibson, and Arms, p. 44. (Teacher's Manual)

_____. "Ballad of the Flood"
Hoffman, Barbarous Knowledge, pp. 241-242.

_____. "Ballad of Hector in Hades"
Feder, Ancient Myth in Modern Poetry, pp. 370-372.

_____. "Ballad of the Soul"
James Aitchison, "The Limits of Experience: Edwin Muir's 'Ballad of the
Soul,'" English, 24 (Spring, 1975), 10-15.

_____. "The Combat"
Hoffman, Barbarous Knowledge, pp. 224-246.

_____. "The Covenant"
Frederick Garber, "Edwin Muir's Heraldic Mode," TCL, 12 (July, 1966),
97.

_____. "The Days"
Ralph J. Mills, Jr., "Edwin Muir: A Speech from Darkness Grown," Accent,
19 (Winter, 1959), 66-67.

_____. "Dialogue"
Tschumi, Thought in Twentieth-Century English Poetry, pp. 113-114.

_____. "The Enchanted Knight"
R. P. Blackmur, "Edwin Muir: Between the Tiger's Paws," in Four Poets
on Poetry, pp. 36-37.

_____. "The Gate"
Felver and Nurmi, Poetry: An Introduction and Anthology, p. 130.

Kimon Friar, "The Circular Route," Poetry, 84 (April, 1954), 29.

Elizabeth Huberman, "Initiation and Tragedy: A New Look at Edwin Muir's
'The Gate,'" PMLA, 87 (Jan., 1972), 75-79.

_____. "The Groove"
Ralph J. Mills, Jr., "Edwin Muir: A Speech from Darkness Grown," Accent,
19 (Winter, 1959), 60-62.

_____. "The Horses"
Ralph J. Mills, Jr., "Edwin Muir: A Speech from Darkness Grown," Accent,
19 (Winter, 1959), 68-69.

_____. "The Human Fold"
Tschumi, Thought in Twentieth-Century English Poetry, pp. 105-106.

_____. "The Journey Back"
Peter H. Butter, "Edwin Muir: The Journey Back," English, 16 (Autumn,
1967), 218-222.

_____. "The Labyrinth"
Feder, Ancient Myth in Modern Poetry, pp. 373-374.

Ralph J. Mills, Jr., "Edwin Muir: A Speech from Darkness Grown," Accent,
19 (Winter, 1959), 64-65.

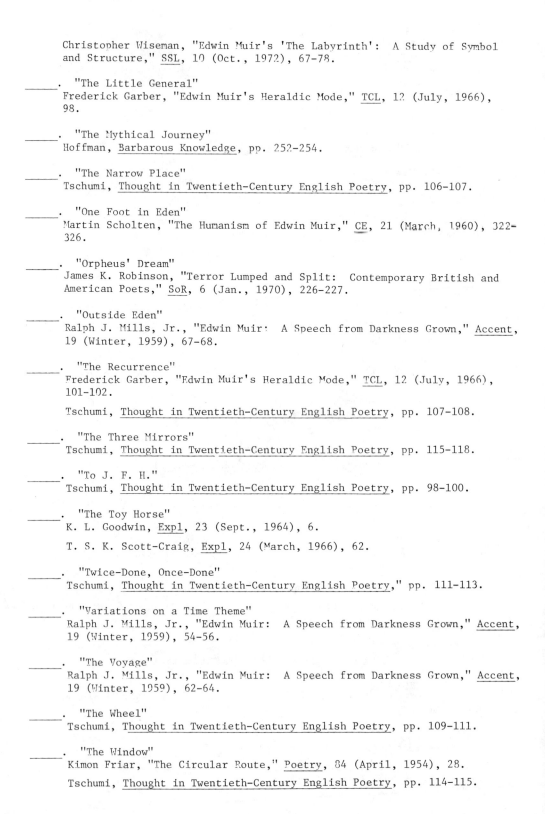

Christopher Wiseman, "Edwin Muir's 'The Labyrinth': A Study of Symbol and Structure," _SSL_, 10 (Oct., 1972), 67-78.

_____. "The Little General"
Frederick Garber, "Edwin Muir's Heraldic Mode," _TCL_, 12 (July, 1966), 98.

_____. "The Mythical Journey"
Hoffman, _Barbarous Knowledge_, pp. 252-254.

_____. "The Narrow Place"
Tschumi, _Thought in Twentieth-Century English Poetry_, pp. 106-107.

_____. "One Foot in Eden"
Martin Scholten, "The Humanism of Edwin Muir," _CE_, 21 (March, 1960), 322-326.

_____. "Orpheus' Dream"
James K. Robinson, "Terror Lumped and Split: Contemporary British and American Poets," _SoR_, 6 (Jan., 1970), 226-227.

_____. "Outside Eden"
Ralph J. Mills, Jr., "Edwin Muir: A Speech from Darkness Grown," _Accent_, 19 (Winter, 1959), 67-68.

_____. "The Recurrence"
Frederick Garber, "Edwin Muir's Heraldic Mode," _TCL_, 12 (July, 1966), 101-102.

Tschumi, _Thought in Twentieth-Century English Poetry_, pp. 107-108.

_____. "The Three Mirrors"
Tschumi, _Thought in Twentieth-Century English Poetry_, pp. 115-118.

_____. "To J. F. H."
Tschumi, _Thought in Twentieth-Century English Poetry_, pp. 98-100.

_____. "The Toy Horse"
K. L. Goodwin, _Expl_, 23 (Sept., 1964), 6.

T. S. K. Scott-Craig, _Expl_, 24 (March, 1966), 62.

_____. "Twice-Done, Once-Done"
Tschumi, _Thought in Twentieth-Century English Poetry_," pp. 111-113.

_____. "Variations on a Time Theme"
Ralph J. Mills, Jr., "Edwin Muir: A Speech from Darkness Grown," _Accent_, 19 (Winter, 1959), 54-56.

_____. "The Voyage"
Ralph J. Mills, Jr., "Edwin Muir: A Speech from Darkness Grown," _Accent_, 19 (Winter, 1959), 62-64.

_____. "The Wheel"
Tschumi, _Thought in Twentieth-Century English Poetry_, pp. 109-111.

_____. "The Window"
Kimon Friar, "The Circular Route," _Poetry_, 84 (April, 1954), 28.

Tschumi, _Thought in Twentieth-Century English Poetry_, pp. 114-115.

MUNDAY, Anthony. "I Serve a Mistress Whiter than the Snow"
     Beaty and Matchett, Poetry: From Statement to Meaning, p. 199.

NASH, Ogden. "Literary Reflection"
     Warren Beck, "Boundaries of Poetry," CE, 4 (March, 1943), 347.

_____. "The Turtle"
     Perrine, Sound and Sense, pp. 135-136.
          Rpt. second edition, pp. 148-149.

NASHE, Thomas. "If I Must Die" (from The Unfortunate Traveller)
     Dorothy Jones, "An Example of Anti-Petrarchan Satire in Nashe's 'The
     Unfortunate Traveller,'" YES, 1 (1971), 48-54.

_____. "Litany in Time of Plague"
     Hennig Cohen, Expl, 31 (April, 1973), 63.

     Cunningham, Tradition and Poetic Structure, pp. 53-58.

     Empson, Seven Types of Ambiguity, pp. 32-35, 145-147; (1947 ed.),
     pp. 25-27, 115-116.

     Judith Little, Expl, 30 (Nov., 1971), 19.

     Fred C. Robinson, "'Strength Stoops unto the Grave': Nashe's 'Adieu,
     Farewell Earth's Bliss,' L. 22," PLL, 6 (Winter, 1970), 89-92.

     Wesley Trimpi, "The Practice of Historical Interpretation and Nashe's
     'Brightnesse Falls from the Ayre,'" JEGP, 66 (Oct., 1967), 501-518.

_____. "Spring, the Sweete Spring, Is the Yere's Pleasant King"
     Beaty and Matchett, Poetry: From Statement to Meaning, pp. 195-196.

NEMEROV. "Painting a Mountain Stream"
     Raymond Smith, "Nemerov and Nature: 'The Stillness In Moving Things,'"
     SoR, 10 (Jan., 1974), 155-158.

_____. "Runes"
     Raymond Smith, "Nemerov and Nature: 'The Stillness In Moving Things,'"
     SoR, 10 (Jan., 1974), 163-168.

_____. "The Sanctuary"
     Raymond Smith, "Nemerov and Nature: 'The Stillness In Moving Things,'"
     SoR, 10 (Jan., 1974), 159-160.

_____. "Santa Claus"
     Perrine and Reid, 100 American Poems, pp. 252-253.

_____. "The View"
     Raymond Smith, "Nemerov and Nature: 'The Stillness In Moving Things,'"
     SoR, 10 (Jan., 1974), 161-163.

NEWMAN. "Dream of Gerontius"
     Esther R. B. Pese, "A Suggested Background for Newman's Dream of Geron-
     tius," MP, 47 (Nov., 1949), 108-116.

_____. "Lead, Kindly Light"
     Paull F. Baum, "The Road to Palermo," SAQ, 55 (April, 1956), 192-197.

_____. "The Pillar of the Cloud"
     Cooper and Holmes, Preface to Poetry, pp. 278-281.

NEWTON, John. "How Sweet the Name of Jesus Sounds"
     Sr. Pauline Parker, "The Hymn as a Literary Form," ECS, 8 (Summer, 1975),
     414-415.

NICHOLAS, Robert. "Sunrise Poem"
     Robert Nichols, "The Birth of a Poem," in Rosamond E. M. Harding, An
     Anatomy of Inspiration (3rd ed.; Cambridge: W. Heffer & Sons, 1948),
     pp. 147-168.

NIMS. "Love Poem"
     Perrine and Reid, 100 American Poems, pp. 234-235.

_____. "The Magical View of Nature"
     William Elton, Poetry: A Critical Supplement, Oct., 1949, pp. 10-12.

_____. "Penny Arcade"
     Robert Shelley, "A Palmtree of Steel," Western Review, 15 (Winter, 1951),
     141-142.

_____. "Winter in the Park"
     Robert Shelley, "A Palmtree of Steel," Western Review, 15 (Winter, 1951),
     140.

NOLL, Bink. "Quaker Hero, Burning"
     Harry M. Campbell, Expl, 29 (May, 1971), 75.

NORRIS, John. "My Estate"
     W. B. Carnochan, Confinement and Flight: An Essay on English Literature
     of the Eighteenth Century (Berkeley: Univ. of California Press, 1977),
     pp. 178-183.

NOYES. "For the Eightieth Birthday of George Meredith"
     Richards, Practical Criticism, pp. 118-129 et passim.

O'DONNELL, George Marion. "Return"
     John Crowe Ransom, "The Making of a Modern," SoR, 1 n.s. (Spring, 1963)
     869-870.

O'HARA, Frank. "The Day Lady Died"
     Charles Altieri, "The Significance of Frank O'Hara," IowaR, 4 (Winter,
     1973), 102-104.

     Carroll, The Poem In Its Skin, pp. 157-164.

_____. "Early on Sunday"
     Marjorie G. Perloff, "New Thresholds, Old Anatomies: Contemporary
     Poetry and the Limits of Exegesis," IowaR, 5 (Winter, 1974), 98-99.

_____. "Essay on Style"
     Marjorie G. Perloff, "New Thresholds, Old Anatomies: Contemporary Poetry
     and the Limits of Exegis," IowaR, 5 (Winter, 1974), 91-95.

_____. "Music"
     Marjorie Perloff, "Frank O'Hara and the Aesthetics of Attention,"
     Boundary 2, 4 (Spring, 1976), 780-785.

_____. "A Step Away From Them"
     Marjorie G. Perloff, "Poetry Chronicle: 1970-71," ConL, 14 (Winter,
     1973), 99-103.

OLDHAM. "Satyr Addressed to a Friend"
>Miner, The Restoration Mode from Milton to Dryden, pp. 429-430.

_____. "A Satyr Upon a Woman"
>Miner, The Restoration Mode from Milton to Dryden, pp. 425-427.

OLSON, Charles. "The Death of Europe (a Funeral Poem for Rainer M. Gerhardt)"
>Philip E. Smith, II, "Descent Into Polis: Charles Olson's Search for
>Community," MPS, 8 (Spring, 1977), 17-20.

_____. "The Kingfishers"
>Guy Davenport, "Scholia and Conjectures for Olson's 'The Kingfishers,'"
>Boundary 2, 2 (Fall, 1973-Winter, 1974), pp. 250-262.

>Thomas F. Merrill, "'The Kingfishers': Charles Olson's 'Marvelous Man-
>euver,'" ConL, 17 (Autumn, 1976), 506-528.

_____. "The Moon is the Number 18"
>Richard G. Ingher, "Number, Image, Sortilege: A Short Analysis of
>'The Moon is the Number 18,'" Boundary 2, 2 (Fall, 1973-Winter, 1974),
>269-272.

_____. "On First Looking out Through Juan de la Cosa's Eyes"
>Daniel G. Hise, "Noticing Juan De La Cosa," Boundary 2, (Fall, 1973-
>Winter, 1974), 323-332.

_____. "The Praises"
>Maxine Apsel, "The Praises," Boundary 2, 2 (Fall, 1973-Winter, 1974),
>263-268.

_____. "Variations Done for Gerald Van de Wiele"
>Charles Altieri, "Olson's Poetics and the Tradition," Boundary 2, 2
>(Fall, 1973-Winter, 1974), 183-188.

OLSON, Lawrence. "Great Abaco"
>Macha Rosenthal, "Sailing for Great Abaco," Poetry, 72 (April, 1948),
>51-53.

O'REILLY, John Boyle. "A White Rose"
>Laurence Perrine, "The Untranslatable Language," EJ, 60 (Jan., 1971),
>60.
>>Rpt. The Art of Total Relevance, p. 45.

O'SULLIVAN, Seumas. "Birds"
>Clark, Lyric Resonance, pp. 79-82.

_____. "Nelson Street"
>Clark, Lyric Resonance, pp. 77-79.

_____. "The Sheep"
>Clark, Lyric Resonance, pp. 82-84.

OWEN, Wilfred. "Anthem for Doomed Youth"
>Bloom, Philbrick, and Blistein, The Order of Poetry, pp. 135-138.

>Samuel J. Hazo, "The Passion of Wilfred Owen," Renascence, 11 (Summer,
>1959), 205-206.

>Horace G. Posey, Jr., "Muted Satire in 'Anthem for Doomed Youth,'"
>EIC, 21 (Oct., 1971), 377-381.

_____. "Dulce et Decorum Est"
Brown and Olmstead, Language and Literature, pp. 6-7, 26-27.

Samuel J. Hazo, "The Passion of Wilfred Owen," Renascence, 11 (Summer, 1959), 202.

_____. "Greater Love"
Roland Bartel, "Teaching Wilfred Owen's War Poems and the Bible," EJ, 61 (Jan., 1972), 39-41.

Jennifer Breen, "Wilfred Owen: 'Greater Love' and Late Romanticism," ELT, 17, No. 3 (1974), 177-181.

Rosemary Freeman, "Wilfred Owen's 'Greater Love,'" EIC, 16 (Jan., 1966), 132-133.

Samuel J. Hazo, "The Passion of Wilfred Owen," Renascence, 11 (Summer, 1959), 204-205.

James J. Hill, "Wilfred Owen's 'Greater Love,'" EIC, 15 (Oct., 1965), 476-477.

Hilda D. Spear, "'I Too Saw God': The Religious Allusions in Wilfred Owen's Poetry," English, 24 (Summer, 1975), 36-37.

_____. "Miners"
William Cooke, "Wilfred Owen's 'Miners' and the Minnie Pit Disaster," English, 26 (Autumn, 1977), 213-217.

_____. "The Parable of the Old Man and the Young"
Roland Bartel, "Teaching Wilfred Owen's War Poems and the Bible," EJ, 61 (Jan., 1972), 36-39.

Timothy O'Keeffe, "Ironic Allusion in the Poetry of Wilfred Owen," ArielE, 3 (Oct., 1972), 79-80.

_____. "The Show"
Joseph Cohen, Expl, 16 (Nov., 1957), 8.
    Rpt. The Explicator Cyclopedia, I, pp. 229-230.

_____. "Strange Meeting"
Roland Bartel, "Teaching Wilfred Owen's War Poems and the Bible," EJ, 61 (Jan., 1972), 41-42.

Elliott B. Gose, Jr., "Digging in: An Interpretation of Wilfred Owen's 'Strange Meeting,'" CE, 22 (March, 1961), 417-419.

Samuel J. Hazo, "The Passion of Wilfred Owen," Renascence, 11 (Summer, 1959), 206-208.

Rosenthal and Smith, Exploring Poetry, pp. 546-547.

D. S. Savage, "Two Prophetic Poems," Western Review, 13 (Winter, 1949), 67-78.

Skelton, The Poetic Pattern, pp. 113-114.

PARKER, Dorothy. "The Actress"
Daniels, The Art of Reading Poetry, pp. 353-354.

PARNELL. "Hymn to Contentment"
Raymond D. Havens, "Parnell's 'Hymn to Contentment,'" MLN, 59 (May, 1944), 320-331.

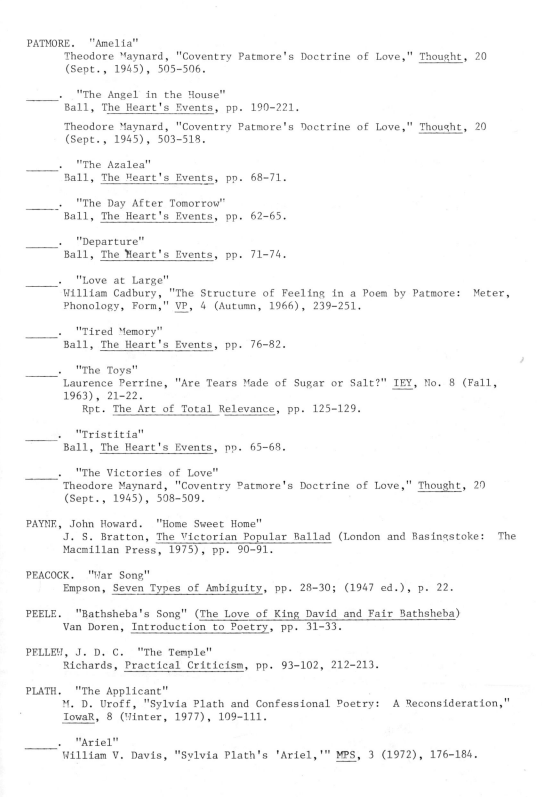

PATMORE.   "Amelia"
    Theodore Maynard, "Coventry Patmore's Doctrine of Love," <u>Thought</u>, 20
    (Sept., 1945), 505-506.

_____.   "The Angel in the House"
    Ball, <u>The Heart's Events</u>, pp. 190-221.

    Theodore Maynard, "Coventry Patmore's Doctrine of Love," <u>Thought</u>, 20
    (Sept., 1945), 503-518.

_____.   "The Azalea"
    Ball, <u>The Heart's Events</u>, pp. 68-71.

_____.   "The Day After Tomorrow"
    Ball, <u>The Heart's Events</u>, pp. 62-65.

_____.   "Departure"
    Ball, <u>The Heart's Events</u>, pp. 71-74.

_____.   "Love at Large"
    William Cadbury, "The Structure of Feeling in a Poem by Patmore: Meter,
    Phonology, Form," <u>VP</u>, 4 (Autumn, 1966), 239-251.

_____.   "Tired Memory"
    Ball, <u>The Heart's Events</u>, pp. 76-82.

_____.   "The Toys"
    Laurence Perrine, "Are Tears Made of Sugar or Salt?" <u>IEY</u>, No. 8 (Fall,
    1963), 21-22.
       Rpt. <u>The Art of Total Relevance</u>, pp. 125-129.

_____.   "Tristitia"
    Ball, <u>The Heart's Events</u>, pp. 65-68.

_____.   "The Victories of Love"
    Theodore Maynard, "Coventry Patmore's Doctrine of Love," <u>Thought</u>, 20
    (Sept., 1945), 508-509.

PAYNE, John Howard.   "Home Sweet Home"
    J. S. Bratton, <u>The Victorian Popular Ballad</u> (London and Basingstoke: The
    Macmillan Press, 1975), pp. 90-91.

PEACOCK.   "War Song"
    Empson, <u>Seven Types of Ambiguity</u>, pp. 28-30; (1947 ed.), p. 22.

PEELE.   "Bathsheba's Song" (<u>The Love of King David and Fair Bathsheba</u>)
    Van Doren, <u>Introduction to Poetry</u>, pp. 31-33.

PELLEW, J. D. C.   "The Temple"
    Richards, <u>Practical Criticism</u>, pp. 93-102, 212-213.

PLATH.   "The Applicant"
    M. D. Uroff, "Sylvia Plath and Confessional Poetry: A Reconsideration,"
    <u>IowaR</u>, 8 (Winter, 1977), 109-111.

_____.   "Ariel"
    William V. Davis, "Sylvia Plath's 'Ariel,'" <u>MPS</u>, 3 (1972), 176-184.

D. F. McKay, "Aspects of Energy in the Poetry of Dylan Thomas and Sylvia Plath," CritQ, 16 (Spring, 1974), 54-56.

Marjorie Perloff, "Angst and Animism in the Poetry of Sylvia Plath," JML, 1, No. 1 (1970), 66-67.

Linda Wagner, "Plath's 'Ariel': 'Auspicious Gales,'" CP, 10 (Fall, 1977), 5-7.

_____. "Arrival of the Bee Box"
Rose Kamel, "'A Self to Recover': Sylvia Plath's Bee Cycle Poems," MPS, 4 (Winter, 1973), 310-311.

Lawrence R. Ries, Wolf Masks: Violence in Contemporary Poetry (Port Washington, N.Y.: Kennikat Press, 1977), pp. 42-44.

_____. "The Beekeeper's Daughter"
Rose Kamel, "'A Self to Recover': Sylvia Plath's Bee Cycle Poems," MPS, 4 (Winter, 1973), 308-310.

_____. "The Bee Meeting"
Rose Kamel, "'A Self to Recover': Sylvia Plath's Bee Cycle Poems," MPS, 4 (Winter, 1973), 306-308.

_____. "Black Rook in Rainy Weather"
Judith B. Herman, "Reflections on a Kitchen Table: A Note on Sylvia Plath's 'Black Rook in Rainy Weather,'" NConL, 7 (Dec., 1977), 5.

_____. "Brasilia"
Margaret D. Uroff, "Sylvia Plath on Motherhood," MQ, 15 (Autumn, 1973), 88-89.

_____. "The Couriers"
Jon Rosenblatt, Expl, 34 (Dec., 1975), 28.

_____. "Cut"
Joan Bobbitt, "Lowell and Plath: Objectivity and the Confessional Mode," ArQ, 33 (Autumn, 1977), 315.

Robert Boyers, "Sylvia Plath: The Trepanned Veteran," CentR, 13 (Spring, 1969), 142-146.

Marjorie Perloff, "Angst and Animism in the Poetry of Sylvia Plath," JML, 1, No. 1 (1970), 70-72.

R. J. Spendal, "Sylvia Plath's 'Cut,'" MPS, 6 (Autumn, 1975), 128-134.

_____. "Daddy"
Robert Boyers, "Sylvia Plath: The Trepanned Veteran," CentR, 13 (Spring, 1969), 148-152.

Dickinson, Suggestions for Teachers of "Introduction to Literature," fifth edition, ed. Locke, Gibson, and Arms, pp. 54-55. (Teacher's Manual)

Philip Hobsbaum, "The Temptation of Giant Despair," HudR, 25 (Winter, 1972-73), 605-606.

M. D. Uroff, "Sylvia Plath and Confessional Poetry: A Reconsideration," IowaR, 8 (Winter, 1977), 113-115.

_____. "The Disquieting Muses"
Margaret D. Uroff, "Sylvia Plath on Motherhood," MQ, 15 (Autumn, 1973), 72-75.

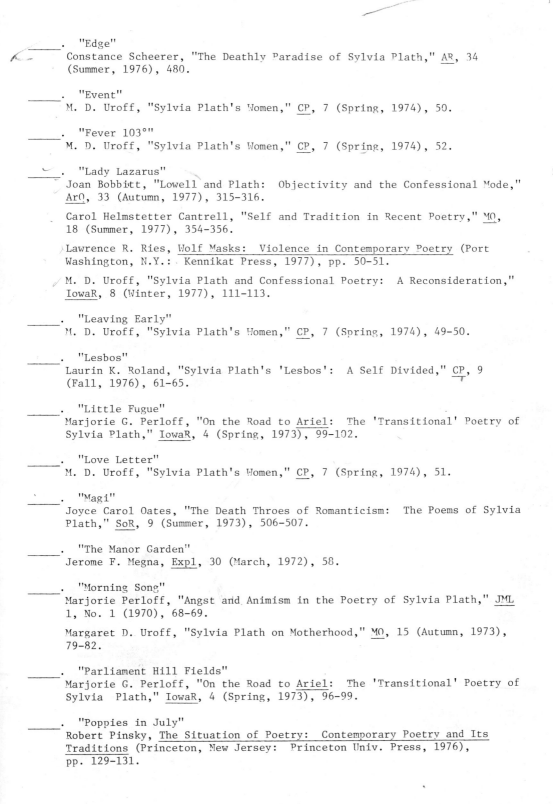

_____. "Edge"
Constance Scheerer, "The Deathly Paradise of Sylvia Plath," AR, 34
(Summer, 1976), 480.

_____. "Event"
M. D. Uroff, "Sylvia Plath's Women," CP, 7 (Spring, 1974), 50.

_____. "Fever 103°"
M. D. Uroff, "Sylvia Plath's Women," CP, 7 (Spring, 1974), 52.

_____. "Lady Lazarus"
Joan Bobbitt, "Lowell and Plath: Objectivity and the Confessional Mode,"
ArQ, 33 (Autumn, 1977), 315-316.

Carol Helmstetter Cantrell, "Self and Tradition in Recent Poetry," MQ,
18 (Summer, 1977), 354-356.

Lawrence R. Ries, Wolf Masks: Violence in Contemporary Poetry (Port
Washington, N.Y.: Kennikat Press, 1977), pp. 50-51.

M. D. Uroff, "Sylvia Plath and Confessional Poetry: A Reconsideration,"
IowaR, 8 (Winter, 1977), 111-113.

_____. "Leaving Early"
M. D. Uroff, "Sylvia Plath's Women," CP, 7 (Spring, 1974), 49-50.

_____. "Lesbos"
Laurin K. Roland, "Sylvia Plath's 'Lesbos': A Self Divided," CP, 9
(Fall, 1976), 61-65.

_____. "Little Fugue"
Marjorie G. Perloff, "On the Road to Ariel: The 'Transitional' Poetry of
Sylvia Plath," IowaR, 4 (Spring, 1973), 99-102.

_____. "Love Letter"
M. D. Uroff, "Sylvia Plath's Women," CP, 7 (Spring, 1974), 51.

_____. "Magi"
Joyce Carol Oates, "The Death Throes of Romanticism: The Poems of Sylvia
Plath," SoR, 9 (Summer, 1973), 506-507.

_____. "The Manor Garden"
Jerome F. Megna, Expl, 30 (March, 1972), 58.

_____. "Morning Song"
Marjorie Perloff, "Angst and Animism in the Poetry of Sylvia Plath," JML
1, No. 1 (1970), 68-69.

Margaret D. Uroff, "Sylvia Plath on Motherhood," MQ, 15 (Autumn, 1973),
79-82.

_____. "Parliament Hill Fields"
Marjorie G. Perloff, "On the Road to Ariel: The 'Transitional' Poetry of
Sylvia Plath," IowaR, 4 (Spring, 1973), 96-99.

_____. "Poppies in July"
Robert Pinsky, The Situation of Poetry: Contemporary Poetry and Its
Traditions (Princeton, New Jersey: Princeton Univ. Press, 1976),
pp. 129-131.

_____. "Private Ground"
Robert N. Mollinger, "Sylvia Plath's 'Private Ground,'" NConL, 5 (March, 1975), 14-15.

_____. "Sheep in Fog"
Jon Rosenblatt, "The Limits of the 'Confessional Mode' in Recent American Poetry," Genre, 9 (Summer, 1976), 157-158.

_____. "Snakecharmer"
Constance Scheerer, "The Deathly Paradise of Sylvia Plath," AR, 34 (Summer, 1976), 471-472.

_____. "Stings"
Rose Kamel, "'A Self to Recover': Sylvia Plath's Bee Cycle Poems," MPS, 4 (Winter, 1973), 313-316.

_____. "The Surgeon at 2 A. M."
Joan Bobbitt, "Lowell and Plath: Objectivity and the Confessional Mode," ArQ, 33 (Autumn, 1977), 316-317.

Constance Scheerer, "The Deathly Paradise of Sylvia Plath," AR, 34 (Summer, 1976), 473-475.

_____. "The Swarm"
Rose Kamel, "'A Self to Recover': Sylvia Plath's Bee Cycle Poems," MPS, 4 (Winter, 1973), 311-313.

_____. "The Tour"
M. D. Uroff, "Sylvia Plath and Confessional Poetry: A Reconsideration," IowaR, 8 (Winter, 1977), 108-109.

_____. "Tulips"
Marjorie Perloff, "Angst and Animism in the Poetry of Sylvia Plath," JML, 1, No. 1 (1970), 69-70.

Constance Scheerer, "The Deathly Paradise of Sylvia Plath," AR, 34 (Summer, 1976), 476.

M. D. Uroff, "Sylvia Plath and Confessional Poetry: A Reconsideration," IowaR, 8 (Winter, 1977), 107-108.

M. D. Uroff, "Sylvia Plath's Women," CP, 7 (Spring, 1974), 51-52.

_____. "Wintering"
Rose Kamel, "'A Self to Recover': Sylvia Plath's Bee Cycle Poems," MPS, 4 (Winter, 1973), 316-317.

_____. "You're"
Margaret D. Uroff, "Sylvia Plath on Motherhood," MQ, 15 (Autumn, 1973), 77-78.

_____. "Zoo Keeper's Wife"
M. D. Uroff, "Sylvia Plath's Women," CP, 7 (Spring, 1974), 48-49.

POE. "Al Aaraaf"
Sharon Furrow, "Psyche and Setting: Poe's Picturesque Landscapes," Criticism, 15 (Winter, 1973), 23-24.

R. C. and M. M. Pettigrew, "A Reply to Floyd Stovall's Interpretation of 'Al Aaraaf,'" AL, 8 (Jan., 1937), 439-445.

Floyd Stovall, "An Interpretation of Poe's 'Al Aaraaf,'" Studies in English (Austin: Univ. of Texas, 1929), 9, 106-133.

_____. "Annabel Lee"
Bradford Booth, "The Identity of Annabel Lee," CE, 7 (Oct., 1945), 17-19.

Wallace C. Brown, "The English Professor's Dilemma," CE, 5 (April, 1944), 380-382.

_____. "The Bells"
Arthur E. Du Bois, "The Jazz Bells of Poe," CE, 2 (Dec., 1940), 230-244.

_____. "The City in the Sea"
Richard E. Amacher, Expl, 19 (May, 1961), 60.
    Rpt. The Explicator Cyclopedia, II, pp. 235-237.

Roy P. Basler, Expl, 4 (Feb., 1946), 30.
    Rpt. The Explicator Cyclopedia, II, p. 235.

Basler, Sex, Symbolism, and Psychology in Literature, pp. 192-195.

Bowra, The Romantic Imagination, pp. 183-184.

Wilson O. Clough, "Poe's 'The City in the Sea' Revisited," in Essays on American Literature, ed. Clarence Gohdes, pp. 81-89.

T. Frederick Keefer, "'The City in the Sea': A Re-Examination," CE, 25 (March, 1964), 436-439.

T. O. Mabbott, Expl, 4 (Oct., 1945), 1.
    Rpt. The Explicator Cyclopedia, II, pp. 233-235.

Eric W. Stockton, "Celestial Inferno: Poe's 'The City in the Sea,'" TSL, 8 (1963), 99-105.

_____. "The Conqueror Worm"
Klaus Lubbers, "Poe's 'The Conqueror Worm,'" AL, 39 (Nov., 1967), 375-379.

Donald R. Swanson, Expl, 19 (April, 1961), 52.
    Rpt. The Explicator Cyclopedia, II, pp. 237-238.

_____. "Dream-Land"
J. O. Bailey, "The Geography of Poe's 'Dream-Land' and 'Ulalume,'" SP, 45 (July, 1948), 517-518.

_____. "Eldorado"
Eric W. Carlson, "Poe's 'Eldorado,'" MLN, 76 (March, 1961), 232-234.

O. S. Coad, "The Meaning of Poe's 'Eldorado,'" MLN, 59 (Jan., 1944), 59-61.

T. O. Mabbott, "The Sources of Poe's 'Eldorado,'" MLN, 60 (June, 1945), 312-314.

Burton R. Pollin, "Poe's 'Eldorado' Viewed as a Song of the West," PrS, 46 (Fall, 1972), 228-235.

W. Stephen Sanderlin, Jr., "Poe's 'Eldorado' Again," MLN, 71 (March, 1956), 189-192.

_____. "An Enigma"
W. T. Bandy, Expl, 20 (Dec., 1961), 35.
    Rpt. The Explicator Cyclopedia, II, p. 238.

_____. "Evening Star"
Patrick E. Kilburn, Expl, 28 (May, 1970), 76.

_____. "For Annie"
Bowra, The Romantic Imagination, pp. 188-189.

_____. "The Haunted Palace"
Richard Wilbur, "The House of Poe," Anniversary Lectures 1959, pp. 26-28.

_____. "Introduction"
David M. Rein, Expl, 29 (Sept., 1961), 8.
    Rpt. The Explicator Cyclopedia, II, pp. 238-239.

_____. "Israfel"
T. O. Mabbott, Expl, 2 (June, 1944), 57.
    Rpt. The Explicator Cyclopedia, II, pp. 239-240.

W. L. Werner, Expl, 2 (April, 1944), 44.
    Rpt. The Explicator Cyclopedia, II, p. 239.

_____. "The Lake: To_____"
Robert Morrison, Expl, 7 (Dec., 1948), 22.
    Rpt. The Explicator Cyclopedia, II, pp. 240-241.

_____. "Lenore"
J. C. Broderick, "Poe's Revisions of 'Lenore,'" AL, 35 (Jan., 1964), 504-509.

_____. "The Raven"
Howard Mumford Jones, "Poe, 'The Raven,' and the Anonymous Young Man," WHR, 9 (Spring, 1955), 132-138.

Roman Jakobson, "Linguistics and Poetics," in Essays on the Language of Literature, ed. Seymour Chatman and Samuel R. Levin (Boston: Houghton Mifflin Company, 1967), pp. 316-317.

Barton Levi St. Armand, "Poe's Emblematic Raven: A Pictorial Approach," ESQ, No. 22 (4th Quarter, 1976), 191-210.

John J. Teunissen and Evelyn J. Hinz, "'Quaint and curious': Backgrounds for Poe's 'Raven,'" SHR, 7 (Fall, 1973), 411-419.

_____. "The Sleeper"
W. B. Hunter, Jr., "Poe's 'The Sleeper' and Macbeth," AL, 20 (March, 1948), 55-57.

T. O. Mabbott, "Poe's 'The Sleeper' Again," AL, 21 (Nov., 1949), 339-340.

_____. "Stanzas"
Michael Hinden, "Poe's Debt to Wordsworth: A Reading of 'Stanzas,'" SIR, 8 (Winter, 1969), 109-120.

_____. "To Helen"
Bowra, The Romantic Imagination, pp. 185-186, 192.

Wallace C. Brown, "The English Professor's Dilemma," CE, 5 (April, 1944), 382-385.

Alice Moser Claudel, "Poe as Voyager in 'To Helen,'" ESQ, No. 60 (Fall, 1970), Supplement, 33-37.

Cohen, Writing About Literature, pp. 3-7, 95-97.

Robert A. Colby, "Poe's Philosophy of Composition," The University of Kansas City Review, 20 (Spring, 1954), 211-214.

Drew, Poetry: A Modern Guide, p. 209.

T. O. Mabbott, Expl, 1 (June, 1943), 60.
    Rpt. Readings for Liberal Education, II, 209-210.
    Rpt. The Explicator Cyclopedia, II, p. 241.

Rosenthal and Smith, Exploring Poetry, pp. 603-604.

Satin, Reading Poetry, pp. 1080-1081.

_____. "To One in Paradise"
R. P. Basler, "Byronism in Poe's 'To One in Paradise,'" AL, 9 (May, 1937), 232-236.

_____. "Ulalume"
J. O. Bailey, "The Geography of Poe's 'Dream-Land' and 'Ulalume,'" SP, 45 (July, 1948), 518-523.

Roy P. Basler, Expl, 2 (May, 1944), 49.
    Rpt. The Explicator Cyclopedia, II, pp. 243-244.

Basler, Sex, Symbolism, and Psychology in Literature, pp. 184-187.
    Rpt. Stallman and Watters, The Creative Reader, pp. 861-862.

J. M. Blumenfield, "Poe's 'Ulalume,' Line 43," N&Q, 197 (March 29, 1952), 147.

Brooks and Warren, Understanding Poetry, Revised Edition, pp. 197-201.

Eric W. Carlson, Expl, 11 (June, 1953), 56.
    Rpt. The Explicator Cyclopedia, II, p. 245.

Eric W. Carlson, "Symbol and Sense in Poe's 'Ulalume,'" AL, 35 (March, 1963), 22-37.

Thomas E. Connolly, Expl, 22 (Sept., 1963), 4.

J. P. Kirby, Expl, 1 (Oct., 1942), 8.
    Rpt. The Explicator Cyclopedia, II, pp. 241-242.

Lewis Leary, Expl, 6 (Feb., 1948), 25.
    Rpt. The Explicator Cyclopedia, II, p. 244.

T. O. Mabbott, Expl, 1 (Feb., 1943), 25.
    Rpt. The Explicator Cyclopedia, II, pp. 242-243.

T. O. Mabbott, Expl, 6 (June, 1948), 57.
    Rpt. Stallman and Watters, The Creative Reader, pp. 860-861.
    Rpt. The Explicator Cyclopedia, II, pp. 244-245.

James E. Miller, Jr., "'Ulalume' Resurrected," PQ, 34 (April, 1955), 197-205.

Edward Strickland, Expl, 34 (Nov., 1975), 19.

Unger and O'Connor, Poems for Study, pp. 468-472.

Yvor Winters, "A Crisis in the History of American Obscurantism," AL, 8 (Jan., 1937), 394-395.
    Rpt. Maule's Curse, pp. 112-113.
    Rpt. In Defense of Reason, pp. 252-253.

_____. "The Valley of Unrest"
Roy P. Basler, Expl, 5 (Dec., 1946), 25.
   Rpt. The Explicator Cyclopedia, II, pp. 245-246.

Basler, Sex, Symbolism and Psychology in Literature, pp. 197-200.
   Rpt. Locke, Gibson and Arms, Introduction to Literature, third edi-
   tion, pp. 121-122.
   Rpt. fourth edition, pp. 120-121.
   Rpt. fifth edition, pp. 111-112.

POPE. "Autumn"
Martin C. Battestin, The Providence of Wit: Aspects of Form in Augustun
Literature and the Arts (London: Oxford Univ. Press, 1974), pp. 69-71.

_____. "The Dunciad"
Martin C. Battestin, The Providence of Wit: Aspects of Form in Augustun
Literature and the Arts (London: Oxford Univ. Press, 1974), pp. 102-118.

Sanford Budick, Poetry of Civilization: Mythopoeic Displacement in the
Verse of Milton, Dryden, Pope and Johnson (New Haven and London: Yale
Univ. Press, 1974), pp. 130-155.

Max Byrd, Visits to Bedlam: Madness and Literature in the Eighteenth
Century (Columbia: Univ. of South Carolina Press, 1974), pp. 12-36.

Teona Tone Gneiting, "Pictorial Imagery and Satiric Inversion in Pope's
Dunciad," ECS, 8 (Summer, 1975), 420-430.

Knight, The Burning Oracle, pp. 174-182.

C. R. Kropf, "Education and the Neoplatonic Idea of Wisdom in Pope's
Dunciad," TSLL, 14 (Winter, 1973), 593-604.

C. R. Kropf, "Miscreation: Another Miltonic Allusion in The Dunciad,"
PLL, 10 (Fall, 1974), 425-427.

F. R. Leavis, "The Dunciad," Scrutiny, 12 (Winter, 1943), 74-80.

Barbara Kiefer Lewalski, "On Looking into Pope's Milton," EA, 27 (Oct.-
Dec., 1974), 494-498.

Nancy Conrad Martinez, "Little Epics: More Lively and Choleric," Diss.
Univ. of New Mexico, 1976, pp. 133-144.

Elias F. Mengel, Jr., "The Dunciad Illustrations," ECS, 7 (Winter,
1973-74), 161-178.

David B. Morris, "The Kinship of Madness in Pope's Dunciad," PQ, 51
(Oct., 1972), 813-831.

John V. Regan, "Orpheus and the Dunciad's Narrator," ECS, 9 (Fall,
1975), 87-101.

B. L. Reid, "Ordering Chaos: The Dunciad," in Quick Springs of Sense
Studies in the Eighteenth Century, ed. Larry S. Champion (Athens: Univ.
of Georgia, 1974), pp. 75-96.

Arthur Sherbo, "No Single Scholiast: Pope's 'The Dunciad,'" MLR, 65
(July, 1970), 503-516.

George Sherburn, The Dunciad, Book IV," Studies in English 1944 (Austin:
Univ. of Texas Press, 1944), pp. 174-190.

Donald T. Siebert, "Cibber and Satan: The Dunciad and Civilization,"
ECS, 10 (Winter, 1976-77), 203-221.

_____. "The Dunciad," III
Daniel P. Deneau, "Pope's 'Iv'ry Gate': The Dunciad, III, 349," MLN, 74 (March, 1959), 208-212.

_____. "The Dunciad," IV
Max Bluestone, Expl, 20 (Jan., 1962), 40.
    Rpt. The Explicator Cyclopedia, II, pp. 247-248.

Jessie R. Chambers, "The Episode of Annius and Mummius: 'Dunciad' IV, 347-96," PQ, 43 (April, 1964), 185-192.

Thomas R. Edwards, Jr., Expl, 16 (May, 1958), 50.
    Rpt. The Explicator Cyclopedia, II, pp. 246-247.

William Kinsley, "Physico-Demonology in Pope's 'Dunciad,'" MLR, 70 (Jan., 1975), 20-31.

C. R. Kropf, "Education and the Neoplatonic Idea of Wisdom in Pope's Dunciad," TSLL, 14 (Winter, 1973), 593-604.

F. R. Leavis, "The Responsible Critic: Or the Function of Criticism at Any Time," Scrutiny, 19 (Spring, 1953), 171-172.

David M. Vieth, Expl, 25 (Dec., 1966), 36.

_____. "Elegy to the Memory of an Unfortunate Lady"
Christopher Gillie, Interpretations, ed. John Wain, pp. 77-85.

F. R. Leavis, "The Poetry of Pope (Revaluations II)," Scrutiny, 2 (Dec., 1933), 269-274, 276-277.
    Rpt. Revaluation, pp. 69-73, 80-81.

Howard D. Weinbrot, "Pope's 'Elegy to the Memory of an Unfortunate Lady,'" MLQ, 32 (Sept., 1971), 255-267.

_____. "Eloisa to Abelard"
W. B. Carnochan, Confinement and Flight: An Essay on Flight: An Essay on English Literature of the Eighteenth Century (Berkeley: Univ. of California Press, 1977), pp. 81-87.

Evelyn Hooven, "Racine and Pope's Eloisa," EIC, 24 (Oct., 1974), 368-374.

David K. Jeffrey, "A 'Strange Itch in the Flesh of a Nun': The Dramatic Movement and the Imagery of Pope's 'Eloisa to Abelard,'" BSUF, 16 (Autumn, 1975), 28-35.

Robert P. Kalmey, "Rhetoric, Language, and Structure in Eloisa to Abelard," ECS, 5 (Winter, 1971-72), 314-318.

Knight, The Burning Oracle, pp. 148-155.

Murray Krieger, "Ekphrasis and the Still Movement of Poetry; or, Laokoön Revisited," in The Poet as Critic, pp. 9-10, 16.

Murray Krieger, "'Eloisa to Abelard': The Escape from Body or the Embrace of Body," ECS, 3 (Fall, 1969), 30-47.

Murray Krieger, "Reply to Robert Kalmey," ECS, 5 (Winter, 1971-72), 318-320.

Langbaum, The Poetry of Experience, pp. 146-148.

Miles, Major Adjectives in English Poetry, pp. 341-346.

David B. Morris, "'The Visionary Maid': Tragic Passion and Redemptive Sympathy in Pope's 'Eloisa to Abelard,'" MLQ, 34 (Sept., 1973), 247-271.

Henry Pettit, "Pope's 'Eloisa to Abelard': An Interpretation," USCLL, No. 4 (July, 1953), 72-79.

Hoyt Trowbridge, "Pope's Eloisa and the Heroides of Ovid," in Studies in Eighteenth-Century Culture, ed. Harold Pagliaro, III (Cleveland and London: Case Western Reserve Univ. Press, 1973), pp. 11-34.
  Rpt. Hoyt Trowbridge, From Dryden to Jane Austen: Essays on English Critics and Writers, 1660-1818, (Albuquerque: Univ. of New Mexico Press, 1977), pp. 140-149.

_____. "Epilogue to the Satires"
Donald J. Greene, "'Dramatic Texture' in Pope," in From Sensibility to Romanticism, pp. 42-47.

Malcolm Kelsall, "Augustus and Pope," HLQ, 39 (Feb., 1976), 127-130.

_____. "Epilogue to the Satires, Dialogue I"
Edwards, Imagination and Power, pp. 107-118.

Maynard Mack, English Masterpieces, Vol. V, The Augustans, pp. 32-34.

Rebecca Price Parkin, "The Quality of Alexander Pope's Humor," CE, 14 (Jan., 1953), 200-201.

Hugo M. Reichard, "The Drift of Pope's First 'Epilogue,'" Boston University Studies in English, 4 (Summer, 1960), 106-113.

Howard D. Weinbrot, "History, Horace, and Augustus Caesar: Some Implications for Eighteenth-Century Satire," ECS, 7 (Summer, 1974), 408-410.

_____. "Epilogue to the Satires, Dialogue II"
Purvis E. Boyette, Expl, 24 (Jan., 1966), 46.

_____. "Epistle to Dr. Arbuthnot"
Jo Allen Bradham, Expl, 26 (Feb., 1968), 50.

Wallace Brown, "Dramatic Tension in Neoclassic Satire," CE, 6 (Feb., 1945), 265-266.

Lawrence Lee Davidow, "Pope's Verse Epistles: Friendship and the Private Sphere of Life," HLQ, 40 (Feb., 1977), 155-168.

Betty Coslow Dodd, Expl, 19 (Dec., 1960), 17.
  Rpt. The Explicator Cyclopedia, II, pp. 248-249.

Richard H. Douglass, "More on the Rhetoric and Imagery of Pope's Arbuthnot," SEL, 13 (Summer, 1973), 488-502.

Donald J. Greene, "'Dramatic Texture' in Pope," in From Sensibility to Romanticism, pp. 38-41.

F. T. Griffiths, "Puns on Poetry and Pope in 'An Epistle to Dr. Arbuthnot,'" N&Q, 24 (May-June, 1977), 239-240.

J. P. Hardy, Reinterpretations: Essays on Poems by Milton, Pope and Johnson (London: Routledge & Kegan Paul, 1971), pp. 81-102.

Ripley Hotch, "The Dilemma of an Obedient Son: Pope's Epistle to Dr. Arbuthnot," ELWIU, 1 (Spring, 1974), 37-45.

U. C. Knoepflmacher, "The Poet as Physician: Pope's Epistle to Dr. Arbuthnot," MLQ, 31 (Dec., 1970), 440-449.

Maynard Mack, English Masterpieces, Vol. V, The Augustans, pp. 30-32.

Elder Olson, "Rhetoric and the Appreciation of Pope," MP, 37 (August, 1939), 21-35.

Patricia Meyer Spacks, "In Search of Sincerity," CE, 29 (May, 1968), 596-598.

_____. "Epistle to Miss Blount"
John D. Boyd, Expl, 35 (Fall, 1977), 21-23.

_____. "An Essay on Criticism"
John M. Aden, "'First Follow Nature': Strategy and Stratification in An Essay on Criticism," JEGP, 55 (Oct., 1956), 604-617.

John M. Aden, "The Doctrinal Design of An Essay on Criticism," CE, 22 (Feb., 1961), 311-315.

Tuvia Bloch, Expl, 30 (April, 1972), 68.

Empson, The Structure of Complex Words, pp. 84-100.

William Empson, "Wit in the 'Essay on Criticism,'" HudR, 2 (Winter, 1950), 559-577.

Alan S. Fisher, "Cheerful Noonday, Gloomy Twilight: Pope's Essay on Criticism," PQ, 51 (Oct., 1972), 832-844.

Ripley Hotch, "Pope Surveys His Kingdom: An Essay on Criticism," SEL, 13 (Summer, 1973), 474-487.

Martin Kallich, "Pegasus on the Seesaw: Balance and Antithesis in Pope's Essay on Criticism," TSL, 12 (1967), 57-66.

Maynard Mack, English Masterpieces, Vol. V, The Augustans, pp. 20-23.

Douglas B. Park, "'At Once the Source and End': Nature's Defining Pattern in An Essay on Criticism," PMLA, 90 (Oct., 1975), 861-873.

Rebecca P. Parkin, "Alexander Pope's Use of the Implied Dramatic Speaker," CE, 11 (Dec., 1949), 140-141.

Rebecca Price Parkin, "The Quality of Alexander Pope's Humor," CE, 14 (Jan., 1953), 197-199.

Hugo M. Reichard, "Pope's Exacting Course in Criticism," SAQ, 75 (Autumn, 1976), 470-482.

Patricia Meyer Spacks, "Imagery and Method in An Essay on Criticism," PMLA, 85 (Jan., 1970), 97-106.

James Edward Tobin, "Alexander Pope, 1744-1944," Thought, 19 (June, 1944), 250-261.

_____. "An Essay on Man"
George Arms, Expl, 1 (April, 1943), 44.
   Rpt. The Explicator Cyclopedia, II, p. 250.

A. Barbeau, "The Wild and the Garden: A Double Focus on Reality in Pope's An Essay on Man," TSL, 22 (1977), 73-84.

Brett, Reason and Imagination, pp. 51-77.

Allen Barry Cameron, Expl, 26 (Nov., 1967), 23.

J. M. Cameron, "Doctrinal to an Age: Notes Towards a Revaluation of Pope's Essay on Man," The Dublin Review, 225 (Second Quarter, 1951), 54-69.

Peter Dixon, Expl, 23 (Nov., 1964), 21.

Br. Roland Faley, T.O.R., Expl, 9 (May, 1951), 51.
   Rpt. The Explicator Cyclopedia, II, pp. 251-252.

William Frost, Expl, 6 (Nov., 1947), 11.
   Rpt. The Explicator Cyclopedia, II, pp. 250-251.

R. E. Hughes, "Pope's Essay on Man: The Rhetorical Structure of Epistle I," MLN, 80 (March, 1955), 177-181.

Martin Kallick, Expl, 25 (Oct., 1966), 17.

J. P. Kirby, Expl, 1 (Nov., 1942), 12.
   Rpt. The Explicator Cyclopedia, II, p. 249.

Knight, The Burning Oracle, pp. 159-174.

John Laird, "Pope's Essay on Man," RES, 20 (Oct., 1944), 286-298.

Maynard Mack, English Masterpieces, Vol. V, The Augustans, pp. 26-29.

Maynard Mack, "On Reading Pope," CE, 7 (Feb., 1946), 271-272.

Francis Manley, Expl, 15 (April, 1957), 44.
   Rpt. The Explicator Cyclopedia, II, p. 252.

Miles, Major Adjectives in English Poetry, pp. 340-345.

Berna Moran, "Pope and Thomas Vaughan," TLS, May 4, 1951, p. 277.

Rebecca P. Parkin, "Alexander Pope's Use of the Implied Dramatic Speaker," CE, 11 (Dec., 1949), 139-140.

Rebecca Price Parkin, "The Quality of Alexander Pope's Humor," CE, 14 (Jan., 1953), 199-200.

F. E. L. Priestley, "'Order, Union, Full Consent of Things!'" UTQ, 42 (Fall, 1972), 1-13.

Irène Simon, "'An Essay on Man' III, 109-146: a Footnote," ES, 50 (Feb., 1969), 93-98.

John Sutherland, "Wit, Reason, Vision, and An Essay on Man," MLQ, 30 (Sept., 1969), 356-369.

James Edward Tobin, "Alexander Pope, 1744-1944," Thought, 19 (June, 1944), 259.

Henry Wasser, Expl, 7 (Nov., 1948), 12.
   Rpt. The Explicator Cyclopedia, II, pp. 249-250.

_____. "Essay on Man, Epistle II"
Thomas R. Edwards, "Visible Poetry: Pope and Modern Criticism," in Twentieth-Century Literature in Retrospect, ed. Reuben A. Brower (Cambridge: Harvard Univ. Press, 1971), 304-317.

_____. "Ode for Musick on St. Cecilia's Day"
Earl R. Wasserman, "Pope's 'Ode for Musick,'" ELH, 28 (June, 1961), 169-186.

_____. "Ode on Solitude"
Stauffer, The Nature of Poetry, pp. 160-162.

_____. "Pastorals"
Martin C. Battestin, "The Transforming Power: Nature and Art in Pope's Pastorals," ECS, 2 (Fall, 1968), 183-204.

David S. Durant, "Man and Nature in Alexander Pope's Pastorals," SEL, 11 (Summer, 1971), 469-485.

_____. "The Rape of the Lock"

Kent Beyette, "Ovid and Pope's Rape of the Lock," CEA, 37 (Jan., 1975), 23-24.

Cleanth Brooks, "The Case of Miss Arabella Fermor: A Re-Examination," SR, 51 (Autumn, 1943), 505-524.

Brooks, The Well Wrought Urn, pp. 74-95.

W. B. Carnochan, Expl, 22 (Feb., 1964), 45.

Arthur E. Case, "The Game of Ombre in 'The Rape of the Lock,'" Studies in English, 1944 (Austin: Univ. of Texas Press, 1944), pp. 191-196.

Murray Cohen, "Versions of the Lock: Readers of 'The Rape of the Lock,'" ELH, 43 (Spring, 1976), 53-73.

Ralph Cohen, "Transformation in The Rape of the Lock," ECS, 2 (Fall, 1968), 205-224.

Michael G. Cooke, The Romantic Will (New Haven and London: Yale Univ. Press, 1976), pp. 70-74.

Marie Cornelia, "The Rape of the Lock and the Romance Tradition," ConnR, 8 (Oct., 1974), 84-89.

J. R. Crider, Expl, 27 (Sept., 1968), 3.

Maureen Duffy, The Erotic World of Faery (London: Hodder and Stoughton, 1972), pp. 202-206.

Dyson and Lovelock, Masterful Images, pp. 97-123.

Robert Folkenflik, "Metamorphosis in The Rape of the Lock," ArielE, 5 (April, 1974), 27-36.

Samuel A. Golden, Expl, 22 (Oct., 1963), 12.

J. P. Hardy, Reinterpretations: Essays on Poems by Milton, Pope and Johnson (London: Routledge & Kegan Paul, 1971), pp. 50-80.

Arthur W. Hoffman, "Spenser and The Rape of the Lock," PQ, 49 (Oct., 1970), 530-546.

James L. Jackson, "Pope's The Rape of the Lock Considered as a Five-Act Epic," PMLA, 65 (Dec., 1950), 1283-1287.

J. G. Keogh, Expl, 30 (Dec., 1971), 31.

Knight, The Burning Oracle, pp. 136-148.

Murray Krieger, "Ekphrasis and the Still Movement of Poetry; or, Laokoön Revisited," in The Poet as Critic, pp. 12-15.

Murray Kreiger, "The 'Frail China Jar' and the Rude Hand of Chaos," CentR, 5 (Spring, 1961), 176-194.
     Rpt. Krieger, The Play and Place of Criticism, pp. 54-68.

Louis A. Landa, "Pope's Belinda, the General Emporie of the World, and the Wondrous Worm," SAQ, 70 (Spring, 1971), 215-235.

Maynard Mack, English Masterpieces, Vol. V, The Augustans, pp. 23-26.

John B. McKee, "The 'Outside World' and the Game of Omber in Pope's The Rape of the Lock: An Experiment in the Use of Evolutionary Evidence," CP, 9 (Fall, 1976), 47-52.

Thomas E. Maresca, "Language and Body in Augustan Poetic," ELH, 37 (Sept., 1970), 381-384.

Nancy Conrad Martinez, "Little Epics: More Lively and Choleric," Diss. Univ. of New Mexico, 1976, pp. 121-132.

Rebecca Price Parkin, "The Quality of Alexander Pope's Humor," CE, 14 (Jan., 1953), 199.

Ricardo Quintana, "'The Rape of the Lock' as a Comedy of Continuity," A Review of English Literature, 7 (April, 1966), 9-19.

Hugo M. Reichard, "The Love Affair in Pope's Rape of the Lock," PMLA, 69 (Sept., 1954), 887-902.

Pat Rogers, "Faery Lore and The Rape of the Lock," RES, 25 (Feb., 1974), 25-38.

Pat Rogers, "Wit and Grammar in The Rape of the Lock," JEGP, 72 (Jan., 1973), 17-31.

Wolfgang E. H. Rudat, "Belinda's 'Painted Vessel': Allusive Technique in The Rape of the Lock," TSL, 19 (1974), 49-55.

Wolfgang E. H. Rudat, Expl, 32 (Nov., 1973), 23.

Wolfgang E. H. Rudat, Expl, 34 (Oct., 1975), 13.

Wolfgang E. H. Rudat, "Pope's Clarissa, the Trojan Horse, and Swift's Houyhnhnms," FMLS, 13 (Jan., 1977), 6-11.

Harold E. Toliver, Pastoral: Forms and Attitudes (Berkeley: Univ. of California Press, 1971), pp. 177-184, 187-189.

Harold Toliver, "The Augustan Balance of Nature and Art in 'The Rape of the Lock,'" CP, 1 (Spring, 1968), 58-68.

John Trimble, "Clarissa's Role in The Rape of the Lock," TSLL, 15 (Winter, 1974), 673-691.

Warren, Rage for Order, pp. 46-49.
   Rpt. Modern Literary Criticism, pp. 333-335.
   Rpt. West, Essays in Modern Literary Criticism, pp. 371-373.

Austin Warren, "The Mask of Pope," SR, 54 (Winter, 1946), 27-31.

Earl R. Wasserman, "The Limits of Allusion in The Rape of the Lock," JEGP, 65 (July, 1966), 425-444.

Wheeler, The Design of Poetry, pp. 96-99.

Robert F. Willson, Jr., "The Rape's Muse: Pope's Ironic Invocation," AN&Q, 14 (Jan., 1976), 72.

W. K. Wimsatt, "Belinda Ludens: Strife and Play in The Rape of the Lock," NLH, 4 (Winter, 1973), 357-374.
   Rpt. Day of the Leopards: Essays in Defense of Poems (New Haven and London: Yale Univ. Press, 1976), pp. 99-116.

_____. "Satire II"
Cedric D. Reverend, II, "Ut pictura poesis and Pope's 'Satire II,'" ECS, 9 (Summer, 1976), 553-568.

_____. "Solitude"
W. B. Carnochan, Confinement and Flight: An Essay on English Literature of the Eighteenth Century (Berkeley: Univ. of California Press, 1977), pp. 173-178.

_____. "Spring"
Martin C. Battestin, The Providence of Wit: Aspects of Form in Augustan Literature and the Arts (London: Oxford Univ. Press, 1974), pp. 66-67.

_____. "Summer"
Martin C. Battestin, The Providence of Wit: Aspects of Form in Augustan Literature and the Arts (London: Oxford Univ. Press, 1974), pp. 67-69.

Wolfgang E. H. Rudat, Expl, 35 (Spring, 1977), 9-11.

_____. "Timon's Villa" (From "To the Right Honourable Richard Earl of Burlington")
Packham and Chatman, Word, Meaning, Poem, pp. 38-58.

_____. "To a Lady" ("Moral Essays, Epistle II")
Douglas, Lamson, and Smith, The Critical Reader, pp. 25-31.
     Rpt. Locke, Gibson, and Arms, Introduction to Literature, third edition, pp. 68-72.
     Revised edition, pp. 635-641.
     Rpt. fourth edition, pp. 63-67.
     Rpt. fifth edition, pp. 64-68.

J. G. Keogh, Expl, 31 (Jan., 1973), 37.

Maynard Mack, English Masterpieces, Vol. V, The Augustans, pp. 29-30.

Felicity A. Nussbaum, "Pope's 'To a Lady' and the Eighteenth-Century Woman," PQ, 54 (Spring, 1975), 444-456.

Thomas A. Stumpf, "Pope's To Cobham, To a Lady, and the Traditions of Inconstancy," SP, 67 (July, 1970), 355-358.

Unger and O'Connor, Poems for Study, pp. 254-262.

_____. "To Allen, Lord Bathurst" ("Moral Essays, Epistle III")
Thomas R. Edwards, Jr., "'Reconcil'd Extremes': Pope's 'Epistle to Bathurst,'" EIC, 11 (July, 1961), 290-308.

Maynard Mack, "On Reading Pope," CE, 7 (Feb., 1946), 269-271.

Steven N. Zwicker, "Politics and Panegyric: The Figural Mode from Marvell to Pope," in Literary Uses of Typology from the Late Middle Ages to the Present, pp. 141-143.

_____. "To Augustus" ("The First Epistle of the Second Book of Horace Imitated")
John M. Aden, Expl, 26 (May, 1968), 70.

Malcolm Kelsall, "Augustus and Pope," HLQ, 39 (Feb., 1976), 119-127.

Manuel Schonhorn, "Pope's Epistle to Augustus: Notes Toward a Mythology," TSL, 16 (1971), 15-33.

_____. "To Lord Bolingbroke" ("The First Epistle of the First Book of Horace Imitated")

Barbara Lauren, "Pope's Epistle to Bolingbroke: Satire from the Vantage of Retirement," SEL, 15 (Summer, 1975), 419-430.

_____. "To Mr. Addison" ("Moral Essays, Epistle V")
Thomas O. Mabbott, Expl, 10 (Nov., 1951), 11.
     Rpt. The Explicator Cyclopedia, II, pp. 253-254.

_____. "To Mr. Bethel" ("The Second Satire of the Second Book of Horace")
Donald J. Greene, "'Dramatic Texture' in Pope," in From Sensibility to Romanticism, pp. 32-37.

_____. "To Mr. Fortescue" (The First Satire of the Second Book of Horace Imitated)
Thomas E. Maresca, "Pope's Defense of Satire: 'The First Satire of the Second Book of Horace Imitated,'" ELH, 31 (Dec., 1964), 366-394.

_____. "To Richard Boyle, Earl of Burlington" ("Moral Essays, Epistle IV, Of the Use of Riches")
Brower, The Fields of Light, pp. 144-163.

William A. Gibson, "Three Principles of Renaissance Architectural Theory in Pope's Epistle to Burlington," SEL, 11 (Summer, 1971), 487-505.

Avril Henry and Peter Dixon, "A Note on the Epistle to Burlington," ES, 51 (Oct., 1970), 437-441.

John P. Kirby, Expl, 1 (Oct., 1942), 3.
   Rpt. The Explicator Cyclopedia, II, pp. 252-253.

Donald M. Korte, Expl, 28 (Dec., 1969), 34.

F. R. Leavis, "The Poetry of Pope (Revaluations II)," Scrutiny, 2 (Dec., 1933), 274-276.
   Rpt. Revaluation, pp. 77-80, 92-100.

Ribner and Morris, Poetry, pp. 203-206.

_____. "To Sir Richard Temple, Lord Cobham" ("Moral Essays, Epistle I")

Rodney M. Baine, Expl, 30 (Oct., 1971), 14.

Thomas A. Stumpf, "Pope's To Cobham, To A Lady and the Traditions of Inconstancy," SP, 67 (July, 1970), 345-355.

_____. "To Venus" ("The First Ode of the Fourth Book of Horace Imitated")
Robert F. Fleissner, Expl, 34 (Feb., 1976), 42.

_____. "Windsor Forest"
Sanford Budick, Poetry of Civilization: Mythopoeic Displacement in the Verse of Milton, Pope and Johnson (New Haven and London: Yale Univ. Press, 1974), pp. 111-124.

Frances M. Clements, "Lansdowne, Pope, and the Unity of Windsor-Forest," MLQ, 33 (March, 1972), 44-53.

James King, Expl, 31 (May, 1973), 71.

Knight, The Burning Oracle, pp. 131-136.

Karl Kroeber, Romantic Landscape Vision: Constable and Wordsworth (Madison: Univ. of Wisconsin Press, 1975), pp. 93-97.

Maynard Mack, "On Reading Pope," CE, 7 (Feb., 1946), 264-268.

David B. Morris, "Virgilian Attitudes in Pope's Windsor-Forest," TSLL, 15 (Summer, 1973), 231-250.

Pottle, The Idiom of Poetry, pp. 113-122; (1946 ed.), pp. 121-129.

Wasserman, The Subtler Language, pp. 101-168.

_____. "Winter"
Martin C. Battestin, The Providence of Wit: Aspects of Form in Augustan Literature and the Arts (London: Oxford Univ. Press, 1974), pp. 71-74.

Gary A. Boire, "The Context of Allusion and Pope's 'Winter' Pastoral," CP, 10 (Spring, 1977), 79-84.

PORTER, Peter. "A Christmas Recalled"
　　　Philip Hobsbaum, Theory of Criticism (Bloomington and London: Indiana
　　　Univ. Press, 1970), pp. 180-184.

POUND. "The Alchemist"
　　　Rosenthal, The Modern Poets, p. 53.

_____. "Ballad of the Goodly Fere"
　　　Abad, A Formal Approach to Lyric Poetry, pp. 172-173, 175-176.

　　　Riding and Graves, A Survey of Modernist Poetry, pp. 140-142.

_____. "Ballatetta"
　　　Satin, Reading Poetry, pp. 1070-1071.

_____. "Canto 2"
　　　William Cookson, "Ezra Pound & Myth: A Reader's Guide to Canto II,"
　　　Agenda, 15, No. 2 (1977), 87-92.

_____. "Canto 20"
　　　Stephen J. Adams, "The Soundscape of the Cantos: Some Ideas of Music in
　　　the Poetry of Ezra Pound," HAB, 28 (Spring, 1977), 177-181.

_____. "Canto 75"
　　　Stephen J. Adams, "The Soundscape of the Cantos: Some Ideas of Music in
　　　the Poetry of Ezra Pound," HAB, 28 (Spring, 1977), 181-185.

_____. "Canto 86"
　　　Daniel D. Pearlman, "The Blue-eyed Eel Dame Fortune in Pound's Later
　　　Cantos," Agenda, 10 (Autumn-Winter, 1971-72), 60-62.

_____. "Cantos 88"
　　　James J. Wilhelm, "The Dragon and the Duel: A Defense of Pound's Canto
　　　88," TCL, 20 (April, 1974), 114-125.

_____. "Canto 91"
　　　Daniel D. Pearlman, "The Blue-eyed Eel Dame Fortune in Pound's Later
　　　Cantos," Agenda, 10 (Autumn-Winter, 1971-72), 62-66.

　　　P. L. Surette, "Having His Own Mind to Stand by Him," HudR, 27 (Winter,
　　　1974-75), 496-497, 500-502, 508.

_____. "Canto 93"
　　　Peter Whigham, "Il Suo Paradiso Terrestre," Agenda, 8 (Spring, 1970),
　　　31-34.

_____. "Canto 97"
　　　Daniel D. Pearlman, "The Blue-eyed Eel Dame Fortune in Pound's Later
　　　Cantos," Agenda, 10 (Autumn-Winter, 1971-72), 71-76.

_____. "Canto 101"
　　　John Peck, "Landscape as Ceremony in the Later Cantos: From 'The Roads
　　　of France' to 'Rock's World,'" Agenda, 9 (Spring-Summer, 1971), 46-51.

_____. "Canto 110"
　　　Donald Davie, "Cypress Versus Rock-Slide: An Appreciation of Canto 110,"
　　　Agenda, 8 (Spring, 1970), 19-26.

　　　John Peck, "Landscape as Ceremony in the Later Cantos: From 'The Roads
　　　of France' to 'Rock's World,'" Agenda, 9 (Spring-Summer, 1971), 52-61.

_____. "Canto 112"
John Peck, "Landscape as Ceremony in the Later Cantos: From 'The Roads of France' to 'Rock's World,'" Agenda, 9 (Spring-Summer, 1971), 63-66.

_____. "Effects of Music upon a Company of People"
Stephen J. Adams, "The Soundscape of the Cantos: Some Ideas of Music in the Poetry of Ezra Pound," HAB, 28 (Spring, 1977), 175-177.

_____. "Fan Piece for Her Imperial Lord"
Earl Miner, "Pound, Haiku and the Image," HudR, 9 (Winter, 1975), 580-581.

_____. "The Garden"
Van Doren, Introduction to Poetry, pp. 46-49.

_____. "Homage to Sextus Propertius"
R. P. Blackmur, "Masks of Ezra Pound," Hound and Horn, 7 (Jan.-March, 1934), 184-191.
    Rpt. Language as Gesture, pp. 130-136.

Thomas Drew-Bear, "Ezra Pound's 'Homage to Sextus Propertius,'" AL, 37 (May, 1965), 204-210.

Vincent E. Miller, "The Serious Wit of Pound's Homage to Sextus Propertius," ConL, 16 (Autumn, 1975), 452-462.

Rosenthal, The Modern Poets, pp. 55-56.

John Speirs, "Mr. Pound's Propertius," Scrutiny, 3 (Sept., 1934), 409-418.

J. P. Sullivan, "Pound's 'Homage to Propertius': The Structure of a Mask," EIC, 10 (July, 1960), 239-249.

J. P. Sullivan, "The Poet as Translater: Ezra Pound and Sextus Propertius," The Kenyon Review, 23 (Summer, 1961), 462-481.

_____. "Hugh Selwyn Mauberley"
R. P. Blackmur, "Masks of Ezra Pound," Hound and Horn, 7 (Jan.-March, 1934), 180-184.
    Rpt. Language as Gesture, pp. 126-130.

Thomas E. Connolly, "Further Notes on Mauberley," Accent, 16 (Winter, 1956), 59-67.

Deutsch, This Modern Poetry, pp. 115-118.

MacDonald Emslie, Expl, 14 (Jan., 1956), 26.
    Rpt. The Explicator Cyclopedia, I, pp. 231-232.

Feder, Ancient Myth in Modern Poetry, pp. 99-105.

A. L. French, "Mauberley: A Rejoinder," EIC, 16 (July, 1966), 356-359.

A. L. French, "'Olympian Apathein': Pound's 'Hugh Selwyn Mauberley' and Modern Poetry," EIC, 15 (Oct., 1965), 428-445.

Friar and Brinnin, Modern Poetry, pp. 527-531.

G. Giovannini, Expl, 16 (March, 1958), 35.
    Rpt. The Explicator Cyclopedia, I, pp. 232-233.

Hoffman, The Twenties, pp. 37-46.

David Holbrook, Lost Bearings in English Poetry (London: Vision Press, 1977), pp. 64-91.

George Knox, "Glaucus in 'Hugh Selwyn Mauberley,'" ES, 45 (June, 1964), 236-237.

Leavis, New Bearings on English Poetry, pp. 141-143.

Richard A. Long, Expl, 10 (June, 1952), 56.
     Rpt. The Explicator Cyclopedia, I, p. 231.

Karl Malkoff, "Allusion as Irony: Pound's Use of Dante in Hugh Selwyn Mauberley," MinnR, 7, No. 1 (1967), 81-88.

Christopher Reiss, "In Defense of Mauberley," EIC, 16 (July, 1966), 351-353.

Rosenthal, The Modern Poets, pp. 61-66.

_____. "In a Station of the Metro"
Warren Beck, "Boundaries of Poetry," CE, 4 (March, 1943), 346-347.

Ralph Bevilaqua, "Pound's 'In a Station of the Metro': A Textual Note," ELN, 8 (June, 1971), 293-296.

Brooks and Warren, Understanding Poetry, pp. 175-176. Revised edition, pp. 78-80.

John J. Espy, Expl, 11 (June, 1953), 59. Abridged in The Case for Poetry, p. 287.
     Rpt. The Explicator Cyclopedia, I, pp. 233-234.

Joseph H. Friend, "Teaching the 'Grammar of Poetry," CE, 27 (Feb., 1966), 362-363.

Thomas A. Hanzo, Expl, 11 (Feb., 1953), 26. Abridged in The Case for Poetry, p. 287.
     Rpt. The Explicator Cyclopedia, I, p. 233.

Yoshiyuki Iwamoto, Expl, 29 (Feb., 1961), 30.
     Rpt. The Explicator Cyclopedia, I, p. 235.

Michael L. Lasser, Expl, 19 (Feb., 1961), 30.
     Rpt. The Explicator Cyclopedia, I, p. 234.

Rosenthal and Smith, Exploring Poetry, pp. 157-158.

_____. "Liu Ch'e"
Suzanne Juhasz, Metaphor and the Poetry of Williams, Pound and Stevens (Lewisburg: Bucknell Univ. Press, 1974), p. 26.

_____. "Near Perigord"
Thomas E. Connolly, "Ezra Pound's 'Near Perigord': The Background of a Poem," CL, 8 (Spring, 1956), 110-116.

_____. "A Pact"
Mario L. D'Avanzo, Expl, 24 (Feb., 1966), 51.

_____. "Papyrus"
Daniels, The Art of Reading Poetry, p. 9.

Christopher M. Dawson, Expl, 9 (Feb., 1951), 30.
     Rpt. The Explicator Cyclopedia, I, p. 236.

Gilbert Highet, The Classical Tradition (New York: Oxford Univ. Press, 1949), p. 517.

John Hollander, "The Poem in the Eye," Shenandoah, 23 (Spring, 1972), 24.

_____. "Portrait d'une Femme"
Richard J. Giannone, "Eliot's 'Portrait of a Lady' and Pound's 'Portrait
d'une Femme,'" TCL, 5 (Oct., 1959), 131-134.

Perrine and Reid, 100 American Poems, pp. 82-83.

_____. "The Return"
Anonymous, "Experiment in Verse," TLS, Aug. 17, 1956, (Special Number),
iii.

Deutsch, Poetry in Our Time, pp. 124-125.

Rosenthal, The Modern Poets, pp. 51-53.

PRATT, E. J. "The Shark"
Bert Case Diltz, Sense or Nonsense: Contemporary Education at the
Crossroads (Toronto: McClelland and Stewart, 1972), pp. 90-93.

PRINCE, F. T. "The Old Age of Michelangelo"
Fred Inglis, "F. T. Prince and the Prospect for Poetry," UDQ, 1 (Autumn,
1966), 34-39.

PRIOR. "The Lady Who Offers Her Looking Glass to Venus"
Bateson, English Poetry, pp. 83-84.

_____. "An Ode"
Ribner and Morris, Poetry, pp. 219-220.

Van Doren, Introduction to Poetry, pp. 17-21.

_____. "To a Child of Quality of Five Years Old, the Author Supposed Forty"
Wheeler, The Design of Poetry, pp. 105-107.

_____. "To the Honourable Charles Montague, Esq."
Leonard E. Held, Jr., Expl, 28 (May, 1970), 75.

_____. "Written in the Beginning of Mezeray's History of France"
Daiches, A Study of Literature, pp. 168-170.

PROCTOR. "The Pilgrims"
Brooks and Warren, Understanding Poetry, pp. 334-336. Revised edition,
pp. 181-183.

PUTNAM. "Ballad of a Strange Thing"
F. O. Matthiessen, "Phelps Putnam (1894-1948)," The Kenyon Review, 11
(Winter, 1949), 80-82.
    Rpt. The Responsibilities of the Critic, pp. 274-276.

_____. "The Five Seasons"
Morton D. Zabel, "Phelps Putnam and America," Poetry, 40 (Sept., 1932),
335-344.

_____. "Hasbrouck and the Rose"
F. O. Mattheissen, "Phelps Putnam (1894-1948)," The Kenyon Review, 11
(Winter, 1949), 78-80.
    Rpt. The Responsibilities of the Critic, pp. 273-274.

RAINE, Kathleen. "The Invisible Spectrum"
    Dudley Fitts, "In Minute Particulars," The New Republic, 127 (Oct. 6,
1952), 27-28.

_____. "Pythoness"
Dudley Fitts, "In Minute Particulars," The New Republic, 127 (Oct. 6, 1952), 27.

_____. "Winter Fire"
Dudley Fitts, "In Minute Particulars," The New Republic, 127 (Oct. 6, 1952), 28.

RAKOSI, Carl. "A Journey Far Away"
Philip Wheelwright, "On the Semantics of Poetry," in Essays on the Language of Literature, ed. Seymour Chatman and Samuel R. Levin (Boston: Houghton Mifflin Company, 1967), pp. 257-258.

RALEGH. "As You Came from the Holy Land"
Felver and Nurmi, Poetry: An Introduction and Anthology, pp. 89-90.

_____. "The Lie"
George Arms and R. W. Whidden, Expl, 3 (April, 1945), 50.
    Rpt. The Explicator Cyclopedia, II, pp. 254-255.

Unger and O'Connor, Poems for Study, pp. 99-100.

_____. "The Ocean's Love to Cynthia"
Donald Davie, "A Reading of 'The Ocean's Love to Cynthia,'" in Elizabethan Poetry, pp. 71-89.

_____. "The Pilgrimage"
Melvin W. Adkew, Expl, 13 (Nov., 1954), 9.
    Rpt. The Explicator Cyclopedia, II, p. 258.

_____. "Walsingham"
O. C. Williams, Expl, 9 (Feb., 1951), 27.
    Rpt. The Explicator Cyclopedia, II, pp. 255-256.

RANSOM. "Amphibious Crocodile"
Richmond C. Beatty, "John Crowe Ransom as Poet," SR, 52 (Summer, 1944), 362-363.

_____. "Antique Harvesters"
Gray, American Poetry, pp. 210-211.

Richard Gray, "The 'Compleat Gentleman': An Approach to John Crowe Ransom," SoR, 12 (July, 1976), 628-631.

Vivienne Koch, "The Achievement of John Crowe Ransom," SR, 58 (Spring, 1950), 252-255.

Vivienne Koch, "The Poetry of John Crowe Ransom," in Modern American Poetry, ed. B. Rajan, pp. 58-61.

F. O. Matthiessen, "Primarily Language," SR, 56 (Summer, 1948), 394-395.
    Rpt. The Responsibilities of the Critic, pp. 43-44.

Louis D. Rubin, Jr., "The Concept of Nature in Modern Poetry," AQ, 9 (Spring, 1957), 69-70.

_____. "Bells for John Whiteside's Daughter"
Adams, The Contexts of Poetry, pp. 12-15.

Brooks, Lewis, and Warren, American Literature, p. 2654.

Gray, American Poetry, pp. 207-208.

Robert Heilman, "Poetic and Prosaic: Program Notes on Opposite Numbers," Pacific Spectator, 5 (Autumn, 1951), 485-460. Abridged in The Case for Poetry, p. 293.

Vivienne Koch, "The Poetry of John Crowe Ransom," in Modern American Poetry, ed. B. Rajan, pp. 43-44.

Donald A. Stauffer, "Portrait of the Critic Poet as Equilibrist," SR, 56 (Summer, 1948), 430.

R. P. Warren, "John Crowe Ransom: A Study in Irony," VQR, 11 (Jan., 1935), 106. Abridged in The Case for Poetry, p. 293.

R. P. Warren, "Pure and Impure Poetry," The Kenyon Review, 5 (Spring, 1943), 237-240.
    Rpt. Criticism, pp. 370-372.
    Rpt. Critiques, pp. 92-94.
    Rpt. The Kenyon Critics, pp. 26-29.
    Rpt. Engle and Carrier, Reading Modern Poetry, 69-71.
    Rpt. West, Essays in Modern Literary Criticism, pp. 253-255.

_____. "Blackberry Winter"
G. P. Wasserman, "The Irony of John Crowe Ransom," The University of Kansas City Review, 23 (Winter, 1956), 154-155.

_____. "Blue Girls"
Ciardi, How Does a Poem Mean? pp. 802-803.

Vivienne Koch, "The Achievement of John Crowe Ransom," SR, 58 (Spring, 250-252.

Vivienne Koch, "The Poetry of John Crowe Ransom," in Modern American Poetry, ed. B. Rajan, pp. 56-58.

Howard Nemerov, "Summer's Flare and Winter's Flaw," SR, 56 (Summer, 1948), 418.

Scott C. Osborn, Expl, 21 (Nov., 1962), 22.

William R. Osborne, Expl, 19 (May, 1961), 53.
    Rpt. The Explicator Cyclopedia, I, pp. 237-238.

Perrine and Reid, 100 American Poems, p. 138.

Hyatt H. Waggoner, Expl, 18 (Oct., 1959), 6.
    Rpt. The Explicator Cyclopedia, I, pp. 236-237.

_____. "Captain Carpenter"
Brooks, Modern Poetry and the Tradition, pp. 35-37.

Vernon Hall, Expl, 26 (Nov., 1967), 28.

Richard Kelly, Expl, 25 (March, 1967), 57.

Riding and Graves, A Survey of Modernist Poetry, pp. 103-109.

_____. "Conrad in Twilight"
Charles Crupi, Expl, 29 (Nov., 1970), 20.

Nat Henry, Expl, 34 (April, 1976), 62.

Karl F. Knight, Expl, 30 (May, 1972), 75.

Delmore Schwartz, "Instructed of Much Mortality," SR, 54 (Summer, 1946), 445-446.

_____. "Dead Boy"
Richard Gray, "The 'Compleat Gentleman': An Approach to John Crowe Ransom," SoR, 12 (July, 1976), 626-627.

Vivienne·Koch, "The Achievement of John Crowe Ransom," SR, 58 (Spring, 1950), 239.

Vivienne Koch, "The Poetry of John Crowe Ransom," in Modern American Poetry, ed. B. Rajan, p. 46.

F. O. Matthiessen, "Primarily Language," SR, 56 (Summer, 1948), 398-400. Rpt. The Responsibilities of the Critic, pp. 47-49.

Stageberg and Anderson, Poetry as Experience, pp. 26-27.

G. P. Wasserman, "The Irony of John Crowe Ransom," The University of Kansas City Review, 23 (Winter, 1956), 157-158.

_____. "The Equilibrists"
Richmond C. Beatty, "John Crowe Ransom as Poet," SR, 52 (Summer, 1944), 359-360.

Bernard Bergonzi, "A Poem about the History of Love," CritQ, 4 (Summer, 1962), 127-137.

Drew and Sweeney, Directions in Modern Poetry, pp. 208-211.

Howard Nemerov, "Summer's Flare and Winter's Flaw," SR, 56 (Summer, 1948), 419-420.

Thornton H. Parsons, "Ransom and the Poetics of Monastic Ecstasy," MLQ, 26 (Dec., 1965), 575-581.

Perrine and Reid, 100 American Poems, p. 137.

G. P. Wasserman, "The Irony of John Crowe Ransom," The University of Kansas City Review, 23 (Winter, 1956), 158-159.

_____. "The First Travels of Max"
Vivienne Koch, "The Achievement of John Crowe Ransom," SR, 58 (Spring, 1950), 237.

Vivienne Koch, "The Poetry of John Crowe Ransom," in Modern American Poetry, ed. B. Rajan, pp. 44-45.

_____. "Grace"
Richmond C. Beatty, "John Crowe Ransom as Poet," SR, 52 (Summer, 1944), 347-348.

G. P. Wasserman, "The Irony of John Crowe Ransom," The University of Kansas City Review, 23 (Winter, 1956), 152-153.

_____. "Here Lies a Lady"
William Bleifuss, Expl, 11 (May, 1953), 51. Rpt. The Explicator Cyclopedia, I, pp. 239-240.

John M. Bradbury, "Ransom as Poet," Accent, 11 (Winter, 1951), 52-54.

Kilby, Poetry and Life, pp. 16-17.

F. H. Stocking and Ellsworth Mason, Expl, 8 (Oct., 1949), 1. Rpt. The Explicator Cyclopedia, I, pp. 238-239.

_____. "Janet Waking"
Brooks, Modern Poetry and the Tradition, pp. 92-93.

Deutsch, Poetry in Our Time, pp. 206-207.

Vivienne Koch, "The Achievement of John Crowe Ransom," SR, 58 (Spring, 1950), 249-250.

Vivienne Koch, "The Poetry of John Crowe Ransom," in Modern American Poetry, ed. B. Rajan, pp. 55-56.

O'Connor, Sense and Sensibility in Modern Poetry, pp. 140-141.

Rosenthal and Smith, Exploring Poetry, pp. 7-8.

G. P. Wasserman, "The Irony of John Crowe Ransom," The University of Kansas City Review, 23 (Winter, 1956), 155-156.

Wheeler, The Design of Poetry, pp. 110-120.

_____. "Lady Lost"
Vivienne Koch, "The Achievement of John Crowe Ransom," SR, 58 (Spring, 1950), 247-249.

Vivienne Koch, "The Poetry of John Crowe Ransom," in Modern American Poetry, ed B. Rajan, pp. 54-55.

_____. "Little Boy Blue"
Charles Mitchell, Expl, 22 (Sept., 1963), 5.

_____. "Miller's Daughter"
Richmond C. Beatty, "John Crowe Ransom as Poet," SR, 52 (Summer, 1944), 357-358.

_____. "Miriam Tazewell"
Robert Flynn, Expl, 12 (May, 1954), 45.
    Rpt. The Explicator Cyclopedia, I, pp. 240-241.

Vivienne Koch, "The Achievement of John Crowe Ransom," SR, 58 (Spring, 1950), 239-240.

Vivienne Koch, "The Poetry of John Crowe Ransom," in Modern American Poetry, ed. B. Rajan, pp. 46-47.

G. P. Wasserman, "The Irony of John Crowe Ransom," The University of Kansas City Review, 23 (Winter, 1956), 156-157.

_____. "Night Voices"
Richmond C. Beatty, "John Crowe Ransom as Poet," SR, 52 (Summer, 1944), 354-355.

_____. "Noonday Grace"
Richmond C. Beatty, "John Crowe Ransom as Poet," SR, 52 (Summer, 1944), 345-346.

_____. "Old Mansion"
Vivienne Koch, "The Achievement of John Crowe Ransom," SR, 58 (Spring, 1950), 245-247.

Vivienne Koch, "The Poetry of John Crowe Ransom," in Modern American Poetry, ed. B. Rajan, pp. 52-53.

_____. "Painted Head"
Richmond C. Beatty, "John Crowe Ransom as Poet," SR, 52 (Summer, 1944), 365-366.

John M. Bradbury, "Ransom as Poet," Accent, 11 (Winter, 1951), 55-56.

Brooks, Lewis, and Warren, American Literature, pp. 2657-2658.

Brooks, Modern Poetry and the Tradition, pp. 94-95.

Vivienne Koch, "The Poetry of John Crowe Ransom," in Modern American Poetry, ed. B. Rajan, pp. 62-64.

Charles Moorman, Expl, 10 (Dec., 1951), 15.
    Rpt. The Explicator Cyclopedia, I, pp. 241-243.

Virginia Wallach, Expl, 14 (April, 1956), 45.
    Rpt. The Explicator Cyclopedia, I, pp. 243-244.

_____. "Parting, without a Sequel"
Perrine and Reid, 100 American Poems, pp. 138-141.

_____. "Philomela"
Edwin Fussell, "The Meter-Making Argument," in Aspects of American Poetry, pp. 3-4.

Delmore Schwartz, "Instructed of Much Mortality," SR, 54 (Summer, 1946), 443-444.

Samuel H. Woods, Jr., "'Philomela': John Crowe Ransoms' Ars Poetica," CE, 27 (Feb., 1966), 408-413.

_____. "Piazza Piece"
Ribner and Morris, Poetry, pp. 479-481.

_____. "Prelude to an Evening"
Brooks, A Shaping Joy, pp. 279-281.

Cleanth Brooks, "The Doric Delicacy," SR, 56 (Summer, 1948), 412-414.

Vivienne Koch, "The Poetry of John Crowe Ransom," in Modern American Poetry, ed. B. Rajan, pp. 62-64.

Virginia L. Peck, Expl, 20 (Jan., 1962), 41.
    Rpt. The Explicator Cyclopedia, I, p. 244.

_____. "The School"
Richmond C. Beatty, "John Crowe Ransom as Poet," SR, 52 (Summer, 1944), 350.

_____. "Spectral Lovers"
Richmond C. Beatty, "John Crowe Ransom as Poet," SR, 52 (Summer, 1944), 353-354.

Brooks, A Shaping Joy, pp. 277-279.

Cleanth Brooks, "The Doric Delicacy," SR, 56 (Summer, 1948), 410-412.

Vivienne Koch, "The Achievement of John Crowe Ransom," SR, 58 (Spring, 1950), 240-243.

Vivienne Koch, "The Poetry of John Crowe Ransom," in Modern American Poetry, ed. B. Rajan, pp. 47-50.

Thornton H. Parsons, "Ransom and the Poetics of Monastic Ecstasy," MLQ, 26 (Dec., 1965), 572-575.

_____. "Spiel of Three Mountebanks"
Howard Nemerov, "Summer's Flare and Winter's Flaw," SR, 56 (Summer, 1948), 422.

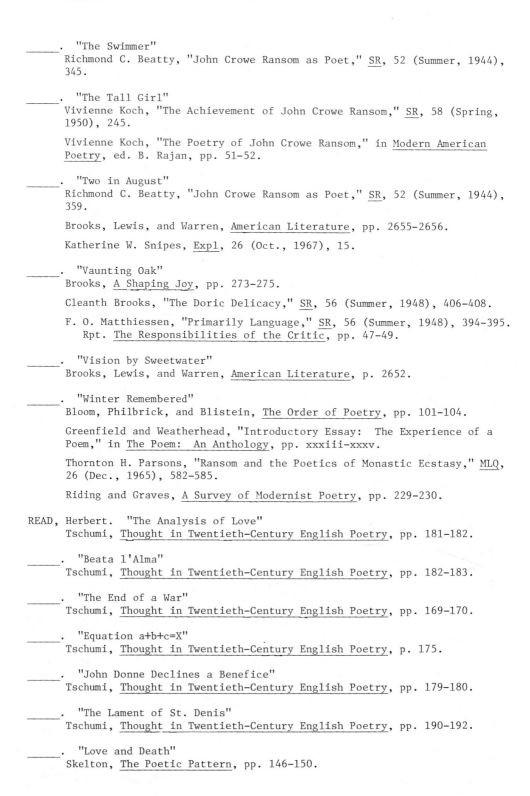

_____. "The Swimmer"
Richmond C. Beatty, "John Crowe Ransom as Poet," SR, 52 (Summer, 1944),
345.

_____. "The Tall Girl"
Vivienne Koch, "The Achievement of John Crowe Ransom," SR, 58 (Spring,
1950), 245.

Vivienne Koch, "The Poetry of John Crowe Ransom," in Modern American
Poetry, ed. B. Rajan, pp. 51-52.

_____. "Two in August"
Richmond C. Beatty, "John Crowe Ransom as Poet," SR, 52 (Summer, 1944),
359.

Brooks, Lewis, and Warren, American Literature, pp. 2655-2656.

Katherine W. Snipes, Expl, 26 (Oct., 1967), 15.

_____. "Vaunting Oak"
Brooks, A Shaping Joy, pp. 273-275.

Cleanth Brooks, "The Doric Delicacy," SR, 56 (Summer, 1948), 406-408.

F. O. Matthiessen, "Primarily Language," SR, 56 (Summer, 1948), 394-395.
    Rpt. The Responsibilities of the Critic, pp. 47-49.

_____. "Vision by Sweetwater"
Brooks, Lewis, and Warren, American Literature, p. 2652.

_____. "Winter Remembered"
Bloom, Philbrick, and Blistein, The Order of Poetry, pp. 101-104.

Greenfield and Weatherhead, "Introductory Essay: The Experience of a
Poem," in The Poem: An Anthology, pp. xxxiii-xxxv.

Thornton H. Parsons, "Ransom and the Poetics of Monastic Ecstasy," MLQ,
26 (Dec., 1965), 582-585.

Riding and Graves, A Survey of Modernist Poetry, pp. 229-230.

READ, Herbert. "The Analysis of Love"
Tschumi, Thought in Twentieth-Century English Poetry, pp. 181-182.

_____. "Beata l'Alma"
Tschumi, Thought in Twentieth-Century English Poetry, pp. 182-183.

_____. "The End of a War"
Tschumi, Thought in Twentieth-Century English Poetry, pp. 169-170.

_____. "Equation a+b+c=X"
Tschumi, Thought in Twentieth-Century English Poetry, p. 175.

_____. "John Donne Declines a Benefice"
Tschumi, Thought in Twentieth-Century English Poetry, pp. 179-180.

_____. "The Lament of St. Denis"
Tschumi, Thought in Twentieth-Century English Poetry, pp. 190-192.

_____. "Love and Death"
Skelton, The Poetic Pattern, pp. 146-150.

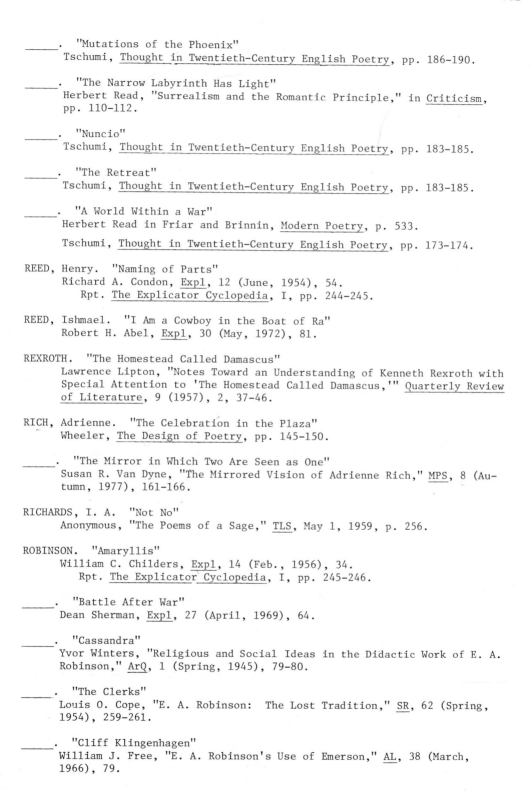

_____. "Mutations of the Phoenix"
Tschumi, Thought in Twentieth-Century English Poetry, pp. 186-190.

_____. "The Narrow Labyrinth Has Light"
Herbert Read, "Surrealism and the Romantic Principle," in Criticism,
pp. 110-112.

_____. "Nuncio"
Tschumi, Thought in Twentieth-Century English Poetry, pp. 183-185.

_____. "The Retreat"
Tschumi, Thought in Twentieth-Century English Poetry, pp. 183-185.

_____. "A World Within a War"
Herbert Read in Friar and Brinnin, Modern Poetry, p. 533.

Tschumi, Thought in Twentieth-Century English Poetry, pp. 173-174.

REED, Henry. "Naming of Parts"
Richard A. Condon, Expl, 12 (June, 1954), 54.
   Rpt. The Explicator Cyclopedia, I, pp. 244-245.

REED, Ishmael. "I Am a Cowboy in the Boat of Ra"
Robert H. Abel, Expl, 30 (May, 1972), 81.

REXROTH. "The Homestead Called Damascus"
Lawrence Lipton, "Notes Toward an Understanding of Kenneth Rexroth with
Special Attention to 'The Homestead Called Damascus,'" Quarterly Review
of Literature, 9 (1957), 2, 37-46.

RICH, Adrienne. "The Celebration in the Plaza"
Wheeler, The Design of Poetry, pp. 145-150.

_____. "The Mirror in Which Two Are Seen as One"
Susan R. Van Dyne, "The Mirrored Vision of Adrienne Rich," MPS, 8 (Autumn, 1977), 161-166.

RICHARDS, I. A. "Not No"
Anonymous, "The Poems of a Sage," TLS, May 1, 1959, p. 256.

ROBINSON. "Amaryllis"
William C. Childers, Expl, 14 (Feb., 1956), 34.
   Rpt. The Explicator Cyclopedia, I, pp. 245-246.

_____. "Battle After War"
Dean Sherman, Expl, 27 (April, 1969), 64.

_____. "Cassandra"
Yvor Winters, "Religious and Social Ideas in the Didactic Work of E. A.
Robinson," ArQ, 1 (Spring, 1945), 79-80.

_____. "The Clerks"
Louis O. Cope, "E. A. Robinson: The Lost Tradition," SR, 62 (Spring,
1954), 259-261.

_____. "Cliff Klingenhagen"
William J. Free, "E. A. Robinson's Use of Emerson," AL, 38 (March,
1966), 79.

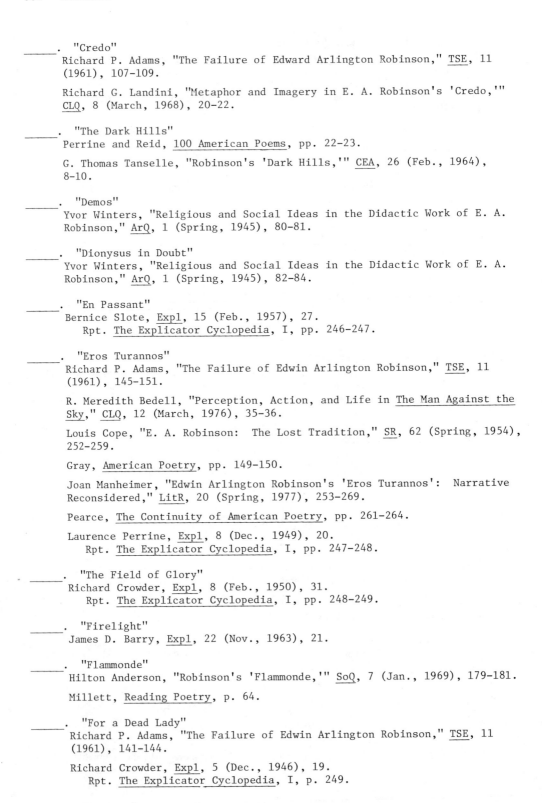

_____. "Credo"
Richard P. Adams, "The Failure of Edward Arlington Robinson," TSE, 11 (1961), 107-109.

Richard G. Landini, "Metaphor and Imagery in E. A. Robinson's 'Credo,'" CLQ, 8 (March, 1968), 20-22.

_____. "The Dark Hills"
Perrine and Reid, 100 American Poems, pp. 22-23.

G. Thomas Tanselle, "Robinson's 'Dark Hills,'" CEA, 26 (Feb., 1964), 8-10.

_____. "Demos"
Yvor Winters, "Religious and Social Ideas in the Didactic Work of E. A. Robinson," ArQ, 1 (Spring, 1945), 80-81.

_____. "Dionysus in Doubt"
Yvor Winters, "Religious and Social Ideas in the Didactic Work of E. A. Robinson," ArQ, 1 (Spring, 1945), 82-84.

_____. "En Passant"
Bernice Slote, Expl, 15 (Feb., 1957), 27.
    Rpt. The Explicator Cyclopedia, I, pp. 246-247.

_____. "Eros Turannos"
Richard P. Adams, "The Failure of Edwin Arlington Robinson," TSE, 11 (1961), 145-151.

R. Meredith Bedell, "Perception, Action, and Life in The Man Against the Sky," CLQ, 12 (March, 1976), 35-36.

Louis Cope, "E. A. Robinson: The Lost Tradition," SR, 62 (Spring, 1954), 252-259.

Gray, American Poetry, pp. 149-150.

Joan Manheimer, "Edwin Arlington Robinson's 'Eros Turannos': Narrative Reconsidered," LitR, 20 (Spring, 1977), 253-269.

Pearce, The Continuity of American Poetry, pp. 261-264.

Laurence Perrine, Expl, 8 (Dec., 1949), 20.
    Rpt. The Explicator Cyclopedia, I, pp. 247-248.

_____. "The Field of Glory"
Richard Crowder, Expl, 8 (Feb., 1950), 31.
    Rpt. The Explicator Cyclopedia, I, pp. 248-249.

_____. "Firelight"
James D. Barry, Expl, 22 (Nov., 1963), 21.

_____. "Flammonde"
Hilton Anderson, "Robinson's 'Flammonde,'" SoQ, 7 (Jan., 1969), 179-181.

Millett, Reading Poetry, p. 64.

_____. "For a Dead Lady"
Richard P. Adams, "The Failure of Edwin Arlington Robinson," TSE, 11 (1961), 141-144.

Richard Crowder, Expl, 5 (Dec., 1946), 19.
    Rpt. The Explicator Cyclopedia, I, p. 249.

E. S. Fussell, Expl, 9 (March, 1951), 33.
Rpt. The Explicator Cyclopedia, I, p. 250.

Clyde L. Grimm, "Robinson's 'For a Dead Lady': An Exercise in Evaluation," CLQ, 7 (Dec., 1967), 535-547.

Sylvia Hart and Estelle Paige, Expl, 10 (May, 1952), 51.
Rpt. The Explicator Cyclopedia, I, p. 250.

R. H. Super, Expl, 3 (June, 1945), 60.
Rpt. The Explicator Cyclopedia, I, p. 249.

R. H. Super, Expl, 5 (June, 1947), 60.
Rpt. The Explicator Cyclopedia, I, pp. 249-250.

_____. "The Gift of God"
R. Meredith Bedell, "Perception, Action, and Life in The Man Against the Sky," CLQ, 12 (March, 1976), 33-35.

Louis O. Cope, "E. A. Robinson: The Lost Tradition," SR, 62 (Spring, 1954), 261-265.

_____. "The Growth of 'Lorraine'"
Ronald Moran, "Lorraine and the Sirens: Courtesans in Two Poems by E. A. Robinson," in Essays in Honor of Esmond Linworth Marilla, pp. 312-315.

_____. "The House on the Hill"
James G. Hepburn, "E. A. Robinson's System of Opposites," PMLA, 80 (June, 1965), 269-270.

_____. "How Annandale Went Out"
Charles V. Genthe, "E. A. Robinson's 'Annandale' Poems," CLQ, 7 (March, 1967), 395-397.

Gray, American Poetry, pp. 147-148.

_____. "Isaac and Archibald"
Perrine and Reid, 100 American Poems, pp. 20-22.

_____. "Karma"
Brown and Milstead, Patterns in Poetry, p. 143.

_____. "Lost Anchor"
S. A. Cowan, Expl, 24 (April, 1966), 68.

James Grimshaw, Expl, 30 (Dec., 1971), 36.

Ralph E. Jenkins, Expl, 23 (April, 1965), 64.

Richard Tuerk, Expl, 32 (Jan., 1974), 37.

Celeste Turner Wright, Expl, 11 (June, 1953), 57.
Rpt. The Explicator Cyclopedia, I, pp. 250-251.

_____. "Luke Havergal"
Richard P. Adams, "The Failure of Edward Arlington Robinson," TSE, 11 (1961), 129-136.

Richard Crowder, Expl, 7 (Nov., 1948), 15.
Rpt. The Explicator Cyclopedia, I, p. 254.

N. E. Dunn, "Riddling Leaves: Robinson's 'Luke Havergal,'" CLQ, 10 (March, 1973), 17-25.

Walter Gierasch, Expl, 3 (Oct., 1944), 8. Abridged in The Case for Poetry, p. 297.
    Rpt. The Explicator Cyclopedia, I, pp. 251-252.

James G. Hepburn, "E. A. Robinson's System of Opposites," PMLA, 80 (June, 1965), 270-272.

Ronald E. McFarland, "Robinson's 'Luke Havergal,'" CLQ, 10 (June, 1974), 365-372.

Ronald Moran, "Meaning and Value in 'Luke Havergal,'" CLQ, 7 (March, 1967), 385-392.

Mathilde M. Parlett, Expl, 3 (June, 1945), 57.
    Rpt. The Explicator Cyclopedia, I, pp. 253-254.

A. A. Raven, Expl, 3 (Dec., 1944), 24.
    Rpt. The Explicator Cyclopedia, I, pp. 252-253.

Bertrand F. Richards, "No, There Is Not a Dawn....," CLQ, 9 (Sept., 1971), 367-374.

_____. "The Man Against the Sky"
Richard P. Adams, "The Failure of Edward Arlington Robinson," TSE, 11 (1961), 136-141.

R. Meredith Bedell, "Perception, Action, and Life in The Man Against the Sky," CLQ, 12 (March, 1976), 36-37.

Richard Crowder, "'Man Against the Sky,'" CE, 14 (Feb., 1953), 269-276.

Robert S. Fish, "The Tempering of Faith in E. A. Robinson's 'The Man Against the Sky,'" CLQ, 9 (March, 1972), 456-468.

Gray, American Poetry, pp. 150-152.

Pearce, The Continuity of American Poetry, pp. 265-267.

Arthur M. Read, II, Expl, 26 (Feb., 1968), 49.

John Newell Sanborn, "Juxtaposition as Structure in 'The Man Against the Sky,'" CLQ, 10 (Dec., 1974), 486-494.

Winfield Townley Scott, "To See Robinson," New Mexico Quarterly Review, 26 (Summer, 1956), 169.

Waggoner, The Heel of Elohim, pp. 29-36.

Yvor Winters, "Religious and Social Ideas in the Didactic Work of E. A. Robinson," ArQ, 1 (Spring, 1945), 74-75 et passim.

_____. "The Man Who Died Twice"
Richard Crowder, "E. A. Robinson's Symphony: 'The Man Who Died Twice,'" CE, 11 (Dec., 1949), 141-144.

_____. "Miniver Cheevy"
Abad, A Formal Approach to Lyric Poetry, pp. 166-167, 174-175.

Michael G. Miller, "Miniver Grows Lean," CLQ, 12 (Sept., 1976), 149-150.

Perrine and Reid, 100 American Poems, pp. 4-5.

Laurence Perrine, "A Reading of 'Miniver Cheevy,'" CLQ, 6 (June, 1962), 65-74.
    Rpt. The Art of Total Relevance, pp. 89-96.

___. "Mr. Flood's Party"
James L. Allen, Jr., "Symbol and Theme in 'Mr. Flood's Party,'" MissQ, 15 (Fall, 1962), 139-143.

Ciardi, How Does a Poem Mean?, p. 712.

Richard Allan Davison, Expl, 29 (Feb., 1971), 45.

Gray, American Poetry, pp. 152-153.

Willis D. Jacobs, "E. A. Robinson's 'Mr. Flood's Party,'" CE, 12 (Nov., 1950), 110.

E. Sydnor Ownbey, Expl, 8 (April, 1950), 47.
    Rpt. The Explicator Cyclopedia, I, pp. 254-255.

John E. Parish, "The Rehabilitation of Eben Flood," EJ, 55 (Sept., 1966), 696-699.

Perrine and Reid, 100 American Poems, pp. 7-8.

Walsh, Doors into Poetry, pp. 136-139.

Wheeler, The Design of Poetry, pp. 99-102.

___. "New England"
Richard E. Amacher, Expl, 10 (March, 1952), 33.
    Rpt. The Explicator Cyclopedia, I, p. 256.

W. R. Robinson, "E. A. Robinson's Yankee Conscience," CLQ, 8 (Sept., 1969), 371-376.

H. H. Waggoner, Expl, 10 (March, 1952), 33.
    Rpt. The Explicator Cyclopedia, I, pp. 256-257.

___. "An Old Story"
Richard Crowder, Expl, 4 (Dec., 1945), 22.
    Rpt. The Explicator Cyclopedia, I, pp. 256-257.

___. "On the Way"
Yvor Winters, "Religious and Social Ideas in the Didactic Work of E. A. Robinson," ArQ, 1 (Spring, 1945), 81-82.

___. "Richard Cory"
Charles Burkhart, Expl, 19 (Nov., 1960), 9.
    Rpt. The Explicator Cyclopedia, I, pp. 257-258.

William J. Free, "E. A. Robinson's Use of Emerson," AL, 38 (March, 1966), 77-79.

Harry R. Garvin, "Poems Pickled in Anthological Brine," CEA, 20 (Oct., 1958), 4.

L. Kart, "Richard Cory: Artist Without An Art," CLQ, 11 (Sept., 1975), 160-161.

J. Kavka, "Richard Cory's Suicide: A Psychoanalysts's View," CLQ, 11 (Sept., 1975), 150-159.

Charles R. Morris, Expl, 23 (March, 1965), 52.

Laurence Perrine, "Interpreting Poetry--Two Ways of Going Wrong," CEJ, 1 (Winter, 1965), 47-49.
    Rpt. The Art of Total Relevance, pp. 97-99.

Perrine and Reid, 100 American Poems, pp. 1-2.

Stageberg and Anderson, Poetry as Experience, pp. 189-192.

Charles A. Sweet, Jr., "A Re-examination of 'Richard Cory,'" CLQ, 9 (Sept., 1972), 579-582.

Steven Turner, Expl, 28 (May, 1970), 73.

_____. "The Sheaves"
Richard Crowder, Expl, 4 (March, 1946), 38.
    Rpt. The Explicator Cyclopedia, I, p. 258.

M. S. Mattfield, "Edwin Arlington Robinson's 'The Sheaves,'" CEA, 21 (Nov., 1968), 10.

_____. "Sonnet: Oh for a Poet"
M. N. O., Expl, 5 (Mary, 1947), Q21.

_____. "The Tree in Pamela's Garden"
Marvin Klotz, Expl, 20 (Jan., 1962), 42.
    Rpt. The Explicator Cyclopedia, I, pp. 258-259.

Laurence Perrine, Expl, 30 (Nov., 1971), 18.

Elizabeth Wright, Expl, 21 (Feb., 1963), 47.

Brian M. Barbour, Expl, 28 (Nov., 1969), 20.

_____. "Veteran Sirens"
Ronald Moran, "Lorraine and the Sirens: Courtesans in Two Poems by E. A. Robinson," in Essays in Honor of Esmond Linworth Marilla, pp. 315-319.

Laurence Perrine, Expl, 6 (Nov., 1947), 13.
    Rpt. The Explicator Cyclopedia, I, pp. 260-261.

_____. "The Whip"
Henry Pettit, Expl, 1 (April, 1943), 50.
    Rpt. The Explicator Cyclopedia, I, pp. 261-262.

ROETHKE. "The Abyss"
    William Heyen, "The Divine Abyss: Theodore Roethke's Mysticism," TSLL, 11 (Summer, 1969), 1052-1068.

_____. "The Auction"
    James McMichael, "The Poetry of Theodore Roethke," SoR, 5, n.s. (Winter, 1969), 5.

_____. "The Big Wind"
    Kenneth Burke, "The Vegetal Radicalism of Theodore Roethke," SR, 58 (Winter, 1950), 70-71.
        Rpt. Language as Symbolic Action, pp. 255-256.

John D. Boyd, "Texture and Form in Theodore Roethke's Greenhouse Poems," MLQ, 32 (Dec., 1971), 415-418.

Phillips, The Confessional Poets, p. 114.

_____. "The Boy and the Bush"
    Del Ivan Janik, Expl, 32 (Nov., 1973), 20.

_____. "Bring the Day"
    Hilton Kramer, "The Poetry of Theodore Roethke," The Western Review, 18 (Winter, 1954), 137.

_____. "Child on Top of a Greenhouse"
    H. G. Widdowson, Stylistics and the Teaching of Literature (London: Longman Group, 1975), 54-57, 108-114.

_____. "Cuttings (later)"
John D. Boyd, "Texture and Form in Theodore Roethke's Greenhouse Poems,"
MLQ, 32 (Dec., 1971), 422-424.

_____. "The Dance"
Carroll Arnett, "Minimal to Maximal: Theodore Roethke's Dialectic," CE,
18 (May, 1957), 415-416.

David L. Vanderwerken, "Roethke's 'Four for Sir John Davies' and 'The
Dying Man,'" RS, 41 (June, 1973), 125-127.

_____. "The Decision"
Richard A. Blessing, "Theodore Roethke's Sometimes Metaphysical Motion,"
TSLL, 14 (Winter, 1973), 741-742.

_____. "The Donkey"
Penelope Scambly Schoot, "'I Am!' Says Theodore Roethke: A Reading of
the Nonsense Poems," RS, 43 (June, 1975), 110.

_____. "The Dying Man"
David L. Vanderwerken, "Roethke's 'Four for Sir John Davies' and 'The
Dying Man,'" RS, 41 (June, 1973), 130-134.

_____. "Elegy"
Richard A. Blessing, "Theodore Roethke: A Celebration," TSE, 20 (1972),
176-179.

_____. "Elegy for Jane"
Richard A. Blessing, "Theodore Roethke: A Celebration," TSE, 20 (1972),
173-174.

Perrine and Reid, 100 American Poems, pp. 205-206.

_____. "The Far Field"
Hugh B. Staples, "The Rose in the Sea-Wind: A Reading of Theodore
Roethke's 'North American Sequence,'" AL, 36 (May, 1964), 201-202.

_____. "A Field of Light"
Kenneth Burke, "The Vegetal Radicalism of Theodore Roethke," SR, 58
(Winter, 1950), 94-95.
    Rpt. Language as Symbolic Action, pp. 272-273.

Hilton Kramer, "The Poetry of Theodore Roethke," The Western Review, 18
(Winter, 1954), 141-142.

_____. "Four for Sir John Davies"
James McMichael, "The Poetry of Theodore Roethke," SoR, 5, n.s. (Winter,
1969), 11-14.

Mills, Contemporary American Poetry, pp. 61-62.

_____. "Frau Bauman, Frau Schmidt, and Frau Schwartze"
Richard A. Blessing, "Theodore Roethke: A Celebration," TSE, 20 (1972),
174-176.

_____. "The Gentle"
D. L. Colussi, Expl, 27 (May, 1969), 73.

_____. "Give Way, Ye Gates"
Hilton Kramer, "The Poetry of Theodore Roethke," The Western Review, 18
(Winter, 1954), 138.

Rosenthal, The Modern Poets, pp. 241-242.

John Vernon, The Garden and the Map: Schizophrenia in Twentieth Century
Literature and Culture (Urbana: Univ. of Illinois Press, 1973),
pp. 179-181.

John Vernon, "Theodore Roethke's Praise to the End! Poems," IowaR, 2
(Fall, 1971), 72-74.

_____. "I Knew a Woman"
Nicholas Ayo, "Jonson's Greek Ode in Roethke," AN&Q, 13 (March, 1975),
107.

Helen T. Buttell, Expl, 24 (May, 1966), 78.

Nat Henry, Expl, 27 (Jan., 1969), 31.

Jenijoy La Belle, Expl, 32 (Oct., 1973), 15.

Virginia L. Peck, Expl, 22 (April, 1964), 66.

_____. "In a Dark Time"
Richard A. Blessing, "Theodore Roethke's Sometimes Metaphysical Motion,"
TSLL, 14 (Winter, 1973), 732-735.

John Hobbs, "The Poet as His Own Interpreter: Roethke on 'In a Dark
Time,'" CE, 33 (Oct., 1971), 55-66.

_____. "I Need, I Need"
John Vernon, The Garden and the Map: Schizophrenia in Twentieth Century
Literature and Culture (Urbana: Univ. of Illinois Press, 1973),
pp. 175-177.

John Vernon, "Theodore Roethke's Praise to the End! Poems," IowaR, 2
(Fall, 1971), 70-71.

_____. "In Evening Air"
Richard A. Blessing, "Theodore Roethke's Sometimes Metaphysical Motion,"
TSLL, 14 (Winter, 1973), 735-737.

_____. "Infirmity"
Richard A. Blessing, "Theodore Roethke's Sometimes Metaphysical Motion,"
TSLL, 14 (Winter, 1973), 740-741.

_____. "I Waited"
Richard A. Blessing, "Theodore Roethke's Sometimes Metaphysical Motion,"
TSLL, 14 (Winter, 1973), 743-744.

_____. "Journey to the Interior"
Hugh B. Staples, "The Rose in the Sea-Wind: A Reading of Theodore
Roethke's 'North American Sequence,'" AL, 26 (May, 1964), 198-200.

_____. "The Kitty-Cat Bird"
Penelope Scambly Schott, "'I Am!' Says Theodore Roethke: A Reading of
the Nonsense Poems," RS, 43 (June, 1975), 104-105.

_____. "The Lamb"
Penelope Scambly Schott, "'I Am!' Says Theodore Roethke: A Reading of the
Nonsense Poems," RS, 43 (June, 1975), 104.

_____. "A Light Breather"
Wheeler, The Design of Poetry, pp. 195-197.

_____. "The Long Alley"
Kenneth Burke, "The Vegetal Radicalism of Theodore Roethke," SR, 58
(Winter, 1950), 85-86, 93-94.
    Rpt. Language as Symbolic Action, pp. 271-272.

Phillips, The Confessional Poets, pp. 122-124.

_____. "The Longing"
Hugh B. Staples, "The Rose in the Sea-Wind: A Reading of Theodore
Roethke's 'North American Sequence,'" AL, 36 (May, 1964), 193-195.

_____. "The Long Waters"
Hugh B. Staples, "The Rose in the Sea-Wind: A Reading of Theodore
Roethke's 'North American Sequence,'" AL, 36 (May, 1964), 200-201.

_____. "The Lost Son"
Carroll Arnett, "Minimal to Maximal: Theodore Roethke's Dialectic,"
CE, 18 (May, 1957), 415.

Kenneth Burke, "The Vegetal Radicalism of Theodore Roethke," SR, 58
(Winter, 1950), 87-93.
    Rpt. Language as Symbolic Action, pp. 266-271.

Deutsch, Poetry in Our Time, pp. 184-185.

Brendan Galvin, "Kenneth Burke and Theodore Roethke's 'Lost Son' Poems,"
The Northwest Review, 2 (Summer, 1971), 73-96.

Hilton Kramer, "The Poetry of Theodore Roethke," The Western Review, 18
(Winter, 1954), 138-141.

Mills, Contemporary American Poetry, pp. 56-60.

Phillips, The Confessional Poets, pp. 119-121.

Theodore Roethke, "Open Letter," in Mid-Century American Poets,
pp. 68-72.

Fred C. Schutz, "Antecedents of Roethke's 'The Lost Son' in an Unpublished Poem," NConL, 5 (May, 1975), 4-6.

_____. "The Marrow"
Richard A. Blessing, "Theodore Roethke's Sometimes Metaphysical Motion,"
TSLL, 14 (Winter, 1973), 742-743.

_____. "Meditation at Oyster River"
Hugh B. Staples, "The Rose in the Sea-Wind: A Reading of Theodore
Roethke's 'North American Sequence,'" AL, 36 (May, 1964), 196-198.

_____. "Meditations of an Old Woman"
Mills, Contemporary American Poetry, pp. 63-66.

_____. "The Motion"
Richard A. Blessing, "Theodore Roethke's Sometimes Metaphysical Motion,"
TSLL, 14 (Winter, 1973), 739.

_____. "My Papa's Waltz"
Ciardi, How Does a Poem Mean?, pp. 1003-1004.

_____. "North American Sequence"
James McMichael, "The Poetry of Theodore Roethke," SoR, 5, n.s. (Winter, 1969), 15-25.

Hugh B. Staples, "The Rose in the Sea-Wind: A Reading of Theodore Roethke's 'North American Sequence,'" AL, 36 (May, 1964), 189-203.

_____. "O Lull Me, Lull Me"
John Vernon, The Garden and the Map: Schizophrenia in Twentieth Century Literature and Culture (Urbana: Univ. of Illinois Press, 1973), pp. 183-184.

_____. "Once More, the Round"
Richard A. Blessing, "Theodore Roethke's Sometimes Metaphysical Motion," TSLL, 14 (Winter, 1973), 748.

_____. "Open House"
Gerald M. Garmon, Expl, 28 (Nov., 1969), 28.

_____. "Orchids"
John D. Boyd, "Texture and Form in Theodore Roethke's Greenhouse Poems," MLQ, 32 (Dec., 1971), 419-420.

_____. "The Partner"
David L. Vanderwerken, "Roethke's 'Four for Sir John Davies' and 'The Dying Man,'" RS, 41 (June, 1973), 127.

_____. "The Restored"
Richard A. Blessing, "Theodore Roethke's Sometimes Metaphysical Motion," TSLL, 14 (Winter, 1973), 745-746.

_____. "The Right Thing"
Richard A. Blessing, "Theodore Roethke's Sometimes Metaphysical Motion," TSLL, 14 (Winter, 1973), 746-748.

_____. "Root Cellar"
George Wolff, Expl, 29 (Feb., 1971), 47.

_____. "The Rose"
Hugh B. Staples, "The Rose in the Sea-Wind: A Reading of Theodore Roethke's 'North American Sequence,'" AL, 36 (May, 1964), 202-203.

_____. "The Sequel"
Richard A. Blessing, "Theodore Roethke's Sometimes Metaphysical Motion," TSLL, 14 (Winter, 1973), 737-739.

_____. "The Serpent"
Penelope Scambly Schott, "'I Am!' Says Theodore Roethke: A Reading of the Nonsense Poems," RS, 43 (June, 1975), 106-107.

_____. "The Shape of Fire"
Kenneth Burke, "The Vegetal Radicalism of Theodore Roethke," SR, 58 (Winter, 1950), 95-97, 100.
    Rpt. Language as Symbolic Action, pp. 272-276.

Phillips, The Confessional Poets, pp. 125-127.

Rosenthal, The Modern Poets, pp. 242-243.

_____. "Song"
W. R. Slaughter, "Roethke's 'Song,'" MinnR, 8, No. 4 (1968), 342-344.

_____. "The Tree, the Bird"
Richard A. Blessing, "Theodore Roethke's Sometimes Metaphysical Motion,"
TSLL, 14 (Winter, 1973), 744-745.

_____. "Unfold! Unfold!"
James G. Southworth, "The Poetry of Theodore Roethke," CE, 21 (March,
1960), 337.

_____. "The Vigil"
David L. Vanderwerken, "Roethke's 'Four for Sir John Davies' and 'The
Dying Man,'" RS, 41 (June, 1973), 128-130.

_____. "The Visitant"
Kenneth Burke, "The Vegetal Radicalism of Theodore Roethke," SR, 58
(Winter, 1950), 71-72.
      Rpt. Language as Symbolic Action, pp. 256-257.

_____. "The Waking"
Richard A. Blessing, "The Shaking That Steadies: Theodore Roethke's
'The Waking,'" BSUF, 12 (Autumn, 1971), 17-19.

William V. Davis, "The Escape into Time: Theodore Roethke's 'The
Waking,'" NConL, 5 (March, 1975), 2-10.

Robert Ely, Expl, 34 (March, 1976), 54.

_____. "A Walk in Late Summer"
James McMichael, "The Poetry of Theodore Roethke," SoR, 5 n.s. (Winter,
1969), 6-7.

_____. "Where Knock Is Open Wide"
Kenneth Burke, "The Vegetal Radicalism of Theodore Roethke," SR, 58
(Winter, 1950), 105-107.
      Rpt. Language as Symbolic Action, pp. 279-281.

Hilton Kramer, "The Poetry of Theodore Roethke," The Western Review, 18
(Winter, 1954), 135-136.

Ronald Reichertz, Expl, 26 (Dec., 1967), 34.

John Vernon, The Garden and the Map: Schizophrenia in Twentieth Century
Literature and Culture (Urbana: Univ. of Illinois Press, 1973),
pp. 164-175.

John Vernon, "Theodore Roethke's Praise to the End! Poems," IowaR, 2
(Fall, 1971), 62-70.

_____. "The Wraith"
David L. Vanderwerken, "Roethke's 'Four for Sir John Davies' and 'The
Dying Man,'" RS, 41 (June, 1973), 128.

ROLLE, Richard. "Jhesu, God Sonn"
William Elford Rogers, Image and Abstraction: Six Middle English Re-
ligous Lyrics (Copenhagen: Rosenkilde and Bagger, 1972), pp. 69-81.

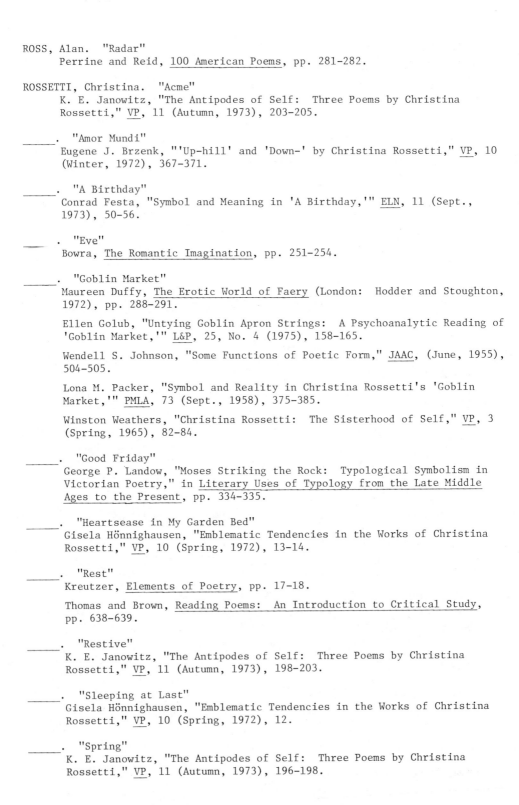

ROSS, Alan. "Radar"
Perrine and Reid, 100 American Poems, pp. 281-282.

ROSSETTI, Christina. "Acme"
K. E. Janowitz, "The Antipodes of Self: Three Poems by Christina
Rossetti," VP, 11 (Autumn, 1973), 203-205.

_____. "Amor Mundi"
Eugene J. Brzenk, "'Up-hill' and 'Down-' by Christina Rossetti," VP, 10
(Winter, 1972), 367-371.

_____. "A Birthday"
Conrad Festa, "Symbol and Meaning in 'A Birthday,'" ELN, 11 (Sept.,
1973), 50-56.

_____. "Eve"
Bowra, The Romantic Imagination, pp. 251-254.

_____. "Goblin Market"
Maureen Duffy, The Erotic World of Faery (London: Hodder and Stoughton,
1972), pp. 288-291.

Ellen Golub, "Untying Goblin Apron Strings: A Psychoanalytic Reading of
'Goblin Market,'" L&P, 25, No. 4 (1975), 158-165.

Wendell S. Johnson, "Some Functions of Poetic Form," JAAC, (June, 1955),
504-505.

Lona M. Packer, "Symbol and Reality in Christina Rossetti's 'Goblin
Market,'" PMLA, 73 (Sept., 1958), 375-385.

Winston Weathers, "Christina Rossetti: The Sisterhood of Self," VP, 3
(Spring, 1965), 82-84.

_____. "Good Friday"
George P. Landow, "Moses Striking the Rock: Typological Symbolism in
Victorian Poetry," in Literary Uses of Typology from the Late Middle
Ages to the Present, pp. 334-335.

_____. "Heartsease in My Garden Bed"
Gisela Hönnighausen, "Emblematic Tendencies in the Works of Christina
Rossetti," VP, 10 (Spring, 1972), 13-14.

_____. "Rest"
Kreutzer, Elements of Poetry, pp. 17-18.

Thomas and Brown, Reading Poems: An Introduction to Critical Study,
pp. 638-639.

_____. "Restive"
K. E. Janowitz, "The Antipodes of Self: Three Poems by Christina
Rossetti," VP, 11 (Autumn, 1973), 198-203.

_____. "Sleeping at Last"
Gisela Hönnighausen, "Emblematic Tendencies in the Works of Christina
Rossetti," VP, 10 (Spring, 1972), 12.

_____. "Spring"
K. E. Janowitz, "The Antipodes of Self: Three Poems by Christina
Rossetti," VP, 11 (Autumn, 1973), 196-198.

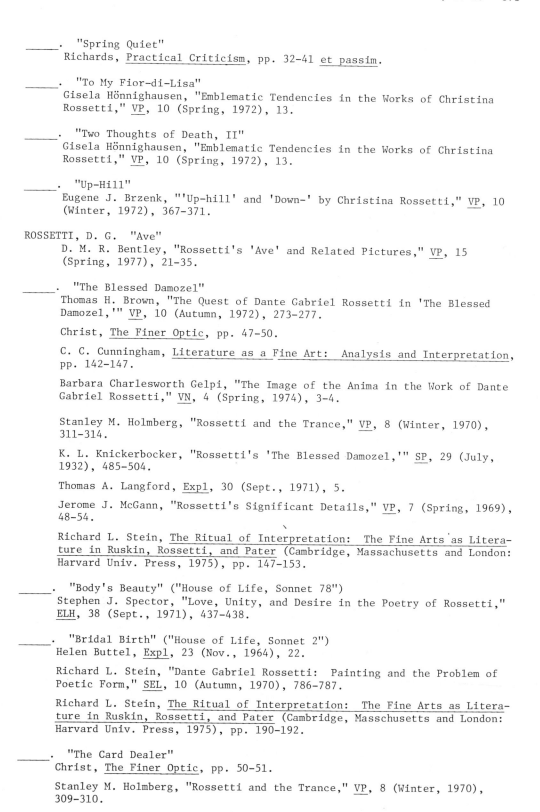

_____. "Spring Quiet"
Richards, Practical Criticism, pp. 32-41 et passim.

_____. "To My Fior-di-Lisa"
Gisela Hönnighausen, "Emblematic Tendencies in the Works of Christina
Rossetti," VP, 10 (Spring, 1972), 13.

_____. "Two Thoughts of Death, II"
Gisela Hönnighausen, "Emblematic Tendencies in the Works of Christina
Rossetti," VP, 10 (Spring, 1972), 13.

_____. "Up-Hill"
Eugene J. Brzenk, "'Up-hill' and 'Down-' by Christina Rossetti," VP, 10
(Winter, 1972), 367-371.

ROSSETTI, D. G. "Ave"
D. M. R. Bentley, "Rossetti's 'Ave' and Related Pictures," VP, 15
(Spring, 1977), 21-35.

_____. "The Blessed Damozel"
Thomas H. Brown, "The Quest of Dante Gabriel Rossetti in 'The Blessed
Damozel,'" VP, 10 (Autumn, 1972), 273-277.

Christ, The Finer Optic, pp. 47-50.

C. C. Cunningham, Literature as a Fine Art: Analysis and Interpretation,
pp. 142-147.

Barbara Charlesworth Gelpi, "The Image of the Anima in the Work of Dante
Gabriel Rossetti," VN, 4 (Spring, 1974), 3-4.

Stanley M. Holmberg, "Rossetti and the Trance," VP, 8 (Winter, 1970),
311-314.

K. L. Knickerbocker, "Rossetti's 'The Blessed Damozel,'" SP, 29 (July,
1932), 485-504.

Thomas A. Langford, Expl, 30 (Sept., 1971), 5.

Jerome J. McGann, "Rossetti's Significant Details," VP, 7 (Spring, 1969),
48-54.

Richard L. Stein, The Ritual of Interpretation: The Fine Arts as Literature in Ruskin, Rossetti, and Pater (Cambridge, Massachusetts and London:
Harvard Univ. Press, 1975), pp. 147-153.

_____. "Body's Beauty" ("House of Life, Sonnet 78")
Stephen J. Spector, "Love, Unity, and Desire in the Poetry of Rossetti,"
ELH, 38 (Sept., 1971), 437-438.

_____. "Bridal Birth" ("House of Life, Sonnet 2")
Helen Buttel, Expl, 23 (Nov., 1964), 22.

Richard L. Stein, "Dante Gabriel Rossetti: Painting and the Problem of
Poetic Form," SEL, 10 (Autumn, 1970), 786-787.

Richard L. Stein, The Ritual of Interpretation: The Fine Arts as Literature in Ruskin, Rossetti, and Pater (Cambridge, Masschusetts and London:
Harvard Univ. Press, 1975), pp. 190-192.

_____. "The Card Dealer"
Christ, The Finer Optic, pp. 50-51.

Stanley M. Holmberg, "Rossetti and the Trance," VP, 8 (Winter, 1970),
309-310.

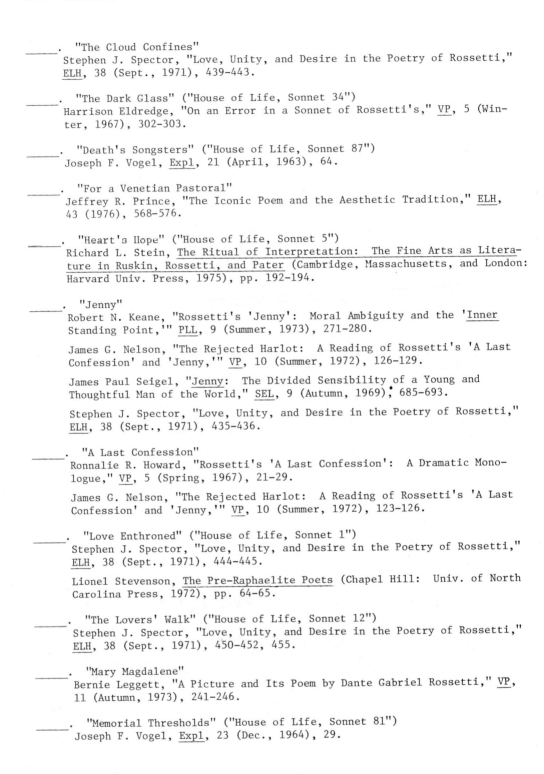

_____. "The Cloud Confines"
Stephen J. Spector, "Love, Unity, and Desire in the Poetry of Rossetti,"
ELH, 38 (Sept., 1971), 439-443.

_____. "The Dark Glass" ("House of Life, Sonnet 34")
Harrison Eldredge, "On an Error in a Sonnet of Rossetti's," VP, 5 (Winter, 1967), 302-303.

_____. "Death's Songsters" ("House of Life, Sonnet 87")
Joseph F. Vogel, Expl, 21 (April, 1963), 64.

_____. "For a Venetian Pastoral"
Jeffrey R. Prince, "The Iconic Poem and the Aesthetic Tradition," ELH,
43 (1976), 568-576.

_____. "Heart's Hope" ("House of Life, Sonnet 5")
Richard L. Stein, The Ritual of Interpretation: The Fine Arts as Literature in Ruskin, Rossetti, and Pater (Cambridge, Massachusetts, and London: Harvard Univ. Press, 1975), pp. 192-194.

_____. "Jenny"
Robert N. Keane, "Rossetti's 'Jenny': Moral Ambiguity and the 'Inner Standing Point,'" PLL, 9 (Summer, 1973), 271-280.

James G. Nelson, "The Rejected Harlot: A Reading of Rossetti's 'A Last Confession' and 'Jenny,'" VP, 10 (Summer, 1972), 126-129.

James Paul Seigel, "Jenny: The Divided Sensibility of a Young and Thoughtful Man of the World," SEL, 9 (Autumn, 1969), 685-693.

Stephen J. Spector, "Love, Unity, and Desire in the Poetry of Rossetti,"
ELH, 38 (Sept., 1971), 435-436.

_____. "A Last Confession"
Ronnalie R. Howard, "Rossetti's 'A Last Confession': A Dramatic Monologue," VP, 5 (Spring, 1967), 21-29.

James G. Nelson, "The Rejected Harlot: A Reading of Rossetti's 'A Last Confession' and 'Jenny,'" VP, 10 (Summer, 1972), 123-126.

_____. "Love Enthroned" ("House of Life, Sonnet 1")
Stephen J. Spector, "Love, Unity, and Desire in the Poetry of Rossetti,"
ELH, 38 (Sept., 1971), 444-445.

Lionel Stevenson, The Pre-Raphaelite Poets (Chapel Hill: Univ. of North Carolina Press, 1972), pp. 64-65.

_____. "The Lovers' Walk" ("House of Life, Sonnet 12")
Stephen J. Spector, "Love, Unity, and Desire in the Poetry of Rossetti,"
ELH, 38 (Sept., 1971), 450-452, 455.

_____. "Mary Magdalene"
Bernie Leggett, "A Picture and Its Poem by Dante Gabriel Rossetti," VP,
11 (Autumn, 1973), 241-246.

_____. "Memorial Thresholds" ("House of Life, Sonnet 81")
Joseph F. Vogel, Expl, 23 (Dec., 1964), 29.

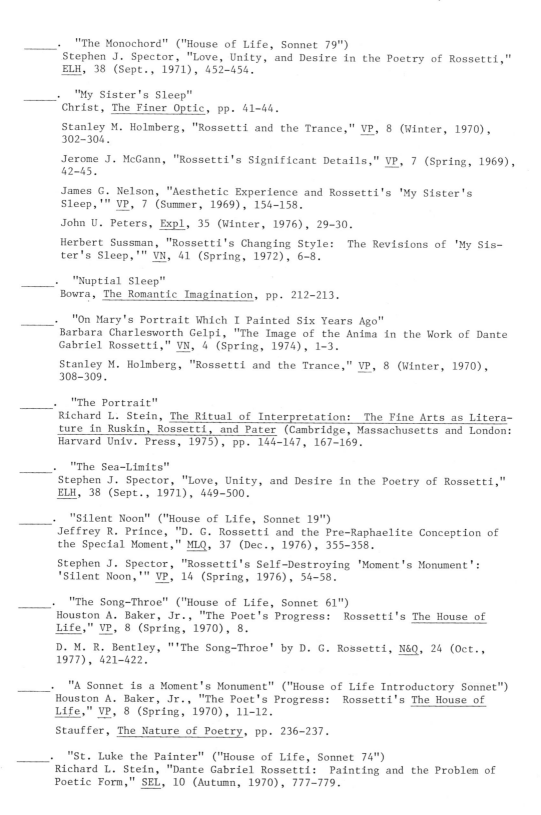

_____. "The Monochord" ("House of Life, Sonnet 79")
Stephen J. Spector, "Love, Unity, and Desire in the Poetry of Rossetti,"
ELH, 38 (Sept., 1971), 452-454.

_____. "My Sister's Sleep"
Christ, The Finer Optic, pp. 41-44.

Stanley M. Holmberg, "Rossetti and the Trance," VP, 8 (Winter, 1970),
302-304.

Jerome J. McGann, "Rossetti's Significant Details," VP, 7 (Spring, 1969),
42-45.

James G. Nelson, "Aesthetic Experience and Rossetti's 'My Sister's
Sleep,'" VP, 7 (Summer, 1969), 154-158.

John U. Peters, Expl, 35 (Winter, 1976), 29-30.

Herbert Sussman, "Rossetti's Changing Style: The Revisions of 'My Sister's Sleep,'" VN, 41 (Spring, 1972), 6-8.

_____. "Nuptial Sleep"
Bowra, The Romantic Imagination, pp. 212-213.

_____. "On Mary's Portrait Which I Painted Six Years Ago"
Barbara Charlesworth Gelpi, "The Image of the Anima in the Work of Dante
Gabriel Rossetti," VN, 4 (Spring, 1974), 1-3.

Stanley M. Holmberg, "Rossetti and the Trance," VP, 8 (Winter, 1970),
308-309.

_____. "The Portrait"
Richard L. Stein, The Ritual of Interpretation: The Fine Arts as Litera-
ture in Ruskin, Rossetti, and Pater (Cambridge, Massachusetts and London:
Harvard Univ. Press, 1975), pp. 144-147, 167-169.

_____. "The Sea-Limits"
Stephen J. Spector, "Love, Unity, and Desire in the Poetry of Rossetti,"
ELH, 38 (Sept., 1971), 449-500.

_____. "Silent Noon" ("House of Life, Sonnet 19")
Jeffrey R. Prince, "D. G. Rossetti and the Pre-Raphaelite Conception of
the Special Moment," MLQ, 37 (Dec., 1976), 355-358.

Stephen J. Spector, "Rossetti's Self-Destroying 'Moment's Monument':
'Silent Noon,'" VP, 14 (Spring, 1976), 54-58.

_____. "The Song-Throe" ("House of Life, Sonnet 61")
Houston A. Baker, Jr., "The Poet's Progress: Rossetti's The House of
Life," VP, 8 (Spring, 1970), 8.

D. M. R. Bentley, "'The Song-Throe' by D. G. Rossetti, N&Q, 24 (Oct.,
1977), 421-422.

_____. "A Sonnet is a Moment's Monument" ("House of Life Introductory Sonnet")
Houston A. Baker, Jr., "The Poet's Progress: Rossetti's The House of
Life," VP, 8 (Spring, 1970), 11-12.

Stauffer, The Nature of Poetry, pp. 236-237.

_____. "St. Luke the Painter" ("House of Life, Sonnet 74")
Richard L. Stein, "Dante Gabriel Rossetti: Painting and the Problem of
Poetic Form," SEL, 10 (Autumn, 1970), 777-779.

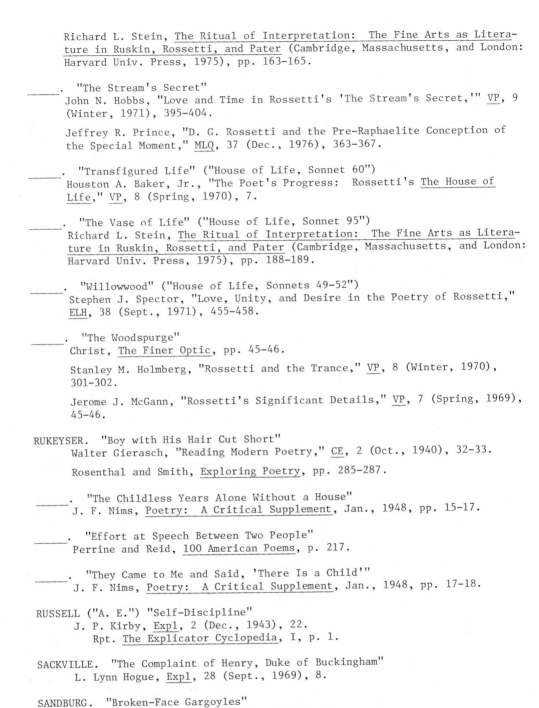

Richard L. Stein, The Ritual of Interpretation: The Fine Arts as Literature in Ruskin, Rossetti, and Pater (Cambridge, Massachusetts, and London: Harvard Univ. Press, 1975), pp. 163-165.

_____. "The Stream's Secret"
John N. Hobbs, "Love and Time in Rossetti's 'The Stream's Secret,'" VP, 9 (Winter, 1971), 395-404.

Jeffrey R. Prince, "D. G. Rossetti and the Pre-Raphaelite Conception of the Special Moment," MLQ, 37 (Dec., 1976), 363-367.

_____. "Transfigured Life" ("House of Life, Sonnet 60")
Houston A. Baker, Jr., "The Poet's Progress: Rossetti's The House of Life," VP, 8 (Spring, 1970), 7.

_____. "The Vase of Life" ("House of Life, Sonnet 95")
Richard L. Stein, The Ritual of Interpretation: The Fine Arts as Literature in Ruskin, Rossetti, and Pater (Cambridge, Massachusetts, and London: Harvard Univ. Press, 1975), pp. 188-189.

_____. "Willowwood" ("House of Life, Sonnets 49-52")
Stephen J. Spector, "Love, Unity, and Desire in the Poetry of Rossetti," ELH, 38 (Sept., 1971), 455-458.

_____. "The Woodspurge"
Christ, The Finer Optic, pp. 45-46.

Stanley M. Holmberg, "Rossetti and the Trance," VP, 8 (Winter, 1970), 301-302.

Jerome J. McGann, "Rossetti's Significant Details," VP, 7 (Spring, 1969), 45-46.

RUKEYSER. "Boy with His Hair Cut Short"
Walter Gierasch, "Reading Modern Poetry," CE, 2 (Oct., 1940), 32-33.

Rosenthal and Smith, Exploring Poetry, pp. 285-287.

_____. "The Childless Years Alone Without a House"
J. F. Nims, Poetry: A Critical Supplement, Jan., 1948, pp. 15-17.

_____. "Effort at Speech Between Two People"
Perrine and Reid, 100 American Poems, p. 217.

_____. "They Came to Me and Said, 'There Is a Child'"
J. F. Nims, Poetry: A Critical Supplement, Jan., 1948, pp. 17-18.

RUSSELL ("A. E.") "Self-Discipline"
J. P. Kirby, Expl, 2 (Dec., 1943), 22.
Rpt. The Explicator Cyclopedia, I, p. 1.

SACKVILLE. "The Complaint of Henry, Duke of Buckingham"
L. Lynn Hogue, Expl, 28 (Sept., 1969), 8.

SANDBURG. "Broken-Face Gargoyles"
Bernard S. Oldsey, Expl, 7 (May, 1949), 50.
Rpt. The Explicator Cyclopedia, I, pp. 262-263.

_____. "Caboose Thoughts"
Richard Crowder, Expl, 4 (June, 1946), 52.
  Rpt. The Explicator Cyclopedia, I, pp. 263-264.

_____. "Chicago"
Charles Allen, "Cadenced Free Verse," CE, 9 (Jan., 1948), 197-198.

Walter Blair, Literature of the United States, II, 962.

Perrine and Reid, 100 American Poems, pp. 53-54.

_____. "Cool Tombs"
Daniel G. Hoffman, Expl, 9 (May, 1951), 46.
  Rpt. The Explicator Cyclopedia, I, p. 264.

_____. "Early Lynching"
Ralph P. Boas, Expl, 1 (June, 1943), 67.
  Rpt. The Explicator Cyclopedia, I, pp. 264-265.

_____. "A Fence"
Selma Wagner, Expl, 27 (Feb., 1969), 42.

_____. "Fog"
Thomas and Brown, Reading Poems: An Introduction to Critical Study,
pp. 646-647.

_____. "Lost"
Hill, Constitutent and Pattern in Poetry, pp. 49-50.

_____. "Nocturne in a Deserted Brickyard"
Charles Allen, "Cadenced Free Verse," CE, 9 (Jan., 1948), 195-197.

_____. "Number Man"
J. F. Nims, Poetry: A Critical Supplement, Oct., 1947, pp. 1-4.

_____. "On a Flimmering Flume You Shall Ride"
J. F. Nims, Poetry: A Critical Supplement, Oct., 1947, pp. 4-5.

_____. "To the Ghost of John Milton"
Paul Engle, Engle and Carrier, Reading Modern Poetry, pp. 32-34.

_____. "Wind Song"
Perrine and Reid, 100 American Poems, p. 55.

SANDERS, Thomas E. "Legacy"
Sanders, The Discovery of Poetry, p. 170.

SANTAYANA. "I Sought on Earth a Garden of Delight"
Philip Blair Rice, "George Santayana," The Kenyon Review, 2 (Autumn,
1940), 469-471.

_____. "O World"
Bert Case Diltz, Sense or Nonsense: Contemporary Education at the Cross-
roads (Toronto: McClelland and Stewart, 1972), pp. 94-96.

SASSOON. "Acceptance"
C. E. Maguire, "Harmony Unheard: The Poetry of Siegfried Sassoon,"
Renascence, 11 (Spring, 1959), 119.

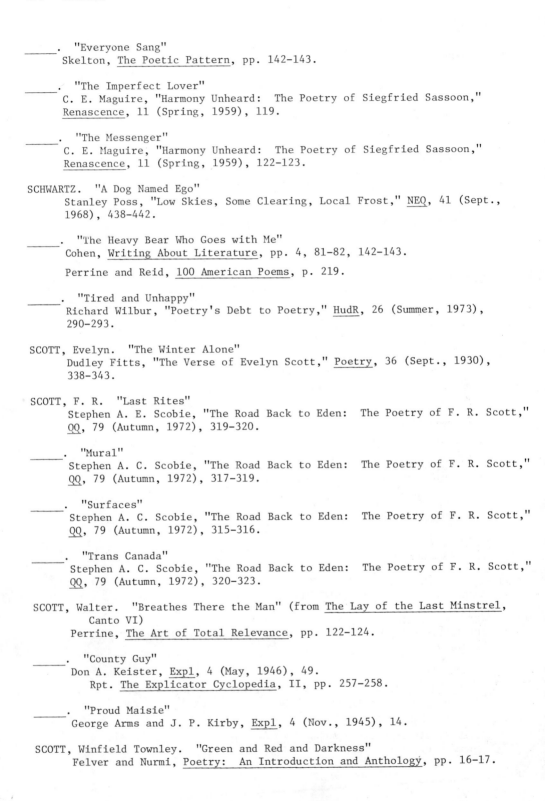

_____. "Everyone Sang"
Skelton, The Poetic Pattern, pp. 142-143.

_____. "The Imperfect Lover"
C. E. Maguire, "Harmony Unheard: The Poetry of Siegfried Sassoon,"
Renascence, 11 (Spring, 1959), 119.

_____. "The Messenger"
C. E. Maguire, "Harmony Unheard: The Poetry of Siegfried Sassoon,"
Renascence, 11 (Spring, 1959), 122-123.

SCHWARTZ. "A Dog Named Ego"
Stanley Poss, "Low Skies, Some Clearing, Local Frost," NEQ, 41 (Sept.,
1968), 438-442.

_____. "The Heavy Bear Who Goes with Me"
Cohen, Writing About Literature, pp. 4, 81-82, 142-143.

Perrine and Reid, 100 American Poems, p. 219.

_____. "Tired and Unhappy"
Richard Wilbur, "Poetry's Debt to Poetry," HudR, 26 (Summer, 1973),
290-293.

SCOTT, Evelyn. "The Winter Alone"
Dudley Fitts, "The Verse of Evelyn Scott," Poetry, 36 (Sept., 1930),
338-343.

SCOTT, F. R. "Last Rites"
Stephen A. E. Scobie, "The Road Back to Eden: The Poetry of F. R. Scott,"
QQ, 79 (Autumn, 1972), 319-320.

_____. "Mural"
Stephen A. C. Scobie, "The Road Back to Eden: The Poetry of F. R. Scott,"
QQ, 79 (Autumn, 1972), 317-319.

_____. "Surfaces"
Stephen A. C. Scobie, "The Road Back to Eden: The Poetry of F. R. Scott,"
QQ, 79 (Autumn, 1972), 315-316.

_____. "Trans Canada"
Stephen A. C. Scobie, "The Road Back to Eden: The Poetry of F. R. Scott,"
QQ, 79 (Autumn, 1972), 320-323.

SCOTT, Walter. "Breathes There the Man" (from The Lay of the Last Minstrel,
        Canto VI)
Perrine, The Art of Total Relevance, pp. 122-124.

_____. "County Guy"
Don A. Keister, Expl, 4 (May, 1946), 49.
    Rpt. The Explicator Cyclopedia, II, pp. 257-258.

_____. "Proud Maisie"
George Arms and J. P. Kirby, Expl, 4 (Nov., 1945), 14.

SCOTT, Winfield Townley. "Green and Red and Darkness"
Felver and Nurmi, Poetry: An Introduction and Anthology, pp. 16-17.

_____. "The U.S. Sailor with the Japanese Skull"
      Perrine and Reid, 100 American Poems, pp. 208-210.

SCRIBLERIANS. The Lamentation of Glumdalclitch for the Loss of Grildig. A
        Pastoral"
      Alan T. MacKenzie, "'The Lamentation of Glumdalclitch for the Loss of
      Grildrig. A Pastoral': What We Have Been Missing," TSLL, 12 (Winter,
      1971), 583-594.

SCULLY, James. "Midsummer"
      Perrine and Reid, 100 American Poems, p. 272.

SEAY, James. "It All Comes Together Outside the Restroom in Hogansville"
      David Bottoms, "Note on the Structure of James Seay's 'It all Comes
      Together Outside the Restroom In Hogansville,'" NConL, 7 (Sept., 1977),
      6-7.

SEDLEY, Sir Charles. "Child and Maiden"
      Denis Donoghue, "Notes Towards a Critical Method," Studies, 44 (Summer,
      1955), 182-183.

_____. "To Phyllis"
      Allan Rodway, English Comedy: Its Role and Nature from Chaucer to the
      Present Day (London: Chatto & Windus, 1975), pp. 121-122.

SEXTON, Anne. "The Division of Parts"
      Lacey, The Inner War, pp. 19-21.

_____. "For God While Sleeping"
      Mills, Contemporary American Poetry, pp. 232-233.

_____. "For My Lover, Returning to His Wife"
      Ira Shor, "Anne Sexton's 'For My Love...': Feminism in the Classroom,"
      CE, 34 (May, 1973), 1085-1090.

_____. "For the Year of the Insane"
      Lacey, The Inner War, pp. 26-27.

_____. "In Celebration of My Uterus"
      Myra Stark, "Walt Whitman and Anne Sexton: A Note on the Uses of Tradi-
      tion," NConL, 8 (Sept., 1978), 7-8.

_____. "Little Girly, My String Bean, My Lovely Woman"
      Lacey, The Inner War, pp. 23-24.

_____. "The Lost Ingredient"
      Lacey, The Inner War, p. 23.

_____. "The Operation"
      Mills, Contemporary American Poetry, pp. 228-230.

_____. "Some Foreign Letters"
      Mills, Contemporary American Poetry, pp. 224-227.

_____. "To a Friend Whose Work Has Come to Triumph"
      Laurence Perrine, "Theme and Tone in Anne Sexton's 'To a Friend Whose
      Work Has Come to Triumph,'" NConL, 7 (May, 1977), 2-3.

_____. "The Truth the Dead Know"
Mills, Contemporary American Poetry, pp. 227-228.

_____. "You, Dr. Martin"
Lacey, The Inner War, pp. 16-17.

SHAKESPEARE. "But When I Came Alas to Wive" (Twelfth Night)
Leslie Hotson, "Twelfth Night," TLS, July 12, 1947, p. 351.

J. Dover Wilson, "Twelfth Night," TLS, July 26, 1947, p. 379.

_____. "Doubt Thou the Stars are Fire" (Hamlet, II, ii, 116-119)
Frank Doggett, Expl, 16 (Jan., 1958), 25.
    Rpt. The Explicator Cyclopedia, II, pp. 265-266.

_____. "Fear No More the Heat o' the Sun" (Cymbeline)
Bloom, Philbrick, and Blistein, The Order of Poetry, pp. 6-7, 54.

W. W. Main, Expl, 9 (March, 1951), 36.
    Rpt. The Explicator Cyclopedia, II, p. 261.

Edward F. Nolan, Expl, 11 (Oct., 1952), 4.
    Rpt. The Explicator Cyclopedia, II, pp. 261-263.

George L. Phillips, Expl, 12 (Oct., 1953), 2.
    Rpt. The Explicator Cyclopedia, II, pp. 263-264.

Wheelwright, The Burning Fountain, pp. 149-150.

_____. "The Phoenix and the Turtle"
A. Alvarez, Interpretations, ed. John Wain, pp. 1-16.

Ronald Bates, "Shakespeare's 'The Phoenix and the Turtle,'" SQ, 6
(Winter, 1955), 19-30.

Sr. Mary Bonaventura, "The Phoenix Renewed," Ball State Teachers College
Forum, 5 (Autumn, 1964), 72-76.

M. C. Bradbrook, "'The Phoenix and the Turtle,'" SQ, 6 (Summer, 1955),
356-358.

Cleanth Brooks, "The Language of Paradox," in The Language of Poetry,
ed. Allen Tate, pp. 59-61.
    Rpt. Criticism, pp. 365-366.

Brooks, The Well Wrought Urn, pp. 17-20.
    Rpt. Critiques, pp. 76-77.
    Rpt. American Literary Criticism, pp. 529-531.

Murray Copland, "The Dead Phoenix," EIC, 15 (July, 1965), 279-287.

J. V. Cunningham, "'Essence' and the Phoenix and the Turtle," ELH, 19
(Dec., 1952), 265-276.
    Rpt. Tradition and Poetic Structure, pp. 76-89.

Frank Kermode, Shakespeare, Spenser, Donne: Renaissance Essays (New
York: The Viking Press, 1971), pp. 190-199.

W. J. Ong, "Metaphor and the Twinned Vision (The Phoenix and the Turtle),"
SR, 63 (Spring, 1955), 199-201.

Elias Schwartz, "Shakespeare's Dead Phoenix," ELN, 7 (Sept., 1969), 25-
30.

Daniel Seltzer, "Their Tragic Scene: The Phoenix and Turtle and Shakespeare's Love Tragedies," SQ, 12 (Spring, 1961), 94-101.

_____. Sonnet 1, "From Fairest Creatures We Desire Increase"
Chatman, An Introduction to the Language of Poetry, pp. 39-43.

_____. Sonnet 2, "When Forty Winters Shall Besiege Thy Brow"
M. M. Mahood, "The Fatal Cleopatra: Shakespeare and the Pun," EIC, 1
(July, 1951), 193-207.

_____. Sonnet 3, "Look in Thy Glass, and Tell the Face Thou Viewest"
Ferry, All in War with Time, pp. 60-62.

David Parker, "Verbal Moods in Shakespeare's Sonnets," MLQ, 30 (Sept.,
1969), 332-335.

_____. "Sonnet 5, "Those Hours, That with Gentle Work Did Frame"
Paul Elman, "Shakespeare's Gentle Hours," SQ, 4 (July, 1953), 301-309.

Peterson, The English Lyric from Wyatt to Donne, pp. 219-220.

_____. Sonnet 7, "Lo, in the Orient When the Gracious Light"
Ferry, All in War with Time, pp. 22-23.

_____. Sonnet 8, "Music to Hear, Why Hear'st Thou Music Sadly?"
Theodore H. Banks, "Shakespeare's Sonnet No. 8," MLN, 63 (Dec., 1948),
541-542.

_____. Sonnet 12, "When I Do Count the Clock that Tells the Time"
J. Wilkes Berry, Expl, 27 (Oct., 1968), 13.

T. Walter Herbert, "Sound and Sense in Two Shakespeare Sonnets," TSL, 3
(1958), 45-47.

Krieger, The Play and Place of Criticism, pp. 22-25.

William Bowman Piper, "A Poem Turned in Process," ELH, 43 (Winter, 1976),
451-453.

_____. Sonnet 15, "When I Consider Everything That Grows"
Ferry, All in War with Time, pp. 3-10.

Kirk and McCutcheon, An Introduction to the Study of Poetry, pp. 39-41.

Krieger, The Play and Place of Criticism, pp. 26-27.

Raymond B. Waddington, "Shakespeare's Sonnet 15 and the Art of Memory,"
in The Rhetoric of Renaissance Poetry, pp. 96-122.

_____. Sonnet 16, "But Wherefore Do Not You a Mightier Way"
Empson, Seven Types of Ambiguity, pp. 70-74; (1947 ed.), pp. 54-57.

_____. Sonnet 18, "Shall I Compare Thee to a Summer's Day?"
Ferry, All in War with Time, pp. 10-13.

Smith, Elizabethan Poetry, p. 178.

_____. Sonnet 19, "Devouring Time, Blunt Thou the Lion's Paws"
Ferry, All in War with Time, pp. 13-15.

Partridge, The Language of Renaissance Poetry, pp. 123-125.

_____. Sonnet 20, "A Woman's Face with Nature's Own Hand Painted"
Martin B. Friedman, "Shakespeare's 'Master Mistris': Image and Tone in
Sonnet 20," SQ, 22 (Spring, 1971), 189-191..

David Toor, Expl, 32 (Jan., 1974), 38.

_____. Sonnet 29, "When in Disgrace with Fortune and Men's Eyes"
Abad, A Formal Approach to Lyric Poetry, pp. 125-127.

Malcolm Brown, "The Sweet Crystalline Cry," The Western Review, 16 (Summer, 1952), 264-265.

Chatman, An Introduction to the Language of Poetry, pp. 47-54.

Frankenberg, Invitation to Poetry, p. 239.

Homer Nearing, Jr., "Shakespeare as a Nondramatic Poet: Sonnet XXIX," SQ, 13 (Winter, 1962), 15-20.

_____. Sonnet 30, "When to the Sessions of Sweet Silent Thought"
Leonard Dean, English Masterpieces, Vol. III, Renaissance Poetry, p. 9.

Ferry, All in War with Time, pp. 20-22.

Donald Hall, The Pleasures of Poetry (New York: Harper & Row, 1971), pp. 25-26.

T. Walter Herbert, "Sound and Sense in Two Shakespeare Sonnets," TSL, 3 (1958), 48-50.

Knights, Explorations, pp. 74-75.

L. C. Knights, "Shakespeare's Sonnets," Scrutiny, 3 (Sept., 1934), 153.

Kreuzer, Elements of Poetry, pp. 67-70.

Partridge, The Language of Renaissance Poetry, pp. 128-130.

S. C. Pepper, The Basis of Criticism in the Arts (Cambridge: Harvard Univ. Press, 1945), pp. 115-127. Abridged in The Case for Poetry, pp. 307-309.
    Rpt. in part Stageberg and Anderson, Poetry as Experience, p. 461.

_____. Sonnet 31, "Thy Bosom Is Endeared with All Hearts"
H. W. Piper, "Shakespeare's Thirty-First Sonnet," TLS, April 13, 1951, p. 229.

Donald A. Sears, "The Translacer: A Rhetorical Thread of a Shakespearean Sonnet," CEA, 35 (March, 1973), 12-15.

_____. Sonnet 33, "Full Many a Glorious Morning Have I Seen"
Leonard Dean, English Masterpieces, Vol. III, Renaissance Poetry, p. 10.

Ransom, The World's Body, pp. 279-282.

_____. Sonnet 34, "Why Didst Thou Promise Such a Beauteous Day"
C. R. B. Combellack, Expl, 29 (Dec., 1970), 30.

T. J. Kallsen, Expl, 27 (April, 1969), 63.

Krieger, The Play and Place of Criticism, pp. 28-29.

Richard Levin, Expl, 29 (Feb., 1971), 49.

_____. Sonnet 35, "No More Be Grieved at That Which Thou Hast Done"
Knights, Explorations, pp. 64-66.

L. C. Knights, "Shakespeare's Sonnets," Scrutiny, 3 (Sept., 1934), 142-143.
    Rpt. Brooks and Warren, Understanding Poetry, pp. 292-293. Revised edition, pp. 152-153.

Peterson, The English Lyric from Wyatt to Donne, pp. 238-240.

_____. Sonnet 36, "Let Me Confess That We Two Must be Twain"
David K. Weiser, "'I' and 'Thou' in Shakespeare's Sonnets," JEGP, 76 (Oct., 1977), 517-520.

_____. Sonnet 46, "Mine Eye and Heart Are at a Mortal War"
P. S. Clarkson and C. T. Warren, "Pleading and Practice in Shakespeare's Sonnet XLVI," MLN, 62 (Feb., 1947), 102-110.

_____. Sonnet 51, "Thus Can My Love Excuse the Slow Offence"
A. Davenport, "Shakespeare's Sonnet 51 Again," N&Q, 198 (Jan., 1953), 15-16.

_____. Sonnet 54, "Oh, How Much More Doth Beauty Beauteous Seem"
Ferry, All in War with Time, pp. 29-35.

_____. Sonnet 55, "Not Marble, nor the Gilded Monuments"
Smith, Elizabethan Poetry, pp. 178-181.

_____. Sonnet 60, "Like as the Waves Make Towards the Pebbled Shore"
Douglas Lamson, and Smith, The Critical Reader, pp. 56-59. Revised edition, pp. 668-671.

John Crowe Ransom, "Shakespeare's Sonnets," SoR, 3 (Winter, 1938), 548-549.

Ransom, The World's Body, pp. 296-297.

Harold E. Toliver, "Shakespeare and the Abyss of Time," JEGP, 64 (April, 1965), 236-237.

_____. Sonnet 61, "Is It Thy Will Thy Image Should Keep Open"
David K. Weiser, "'I' and 'Thou' in Shakespeare's Sonnets," JEGP, 76 (Oct., 1976), 521-522.

_____. Sonnet 64, "When I Have Seen By Time's Fell Hand Defaced"
Ferry, All in War with Time, pp. 25-28.

James Grimshaw, "Amphibology in Shakespeare's Sonnet 64," SQ, 25 (Winter, 1974), 127-129.

Krieger, The Play and Place of Criticism, pp. 25-26.

Richard Levin, Expl, 24 (Dec., 1965), 39.

Partridge, The Language of Renaissance Poetry, pp. 130-133.

William Bowman Piper, "A Poem Turned in Process," ELH, 43 (Winter, 1976), 446-447.

Jon R. Russ, Expl, 30 (Jan., 1972), 38.

Van Doren, Introduction to Poetry, pp. 117-120.

_____. Sonnet 65, "Since Brass, Nor Stone, Nor Earth, Nor Boundless Sea"
Ferry, All in War with Time, pp. 15-19.

Krieger, The Play and Place of Criticism, p. 30.

Millett, Reading Poetry, pp. 60-61.

_____. Sonnet 66, "Tir'd with All These, for Restful Death I Cry"
Richard Levin, Expl, 22 (Jan., 1964), 36.

_____. Sonnet 71, "No Longer Mourn for Me When I Am Dead"
Krieger, The Play and Place of Criticism, pp. 31-32.

Van Doren, Introduction to Poetry, pp. 117-120.

_____. Sonnet 73, "That Time of Year Thou May'st in Me Behold"
Melvin W. Askew, "Form and Process in Lyric Poetry," SR, 62 (April-
June, 1964), 285-288.

Robert Berkelman, "The Drama in Shakespeare's Sonnets," CE, 10 (Dec.,
1948), 139.

Alan Taylor Bradford, "A Note on Sonnet 73, Line 12," SQ, 26 (Winter,
1975), 48-49.

Alan T. Bradford, "Mirrors of Mutability: Winter Landscapes in Tudor
Poetry," ELR, 4 (Winter, 1974), 28-33.

Cohen, Writing About Literature, pp. 99-101, 120-121.

Fred M. Fetrow, "Strata and Structure: A Reading of Shakespeare's Sonnet
73," CP, 9 (Fall, 1976), 23-25.

Donald Hall, The Pleasures of Poetry (New York: Harper & Row, 1971),
26-28.

Richard B. Hovey, James Schroeter, and Robert Berkelman, "Sonnet 73,"
CE, 23 (May, 1962), 672-675.

Joseph Kau, "Daniel's Influence on an Image in Pericles and Sonnet 73:
An Impresa of Destruction," SQ, 26 (Winter, 1975), 51-53.

J. G. Keogh, Expl, 28 (Sept., 1969), 6.

Kreuzer, Elements of Poetry, pp. 150-151.

R. M. Lumiansky, Expl, 6 (June, 1948), 55.
    Rpt. The Explicator Cyclopedia, II, p. 287.

Winifred Lynskey, "A Critic in Action: Mr. Ransom," CE, 5 (Feb., 1944),
244-245.

Carlisle Moore, Expl, 8 (Oct., 1949), 2.
    Rpt. The Explicator Cyclopedia, II, pp. 288-289.

Edward F. Nolan, Expl, 7 (Nov., 1948), 13.
    Rpt. The Explicator Cyclopedia, II, pp. 287-288.

Peterson, The English Lyric from Wyatt to Donne, pp. 223-224.

William Bowman Piper, "A Poem Turned in Process," ELH, 43 (Winter, 1976),
447-449.

René Rapin, Expl, 30 (Sept., 1971), 3.

Ransom, The World's Body, pp. 297-298.

Rosenthal and Smith, Exploring Poetry, pp. 91-94.

Claes Schaar, "Qui Me Alit Me Extinguit," ES, 49 (Aug., 1968), 326-327.

James Schroeter, "Shakespeare's Not 'To-Be-Pitied Lover,'" CE, 23 (Jan.,
1962), 250-255.

Smith, Elizabethan Poetry, pp. 182-185.

Thomas and Brown, Reading Poems: An Introduction to Critical Study,
pp. 744-748.

_____. Sonnet 74, "But Be Contented When That Fell Arrest"
Longworth Chambrun, "The Rival Poet," TLS, Feb. 2, 1951, p. 69.

_____. Sonnet 77, "Thy Glass Will Show Thee How Thy Beauties Wear"
Ferry, All in War with Time, pp. 62-63.

Yvor Winters, "The Sixteenth Century Lyric in England," Poetry, 54
(April, 1939), 49-51.
   Rpt. Four Poets on Poetry, pp. 58-60.
   Rpt. Forms of Discovery, pp. 61-63.

_____. Sonnet 81, "Or I Shall Live Your Epitaph to Make"
Empson, Seven Types of Ambiguity, pp. 69-70; (1947 ed.), pp. 53-54.

_____. Sonnet 83, "I Never Saw That You Did Painting Need"
Empson, Seven Types of Ambiguity, pp. 168-175; (1947 ed.), pp. 133-139.

Ferry, All in War with Time, pp. 52-54.

_____. Sonnet 86, "Was It the Proud Full Sail of His Great Verse"
Frankenberg, Invitation to Poetry, pp. 94-95.

_____. Sonnet 87, "Farewell! Thou Art Too Dear for My Possessing"
Daniels, The Art of Reading Poetry, p. 212.

Krieger, The Play and Place of Criticism, pp. 34-35.

_____. Sonnet 90, "Then Hate Me When Thou Wilt! If Ever, Now"
Virginia Jorgenson, "Of Love and Hate," EJ, 53 (Sept., 1964), 459-461.

_____. Sonnet 92, "But Do Thy Worst to Steal Thyself Away"
Richard P. Wheeler, "Poetry and Fantasy in Shakespeare's Sonnets 88-96,"
L&P, 22, No. 3 (1972), 156, 157-158.

_____. Sonnet 93, "So Shall I Live Supposing Thou Art True"
Empson, English Pastoral Poetry, pp. 89-101.

Richard P. Wheeler, "Poetry and Fantasy in Shakespeare's Sonnets 88-96,"
L&P, 22, No. 3 (1972), 158-159.

_____. Sonnet 94, "They That Have Pow'r to Hurt and Will Do None"
Empson, English Pastoral Poetry, pp. 89-101.

Knights, Explorations, pp. 69-70.

L. C. Knights, "Shakespeare's Sonnets," Scrutiny, 3 (Sept., 1934), 147-
149.

Carol Thomas Neely, "Detachment and Engagement in Shakespeare's Sonnets:
94, 116, and 129," PMLA, 92 (Jan., 1977), 83-86.

Smith, Elizabethan Poetry, pp. 188-191.

_____. Sonnet 95, "How Sweet and Lovely Dost Thou Make the Shame"
Empson, English Pastoral Poetry, pp. 89-101.

_____. Sonnet 97, "How Like a Winter Hath My Absence Been"
E. C. Evans, "Shakespeare's Sonnet 97," RES, 14 (Nov., 1963), 379-380.

Fowler, Conceitful Thought, pp. 109-113.

Kreuzer, Elements of Poetry, pp. 10-11.

Jack E. Reese, "Sound and Sense: The Teaching of Prosody," CE, 27
(Feb., 1966), 372-373.

_____. Sonnet 100, "Where Art Thou, Muse, That Thou Forget'st So Long"
Ferry, All in War with Time, pp. 37-39.

_____. Sonnet 101, "O Truant Muse, What Shall Be Thy Amends"
Ferry, All in War with Time, pp. 36-37.

_____. Sonnet 104, "To Me, Fair Friend, You Never Can Be Old"
Ferry, All in War with Time, pp. 41-47.

William Bowman Piper, "A Poem Turned in Process," ELH, 43 (Winter, 1976), 444-460.

_____. Sonnet 106, "When in the Chronicle of Wasted Time"
Chatman, An Introduction to the Language of Poetry, pp. 22-24.

Partridge, The Language of Renaissance Poetry, pp. 133-135.

_____. Sonnet 107, "Not Mine Own Fears, Nor the Prophetic Soul"
F. W. Bateson, "Elementary, My Dear Hotson," EIC, 1 (Jan., 1951), 81-88.

F. W. Bateson, Essays in Critical Dissent (London: Longman Group, 1972), pp. 49-56.

Lawrence Michel, "Shakespeare's Sonnet CVII," JEGP, 54 (April, 1955), 301-305.

Ransom, The World's Body, pp. 298-299.

Yvor Winters, "Poetic Styles, Old and New," in Four Poets on Poetry, pp. 51-55.
   Rpt. Forms of Discovery, pp. 56-59.

_____. Sonnet 108, "What's in the Brain That Ink May Character"
Ferry, All in War with Time, pp. 47-49.

_____. Sonnet 110, "Alas, 'Tis True I Have Gone Here and There"
V. L. Radley and David C. Redding, "Shakespeare: Sonnet 110, A New Look," SQ, 12 (Summer, 1961), 462-463.

_____. Sonnet 113, "Since I Left You, Mine Eye Is in My Mind"
Doniphan Louthan, "Sonnet 113," TLS, July 6, 1951, p. 421.

_____. Sonnet 116, "Let Me Not to the Marriage of True Minds"
Abad, A Formal Approach to Lyric Poetry, pp. 125-127.

Brown and Olmstead, Language and Literature, pp. 197-198.

Sigurd Burckhardt, "The Poet as Fool and Priest," ELH, 23 (Dec., 1956), 289-298.

Peter M. Daly, "A Note on Sonnet 116: A Case of Emblematic Association," SQ, 28 (Autumn, 1977), 515-516.

Frankenberg, Invitation to Poetry, pp. 398-399.

Hilton Landry, "The Marriage of True Minds: Truth and Error in Sonnet 116," ShakS, 3 (1968), 98-110.

Charles Matthews and Margaret M. Blum, "To the Student of Poetry: An Essay on Essays," CEA, 35 (Jan., 1973), 24-27.

Carol Thomas Neely, "Detachment and Engagement in Shakespeare's Sonnets: 94, 116, and 129," PMLA, 92 (Jan., 1977), 88-89.

Peckham and Chatman, Word, Meaning, Poem, pp. 296-302.

Smith, Elizabethan Poetry, pp. 172-176.

Yvor Winters, "Poetic Styles, Old and New," in Four Poets on Poetry, pp. 50-51.
    Rpt. Forms of Discovery, pp. 54-56.

_____. Sonnet 120, "That You Were Once Unkind Befriends Me Now"
Ferry, All in War with Time, pp. 55-58.

Frankenberg, Invitation to Poetry, p. 285.

David K. Weiser, "'I' and 'Thou' in Shakespeare's Sonnets," JEGP, 76 (Oct., 1976), 523-524.

_____. Sonnet 121, "Tis Better to be Vile Than Vile Esteemed"
L. C. Knights, "Shakespeare's Sonnets," Scrutiny, 3 (Sept., 1930), 155-156.

David Parker, "Verbal Moods in Shakespeare's Sonnets," MLQ, 30 (Sept., 1969), 337-338.

_____. Sonnet 122, "Thy Gift, Thy Tables, Are Within My Brain"
Ferry, All in War with Time, pp. 49-50.

_____. Sonnet 123, "No, Time, Thou Shalt Not Boast That I Do Change"
Ferry, All in War with Time, pp. 50-52.

Knights, Explorations, pp. 79-80.

L. C. Knights, "Shakespeare's Sonnets," Scrutiny, 3 (Sept., 1934), 158-160.

_____. Sonnet 124, "If My Dear Love Were But the Child of State"
Sacvan Bercovitch, Expl, 27 (Nov., 1968), 22.

Arthur Mizener, "The Structure of Figurative Language in Shakespeare's Sonnets," SoR, 5 (Spring, 1940), 734-747.

_____. Sonnet 125, "Were't Aught to Me I Bore the Canopy"
Heather Dubrow Ousby, Expl, 35 (Spring, 1977), 23.

_____. Sonnet 126, "O Thou, My Lovely Boy, Who in Thy Power"
Ferry, All in War with Time, pp. 59-62.

John R. Russ, "Time's Attributes in Shakespeare's Sonnet 126," ES, 52 (Aug., 1971), 318-323.

S. Viswanathan, "'Time's Fickle Glass' in Shakespeare's Sonnet 126," ES, 57 (June, 1976), 211-214.

_____. Sonnet 128, "How Oft When Thou, My Music Play'st"
Richard Purdum, "Shakespeare's Sonnet 128," JEGP, 63 (April, 1964), 235-239.

_____. Sonnet 129, "The Expense of Spirit in a Waste of Shame"
J. Bunselmeyer, "Appearances and Verbal Paradox: Sonnets 129 and 138," SQ, 25 (Winter, 1974), 104-105.

Jerome, Poetry: Premeditated Art, pp. 174-178.

C. W. M. Johnson, Expl, 7 (April, 1949), 41.
    Rpt. The Explicator Cyclopedia, II, pp. 290-291.

Carol Thomas Neely, "Detachment and Engagement in Shakespeare's Sonnets: 94, 116, and 129," PMLA, 92 (Jan., 1977), 90-92.

Riding and Graves, _A Survey of Modernist Poetry_, pp. 63-75, 78-80.

Richard Levin, "Sonnet CXXIX as a 'Dramatic' Poem," _SQ_, 14 (Spring, 1965), 175-181.

Peterson, _The English Lyric from Wyatt to Donne_, pp. 227-231.

Smith, _Elizabethan Poetry_, pp. 187-188.

Karl F. Thompson, _Expl_, 7 (Feb., 1949), 27.
   Rpt. _The Explicator Cyclopedia_, II, pp. 289-290.

_____. Sonnet 130, "My Mistress' Eyes are Nothing Like the Sun"
Wayne C. Booth, _A Rhetoric of Irony_ (Chicago and London: Univ. of Chicago Press, 1974), pp. 123-127.

Joseph H. Friend, "Teaching the 'Grammar of Poetry,'" _CE_, 27 (Feb., 1966), 365-366.

Partridge, _The Language of Renaissance Poetry_, pp. 135-137.

_____. Sonnet 131, "Thou Art as Tyranous, So as Thou Art"
Peterson, _The English Lyric from Wyatt to Donne_, pp. 212-213.

_____. Sonnet 132, "Thine Eyes I Love, and They as Pitying Me"
Peterson, _The English Lyric from Wyatt to Donne_, pp. 213-214.

_____. Sonnet 137, "Thou Blind Fool, Love, What Dost Thou to Mine Eyes"
Robert Fleissner, _Expl_, 35 (Spring, 1977), 21-22.

_____. Sonnet 138, "When My Love Swears That She Is Made of Truth"
J. Bunselmeyer, "Appearances and Verbal Paradox: Sonnets 129 and 138," _SQ_, 25 (Winter, 1974), 105-106.

C. R. B. Combellack, _Expl_, 30 (Dec., 1971), 33.

Richard Helgerson, _Expl_, 28 (Feb., 1970), 48.

Samuel Hux, _Expl_, 25 (Jan., 1967), 45.

_____. Sonnet 142, "Love Is My Sin, and Thy Dear Virtue Hate"
David K. Weiser, "'I' and 'Thou' in Shakespeare's Sonnets," _JEGP_, 76 (Oct., 1976), 520-521.

T. Walter Herbert, _Expl_, 13 (April, 1955), 38.
   Rpt. _The Explicator Cyclopedia_, II, pp. 291-292.

_____. Sonnet 144, "Two Loves I Have of Comfort and Despair"
John M. Steadman, "'Like Two Spirits': Shakespeare and Ficino," _SQ_, 10 (Spring, 1959), 244-246.

_____. Sonnet 145, "Those Lips That Love's Own Hand Did Make"
Andrew Gurr, "Shakespeare's First Poem: Sonnet 145," _EIC_, 21 (July, 1971), 221-226.

Hilda Hume, "Sonnet 145: 'I Hate, From Hathaway She Threw,'" _EIC_, 21 (Oct., 1971), 427-429.

_____. Sonnet 146, "Poor Soul, the Center of My Sinful Earth"
Beaty and Matchett, _Poetry: From Statement to Meaning_, pp. 14-15, 46-47, 77-79.

Robert Berkelman, "The Drama in Shakespeare's Sonnets," _CE_, 10 (Dec., 1948), 139-141.

Brooks, Purser, and Warren, An Approach to Literature, fourth edition, p. 393.

Charles A. O. Fox, "Shakespeare's Sonnet 146," N&Q, 1 n.s. (Feb., 1954), 83.

C. A. Huttar, "The Christian Basis of Shakespeare's Sonnet 146," SQ, 19 (Autumn, 1968), 355-365.

Kreuzer, Elements of Poetry, pp. 91-92.

Sanders, The Discovery of Poetry, pp. 350-352.

B. C. Southam, "Shakespeare's Christian Sonnet? Number 146," SQ, 11 (Winter, 1960), 67-72.

Donald A. Stauffer, et al., "Critical Principles and a Sonnet," ASch, 12 (Winter, 1942), 52-62. Abridged in The Case for Poetry, pp. 317-319.

Michael West, "The Internal Dialogue of Shakespeare's Sonnet 146," SQ, 25 (Winter, 1974), 109-122.

_____. Sonnet 147, "My Love Is as a Fever, Longing Still,"
Smith, Elizabethan Poetry, pp. 186-187.

_____. Sonnet 153, "Cupid Laid by His Brand and Fell Asleep"
James Hutton, "Analogues of Shakespeare's Sonnets, 153-154," MP, 38 (May, 1941), 399-403.

_____. Sonnet 154, "The Little Love-God Lying Once Asleep"
James Hutton, "Analogues of Shakespeare's Sonnets 153-154," MP, 38 (May, 1941), 399-403.

_____. "Take Oh Take Those Lips Away" (Measure for Measure)
Empson, Seven Types of Ambiguity, pp. 229-230; (1947 ed.), pp. 180-182.

Stauffer, The Nature of Poetry, p. 107.

_____. "What Shall He Have That Kill'd the Deer?" (As You Like It)
Peter J. Seng, "The Foresters' Song in As You Like It," SQ, 10 (Spring, 1959), 246-249.

_____. "When Daisies Pied and Violets Blue" (Love's Labour's Lost)
Bertrand H. Bronson, "Daisies Pied and Icicles," MLN, 63 (Jan., 1948), 35-38.

Laurence Perrine, "The Art of Total Relevance," CEA, 36 (Nov., 1973), 10-12.
    Rpt. The Art of Total Relevance, pp. 7-10.

_____. "When Icicles Hang by the Wall" (Love's Labour's Lost)
Bertrand H. Bronson, "Daisies Pied and Icicles," MLN, 63 (Jan., 1948), 35-38.

Daniels, The Art of Reading Poetry, pp. 50-51.

Perrine, Sound and Sense, pp. 7-8.
    Rpt. second edition, pp. 7-8.

_____. "Who Is Silvia? What Is She?" (The Two Gentlemen of Verona)
Cleanth Brooks, "Irony and 'Ironic' Poetry," CE, 9 (Feb., 1948), 234-235; EJ, 37 (Feb., 1948), 60-61.
    Rpt. Zabel, Literary Opinion in America, revised edition, pp. 733-734.

Paul R. Sullivan, "Untheological Grace," CE, 10 (Dec., 1948), 164-165.

SHAPIRO. "Auto Wreck"
   Bloom, Philbrick, and Blistein, The Order of Poetry, pp. 24-28.

   Alice Coleman, "Doors Leap Open," EJ, 53 (Nov., 1964), 631-633.

   Mills, Contemporary American Poetry, pp. 110-113.

   Perrine and Reid, 100 American Poems, p. 35.

_____. "Christmas Eve: Australia"
   David Daiches, "The Poetry of Karl Shapiro," Poetry, 66 (Aug., 1945), 267-269.
      Rpt. Engle and Carrier, Reading Modern Poetry, pp. 250-251.

_____. "The Dome of Sunday"
   Edwin Fussell, "Karl Shapiro: The Paradox of Prose and Poetry," The Western Review, 18 (Spring, 1954), 240-242.

_____. "Drug Store"
   Perrine and Reid, 100 American Poems, pp. 226-227.

_____. "Elegy for a Dead Soldier"
   Paul Engle, "Five Years of Pulitzer Poets," EJ, 38 (Feb., 1949), 62-63.

   Edwin Fussell, "Karl Shapiro: The Paradox of Prose and Poetry," The Western Review, 18 (Spring, 1954), 239-240.

_____. "The Leg"
   Mills, Contemporary American Poetry, pp. 113-115.

_____. "Poet"
   Michel Vinavert, Expl, 4 (Dec., 1945), 23.
      Rpt. The Explicator Cyclopedia, I, p. 265.

_____. "The Progress of Faust"
   Perrine and Reid, 100 American Poems, pp. 221-223.

SHELLEY. "Adonais"
   George Arms, Expl, 1 (Dec., 1942), 22.
      Rpt. The Explicator Cyclopedia, II, p. 299.

   Bloom, The Visionary Company, pp. 333-341.

   Bostetter, The Romantic Ventriloquists, pp. 224-229.

   Daiches and Charvat, Poems in English, p. 704.

   Richard H. Fogle, "Dante and Shelley's Adonais," BuR, 15 (1967), 11-21.
      Rpt. The Permanent Pleasure, pp. 87-99.

   Roberts W. French, Expl, 29 (Oct., 1970), 16.

   Hungerford, Shores of Darkness, pp. 216-239.

   Michael Macklem, "The Elegiac Theme in Housman," QQ, 59 (Spring, 1952), 47-48.

   Elizabeth Nitchie and T. O. Mabbott, Expl, 1 (March, 1943), 39.
      Rpt. The Explicator Cyclopedia, II, pp. 299-300.

John P. O'Neill and Stewart C. Wilcox, Expl, 12 (Oct., 1953), 5.
    Rpt. The Explicator Cyclopedia, II, p. 299.

Perkins, The Quest for Permanence, pp. 130-136.

Eric Smith, By Mourning Tongues: Studies in English Elegy (Ipswich and
Totowa: The Boydell Press and Rowan and Littlefield, 1977), pp. 55-78.

Tillyard, Poetry Direct and Oblique, pp. 172-173.

Earl R. Wasserman, "'Adonias': Progressive Revelation as a Poetic Mode,"
ELH, 21 (Dec., 1954), 278-326.

Wasserman, The Subtler Language, pp. 305-361.

S. C. Wilcox, Expl, 8 (Nov., 1949), 13.
    Rpt. The Explicator Cyclopedia, II, pp. 297-299.

Stewart C. Wilcox, Expl, 9 (April, 1951), 39.
    Rpt. The Explicator Cyclopedia, II, pp. 295-297.

_____. "Alastor"
John C. Bean, "The Poet Borne Darkly: The Dream-Voyage Allegory in Shelley's Alastor," KSJ, 23 (1974), 60-76.

Bloom, The Visionary Company, pp. 277-282.

Leonard Brown, "The Genesis, Growth, and Meaning of 'Endymion,'" SP, 30
(Oct., 1933), 623-653 et passim.

Kenneth Neill Cameron, "Rasselas and Alastor: A Study in Transmutation,"
SP, 40 (Jan., 1943), 58-78.

Bryan Cooper, "Shelley's Alastor: The Quest for a Vision," KSJ, 19
(1970), 63-76.

A. E. DuBois, "Alastor: The Spirit of Solitude," JEGP, 35 (1936), 530-
545.

Albert Gerard, "Alastor, or the Spirit of Solipsism," PQ, 33 (April,
1954), 164-177.

Evan K. Gibson, "Alastor: A Reinterpretation," PMLA, 62 (Dec., 1947),
1022-1045.

Raymond D. Havens, "Shelley's 'Alastor,'" PMLA, 45 (Dec., 1930), 1098-
1115.

W. H. Hildebrand, "Shelley's Early Vision Poems," SIR, 8 (Summer, 1969),
207-211.

A. M. D. Hughes, "'Alastor, or the Spirit of Solitude,'" MLR, 43 (Oct.,
1948), 465-470.

Parks C. Hunter, Jr., Expl, 29 (Jan., 1971), 40.

F. L. Jones, "The Inconsistency of Shelley's Alastor," ELH, 13 (Dec.,
1946), 291-298.

F. L. Jones, "The Vision Theme in Shelley's Alastor and Related Works,"
SP, 44 (Jan., 1947), 108-125.

Marcel Kessel, Paul Mueschke and E. L. Griggs, "The Poet in Shelley's
Alastor: A Criticism and a Reply," PMLA, 51 (March, 1936), 302-312.

Seraphia Leyda, "'Love's Rare Universe': Eros in Shelley's Poetry," in
Explorations of Literature, ed. Rima Drell Reck, pp. 44-49, 66-69 et
passim.

Norman Thurston, "Author, Narrator, and Hero in Shelley's Alastor," SIR,
14 (Spring, 1975), 119-131.

Timothy Webb, "Coleridge and Shelley's Alastor: A Reply," RES, 18 (Nov., 1967), 402-441.

Robert A. Wickert, Expl, 12 (Nov., 1953), 11.
   Rpt. The Explicator Cyclopedia, II, p. 300.

_____. "The Cloud"
Brooks, Purser, and Warren, An Approach to Literature, pp. 471-473.

Mignonette E. Harrison, Expl, 12 (Nov., 1953), 10.
   Rpt. The Explicator Cyclopedia, II, pp. 300-301.

Knight, The Starlit Dome, pp. 198-199.

Donald Pearce, "The Riddle of Shelley's Cloud," YR, 62 (Winter, 1973), 202-220.

_____. "Epipsychidion"
Bloom, The Visionary Company, pp. 327-333.

Bostetter, The Romantic Ventriloquists, pp. 198-218.

K. N. Cameron, "The Planet-Tempest Passage in Epipsychidion," PMLA, 63 (Sept., 1948), 950-972.

D. J. Hughes, "Coherence and Collapse in Shelley, with Particular Reference to 'Epipsychidion,'" ELH, 28 (Sept., 1961), 264-283.

Seraphia Leyda, "'Love's Rare Universe': Eros in Shelley's Poetry," in Explorations of Literature, ed. Rima Drell Reck, pp. 54-66, 67-69 et passim.

Perkins, The Quest for Permanence, pp. 171-179.

John Hawley Roberts, Expl, 1 (April, 1943), 49.
   Rpt. The Explicator Cyclopedia, II, pp. 301-302.

John F. Slater, "Self-Concealment and Self-Revelation in Shelley's 'Epipsychidion,'" PLL, 11 (Summer, 1975), 279-292.

Vivante, English Poetry, pp. 174-177.

_____. "Fragment Supposed to Be an Epithalamium of Francis Ravaillac and Charlotte Corday"
W. H. Hildebrand, "Shelley's Early Vision Poems," SIR, 8 (Summer, 1969), 198-200.

_____. "Ginevra"
Ben W. Griffith, Jr., "Shelley's 'Ginevra,'" TLS, Jan. 15, 1954, p. 41.

_____. "Hymn to Intellectual Beauty"
Bloom, The Visionary Company, pp. 283-285.

W. H. Hildebrand, "Shelley's Early Vision Poems," SIR, 8 (Summer, 1969), 211-214.

F. L. Jones, "Shelley's On Life," PMLA, 72 (Sept., 1947), 775-778.

Gerald McNiece, "The Poet as Ironist in 'Mont Blanc' and 'Hymn to Intellectual Beauty,'" SIR, 15 (Fall, 1975), 327-334.

Peter Mortenson, "Image and Structure in Shelley's Longer Lyrics," SIR, 4 (Winter, 1965), 106-107.

Elizabeth Nitchie, PMLA, 63 (June, 1948), 752-753.

Perkins, The Quest for Permanence, pp. 138-139.

_____. "The Indian Serenade"
Brooks and Warren, Understanding Poetry, pp. 320-323. Revised edition, pp. 174-176.

Richard Levin, "Shelley's 'Indian Serenade': A Re-Revaluation," CE, 24 (Jan., 1963), 305-307.

_____. "Julian and Maddalo"
Carlos Baker, "Shelley's Farrarese Maniac," in English Institute Essays 1946, pp. 41-73.

James L. Hill, "Dramatic Structure in Shelley's Julian and Maddalo," ELH, 35 (March, 1968), 84-93.

Seraphia Leyda, "'Love's Rare Universe': Eros in Shelley's Poetry," in Explorations of Literature, ed. Rima Drell Reck, pp. 53-54.

_____. "Lamia"
John H. Roberts, "The Significance of Lamia," PMLA, 50 (June, 1935), 550-561.
_____. "Lines: When the Lamp is Shattered"
Beach, A Romantic View of Poetry, pp. 76-81.

Louise Schutz Boas, Expl, 1 (April, 1943), 48.
    Rpt. The Explicator Cyclopedia, II, pp. 302-303.

R. H. Fogle, "Romantic Bards and Metaphysical Reviewers," ELH, 12 (Sept., 1945), 234-235.

Robert M. Gay, Expl, 2 (Oct., 1943), 6.
    Rpt. The Explicator Cyclopedia, II, p. 302.

Daniel Gibson, F. A. Philbrick, and Gilbert MacBeth, Expl, 1 (May, 1943), 51.
    Rpt. The Explicator Cyclopedia, II, pp. 303-304.

Marcel Kessel, Expl, 3 (Nov., 1944), 13.
    Rpt. The Explicator Cyclopedia, II, pp. 304-305.

F. R. Leavis, "Shelley (Revaluations VIII)," Scrutiny, 4 (Sept., 1935), 168-171.
    Rpt. Revaluation, pp. 216-220.
    Rpt. Critiques, pp. 169-172.

Norman Nathan, "Shelley's 'Eagle Home,'" N&Q, 1, n.s. (Jan., 1954), 30.

Tate, On the Limits of Poetry, pp. 126-127.

Tate, Reason in Madness, pp. 96-97.

Allen Tate, "Understanding Modern Poetry," CE, 1 (April, 1940), 570-571.

René Wellek, "A Letter," in The Importance of Scrutiny, p. 28. First published in Scrutiny, 1937.

_____. "Lines Written Among the Euganean Hills"
Louise Schutz Boas, Expl, 3 (Nov., 1944), 14.
    Rpt. The Explicator Cyclopedia, II, pp. 305-306.

J. P. Kirby, Expl, 1 (Oct., 1942), 5.
    Rpt. The Explicator Cyclopedia, II, p. 305.

Donald H. Reiman, "Structure, Symbol, and Theme in 'Lines Written Among the Euganean Hills,'" PMLA, 77 (Sept., 1962), 404-413.

_____.   "Mont Blanc"
Bloom, The Visionary Company, pp. 285-289.

Spencer Hall, "Shelley's 'Mont Blanc,'" SP, 70 (April, 1973), 199-221.

I. J. Kapstein, "The Meaning of Shelley's 'Mont Blanc,'" PMLA, 62 (Dec., 1947), 1046-1060.

John Kinnaird, "'But for Such Faith': A Controversial Phrase in Shelley's 'Mont Blanc,'" N&Q, 15 (Sept., 1968), 332-334.

Leavis, Revaluation, pp. 212-214.
    Rpt. Critiques, pp. 167-168.

F. R. Leavis, "A Reply," in The Importance of Scrutiny, p. 39. First published in Scrutiny, 1937.

Gerald McNiece, "The Poet as Ironist in 'Mont Blanc' and 'Hymn to Intellectual Beauty,'" SIR, 15 (Fall, 1975), 313-327.

Peter Mortenson, "Image and Structure in Shelley's Longer Lyrics," SIR, 4 (Winter, 1965), 104-106.

E. B. Murray, "Mont Blanc's Unfurled Veil," KSJ, 18 (1969), 39-45.

Perkins, The Quest for Permanence, pp. 127-129.

Joan Rees, "'But for Such Faith,' A Shelley Crux," RES, 15 (May, 1964), 185-186.

Charles H. Vivian, "The One 'Mont Blanc,'" KSJ, 4 (1955), 55-65.

Wasserman, The Subtler Language, pp. 195-240.

René Wellek, "A Letter," in The Importance of Scrutiny, pp. 27-28. First published in Scrutiny, 1937.

Yeats, Essays, pp. 104-107.

_____.   "Ode to Heaven"
Peckham and Chatman, Word, Meaning, Poem, pp. 154-170.

_____.   "Ode to Liberty"
William P. Albrecht, Expl, 5 (Dec., 1946), 23.
    Rpt. The Explicator Cyclopedia, II, pp. 306-307.

Louise Schutz Boas, Expl, 2 (June, 1944), 59.
    Rpt. The Explicator Cyclopedia, II, p. 306.

_____.   "Ode to the West Wind"
Adams, The Context of Poetry, pp. 132-134.

Melvin W. Askew, "Form and Process in Lyric Poetry," SR, 62 (April-June, 1964), 292-293.

Eben Bass, "The Fourth Element in 'Ode to the West Wind,'" PLL, 3 (Fall, 1967), 327-338.

Bateson, English Poetry, pp. 213-217. Abridged in The Case for Poetry, pp. 325-327.

Bloom, A Map of Misreading, pp. 149-152.

Bloom, The Visionary Company, pp. 289-294.

Irene H. Chayes, "Rhetoric as Drama: An Approach to the Romantic Ode," PMLA, 79 (March, 1964), 71-74.

Dyson and Lovelock, Masterful Images, pp. 193-203.

Richard H. Fogle, Expl, 6 (Oct., 1947).
   Rpt. The Explicator Cyclopedia, II, pp. 308-309.

R. H. Fogle, "Romantic Bards and Metaphysical Reviewers," ELH, 12 (Sept., 1945), 236-238, 249-250.

R. H. Fogle, "The Imaginal Design of Shelley's 'Ode to the West Wind,'" ELH, 15 (Sept., 1948), 219-226. Abridged in The Case for Poetry, pp. 323-325.
   Rpt. The Permanent Pleasure, pp. 60-68.

Philip Hobsbaum, Theory of Criticism (Bloomington and London: Indiana Univ. Press, 1970), pp. 62-67.

I. J. Kapstein, "The Symbolism of the Wind and the Leaves in Shelley's 'Ode to the West Wind,'" PMLA, 51 (Dec., 1936), 1069-1079.

F. R. Leavis, "A Reply," in The Importance of Scrutiny, p. 38. First published in Scrutiny, 1937.

F. R. Leavis, "Shelley (Revaluations VIII)," Scrutiny, 4 (Sept., 1935), 159-163 et passim.
   Rpt. Revaluation, pp. 204-206.
   Rpt. Critiques, pp. 162-163.

Douglass S. Mead, Expl, 5 (May, 1947), Q20.
   Rpt. The Explicator Cyclopedia, II, p. 307.

Coleman O. Parsons, "Shelley's Prayer to the West Wind," KSJ, 11 (Winter, 1962), 31-37.

Perkins, The Quest for Permanence, pp. 163-167.

Tate, Reactionary Essays on Poetry and Ideas, pp. 95-97 et passim.

William I. Thompson, "Collapsed Universe and Structural Poem: An Essay in Whiteheadian Criticism," CE, 28 (Oct., 1966), 32-33.

S. Viswanathan, "Antiphonal Patterns in Shelley's 'Ode to the West Wind,'" PLL, 8 (Summer, 1972), 307-311.

Vivante, English Poetry, pp. 164-169.

René Wellek, "A Letter," in The Importance of Scrutiny, pp. 26-27. First published in Scrutiny, 1937.

Stewart C. Wilcox, "Imagery, Ideas, and Design in Shelley's 'Ode to the West Wind,'" SP, 47 (Oct., 1950), 634-649. Abridged in The Case for Poetry, p. 325.

Arthur Wormhoudt and R. H. Fogle, Expl, 6 (Oct., 1947), 1.
   Rpt. The Explicator Cyclopedia, II, pp. 307-308.

_____. "On the Medusa of Leonardo da Vinci in the Florentine Gallery"
Daniel Hughes, "Shelley, Leonardo, and the Monsters of Thought," Criticism, 12 (Summer, 1970), 201-205.

_____. "Ozymandias"
Abad, A Formal Approach to Lyric Poetry, p. 227.

William B. Bache, "Vanity and Art in 'Ozymandias,'" CEA, 31 (Feb., 1969), 20.
   College English Association

Brown and Olmstead, Language and Literature, pp. 189-190.

Dickinson, Suggestions for Teachers of "Introduction to Literature," fifth edition, ed. Locke, Gibson, and Arms, pp. 22-23. (Teacher's Manual)

Robert B. Heilman, "Poetic and Prosaic: Program Notes of Opposite Numbers," Pacific Spectator, 5 (Autumn, 1951), 456-457.

Kirk and McCutcheon, An Introduction to the Study of Poetry, pp. 37-39.
    Rpt. Readings for Liberal Education, II, 309-310.

William V. Spanos, "Shelley's 'Ozymandias' and the Problem of the Persona," CEA, 30 (Jan., 1968), 14-15.

Wheeler, The Design of Poetry, pp. 103-105.

_____. "Prince Athanase"
Seraphia Leyda, "'Love's Rare Universe': Eros in Shelley's Poetry," in Explorations of Literature, ed. Rima Drell Reck, pp. 49-51.

_____. "The Sensitive Plant"
Richard S. Caldwell, "'The Sensitive Plant' as Original Fantasy," SIR, 15 (Spring, 1976), 221-252.

Frederick L. Jones, "Shelley and Spenser," SP, 39 (Oct., 1942), 667-669.

Robert M. Maniquis, "The Puzzling Mimosa: Sensitivity and Plant Symbols in Romanticism," SIR, 8 (Spring, 1969), 144-150.

Elizabeth Nitchie, Expl, 15 (Dec., 1956), 15.
    Rpt. The Explicator Cyclopedia, II, p. 310.

Perkins, The Quest for Permanence, pp. 147-153.

William H. Pixton, "The Sensitive Plant: Shelley's Acquiescence to Agnosticism," BSUF, 14 (Autumn, 1973), 35-44.

Priscilla P. St. George, "The Styles of Good and Evil in 'The Sensitive Plant,'" JEGP, 64 (July, 1965), 479-488.

Wasserman, The Subtler Language, pp. 251-284.

_____. "Stanzas Written in Dejection, Near Naples"
Fred A. Dudley, Expl, 1 (Feb., 1943), 31.
    Rpt. The Explicator Cyclopedia, II, p. 310.

Leonard A. Waters, Expl, 18 (June, 1960), 54.
    Rpt. The Explicator Cyclopedia, II, pp. 310-311.

_____. "To Ianthe"
Brooks, Purser, and Warren, An Approach to Literature, p. 463.
    Rpt. third edition, pp. 333-334.
    Rpt. fourth edition, pp. 331.

_____. "To Jane, the Recollection"
Vivante, English Poetry, pp. 177-181.

_____. "To Music, When Soft Voices Die"
Boulton, The Anatomy of Poetry, pp. 123-125.

John Crossett, Expl, 14 (Feb., 1956), 32.
    Rpt. The Explicator Cyclopedia, II, pp. 311-312.

Ben W. Griffith, Jr., Expl, 15 (Jan., 1957), 26.
    Rpt. The Explicator Cyclopedia, II, pp. 312-313.

E. D. Hirsch, Jr., "Further Comment on 'Music, When Soft Voices Die,'" JEGP, 60 (April, 1961), 296-298.

William Howard, Expl, 15 (Jan., 1957), 26.
    Rpt. The Explicator Cyclopedia, II, pp. 313-314.

F. R. Leavis, "'Thought' and Emotional Quality," Scrutiny, 13 (Spring, 1945), 66-67.

Irving Massey, "Shelley's 'Music, When Soft Voices Die': Text and Meaning," JEGP, 59 (July, 1960), 430-438.

John Unterecker, Expl, 15 (Jan., 1957), 26.
    Rpt. The Explicator Cyclopedia, II, p. 313.

_____. "To Night"
Daniels, The Art of Reading Poetry, pp. 354-358.

_____. "To a Skylark"
James V. Baker, "The Lark in English Poetry," PrS, 24 (Spring, 1950), 71-74.

Bloom, The Visionary Company, pp. 294-297.

Empson, Seven Types of Ambiguity, pp. 197-202; (1947 ed.), pp. 156-159.

Newell F. Ford, "Shelley's 'To a Skylark,'" KSMB, No. 11 (1960), 6-12.

Frankenberg, Invitation to Poetry, pp. 82-83.

A. E. Housman in Grant Richards, Housman, 1897-1936, p. 246. First printed in TLS, Dec. 20, 1927.

Knight, The Starlit Dome, pp. 199-200.

E. Wayne Marjarum, "The Symbolism of Shelley's 'To a Skylark,'" PMLA, 52 (Sept., 1937), 911-913.

T. S. Moore, "Mr. T. S. Eliot and Shelley's Skylark," TLS, Nov. 16, 1928, p. 991; Jan. 3, 1929, p. 12.

Peter Mortenson, "Image and Structure in Shelley's Longer Lyrics," SIR, 4 (Winter, 1965), 107-108.

Perkins, The Quest for Permanence, pp. 141-147.

Tillyard, Poetry Direct and Oblique, pp. 163-166.

Vivante, English Poetry, pp. 169-174.

S. C. Wilcox, "The Sources, Symbolism, and Unity of Shelley's Skylark," SP, 46 (Oct., 1949), 560-576.

_____. "The Triumph of Life"
Kenneth Allott, "Bloom on 'The Triumph of Life,'" EIC, 10 (April, 1960), 222-228.

Bloom, Poetry and Repression, pp. 98-111.

Bloom, The Visionary Company, pp. 344-353.

Bostetter, The Romantic Ventriloquists, pp. 181-192.

P. H. Butter, "Sum and Shape in Shelley's 'The Triumph of Life,'" RES, 13 (Spring, 1962), 40-51.

William Cherubini, "Shelley's 'Own Symposium': 'The Triumph of Life,'" SP, 39 (July, 1942), 559-570.

David Eggenschwiler, "Sexual Parody in 'The Triumph of Life,'" CP, 5 (Fall, 1972), 28-36.

G. M. Matthews, "'The Triumph of Life,'" EIC, 18 (July, 1968), 352-356.

Perkins, The Quest for Permanence, pp. 121-126.

S. R. Swaminathan, "Shelley's 'Triumph of Life,'" N&Q, 14 (Aug., 1967), 305-306.

Yeats, Essays, pp. 92-94.

_____. "The Two Spirits: An Allegory"
Bloom, The Visionary Company, pp. 315-317.

_____. "The Witch of Atlas"
Bloom, The Visionary Company, pp. 318-327.

David Rubin, "A Study of Antinomies in Shelley's The Witch of Atlas," SIR, 8 (Summer, 1969), 216-228.

_____. "The World's Great Age Begins Anew" (from Hellas)
Empson, Seven Types of Ambiguity (1947 ed.), pp. 159-160.

SHIRLEY. "Death the Leveler"
Cleanth Brooks, "In Defence of 'Interpretation' and 'Literary History," Mosaic, 8 (Winter, 1975), 6-8.

_____. "The Glories of Our Blood and State" (The Contention of Ajax and Ulysses for the Armor of Achilles)

Boulton, The Anatomy of Poetry, pp. 165-167.

E. Sydnor Ownbey, Expl, 10 (Feb., 1952), 30.
   Rpt. The Explicator Cyclopedia, II, pp. 314-315.

Tillyard, Poetry Direct and Oblique, pp. 122-124.

Wheeler, The Design of Poetry, pp. 183-185.

SIDNEY. "Astrophil and Stella, Fourth Song: Onely Joy, Now Here You Are"
Russell M. Brown, Expl, 29 (Feb., 1971), 48.

Mariann S. Regan, "Astrophel: Full of Desire, Emptie of Wit," ELN, 14 (June, 1977), 255.

_____. "Astrophil and Stella, Eighth Song: In a Grove Most Rich of Shade"
Mariann S. Regan, "Astrophel: Full of Desire, Emptie of Wit," ELN, 14 (June, 1977), 255-256.

Andrew D. Weiner, "'In a grove most rich of shade': A Figurative Reading of the Eighth Song of Astrophil and Stella," TSLL, 18 (Fall, 1976), 341-361.

_____. "Astrophil and Stella, Tenth Song: O Deare Life, When Shall It Be"
Alan Sinfield, "Sexual Puns in Astrophel and Stella," EIC, 24 (Oct., 1974), 353-355.

_____. "Astrophil and Stella, Sonnet 1: Loving in Truth and Fain in Verse My Love to Show"
Adams, Strains of Discord, pp. 4-6.

Leonard Barkan, Nature's Work of Art: The Human Body as Image of the World (New Haven and London: Yale Univ. Press, 1975), pp. 181-183.

Russell M. Brown, Expl, 32 (Nov., 1973), 21.

Arthur Dickson, Expl, 3 (Oct., 1944), 3.
   Rpt. The Explicator Cyclopedia, II, pp. 315-316.

Fowler, Conceitful Thought, pp. 100-101.

Fowler, Conceitful Thought, pp. 100-101.

David Kalstone, "Sir Philip Sidney and 'Poore Petrarch's Long Deceased Woes,'" JEGP, 63 (Jan., 1964), 30-31.

Richard A. Lanham, "Astrophil and Stella: Pure and Impure Persuasion," ELR, 2 (Winter, 1972), 101-102.

Henry Pettit and Gerald Sanders, Expl, 1 (Feb., 1943), 26.
    Rpt. The Explicator Cyclopedia, II, p. 315.

Thomas O. Sloan, "The Crossing of Rhetoric and Poetry in the English Renaissance," in The Rhetoric of Renaissance Poetry, pp. 234-237.

Andrew D. Weiner, "Structure and 'Fore Conceit' in Astrophil and Stella," TSLL, 16 (Spring, 1974), 3-4.

_____. "Astrophil and Stella, Sonnet 2: Not at First Sight, Nor with a Dribbed Shot"
Andrew D. Weiner, "Structure and 'Fore Conceit' in Astrophil and Stella," TSLL, 16 (Spring, 1974), 4-5.

_____. "Astrophil and Stella, Sonnet 3: Let Daintie Wits Crie on the Sisters Nine"
Andrew D. Weiner, "Structure and 'Fore Conceit' in Astrophil and Stella," TSLL, 16 (Spring, 1974), 5-6.

_____. "Astrophil and Stella, Sonnet 4: Vertue Alas, Now Let Me Take Some Rest"
James J. Scanlon, "Sidney's Astrophil and Stella: 'See what it is to Love' Sensually!" SEL, 16 (Winter, 1976), 68-69.

Andrew D. Weiner, "Structure and 'Fore Conceit' in Astrophil and Stella," TSLL, 16 (Spring, 1974), 6.

Richard B. Young, "English Petrarke: A Study of Sidney's Astrophel and Stella," in Three Studies in the Renaissance, pp. 33-34.

_____. "Astrophil and Stella, Sonnet 5: It Is Most True that Eyes Are Formed to Serve"
De Mourgues, Metaphysical Baroque & Precieux Poetry, pp. 14-15.

Robert L. Montgomery, Jr., "Reason, Passion, and Introspection in Astrophel and Stella," University of Texas Studies in English, 36 (1957), 132-133.

James J. Scanlon, "Sidney's Astrophil and Stella: 'See what it is to Love' Sensually!" SEL, 16 (Winter, 1976), 66-67.

Andrew D. Weiner, "Structure and 'Fore Conceit' in Astrophil and Stella," TSLL, 16 (Spring, 1974), 7-8.

_____. "Astrophil and Stella, Sonnet 9: Queene Vertue's Court, Which Some Call Stella's Face"
Leonard Barkan, Nature's Work of Art: The Human Body as Image of the World (New Haven and London: Yale Univ. Press, 1975), pp. 189-190.

Stanley A. Cowan, Expl, 20 (May, 1962), 76.
    Rpt. The Explicator Cyclopedia, II, p. 317.

Fred A. Dudley, Expl, 20 (May, 1962), 76.
    Rpt. The Explicator Cyclopedia, II, p. 317.

Fowler, Conceitful Thought, pp. 98-100.

Peterson, The English Lyric from Wyatt to Donne, pp. 188-189.

Max Putzel, Expl, 29 (Jan., 1961), 25.
  Rpt. The Explicator Cyclopedia, II, pp. 316-317.

Raymond Southall, "Love Poetry in the Sixteenth Century," EIC, 22 (Oct., 1972), 371-373.

Richard B. Young, "English Petrarke: A Study of Sidney's Astrophel and Stella," in Three Studies in the Renaissance, p. 11.

_____. "Astrophil and Stella, Sonnet 11: In Truth, O Love, With What A Boyish Kind"
Leonard Barkan, Nature's Work of Art: The Human Body as Image of the World (New Haven and London: Yale Univ. Press, 1975), pp. 184-188.

_____. "Astrophil and Stella, Sonnet 12: Cupid, Because Thou Shin'st in Stella's Eyes"
Robert S. Kinsman, Expl, 8 (June, 1950), 56.
  Rpt. The Explicator Cyclopedia, II, pp. 317-319.

Leonard Barkan, Nature's Work of Art: The Human Body as Image of the World (New Haven and London: Yale Univ. Press, 1975), pp. 187-188.

_____. "Astrophil and Stella, Sonnet 13: Phoebus Was Judge Between Jove, Mars, and Love"
Richard B. Young, "English Petrarke: A Study of Sidney's Astrophel and Stella," in Three Studies in the Renaissance, pp. 20-22.

_____. "Astrophil and Stella, Sonnet 14: Alas Have I Not Paine Enough My Friend"
Robert Emmet Finnegan, Expl, 35 (Winter, 1976), 22-23.

Alan Sinfield, "Sexual Puns in Astrophel and Stella," EIC, 24 (Oct., 1974), 344-346.

Andrew D. Weiner, "Structure and 'Fore Conceit' in Astrophil and Stella," TSLL, 16 (Spring, 1974), 10-11.

_____. "Astrophil and Stella, Sonnet 18: With What Sharpe Checkes I in My Selfe Am Shent"

Richard A. Lanham, "Astrophil and Stella: Pure and Impure Persuasion," ELR, 2 (Winter, 1972), 105-106.

Alan Sinfield, "Sexual Puns in Astrophel and Stella," EIC, 24 (Oct., 1974), 347-349.

_____. "Astrophil and Stella, Sonnet 22: In Highest Way of Heav'n the Sunne Did Ride"
Alan Sinfield, "Sexual Puns in Astrophel and Stella," EIC, 24 (Oct., 1974), 350-352.

_____. "Astrophil and Stella, Sonnet 24: "Rich Fooles There Be, Whose Base and Filthy Hart"
Alan Sinfield, "Sexual Puns in Astrophel and Stella," EIC, 24 (Oct., 1974), 349-350.

Richard B. Young, "English Petrarke: A Study of Sidney's Astrophel and Stella," in Three Studies in the Renaissance, pp. 29-30.

_____. "Astrophil and Stella, Sonnet 28: Because I Oft in Dark Abstracted Guise"
Tuve, Elizabethan and Metaphysical Imagery, p. 320.

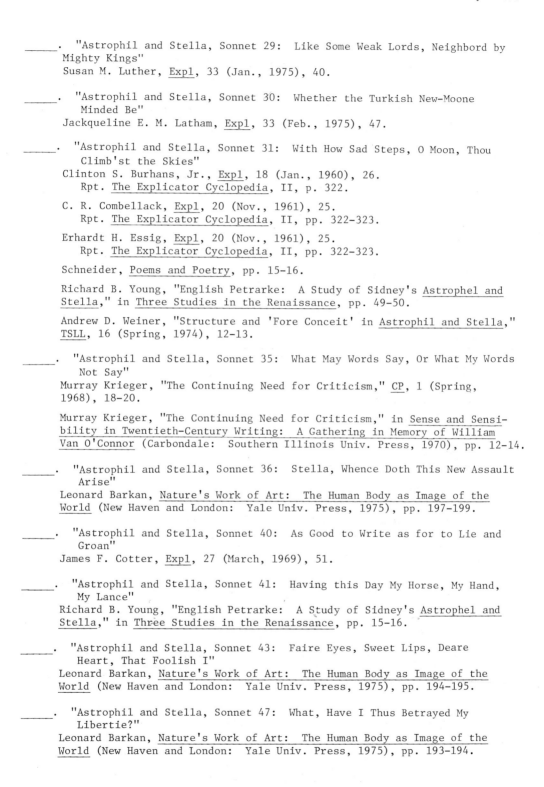

_____. "Astrophil and Stella, Sonnet 29: Like Some Weak Lords, Neighbord by
Mighty Kings"
Susan M. Luther, Expl, 33 (Jan., 1975), 40.

_____. "Astrophil and Stella, Sonnet 30: Whether the Turkish New-Moone
     Minded Be"
Jackqueline E. M. Latham, Expl, 33 (Feb., 1975), 47.

_____. "Astrophil and Stella, Sonnet 31: With How Sad Steps, O Moon, Thou
     Climb'st the Skies"
Clinton S. Burhans, Jr., Expl, 18 (Jan., 1960), 26.
     Rpt. The Explicator Cyclopedia, II, p. 322.

C. R. Combellack, Expl, 20 (Nov., 1961), 25.
     Rpt. The Explicator Cyclopedia, II, pp. 322-323.

Erhardt H. Essig, Expl, 20 (Nov., 1961), 25.
     Rpt. The Explicator Cyclopedia, II, pp. 322-323.

Schneider, Poems and Poetry, pp. 15-16.

Richard B. Young, "English Petrarke: A Study of Sidney's Astrophel and
Stella," in Three Studies in the Renaissance, pp. 49-50.

Andrew D. Weiner, "Structure and 'Fore Conceit' in Astrophil and Stella,"
TSLL, 16 (Spring, 1974), 12-13.

_____. "Astrophil and Stella, Sonnet 35: What May Words Say, Or What My Words
     Not Say"
Murray Krieger, "The Continuing Need for Criticism," CP, 1 (Spring,
1968), 18-20.

Murray Krieger, "The Continuing Need for Criticism," in Sense and Sensibility in Twentieth-Century Writing: A Gathering in Memory of William
Van O'Connor (Carbondale: Southern Illinois Univ. Press, 1970), pp. 12-14.

_____. "Astrophil and Stella, Sonnet 36: Stella, Whence Doth This New Assault
     Arise"
Leonard Barkan, Nature's Work of Art: The Human Body as Image of the
World (New Haven and London: Yale Univ. Press, 1975), pp. 197-199.

_____. "Astrophil and Stella, Sonnet 40: As Good to Write as for to Lie and
     Groan"
James F. Cotter, Expl, 27 (March, 1969), 51.

_____. "Astrophil and Stella, Sonnet 41: Having this Day My Horse, My Hand,
     My Lance"
Richard B. Young, "English Petrarke: A Study of Sidney's Astrophel and
Stella," in Three Studies in the Renaissance, pp. 15-16.

_____. "Astrophil and Stella, Sonnet 43: Faire Eyes, Sweet Lips, Deare
     Heart, That Foolish I"
Leonard Barkan, Nature's Work of Art: The Human Body as Image of the
World (New Haven and London: Yale Univ. Press, 1975), pp. 194-195.

_____. "Astrophil and Stella, Sonnet 47: What, Have I Thus Betrayed My
     Libertie?"
Leonard Barkan, Nature's Work of Art: The Human Body as Image of the
World (New Haven and London: Yale Univ. Press, 1975), pp. 193-194.

Robert L. Montgomery, Jr., "Reason, Passion, and Introspection in Astrophel and Stella," University of Texas Studies in English, 36 (1957), 136-137.

Richard B. Young, "English Petrarke: A Study of Sidney's Astrophel and Stella," in Three Studies in Renaissance, pp. 23-24.

_____. "Astrophil and Stella, Sonnet 50: Stella, the Fulnesse of My Thoughts of Thee"
Leonard Barkan, Nature's Work of Art: The Human Body as Image of the World (New Haven and London: Yale Univ. Press, 1975), pp. 183-184.

_____. "Astrophil and Stella, Sonnet 51: Pardon Mine Eares, Both I and They Do Pray"
Andrew D. Weiner, "Structure and 'Fore Conceit' in Astrophil and Stella," TSLL, 16 (Spring, 1974), 15.

_____. "Astrophil and Stella, Sonnet 52: A Strife Is Growne Betweene Vertue and Love"
Andrew D. Weiner, "Structure and 'Fore Conceit' in Astrophil and Stella," TSLL, 16 (Spring, 1974), 15.

_____. "Astrophil and Stella, Sonnet 53: In Martial Sports I Had My Cunning Trade"
Leonard Barkan, Nature's Work of Art: The Human Body as Image of the World (New Haven and London: Yale Univ. Press, 1975), pp. 178-181.

_____. "Astrophil and Stella, Sonnet 59: Dear, Why Make You More of a Dog Than Me"
Tuve, Elizabethan and Metaphysical Imagery, p. 321.

_____. Astrophil and Stella, Sonnet 60: When My Good Angel Guides Me to the Place"
De Morgues, Metaphysical Baroque & Precieux Poetry, pp. 15-16.

_____. "Astrophil and Stella, Sonnet 64: No More, My Dear, No More These Counsels Try"
Robert L. Montgomery, Jr., "Reason, Passion, and Introspection in Astrophel and Stella," University of Texas Studies in English, 36 (1957), 137.

_____. "Astrophil and Stella, Sonnet 64: Love By Sure Proof I May Call Thee Unkind"
Leonard Barkan, Nature's Work of Art: The Human Body as Image of the World (New Haven and London: Yale Univ. Press, 1975), pp. 191-192.

Richard B. Young, "English Petrarke: A Study of Sidney's Astrophel and Stella," in Three Studies in the Renaissance, pp. 18-20.

_____. "Astrophil and Stella, Sonnet 68: Stella, the Only Planet of My Light"
Richard B. Young, "English Petrarke: A Study of Sidney's Astrophel and Stella," in Three Studies in the Renaissance, pp. 35-36.

_____. "Astrophil and Stella, Sonnet 71"
David Kalstone, "Sir Philip Sidney and 'Poore Petrarchs Long Deceased Woes,'" JEGP, 63 (Jan., 1964), 26-30.

_____. "Astrophil and Stella, Sonnet 73: Love Still a Boy, and Oft a Wanton Is"
Leonard Barkan, Nature's Work of Art: The Human Body as Image of the World (New Haven and London: Yale Univ. Press, 1975), pp. 199-200.

James Finn Cotter, "The 'Baiser' Group in Sidney's Astrophil and Stella," TSLL, 12 (Fall, 1970), 390-392.

_____. "Astrophil and Stella, Sonnet 74: I Never Dranke of Aganippe Well"
James Finn Cotter, "The 'Baiser' Group in Sidney's Astrophil and Stella," TSLL, 12 (Fall, 1970), 392-393.

Richard B. Young, "English Petrarke: A Study of Sidney's Astrophel and Stella," in Three Studies in the Renaissance, pp. 7-8.

_____. "Astrophil and Stella, Sonnet 75, "Of All the Kings That Ever Did Here Reign"

John Finn Cotter, Expl, 27 (May, 1969), 70.

_____. "Astrophil and Stella, Sonnet 76: She Comes, and Streight Therewith Her Shining Twins Do Move"
James Finn Cotter, "The 'Baiser' Group in Sidney's Astrophil and Stella," TSLL, 12 (Fall, 1970), 393-394.

_____. "Astrophil and Stella, Sonnet 77: "Those Lookes, Whose Beames Be Joy, Whose Motion Is Delight"
James Finn Cotter, "The 'Baiser' Group in Sidney's Astrophil and Stella," TSLL, 12 (Fall, 1970), 394-395.

_____. "Astrophil and Stella, Sonnet 78: O How the Pleasant Aires of True Love Be"
James Finn Cotter, "The 'Baiser' Group in Sidney's Astrophil and Stella," TSLL, 12 (Fall, 1970), 395-396.

Harold S. Wilson, Expl, 2 (Nov., 1943), 17.
    Rpt. The Explicator Cyclopedia, II, p. 319.

_____. "Astrophil and Stella, Sonnet 79: Sweet Kisse, Thy Sweets I Faine Would Sweetly Endite"
James Finn Cotter, "The 'Baiser' Group in Sidney's Astrophil and Stella," TSLL, 12 (Fall, 1970), 396-397.

_____. "Astrophil and Stella, Sonnet 80: Sweet Swelling Lip, Well Maist Thou Swell in Pride"
James Finn Cotter, "The 'Baiser' Group in Sidney's Astrophil and Stella," TSLL, 12 (Fall, 1970), 397-398.

_____. "Astrophil and Stella, Sonnet 81: O Kisse Which Those Ruddie Gemmes Impart"
James Finn Cotter, "The 'Baiser' Group in Sidney's Astrophil and Stella," TSLL, 12 (Fall, 1970), 398-399.

_____. "Astrophil and Stella, Sonnet 82: "Nymph of the Garden, Where All Beauties Be"
James Finn Cotter, "The 'Baiser' Group in Sidney's Astrophil and Stella," TSLL, 12 (Fall, 1970), 399-400.

_____. "Astrophil and Stella, Sonnet 83: Good Brother Philip, I Have Borne You Long"
James Finn Cotter, "The 'Baiser' Group in Sidney's Astrophil and Stella," TSLL, 12 (Fall, 1970), 400-401.

_____. "Astrophil and Stella, Sonnet 84: Highway Since You My Chiefe Pernas-
      sus Be"
James Finn Cotter, "The 'Baiser' Group in Sidney's Astrophil and Stella,"
TSLL, 12 (Fall, 1970), 401-402.

Curtis Dahl, Expl, 6 (May, 1948), 46.
      Rpt. The Explicator Cyclopedia, II, pp. 319-320.

Mariann S. Regan, "Astrophel: Full of Desire, Emptie of Wit," ELN, 14
(June, 1977), 254.

Yvor Winters, "The Sixteenth-Century Lyric in England," Poetry, 53
(April, 1939), 328-329.
      Rpt. Forms of Discovery, pp. 30-32.

_____. "Astrophil and Stella, Sonnet 96: Thought With Good Cause Thou Likest
      So Well the Night"
Andrew D. Weiner, "Structure and 'Fore Conceit' in Astrophil and Stella,"
TSLL, 16 (Spring, 1974), 19.

_____. "Astrophil and Stella, Sonnet 97: Dian That Faine Would Cheare Her
      Friend the Night"
Andrew D. Weiner, "Structure and 'Fore Conceit' in Astrophil and Stella,
TSLL, 16 (Spring, 1974), 19-20.

_____. "Astrophil and Stella, Sonnet 98: Ah Bed, the Field Where Joye's
      Peace Some Do See"
Andrew D. Weiner, "Structure and 'Fore Conceit' in Astrophil and Stella,
TSLL, 16 (Spring, 1974), 20-21.

_____. "Astrophil and Stella, Sonnet 99: When Far Spent Night Persuades Each
      Mortal Eye"
Richard B. Young, "English Petrarke: A Study of Sidney's Astrophel and
Stella," in Three Studies in the Renaissance, p. 85.

_____. "Astrophil and Stella, Sonnet 102: Where Be Those Roses Gone Which
      Sweetned So Our Eyes?"

Leonard Barkan, Nature's Work of Art: The Human Body as Image of the
World (New Haven and London: Yale Univ. Press, 1975), pp. 185-186.

_____. "Astrophil and Stella, Sonnet 105: Unhappie Sight, and Hath She Ban-
      isht By"
Leonard Barkan, Nature's Work of Art: The Human Body as Image of the
World (New Haven and London: Yale Univ. Press, 1975), pp. 192-193.

_____. "Certaine Sonnets, 4: And Have I heard Her Say? O Cruell Paine"
Paul K. Dempsey, Expl, 25 (Feb., 1967), 51.

_____. "Certaine Sonnets, 31: Thou Blind Man's Mark, Thou Fool's Self-
      Chosen Snare"
Dan G. Hoffman, Expl, 8 (Feb., 1950), 29.
      Rpt. The Explicator Cyclopedia, II, pp. 321-322.

Peterson, The English Lyric from Wyatt to Donne, pp. 199-201.

_____. "Certaine Sonnets, 32: Leave Me, O Love Which Reachest But to Dust"
Leland Ryken, Expl, 26 (Sept., 1967), 9.

W. K. Thomas, Expl, 28 (Jan., 1970), 45.

Harold S. Wilson, Expl, 2 (April, 1944), 47.
     Rpt. Locke, Gibson, and Arms, Introduction to Literature, third edi-
     tion, pp. 23-24.
     Rpt. The Explicator Cyclopedia, II, pp. 320-321.

Winters, Forms of Discovery, pp. 33-34.

_____. "A Litany"
Brooks and Warren, Understanding Poetry, pp. 342-345. Revised edition,
pp. 206-210.

_____. "Psalm 8"
G. F. Waller, "'This Matching of Contraries': Calvanism and Courtly
Philosophy in the Sidney Psalms," ES, 55 (Feb, 1974), 30-31.

_____. "Psalm 45"
G. F. Waller, "'This Matching of Contraries': Calvanism and Courtly
Philosophy in the Sidney Psalms," ES, 55 (Feb., 1974), 29.

_____. "Psalm 81"
G. F. Waller, "'This Matching of Contraries': Calvinism and Courtly
Philosophy in the Sidney Psalms," ES, 55 (Feb., 1974), 28-29.

_____. "What Toong Can Her Perfections Tell"
Dorothy Jones, "Sidney's Erotic Pen: An Interpretation of One of the
Arcadia Poems," JEGP, 73 (Jan., 1974), 32-47.

_____. "Ye Goatherd Gods"
Fowler, Conceitful Thought, pp. 38-52.

Empson, Seven Types of Ambiguity, pp. 45-50; (1947 ed.), pp. 34-38.

Ransom, The New Criticism, pp. 108-114.

SILKIN, Jon. "Amana Grass"
Merle E. Brown, "On Jon Silin's 'Amana Grass,'" IowaR, 1 (Winter, 1970),
115-125.

_____. "Carved"
Merle Brown, "Stress in Silkin's Poetry and the Healing Emptiness of
America," ConL, 18 (Summer, 1977), 367-368.

_____. "Concerning Strength"
Merle Brown, "Stress in Silkin's Poetry and the Healing Emptiness of
America," ConL, 18 (Summer, 1977), 388-389.

_____. "Death of a Son (Who Died in a Mental Hospital Aged One)"
Merle Brown, "Stress in Silkin's Poetry on the Healing Emptiness of
America," ConL, 18 (Summer, 1977), 368-372.

_____. "A Death to Us"
Merle Brown, "Stress in Silkin's Poetry and the Healing Emptiness of
America," ConL, 18 (Summer, 1977), 364-366.

_____. "From the Road I Saw a Small Rounded Bluff"
Merle Brown, "Stress in Silkin's Poetry on the Healing Emptiness of
America," ConL, 18 (Summer, 1977), 382-383.

_____. "Small Hills Among the Fells Come Apart from the Large"
Merle Brown, "Stress in Silkin's Poetry on the Healing Emptiness of
America," ConL, 18 (Summer, 1977), 385-388.

_____. "The Two Freedoms"
Satin, Reading Poetry, pp. 1140-1142.

SIMIC, Charles. "The Variant"
David Walker, "O What Solitude: The Recent Poetry of Charles Simic,"
Ironwood, 7-8, 66-67.

SIMPSON, Louis. "The Green Shepherd"
Perrine and Reid, 100 American Poems, pp. 266-267.

_____. "Walt Whitman at Bear Mountain"
Ronald Moran, "'Walt Whitman at Bear Mountain' and the American Illusion,"
CP, 2 (Spring, 1969), 5-9.

SITWELL, Edith. "Aubade"
Eastman, The Literary Mind, pp. 73-76 (quoting from Sitwell).

Stageberg and Anderson, Poetry as Experience, pp. 497-498.

_____. "The Canticle of the Rose"
Keith D. Cuffel, "The Shadow of Cain: Themes in Dame Edith Sitwell's
Later Poetry," The Personalist," 46 (Autumn, 1965), 524-525.

_____. "Dirge for the New Sunrise"
Keith D. Cuffel, "The Shadow of Cain: Themes in Dame Edith Sitwell's
Later Poetry," The Personalist, 46 (Autumn, 1965), 520-521.

_____. "Fantasia for Mouth Organ"
Riding and Graves, A Survey of Modernist Poetry, pp. 247-249.

_____. "Gold Coast Customs"
Sr. M. Jeremy, "Clown and Canticle: The Achievement of Edith Sitwell,"
Renascence, 3 (Spring, 1951), 133-134.

_____. "The Shadow of Cain"
Keith D. Cuffel, "The Shadow of Cain: Themes in Dame Edith Sitwell's
Later Poetry," The Personalist, 46 (Autumn, 1965), 520-521.

Sr. M. Jeremy, "Clown and Canticle: The Achievement of Edith Sitwell,"
Renascence, 3 (Spring, 1951), 135-136.

Jack Lindsay, "The Poetry of Edith Sitwell," Life and Letters, 64 (Jan.,
1950), 51-52.

_____. "The Sleeping Beauty"
Deutsch, Poetry in Our Time, pp. 223-225.

_____. "Spring Morning"
Sr. M. Jeremy, "Clown and Canticle: The Achievement of Edith Sitwell,"
Renascence, 3 (Spring, 1951), 136-137.

_____. "Still Falls the Rain"
James Brophy, Expl, 29 (Dec., 1970), 36.

Willis D. Jacobs, Expl, 31 (Sept., 1972), 5.

_____. "When Sir Beelzebub"
Daniels, The Art of Reading Poetry, pp. 400-401.

_____. "The Winds Bastinado Whipt on the Calico"
Riding and Graves, A Survey of Modernist Poetry, pp. 231-233.

SITWELL, Sacheverell. "Doctor Donne and Gargantua: The First of Six Cantos"
R. P. Blackmur, "A Poet's Lent," Poetry, 38 (June, 1931), 162-166.

_____. "The Lady and the Rooks"
Joseph Warren Beach, "Rococo: The Poetry of Sacheverell Sitwell,"
Poetry, 74 (July, 1949), 229-231.

_____. "New Water Music"
Joseph Warren Beach, "Rococo: The Poetry of Sacheverell Sitwell,"
Poetry, 74 (July, 1949), 227.

SKELTON, John. "Manerly Margery Mylk and Ale"
David V. Harrington, Expl, 25 (Jan., 1967), 42.

_____. "Speke, Parrot"
F. W. Brownlow, "The Boke Compiled by Maister Skelton, Poet Laureate,
Called Speake Parrot," ELR, 1 (Winter, 1971), 3-26.

William Nelson, "Skelton's 'Speak, Parrot,'" PMLA, 51 (March, 1936),
59-82.

_____. "With Lullay, Lullay, Like a Child"
Frankenberg, Invitation to Poetry, pp. 151-152.

SKELTON, Robin. "The Shell"
Skelton, The Poetic Pattern, pp. 152-153.

_____. "Temple Flower"
Skelton, The Poetic Pattern, pp. 150-152.

SMART. "The Author Apologizes to a Lady for His Being a Little Man"
Spacks, The Poetry of Vision, pp. 151-152.

_____. "The Circumcision"
Darina Williamson, "Christopher Smart's Hymns and Spiritual Songs," PQ,
38 (Oct., 1959), 416-422.

_____. "For I Will Consider My Cat Jeoffry"
Rebecca P. Parkin, "Christopher Smart's Sacramental Cat," TSLL, 11
(Fall, 1969), 1191-1196.

Max Keith Sulton, "Smart's 'Compleat Cat,'" CE, 24 (Jan., 1963), 302-304.

_____. "The Hop-Garden"
Spacks, The Poetry of Vision, pp. 153-156.

_____. Hymn VI: "The Presentation of Christ in the Temple"
Spacks, The Poetry of Vision, pp. 158-159.

_____. Hymn XI: "Easter Day"
Spacks, The Poetry of Vision, pp. 159-160.

_____. Hymn XIII: "St. Philip and St. James"
Spacks, The Poetry of Vision, pp. 162-163.

_____. "Jubilate Agno"
   Allan C. Christensen, "Liturgical Order in Smart's Jubilate Agno: A
   Study of Fragment C," PLL, 6 (Fall, 1970), 366-373.

   John Over, Expl, 30 (April, 1972), 72.

_____. "A Noon-Piece, or, The Mowers at Dinner"
   Spacks, The Poetry of Vision, pp. 150-151.

_____. "A Song to David"
   R. D. Havens, "The Structure of Smart's Song to David," RES, 14 (April,
   1938), 178-182.

   Spacks, The Poetry of Vision, pp. 124-139.

LUCIE-SMITH, Edward. "Rook-Shooting at Sunset"
   Philip Hobsbaum, Theory of Criticism (Bloomington and London: Indiana
   Univ. Press, 1970), pp. 176-180.

SMITH, Iain Crichton. "On a Summer's Day"
   Robin Fulton, Contemporary Scottish Poetry: Individuals and Contexts
   (Loanhead, Midlothian: MacDonald Publishers, 1974), pp. 49-51.

SMITH, William Jay. "American Primitive"
   C. F. Burgess, "William Jay Smith's 'American Primitive': Toward a
   Reading," ArQ, 26 (Spring, 1970), 71-75.

SNODGRASS, W. D. "April Inventory"
   Carroll, The Poem In Its Skin, pp. 174-185.

_____. "A Cardinal"
   Phillips, Confessional Poets, pp. 54-55; first published "Snodgrass and
   the Sad Hospital of the World," UWR, 4 (Spring, 1969).

_____. "Heart's Needle"
   Phillips, Confessional Poets, pp. 57-62; first published "Snodgrass and
   the Sad Hospital of the World," UWR, 4 (Spring, 1969).

_____. "The Operation"
   Phillips, Confessional Poets, pp. 52-53; first published "Snodgrass and
   the Sad Hospital of the World," UWR, 4 (Spring, 1969).

_____. "Powwow"
   Perrine and Reid, 100 American Poems, pp. 269-270.

SNYDER, Gary. "After Work"
   Anthony Hunt, Expl, 32 (April, 1974), 61.

_____. "I Went into the Maverick Bar"
   Sherman Paul, "Noble and Simple," Parnassus: Poetry in Review, 3
   (Spring-Summer, 1975), 217-220.

_____. "Marin-An"
   Cheng Lok Chua & N. Sasaki, "Zen and the Title of Gary Snyder's 'Marin-
   An,'" NConL, 8 (May, 1978), 2-3.

_____. "Mid August at Sourdough Mountain Lookout"
   Robert Kern, "Toward a New Nature Poetry," CentR, 19 (Summer, 1975),
   213-216.

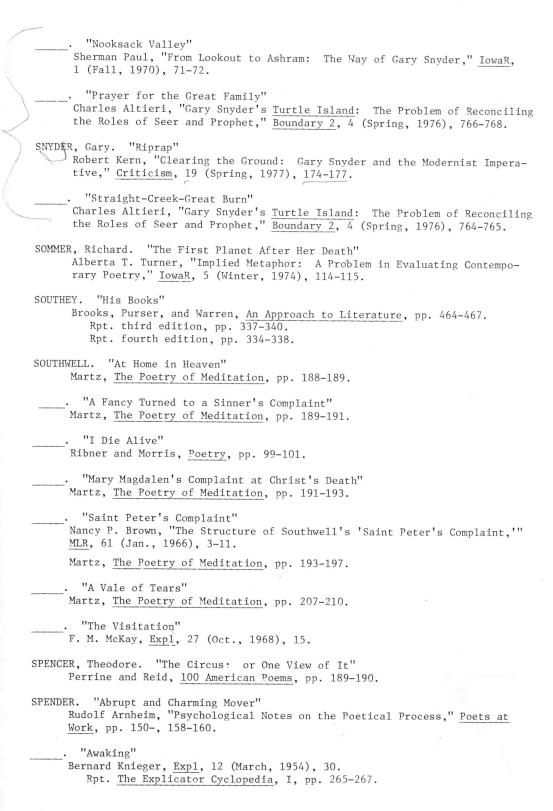

_____. "Nooksack Valley"
Sherman Paul, "From Lookout to Ashram: The Way of Gary Snyder," IowaR, 1 (Fall, 1970), 71-72.

_____. "Prayer for the Great Family"
Charles Altieri, "Gary Snyder's Turtle Island: The Problem of Reconciling the Roles of Seer and Prophet," Boundary 2, 4 (Spring, 1976), 766-768.

SNYDER, Gary. "Riprap"
Robert Kern, "Clearing the Ground: Gary Snyder and the Modernist Imperative," Criticism, 19 (Spring, 1977), 174-177.

_____. "Straight-Creek-Great Burn"
Charles Altieri, "Gary Snyder's Turtle Island: The Problem of Reconciling the Roles of Seer and Prophet," Boundary 2, 4 (Spring, 1976), 764-765.

SOMMER, Richard. "The First Planet After Her Death"
Alberta T. Turner, "Implied Metaphor: A Problem in Evaluating Contemporary Poetry," IowaR, 5 (Winter, 1974), 114-115.

SOUTHEY. "His Books"
Brooks, Purser, and Warren, An Approach to Literature, pp. 464-467.
    Rpt. third edition, pp. 337-340.
    Rpt. fourth edition, pp. 334-338.

SOUTHWELL. "At Home in Heaven"
Martz, The Poetry of Meditation, pp. 188-189.

_____. "A Fancy Turned to a Sinner's Complaint"
Martz, The Poetry of Meditation, pp. 189-191.

_____. "I Die Alive"
Ribner and Morris, Poetry, pp. 99-101.

_____. "Mary Magdalen's Complaint at Christ's Death"
Martz, The Poetry of Meditation, pp. 191-193.

_____. "Saint Peter's Complaint"
Nancy P. Brown, "The Structure of Southwell's 'Saint Peter's Complaint,'" MLR, 61 (Jan., 1966), 3-11.

Martz, The Poetry of Meditation, pp. 193-197.

_____. "A Vale of Tears"
Martz, The Poetry of Meditation, pp. 207-210.

_____. "The Visitation"
F. M. McKay, Expl, 27 (Oct., 1968), 15.

SPENCER, Theodore. "The Circus: or One View of It"
Perrine and Reid, 100 American Poems, pp. 189-190.

SPENDER. "Abrupt and Charming Mover"
Rudolf Arnheim, "Psychological Notes on the Poetical Process," Poets at Work, pp. 150-, 158-160.

_____. "Awaking"
Bernard Knieger, Expl, 12 (March, 1954), 30.
    Rpt. The Explicator Cyclopedia, I, pp. 265-267.

_____. "An Elementary School Class Room in a Slum"
Phyllis Bartlett, Poems in Process, pp. 217-219.

_____. "The Exiles"
Beach, Obsessive Images, pp. 148-151.

_____. "The Express"
Douglas, Lamson and Smith, The Critical Reader, 134-136. Revised edition, pp. 746-748.

James L. Potter, "The 'Destined Pattern' of Spender's 'Express,'" CE, 27
(Feb., 1966), 426-428.

Karl Shapiro, "The Meaning of the Discarded Poem," Poems at Work,
pp. 94-101.

_____. "The Funeral"
Willis D. Jacobs, "The Moderate Poetical Success of Stephen Spender,"
CE, 17 (April, 1956), 376.

Karl Shapiro, "The Meaning of the Discarded Poem," in Poets at Work,
pp. 101-105.

_____. "He Will Watch the Hawk with an Indifferent Eye"
S. A. Cowan, Expl, 28 (April, 1970), 67.

_____. "I Think Continually of Those"
Willis D. Jacobs, "Spender's 'I Think Continually of Those,'" MLN, 65
(Nov., 1950), 491-492.

Hallett Smith, Expl, 2 (Feb., 1944), 33.
    Rpt. The Explicator Cyclopedia, I, p. 267.

Donald A. Stauffer, "Genesis, of the Poet as Maker," in Poets at Work,
pp. 76-80.

_____. "The Landscape Near an Aerodrome"
Willis D. Jacobs, "The Moderate Poetical Success of Stephen Spender," CE,
17 (April, 1956), 375-376.

C. C. Walcutt, Expl, 5 (March, 1947), 37.
    Rpt. Engle and Carrier, Reading Modern Poetry, pp. 85-86.
    Rpt. The Explicator Cyclopedia, I, p. 267.

_____. "Not Palaces"
Willis D. Jacobs, "The Moderate Poetical Success of Stephen Spender," CE,
17 (April, 1956), 376-377.

_____. "Oh What Is the Use Now of Our Meeting and Speaking"
Rudolf Arnheim, "Psychological Notes on the Poetical Process," Poets at
Work, pp. 146-147.

_____. "Oh Young Men Oh Young Comrades"
Ralph Lynn, Jr., English "A" Analyst, No. 13, pp. 1-5.

_____. "The Pylons"
Charles D. Abbott, "Poetry in the Making," Poetry, 55 (Feb., 1940),
262-266.

_____. "Rolled Over on Europe"
Daniels, The Art of Reading Poetry, pp. 293-294.

_____. "Seascape"
Barbara Gibbs, "'Where Thoughts Lash Tail and Fin,'" _Poetry_, 86 (July, 1955), 239-240.

Day Lewis, _The Poetic Image_, pp. 136-140 (with quotations from Spender's remarks).

_____. "There Are Some Days the Happy Ocean Lies"
Stephen Spender, "The Making of a Poem," _PR_, 13 (Summer, 1946), 297-300.
    Rpt. _Criticism_, pp. 189-190.
    Rpt. _Critiques_, pp. 20-22.

_____. "Tom's A-Cold"
J. F. Nims, _Poetry: A Critical Supplement_, Oct., 1948, pp. 1-7.

_____. "Vienna"
Beach, _Obsessive Images_, pp. 28-32.

SPENSER. "Amoretti, Sonnet 1: 'Happy Ye Leaves When as Those Lilly Hands"
Peter M. Cummings, "Spenser's _Amoretti_ as an Allegory of Love," _TSLL_, 12 (Summer, 1970), 165.

Fowler, _Conceitful Thought_, pp. 92-95.

_____. "Amoretti, Sonnet 2: Unquiet Thought, Whom at the First I Bred"
Peter M. Cummings, "Spenser's _Amoretti_ as an Allegory of Love," _TSLL_, 12 (Summer, 1970), 165-166.

_____. "Amoretti, Sonnet 6: Be Nought Dismayd That Her Unmoved Mind"
Fowler, _Conceitful Thought_, pp. 89-91.

William C. Johnson, _Expl_, 29 (Jan., 1971), 38.

_____. "Amoretti, Sonnet 10: Unrighteous Lord of Love, What Law Is This"
Peter M. Cummings, "Spenser's _Amoretti_ as an Allegory of Love," _TSLL_, 12 (Summer, 1970), 167-168.

_____. "Amoretti, Sonnet 15: Ye Tradeful Merchants, That with Weary Toil"
Fowler, _Conceitful Thought_, pp. 95-97.

Tuve, _Elizabethan and Metaphysical Imagery_, pp. 64-65.

_____. "Amoretti, Sonnet 22: Penelope for Her Ulysses' Sake"
Kreuzer, _Elements of Poetry_, pp. 83-84.

_____. "Amoretti, Sonnet 34: Like as a Ship That Through the Ocean Wide"
Unger and O'Connor, _Poems for Study_, pp. 60-62.

_____. "Amoretti, Sonnet 35: My Hungry Eyes Through Greedy Covetize"
William Elford Rogers, "Narcissus in _Amoretti_ XXXV," _AN&Q_, 15 (Oct., 1976), 18-20.

_____. "Amoretti, Sonnet 41: It Is Her Nature, or Is It Her Will"
Tuve, _Elizabethan and Metaphysical Imagery_, pp. 63-64.

_____. "Amoretti, Sonnet 46: When My Abodes Prefixed Time is Spent"
Tuve, _Elizabethan and Metaphysical Imagery_, pp. 325-327.

_____. "Amoretti, Sonnet 54: When Those Renoumed Noble Peres of Greece"
Peter M. Cummings, "Spenser's _Amoretti_ as an Allegory of Love," _TSLL_, 12 (Summer, 1970), 169-170.

_____. "Amoretti, Sonnet 56: Fair Ye Be Sure, But Cruel and Unkind"
Winifred Lynskey, "A Critic in Action: Mr. Ransom," CE, 5 (Feb., 1944),
244 245.

_____. "Amoretti, Sonnet 59: Thrice Happy She, That Is So Well Assured"
Bateson, English Poetry and the English Language, pp. 32-33.

_____. "Amoretti, Sonnet 61: The Glorious Image of the Maker's Beautie"
Peter M. Cummings, "Spenser's Amoretti as an Allegory of Love," TSLL, 12
(Summer, 1970), 171.

_____. "Amoretti, Sonnet 62: The Weary Yeare His Race Now Having Run"
Josephine Waters Bennett, "Spenser's Amoretti LXII and the Date of the
New Year," RenQ, 26 (Winter, 1973), 433-436.

_____. "Amoretti, Sonnet 64: Comming to Kisse Her Lips (Such Grace I Found)"
Peter M. Cummings, "Spenser's Amoretti as an Allegory of Love," TSLL, 12
(Summer, 1970), 172.

_____. "Amoretti, Sonnet 65: The Doubt Which Ye Misdeeme, Fair Love is Vaine"
Peter M. Cummings, "Spenser's Amoretti as an Allegory of Love," TSLL, 12
(Summer, 1970), 172.

_____. "Amoretti, Sonnet 66"
"To All Those Happy Blessings Which Ye Have"
Peter M. Cummings, "Spenser's Amoretti as an Allegory of Love," TSLL, 12
(Summer, 1970), 172.

_____. "Amoretti, Sonnet 67: Lyke As a Huntsman After Weary Chace"
Peter M. Cummings, "Spenser's Amoretti as an Allegory of Love," TSLL, 12
(Summer, 1970), 172-173.
William Bowman Piper, "Spenser's 'Lyke as a Huntsman,'" CE, 22 (March,
1961), 405.

_____. "Amoretti, Sonnet 68: Most Glorious Lord of Lyfe, That on This Day"
Peter M. Cummings, "Spenser's Amoretti as an Allegory of Love," TSLL, 12
(Summer, 1970), 173.

_____. "Amoretti, Sonnet 71: I Joy To See How in Your Drawen Work"
Peter M. Cummings, "Spenser's Amoretti as an Allegory of Love," TSLL, 12
(Summer, 1970), 174.

_____. "Amoretti, Sonnet 72: Oft When My Spirit Doth Spred Her Bolder Winges"
Peter M. Cummings, "Spenser's Amoretti as an Allegory of Love," TSLL, 12
(Summer, 1970), 174.
W. B. C. Watkins, "The Kingdom of Our Language," HudR, 2 (Autumn, 1949),
343-344.

_____. "Amoretti, Sonnet 78: Lacking My Love I Go From Place to Place"
Peter M. Cummings, "Spenser's Amoretti as an Allegory of Love," TSLL, 12
(Summer, 1970), 175-176.

_____. "Amoretti, Sonnet 79: Men Call You Fayre, and You Doe Credit It"
Jack F. Stewart, Expl, 27 (May, 1969), 74.

_____. "Amoretti, Sonnet 81: Fayre Is My Love, When Her Fayre Golden Heares"
Peter M. Cummings, "Spenser's Amoretti as an Allegory of Love," TSLL, 12
(Summer, 1970), 176.

_____. "Amoretti, Sonnet 85: The World That Cannot Deeme of Worthy Things"
Peter M. Cummings, "Spenser's Amoretti as an Allegory of Love," TSLL, 12
(Summer, 1970), 177.

_____. "Astrophel"
Peter E. Bondanella and Julia Conaway, "Two Kinds of Renaissance Love:
Spenser's 'Astrophel' and Ronsard's 'Adonis,'" ES, 52 (Aug., 1971), 311-
318.

Michael O' Connell, "Astrophel: Spenser's Double Elegy," SEL, 11 (Winter,
1971), 27-35.

Leonard D. Tourney, "Spenser's Astrophel: Myth and the Critique of Values," ELWIU, 3 (Fall, 1976), 145-151.

_____. "Epithalamion"
Thomas H. Cain, "Spenser and the Renaissance Orpheus," UTQ, 41 (Autumn,
1971), 42-45.

Albert R. Cirillo, "Spenser's Epithalamion: The Harmonious Universe of
Love," SEL, 8 (Winter, 1968), 19-34.

J. C. Eade, "The Pattern in the Astronomy of Spenser's Epithalamion,"
RES, 23 (May, 1972), 173-178.

Lawrence W. Hyman, "Structure and Meaning in Spenser's Epithalamion,"
TSL, 3 (1958), 37-42.

Richard Neuse, "The Triumph over Hasty Accidents: A Note on the Symbolic
Mode of the Epithalamion," MLR, 61 (April, 1966), 163-174.

W. H. Stevenson, "The Spaciousness of Spenser's 'Epithalamion,'" A Review
of English Literature, 5 (July, 1964), 61-69.

Max A. Wickert, "Structure and Ceremony in Spenser's Epithalamion," ELH,
35 (June, 1968), 135-157.

Frank B. Young, "Medusa and the Epithalamion: A Problem in Spenserian
Imagery," ELN, 11 (Sept., 1973), 21-29.

_____. "Four Hymns"
Philip B. Rollinson, "A Generic View of Spenser's Four Hymns," SP, 68
(July, 1971), 292-304.

_____. "Hymn in Honor of Beautie"
Einar Bjorvand, "Spenser's Defence of Poetry: Some Structural Aspects of
the Fowre Hymnes," in Fair Forms: Essays in English Literature from
Spenser to Jane Austen, ed. Maren-Sofen Røstvig (Totowa, New Jersey:
Rowan and Littlefield, 1975), pp. 34-45.

_____. "Hymn of Heavenly Beautie"
Einar Bjorvand, "Spenser's Defence of Poetry: Some Structural Aspects of
the Fowre Hymnes," in Fair Forms: Essays in English Literature from
Spenser to Jane Austen, ed. Maren-Sofie Røstvig (Totowa, New Jersey:
Rowan and Littlefield, 1975), pp. 34-45.

A. Leigh DeNeef, "Spenserian Meditation: The Hymne of Heavenly Beautie,
ABR," 25 (Sept., 1974), 317-324.

_____. "Hymn in Honour of Love"
Einar Bjorvand, "Spenser's Defence of Poetry: Some Structural Aspects of
the Fowre Hymnes," in Fair Forms: Essays in English Literature from
Spenser to Jane Austen, ed. Maren-Sofie Røstvig (Totowa, New Jersey:
Rowan and Littlefield, 1975), pp. 16-34.

_____. "Hymn of Heavenly Love"
Einar Bjorvand, "Spenser's Defence of Poetry: Some Structural Aspects of
the Fowre Hymnes," in Fair Forms: Essays in English Literature from
Spenser to Jane Austen, ed. Maren-Sofie Røstvig (Totowa, New Jersey:
Rowan and Littlefield, 1975), pp. 16-34.

_____. "A Hymn to Venus" (The Faerie Queene, Book IV, Canto X, Stanzas 44-47)
Peckham and Chatman, Word, Meaning, Poem, pp. 68-78.

_____. "Muiopotmos"
Don Cameron Allen, "On Spenser's Muiopotmos," SP, 53 (April, 1956),
141-158.
    Rpt. Image and Meaning, pp. 20-40; new enlarged edition, pp. 20-41.

Franklin E. Court, "The Theme and Structure of Spenser's Muiopotmos,"
SEL, 10 (Winter, 1970), 1-15.

Judith Dundas, "Muiopotmos: A World of Art," YES, 5 (1975), 30-38.

_____. "Prothalamion"
George Arms, Expl, 1 (March, 1943), 36.
    Rpt. The Explicator Cyclopedia, II, pp. 324-325.

Harry Berger, "Spenser's 'Prothalamion': An Interpretation," EIC, 15
(Oct., 1965), 363-380.

Daiches and Charvat, Poems in English, pp. 650-652.

Fowler, Conceitful Thought, pp. 59-86.

Jay L. Halio, "'Prothalamion,' 'Ulysses,' and Intention in Poetry," CE,
22 (March, 1961), 390-392.

Dan S. Norton, "Queen Elizabeth's 'Brydale Day,'" MLQ, 5 (1944), 149-154.

William Elford Rogers, "Proserpina in the Prothalamion," AN&Q, 15
(May, 1977), 131-135.

M. L. Wine, "Spenser's 'Sweete Themmes': Of Time and the River," SEL, 2
(Winter, 1962), 111-117.

Daniel H. Woodward, "Some Themes in Spenser's 'Prothalamion,'" ELH, 29
(March, 1962), 34-46.

_____. "Aprill" (from The Shepherd's Calendar)
Virginia Tufte, The Poetry of Marriage: The Epithalamium in Europe and
Its Development in England (Los Angeles: Tinnon-Brown, 1970), 167-178.

_____. "January" (from The Shepherd's Calendar)
John W. Moore, Jr., "Colin Breaks His Pipe: A Reading of the 'January'
Eclogue," ELR, 5 (Winter, 1975), 3-24.

_____. "November" (from The Shepherd's Calendar)
C. R. B. Combellack, Expl, 33 (Sept., 1974), 5.

Ellen Zetzel Lambert, Placing Sorrow: A Study of the Pastoral Elegy
Convention from Theocritus to Milton (Chapel Hill: Univ. of North
Carolina Press, 1976), 127-136.

Partridge, The Language of Renaissance Poetry, pp. 62-83.

_____. "October," (from The Shepherd's Calendar)
James Neil Brown, Expl, 34 (Nov., 1975), 21.

Richard F. Hardin, "The Resolved Debate of Spenser's 'October,'" MP, 73
(Feb., 1976), 257-263.

_____. "The Teares of the Muses"
    Gerald Snare, "The Muses on Poetry: Spenser's 'The Teares of the Muses,'"
    TSE, 17 (1969), 31-52.

_____. "To the Right Honourable the Earle of Cumberland"
    Earl John Clark, Expl, 27 (Oct., 1968), 10.

SPICER, Jack. "Billy the Kid"
    Frank Sadler, "The Frontier in Jack Spicer's 'Billy the Kid,'" CP, 9
    (Fall, 1976), 15-21.

STAATS. "Spring Thaw"
    Sanders, The Discovery of Poetry, pp. 77-79.

STAFFORD. "Connections"
    George S. Lensing and Ronald Moran, Four Poets and the Emotive Imagina-
    tion: Robert Bly, James Wright, Louis Simpson, and William Stafford
    (Baton Rouge: Louisiana State Univ., 1976), pp. 205-207.

    George S. Lensing, "William Stafford, Mythmaker," MPS, 6 (Spring, 1975),
    7-9.

_____. "At Cove on the Crooked River"
    John Lauber, "World's Guest--William Stafford," IowaR, 5 (Spring, 1974),
    91-92.

_____. "The Farm on the Great Plains"
    Richard Hugo, "Problems with Landscapes in Early Stafford Poems," KanQ,
    2 (Spring, 1970), 35.

_____. "Fifteen"
    Dennis Daley Lunch, "Journeys in Search of Oneself: The Metaphor of the
    Road in William Stafford's Traveling Through the Dark and The Rescued
    Year," MPS, 7 (Autumn, 1976), 129-130.

_____. "In California"
    John Lauber, "World's Guest--William Stafford," IowaR, 5 (Spring, 1974),
    94.

_____. "One Home"
    John Lauber, "World's Guest--William Stafford," IowaR, 5 (Spring, 1974),
    90-91.

_____. "Our People"
    John Lauber, "World's Guest--William Stafford," IowaR, 5 (Spring, 1974),
    88-89.

_____. "Shadows"
    George S. Lensing, "William Stafford, Mythmaker," MPS, 6 (Spring, 1975),
    9-13.

_____. "Summer Will Rise"
    John Lauber, "World's Guest--William Stafford," IowaR, 5 (Spring, 1974),
    96.

_____. "Traveling Through the Dark"
    George S. Lensing and Ronald Moran, Four Poets and the Emotive Imagina-
    tion: Robert Bly, James Wright, Louis Simpson, and William Stafford
    (Baton Rouge: Louisiana State Univ., 1976), pp. 198-200.

Dennis Daley Lynch, "Journeys in Search of Oneself: The Metaphor of the Road in William Stafford's Traveling Through the Dark and The Rescued Year," MPS, 7 (Autumn, 1976), 127-129.

STANTON. "Dandelion"
    Perrine and Reid, 100 American Poems, pp. 283-284.

STAUFFER, Donald. "The Lemmings"
    Adams, The Contexts of Poetry, pp. 109-111.

STEIN. "A Box"
    Jonathan C. George, Expl, 31 (Feb., 1973), 42.

_____. "Lipschitz"
    Harry R. Garvin, Expl, 14 (Dec., 1955), 18.
        Rpt. The Explicator Cyclopedia, I, pp. 267-268.

_____. "A Long Dress"
    Ruth H. Brady, Expl, 34 (Feb., 1976), 47.

STEPHENS, Alan. "The Dragon of Things"
    Donald W. Markos," Alan Stephens: The Lineaments of the Real," SoR, 11 (April, 1975), 346-347.

_____. "First Twenty-four Hours"
    Donald W. Markos, "Alan Stephens: The Lineaments of the Real," SoR, 11 (April, 1975), 351-353.

_____. "The Green Cape"
    Donald W. Markos, "Alan Stephens: The Lineaments of the Real," SoR, 11 (April, 1975), 349-351.

_____. "Homily"
    Donald W. Markos, "Alan Stephens: The Lineamaents of the Real," SoR, 11 (April, 1975), 335-336.

_____. "Little Things"
    Nat Henry, Expl, 11 (Dec., 1950), 20.
        Rpt. The Explicator Cyclopedia, II, pp. 325-326.

    Lysander Kemp, Expl, 8 (May, 1950), 50.
        Rpt. The Explicator Cyclopedia, II, p. 325.

_____. "The Main Deep"
    Brooks and Warren, Understanding Poetry, pp. 170-173. Revised edition, pp. 74-77.

_____. "The Open World"
    Donald W. Markos, "Alan Stephens: The Lineaments of the Real," SoR, 11 (April, 1975), 338-340.

_____. "Prologue: Moments in a Glade"
    Winters, Forms of Discovery, pp. 339-341.

_____. "The Rivals"
    Frankenberg, Invitation to Poetry, p. 58.

_____. "The Three Sisters"
    Donald W. Markos, "Alan Stephens: The Lineaments of the Real," SoR, 11 (April, 1975), 347-348.

_____. "Tree Meditation"
    Donald W. Markos, "Alan Stephens: The Lineaments of the Real," SoR, 11
    (April, 1975), 353-355.

_____. "A Walk in the Void"
    Donald W. Markos, "Alan Stephens: The Lineaments of the Real," SoR, 11
    (April, 1975), 333-335.

STEVENS. "Academic Discourse at Havana"
    Friar and Brinnin, Modern Poetry, p. 537.

_____. "Anecdote of the Jar"
    Abad, A Formal Approach to Lyric Poetry, pp. 145-147.

    Howard Baker, "Wallace Stevens and Other Poetry," SoR, 1 (Autumn, 1935),
    376-377.

    Bornstein, Transformations of Romanticism, pp. 171-172.

    Brooks, Lewis, and Warren, American Literature, pp. 2156-2157.

    Sr. Madeline DeFrees, "Pegasus and Six Blind Indians," EJ, 59 (Oct.,
    1970), 935.

    Don Geiger, "Wallace Stevens' Wealth," Perspective, 7 (Autumn, 1954), 160.

    Gray, American Poetry, pp. 167-168.

    Robert Hass, "Wendell Berry: Finding the Land," MPS, 2, No. 1 (1971),
    32-34.

    Samuel Jay Keyser, "Wallace Stevens: Form and Meaning in Four Poems," CE,
    37 (Feb., 1976), 585-589.

    J. P. Kirby, Expl, 3 (Nov., 1944), 16.
      Rpt. The Explicator Cyclopedia, I, pp. 268-269.

    Murray Krieger, "Ekphrasis and the Still Movement of Poetry; or, Laokoön
    Revisited," in The Poet as Critic, pp. 24-25.

    Patricia Merivale, "Wallace Stevens' 'Jar': The Absurd Detritus of Ro-
    mantic Myth," CE, 26 (April, 1965), 527-532.

    C. D. Narasimhaiah, "Wallace Stevens," in Studies in American Literature:
    Essays in Honor of William Mulder, ed. Jagdish Cander and Narindar S.
    Pradhan (Delhi: Oxford Univ. Press, 1976), pp. 227-228.

    Rosenthal, The Modern Poets, pp. 125-126.

    Charles C. Walcutt, "Interpreting the Symbol," CE, 14 (May, 1953),
    449-451.

    T. Weiss, "The Nonsense of Winters' Anatomy," Quarterly Review of Litera-
    ture, 1 (Spring, 1944), 228.

    Winters, Anatomy of Nonsense, pp. 93-95. Also In Defense of Reason,
    pp. 435-437.

_____. "Anecdote of Men by the Thousand"
    Quinn, The Metamorphic Tradition, p. 77.

_____. "The Apostrophe to Vincentine"
    Frank Doggett, "Wallace Stevens and the World We Know," EJ, 48 (Oct.,
    1959), 369-370.

    Sr. M. Bernetta Quinn, O.S.F., "Metamorphosis in Wallace Stevens," SR,
    60 (Spring, 1952), 243-244.

    Quinn, The Metamorphic Tradition, pp. 75-76.

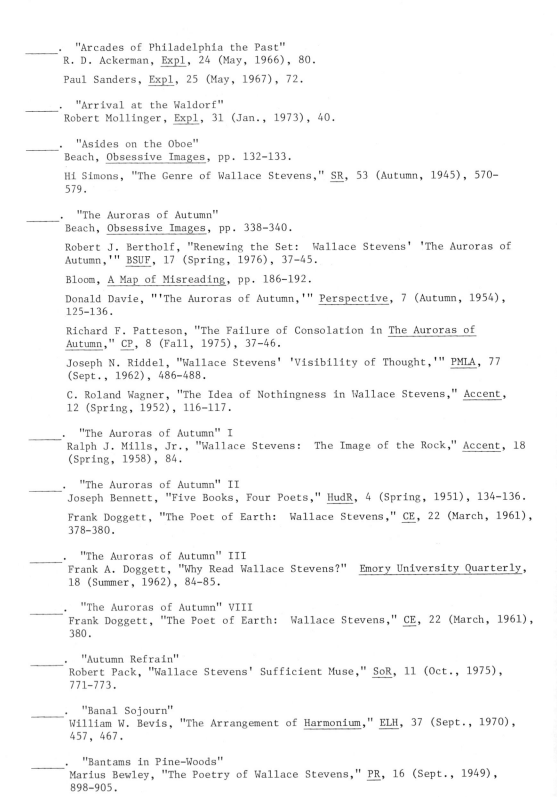

_____. "Arcades of Philadelphia the Past"
R. D. Ackerman, Expl, 24 (May, 1966), 80.

Paul Sanders, Expl, 25 (May, 1967), 72.

_____. "Arrival at the Waldorf"
Robert Mollinger, Expl, 31 (Jan., 1973), 40.

_____. "Asides on the Oboe"
Beach, Obsessive Images, pp. 132-133.

Hi Simons, "The Genre of Wallace Stevens," SR, 53 (Autumn, 1945), 570-
579.

_____. "The Auroras of Autumn"
Beach, Obsessive Images, pp. 338-340.

Robert J. Bertholf, "Renewing the Set: Wallace Stevens' 'The Auroras of
Autumn,'" BSUF, 17 (Spring, 1976), 37-45.

Bloom, A Map of Misreading, pp. 186-192.

Donald Davie, "'The Auroras of Autumn,'" Perspective, 7 (Autumn, 1954),
125-136.

Richard F. Patteson, "The Failure of Consolation in The Auroras of
Autumn," CP, 8 (Fall, 1975), 37-46.

Joseph N. Riddel, "Wallace Stevens' 'Visibility of Thought,'" PMLA, 77
(Sept., 1962), 486-488.

C. Roland Wagner, "The Idea of Nothingness in Wallace Stevens," Accent,
12 (Spring, 1952), 116-117.

_____. "The Auroras of Autumn" I
Ralph J. Mills, Jr., "Wallace Stevens: The Image of the Rock," Accent, 18
(Spring, 1958), 84.

_____. "The Auroras of Autumn" II
Joseph Bennett, "Five Books, Four Poets," HudR, 4 (Spring, 1951), 134-136.

Frank Doggett, "The Poet of Earth: Wallace Stevens," CE, 22 (March, 1961),
378-380.

_____. "The Auroras of Autumn" III
Frank A. Doggett, "Why Read Wallace Stevens?" Emory University Quarterly,
18 (Summer, 1962), 84-85.

_____. "The Auroras of Autumn" VIII
Frank Doggett, "The Poet of Earth: Wallace Stevens," CE, 22 (March, 1961),
380.

_____. "Autumn Refrain"
Robert Pack, "Wallace Stevens' Sufficient Muse," SoR, 11 (Oct., 1975),
771-773.

_____. "Banal Sojourn"
William W. Bevis, "The Arrangement of Harmonium," ELH, 37 (Sept., 1970),
457, 467.

_____. "Bantams in Pine-Woods"
Marius Bewley, "The Poetry of Wallace Stevens," PR, 16 (Sept., 1949),
898-905.

R. P. Blackmur, "Wallace Stevens," Hound and Horn, 5 (Jan.-March, 1932), 247-248.
    Rpt. Language as Gesture, pp. 242-243.

Brooks, Lewis, and Warren, American Literature, p. 2157.

Mario L. D'Avanzo, "Emerson and Shakespeare in Stevens's 'Bantams in Pine-Woods,'" AL, 49 (March, 1977), 103-107.

Gray, American Poetry, pp. 166-167.

Mildred E. Hartsock, Expl, 18 (March, 1960), 33.
    Rpt. The Explicator Cyclopedia, I, pp. 270-271.

William Van O'Connor, "Wallace Stevens on 'The Poems of Our Climate,'" The University of Kansas City Review, 15 (Winter, 1948), 106-107.

Fred H. Stocking, Expl, 3 (April, 1945), 45.
    Rpt. The Explicator Cyclopedia, I, p. 269.

_____. "The Bird with the Coppery, Keen Claws"
Louis H. Leiter, "Sense in Nonsense: Wallace Stevens' 'The Bird with the Coppery, Keen Claws,'" CE, 26 (April, 1965), 551-554.

_____. "Blanche McCarthy"
Harold Bloom, "Poetic Crossing II: American Stances," GaR, 30 (Winter, 1976), 790-792.

_____. "The Bouquet"
George McFadden, "Poet, Nature, and Society in Wallace Stevens," MLQ, 23 (Sept., 1962), 269-270.

_____. "Bouquet of Roses in Moonlight"
J. F. Nims, Poetry: A Critical Supplement, Oct., 1947, p. 9.

_____. "Certain Phenomena of Sound"
William W. Heath, Expl, 12 (Dec., 1953), 16.
    Rpt. The Explicator Cyclopedia, I, pp. 271-272.

_____. "Chocorua to Its Neighbor"
Robert Pact, "The Abstracting Imagination of Wallace Stevens: Nothingness and the Hero," ArQ, 11 (Autumn, 1955), 206-208.

_____. "A Clear Day and No Memories"
William Bevis, "Stevens' Toneless Poetry," ELH, 41 (Summer, 1974), 269-272.

Richard Blessing, "Wallace Stevens and the Necessary Reader: A Technique of Dynamism," TCL, 18 (Oct., 1972), 255-256.

_____. "The Comedian as the Letter C"
Richard P. Adams, "'The Comedian as the Letter C': A Somewhat Literal Reading," TSE, 18 (1970), 95-114.

Howard Baker, "Wallace Stevens," SoR, 1 (Autumn, 1935), 377-381.

R. P. Blackmur, "Wallace Stevens," Hound and Horn, 5 (Jan.-March, 1932), 248-255.
    Rpt. The Double Agent, pp. 94-102.
    Rpt. Language as Gesture, pp. 243-249.

M. J. Collie, "The Rhetoric of Accurate Speech: A Note on the Poetry of Wallace Stevens," EIC, 12 (Jan., 1962), 59-60.

Eleanor Cook, "Wallace Stevens: 'The Comedian as the Letter C,'" AL, 49 (May, 1977), 192-205.

J. V. Cunningham, "The Poetry of Wallace Stevens," Poetry, 75 (Dec., 1949), 151-159.
  Rpt. Modern Literary Criticism, pp. 356-360.
  Rpt. Tradition and Poetic Structure, pp. 111-116.

Guy Davenport, "Spinoza's Tulips: A Commentary on 'The Comedian as the Letter C,'" Perspective, 7 (Autumn, 1954), 147-154.

Frank Doggett, "Our Nature Is Her Nature," in The Twenties, pp. 39-40.

Carol Flake, Expl, 30 (Nov., 1971), 26.

Frankenberg, Pleasure Dome, pp. 210-215.

Don Geiger, "Wallace Stevens' Wealth," Perspective, 7 (Autumn, 1954), 165.

Edward Guereschi, "'The Comedian as the Letter C': Wallace Stevens' Anti-Mythological Poem," CentR, 8 (Fall, 1964), 465-477.

Hoffman, The Twenties, pp. 183-185.

George McFadden, "Poet, Nature, and Society in Wallace Stevens," MLQ, 23 (Sept., 1962), 263-264.

K. E. Marre, "Narrative Comedy in Wallace Stevens' 'The Comedian as the Letter C,'" UDR, 12 (Summer, 1976), 133-149.

Miller, Poets of Reality, pp. 220-221.

Samuel French Morse, "Wallace Stevens, Bergson, Pater," ELH, 31 (March, 1964), 17-34.

James E. Mulqueen, "A Reading of Wallace Stevens' 'The Comedian As the Letter C,'" CimR, 13 (Oct., 1970), 35-42.

James E. Mulqueen, "Wallace Stevens: Radical Transcendentalist," MQ, 11 (Spring, 1970), pp. 336-339.

Francis Murphy, "'The Comedian as the Letter C,'" Wisconsin Studies in Contemporary Literature, 2 (Spring-Summer, 1962), 80-99.

O'Connor, Sense and Sensibility in Modern Poetry, pp. 141-142.

William Van O'Connor, "Wallace Stevens on 'The Poems of Our Climate,'" The University of Kansas City Review, 15 (Winter, 1948), 109.

Pearce, The Continuity of American Poetry, pp. 387-389.

A. Poulin, Jr., "Crispin as Everyman as Adam: 'The Comedian as the Letter C,'" CP, 5 (Spring, 1972), 5-23.

John N. Serio, "'The Comedian' as the Idea of Order in Harmonium," PLL, 12 (Winter, 1976), 87-101.

Hi Simons, "'The Comedian as the Letter C': Its Sense and Its Significance," SoR, 5 (Winter, 1940), 453-468.

Fred H. Stocking, Expl, 3 (March, 1945), 43.
  Rpt. The Explicator Cyclopedia, I, pp. 272-273.

T. Weiss, "The Nonsense of Winters' Anatomy," Quarterly Review of Literature, 1 (Spring, 1944), 229.

Winters, <u>Anatomy of Nonsense</u>, pp. 98-103. Also <u>In Defense of Reason</u>, pp. 439-444.

_____. "Connoisseur of Chaos"
Abad, <u>A Formal Approach to Lyric Poetry</u>, pp. 148-151.

Bornstein, <u>Transformation of Romanticism</u>, pp. 202-203.

Beverly Cole, "An Anchorage of Thought: Defining the Role of Aphorism in Wallace Stevens' Poetry," <u>PMLA</u>, 91 (March, 1976), 213-215.

_____. "Cortége for Rosenbloom"
Richard Ellman, "Wallace Stevens' Ice Cream," <u>The Kenyon Review</u>, 19 (Winter, 1957), 90-92.

_____. "The Course of a Particular"
William Bevis, "Stevens' Toneless Poetry," <u>ELH</u>, 41 (Summer, 1974), 273-275.

Richard Blessing, "Wallace Stevens and the Necessary Reader: A Technique of Dynamism," <u>TCL</u>, 18 (Oct., 1972), 256.

Sigurd Burckhardt and Roy Harvey Pearce, "Poetry, Language, and the Condition of Modern Man," <u>CentR</u>, 4 (Winter, 1960), 9-13.

Gerald Graff, <u>Poetic Statement and Critical Dogma</u> (Evanston: Northwestern Univ. Press, 1970), 27-30, 144-145.

Robert Pack, "The Abstracting Imagination of Wallace Stevens: Nothingness and the Hero," <u>ArQ</u>, 11 (Autumn, 1955), 198-199.

_____. "Credences of Summer"
Sandy Cohen, "A Calculus of the Cycle: Wallace Stevens' 'Credences of Summer,' An Alternative View," <u>BSUF</u>, 17 (Spring, 1976), 31-36.

Bernard Heringman, "The Poetry of Synthesis," <u>Perspective</u>, 7 (Autumn, 1954), 171-174.

J. Dennis Huston, "'Credences of Summer': An Analysis," <u>MP</u>, 67 (Feb., 1970), 263-272.

Isabel G. MacCaffrey, "The Other Side of Silence: 'Credences of Summer' as an Example," <u>MLQ</u>, 30 (Sept., 1969), 417-438.

Ralph J. Mills, Jr., "Wallace Stevens: The Image of the Rock," <u>Accent</u>, 17 (Spring, 1958), 77-78, 81.

Harold H. Watts, "Wallace Stevens and the Rock of Summer," <u>The Kenyon Review</u>, 14 (Winter, 1952), 122-124.

_____. "The Death of a Soldier"
R. P. Blackmur, "Wallace Stevens," <u>Hound and Horn</u>, 5 (Jan.-March, 1932), 229-230.
    Rpt. <u>The Double Agent</u>, pp. 74-75.

Samuel Joy Keyser, "Wallace Stevens: Form and Meaning in Four Poems," <u>CE</u>, 37 (Feb., 1976), 578-584.

_____. "Depression before Spring"
William W. Bevis, "The Arrangement of <u>Harmonium</u>," <u>ELH</u>, 37 (Sept., 1970), 457-467.

Frank Doggett, "Our Nature Is Her Nature," in <u>The Twenties</u>, pp. 37-38.

_____. "Description Without Place"
Michael T. Beehler, "Meteoric Poetry: Wallace Stevens' 'Description Without Place,'" Criticism, 19 (Summer, 1977), 241-259.

Robert Pack, "The Abstracting Imagination of Wallace Stevens: Nothingness and the Hero," ArQ, 11 (Autumn, 1955), 199-200.

_____. "Disillusionment of Ten O'Clock"
R. P. Blackmur, "Examples of Wallace Stevens," Hound and Horn, 5 (Jan.-March, 1932), 228-229.
    Rpt. The Double Agent, pp. 73-74.
    Rpt. Language as Gesture, pp. 226-227.

Randall Jarrell, "Reflections on Wallace Stevens," PR, 18 (May-June, 1951), 337-338.

_____. "Domination of Black"
Harold Bloom, "Poetic Crossing: Rhetoric and Psychology," GaR, 30 (Fall, 1976), 495-524.

Bornstein, Transformations of Romanticism, pp. 195-197.

Frank Doggett, "Our Nature Is Her Nature," in The Twenties, pp. 36-37.

Dorothy Pettit, "'Domination of Black': A Study in Involvement," EJ, 51 (May, 1962), 347-348.

William J. Rooney, "'Spelt from Sibyl's Leaves'--A Study in Contrasting Methods of Evaluation," JAAC, 13 (June, 1955), 512-514.

_____. "The Dwarf"
Robert Pack, "The Abstracting Imagination of Wallace Stevens: Nothingness and the Hero," ArQ, 11 (Autumn, 1955), 197-198.

_____. "Earthy Anecdote"
George Betar, Expl, 22 (Feb., 1964), 43.

Frankenberg, Pleasure Dome, pp. 198-199.

Miller, Poets of Reality, pp. 234-235.

Rosenthal, The Modern Poets, pp. 122-123.

Hugh L. Smith, Expl, 24 (Dec., 1965), 37.

_____. "The Emperor of Ice-Cream"
R. P. Blackmur, "Wallace Stevens," Hound and Horn, 5 (Jan.-March, 1932), 230-232.
    Rpt. The Double Agent, pp. 75-77.
    Rpt. Language as Gesture, pp. 227-229.

Warren Carrier, "Commonplace Costumes and Essential Gaudiness: Wallace Stevens' 'Emperor of Ice-Cream,'" CollL, 1 (Fall, 1974), 230-235.

Beverly Coyle, "An Anchorage of Thought: Defining the Role of Aphorism in Wallace Stevens' Poetry," PMLA, 91 (March, 1976), 212-213.

Taylor Culbert and John M. Violette, "Wallace Stevens' Emperor," Criticism, 2 (Winter, 1960), 38-47.

Sr. Madeline DeFrees, "Pegasus and Six Blind Indians," EJ, 59 (Oct., 1970), 933-934.

Dickinson, Suggestions for Teachers of "Introduction to Literature," fifth edition, ed. Locke, Gibson, and Arms, pp. 42-43. (Teacher's Manual)

Drew and Sweeney, Directions in Modern Poetry, pp. 227-231. Abridged in The Case for Poetry, p. 341.

Richard Ellmann, "Wallace Stevens' Ice Cream," The Kenyon Review, 19 (Winter, 1957), 92-95.
     Rpt. Aspects of American Poetry, pp. 203-222.

Robert F. Fleissner, "Stevens in Wittenberg: 'The Emperor of Ice-Cream,'" RS, 42 (Dec., 1974), 256-260.

Friar and Brinnin, Modern Poetry, p. 538.

Max Herzberg and Wallace Stevens, Expl, 7 (Nov., 1948), 18.
   Rpt. The Explicator Cyclopedia, I, p. 275.

Kenneth Lash and Robert Thackaberry, Expl, 6 (April, 1948), 36. Abridged in The Case for Poetry, p. 342.
     Rpt. The Explicator Cyclopedia, I, pp. 273-274.

James E. Mulqueen, "Wallace Stevens: Radical Transcendentalist," MQ, 11 (Spring, 1970), 330-331.

C. D. Narasimhaiah, "Wallace Stevens," in Studies in American Literature: Essays in Honor of William Mulder, ed. Jagdish Chander and Narindar S. Pradhan (Delhi: Oxford Univ. Press, 1976), pp. 221-225.

Ralph Nash, "About 'The Emperor of Ice-Cream,'" Perspective, 7 (Autumn, 1954), 122-124.

Edward Neill, "The Melting Moment: Stevens' Rehabilitation of Ice Cream," ArielE, 4 (Jan., 1973), 88-96.

Elder Oson, "The Poetry of Wallace Stevens," CE, 16 (April, 1955), 397-398.

Rosenthal, The Modern Poets, pp. 129-130.

Stuart Silverman, "The Emperor of Ice-Cream," WHR, 26 (Spring, 1972), 165-168.

Kermit Vanderbilt, "More Stevens and Shakespeare," CollL, 2 (Spring, 1975), 143-145.

T. Weiss, "The Nonsense of Winters' Anatomy," Quarterly Review of Literature, 1 (Spring, 1944), 226.

Michael Zimmerman, "Wallace Stevens' Emperor," ELN, 4 (Dec., 1966), 119-123.

_____. "Esthétique du Mal"
Robert J. Bertholf, Parables and Wallace Stevens' 'Esthétique du Mal,'" ELH, 42 (Winter, 1975), 669-689.

Frank Doggett, "The Poet of Earth: Wallace Stevens," CE, 22 (March, 1961), 376.

Richard Ellmann, "Wallace Stevens' Ice Cream," The Kenyon Review, 19 (Winter, 1957), 100-101.

Frankenberg, Pleasure Dome, pp. 249-251.

Ellwood Johnson, "Title and Substance of Wallace Stevens' 'Esthétique du Mal,'" NConL, 8 (Nov., 1978), 2-3.

Janet McCann, "Wallace Stevens' 'Esthétique du Mal,' Section X," AN&Q, 15 (April, 1977), 111-113.

Martz, The Poem of the Mind, pp. 196-197.

Louis L. Martz, "The World of Wallace Stevens," in Modern American Poetry, ed. B. Rajan, p. 106.

Pearce, The Continuity of American Poetry, pp. 400-404, 425-426.

Wylie Sypher, "Connoisseur of Chaos: Wallace Stevens," PR, 13 (Winter, 1946), 84-86.

_____. "Esthétique du Mal" VII
Ralph J. Mills, Jr., "Wallace Stevens: The Image of the Rock," Accent, 18 (Spring, 1958), 82-83.

_____. "Evening Without Angels"
Griar and Brinnin, Modern Poetry, p. 537.

_____. "The Examination of the Hero in Time of War"
James E. Mulqueen, "Wallace Stevens: Radical Transcendentalist," MQ, 11 (Spring, 1970), 333-334.

_____. "Farewell to Florida"
Adelyn Dougherty, "Structures of Sound in Wallace Stevens' 'Farewell to Florida,'" TSLL, 16 (Winter, 1975), 755-764.

Dwight Eddins, "Wallace Stevens: America the Primordial," MLQ, 32 (March, 1971), 85-86.

_____. "Final Soliloquy of the Interior Paramour"
Charles Altieri, "The Poem as Act: A Way to Reconcile Presentational and Mimetic Theories," IowaR, 6 (Summer-Fall, 1975), 116-122.

Sharon Cameron, "'The Sense Against Calamity': Ideas of a Self in Three Poems by Wallace Stevens," ELH, 43 (Winter, 1976), 593-603.

Gray, American Poetry, pp. 180-181.

Judith McDaniel, "Wallace Stevens and the Scientific Imagination," ConL, 15 (Spring, 1974), 230.

Robert Pack, "Wallace Stevens' Sufficient Muse," SoR, 11 (Oct., 1975), 767-770.

_____. "Flyer's Fall"
Harold H. Watts, "Wallace Stevens and the Rock of Summer," The Kenyon Review, 14 (Winter, 1952), 133-134.

_____. "Frogs Eat Butterflies"
Don Geiger, "Wallace Stevens' Wealth," Perspective, 7 (Autumn, 1954), 158-160.

Robert McIlvaine, Expl, 33 (Oct., 1974), 14.

John N. Serio, "'The Comedian' as the Idea of Order in Harmonium," PLL, 12 (Winter, 1976), 102-103.

_____. "The Glass of Water"
Warren G. French, Expl, 19 (Jan., 1961), 23.
     Rpt. The Explicator Cyclopedia, I, pp. 276-277.

David H. Owen, "'The Glass of Water,'" Perspective, 7 (Autumn, 1954), 181-183.

Eric Sellin, Expl, 17 (Jan., 1959), 28.
     Rpt. The Explicator Cyclopedia, I, p. 276.

Sr. Therese, S.N.D., Expl, 21 (March, 1963), 56.

_____. "God Is Good. It Is a Beautiful Night"
Frank A. Doggett, "Why Read Stevens?" Emory University Quarterly, 18 (Summer, 1962), 89-91.

_____. "The Good Man Has No Shape"
Richard Gustafson, "The Practick of the Maker in Wallace Stevens," TCL, 9 (July, 1963), 88.

Janet McCann, "Wallace Stevens' 'The Good Man Has No Shape,'" NConL, 6 (March, 1976), 9-10.

_____. "The Green Plant"
Marjorie Perloff, "Irony in Wallace Stevens's The Rock," AL, 36 (Nov., 1964), 335-336.

_____. "The Hermitage at the Center"
Marjorie Perloff, "Irony in Wallace Stevens's The Rock," AL, 36 (Nov., 1964), 338-339.

_____. "A High-Toned Old Christian Woman"
Gray, American Poetry, pp. 159-160.

William Van O'Connor, "Wallace Stevens on 'The Poems of Our Climate,'" The University of Kansas City Review, 15 (Winter, 1948), 110.

Perrine and Reid, 100 American Poems, pp. 72-73.

A. E. Waterman, "Poetry as Play: 'A High-toned Old Christian Woman,'" CEA, 26 (Jan., 1964), 7.

_____. "Holiday in Reality"
Bernard Heringman, "The Poetry of Synthesis," Perspective, 7 (Autumn, 1954), 169-171.

_____. "Homunculus et La Belle Étoile"
Norman Silverstein, Expl, 13 (May, 1955), 40.
     Rpt. The Explicator Cyclopedia, I, pp. 277-278.

_____. "The House Was Quiet and the World Was Calm"
J. V. Cunningham, "The Poetry of Wallace Stevens," Poetry, 75 (Dec., 1949), 164-165.
     Rpt. Modern Literary Criticism, pp. 365-366.

Quinn, The Metamorphic Tradition, p. 76.

_____. "How to Live. What to Do"
Ralph J. Mills, Jr., "Wallace Stevens: The Image of the Rock," Accent, 18 (Spring, 1958), 76-77.

_____. "The Idea of Order at Key West"
Bornstein, Transformations of Romanticism, pp. 197-202.

Brooks, Lewis, and Warren, American Literature, pp. 2158-2161.

Deutsch, Poetry in Our Time, pp. 248-250.

Frank Doggett, "Wallace Stevens and the World We Know," EJ, 48 (Oct., 1959), 370-371.

Drew, Discovering Poetry, pp. 261-262.

Friar and Brinnin, Modern Poetry, pp. 537-538.

Gray, <u>American Poetry</u>, pp. 169-170.

Richard Gustafson, "The Practick of the Maker in Wallace Stevens," <u>TCL</u>, 9 (July, 1963), 84-85.

Todd M. Lieber, "Robert Frost and Wallace Stevens: 'What to Make of a Diminished Thing,'" <u>AL</u>, 47 (March, 1975), 71-73.

Louis L. Martz, "The World of Wallace Stevens," in <u>Modern American Poetry</u>, ed. B. Rajan, pp. 101-103.
    Rpt. Martz, <u>The Poem of the Mind</u>, pp. 191-193, 205-206.

Louis L. Martz, "Wallace Stevens: The World as Meditation," <u>YR</u>, 47 (Summer, 1958), 521-522.

Kenneth Walker, <u>Expl</u>, 32 (April, 1974), 59.

_____. "In a Bad Time"
C. Roland Wagner, "The Idea of Nothingness in Wallace Stevens," <u>Accent</u>, 12 (Spring, 1952), 119.

_____. "Infanta Marina"
Marius Bewley, "The Poetry of Wallace Stevens," <u>PR</u>, 16 (Sept., 1949), 906.

_____. "The Irish Cliffs of Moher"
Judith McDaniel, "Wallace Stevens and the Scientific Imagination," <u>ConL</u>, 15 (Spring, 1974), 227-228.

_____. "July Mountain"
Beverly Coyle, "An Anchorage of Thought: Defining the Role of Aphorism in Wallace Stevens' Poetry," <u>PMLA</u>, 91 (March, 1976), 215-216.

_____. "Landscape with Boat"
Watts, <u>Hound and Quarry</u>, pp. 48-49.

Harold H. Watts, "Wallace Stevens and the Rock of Summer," <u>The Kenyon Review</u>, 14 (Winter, 1952), 128-130.

_____. "Large Red Man Reading"
Frank Doggett, "Wallace Stevens and the World We Know," <u>EJ</u>, 48 (Oct., 1959), 371-373.

_____. "Last Looks at the Lilacs"
Frank Doggett, "Our Nature Is Her Nature," in <u>The Twenties</u>, p. 38.

James Rother, "Modernism and the Nonsense Style," <u>ConL</u>, 15 (Spring, 1974), 192-195.

_____. "Lebensweisheitspielerei"
Marjorie Perloff, "Irony in Wallace Stevens's <u>The Rock</u>," AL, 36 (Nov., 1964), 341.

_____. "Le Monocle de Mon Oncle"
R. P. Blackmur, "Wallace Stevens," <u>Hound and Horn</u>, 5 (Jan.-March, 1932), 232-233, 245-246.
    Rpt. <u>The Double Agent</u>, pp. 77-78, 91-93.
    Rpt. <u>Language as Gesture</u>, pp. 229-230.

Beverly Coyle, "An Anchorage of Thought: Defining the Role of Aphorism in Wallace Stevens' Poetry," <u>PMLA</u>, 91 (March, 1976), 211-212.

Donald Davie, "'Essential Gaudiness': The Poems of Wallace Stevens," TC, 153 (June, 1953), 455-462.

Frank Doggett, "Our Nature Is Her Nature," in The Twenties, pp. 38-39.

Richard Ellmann, "Wallace Stevens' Ice Cream," The Kenyon Review, 19 (Winter, 1957), 97-99.

William A. Fahey, Expl, 15 (Dec., 1956), 16.
    Rpt. The Explicator Cyclopedia, I, pp. 280-281.

Frankenberg, Pleasure Dome, pp. 205-207.

R. M. Gay, Expl, 6 (Feb., 1948), 27.
    Rpt. The Explicator Cyclopedia, I, pp. 279-280.

Frank Lentricchia, Jr., "Wallace Stevens: The Ironic Eyes," YR, 56 (Spring, 1967), 344-345.

Earl Roy Miner, Expl, 13 (March, 1955), 28.
    Rpt. The Explicator Cyclopedia, I, pp. 281-282.

Robert Pack, "Wallace Stevens: The Secular Mystery and the Comic Spirit," The Western Review, 20 (Autumn, 1955), 57-59.

Delmore Schwartz, "In the Orchards of Imagination," The New Republic, 131 (Nov. 1, 1954), 17.

T. Weiss, "The Nonsense of Winters' Anatomy," Quarterly Review of Literature, 1 (Spring, 1944), 225-226.

_____. "Less and Less Human, O Savage Spirit"
C. Roland Wagner, "The Idea of Nothingness in Wallace Stevens," Accent, 12 (Spring, 1952), 113-114.

_____. "Life Is Motion"
Elder Olson, "The Poetry of Wallace Stevens," CE, 16 (April, 1955), 396-397.

Hugh L. Smith, Jr., Expl, 19 (April, 1961), 48.
    Rpt. The Explicator Cyclopedia, I, pp. 282-283.

_____. "Life on a Battleship"
Frankenberg, Pleasure Dome, pp. 240-242.

William Van O'Connor, "The Politics of a Poet," Perspective, 1 (Summer, 1948), 206-207.

_____. "Like Decorations in a Nigger Cemetery"
Ardyth Bradley, "Wallace Stevens' Decorations," TCL, 7 (Oct., 1961), 114-117.

Paul McBrearty, "Wallace Stevens's 'Like Decorations in a Nigger Cemetery,': Notes toward an Explication," TSLL, 15 (Summer, 1973), 341-356.

Helen Hennessy Vendler, "Stevens' 'Like Decorations in a Nigger Cemetery,'" MR, 7 (Winter, 1966), 136-146.

_____. Lions in Sweden"
Ramon Guthrie, Expl, 20 (Dec., 1961), 32.
    Rpt. The Explicator Cyclopedia, I, p. 283.

_____. "The Load of Sugar-Cane"
Don Geiger, "Wallace Stevens' Wealth," Perspective, 7 (Autumn, 1954), 157-158.

_____. Loneliness in Jersey City"
Dwight Eddins, "Wallace Stevens: America the Primordial," MLQ, 32
(March, 1971), 78-79.

_____. "Long and Sluggish Lines"
Marjorie Perloff, "Irony in Wallace Stevens's The Rock," AL, 36 (Nov.,
1964), 337-338.

_____. "Looking Across the Fields and Watching the Birds Fly"
Marius Bewley, "The Poetry of Wallace Stevens," Commonweal, 62 (Sept. 23,
1955), 620-621.

Marjorie Perloff, "Irony in Wallace Stevens's The Rock," AL, 36 (Nov.,
1964), 334-335.

_____. "Madame La Fleurie"
Judith McDaniel, "Wallace Stevens and the Scientific Imagination," ConL,
15 (Spring, 1974), 233-234.

Marjorie Perloff, "Irony in Wallace Stevens's The Rock," AL, 36 (Nov.,
1964), 336.

_____. "Man and Bottle"
Bornstein, Transformations of Romanticism, pp. 6-7.

_____. "The Man on the Dump"
Harold E. Toliver, Pastoral: Forms and Attitudes (Berkeley: Univ. of
California Press, 1971), pp. 310-312.

_____. "The Man Whose Pharynx Was Bad"
Marius Bewley, "The Poetry of Wallace Stevens," PR, 16 (Sept., 1949),
908-910.

T. Weiss, "The Nonsense of Winters' Anatomy," Quarterly Review of Literature, 1 (Spring, 1944), 230.

_____. "The Man with the Blue Guitar"
Richard P. Adams, "Wallace Stevens and Schopenhauer's The World as Will
and Idea," TSE, 20 (1972), 143-151.

Baker, Syntax in English Poetry, 1870-1930, pp. 160-161.

Merle E. Brown, "Concordia Discors in the Poetry of Wallace Stevens,"
AL, 34 (May, 1962), 249-254.

David Cavitch, Expl, 27 (Dec., 1968), 30.

J. V. Cunningham, "The Styles and Procedures of Wallace Stevens," UDQ,
1 (Spring, 1966), 19-21.

Frankenberg, Pleasure Dome, pp. 222-227.

Miller, Poets of Reality, pp. 252-253, 260-262.

Joseph N. Riddel, "Wallace Stevens--'It Must Be Human,'" EJ, 56 (April,
1967), 526-527.

Hi Simons, "The Genre of Wallace Stevens," SR, 53 (Oct.-Dec., 1945),
571-574.

_____. "Memorandum"
Dwight Eddins, "Wallace Stevens: America the Primordial," MLQ, 32
(March, 1971), 77-78.

_____. "The Men That are Falling"
John C. McCloskey, Expl, 23 (Jan., 1965), 41.

Ralph J. Mills, Jr., "Wallace Stevens: The Image of the Rock," Accent,
18 (Spring, 1958), 78-79.

_____. "Metamorphosis"
Sr. M. Bernetta Quinn, O.S.F., "Metamorphosis in Wallace Stevens," SR,
60 (Spring, 1952), 235-236.

Quinn, The Metamorphic Tradition, pp. 57-58.

_____. "Metaphors of a Magnifico"
Marius Bewley, "The Poetry of Wallace Stevens," PR, 16 (Sept., 1949),
903-904.

Bornstein, Transformations of Romanticism, pp. 213-214.

Don Geiger, "Wallace Stevens' Wealth," Perspective, 7 (Autumn, 1954), 156.

Bruce King, "Wallace Stevens' 'Metaphors of a Magnifico,'" ES, 49 (Oct.,
1969), 450-452.

Alexander S. Liddie, Expl, 21 (Oct., 1962), 15.

_____. "The Motive for Metaphor"
John Crowe Ransom, "The Concrete Universal: Observations on the Understanding of Poetry, II," The Kenyon Review, 17 (Summer, 1955), 400-402.

_____. "Mrs. Alfred Uruguay"
Friar and Brinnin, Modern Poetry, p. 536.

_____. "New England Verses"
Beverly Coyle, "An Achorage of Thought: Defining the Role of Aphorism in
Wallace Stevens' Poetry," PMLA, 91 (March, 1976), 209-211.

_____. "No Possum, No Sop, No Taters"
Merle E. Brown, "Concordia Discors in the Poetry of Wallace Stevens," AL,
34 (May, 1962), 247-249.

_____. "Note on Moonlight"
Robert Pack, "Wallace Stevens' Sufficient Muse," SoR, 11 (Oct., 1975),
778.

_____. "Notes toward a Supreme Fiction"
Richard P. Adams, "Wallace Stevens and Schopenhauer's The World as Will
and Idea," TSE, 20 (1972), 153-167.

Harold Bloom, The Ringers in the Tower: Studies in Romantic Tradition
(Chicago and London: Univ. of Chicago Press, 1971), pp. 235-255.

Bornstein, Transformations of Romanticism, pp. 218-230.

Merle E. Brown, "Concordia Discors in the Poetry of Wallace Stevens,"
AL, 34 (May, 1962), 254-262.

Wilson O. Clough, Expl, 28 (Nov., 1969), 24.

Frank Doggett, Expl, 15 (Feb., 1957), 30.
    Rpt. The Explicator Cyclopedia, I, pp. 278-279.

Frank Doggett, "This Invented World: Stevens' 'Notes Toward a Supreme
Fiction,'" ELH, 28 (Sept., 1961), 284-299.

Frankenberg, Pleasure Dome, pp. 257-267.

Gray, American Poetry, pp. 174-180.

Friar and Brinnin, Modern Poetry, pp. 535-536.

Bernard Heringman, "The Poetry of Synthesis," Perspective, 7 (Autumn, 1954), 167-168.

Suzanne Juhasz, Metaphor and the Poetry of Williams, Pound, and Stevens (Lewisburg: Bucknell Univ. Press, 1974), pp. 140-161.

Frank Lentricchia, Jr., "Wallace Stevens: The Ironic Eye," YR, 56 (Spring, 1967), 348-350.

Louis L. Martz, "The World of Wallace Stevens," in Modern American Poetry, ed. B. Rajan, pp. 98-101.

Miller, Poets of Reality, pp. 248-249.

James E. Mulqueen, "Wallace Stevens: Radical Transcendentalist," MQ, 11 (Spring, 1970), 335-336.

Pearce, The Continuity of American Poetry, pp. 395-400.

Joseph N. Riddel, "Wallace Stevens--'It Must Be Human,'" EJ, 56 (April, 1967), 527-530.

Joseph N. Riddel, "Wallace Stevens' 'Notes Toward a Supreme Fiction,'" Wisconsin Studies in Contemporary Literature, 2 (Spring-Summer, 1961), 23-42.

Andrew Taylor, "Stevens' Notes Toward a Supreme Fiction: A Reading," The Southern Review (Australia), 4, No. 4 (1971), 284-299.

Harold E. Toliver, Pastoral: Forms and Attitudes (Berkeley: Univ. of California, 1971), pp. 313-315.

_____. "Not Ideas about the Thing but the Thing Itself"
William Bevis, "Stevens' Toneless Poetry," ELH, 41 (Summer, 1974), 280-282.

Peckham and Chatman, Word, Meaning, Poem, pp. 312-319.

Marjorie Perloff, "Irony in Wallace Stevens's The Rock," AL, 36 (Nov., 1964), 339-340.

Harold E. Toliver, Pastoral: Forms and Attitudes (Berkeley: Univ. of California Press, 1971), pp. 320-322.

_____. "Nuances of a Theme by Williams"
Rosenthal, The Modern Poets, pp. 121-122.

_____. "Oak Leaves Are Hands"
Sr. M. Bernetta Quinn, O.S.F., "Metamorphosis in Wallace Stevens," SR, 60 (Spring, 1952), 250-251.

Quinn, The Metamorphic Tradition, p. 85.

_____. "Of Hartford in a Purple Light"
Norman Silverstein, Expl, 18 (Dec., 1959), 20.
    Rpt. The Explicator Cyclopedia, I, pp. 283-284.

_____. "Of Ideal Time and Choice"
Kenneth John Atchity, "Wallace Stevens: 'Of Ideal Time and Choice,'" RS, 41 (Sept., 1973), 141-153.

_____. "O Florida, Veneral Soil"
Frank Doggett, "Our Nature Is Her Nature," in The Twenties, p. 38.

_____. "Of Mere Being"
William Bevis, "Stevens' Toneless Poetry," ELH, 41 (Summer, 1974), 279–280.

Frank Doggett, "The Poet of Earth: Wallace Stevens," CE, 22 (March, 1961), 374–375.

_____. "Of Modern Poetry"
Bornstein, Transformations of Romanticism, pp. 2–5.

William Van O'Connor, "Wallace Stevens on 'The Poems of Our Climate,'" The University of Kansas City Review, 15 (Winter, 1948), 108–109.

_____. "Of the Manner of Addressing Clouds"
R. P. Blackmur, "Examples of Wallace Stevens," Hound and Horn, 5 (Jan.–March, 1932), 225–227.
    Rpt. The Double Agent, pp. 70–72.
    Rpt. Language as Gesture, pp. 223–224.

_____. "One of the Inhabitants of the West"
Marjorie Perloff, "Irony in Wallace Stevens's The Rock," AL, 36 (Nov., 1964), 331–332.

_____. "An Ordinary Evening in New Haven"
Bloom, Poetry and Repression, pp. 273–279.

Merle E. Brown, "Concordia Discors in the Poetry of Wallace Stevens," AL, 34 (May, 1962), 262–269.

Beverly Coyle, "An Anchorage of Thought: Defining the Role of Aphorism in Wallace Stevens' Poetry," PMLA, 91 (March, 1976), 216–217.

Frank Lentricchia, Jr., "Wallace Stevens: The Ironic Eye," YR, 56 (Spring, 1967), 339, 346–348.

Joseph N. Riddell, "Wallace Stevens' 'Visibility of Thought,'" PMLA, 77 (Sept., 1962), 493–498.

Lewis Turco, "The Agonism and the Existentity: Stevens," CP, 6 (Spring, 1973), 32–44.

C. Roland Wagner, "The Idea of Nothingness in Wallace Stevens," Accent, 12 (Spring, 1952), 120–121.

_____. "The Ordinary Women"
R. P. Blackmur, "Examples of Wallace Stevens," Hound and Horn, 5 (Jan.–March, 1932), 227–228.
    Rpt. The Double Agent, pp. 72–73.
    Rpt. Language as Gesture, pp. 225–226.

Don Geiger, "Wallace Stevens' Wealth," Perspective, 7 (Autumn, 1954), 160–163.

Fred H. Stocking, Expl, 4 (Oct., 1945), 4.
    Rpt. The Explicator Cyclopedia, I, pp. 284–285.

_____. "The Owl in the Sarcophagus"
Frank Doggett, "The Poet of Earth: Wallace Stevens," CE, 22 (March, 1961), 378.

Miller, Poets of Reality, pp. 268–270.

J. Hillis Miller, "Wallace Stevens' Poetry of Being," <u>ELH</u>, 31 (March, 1964), 86-105.

Ralph J. Mills, Jr., "Wallace Stevens: The Image of the Rock," <u>Accent</u>, 18 (Spring, 1958), 83.

Joseph N. Riddell, "Wallace Stevens' 'Visibility of Thought,'" <u>PMLA</u>, 77 (Sept., 1962), 488.

C. Roland Wagner, "The Idea of Nothingness in Wallace Stevens," <u>Accent</u>, 12 (Spring, 1952), 115-116.

_____. "Owl's Clover"
Frankenberg, <u>Pleasure Dome</u>, pp. 227-231.

Louis L. Martz, "Wallace Stevens: The World as Meditation," <u>YR</u>, 47 (Summer, 1958), 523-526.
    Rpt. Martz, <u>The Poem of the Mind</u>, pp. 209-211.

Leonora Woodman, "'A Giant on the Horizon': Wallace Stevens and the 'Idea of Man,'" <u>TSLL</u>, 15 (Winter, 1974), 771-785.

_____. "The Paltry Nude Starts on a Spring Voyage"
Frank Doggett, "Our Nature Is Her Nature," in <u>The Twenties</u>, p. 37.

_____. "Peter Quince at the Clavier"
Cooper and Holmes, <u>Preface to Poetry</u>, p. 63.

Carol Flake, "Wallace Stevens' 'Peter Quince at the Clavier': Sources and Structure,'" <u>ELN</u>, 12 (Dec., 1974), 116-120.

Newell F. Ford, "Peter Quince's Orchestra," <u>MLN</u>, 75 (May, 1960), 405-411.

Robert G. Goulet and Jean Watson Rosenbaum, "The Perception of Immortal Beauty: 'Peter Quince at the Clavier,'" <u>CollL</u>, 2 (Winter, 1975), 66-72.

Neil D. Isaacs, "The Autoerotic Metaphor," <u>L&P</u>, 15 (Spring, 1965), 103-104.

Wendell S. Johnson, "Some Functions of Poetic Form," <u>JAAC</u>, 13 (June, 1955), 501-503.

Eugene Paul Nassar, "Reply," <u>CE</u>, 27 (Feb., 1966), 431.

Eugene Paul Nassar, "Wallace Stevens: 'Peter Quince at the Clavier,'" <u>CE</u>, 26 (April, 1965), 549-551.

Phyllis E. Nelson, <u>Expl</u>, 24 (Feb., 1966), 52.

O'Connor, <u>Sense and Sensibility in Modern Poetry</u>, pp. 149-150.

William Van O'Connor, "Tension and Structure of Poetry," <u>SR</u>, 51 (Autumn, 1943), 559.

Laurence N. Perrine, "'Peter Quince at the Clavier': A Protest," <u>CE</u>, 27 (March, 1966), 430.

Laurence Perrine, "Rebuttal: 'Peter Quince at the Clavier': A Protest,'" <u>CE</u>, 27 (Feb., 1966), 430.

Perrine and Reid, <u>100 American Poems</u>, pp. 68-70.

Joseph N. Riddel, "Stevens' 'Peter Quince at the Clavier': Immortality as Form," <u>CE</u>, 23 (Jan., 1962), 307-309.

Rosenthal, <u>The Modern Poets</u>, pp. 126-128

Sanders, The Discovery of Poetry, pp. 336-341.

John N. Serio, "'The Comedian' as the Idea of Order in Harmonium," PLL, 12 (Winter, 1976), 97-98.

Fred H. Stocking, Expl, 5 (May, 1947), 47.
   Rpt. The Explicator Cyclopedia, I, pp. 285-286.

Mary Jane Storm, Expl, 14 (Nov., 1955), 9.
   Rpt. The Explicator Cyclopedia, I, pp. 286-287.

Walsh, Doors into Poetry, pp. 146-149.

Charles Wolfe, Expl, 33 (Feb., 1975), 43.

_____. "The Plain Sense of Things"
William Bevis, "Stevens' Toneless Poetry," ELH, 41 (Summer, 1974), 282-283.

Judith McDaniel, "Wallace Stevens and the Scientific Imagination," ConL, 15 (Spring, 1974), 228-229.

Robert Pack, "Wallace Stevens' Sufficient Muse," SoR, 11 (Oct., 1975), 773-776.

Marjorie Perloff, "Irony in Wallace Stevens's The Rock," AL, 36 (Nov., 1964), 340-341.

_____. "The Plot Against the Giant"
Frankenberg, Pleasure Dome, p. 201.

Albert W. Levi, "A Note on Wallace Stevens and the Poem of Perspective," Perspective, 7 (Autumn, 1954), 138-139.

Rosenthal, The Modern Poets, p. 123.

Wheeler, The Design of Poetry, p. 68.

_____. "The Poem as Icon"
Leonora Woodman, "'A Giant on the Horizon': Wallace Stevens and the 'Idea of Man,'" TSLL, 15 (Winter, 1974), 783-784.

_____. "The Poems of Our Climate"
Friar and Brinnin, Modern Poetry, p. 537.

_____. "Poem Written at Morning"
Suzanne Juhasz, Metaphor and the Poetry of Williams, Pound, and Stevens (Lewisburg: Bucknell Univ. Press, 1974), pp. 138-139.

_____. "Poetry Is a Destructive Force"
Samuel Joy Keyser, "Wallace Stevens: Form and Meaning in Four Poems," CE, 37 (Feb., 1976), 584-585.

_____. "A Postcard from the Volcano"
Beaty and Matchett, Poetry: From Statement to Meaning, pp. 204-205.

_____. "A Primitive Like an Orb"
Marius Bewley, "The Poetry of Wallace Stevens," PR, 16 (Sept., 1949), 913-914.

Watts, Hound and Quarry, pp. 54-55.

_____. "Prologues to What Is Possible"
Janet McCann, "'Prologues to What Is Possible,'" BSUF, 17 (Spring, 1976), 46-50.

Judith McDaniel, "Wallace Stevens and the Scientific Imagination," ConL, 15 (Spring, 1974), 231-232.

Marjorie Perloff, "Irony in Wallace Stevens's The Rock," AL, 36 (Nov., 1964), 332-334.

Joseph N. Riddle, "Wallace Stevens--'It Must Be Human,'" EJ, 56 (April, 1967), 532-533.

_____. "Reality"
Richard Blessing, "Wallace Stevens and the Necessary Reader: A Technique of Dynamism," TCL, 18 (Oct., 1972), 257.

_____. "The Red Fern"
Louis L. Martz, "The World of Wallace Stevens," in Modern American Poetry, ed. B. Rajan, pp. 97-98.

C. D. Narasimhaiah, "Wallace Stevens," in Studies in American Literature: Essays in Honor of William Mulder, ed. Jagdish Chander and Narindar S. Pradhan (Delhi: Oxford Univ. Press, 1976), pp. 228-231.

_____. "Repetition of a Young Captain"
Bernard Heringman, "The Poetry of Synthesis," Perspective, 7 (Autumn, 1954), 168-169.

_____. "Restatement of Romance"
Watts, Hound and Quarry, pp. 52-53.

_____. "The Rock"
Isabel G. MacCaffrey, "A Point of Central Arrival: Stevens' The Rock," ELH, 40 (Winter, 1973), 606-633.

Judith McDaniel, "Wallace Stevens and the Scientific Imagination," ConL, 15 (Spring, 1974), 234-236.

J. Hillis Miller, "Stevens' Rock and Criticism as Cure," GaR, 30 (Spring, 1976), 5-31.

Ralph J. Mills, Jr., "Wallace Stevens: The Image of the Rock," Accent, 18 (Spring, 1958), 85-89.

Marjorie Perloff, "Irony in Wallace Stevens' The Rock," AL, 36 (Nov., 1964), 327-342.

_____. "Sad Strains of a Gay Waltz"
Matthiessen, The Responsibilities of the Critic, pp. 15-16.

_____. "Sailing after Lunch"
Bornstein, Transformations of Romanticism, pp. 176-178.

_____. "Sea Surface Full of Clouds"
Harold C. Ackerman, Jr., "Notes Towards an Explication of Stevens' 'Sea Surface Full of Clouds,'" CP, 2 (Spring, 1969), 73-77.

Richard P. Adams, "Pure Poetry: Wallace Stevens' 'Sea Surface Full of Clouds,'" TSE, 21 (1974), 91-122.

R. P. Blackmur, "Wallace Stevens," Hound and Horn, 5 (Jan.-March, 1932), 233-235.
   Rpt. The Double Agent, pp. 79-80.
   Rpt. Language as Gesture, pp. 230-232.

David R. Ferry, Expl, 6 (June, 1948), 56.
    Rpt. The Explicator Cyclopedia, I, pp. 287-288.

Albert W. Levi, "A Note on Wallace Stevens and the Poem of Perspective," Perspective, 7 (Autumn, 1954), 141-142.

Miller, Poets of Reality, pp. 239-241.

Ransom, The World's Body, pp. 58-60.

Joseph N. Riddel, "'Disguised Pronunciamento': Wallace Stevens, 'Sea Surface Full of Clouds,'" University of Texas Studies in English, 37 (1958), 177-186.

M. L. Rosenthal, Expl, 19 (March, 1961), 38.
    Rpt. The Explicator Cyclopedia, I, pp. 288-289.

Rosenthal, The Modern Poets, pp. 130-131.

_____. "The Sense of the Sleight-of-Hand Man"
Perrine and Reid, 100 American Poems, pp. 70-71.

_____. "Six Significant Landscapes"
Albert W. Levi, "A Note on Wallace Stevens and the Poem of Perspective," Perspective, 7 (Autumn, 1954), 142-144.

Charles Moorman, Expl, 17 (Oct., 1958), 1.
    Rpt. The Explicator Cyclopedia, I, pp. 289-290.

_____. "The Snow Man"
Abad, A Formal Approach to Lyric Poetry, pp. 144-145.

Richard P. Adams, "Wallace Stevens and Schopenhauer's The World as Will and Idea," TSE, 20 (1972), 137-139.

William Bevis, "Stevens' Toneless Poetry," ELH, 41 (Summer, 1974), 257-269.

R. P. Blackmur, "Wallace Stevens," Hound and Horn, 5 (Jan.-March, 1932), 242-243.
    Rpt. The Double Agent, pp. 87-89.
    Rpt. Language as Gesture, pp. 237-238.

Richard Blessing, "Wallace Stevens and the Necessary Reader: A Technique of Dynamism," TCL, 18 (Oct., 1972), 252-253.

Bloom, Poetry and Repression, pp. 269-271.

Sharon Cameron, "'The Sense Against Calamity': Ideas of a Self in Three Poems by Wallace Stevens," ELH, 43 (Winter, 1976), 584-587.

Frank A. Doggett, "Why Read Wallace Stevens?" Emory University Quarterly, 18 (Summer, 1962), 88.

Gray, American Poetry, pp. 158-159.

Robert Kern, "Toward a New Nature Poetry," CentR, 19 (Summer, 1975), 210-212.

Samuel Jay Keyser, "Wallace Stevens: Form and Meaning in Four Poems," CE, 37 (Feb., 1976), 589-597.

Frank Lentricchia, Jr., "Wallace Stevens: The Ironic Eye," YR, 56 (Spring, 1967), 342-343.

Robert Pinsky, The Situation of Poetry: Contemporary Poetry and Its Traditions (Princeton, New Jersey: Princeton Univ. Press, 1976), 71-74.

C. Roland Wagner, "The Idea of Nothingness in Wallace Stevens," Accent, 12 (Spring, 1952), 118.

_____. "So-and-So Reclining on Her Couch"
Robert M. Farnsworth, Expl, 10 (June, 1952), 60.
   Rpt. The Explicator Cyclopedia, I, pp. 290-291.

Richard Gustafson, "The Practick of the Maker in Wallace Stevens," TCL, 9 (July, 1963), 83-85.

_____. "Some Friends from Pascagoula"
J. M. Linebarger, Expl, 35 (Winter, 1976), 12-13.

_____. "Someone Puts a Pineapple Together"
Miller, Poets of Reality, pp. 242-244.

_____. "Somnambulisma"
Janet McCann, Expl, 35 (Winter, 1976), 6-8.

_____. "Sonatina to Hans Christian"
Frank Doggett, "Wallace Stevens and the World We Know," EJ, 48 (Oct., 1959), 367.

_____. "Study of Images"
Warren Carrier, "Wallace Stevens' Pagan Vantage," Accent, 13 (Summer, 1953), 165-168.
   Rpt. Engle and Carrier, Reading Modern Poetry, pp. 361-364.

_____. "Study of Two Pears"
Richard Blessing, "Wallace Stevens and the Necessary Reader: A Technique of Dynamism," TCL, 18 (Oct., 1972), 253-254.

Suzanne Juhasz, Metaphor and the Poetry of Williams, Pound, and Stevens (Lewisburg: Bucknell Univ. Press, 1974), pp. 35-37.

Miller, Poets of Reality, pp. 250-251.

_____. "Sunday Morning"
R. P. Blackmur, "Wallace Stevens," Hound and Horn, 5 (Jan.-March, 1932), 240-241, 244.
   Rpt. The Double Agent, pp. 85-87, 90.
   Rpt. Language as Gesture, pp. 236-237.

Brooks, Lewis, and Warren, American Literature, pp. 2155-2156.

J. V. Cunningham, "The Poetry of Wallace Stevens," Poetry, 75 (Dec., 1949), 159-164.
   Rpt. Modern Literary Criticism, pp. 360-365.
   Rpt. Tradition and Poetic Structure, pp. 117-122.

Frank Doggett, "Our Nature Is Her Nature," in The Twenties, pp. 40-41.

Drew, Poetry: A Modern Guide, pp. 217-221.

Dwight Eddins, "Wallace Stevens: America the Primordial," MLQ, 32 (March, 1971), 75-77.

Richard Ellman, "Wallace Stevens' Ice Cream," The Kenyon Review, 19 (Winter, 1957), 95-97.

Frankenberg, Pleasure Dome, pp. 215-217.

Philip Furia, "Nuances of a Theme by Milton: Wallace Stevens's 'Sunday Morning,'" AL, 46 (March, 1974), 83-87.

Don Geiger, "Wallace Stevens' Wealth," Perspective, 7 (Autumn, 1954), 164-165.

Gray, American Poetry, pp. 160-166.

Richard Gustafson, "The Practick of the Maker in Wallace Stevens," TCL, 9 (July, 1963), 85-86.

James L. Hill, "The Frame for the Mind: Landscape in 'Lines Composed a Few Miles Above Tintern Abbey,' 'Dover Beach,' and 'Sunday Morning,'" CentR, 18 (Winter, 1974), 43-48.

Frank Lentricchia, Jr., "Wallace Stevens: The Ironic Eye," YR, 56 (Spring, 1967), 339-342.

Martz, The Poem of the Mind, pp. 197-199.

Louis L. Martz, "The World of Wallace Stevens," in Modern American Poetry, ed. B. Rajan, pp. 107-108.

Miller, Poets of Reality, pp. 222-223.

Robert Pack, "Wallace Stevens: The Secular Mystery and the Comic Spirit," The Western Review, 20 (Autumn, 1955), 53-55.

Joseph N. Riddel, "Walt Whitman and Wallace Stevens: Functions of a 'Literatus,'" SAQ, 61 (Autumn, 1962), 512-513.

Schneider, Poems and Poetry, p. 488.

Carol Kyros Walker, "The Subject as Speaker in 'Sunday Morning,'" CP, 10 (Spring, 1977), 25-31.

T. Weiss, "The Nonsense of Winters' Anatomy," Quarterly Review of Literature, 1 (Spring, 1944), 232-233.

Yvor Winters, "Poetic Styles, Old and New," in Four Poets on Poetry, pp. 72-75.

Winters, The Anatomy of Nonsense, pp. 88-91, 105-108. Also In Defense of Reason, pp. 431-434, 447-456.
    Rpt. Readings for Liberal Education, II, pp. 530-533.
    Rpt. Locke, Gibson, and Arms, Introduction to Literature, third edition, pp. 193-196.
    Rpt. fourth edition, pp. 194-197.
    Rpt. fifth edition, pp. 174-177.
    Rpt. Forms of Discovery, pp. 274-277.

Michael Zimmerman, "The Pursuit of Pleasure and the Uses of Death: Wallace Stevens' 'Sunday Morning,'" The University of Kansas City Review, 33 (Winter, 1966), 113-123.

_____. "Tattoo"
R. P. Blackmur, "Wallace Stevens," Hound and Horn, 5 (Jan.-March, 1932), 235-236.
    Rpt. The Double Agent, pp. 81-82.
    Rpt. Language as Gesture, pp. 232-233.

_____. "Tea at the Palaz of Hoon"
Samuel French Morse, "Wallace Stevens, Bergson, Pater," ELH, 31 (March, 1964), 13-14.

_____. "That Which Cannot Be Fixed"
Marius Bewley, "The Poetry of Wallace Stevens," PR, 16 (Sept., 1949), 910-911.

_____. "Things of August"
John Berryman, Poetry: A Critical Supplement, Dec., 1949, pp. 1-9.

_____. "Thirteen Ways of Looking at a Blackbird"
Price Caldwell, "Metaphoric Structures in Wallace Stevens' 'Thirteen Ways of Looking at a Blackbird,'" JEGP, 71 (July, 1972), 321-335.

Beverly Coyle, "An Anchorage of Thought: Defining the Role of Aphorism in Wallace Stevens' Poetry," PMLA, 91 (March, 1976), 207-209.

Frank Doggett, "Wallace Stevens and the World We Know," EJ, 48 (Oct., 1959), 368.

John J. Hafner, "One Way of Looking at 'Thirteen Ways of Looking at a Blackbird,'" CP, 3 (Spring, 1970), 61-65.

John V. Hagopian, "Thirteen Ways of Looking at a Blackbird," AN&Q, 1 (Feb., 1963), 84-85.

Albert W. Levi, "A Note on Wallace Stevens and the Poem of Perspective," Perspective, 7 (Autumn, 1954), 144-146.

Peter L. McNamara, "The Multi-Faceted Blackbird and Wallace Stevens' Poetic Vision," CE, 25 (March, 1964), 446-448.

Willis Monie, Expl, 34 (Sept., 1975), 2.

Rosenthal, The Modern Poets, pp. 125-129.

Robert S. Ryf, "X Ways of Looking at Y: Stevens' Elusive Blackbirds," Mosaic, 11 (Fall, 1977), 93-101.

Unger and O'Connor, Poems for Study, pp. 608-616.

_____. "A Thought Revolved"
Robert Mollinger, Expl, 33 (Sept., 1974), 1.

_____. "To the One of Fictive Music"
Richard E. Amacher, Expl, 11 (April, 1953), 43.
    Rpt. The Explicator Cyclopedia, I, pp. 291-292.

Louis L. Martz, "The World of Wallace Stevens," in Modern American Poetry, ed. B. Rajan, p. 95.

John N. Serio, "'The Comedian' as the Idea of Order in Harmonium," PLL, 12 (Winter, 1976), 98-99.

_____. "To the Roaring Wind"
Abad, A Formal Approach to Lyric Poetry, pp. 40-41, 180.

_____. "Two Figures in Dense Violet Light"
Robert W. Buttel, Expl, 9 (May, 1951), 45.
    Rpt. The Explicator Cyclopedia, I, p. 293.

_____. "Two Illustrations that the World Is What You Make of It"
Marjorie Perloff, "Irony in Wallace Stevens's The Rock," AL, 36 (Nov., 1964), 337, 341.

_____. "Two Tales of Liadoff"
Frankenberg, Pleasure Dome, pp. 254-256.

_____. "The Ultimate Poem Is Abstract"
J. F. Nims, Poetry: A Critical Supplement, Oct., 1947, pp. 7-9.

_____. "Variations on a Summer Day"
Edward Butscher, "Wallace Stevens' Neglected Fugue: 'Variations on a Summer Day,'" TCL, 19 (July, 1973), 153-164.

_____. "The Virgin Carrying a Lantern"
Howard Baker, "Wallace Stevens and Other Poets," SoR, 1 (Autumn, 1935), 374-376.

_____. "The Weeping Burgher"
Samuel French Morse, "Wallace Stevens, Bergson, Pater," ELH, 31 (March, 1964), 4-5.

_____. "The Well Dressed Man with A Beard"
Frank Doggett, "The Poet of Earth: Wallace Stevens," CE, 22 (March, 1961), 377-378.

_____. "What We See Is What We Think"
Baker, Syntax in English Poetry, 1870-1930, pp. 162-165.

_____. "The Woman in Sunshine"
Richard Blessing, "Wallace Stevens and the Necessary Reader: A Technique of Dynamism," TCL, 18 (Oct., 1972), 254-255.

Bornstein, Transformations of Romanticism, pp. 215-216.

Robert Pack, "Wallace Stevens' Sufficient Muse," SoR, 11 (Oct., 1975), 776-777.

_____. "Woman Looking at a Vase of Flowers"
Frank Doggett, Expl, 19 (Nov., 1960), 7.
    Rpt. The Explicator Cyclopedia, I, pp. 293-294.

Ralph Freedman, "Wallace Stevens and Rainer Maria Rilke," in The Poet as Critic, p. 63.

_____. "The World as Meditation"
Sharon Cameron, "'The Sense Against Calamity': Ideas of a Self in Three Poems by Wallace Stevens," ELH, 43 (Winter, 1976), 587-592.

Louis L. Martz, "Wallace Stevens: The World as Meditation," YR, 47 (Summer, 1958), 517-518, 534.
    Rpt. The Poem of the Mind, pp. 200-202, 218-220.

Marjorie Perloff, "Irony in Wallace Stevens's The Rock," AL, 36 (Nov., 1964), 330-331.

STICKNEY, Trumball. "In Ampezzo"
Ross C. Murfin, "The Poetry of Trumball Stickney," NEQ, 48 (Dec., 1975), 543-546, 553.

_____. "Lakeward"
Ross C. Murfin, "The Poetry of Trumball Stickney," NEQ, 48 (Dec., 1975), 547-549.

STRAND, Mark. "The Man in the Mirror"
Harold Bloom, "Dark and Radiant Peripheries: Mark Strand and A. P. Ammons," SoR, 8 (Winter, 1972), 136-138.

SUCKLING. "A Ballad Upon a Wedding"
Raymond A. Anselment, "'Men Most of All Enjoy, When Least They Do,': The Love Poetry of John Suckling," TSLL, 14 (Spring, 1972), 29-32.

_____. "Out Upon It"
Raymond A. Anselment, "'Men Most of All Enjoy, When Least They Do': The
Love Poetry of John Suckling," <u>TSLL</u>, 14 (Spring, 1972), 17-19.

_____. "Song: Why So Pale and Wan, Fond Lover?"
Schneider, <u>Poems and Poetry</u>, pp. 12-14.

_____. "There Never Yet Was Woman Made"
Raymond A. Anselment, "'Men Most of All Enjoy When Least They Do': The
Love Poetry of John Suckling," <u>TSLL</u>, 14 (Spring, 1972), 23-24.

_____. "'Tis Now, Since I Sate Down Before"
Raymond A. Anselment, "'Men Most of All Enjoy When Least They Do': The
Love Poetry of John Suckling," <u>TSLL</u>, 14 (Spring, 1972), 28-29.

SURREY. "Dyvers Thy Death"
C. W. Jentoft, "Surrey's Five Elelgies: Rhetoric, Structure, and the
Poetry of Praise," <u>PMLA</u>, 91 (Jan., 1976), 27-28.

_____. "Give Place Ye Lovers"
C. W. Jentoft, "Surrey's Four 'Orations' and the Influence of Rhetoric
on Dramatic Effect," <u>PLL</u>, 9 (Summer, 1973), 253-256.

_____. "Good Ladies"
C. W. Jentoft, "Surrey's Four 'Orations' and the Influence of Rhetoric on
Dramatic Effect," <u>PLL</u>, 9 (Summer, 1973), 253-255.

_____. "How Each Thing Save the Lover in Spring Reviveth to Pleasure" ("When
     Windesor Walles Sustained My Wearied Arme")
Alicia Ostriker, "Thomas Wyatt and Henry Surrey: Dissonance and Harmony
in Lyric Form," <u>NLH</u>, 1 (Spring, 1970), 395-397.

_____. "In the Rude Age"
C. W. Jentoft, "Surrey's Five Elegies: Rhetoric, Structure, and the
Poetry of Praise," <u>PMLA</u>, 91 (Jan., 1976), 28-29.

_____. "London Hast Thou Accused Me"
C. W. Jentoft, "Surrey's Four 'Orations' and the Influence of Rhetoric
on Dramatic Effect," <u>PLL</u>, 9 (Summer, 1973), 257-262.

_____. "Love That Doth Reign and Live within My Thought"
Adams, <u>The Contexts of Poetry</u>, pp. 57-59.

Leonard Barkan, <u>Nature's Work of Art: The Human Body as Image of the
World</u> (New Haven and London: Yale Univ. Press, 1975), pp. 177-178.

William O. Harris, "'Love that Doth Raine': Surrey's Creative Imitation," <u>MP</u>, 66 (May, 1969), 298-305.

Miles, <u>Major Adjectives in English Poetry</u>, pp. 326-327.

Alicia Ostriker, "Thomas Wyatt and Henry Surrey: Dissonance and Harmony
in Lyric Form," <u>NLH</u>, 1 (Spring, 1970), 391-394.

Hallett Smith, "The Art of Sir Thomas Wyatt," <u>HLQ</u>, 9 (Aug., 1946), 334-
337.

_____. "The Means to Attain Happy Life"
George Arms, <u>Expl</u>, 1 (Nov., 1942), 10.

Thee" (Thomas Clere Sonnet)
l Thought, pp. 31-37.

urrey's Five Elegies: Rhetoric, Structure, and the
" PMLA, 91 (Jan., 1976), 25.

urrey's Four 'Orations' and the Influence of Rhetoric on
PLL, 9 (Summer, 1973), 253-255.

dsor, He Recounteth His Pleasure There Passed"
, 27 (Oct., 1968), 11.

rrey's Five Elegies: Rhetoric, Structure, and the
' PMLA, 91 (Jan., 1976), 30-32.

n"
Thought, pp. 22-25.

ere"
Thought, pp. 25-30.

urrey's Five Elegies: Rhetoric, Structure, and the
Poetry of Praise," PMLA, 91 (Jan., 1976), 25-27.

SWAN, Jon. "The Magpie"
Perrine and Reid, 100 American Poems, pp. 286-287.

SWENSON, May. "Lion"
Perrine and Reid, 100 American Poems, pp. 250-251.

SWIFT. "Baucis and Philemon"
Rebecca Price Parkin, "Swift's Baucis and Philemon: A Sermon in the
Burlesque Mode," Satire Newsletter, 7 (Spring, 1970), 109-114.

_____. "A Beautiful Young Nymph Going to Bed"
Thomas B. Gilmore, Jr., "The Comedy of Swift's Scatological Poems," PMLA,
91 (Jan., 1976), 34-35.

Felicity Nussbaum, "Juvenal, Swift, and The Folly of Love," ECS, 9 (Summer, 1976), 549-551.

John F. Sena, "Swift as Moral Physician: Scatalogy and the Tradition of
Love Melancholy," JEGP, 76 (July, 1977), 358-359.

Robert W. Uphaus, "Swift's Poetry: The Making of Meaning," ECS, 5
(Summer, 1972), 578-581.

_____. "Cassinus and Peter"
John M. Aden, "Those Gaudy Tulips: Swift's 'Unprintables,'" in Quick
Springs of Sense: Studies in the Eighteenth Century, ed. Larry S. Cham-
pion (Athens: Univ. of Georgia, 1974), pp. 28-31.

Thomas B. Gilmore, Jr., "The Comedy of Swift's Scatological Poems," PMLA,
91 (Jan., 1976), 38-39.

_____. "The Day of Judgement"
T. Henry Smith, Expl, 22 (Sept., 1963), 6.

_____. "Description of a City Shower"
Abad, A Formal Approach to Lyric Poetry, pp. 254-258.

John I. Fischer, "Apparent Contraries: A Reading of Swift's 'A Description of a City Shower,'" TSL, 19 (1974), 21-34.

Brendan O. Hehir, "Meaning in Swift's 'Description of a City Shower,'" _ELH_, 27 (Sept., 1960), 194-207.

_____. "Description of the Morning"
Bateson, _English Poetry_, pp. 175-178.

David M. Vieth, "_Fiat Lux_: Logos Versus Chaos in Swift's 'A Description of the Morning,'" _PLL_, 8 (Summer, 1972), 302-307.

_____. "The Description of a Salamander"
A. B. England, "The Subversion of Logic in Some Poems by Swift," _SEL_, 15 (Summer, 1975), 410-412.

Robert W. Uphaus, "Swift's Poetry: The Making of Meaning," _ECS_, 5 (Summer, 1972), 572-574.

_____. "The Fable of Midas"
A. B. England, "The Subversion of Logic in Some Poems by Swift," _SEL_, 15 (Summer, 1975), 412-413.

_____. "The Journal" or "The Country Life"
Aubrey Williams, "Swift and the Poetry of Allusion: 'The Journal,'" in _Literary Theory and Structure: Essays in Honor of William K. Wimsatt_ (New Haven: Yale Univ. Press, 1973), pp. 227-243.

_____. "The Lady's Dressing Room"
John M. Aden, "Those Gaudy Tulips: Swift's 'Unprintables,'" in _Quick Springs of Sense: Studies in the Eighteenth Century_, ed. Larry S. Champion (Athens: Univ. of Georgia, 1974), pp. 19-23.

Louise K. Barnett, "The Mysterious Narrator: Another Look at 'The Lady's Dressing Room,'" _CP_, 9 (Fall, 1976), 29-32.

Thomas B. Gilmore, Jr., "The Comedy of Swift's Scatological Poems," _PMLA_, 91 (Jan., 1976), 36-37, 39.

John F. Sena, "Swift as Moral Physician: Scatology and the Tradition of Love Melancholy," _JEGP_, 76 (July, 1977), 355-358.

_____. "The Legion Club"
Peter J. Schakel, "Virgil and the Dean: Christian and Classical Allusion in The Legion Club," _SP_, 70 (Oct., 1973), 427-438.

_____. "Ode to Sancroft"
David P. French, "Swift, the Non-Jurors, and Jacobitism," _MLN_, 72 (April, 1957), 258-264.

Edward W. Rosenheim, Jr., "Swift's _Ode to Sancroft_: Another Look," _MP_, 73 (May, 1976), Supplement, S24-S39.

_____. "On Poetry: A Rapsody"
James L. Tyne, S.J., "Swift's Mock Panegyrics in 'On Poetry: A Rapsody,'" _PLL_, 10 (Summer, 1974), 279-286.

Robert W. Uphaus, "Swift's Poetry: The Making of Meaning," _ECS_, 5 (Summer, 1972), 582-586.

_____. "A Panegyrick on the D--n, in the Person of a Lady in the North"
Thomas B. Gilmore, Jr., "The Comedy of Swift's Scatological Poems," _PMLA_, 91 (Jan., 1976), 40-41.

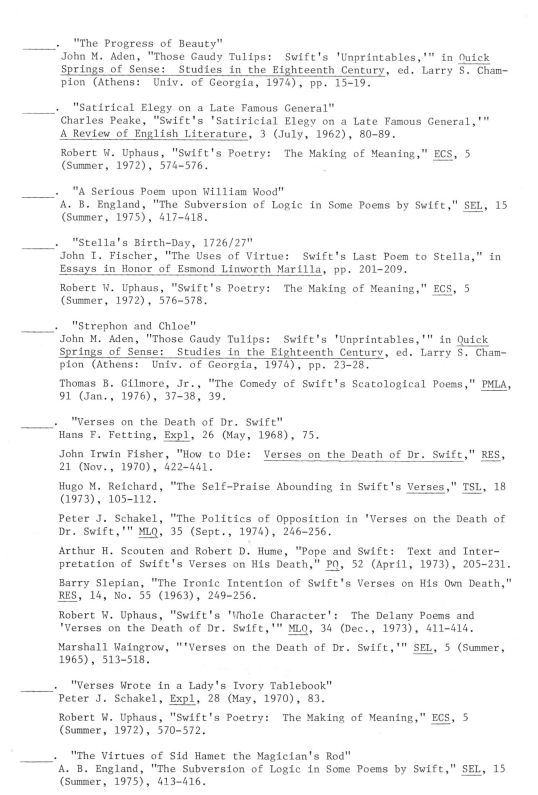

_____. "The Progress of Beauty"
John M. Aden, "Those Gaudy Tulips: Swift's 'Unprintables,'" in Quick
Springs of Sense: Studies in the Eighteenth Century, ed. Larry S. Cham-
pion (Athens: Univ. of Georgia, 1974), pp. 15-19.

_____. "Satirical Elegy on a Late Famous General"
Charles Peake, "Swift's 'Satiricial Elegy on a Late Famous General,'"
A Review of English Literature, 3 (July, 1962), 80-89.

Robert W. Uphaus, "Swift's Poetry: The Making of Meaning," ECS, 5
(Summer, 1972), 574-576.

_____. "A Serious Poem upon William Wood"
A. B. England, "The Subversion of Logic in Some Poems by Swift," SEL, 15
(Summer, 1975), 417-418.

_____. "Stella's Birth-Day, 1726/27"
John I. Fischer, "The Uses of Virtue: Swift's Last Poem to Stella," in
Essays in Honor of Esmond Linworth Marilla, pp. 201-209.

Robert W. Uphaus, "Swift's Poetry: The Making of Meaning," ECS, 5
(Summer, 1972), 576-578.

_____. "Strephon and Chloe"
John M. Aden, "Those Gaudy Tulips: Swift's 'Unprintables,'" in Quick
Springs of Sense: Studies in the Eighteenth Century, ed. Larry S. Cham-
pion (Athens: Univ. of Georgia, 1974), pp. 23-28.

Thomas B. Gilmore, Jr., "The Comedy of Swift's Scatological Poems," PMLA,
91 (Jan., 1976), 37-38, 39.

_____. "Verses on the Death of Dr. Swift"
Hans F. Fetting, Expl, 26 (May, 1968), 75.

John Irwin Fisher, "How to Die: Verses on the Death of Dr. Swift," RES,
21 (Nov., 1970), 422-441.

Hugo M. Reichard, "The Self-Praise Abounding in Swift's Verses," TSL, 18
(1973), 105-112.

Peter J. Schakel, "The Politics of Opposition in 'Verses on the Death of
Dr. Swift,'" MLQ, 35 (Sept., 1974), 246-256.

Arthur H. Scouten and Robert D. Hume, "Pope and Swift: Text and Interpretation of Swift's Verses on His Death," PQ, 52 (April, 1973), 205-231.

Barry Slepian, "The Ironic Intention of Swift's Verses on His Own Death,"
RES, 14, No. 55 (1963), 249-256.

Robert W. Uphaus, "Swift's 'Whole Character': The Delany Poems and
'Verses on the Death of Dr. Swift,'" MLQ, 34 (Dec., 1973), 411-414.

Marshall Waingrow, "'Verses on the Death of Dr. Swift,'" SEL, 5 (Summer,
1965), 513-518.

_____. "Verses Wrote in a Lady's Ivory Tablebook"
Peter J. Schakel, Expl, 28 (May, 1970), 83.

Robert W. Uphaus, "Swift's Poetry: The Making of Meaning," ECS, 5
(Summer, 1972), 570-572.

_____. "The Virtues of Sid Hamet the Magician's Rod"
A. B. England, "The Subversion of Logic in Some Poems by Swift," SEL, 15
(Summer, 1975), 413-416.

SWINBURNE. "Anactoria"
    David A. Cook, "The Content and Meaning of Swinburne's 'Anactoria,'" <u>VP</u>,
    9 (Spring-Summer, 1971), 77-93.

_____. "Autumn in Cornwall"
    J. P. Kirby, <u>Expl</u>, 1 (May, 1943), 56.
      Rpt. <u>The Explicator Cyclopedia</u>, II, pp. 326-327.

_____. "Ave Atque Vale"
    Jerome J. McGann, "'Ave atque Vale': An Introduction to Swinburne," <u>VP</u>,
    9 (Spring-Summer, 1971), 145-163.

_____. "A Ballad of Death"
    Julian Baird, "Swinburne, Sade, and Blake: The Pleasure-Pain Paradox,"
    <u>VP</u>, 9 (Spring-Summer, 1971), 60-63.

_____. "A Ballad of Dreamland"
    Peckham and Chatman, <u>Word, Meaning, Poem</u>, pp. 262-272.

_____. "Before the Mirror"
    Jeffrey R. Prince, "The Iconic Poem and the Aesthetic Tradition," <u>ELH</u>, 43
    (Winter, 1976), 571-574.

_____. "Between the Sunset and the Sea"
    Daniels, <u>The Art of Reading Poetry</u>, pp. 450-453.

_____. "By the North Sea"
    Kerry McSweeney, "Swinburne's 'By the North Sea,'" <u>YES</u>, 3 (1973), 222-
    231.

_____. "A Cameo"
    Brooks Wright, <u>Expl</u>, 12 (Nov., 1953), 13.
      Rpt. <u>The Explicator Cyclopedia</u>, II, p. 327.

_____. "Faustine"
    Jeffrey R. Prince, "The Iconic Poem and the Aesthetic Tradition," <u>ELH</u>, 43
    (Winter, 1976), 578-580.

_____. "The Garden of Proserpine"
    William Empson, "Basic English and Wordsworth," <u>The Kenyon Review</u>, 2
    (Autumn, 1940), 450-452.

    Douglas C. Fricke, "The Proserpine Figure in Swinburne's <u>Poems and Bal-
    lads I</u>," in <u>Aeolian Harps: Essays in Honor of Maurice Browning</u>, ed.
    Donna G. Fricke and Douglas C. Fricke (Bowling Green, Ohio: Bowling
    Green Univ. Press, 1976), pp. 193-197.

    William Frost, <u>English Masterpieces</u>, Vol. VI, <u>Romantic and Victorian
    Poetry</u>, pp. 19-20.

    Thomas and Brown, <u>Reading Poems: An Introduction to Critical Study</u>,
    pp. 640-641.

_____. "Hertha"
    C. C. Cunningham, <u>Literature as a Fine Art: Analysis and Interpretation</u>,
    pp. 101-106.

    Tillyard, <u>Five Poems, 1470-1870</u>, pp. 87-103.

_____. "The Hounds of Spring"
Leavis, Revaluation, pp. 238-240.
    Rpt. Critiques, pp. 179-180.

Unger and O'Connor, Poems for Study, pp. 555-556.

_____. "Hymn to Proserpine"
Curtis Dahl, "A Double Frame for Tennyson's Demeter?" VS, 1 (June, 1958),
360-361.

Douglas C. Fricke, "The Proserpine Figure in Swinburne's Poems and Bal-
lads I," in Aeolian Harps: Essays in Honor of Maurice Browning, ed.
Donna G. Fricke and Douglas C. Fricke (Bowling Green, Ohio: Bowling
Green Univ. Press, 1976), pp. 197-204.

_____. "The Lake of Gaube"
Kerry McSweeney, "Swinburne's 'A Nympholept' and 'The Lake of Gaube,'"
VP, 9 (Spring-Summer, 1971), 212-215.

Meredith B. Raymond, "'The Lake of Gaube': Swinburne's Dive in the Dark
and the 'Indeterminate Moment,'" VP, 9 (Spring-Summer, 1971), 185-199.

_____. "Laus Veneris"
Julian Baird, "Swinburne, Sade, and Blake: The Pleasure-Pain Paradox,"
VP, 9 (Spring-Summer, 1971), 63-74.

Empson, Seven Types of Ambiguity, pp. 205-207.

Gerald Levin, "Swinburne's 'End of the World' Fantasy," L&P, 24, No. 3
(1974), 110-111.

_____. "Nephelidia"
Ciardi, How Does a Poem Mean? pp. 934-936.

_____. "A Nympholept"
Paull F. Baum, "Swinburne's 'A Nympholept,'" SAQ, 57 (Winter, 1958), 58-
68.

Kerry McSweeney, "Swinburne's 'A Nympholept,' and 'The Lake of Gaube,'"
VP, 9 (Spring-Summer, 1971), 204-212.

F. A. C. Wilson, "Indian and Mithraic Influences on Swinburne's Panthe-
ism: 'Hertha' and 'A Nympholept,'" PLL, 8, Supplement (Fall, 1972),
61-66.

_____. "On the Cliffs"
Meredith B. Raymond, "Swinburne Among the Nightingales," VP, 6 (Summer,
1968), 125-141.

_____. "Prelude" to Songs Before Sunrise
Donald C. Stuart, "Swinburne: The Composition of a Self-Portrait," VP,
9 (Spring-Summer, 1971), 116-117.

_____. "A Solitude"
Bloom, Philbrick, and Blistein, The Order of Poetry, pp. 127-129.

_____. "The Sundew"
Douglas C. Fricke, "The Idea of Love in Swinburne's 'The Sundew,'" ELN,
13 (March, 1976), 194-201.

_____. "Thalassius"
Richard D. McGhee, "'Thalassius': Swinburne's Poetic Myth," VP, 5
(Summer, 1967), 127-136.

Donald C. Stuart, "Swinburne: The Composition of a Self-Portrait," _VP_, 9 (Spring-Summer, 1971), 118-128.

_____. "The Triumph of Time"
Gerald Levin, "Swinburne's 'End of the World' Fantasy," _L&P_, 24, No. 3 (1974), 112-113.

Donald C. Stuart, "Swinburne: The Composition of a Self-Portrait," _VP_, 9 (Spring-Summer, 1971), 112-115.

SYMONS, Arthur. "Liber Amoris"
Jan B. Gordon, "The Dance Macabre of Arthur Symons' _London Nights_," _VP_, 9 (Winter, 1971), 440-441.

_____. "La Mêlinite: Moulin Rouge"
Kerry Powell, "Arthur Symons, Symbolism, and the Aesthetics of Escape," _Renascence_, 29 (Spring, 1977), 161-164.

_____. "Nora on the Pavement"
Jan B. Gordon, "The Dance Macabre of Arthur Symons' _London Nights_," _VP_, 9 (Winter, 1971), 432-433.

_____. "Prologue" to _London Nights_
Jan B. Gordon, "The Dance Macabre of Arthur Symons' _London Nights_," _VP_, 9 (Winter, 1971), 430-431.

_____. "Rosa Mundi"
Jan B. Gordon, "The Dance Macabre of Arthur Symons' _London Nights_," _VP_, 9 (Winter, 1971), 435.

_____. "Stella Maris"
Jan B. Gordon, "The Dance Macabre of Arthur Symons' _London Nights_," _VP_, 9 (Winter, 1971), 435-436.

_____. "To a Dancer"
Jan B. Gordon, "The Dance Macabre of Arthur Symons' _London Nights_," _VP_, 9 (Winter, 1971), 431-432.

TAFT, Robert W. "Attack on Barbados at Sandy Point"
Rolfe Humphries, _Expl_, 18 (April, 1960), 44.

TAGGARD. "The Four Songs"
Donald A. Stauffer, "Genesis, or the Poet as Maker," in _Poets at Work_, pp. 63-70.

TATE, Allen. "Again the Native Hour"
August H. Mason, _Expl_, 7 (Dec., 1948), 23.
    Rpt. _The Explicator Cyclopedia_, I, pp. 295-296.

Samuel H. Monk, _Expl_, 6 (June, 1948), 58.
    Rpt. _The Explicator Cyclopedia_, I, pp. 294-295.

_____. "The Buried Lake"
Alan Williamson, "Allen Tate and the Personal Epic," _SoR_, 12 (Oct., 1976), 727-732.

_____. "Causerie"
Vivienne Koch, "The Poetry of Allen Tate," _The Kenyon Review_, 11 (Summer, 1949), 366-367.
    Rpt. _The Kenyon Critics_, pp. 174-175.
    Rpt. _Modern American Poetry_, ed. B. Rajan, pp. 20-21.

_____. "The Cross"
Sr. Mary Bernetta, O.S.F., "Allen Tate's Inferno," Renascence, 3 (Spring, 1951), 118.

Robert Dupree, "The Mirrors of Analogy: Three Poems of Allen Tate," SoR, 8 (Oct., 1972), 778-785.

Frederick Morgan, "Recent Verse," HudR, 1 (Summer, 1948), 263-264.

Richard J. O'Dea, "Allen Tate's 'The Cross,'" Renascence, 18 (Spring, 1966), 156-160.

Charles C. Walcutt, Expl, 6 (April, 1948), 41.
    Rpt. The Explicator Cyclopedia, I, pp. 296-297.

Winters, Forms of Discovery, pp. 322-323.

_____. "Death of Little Boys"
David V. Harrington and Carole Schneider, Expl, 26 (Oct., 1967), 16.

Vivienne Koch, "The Poetry of Allen Tate," The Kenyon Review, 11 (Summer, 1949), 357-360.
    Rpt. The Kenyon Critics, pp. 172-174.
    Rpt. Modern American Poetry, ed. B. Rajan, pp. 12-14.

Roy Harvey Pearce, "A Small Crux in Allen Tate's 'Death of Little Boys': Postcript," MLN, 75 (March, 1960), 213-214.

Southworth, More Modern American Poets, p. 97.

Radcliffe Squires, "Mr. Tate: Whose Wreath Should be a Moral," in Aspects of American Poetry, pp. 265-266, 268.

Thompson Uhlman, Expl, 28 (March, 1970), 58.

Winters, The Anatomy of Nonsense, pp. 198-202. Also In Defense of Reason, pp. 529-533.

_____. "Fragment of a Meditation"
Vivienne Koch, "The Poetry of Allen Tate," The Kenyon Review, 11 (Summer, 1949), 363-364.
    Rpt. Modern American Poetry, ed. B. Rajan, pp. 17-18.

_____. "Last Days of Alice"
Sr. Mary Bernetta, O.S.F., "Allen Tate's Inferno," Renascence, 3 (Spring, 1951), 117.

Brooks, Modern Poetry and the Tradition, p. 104.

Robert Dupree, "The Mirrors of Analogy: Three Poems of Allen Tate," SoR, 8 (Oct., 1972), 774-778.

Delmore Schwartz, "The Poetry of Allen Tate," SoR, 5 (Winter, 1940), 427-430.

_____. "The Maimed Man"
Alan Williamson, "Allen Tate and the Personal Epic," SoR, 12 (Oct., 1976), 726-727.

_____. "The Meaning of Death"
Brooks, Modern Poetry and the Tradition, pp. 106-108.

Brooks, Lewis, and Warren, American Literature, pp. 2666-2667.

Howard Nemerov, "The Current of the Frozen Stream," Furioso, 3 (Fall, 1948), 55-56.

Howard Nemerov, "The Current of the Frozen Stream," SR, 67 (Autumn, 1959), 590-592.

_____. "The Meaning of Life"
Brooks, Lewis, and Warren, American Literature, pp. 2665-2666.

Brooks, Modern Poetry and the Tradition, pp. 105-106.

R. K. Meiners, Expl, 19 (June, 1961), 63.
   Rpt. The Explicator Cyclopedia, I, pp. 297-299.

Howard Nemerov, "The Current of the Frozen Stream," Furioso, 3 (Fall, 1948), 54-55.

Howard Nemerov, "The Current of the Frozen Stream," SR, 67 (Autumn, 1959), 589-592.

_____. "The Mediterranean"
Robert Dupree, "The Mirrors of Analogy: Three Poems of Allen Tate," SoR, 8 (Oct., 1972), 785-790.

R. K. Meiners, "The Art of Allen Tate: A Reading of 'The Mediterranean,'" The University of Kansas City Review, 27 (Winter, 1960), 155-159.

Louis D. Rubin, Jr., "The Concept of Nature in Modern Southern Poetry," AQ, 9 (Spring, 1957), 64-65.

_____. "Message from Abroad"
Vivienne Koch, "The Poetry of Allen Tate," The Kenyon Review, 11 (Summer, 1949), 364-365.
      Rpt. The Kenyon Critics, p. 174.
      Rpt. Modern American Poetry, ed. B. Rajan, pp. 18-20.

_____. "More Sonnets at Christmas, I" "Again the native hour lets down the
      locks"
Radcliffe Squires, "Allen Tate: A Season at Monteagle," MQR, 10 (Winter, 1971), 58.

_____. "More Sonnets at Christmas, IV" "Gay citizen, myself, and thoughtful
      friend"
Radcliffe Squires, "Allen Tate: A Season at Monteagle," MQR, 10 (Winter, 1971), 58-59.

_____. "Mother and Son"
Sr. Mary Bernetta, O.S.F., "Allen Tate's Inferno," Renascence, 3 (Spring, 1951), 114-115.

Denis Donoghue, "Nuances of a Theme by Allen Tate," SoR, 12 (Oct., 1976), 711-713.

Southworth, More Modern American Poets, p. 99.

_____. "Mr. Pope"
Margaret Morton Blum, "Allen Tate's 'Mr. Pope': A Reading," MLN, 74 (Dec., 1959), 706-709.

Daniels, The Art of Reading Poetry, pp. 312-314.

Felver and Nurmi, Poetry: An Introduction and Anthology, pp. 123-124, 128.

James Edward Tobin, Expl, 15 (March, 1957), 35.
   Rpt. The Explicator Cyclopedia, I, pp. 299-300.

_____. "The Oath"
Brooks, <u>Modern Poetry and the Tradition</u>, pp. 108-109.

_____. "Ode to Our Young Pro-Consuls of the Air"
Hoffman, <u>The Twenties</u>, pp. 385-388.

_____. "Ode to the Confederate Dead"
Brooks, Lewis, and Warren, <u>American Literature</u>, pp. 2663-2664.

Denis Donoghue, "Technique in Hopkins," <u>Studies</u>, 44 (Winter, 1955), 449-450.

Lillian Feder, "Allen Tate's Use of Classical Literature," <u>CentR</u>, 4 (Winter, 1960), 98-103.

Hoffman, <u>The Twenties</u>, pp. 151-153.

Vivienne Koch, "The Poetry of Allen Tate," <u>The Kenyon Review</u>, 11 (Summer, 1949), 370-372.
    Rpt. <u>Modern American Poetry</u>, ed. B. Rajan, pp. 24-26.

Louis D. Rubin, Jr., "The Concept of Nature in Modern Poetry," <u>AQ</u>, 9 (Spring, 1957), 70-71.

Louis D. Rubin, Jr., "The Serpent in the Mulberry Bush Again," <u>SoR</u>, 12 (Oct., 1976), 744-757.

Schlauch, <u>Modern English and American Poetry</u>, pp. 97-98.

Southworth, <u>More Modern American Poets</u>, pp. 100-101.

Allen Tate in Friar and Brinnin, <u>Modern Poetry</u>, pp. 538-539.

Allen Tate, "Narcissus as Narcissus," <u>VQR</u>, 14 (Jan., 1938), 108-122.

Tate, <u>Reason in Madness</u>, pp. 136-151.
    Rpt. <u>On the Limits of Poetry</u>, pp. 248-262.
    Rpt. Engle and Carrier, <u>Reading Modern Poetry</u>, pp. 207-219.

Alan Williamson, "Allen Tate and the Personal Epic," <u>SoR</u>, 12 (Oct., 1976), 717-720.

_____. "Retroduction to American History"
Southworth, <u>More Modern American Poets</u>, pp. 99-100.

_____. "Seasons of the Soul"
Richmond C. Beatty, "Allen Tate as a Man of Letters," <u>SAQ</u>, 47 (April, 1948), 233-234.

Alwyn Berland, "Violence in the Poetry of Allen Tate," <u>Accent</u>, 11 (Summer, 1951), 165-171.

Brooks, Lewis, and Warren, <u>American Literature</u>, pp. 2670-2674.

Deutsch, <u>Poetry in Our Time</u>, pp. 199-202.

Vivienne Koch, "The Poetry of Allen Tate," <u>The Kenyon Review</u>, 11 (Summer, 1949), 374-378.
    Rpt. <u>The Kenyon Review</u>, pp. 177-181.
    Rpt. <u>Modern American Poetry</u>, ed. B. Rajan, pp. 28-30.

Radcliffe Squires, "Allen Tate: A Season at Monteagle," <u>MQR</u>, 10 (Winter, 1971), 62-65.

Alan Williamson, "Allen Tate and the Personal Epic," <u>SoR</u>, 12 (Oct., 1976), 721-725.

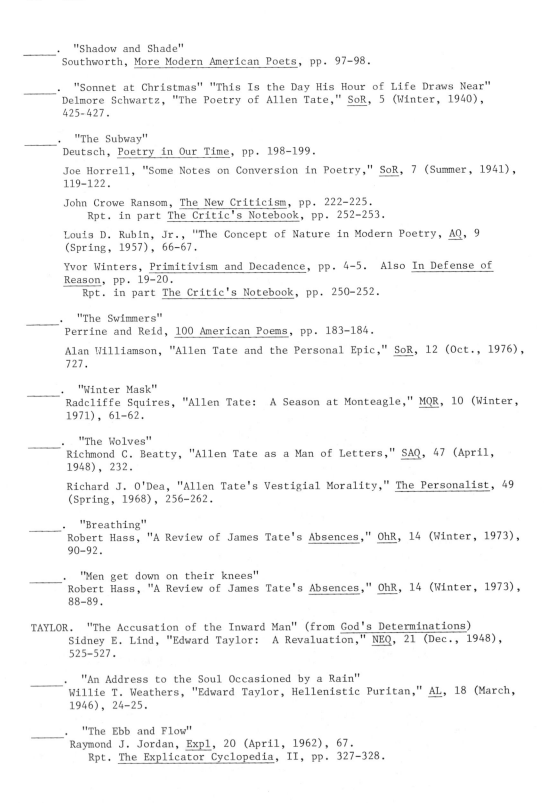

_____. "Shadow and Shade"
Southworth, More Modern American Poets, pp. 97-98.

_____. "Sonnet at Christmas" "This Is the Day His Hour of Life Draws Near"
Delmore Schwartz, "The Poetry of Allen Tate," SoR, 5 (Winter, 1940),
425-427.

_____. "The Subway"
Deutsch, Poetry in Our Time, pp. 198-199.

Joe Horrell, "Some Notes on Conversion in Poetry," SoR, 7 (Summer, 1941),
119-122.

John Crowe Ransom, The New Criticism, pp. 222-225.
      Rpt. in part The Critic's Notebook, pp. 252-253.

Louis D. Rubin, Jr., "The Concept of Nature in Modern Poetry, AQ, 9
(Spring, 1957), 66-67.

Yvor Winters, Primitivism and Decadence, pp. 4-5. Also In Defense of
Reason, pp. 19-20.
      Rpt. in part The Critic's Notebook, pp. 250-252.

_____. "The Swimmers"
Perrine and Reid, 100 American Poems, pp. 183-184.

Alan Williamson, "Allen Tate and the Personal Epic," SoR, 12 (Oct., 1976),
727.

_____. "Winter Mask"
Radcliffe Squires, "Allen Tate: A Season at Monteagle," MQR, 10 (Winter,
1971), 61-62.

_____. "The Wolves"
Richmond C. Beatty, "Allen Tate as a Man of Letters," SAQ, 47 (April,
1948), 232.

Richard J. O'Dea, "Allen Tate's Vestigial Morality," The Personalist, 49
(Spring, 1968), 256-262.

_____. "Breathing"
Robert Hass, "A Review of James Tate's Absences," OhR, 14 (Winter, 1973),
90-92.

_____. "Men get down on their knees"
Robert Hass, "A Review of James Tate's Absences," OhR, 14 (Winter, 1973),
88-89.

TAYLOR. "The Accusation of the Inward Man" (from God's Determinations)
      Sidney E. Lind, "Edward Taylor: A Revaluation," NEQ, 21 (Dec., 1948),
      525-527.

_____. "An Address to the Soul Occasioned by a Rain"
      Willie T. Weathers, "Edward Taylor, Hellenistic Puritan," AL, 18 (March,
      1946), 24-25.

_____. "The Ebb and Flow"
      Raymond J. Jordan, Expl, 20 (April, 1962), 67.
          Rpt. The Explicator Cyclopedia, II, pp. 327-328.

_____. "The Experience"
W. C. Brown, "Edward Taylor: An American 'Metaphysical,'" AL, 16 (Nov.,
1944), 191, 196–197.

_____. "The Glory of and Grace in the Church Set Out'
G. Giovannini, Expl, 6 (Feb., 1948), 26.
    Rpt. The Explicator Cyclopedia, II, pp. 328–329.

_____. "God's Determinations"
Michael J. Colacurcio, "God's Determinations Touching Half-Way Member-
ship: Occasion and Audience in Edward Taylor," AL, 39 (Nov., 1967),
298–314.

Evan Prosser, "Edward Taylor's Poetry," NEQ, 40 (Sept., 1967), 392–398.

Jean L. Thomas, "Drama and Doctrine in 'Gods Determinations,'" AL, 36
(Jan., 1965), 452–462.

Austin Warren, "Edward Taylor's Poetry: Colonial Baroque," The Kenyon
Review, 3 (Summer, 1941), 362–365.

Warren, Rage for Order, pp. 8–12.

_____. "Huswifery"
Anonymous, "More Than Enough There," TLS, Nov. 6, 1959, p. xiv.

Norman S. Grabo, "Edward Taylor's Spiritual Huswifery," PMLA, 89 (Dec.,
1964), 554–560.

John Higby, Expl, 30 (March, 1972), 60.

_____. "Meditation 1.1: What Love is This of Thine, That Cannot Be"
W. C. Brown, "Edward Taylor: An American 'Metaphysical,'" AL, 16
(Nov., 1944), 194–195.

Allen Richard Penner, "Edward Taylor's 'Meditation One,'" AL, 39 (May,
1967), 193–199.

_____. "Meditation 1.3: How Sweet a Lord Is Mine?"
Joel R. Kehler, "Physiology and Metaphor in Edward Taylor's 'Meditation.
Can. I.3,'" EAL, 9 (Winter, 1975), 315–320.

_____. "Meditation 1.6: Am I Thy Gold? Or Purse, Lord, for Thy Wealth;"
Kent Bales and William J. Aull, "Touching Taylor Overly: A Note on
'Meditation Six,'" EAL, 5 (Fall, 1970), 57–59.

William K. Bottorff, "Edward Taylor, an Explication: Another Meditation
at the Same Time," EAL, 3 (Spring, 1968), 17–21.

Norman S. Grabo, Expl, 18 (April, 1960), 40.
    Rpt. The Explicator Cyclopedia, II, pp. 331–332.

Anne Marie McNamara, Expl, 17 (Oct., 1958), 3.
    Rpt. The Explicator Cyclopedia, II, pp. 330–331.

Roy Harvey Pearce, "Edward Taylor: The Poet as Puritan," NEQ, 23
(March, 1950), 34–35.

Donald E. Stanford, "Edward Taylor," in Major Writers of Early American
Literature, ed. Everett Emerson (Madison, Wisconsin: Univ. of Wisconsin
Press, 1972), pp. 77–79.

_____. "Meditation 1.8: I Kenning Through Astronomy Divine"
Gerhard T. Alexis, Expl, 24 (May, 1966), 77.

George Monteiro, Expl, 27 (Feb., 1969), 45.

Roy Harvey Pearce, "Edward Taylor: The Poet as Puritan," NEQ, 23 (March, 1950), 44-45.

Austin Warren, "Edward Taylor's Poetry: Colonial Baroque," The Kenyon Review, 3 (Summer, 1941), 365-368.

Warren, Rage for Order, pp. 12-16.

_____. "Meditation 1.28: When I, Lord, Send Some Bits of Glory Home"
W. C. Brown, "Edward Taylor: An American 'Metaphysical,'" AL, 16 (Nov., 1944), 192-193.

_____. "Meditation 1.29: My Shattred Phancy Stole Away From Mee"
Ursula Brumm, "The 'Tree of Life' in Edward Taylor's Meditations," EAL, 3 (Fall, 1968), 74-80.

Cecilia L. Halbert, "Tree of Life Imagery in the Poetry of Edward Taylor," AL, 38 (March, 1966), 25-27.

_____. "Meditation 1.30: The Daintiest Draught Thy Pensill Ever Drew"
Cecilia L. Halbert, "Tree of Life Imagery in the Poetry of Edward Taylor," AL, 38 (March, 1966), 31-52.

_____. "Meditation 1.32: Thy Grace, Deare Lord's My Golden Wrack, I Finde"
Martz, The Poem of the Mind, pp. 60-62.

_____. "Meditation 1.33: My Lord, My Life, Can Envy Ever Be"
W. C. Brown, "Edward Taylor: An American 'Metaphysical,'" AL, 16 (Nov., 1944), 193.

_____. "Meditation 1.34: My Lord I Fain Would Praise Thee Well But Finde"
Evan Prosser, "Edward Taylor's Poetry," NEQ, 40 (Sept., 1967), 387-388.

_____. "Meditation 1.39: My Sin! My Sin, My God, These Cursed Dregs"
William J. Scheick, "'The Inward Tacles and the Outward Traces': Edward Taylor's Elusive Transitions," EAL, 12 (Fall, 1977), 164-169.

_____. "Meditation 1.40: Still I Complain; I Am Complaining Still"
Robert D. Arner, "Folk Metaphors in Edward Taylor's 'Meditation 1.40,'" SCN, 31 (Spring, 1973), 6-9.

_____. "Meditation 1.42: Apples of Gold, in Silver Pictures Shrin'de"
Sr. M. Laurentia C.J.S., Expl, 8 (Dec., 1949), 19.
    Rpt. The Explicator Cyclopedia, II, p. 329.

_____. "Meditation 2.1: Oh Leaden Heeld. Lord, Give, Forgive I Pray"
Robert E. Reiter, "Edward Taylor's Preparatory Meditations, Second Series, Numbers 1-30," EAL, 5 (Spring, 1970), 113-114.

_____. "Meditation 2.3: Like to the Marigold, I Blushing Close"
Robert E. Reiter, "Edward Taylor's Preparatory Meditations, Second Series, Numbers 1-30," EAL, 5 (Spring, 1970), 115-116.

William J. Scheick, "'The Inward Tacles and the Outward Traces': Edward Taylor's Elusive Transitions," EAL, 12 (Fall, 1977), 169-173.

_____. "Meditation 2.7: All Dull, My Lord, My Spirits Flat, and Dead"
Robert E. Reiter, "Edward Taylor's Preparatory Meditations, Second Series, Numbers 1-30," EAL, 5 (Spring, 1970), 116-118.

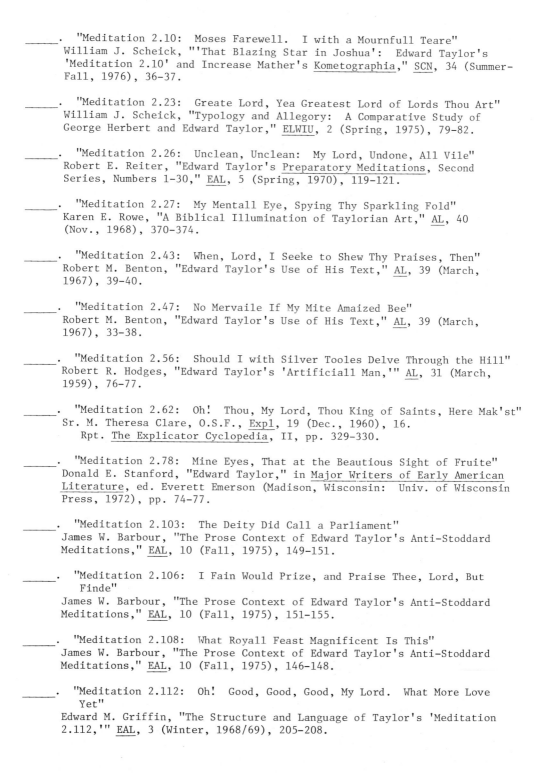

_____. "Meditation 2.10: Moses Farewell. I with a Mournfull Teare"
William J. Scheick, "'That Blazing Star in Joshua': Edward Taylor's
'Meditation 2.10' and Increase Mather's Kometographia," SCN, 34 (Summer-
Fall, 1976), 36-37.

_____. "Meditation 2.23: Greate Lord, Yea Greatest Lord of Lords Thou Art"
William J. Scheick, "Typology and Allegory: A Comparative Study of
George Herbert and Edward Taylor," ELWIU, 2 (Spring, 1975), 79-82.

_____. "Meditation 2.26: Unclean, Unclean: My Lord, Undone, All Vile"
Robert E. Reiter, "Edward Taylor's Preparatory Meditations, Second
Series, Numbers 1-30," EAL, 5 (Spring, 1970), 119-121.

_____. "Meditation 2.27: My Mentall Eye, Spying Thy Sparkling Fold"
Karen E. Rowe, "A Biblical Illumination of Taylorian Art," AL, 40
(Nov., 1968), 370-374.

_____. "Meditation 2.43: When, Lord, I Seeke to Shew Thy Praises, Then"
Robert M. Benton, "Edward Taylor's Use of His Text," AL, 39 (March,
1967), 39-40.

_____. "Meditation 2.47: No Mervaile If My Mite Amaized Bee"
Robert M. Benton, "Edward Taylor's Use of His Text," AL, 39 (March,
1967), 33-38.

_____. "Meditation 2.56: Should I with Silver Tooles Delve Through the Hill"
Robert R. Hodges, "Edward Taylor's 'Artificiall Man,'" AL, 31 (March,
1959), 76-77.

_____. "Meditation 2.62: Oh! Thou, My Lord, Thou King of Saints, Here Mak'st"
Sr. M. Theresa Clare, O.S.F., Expl, 19 (Dec., 1960), 16.
   Rpt. The Explicator Cyclopedia, II, pp. 329-330.

_____. "Meditation 2.78: Mine Eyes, That at the Beautious Sight of Fruite"
Donald E. Stanford, "Edward Taylor," in Major Writers of Early American
Literature, ed. Everett Emerson (Madison, Wisconsin: Univ. of Wisconsin
Press, 1972), pp. 74-77.

_____. "Meditation 2.103: The Deity Did Call a Parliament"
James W. Barbour, "The Prose Context of Edward Taylor's Anti-Stoddard
Meditations," EAL, 10 (Fall, 1975), 149-151.

_____. "Meditation 2.106: I Fain Would Prize, and Praise Thee, Lord, But
   Finde"
James W. Barbour, "The Prose Context of Edward Taylor's Anti-Stoddard
Meditations," EAL, 10 (Fall, 1975), 151-155.

_____. "Meditation 2.108: What Royall Feast Magnificent Is This"
James W. Barbour, "The Prose Context of Edward Taylor's Anti-Stoddard
Meditations," EAL, 10 (Fall, 1975), 146-148.

_____. "Meditation 2.112: Oh! Good, Good, Good, My Lord. What More Love
   Yet"
Edward M. Griffin, "The Structure and Language of Taylor's 'Meditation
2.112,'" EAL, 3 (Winter, 1968/69), 205-208.

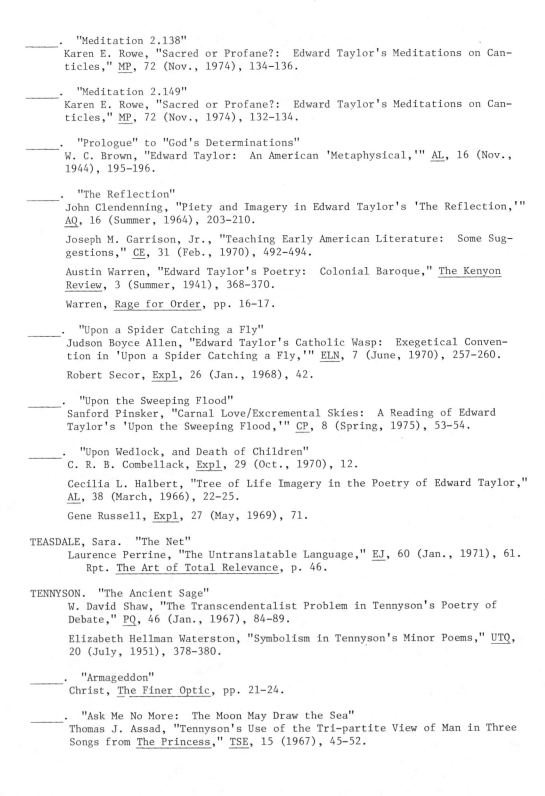

_____. "Meditation 2.138"
Karen E. Rowe, "Sacred or Profane?: Edward Taylor's Meditations on Can-
ticles," MP, 72 (Nov., 1974), 134-136.

_____. "Meditation 2.149"
Karen E. Rowe, "Sacred or Profane?: Edward Taylor's Meditations on Can-
ticles," MP, 72 (Nov., 1974), 132-134.

_____. "Prologue" to "God's Determinations"
W. C. Brown, "Edward Taylor: An American 'Metaphysical,'" AL, 16 (Nov.,
1944), 195-196.

_____. "The Reflection"
John Clendenning, "Piety and Imagery in Edward Taylor's 'The Reflection,'"
AQ, 16 (Summer, 1964), 203-210.

Joseph M. Garrison, Jr., "Teaching Early American Literature: Some Suggestions," CE, 31 (Feb., 1970), 492-494.

Austin Warren, "Edward Taylor's Poetry: Colonial Baroque," The Kenyon
Review, 3 (Summer, 1941), 368-370.

Warren, Rage for Order, pp. 16-17.

_____. "Upon a Spider Catching a Fly"
Judson Boyce Allen, "Edward Taylor's Catholic Wasp: Exegetical Convention in 'Upon a Spider Catching a Fly,'" ELN, 7 (June, 1970), 257-260.

Robert Secor, Expl, 26 (Jan., 1968), 42.

_____. "Upon the Sweeping Flood"
Sanford Pinsker, "Carnal Love/Excremental Skies: A Reading of Edward
Taylor's 'Upon the Sweeping Flood,'" CP, 8 (Spring, 1975), 53-54.

_____. "Upon Wedlock, and Death of Children"
C. R. B. Combellack, Expl, 29 (Oct., 1970), 12.

Cecilia L. Halbert, "Tree of Life Imagery in the Poetry of Edward Taylor,"
AL, 38 (March, 1966), 22-25.

Gene Russell, Expl, 27 (May, 1969), 71.

TEASDALE, Sara. "The Net"
Laurence Perrine, "The Untranslatable Language," EJ, 60 (Jan., 1971), 61.
        Rpt. The Art of Total Relevance, p. 46.

TENNYSON. "The Ancient Sage"
W. David Shaw, "The Transcendentalist Problem in Tennyson's Poetry of
Debate," PQ, 46 (Jan., 1967), 84-89.

Elizabeth Hellman Waterston, "Symbolism in Tennyson's Minor Poems," UTQ,
20 (July, 1951), 378-380.

_____. "Armageddon"
Christ, The Finer Optic, pp. 21-24.

_____. "Ask Me No More: The Moon May Draw the Sea"
Thomas J. Assad, "Tennyson's Use of the Tri-partite View of Man in Three
Songs from The Princess," TSE, 15 (1967), 45-52.

_____. "Aylmer's Field"
Thomas J. Assad, "On the Major Poems of Tennyson's 'Enoch Arden' Volume,"
TSE, 14 (1965), 40-44.

_____. "Break, Break, Break"
Abad, A Formal Approach to Lyric Poetry, pp. 321-322, 326-327.

Thomas J. Assad, "Tennyson's 'Break, Break, Break,'" TSE, 12 (1967), 71-
80.

Brooks, The Well Wrought Urn, pp. 160-162.

Daiches and Charvat, Poems in English, pp. 712-713.

Daniels, The Art of Reading Poetry, p. 272.

Bert G. Hornback, "Tennyson's 'Break, Break, Break' Again," VN, No. 3
(Spring, 1968), 47-48.

Kreuzer, Elements of Poetry, pp. 41-43.

O'Connor, Sense and Sensibility in Modern Poetry, pp. 151-152.

Phyllis Rackin, "Recent Misreadings of 'Break, Break, Break' and their
implications for Poetic Theory," JEGP, 65 (April, 1966), 217-228.

_____. "Bugle Song"
Thomas J. Assad, "Tennyson's Use of the Tri-partite View of Man in Three
Songs from The Princess," TSE, 15 (1967), 35-45.

Brooks, Purser, and Warren, An Approach to Literature, pp. 458-459.
     Rpt. third edition, pp. 311-312.
     Rpt. fourth edition, p. 308

_____. "The Coming of Arthur"
J. M. Gray, "The Purpose of an Epic List in 'The Coming of Arthur,'" VP,
8 (Winter, 1970), 339-341.

_____. "Courage, Poor Heart of Stone" (from Maud, sect. III, Pt. II)
Thomas J. Assad, "Tennyson's 'Courage, Poor Heart of Stone,'" TSE, 18
(1970), 73-80.

_____. "Crossing the Bar"
Thomas J. Assad, "Analogy in Tennyson's 'Crossing the Bar,'" TSE, 8
(1958), 153-164.

Paull F. Baum, "Crossing the Bar," ELN, 1 (Dec., 1963), 115-116.

Lord Dunsany, "The Food of Imagination," Poetry Review, 41 (July-Aug.,
1950), 197-198.

John Tyree Fain and G. Geoffrey Langsam, Expl, 10 (April, 1952), 40.
     Rpt. The Explicator Cyclopedia, II, pp. 334-335.

Frederick L. Jones, Expl, 19 (Dec., 1951), 19.
     Rpt. The Explicator Cyclopedia, II, pp. 332-334.

James R. Kincaid, "Tennyson's 'Crossing the Bar': A Poem of Frustration,"
VP, 3 (Winter, 1965), 57-61.

Dale Kramer, "Metaphor and Meaning in 'Crossing the Bar,'" BSUF, 10 (Summer, 1969), 44-47.

Milton Millhauser, "Structure and Symbol in 'Crossing the Bar,'" VP, 4
(Winter, 1966), 34-39.

Laurence Perrine, "The Poetry and the Pulpit," SWR, 69 (Spring, 1974), 113-123.
> Rpt. The Art of Total Relevance, pp. 138-139.

✝ Laurence Perrine, "When Does Hope Mean Doubt?: The Tone of 'Crossing the Bar,'" VP, 4 (Spring, 1966), 127-131.

Harry W. Rudman, Expl, 8 (April, 1950), 45.
> Rpt. The Explicator Cyclopedia, II, p. 332.

David Sonstroem, "'Crossing the Bar' as Last Word," VP, 8 (Spring, 1970), 55-60.

_____. "The Defence of Lucknow"
Baker, Syntax in English Poetry, 1870-1930, pp. 43-45.

_____. "Demeter and Persephone"
Curtis Dahl, "A Double Frame for Tennyson's Demeter?" VS, 1 (June, 1958), 356-362.

Christine Gallant, "Tennyson's Use of the Nature Goddess in 'The Hesperides,' 'Tithonus,' and 'Demeter and Persephone,'" VP, 14 (Summer, 1976), 158-160.

Gerhard Joseph, "Tennyson's Death in Life in Lyric and Myth," VN, No. 34 (Fall, 1968), 15-18.

G. Robert Strange, "Tennyson's Mythology: A Study of Demeter and Persephone," ELH, 21 (March, 1954), 67-80.

_____. "A Dream of Fair Women"
Arthur J. Carr, "Tennyson as a Modern Poet," UTQ, 19 (July, 1950), 368-369.

Clyde de L. Ryals, "The 'Fatal Woman' Symbol in Tennyson," PMLA, 74 (Sept., 1959), 441.

_____. "The Eagle"
Brooks, Purser, and Warren, An Approach to Literature, pp. 447-448.
> Rpt. third edition, pp. 302-303.
> Rpt. fourth edition, pp. 301-303.

Sanders, The Discovery of Poetry, p. 158.

_____. "Eleanore"
Clyde de L. Ryals, "The 'Fatal Woman' Symbol in Tennyson," PMLA, 74 (Sept., 1959), 439.

_____. "The Epic"
J. S. Lawry, "Tennyson's 'The Epic': A Gesture of Recovered Faith," MLN, 74 (May, 1959), 400-404.

_____. "A Farewell"
Thomas J. Assad, "Time and Eternity: Tennyson's 'The Farewell' and 'In the Valley of Cauteretz,'" TSE, 17 (1969), 96-102.

_____. "The Grandmother"
Thomas J. Assad, "On the Major Poems of Tennyson's 'Enoch Arden' Volume," TSE, 14 (1965), 34-36.

_____. "The Hesperides"
Christine Gallant, "Tennyson's Use of the Nature Goddess in 'The Hesperides,' 'Tithonus,' and 'Demeter and Persephone,'" VP, 14 (Summer, 1976), 156-158.

Ernest Fontana, "Virginal Hysteria in Tennyson's The Hesperides," CP, 8 (Fall, 1975), 17-20.

James D. Merriam, "The Poet as Heroic Thief: Tennyson's 'The Hesperides' Re-Examined," VN, No. 35 (Spring, 1969), 25.

G. Robert Strange, "Tennyson's Garden of Art: A Study of The Hesperides," PMLA, 67 (Sept., 1952), 732-743.

R. B. Wilkenfeld, "The Shape of Two Voices," VP, 4 (Summer, 1966), 166-167.

_____. "In Memoriam"
Winston Collins, "Tennyson and Hopkins," UTQ, 38 (Oct., 1968), 92-95.

J. C. C. Mays, "In Memoriam': An Aspect of Form," UTQ, 35 (Oct., 1965), 22-46.

Carlisle Moore, "Faith, Doubt, and Mystical Experience in 'In Memoriam,'" VS, 7 (Dec., 1963), 155-169.

W. David Shaw, "The Transcendentalist Problem in Tennyson's Poetry of Debate," PQ, 46 (Jan., 1967), 89-93.

Marvel Shmiefsky, "'In Memoriam': Its Seasonal Imagery Reconsidered," SEL, 7 (Autumn, 1967), 721-740.

Martin Svaglic, "A Framework for Tennyson's In Memoriam," JEGP, 61 (Oct., 1962), 810-825.

James G. Taafe, "Circle Imagery in Tennyson's In Memoriam," VP, 1 (Summer, 1963), 123-131.

_____. "In Memoriam, 'Prologue'"
Daniel D. Moews, "The 'Prologue' to In Memoriam: A Commentary on Lines 5, 17, and 32," VP, 6 (Summer, 1968), 185-187.

_____. "In Memoriam, 7: Dark House, By Which Once More I Stand"
Francis P. Devlin, "Dramatic Irony in the Early Sections of Tennyson's In Memoriam," PLL, 8 (Spring, 1972), 178.

_____. "In Memoriam, 9: Fair Ship, That From the Italian Shore"
Francis P. Devlin, "Dramatic Irony in the Early Sections of Tennyson's In Memoriam," PLL, 8 (Spring, 1972), 175-176.

_____. "In Memoriam, 11: Calm Is the Morn Without a Sound"
Brower, The Fields of Light, pp. 34-35.

Ben W. Fuson, Expl, 4 (March, 1946), 34.
   Rpt. The Explicator Cyclopedia, II, pp. 335-336.

Riding and Graves, A Survey of Modernist Poetry, p. 49.

_____. "In Memoriam, 12: Lo, As a Dove When Up She Springs"
Francis P. Devlin, "Dramatic Irony in the Early Sections of Tennyson's In Memoriam," PLL, 8 (Spring, 1972), 177-178.

_____. "In Memoriam, 14: If One Should Bring Me This Report"
W. David Shaw, "In Memoriam and the Rhetoric of Confession," ELH, 38 (March, 1971), 86-87.

_____. "In Memoriam, 15: Tonight the Winds Begin to Rise"
Beaty and Matchett, Poetry: From Statement to Meaning, pp. 294-296.

Raymond G. Malbone, Expl, 35 (Spring, 1977), 6-8.

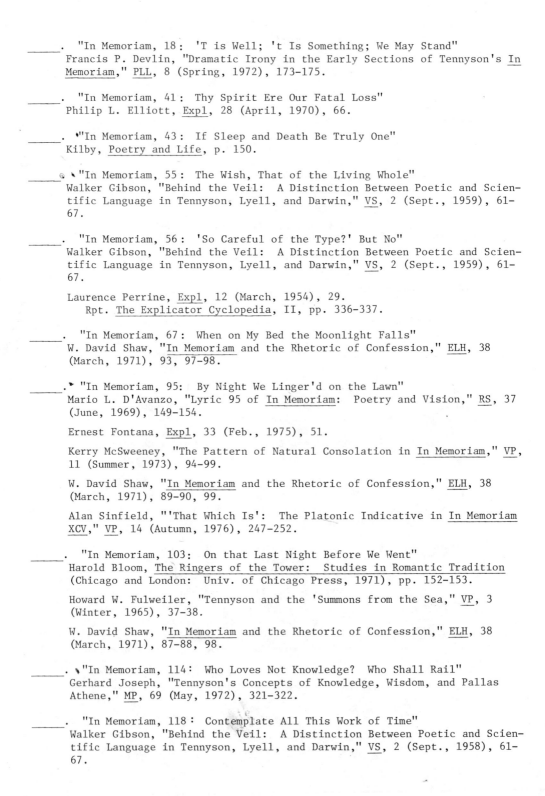

_____. "In Memoriam, 18: 'T is Well; 't Is Something; We May Stand"
Francis P. Devlin, "Dramatic Irony in the Early Sections of Tennyson's In Memoriam," PLL, 8 (Spring, 1972), 173-175.

_____. "In Memoriam, 41: Thy Spirit Ere Our Fatal Loss"
Philip L. Elliott, Expl, 28 (April, 1970), 66.

_____. "In Memoriam, 43: If Sleep and Death Be Truly One"
Kilby, Poetry and Life, p. 150.

_____. "In Memoriam, 55: The Wish, That of the Living Whole"
Walker Gibson, "Behind the Veil: A Distinction Between Poetic and Scientific Language in Tennyson, Lyell, and Darwin," VS, 2 (Sept., 1959), 61-67.

_____. "In Memoriam, 56: 'So Careful of the Type?' But No"
Walker Gibson, "Behind the Veil: A Distinction Between Poetic and Scientific Language in Tennyson, Lyell, and Darwin," VS, 2 (Sept., 1959), 61-67.

Laurence Perrine, Expl, 12 (March, 1954), 29.
    Rpt. The Explicator Cyclopedia, II, pp. 336-337.

_____. "In Memoriam, 67: When on My Bed the Moonlight Falls"
W. David Shaw, "In Memoriam and the Rhetoric of Confession," ELH, 38 (March, 1971), 93, 97-98.

_____. "In Memoriam, 95: By Night We Linger'd on the Lawn"
Mario L. D'Avanzo, "Lyric 95 of In Memoriam: Poetry and Vision," RS, 37 (June, 1969), 149-154.

Ernest Fontana, Expl, 33 (Feb., 1975), 51.

Kerry McSweeney, "The Pattern of Natural Consolation in In Memoriam," VP, 11 (Summer, 1973), 94-99.

W. David Shaw, "In Memoriam and the Rhetoric of Confession," ELH, 38 (March, 1971), 89-90, 99.

Alan Sinfield, "'That Which Is': The Platonic Indicative in In Memoriam XCV," VP, 14 (Autumn, 1976), 247-252.

_____. "In Memoriam, 103: On that Last Night Before We Went"
Harold Bloom, The Ringers of the Tower: Studies in Romantic Tradition (Chicago and London: Univ. of Chicago Press, 1971), pp. 152-153.

Howard W. Fulweiler, "Tennyson and the 'Summons from the Sea," VP, 3 (Winter, 1965), 37-38.

W. David Shaw, "In Memoriam and the Rhetoric of Confession," ELH, 38 (March, 1971), 87-88, 98.

_____. "In Memoriam, 114: Who Loves Not Knowledge? Who Shall Rail"
Gerhard Joseph, "Tennyson's Concepts of Knowledge, Wisdom, and Pallas Athene," MP, 69 (May, 1972), 321-322.

_____. "In Memoriam, 118: Contemplate All This Work of Time"
Walker Gibson, "Behind the Veil: A Distinction Between Poetic and Scientific Language in Tennyson, Lyell, and Darwin," VS, 2 (Sept., 1958), 61-67.

_____. "In Memoriam, 121: Sad Hesper O'er the Buried Sun"
John D. Boyd, "In Memoriam, Section CXXI," VP, 14 (Summer, 1976), 161-164.

Francis P. Devlin, "Dramatic Irony in the Early Sections of Tennyson's In Memoriam," PLL, 8 (Spring, 1972), 182-183.

Kerry McSweeney, "The Pattern of Natural Consolation in In Memoriam," VP, 11 (Summer, 1973), 93-94.

_____. "In Memoriam, 122: O, Wast Thou with Me, Dearest, Then,"
Walker Gibson, "Behind the Veil: A Distinction Between Poetic and Scientific Language in Tennyson, Lyell, and Darwin," VS, 2 (Sept., 1958), 61-67.

_____. "In Memoriam, 123: There Rolls the Deep Where Grew the Tree"
W. David Shaw, "Consolation and Catharsis in In Memoriam," MLQ, 37 (March, 1976), 61-63.

_____. "In Memoriam, 130: Thy Voice Is on the Rolling Air"
Louise D. Wiggins, "Tennyson's Veiled Status," ES, 49 (Oct., 1968), 444-445.

_____. "In Memoriam, 131: O Living Will that Shalt Endure"
George P. Landow, "Moses Striking the Rock: Typological Symbolism in Victorian Poetry," in Literary Uses of Typology from the Late Middle Ages to the Present, pp. 335-336.

_____. "In the Valley of Cauteretz"
Thomas J. Assad, "Time and Eternity: Tennyson's 'The Farewell' and 'In the Valley of Cauteretz,'" TSE, 17 (1969), 105-111.

_____. "The Kraken"
James Donald Welch, "Tennyson's Landscapes of Time and a Reading of 'The Kraken,'" VP, 14 (Autumn, 1976), 201-204.

_____. "Lady Clara Vere de Vere"
Clyde de L. Ryals, "The 'Fatal Woman' Symbol in Tennyson," PMLA, 74 (Sept., 1959), 440.

_____. "The Lady of Shalott"
Flavia M. Alaya, "Tennyson's 'The Lady of Shalott': The Triumph of Art," VP, 8 (Winter, 1970), 273-289.

June Steffenson Hagen, "Reality and Reflection in "The Lady of Shalott,'" AN&Q, 14 (Sept., 1975), 7-8.

James L. Hill, "Tennyson's 'The Lady of Shalott': The Ambiguity of Commitment," CentR, 12 (Fall, 1968), 415-429.

Johnson, The Alien Vision of Victorian Poetry, p. 9.

David M. Martin, "Romantic Perspectivism in Tennyson's 'The Lady of Shalott,'" VP, 11 (Autumn, 1973), 255-256.

Lona Mosk Packer, "Sun and Shadow: The Nature of Experience in Tennyson's 'The Lady of Shalott,'" VN, No. 25 (Spring, 1964), 4-8.

Lionel Stevenson, "Tennyson, Browning, and a Romantic Fallacy," UTQ, 13 (Jan., 1944), 184.

Richard C. Tobias, "Tennyson's Painted Shell," VN, No. 39 (Spring, 1971), 7-10.

Elizabeth H. Waterston, "Symbolism in Tennyson's Minor Poems," UTQ, 20 (July, 1951), 375-376.

R. B. Wilkenfeld, "The Shape of Two Voices," VP, 4 (Summer, 1966), 163-173.

_____. "Locksley Hall"
E. C. Bufkin, "Imagery in 'Locksley Hall,'" VP, 2 (Spring, 1964), 21-28.

June Steffensen Hagen, "The 'Crescent Promise' of 'Locksley Hall': A Crisis in Poetic Creativity," VP, 11 (Summer, 1973), 169-171.

Kaplan, Miracles of Rare Device, pp. 62-77.

F. E. L. Priestley, "Locksley Hall Revisited," QQ, 81 (Winter, 1974), 512-524.

_____. "Locksley Hall-Sixty Years After"
F. E. L. Priestley, "Locksley Hall Revisited," QQ, 81 (Winter, 1974), 524-532.

_____. "The Lotus-Eaters"
Alan Grob, "Tennyson's 'The Lotus-Eaters': Two Versions of Art," MP, 62 (Nov., 1964), 118-129.

Johnson, The Alien Vision of Victorian Poetry, pp. 9-10.

James R. Kincaid, "Rhetorical Irony, the Dramatic Monologue, and Tennyson's Poems (1842)," PQ, 52 (April, 1974), 224-227.

James R. Kincaid, "Tennyson's Mariners and Spenser's Despair: The Argument of 'The Lotos-Eaters,'" PLL, 5 (Summer, 1969), 273-281.

R. B. Wilkenfeld, "The Shape of Two Voices," VP, 4 (Summer, 1966), 168-170.

_____. "Lucretius"
James A. Freeman, "Tennyson, 'Lucretius,' and the 'Breasts of Helen,'" VP, 11 (Spring, 1973), 69-75.

Johnson, The Alien Vision of Victorian Poetry, pp. 31-34.

W. David Shaw, "Imagination and Intellect in Tennyson's 'Lucretius,'" MLQ, 33 (June, 1972), 130-139.

_____. "Mariana"
Bloom, Poetry and Repression, pp. 149-155.

Christ, The Finer Optic, pp. 18-20, 24.

_____. "Mariana in the South"
Elizabeth H. Waterston, "Symbolism in Tennyson's Minor Poems," UTQ, 20 (July, 1951), 376.

_____. "Merlin and the Gleam"
Gordon S. Haight, "Tennyson's Merlin," SP, 44 (July, 1947), 560-566.

_____. "Move Eastward, Happy Earth, and Leave"
James Donald Welch, "Tennyson's Landscapes of Time and a Reading of 'The Kraken,'" VP, 14 (Autumn, 1976), 199.

_____. "Northern Farmer: New Style"
Thomas J. Assad, "On the Major Poems of Tennyson's 'Enoch Arden' Volume,"
TSE, 14 (1965), 31-34.

_____. "Now Sleeps the Crimson Petal, Now the White"
Thomas J. Assad, "Tennyson's Use of the Tripartite View of Man in Three
Songs from The Princess," TSE, 15 (1967), 52-58.

_____. "Ode: O Basky Brook"
Andrew Fichter, "Ode and Elegy: Idea and Form in Tennyson's Early
Poetry," ELH, 40 (Fall, 1973), 408-410.

_____. "Ode to Memory"
Andrew Fichter, "Ode and Elegy: Idea and Form in Tennyson's Early
Poetry," ELH, 40 (Fall, 1973), 406-408.

_____. "Ode on the Death of the Duke of Wellington"
Margery Stricker Durham, "Tennyson's Wellington Ode and the Cosmology of
Love," VP, 14 (Winter, 1976), 277-292

_____. "Oenone"
Arthur J. Carr, "Tennyson as a Modern Poet," UTQ, 19 (July, 1950), 371.

Gerhard Joseph, "Tennyson's Concepts of Knowledge, Wisdom, and Pallas
Athene," MP, 69 (May, 1972), 317-318.

James R. Kincaid, "Rhetorical Irony, the Dramatic Monologue, and Tennyson's Poems (1842)," PQ, 52 (April, 1974), 222-224.

Paul Turner, "Some Ancient Light on Tennyson's 'Oenone,'" JEGP, 61
(Jan., 1962), 57-72.

James Walton, "Tennyson's Patrimony: From 'The Outcast' to 'Mud,'" TSLL,
11 (Spring, 1969), 746-747.

Elizabeth H. Waterston, "Symbolism in Tennyson's Minor Poems," UTQ, 20
(July, 1951), 376.

_____. "On a Mourner"
Sir Charles Tennyson, "The Dream in Tennyson's Poetry," VQR, 40 (Spring,
1964), 244-246.

_____. "The Palace of Art"
Andy P. Antippas, "Tennyson's Sinful Soul: Poetic Tradition and 'Keats
Turned Imbecile,'" TSE, 17 (1969), 113-134.

John Britton, Expl, 20 (Oct., 1961), 17.
    Rpt. The Explicator Cyclopedia, II, p. 337.

William Cadbury, "Tennyson's 'The Palace of Art' and the Rhetoric of
Structures," Criticism, 7 (Winter, 1965), 23-44.

A. C. Howell, "Tennyson's 'Palace of Art'--An Interpretation," SP, 33
(July, 1936), 507-522.

Clyde de L. Ryals, "The 'Fatal Woman' Symbol in Tennyson," PMLA, 74
(Sept., 1959), 440-441.

Joseph Sendry, "'The Palace of Art' Revisited," VP, 4 (Summer, 1966),
149-162.

Lionel Stevenson, "Tennyson, Browning, and a Romantic Fallacy," UTQ, 13
(Jan., 1944), 182-184.

Elizabeth H. Waterston, "Symbolism in Tennyson's Minor Poems," UTQ, 20 (July, 1951), 376-377.

_____. "The Poet"
T. O. Mabbott, Expl, 3 (Oct., 1944), 9.
   Rpt. The Explicator Cyclopedia, II, p. 339.

W. D. Paden, Expl, 2 (June, 1944), 56.
   Rpt. The Explicator Cyclopedia, II, pp. 337-339.

_____. "The Poet's Mind"
Thomas J. Assad, "Time and Eternity: Tennyson's 'The Farewell' and 'In the Valley of Cauteretz,'" TSE, 17 (1969), 94-95.

_____. "The Poet's Song"
Thomas J. Assad, "Time and Eternity: Tennyson's 'The Farewell' and 'In the Valley of Cauteretz,'" TSE, 17 (1969), 93-96.

_____. "The Progress of Spring"
Andrew Fichter, "Ode and Elegy: Idea and Form in Tennyson's Early Poetry," ELH, 40 (Fall, 1973), 410-412.

_____. "Recollections of the Arabian Nights"
Brian John, "Tennyson's 'Recollections of the Arabian Nights' and the Individuation Process," VP, 4 (Autumn, 1966), 275-279.

_____. "Sea Dreams"
Thomas J. Assad, "On the Major Poems of Tennyson's 'Enoch Arden' Volume," TSE, 14 (1965), 36-40.

_____. "The Sea-Fairies"
R. B. Wilkenfeld, "The Shape of Two Voices," VP, 4 (Summer, 1966), 167-168.

_____. "Sir Galahad"
George Arms, "'Childe Roland' and 'Sir Galahad,'" CE, 6 (Feb., 1945), 258-262.

Mary J. Donahue, "The Revision of Tennyson's Sir Galahad," PQ, 18 (April, 326-329.

_____. "A Spirit Haunts the Year's Last Hours"
R. B. Wilkenfeld, "The Shape of Two Voices," VP, 4 (Summer, 1966), 163-165.

_____. "The Splendor Falls on Castle Walls"
Daiches and Charvat, Poems in English, p. 713.

_____. "St. Simeon Stylites"
William E. Fredeman, "'A Sign Betwixt the Meadow and the Cloud': The Ironic Apotheosis of Tennyson's St. Simeon Stylites," UTQ, 38 (Oct., 1968), 69-80.

James R. Kincaid, "Rhetorical Irony, the Dramatic Monologue, and Tennyson's Poems (1842)," PQ, 52 (April, 1974), 234-236.

_____. "Sweet and Low"
Satin, Reading Poetry, pp. 1050-1051.

_____. "Tears, Idle Tears"
Thomas J. Assad, "Tennyson's 'Tears, Idle Tears,'" TSE, 13 (1963), 71-83.

Bateson, English Poetry, pp. 225-233.

Bloom, Poetry and Repression, pp. 161-163.

Cleanth Brooks, "The New Criticism: A Brief for the Defense," ASch, 13 (Summer, 1944), 286-293.

Brooks, The Well Wrought Urn, pp. 153-162.
    Rpt. Readings for Liberal Education, II, 122-126. Abridged in The Case for Poetry, p. 355.
    Rpt. Locke, Gibson, and Arms, Introduction to Literature, third edition, pp. 125-129.
    Rpt. fourth edition, pp. 124-128.

William Empson, "Thy Darling in an Urn," SR, 55 (Autumn, 1947), 691-692.

Graham Hough, "'Tears, Idle Tears,'" The Hopkins Review, 4 (Spring, 1951), 31-36.

Gerhard Joseph, "Tennyson's Death in Life in Lyric and Myth," VN, No. 34 (Fall, 1968), 13-15.

F. R. Leavis, "'Thought' and Emotional Quality," Scrutiny, 13 (Spring, 1945), 59.

John Crowe Ransom, "The Tense of Poetry," SoR, 1 (Autumn, 1935), 221-222.

Ransom, The World's Body, pp. 233-234.

Leo Spitzer, "'Tears, Idle Tears' Again," The Hopkins Review, 5 (Spring, 1952), 71-80.
    Rpt. Essays on English and American Literature by Leo Spitzer, pp. 37-50.

Fred H. Stocking, Expl, 5 (June, 1947), 54. Abridged in The Case for Poetry, p. 355.
    Rpt. The Explicator Cyclopedia, II, pp. 339-340.

Edward P. Vandiver, Jr., Expl, 21 (March, 1963), 53.

W. K. Wimsatt, Jr. and M. C. Beardsley, "The Affective Fallacy," SR, 57 (Winter, 1949), 46-47.

Herbert G. Wright, "Tennyson and Wales," Essays and Studies, 14 (1928), 75.

_____. "Timbuctoo"
Andrew Fichter, "Ode and Elegy: Idea and Form in Tennyson's Early Poetry," ELH, 40 (Fall, 1973), 404-406.

_____. "Time: An Ode"
Andrew Fichter, "Ode and Elegy: Idea and Form in Tennyson's Early Poetry," ELH, 40 (Fall, 1973), 403-404.

_____. "Tiresias"
Gerhard Joseph, "Tennyson's Concepts of Knowledge, Wisdom, and Pallas Athene," MP, 69 (May, 1972), 319-321.

_____. "Tithonus"
Bloom, Poetry and Repression, pp. 163-168.

Mary J. Donahue, "Tennyson's Hail, Briton! and Tithon in the Heath Manuscript," PMLA, 64 (June, 1949), 400-415.

Douglas, Lamson, and Smith, The Critical Reader, pp. 96–100. Revised edition, pp. 720–724.

Christine Gallant, "Tennyson's Use of the Nature Goddess in 'The Hesperides,' 'Tithonus,' and 'Demeter and Persephone,'" VP, 14 (Summer, 1976), 158.

James R. Kincaid, "Rhetorical Irony, the Dramatic Monologue, and Tennyson's Poems (1842)," PQ, 52 (April, 1974), 232–234.

Phyllis Rackin, "Tennyson's Art that Conceals Itself," CEA, 28 (Jan., 1966), 9–10.

Ribner and Morris, Poetry, pp. 336–337.

W. David Shaw, "Tennyson's 'Tithonus' and the Problem of Mortality," PQ, 52 (April, 1973), 274–285.

Arthur L. Simpson, Jr., "Aurora as Artist: A Reinterpretation of Tennyson's Tithonus," PQ, 51 (Oct., 1972), 905–921.

Carl Robinson Sonn, "Poetic Vision and Religious Certainty in Tennyson's Earlier Poetry," MP, 57 (Nov., 1959), 88–90.

Arthur D. Ward, "'Ulysses' and 'Tithonus': Tunnel-Vision and Idle Tears," VP, 12 (Autumn, 1974), 311–319.

_____. "To E. L., On His Travels in Greece"
Hugh Kenner, "Some Post-Symbolist Structures," in Literary Theory and Structure: Essays in Honor of William K. Wimsatt, ed. Frank Brady, John Palmer, and Martin Price (New Haven: Yale Univ. Press, 1973), pp. 380–382.

_____. "The Two Voices"
William R. Brashear, "Tennyson's Third Voice: A Note," VP, 2 (Winter, 1964), 283–286.

Wendell Stacy Johnson, Sex and Marriage in Victorian Poetry (Ithaca and London: Cornell Univ. Press, 1975), pp. 119–124.

Wendell S. Johnson, "Some Functions of Poetic Form," JAAC, 13 (June, 1955), 504.

W. David Shaw, "The Transcendentalist Problem in Tennyson's Poetry of Debate," PQ, 46 (Jan., 1967), 80–84.

_____. "Ulysses"
Roy P. Basler and William Frost, Expl, 4 (May, 1946), 48.
    Rpt. The Explicator Cyclopedia, II, pp. 341–342.

Harold Bloom, A Map of Misreading, pp. 156–159.

E. J. Chaisson, "Tennyson's 'Ulysses'--A Reinterpretation," UTQ, 23 (July, 1954), 402–409.

A. Dwight Culler, "Monodrama and the Dramatic Monologue," PMLA, 90 (May, 1975), 382–383.

Edgar Hill Duncan, "Tennyson: A Modern Appraisal," TSL, 4 (1959), 17–28.

William Frost, Expl, 4 (May, 1946), 48.
    Rpt. The Explicator Cyclopedia, II, p. 387.

Howard W. Fulweiler, "Tennyson and the 'Summons from the Sea,'" VP, 3 (Winter, 1965), 34–35.

Royal A. Gettmann and John Robert Moore, Expl, 1 (Feb., 1943), 33.
  Rpt. The Explicator Cyclopedia, II, p. 342.

Jay L. Halio, "Prothalamion,' 'Ulysses,' and Intention in Poetry," CE,
22 (March, 1961), 392-394.

Willis D. Jacobs, "Tennyson's 'Ulysses,'" Rocky Mountain Modern Language
Association Bulletin, 4 (Oct., 1951), 4.

Gerhard Joseph, "Tennyson's Concepts of Knowledge, Wisdom, and Pallas
Athene," MP, 69 (May, 1972), 315-317.

James P. Kincaid, "Rhetorical Irony, the Dramatic Monologue, and Tennyson's Poems (1842)," PQ, 52 (April, 1974), 227-232.

Langbaum, The Poetry of Experience, pp. 90-92.

B. J. Leggett, "Dante, Byron, and Tennyson's Ulysses," TSL, 15 (1970),
143-159.

George O. Marshall, Jr., Expl, 21 (Feb., 1963), 50.

Charles Mitchell, "The Undying Will of Tennyson's 'Ulysses,'" VP, 2
(Summer, 1964), 87-95.

Perrine, Sound and Sense, pp. 172-174.

John Pettigrew, "Tennyson's 'Ulysses': A Reconciliation of Opposites,"
VP, 1 (Spring, 1963), 27-45.

Tony Robbins, "Tennyson's 'Ulysses': The Significance of the Homeric and
Dantesque Backgrounds," VP, 11 (Autumn, 1973), 177-193.

R. Roppen, "'Ulysses' and Tennyson's Sea-Quest," ES, 40 (April, 1959),
77-90.

Carl Robinson Sonn, "Poetic Vision and Religious Certainty in Tennyson's
Earlier Poetry," MP, 57 (Nov., 1959), 87-88.

Charles C. Walcutt, Expl, 4 (Feb., 1946), 28.
  Rpt. The Explicator Cyclopedia, II, pp. 340-341.

Arthur D. Ward, "'Ulysses' and 'Tithonus': Tunnel-Vision and Idle Tears,"
VP, 12 (Autumn, 1974), 311-319.

_____. "Vastness"
Winston Collins, "Tennyson and Hopkins," UTQ, 38 (Oct., 1968), 84-87.

THOMAS, Dylan. "After the Funeral (In Memory of Ann Jones)"
  Daiches and Charvat, Poems in English, pp. 744-745.

Day Lewis, The Poetic Image, pp. 123-125.

Deutsch, Poetry in Our Time, p. 342.

Friar and Brinnin, Modern Poetry, p. 541.

Graham Dunstan Martin, Language, Truth, and Poetry: Notes towards a
Philosophy of Literature (Edinburgh: Edinburgh Univ. Press, 1975),
pp. 85-86.

Myron Ochshorn, "The Love Song of Dylan Thomas," New Mexico Quarterly
Review, 24 (Spring, 1954), 51.

Robert S. Phillips, "Death and Resurrection: Tradition in Thomas's
'After the Funeral,'" McNR, 15 (Sept., 1964), 3-10.

Schneider, <u>Poems and Poetry</u>, pp. 455-457.

Marshall W. Stearns, <u>Expl</u>, 3 (May, 1945), 52.
   Rpt. <u>The Explicator Cyclopedia</u>, I, pp. 300-301.
   Rpt. Engle and Carrier, <u>Reading Modern Poetry</u>, pp. 313-314.

_____. "All All and All the Dry Worlds Lever"
Jacob Korg, "Imagery and Universe in Dylan Thomas's '18 Poems,'" <u>Accent</u>,
22 (Winter, 1957), 12-15.

_____. "Altar-Wise by Owl Light"
Monroe C. Beardsley and Sam Hynes, "Misunderstanding Poetry: Notes on
Some Readings of Dylan Thomas," <u>CE</u>, 21 (March, 1960), 315-322.

Erhardt H. Essig, <u>Expl</u>, 16 (June, 1958), 53.
   Rpt. <u>The Explicator Cyclopedia</u>, I, pp. 323-325.

W. Nelson Francis, "Syntax and Literary Interpretation," in <u>Essays on the
Language of Literature</u>, ed. Seymour Chatman and Samuel R. Levin (Boston:
Houghton Mifflin Company, 1967), pp. 211-216.

Brewster Ghiselin, "The Extravagant Energy of Genius," <u>The Western Review</u>,
18 (Spring, 1954), 248.

M. E. Grenander, "Sonnet V from Dylan Thomas' 'Altarwise by Owl-Light'
Sequence," <u>N&Q</u>, 5 (June, 1958), 263.

Bernard Knieger, "Dylan Thomas: The Christianity of the 'Altarwise by
Owl-Light' Sequence," <u>CE</u>, 23 (May, 1962), 623-628.

Bernard Knieger, <u>Expl</u>, 15 (Dec., 1956), 18.
   Rpt. <u>The Explicator Cyclopedia</u>, I, pp. 322-323, 325-327.

D. F. McKay, "Aspects of Energy in the Poetry of Dylan Thomas and Sylvia
Plath," <u>CritQ</u>, 16 (Spring, 1974), 59-60.

Ralph N. Maud, <u>Expl</u>, 14 (Dec., 1955), 16.
   Rpt. <u>The Explicator Cyclopedia</u>, I, pp. 321-322.

Schlauch, <u>Modern English and American Poetry</u>, pp. 84-85.

_____. "Among Those Killed in the Dawn Raid Was a Man Aged a Hundred"
Phyllis Bartlett, <u>Expl</u>, 12 (Dec., 1953), 21.
   Rpt. <u>The Explicator Cyclopedia</u>, I, p. 301.

Elmer L. Brooks, <u>Expl</u>, 12 (June, 1954), 49.
   Rpt. <u>The Explicator Cyclopedia</u>, I, pp. 301-302.

_____. "Author's Prologue"
David Middleton, <u>Expl</u>, 34 (Oct., 1975), 12.

_____. "The Ballad of the Long-Legged Bait"
Richard A. Condon, <u>Expl</u>, 16 (March, 1958), 37.
   Rpt. <u>The Explicator Cyclopedia</u>, I, pp. 303-304.

Suzanne Ferguson, "Fishing the Deep Sea: Archetypal Patterns in Thomas'
'Ballad of the Long-Legged Bait,'" <u>MPS</u>, 6 (Autumn, 1975), 102-114.

William T. Moynihan, "Dylan Thomas and the 'Biblical Rhythm,'" <u>PMLA</u>, 79
(Dec., 1964), 641-642.

A. Richmond Neuville, <u>Expl</u>, 23 (Feb., 1965), 43.

Elder Olson, "The Poetry of Dylan Thomas," <u>Poetry</u>, 83 (Jan., 1954), 214-
215.

Lee J. Richmond, <u>Expl</u>, 23 (Feb., 1965), 43.

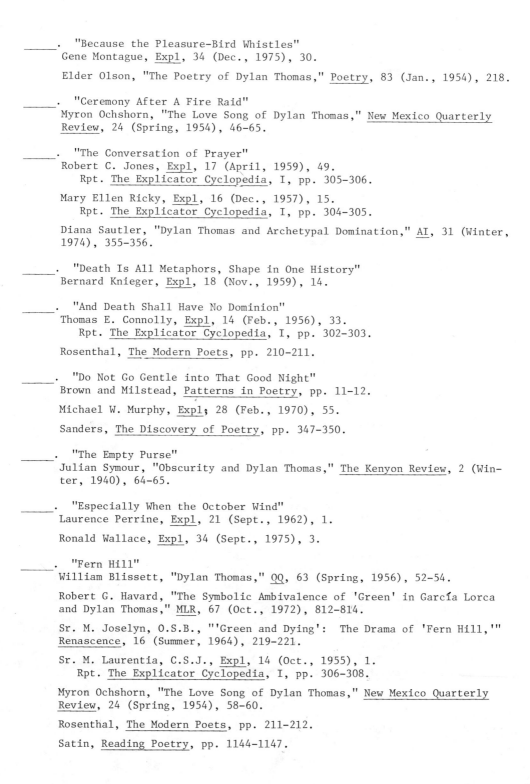

_____. "Because the Pleasure-Bird Whistles"
Gene Montague, Expl, 34 (Dec., 1975), 30.

Elder Olson, "The Poetry of Dylan Thomas," Poetry, 83 (Jan., 1954), 218.

_____. "Ceremony After A Fire Raid"
Myron Ochshorn, "The Love Song of Dylan Thomas," New Mexico Quarterly
Review, 24 (Spring, 1954), 46-65.

_____. "The Conversation of Prayer"
Robert C. Jones, Expl, 17 (April, 1959), 49.
    Rpt. The Explicator Cyclopedia, I, pp. 305-306.

Mary Ellen Ricky, Expl, 16 (Dec., 1957), 15.
    Rpt. The Explicator Cyclopedia, I, pp. 304-305.

Diana Sautler, "Dylan Thomas and Archetypal Domination," AI, 31 (Winter,
1974), 355-356.

_____. "Death Is All Metaphors, Shape in One History"
Bernard Knieger, Expl, 18 (Nov., 1959), 14.

_____. "And Death Shall Have No Dominion"
Thomas E. Connolly, Expl, 14 (Feb., 1956), 33.
    Rpt. The Explicator Cyclopedia, I, pp. 302-303.

Rosenthal, The Modern Poets, pp. 210-211.

_____. "Do Not Go Gentle into That Good Night"
Brown and Milstead, Patterns in Poetry, pp. 11-12.

Michael W. Murphy, Expl, 28 (Feb., 1970), 55.

Sanders, The Discovery of Poetry, pp. 347-350.

_____. "The Empty Purse"
Julian Symour, "Obscurity and Dylan Thomas," The Kenyon Review, 2 (Winter, 1940), 64-65.

_____. "Especially When the October Wind"
Laurence Perrine, Expl, 21 (Sept., 1962), 1.

Ronald Wallace, Expl, 34 (Sept., 1975), 3.

_____. "Fern Hill"
William Blissett, "Dylan Thomas," QQ, 63 (Spring, 1956), 52-54.

Robert G. Havard, "The Symbolic Ambivalence of 'Green' in García Lorca
and Dylan Thomas," MLR, 67 (Oct., 1972), 812-814.

Sr. M. Joselyn, O.S.B., "'Green and Dying': The Drama of 'Fern Hill,'"
Renascence, 16 (Summer, 1964), 219-221.

Sr. M. Laurentia, C.S.J., Expl, 14 (Oct., 1955), 1.
    Rpt. The Explicator Cyclopedia, I, pp. 306-308.

Myron Ochshorn, "The Love Song of Dylan Thomas," New Mexico Quarterly
Review, 24 (Spring, 1954), 58-60.

Rosenthal, The Modern Poets, pp. 211-212.

Satin, Reading Poetry, pp. 1144-1147.

_____. "First There Was the Lamb of Knocking Knees"
Bernard Knieger, Expl, 18 (Jan., 1960), 25.
    Rpt. The Explicator Cyclopedia, I, PP. 326-327.

_____. "The Force That Through the Green Fuse Drives the Flower"
Bloom, Philbrick, and Blistein, The Order of Poetry, pp. 60-62.

Drew, Poetry: A Modern Guide, pp. 181-183.

Frankenberg, Pleasure Dome, pp. 318-319.

G. Giovannini, Expl, 8 (June, 1950), 59.
    Rpt. Locke, Gibson, and Arms, Introduction to Literature, third
    edition, pp. 260-263.
    Rpt. fourth edition, pp. 253-254.
    Rpt. The Explicator Cyclopedia, I, pp. 308-309.

Jerome, Poetry: Premeditated Art, pp. 49-50.

S. F. Johnson, Expl, 8 (June, 1950), 60.
    Rpt. Locke, Gibson, and Arms, Introduction to Literature, fourth
    edition, pp. 254-256.
    Rpt. The Explicator Cyclopedia, I, pp. 309-310.

S. F. Johnson, Expl, 10 (Feb., 1952), 26.
    Rpt. The Explicator Cyclopedia, I, p. 310.

Myron Ochshorn, "The Love Song of Dylan Thomas," New Mexico Quarterly
Review, 24 (Spring, 1954), 51-53.

Peter F. Parshall, Expl, 29 (April, 1971), 65.

Rosenthal, The Modern Poets, pp. 209-210.

_____. "From Love's First Fever to Her Plague"
Sam Hynes, Expl, 9 (Dec., 1950), 18.
    Rpt. The Explicator Cyclopedia, I, pp. 311-312.

Diana Sautler, "Dylan Thomas and Archetypal Domination," AI, 31 (Winter,
1974), 347-348.

_____. "Hold Hard, These Ancient Minutes in the Cuckoo's Month"
Howard Nemerov, "The Generation of Violence," The Kenyon Review, 15
(Summer, 1953), 478-480.

_____. "How Soon the Servant Sun"
Max Halpern, Expl, 23 (April, 1965), 65.

_____. "The Hunchback in the Park"
Sr. Helena Brand, SNJM, "Structure Signals in 'The Hunchback in the
Park,'" EJ, 59 (Feb., 1970), 195-200.

Deutsch, Poetry in Our Time, pp. 340-341.

S. F. Johnson, Expl, 10 (Feb., 1952), 27.
    Rpt. The Explicator Cyclopedia, I, p. 312.

Laurence Perrine, Expl, 20 (Jan., 1962), 45.
    Rpt. The Explicator Cyclopedia, I, pp. 312-313.

_____. "If I Were Tickled by the Rub of Love"
Max Halpern, Expl, 21 (Nov., 1962), 25.

_____. "I in My Intricate Image," or "A Poem in Three Parts"
Alan Young, "Image as Structure: Dylan Thomas and Poetic Meaning,"
CritQ, 17 (Winter, 1975), 333-345.

_____. "In Country Heaven"
William T. Moynihan, "Dylan Thomas and the 'Biblical Rhythm,'" PMLA, 79
(Dec., 1964), 645.

_____. "In Country Sleep"
Helen Bevington, in When Found Make a Verse of (New York: Simon and
Schuster, 1961), pp. 58-60.

Martin E. Gingerich, "The Timeless Narrators of Dylan Thomas' 'In Country
Heaven,'" MPS, 7 (Autumn, 1976), 116-120.

William T. Moynihan, "Dylan Thomas and the 'Biblical Rhythm,'" PMLA, 71
(Dec., 1964), 645-646.

_____. "In My Craft or Sullen Art"
Frankenberg, Invitation to Poetry, pp. 99-101.

Barbara T. Gates, Expl, 32 (May, 1974), 68.

D. R. Howard, Expl, 12 (Feb., 1954), 22.
    Rpt. The Explicator Cyclopedia, I, pp. 313-314.

Rosenthal, The Modern Poets, pp. 203-240.

Patricia Meyer Spacks, Expl, 18 (Dec., 1959), 21.
    Rpt. The Explicator Cyclopedia, I, pp. 314-315.

_____. "In the Beginning Was the Three-Pointed Star"
Diana Sautler, "Dylan Thomas and Archetypal Domination," AI, 31 (Winter,
1974), 346-347.

_____. "In the White Giant's Thigh"
Marlene Chambers, Expl, 19 (Oct., 1960), 1.
    Rpt. The Explicator Cyclopedia, I, pp. 316-317.

Marlene Chambers, Expl, 19 (March, 1961), 39.
    Rpt. The Explicator Cyclopedia, I, pp. 317-318.

Martin E. Gingerich, "The Timeless Narrators of Dylan Thomas' 'In Country
Heaven,'" MPS, 7 (Autumn, 1976), 113-116.

William T. Moynihan, "Dylan Thomas and the 'Biblical Rhythm,'" PMLA, 79
(Dec., 1964), 646-647.

William T. Moynihan, Expl, 17 (May, 1959), 59.
    Rpt. The Explicator Cyclopedia, I, pp. 315-316.

Robert R. Singleton, Expl, 31 (Jan., 1973), 34.

_____. "I See the Boys of Summer"
Brewster Ghislein, "The Extravagant Energy of Genius," The Western Review, 18 (Spring, 1954), 246.

Rob Jackaman, "Man and Mandala: Symbol as Structure in a Poem by Dylan
Thomas," ArielE, 7 (Oct., 1976), 22-23.

Myron Ochshorn, "The Love Song of Dylan Thomas," New Mexico Quarterly
Review, 24 (Spring, 1954), 47-49.

_____. "Light Breaks Where No Sun Shines"
Bernard Knieger, Expl, 15 (Feb., 1957), 32.
    Rpt. The Explicator Cyclopedia, I, p. 318.

William T. Moynihan, Expl, 16 (Feb., 1958), 28.
    Rpt. The Explicator Cyclopedia, I, pp. 318-319.

Marshall W. Stearns, "Unsex the Skeleton," SR, 52 (July-Sept., 1944),
435-440.

_____. "Love in the Asylum"
Brewster Ghiselin, "Use of a Mango," Rocky Mountain Review, 8 (Spring,
1944), 112.

Bernard Knieger, Expl, 20 (Oct., 1961), 13.
    Rpt. The Explicator Cyclopedia, I, 319-320.

Diana Sautler, "Dylan Thomas and Archetypal Domination," AI, 31 (Winter,
1974), 351-352.

_____. "The Map of Love: No. 4"
Henry Gibson, "A Comment," The Critic, 1 (Autumn, 1947), 20.

Edith Sitwell, "Comment on Dylan Thomas," The Critic, 1 (Autumn, 1947),
18.

_____. "O Make Me a Mask"
Olga de Hart Darvill, Expl, 26 (Oct., 1967), 12.

_____. "On the Marriage of a Virgin"
Daiches and Charvat, Poems in English, p. 745.

Brewster Ghiselin, "The Extravagant Energy of Genius," The Western Review,
18 (Spring, 1954), 249.

S. F. Johnson, Expl, 10 (Feb., 1952), 27.
    Rpt. The Explicator Cyclopedia, I, p. 312.

Bernard Knieger, Expl, 19 (May, 1961), 61.
    Rpt. The Explicator Cyclopedia, I, p. 320.

Diana Sautler, "Dylan Thomas and Archetypal Domination," AI, 31 (Winter,
1974), 352.

_____. "Our Eunuch Dreams"
A. J. Smith, "Ambiguity or Poetic Shift," CritQ, 4 (Spring, 1962), 68-74.

_____. "Out of the Sighs"
Diana Sautler, "Dylan Thomas and Archetypal Domination," AI, 31 (Winter,
1974), 354-355.

_____. "Over Sir John's Hill"
Chatman, Introduction to the Language of Poetry, pp. 80-83.

Martin E. Gingerich, "The Timeless Narrators of Dylan Thomas' 'In Country
Heaven,'" MPS, 7 (Autumn, 1976), 111-112.

William T. Moynihan, "Dylan Thomas and the 'Biblical Rhythm,'" PMLA, 79
(Dec., 1964), 646.

David Ormerod, "The Central Image in Dylan Thomas' 'Over Sir John's Hill,'"
ES, 49 (Oct., 1968), 449-450.

Carroll F. Terrell, Expl, 35 (Fall, 1977), 24-26.

_____. "Poem 40: Twenty-Four Years Remind the Tears of My Eyes"
Andrews Wanning, "Criticism and Principles: Poetry of the Quarter, SoR,
6 (Spring, 1941), 806-809.

_____. "Poem in October"
David Daiches, "The Poetry of Dylan Thomas," CE, 16 (Oct., 1954), 7.
  Rpt. EJ, 43 (Oct., 1954), 355.

Deutsch, Poetry in Our Time, pp. 332-333.

Sr. M. Roberta Jones, O.S.R., "The Well-spring of Dylan," EJ, 55 (Jan., 1966), 78-79.

Laurence Perrine, Expl, 27 (Feb., 1969), 43.

_____. "A Refusal to Mourn the Death, by Fire, of a Child in London"
John A. Clair, Expl, 17 (Dec., 1958), 25.
  Rpt. The Explicator Cyclopedia, I, pp. 320-321.

David Daiches, "The Poetry of Dylan Thomas," CE, 16 (Oct., 1954), 3-5.
  Rpt. EJ, 43 (Oct., 1954), 351-352.

William Virgil Davis, "Several Comments on 'A Refusal to Mourn the Death, by Fire, of a Child in London,'" CP, 2 (Fall, 1969), 45-48.

Deutsch, Poetry in Our Time, pp. 335-337.

Henry Gibson, "A Comment," The Critic, 1 (Autumn, 1947), 19-20.

Br. Benilde Montgomery, O.S.F., "The Function of Ambiguity in 'A Refusal to Mourn the Death, by Fire, of a Child in London,'" CP, 8 (Fall, 1975), 77-81.

Rosenthal, The Modern Poets, pp. 215-216.

Edith Sitwell, "Comment on Dylan Thomas," The Critic, 1 (Autumn, 1947), 18.

Edith Sitwell, "Dylan Thomas," The Atlantic Monthly, 193 (Feb., 1954), 44-45.

Edith Sitwell, "The Love of Man, the Praise of God," Herald Tribune Book Review, 29 (May 10, 1953), 14.

Paula Sunderman, "Dylan Thomas' 'A Refusal to Mourn': A Syntactic and Semantic Interpretation," Lang&S, 7 (Winter, 1974), 20-35.

_____. "This Bread I Break"
Geoffrey Leech, "'This Bread I Break,'--Language and Interpretation," A Review of English Literature (Leeds), 6 (April, 1965), 66-75.

_____. "This Was the Crucifixion on the Mountain"
D. F. McKay, "Aspects of Energy in the Poetry of Dylan Thomas and Sylvia Plath," CritQ, 16 (Spring, 1974), 58-59.

Marshall W. Stearns, "Unsex the Skeleton: Notes on the Poetry of Dylan Thomas," SR, 52 (July-Sept., 1944), 430-433.

_____. "To-day, This Insect"
Bill Casey, Expl, 17 (March, 1959), 43.
  Rpt. The Explicator Cyclopedia, I, pp. 327-328.

Gene Montague, Expl, 19 (Dec., 1960), 15.
  Rpt. The Explicator Cyclopedia, I, pp. 328-329.

William T. Moynihan, "Dylan Thomas and the 'Biblical Rhythm,'" PMLA, 79 (Dec., 1964), 639.

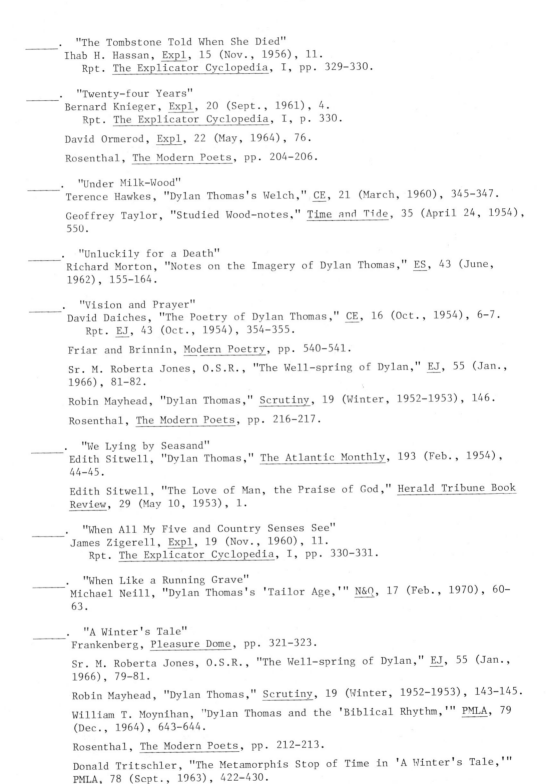

_____. "The Tombstone Told When She Died"
Ihab H. Hassan, Expl, 15 (Nov., 1956), 11.
    Rpt. The Explicator Cyclopedia, I, pp. 329-330.

_____. "Twenty-four Years"
Bernard Knieger, Expl, 20 (Sept., 1961), 4.
    Rpt. The Explicator Cyclopedia, I, p. 330.

David Ormerod, Expl, 22 (May, 1964), 76.

Rosenthal, The Modern Poets, pp. 204-206.

_____. "Under Milk-Wood"
Terence Hawkes, "Dylan Thomas's Welch," CE, 21 (March, 1960), 345-347.

Geoffrey Taylor, "Studied Wood-notes," Time and Tide, 35 (April 24, 1954),
550.

_____. "Unluckily for a Death"
Richard Morton, "Notes on the Imagery of Dylan Thomas," ES, 43 (June,
1962), 155-164.

_____. "Vision and Prayer"
David Daiches, "The Poetry of Dylan Thomas," CE, 16 (Oct., 1954), 6-7.
    Rpt. EJ, 43 (Oct., 1954), 354-355.

Friar and Brinnin, Modern Poetry, pp. 540-541.

Sr. M. Roberta Jones, O.S.R., "The Well-spring of Dylan," EJ, 55 (Jan.,
1966), 81-82.

Robin Mayhead, "Dylan Thomas," Scrutiny, 19 (Winter, 1952-1953), 146.

Rosenthal, The Modern Poets, pp. 216-217.

_____. "We Lying by Seasand"
Edith Sitwell, "Dylan Thomas," The Atlantic Monthly, 193 (Feb., 1954),
44-45.

Edith Sitwell, "The Love of Man, the Praise of God," Herald Tribune Book
Review, 29 (May 10, 1953), 1.

_____. "When All My Five and Country Senses See"
James Zigerell, Expl, 19 (Nov., 1960), 11.
    Rpt. The Explicator Cyclopedia, I, pp. 330-331.

_____. "When Like a Running Grave"
Michael Neill, "Dylan Thomas's 'Tailor Age,'" N&Q, 17 (Feb., 1970), 60-
63.

_____. "A Winter's Tale"
Frankenberg, Pleasure Dome, pp. 321-323.

Sr. M. Roberta Jones, O.S.R., "The Well-spring of Dylan," EJ, 55 (Jan.,
1966), 79-81.

Robin Mayhead, "Dylan Thomas," Scrutiny, 19 (Winter, 1952-1953), 143-145.

William T. Moynihan, "Dylan Thomas and the 'Biblical Rhythm,'" PMLA, 79
(Dec., 1964), 643-644.

Rosenthal, The Modern Poets, pp. 212-213.

Donald Tritschler, "The Metamorphis Stop of Time in 'A Winter's Tale,'"
PMLA, 78 (Sept., 1963), 422-430.

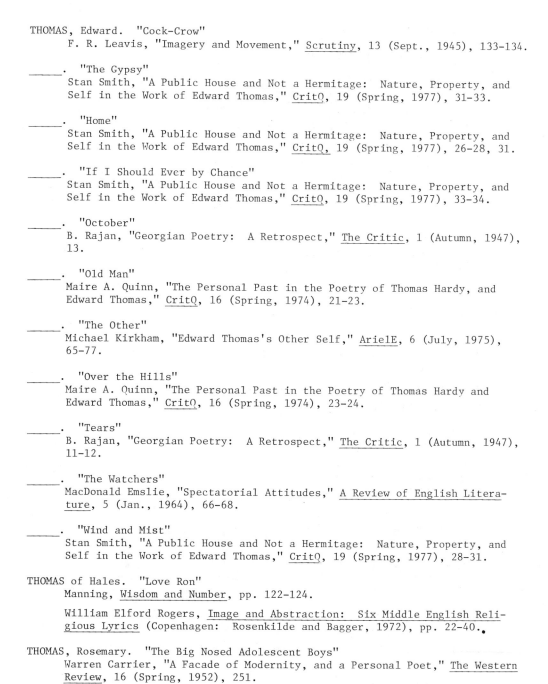

THOMAS, Edward. "Cock-Crow"
    F. R. Leavis, "Imagery and Movement," Scrutiny, 13 (Sept., 1945), 133-134.

_____. "The Gypsy"
    Stan Smith, "A Public House and Not a Hermitage: Nature, Property, and
    Self in the Work of Edward Thomas," CritQ, 19 (Spring, 1977), 31-33.

_____. "Home"
    Stan Smith, "A Public House and Not a Hermitage: Nature, Property, and
    Self in the Work of Edward Thomas," CritQ, 19 (Spring, 1977), 26-28, 31.

_____. "If I Should Ever by Chance"
    Stan Smith, "A Public House and Not a Hermitage: Nature, Property, and
    Self in the Work of Edward Thomas," CritQ, 19 (Spring, 1977), 33-34.

_____. "October"
    B. Rajan, "Georgian Poetry: A Retrospect," The Critic, 1 (Autumn, 1947),
    13.

_____. "Old Man"
    Maire A. Quinn, "The Personal Past in the Poetry of Thomas Hardy, and
    Edward Thomas," CritQ, 16 (Spring, 1974), 21-23.

_____. "The Other"
    Michael Kirkham, "Edward Thomas's Other Self," ArielE, 6 (July, 1975),
    65-77.

_____. "Over the Hills"
    Maire A. Quinn, "The Personal Past in the Poetry of Thomas Hardy and
    Edward Thomas," CritQ, 16 (Spring, 1974), 23-24.

_____. "Tears"
    B. Rajan, "Georgian Poetry: A Retrospect," The Critic, 1 (Autumn, 1947),
    11-12.

_____. "The Watchers"
    MacDonald Emslie, "Spectatorial Attitudes," A Review of English Litera-
    ture, 5 (Jan., 1964), 66-68.

_____. "Wind and Mist"
    Stan Smith, "A Public House and Not a Hermitage: Nature, Property, and
    Self in the Work of Edward Thomas," CritQ, 19 (Spring, 1977), 28-31.

THOMAS of Hales. "Love Ron"
    Manning, Wisdom and Number, pp. 122-124.

    William Elford Rogers, Image and Abstraction: Six Middle English Reli-
    gious Lyrics (Copenhagen: Rosenkilde and Bagger, 1972), pp. 22-40.

THOMAS, Rosemary. "The Big Nosed Adolescent Boys"
    Warren Carrier, "A Facade of Modernity, and a Personal Poet," The Western
    Review, 16 (Spring, 1952), 251.

_____. "St. Francis of Assisi"
Warren Carrier, "A Facade of Modernity, and a Personal Poet, The Western
Review, 16 (Spring, 1952), 252.

THOMAS, R. S. "The Labourer"
Laurence Lerner, "An Essay on Pastoral," EIC, 20 (July, 1970), 277-279.

Laurence Lerner, The Uses of Nostalgia: Studies in Pastoral Poetry
(New York: Schocken Books, 1972), pp. 13-15.

THOMPSON, Francis. "Grace of the Way"
Terence L. Connolly, S.J., Expl, 9 (June, 1951), 56.
    Rpt. The Explicator Cyclopedia, I, pp. 332-333.

George G. Williams, Expl, 9 (Nov., 1950), 16.
    Rpt. The Explicator Cyclopedia, I, p. 332.

_____. "The Hound of Heaven"
Brooks and Warren, Understanding Poetry, revised edition, pp. 283-285.

_____. "New Year's Chimes"
W. G. Wilson, "Francis Thompson's Outlook on Science," ContempR, 192
(Nov., 1957), 266.

_____. "The Nineteenth Century"
W. G. Wilson, "Francis Thompson's Outlook on Science," ContempR, 192
(Nov., 1957), 264.

_____. "Sad Semele"
Myrtle Pihlman Pope, Expl, 17 (Feb., 1959), 35.
    Rpt. The Explicator Cyclopedia, I, pp. 333-334.

THOMSON, James (B.V.). "The City of Dreadful Night"
David DeCamp, Expl, 7 (Feb., 1949), 29.
    Rpt. The Explicator Cyclopedia, II, pp. 342-343.

_____. "The Vine"
Tate, Reason in Madness, pp. 66-71.
    Rpt. On the Limits of Poetry, pp. 78-82.
    Rpt. Critiques, pp. 57-60.

Allen Tate, "Tension in Poetry," SoR, 4 (Summer, 1938), 104-108.

THOREAU. "All Things Are Current Found"
Carl Dennis, "Correspondence in Thoreau's Nature Poetry," ESQ, No. 58
(Part 3, 1970), 105.

_____. "The Cliffs & Springs"
Arthur L. Ford, "The Poetry of Henry David Thoreau," ESQ, No. 61 (1970),
18-19.

_____. "It Is No Dream of Mine"
Carl Dennis, "Correspondence in Thoreau's Nature Poetry," ESQ, No. 58
(Part 3, 1970), 107.

_____. "I Was Born Upon Thy Bank River"
Carl Dennis, "Correspondence in Thoreau's Nature Poetry," ESQ, No. 58
(Part 3, 1970), 107.

_____. "Light-winged Smoke"
Carl Dennis, "Correspondence in Thoreau's Nature Poetry," ESQ, No. 58
(Part 3, 1970), 108.

_____. "May Morning"
Douglas V. Noverr, "Thoreau's 'May Morning': Nature, Poetic Vision, and
the Poet's Publication of His Truth," TJQ, 2 (July 15, 1970), 7-10.

_____. "My Boots"
Arthur L. Ford, "The Poetry of Henry David Thoreau," ESQ, No. 61 (1970),
19.

_____. "Poem No. 189"
Mary S. Mattfield, "Thoreau's Poem #189: An Emended Reading," CEA, 33
(Nov., 1970), 10-12.

_____. "The Sluggish Smoke"
Arthur L. Ford, "The Poetry of Henry David Thoreau," ESQ, No. 61 (1970),
16-18.

_____. "Smoke"
Delmer Rodabaugh, Expl, 17 (April, 1959), 47.
    Rpt. The Explicator Cyclopedia, II, pp. 343-344.

_____. "Smoke in the Winter"
Matthiessen, The American Renaissance, pp. 165-166.

TODD, Ruthven. "Rivers: On Living in Brooklyn"
J. F. Nims, Poetry: A Critical Supplement, May, 1948, pp. 18-20.

TOMLINSON. "After a Death"
Evan Watkins, The Critical Act: Criticism and Community (New Haven:
Yale Univ. Press, 1978), 126-129.

TOMLINSON. "At Holwell Farm"
Michael Edwards, "The Poetry of Charles Tomlinson," Agenda, 9 (Spring-
Summer, 1971), 131-132.

_____. "The Dream"
Evan Watkins, The Critical Act: Criticism and Community (New Haven:
Yale Univ. Press, 1978), 124-126.

_____. "Foxes' Moon"
Evan Watkins, The Critical Act: Criticism and Community (New Haven:
Yale Univ. Press, 1978), 122-124.

_____. "In the Fullness of Time"
Evan Watkins, The Critical Act: Criticism and Community (New Haven:
Yale Univ. Press, 1978), 104-107.

_____. "Prometheus"
Evan Watkins, The Critical Act: Criticism and Community (New Haven:
Yale Univ. Press, 1978), 107-115.

_____. "Reflections"
Robert Pinsky, The Situation of Poetry: Contemporary Poetry and Its
Traditions (Princeton, New Jersey: Princeton Univ. Press, 1976),
pp. 90-91.

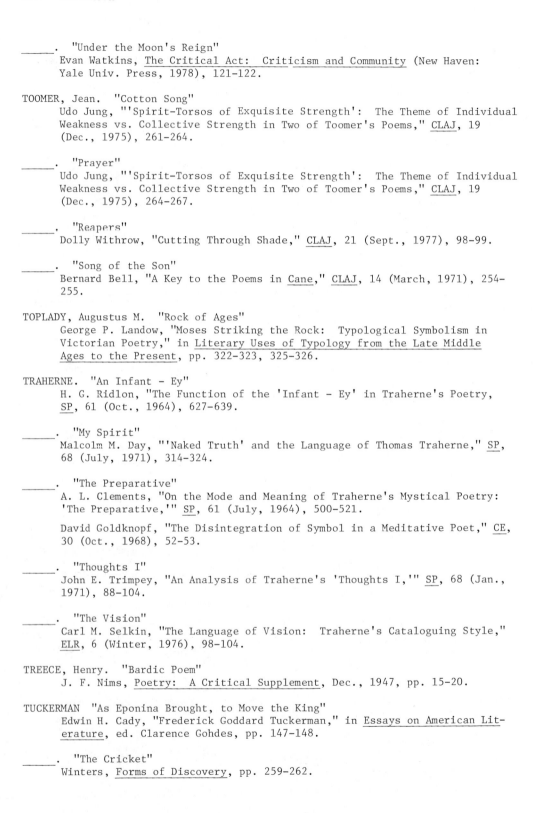

_____. "Under the Moon's Reign"
    Evan Watkins, The Critical Act: Criticism and Community (New Haven:
    Yale Univ. Press, 1978), 121-122.

TOOMER, Jean. "Cotton Song"
    Udo Jung, "'Spirit-Torsos of Exquisite Strength': The Theme of Individual
    Weakness vs. Collective Strength in Two of Toomer's Poems," CLAJ, 19
    (Dec., 1975), 261-264.

_____. "Prayer"
    Udo Jung, "'Spirit-Torsos of Exquisite Strength': The Theme of Individual
    Weakness vs. Collective Strength in Two of Toomer's Poems," CLAJ, 19
    (Dec., 1975), 264-267.

_____. "Reapers"
    Dolly Withrow, "Cutting Through Shade," CLAJ, 21 (Sept., 1977), 98-99.

_____. "Song of the Son"
    Bernard Bell, "A Key to the Poems in Cane," CLAJ, 14 (March, 1971), 254-
    255.

TOPLADY, Augustus M. "Rock of Ages"
    George P. Landow, "Moses Striking the Rock: Typological Symbolism in
    Victorian Poetry," in Literary Uses of Typology from the Late Middle
    Ages to the Present, pp. 322-323, 325-326.

TRAHERNE. "An Infant - Ey"
    H. G. Ridlon, "The Function of the 'Infant - Ey' in Traherne's Poetry,
    SP, 61 (Oct., 1964), 627-639.

_____. "My Spirit"
    Malcolm M. Day, "'Naked Truth' and the Language of Thomas Traherne," SP,
    68 (July, 1971), 314-324.

_____. "The Preparative"
    A. L. Clements, "On the Mode and Meaning of Traherne's Mystical Poetry:
    'The Preparative,'" SP, 61 (July, 1964), 500-521.

    David Goldknopf, "The Disintegration of Symbol in a Meditative Poet," CE,
    30 (Oct., 1968), 52-53.

_____. "Thoughts I"
    John E. Trimpey, "An Analysis of Traherne's 'Thoughts I,'" SP, 68 (Jan.,
    1971), 88-104.

_____. "The Vision"
    Carl M. Selkin, "The Language of Vision: Traherne's Cataloguing Style,"
    ELR, 6 (Winter, 1976), 98-104.

TREECE, Henry. "Bardic Poem"
    J. F. Nims, Poetry: A Critical Supplement, Dec., 1947, pp. 15-20.

TUCKERMAN "As Eponina Brought, to Move the King"
    Edwin H. Cady, "Frederick Goddard Tuckerman," in Essays on American Lit-
    erature, ed. Clarence Gohdes, pp. 147-148.

_____. "The Cricket"
    Winters, Forms of Discovery, pp. 259-262.

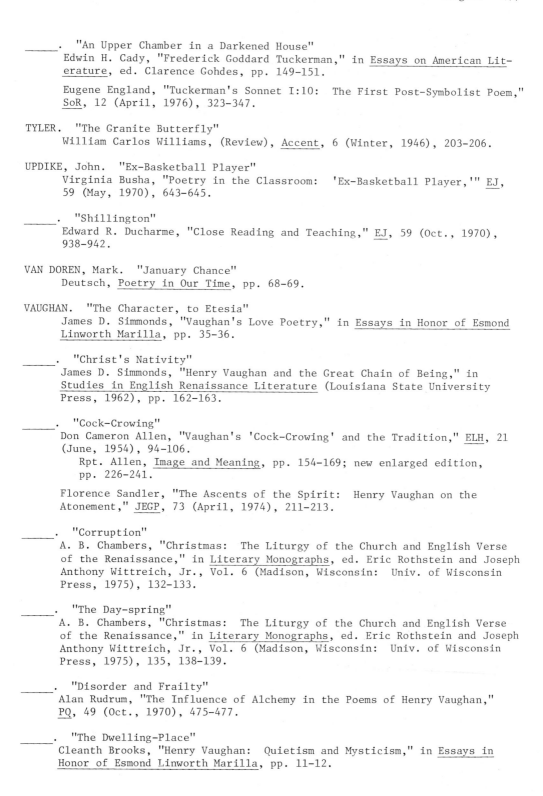

_____. "An Upper Chamber in a Darkened House"
Edwin H. Cady, "Frederick Goddard Tuckerman," in Essays on American Literature, ed. Clarence Gohdes, pp. 149-151.

Eugene England, "Tuckerman's Sonnet I:10: The First Post-Symbolist Poem,"
SoR, 12 (April, 1976), 323-347.

TYLER. "The Granite Butterfly"
William Carlos Williams, (Review), Accent, 6 (Winter, 1946), 203-206.

UPDIKE, John. "Ex-Basketball Player"
Virginia Busha, "Poetry in the Classroom: 'Ex-Basketball Player,'" EJ,
59 (May, 1970), 643-645.

_____. "Shillington"
Edward R. Ducharme, "Close Reading and Teaching," EJ, 59 (Oct., 1970),
938-942.

VAN DOREN, Mark. "January Chance"
Deutsch, Poetry in Our Time, pp. 68-69.

VAUGHAN. "The Character, to Etesia"
James D. Simmonds, "Vaughan's Love Poetry," in Essays in Honor of Esmond
Linworth Marilla, pp. 35-36.

_____. "Christ's Nativity"
James D. Simmonds, "Henry Vaughan and the Great Chain of Being," in
Studies in English Renaissance Literature (Louisiana State University
Press, 1962), pp. 162-163.

_____. "Cock-Crowing"
Don Cameron Allen, "Vaughan's 'Cock-Crowing' and the Tradition," ELH, 21
(June, 1954), 94-106.
     Rpt. Allen, Image and Meaning, pp. 154-169; new enlarged edition,
     pp. 226-241.

Florence Sandler, "The Ascents of the Spirit: Henry Vaughan on the
Atonement," JEGP, 73 (April, 1974), 211-213.

_____. "Corruption"
A. B. Chambers, "Christmas: The Liturgy of the Church and English Verse
of the Renaissance," in Literary Monographs, ed. Eric Rothstein and Joseph
Anthony Wittreich, Jr., Vol. 6 (Madison, Wisconsin: Univ. of Wisconsin
Press, 1975), 132-133.

_____. "The Day-spring"
A. B. Chambers, "Christmas: The Liturgy of the Church and English Verse
of the Renaissance," in Literary Monographs, ed. Eric Rothstein and Joseph
Anthony Wittreich, Jr., Vol. 6 (Madison, Wisconsin: Univ. of Wisconsin
Press, 1975), 135, 138-139.

_____. "Disorder and Frailty"
Alan Rudrum, "The Influence of Alchemy in the Poems of Henry Vaughan,"
PQ, 49 (Oct., 1970), 475-477.

_____. "The Dwelling-Place"
Cleanth Brooks, "Henry Vaughan: Quietism and Mysticism," in Essays in
Honor of Esmond Linworth Marilla, pp. 11-12.

_____. "Etesia Absent"
James D. Simmonds, "Vaughan's Love Poetry," in Essays in Honor of Esmond Linworth Marilla, pp. 38-39.

_____. "FIDA: Or the Country-beauty"
James D. Simmonds, "Vaughan's Love Poetry," in Essays in Honor of Esmond Linworth Marilla, pp. 32-33.

_____. "In Amicum Foeneratorem"
A. U. Chapman, "Henry Vaughan and Magnetic Philosophy," The Southern Review (Australia), No. 3 (1971), 219-220.

_____. "Isaacs Marriage"
Frances M. Malpezzi, "An Approach to Vaughan's 'Isaacs Marriage,'" ELN, 14 (Dec., 1976), 112-117.

_____. "I Walked the Other Day (to Spend My Hour)"
Martz, The Poetry of Meditation, pp. 64-67.

Florence Sandler, "The Ascents of the Spirit: Henry Vaughan on the Atonement," JEGP, 73 (April, 1974), 210-211.

Wanamaker, Discordia Concors, pp. 65-66.

Melissa Cynthia Wanamaker, "Discordia Concors: The Metaphysical Wit of Henry Vaughan's Silex Scintillans," TSLL, 16 (Fall, 1974), 473.

_____. "The Lamp"
Winters, Forms of Discovery, pp. 98-100.

_____. "L'Envoy"
Florence Sandler, "The Ascents of the Spirit: Henry Vaughan on the Atonement," JEGP, 73 (April, 1974), 225-226.

_____. "Man"
Cleanth Brooks, "Henry Vaughan: Quietism and Mysticism," in Essays in Honor of Esmond Linworth Marilla, pp. 6-9.

Kester Svendsen, Expl, 2 (June, 1944), 58.
    Rpt. The Explicator Cyclopedia, II, p. 344.

_____. "Man's Fall and Recovery"
Florence Sandler, "The Ascents of the Spirit: Henry Vaughan on the Atonement," JEGP, 73 (April, 1974), 221-222.

_____. "The Morning-Watch"
Conrad Hilberry, Expl, 14 (April, 1956), 44.
    Rpt. The Explicator Cyclopedia, II, pp. 344-345.

Anthony Low, Expl, 26 (Oct., 1967), 13.

Florence Sandler, "The Ascents of the Spirit: Henry Vaughan on the Atonement," JEGP, 73 (April, 1974), 212-213.

Wanamaker, Discordia Concors, pp. 64-65.

Melissa Cynthia Wanamaker, "Discordia Concors: The Metaphysical Wit of Henry Vaughan's Silex Scintillans," TSLL, 16 (Fall, 1974), 472.

_____. "The Nativity Written in the Year 1656"
A. B. Chambers, "Christmas: The Liturgy of the Church and English Verse of the Renaissance," in Literary Monographs, ed. Eric Rothstein and Joseph Anthony Wittreich, Jr., Vol. 6 (Madison, Wisconsin: Univ. of Wisconsin Press, 1975), 134-135.

_____. "The Night"
Cleanth Brooks, "Henry Vaughan: Quietism and Mysticism," in Essays in Honor of Esmond Linworth Marilla, pp. 19-26.

Leland H. Chambers, "Henry Vaughan's Allusive Technique: Biblical Allusions in 'The Night,'" MLQ, 27 (Dec., 1966), 371-387.

R. A. Durr, "Vaughan's 'The Night,'" JEGP, 59 (Jan., 1960), 34-40.

Fern Farnham, "The Imagery of Henry Vaughan's 'The Night,'" PQ, 38 (Oct., 1959), 425-435.

John J. Pollock, "The Divided Consciousness of Henry Vaughan," PLL, 10 (Fall, 1974), 422-424.

Alan W. Rudrum, "Vaughan's 'The Night': Some Hermetic Notes," MLR, 64 (Jan., 1969), 11-19.

Florence Sandler. "The Ascents of the Spirit: Henry Vaughan on the Atonement," JEGP, 73 (April, 1974), 223-224.

Bain Tate Stewart, "Hermetic Symbolism in Henry Vaughan's 'The Night,'" PQ, 29 (Oct., 1950), 417-422.

Wanamaker, Discordia Concors, pp. 57-59, 69-70.

Melissa Cynthia Wanamaker, "Discordia Concors: The Metaphysical Wit of Henry Vaughan's Silex Scintillans," TSLL, 16 (Fall, 1974), 466-467, 476-477.

_____. "The Passion"
Florence Sandler, "The Ascents of the Spirit: Henry Vaughan on the Atonement," JEGP, 73 (April, 1974), 222-223.

_____. "Peace"
L. C. Locke, Expl, 1 (April, 1943), 43.
    Rpt. The Explicator Cyclopedia, II, pp. 345-346.

_____. "The Proffer"
R. A. Durr, "Vaughan's Pilgrim and the Birds of Night: 'The Proffer,'" MLQ, 21 (March, 1960), 45-58.

_____. "The Pursuite"
Jonathan George, Expl, 35 (Spring, 1977), 2-3.

_____. "The Queer"
Macdonald Emslie, Expl, 13 (March, 1955), 29.
    Rpt. Th Explicator Cyclopedia, II, pp. 346-347.

Laurence Perrine, Expl, 13 (March, 1955), 29.
    Rpt. The Explicator Cyclopedia, II, p. 346.

Celeste Turner Wright, Expl, 13 (March, 1955), 29.
    Rpt. The Explicator Cyclopedia, II, p. 347.

_____. "Quickness"
Cleanth Brooks, "Henry Vaughan: Quietism and Mysticism," in Essays in Honor of Esmond Linworth Marilla, pp. 13-14.

Drew, Poetry: A Modern Guide, pp. 244-245.

E. C. Pettet, "A Simile in Vaughan," TLS, Jan. 27, 1956, p. 53.

Florence Sandler, "The Ascents of the Spirit: Henry Vaughan on the Atonement," JEGP, 73 (April, 1974), 220.

_____. "Regeneration"
Edgar F. Daniels, "Vaughan's 'Regeneration': An Emendation," AN&Q, 9 (Oct., 1970), 19-20.

Robert Allen Durr, "Vaughan's Theme and Its Pattern: 'Regeneration,'" SP, 54 (Jan., 1957), 14-28.

Barbara K. Lewalski, "Typology and Poetry: A Consideration of Herbert, Vaughan, and Marvell," in Illustrious Evidence: Approaches to English Literature of the Early Seventeenth Century, ed. Earl Miner (Berkeley: Univ. of Calif. Press, 1975), pp. 59-61.

Louis L. Martz, "Henry Vaughan: The Man Within," PMLA, 78 (March, 1963), 41-42.

Claude J. Summers and Ted-Larry Pebworth, "Vaughan's Temple in Nature and the Context of 'Regeneration,'" JEGP, 74 (July, 1975), 351-360.

Wanamaker, Discordia Concors, pp. 59-60.

Melissa Cynthia Wanamaker, "Discordia Concors: The Metaphysical Wit of Henry Vaughan's Silex Scintillans," TSLL, 16 (Fall, 1974), 467-469.

Thomas J. Wyly, "Vaughan's 'Regeneration' Reconsidered," PQ, 55 (Summer, 1976), 340-353.

_____. "Religion"
Wanamaker, Discordia Concors, pp. 60-61.

Melissa Cynthia Wanamaker, "Discordia Concors: The Metaphysical Wit of Henry Vaughan's Silex Scintillans," TSLL, 16 (Fall, 1974), 469.

_____. "The Retreat"
Cleanth Brooks, "Henry Vaughan: Quietism and Mysticism," in Essays in Honor of Esmond Linworth Marilla, pp. 15-19.

M. Y. Hughes, "The Theme of Pre-Existence and Infancy in The Retreate," PQ, 20 (July, 1941), 484-500.

Kreuzer, Elements of Poetry, pp. 159-161.

_____. "The Sap"
Alan Rudrum, "The Influence of Alchemy in the Poems of Henry Vaughan," PQ, 44 (Oct., 1970), 473.

_____. "The Search"
Martz, The Poetry of Meditation, pp. 86-90.

_____. "Silence, and stealth of dayes!"
Melissa Cynthia Wanamaker, "Discordia Concors: The Metaphysical Wit of Henry Vaughan's Silex Scintillans," TSLL, 16 (Fall, 1974), 475.

_____. "Song to Amoret"
James D. Simmonds, "Vaughan's Love Poetry," in Essays in Honor of Esmond Linworth Marilla, pp. 41-42.

_____. "The Starre"
Alan Rudrum, "An Aspect of Vaughan's Hermeticism: The Doctrine of Cosmic Sympathy," SEL, 14 (Winter, 1974), 135-136.

_____. "Sure, there's a type of Bodyes"
Alan Rudrum, "An Aspect of Vaughan's Hermeticism: The Doctrine of Cosmic Sympathy," SEL, 14 (Winter, 1974), 133-135.

Wanamaker, Discordia Concors, pp. 61-63.

Melissa Cynthia Wanamaker, "Discordia Concors: The Metaphysical Wit of Henry Vaughan's Silex Scintillans," TSLL, 16 (Fall, 1974), 470-471.

_____. "The Tempest"
James D. Simmonds, "Henry Vaughan and the Great Chain of Being," in Studies in English Renaissance Literature (Louisiana State University Press, 1962).

_____. "To Amoret of the difference"
A. U. Chapman, "Henry Vaughan and Magnetic Philosophy," The Southern Review (Australia), No. 3 (1971), 216-217.

_____. "To Estesia parted from him, and looking back"
James D. Simmonds, "Vaughan's Love Poetry," in Essays in Honor of Esmond Linworth Marilla, pp. 36-37.

_____. "To His Books"
Winters, Forms of Discovery, pp. 100-102.

_____. "To I. Morgan...upon his sudden Journey and succeeding Marriage"
James D. Simmonds, "Vaughan's Love Poetry," in Essays in Honor of Esmond Linworth Marilla, pp. 29-30.

_____. "To the River Isca"
James D. Simmonds, "Vaughan's Love Poetry," in Essays in Honor of Esmond Linworth Marilla, p. 30.

_____. "Vanity of Spirit"
Martz, The Poetry of Meditation, pp. 150-152.

James D. Simmonds, "Henry Vaughan and the Great Chain of Being," in Studies in English Renaissance Literature (Louisiana State University Press, 1962), pp. 164-165.

_____. "The Waterfall"
W. Nelson Francis, Expl, 14 (June, 1956), 57.
    Rpt. The Explicator Cyclopedia, II, pp. 347-348.

Ted-Larry Pebworth, "The Problem of Restagnotes in Henry Vaughan's 'The Waterfall,'" PLL, 3 (Summer, 1967), 258-259.

_____. "The World"
Edgar F. Daniels, Expl, 22 (May, 1964), 70.

Paul A. Olson, "Vaughan's 'The World': The Pattern of Meaning and Tradition," CL, 13 (Winter, 1961), 26-32.

Maren-Sofie Røstvig, "Syncretistic Imagery and the Unity of Vaughan's 'The World,'" PLL, 5 (Fall, 1969), 415-422.

Florence Sandler, "The Ascents of the Spirit: Henry Vaughan on the Atonement," <u>JEGP</u>, 73 (April, 1974), 220-221.

James D. Simmonds, "Vaughan's Masterpiece and Its Critics: 'The World' Revaluated," <u>SEL</u>, 2 (Winter, 1962), 77-93.

VERY.   "The Baker's Island Lights"
Carl Dennis, "Correspondence in Very's Nature Poetry," <u>NEQ</u>, 43 (June, 1970), 265-266.

_____.   "The Columbine"
Carl Dennis, "Correspondence in Very's Nature Poetry," <u>NEQ</u>, 43 (June, 1970), 263-265.

_____.   "The Hand and Foot"
Winters, "Jones Very: A New England Mystic," <u>American Review</u>, 7 (May, 1936), 161-163.

Winters, <u>Maule's Curse</u>, pp. 127-129. Also <u>In Defense of Reason</u>, pp. 264-266.

_____.   "The Lost"
Carl Dennis, "Correspondence in Very's Nature Poetry," <u>NEQ</u>, 43 (June, 1970), 268-270.

Winters, "Jones Very: A New England Mystic," <u>American Review</u>, 7 (May, 1936), 171-172.

Winters, <u>Maule's Curse</u>, pp. 138-139. Also <u>In Defense of Reason</u>, pp. 274-276.

_____.   "Man in Harmony with Nature"
Carl Dennis, "Correspondence in Very's Nature Poetry," <u>NEQ</u>, 43 (June, 1970), 257-258.

_____.   "The New Birth"
Carl Dennis, "Correspondence in Very's Nature Poetry," <u>NEQ</u>, 43 (June, 1970), 259.

_____.   "The Revelation of the Spirit Through the Material World"
Carl Dennis, "Correspondence in Very's Nature Poetry," <u>NEQ</u>, 43 (June, 1970), 259-260.

_____.   "To the Canary Bird"
Carl Dennis, "Correspondence in Very's Nature Poetry," <u>NEQ</u>, 43 (June, 1970), 261-262.

_____.   "The Tree" (p. 70 of <u>Poems and Essays</u>, 1886)
Carl Dennis, "Correspondence in Very's Nature Poetry," <u>NEQ</u>, 43 (June, 1970), 262-263.

_____.   "The Tree (p. 121 of <u>Poems and Essays</u>, 1886)
Carl Dennis, "Correspondence in Very's Nature Poetry," <u>NEQ</u>, 43 (June, 1970), 267-268.

_____.   "The True Light"
Carl Dennis, "Correspondence in Very's Nature Poetry," <u>NEQ</u>, 43 (June, 1970), 258-259.

VIERECK. "Better Come Quietly"
    J. F. Nims, Poetry: A Critical Supplement, Dec., 1947, pp. 1-4.

_____. "Blindman's Buff"
    J. F. Nims, Poetry: A Critical Supplement, Dec., 1947, pp. 6-8.

_____. "Crass Times Redeemed by Dignity of Souls"
    Ciardi, How Does a Poem Mean? p. 952-953.

_____. "Don't Look Now but Mary is Everybody"
    Richard P. Benton, Expl, 20 (Dec., 1961), 30.
        Rpt. The Explicator Cyclopedia, I, pp. 334-336.

_____. "Game Called on Account of Darkness"
    J. F. Nims, Poetry: A Critical Supplement, Dec., 1947, pp. 9-10.

_____. "Like a Sitting Breeze"
    Peter Viereck, "Correspondence Relating to 'Like a Sitting Breeze,'"
    ASch, 20 (Spring, 1951), 216-217.

_____. "Six Theological Cradle Songs"
    Peter Viereck, "My Kind of Poetry," in Mid-Century American Poets,
    pp. 26-27.

_____. "Some Lines in Three Parts"
    Peter Viereck, "My Kind of Poetry," in Mid-Century American Poets,
    pp. 26-27.

_____. "Vale from Carthage (Spring, 1944)"
    Kreuzer, Elements of Poetry, pp. 93-96.

    Perrine and Reid, 100 American Poems, p. 241.

WALLER. "An Apologie for Having Loved Before"
    Karl Josef Holtger, "Why Was Man Created in the Evening? On Waller's
    'An Apologie for Having Loved Before,'" MLR, 69 (Jan., 1974), 23-28.

_____. "At Pens-hurst"
    Miner, The Cavalier Mode from Jonson to Cotton, pp. 17-22.

_____. "Go, Lovely Rose"
    Kreuzer, Elements of Poetry, pp. 157-158.

    Miner, The Cavalier Mode from Jonson to Cotton, pp. 39-41.

    Rosenthal and Smith, Exploring Poetry, pp. 695-697.

_____. "Of a Fair Lady Playing with a Snake"
    Miner, The Cavalier Mode from Jonson to Cotton, pp. 115-117.

_____. "On a Girdle"
    L. G. Locke, Expl, 1 (May, 1943), 52.
        Rpt. The Explicator Cyclopedia, II, p. 348.

    Williamson, The Proper Wit of Poetry, pp. 103-104.

_____. "On St. James's Park as Lately Improved by His Majesty"
    Miner, The Cavalier Mode from Jonson to Cotton, pp. 24-39.

_____. "Panegyric to My Lord Protector"
Warren L. Chernaik, "Waller's Panegyric to My Lord Protector and the Poetry of Praise," SEL, 4 (Winter, 1964), 113-124.

_____. "The Story of Phoebus and Daphne Applied"
Bateson, English Poetry, pp. 169-170.

_____. "Upon Her Majesty's New Buildings at Somerset House"
Charles Larson, "The Somerset House Poems of Cowley and Waller," PLL, 10 (Spring, 1974), 131-135.

WARREN.   "Aged Man Surveys the Past Time"
Brooks, Modern Poetry and the Tradition, pp. 78-79.

W. P. Southard, "Speculation," The Kenyon Review, 7 (Autumn, 1945), 666-667.

_____. "The Ballad of Billie Potts"
Deutsch, Poetry in Our Time, pp. 202-203.

Ruth Herschberger, "Poised Between the Two Alarms...,'" Accent, 4 (Summer, 1944), 245.

Sam Hynes, "Robert Penn Warren: The Symbolic Journey," The University of Kansas City Review, 17 (Summer, 1951), 280-281.

M. L. Rosenthal, "Robert Penn Warren's Poetry," SAQ, 62 (Autumn, 1963), 501-503.

W. P. Southard, "Speculation," The Kenyon Review, 7 (Autumn, 1945), 670-673.

John L. Stewart, "Robert Penn Warren and the Knot of History," ELH, 26 (March, 1959), 117, 120-122.

John L. Stuart, "The Achievement of Robert Penn Warren," SAQ, 47 (Oct., 1948), 570-574.

_____. "Bearded Oaks"
Beach, Obsessive Images, pp. 324-325.

Brooks, Modern Poetry and the Tradition, pp. 81-82.
    Rpt. Engle and Carrier, Reading Modern Poetry, pp. 106-108.

O'Connor, Sense and Sensibility in Modern Poetry, pp. 154-155.

_____. "Blow West Wind, Blow"
Sr. M. Bernetta Quinn, O.S.F., "Robert Penn Warren's Promised Land," SoQ, 8 (April, 1972), 337-339.

_____. "The Child Next Door"
James Wright, "The Stiff Smile of Mr. Warren," The Kenyon Review, 20 (Autumn, 1958), 648-655.

_____. "Composition in Red and Gold"
Sr. M. Bernetta Quinn, O.S.F., "Robert Penn Warren's Promised Land," SoQ, 8 (April, 1972), 335-336.

_____. "Crime"
W. P. Southard, "Speculation," The Kenyon Review, 7 (Autumn, 1945), 661-662.

_____. "Dragon Country: To Jacob Boehme"
Brooks, A Shaping Joy, pp. 223-224.

Perrine and Reid, 100 American Poems, pp. 203-204.

_____. "The Garden"
W. P. Southard, "Speculation," The Kenyon Review, 7 (Autumn, 1945), 668.

_____. "Gold Glade"
Sr. M. Bernetta Quinn, O.S.F., "Robert Penn Warren's Promised Land," SoQ, 8 (April, 1972), 354-355.

_____. "History"
Brooks, Modern Poetry and the Tradition, pp. 85-87.

_____. "History Among the Rocks"
Brooks, Modern Poetry and the Tradition, pp. 77-78.

_____. "Letter from a Coward to a Hero"
Brooks, Modern Poetry and the Tradition, pp. 82-85.

W. P. Southard, "Speculation," The Kenyon Review, 7 (Autumn, 1945), 659-660.

_____. "Love's Parable"
Howard Nemerov, "The Phoenix in the World," Furioso, 3 (Spring, 1948), 36-46.

_____. "Man Coming of Age"
W. P. Southard, "Speculation," The Kenyon Review, 7 (Autumn, 1945), 657-658.

_____. "The Mango on the Mango Tree"
Frederick Brantley, "The Achievement of Robert Penn Warren," in Modern American Poetry, ed. B. Rajan, pp. 78-79.

_____. "Mexico Is a Foreign Country"
W. P. Southard, "Speculation," The Kenyon Review, 7 (Autumn, 1945), 668-670.

_____. "Monologue at Midnight"
Beach, Obsessive Images, pp. 315-316.

Frederick Brantley, "The Achievement of Robert Penn Warren," in Modern American Poetry, ed. B. Rajan, pp. 76-77.

_____. "Original Sin: A Short Story"
Richard E. Amacher, Expl, 8 (May, 1950), 52.
   Rpt. The Explicator Cyclopedia, I, pp. 336-337.

Frederick Brantley, "The Achievement of Robert Penn Warren," in Modern American Poetry, ed. B. Rajan, pp. 77-78.

Clifford M. Gordon, Expl, 9 (Dec., 1950), 21.
   Rpt. The Explicator Cyclopedia, I, pp. 337-338.

_____. "Pondy Woods"
M. L. Rosenthal, "Robert Penn Warren's Poetry," SAQ, 62 (Autumn, 1963), 500-501.

_____. "Pursuit"
William Frost, Expl, 11 (Feb., 1953), 22.
   Rpt. The Explicator Cyclopedia, I, pp. 338-339.

W. P. Southard, "Speculation," The Kenyon Review, 7 (Autumn, 1945), 662-665.

Robert Penn Warren in Friar and Brinnin, Modern Poetry, p. 542.

_____. "The Return: An Elegy"
Frederick Brantley, "The Achievement of Robert Penn Warren," in Modern American Poetry, ed. B. Rajan, pp. 75-76.

Brooks, Modern Poetry and the Tradition, pp. 79-80.

_____. "Revelation"
Robert Penn Warren in Friar and Brinnin, Modern Poetry, pp. 541-542.

_____. "Sunset Walk in Thaw-Time in Vermont"
Bloom, A Map of Misreading, pp. 193-198.

_____. "Terror"
Robert Penn Warren in Friar and Brinnin, Modern Poetry, pp. 542-543.

_____. "Variation: Ode to Fear"
Beach, Obsessive Images, pp. 216-218.

WARTON, Joseph. "The Enthusiast"
David B. Morris, "Joseph Warton's Figure of Virtue: Poetic Indirection in 'The Enthusiast,'" PQ, 50 (Oct., 1971), 678-683.

WATKINS, Vernon. "Arakhova and the Daemon"
J. F. Nims, Poetry: A Critical Supplement, March, 1947, pp. 1-3.

_____. "Ballad of the Mari Lwyd"
Robert Gorham Davis, "Eucharist and Roasting Pheasant," Poetry, 73 (Dec., 1948), 171.

_____. "Music of Colours: The Blossom Scattered"
John Berryman, Poetry: A Critical Supplement, Dec., 1949, pp. 14-16.

WATTS. "Come, Holy Spirit, Heavenly Dove"
Daniels, The Art of Reading Poetry, pp. 207-208.

Helen S. and J. D. Thomas, Expl, 10 (April, 1952), 39.
    Rpt. The Explicator Cyclopedia, pp. 348-349.

WELLESLEY. "Poem"
W. B. Yeats, Letters on Poetry from W. B. Yeats to Dorothy Wellesley, pp. 170-175.

WESLEY, John. "Christ, Whose Glory Fills the Skies"
Sr. M. Pauline Parker, "The Hymn as a Literary Form," ECS, 8 (Summer, 1975), 410-411.

WHEELWRIGHT, John Brooks. "Father"
Austin Warren, New England Saints (Ann Arbor: Univ. of Michigan Press, 1956), pp. 174-175.

WHITMAN. "Aboard at a Ship's Helm"
Robert LaRue, "Whitman's Sea: Large enough for Moby Dick," WWR, 12 (Sept., 1966), 57.

Douglas A. Noverr, "'Aboard at a Ship's Helm': A Minor Sea Drama, The Poet, and The Soul," WWR, 17 (March, 1971), 23-25.

_____. "As I Ebb'd with the Ocean of Life"
Melvin W. Askew, "Whitman's 'As I Ebb'd with the Ocean of Life,'" WWR,
10 (Dec., 1964), 87-92.

Stephen A. Black, "Radical Utterances from the Soul's Abysms: Toward a
New Sense of Whitman," PMLA, 88 (Jan., 1973), 103-104.

Bloom, A Map of Misreading, pp. 178-184.

Harold Bloom, "The Central Man: Emerson, Whitman, Wallace Stevens," MR,
7 (Winter, 1966), 34-36.

Harold Bloom, The Ringers in the Tower: Studies in Romantic Tradition
(Chicago and London: Univ. of Chicago Press, 1971), pp. 226-228.

Robert LaRue, "Whitman's Sea: Large enough for Moby Dick," WWR, 12
(Sept., 1966), 52-54.

_____. "The Base of All Metaphysics"
R. Galen Hanson, "A Critical Reflection on Whitman's 'The Base of All
Metaphysics,'" WWR, 18 (June, 1972), 67-70.

_____. "A Boston Ballad (1854)"
Stephen D. Malin, "'A Boston Ballad' and the Boston Riot," WWR, 9 (Sept.,
1963), 51-57.

Edward A. Martin, "Whitman's 'A Boston Ballad (1854),'" WWR, 11 (Sept.,
1965), 61-69.

_____. "By Blue Ontario's Shore" ("Poem of Many in One")
Gary A. Culbert, "Whitman's Revisions of 'By Blue Ontario's Shore,'" WWR,
23 (March, 1977), 35-45.

Willie T. Weathers, "Whitman's Poetic Translations of His 1855 Preface,"
AL, 19 (March, 1947), 24-27.

_____. "A Broadway Pageant"
Richard P. Sugg, "Whitmans' Symbolic Circle and 'A Broadway Pageant,'"
WWR, 16 (June, 1970), 35-40.

_____. "Calamus"
Lawrence Buell, "Transcendental Catalogue Rhetoric: Vision Versus Form,"
AL, 40 (Nov., 1968), 326-328.

Russell A. Hunt, "Whitman's Poetics and the Unity of 'Calamus,'" AL, 46
(Jan., 1975), 482-494.

Minor W. Major, "A New Interpretation of Whitman's Calamus Poems," WWR,
13 (June, 1967), 51-54.

James E. Miller, Jr., "Whitman's 'Calamus': The Leaf and the Root,"
PMLA, 72 (March, 1957), 249-271.

_____. "Calamus," No. 9
R. Galen Hanson, "Anxiety as Human Predicament: Whitman's 'Calamus' No.
9," WWR, 21 (June, 1975), 73-75.

_____. "Cavalry Crossing a Ford"
Richard Allan Davison, "Mixed Tone in 'Cavalry Crossing a Ford,'" WWR,
16 (Dec., 1970), 114-117.

Dale Doepke, "Whitman's Theme in 'Cavalry Crossing a Ford,'" WWR, 18
(Dec., 1972), 132-136.

_____. "Chanting the Square Deific"
Alfred H. Marks, "Whitman's Triadic Imagery," AL, 23 (March, 1951), 112-118.

G. L. Sixbey, "'Chanting the Square Deific'--A Study in Whitman's Religion," AL, 9 (May, 1937), 171-195.

_____. "Clef Poem"
Stephen A. Black, "Radical Utterances from the Soul's Abysms: Toward a New Sense of Whitman," PMLA, 88 (Jan., 1973), 101-102.

_____. "Crossing Brooklyn Ferry"
Richard P. Adams, "Whitman: A Brief Revaluation," TSE, 5 (1955), 135-138.

John E. Byron, "Significance of T, I, and O in 'Crossing Brooklyn Ferry,'" WWR, 9 (Dec., 1963), 89-90.

F. C. Cronin, "Modern Sensibility in Stanza 2 of 'Crossing Brooklyn Ferry,'" WWR, 15 (March, 1969), 56-57.

Wilson F. Engel, III, "Two Biblical Echoes in 'Crossing Brooklyn Ferry,'" WWR, 23 (June, 1977), 88-90.

Marvin Felheim, "The Problem of Structure in Some Poems by Whitman," in Aspects of American Poetry, pp. 91-94.

James W. Gargano, "Technique in 'Crossing Brooklyn Ferry': The Everlasting Moment," JEGP, 62 (April, 1963), 262-269.

Eugene R. Kanjo, "Time and Eternity in 'Crossing Brooklyn Ferry,'" WWR, 18 (Sept., 1972), 82-90.

Barbara Kroll, "The 'Confession' in 'Crossing Brooklyn Ferry' and the Jewish Day of Atonement Prayers," WWR, 23 (Sept., 1977), 125-129.

_____. "The Dismantled Ship"
Sutton, American Free Verse, pp. 22-23.

_____. "Eidólons"
Lois A. Cuddy, "Exploration of Whitman's 'Eidólons,'" WWR, 19 (Dec., 1973), 153-157.

Phillipa P. Harrison, "'Eidólons': An Entrance-Song," WWR, 17 (June, 1971), 35-45.

_____. "Ethiopia Saluting the Colors"
J. R. LeMaster, "Some Traditional Poems from Leaves of Grass," WWR, 13 (June, 1967), 44-51.

_____. "Excelsior"
Thomas W. Ford, "Whitman's 'Excelsior': The Poem as Microcosm," TSLL, 17 (Winter, 1976), 778-785.

_____. "Faces"
Harold Aspiz, "A Reading of Whitman's 'Faces,'" WWR, 19 (June, 1973), 37-48.

_____. "Give Me the Splendid Silent Sun"
J. Thomas Chaffin, Jr., "Give Me Faces and Streets: Walt Whitman and the City," WWR, 23 (Sept., 1977), 114-116.

_____. "Good-bye My Fancy!"
Rose Cherie Reissman, "Recurrent Motifs in Good-bye My Fancy," WWR, 21 (March, 1975), 29-30, 33.

_____. "I Hear It Was Charged Against Me"
J. Thomas Chaffin, Jr., "Give Me Faces and Streets: Walt Whitman and the City," WWR, 23 (Sept., 1977), 116.

_____. "I Sing the Body Electric"
Robert Coskren, "A Reading of Whitman's 'I Sing the Body Electric,'" WWR, 22 (Sept., 1976), 125-132.

John H. Matle, "The Body Acclaimed," WWR, 16 (Dec., 1970), 110-114.

_____. "Lingering Last Drops"
Rose Cherie Reissman, "Recurrent Motifs in Good-bye My Fancy," WWR, 21 (March, 1975), 32-33.

_____. "A March in the Ranks Hard-Prest, and the Road Unknown"
Dominick A. Labianca and William J. Reeves, "'A March in the Ranks Hard-Prest, and the Road Unknown': A Chemical Analysis," AN&Q, 15 (April, 1977), 110-111.

_____. "The Mystic Trumpeter"
W. L. Werner, "Whitman's 'The Mystic Trumpeter' as Autobiography," AL, 7 (Jan., 1936), 455-460.

_____. "A Noiseless, Patient Spider"
Bert Case Diltz, Sense or Nonsense: Contemporary Education at the Crossroads (Toronto: McClelland and Stewart, 1972), pp. 100-101.

Wilton Eckley, Expl, 22 (Nov., 1963), 20.

Arnold Mersch, "Teilhard de Chardin and Whitman's 'A Noiseless Patient Spider,'" WWR, 17 (Sept., 1971), 99-100.

Van Doren, Introduction to Poetry, pp. 43-45.

Fred D. White, "Whitman's Cosmic Spider," WWR, 23 (June, 1977), 85-88.

_____. "On Journeys Through the States"
B. J. Leggett, "The Structure of Whitman's 'On Journeys Through the States,'" WWR, 14 (June, 1968), 58-59.

_____. "On the Beach at Night"
Matthiessen, American Renaissance, pp. 575-577.

_____. "Our Old Feuillage"
Robert J. Griffin, "Notes on Structural Devices in Whitman's Poetry," TSL, 6 (1961), 18-19.

Robin P. Hoople, "'Chants Democratic and Native American': A Neglected Sequence in the Growth of Leaves of Grass," AL, 42 (May, 1970), 188-189.

Douglas A. Noverr, "Poetic Vision and Locus in Whitman's 'Our Old Feuillage,'" WWR, 22 (Sept., 1976), 118-122.

_____. "Out of the Cradle Endlessly Rocking"
Richard P. Adams, "Whitman: A Brief Revaluation," TSE, 5 (1955), 138-140, 146-149.

Roy P. Basler, Expl, 5 (June, 1947), 59.
    Rpt. The Explicator Cyclopedia, II, p. 352.

Stephen A. Black, "Radical Utterances from the Soul's Abysms: Toward a New Sense of Whitman," PMLA, 88 (Jan., 1973), 107-110.

Brooks, Lewis, and Warren, American Literature, pp. 941-942.

C. C. Cunningham, Literature as a Fine Art: Analysis and Interpretation, pp. 176-185.

Dickinson, Suggestions for Teachers of "Introduction to Literature," fifth edition, ed. Locke, Gibson, and Arms, p. 32. (Teacher's Manual)

Marvin Felheim, "The Problem of Structure in Some Poems by Whitman," in Aspects of American Poetry, pp. 84-87.

Neil D. Isaacs, "The Autoerotic Metaphor," L&P, 15 (Spring, 1965), 104-106.

C. W. M. Johnson, Expl, 5 (May, 1947), 52.
    Rpt. The Explicator Cyclopedia, II, pp. 351-352.

Robert LaRue, "Whitman's Sea: Large enough for Moby Dick," WWR, 12 (Sept., 1966), 54-56.

Alfred H. Marks, "Whitman's Triadic Imagery," AL, 23 (March, 1951), 120-126.

Tracey R. Miller, "The Boy, the Bird, and the Sea: An Archetypal Reading of 'Out of the Cradle,'" WWR, 19 (Sept., 1973), 93-103.

Pearce, The Continuity of American Poetry, pp. 170-172.

Louise Pound, "Note on Walt Whitman and Bird Poetry," EJ, 19 (Jan., 1930), 34-36.

Joseph N. Riddel, "Walt Whitman and Wallace Stevens: Functions of a 'Literatus,'" SAQ, 61 (Autumn, 1962), 515-517.

Rosenthal and Smith, Exploring Poetry, 695-696.

Leo Spitzer, "'Explication de Texte' Applied to Whitman's 'Out of the Cradle Endlessly Rocking,'" ELH, 16 (Sept., 1949), 229-249.
    Rpt. Essays on English and American Literature by Leo Spitzer,
        pp. 14-36.

Floyd Stovall, "Main Drifts in Whitman's Poetry," AL, 4 (March, 1932), 8-10.

Beverly Luzietti Strohl, "An Interpretation of 'Out of the Cradle,'" WWR, 10 (Dec., 1964), 83-87.

Sutton, American Free Verse, pp. 16-19.

Charles C. Walcutt, "Whitman's 'Out of the Cradle Endlessly Rocking,'" CE, 10 (Feb., 1949), 277-279.

Harry R. Warfel, "'Out of the Cradle Endlessly Rocking,'" TSL, 3 (1958), 83-87.

S. E. Whicher, Expl, 5 (Feb., 1947), 28.
    Rpt. The Explicator Cyclopedia, II, pp. 350-351.

_____. "Passage to India"
Richard P. Adams, "Whitman: A Brief Revaluation," TSE, 5 (1955), 141-143.

Richard E. Amacher, Expl, 9 (Dec., 1950), Q2.
    Rpt. The Explicator Cyclopedia, II, pp. 352-353.

S. K. Coffman, Jr., "Form and Meaning in Whitman's 'Passage to India,'" PMLA, 70 (June, 1955), 337-349.

Marvin Felheim, "The Problem of Structure in Some Poems by Whitman," in Aspects of American Poetry, pp. 94-97.

Arthur Golden, "Passage to Less than India: Structure and Meaning in Whitman's 'Passage to India,'" PMLA, 88 (Oct., 1973), 1095-1103.

Clare R. Goldfarb, "The Poet's Role in 'Passage to India,'" WWR, 8 (Dec., 1962), 75-79.

Joel R. Kehler, "A Typological Reading of 'Passage to India,'" ESQ, 23 (Second Quarter, 1977), 123-129.

Judge M. Schonfeld, "No Exit in 'Passage to India': Existence Precedes Essence in Section 5," WWR, 19 (Dec., 1973), 147-151.

Som P. Sharma, "Self, Soul, and God in 'Passage to India,'" CE, 27 (Feb., 1966), 394-399.

Ruth Slonim, "Walt Whitman's 'Open Road,'" RS, 25 (March, 1957), 72-74.

Ruth Stauffer, Expl, 9 (May, 1951), 50.
    Rpt. The Explicator Cyclopedia, II, p. 353.

Randall Stewart, The Literature of the United States, II, p. 217.

Floyd Stovall, "Main Drifts in Whitman's Poetry," AL, 4 (March, 1932), 1-21.

Charles Stubblefield, "The Great Circle: Whitman's 'Passage to India,'" PrS, 49 (Spring, 1975), 19-30.

_____. "Patroling Barnegat"
Raymond G. Malbone, "Organic Language in 'Patroling Barnegat,'" WWR, 13 (Dec., 1967), 125-127.

_____. "Pictures"
George H. Soule, Jr., "Walt Whitman's 'Pictures': An Alternative to Tennyson's 'Palace of Art,'" ESQ, No. 22 (First Quarter, 1976), 39-47.

_____. "Pioneers! O Pioneers!
Gay Wilson Allen, "On the Trochaic Meter of 'Pioneers! O Pioneers!'" AL, 20 (Jan., 1949), 449-451.

Edward G. Fletcher, "Pioneers! O Pioneers!" AL, 19 (Nov., 1947), 259-261.

_____. "Proud Music of the Storm"
Sydney J. Krause, "Whitman, Music, and Proud Music of the Storm," PMLA, 72 (Sept., 1957), 707-716.

James C. McCullagh, "'Proud Music of the Storm': A Study in Dynamics," WWR, 21 (June, 1975), 66-73.

_____. "A Riddle Song"
C. Scott Pugh, "The End as Means in 'A Riddle Song,'" WWR, 23 (Sept., 1977), 82-85.

_____. "Sail Out for Good, Eidólon Yacht!"
Rose Cherie Reissman, "Recurrent Motifs in Good-bye My Fancy," WWR, 21 (March, 1975), 29, 32-33.

_____. "Salut au Monde"
Alvin Rosenfeld, "The Poem as Dialogical Process: A New Reading of 'Salut au Monde,'" WWR, 10 (June, 1964), 34-40.

_____. "Scented Herbage of My Breast"
Philip V. Coleman, "Walt Whitman's Ambiguities of 'I,'" PLL, 5 (Summer, 1969), Supplement, 41-42.

_____. "A Sight in Camp in the Daybreak Gray and Dim"
Sutton, American Free Verse, pp. 21-22.

Robert B. Sweet, "A Writer Looks at Whitman's 'A Sight in Camp in the Daybreak Gray and Dim,'" WWR, 17 (June, 1971), 58-62.

James T. F. Tanner, "A Note on Whitman's 'A Sight in Camp,'" ESQ, No. 58 (Part 4, 1970), 123-124.

William A. Wortman, "Spiritual Progression in 'A Sight in Camp,'" WWR, 14 (March, 1968), 24-26.

_____. "The Sleepers"
Robert E. Abrams, "The Function of Dreams and Dream-Logic in Whitman's Poetry," TSLL, 17 (Fall, 1975), 605-611.

Matlu Blasing, "'The Sleepers': The Problem of the Self in Whitman," WWR, 21 (Sept., 1975), 111-119.

Harry James Cook, "The Individuation of a Poet: The Process of Becoming in Whitman's 'The Sleepers,'" WWR, 21 (Sept., 1975), 101-111.

Joyce Kornblatt, "Whitman's Vision of the Past in 'The Sleepers,'" WWR, 16 (Sept., 1970), 86-89.

Robert K. Martin, Expl, 33 (Oct., 1974), 13.

Sr. Eva Mary, "Shades of Darkness in 'The Sleepers,'" WWR, 15 (Sept., 1969), 187-190.

Matthiessen, American Renaissance, pp. 572-573.

Pearce, The Continuity of American Poetry, pp. 168-170.

Francis E. Skipp, "Whitman's Lucifer: A Footnote to 'The Sleepers,'" WWR, 11 (June, 1965), 52-53.

R. W. Vince, "A Reading of 'The Sleepers,'" WWR, 18 (March, 1972), 17-28.

_____. "Song for Occupations"
Robin P. Hoople, "'Chants Democratic and Native American': A Neglected Sequence in the Growth of Leaves of Grass," AL, 42 (May, 1970), 187-188.

_____. "Song of Myself"
Richard P. Adams, "Whitman: A Brief Revaluation," TSE, 5 (1955), 144-145.

Richard R. Adicks, "The Sea-Fight Episode in 'Song of Myself,'" WWR, 13 (March, 1967), 16-21.

Sally Ann Batchelor, "Whitman's Yawp and How He Yawped It," WWR, 18 (Sept., 1972), 97-101.

Adrianne Baytop, "'Song of Myself' 52: Motion as Vehicle for Meaning," WWR, 18 (Sept., 1972), 101-103.

Joel Jay Belson, "Whitman's 'Overstaid Fraction,'" WWR, 17 (June, 1971), 63-65.

Bloom, Poetry and Repression, pp. 248-266.

Eric W. Carlson, Expl, 18 (Nov., 1959), 13.
    Rpt. The Explicator Cyclopedia, II, pp. 353-354.

Philip Y. Coleman, "Walt Whitman's Ambiguities of 'I,'" PLL, 5 (Summer, 1969), Supplement, 45-59.

Malcolm Cowley, "Walt Whitman's Buried Masterpiece," The Saturday Review, 42 (Oct. 31, 1959), 11-13, 32-34.

Joseph M. DeFalco, "The Narrative Shift in Whitman's 'Song of Myself,'" WWR, 9 (Dec., 1963), 82-84.

Griffith Dudding, "The Function of Whitman's Imagery in 'Song of Myself,' 1885," WWR, 13 (March, 1967), 3-11.

Massud Farzan, "Whitman and Sufism: Towards 'A Persian Lesson,'" AL, 47 (Jan., 1976), 574-581.

Ida Fasel, "'Song of Myself' as Prayer," WWR, 17 (March, 1971), 19-22.

Richard J. Fein, "Whitman and the Emancipated Self," CentR, 20 (Winter, 1976), 36-49.

Albert Gelpi, The Tenth Muse: The Psyche of the American Poet (Cambridge and London: Harvard Univ. Press, 1975), pp. 169-209.

Sam B. Girgus, "Culture and Post-Culture in Walt Whitman," CentR, 18 (Fall, 1974), 398-400.

Clarence Gohdes, "Section 50 of Whitman's 'Song of Myself,'" MLN, 75 (Dec., 1960), 654-656.

Robert J. Griffin, Expl, 21 (Oct., 1962), 16.

Robert J. Griffin, "Notes on Structural Devices in Whitman's Poetry," TSL, 6 (1961), 15-16.

Chaviva Hosek, "The Rhetoric of Whitman's 1855 'Song of Myself,'" 20 (Summer, 1976), 263-277.

David J. Johnson, "The Effect of Suspension Dots, Parentheses, and Italics on Lyricism of 'Song of Myself,'" WWR, 21 (June, 1975), 47-58.

Kenneth G. Johnston and John O. Rees, Jr., "Whitman and the Foo-Foos: An Experiment in Language," WWR, 17 (March, 1971), 3-10.

Dwight Kalita, "Walt Whitman: Ecstatic Sea-Voyager," WWR, 21 (March, 1975), 14-21.

T. J. Kallsen, "'Song of Myself': Logical Unity Through Analogy," WVUPP, 9 (June, 1953), 33-40.

T. J. Kallsen, "The Improbabilities in Section 11 of 'Song of Myself,'" WWR, 15 (Sept., 1967), 87-92.

Karl Keller, "Alephs, Zahirs, and the Triumph of Ambiguity: Typology in Nineteenth-Century American Literature," in Literary Uses of Typology from the Late Middle Ages to the Present, pp. 290-291.

James A. Kilby, "Walt Whitman's 'Trippers and Askers,'" AN&Q, 4 (Nov., 1965), 37-39.

John Kinnaird, "The Paradox of an American 'Identity,'" PR, 25 (Summer, 1958), 385-394.

Donald D. Kummings, "The Vernacular Hero in Whitman's 'Song of Myself,'" WWR, 23 (March, 1977), 23-34.

T. O. Mabbott, Expl, 5 (April, 1947), 43.
   Rpt. The Explicator Cyclopedia, II, p. 354.

T. O. Mabbott, _Expl_, 11 (March, 1953), 34.
  Rpt. The Explicator Cyclopedia, II, pp. 354-355.

Robin Magowan, "The Horse of Gods: Possession in 'Song of Myself,'"
WWR, 15 (June, 1969), 67-76.

John B. Mason, "Walt Whitman's Catalogues: Rhetorical Means for Two
Journeys in 'Song of Myself,'" _AL_, 45 (March, 1973), 34-49.

Matthiessen, _American Renaissance_, pp. 535 ff., 547-549.

James E. Miller, Jr., "'Song of Myself' as Inverted Mystical Experience,"
PMLA, 70 (Sept., 1955), 636-661.

James E. Miller, Jr., "Whitman and Eliot: The Poetry of Mysticism," _SWR_,
73 (Spring, 1958), 114-123.

James E. Mulqueen, "'Song of Myself': Whitman's Hymn to Eros," _WWR_, 20
(June, 1974), 60-66.

J. M. Nagle, "Toward Theory of Structure in 'Song of Myself,'" _WWR_, 15
(Sept., 1969), 162-171.

Mary A. Neuman, "'Song of Myself,' Section 21: An Explication," _WWR_,
13 (Sept., 1967), 98-99.

Michael Orth, "Walt Whitman, Metaphysical Teapot: The Structure of 'Song
of Myself,'" _WWR_, 14 (March, 1968), 16-24.

Pearce, _The Continuity of American Poetry_, pp. 72-83, 167-168.

Roy Harvey Pearce, "Toward an American Epic," _HudR_, 12 (Autumn, 1959),
366-370.

Elizabeth Phillips, "'Song of Myself': The Numbers of the Poem in Relation to its Form," _WWR_, 16 (Sept., 1970), 67-81.

Michael D. Reed, "First Person Persona and the Catalogue in 'Song of
Myself,'" _WWR_, 23 (Dec., 1977), 147-155.

Alfred S. Reid, "The Structure of 'Song of Myself' Reconsidered," _SHR_, 7
(Fall, 1973), 507-514.

A. H. Rose, "Destructive Vision in the First and Last Versions of 'Song
of Myself,'" _WWR_, 15 (Dec., 1969), 215-222.

P. Z. Rosenthal, "'Dilation' in Whitman's Early Writing," _WWR_, 20 (March,
1974), 3-14.

Thomas J. Roundtree, "Whitman's Indirect Expression and Its Application
to 'Song of Myself,'" _PMLA_, 73 (Dec., 1958), 549-555.

Carl F. Strauch, "The Structure of Walt Whitman's 'Song of Myself,'"
_EJ_, (college ed.), 27 (Sept., 1938), 597-607.

George Y. Trail, "Whitman's Spear of Summer Grass: Epic Invocations in
'Song of Myself,'" _WWR_, 23 (Sept., 1977), 120-125.

_____. "Song of the Broad-Axe"
Stanley Coffman, Jr., _Expl_, 12 (April, 1954), 39.

Robin P. Hoople, "'Chants Democratic and Native American': A Neglected
Sequence in the Growth of _Leaves of Grass_," _AL_, 42 (May, 1970), 185-187.

Linda S. Peavy, "'Wooded Flesh and Metal Bone': A Look at the Riddle of
the Broad-Axe," _WWR_, 20 (Dec., 1974), 152-154.

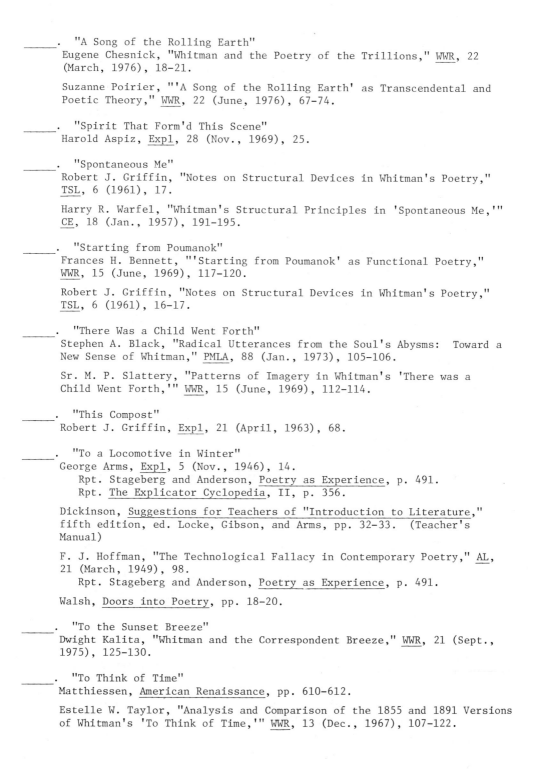

_____. "A Song of the Rolling Earth"
Eugene Chesnick, "Whitman and the Poetry of the Trillions," WWR, 22
(March, 1976), 18-21.

Suzanne Poirier, "'A Song of the Rolling Earth' as Transcendental and
Poetic Theory," WWR, 22 (June, 1976), 67-74.

_____. "Spirit That Form'd This Scene"
Harold Aspiz, Expl, 28 (Nov., 1969), 25.

_____. "Spontaneous Me"
Robert J. Griffin, "Notes on Structural Devices in Whitman's Poetry,"
TSL, 6 (1961), 17.

Harry R. Warfel, "Whitman's Structural Principles in 'Spontaneous Me,'"
CE, 18 (Jan., 1957), 191-195.

_____. "Starting from Poumanok"
Frances H. Bennett, "'Starting from Poumanok' as Functional Poetry,"
WWR, 15 (June, 1969), 117-120.

Robert J. Griffin, "Notes on Structural Devices in Whitman's Poetry,"
TSL, 6 (1961), 16-17.

_____. "There Was a Child Went Forth"
Stephen A. Black, "Radical Utterances from the Soul's Abysms: Toward a
New Sense of Whitman," PMLA, 88 (Jan., 1973), 105-106.

Sr. M. P. Slattery, "Patterns of Imagery in Whitman's 'There was a
Child Went Forth,'" WWR, 15 (June, 1969), 112-114.

_____. "This Compost"
Robert J. Griffin, Expl, 21 (April, 1963), 68.

_____. "To a Locomotive in Winter"
George Arms, Expl, 5 (Nov., 1946), 14.
        Rpt. Stageberg and Anderson, Poetry as Experience, p. 491.
        Rpt. The Explicator Cyclopedia, II, p. 356.

Dickinson, Suggestions for Teachers of "Introduction to Literature,"
fifth edition, ed. Locke, Gibson, and Arms, pp. 32-33. (Teacher's
Manual)

F. J. Hoffman, "The Technological Fallacy in Contemporary Poetry," AL,
21 (March, 1949), 98.
        Rpt. Stageberg and Anderson, Poetry as Experience, p. 491.

Walsh, Doors into Poetry, pp. 18-20.

_____. "To the Sunset Breeze"
Dwight Kalita, "Whitman and the Correspondent Breeze," WWR, 21 (Sept.,
1975), 125-130.

_____. "To Think of Time"
Matthiessen, American Renaissance, pp. 610-612.

Estelle W. Taylor, "Analysis and Comparison of the 1855 and 1891 Versions
of Whitman's 'To Think of Time,'" WWR, 13 (Dec., 1967), 107-122.

_____. "Transpositions"
Robin P. Hoople, "'Chants Democratic and Native American': A Neglected
Sequence in the Growth of Leaves of Grass," AL, 42 (May, 1970), 189-190.

_____. "Twenty-eight Young Men"
James Davidson, "Whitman's 'Twenty-eight Young Men,'" WWR, 12 (Dec.,
1966), 100-101.

_____. "Two Rivulets"
Alfred H. Marks, "Whitman's Triadic Imagery," AL, 23 (March, 1951), 105-
106.

_____. "Unfolded Out of the Folds"
Harold Aspiz, "Unfolding the Folds," WWR, 12 (Dec., 1966), 81-87.

_____. "A Voice From Death"
Rose Cherie Reissman, "Recurrent Motifs in Good-bye My Fancy," WWR, 21
(March, 1975), 32.

_____. "When I Heard the Learn'd Astronomer"
Blair and Gerber, Better Reading 2: Literature, p. 114.

Bernth Lindfors, "Whitman's 'When I heard the Learn'd Astronomer,'" WWR,
10 (March, 1964), 19-21.

_____. "When Lilacs Last in the Dooryard Bloom'd"
Richard P. Adams, "Whitman's 'Lilacs' and the Tradition of Pastoral
Elegy," PMLA, 72 (June, 1957), 479-487.

Harsharan Singh Ahluwalia, "The Private Self and the Public Self in
Whitman's 'Lilacs,'" WWR, 23 (Dec., 1977), 166-175.

Gay Wilson Allen, Expl, 10 (June, 1952), 55.
    Rpt. The Explicator Cyclopedia, II, pp. 358-359.

Brooks, Lewis, and Warren, American Literature, pp. 942-943.

Calvin S. Brown, Music and Literature (Athens: Univ. of Georgia Press,
1948).
    Rpt. Feidelson and Brodtkorb, Interpretations of American Literature,
    pp. 187-196.

Robert Emerson Carlile, "Leitmotif and Whitman's 'When Lilacs Last in the
Dooryard Bloom'd,'" Criticism, 13 (Fall, 1971), 329-339.

Richard A. Davison, "Ambivalent Imagery in Whitman's 'Lilacs,'" WWR, 14
(June, 1968), 54-56.

Lyle Domina, "Whitman's 'Lilacs': Process of Self-Realization," ESQ,
No. 58 (Part 4, 1970), 124-127.

Charles C. Doyle, "Poetry and Pastoral: A Dimension of Whitman's
'Lilacs,'" WWR, 15 (Dec., 1969), 242-245.

W. P. Elledge, "Whitman's 'Lilacs' As Romantic Narrative," WWR, 12
(Sept., 1966), 59-67.

Marvin Felheim, "The Problem of Structure in Some Poems by Whitman," in
Aspects of American Poetry, pp. 88-91.

Evelyn J. Hinz, "Whitman's 'Lilacs': The Power of Elegy," BuR, 20
(Fall, 1972), 35-54.

Joseph Jones, Expl, 9 (April, 1951), 42.
    Rpt. The Explicator Cyclopedia, II, pp. 356-358.

Oswald LeWinter, "Whitman's 'Lilacs,'" WWR, 10 (March, 1964), 10-14.

Matthiessen, American Renaissance, pp. 618-623.
    Rpt. Readings for Liberal Education, II, 543-547.

James A. Nelson, "Ecstasy and Transformation in Whitman's 'Lilacs,'" WWR, 18 (Dec., 1972), 113-123.

Ferner Nuhn, "Leaves of Grass Viewed as an Epic," ArQ, 7 (Winter, 1951), 335-336.

Margaret C. Patterson, "'Lilacs,' a Sonata," WWR, 14 (June, 1968), 46-50.

Joseph Pici, "An Editing of Walt Whitman's 'When Lilacs Last in the Dooryard Bloom'd,'" UDR, 9 (Summer, 1972), 35-35.

Floyd Stovall, "Main Drifts in Whitman's Poetry," AL, 4 (March, 1932), 13-15.

_____. "Whispers of Heavenly Death"
J. T. Ledbetter, "Whitman's Power in the Short Poem: A Discussion of 'Whispers of Heavenly Death,'" WWR, 21 (Dec., 1975), 155-158.

_____. "Whoever You Are Holding Me Now in Hand"
Philip Y. Coleman, "Walt Whitman's Ambiguities of 'I,'" PLL, 5 (Summer, 1969), Supplement, 42-45.

Frankenberg, Invitation to Poetry, pp. 97-99.

_____. "The World Below the Brine"
Ida Fasel, Expl, 25 (Sept., 1966), 7.

William A. Freedman, Expl, 23 (Jan., 1965), 39.

_____. "The Wound-Dresser"
Agnes Dicken Cannon, "Fervid Atmosphere and Typical Events: Autobiography in Drum-Taps," WWR, 20 (Sept., 1974), 86-87.

WHITTEMORE, Reed. "A Closet Drama"
Hayden Carruth, Poetry: A Critical Supplement, Jan., 1949, pp. 1-10.

_____. "The Primitives"
J. F. Nims, Poetry: A Critical Supplement, Oct., 1947, pp. 13-14.

WHITTIER. "Barbara Frietchie"
Arms, The Fields Were Green, pp. 43-44.

_____. "Birchbrook Mill"
Arms, The Fields Were Green, pp. 37-38.

_____. "Ichabod"
Arms, The Fields Were Green, pp. 39-40.

Wayne R. Kime, Expl, 28 (March, 1970), 59.

Notley Sinclair Maddox, Expl, 18 (Apil, 1960), 38.
    Rpt. The Explicator Cyclopedia, II, pp. 359-360.

Notley Sinclair Maddox, Expl, 30 (March, 1972), 59.

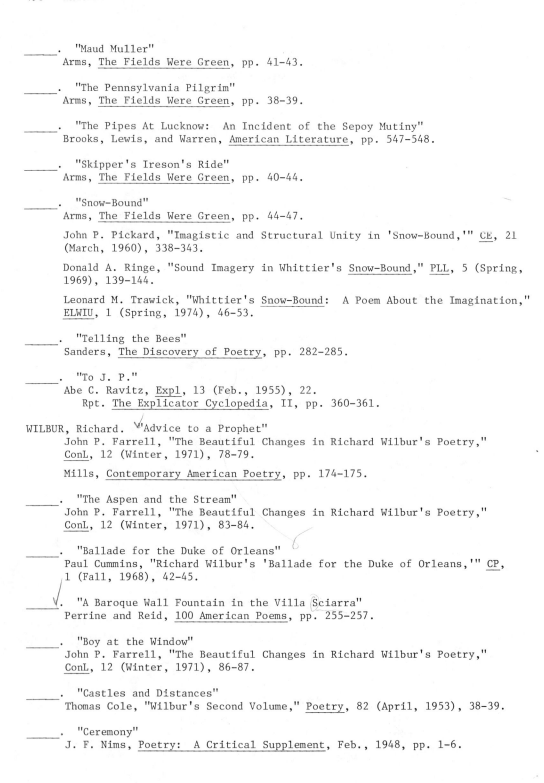

_____. "Maud Muller"
Arms, The Fields Were Green, pp. 41-43.

_____. "The Pennsylvania Pilgrim"
Arms, The Fields Were Green, pp. 38-39.

_____. "The Pipes At Lucknow: An Incident of the Sepoy Mutiny"
Brooks, Lewis, and Warren, American Literature, pp. 547-548.

_____. "Skipper's Ireson's Ride"
Arms, The Fields Were Green, pp. 40-44.

_____. "Snow-Bound"
Arms, The Fields Were Green, pp. 44-47.

John P. Pickard, "Imagistic and Structural Unity in 'Snow-Bound,'" CE, 21 (March, 1960), 338-343.

Donald A. Ringe, "Sound Imagery in Whittier's Snow-Bound," PLL, 5 (Spring, 1969), 139-144.

Leonard M. Trawick, "Whittier's Snow-Bound: A Poem About the Imagination," ELWIU, 1 (Spring, 1974), 46-53.

_____. "Telling the Bees"
Sanders, The Discovery of Poetry, pp. 282-285.

_____. "To J. P."
Abe C. Ravitz, Expl, 13 (Feb., 1955), 22.
    Rpt. The Explicator Cyclopedia, II, pp. 360-361.

WILBUR, Richard. "Advice to a Prophet"
John P. Farrell, "The Beautiful Changes in Richard Wilbur's Poetry," ConL, 12 (Winter, 1971), 78-79.

Mills, Contemporary American Poetry, pp. 174-175.

_____. "The Aspen and the Stream"
John P. Farrell, "The Beautiful Changes in Richard Wilbur's Poetry," ConL, 12 (Winter, 1971), 83-84.

_____. "Ballade for the Duke of Orleans"
Paul Cummins, "Richard Wilbur's 'Ballade for the Duke of Orleans,'" CP, 1 (Fall, 1968), 42-45.

_____. "A Baroque Wall Fountain in the Villa Sciarra"
Perrine and Reid, 100 American Poems, pp. 255-257.

_____. "Boy at the Window"
John P. Farrell, "The Beautiful Changes in Richard Wilbur's Poetry," ConL, 12 (Winter, 1971), 86-87.

_____. "Castles and Distances"
Thomas Cole, "Wilbur's Second Volume," Poetry, 82 (April, 1953), 38-39.

_____. "Ceremony"
J. F. Nims, Poetry: A Critical Supplement, Feb., 1948, pp. 1-6.

_____. "The Death of a Toad"
Abbe, You and Contemporary Poetry, pp. 73-76.

Sanders, The Discovery of Poetry, pp. 182-186.

_____. "Driftwood"
John P. Farrell, "The Beautiful Changes in Richard Wilbur's Poetry,"
ConL, 12 (Winter, 1971), 84-85.

J. F. Nims and Richard Wilbur, Poetry: A Critical Supplement, Dec.,
1948, pp. 1-7.

_____. "Epistemology"
R. H. Miller, Expl, 34 (Jan., 1976), 37.

_____. "Exeunt"
Philip C. Kolin, "The Subtle Drama of Richard Wilbur's 'Exeunt,'" NConL,
5 (Jan., 1975), 11-13.

_____. "For the New Railway Station in Rome"
Perrine and Reid, 100 American Poems, pp. 258-259.

_____. "Grasse: The Olive Trees"
Thomas Cole, "Wilbur's Second Volume," Poetry, 82 (April, 1953), 37-38.

_____. "Junk"
Mills, Contemporary American Poetry, pp. 163-166.

_____. "Looking into History"
John P. Farrell, "The Beautiful Changes in Richard Wilbur's Poetry,"
ConL, 12 (Winter, 1971), 79-83.

_____. "Love Calls Us to the Things of this World"
Jerome, Poetry: Premeditated Art, pp. 180-183.

_____. "The Mill"
Perrine and Reid, 100 American Poems, pp. 260-261.

_____. "A Plain Song for Comadre"
William Heyen, "On Richard Wilbur," SoR, 9 (Summer, 1973), 629-630.

_____. "Poplar, Sycamore"
Mills, Contemporary American Poetry, pp. 161-162.

_____. "The Puritans"
Mary S. Mattfield, Expl, 28 (Feb., 1970), 53.

_____. "A Simile for Her Smile"
J. F. Nims, Poetry: A Critical Supplement, Feb., 1948, pp. 6-9.

_____. "Statues"
John P. Farrell, "The Beautiful Changes in Richard Wilbur's Poetry,
ConL, 12 (Winter, 1971), 85-86.

_____. Still, Citizen Sparrow"
Dickinson, Suggestions for Teachers of "Introduction to Literature,"
fifth edition, ed. Locke, Gibson, and Arms, pp. 51-52. (Teacher's
Manual)

Charles R. Woodard, Expl, 34 (Feb., 1976), 46.

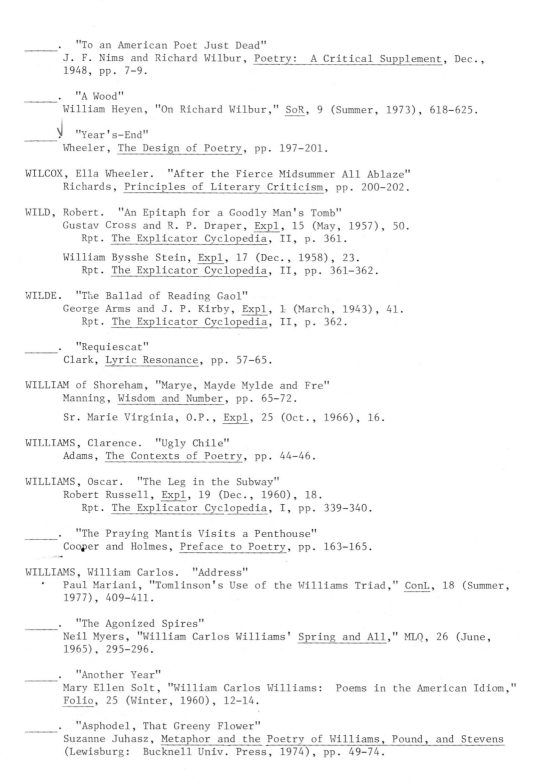

_____. "To an American Poet Just Dead"
J. F. Nims and Richard Wilbur, <u>Poetry: A Critical Supplement</u>, Dec.,
1948, pp. 7-9.

_____. "A Wood"
William Heyen, "On Richard Wilbur," <u>SoR</u>, 9 (Summer, 1973), 618-625.

_____. "Year's-End"
Wheeler, <u>The Design of Poetry</u>, pp. 197-201.

WILCOX, Ella Wheeler. "After the Fierce Midsummer All Ablaze"
Richards, <u>Principles of Literary Criticism</u>, pp. 200-202.

WILD, Robert. "An Epitaph for a Goodly Man's Tomb"
Gustav Cross and R. P. Draper, <u>Expl</u>, 15 (May, 1957), 50.
    Rpt. <u>The Explicator Cyclopedia</u>, II, p. 361.

William Bysshe Stein, <u>Expl</u>, 17 (Dec., 1958), 23.
    Rpt. <u>The Explicator Cyclopedia</u>, II, pp. 361-362.

WILDE. "The Ballad of Reading Gaol"
George Arms and J. P. Kirby, <u>Expl</u>, 1 (March, 1943), 41.
    Rpt. <u>The Explicator Cyclopedia</u>, II, p. 362.

_____. "Requiescat"
Clark, <u>Lyric Resonance</u>, pp. 57-65.

WILLIAM of Shoreham, "Marye, Mayde Mylde and Fre"
Manning, <u>Wisdom and Number</u>, pp. 65-72.

Sr. Marie Virginia, O.P., <u>Expl</u>, 25 (Oct., 1966), 16.

WILLIAMS, Clarence. "Ugly Chile"
Adams, <u>The Contexts of Poetry</u>, pp. 44-46.

WILLIAMS, Oscar. "The Leg in the Subway"
Robert Russell, <u>Expl</u>, 19 (Dec., 1960), 18.
    Rpt. <u>The Explicator Cyclopedia</u>, I, pp. 339-340.

_____. "The Praying Mantis Visits a Penthouse"
Cooper and Holmes, <u>Preface to Poetry</u>, pp. 163-165.

WILLIAMS, William Carlos. "Address"
  Paul Mariani, "Tomlinson's Use of the Williams Triad," <u>ConL</u>, 18 (Summer,
1977), 409-411.

_____. "The Agonized Spires"
Neil Myers, "William Carlos Williams' <u>Spring and All</u>," MLQ, 26 (June,
1965), 295-296.

_____. "Another Year"
Mary Ellen Solt, "William Carlos Williams: Poems in the American Idiom,"
<u>Folio</u>, 25 (Winter, 1960), 12-14.

_____. "Asphodel, That Greeny Flower"
Suzanne Juhasz, <u>Metaphor and the Poetry of Williams, Pound, and Stevens</u>
(Lewisburg: Bucknell Univ. Press, 1974), pp. 49-74.

Paul L. Mariani, "The Satyr's Defense: Williams' 'Asphodel,'" ConL, 14 (Winter, 1973), 1-18.

Miller, Poets of Reality, pp. 356-358.

Helge N. Nilsen, "Notes on the Theme of Love in the Later Poetry of William Carlos Williams," ES, 50 (June, 1969), 273-283.

Linda Welshimer Wagner, "The Last Poems of William Carlos Williams," Criticism, 6 (Fall, 1964), 362-365.

_____. "The Attic Which Is Desire"
Willis D. Jacobs, Expl, 25 (March, 1967), 61.

_____. "Between Walls"
Willis D. Jacobs, Expl, 28 (April, 1970), 68.

Miller, Poets of Reality, pp. 345-347.

Alfred F. Rosa, Expl, 30 (Nov., 1971), 21.

John L. Simons, "The Lying Cinders: Patterns of Linguistic Unity in W. C. Williams' 'Between Walls,'" CP, 10 (Spring, 1977), 63-70.

_____. "Blizzard"
Suzanne Juhasz, Metaphor and the Poetry of Williams, Pound, and Stevens (Lewisburg: Bucknell Univ. Press, 1974), pp. 45-46.

_____. "The Botticellian Trees"
Sutton, American Free Verse, pp. 126-128.

_____. "Burning the Christmas Greens"
James K. Guimond, "William Carlos Williams and the Past: Some Clarifications," JML, 1 (May, 1971), 496-498.

William Carlos Williams in Friar and Brinnin, Modern Poetry, p. 546.

_____. "By the Road to the Contagious Hospital"
Charles V. Hartung, "A Poetry of Experience," The University of Kansas City Review, 25 (Autumn, 1958), 67-68.

John Hollander, "The Poem in the Eye," Shenandoah, 23 (Spring, 1972), 30-32.

Winters, Primitivism and Decadence, pp. 67-70.
    Rpt. In Defense of Reason, pp. 78-82.

_____. "Catastrophic Birth"
Miller, Poets of Reality, pp. 354-355.

_____. "Classic Scene"
Abad, A Formal Approach to Lyric Poetry, pp. 271-272.

_____. "The Clouds"
Burke, Language as Symbolic Action, pp. 288-290.

William Carlos Williams in Friar and Brinnin, Modern Poetry, p. 545.

_____. "The Cold Night"
Charles V. Hartung, "A Poetry of Experience," The University of Kansas City Review, 25 (Autumn, 1958), 66-67.

_____. "A Coronal"
Willis D. Jacobs, Expl, 29 (April, 1971), 64.

_____. "Death the Barber"
Neil Myers, "William Carlos Williams' Spring and All," MLQ, 26 (June, 1965), 291.

_____. "The Descent" (from Paterson)
Neil Myers, "Decreation in Williams' 'The Descent,'" Criticism, 14 (Fall, 1972), 315-327.

_____. "The Desert Music"
Neil Myers, "Williams' Imitation of Nature in 'The Desert Music,'" Criticism, 12 (Winter, 1970), 38-50.

Mary Ellen Solt, "William Carlos Williams: Poems in the American Idiom," Folio, 25 (Winter, 1960), 9-11.

_____. "Elaine"
Linda Welshimer Wagner, "The Last Poems of William Carlos Williams," Criticism, 6 (Fall, 1964), 368-370.

_____. "An Elegy for D. H. Lawrence"
Mary Ellen Solt, "William Carlos Williams: Poems in the American Idiom," Folio, 25 (Winter, 1960), 14-16.

_____. "El Hombre"
Rosenthal, The Modern Poets, p. 121.

_____. "Flowers by the Sea"
Rosenthal and Smith, Exploring Poetry, pp. 51-53.

A. J. M. Smith, "Refining Fire: The Meaning and Use of Poetry," QQ, 61 (Autumn, 1954), 355-356.

_____. "A Flowing River"
Marshall W. Stearns, "Syntax, Sense, Sound, and Dr. Williams," Poetry, 66 (April, 1945), 36-37.

_____. "Full Moon"
Emerson Brown, Jr., "William Carlos Williams' 'Full Moon' and the Medieval Dawn Song," SHR, 11 (Winter, 1977), 175-183.

_____. "The Gift"
Perrine and Reid, 100 American Poems, pp. 78-79.

_____. "The Great Figure"
James E. Breslin, "William Carlos Williams and Charles Demuth: Cross-Fertilization in the Arts," JML, 6 (April, 1977), 258-261.

_____. "Great Mullen"
Willis D. Jacobs, Expl, 28 (March, 1970), 63.

_____. "The Horse Show"
Perrine and Reid, 100 American Poems, pp. 80-81.

_____. "The Hunter"
Willis D. Jacobs, Expl, 29 (March, 1971), 60.

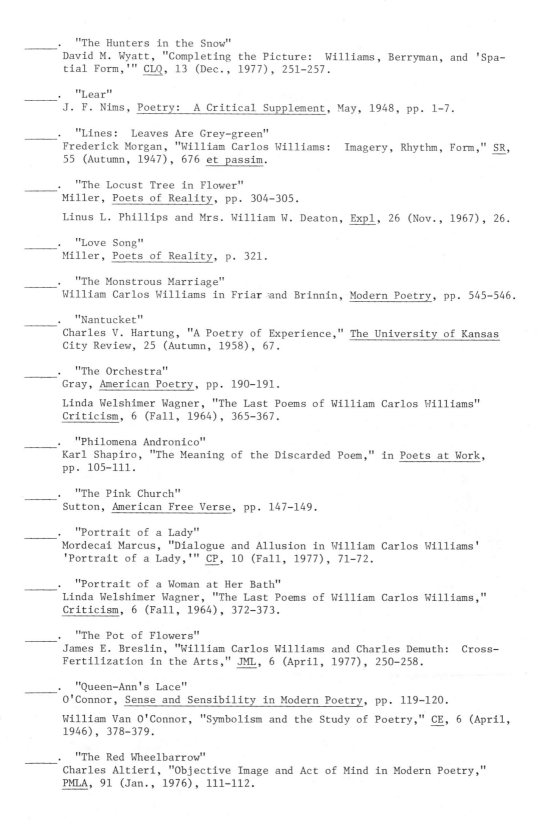

_____. "The Hunters in the Snow"
David M. Wyatt, "Completing the Picture: Williams, Berryman, and 'Spatial Form,'" CLQ, 13 (Dec., 1977), 251-257.

_____. "Lear"
J. F. Nims, Poetry: A Critical Supplement, May, 1948, pp. 1-7.

_____. "Lines: Leaves Are Grey-green"
Frederick Morgan, "William Carlos Williams: Imagery, Rhythm, Form," SR,
55 (Autumn, 1947), 676 et passim.

_____. "The Locust Tree in Flower"
Miller, Poets of Reality, pp. 304-305.

Linus L. Phillips and Mrs. William W. Deaton, Expl, 26 (Nov., 1967), 26.

_____. "Love Song"
Miller, Poets of Reality, p. 321.

_____. "The Monstrous Marriage"
William Carlos Williams in Friar and Brinnin, Modern Poetry, pp. 545-546.

_____. "Nantucket"
Charles V. Hartung, "A Poetry of Experience," The University of Kansas
City Review, 25 (Autumn, 1958), 67.

_____. "The Orchestra"
Gray, American Poetry, pp. 190-191.

Linda Welshimer Wagner, "The Last Poems of William Carlos Williams"
Criticism, 6 (Fall, 1964), 365-367.

_____. "Philomena Andronico"
Karl Shapiro, "The Meaning of the Discarded Poem," in Poets at Work,
pp. 105-111.

_____. "The Pink Church"
Sutton, American Free Verse, pp. 147-149.

_____. "Portrait of a Lady"
Mordecai Marcus, "Dialogue and Allusion in William Carlos Williams'
'Portrait of a Lady,'" CP, 10 (Fall, 1977), 71-72.

_____. "Portrait of a Woman at Her Bath"
Linda Welshimer Wagner, "The Last Poems of William Carlos Williams,"
Criticism, 6 (Fall, 1964), 372-373.

_____. "The Pot of Flowers"
James E. Breslin, "William Carlos Williams and Charles Demuth: Cross-
Fertilization in the Arts," JML, 6 (April, 1977), 250-258.

_____. "Queen-Ann's Lace"
O'Connor, Sense and Sensibility in Modern Poetry, pp. 119-120.

William Van O'Connor, "Symbolism and the Study of Poetry," CE, 6 (April,
1946), 378-379.

_____. "The Red Wheelbarrow"
Charles Altieri, "Objective Image and Act of Mind in Modern Poetry,"
PMLA, 91 (Jan., 1976), 111-112.

Stanley Archer, "Glazed in Williams's 'The Red Wheelbarrow,'" CP, 9 (Fall, 1976), 27.

Beaty and Matchett, Poetry: From Statement to Meaning, pp. 181-182.

Donald Hall, The Pleasures of Poetry (New York: Harper & Row, 1971), 41-44.

Homer Hogan, Poetry of Relevance 2 (Toronto: Methuen, 1970), pp. 7-10.

John Hollander, "Sense Variously Drawn Out': Some Observations on English Enjambment," in Literary Theory and Structure: Essays in Honor of William K. Wimsatt (New Haven: Yale Univ. Press, 1973), pp. 217-218.

John Hollander, "The Poem in the Eye," Shenandoah, 23 (Spring, 1972), 25.

Rosenthal, The Modern Poets, pp. 113-114.

Sutton, American Free Verse, pp. 120-121.

_____. "The Revelation"
Gray, American Poetry, pp. 181-182.

_____. "The Right of Way"
Neil Myers, "William Carlos Williams' Spring and All," MLQ, 26 (June, 1965), 293-294.

_____. "The Rose"
Neil Myers, "William Carlos Williams' Spring and All," MLQ, 26 (June, 1965), 297-299.

_____. "Sea-Trout and Butterfish"
Gray, American Poetry, pp. 182-183.

_____. "Song"
Brooks, Lewis, and Warren, American Literature, p. 2146.

Suzanne Juhasz, Metaphor and the Poetry of Williams, Pound, and Stevens (Lewisburg: Bucknell Univ. Press, 1974), p. 46.

_____. "A Sort of a Song"
Brooks, Lewis, and Warren, American Literature, pp. 2145-2146.

_____. "St. Francis Einstein of the Daffodils"
William Carlos Williams in Friar and Brinnin, Modern Poetry, p. 546.

_____. "Struggle of Wings"
Riding and Graves, A Survey of Modernist Poetry, pp. 201-204.

_____. "The Term"
Willis D. Jacobs, Expl, 25 (May, 1967), 73.

Robert Pinsky, The Situation of Poetry: Contemporary Poetry and Its Traditions (Princeton, New Jersey: Princeton Univ. Press, 1976), 62-65.

_____. "This Is Just to Say"
Wheeler, The Design of Poetry, pp. 63-68, 70-72, 79-80, 82-87, 282-283.

_____. "The Three Graces"
Frank Jones, Poetry: A Critical Supplement, Nov., 1949, pp. 16-17.

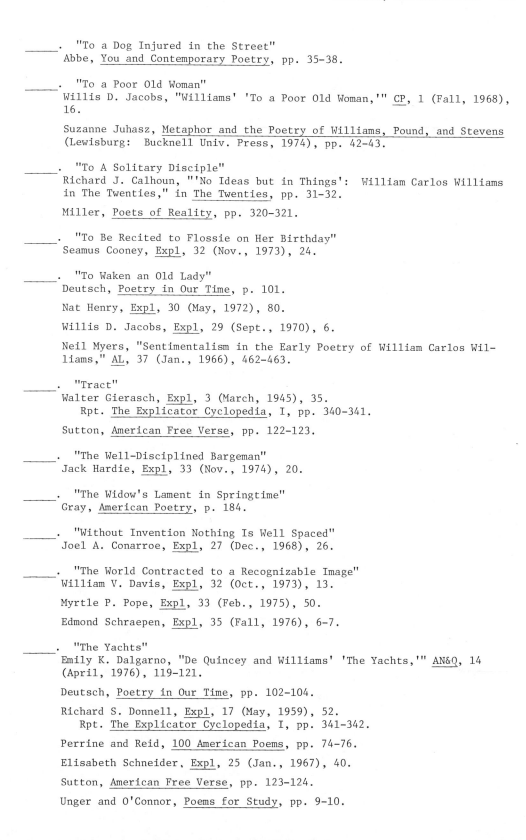

_____. "To a Dog Injured in the Street"
Abbe, You and Contemporary Poetry, pp. 35–38.

_____. "To a Poor Old Woman"
Willis D. Jacobs, "Williams' 'To a Poor Old Woman,'" CP, 1 (Fall, 1968), 16.

Suzanne Juhasz, Metaphor and the Poetry of Williams, Pound, and Stevens (Lewisburg: Bucknell Univ. Press, 1974), pp. 42–43.

_____. "To A Solitary Disciple"
Richard J. Calhoun, "'No Ideas but in Things': William Carlos Williams in The Twenties," in The Twenties, pp. 31–32.

Miller, Poets of Reality, pp. 320–321.

_____. "To Be Recited to Flossie on Her Birthday"
Seamus Cooney, Expl, 32 (Nov., 1973), 24.

_____. "To Waken an Old Lady"
Deutsch, Poetry in Our Time, p. 101.

Nat Henry, Expl, 30 (May, 1972), 80.

Willis D. Jacobs, Expl, 29 (Sept., 1970), 6.

Neil Myers, "Sentimentalism in the Early Poetry of William Carlos Williams," AL, 37 (Jan., 1966), 462–463.

_____. "Tract"
Walter Gierasch, Expl, 3 (March, 1945), 35.
    Rpt. The Explicator Cyclopedia, I, pp. 340–341.

Sutton, American Free Verse, pp. 122–123.

_____. "The Well-Disciplined Bargeman"
Jack Hardie, Expl, 33 (Nov., 1974), 20.

_____. "The Widow's Lament in Springtime"
Gray, American Poetry, p. 184.

_____. "Without Invention Nothing Is Well Spaced"
Joel A. Conarroe, Expl, 27 (Dec., 1968), 26.

_____. "The World Contracted to a Recognizable Image"
William V. Davis, Expl, 32 (Oct., 1973), 13.

Myrtle P. Pope, Expl, 33 (Feb., 1975), 50.

Edmond Schraepen, Expl, 35 (Fall, 1976), 6–7.

_____. "The Yachts"
Emily K. Dalgarno, "De Quincey and Williams' 'The Yachts,'" AN&Q, 14 (April, 1976), 119–121.

Deutsch, Poetry in Our Time, pp. 102–104.

Richard S. Donnell, Expl, 17 (May, 1959), 52.
    Rpt. The Explicator Cyclopedia, I, pp. 341–342.

Perrine and Reid, 100 American Poems, pp. 74–76.

Elisabeth Schneider, Expl, 25 (Jan., 1967), 40.

Sutton, American Free Verse, pp. 123–124.

Unger and O'Connor, Poems for Study, pp. 9–10.

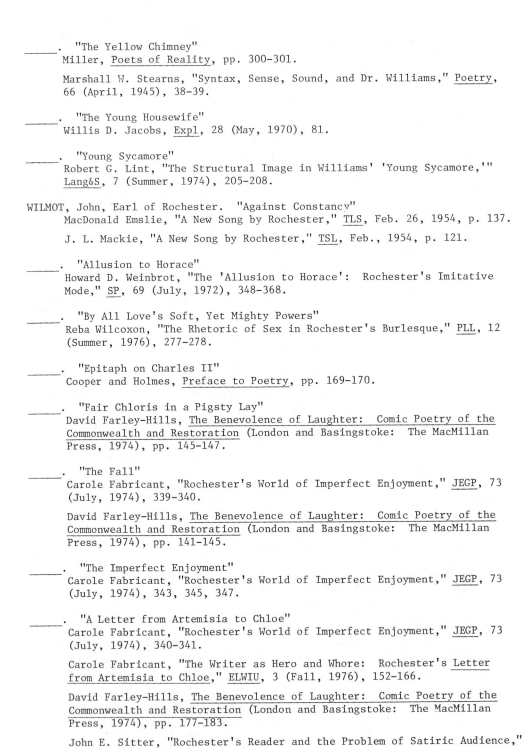

_____. "The Yellow Chimney"
Miller, Poets of Reality, pp. 300–301.

Marshall W. Stearns, "Syntax, Sense, Sound, and Dr. Williams," Poetry, 66 (April, 1945), 38–39.

_____. "The Young Housewife"
Willis D. Jacobs, Expl, 28 (May, 1970), 81.

_____. "Young Sycamore"
Robert G. Lint, "The Structural Image in Williams' 'Young Sycamore,'" Lang&S, 7 (Summer, 1974), 205–208.

WILMOT, John, Earl of Rochester. "Against Constancy"
MacDonald Emslie, "A New Song by Rochester," TLS, Feb. 26, 1954, p. 137.

J. L. Mackie, "A New Song by Rochester," TSL, Feb., 1954, p. 121.

_____. "Allusion to Horace"
Howard D. Weinbrot, "The 'Allusion to Horace': Rochester's Imitative Mode," SP, 69 (July, 1972), 348–368.

_____. "By All Love's Soft, Yet Mighty Powers"
Reba Wilcoxon, "The Rhetoric of Sex in Rochester's Burlesque," PLL, 12 (Summer, 1976), 277–278.

_____. "Epitaph on Charles II"
Cooper and Holmes, Preface to Poetry, pp. 169–170.

_____. "Fair Chloris in a Pigsty Lay"
David Farley-Hills, The Benevolence of Laughter: Comic Poetry of the Commonwealth and Restoration (London and Basingstoke: The MacMillan Press, 1974), pp. 145–147.

_____. "The Fall"
Carole Fabricant, "Rochester's World of Imperfect Enjoyment," JEGP, 73 (July, 1974), 339–340.

David Farley-Hills, The Benevolence of Laughter: Comic Poetry of the Commonwealth and Restoration (London and Basingstoke: The MacMillan Press, 1974), pp. 141–145.

_____. "The Imperfect Enjoyment"
Carole Fabricant, "Rochester's World of Imperfect Enjoyment," JEGP, 73 (July, 1974), 343, 345, 347.

_____. "A Letter from Artemisia to Chloe"
Carole Fabricant, "Rochester's World of Imperfect Enjoyment," JEGP, 73 (July, 1974), 340–341.

Carole Fabricant, "The Writer as Hero and Whore: Rochester's Letter from Artemisia to Chloe," ELWIU, 3 (Fall, 1976), 152–166.

David Farley-Hills, The Benevolence of Laughter: Comic Poetry of the Commonwealth and Restoration (London and Basingstoke: The MacMillan Press, 1974), pp. 177–183.

John E. Sitter, "Rochester's Reader and the Problem of Satiric Audience," PLL, 12 (Summer, 1976), 293–297.

Howard D. Weinbrot, "The Swelling Volume: The Apocalyptic Satire of Rochester's Letter From Artemisia In The Town To Chloe In The Country," SLitI, 5 (Oct., 1972), 19-37.

_____. "Love and Life"
Reba Wilcoxon, "Rochester's Philosophical Premises: A Case for Consistency," ECS, 8 (Winter, 1974/75), 198-200.

_____. "The Maim'd Debauchee"
Carole Fabricant, "Rochester's World of Imperfect Enjoyment," JEGP, 73 (July, 1974), 342.

David Farley-Hills, The Benevolence of Laughter: Comic Poetry of the Commonwealth and Restoration (London and Basingstoke: The MacMillan Press, 1974), pp. 139-141.

Williamson, The Proper Wit of Poetry, pp. 127-129.

_____. "A Ramble in St. James's"
Carole Fabricant, "Rochester's World of Imperfect Enjoyment," JEGP, 73 (July, 1974), 341-342, 348-350.

Kristoffer F. Paulson, "The 'Dog-Drawn Bitch' of Rochester's Ramble," Satire Newsletter, 10 (1972), 28-29.

Reba Wilcoxon, "The Rhetoric of Sex in Rochester's Burlesque," PLL, 12 (Summer, 1976), 279-284.

_____. "Satire Against Reason and Mankind"

Thomas H. Fijimura, "Rochester's 'Satyr Against Mankind': An Analysis," SP, 55 (Oct., 1958), 576-590.

Ronald W. Johnson, "Rhetoric and Drama in Rochester's "Satyr against Reason and Mankind,'" SEL, 15 (Summer, 1975), 367-373.

Charles A. Knight, "The Paradox of Reason: Argument in Rochester's 'Satyr Against Mankind,'" MLR, 65 (April, 1970), 254-260.

Kristoffer F. Paulson, "The Reverend Edward Stillingfleet and the 'Epilogue' to Rochester's A Satyr against Reason and Mankind," PQ, 50 (Oct., 1971), 657-663.

K. E. Robinson, "Rochester and Hobbes and the Irony of A Satyr against Reason and Mankind," YES, 3 (1973), 108-119.

Reba Wilcoxon, "Rochester's Philosophical Premises: A Case for Consistency," ECS, 8 (Winter, 1974/75), 189-198.

_____. "Song of a Young Lady to Her Ancient Lover"
John R. Clark, "Satiric Singing: An Example from Rochester," EngR, 24 (1973), 16-20.

Carole Fabricant, "Rochester's World of Imperfect Enjoyment," JEGP, 73 (July, 1974), 343-344.

_____. "Timon"
Carole Fabricant, "Rochester's World of Imperfect Enjoyment," JEGP, 73 (July, 1974), 342-343.

_____. "Tunbridge Wells"
Carole Fabricant, "Rochester's World of Imperfect Enjoyment," JEGP, 73 (July, 1974), 340-341.

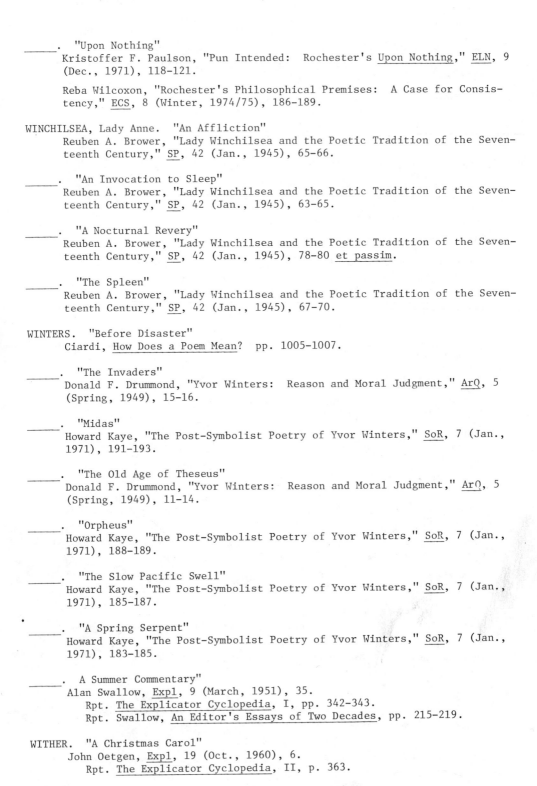

_____. "Upon Nothing"
Kristoffer F. Paulson, "Pun Intended: Rochester's Upon Nothing," ELN, 9 (Dec., 1971), 118-121.

Reba Wilcoxon, "Rochester's Philosophical Premises: A Case for Consistency," ECS, 8 (Winter, 1974/75), 186-189.

WINCHILSEA, Lady Anne. "An Affliction"
Reuben A. Brower, "Lady Winchilsea and the Poetic Tradition of the Seventeenth Century," SP, 42 (Jan., 1945), 65-66.

_____. "An Invocation to Sleep"
Reuben A. Brower, "Lady Winchilsea and the Poetic Tradition of the Seventeenth Century," SP, 42 (Jan., 1945), 63-65.

_____. "A Nocturnal Revery"
Reuben A. Brower, "Lady Winchilsea and the Poetic Tradition of the Seventeenth Century," SP, 42 (Jan., 1945), 78-80 et passim.

_____. "The Spleen"
Reuben A. Brower, "Lady Winchilsea and the Poetic Tradition of the Seventeenth Century," SP, 42 (Jan., 1945), 67-70.

WINTERS. "Before Disaster"
Ciardi, How Does a Poem Mean? pp. 1005-1007.

_____. "The Invaders"
Donald F. Drummond, "Yvor Winters: Reason and Moral Judgment," ArQ, 5 (Spring, 1949), 15-16.

_____. "Midas"
Howard Kaye, "The Post-Symbolist Poetry of Yvor Winters," SoR, 7 (Jan., 1971), 191-193.

_____. "The Old Age of Theseus"
Donald F. Drummond, "Yvor Winters: Reason and Moral Judgment," ArQ, 5 (Spring, 1949), 11-14.

_____. "Orpheus"
Howard Kaye, "The Post-Symbolist Poetry of Yvor Winters," SoR, 7 (Jan., 1971), 188-189.

_____. "The Slow Pacific Swell"
Howard Kaye, "The Post-Symbolist Poetry of Yvor Winters," SoR, 7 (Jan., 1971), 185-187.

_____. "A Spring Serpent"
Howard Kaye, "The Post-Symbolist Poetry of Yvor Winters," SoR, 7 (Jan., 1971), 183-185.

_____. A Summer Commentary"
Alan Swallow, Expl, 9 (March, 1951), 35.
    Rpt. The Explicator Cyclopedia, I, pp. 342-343.
    Rpt. Swallow, An Editor's Essays of Two Decades, pp. 215-219.

WITHER. "A Christmas Carol"
John Oetgen, Expl, 19 (Oct., 1960), 6.
    Rpt. The Explicator Cyclopedia, II, p. 363.

WOODS, John. "Best in the Orchard"
Dave Smith, "Fifty Years, Mrs. Carter: The Poetry of John Woods," MQ, 17 (Summer, 1976), 413-417.

WORDSWORTH. "Animal Tranquillity and Decay"
Cleanth Brooks, "Wordsworth and Human Suffering: Notes on Two Early Poems," in From Sensibility to Romanticism, pp. 380-381.

———. "Anticipation. October, 1803"
Edwards, Imagination and Power, pp. 171-173.

———. "The Brothers"
Stephen M. Parrish, "Dramatic Technique in the Lyrical Ballads," PMLA, 74 (March, 1959), 92.

———. "The Childless Father"
Robert R. Harson, "Wordsworth's Narrator in 'The Childless Father,'" AN&Q, 13 (May, 1975), 138-140.

———. "Composed Among the Ruins of a Castle in North Wales"
Vivante, English Poetry, p. 118.

———. "Composed Upon Westminster Bridge"
Abad, A Formal Approach to Lyric Poetry, pp. 258-259.

Beach, A Romantic View of Poetry, pp. 64-71.

Beaty and Matchett, Poetry: From Statement to Meaning, pp. 18-21.

Cleanth Brooks, "The Language of Paradox," in The Language of Poetry, pp. 39-42.
   Rpt. Criticism, p. 359.

Brooks, The Well Wrought Urn, pp. 5-6.
   Rpt. Critiques, pp. 67-68.
   Rpt. American Literary Criticism, pp. 518-520.

Daiches and Charvat, Poems in English, pp. 697-698.

Charles G. Davis, "The Structure of Wordsworth's Sonnet 'Composed Upon Westminster Bridge,'" English, 19 (Spring, 18-21.

Joseph M. Garrison, Jr., "Knowledge and Beauty in Wordsworth's 'Composed Upon Westminster Bridge,'" RS, 40 (March, 1972), 46-47.

Charles V. Hartung, "Wordsworth on Westminster Bridge: Paradox or Harmony?" CE, 13 (Jan., 1952), 201-203.

G. M. Harvey, "The Design of Wordsworth's Sonnets," ArielE, 6 (July, 1975), 80.

Hill, Constituent and Pattern in Poetry, pp. 50-52.

F. R. Leavis, "Imagery and Movement," Scrutiny, 13 (Sept., 1945), 127-130.

Millet, Reading Poetry, pp. 19-20.

Harvey Peter Sucksmith, "Ultimate Affirmation: A Critical Analysis of Wordsworth's Sonnet, 'Composed upon Westminster Bridge,' and the Image of the City in The Prelude," YES, 6 (1976), 113-115.

Van Doren, Introduction to Poetry, pp. 55-58.

Wheeler, The Design of Poetry, pp. 51-52, 163-168, 225-226.

C. V. Wicker, "On Wordsworth's Westminster Bridge Sonnet," Rocky Mountain Modern Language Association Bulletin, 9 (Oct., 1955), 4.

____. "The Danish Boy"
Geoffrey H. Hartman, "Wordsworth and Goethe in Literary History," NLH, 6 (Winter, 1975), 396-403.

____. "Elegiac Stanzas"
Ernest Bernhardt-Kabisch, Expl, 23 (May, 1965), 71.

Bloom, The Visionary Company, pp. 179-182.

Bostetter, The Romantic Ventriloquists, pp. 40-41.

Joseph M. Griska, Jr., "Wordsworth's Mood Disturbance: A Psychoanalytic Approach to Three Poems," L&P, 24, No. 4 (1974), 151.

Charles I. Patterson, "The Meaning and Significance of Wordsworth's 'Peele Castle,'" JEGP, 56 (Jan., 1957), 1-9.

Charles J. Smith, "The Contrarieties: Wordsworth's Dualistic Imagery," PMLA, 69 (Dec., 1954), 1188-1189.

____. "Elegiac Stanzas Suggested by a Picture of Peele Castle"
Karl Kroeber, Romantic Landscape Vision: Constable and Wordsworth (Madison: Univ. of Wisconsin Press, 1975), pp. 44-60.

____. "An Evening Walk"
Pottle, The Idiom of Poetry, pp. 105-122; (1946 ed.), pp. 111-121.

____. "The Fountain"
Adams, The Contexts of Poetry, pp. 32-34.

Anne Kostelanetz, "Wordsworth's 'Conversations': A Reading of 'The Two April Mornings' and 'The Fountain, a Conversation,'" ELH, 33 (March, 1966), 43-52.

Harold E. Toliver, Pastoral: Forms and Attitudes (Berkeley: Univ. of California Press, 1971), pp. 249-251.

____. "Goody Blake and Harry Gill"
Paul Edwards, "The Narrator's Voice in 'Goody Blake and Harry Gill,'" English, 19 (Spring, 1970), 13-17.

John F. Jordan, "Wordsworth's Humor," PMLA, 73 (March, 1958), 89.

____. "Hart-Leap Well"
James B. Twitchell, "'Hart-Leap Well': Wordsworth's Crucifixion Poem," TSL, 20 (1975), 11-16.

____. "The Idiot Boy"
Alan R. Jones, "The Compassionate World: Some Observations on Wordsworth's Lyrical Ballads of 1798," English, 19 (Spring, 1970), 9-12.

John E. Jordan, "Wordsworth's Humor," PMLA, 73 (March, 1/58), 88-89.

Roger Murray, "Betty Foy: An Early Mental Traveler," JEGP, 70 (Jan., 1971), 51-61.

Stephen M. Parrish, "Dramatic Technique in the Lyrical Ballads," PMLA, 74 (March, 1959), 87-88.

Albert E. Wilhelm, "The Dramatized Narrator in Wordsworth's The Idiot Boy," JNT, 5 (Jan., 1975), 16-23.

_____. "I Grieved for Buonaparte"
Dell H. Hymes, "Phonological Aspects of Style: Some English Sonnets," in Essays on the Language of Literature, ed. Seymour Chatman and Samuel R. Levin (Boston: Houghton Mifflin Company, 1967), p. 42.

_____. "I Thought of Thee, My Partner and My Guide"
Stewart C. Wilcox, "Wordsworth's River Duddon Sonnets," PMLA, 69 (March, 1954), 139-141.

_____. "It Is a Beauteous Evening"
T. O. Beachcroft, "Nicholas Ferror and George Herbert," The Criterion, 12 (Oct., 1932), 30-31.

Cleanth Brooks, "The Language of Paradox," in The Language of Poetry, pp. 38-39 et passim.
     Rpt. Criticism, pp. 358-359.

Brooks, The Well Wrought Urn, pp. 4-5, 8-9.
     Rpt. Critiques, pp. 66-67, 70.
     Rpt. American Literary Criticism, p. 518, 522.

F. R. Leavis, "Imagery and Movement," Scrutiny, 13 (Sept., 1945), 125-127.

N. F. MacLean, "An Analysis of a Lyric Poem," The University of Kansas City Review, 8 (Spring, 1942), 202-209.

_____. "It Is Not to Be Thought of"
Dell H. Hymes, "Phonological Aspects of Style: Some Sonnets," in Essays on the Language of Literature, ed. Seymour Chatman and Samuel R. Levin (Boston: Houghton Mifflin Company, 1967), p. 43.

_____. "I Travelled Among Unknown Men"
Ball, The Heart's Events, pp. 14-15.

Francis C. Ferguson, "The Lucy Poems: Wordsworth's Quest for a Poetic Object," ELH, 40 (Winter, 1973), 541-543.

Walter Gierasch, Expl, 1 (June, 1943), 65.
     Rpt. The Explicator Cyclopedia, II, pp. 363-364.

James G. Taafe, "Poet and Lover in Wordsworth's 'Lucy Poems,'" MLR, 61 (April, 1966), 178.

_____. "I Wandered Lonely As a Cloud"
Drew, Poetry: A Modern Guide, pp. 88-92.

Frederick Garber, "Wordswroth at the Universal Dance," SIR, 8 (Spring, 1969), 168-182.

Greene, The Arts and the Art of Criticism, pp. 114-115.

Donald Hall, The Pleasures of Poetry (New York: Harper & Row, 1971), 52-55.

Frederick A. Pottle, "The Eye and the Object in the Poetry of Wordsworth," YR, 40 (Sept., 1950), 29-40.
     Rpt. Locke, Gibson, and Arms, Introduction to Literature, third edition, pp. 88-92.
     Rpt. fourth edition, pp. 79-83.

Rosenheim, What Happens in Literature, pp. 140-145.

Scott, The Poet's Craft, pp. 60-63.

Stageberg and Anderson, Poetry as Experience, pp. 194-195.

Harvey Peter Sucksmith, "Orchestra and the Golden Flower: A Critical Interpretation of the Two Versions of Wordsworth's 'I Wandered Lonely as a Cloud,'" YES, 4 (1974), 149-158.

_____. "I Watch and Long Have Watched with Calm Regret"
G. M. Harvey, "The Design of Wordsworth's Sonnets," ArielE, 6 (July, 1975), 83-85.

_____. "Laodamia"
Bloom, The Visionary Company, pp. 183-188.

Richard D. McGhee, "'Conversant with Infinity': Form and Meaning in Wordsworth's 'Laodamia,'" SP, 68 (July, 1971), 357-369.

Wormhoudt, The Demon Lover, pp. 63-67.

_____. "Lines Composed a Few Miles Above Tintern Abbey"
John Alexander Alford, "Wordsworth's Use of the Present Perfect," MLQ, 33 (June, 1972), 124-129.

James Benzigner, "Tintern Abbey Revisited," PMLA, 65 (March, 1950), 154-162.

Bloom, Poetry and Repression, pp. 53-82.

Bloom, The Visionary Company, pp. 127-136.

Dennis Camp, Expl, 29 (March, 1971), 57.

Frederick M. Combellack, Expl, 14 (June, 1956), 61.
    Rpt. The Explicator Cyclopedia, II, p. 365.

Michael G. Cooke, The Romantic Will (New Haven and London: Yale Univ. Press, 1976), pp. 47-50.

Empson, Seven Types of Ambiguity, pp. 192-194; (1947 ed.), pp. 151-154.

Albert S. Gerard, "Dark Passage: Exploring Tintern Abbey," SIR, 3 (Autumn, 1963), 10-23.

Morris Golden, The Self Observed: Swift, Johnson, and Wordsworth (Baltimore: Johns Hopkins Press, 1972), pp. 127-128.

Hartman, The Unmediated Vision, pp. 3-12, 23-26.

James L. Hill, "The Frame for the Mind: Landscape in 'Lines Composed a Few Miles Above Tintern Abbey,' 'Dover Beach,' and 'Sunday Morning,'" CentR, 18 (Winter, 1974), 33-38.

John A. Hodgson, "Wordsworth's Dialectical Transcendentalism, 1798: 'Tintern Abbey,'" Criticism, 18 (Fall, 1976), 367-380.

Kaplan, Miracles of Rare Device, pp. 30-43.

Langbaum, The Poetry of Experience, pp. 43-45, 48.

Robert M. Maniquis, "Comparison, Intensity, and Time in 'Tintern Abbey,'" Criticism, 11 (Fall, 1969), 358-382.

John R. Nabholtz, "The Integrity of Wordsworth's 'Tintern Abbey,'" JEGP, 73 (April, 1974), 227-238.

Frederick A. Pottle, Expl, 16 (March, 1958), 36.
Rpt. The Explicator Cyclopedia, II, pp. 365-366.

Ransom, The New Criticism, pp. 115-119.

Charles J. Smith, "The Contrarieties: Wordsworth's Dualistic Imagery,"
PMLA, 69 (Dec., 1954), 1184-1185.

Roy Arthur Swanson, Expl, 14 (Feb., 1956), 31.
Rpt. The Explicator Cyclopedia, II, pp. 364-365.

William I. Thompson, "Collapsed Universe and Structural Poem: An Essay
in Whiteheadian Criticism," CE, 28 (Oct., 1966), 29-32.

René Wellek, "A Letter," in The Importance of Scrutiny, pp. 25-26.
First published in Scrutiny, 1937.

Donald Wesling, "The Inevitable Ear: Freedom and Necessity in Lyric
Form, Wordsworth and After," ELH, 36 (Sept., 1969), 553-557.

Wormhoudt, The Demon Lover, pp. 52-55.

_____. "Lines Written in Early Spring"
Kirk and McCutcheon, An Introduction to the Study of Poetry, pp. 76-79.

_____. "London, 1802"
Brooks, Purser, and Warren, An Approach to Literature, pp. 496-498.
Rpt. third edition, pp. 387-390.
Rpt. fourth edition, pp. 383-385.

Walter Gierasch, Expl, 2 (April, 1944), 42.
Rpt. The Explicator Cyclopedia, II, pp. 366-367.

Dell H. Hymes, "Phonological Aspects of Style: Some English Sonnets,"
in Essays on the Language of Literature, ed. Seymour Chatman and Samuel
R. Levin (Boston: Houghton Mifflin Company, 1967), p. 43.

M. J. Wagner, English "A" Analyst, No. 1.

_____. "Lucy Gray, or Solitude"
Unger and O'Connor, Poems for Study, pp. 363-365.

_____. "The Mad Mother"
Stephen M. Parrish, "Dramatic Technique in the Lyrical Ballads," PMLA,
74 (March, 1959), 96-97.

_____. "Matthew"
Harold E. Toliver, Pastoral: Forms and Attitudes (Berkeley: Univ. of
California Press, 1971), p. 249.

_____. "Michael"
Bloom, The Visionary Company, pp. 178-179.

Brooks and Warren, Understanding Poetry, pp. 83-85. Revised edition,
pp. 36-37.

Frederick Garber, "Point of View and the Egotistical Sublime," ES, 49
(Oct., 1968), 415-417.

Peter J. Manning, "'Michael,' Luke, and Wordsworth," Criticism, 19 (Summer, 1977), 195-211.

Lore Metzger, "Wordsworth's Pastoral Covenant,". MLQ, 37 (Dec., 1976), 307-323.

James Smith, Wordsworth: A Preliminary Survey," Scrutiny, 7 (June, 1938), 52-55.

Wormhoudt, The Demon Lover, pp. 55-58.

_____. "Mutability"
John Wain, "The Liberation of Wordsworth," TC, 157 (Jan., 1955), 72-73.

Winters, Forms of Discovery, pp. 169-171.

_____. "My Heart Leaps Up When I Behold"
Richard Greenleaf, "Emerson and Wordsworth," Science and Society, 22 (Summer, 1958), 228-229.

Abbie Findlay Potts, "The Spenserian and Miltonic Influence in Wordsworth's 'Ode' and 'Rainbow,'" SP, 29 (Oct., 1932), 607-616.

Harold E. Toliver, Pastoral: Forms and Attitudes (Berkeley: Univ. of California Press, 1971), pp. 242-243.

_____. "A Night-Piece"
Neil H. Hartz, "Wordsworth and the Tears of Adam," SIR, 7 (Autumn, 1967), 17-21.

James Kissane, "'A Night-Piece,': Wordsworth's Emblem of the Mind," MLN, 71 (March, 1956), 183-186.

L. J. Swingle, "Wordsworth's Contrarieties: A Prelude to Wordsworthian Complexity," ELH, 44 (Summer, 1977), 345-349.

_____. "Nutting"
Bloom, The Visionary Company, pp. 124-127.

Alan Grob, "Wordsworth's 'Nutting,'" JEGP, 61 (Oct., 1962), 826-832.

_____. "October, 1803" ("When Looking on the Present Face of Things")
Edwards, Imagination and Power, pp. 173-176.

René Rapin, Expl, 24 (Sept., 1965), 10.

_____. "Ode: Intimations of Immortality"
Bateson, English Poetry, pp. 196-205.

Bloom, A Map of Misreading, pp. 145-149.

Bloom, The Visionary Company, pp. 166-173.

Bostetter, The Romantic Ventriloquists, pp. 36-39.

Bowra, The Romantic Imagination, pp. 76-102.

Brooks and Warren, Understanding Poetry, revised edition, pp. 639-645.

Cleanth Brooks, "The Intimations of the Ode (Reconsiderations V)," The Kenyon Review, 8 (Winter, 1946), 80-102.

Brooks, The Well Wrought Urn, pp. 114-138, 163-165.

Irene H. Chayes, "Rhetoric as Drama: An Approach to the Romantic Ode," PMLA, 79 (March, 1964), 77.

Roger L. Cox, Expl, 19 (March, 1961), 34.
    Rpt. The Explicator Cyclopedia, II, pp. 367-368.

Gilbert R. Davis, Expl, 13 (May, 1955), 45.
    Rpt. The Explicator Cyclopedia, II, p. 369.

Wallace W. Douglas, "The Professor and the Ode," The Western Review, 13 (Autumn, 1948), 4-14. (Cleanth Brooks replies, Ibid., 14-15.)

David Eggenschwiler, "Wordsworth's Discordia Discors," SIR, 8 (Winter, 1969), 89-94.

Joseph M. Griska, Jr., "Wordsworth's Mood Disturbance: A Psychoanalytic Approach to Three Poems," L&P, 24, No. 4 (1974), 150-151.

Victor M. Hamm, Expl, 12 (April, 1954), 38.
    Rpt. The Explicator Cyclopedia, II, p. 368.

Hartman, The Unmediated Vision, pp. 40-44.

Knight, The Starlit Dome, pp. 37-49 et passim.

Kenneth R. Lincoln, "Wordsworth's Mortality Ode," JEGP, 71 (April, 1972), 211-225.

Florence G. Marsh, "Wordsworth's Ode: Obstinate Questionings," SIR, 5 (Summer, 1966), 219-230.

J. K. Matthison, "Wordsworth's Ode," SP, 46 (July, 1949), 419-439.

George W. Meyer, "A Note on the Sources and Symbolism of the Intimations Ode," TSE, 3 (1953), 33-46.

Robert Meyers, Expl, 28 (Sept., 1969), 3.

Frederick A. Pottle, Expl, 13 (Feb., 1955), 23.
    Rpt. The Explicator Cyclopedia, II, pp. 368-369.

Abbie Findlay Potts, "The Spenserian and Miltonic Influence in Words-worth's 'Ode' and 'Rainbow,'" SP, 29 (Oct., 1932), 607-616.

C. E. Pulos, "The Unity of Wordsworth's Immortality Ode," SIR, 13 (Sum-mer, 1974), 179-188.

John Crowe Ransom, "William Wordsworth: Notes Toward an Understanding of Poetry," The Kenyon Review, 12 (Summer, 1950), 514-518.

Thomas M. Raysor, "The Themes of Immortality and Natural Piety in Words-worth's Immortality Ode," PMLA, 69 (Sept., 1954), 861-875.

Elisabeth Schneider, Expl, 5 (Feb., 1947), 30.
    Rpt. The Explicator Cyclopedia, II, p. 369.

Robert L. Schneider, "Failure of Solitude: Wordsworth's Immortality Ode," JEGP, 54 (Oct., 1955), 625-633.

Charles J. Smith, "The Contrarieties: Wordsworth's Dualistic Imagery," PMLA, 69 (Dec., 1954), 1186-1188.

D. A. Stauffer, "Cooperative Criticism," The Kenyon Review, 4 (Winter, 1942), 133-144.

Swallow, An Editor's Essays of Two Decades, pp. 66-69.

Lionel Trilling, "Wordsworth's 'Ode: Intimations of Immortality,'" English Institute Annual 1941, pp. 1-28.

Wormhoudt, The Demon Lover, pp. 58-62.

. "Ode to Duty"
Bloom, The Visionary Company, pp. 182-183.

Perkins, The Quest for Permanence, pp. 87-88.

_____.   "The Old Cumberland Beggar"
Bloom, The Visionary Company, pp. 173-178.

Brooks, A Shaping Joy, pp. 317-321.

Cleanth Brooks, "Wordsworth and Human Suffering: Notes on Two Early
Poems," in From Sensibility to Romanticism, pp. 373-380.

Frederick Garber, "Point of View and the Egotistical Sublime," ES, 49
(Oct., 1968), 411-414.

Stephen C. Gill, "Wordsworth's Breeches Pocket: Attitudes to the Didactic Poet," EIC, 19 (Oct., 1969), 387-393.

_____.   "On the Extinction of the Venetian Republic"
Z. S. Fink, "Wordsworth and the English Republican Tradition," JEGP, 47
(April, 1948), 118-119.

_____.   "On the Power of Sound"
Knight, The Starlit Dome, pp. 78-81.

Sewell, The Orphic Voice, pp. 320-327.

_____.   "A POET!--He Hath Put His Heart to School"
Paul Fussell, Jr., "Some Observations on Wordsworth's 'A POET!--He Hath
Put His Heart to School,'" PQ, 37 (Oct., 1958), 454-464.

_____.   "A Poet's Epitaph"
Brooks and Warren, Understanding Poetry, pp. 579-582. Revised edition,
pp. 423-427, 632.

_____.   "Power of Music"
Sewell, The Orphic Voice, pp. 316-320.

_____.   "Resolution and Independence"
Gorman Beauchamp, "Wordsworth's Archetypal Resolution," CP, 7 (Fall,
1974), 13-19.

Bloom, The Visionary Company, pp. 160-166.

Bostetter, The Romantic Ventriloquists, pp. 34-35.

Michael G. Cooke, The Romantic Will (New Haven and London: Yale Univ.
Press, 1976), pp. 210-214.

David Eggenschwiler, "Wordsworth's Discordia Discors," SIR, 8 (Winter,
1969), 79-89.

Frederick Garber, "Point of View and the Egotistical Sublime," ES, 49
(Oct., 1968), 409-411.

Joseph M. Griska, Jr., "Wordsworth's Mood Disturbance: A Psychoanalytic
Approach to Three Poems," L&P, 24, No. 4 (1974), 148-150.

Alan Grob, "Process and Permanence in 'Resolution and Independence,'"
ELH, 28 (March, 1961), 89-100.

Stanley Edgar Hyman, "A Poem of Resolution," CentR, 5 (Spring, 1961),
195-205.

Langbaum, The Poetry of Experience, pp. 54-55.

W. W. Robson, Interpretations, ed. John Wain, pp. 117-128.

Charles J. Smith, "The Contrarieties: Wordsworth's Dualistic Imagery,"
PMLA, 69 (Dec., 1954), 1185-1186.

Milton Teichman, "Wordsworth's Two Replies to Coleridge's 'Dejection: An Ode,'" <u>PMLA</u>, 86 (Oct., 1971), 983-986.

James B. Twitchell, "The Character of Wordsworth's Leech Gatherer," <u>RS</u>, 43 (Dec., 1975), 253-259.

_____. "The Ruined Cottage"
James H. Averill, "Suffering and Calm in Wordsworth's Early Poetry," <u>PMLA</u>, 91 (March, 1976), 223-224, 227-230.

Bostetter, <u>The Romantic Ventriloquists</u>, pp. 61-65.

Cleanth Brooks, "Wordsworth and Human Suffering: Notes on Two Early Poems," in <u>From Sensibility to Romanticism</u>, pp. 382-387.

_____. "Salisbury Plain"
James H. Averill, "Suffering and Calm in Wordsworth's Early Poetry," <u>PMLA</u>, 91 (March, 1976), 226-227.

_____. "The Sea Was Laughing at a Distance, All"
William Empson, "Basic English and Wordsworth," <u>The Kenyon Review</u>, 2 (Autumn, 1940), 450-457.

_____. "She Dwelt Among Untrodden Ways"
Ball, <u>The Heart's Events</u>, pp. 13-14.

Cleanth Brooks, <u>A Shaping Joy</u>, pp. 55-56.

Edwin B. Burgum, "The Cult of the Complex in Poetry," <u>Science and Society</u>, 15 (Winter, 1951), 37-41.

Daniels, <u>The Art of Reading Poetry</u>, pp. 222-224.

Frances C. Ferguson, "The Lucy Poems: Wordsworth's Quest for a Poetic Object," <u>ELH</u>, 40 (Winter, 1973), 540-541.

Greenfield and Weatherhead, ed., "Introductory Essay: The Experience of a Poem," in <u>The Poem: An Anthology</u>, pp. xxxi-xxxiii.

Roger L. Slakey, "At Zero: A Reading of Wordsworth's 'She Dwelt Among the Untrodden Ways,'" <u>SEL</u>, 12 (Autumn, 1972), 629-638.

James G. Taafe, "Poet and Lover in Wordsworth's 'Lucy Poems,'" <u>MLR</u>, 61 (April, 1966), 177-178.

J. R. Watson, "Lucy and the Earth-Mother," <u>EIC</u>, 27 (July, 1977), 189-191.

_____. "She Was a Phantom of Delight"
Walter Houghton, <u>Expl</u>, 3 (Dec., 1944), 20.
    Rpt. <u>The Explicator Cyclopedia</u>, II, pp. 372-373.

Monroe M. Stearns, <u>Expl</u>, 1 (June, 1943), 68.
    Rpt. <u>The Explicator Cyclopedia</u>, II, p. 373.

J. E. Whitesell, <u>Expl</u>, 1 (April, 1943), 46.
    Rpt. <u>The Explicator Cyclopedia</u>, II, p. 372.

_____. "Simon Lee"
Andrew L. Griffin, "Wordsworth and the Problem of Imaginative Story: The Case of 'Simon Lee,'" <u>PMLA</u>, 92 (May, 1977), 392-409.

Alun R. Jones, "The Compassionate World: Some Observations on Wordsworth's Lyrical Ballads of 1798," <u>English</u>, 19 (Spring, 1970), 8-9.

_____. "A Slumber Did My Spirit Seal"
Ball, <u>The Heart's Events</u>, pp. 17-18.

Bateson, English Poetry, pp. 32–34.

Blair and Chandler, Approaches to Poetry, p. 262.

Brooks, A Shaping Joy, pp. 56–57.

Cleanth Brooks, "Irony and 'Ironic' Poetry," CE, 9 (Feb., 1948), 235–237; EJ, 37 (Feb., 1948), 61–63.
    Rpt. Zabel, Literary Opinion in America, revised edition, pp. 735–737.

Hugh Sykes Davies, "Another New Poem by Wordsworth," EIC, 15 (April, 1965), 135–161.

Drew, Poetry: A Modern Guide, pp. 132–133.

Frances C. Ferguson, "The Lucy Poems: Wordsworth's Quest for a Poetic Object," ELH, 40 (Winter, 1973), 546–547.

Spencer Hall, "Wordsworth's 'Lucy' Poems: Context and Meaning," SIR, 10 (Summer, 1971), 168–173.

Kreuzer, Elements of Poetry, pp. 200–204.

F. R. Leavis, "'Thought' and Emotional Quality," Scrutiny, 13 (Spring, 1945), 53–55.
    Rpt. Stallman and Watters, The Creative Reader, p. 851.

Walter S. Minot, "Wordsworth's Use of diurnal in 'A Slumber Did My Spirit Seal,'" PLL, 9 (Summer, 1975), 319–322.

Rosenthal and Smith, Exploring Poetry, pp. 89–90.

Gene W. Ruoff, "Another Poem by Wordsworth," EIC, 16 (July, 1966), 359–360.

Skelton, The Poetic Pattern, pp. 182–185.

R. F. Storch, "Another New Poem by Wordsworth," EIC, 15 (Oct., 1965), 473–476.

Thomas and Brown, Reading Poems: An Introduction to Critical Study, pp. 642–643.

Harold E. Toliver, Pastoral: Forms and Attitudes (Berkeley: Univ. of California Press, 1971), p. 246.

J. R. Watson, "Lucy and the Earth-Mother," EIC, 27 (July, 1977), 199–201.

_____. "Sole Listener, Duddon! to the Breeze that Played"
Richards, Principles of Literary Criticism, pp. 207–208.

_____. "Solitary Reaper"
Melvin W. Askew, "Form and Process in Lyric Poetry," SR, 72 (April–June, 1964), 291.

Michael G. Cooke, The Romantic Will (New Haven and London: Yale Univ. Press, 1976), pp. 41–47.

Geoffrey J. Finch, "Wordsworth's Solitary Song: The Substance of 'true art' in 'The Solitary Reaper,'" ArielE, 6 (July, 1975), 91–100.

Hardy, The Curious Frame, pp. 62–81.

G. Ingli James, "Wordsworth's 'Solitary Reaper,'" EIC, 15 (Jan., 1965), 65–76.

Shun-ichi Maekawa, "Understanding 'The Solitary Reaper,'" Bulletin of the Faculty of Literature, Kyushu University, No. 12, 1968, 19–31.

Malcolm Pittock, "'The Solitary Reaper,'" EIC, 15 (April, 1965), 243-245.

Frederick A. Pottle, "The Eye and the Object in the Poetry of Wordsworth," YR, 40 (Sept., 1950), 29-40.

John Preston, "'The Moral Qualities and Scope of Things,': The Structure of The Solitary Reaper," EIC, 19 (Jan., 1969), 60-66.

Ribner and Morris, Poetry, pp. 266-268.

Donald J. Ryan, "Scansion Scanned," CE, 2 (Jan., 1941), 390-393.

Van Doren, Introduction to Poetry, pp. 51-55.

W. K. Wimsatt, Jr., "The Structure of the 'Concrete Universal' in Literature," PMLA, 62 (March, 1947), 274-275.
    Rpt. Criticism, pp. 399-400.

Wimsatt, The Verbal Icon, p. 80.
    Rpt. Locke, Gibson, and Arms, Introduction to Literature, third edition, pp. 86-87.
    Rpt. fourth edition, pp. 77-78.
    Rpt. fifth edition, pp. 77-78.

_____. "Stanzas Written in My Pocket-Copy of Thomson's 'Castle of Indolence'"
Milton Teichman, "Wordsworth's Two Replies to Coleridge's 'Dejection: An Ode,'" PMLA, 86 (Oct., 1971), 986-988.

_____. "Stepping Westward"
Beach, A Romantic View of Poetry, pp. 74-75.

_____. "Strange Fits of Passion Have I Known"
Adams, The Context of Poetry, pp. 35-36.

Ball, The Heart's Events, pp. 11-13.

Kent Begette, "Wordsworth's Medical Muse: Erasmus Darwin and Psychology in 'Strange Fits of Passion Have I Known,'" L&P, 23, No. 2 (1973), 93-101.

Frances C. Ferguson, "The Lucy Poems: Wordsworth's Quest for a Poetic Object," ELH, 40 (Winter, 1973), 538-540.

Spencer Hall, "Wordsworth's 'Lucy' Poems: Context and Meaning," SIR, 10 (Summer, 1971), 163-165.

Leavis, Revaluation, pp. 199-202.

John Price, "Wordsworth's Lucy," AI, 31 (Winter, 1974), 360-377.

James G. Taafe, "Poet and Lover in Wordsworth's 'Lucy Poems,'" MLR, 61 (April, 1966), 176-177.

J. R. Watson, "Lucy and the Earth-Mother," EIC, 27 (July, 1977), 196-198.

_____. "Surprised by Joy--Impatient as the Wind"
Brower, The Fields of Light, pp. 75-76.

Drew, Poetry: A Modern Guide, pp. 123-124.

F. R. Leavis, "Imagery and Movement," Scrutiny, 13 (Sept., 1945), 125-127.

_____. "The Thorn"
Thomas L. Ashton, "The Thorn: Wordsworth's Insensitive Plant," HLQ, 35 (Feb., 1972), 171-187.

Albert S. Gerard, "Of Trees and Men: The Unity of Wordsworth's 'The Thorn,'" EIC, 14 (July, 1964), 237-255.

Michael Kirkham, "Innocence and Experience in Wordsworth's 'The Thorn,'" ArielE, 5 (Jan., 1974), 66-80.

Stephen M. Parrish, "'The Thorn': Wordsworth's Dramatic Monologue," ELH, 24 (June, 1957), 153-163.

Donald G. Priestman, "Superstition and Imagination: Complementary Faculties of Wordsworth's Narrator in 'The Thorn,'" JNT, 5 (Sept., 1975), 196-207.

_____. "Three Years She Grew in Sun and Shower"
Ball, The Heart's Events, pp. 15-17.

Francis Christensen, Expl, 4 (Dec., 1945), 18.
    Rpt. The Explicator Cyclopedia, II, p. 374.

Fred A. Dudley, Expl, 2 (Feb., 1944), Q19.
    Rpt. The Explicator Cyclopedia, II, pp. 373-374.

Frances C. Ferguson, "The Lucy Poems: Wordsworth's Quest for a Poetic Object," ELH, 40 (Winter, 1973), 543-546.

Spencer Hall, "Wordsworth's 'Lucy' Poems: Context and Meaning," SIR, 10 (Summer, 1971), 166-168.

Charles J. Smith, "The Contrarieties: Wordsworth's Dualistic Imagery," PMLA, 69 (Dec., 1954), 1185.

James G. Taafe, "Poet and Lover in Wordsworth's 'Lucy Poems,'" MLR, 61 (April, 1966), 178-179.

Harold E. Toliver, Pastoral: Forms and Attitudes (Berkeley: Univ. of California Press, 1971), pp. 247-248.

J. R. Watson, "Lucy and the Earth-Mother," EIC, 27 (July, 1977), 191-193.

J. E. Whitesell, Expl, 2 (Nov., 1943), Q7.

_____. "To My Sister"
L. J. Swingle, "Wordsworth's Contrarieties: A Prelude to Wordsworthian Complexity," ELH, 44 (Summer, 1977), 349-350.

_____. "To the Cuckoo"
Beaty and Matchett, Poetry: From Statement to Meaning, pp. 251-254.

Murray Krieger, "Ekphrasis and the Still Movement of Poetry; or, Laokoön Revisited," in The Poet as Critic, pp. 18-19.

_____. "The Tuft of Primroses"
Laurence Goldstein, "The Auburn Syndrome: Change and Loss in 'The Deserted Village' and Grasmere," ELH, 40 (Fall, 1973), 365-369.

_____. "The Two April Mornings"
Anne Kostelanetz, "Wordsworth's 'Conversations': A Reading of 'The Two April Mornings' and 'The Fountain, A Conversation,'" ELH, 33 (March, 1966), 43-52.

Harold E. Toliver, Pastoral: Forms and Attitudes (Berkeley: Univ. of California Press, 1971), pp. 252-254.

_____. "Vernal Ode"
Richard D. McGhee, "'And Earth and Stars Composed a Universal Heaven':
A View of Wordsworth's Later Poetry," SEL, 11 (Autumn, 1971), 641-657.

_____. "We Are Seven"
Marcel Kessel, Expl, 2 (April, 1944), 43.
    Rpt. The Explicator Cyclopedia, II, p. 374.

Arthur K. Moore, "A Folk Attitude in Wordsworth's 'We are Seven,'" RES,
23 (July, 1947), 260-262.

Perkins, The Quest for Permanence, pp. 69-80.

_____. "The Winds Come to Me from the Fields of Sleep"
Nowell Smith, "Wordsworth's 'Fields of Sleep,'" TLS, Sept. 17, 1954,
p. 591.

_____. "The World Is Too Much With Us"
George Arms, Expl, 1 (Oct., 1942), 4.
    Rpt. The Explicator Cyclopedia, II, p. 375.

G. M. Harvey, "The Design of Wordsworth's Sonnets," ArielE, 6 (July,
1975), 85-89.

Karl Kroeber, "A New Reading of 'The World Is Too Much With Us,'" SIR,
2 (Spring, 1963), 183-188.

Peckham and Chatman, Word, Meaning, Poem, pp. 372-380.

_____. "Written in Very Early Youth"
Michael G. Cooke, The Romantic Will (New Haven and London: Yale Univ.
Press, 1976), pp. 208-210.

_____. "Yarrow Revisited"
Ronald Schleifer, "Wordsworth's Yarrow and the Poetics of Repetition,"
MLQ, 38 (Dec., 1977), 362-366.

_____. "Yarrow Unvisited"
Ronald Schleifer, "Wordsworth's Yarrow and the Poetics of Repetition,"
MLQ, 38 (Dec., 1977), 348-360.

_____. "Yarrow Visited"
Ronald Schleifer, "Wordsworth's Yarrow and the Poetics of Repetition,"
MLQ, 38 (Dec., 1977), 360-362.

_____. "Yew-Trees"
Michael Riffaterre, "Interpretation and Descriptive Poetry: A Reading of
Wordsworth's 'Yew-Trees,'" NLH, 4 (Winter, 1973), 229-256.

Gene W. Ruoff, "Wordsworth's 'Yew-trees' and Romantic Perception," MLQ,
34 (June, 1973), 146-160.

George Rylands, "English Poets and Abstract Words," Essays and Studies,
16 (1930), 64-65.

WOOTON. "A Hymn to My God..."
Daniels, The Art of Reading Poetry, pp. 438-442.

WRIGHT, James. "The Accusation"
Phyllis Hoge Thompson, "James Wright: His Kindliness," Ironwood, 10
Special Issue, 97-98.

_____. "Ars Poetica: Some Recent Criticism"
Dave Smith, "That Halting, Stammering Movement," Ironwood, 10, Special
Issue, 123-125.

_____. "As I Step over a Puddle at the End of Winter, I Think of an Ancient
      Chinese Governor"
Carroll, The Poem In Its Skin, pp. 190-198.

_____. "At the Slackening of the Tide"
William B. Toole, III, Expl, 22 (Dec., 1963), 29.

_____. "Autumn Begins in Martin's Ferry, Ohio"
Robert Hass, "James Wright," Ironwood, 10, Special Issue, 86-89.

_____. "A Centenary Ode: Inscribed to Little Crow, Leader of the Sioux
      Rebellion in Minnesota, 1862"
Peter Stitt, "James Wright--Poetry of the Present," Ironwood, 10, Special
Issue, 148-150.

_____. "A Dream of Burial"
Mills, Contemporary American Poetry, pp. 216-217.

_____. "Gambling in Stateline, Nevada"
Leonard Nathan, "The Private 'I' in Contemporary Poetry," Shenandoah, 22
(Summer, 1971), 90-96.

_____. "The Idea of the Good"
Leonard Nathan, "The Traditional James Wright," Ironwood, 10, Special
Issue, 131-137.

_____. "I Try to Waken and Greet the World Once Again"
Edward Butscher, "The Rise and Fall of James Wright," GaR, 28 (Summer,
1974), 259-263.

_____. "Lying in a Hammock at William Duffy's Farm in Pine Island, Minnesota"
Bruce Henricksen, Expl, 32 (Jan., 1974), 40.

George S. Lensing and Ronald Moran, Four Poets and the Emotive Imagination: Robert Bly, James Wright, Louis Simpson, and William Stafford
(Baton Rouge: Louisiana State Univ., 1976), pp. 108-110.

R. J. Spendal, Expl, 34 (May, 1976), 64.

_____. "Many of Our Waters: Variations on a Poem by a Black Child"
Lacey, The Inner War, pp. 78-81.

_____. "The Morality of Poetry"
Lacey, The Inner War, pp. 60-62.

Mills, Contemporary American Poetry, pp. 204-206.

_____. "The Old WPA Swimming Pool In Martins Ferry, Ohio"
Dave Smith, "That Halting, Stammering Movement," Ironwood, 10, Special
Issue, 127-128.

Peter Stitt, "James Wright--Poetry of the Present," Ironwood, 10, Special
Issue, 151-153.

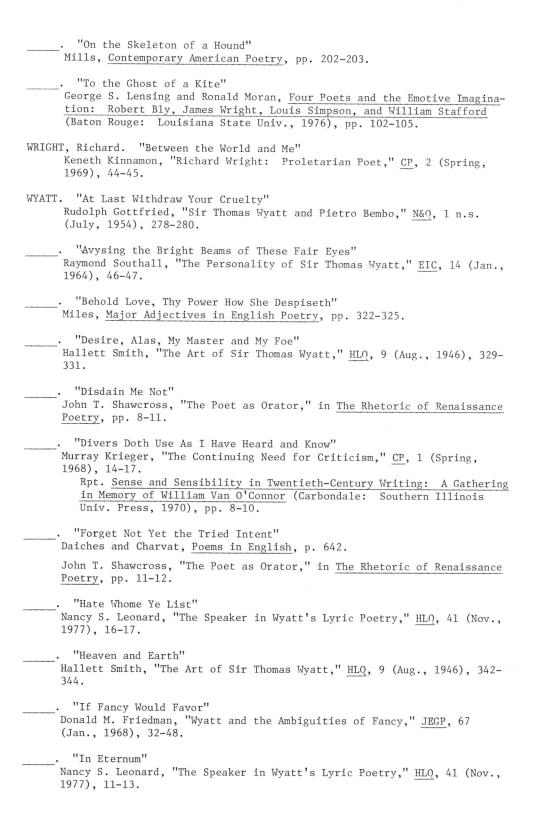

_____. "On the Skeleton of a Hound"
Mills, <u>Contemporary American Poetry</u>, pp. 202-203.

_____. "To the Ghost of a Kite"
George S. Lensing and Ronald Moran, <u>Four Poets and the Emotive Imagina-</u>
<u>tion: Robert Bly, James Wright, Louis Simpson, and William Stafford</u>
(Baton Rouge: Louisiana State Univ., 1976), pp. 102-105.

WRIGHT, Richard. "Between the World and Me"
Keneth Kinnamon, "Richard Wright: Proletarian Poet," <u>CP</u>, 2 (Spring,
1969), 44-45.

WYATT. "At Last Withdraw Your Cruelty"
Rudolph Gottfried, "Sir Thomas Wyatt and Pietro Bembo," <u>N&Q</u>, 1 n.s.
(July, 1954), 278-280.

_____. "Avysing the Bright Beams of These Fair Eyes"
Raymond Southall, "The Personality of Sir Thomas Wyatt," <u>EIC</u>, 14 (Jan.,
1964), 46-47.

_____. "Behold Love, Thy Power How She Despiseth"
Miles, <u>Major Adjectives in English Poetry</u>, pp. 322-325.

_____. "Desire, Alas, My Master and My Foe"
Hallett Smith, "The Art of Sir Thomas Wyatt," <u>HLQ</u>, 9 (Aug., 1946), 329-
331.

_____. "Disdain Me Not"
John T. Shawcross, "The Poet as Orator," in <u>The Rhetoric of Renaissance</u>
<u>Poetry</u>, pp. 8-11.

_____. "Divers Doth Use As I Have Heard and Know"
Murray Krieger, "The Continuing Need for Criticism," <u>CP</u>, 1 (Spring,
1968), 14-17.
    Rpt. <u>Sense and Sensibility in Twentieth-Century Writing: A Gathering</u>
    <u>in Memory of William Van O'Connor</u> (Carbondale: Southern Illinois
    Univ. Press, 1970), pp. 8-10.

_____. "Forget Not Yet the Tried Intent"
Daiches and Charvat, <u>Poems in English</u>, p. 642.

John T. Shawcross, "The Poet as Orator," in <u>The Rhetoric of Renaissance</u>
<u>Poetry</u>, pp. 11-12.

_____. "Hate Whome Ye List"
Nancy S. Leonard, "The Speaker in Wyatt's Lyric Poetry," <u>HLQ</u>, 41 (Nov.,
1977), 16-17.

_____. "Heaven and Earth"
Hallett Smith, "The Art of Sir Thomas Wyatt," <u>HLQ</u>, 9 (Aug., 1946), 342-
344.

_____. "If Fancy Would Favor"
Donald M. Friedman, "Wyatt and the Ambiguities of Fancy," <u>JEGP</u>, 67
(Jan., 1968), 32-48.

_____. "In Eternum"
Nancy S. Leonard, "The Speaker in Wyatt's Lyric Poetry," <u>HLQ</u>, 41 (Nov.,
1977), 11-13.

_____. "Ys Yt Possyble"
Thomas A. Hannen, "The Humanism of Sir Thomas Wyatt," in The Rhetoric of Renaissance Poetry, pp. 45-51.

_____. "It May Be Good Like It Who List"
Thomas A. Hannen, "The Humanism of Sir Thomas Wyatt," in The Rhetoric of Renaissance Poetry, pp. 51-55.

Raymond Southall, "The Personality of Sir Thomas Wyatt," EIC, 14 (Jan., 1964), 50-52.

_____. "It Was My Choice, It Was No Chance"
Peterson, The English Lyric from Wyatt to Donne, pp. 106-110.

_____. "The Long Love That in My Thought Doth Harbor"
Adams, The Contexts of Poetry, pp. 57-59.

Miles, Major Adjectives in English Poetry, pp. 325-326.

Alicia Ostriker, "Thomas Wyatt and Henry Surrey: Dissonance and Harmony in Lyric Form," NLH, 1 (Spring, 1970), 390-394.

Hallet Smith, "The Art of Sir Thomas Wyatt," HLQ, 9 (Aug., 1946), 333-337.

Raymond Southall, "The Personality of Sir Thomas Wyatt," EIC, 14 (Jan., 1964), 55-57.

_____. "The Lover Compareth His State to a Ship in a Perilous Storm Tossed on on the Sea"
S. F. Johnson and William P. Orwen, Expl, 5 (April, 1947), 40.
    Rpt. The Explicator Cyclopedia, II, pp. 375-376.

Maxwell S. Luria, "Wyatt's 'The Lover Compareth His State' and the Petrarchan Commentators," TSLL, 12 (Winter, 1971), 531-535.

Peterson, The English Lyric from Wyatt to Donne, pp. 99-100.

_____. "My Galy Charged with Forgetfulnes"
Nancy S. Leonard, "The Speaker in Wyatt's Lyric Poetry," HLQ, 41 (Nov., 1977), 6-8.

_____. "My Lute Awake"
Hallet Smith, "The Art of Sir Thomas Wyatt," HLQ, 9 (Aug., 1946), 344-345.

_____. "Ons as Me Thought Fortune Me Kyst"
Michael Bath, "Wyatt and 'Liberty,'" EIC, 23 (July, 1973), 322-328.

_____. "Patience, Though I Have Not"
John T. Shawcross, "The Poet as Orator," in The Rhetoric of Renaissance Poetry, pp. 14-16.

_____. "Processe of Tyme Worketh Suche Wounder"
Nancy S. Leonard, "The Speaker in Wyatt's Lyric Poetry," HLQ, 41 (Nov., 1977), 5-6.

_____. "Psalm 6"
Robert G. Twombly, "Wyatt's Paraphrase of the Penitential Psalms," TSLL, 12 (Fall, 1970), 352-364.

_____. "Psalm 32"
Robert G. Twombly, "Wyatt's Paraphrase of the Penitential Psalms," TSLL,
12 (Fall, 1970), 364-366.

_____. "Psalm 38"
Robert G. Twombly, "Wyatt's Paraphrase of the Penitential Psalms," TSLL,
12 (Fall, 1970), 366-369.

_____. Psalm 51"
Robert G. Twombly, "Wyatt's Paraphrase of the Penitential Psalms," TSLL,
12 (Fall, 1970), 345-347, 369-376.

_____. "Psalm 102"
Robert G. Twombly, "Wyatt's Paraphrase of the Penitential Psalms," TSLL,
12 (Fall, 1970), 376-379.

_____. "Psalm 143"
Robert G. Twombly, "Wyatt's Paraphrase of the Penitential Psalms," TSLL,
12 (Fall, 1970), 379-380.

_____. "Resound My Voyse; Ye Wodes That Here Me Plain"
Raymond Southall, "The Personality of Sir Thomas Wyatt," EIC, 14 (Jan.,
1964), 53-54.

_____. "There Was Never Nothing More Me Payned"
John Douglas Boyd, "Literary Interpretation and the Subjective Correlative: An Illustration from Wyatt," EIC, 21 (Oct., 1971), 327-346.

Joost Daalder, "Wyatt's 'There Was Never Nothing More Me Payned': A
Reply to John Douglas Boyd," EIC, 21 (Oct., 1971), 418-424.

_____. "They Flee from Me"
Bateson, English Poetry, pp. 142-146.

Bateson, English Poetry and the English Language, pp. 59-60.

Ann Berthoff, "The Falconer's Dream of Trust: Wyatt's 'They Fle From
Me,'" SR, 71 (July-Sept., 1963), 477-494.

Frederick M. Combellack, Expl, 17 (Feb., 1959), 36.
   Rpt. The Explicator Cyclopedia, II, pp. 378-379.

Daiches and Charvat, Poems in English, pp. 642-644.

Leonard Dean, English Masterpieces, Vol. III, Renaissance Poetry,
pp. 3-4.

E. E. Duncan-Jones, Expl, 12 (Nov., 1953), 9.
   Rpt. The Explicator Cyclopedia, II, p. 378.

Fowler, Conceitful Thought, pp. 11-17.

Donald M. Friedman, "The Mind in the Poem: Wyatt's 'They Fle From Me,'"
SEL, 7 (Winter, 1967), 1-13.

Albert S. Gerard, "'They Fle From Me,'" EIC, 11 (July, 1961), 359-366.

J. O. Hainsworth, "Sir Thomas Wyatt's Use of the Love Convention," EIC,
7 (Jan., 1957), 90-95.

J. D. Hainsworth, "Wyatt's 'They Fle From Me,'" EIC, 11 (July, 1961),
366-368.

Donald Hall, <u>The Pleasures of Poetry</u> (New York: Harper & Row, 1971), 16-18.

Philip Hobsbaum, <u>Theory of Criticism</u> (Bloomington and London: Indiana Univ. Press, 1970), pp. 124-131.

S. F. Johnson, <u>Expl</u>, 11 (April, 1953), 39.
    Rpt. <u>The Explicator Cyclopedia</u>, II, p. 377.

Arthur K. Moore, "The Design of Wyatt's <u>They Fle from Me</u>," <u>Anglia</u>, 71 (1953), 102-111.

Harry Morris, "Birds, Does, and Manliness in 'They Fle from Me,'" <u>EIC</u>, 10 (Oct., 1960), 484-492.

Alicia Ostriker, "Thomas Wyatt and Henry Surrey: Dissonance and Harmony in Lyric Form," <u>NLH</u>, 1 (Spring, 1970), 397-399.

Arnold Stein, "Wyatt's 'They Flee From Me,'" <u>SR</u>, 67 (Winter, 1959), 28-44.

George W. Whiting, "Fortune in Wyatt's 'They Flee From Me,'" <u>EIC</u>, 10 (April, 1960), 220-222.

Leigh Winser, "The Question of Love Tradition in Wyatt's 'They Flee from Me,'" <u>ELWIU</u>, 2 (Spring, 1975), 3-9.

_____. "Tho I Cannot Your Crueltie Constrain"
Nancy S. Leonard, "The Speaker in Wyatt's Lyric Poetry," <u>HLQ</u>, 41 (Nov., 1977), 8-10.

_____. "To Wisshe and Want and Not Obtain"
Nancy S. Leonard, "The Speaker in Wyatt's Lyric Poetry," <u>HLQ</u>, 41 (Nov., 1977), 3-5.

_____. "Unstable Dream, According to the Place"
Raymond Southall, "The Personality of Sir Thomas Wyatt," <u>EIC</u>, 14 (Jan., 1964), 59-60.

_____. "What Menythe Thys?"
Nancy S. Leonard, "The Speaker in Wyatt's Lyric Poetry," <u>HLQ</u>, 41 (Nov., 1977), 10-11.

_____. "What Word Is That"
Anthony Low, "Wyatt's 'What Word Is That,'" <u>ELN</u>, 10 (Dec., 1972), 89-90.

_____. "Who So List to Hunt"
Fowler, <u>Conceitful Thought</u>, pp. 2-6.

Nancy S. Leonard, "The Speaker in Wyatt's Lyric Poetry," <u>HLQ</u>, 41 (Nov., 1977), 13-16.

Raymond Southall, "Love Poetry in the Sixteenth Century," <u>EIC</u>, 22 (Oct., 1972), 368-369.

Raymond Southall, "The Personality of Sir Thomas Wyatt," <u>EIC</u>, 14 (Jan., 1964), 60-62.

WYLIE. "Castilian"
    Richard E. Amacher, <u>Expl</u>, 7 (Nov., 1948), 16.
        Rpt. <u>The Explicator Cyclopedia</u>, I, p. 344.

_____. "Cold-Blooded Creatures"
    C. C. Walcutt, "Critic's Taste or Artist's Intention," <u>The University of Kansas City Review</u>, 12 (Summer, 1946), 279-282.

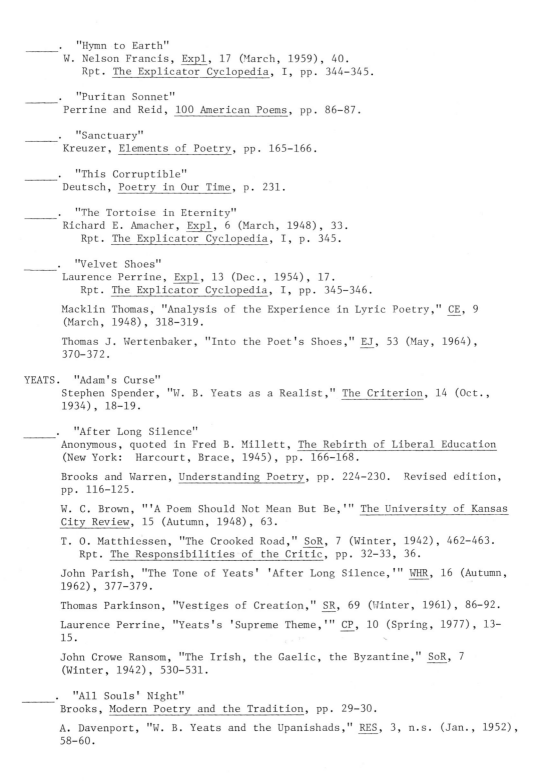

_____. "Hymn to Earth"
W. Nelson Francis, Expl, 17 (March, 1959), 40.
    Rpt. The Explicator Cyclopedia, I, pp. 344-345.

_____. "Puritan Sonnet"
Perrine and Reid, 100 American Poems, pp. 86-87.

_____. "Sanctuary"
Kreuzer, Elements of Poetry, pp. 165-166.

_____. "This Corruptible"
Deutsch, Poetry in Our Time, p. 231.

_____. "The Tortoise in Eternity"
Richard E. Amacher, Expl, 6 (March, 1948), 33.
    Rpt. The Explicator Cyclopedia, I, p. 345.

_____. "Velvet Shoes"
Laurence Perrine, Expl, 13 (Dec., 1954), 17.
    Rpt. The Explicator Cyclopedia, I, pp. 345-346.

Macklin Thomas, "Analysis of the Experience in Lyric Poetry," CE, 9
(March, 1948), 318-319.

Thomas J. Wertenbaker, "Into the Poet's Shoes," EJ, 53 (May, 1964),
370-372.

YEATS. "Adam's Curse"
Stephen Spender, "W. B. Yeats as a Realist," The Criterion, 14 (Oct.,
1934), 18-19.

_____. "After Long Silence"
Anonymous, quoted in Fred B. Millett, The Rebirth of Liberal Education
(New York: Harcourt, Brace, 1945), pp. 166-168.

Brooks and Warren, Understanding Poetry, pp. 224-230. Revised edition,
pp. 116-125.

W. C. Brown, "'A Poem Should Not Mean But Be,'" The University of Kansas
City Review, 15 (Autumn, 1948), 63.

T. O. Matthiessen, "The Crooked Road," SoR, 7 (Winter, 1942), 462-463.
    Rpt. The Responsibilities of the Critic, pp. 32-33, 36.

John Parish, "The Tone of Yeats' 'After Long Silence,'" WHR, 16 (Autumn,
1962), 377-379.

Thomas Parkinson, "Vestiges of Creation," SR, 69 (Winter, 1961), 86-92.

Laurence Perrine, "Yeats's 'Supreme Theme,'" CP, 10 (Spring, 1977), 13-
15.

John Crowe Ransom, "The Irish, the Gaelic, the Byzantine," SoR, 7
(Winter, 1942), 530-531.

_____. "All Souls' Night"
Brooks, Modern Poetry and the Tradition, pp. 29-30.

A. Davenport, "W. B. Yeats and the Upanishads," RES, 3, n.s. (Jan., 1952),
58-60.

_____. "Among School Children"
Bornstein, Transformations of Romanticism, pp. 69-71.

James L. Allen, Jr., "Yeats's Use of the Serious Pun," SoQ, 1 (Jan., 1963), 161-163.

Bowra, The Heritage of Symbolism, pp. 211-212.

Brooks, The Well Wrought Urn, pp. 163-175.

Richard Chase, "Myth As Literature," in English Institute Essays 1947, pp. 18-21.

Deutsch, Poetry in Our Time, p. 269.

Richard Ellmann, "The Art of Yeats: Affirmative Capability," The Kenyon Review, 15 (Summer, 1953), 369-371.

Stephen Feinberg, Expl, 33 (Feb., 1975), 45.

Michael P. Gallagher, "Yeats, Syntax, and the Self," ArQ, 26 (Spring, 1970), 5-16.

David Holbrook, Lost Bearings in English Poetry (London: Vision Press, 1977), pp. 194-203.

Kermode, Romantic Image, pp. 83-84.

Knights, Explorations, pp. 200-202.

L. C. Knights, "W. B. Yeats: The Assertion of Values," SoR, 7 (Winter, 1942), 436-438.

Kremen, The Imagination of the Resurrection, pp. 278-281.

Maynard Mack, Leonard Dean, and William Frost, English Masterpieces, Vol. III, Modern Poetry, p. 8.

Leven Magruder Dawson, "'Among School Children': 'Labour' and 'Play,'" PQ, 52 (April, 1973), 286-295.

Arthur Mizener, "The Romanticism of W. B. Yeats," SoR, 7 (Winter, 1942), 618-620.

Thomas Parkinson, "The Indivuality of Yeats," Pacific Spectator, 6 (Autumn, 1952), 492-493, 496.

Thomas Parkinson, "Vestiges of Creation," SR, 69 (Winter, 1961), 92-111.

V. De Sola Pinto, Crisis in English Poetry, pp. 108-109.

Charles A. Raines, "Yeats' Metaphors of Permanence," TCL, 5 (April, 1959), 18-19.

John Crowe Ransom, "The Irish, the Gaelic, the Byzantine," SoR, 7 (Winter, 1942), 536-538.

S. P. Rosenbaum, Expl, 23 (Oct., 1964), 14.

Robert S. Ryf, "Yeats's Major Metaphysical Poems," JML, 4 (Feb., 1975), 617-620.

Schneider, Poems and Poetry, pp. 481-483.

Delmore Schwartz, "An Unwritten Book," SoR, 7 (Winter, 1942), 488-491.

Donald A. Stauffer, "The Reading of a Lyric Poem," The Kenyon Review, 11 (Summer, 1949), 436-437.

Patricia J. Terwilliger, "A Re-Interpretation of Stanzas VII and VIII of W. B. Yeats's 'Among School Children,'" Boston University Studies in English, 5 (Spring, 1961), 29-34.

William I. Thompson, "Collapsed Universe and Structured Poem: An Essay in Whiteheadian Criticism," CE, 28 (Oct., 1966), 35-39.

John Wain, Interpretations, ed. John Wain, pp. 196-210.

Charles C. Walcutt, Expl, 8 (April, 1950), 42.
    Rpt. The Explicator Cyclopedia, I, pp. 346-347.

Charles Child Walcutt, Expl, 26 (May, 1968), 72.

Charles Child Walcutt, "Introduction," The Explicator Cyclopedia, I, pp. xv-xvi.

Yvor Winters, "The Poetry of W. B. Yeats," TCL, 6 (April, 1960), 12-14.
    Rpt. Forms of Discovery, pp. 218-220.

Wright, The Poet in the Poem, pp. 110-111.

_____. "An Acre of Grass"
Drew, Poetry: A Modern Guide, pp. 116-118.

Bryant E. Hoffman, "Myself Must I Remake: Yeats's Last Poems (1936-1939)," LitR, 20 (Summer, 1977), 407-408.

D. C. Nimmo, Expl, 29 (Feb., 1971), 50.

Laurence Perrine, Expl, 22 (April, 1964), 64.

William V. Spanos, "The Sexual Imagination in Yeats's Late Poetry: A Reading of 'An Acre of Grass,'" CEA, 32 (Oct., 1969), 16-18.

Myron Taube, Expl, 26 (Jan., 1968), 40.

_____. "The Apparitions"
R. P. Blackmur, "Between Myth and Philosophy: Fragments of W. B. Yeats," SoR, 7 (Winter, 1942), 412-413.
    Rpt. Language as Gesture, pp. 110-112.

Robin Skelton, "The Workshop of W. B. Yeats," CP, 1 (Fall, 1968), 18-19.

_____. "At Algeciras--A Meditation upon Death"
Deutsch, Poetry in Our Time, p. 267.

_____. "The Ballad of Father Gilligan"
Van Doren, Introduction to Poetry, pp. 131-133.

_____. "Before the World Was Made"
Bert Case Diltz, Sense or Nonsense: Contemporary Education at the Crossroads (Toronto: McClelland and Stewart, 1972), pp. 104-105.

_____. "Beggar to Beggar Cried"
Hoffman, Barbarous Knowledge, pp. 41-44.

_____. "The Black Tower"
Felver and Nurmi, Poetry: An Introduction and Anthology, pp. 112-114.

T. R. Henn, "The Accent of Yeats's Last Poems," Essays and Studies, 9 (1956), 68-69.

W. J. Keith, "Yeats' Arthurian Black Tower," MLN, 75 (Feb., 1960), 119-123.

Susan Matthews, "Defiance and Defeat in W. B. Yeats' 'The Black Tower,'"
CP, 5 (Fall, 1972), 22-26.

_____. "Blood and the Moon"
Cleanth Brooks, "The Vision of William Butler Yeats," SoR, 4 (Summer,
1938), 121-123.

Denis Donoghue, "Notes Towards a Critical Method: Language as Order,"
Studies, 44 (Summer, 1955), 186-187.

Feder, Ancient Myth in Modern Poetry, pp. 286-288.

Jeffrey Meyers, Expl, 30 (Feb., 1972), 50.

James Olney, "'A Powerful Emblem': The Towers of Yeats and Jung," SAQ,
72 (Autumn, 1973), 513-515.

_____. "A Bronze Head"
Robert D. Denham, Expl, 29 (Oct., 1970), 14.

Edward Engelberg, "Picture and Gesture in the Yeatsian Aesthetic,"
Criticism, 3 (Spring, 1961), 119.

_____. "Byzantium"
R. M. Adams, "Now That My Ladder's Gone--Yeats Without Myth," Accent, 13
(Summer, 1953), 143-148.

James L. Allen, Jr., "Miraculous Birds, Another and the Same: Yeats's
Golden Image and the Phoenix," ES, 48 (June, 1967), 215-226, et passim.

R. A. Auty, "Byzantium," TLS, Aug. 11, 1950, p. 501.

Michael Bell, "The Assimilation of Doubt in Yeats's Visionary Poems,"
QQ, 80 (Autumn, 1973), 393-394.

Blackmur, The Expense of Greatness, pp. 98-99.
    Rpt. Critiques, pp. 372-373.
    Rpt. Language as Gesture, pp. 98-99.

Curtis Bradford, "Yeats's Byzantium Poems: A Study of Their Development," PMLA, 75 (March, 1960), 119-125.

Brooks, Modern Poetry and the Tradition, pp. 192-200.

Cleanth Brooks, "The Vision of William Butler Yeats," SoR, 4 (Summer,
1938), 133-140.

John Christopherson, "Byzantium," TLS, Sept. 15, 1950, p. 581.

Ethel Cornwell, The "Still Point," pp. 106-107.

Daiches and Charvat, Poems in English, pp. 733-735.

Daiches, Poetry and the Modern World, pp. 181-185.

A. Davenport, "W. B. Yeats and the Upanishads," RES, 3, n.s. (Jan.,
1952), 59-60.

Bonamy Dobree, "Byzantium," TLS, Sept. 22, 1950, p. 597.

Drew and Sweeney, Directions in Modern Poetry, pp. 166-171.

Richard Ellmann in Locke, Gibson, and Arms, Introduction to Literature,
third edition, pp. 168-170.
    Rpt. from Ellmann, The Identity of Yeats (New York: Oxford Univ.
    Press, 1954), pp. 219-222.
    Rpt. fourth edition, pp. 173-175.
    Rpt. fifth edition, pp. 155-157.

Richard Ellmann, "The Art of Yeats: Affirmative Capability," The Kenyon Review, 15 (Summer, 1953), 360-366.

William Empson, "Donne and the Rhetorical Tradition," The Kenyon Review, 11 (Autumn, 1949), 576-577.

Feder, Ancient Myth in Modern Poetry, pp. 85-86, 190.

Friar and Brinnin, Modern Poetry, pp. 552-554.

F. L. Gwynn, "Yeats's 'Byzantium' and Its Sources," PQ, 32 (Jan., 1953), 9-21.

Elizabeth Huberman, "To Byzantium Once More: A Study of the Structure of Yeats's 'Byzantium,'" ELWIU, 1 (Fall, 1974), 193-205.

A. N. Jeffares, "The Byzantine Poems of W. B. Yeats," RES, 22 (Jan., 1946), 49-52.

Anne Kostelanetz, "Irony in Yeats's Byzantium Poems," TSL, 9 (1964), 134-141.

Kremen, The Imagination of the Resurrection, pp. 292-295.

Joan Towey Mitchell, "'Byzantium': Vision as Drama," CP, 6 (Spring, 1973), 66-71.

Gwendolyn Murphy, "Byzantium," TLS, Aug. 25, 1950, p. 533.

Gwendolyn Murphy, "Byzantium," TLS, Sept. 15, 1950, p. 581.

Gwendolyn Murphy, "Byzantium," TLS, Nov. 3, 1950, p. 693.

Richard Murphy, "Byzantium," TLS, Sept. 1, 1950, p. 548.

Ruth Nevo, "Again, Byzantium," Lang&S, 9 (Fall, 1976), 247-259.

Robert S. Ryf, "Yeats's Major Metaphysical Poems," JML, 4 (Feb., 1975), 620-623.

Schneider, Poems and Poetry, pp. 484-485.

Stauffer, The Nature of Poetry, pp. 172-175.

Thomas and Brown, Reading Poems: An Introduction to Critical Study, pp. 714-715.

Tschumi, Thought in Twentieth-Century English Poetry, pp. 69-73.

Leonard Unger, "The New Collected Yeats," Poetry, 80 (April, 1952), 47-48.

Vernon Watkins, "Byzantium," TLS, Sept. 22, 1950, p. 597.

Alison White, Expl, 13 (Nov., 1954), 8.
    Rpt. The Explicator Cyclopedia, I, p. 347.

Yvor Winters, "The Poetry of W. B. Yeats," TCL, 6 (April, 1960), 11-12.
    Rpt. Forms of Discovery, pp. 216-218.

_____. "The Cap and Bells"
Bowra, The Heritage of Symbolism, pp. 192-193.

George S. Fraser, Essays on Twentieth-Century Poets (Great Britain: Leicester Univ. Press, 1977), pp. 71-75.

J. H. Natterstad, Expl, 25 (May, 1967), 75.

Morton Irving Seiden, "A Psychoanalytical Essay on William Butler Yeats," Accent, 6 (Spring, 1946), 179-180.

_____. "Cast a Cold Eye"
James Lovic Allen, "'Horseman, Pass By!' Metaphor and Meaning in Yeats's Epitaph," CP, 10 (Spring, 1977), 17-22.

_____. "The Cat and the Moon"
Grover Smith, "Yeats, Minnaloushe, and the Moon," Western Review, 11 (Summer, 1947), 241-244.

Van Doren, Introduction to Poetry, pp. 86-89.

_____. "The Chambermaid's First Song"
Arra M. Garab, "Fabulous Artifice: Yeats's 'Three Bushes' Sequence," Criticism, 7 (Summer, 1965), 245-246.

_____. "The Chambermaid's Second Song"
Arra M. Garab, "Fabulous Artifice: Yeats's 'Three Bushes' Sequence," Criticism, 7 (Summer, 1965), 246-247.

_____. "The Choice"
W. C. Brown, "'A Poem Should Not Mean But Be,'" The University of Kansas City Review, 15 (Autumn, 1948), 59-60.

_____. "The Circus Animals' Desertion"
Claire Hahn, "The Moral Center of Yeats's 'Last Poems,'" Thought, 50 (Sept. 1975), 307-309.

Bryant E. Hoffman, "Myself Must I Remake: Yeats' Last Poems (1936-1939)," LitR, 20 (Summer, 1977), 421-423.

_____. "The Cold Heaven"
Gary and Linda Storhoff, "'A Mind of Winter': Yeats's Early Vision of Old Age," CLAJ, 21 (Sept., 1977), 94-97.

_____. "The Collar-Bone of a Hare"
Hugh Kenner, "The Sacred Book of the Arts," SR, 64 (Autumn, 1956), 580-581.

Marion Witt, Expl, 7 (Dec., 1948), 21.
    Rpt. The Explicator Cyclopedia, I, pp. 347-348.

_____. "Come Gather Round Me Parnellites"
Clark, Lyric Resonance, pp. 22-24.

_____. "The Coming of Wisdom with Time"
Brown and Olmstead, Language and Literature, pp. 63-64.

_____. "Coole Park"
Yvor Winters, "The Poetry of W. B. Yeats," TCL, 6 (April, 1960), 16-17.

_____. "Coole Park and Ballylee, 1931"
Charles Altieri, "From a Comic to a Tragic Sense of Language in Yeats's Mature Poetry," MLQ, 33 (June, 1972), 166-168.

D. S. Carne-Ross, "A Commentary on Yeats' 'Coole and Ballylee, 1931,'" Nine, No. 1 (Autumn, 1949), 21-24.

Marjorie Perloff, "'Another Emblem There': Theme and Convention in Yeats's 'Coole Park and Ballylee, 1931,'" JEGP, 69 (April, 1970), 223-240.

Donald A. Stauffer, "The Reading of a Lyric Poem," The Kenyon Review, 11 (Summer, 1949), 437-438.

_____. "Crazy Jane and Jack the Journeyman"
Laurence Perrine, "Yeats's 'Crazy Jane and Jack the Journeyman,'" CEA, 34 (March, 1972), 22-23.

_____. "Crazy Jane and the Bishop"
Wright, The Poet in the Poem, p. 109.

_____. "Crazy Jane Grown Old Looks at the Dancers"
Andy P. Antippas, "A Note on Yeats's 'Crazy Jane' Poems," ES, 49 (Dec., 1968), 558-559.

_____. "Crazy Jane on God"
Andy P. Antippas, "A Note on Yeats's 'Crazy Jane' Poems," ES, 49 (Dec., 1968), 558.

Walter E. Houghton, "Yeats and Crazy Jane," MP, 40 (May, 1943), 326-327.

_____. "Crazy Jane on the Day of Judgment"
Andy P. Antippas, "A Note on Yeats's 'Crazy Jane' Poems," ES, 49 (Dec., 1968), 557.

_____. "Crazy Jane on the Mountain"
Barbara L. Estrin, "Alternating Personae in Yeats' 'Lapis Lazuli' and 'Crazy Jane on the Mountain,'" Criticism, 16 (Winter, 1974), 20-22.

_____. "Crazy Jane Talks With the Bishop"
R. P. Blackmur, "Between Myth and Philosophy: Fragments of W. B. Yeats," SoR, 7 (Winter, 1942), 423-424.
    Rpt. Language as Gesture, pp. 121-122.

_____. "Cuchulain Comforted"
T. R. Henn, "The Accent of Yeats's Last Poems," Essays and Studies, 9 (1956), 67-68.

Joan Towey Mitchell, "Hero and Poet Reconciled," English, 23 (Spring, 1974), 30-33.

Kathleen Raine, "Life in Death and Death in Life: Yeats's 'Cuchulain Comforted' and 'News for the Delphic Oracle,'" SoR, 9 (Summer, 1973), 562-573.

_____. "The Curse of Cromwell"
Hoffman, Barbarous Knowledge, pp. 57-58.

_____. "Death"
R. P. Blackmur, "Between Myth and Philosophy: Fragments of W. B. Yeats," SoR, 7 (Winter, 1942), 418.
    Rpt. Language as Gesture, p. 116.

_____. "The Death of the Hare"
John Somer, "Unageing Monuments: A Study of W. B. Yeats' Poetry Sequence, 'A Man Young and Old,'" BSUF, 12 (Autumn, 1971), 30-31.

_____. "A Deep-Sworn Vow"
Brooks and Warren, Understanding Poetry, pp. 294-297. Revised edition, pp. 148-152.

_____. "The Delphic Oracle upon Plotinus"
William C. Barnwell, "The Blandness of Yeats's Rhadamanthus," ELN, 14
(March, 1977), 206-210.

Clark, Lyric Resonance, pp. 48-54.

Donald Pearce, "Yeats's 'The Delphic Oracle upon Plotinus,'" N&Q, 1,
n.s. (April, 1954), 175-176.

_____. "Demon and Beast"
James L. Allen, Jr., "Yeats's Use of the Serious Pun," SoR, 1 n.s.
(Jan., 1963), 163-164.

Brooks, Modern Poetry and the Tradition, pp. 188-189.

Cleanth Brooks, "The Vision of William Butler Yeats," SoR, 4 (Summer,
1938), 129-130.

_____. "A Dialogue of Self and Soul"
Stella Revard, "Verlaine and Yeats's 'A Dialogue of Self and Soul,'"
PLL, 7 (Summer, 1971), 272-278.

Marion Witt, Expl, 5 (May, 1947), 48.
   Rpt. The Explicator Cyclopedia, I, p. 348.

_____. "The Dolls"
Conrad A. Balliet, "'The Dolls' of Yeats and the Cradle of Christ," RS,
38 (March, 1970), 54-57.

_____. "The Double Vision of Michael Robartes"
Bowra, The Heritage of Symbolism, p. 207.

Kermode, Romantic Image, pp. 59-60.

Tschumi, Thought in Twentieth-Century English Poetry, pp. 45-47.

Thomas R. Whitaker, "The Dialectic of Yeats's Vision of History," MP, 57
(Nov., 1959), 109-112.

_____. "Easter 1916"
Bowra, The Heritage of Symbolism, pp. 202-203.

Terry Eagleton, "History and Myth in Yeats's 'Easter 1916,'" EIC, 21
(July, 1971), 248-260.

Edwards, Imagination and Power, pp. 185-197.

Stephen Maloney, "Yeats's Meaningful Words: The Role of 'Easter 1916'
in His Poetic Development," EngR, 22 (Fall, 1971), 11-18.

Marjorie Perloff, "Yeats and the Occasional Poem: 'Easter 1916,'" PLL,
4 (Summer, 1968), 320-328.

Charles A. Raines, "Yeats' Metaphors of Permanence," TCL, 5 (April,
1959), 13-14.

John Crowe Ransom, "The Irish, the Gaelic, the Byzantine," SoR, 7
(Winter, 1942), 535-536.

Rosenthal, The Modern Poets, pp. 30-32.

Arnold Stein, "Yeats: A Study in Recklessness," SR, 57 (Autumn, 1949),
623-626.

Yvor Winters, "The Poetry of W. B. Yeats," TCL, 6 (April, 1960), 18-19.

_____. "Ego Dominus Tuus"
Stuart Hirschberg, "A Dialogue Between Realism and Idealism in Yeats's
'Ego Dominus Tuus,'" CLQ, 11 (June, 1975), 129-132.

Robert Langbaum, "The Exteriority of Self in Yeats's Poetry and Thought,"
NLH, 7 (Spring, 1976), 589-590.

Tschumi, Thought in Twentieth-Century English Poetry, pp. 38-40.

Marion Witt, "William Butler Yeats," English Institute Essays 1946,
pp. 92-99.

_____. "The Empty Cup"
John Somer, "Unageing Monuments: A Study of W. B. Yeats' Poetry Sequence,
'A Man Young and Old,'" BSUF, 12 (Autumn, 1971), 31-32.

_____. "Father and Child"
Delmore Schwartz, "An Unwritten Book," SoR, 7 (Winter, 1942), 484-485.

_____. "First Love"
John Somer, "Unageing Monuments: A Study of W. B. Yeats' Poetry Sequence,
'A Man Young and Old,'" BSUF, 12 (Autumn, 1971), 29-30.

_____. "The Fisherman"
Deutsch, Poetry in Our Time, pp. 259-260.

Deutsch, This Modern Poetry, pp. 201-203.

_____. "The Folly of Being Comforted"
Paul R. Maixner, Expl, 13 (Oct., 1954), 1.
     Rpt. The Explicator Cyclopedia, I, pp. 348-349.

Peter J. Seng, Expl, 17 (April, 1959), 48.
     Rpt. The Explicator Cyclopedia, I, pp. 349-350.

_____. "For Anne Gregory"
Richard Zlogar, Expl, 35 (Winter, 1976), 16-17.

_____. "Friends"
Samuel Hynes, "All the Wild Witches: The Women in Yeats's Poems," SR, 85
(Oct.-Dec., 1977), 566-568.

_____. "The Friends of His Youth"
John Somer, "Unageing Monuments: A Study of W. B. Yeats' Poetry Sequence,
'A Man Young and Old,'" BSUF, 12 (Autumn, 1971), 32-33.

_____. "The Gyres"
Robert M. Adams, "Now That My Ladder's Gone--Yeats Without Myth," Accent,
13 (Summer, 1953), 141.

Robert Bierman, Expl, 19 (April, 1961), 44.
     Rpt. The Explicator Cyclopedia, I, pp. 350-351.

Richard Ellmann, "Three Ways of Looking at a Briton," SR, 61 (Winter,
1953), 154.

Feder, Ancient Myth in Modern Poetry, pp. 289-291.

Claire Hahn, "The Moral Center of Yeats's 'Last Poems,'" Thought, 50
(Sept., 1975), 303-305.

Stuart Hirschberg, "Beyond Tragedy: Yeats's View of History in 'The Gyres,'" RS, 42 (March, 1974), 50–55.

A. Norman Jeffares, "Yeats's 'The Gyres': Sources and Symbolism," HLQ, 15 (Nov., 1951), 88–97.

Eleanor M. Sickles, Expl, 15 (June, 1957), 60.
   Rpt. The Explicator Cyclopedia, I, pp. 350–351.

Donald A. Stauffer, "W. B. Yeats and the Medium of Poetry," ELH, 15 (Sept., 1948), 244–245.

Tschumi, Thought in Twentieth-Century English Poetry, pp. 53–55.

Leonard Unger, "The New Collected Yeats," Poetry, 80 (April, 1952), 44–45.

_____. "The Happy Townland"
Bowra, The Heritage of Symbolism, pp. 190–191.

_____. "The Hawk"
Schneider, Poems and Poetry, pp. 479–480.

_____. "He Bids His Beloved Be at Peace"
Clark, Lyric Resonance, pp. 31–38.

_____. "Her Vision in the Wood"
James L. Allen, Jr., Expl, 18 (May, 1960), 45.
   Rpt. The Explicator Cyclopedia, I, pp. 351–353.

Michael Ragussis, The Subterfuge of Art: Language and the Romantic Tradition (Baltimore and London: The Johns Hopkins Univ. Press, 1978), pp. 112–132.

_____. "He Thinks of His Past Greatness When a Part of the Constellation of Heaven"
Quinn, The Metamorphic Tradition, p. 229.

_____. "High Talk"
Bryant E. Hoffman, "Myself Must I Remake: Yeats' Last Poems (1936–1939)," LitR, 20 (Summer, 1977), 420–421.

Brian John, Expl, 29 (Nov., 1970), 22.

Bernard Levine, "'High Talk': A Concentrative Analysis of a Poem by Yeats," JJQ, 3 (Winter, 1966), 124–129.

Victor Reed, Expl, 26 (Feb., 1968), 52.

_____. "His Dream"
George S. Fraser, Essays on Twentieth-Century Poets (Great Britain: Leicester Univ. Press, 1977), pp. 75–78.

_____. "His Memories"
Samuel Hynes, "All the Wild Witches: The Women in Yeats's Poems," SR, 85 (Oct.-Dec., 1977), 577–578.

John Somer, "Unageing Monuments: A Study of W. B. Yeats' Poetry Sequence, 'A Man Young and Old,'" BSUF, 12 (Autumn, 1971), 32.

_____. "The Hosting of the Sidhe"
Kermode, Romantic Image, pp. 74–76.

_____. "The Hour-Glass"
Otto Reinert, Expl, 15 (Dec., 1956), 19.
    Rpt. The Explicator Cyclopedia, I, p. 353.

_____. "Human Dignity"
John Somer, "Unageing Monuments: A Study of W. B. Yeats' Poetry Sequence,
'A Man Young and Old,'" BSUF, 12 (Autumn, 1971), 30.

_____. "I Am of Ireland"
Martha Gross, Expl, 17 (Nov., 1958), 15.
    Rpt. The Explicator Cyclopedia, I, pp. 354-355.

Hoffman, Barbarous Knowledge, pp. 49-56.

Walter E. Houghton, "Yeats and Crazy Jane," MP, 40 (May, 1943), 324-325.

F. O. Matthiessen, "The Crooked Road," SoR, 7 (Winter, 1942), 459-462.
    Rpt. The Responsibilities of the Critic, pp. 30-32.

Eleanor M. Sickels, Expl, 15 (Nov., 1956), 10.
    Rpt. The Explicator Cyclopedia, I, pp. 353-354.

_____. "The Indian to His Love"
Nandini Pillai Kuehn, Expl, 33 (Nov., 1974), 23.

_____. "In Memory of Major Robert Gregory"
James Olney, "'A Powerful Emblem': The Towers of Yeats and Jung," SAQ,
72 (Autumn, 1973), 505-510.

Kermode, Romantic Image, pp. 30-42.

Marjorie Perloff, "The Consolation of Major Robert Gregory," MLQ, 27
(Sept., 1966), 306-322.

Yvor Winters, "The Poetry of W. B. Yeats," TCL, 6 (April, 1960), 15-16.
    Rpt. Forms of Discovery, pp. 222-225.

Marion Witt, "The Making of an Elegy: Yeats's 'In Memory of Major Robert
Gregory,'" MP, 48 (Nov., 1950), 112-121.

_____. "In Memory of Eva Gore-Booth and Con Markiewicz"
Marjorie Perloff, "Spatial Form in the Poetry of Yeats: The Two Lissa-
dell Poems," PMLA, 92 (Oct., 1967), 449-454.

_____. "In the Seven Woods"
Herbert Howarth, Expl, 17 (Nov, 1958), 14.
    Rpt. The Explicator Cyclopedia, I, pp. 355-356.

_____. "Into the Twilight"
Thomas Parkinson, "The Sun and the Moon in Yeats's Early Poetry," MP, 50
(Aug., 1952), 55.

_____. "An Irish Airman Foresees His Death"
H. G. Widdowson, Stylistics and the Teaching of Literature (London:
Longman Group, 1975), 40-41.

_____. "I Wander by the Edge"
Deutsch, This Modern Poetry, pp. 201-203.

_____. "John Kinsella's Lament for Mrs. Mary Moore"
Clark, Lyric Resonance, pp. 28-30.

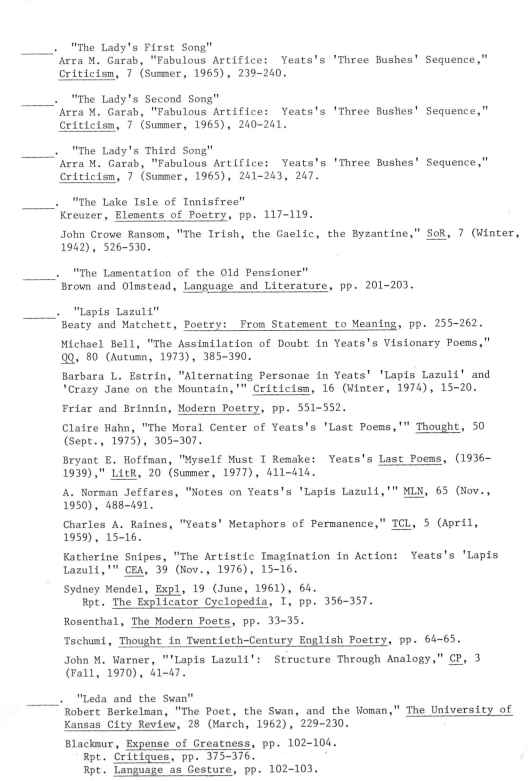

_____. "The Lady's First Song"
Arra M. Garab, "Fabulous Artifice: Yeats's 'Three Bushes' Sequence,"
Criticism, 7 (Summer, 1965), 239-240.

_____. "The Lady's Second Song"
Arra M. Garab, "Fabulous Artifice: Yeats's 'Three Bushes' Sequence,"
Criticism, 7 (Summer, 1965), 240-241.

_____. "The Lady's Third Song"
Arra M. Garab, "Fabulous Artifice: Yeats's 'Three Bushes' Sequence,"
Criticism, 7 (Summer, 1965), 241-243, 247.

_____. "The Lake Isle of Innisfree"
Kreuzer, Elements of Poetry, pp. 117-119.

John Crowe Ransom, "The Irish, the Gaelic, the Byzantine," SoR, 7 (Winter,
1942), 526-530.

_____. "The Lamentation of the Old Pensioner"
Brown and Olmstead, Language and Literature, pp. 201-203.

_____. "Lapis Lazuli"
Beaty and Matchett, Poetry: From Statement to Meaning, pp. 255-262.

Michael Bell, "The Assimilation of Doubt in Yeats's Visionary Poems,"
QQ, 80 (Autumn, 1973), 385-390.

Barbara L. Estrin, "Alternating Personae in Yeats' 'Lapis Lazuli' and
'Crazy Jane on the Mountain,'" Criticism, 16 (Winter, 1974), 15-20.

Friar and Brinnin, Modern Poetry, pp. 551-552.

Claire Hahn, "The Moral Center of Yeats's 'Last Poems,'" Thought, 50
(Sept., 1975), 305-307.

Bryant E. Hoffman, "Myself Must I Remake: Yeats's Last Poems, (1936-
1939)," LitR, 20 (Summer, 1977), 411-414.

A. Norman Jeffares, "Notes on Yeats's 'Lapis Lazuli,'" MLN, 65 (Nov.,
1950), 488-491.

Charles A. Raines, "Yeats' Metaphors of Permanence," TCL, 5 (April,
1959), 15-16.

Katherine Snipes, "The Artistic Imagination in Action: Yeats's 'Lapis
Lazuli,'" CEA, 39 (Nov., 1976), 15-16.

Sydney Mendel, Expl, 19 (June, 1961), 64.
   Rpt. The Explicator Cyclopedia, I, pp. 356-357.

Rosenthal, The Modern Poets, pp. 33-35.

Tschumi, Thought in Twentieth-Century English Poetry, pp. 64-65.

John M. Warner, "'Lapis Lazuli': Structure Through Analogy," CP, 3
(Fall, 1970), 41-47.

_____. "Leda and the Swan"
Robert Berkelman, "The Poet, the Swan, and the Woman," The University of
Kansas City Review, 28 (March, 1962), 229-230.

Blackmur, Expense of Greatness, pp. 102-104.
   Rpt. Critiques, pp. 375-376.
   Rpt. Language as Gesture, pp. 102-103.

R. P. Blackmur, "The Later Poetry of W. B. Yeats," SoR, 2 (Autumn, 1936), 360-362.

Kenneth Burke, "On Motivation in Yeats," SoR, 7 (Winter, 1942), 554-555.

E. R. Cole, "Three Cycle Poems of Yeats and His Mystico-Historical Thought," The Personalist, 46 (Winter, 1965), 75-77.

Deutsch, Poetry in Our Time, pp. 260-262.

Drew, Poetry: A Modern Guide, pp. 65-67.

Drew and Sweeney, Directions in Modern Poetry, pp. 164-166.

Cecil H. DuVall and John B. Humma, "The Opening Phrase of Yeats' 'Leda and Swan,'" RS, 40 (June, 1972), 131-132.

Richard Ellman, "Yeats Without Analogues," The Kenyon Review, 26 (Winter, 1964), 31-33.

Feder, Ancient Myth in Modern Poetry, pp. 193-194.

Bernard Levine, "A Psychopoetic Analysis of Yeats's 'Leda and the Swan,'" BuR, 17 (March, 1969), 85-111.

Joseph Margolis, Expl, 13 (April, 1955), 34.
    Rpt. The Explicator Cyclopedia, I, pp. 357-358.

Quinn, The Metamorphic Tradition, pp. 233-235.

Charles A. Raines, "Yeats' Metaphors of Permanence," TCL, 5 (April, 1959), 16-17.

Jane D. Reid, "Leda, Twice Assaulted," JAAC, 11 (June, 1953), 378-389.

Rosenthal, The Modern Poets, pp. 41-42.

Leo Spitzer, "On Yeats's Poem 'Leda and the Swan,'" MP, 51 (May, 1954), 271-276.
    Rpt. Essays on English and American Literature by Leo Spitzer, pp. 3-13.

Arnold Stein, "Yeats: A Study in Recklessness," SR, 57 (Autumn, 1949), 617-620.

Hoyt Trowbridge, "'Leda and the Swan': A Longinian Analysis," MP, 51 (Nov., 1953), 120-129.

Yvor Winters, "The Poetry of W. B. Yeats," TCL, 6 (April, 1960), 7-8.
    Rpt. Forms of Discovery, pp. 210-212.

_____. "Line Written in Dejection"
Thomas Parkinson, "The Sun and the Moon in Yeats's Early Poetry," MP, 50 (Aug., 1952), 50, 53-55.

_____. "The Living Beauty"
Gary and Linda Storhoff, "'A Mind of Winter'" Yeats's Early Vision of Old Age," CLAJ, 21 (Sept., 1977), 91-94.

_____. "Long-Legged Fly"
James L. Allen, Jr., Expl, 21 (Feb., 1963), 51.

Daiches and Charvat, Poems in English, pp. 735-736.

Mario L. D'Avanzo, Expl, 34 (Nov., 1975), 23.

Robert R. Hodges, "The Irony of Yeats's 'Long-Legged Fly,'" TCL, 12 (April, 1966), 27-30.

William Elford Rogers, "Yeats' 'Long-Legged Fly' and Coleridge's Bio-graphia Literaria," CP, 8 (Spring, 1975), 11-21.

B. C. Southam, Expl, 22 (May, 1964), 73.

B. C. Southam, "Yeats: Life and the Creator in 'The Long-Legged Fly,'" TCL, 6 (Jan., 1961), 175-179.

Jon Stallworthy, "Two of Yeats's Last Poems," A Review of English Literature, 4 (July, 1963), 48-69.

Tschumi, Thought in Twentieth-Century English Poetry, pp. 61-63.

Yvor Winters, "The Poetry of W. B. Yeats," TCL, 6 (April, 1960), 21.

_____. "The Lover Mourns for the Change That Has Come upon Him and His Beloved
    and Longs for the End of the World"
Stauffer, The Nature of Poetry, pp. 170-171.

_____. "The Lover's Song"
Arra M. Garab, "Fabulous Artifice: Yeats's 'Three Bushes' Sequence,"
Criticism, 7 (Summer, 1965), 243-245.

_____. "The Magi"
E. R. Cole, "Three Cycle Poems of Yeats and His Mystico-Historical
Thought," The Personalist, 46 (Winter, 1965), 79-80.

Wayne D. McGinnis, "Giotto and Yeats' 'The Magi,'" RS, 42 (Sept., 1974),
182-185.

Paul Sanders, Expl, 25 (March, 1967), 53.

Helen Vendler, "Sacred and Profane Perfection in Yeats," SoR, 9 (Winter,
1973), 107.

Thomas R. Whitaker, "The Dialectic of Yeats's Vision of History," MP, 57
(Nov., 1959), 108.

_____. "The Man and the Echo"
Feder, Ancient Myth in Modern Poetry, pp. 291-293.

Thomas Parkinson, "The Individuality of Yeats," Pacific Spectator, 6
(Autumn, 1952), 497-498.

Charles A. Raines, "Yeats' Metaphors of Permanence," TCL, 5 (April,
1959), 14-15.

_____. "The Man Who Dreamed of Faeryland"
Rosenthal, The Modern Poets, pp. 36-37.

_____. "The Mask"
Robert Langbaum, "The Exteriority of Self in Yeats's Poetry and Thought,"
NLH, 7 (Spring, 1976), 582.

_____. "Meditations in Time of Civil War"
Michael North, "Symbolism and Obscurity in 'Meditations in Time of Civil
War,'" CritQ, 19 (Spring, 1977), 5-18.

Sarah Youngblood, "The Structure of Yeats's Long Poems," Criticism, 5
(Fall, 1963), 328-335.

_____. "Memory"
Zitner, Kissane, Liberman, <u>A Preface to Literary Analysis</u>, pp. 29-31.

_____. "Men Improve with Years"
Hugh Kenner, "The Sacred Book of the Arts," <u>SR</u>, 64 (Autumn, 1956), 578-580.

_____. "The Mermaid"
John Somer, "Unageing Monuments: A Study of W. B. Yeats' Poetry Sequence, 'A Man Young and Old,'" <u>BSUF</u>, 12 (Autumn, 1971), 30.

_____. "Meru"
Richard Ellmann, "The Art of Yeats: Affirmative Capability," <u>The Kenyon Review</u>, 15 (Summer, 1953), 373-376.

_____. "Michael Robartes and the Dancer"
Kermode, <u>Romantic Image</u>, pp. 52-55.

_____. "Mohini Chatterjee"
Marion Witt, <u>Expl</u>, 4 (June, 1946), 60.
    Rpt. <u>The Explicator Cyclopedia</u>, I, pp. 358-359.

_____. "The Moods"
Marion Witt, <u>Expl</u>, 6 (Dec., 1947), 15.
    Rpt. <u>The Explicator Cyclopedia</u>, I, p. 359.

_____. "Mother of God"
Peter Allt, "Yeats, Religion, and History," <u>SR</u>, 60 (Autumn, 1952), 647-651.

E. R. Cole, "Three Cycle Poems of Yeats and His Mystico-Historical Thought," <u>The Personalist</u>, 46 (Winter, 1965), 77.

_____. "The Municipal Gallery Revisited"
Bryant E. Hoffman, "Myself Must I Remake: Yeats's <u>Last Poems</u> (1936-1939)," <u>LitR</u>, 20 (Summer, 1977), 414-416.

Robin Skelton, "The Workshop of W. B. Yeats," <u>CP</u>, 1 (Fall, 1968), 22-24.

Yvor Winters, "The Poetry of W. B. Yeats," <u>TCL</u>, 6 (April, 1960), 17-18.

_____. "The New Faces"
A. N. Jeffares, "'The New Faces': A New Explanation," <u>RES</u>, 23 (Oct., 1947), 349-353.

_____. "News for the Delphic Oracle"
Clark, <u>Lyric Resonance</u>, pp. 39-54.

David R. Clark, Poussin and Yeats's 'News for the Delphic Oracle,'" <u>WascanaR</u>, 2, No. 1, 33-44.

Feder, <u>Ancient Myth in Modern Poetry</u>, pp. 88-89.

Friar and Brinnin, <u>Modern Poetry</u>, pp. 550-551.

Joyce Carol Oates, "Yeats: Violence, Tragedy, Mutability," <u>BuR</u>, 17 (Dec., 1969), 6-7.

John Ower, <u>Expl</u>, 28 (Sept., 1969), 7.

Kathleen Raine, "Life in Death and Death in Life: Yeats's 'Cuchulain Comforted' and 'News for the Delphic Oracle,'" <u>SoR</u>, 9 (Summer, 1973), 573-577.

Charles A. Raines, "Yeats' Metaphors of Permanence," <u>TCL</u>, 5 (April, 1959), 12-13.

_____. "Nineteen Hundred and Nineteen"
Friar and Brinnin, <u>Modern Poetry</u>, pp. 559-560.

Michael Ragussis, <u>The Subterfuge of Art: Language and the Romantic Tradition</u> (Baltimore and London: The Johns Hopkins Univ. Press, 1978), pp. 91-108.

Donald A. Stauffer, "The Reading of a Lyric Poem," <u>The Kenyon Review</u>, 11 (Summer, 1949), 435-436.

Tschumi, <u>Thought in Twentieth-Century English Poetry</u>, pp. 55-56.

_____. "Old Tom Again"
Donald A. Stauffer, "W. B. Yeats and the Medium of Poetry," <u>ELH</u>, 15 (Sept., 1948), 241-242.

_____. "On a Picture of a Black Centaur by Edmund Dulac"
Harry Goldgar, "Yeats and the Black Centaur in French," <u>Western Review</u>, 15 (Winter, 1951), 113-122.

John Crowe Ransom, "The Irish, the Gaelic, the Byzantine," <u>SoR</u>, 7 (Winter, 1942), 522-524.

_____. "On a Political Prisoner"
James L. Allen, Jr., "Yeats's Use of the Serious Pun," <u>SoQ</u>, 1 (Jan., 1963), 158-159.

Marjorie Perloff, "Spatial Form in the Poetry of Yeats: The Two Lissa-dell Poems," <u>PMLA</u>, 82 (Oct., 1967), 446-449.

Laurence Perrine, <u>Expl</u>, 32 (April, 1974), 64.

_____. "Parnell's Funeral"
F. A. C. Wilson, <u>Expl</u>, 27 (May, 1969), 72.

_____. "The Phases of the Moon"
Stuart Hirschberg, <u>Expl</u>, 32 (May, 1974), 75.

Tschumi, <u>Thought in Twentieth-Century English Poetry</u>, pp. 42-45.

_____. "Prayer for My Daughter"
Charles Altieri, "From a Comic to a Tragic Sense of Language in Yeats's Mature Poetry," <u>MLQ</u>, 33 (June, 1972), 159-165.

Warren Beck, "Boundaries of Poetry," <u>CE</u>, 4 (March, 1943), 349-350.

Brooks, <u>A Shaping Joy</u>, pp. 195-197.

Brooks, Purser, and Warren, <u>An Approach to Literature</u>, third edition, pp. 368-371.
    Rpt. fourth edition, pp. 360-363.

Cleanth Brooks, "Yeats: His Poetry and His Prose," <u>English</u>, 15 (Summer, 1965), 177-180.

Cal Clothier, "Some Observations on Yeats' 'A Prayer for My Daughter,'" <u>Agenda</u>, 10 (Autumn-Winter, 1971/72), 39-45.

Hardy, <u>The Curious Frame</u>, pp. 118-150.

Marjorie Perloff, "Spatial Form in the Poetry of Yeats: The Two Lissa-
dell Poems," PMLA, 82 (Oct., 1967), 449.

Marjorie Perloff, "'The Tradition of Myself': The Autobiographical Mode
of Yeats," JML, 4 (Feb., 1975), 552-553.

_____. "Red Hanrahan's Song About Ireland"
Sr. M. Bernetta Quinn, O.S.F., "Yeats and Ireland," EJ, 54 (May, 1965),
449-450.

_____. "The Results of Thought"
Richard Ellmann, "The Art of Yeats: Affirmative Capability," The Kenyon
Review, 15 (Summer, 1953), 368-369.

_____. "Ribh at the Tomb of Baile and Aillinn"
T. K. Dunseath, "Yeats and the Genesis of Supernatural Song," ELH, 28
(Dec., 1961), 399-416.

Peter Ure, "Yeats's Supernatural Songs," RES, 7, n.s. (Jan., 1956), 39-46.

_____. "Ribh Denounces Patrick"
Peter Ure, "Yeats's Supernatural Songs," RES, 7, n.s. (Jan., 1956), 46-48.

_____. "Ribh in Ecstasy"
Peter Ure, "Yeats's Supernatural Songs," RES, 7, n.s. (Jan., 1956), 40-41,
48-50.

_____. "The Rose"
Hiram Haydn, "The Last of the Romantics: An Introduction to the Symbolism
of William Butler Yeats," SR, 55 (Spring, 1947), 308-309.

_____. "The Rose of Battle"
Thomas Parkinson, "The Sun and the Moon in Yeats's Early Poetry," MP, 50
(Aug., 1952), 55.

_____. "The Rose Tree"
Bowra, The Heritage of Symbolism, p. 204.

_____. "Running to Paradise"
Hoffman, Barbarous Knowledge, pp. 44-46.

_____. "The Sad Shepherd"
Michael Ragussis, The Subterfuge of Art: Language and the Romantic
Tradition (Baltimore and London: The Johns Hopkins Univ. Press, 1978),
pp. 89-90.

_____. "Sailing to Byzantium"
Abad, A Formal Approach to Lyric Poetry, pp. 358-360.

James L. Allen, Jr., "Miraculous Birds, Another and the Same: Yeats's
Golden Image and the Phoenix," ES, 48 (June, 1967), 215-226, et passim.

James L. Allen, Jr., "Yeats's Use of the Serious Pun," SoQ, 1 (Jan.,
1963), 159-160.

Blackmur, Expense of Greatness, pp. 98-99.
   Rpt. Language as Gesture, pp. 98-99.

Curtis Bradford, "Yeats's Byzantium Poems: A Study of Their Development," PMLA, 75 (March, 1960), 110-118.

Cleanth Brooks, "A Note on Symbol and Conceit," The American Review, 3 (May, 1934), 209-211.

Brooks, Modern Poetry and the Tradition, pp. 62-64, 190-192. Abridged in The Case for Poetry, p. 401.

Cleanth Brooks, "The Vision of William Butler Yeats," SoR, 4 (Summer, 1938), 131-133.

H. M. Campbell, "Yeats's 'Sailing to Byzantium,'" MLN, 70 (Dec., 1955), 585-589.

Frederic I. Carpenter, "A Lesser 'Byzantium,'" CE, 28 (May, 1967), 614-615.

Ethel F. Cornwell, The "Still Point," pp. 104-105.

A. Davenport, "W. B. Yeats and the Upanishads," RES, 3 n.s. (Jan., 1952), 56-57.

Dickinson, Suggestions for Teachers of "Introduction to Literature," fifth edition, ed. Locke, Gibson, and Arms, p. 39. (Teacher's Manual)

Allan Donaldson, "A Note on W. B. Yeats' 'Sailing to Byzantium,'" N&Q, 1 n.s. (Jan., 1954), 34-35.

Douglas, Lamson, and Smith, The Critical Reader, pp. 115-118. Revised edition, pp. 726-729.

Drew, Poetry: A Modern Guide, pp. 262-267.

Feder, Ancient Myth in Modern Poetry, pp. 82-85.

D. C. Fowler, "Lesser on Yeats's 'Sailing to Byzantium,'" CE, 28 (May, 1967), 614.

Frankenberg, Invitation to Poetry, p. 383.

Friar and Brinnin, Modern Poetry, pp. 554-555.

F. L. Gwynn, "Yeats's Byzantium and Its Sources," PQ, 32 (Jan., 1953), 9-21.

Jeremy Hawthorn, Identity and Relationship: A Contribution to Marxist Theory of Literary Criticism (London: Lawrence & Wishart, 1973), pp. 50-54.

Archibald A. Hill, "Method in Source Study: Yeats' Golden Bird of Byzantium as a Test Case," TSLL, 17 (Summer, 1o75), 525-538.

Stanley M. Holberg, "'Sailing to Byzantium': A New Source and a New Reading," ELN, 12 (Dec., 1974), 111-116.

Rob Jackaman, "Byzantium Revisited: A Look at the Direction of Yeats's Philosophical Journey in the Poem 'Byzantium,'" The Southern Revew (Australia), 8 (Nov., 1975), 236-246.

A. N. Jeffares, "The Byzantine Poems of W. B. Yeats," RES, 22 (Jan., 1946), 44-49.

Knights, Explorations, pp. 202-203.

L. C. Knights, "W. B. Yeats: The Assertion of Values," SoR, 7 (Winter, 1942), 438-439.

Anne Kostelanetz, "Irony in Yeats's Byzantium Poems," TSL, 9 (1964), 130-134.

Kremen, The Imagination of the Resurrection, pp. 289-292.

Simon O. Lesser, "Reply," CE, 28 (May, 1967), 615-617.

Simon O. Lesser, "'Sailing to Byzantium'--Another Voyage, Another Reading," CE, 28 (Jan., 1967), 291-310.

Maynard Mack, Leonard Dean, and William Frost, English Masterpieces, Vol. VII, Modern Poetry, p. 7.

Elder Olson, The University of Kansas City Review, 8 (Spring, 1942), 209-219.
    Rpt. in part, Critiques, pp. 284-288.
    Rpt. Engle and Carrier, Reading Modern Poetry, pp. 139-149. Abridged in The Case for Poetry, p. 401.

L. C. Parks, "The Hidden Aspect of 'Sailing to Byzantium,'" EA, 16 (Oct.-Dec., 1963), 333-344.

Peckham and Chatman, Word, Meaning, Poem, pp. 274-285.

Robert S. Phillips, Expl, 22 (Oct., 1963), 11.

Charles A. Raines, "Yeats' Metaphors of Permanence," TCL, 5 (April, 1959), 18.

John Crowe Ransom, "The Irish, the Gaelic, the Byzantine," SoR, 7 (Winter, 1942), 518-522.

John Crowe Ransom, "Yeats and His Symbols," The Kenyon Review, 1 (Summer, 1939), 318-320.

William O. Raymond, "'The Mind's Internal Heaven' in Poetry," UTQ, 20 (April, 1951), 231-232.

Rosenthal and Smith, Exploring Poetry, pp. 577-582.

Rosenthal, The Modern Poets, p. 40.

Norman E. Stageberg, "Yeats' 'Sailing to Byzantium,'" Expl, 6 (Nov., 1947), 14.
    Rpt. The Explicator Cyclopedia, I, p. 360.

Stauffer, The Nature of Poetry, pp. 243-246. Abridged in The Case for Poetry, pp. 401-403.

Richard Studing, "'That Is No Country for Old Men'--A Yeatsian Ambiguity?" RS, 41 (March, 1973), 60-61.

Ruth Elizabeth Sullivan, "Backward to Byzantium," L&P, 17, No. 1 (1967), 13-18.

Thomas and Brown, Reading Poems: An Introduction to Critical Study, pp. 712-714.

Tschumi, Thought in Twentieth-Century English Poetry, pp. 67-69.

Helen Vendler, "Sacred and Profane Perfection in Yeats," SoR, 9 (Winter, 1973), 109-110.

Walsh, Doors into Poetry, pp. 55-56.

Geoffrey Walton, "Yeats's 'Perne': Bobbin or Bird?" EIC, 13 (April, 1966), 255-258.

Aileen Ward, "The Psychoanalytic Theory of Poetic Form: A Comment," L&P, 17, No. 1 (1967), 31-33.

Alison White, Expl, 13 (Nov., 1954), 8.
    Rpt. The Explicator Cyclopedia, I, p. 347.

W. K. Wimsatt, "Comment on 'Two Essays in Practical Criticism,'" The University of Kansas City Review, 9 (Winter, 1952), 142.

Yvor Winters, "The Poetry of W. B. Yeats," TCL, 6 (April, 1960), 10-11.
   Rpt. Forms of Discovery, pp. 215-216.

_____. "The Second Coming"

Michael Bell, "The Assimilation of Doubt in Yeats's Visionary Poems," QQ, 80 (Autumn, 1973), 390-391.

Blackmur, Expense of Greatness, pp. 79-85.
   Rpt. Critiques, pp. 361-364.

R. P. Blackmur, "The Later Poetry of W. B. Yeats," SoR, 2 (Autumn, 1936), 343-347.
   Rpt. Language as Gesture, pp. 84-89.

Bloom, Philbrick, and Blistein, The Order of Poetry, p. 43-52.

Bloom, Poetry and Repression, pp. 216-222.

Edward A. Bloom, "Yeats' 'Second Coming': An Experiment in Analysis," The University of Kansas City Review, 21 (Winter, 1954), 103-110.

Bornstein, Transformations of Romanticism, pp. 62-64.

Bowra, The Heritage of Symbolism, pp. 208-209.

Daiches and Charvat, Poems in English, pp. 732-733.

Deutsch, Poetry in Our Time, pp. 273-274.

R. F. Fleissner, "The Second Coming of Guess Who?: The 'Rough Beast' as Africa in The Second Coming," NConL, 6 (Nov., 1976), 7-9.

A. M. Gibbs, "The 'Rough Beasts' of Yeats and Shakespeare," N&Q, 17 (Feb., 1970), 48-49.

Hiram Haydn, "The Last of the Romantics: An Introduction to the Symbolism of William Butler Yeats," SR, 55 (Spring, 1947), 314-315.

Joe Horrell, "Some Notes on Conversion in Poetry," SoR, 7 (Summer, 1942), 123-126.

Judson Jerome, "Six Senses of the Poet," ColQ, 10 (Winter, 1962), 225-240.

Wendell S. Johnson, "Some Functions of Poetic Form," JAAC, 13 (June, 1955), 505.

Jerome L. Mazzaro, Expl, 16 (Oct., 1957), 6.
   Rpt. The Explicator Cyclopedia, I, p. 360.

John Crowe Ransom, "Yeats and His Symbols," The Kenyon Review, 1 (Summer, 1939), 317-318.

Rosenthal, The Modern Poets, pp. 42-44.

D. S. Savage, "Two Prophetic Poems," Western Review, 13 (Winter, 1949), 67-78.

Jon Stallworthy, "The Second Coming," Agenda, 10 (Autumn-Winter, 1971/72), 24-33.

Thomas and Brown, Reading Poems: An Introduction to Critical Study, pp. 715-716.

Tschumi, Thought in Twentieth-Century English Poetry, pp. 56-57.

Unger and O'Connor, Poems for Study, pp. 582-584.

Van Doren, Introduction to Poetry, pp. 81-85.

Donald Weeks, "Image and Idea in Yeats' The Second Coming," PMLA, 63 (March, 1948), 281-292.

Wheeler, The Design of Poetry, pp. 52, 54.

Richard P. Wheeler, "Yeats' 'Second Coming': What Rough Beast?" AI, 31 (Fall, 1974), 233-251.
    Rpt. The Practice of Psychoanalytic Criticism, ed. Leonard Tennenhouse (Detroit: Wayne State Univ. Press, 1976), pp. 152-170.

_____. "The Secret Rose"
Bowra, The Heritage of Symbolism, p. 191.

_____. "September 1913"
Adele M. Dalsimer, "By Memory Inspired: W. B. Yeats's 'September 1913,'" CLQ, 12 (March, 1976), 38-49.

_____. "The Song of the Happy Shepherd"
Michael Ragussis, The Subterfuge of Art: Language and the Romantic Tradition (Baltimore and London: The Johns Hopkins Univ. Press, 1978), pp. 86-88.

Marion Witt, "Yeats's 'The Song of the Happy Shepherd,'" PQ, 32 (Jan., 1953), 1-8.

_____. "The Song of Wandering Aengus"
Bowra, The Heritage of Symbolism, pp. 189-190.

Valerie J. Goldzung, "Yeats's Traditional 'The Song of Wandering Aengus," MSE, 1 (Spring, 1967), 8-15.

Thomas Parkinson, "The Sun and the Moon in Yeats's Early Poetry," MP, 50 (Aug., 1952), 55.

Bruce A. Rosenberg, "Irish Folklore and 'The Song of Wandering Aengus,'" PQ, 46 (Oct., 1967), 527-535.

_____. "The Sorrow of Love"
Bartlett, Poems in Process, pp. 193-195.

Herbert Read, "The Collected Poems of W. B. Yeats," The Criterion, 13 (April, 1934), 468-472.

_____. "The Spur"
Hanford Henderson, Expl, 15 (March, 1957), 41.
    Rpt. The Explicator Cyclopedia, I, p. 360.

_____. "The Statues"
Hazard Adams, "Yeatsian Art and Mathematic Form," CentR, 4 (Winter, 1960), 78-85.

Richard Ellmann, "Three Ways of Looking at a Briton," SR, 61 (Winter, 1953), 154.

Bryant E. Hoffman, "Myself Must I Remake: Yeats's Last Poems (1936-1939)," LitR, 20 (Summer, 1977), 416-420.

Joyce Carol Oates, "Yeats: Violence, Tragedy, Mutability," BuR, 17 (Dec., 1969), 5-6.

Jon Stallworthy, "Two of Yeats's Last Poems," A Review of English Literature, 4 (July, 1963), 48-69.

Helen Vendler, "Sacred and Profane Perfection in Yeats," SoR, 9 (Winter, 1973), 114-116.

Sarah Youngblood, "The Structure of Yeats's Long Poems," Criticism, 5 (Fall, 1963), 324-327.

_____. "The Stolen Child"
Robert W. Caswell, Expl, 25 (April, 1967), 64.

Rosenthal, The Modern Poets, pp. 35-36.

_____. "Summer and Spring"
John Somer, "Unageing Monuments: A Study of W. B. Yeats' Poetry Sequence, 'A Man Young and Old,'" BSUF, 12 (Autumn, 1971), 33-34.

_____. "Symbols"
Daiches, The Place of Meaning in Poetry, pp. 43-44.

_____. "That the Night Come"
Brooks, Purser, and Warren, An Approach to Literature, pp. 469-471.
    Rpt. third edition, pp. 319-321.
    Rpt. fourth edition, pp. 317-319.

H. L. Dean, Expl, 31 (Feb., 1973), 44.

Leonard Unger, "Yeats and Hamlet," SoR, 6 (July, 1960), 698-709.

_____. "There"
Peter Ure, "Yeats's Supernatural Songs," RES, 7, n.s. (Jan., 1956), 50-51.

_____. "The Three Bushes"
Arra M. Garab, "Fabulous Artifice: Yeats's 'Three Bushes' Sequence," Criticism, 7 (Summer, 1965), 235-239, 247-249.

Hoffman, Barbarous Knowledge, pp. 52-53.

Edward B. Partridge, "Yeats's 'The Three Bushes'--Genesis and Structure," Accent, 17 (Spring, 1957), 67-80.

Leonard Unger, "The New Collected Yeats," Poetry, 80 (April, 1952), 48-49.

_____. "The Three Hermits"
Deutsch, Poetry in Our Times, pp. 269-270.

_____. "Three Things"
Nat Henry, Expl, 33 (Jan., 1975), 38.

Laurence Perrine, Expl, 32 (Sept., 1973), 4.

Thomas J. Wertenbaker, Jr., Expl, 34 (May, 1976), 67.

_____. "A Thought from Propertius"
Delmore Schwartz, "An Unwritten Book," SoR, 7 (Winter, 1942), 487.

_____. "To a Friend Whose Work Has Come to Nothing"
Malcolm Brown, "The Sweet Crystalline Cry," The Western Review, 16 (Summer, 1952), 265.

_____. "To a Shade"
David Daiches in Locke, Gibson, and Arms, Introduction to Literature, fifth edition, pp. 148-151.

_____. "To a Young Beauty"
Laurence Perrine, "Yeats and Landor: 'To a Young Beauty,'" N&Q, 19 (Sept., 1972), 330.

_____. "To D. W."
Yeats, Letters on Poetry from W. B. Yeats to Dorothy Wellesley, pp. 93-95.

_____. "To His Heart, Bidding It Have No Fear"
Marion Witt, Expl, 9 (March, 1951), 32.
     Rpt. The Explicator Cyclopedia, I, pp. 360-361.

_____. "The Tower"
A. Davenport, "W. B. Yeats and the Upanishads," RES, 3, n.s. (Jan., 1952), 60-62.

Richard Ellmann, "The Art of Yeats: Affirmative Capability," The Kenyon Review, 15 (Summer, 1953), 364-366.

Friar and Brinnin, Modern Poetry, pp. 557-559.

Hoffman, Barbarous Knowledge, pp. 62-83.

James H. O'Brien, "Yeats' Dark Night of Self and The Tower," BuR, 15 (May, 1967), 10-25.

Marjorie Perloff, "'The Tradition of Myself': The Autobiographical Mode of Yeats," JML, 4 (Feb., 1975), 566-573.

John Crowe Ransom, "The Irish, the Gaelic, the Byzantine," SoR, 7 (Winter, 1942), 542-543.

Donald A. Stauffer, "The Reading of a Lyric Poem," The Kenyon Review, 11 (Summer, 1949), 434-435.

Tschumi, Thought in Twentieth-Century English Poetry, pp. 47-49.

Tuve, Elizabethan and Metaphysical Imagery, pp. 269-271.

Sarah Youngblood, "A Reading of 'The Tower,'" TCL, 5 (July, 1959), 74-84.

_____. "Two Songs from a Play"
Brooks and Warren, Understanding Poetry, pp. 615-621. Revised edition, pp. 458-464.

Cleanth Brooks, "The Vision of William Butler Yeats," SoR, 4 (Summer, 1938), 123-124.

Brower, Fields of Light, pp. 84-88.

Friar and Brinnin, Modern Poetry, pp. 555-557.

Yvor Winters, "The Poetry of W. B. Yeats," TCL, 6 (April, 1960), 8-9.
     Rpt. Forms of Discovery, pp. 212-213.

_____. "The Two Trees"
Kermode, Romantic Iamge, pp. 96-99.

_____. "Under Ben Bulben"
R. P. Blackmur, "Between Myth and Philosophy: Fragments of W. B. Yeats," SoR, 7 (Winter, 1942), 415-417.

Curtis B. Bradford, "Journeys to Byzantium," VQR, 25 (Spring, 1949), 212-214.

Joseph J. Comprone, "Unity of Being and W. B. Yeats' 'Under Ben Bulben,'" BSUF, 11 (Summer, 1970), 41-49.

Claire Hahn, "The Moral Center of Yeats's 'Last Poems,'" Thought, 50 (Sept., 1975), 309-311.

Bryant E. Hoffman, "Myself Must I Remake: Yeats' Last Poems (1936-1939)," LitR, 20 (Summer, 1977), 423-426.

Jon Stallworthy, "W. B. Yeats's 'Under Ben Bulben,'" RES, 17 (Feb., 1966), 30-53.

Tschumi, Thought in Twentieth-Century English Poetry, pp. 59-61.

_____. "Under the Moon"
Thomas Parkinson, "The Sun and the Moon in Yeats's Early Poetry," MP, 50 (Aug., 1952), 56.

_____. "Under the Round Tower"
Thomas Parkinson, "The Sun and the Moon in Yeats's Early Poetry," MP, 50 (Aug., 1952), 55-56.

_____. "Vacillation"
James L. Allen, Jr., "Yeats's Use of the Serious Pun," SoQ, 1 (Jan., 1963), 157-158.

Feder, Ancient Myth in Modern Poetry, pp. 196-198.

_____. "The Valley of the Black Pig"
Thomas R. Whitaker, "The Dialectic of Yeats's Vision of History," MP, 57 (Nov., 1959), 101-102.

_____. "A Vision"
Cleanth Brooks, "The Vision of William Butler Yeats," SoR, 4 (Summer, 1938), 116-142.

Drew and Sweeney, Directions in Modern Poetry, pp. 154-155.

Morton Irving Seiden, "A Psychoanalytical Essay on William Butler Yeats," Accent, 6 (Winter, 1946), 189-190.

_____. "The Wanderings of Oisin"
Russell K. Alspach, "Some Sources of Yeats's 'The Wanderings of Oisin,'" PMLA, 58 (Sept., 1943), 849-866.

Morton Irving Seiden, "A Psychoanalytical Essay on William Butler Yeats," Accent, 6 (Winter, 1946), 180-189.

_____. "What Magic Drum?"
Dennic E. Smith and F. A. C. Wilson, "The Source of Yeats's 'What Magic Drum,'" PLL, 9 (Spring, 1973), 197-201.

_____. "What Then?"
Bryant E. Hoffman, "Myself Must I Remake: Yeats's Last Poems (1936-1939)," LitR, 20 (Summer, 1977), 409.

_____. "When You Are Old"
Arthur Minton, Expl, 5 (May, 1947), 49.
    Rpt. The Explicator Cyclopedia, I, pp. 361-362.

Elisabeth Schneider, Expl, 6 (May, 1948), 50.
    Rpt. The Explicator Cyclopedia, I, pp. 362-364.

Marion Witt, Expl, 6 (Oct., 1947), 6.
    Rpt. The Explicator Cyclopedia, I, p. 362.

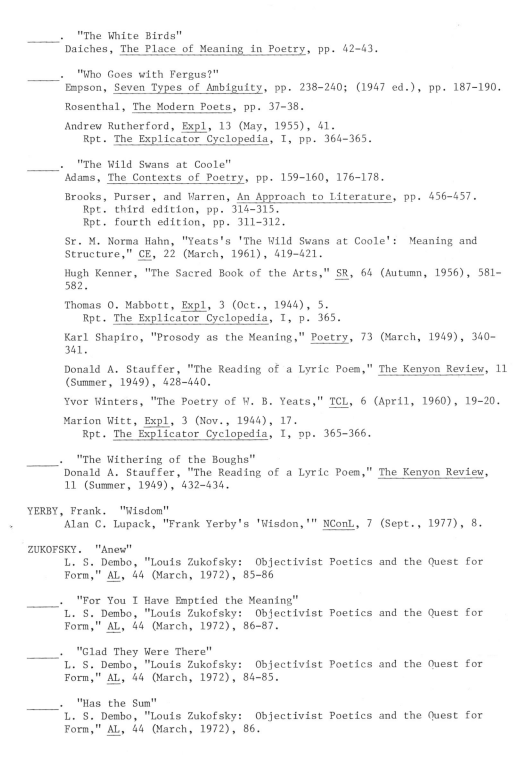

_____. "The White Birds"
Daiches, _The Place of Meaning in Poetry_, pp. 42-43.

_____. "Who Goes with Fergus?"
Empson, _Seven Types of Ambiguity_, pp. 238-240; (1947 ed.), pp. 187-190.

Rosenthal, _The Modern Poets_, pp. 37-38.

Andrew Rutherford, _Expl_, 13 (May, 1955), 41.
   Rpt. _The Explicator Cyclopedia_, I, pp. 364-365.

_____. "The Wild Swans at Coole"
Adams, _The Contexts of Poetry_, pp. 159-160, 176-178.

Brooks, Purser, and Warren, _An Approach to Literature_, pp. 456-457.
   Rpt. third edition, pp. 314-315.
   Rpt. fourth edition, pp. 311-312.

Sr. M. Norma Hahn, "Yeats's 'The Wild Swans at Coole': Meaning and Structure," _CE_, 22 (March, 1961), 419-421.

Hugh Kenner, "The Sacred Book of the Arts," _SR_, 64 (Autumn, 1956), 581-582.

Thomas O. Mabbott, _Expl_, 3 (Oct., 1944), 5.
   Rpt. _The Explicator Cyclopedia_, I, p. 365.

Karl Shapiro, "Prosody as the Meaning," _Poetry_, 73 (March, 1949), 340-341.

Donald A. Stauffer, "The Reading of a Lyric Poem," _The Kenyon Review_, 11 (Summer, 1949), 428-440.

Yvor Winters, "The Poetry of W. B. Yeats," _TCL_, 6 (April, 1960), 19-20.

Marion Witt, _Expl_, 3 (Nov., 1944), 17.
   Rpt. _The Explicator Cyclopedia_, I, pp. 365-366.

_____. "The Withering of the Boughs"
Donald A. Stauffer, "The Reading of a Lyric Poem," _The Kenyon Review_, 11 (Summer, 1949), 432-434.

YERBY, Frank. "Wisdom"
Alan C. Lupack, "Frank Yerby's 'Wisdon,'" _NConL_, 7 (Sept., 1977), 8.

ZUKOFSKY. "Anew"
L. S. Dembo, "Louis Zukofsky: Objectivist Poetics and the Quest for Form," _AL_, 44 (March, 1972), 85-86

_____. "For You I Have Emptied the Meaning"
L. S. Dembo, "Louis Zukofsky: Objectivist Poetics and the Quest for Form," _AL_, 44 (March, 1972), 86-87.

_____. "Glad They Were There"
L. S. Dembo, "Louis Zukofsky: Objectivist Poetics and the Quest for Form," _AL_, 44 (March, 1972), 84-85.

_____. "Has the Sum"
L. S. Dembo, "Louis Zukofsky: Objectivist Poetics and the Quest for Form," _AL_, 44 (March, 1972), 86.

_____. "A Last Cigarette"
L. S. Dembo, "Louis Zukofsky: Objectivist Poetics and the Quest for
Form," <u>AL</u>, 44 (March, 1972), 82-83.

_____. "Mantis" and "'Mantis' an Interpretation"
L. S. Dembo, "Louis Zukofsky: Objectivist Poetics and the Quest for
Form," <u>AL</u>, 44 (March, 1972), 87-91.

_____. "Poem Beginning 'The'"
L. S. Dembo, "Louis Zukofsky: Objectivist Poetics and the Quest for
Form," <u>AL</u>, 44 (March, 1972), 91-94.

Main Sources Consulted

Note: When explication might generally be assumed to
appear in a book that we have examined, we have
listed that book even though no explication has
been found in it. We have, however, added the
parenthetical comment that it contains "no
explication."

ABAD, Gémino H. A Formal Approach to Lyric Poetry. Quezon City, Philippines:
Univ. of the Philippines Press, 1978.

ABBE, George. You and Contemporary Poetry. North Guilford, Connecticut:
Author-Audience Publication, 1957.

Accent: A Quarterly of New Literature, 1 (Autumn, 1940)-20, No. 4 (Autumn,
1960).

ADAMS, Hazard. The Contexts of Poetry. Boston, Massachusetts: Little, Brown
and Company, 1963.

ADAMS, Robert M. Strains of Discord; Studies in Literary Openness. Ithaca,
New York: Cornell Univ. Press, 1958.

ALLEN, Don Cameron. Image and Meaning: Metaphoric Traditions in Renaissance
Poetry. Baltimore: The Johns Hopkins Press, 1960. New enlarged edition, 1968.

American Literary Criticism, 1900-1950. Ed. Charles I. Blicksberg. New York:
Hendricks House, Inc., 1951.

American Literature: A Journal of Literary History, Criticism, and Bibliography, 1 (1929)-49, No. 3 (Nov., 1977).

American Poetry of the Twentieth Century. Ed. Richard Gray. London: Cambridge Univ. Press, 1976.

The American Review, 1 (April-Oct., 1933)-9 (Oct., 1937).

Anglo-Saxon Poetry: Essays in Appreciation. Ed. Lewis E. Nicholson and
Dolores Warwick Frese. Notre Dame and London: Univ. of Notre Dame
Press, 1975.

Anniversary Lectures 1959: Robert Burns, 1759, by Robert Hillyer; Edgar Allen
    Poe, 1809, by Richard Wilbur; Alfred Edward Housman, 1859, by Cleanth
    Brooks. Lectures Presented Under the Auspices of the Gertrude Clarke
    Whittall Poetry and Literature Fund. Washington: Reference Department,
    Library of Congress, 1959.

Ariel: A Review of International English Literature, 1, No. 1 (Jan., 1970)-8,
    No. 4 (Oct., 1977).

ARMS, George. The Fields Were Green: A New View of Bryant, Whittier, Holmes,
    Lowell, and Longfellow, with a Selection of Their Poems. Stanford,
    California: Stanford Univ. Press, 1953.

ARNSTEIN, Flora S. Adventure into Poetry. Stanford, California: Stanford
    Univ. Press, 1951. (No explication)

Aspects of American Poetry: Essays Presented to Howard Mumford Jones. Ed.
    Richard M. Ludwig. Columbus, Ohio: Ohio State Univ. Press, 1962.

BAKER, William E. Syntax in English Poetry, 1870-1930. Berkeley and Los
    Angeles: Univ. of California Press, 1967.

BALL, Patricia M. The Heart's Events: The Victorian Poetry of Relationships.
    London: Athlone Press, 1976.

BARTLETT, Phyllis. Poems in Process. New York: Oxford Univ. Press, 1951.

BASLER, Roy P. Sex, Symbolism, and Psychology in Literature. New Brunswick:
    Rutgers Univ. Press, 1948.

BATESON, F. W. English Poetry: A Critical Introduction. London and New York:
    Longman's Green Co., 1950.

_____. English Poetry and the English Language: An Experiment in Literary
    History. Oxford: The Clarendon Press, 1934.

BEACH, Joseph Warren. A Romantic View of Poetry. Minneapolis: The Univ. of
    Minnesota Press, 1944.

_____. Obsessive Images: Symbolism in Poetry of the 1930's and 1940's. Ed.
    William Van O'Connor. Minneapolis: Univ. of Minnesota Press, 1960.

BEATY, Jerome and William H. Matchett. Poetry: From Statement to Meaning.
    New York: Oxford Univ. Press, 1965.

BELGION, Montgomery. Reading for Profit. Chicago: Henry Regnery Company,
    1950.

BLACKMUR, R. P. The Double Agent: Essays in Craft and Elucidation. New York:
    Arrow Editions, 1935.

_____. The Expense of Greatness. New York: Arrow Editions, 1940.

_____. Language as Gesture: Essays in Poetry. New York: Harcourt, Brace and
    Company, 1952.

BLAIR, Walter and W. K. Chandler. Approaches to Poetry. New York:
    D. Appleton-Century Company, 1935.

BLAIR, Walter and John C. Gerber. Better Reading 2: Literature. Chicago: Scott, Foresman and Company, 1948.

BLOOM, Edward A., Charles H. Philbrick, and Elmer M. Blistein. The Order of Poetry: An Introduction. New York: The Odyssey Press, Inc., 1961.

BLOOM, Harold. A Map of Misreading. New York: Oxford Univ. Press, 1975.

_____. Poetry and Repression: Revisionism from Blake to Stevens. New Haven and London: Yale Univ. Press, 1976.

_____. The Visionary Company: A Reading of English Romantic Poetry. Garden City, New York: Doubleday & Company, Inc., 1961.

BODKIN, Maud. Archetypal Patterns in Poetry. London: Oxford Univ. Press, 1934.

BORNSTEIN, George. Transformations of Romanticism in Yeats, Eliot, and Stevens. Chicago and London: Univ. of Chicago Press, 1976.

BOSTETTER, Edward E. The Romantic Ventriloquists: Wordsworth, Coleridge, Keats, Shelley, Byron. Seattle: Univ. of Washington Press, 1963.

BOULTON, Marjorie. The Anatomy of Poetry. London: Routledge & Kegan Paul, 1953.

Boundary 2, 1, No. 1 (Fall, 1972)-5, No. 3 (Spring, 1977).

BOWRA, C. M. The Creative Experiment. London: Macmillan & Company, Ltd., 1949.

_____. The Heritage of Symbolism. London: Macmillan & Company, Ltd., 1947.

_____. The Romantic Imagination. Cambridge, Massachusetts: Harvard Univ. Press, 1949.

BRETT, R. L. Reason and Imagination: A Study of Form and Meaning in Four Poems. London: Oxford Univ. Press, 1960.

BROOKS, Cleanth, Jr., A Shaping Joy: Studies in the Writer's Craft. London: Methuen & Company, Ltd., 1971.

_____. Modern Poetry and the Tradition. Chapel Hill: Univ. of North Carolina Press, 1939.

_____. The Well Wrought Urn. New York: Reynal and Hitchcock, 1947.

BROOKS, Cleanth, Jr., John Thibaut Purser, and Robert Penn Warren. An Approach to Literature. Revised edition. New York: F. S. Crofts & Company, 1942. Third edition, 1952. Fourth edition, 1964.

BROOKS, Cleanth, Jr., and Robert Penn Warren. Understanding Poetry: An Anthology for College Students. New York: Henry Holt and Company, 1938. Revised edition, 1950. Fourth edition, 1964.

BROOKS, Cleanth, R. W. B. Lewis, and Robert Penn Warren. American Literature: The Makers and the Making. New York: St. Martin's Press, 1973.

BROWER, Reuben A. Forms of Lyric: Selected Papers from the English Insti-
     tute. New York: Columbia Univ. Press, 1970.

BROWER, Reuben Arthur. The Fields of Light: An Experiment in Critical Read-
     ing. New York: Oxford Univ. Press, 1951.

BROWN, Harry, and John Milstead. Patterns in Poetry: An Introductory Anthol-
     ogy. Glenview, Illinois: Scott, Foresman and Company, 1968.

BROWN, Wentworth K., and Sterling P. Olmstead. Language and Literature. New
     York: Harcourt, Brace & World, Inc., 1962.

BURKE, Kenneth. Counter-Statement. New York: Harcourt, Brace and Company,
     1931.

_____. Language as Symbolic Action: Essays on Life, Literature, and Method.
     Berkeley and Los Angeles: Univ. of California Press, 1968.

_____. Permanence and Change. New York: New Republic, Inc., 1935. (No
     explication)

_____. The Philosophy of Literary Form. Baton Rouge: Louisiana State Univ.
     Press, 1941.

_____. A Rhetoric of Motives. New York: Prentice-Hall, Inc., 1950. (No
     explication)

CARROLL, Paul. The Poem In Its Skin. Chicago: Follett Publishing Company,
     1968.

The Case for Poetry. Ed. Frederick L. Gwynn, Ralph W. Condee, and Arthur O.
     Lewis. Englewood Cliffs, New Jersey: Prentice-Hall, Inc., 1954.

The CEA Critic, 1, No. 1 (Oct., 1939)-40, No. 1 (Nov., 1977).

The Centennial Review (formerly Centennial Review of Arts and Sciences), 1
     (1957)-21, No. 4 (Fall, 1977).

CHATMAN, Seymour. An Introduction to the Language of Poetry. Boston:
     Houghton Mifflin Company, 1968.

CHRIST, Carol T. The Finer Optic: The Aesthetic of Particularity in Victori-
     an Poetry. New Haven and London: Yale Univ. Press, 1975.

CIARDI, John. How Does a Poem Mean? Boston: Houghton Mifflin Company, 1959.

CLARK, David R. Lyric Resonance: Glosses on Some Poems of Yeats, Frost,
     Crane, Cummings and Others. Amherst: Univ. of Massachusetts Press,
     1972.

COFFMAN, Stanley K. Imagism: A Chapter for the History of Modern Poetry.
     Norman, Oklahoma: Univ. of Oklahoma Press, 1951. (No explication)

COHAN, B. Bernard. Writing About Literature. Chicago, Illinois: Scott,
     Foresman and Company, 1963.

College English, 1 (Oct., 1939)-39, No. 4 (Dec., 1977).

Concerning Poetry, 1, No. 1 (Fall, 1968)-10, No. 2 (Fall, 1977).

COOPER, Charles W., and John Holmes. Preface to Poetry. New York: Harcourt, Brace and Company, Inc., 1946.

CORNWELL, Ethel F. The "Still Point": Theme and Variations in the Writings of T. S. Eliot, Coleridge, Yeats, Henry James, Virginia Woolf, and D. H. Lawrence. New Brunswick, New Jersey: Rutgers Univ. Press, 1962.

Criterion: A Quarterly Review, 1 (Oct., 1922)-18 (Jan., 1939).

The Critic, 1 (Spring, 1947)-1, No. 2 (Autumn, 1947).

Critical Quarterly, 1, No. 1 (Spring, 1959)-19, No. 4 (Winter, 1977).

A Critical Supplement to "Poetry," Oct., 1948-Dec., 1949. (The listing in this checklist is incomplete and limited to poems by widely recognized contemporaries. The poems explicated appear in the corresponding issues of Poetry: A Magazine of Verse.)

Criticism: A Quarterly for Literature and the Arts, 1, No. 1 (Winter, 1959)-19, No. 4 (Fall, 1977).

Critics and Criticism: Ancient and Modern. Ed. R. S. Crane. Chicago: Univ. of Chicago Press, 1952. (No explication)

The Critic's Notebook. Ed. Robert Wooster Stallman. Minneapolis: The Univ. of Minnesota Press, 1950.

Criticism: The Foundations of Modern Literary Judgment. Ed. Mark Schorer, Josephine Miles, and Gordon McKenzie. New York: Harcourt, Brace and Company, 1948.

Critiques and Essays in Criticism, 1920-1948. Selected by Robert Wooster Stallman. New York: The Ronald Press Company, 1949.

CRUTWELL, Patrick. The Shakespearean Moment and Its Place in the Poetry of the 17th Century. New York: Columbia Univ. Press, 1955.

CUNNINGHAM, Cornelius Carman. Literature as a Fine Art: Analysis and Interpretation. New York: Thomas Nelson and Sons, 1941.

CUNNINGHAM, J. V. Tradition and Poetic Structure. Denver, Colorado: Alan Swallow, 1960.

DAICHES, David. The Place of Meaning in Poetry. Edinburgh and London: Oliver and Boyd, 1935.

_____. Poetry and the Modern World: A Study of Poetry in England Between 1900 and 1939. Chicago: The Univ. of Chicago Press, 1940.

_____. A Study of Literature for Readers and Critics. Ithaca: Cornell Univ. Press, 1948.

DAICHES, David, and William Charvat. Poems in English, 1530-1940. New York: The Ronald Press Company, 1950.

DANIELS, Earl. The Art of Reading Poetry. New York: Farrar & Rinehart, Inc., 1941.

DAY LEWIS, C. The Poetic Image. London: Jonathan Cape, 1947.

De MOURGES, Odette. Metaphysical Baroque & Precieux Poetry. Oxford: Oxford Univ. Press, 1953.

Determinations: Critical Essays, by Twelve Contributors with Introduction. Ed. F. R. Leavis. London: Chatto and Windus, 1934.

DEUTSCH, Babette. Poetry in Our Time. New York: Henry Holt and Company, 1952.

_____. This Modern Poetry. New York: W. W. Norton and Company, Inc., 1935.

The Dial, 78 (Jan., 1925)-86 (July, 1929).

DICKINSON, Leon T. Suggestions for Teachers of "Introduction to Literature," fifth edition. Ed. Locke, Gibson, and Arms. New York: Holt, Rinehart and Winston, Inc., 1967.

DOUGLAS, Wallace, Roy Lamson, and Hallett Smith. The Critical Reader. New York: W. W. Norton & Company, 1949. Revised edition, Roy Lamson, Hallett Smith, Hugh N. MacLean, Wallace E. Douglas, 1962.

DREW, Elizabeth. Discovering Poetry. New York: W. W. Norton & Company, 1933.

_____. The Enjoyment of Literature. New York: W. W. Norton & Company, Inc., 1935. (No explication)

DREW, Elizabeth, in collaboration with John L. Sweeney. Directions in Modern Poetry. New York: W. W. Norton & Company, Inc., 1940.

DREW, Elizabeth. Poetry: A Modern Guide to Its Understanding and Enjoyment. New York: W. W. Norton & Company, Inc., 1959

DYSON, A. E. and Julian Lovelock. Masterful Images: English Poetry from Metaphysicals to Romantics. London: The Macmillan Press, Ltd., 1976.

Early American Literature, 2 (Spring, 1967) 12 (Winter, 1977-78).

EASTMAN, Max. Enjoyment of Poetry (Revised). New York: Charles Scribner's Sons, 1930. (No explication)

_____. The Literary Mind. New York: Charles Scribner's Sons, 1931.

EDWARDS, Thomas R. Imagination and Power: A Study of Poetry on Public Themes. New York: Oxford Univ. Press, 1971.

Eighteenth Century Studies, 1 (1968)-9 (Winter, 1977/78).

ELH: A Journal of English Literary History, 1, No. 1 (April, 1934)-44, No. 4 (Winter, 1977).

ELIOT, T. S. Essays, Ancient and Modern. New York: Harcourt, Brace and Company, 1936. (No explication)

_____. The Sacred Wood: Essays on Poetry and Criticism. London: Methuen and Company, Ltd., 1920. (No explication)

_____. Selected Essays. New York: Harcourt, Brace and Company, 1932. (No explication)

_____. The Use of Poetry and the Use of Criticism. New York: Harcourt, Brace and Company, 1933. (No explication)

Elizabethan Poetry. Stratford-upon-Avon Studies 2. Ed. John Russell Brown and Bernard Harris. London: Edward Arnold (Publishers) Ltd., 1960.

EMPSON, William. English Pastoral Poetry. New York: W. W. Norton & Company, 1938.

_____. Seven Types of Ambiguity. London: Chatto and Windus, 1930. (Also revised edition, New York: New Directions, 1947.)

_____. The Structure of Complex Words. Norfolk, Connecticut: New Directions Books, 1951.

ENGLE, Paul and Warren Carrier. Reading Modern Poetry. Chicago: Scott, Foresman and Company, 1955.

English "A" Analyst (Northwestern University), Nos. 1-17 (1947?-1949).

English Institute Annual 1939-1942; English Institute Essays. New York: Columbia Univ. Press, 1940-1943, 1946-1948, 1947-1949, 1950-1952.

The English Journal (High School and College Editions), 14 (Jan., 1925)-66, No. 9 (Dec., 1977).

English Language Notes, 1, No. 1 (Sept., 1963)-15, No. 2 (Dec., 1977).

English Literary Renaissance, 1, Inaugural Issue (Winter, 1971)-7, No. 3 (Autumn, 1977).

English Masterpieces: An Anthology of Imaginative Literature from Chaucer to T. S. Eliot. VII vols.: Ed. Maynard Mack, Leonard Dean, William Frost. New York: Prentice-Hall, Inc., 1950.

English Studies (superseding Essays and Studies...), 1 (1948)-2 (1949).

English Studies in Honor of James Southall Wilson. Ed. Fredson Bowers. University of Virginia Studies, Vol. 4. Charlottesville: Univ. of Virginia Press, 1951.

Essays and Studies by Members of the English Association. Oxford: The Clarendon Press, 11 (1925)-33 (1947). New Series 3 (1950)-20 (1969).

Essays in Criticism, 1, No. 1 (Jan., 1951)-27, No. 4 (Oct., 1977).

Essays in Honor of Esmond Linworth Marilla. Ed Thomas Austin Kirby and William John Olive. Baton Rouge: Louisiana State Univ. Press, 1970.

Essays in Literature (Western Illinois Univ.) 1, No. 1 (Spring, 1974)-4, No. 2 (Fall, 1977).

Essays in Modern Literary Criticism. Ed. Ray B. West, Jr. New York: Rinehart & Company, Inc., 1952.

Essays on American Literature in Honor of Jay B. Hubbell. Ed. Clarence Gohdes. Durham, N.C.: Duke Univ. Press, 1967.

Essays on English and American Literature by Leo Spitzer. Ed. Anna Hatcher.
    Princeton, New Jersey: Princeton Univ. Press, 1962.

Essays on the Teaching of English: Reports of the Yale Conference on the Teach-
    ing of English. Ed. Edward J. Gorden and Edward S. Noyes. New York:
    Appleton-Century-Crofts, Inc., 1960.

The Explicator, 1 (Oct., 1942)-36, No. 1 (Fall, 1977).

The Explicator Cyclopedia. Ed. Charles Child Walcutt and J. Edwin Whitesell.
    Volume I. Modern Poetry. Chicago: Quadrangle Books, 1966.

The Explicator Cyclopedia. Ed. Charles Child Walcutt and J. Edwin Whitesell.
    Volume II. Traditional Poetry: Medieval to Late Victorian. Chicago:
    Quadrangle Books, 1968.

Exploration of Literature. Ed. Rima Drell Reck. Baton Rouge: Louisiana State
    Univ. Press, 1966.

FEDER, Lillian. Ancient Myth in Modern Poetry. Princeton, New Jersey: Prince-
    ton Univ. Press, 1971.

FELVER, Charles S., and Martin K. Nurmi. Poetry: An Introduction and Anthology.
    Columbus, Ohio: Charles E. Marrill Books, Inc., 1967.

FERRY, Anne. All in War with Time: Love Poetry of Shakespeare, Donne, Jonson,
    Marvell. Cambridge, Massachusetts and London: Harvard Univ. Press, 1975.

FOGLE, Richard Harter. The Permanent Pleasure: Essays on Classics of Romanti-
    cism. Athens: Univ. of Georgia Press, 1974.

Four Poets on Poetry. Ed. Don Cameron Allen. Baltimore, Maryland: The Johns
    Hopkins Press, 1959.

FOWLER, Alastair. Conceitful Thought: The Interpretation of English Renais-
    sance Poems. Edinburgh: Edinburgh Univ. Press, 1975.

FRANKENBERG, Lloyd. Invitation to Poetry. New York: Doubleday & Company,
    Inc., 1956.

_____. Pleasure Dome: On Reading Modern Poetry. Boston: Houghton Mifflin
    Company, 1949.

FRIAR, Kimon, and John Malcolm Brinnin. Modern Poetry, American and British.
    New York: Appleton-Century-Crofts, 1951.

FRIEDMAN, Norman and Charles A. McLaughlin. Poetry: An Introduction to Its
    Form and Art. New York: Harper & Brothers, 1961.

From Sensibility to Romanticism: Essays Presented to Frederick A. Pottle. Ed.
    Frederick W. Hilles and Harold Bloom. New York: Oxford Univ. Press,
    1965.

Furioso, 1 (Summer, 1939)-8 (Spring, 1953).

GARDNER, Helen. The Business of Criticism. Oxford: The Clarendon Press, 1959.

GARDNER, John. The Construction of Christian Poetry in Old English. Carbondale: Southern Illinois Univ. Press, 1975.

GOODMAN, Paul. The Structure of Literature. Chicago: The Univ. of Chicago Press, 1954.

GREENE, Theodore M. The Arts and the Art of Criticism. Princeton, New Jersey: Princeton Univ. Press, 1940.

HALL, Donald. The Pleasures of Poetry. New York: Harper & Row, 1971.

HAMILTON, G. Rostrevor. The Tell-Tale Article: A Critical Approach to Modern Poetry. New York: Oxford Univ. Press, 1950. (No explication)

HARDISON, O. B., Jr. The Enduring Monument: A Study of the Idea of Praise in Renaissance Theory and Practice. Chapel Hill: The Univ. of North Carolina Press, 1962.

HARDY, John Edward. The Curious Frame: Seven Poems in Text and Context. Notre Dame, Indiana: The Univ. of Notre Dame Press, 1962.

HOFFMAN, Daniel G. Barbarous Knowledge: Myth in the Poetry of Yeats, Graves, and Muir. New York: Oxford Univ. Press, 1967.

HARTMAN, Geoffrey H. The Unmediated Vision: An Interpretation of Wordsworth, Hopkins, Rilke, and Valery. New Haven: Yale Univ. Press, 1954.

HILL, Archibald A. Constituent and Pattern in Poetry. Austin: Univ. of Texas Press, 1976.

HOFFMAN, Frederick J. The Twenties: American Writing in the Postwar Decade. New York: The Viking Press, 1955.

HOUGHTON, Walter E. The Victorian Frame of Mind, 1830-1870. New Haven: Yale Univ. Press, 1957. (No explication)

The Hudson Review, 1 (Spring, 1948)-30, No. 3 (Autumn, 1977).

Hound and Horn, 1 (Sept., 1927)-7 (July-Sept., 1934).

HUNGERFORD, Edward B. Shores of Darkness. New York: Columbia Univ. Press, 1941.

HUPPÉ, Bernard F. The Web of Words: Structural Analyses of Four Old English Poems. Albany: State Univ. of New York Press, 1970.

The Importance of Scrutiny: Selections from Scrutiny: A Quarterly Review, 1932-1948. Ed. Eric Bentley. New York: George W. Stewart, Publisher, Inc., 1948.

The Intent of the Critic. Ed. Donald A. Stauffer. Princeton, New Jersey: Princeton Univ. Press, 1941. (No explication)

Interpretations: Essays on Twelve English Poems. Ed. John Wain. London: Routledge and Kegan Paul, 1955.

Interpretations of American Literature. Ed. Charles Feidelson, Jr., and Paul Brodtkorb, Jr. New York: Oxford Univ. Press, 1959.

The Iowa Review, 1, No. 1 (Winter, 1970)-8, No. 4 (Fall, 1977).

ISAACS, Neil D. Structural Principles in Old English Poetry. Knoxville: The Univ. of Tennessee Press, 1968.

JEROME, Judson. Poetry: Premeditated Art. Boston: Houghton Mifflin Company, 1968.

JOHNSON, E. D. H. The Alien Vision of Victorian Poetry. Princeton, New Jersey: Princeton Univ. Press, 1952.

Journal of English and Germanic Philology, 24 (1925)-76, No. 4 (Oct., 1977).

Journal of Modern Literature, 1, No. 1 (1970)-6, No. 2 (April, 1977).

KAPLAN, Fred. Miracles of Rare Device: The Poet's Sense of Self in Nineteenth-Century Poetry. Detroit: Wayne State Univ. Press, 1972.

The Kenyon Critics: Studies in Modern Literature from the "Kenyon Review." Ed. John Crowe Ransom. Cleveland and New York: The World Publishing Company, 1951.

The Kenyon Review, 1 (Winter, 1939)-32, No. 1 (1970).

KERMODE, Frank. Romantic Image. London: Routledge and Kegan Paul, 1957.

KILBY, Clyde S. Poetry and Life: An Introduction To Poetry. New York: The Odyssey Press, 1953.

KIRK, Richard Ray, and Roger Philip McCutcheon. An Introduction to the Study of Poetry. New York: American Book Company, 1934.

KNIGHT, G. Wilson. The Burning Oracle: Studies in the Poetry of Action. London, New York, Toronto: Oxford Univ. Press, 1939.

_____. The Starlit Dome: Studies in the Poetry of Vision. London, New York, Toronto: Oxford Univ. Press, 1941.

KNIGHTS, L. C. Explorations: Essays in Criticism. New York: George W. Stewart, 1947.

KREMEN, Kathryn R. The Imagination of the Resurrection: The Poetic Continuity of a Religious Motif in Donne, Blake, and Yeats. Lewisburg: Bucknell Univ. Press, 1972.

KREUZER, James R. Elements of Poetry. New York: The Macmillan Company, 1955.

KRIEGER, Murray. The New Apologists for Poetry. Minneapolis: The Univ. of Minnesota Press, 1956.

_____. The Play and the Place of Criticism. Baltimore: The Johns Hopkins Press, 1967.

LACEY, Paul A. The Inner War: Forms and Themes in Recent American Poetry. Philadelphia: Fortress Press, 1972.

LANGBAUM, Robert. The Poetry of Experience: The Dramatic Monologue in Modern Literary Experience. New York: Random House, 1957.

The Language of Poetry. Ed. Allen Tate. Princeton, New Jersey: Princeton Univ. Press, 1942.

LEAVIS, F. R. *Education and the University: A Sketch for an "English School."* London: Chatto and Windus, 1943; New York: George W. Stewart, Publisher, Inc., 1948.

_____. *New Bearings in English Poetry*. London: Chatto and Windus, 1932.

_____. *Revaluation: Tradition and Development in English Poetry*. London: Chatto and Windus, 1936. (Also, same pagination, New York: George W. Stewart, 1947.)

LEISHMAN, J. B. *The Metaphyscial Poets: Donne, Herbert, Vaughan, Traherne*. Oxford: Oxford Univ. Press, 1934.

Literary Opinion in America. Ed. M. D. Zabel. New York: Harper & Brothers, 1937. Revised edition, 1951.

Literary Scholarship: Its Aims and Methods. Chapel Hill: Univ. of North Carolina Press, 1941. (No explication)

Literary Theory and Structure: Essays in Honor of William K. Wimsatt. Ed. Frank Brady, John Palmer, and Martin Price. New Haven: Yale Univ. Press, 1973.

Literary Uses of Typology from the Late Middle Ages to the Present. Ed. Earl Miner. Princeton, New Jersey: Princeton Univ. Press, 1977.

The Literature of the United States. Ed. Walter Blair, Theodore Hornberger, and Randall Stewart. Chicago: Scott, Foresman and Company, 1947.

LOCKE, Louis G., William M. Gibson, and George Arms. *Introduction to Literature*, third edition. New York: Rinehart & Company, Inc., 1957. Fourth edition. Holt, Rinehart and Winston, Inc., 1962. Fifth edition, 1967.

MANNING, Stephen. *Wisdom and Number: Toward a Critical Appraisal of the Middle English Lyric*. Lincoln: Univ. of Nebraska Press, 1962.

MARTZ, Louis L. *The Poetry of Meditation: A Study in English Religious Literature*. New Haven: Yale Univ. Press, 1954.

_____. *The Poem of the Mind: Essays on Poetry English and American*. New York: Oxford Univ. Press, 1966.

MATTHIESSEN, F. O. *American Renaissance: Art and Expression in the Age of Emerson and Whitman*. New York: Oxford Univ. Press, 1941.

_____. *The Responsibilities of the Critic*. Ed. John Rackliffe. New York: Oxford Univ. Press, 1952.

McCANLES, Michael. *Dialectical Criticism and Renaissance Literature*. Berkeley: Univ. of California Press, 1975.

Mid-Century American Poets. Ed. John Ciardi. New York: Twayne Publishers, Inc., 1950.

MILES, Josephine. *Major Adjectives in English Poetry: From Wyatt to Auden*. Berkeley and Los Angeles: Univ. of California Press, 1946.

_____. The Primary Language of Poetry in the 1640's. Berkeley and Los Angeles: Univ. of California Press, 1948.

MILLER, J. Hillis. Poets of Reality: Six Twentieth-Century Writers. Cambridge: Harvard Univ. Press, 1965.

MILLER, James E., Jr., Karl Shapiro, and Bernice Slote. Start With the Sun: Studies in Cosmic Poetry. Lincoln, Nebraska: Univ. of Nebraska Press, 1960.

MILLET, Fred B. Reading Poetry: A Method of Analysis with Selections for Study. New York: Harper & Brothers, 1950.

MILLS, Ralph J., Jr. Contemporary American Poetry. New York: Random House, Inc., 1965.

MINER, Earl. The Cavalier Mode from Jonson to Cotton. Princeton, New Jersey: Princeton Univ. Press, 1971.

_____. The Metaphysical Mode from Donne to Cowley. Princeton, New Jersey: Princeton Univ. Press, 1969.

_____. The Restoration Mode from Milton to Dryden. Princeton, New Jersey: Princeton Univ. Press, 1974.

Modern American Poetry. Ed. B. Rajan. New York: Roy Publishers, 1950.

Modern Language Notes, 40 (Jan., 1925)-92, No. 5 (Dec., 1977).

Modern Language Quarterly, 1, No. 1 (March, 1940)-38, No. 4 (Dec., 1977).

Modern Literary Criticism. Ed. Irving Howe. Boston: Beacon Press, 1958.

Modern Philology, 22 (Aug., 1924)-75, No. 2 (Nov., 1977).

The Moment of Poetry. Ed. Don Cameron Allen. Baltimore: The Johns Hopkins Press, 1962.

MOORE, Arthur K. The Secular Lyric in Middle English. Lexington: Univ. of Kentucky Press, 1951.

MURRY, John Middleton. Aspects of Literature, 2nd ed. London: W. Collins Sons and Company, Ltd., 1921. (No explication)

_____. Countries of the Mind: Essays in Literary Criticism, First Series. London: Oxford Univ. Press, Humphrey Milford, 1931 (New Edition). (No explication)

_____. Countries of the Mind: Essays in Literary Criticism, Second Series. London: Oxford Univ. Press, Humphrey Milford, 1931. (No explication)

NICOLSON, Marjorie Hope. The Breaking of the Circle. Evanston: Northwestern Univ. Press, 1950.

O'CONNOR, William Van. Sense and Sensibility in Modern Poetry. Chicago: The Univ. of Chicago Press, 1948.

PALMER, Herbert. Post-Victorian Poetry. London: J. M. Dent and Sons, Ltd., 1938.

Papers on Language & Literature, 1, No. 1 (Winter, 1965)-13, No. 4 (Fall, 1977).

PARTRIDGE, A. C. The Language of Renaissance Poetry. London: Andre Deutsch, 1971.

PEARCE, Roy Harvey. The Continuity of American Poetry. Princeton, New Jersey: Princeton Univ. Press, 1961.

PECKHAM, Morse and Seymour Chatman. Word, Meaning, Poem. New York: Thomas Y. Crowell Company, 1961.

PERKINS, David. The Quest for Permanence: The Symbolism of Wordsworth, Shelley, and Keats. Cambridge, Massachusetts: Harvard Univ. Press, 1959.

PERRINE, Laurence. The Art of Total Relevance. Rowley, Massachusetts: Newbury House Publishers, Inc., 1976.

_____. Sound and Sense: An Introduction to Poetry. New York: Harcourt, Brace and Company, 1956. Second edition, 1963.

PERRINE, Laurence and James M. Reid. 100 American Poems of the Twentieth Century. New York: Harcourt Brace & World, Inc., 1966.

PETERSON, Douglas L. The English Lyric from Wyatt to Donne: A History of the Plain and Eloquent Styles. Princeton, New Jersey: Princeton Univ. Press, 1967.

PHILLIPS, Robert. The Confessional Poets. Carbondale: Southern Illinois Univ. Press, 1973.

PINTO, Vivian De Sola. Crisis in English Poetry 1880-1940. London: Hutchinson's Univ. Library, 1951.

The Poem: An Anthology. Ed. Stanley B. Greenfield and A. Kingsley Weatherhead. New York: Appleton-Century-Crofts, 1968.

Poetry: A Critical Supplement. March, 1947-May, 1948. See the note under A Critical Supplement to "Poetry."

The Poet as Critic. Ed. Frederick P. W. McDowell. Evanston, Illinois: Northwestern Univ. Press, 1967.

Poets at Work. Ed. Charles D. Abbott. New York: Harcourt, Brace and Company, 1948.

Politics and Letters (incorporating The Critic), 1 (Summer, 1947)-1, No. 4 (Summer, 1948).

POTTLE, Frederick A. The Idiom of Poetry. Ithaca: Cornell Univ. Press, 1941. (Also, revised edition, 1946).

Publications of the Modern Language Association of America, 40 (March, 1925)-92, No. 6 (Nov., 1977).

Quarterly Review of Literature, 1, No. 1 (Autumn, 1943); 2 (Fall, 1944)-4, No. 4.

QUINN, Sister M. Bernetta. The Metamorphic Tradition in Modern Poetry. New Brunswick, New Jersey: Rutgers Univ. Press, 1955.

RANSOM, John Crowe. God Without Thunder. New York: Harcourt Brace and Company, 1930. (No explication)

_____. The New Criticism. Norfolk, Connecticut: New Directions, 1941.

_____. The World's Body. New York: Charles Scribner's Sons, 1938.

READ, Herbert. Collected Essays in Literary Criticism. London: Faber and Faber, Ltd., 1938. (No explication)

Readings in Applied English Linguistics. Ed. Harold B. Allen. New York: Appleton-Century-Crofts, Inc., 1958.

Readings for Liberal Education, volume II, Introduction to Literature. Ed. Louis G. Locke, William M. Gibson, and George Arms. New York: Rinehart & Company, 1948.

REISS, Edmund. The Art of the Middle English Lyric. Athens: Univ. of Georgia Press, 1972.

Research Studies (formerly Research Studies of the State College of Washington), 1, No. 1 (June 28, 1929)-45 (Dec., 1977).

RIBNER, Irving and Harry Morris. Poetry: A Critical and Historical Introduction. Chicago, Illinois: Scott, Foresman and Company, 1962.

RICHARDS, I. A. Coleridge on Imagination. New York: Harcourt, Brace and Company, 1935. (No explication)

_____. How to Read a Page. New York: W. W. Norton and Company, 1942. (No explication)

_____. The Philosophy of Rhetoric. New York: Oxford Univ. Press, 1936. (No explication)

_____. Practical Criticism. New York: Harcourt, Brace, and Company, 1929.

_____. Principles of Literary Criticism. 2nd ed. London: Kegan Paul, Trench, Trubner & Company, Ltd., 1926.

_____. Science and Poetry, 2nd ed. London: K. Paul, Trench, Trubner and Company, Ltd., 1935. (No explication)

RICHARDS, I. A., C. K. Ogden, and James Wood. The Foundations of Aesthetics, 2nd ed. New York: Lear Publishers, 1948. (No explication)

RIDING, Laura and Robert Graves. A Survey of Modernist Poetry. New York: Doubleday, Doran and Company, 1928.

ROSENTHAL, M. L. and A. J. M. Smith. Exploring Poetry. New York: The Macmillan Company, 1955.

ROSENHEIM, Edward W. What Happens in Literature: A Student's Guide to Poetry, Drama, and Fiction. Chicago, Illinois: The Univ. of Chicago Press, 1960.

ROSENTHAL, M. L. The Modern Poets: A Critical Introduction. New York: Oxford Univ. Press, 1960.

SANDERS, Thomas E. The Discovery of Poetry. Glenview, Illinois: Scott, Fores-man and Company, 1967.

SATIN, Joseph. Reading Poetry (Part Four of Reading Literature). Boston: Houghton Mifflin Company, 1964.

SAVAGE, D. S. The Personal Principle: Studies in Modern Poetry. London: George Routledge and Sons, Ltd., 1944.

SCHLAUCH, Margaret. Modern English and American Poetry: Techniques and Idealo-gies. London: C. A. Watts & Company, Ltds., 1956.

SCHNEIDER, Elisabeth. Aesthetic Motive. New York: The Macmillan Company, 1939.

SCHNEIDER, Elisabeth W. Poems and Poetry. New York: American Book Company, 1964.

SCOTT, A. F. The Poet's Craft. Cambridge: Cambridge Univ. Press, 1957.

SCOTT, Nathan A., Jr. Rehearsals of Discomposure. New York: King's Crown Press, 1952.

Scottish Poetry: A Critical Survey. Ed. James Kinsley. London: Cassell and Company, Ltds., 1955.

Scrutinies, by Various Writers. 2 volumes. Ed. Edgell Rickword. London: Wishart & Company, 1928 and 1931.

Scrutiny: A Quarterly Review, 1 (May, 1932)-19, No. 4 (Oct., 1953).

The Sewanee Review, 33 (Jan., 1925)-85, No. 4 (Oct.-Dec., 1977).

SEWELL, Elizabeth. The Orphic Voice: Poetry and Natural History. New Haven, Connecticut: Yale Univ. Press, 1962.

_____. The Structure of Poetry. London: Routledge and Kegan Paul, 1951.

SKELTON, Robin. The Poetic Pattern. Berkeley and Los Angeles: Univ. of California Press, 1956.

SMITH, Hallett. Elizabethan Poetry: A Study in Conventions, Meaning, and Expression. Cambridge: Harvard Univ. Press, 1952.

The Southern Review, 1 (July, 1935)-7 (Spring, 1942).

The Southern Review, 1, No. 1, n.s. (Jan., 1965)-13, No. 4, n.s. (Oct., 1977).

SOUTHWORTH, James G. More Modern American Poets. New York: The Macmillan Company, 1954.

_____. Some Modern American Poets. Oxford: Basil Blackwell, 1950.

SPACKS, Patricia Meyer. The Poetry of Vision: Five Eighteenth-Century Poets. Cambridge, Massachusetts: Harvard Univ. Press, 1967.

SPITZER, Leo. A Method of Interpreting Literature. Northampton, Massachusetts: Smith College, 1949.

STAGEBERG, Norman C. and Wallace Anderson. Poetry as Experience. New York: American Book Company, 1952.

STALLMAN, R. W. and R. E. Watters. The Creative Reader: An Anthology of Fiction, Drama, and Poetry. New York: The Ronald Press Company, 1954.

STAUFFER, Donald A. The Nature of Poetry. New York: W. W. Norton & Company, Inc., 1946.

STEVENS, Wallace. The Necessary Angel. New York: Alfred A. Knopf, 1951.

STONE, Edward. A Certain Morbidness: A View of American Literature. Carbondale: Southern Illinois Univ. Press, 1969.

Studies in English Literature, 1500-1900, 1, No. 1 (Winter, 1960) 17, No. 4 (Autumn, 1977).

Studies in Honor of John Wilcox. Ed. A. Doyle Wallace and Woodburn O. Ross. Detroit: Wayne State Univ. Press, 1958.

Studies in Philology, 22 (Jan., 1925)-72, No. 1 (Jan., 1975).

Studies in Romanticism, 1, No. 1 (Autumn, 1961)-16, No. 4 (Fall, 1977).

Studies in the Literature of the Augustan Age: Essays Collected in Honor of Arthur Ellicott Case. Ed. Richard C. Boys. Ann Arbor: The George Wahr Publishing Company, 1952. (No explication)

SUTTON, Walter. American Free Verse: The Modern Revolution in Poetry. New York: New Directions, 1973.

SWALLOW, Alan. An Editor's Essays of Two Decades. Seattle and Denver: Experiment Press, 1962.

TATE, Allen. On the Limits of Poetry. New York: The Swallow Press and William Morrow & Company, 1948.

_____. Reactionary Essays on Poetry and Ideas. New York: Charles Scribner's Sons, 1936.

_____. Reason in Madness. New York: G. P. Putnam's Sons, 1941.

Texas Studies in Literature and Language, 1, No. 1 (Spring, 1959)-19, No. 4 (Winter, 1977).

THOMAS, Wright, and Stuart Gerry Brown. Reading Poems: An Introduction to Critical Study. New York: Oxford Univ. Press, 1941.

Three Studies in the Renaissance: Sidney, Jonson, Milton. Ed. Benjamin Christe Nangle. Yale Studies in English, Vol. 138. New Haven: Yale Univ. Press, 1958.

TILLYARD, E. M. W. Five Poems, 1470-1870. London: Chatto and Windus, 1948.

_____. The Metaphysicals and Milton. London: Chatto and Windus, 1956.

_____. Poetry Direct and Oblique. London: Chatto and Windus, 1934.

TOLIVER, Harold E. Pastoral: Forms and Attitudes. Berkeley: Univ. of California Press, 1971.

TSCHUMI, Raymond. Thought in Twentieth-Century English Poetry. London: Routledge and Kegan Paul, Ltd., 1951.

TUVE, Rosemond. Elizabethan and Metaphysical Imagery. Chicago: The Univ. of Chicago Press, 1947.

The Twenties: Poetry and Prose. Ed. Richard E. Langford and William E. Taylor. Deland, Florida: Everett/Edwards, Inc., 1966.

Twentieth Century Literature, 1, No. 1 (Jan., 1956)-23, No. 4 (Dec., 1977).

UNGER, Leonard. The Man in the Name: Essays on the Experience of Poetry. Minneapolis: The Univ. of Minnesota Press, 1956.

UNGER, Leonard, and William Van O'Connor. Poems for Study. New York: Rinehart & Company, Inc., 1953.

VAN DOREN, Mark. Introduction to Poetry. New York: William Sloane Associates, Inc., 1951.

Victorian Poetry, 1, No. 1 (Spring, 1963)-15, No. 4 (Winter, 1977).

Victorian Studies, 1, No. 1 (Sept., 1957)-21, No. 1 (Autumn, 1977).

VIVANTE, Leone. English Poetry and Its Contribution to the Knowledge of a Creative Principle. New York: The Macmillan Company, 1950.

VOGLER, Thomas A. Preludes to Vision: The Epic Venture in Blake, Wordsworth, Keats, and Hart Crane. Berkeley: Univ. of California Press, 1971.

WAGGONER, Hyatt Howe. The Heel of Elohim: Science and Values in Modern American Poetry. Norman: Univ. of Oklahoma Press, 1950.

[The Harvard] Wake, 5 (Spring, 1946); Wake, 7 (Autumn, 1948)-12 (1953).

WALSH, Chad. Doors into Poetry. Englewood Cliffs, New Jersey: Prentice-Hall, Inc., 1962.

WALSH, William. The Use of Imagination: Educational Thought and the Literary Mind. London: Chatto & Windus, 1959.

WANAMAKER, Melissa C. Discordia Concors: The Wit of Metaphysical Poetry. Port Washington, New York: Kennikat Press, 1975.

WARREN, Austin. Rage for Order: Essays in Criticism. Chicago: The Univ. of Chicago Press, 1948.

WASSERMAN, Earl R. The Subtler Language: Critical Readings of Neoclassic and Romantic Poems. Baltimore: The Johns Hopkins Press, 1959.

WATTS, Harold H. Hound and Quarry. London: Routledge and Kegan Paul, 1953.

WEBER, Sarah Appleton. Theology and Poetry in the Middle English Lyric: A Study of Sacred History and Aesthetic Form. Columbus: Ohio State Univ. Press, 1969.

WEITZ, Morris. Philosophy of the Arts. Cambridge: Harvard Univ. Press, 1950.

WELLS, E. K. The Ballad Tree. New York: Ronald Press, 1950.

WELLS, HENRY W. New Poets from Old: A Study in Literary Genetics. New York:
    Columbia Univ. Press, 1940.

The Western Review, 11 (Autumn, 1946)-23 (Spring, 1959).

WHEELER, Charles B. The Design of Poetry. New York: W. W. Norton & Company,
    Inc., 1966.

WHEELWRIGHT, Philip. The Burning Fountain: A Study in the Language of Symbol-
    ism. Bloomington: Indiana Univ. Press, 1954.

WILKIE, Brian. Romantic Poets and Epic Tradition. Madison and Milwaukee: The
    Univ. of Wisconsin Press, 1965.

WILLIAMSON, George. 'he Proper Wit of Poetry. Chicago: The Univ. of Chicago
    Press, 1961.

WILSON, Edmund. Axel's Castle. New York: Charles Scribner's Sons, 1931.

WIMSATT, W. K., Jr. The Verbal Icon: Studies in the Meaning of Poetry.
    Lexington: Univ. of Kentucky Press, 1954.

WINTERS, Yvor. The Anatomy of Nonsense. Norfolk, Connecticut: New Direc-
    tions, 1943.

_____. Forms of Discovery: Critical and Historical Essays on the Forms of
    the Short Poem in English. Chicago: Alan Swallow, 1967.

_____. The Function of Criticism: Problems and Exercises. Denver: Alan
    Swallow, 1957.

_____. In Defense of Reason. New York: The Swallow Press and William Morrow
    and Company, 1947; third ed. Denver: Alan Swallow, 1960.

_____. Maule's Curse. Norfolk, Connecticut: New Directions, 1938.

_____. Primitivism and Decadence. New York: Arrow Editions, 1933.

WORMHOUDT, Arthur. The Demon Lover: A Psychoanalytical Approach to Litera-
    ture. New York: Exposition Press, 1949.

WRIGHT, George T. The Poet in the Poem: The Personae of Eliot, Yeats, Donne.
    Berkeley and Los Angeles: Univ. of California Press, 1960.

The Yearbook of English Studies, 1 (1971)-7 (1977).

YEATS, W. B. Essays. New York: The Macmillan Company, 1924.

_____. Letters on Poetry from W. B. Yeats to Dorothy Wellesley. New York:
    Oxford Univ. Press, 1940.

ZITNER, Sheldon P., James D. Kissane, Myron M. Liberman. A Preface to Literary
    Analysis. Chicago: Scott, Foresman and Company, 1964.